THE BLUE AND THE GRAY

The Second Battle of Bull Run

The Blue
and
the Gray

TWO VOLUMES IN ONE

THE STORY OF THE CIVIL WAR

AS TOLD BY PARTICIPANTS

EDITED BY

Henry Steele Commager

THE FAIRFAX PRESS
NEW YORK

To
the memory of

HENRY STEELE COMMAGER
Colonel, 67th Ohio

DAVID HEDGES COMMAGER
Captain, 184th Ohio

JAMES ALEXANDER WILLIAM THOMAS
Captain, 21st South Carolina

DUNCAN DONALD McCOLL
1st Heavy Artillery, North Carolina

JAMES THOMAS CARROLL
North Carolina Volunteers

and to
my children

HENRY STEELE
NELLIE THOMAS McCOLL
ELISABETH CARROLL

This 1982 edition is published by The Fairfax Press,
distributed by Crown Publishers, Inc.,
by arrangement with Lou Reda.
A Lou Reda Book
Manufactured in the United States of America

Library of Congress Cataloging in Publication Data
Main entry under title:

The Blue and the Gray.

  Reprint. Originally published: Indianapolis : Bobbs-
Merrill, c1950.
  Bibliography: p.
  1. United States—History—Civil War, 1861-1865—
Personal narratives.   I. Commager, Henry Steele,
1902-
E464.B56   1982   973.7'8   82-5021
                                       AACR2
ISBN: 0-517-383799

h g f e d c b a

CONTENTS
VOLUME I

Contents

CONTENTS
VOLUME II

Contents

ILLUSTRATIONS
VOLUME I

ILLUSTRATIONS
VOLUME II

MAPS

FOREWORD

MANY hands filled the storehouse from which Henry Steele Commager drew the treasures that appear in the fascinating pages of this long-desired collection. Some survivors wrote of the eighteen-sixties because they had tarnished reputations to repolish or grudges to satisfy. Other participants set down the history of their old Regiment to please comrades who met annually at a G.A.R. encampment or at a Confederate reunion to live again in memory their great hours. In a few instances, most notably that of General Grant, memoirs were prepared because the public literally demanded them. Hundreds of books and brochures were the work of those who sought, consciously or otherwise, to associate themselves with the mighty men and the decisive conflict of their generation. The failure of some Southern writers to find a publisher was responsible for the private printing of numerous books and for the allegation, never justified, that the North would not give Southern writers a hearing. One forgotten phase of this had its origin in the persistent effort of certain schoolbook publishers to procure the "adoption" in the South of texts on American history written in partisan spirit for Northern readers. This salesmanship was met repeatedly with pleas for the establishment in Richmond, Atlanta or New Orleans of a publishing house that would be "fair to the South." Where a response was made to this appeal, the fruit sometimes was a text as extreme as the one that provoked it. A long-popular Southern school history contained 590 pages, of which more than 200 were devoted to the preliminaries of the War Between the States and to the events of that struggle. A study of the disputes of the eighteen-nineties involving rival books of this type would startle a generation that assumes an author's non-partisan approach as a matter of course.

Many contrasts are offered in the literature of the American war of 1861–65, and most notably in what Mr. Commager remarks in his introduction—that "the Confederate narratives seem to be of a higher literary quality than the Federal." This is meant, of course, to be subject at the outset to qualification as respects some notable books. The list of Union brigade histories, for example, may contain no single volume better than Caldwell's charming story of Gregg's South Carolinians; but Mr. Commager most surely is correct in saying that Charles E. Davis's account of the Thirteenth Massachusetts is definitely the most interesting regimental history on either side.

If there is general, or average superiority in Southern memoirs and personal narratives, this doubtless is due to a number of circumstances that raise no questions of rival "cultures." Nearly always there is glamor to a "lost cause." Cromwell's body on the Tyburn gallows, "Bonnie Prince Charlie" in exile, and Bonaparte dying of cancer at Longwood never fail to arouse sympathy the Puritan Revolution, the Jacobite cause and Napoleonic imperialism cannot stir. It manifestly has been so with the South which had, in addition, a most unusual number of picturesque leaders. These men possessed the "color" and the peculiarities that inspire the *causerie de bivouac* the Little Corporal said every general should provide if he wished to be successful. Lee had a magnificence that awed his soldiers, who seldom cheered him; when Stonewall Jackson came in sight, riding awkwardly on a poor horse, the rebel yell nearly always would be raised. He fired the imagination of his troops as Lee never did until the *post-bellum* years. Albert Sidney Johnston, Forrest, Morgan, "Jeb" Stuart—these, too, were men to arouse enthusiasms that echoed in the memoirs of their followers. The North had soldiers and seamen of like appeal, but somehow the memory of nearly all these leaders was forgotten in the changes of population incident to the Westward movement and to expanded immigration. Static Southern society had longer memory.

Besides this, the South chanced to produce early a "war book" that set a standard which perhaps was considered representative, though actually it could not be maintained. This was Lieutenant General Richard Taylor's *Destruction and Reconstruction,* parts of which appeared in *The North American Review* in January-April 1878, the year before the memoirs were published in book form. Anyone reading that superb narrative would get an exalted conception of the literary skill of Southern military writers, a conception not borne out by later works of other authors. This is not derogatory because Taylor's book remains to this day the most exciting narrative of its kind by an American commander. It would be difficult to find anywhere a better told story of a military movement than Taylor's account of "Stonewall" Jackson's Valley Campaign of 1862 (Vol. I p. 150ff).

If these and other circumstances bear out Mr. Commager's statement regarding the excellence of some Confederate narratives, fair play requires a Southerner to put the emphasis on that word *narratives*. There certainly is not a like superiority in the poetry. Thomas De Leon, from whom Mr. Commager takes several diverting episodes, remarked in his *Four Years in Rebel Capitals* that he had accumulated 1,900 wartime poems of the South, and later added greatly to his list: "There were battle odes, hymns, calls to arms, paeans and dirges and prayers for peace—many of them good, few of them great; and the vast majority, alas! wretchedly poor."

De Leon could have carried his scrutiny of Southern literature twenty years further and would have found few Confederate poems besides those of the Catholic priest, Father Abram Joseph Ryan, that voiced impressively the full emotion of the Southern people. Frequently Theodore O'Hara's "The Bivouac of the Dead" is put forward with Father Ryan's "Conquered Banner," but O'Hara wrote in 1847 of the Kentuckians killed in the Battle of Buena Vista. It is a singular fact that John R. Thompson's verses on the Confederacy, though written, as it were, to the pulsing of the guns on the Richmond defenses, seldom reached the level of his best work. Simms, Hayne, Lanier, Timrod, Randall—none of these wrote of "the war" as their admirers might have expected. No theme seemed to elicit their finest utterance, not even "Marse Robert" himself. Lee remains the demigod of the South and has there a place even Washington does not hold, but where may be found a poem on Lee that anyone would wish to make a permanent part of one's mental acquisition? In contrast, Lowell outdid himself in the "Harvard Commemoration Ode"; Whitman's "O Captain! My Captain!" and his "When Lilacs Last in the Dooryard Bloomed" are among the author's most successful works; and as Mr. Commager says, the North produced the "one great battle hymn of our literature."

Perhaps the most remarkable feature of the 400 and more articles reproduced in this notable collection is the humor that runs through nearly all of them and particularly through those of Southern origin. Doubtless there was an Erich Remarque somewhere on the Rappahannock front; letters written home by Billy Yank and Johnny Reb contained the usual number of complaints and requests; but when the column was in motion, there were more jests than oaths on the lips of the soldiers. Laughter was the medicine for most of the ills visible to the men next in line, though fear and rebellious wrath and homesickness might be gnawing at the heart.

Good cheer was not unnatural in the Union Regiments after July 1863, but its persistence until the autumn of 1864 in most of the Southern forces, and particularly in the Army of Northern Virginia, is a phenomenon of morale. The same thing may be said of the attitude of the men toward the manifest inferiority of Southern military equipment. The graycoats laughed at their wagons and their harness, their tatters and their gaping shoes. Again and again this stirs one who opens these volumes at random and reads the first paragraph on which the eye falls: were these men mocking death as a foe long outwitted, or were they assuming a heroism they did not possess? Were they valiant or merely pretending? It scarcely seemed to matter where some of them were or what they were doing: they laughed their way from Manassas to Appomattox and even through the hospitals. Except for the military prisons, the Confederates, for instance, could have had few places of darker tragedy, written in tears and anguish, than Chimborazo Hospital in Richmond, where as many as 7,000 soldiers sometimes suffered together; yet it was life there that Mrs. Phoebe Pember described in some of the most humorous writing of the war.

These Confederate soldiers and nurses and citizens of beleaguered towns had one inspiration that twentieth-century America has not credited to them—the vigorous Revolutionary tradition. The men who fought at Gettysburg were as close in time to the turning point of that earlier struggle, the Trenton-Princeton campaign of 1777, as readers of 1950 are to the *dies irae* described by Colonel Frank Haskell in his famous account of the repulse of Pickett's charge. Many men in the ranks, North and South, had seen old soldiers of the Continental Army; thousands had heard stories of the sacrifices of 1777 and of the hunger and nakedness at Valley Forge. From its very nature, freedom was born in travail. Ignorant·men sensed this vaguely, if at all; the literate reread William Gordon and Washington Irving and steeled themselves to like hardship. To some of the commanders, and above all to Lee, there daily was an inspiring analogy between the struggle of the Confederacy and that of Revolutionary America under the generalship of Lee's great hero, Washington. Many another Southern soldier told himself the road was no more stony than the one that had carried his father and his grandfather at last to Yorktown. If independence was to be the reward, patience, good cheer and the tonic of laughter would bring it all the sooner.

Those Confederates believed they were as good judges of humor as, say, of horses; and both they and their adversaries in blue regarded themselves as strategists or, at least, as competent critics of strategy. Quick to perceive the aim of the marches they were called upon to make, they discussed by every campfire and on every riverbank the shrewdness or the blunders of the men who led them. After the manner of youth in every land and of every era, they made heroes of the officers they admired and they denounced the martinets, but, in time, most of them learned from their discussion and, considering the paucity of their information, came to broad strategical conclusions their seniors would not have been ashamed to own.

Many of the diarists and letter writers were observant, too, and not infrequently recorded important fact no officer set down in any report. If some of these writers let their vanity adorn their tale, the majority were of honest mind. One somewhat renowned *post-bellum* lecturer who should have been an invaluable witness, progressively lost the truth of his narrative as he made it more and more dramatic and egocentric, but he did not have many fellow offenders outside the ranks of those known and branded prevaricators who bored their comrades of the U.C.V. or the G.A.R. as they told how "they won" the battle or the war. On the other hand, Mr. Commager quotes in these pages several veterans who wrote long after the conflict, without access to records, and yet were so astonishingly accurate that any psychologist, chancing on their memoirs, will wish he might have studied in person the mentality of the authors.

These men and women had no literary inhibitions other than those of a decency that is to be respected both for itself and for the contrasts it suggests with certain later writing on war and warriors. If, incidentally, the restraint and modesty of most of the soldiers' letters of the eighteen-sixties were Victorian, then so much the better for Victorianism. This apart, every man felt free to write of anything—and considered himself as competent as free—with the result that the source materials of the conflict are opulently numerous and almost bewilderingly democratic. Private Casler may dispute in a footnote the pronouncements of the learned Dr. Dabney on the strategy of "Old Jack"; the testimony of a boy who saw Grant once only may be preferred to that of a corps commander who conferred so often with "Unconditional Surrender" that, in retrospect, he confused the details of the various interviews.

Historically, then, it may be hoped that one result of the appearance of this book will be the use of other authorities than the few, such as "Rebel War Clerk" Jones and Mrs. Chesnut, for example, who have been overworked and, on some subjects, have been uncritically cited. The student will find that new witnesses have been made available, and that stirring tales have been assembled and prefaced sagely by an editor whose knowledge of the literature of 1861-65 is unexcelled. Henry Steele Commager has the admiration as well as the personal affection of all students who appreciate the catholicity of his scholarship and the penetrating justice of his judgment. Had members of his profession been asked by the publishers to name the individual best equipped to present "a history of the Civil War in the words of those who fought it," their choice would have been the man who flawlessly has rendered here that welcome service to the American people.

DOUGLAS SOUTHALL FREEMAN

Westbourne,
Richmond, Virginia,

INTRODUCTION

WE have fought five major wars in the last century or so, and three since Appomattox, but of them all it is the Civil War that has left the strongest impression on our minds, our imagination, and our hearts. It is the Civil War songs that we sing—who does not know "Marching Through Georgia" or "Tramp, Tramp, Tramp" or "Dixie"?—and that war gave us the one great battle hymn of our literature. It furnished our best war poetry, both at the time and since; no other war has produced anything as good as "Drum Taps" or the "Harvard Commemoration Ode," nor has any other been celebrated by an epic poem comparable to Stephen Benét's *John Brown's Body*. It has inspired more, and better, novels than any other of our wars and it excites even Hollywood to rise above mediocrity. It has furnished our standards of patriotism, of gallantry, and of fortitude; it has given us our most cherished military heroes—Lee and Jackson, Grant and Sherman, Sheridan and "Beauty" Stuart, and a host of others, and it has given us, too, our greatest national hero and our greatest sectional one, Lincoln and Lee. No other chapter in our history has contributed so much to our traditions and our folklore. The very words—whether they are Civil War or War between the States—conjure up for us a hundred images: Jackson standing like a stone wall; U. S. Grant becoming Unconditional Surrender Grant; Lee astride Traveller, "It is well war is so terrible, or we should get too fond of it"; Barbara Frietchie waving her country's flag; A. P. Hill breaking through the wheat fields at Antietam; Thomas standing like a rock at Chickamauga; Pickett's men streaming up the long slope of Cemetery Ridge; Farragut lashed to the mast at Mobile Bay, "Damn the torpedoes, full steam ahead"; the Army of the Cumberland scrambling up the rugged heights of Missionary Ridge; Hood's Texans forcing Lee to the rear before they would close the gap at Spotsylvania; Sheridan dashing down the Winchester Pike; Lincoln pardoning the sleeping sentinels, reading Artemus Ward to his Cabinet, dedicating the battlefield of Gettysburg; Grant and Lee at Appomattox Court House.

It was, in many respects, a curious war, one in which amenities were preserved. It could not begin until high-ranking officers of the army and navy had been permitted to resign and help organize a rebellion. Southerners tolerated outspoken Unionists, like Petigru or Botts; Northerners permitted Vallandigham to campaign openly against the war, and at the crisis of the conflict almost two million of them voted for a party that had formally pronounced the war a failure. Journalists seemed to circulate at will, and Northern papers had correspondents in the South while Confederates got much of their information about Federal army movements from the Northern newspapers. There was an immense amount of trading back and forth, some of it authorized or at least tolerated by the governments, and Sherman could say that Cincinnati furnished more supplies to the Confederacy than did Charleston.

Officers had been trained in the same schools and fought in the same armies, and most of them knew one another or knew of one another; Mrs. Pickett tells us that when her baby was born Grant's staff celebrated with bonfires. There was a great deal of fraternization—a word which did not have the ugly connotations it achieved after World War II—both among soldiers and civilians. Pickets exchanged tobacco, food, and news; if Yankee officers did not marry Southern beauties as often as novelists imagined, there was at least some basis for the literary emphasis on romance. Confederates cheered Meagher's Irish Brigade as it charged up Marye's Heights, and the Yankees almost outdid the Confederates in admiration for Jackson and Pelham. There were plenty of atrocity stories, but few atrocities. There was a good deal of pillaging and vandalism—as in all wars—but little of that systematic destruction we know from two world wars. On the whole, civilians were safe; there were crimes against property but few against persons, and women everywhere were respected. When Butler affronted the ladies of New Orleans he was transferred to another command, and Sherman engaged in a wordy correspondence with the mayor of Atlanta seeking to justify what he thought a military necessity. Whether Sherman burned Columbia is still a matter of controversy; the interesting thing is that there should be a controversy at all. Both peoples subscribed to the same moral values and observed the same standards of conduct. Both displayed that "decent respect to the opinions of mankind" to which Jefferson had appealed three quarters of a century earlier. Both were convinced that the cause for which they fought was just—and their descendants still are.

Nor did the war come to an end, psychologically or emotionally, with Appomattox. Politicians nourished its issues; patriotic organizations cherished its memories; scholars refought its battles with unflagging enthusiasm. No other war has started so many controversies and for no other do they flourish so vigorously. Every step in the conflict, every major political decision, every campaign, almost every battle, has its own proud set of controversies, and of all the military figures only Lee stands above argument and debate. Was the election of Lincoln a threat to the South, and was secession justified? Was secession a revolutionary or a constitutional act, and was the war a rebellion or an international conflict? Was the choice of Davis a mistake, and did Davis interfere improperly in military affairs? Should the Confederacy have burned its cotton, or exported it? Was the blockade a success, and if so at what point? Should Britain have recognized the Confederacy, or did she go too far toward the assistance of the South as it was? Who was responsible for the attack on Fort Sumter, Lincoln or Beauregard, and was the call for 75,000 men an act of aggression? Was Jackson late at Seven Days? Was Grant surprised at Shiloh? Did the radicals sabotage McClellan's Peninsular campaign? Who was responsible for the disaster of Second Bull Run and was Fitz John Porter a marplot or a scapegoat? Should Lee have persisted in his offensive of the autumn of 1862 even after the discovery of the Lost Order? Should McClellan have renewed battle after Antietam? Why did Pemberton fail to link up with Johnston outside Vicksburg and why did Johnston fail to relieve

Pemberton? Would Gettysburg have been different had Jackson been there, or had Longstreet seized Little Round Top on the morning of the second day, or had Pickett been properly supported on the third? Who was responsible for the Confederate failure at Stones River and who for the debacle of Missionary Ridge, and why did Davis keep Bragg in command so long? Could Johnston have saved Atlanta, and did Hood lose it? Was Hood's Tennessee campaign strategically sound but tactically mismanaged, or was it the other way around? Was Lee deceived during those critical June days when Grant flung his army across the James? And why did the Federals fail to break through the thin lines of Petersburg? Who burned Columbia, and was Sherman's theory of war justified? What really happened at Five Forks, and would the outcome have been different had Pickett been more alert? What explains the failure to have supplies at Amelia Court House and could Lee have made good his escape and linked up with Johnston had the supplies been there? Could the Confederacy ever have won the war, or was defeat foredoomed; if defeat was not foredoomed what caused it? These and a thousand other questions are still avidly debated by a generation that has already forgotten the controversies of the Spanish War and the First World War.

Nor is it by chance that the cause lost on the battlefield should be celebrated in story and in history, or that the whole people, victors and vanquished alike, should exalt its heroism and cherish its leaders. Lee is only less of a hero than Lincoln, and the Federal Army boasts no figure so glamorous as Stonewall Jackson. Novelists have been kinder to the Confederacy than to the Union, and so, too, in our own day, the moving pictures and the radio. There is no literary monument to any Union general comparable to those erected to Lee and Jackson, and for a generation Northern historians found themselves apologizing for Appomattox. Southerners everywhere accept the verdict of the war, and even are thankful for it, but there are none so lacking in filiopietism that they would change a line of history.

From the point of view of the student of military history, too, the Civil War is inexhaustibly interesting, and it is no wonder that English, French, and German strategists and historians have assiduously studied its battles and campaigns. It was, in a sense, the last of the old wars and the first of the new. It had many of the characteristics of earlier wars—the chivalry that animated officers and men, and the mutual esteem in which the combatants held each other, for example; the old-fashioned weapons and tactics such as sabers and cavalry charges; the woeful lack of discipline; the pitiful inadequacy of medical and hospital services, of what we would now call service of supply, of any provision for welfare and morale; the almost total absence of any proper Intelligence service or adequate staff work, and the primitive state of maps; the casual and amateur air that pervaded it all. But it was, too, in many and interesting respects, a modern war, one that anticipated the "total" wars of the twentieth century. It was the first in which the whole nation was involved, and it is probable that a larger proportion of the population, North as well as South, was actually in uniform than in any previous war of modern history. It was the first in which there was an even partial control of the economy—this largely in the South rather than in the more fortunate North. It was the first in which a large-scale blockade was a really effective if not indeed a decisive weapon. It was the first in which the railroad and the telegraph played a major role. It involved almost every known form of warfare: large-scale battles, guerrilla fighting, trench warfare, sieges and investments, bold forays into enemy country and large-scale invasions, amphibious warfare along coastal and inland waters, blockade, privateering, surface and sub-surface naval war, the war of propaganda and of nerves. It produced in Lee one of the supreme military geniuses of history, in Farragut one of the great naval captains; in Grant a major strategist; in Sherman, Hancock, Jackson, A. P. Hill, and Joseph E. Johnston captains whose tactics are still worthy of study; in Thomas a master of artillery; in Forrest and Stuart, Buford, Sheridan and Wilson, cavalry leaders whose exploits have rarely been surpassed.

Every war dramatizes the ordinary and accentuates the characteristic; more than any other in which we have ever been engaged the Civil War brought out in sharp relief those qualities that we think of as distinctively American. The American was practical, experimental, inventive, intelligent, self-reliant, opportunistic, energetic, careless, undisciplined, amateurish, equalitarian, sentimental, humorous, generous and moral. He believed that the civil was superior to the military even in war, and that privates were as good as officers, that it was wrong to begin a war or to fight in a cause that was not just, that a war should be fought according to rules, and that moral standards should obtain in war as in peace. All these qualities and principles were carried over from the civil to the military arena.

Thus the war discovered a people wholly unprepared, and never willing to prepare, either materially or psychologically. Neither side ever really organized for war; neither ever used the whole of its resources—though the South came far closer to this than the North; neither accepted the iron discipline which modern war imposes. The war required the subordination of the individual to the mass, of the particular to the general interest, and of the local to the central government; but both Federals and Confederates indulged their individualism in the army and out, rejected military standards and discipline, selected officers for almost any but military reasons, pursued local and state interest at the expense of the national. The war required organization and efficiency, but both sides conducted the war with monumental inefficiency—witness the shambles of conscription, or of the procurement of ordnance or of finances. The war required the husbanding of resources, but both sides wasted their resources, human and material—witness the medical services, or desertion, or the indulgence of business as usual, especially in the North.

The Americans were an educated, informed, self-reliant and resourceful people, and the Civil War armies undoubtedly boasted the highest level of intelligence of any armies in modern history up to that time. It took foreigners to remark this quality, however; Americans themselves took it for granted. Everyone, as both Dicey and Trollope remarked in wonder, read newspapers, followed political debates, and had opinions on the war, slavery, politics, and everything else; almost everyone—as an editor knows—kept a diary or a journal. Resourcefulness was almost their most striking quality. This resourcefulness appeared in Grant, who kept at it until he had found the road to Vicksburg; it appeared in Lee, who was able to adjust his plans to his shifting opponents, and to count on the understanding and co-operation of his lieutenants; it appeared in the engineers, who built dams and bridges, laid railroad tracks—or tore them up—solved problems of transport and supply that appeared insoluble; it appeared in the privates of both armies, who improvised breastworks or camp shelters, foraged for food and supplies, chose their own officers, voted in the field, provided their own newspapers, theatricals, and religious services, and often fought their own battles with such weapons as they could piece together. It appeared, too, in civilians, especially in the South, who managed somehow to improvise most of the weapons of war and the essentials of domestic economy, to make do with such labor and such materials as they had, and to hold society together through four years of strife and want.

Thus the conduct of the war confounded both the critics and the prophets. It was thought a people as unmilitary as the Americans could not fight a long war, or would not—but they did. It was thought that an agricultural South could not produce the matériel of war, but no single Southern defeat could be ascribed to lack of arms or equipment. It was supposed that neither side could finance a major war, but both managed somehow, and though Confederate finances were a shambles the North emerged from the conflict richer than she had entered it. To blockade thousands of miles of coast line, to invade an area of continental dimensions—these had never been done successfully in modern times, but the Union did them. Curiously, Europe was not convinced; the same basic errors of judgment that plagued England and France during the Civil War reappeared in Germany in 1917 and in Germany, Italy, and France in 1940.

The Americans were a good-natured people, easygoing, careless, and kindly, and in a curious sense these qualities carried over even into war. Lincoln set the tone here, for the North—Lincoln, who somehow managed to mitigate the wrath of war and his own melancholy with his humor, and who never referred to the Confederates as rebels; and Lee for the South, Lee, who always called the enemy "those people." Relations between the two armies were, somehow, good-natured: the very names the combatants had for each other, Johnny Reb and Billy Yank, testified to this. Only occasionally were relations between these enemies who so deeply respected each other exacerbated by official policy or by the prejudices of an officer. The soldiers themselves—boys for the most part, for it was a boys' war—were high-spirited and amiable, and endured endless discomforts and privations with good humor. Their good humor emerged in their songs—"Goober Peas," "Mister, Here's Your Mule," "Grafted into the Army," "We are the Boys of Potomac's Ranks"—their stories, their campfire jokes, so naïve and innocent for the most part; it spilled over into their letters home and into the diaries and journals they so assiduously kept. There was bitterness enough in the war, especially for the South and for the women of the South, but probably no other great civil war was attended by so little bitterness and no other recorded so many acts of kindness and civility between enemies; certainly no other was so magnanimously concluded. Read over, for example, that moving account of the surrender at Appomattox by Joshua Chamberlain:

Before us in proud humiliation stood the embodiment of manhood: men whom neither toils and sufferings, nor the fact of death, nor disaster, nor hopelessness could bend from their resolve; standing before us now, thin, worn, and famished, but erect, and with eyes looking level into ours, waking memories that bound us together as no other bond;—was not such manhood to be welcomed back into a Union so tested and assured? . . . How could we help falling on our knees, all of us together, and praying God to pity and forgive us all!

The Americans were a moral people and carried their ordinary moral standards over into the conduct of war. They thought aggressive warfare wrong and the war could not get under way until Beauregard had fired on Fort Sumter; Southerners insisted that the firing was self-defense against Yankee aggression. Every war is barbarous, but—Sherman, Hunter, and Sheridan to the contrary notwithstanding—there was less barbarism in the Civil than in most other wars. Both peoples, as Lincoln observed, read the same Bible and prayed to the same God; both armies were devout; leaders on both sides managed to convince themselves that they stood at Armageddon and battled for the Lord. When the end came there was no vengeance and no bloodshed; this was probably the only instance in modern history where rebellion was crushed without punishing its leaders.

Above all, the generation that fought the war had that quality which Emerson ascribed pre-eminently to the English—character. It is an elusive word, as almost all great words are elusive—truth, beauty, courage, loyalty, honor—but we know well enough what it means and know it when we see it. The men in blue and in gray who marched thirty miles a day through the blistering heat of the Bayou Teche, went without food for days on end, shivered through rain and snow in the mountains of Virginia and Tennessee, braved the terrors of hospital and prison, charged to almost certain death on the crest of Cemetery Ridge, closed the gap at the Bloody Angle, ran the batteries of Vicksburg and braved the torpedoes of Mobile Bay, threw away their lives on the hills outside Franklin for a cause they held dear—these men had character. They knew what they were fighting for, as well as men ever know this, and they fought with a tenacity and a courage rarely equaled in history. So, too, their leaders, civil and military. It is, in last analysis, grandeur of character that assures immortality to Lincoln as to Lee, and it is character, too, we admire in Grant and Jackson, Sherman and Longstreet, the brave Reynolds and the gallant Pelham, and a thousand others. Winston Churchill tells us, in his account of Pearl Harbor, that there were some in

England who feared the consequences of that fateful blow and doubted the ability of Americans to stand up to the test of modern war. "But I had studied the American Civil War," he says, "fought out to the last desperate inch," and "I went to bed and slept the sleep of the saved and thankful."

But it is a veteran of the war itself who paid the finest tribute to his comrades in blue and in gray. "Through our great good fortune," said Justice Oliver Wendell Holmes—and he spoke for his whole generation—

in our youth our hearts were touched with fire. It was given us to learn at the outset that life is a profound and passionate thing. While we are permitted to scorn nothing but indifference, and do not pretend to undervalue the worldly rewards of ambition, we have seen with our own eyes, beyond and above the gold fields, the snowy heights of honor, and it is for us to bear the report to those who come after us.

What I have tried to do in these volumes is very simple, but the execution of the task has been far from simple. I have tried to present a well-rounded— I cannot call it complete—history of the Civil War in the words of those who fought it. From the four hundred and fifty-odd narratives which are presented here there will emerge, I hope, a picture of the war that is authentic, coherent, and interesting. All depends, to be sure, on the selection and the editing of the material, and it is relevant therefore to say something about the principles that have governed that selection and about editorial practices.

Only those who have worked in the rich fields of Civil War history know how apparently inexhaustible the material is, and how unorganized. Only the Puritan Revolution and the French Revolutionary and Napoleonic wars boast a comparable literature, and even here the literature is not really comparable. For the American Civil War affected the whole population and, as Edward Dicey remarked in astonishment, it was a highly literate population. Almost everyone could write, and almost everyone, it seems, did. Surely no other chapter of modern history has been so faithfully or so elaborately recorded by ordinary men and women; in the American Civil War Everyman was, indeed, his own historian. A disproportionate body of the available material is, to be sure, from officers or from statesmen; these were the more articulate members of the population and those who could better arrange for the publication of what they wanted to say. But to a remarkable degree the privates kept records, and so too did the folks back home. Their reminiscences, recollections, and journals are to be found not in the handsomely published volumes from the great publishing houses, but in the pages of regimental histories, of state, local, and patriotic historical societies, of magazines that printed letters from veterans or from their families. The richness of this literature is the delight and the despair of every student.

The choice of available material is, in short, fabulously wide. For every episode, every battle, every experience of camp life or discipline or prison, every social practice, there are a dozen first-rate accounts, and for some there are many more. During the twelve years in which I have been collecting material for this book I have tried to read all of these that I could lay my hands on; I do not know how many diaries, journals, letters, autobiographies, biographies, battle and campaign histories, regimental histories, volumes of learned societies, of historical societies, of magazines like the _Confederate Veteran_ or the old _Century_ I have read; that the selection here presented represents only a small fraction of the whole will surprise no one familiar with the field.

My point of departure has not, however, been literature but history. My concern has been the particular battle or campaign, the particular military or social institution, and I have worked out from these to the available literature, selecting not primarily what was interesting for its own sake, or dramatic or eloquent, but what illuminated the subject and the problem. I do not mean to imply that I have been immune to the purely literary appeal, or to the appeal of drama or of personality. Needless to say it is not for authenticity alone that I have preferred Haskell's to a score of other accounts of Pickett's charge, or Chamberlain's to a dozen others of the surrender at Appomattox.

I have tried to cover the whole war; not only the military, which has attracted disproportionate attention, and the naval, but the economic, social, political, and diplomatic as well. The war was not all fighting; it was public opinion, it was the draft, it was prison and hospital, it was ordnance and supplies, it was politics and elections, it was religion, and even play. Approximately half the material in these volumes records the actual fighting; another half is devoted to the other aspects of the war. I have tried to hold even the balance between Union and Confederate, the East and the West, the military and the civil, and to give some representation to women and to foreign observers. I cannot suppose that I have wholly succeeded in all this, for the available material has not always lent itself to a balanced picture. As every student knows, good battle accounts are voluminous but accounts of Intelligence or ordnance or supply are meager, and there are at least two capital descriptions of fighting for every one of politics or diplomacy or even of social conditions. Nor is the balance between the material available from officer and private really even. Almost every leading officer wrote his reminiscences or at least contributed them to the _Battles and Leaders_ series or to one of the meetings of the state Loyal Legion or of the Confederate Veterans, and the temptation to draw on these magisterial accounts has been irresistible. Nor do I feel unduly apologetic about drawing on Grant and Sherman, Longstreet and Hood and others; think what we would give for the war memoirs of R. E. Lee!

Even in the matter of proper representation from Federal and Confederate participants and from the East and the West I have not been entirely a free agent. There are considerably more Union than Confederate narratives— quite naturally, considering the relative numbers involved and the mechanics and economy of publishing. On the whole, however—and I know this is a very dangerous thing to say—the Confederate narratives seem to be of a higher literary quality than the Federal, and this somewhat redresses the quantitative balance. Again, the literature on the fighting in the East, especially in Northern Virginia, is far more voluminous and more interesting than that on the fighting in the West; the reasons for this are not wholly clear, but the fact will not, I think, be disputed by any student of the war and it is one to which an editor must accommodate himself as best he can.

Two types of source material have been deliberately neglected, or discriminated against: official reports and newspapers. I have not, to be sure, been consistent here; the reader will find, in these pages, samples of both. Official reports are invaluable to the historian, but they are for the most part altogether too detailed, too technical, and too dull for use in a book of this character. As for newspaper accounts some of them, like those by "Bull Run" Russell or George Townsend, are indispensable, but most of them, again, are too verbose and detailed for our purposes. Scholars will note, and doubtless deplore, the omission of one other body of source material: I refer to manuscripts. I have examined a good many Civil War manuscripts, but, with the single exception of the Ramseur letters, which I could not resist, I have not used manuscript material in these volumes. A carefully edited documentary source book of the Civil War is badly needed, and so, too, a newspaper history of the war, while any number of volumes can be quarried from the vast mines of manuscript sources. But these are formidable tasks, and each one would have called for another decade of intensive work.

There are, of course, many gaps in these volumes, and these will doubtless pain some readers. Those whose grandfathers were wounded at Perryville will object, quite properly, that that battle is neglected; others whose forebears fought at Fort Pillow will wonder why the massacre is not included; students of economic or social history will doubtless feel that these important subjects have been slighted, while military historians, alive to the importance in our own day of Intelligence or logistics, will feel that the fighting war has been overemphasized. In extenuation I can only plead the obvious. Some of the gaps in these volumes are dictated by considerations of space, others by availability of material. I could not put in everything; I could not even put in everything that was important. As with most books of this kind a good deal more was left out, in the final selection, than was put in, and this with the usual heartburnings. That is part of the story. The other part is that many of the things that interest us most did not appear to interest the generation that fought the war—or that read about it. There are descriptions enough of food and cooking, but no systematic account of the services of supply. There must be a hundred narratives of prison life and prison escape for every one of the organization and administration of prisons. If there is any good analysis of what we now call Intelligence, outside voluminous official correspondence, I do not know it.

Again and again I have had to make choices which were painful to me, however they may affect the reader. Should I attempt to cover the whole of the diplomatic history of the war, or be content with relations with Britain? To have covered the whole—to have included the diplomatic relations of both belligerents with France and Mexico and the Vatican, for example—would have resulted in a fragmentary picture. I decided, I think rightly, to concentrate on that country whose policy was, after all, decisive. Again, what of politics, North and South; what of the westward movement and railroad building that went on during the war; what of the life of the mind and the spirit? I consoled myself that these things were either marginal to the war itself, or were adequately covered in the voluminous histories and source books already available such as McPherson's *Political History of the Great Rebellion* or Frank Moore's *Rebellion Record*.

I have tried in every case to get actual participants and observers to contribute to this co-operative history. Most of the contributors were participants in the physical sense; they experienced what Oliver Wendell Holmes called "the crush of Arctic ice." Others, and among them some of the most sagacious, were "behind the lines": poets who interpreted the significance of the war; diplomats who pleaded their country's cause abroad; women who lived "the lives which women have lead since Troy fell"; surgeons who treated the wounded and chaplains who comforted the dying. All these were participants even though they may not have held a musket, and all have something to tell us of the war.

It would be naïve for me, or for the reader, to suppose that the accounts here reproduced are in every case authentic, or that even the most authentic are wholly reliable. Most of those who claimed to be participants undoubtedly were so, but it would strain our imagination to suppose that all of our reporters actually witnessed everything they described. As every student of evidence knows, people do not always see what they think they see and they do not remember what they saw. There are doubtless many instances where soldiers, writing fifteen or twenty years after the event, deluded themselves, as well as their readers. They embroidered on their original stories; they incorporated into their accounts not only what they had experienced but what they had heard or read elsewhere; they went back and consulted official records and doctored their manuscripts. Soldiers whose companies did not actually get into a battle appear, in written recollections, in the thick of it; hangers-on, who have entertained their friends with the gossip of the capital for years, remember through the haze of time that they themselves directed great affairs of state.

All this is a commonplace of historical criticism, and there is no wholly effective safeguard against it. Diaries, journals, and letters are obviously to be preferred to later recollections, but there is no guarantee that diaries and letters conform to the strictest standards of accuracy and objectivity, or that they come to us untouched by the editorial pen, while many volumes of reminiscences, otherwise suspect for age, are based on diaries and letters and have claims on our confidence. Official reports are doubtless more reliable than merely personal accounts, but even official reports were often written months after the event and colored by imagination or wishful thinking, and there is no sound reason for supposing that the average officer, writing an official report, really knew the whole of what he was writing about.

We must keep in mind, too, that the Civil War was a far more casual affair than more recent wars. There was no proper organization for keeping records or for writing history. Even the most elementary facts are in dispute. It is no exaggeration to say that the statistical picture is a chaos. We do not know the numbers of those who fought on either side, or of those who took part in particular battles, or of casualties, and Confederate figures in these fields are mostly guesswork. Take so simple a matter as executions. Our literature tells us of innumerable executions. But Phisterer, author of a statistical handbook of the war, gives us three widely varying official figures, and historians who have gone into the matter accept none of them. Or take the matter of desertion. Both Ella Lonn and Fred Shannon have dealt with this at length, but about the best they can do for us is to give broad estimates. For what was desertion, after all? Were those who failed to register for conscription deserters, or those who having registered failed to show up? Were bounty jumpers deserters, and how often should one of them be counted? Were those who went home to visit their wives or to help get in the crops, and later returned to the army, deserters? Or what shall we say of the blockade? Was it ever really effective? How many blockade-runners were there, and how many of them got through the blockade? With the most elementary facts of the war in this state of confusion it is perhaps excessive to strain overmuch at discrepancies in accounts of the conduct of a company or a regiment in a particular battle.

Something should be said about the principles governing the reproduction of source material in these volumes. There has been no tinkering with the text except in three very minor details. First, in some instances where paragraphs seemed intolerably long, they have been broken up. Second, while I have faithfully indicated all omissions within any excerpt I have not thought it necessary to put the customary dots at the beginning and end of excerpts: these can usually be taken for granted. Third, in deference to modern usage I have capitalized the word Negro wherever it appears. Aside from these insignificant modifications the text appears here as it appears in the original source to which credit is given in the bibliography.

That authors themselves, or editors—often devoted wives or daughters— have sometimes tinkered with the text is, however, painfully clear. There is no protection against this, and nothing to be done about it short of going back to the original manuscript where that is available; ordinarily it is not available. And this leads me to a more important matter. Not only have I not presumed to correct spelling or punctuation, I have not attempted to correct factual statements or misstatements. To have done so would have involved both me and the reader in a wilderness of controversy. There are, after all, hundreds of histories that attempt to set the facts straight. Careful readers will therefore note many glaring errors in these accounts. Almost every soldier, for example, consistently exaggerated enemy strength, and enemy losses, and two accounts of the same battle will confidently submit wholly inconsistent statistical information. The reader must keep in mind that our contributors are not writing as scholarly historians. They are giving their story from their own point of view—a point of view at once circumscribed and biased. They are not only limited in their knowledge; they are often ignorant, prejudiced, and vain. Sometimes they are on the defensive; sometimes they are repeating rumor and gossip; sometimes they are yielding to the temptation of the purple passage; sometimes they are trying to make a good impression on the folks back home, or on posterity. The reader is warned: they are not always to be trusted. But there are some consolations and some safeguards. As we give both Federal and Confederate accounts the errors often cancel out. The vainglorious give themselves away, and so too the ignorant and the timid, while those who write with an eye on the verdict of history proclaim that fact in every line.

An enterprise of this nature, stretching over more than a decade, naturally incurs a great many debts and obligations. I could not have completed this work without the help of the staff of the Columbia University Library, who endured with patience and good humor continuous raids upon their collections and who co-operated generously in making their Civil War collection one of the best in the country. I am indebted, too, to libraries and librarians elsewhere: the Library of Congress, the New York Public Library, the libraries of Harvard University, the University of Virginia, the University of North Carolina, New York University, the University of California, to name but a few. To my graduate students who have helped in the arduous work of tracking down elusive books, transcribing and photostating, I am deeply indebted, and especially to Mrs. Elizabeth Kelley Bauer, Mr. Wilson Smith, and Mr. Leonard Levy. The editorial and production departments of The Bobbs-Merrill Company have co-operated far beyond the call of duty, and I owe a great deal to the sagacious judgment of Mr. Laurance Chambers, the astute editorial eye of Miss Judith Henley, the imaginative co-operation of Mr. Walter Hurley. To the many publishers, historical societies, university presses, and private individuals who have so generously given me permission to reproduce material in their control I am deeply grateful. To my wife, who magnanimously permitted the Yankees to win an occasional victory in these pages, my debt is, of course, beyond expression.

HENRY STEELE COMMAGER

Williamsville, Vermont
1950
Amherst, Massachusetts
1982

THE BLUE AND THE GRAY

VOLUME I

I

Darkening Clouds

WITH *the deeper causes of the Civil War we are not concerned, nor with the question which has commanded so much speculation, whether the war was a repressible or an irrepressible conflict. What is certain is that the leaders of the Deep South had convinced themselves, by December 1860, that separation was essential to the preservation of the "peculiar institution," and to the social and economic prosperity of their section. Whether these views fairly represented majority opinion, even in the Deep South, we do not and cannot know; all we can say is that there were substantial elements in every Southern state which did not subscribe to them and even larger elements which opposed secession. Unionist sentiment was particularly strong in the border states—Maryland, Virginia, Kentucky, Tennessee, and Missouri, and in North Carolina which had never been so deeply committed to slavery or the plantation system as other Southern states.*

The political machinery of most Southern states was in the hands of the secessionists; this was particularly the case in South Carolina, least democratic of states in its political organization. With the triumph of the Republicans in the November elections—a triumph which was far from giving that party a complete control of the government however—Southern hotheads decided to act, and South Carolina led the way. There were frantic efforts at compromise, North and South, but all foundered. One reason for their failure was the unwillingness or inability of Lincoln to accept any compromise which extended the area open to slavery; another was the conviction of Southern extremists that separation was inevitable and that compromise, on no matter what terms, would leave the South in a relatively weaker position for the future. So while Buchanan vacillated and the North marked time, the Deep South seceded and organized as an independent nation. With the secession of Virginia, in April, the capital was moved to Richmond and a permanent government established.

Meantime Lincoln, too, had organized his Cabinet—a Cabinet of all factions rather than all talents—and in his Inaugural Address appealed to "my countrymen, one and all" to sink their differences in a common patriotism. The appeal was in vain.

1. ABRAHAM LINCOLN IS NOMINATED IN THE WIGWAM

It was the nomination and subsequent election of the "Black Republican," Lincoln, that precipitated secession and, in the end, war. Lincoln actually

1

represented no immediate threat to the South, but many leading Southerners were convinced that Republican control of the Presidency and of Congress would, in the end, doom the "peculiar institution" of slavery and that separation was "now or never."

The story of Lincoln's nomination is here told by Murat Halstead, one of the most brilliant journalists of the day and long editor of the Cincinnati Commercial.

THIRD day [May 18, 1860].—After adjournment on Thursday (the second day) there were few men in Chicago who believed it possible to prevent the nomination of Seward. His friends had played their game to admiration and had been victorious on every preliminary skirmish. When the platform had been adopted, inclusive of the Declaration of Independence, they felt themselves already exalted upon the pinnacle of victory. They rejoiced exceedingly, and full of confidence, cried in triumphant tones, "Call the roll of states." But it was otherwise ordered. The opponents of Mr. Seward left the wigwam that evening thoroughly disheartened. Greeley was, as has been widely reported, absolutely "terrified." The nomination of Seward in defiance of his influence would have been a cruel blow. He gave up the ship. . . .

The New Yorkers were exultant. Their bands were playing and the champagne flowing at their headquarters as after a victory.

But there was much done after midnight and before the convention assembled on Friday morning. There were hundreds of Pennsylvanians, Indianians, and Illinoisians who never closed their eyes that night. I saw Henry S. Lane at one o'clock, pale and haggard, with cane under his arm, walking as if for a wager, from one caucus room to another, at the Tremont House. He had been toiling with desperation to bring the Indiana delegation to go as a unit for Lincoln. And then in connection with others, he had been operating to bring the Vermonters and Virginians to the point of deserting Seward.

The Seward men generally abounded in confidence Friday morning. The air was full of rumors of the caucusing the night before, but the opposition of the doubtful states to Seward was an old story; and after the distress of Pennsylvania, Indiana and Company on the subject of Seward's availability had been so freely and ineffectually expressed from the start, it was not imagined their protests would suddenly become effective. The Sewardites marched as usual from their headquarters at the Richmond House after their magnificent band, which was brilliantly uniformed—epaulets shining on their shoulders and white and scarlet feathers waving from their caps—marched under the orders of recognized leaders, in a style that would have done credit to many volunteer military companies. They were about a thousand strong, and protracting their march a little too far, were not all able to get into the wigwam. This was their first misfortune. They were not where they could scream with the best effect in responding to the mention of the name of William H. Seward.

When the convention was called to order, breathless attention was given the proceedings. There was not a space a foot square in the wigwam un-occupied. There were tens of thousands still outside, and torrents of men had rushed in at the three broad doors until not another one could squeeze in.

Everybody was now impatient to begin the work. Mr. Evarts of New York nominated Mr. Seward. Mr. Judd of Illinois nominated Mr. Lincoln.

Everybody felt that the fight was between them and yelled accordingly. The applause when Mr. Evarts named Seward was enthusiastic. When Mr. Judd named Lincoln, the response was prodigious, rising and raging far beyond the Seward shriek. Presently, upon Caleb B. Smith seconding the nomination of Lincoln, the response was absolutely terrific. It now became the Seward men to make another effort, and when Blair of Michigan sec-onded his nomination,

> At once there rose so wild a yell,
> Within that dark and narrow dell;
> As all the fiends from heaven that fell
> Had pealed the banner cry of hell.

The effect was startling. Hundreds of persons stopped their ears in pain. The shouting was absolutely frantic, shrill and wild. No Comanches, no panthers, ever struck a higher note or gave screams with more infernal in-tensity. Looking from the stage over the vast amphitheater, nothing was to be seen below but thousands of hats—a black, mighty swarm of hats—flying with the velocity of hornets over a mass of human heads, most of the mouths of which were open. Above, all around the galleries, hats and handkerchiefs were flying in the tempest together. The wonder of the thing was that the Seward outside pressure should, so far from New York, be so powerful.

Now the Lincoln men had to try it again, and as Mr. Delano of Ohio on behalf "of a portion of the delegation of that state" seconded the nomination of Lincoln, the uproar was beyond description. Imagine all the hogs ever slaughtered in Cincinnati giving their death squeals together, a score of big steam whistles going (steam at a hundred and sixty pounds per inch), and you conceive something of the same nature. I thought the Seward yell could not be surpassed, but the Lincoln boys were clearly ahead and, feeling their vic-tory, as there was a lull in the storm, took deep breaths all round and gave a concentrated shriek that was positively awful, and accompanied it with stamping that made every plank and pillar in the building quiver.

Henry S. Lane of Indiana leaped upon a table, and swinging hat and cane, performed like an acrobat. The presumption is he shrieked with the rest, as his mouth was desperately wide open; but no one will ever be able to testify that he has positive knowledge of the fact that he made a particle of noise. His individual voice was lost in the aggregate hurricane.

The New York, Michigan, and Wisconsin delegations sat together and were in this tempest very quiet. Many of their faces whitened as the Lincoln *yawp* swelled into a wild hosanna of victory.

The convention now proceeded to business. The most significant vote was that of Virginia, which had been expected solid for Seward, and which now gave him but eight and gave Lincoln fourteen. The New Yorkers looked significantly at each other as this was announced. Then Indiana gave her twenty-six votes for Lincoln. This solid vote was a startler. The division of the first vote caused a fall in Seward stock. It was seen that Lincoln, Cameron, and Bates had the strength to defeat Seward, and it was known that the greater part of the Chase vote would go for Lincoln.

The convention proceeded to a second ballot. Every man was fiercely enlisted in the struggle. The partisans of the various candidates were strung up to such a pitch of excitement as to render them incapable of patience, and the cries of "Call the roll" were fairly hissed through their teeth. The first gain for Lincoln was in New Hampshire. The Chase and the Frémont vote from that state were given him. His next gain was the whole vote of Vermont. This was a blighting blow upon the Seward interest. The New Yorkers started as if an Orsini bomb had exploded. And presently the Cameron vote of Pennsylvania was thrown for Lincoln, increasing his strength forty-four votes. The fate of the day was now determined. New York saw "checkmate" next move and sullenly proceeded with the game, assuming unconsciousness of her inevitable doom. On this ballot Lincoln gained seventy-nine votes. Seward had one hundred and eighty-four and a half votes, Lincoln one hundred and eighty-one. . . .

While this [the third] ballot was taken amid excitement that tested the nerves, the fatal defection from Seward in New England still further appeared, four votes going over from Seward to Lincoln in Massachusetts. The latter received four additional votes from Pennsylvania and fifteen additional votes from Ohio. It was whispered about: "Lincoln's the coming man—will be nominated this ballot." When the roll of states and territories had been called, I had ceased to give attention to any votes but those for Lincoln and had his vote added up as it was given. The number of votes necessary to a choice were two hundred and thirty-three, and I saw under my pencil as the Lincoln column was completed the figures 231½—one vote and a half to give him the nomination. In a moment the fact was whispered about. A hundred pencils had told the same story. The news went over the house wonderfully, and there was a pause. There are always men anxious to distinguish themselves on such occasions. There is nothing that politicians like better than a crisis. I looked up to see who would be the man to give the decisive vote. In about ten ticks of a watch, Cartter of Ohio was up. I had imagined Ohio would be slippery enough for the crisis. And sure enough! Every eye was on Cartter, and everybody who understood the matter at all knew what he was about to do. He said: "I rise (eh), Mr. Chairman (eh), to announce the change of four votes of Ohio from Mr. Chase to Mr. Lincoln." The deed was done. There was a moment's silence. The nerves of the thousands, which through the hours of suspense had been subjected to terrible tension, relaxed, and as deep breaths of relief were taken, there was a noise in the wigwam like the rush of a great wind in the van of a storm—and in another breath, the storm was there. There were thousands cheering with the energy of insanity.

A man who had been on the roof and was engaged in communicating the results of the ballotings to the mighty mass of outsiders now demanded, by gestures at the skylight over the stage, to know what had happened. One of the secretaries, with a tally sheet in his hands, shouted: "Fire the salute! Abe Lincoln is nominated!"

The city was wild with delight. The "Old Abe" men formed processions and bore rails through the streets. Torrents of liquor were poured down the hoarse throats of the multitude. A hundred guns were fired from the top of the Tremont House.

I left the city on the night train on the Fort Wayne and Chicago road. The train consisted of eleven cars, every seat full and people standing in the aisles and corners. I never before saw a company of persons so prostrated by continued excitement. The Lincoln men were not able to respond to the cheers which went up along the road for "Old Abe." They had not only done their duty in that respect, but exhausted their capacity. At every station where there was a village, until after two o'clock, there were tar barrels burning, drums beating, boys carrying rails, and guns, great and small, banging away. The weary passengers were allowed no rest, but plagued by the thundering jar of cannon, the clamor of drums, the glare of bonfires, and the whooping of the boys, who were delighted with the idea of a candidate for the Presidency who thirty years ago split rails on the Sangamon River—classic stream now and forevermore—and whose neighbors named him "honest."

—HALSTEAD, *Caucuses of 1860*

2. "FIRST GALLANT SOUTH CAROLINA NOBLY MADE THE STAND"

Immediately upon the election of Lincoln the legislature of South Carolina called a convention to meet on December 17 to consider the question of secession. The convention met first at Columbia, then adjourned to Charleston, where, on December 20, it voted unanimously for secession, issuing at the same time a Declaration of Causes which emphasized above all the threat to slavery. By February 1861, six other states had joined South Carolina—Mississippi, Florida, Alabama, Georgia, Louisiana, and Texas—and delegates from these states shortly met at Montgomery, Alabama, to organize the Confederate States of America, draw up a Constitution, and name Jefferson Davis of Mississippi as provisional President.

A. SOUTH CAROLINA ORDINANCE OF SECESSION
December 20, 1860

AN *Ordinance to Dissolve the Union between the State of South Carolina and other States united with her under the compact entitled the Constitution of the United States of America:*

We, the people of the State of South Carolina, in Convention assembled, do declare and ordain, and it is hereby declared and ordained, that the ordinance adopted by us in Convention, on the 23d day of May, in the year of our Lord 1788, whereby the Constitution of the United States of America was ratified, and also all Acts and parts of Acts of the General Assembly of this State ratifying the amendments of the said Constitution, are hereby repealed, and that the union now subsisting between South Carolina and other States under the name of the United States of America is hereby dissolved.

B. SOUTH CAROLINA DECLARATION OF CAUSES OF SECESSION
December 24, 1860

The people of the State of South Carolina in Convention assembled, on the 2d day of April, A.D. 1852, declared that the frequent violations of the Constitution of the United States by the Federal Government, and its encroachments upon the reserved rights of the States, fully justified this State in their withdrawal from the Federal Union; but in deference to the opinions and wishes of the other Slaveholding States, she forbore at that time to exercise this right. Since that time these encroachments have continued to increase, and further forbearance ceases to be a virtue.

And now the State of South Carolina having resumed her separate and equal place among nations, deems it due to herself, to the remaining United States of America, and to the nations of the world, that she should declare the immediate causes which have led to this act. . . .

We affirm that these ends for which this Government was instituted have been defeated, and the Government itself has been destructive of them by the action of the nonslaveholding States. Those States have assumed the right of deciding upon the propriety of our domestic institutions; and have denied the rights of property established in fifteen of the States and recognized by the Constitution; they have denounced as sinful the institution of Slavery; they have permitted the open establishment among them of societies, whose avowed object is to disturb the peace of and eloin the property of the citizens of other States. They have encouraged and assisted thousands of our slaves to leave their homes; and those who remain, have been incited by emissaries, books, and pictures, to servile insurrection.

For twenty-five years this agitation has been steadily increasing, until it has now secured to its aid the power of the common Government. Observing the *forms* of the Constitution, a sectional party has found within that article establishing the Executive Department, the means of subverting the Constitution itself. A geographical line has been drawn across the Union, and all the States north of that line have united in the election of a man to the high office of President of the United States whose opinions and purposes are hostile to Slavery. He is to be intrusted with the administration of the common Government, because he has declared that "Government cannot endure permanently half slave, half free," and that the public mind must rest in the belief that Slavery is in the course of ultimate extinction.

This sectional combination for the subversion of the Constitution has been aided, in some of the States, by elevating to citizenship persons who, by the supreme law of the land, are incapable of becoming citizens; and their votes have been used to inaugurate a new policy, hostile to the South, and destructive of its peace and safety.

On the 4th of March next this party will take possession of the Government. It has announced that the South shall be excluded from the common territory, that the Judicial tribunal shall be made sectional, and that a war must be waged against Slavery until it shall cease throughout the United States.

The guarantees of the Constitution will then no longer exist; the equal rights of the States will be lost. The Slaveholding States will no longer have the power of self-government, or self-protection, and the Federal Government will have become their enemy.

Sectional interest and animosity will deepen the irritation; and all hope of remedy is rendered vain, by the fact that the public opinion at the North has invested a great political error with the sanctions of a more erroneous religious belief.

We, therefore, the people of South Carolina, by our delegates in Convention assembled, appealing to the Supreme Judge of the world for the rectitude of our intentions, have solemnly declared that the Union heretofore existing between this State and the other States of North America is dissolved, and that the State of South Carolina has resumed her position among the nations of the world, as a separate and independent state, with full power to levy war, conclude peace, contract alliances, establish commerce, and to do all other acts and things which independent States may of right do.

—MOORE, ed., *The Rebellion Record*

3. "SHE HAS LEFT US IN PASSION AND PRIDE"

Although Oliver Wendell Holmes published his first volume of poems in 1836 he devoted himself, for the next twenty years, almost entirely to medicine, serving as professor of anatomy and dean of the Harvard Medical School. With the founding of the Atlantic Monthly *in 1857 he came into his own as essayist and poet. To this magazine he contributed* The Autocrat of the Breakfast Table *and* The Professor at the Breakfast Table, *and in it appeared many of his best-known poems. It was to the* Atlantic, *too, that he contributed his famous "My Hunt after the Captain"—the story of his search for his son, wounded at Antietam.*

This poem is notable chiefly for its expression in poetry of what Lincoln said in his First Inaugural Address.

Brother Jonathan's Lament for Sister Caroline

She has gone,—she has left us in passion and pride,—
Our stormy-browed sister, so long at our side!
She has torn her own star from our firmament's glow,
And turned on her brother the face of a foe!

O Caroline, Caroline, child of the sun,
We can never forget that our hearts have been one,—
Our foreheads both sprinkled in Liberty's name,
From the fountain of blood with the finger of flame!

You were always too ready to fire at a touch;
But we said, "She is hasty,—she does not mean much."
We have scowled, when you uttered some turbulent threat;
But Friendship still whispered, "Forgive and forget!"

Has our love all died out? Have its altars grown cold?
Has the curse come at last which the fathers foretold?
Then Nature must teach us the strength of the chain
That her petulant children would sever in vain.

They may fight till the buzzards are gorged with their spoil,
Till the harvest grows black as it rots in the soil,
Till the wolves and the catamounts troop from their caves,
And the shark tracks the pirate, the lord of the waves:

In vain is the strife! When its fury is past,
Their fortunes must flow in one channel at last,
As the torrents that rush from the mountains of snow
Roll mingled in peace through the valleys below.

Our Union is river, lake, ocean, and sky:
Man breaks not the medal, when God cuts the die!
Though darkened with sulphur, though cloven with steel,
The blue arch will brighten, the waters will heal!

O Caroline, Caroline, child of the sun,
There are battles with Fate that can never be won!
The star-flowering banner must never be furled,
For its blossoms of light are the hope of the world!

Go, then, our rash sister! afar and aloof,
Run wild in the sunshine away from our roof;
But when your heart aches and your feet have grown sore,
Remember the pathway that leads to our door!
                                    —HOLMES, *Poems*

March 25, 1861

4. LINCOLN REFUSES TO COMPROMISE ON SLAVERY

Secession brought frantic efforts to find some compromise which might restore the Union and avoid the danger of a brothers' war. The most prominent of these proposals was the Crittenden Compromise which provided for the extension of the Missouri Compromise line of 36°-30' westward to Cali-

*fornia—a proposal which would have opened new territory in the West to
slavery. It was on this issue that Lincoln, who was otherwise conciliatory,
refused to yield. E. B. Washburne was a representative from the Galena district of Illinois, a friend of both Lincoln and Grant, and one of four brothers
who were in Congress—the others all spelled their name without the final
"e." James T. Hale was a representative from Pennsylvania. Seward, Lincoln's principal rival for the Republican nomination, had already accepted
Lincoln's offer to make him Secretary of State.*

A. Letter to E. B. Washburne
(*Private and Confidential*)

Springfield, Ill., December 13, 1860

Hon. E. B. Washburne.

My Dear Sir:—Yours of the 10th is received. Prevent, as far as possible,
any of our friends from demoralizing themselves and our cause by entertaining propositions for compromise of any sort on "slavery extension." There
is no possible compromise upon it but which puts us under again, and leaves
all our work to do over again. Whether it be a Missouri line or Eli Thayer's
popular sovereignty, it is all the same. Let either be done, and immediately
filibustering and extending slavery recommences. On that point hold firm,
as with a chain of steel.

Yours as ever,

A. Lincoln.

B. Letter to James T. Hale
(*Confidential*)

Springfield, Illinois, January 11, 1861

My Dear Sir: Yours of the 6th is received. I answer it only because I fear
you would misconstrue my silence. What is our present condition? We have
just carried an election on principles fairly stated to the people. Now we are
told in advance the Government shall be broken up unless we surrender to
those we have beaten, before we take the offices. In this they are either
attempting to play upon us or they are in dead earnest. Either way, if
we surrender, it is the end of us and of the Government. They will repeat
the experiment upon us *ad libitum*. A year will not pass till we shall have to
take Cuba as a condition upon which they will stay in the Union. They now
have the Constitution under which we have lived over seventy years, and acts
of Congress of their own framing, with no prospect of their being changed;
and they can never have a more shallow pretext for breaking up the Government, or extorting a compromise, than now. There is in my judgment but
one compromise which would really settle the slavery question, and that
would be a prohibition against acquiring any more territory.

C. LETTER TO W. H. SEWARD
(*Private and Confidential*)

Springfield, Illinois, February 1, 1861

My Dear Sir: . . . I say now . . . as I have all the while said, that on the territorial question—that is, the question of extending slavery under the national auspices—I am inflexible. I am for no compromise which assists or permits the extension of the institution on soil owned by the nation. And any trick by which the nation is to acquire territory, and then allow some local authority to spread slavery over it, is as obnoxious as any other. I take it that to effect some such result as this, and to put us again on the highroad to a slave empire, is the object of all these proposed compromises. I am against it. As to fugitive slaves, District of Columbia, slave trade among the slave States, and whatever springs of necessity from the fact that the institution is amongst us, I care but little, so that what is done be comely and not altogether outrageous. Nor do I care much about New Mexico, if further extension were hedged against.

—*Complete Works of Abraham Lincoln*

5. LINCOLN WRITES HIS INAUGURAL ADDRESS

This account of Lincoln's preparation for his Inauguration is given us by his law partner and friend, William Henry Herndon. It was in 1844 that Herndon joined Lincoln's office; when Lincoln went to Washington he asked Herndon to keep the old sign, Lincoln & Herndon, until he returned. After Lincoln's death Herndon devoted himself to collecting materials for a biography of his great friend. Some of these were sold to Ward Lamon and others were made available to other biographers. As an old man Herndon produced, in association with Jesse Weik, Herndon's Lincoln. The biography was notable for its frankness about Lincoln's early life and his marriage, and for its support to the Ann Rutledge story.

LATE in January Mr. Lincoln informed me that he was ready to begin the preparation of his inaugural address. He had, aside from his law books and the few gilded volumes that ornamented the centre-table in his parlor at home, comparatively no library. He never seemed to care to own or collect books. On the other hand I had a very respectable collection, and was adding to it every day. To my library Lincoln very frequently had access. When, therefore, he began on his inaugural speech he told me what works he intended to consult. I looked for a long list, but when he went over it I was greatly surprised. He asked me to furnish him with Henry Clay's great speech delivered in 1850; Andrew Jackson's proclamation against Nullification; and a copy of the Constitution. He afterwards called for Webster's reply to Hayne, a speech which he read when he lived at New Salem, and which he always regarded as the grandest specimen of American oratory.

With these few "volumes," and no further sources of reference, he locked himself up in a room upstairs over a store across the street from the State House, and there, cut off from all communication and intrusion, he prepared the address. Though composed amid the unromantic surroundings of a dingy, dusty, and neglected back room, the speech has become a memorable document. . . .

Early in February the last item of preparation for the journey to Washington had been made. Mr. Lincoln had disposed of his household goods and furniture to a neighbor, had rented his house; and as these constituted all the property he owned in Illinois there was no further occasion for concern on that score. In the afternoon of his last day in Springfield he came down to our office to examine some papers and confer with me about certain legal matters in which he still felt some interest. On several previous occasions he had told me he was coming over to the office "to have a long talk with me," as he expressed it. We ran over the books and arranged for the completion of all unsettled and unfinished matters. In some cases he had certain requests to make—certain lines of procedure he wished me to observe. After these things were all disposed of he crossed to the opposite side of the room and threw himself down on the old office sofa, which, after many years of service, had been moved against the wall for support.

He lay for some moments, his face towards the ceiling, without either of us speaking. Presently he inquired, "Billy,"—he always called me by that name,—"how long have we been together?" "Over sixteen years," I answered. "We've never had a cross word during all that time, have we?" to which I returned a vehement, "No, indeed we have not." He then recalled some incidents of his early practice and took great pleasure in delineating the ludicrous features of many a lawsuit on the circuit. It was at this last interview in Springfield that he told me of the efforts that had been made by other lawyers to supplant me in the partnership with him. He insisted that such men were weak creatures, who, to use his own language, "hoped to secure a law practice by hanging to his coattail."

I never saw him in a more cheerful mood. He gathered a bundle of books and papers he wished to take with him and started to go; but before leaving he made the strange request that the sign-board which swung on its rusty hinges at the foot of the stairway should remain. "Let it hang there undisturbed," he said, with a significant lowering of his voice. "Give our clients to understand that the election of a President makes no change in the firm of Lincoln and Herndon. If I live I'm coming back some time, and then we'll go right on practicing law as if nothing had ever happened." He lingered for a moment as if to take a last look at the old quarters, and then passed through the door into the narrow hallway.

I accompanied him downstairs. On the way he spoke of the unpleasant features surrounding the Presidential office. "I am sick of office-holding already," he complained, "and I shudder when I think of the tasks that are still ahead." He said the sorrow of parting from his old associates was deeper than most persons would imagine, but it was more marked in his case because of the feeling which had become irrepressible that he would never return alive. I argued against the thought, characterizing it as an illusory notion not in harmony or keeping with the popular ideal of a President. "But it is in keeping with my philosophy," was his quick retort.

Our conversation was frequently broken in upon by the interruptions of passers-by, who, each in succession, seemed desirous of claiming his attention. At length he broke away from them all. Grasping my hand warmly and with a fervent "Good-bye," he disappeared down the street, and never came back to the office again.

—WEIK, *Herndon's Lincoln*

6. LINCOLN IS INAUGURATED

On February 11 Lincoln left Springfield for Washington, planning to make a number of speeches en route. Because of threats of assassination, which his friends took seriously, the last stage of the trip, from Philadelphia to Washington, was made in complete secrecy.

Three descriptions are here given of the Inauguration—one from Herndon; another, written on the day itself, from young Wilder Dwight, member of a distinguished Massachusetts family and major of the 2nd Massachusetts Infantry; and the third from the mysterious Public Man whose identity—if indeed he ever existed—is still a secret. Frank Maloy Anderson, the most careful student of the "Public Man," concludes that the "Diary" itself was a fabrication, and that the author of the fabrication was probably Samuel Ward. Herndon's book was not published until a decade after the appearance, in the North American Review, of the "Diary of a Public Man," and it may have been from this "Diary" that Herndon took his story of Douglas holding Lincoln's hat at the Inauguration. Whether the story is true or not, it belongs to the folklore of our history.

A. HERNDON DESCRIBES THE INAUGURATION

HAVING at last reached his destination in safety, Mr. Lincoln spent the few days preceding his inauguration at Willard's Hotel, receiving an uninterrupted stream of visitors and friends. In the few unoccupied moments allotted him, he was carefully revising his inaugural address. On the morning of the 4th of March he rode from his hotel with Mr. Buchanan in an open barouche to the Capitol. There, slightly pale and nervous, he was introduced to the assembled multitude by his own friend Edward D. Baker, and in a fervid and impressive manner delivered his address. At its conclusion the customary oath was administered by the venerable Chief Justice Taney, and he was now clothed with all the powers and privileges of Chief Magistrate of the nation. He accompanied Mr. Buchanan to the White House and here the historic bachelor of Lancaster bade him farewell, bespeaking for him a peaceful, prosperous, and successful administration.

One who witnessed the impressive scene left the following graphic description of the inauguration and its principal incidents: "Near noon I found myself a member of the motley crowd gathered about the side entrance to Willard's Hotel. Soon an open barouche drove up, and the only occupant stepped out. A large, heavy, awkward-moving man, far advanced in years, short and thin gray hair, full face, plentifully seamed and wrinkled, head curiously inclined to the left shoulder, a low-crowned, broad-brimmed silk hat, an immense white cravat like a poultice, thrusting the old-fashioned standing collar up to the ears, dressed in black throughout, with swallow-tail coat not of the newest style. It was President Buchanan, calling to take his successor to the Capitol. In a few minutes he reappeared, with Mr. Lincoln on his arm; the two took seats side-by-side, and the carriage rolled away, followed by a rather disorderly and certainly not very imposing procession.

"I had ample time to walk to the Capitol, and no difficulty in securing a place where everything could be seen and heard to the best advantage. The attendance at the inauguration was, they told me, unusually small, many being kept away by anticipated disturbance, as it had been rumored—truly, too—that General Scott himself was fearful of an outbreak, and had made all possible military preparations to meet the emergency. A square platform had been built out from the steps to the eastern portico, with benches for distinguished spectators on three sides. Douglas, the only one I recognized, sat at the extreme end of the seat on the right of the narrow passage leading from the steps.

"There was no delay, and the gaunt form of the President-elect was soon visible, slowly making his way to the front. To me, at least, he was completely metamorphosed—partly by his own fault, and partly through the efforts of injudicious friends and ambitious tailors. He was raising (to gratify a very young lady, it is said) a crop of whiskers, of the blacking-brush variety, coarse, stiff, and ungraceful; and in so doing spoiled, or at least seriously impaired, a face which, though never handsome, had in its original state a peculiar power and pathos. On the present occasion the whiskers were reinforced by brand-new clothes from top to toe; black dresscoat, instead of the usual frock, black cloth or satin vest, black pantaloons, and a glossy hat evidently just out of the box. To cap the climax of novelty, he carried a huge ebony cane, with a gold head the size of an egg. In these, to him, strange habiliments, he looked so miserably uncomfortable that I could not help pitying him.

"Reaching the platform, his discomfort was visibly increased by not knowing what to do with hat and cane; and so he stood there, the target for ten thousand eyes, holding cane in one hand and hat in the other, the very picture of helpless embarrassment. After some hesitation he pushed the cane into a corner of the railing, but could not find a place for the hat except on the floor, where I could see he did not like to risk it. Douglas, who fully took in the situation, came to the rescue of his old friend and rival, and held the precious hat until the owner needed it again; a service which, if predicted two years before, would probably have astonished him.

"The oath of office was administered by Chief Justice Taney, whose black robes, attenuated figure, and cadaverous countenance reminded me of a galvanized corpse. Then the President came forward, and read his inaugural address in a clear and distinct voice. It was attentively listened to by all, but the closest listener was Douglas, who leaned forward as if to catch every word, nodding his head emphatically at those passages which most pleased him. There was some applause, not very much nor very enthusiastic.

"I must not forget to mention the presence of a Mephistopheles in the person of Senator Wigfall, of Texas, who stood with folded arms leaning against the doorway of the Capitol, looking down upon the crowd and the ceremony with a contemptuous air, which sufficiently indicated his opinion of the whole performance. To him the Southern Confederacy was already an accomplished fact. He lived to see it the saddest of fictions."

—WEIK, *Herndon's Lincoln*

B. WILDER DWIGHT SEES LINCOLN INAUGURATED

Washington, March 4, 1861

Dear Father,—

This morning broke badly, but at noon the sky cleared. I remained quietly at Willard's, and was present when Mr. Buchanan came to receive the President elect, and saw the interview, which was a formal one; then I saw Lincoln and Buchanan take their carriage, and, by back streets, reached the Capitol grounds, and got a good place.

Soon Lincoln and Judge Taney, followed by Buchanan and the other judges, etc. appeared. The band played Hail Columbia. The crowd was immense. The Capitol steps were covered with uniforms, etc. Baker, of Oregon, for the Committee of Arrangements, announced that Mr. Lincoln would speak; and when Abraham rose and came forward and rang out the words, 'Fellow-citizens of the *United* States,' he loomed and grew and was ugly no longer. I was not very near, but heard him perfectly. The address you will read, and like, I hope. Its effect was very good. An immense concourse—thousands—stood uncovered and silent, except occasional applause; the voice clear and ringing; the manner very good, often impressive, and even solemn; the words I think to the point, direct and clear. The scene itself was of its own kind. And I must say its effect upon me was far greater than I had supposed.

When the address closed and the cheering subsided, Taney rose, and, almost as tall as Lincoln, he administered the oath, Lincoln repeating it; and as the words, 'preserve, protect and defend the Constitution' came ringing out, he bent and kissed the book; and for one, I breathed freer and gladder than for months. The man looked a man, and acted a man and a President. So much for the inauguration.

—DWIGHT, *The Life and Letters of Wilder Dwight*

C. The Public Man Attends the Inauguration

Washington, March 4th.—I am sure we must attribute to the mischievous influence of the Blairs the deplorable display of perfectly unnecessary, and worse than unnecessary, military force which marred the inauguration to-day, and jarred so scandalously upon the tone of the inaugural. Nothing could have been more ill-advised or more ostentatious than the way in which the troops were thrust everywhere upon the public attention, even to the roofs of the houses on Pennsylvania Avenue, on which little squads of sharp-shooters were absurdly stationed. I never expected to experience such a sense of mortification and shame in my own country as I felt to-day, in entering the Capitol through hedges of marines armed to the teeth. ——, of Massachusetts, who felt as I did—indeed, I have yet to find a man who did not—recalled to me, as we sat in the Senate-chamber, the story of old Josiah Quincy, the President of Harvard College, who, having occasion to visit the Boston court-house during one of the fugitive-slave excitements in that city, found the way barred by an iron chain. The sentinels on duty recognized him, and stooped to raise the chain, that he might pass in, but the old man indignantly refused, and turned away, declaring that he would never pass into a Massachusetts court-house by the favor of armed men or under a chain.

It is really amazing that General Scott should have consented to preside over such a pestilent and foolish parade of force at this time, and I can only attribute his doing so to the agitation in which he is kept by the constant pressure upon him from Virginia, of which I heard only too much to-day from ——, who returned yesterday from Richmond. Fortunately, all passed off well, but it is appalling to think of the mischief which might have been done by a single evil-disposed person to-day. A blank cartridge fired from a window on Pennsylvania Avenue might have disconcerted all our hopes, and thrown the whole country into inextricable confusion.

That nothing of the sort was done, or even so much as attempted, is the most conclusive evidence that could be asked of the groundlessness of the rumors and old women's tales on the strength of which General Scott has been led into this great mistake. Even without this the atmosphere of the day would have been depressing enough. It has been one of our disagreeable, clear, windy, Washington spring days. The arrangements within the Capitol were awkward, and very ill attended to. No one was at his ease. Neither Mr. Buchanan nor Mr. Lincoln appeared to advantage. Poor Chief-Justice Taney could hardly speak plainly, in his uncontrollable agitation.

I must, however, except Senator Douglas, whose conduct can not be over-praised. I saw him for a moment in the morning, when he told me that he meant to put himself as prominently forward in the ceremonies as he properly could, and to leave no doubt on any one's mind of his determination to stand by the new Administration in the performance of its first great duty to maintain the Union. I watched him carefully. He made his way not without difficulty—for there was literally no sort of order in the arrangements—

to the front of the throng directly beside Mr. Lincoln, when he prepared to read the address. A miserable little rickety table had been provided for the President, on which he could hardly find room for his hat, and Senator Douglas, reaching forward, took it with a smile and held it during the delivery of the address. It was a trifling act, but a symbolical one, and not to be forgotten, and it attracted much attention all around me.

Mr. Lincoln was pale and very nervous, and did not read his address very well, which is not much to be wondered at under all the circumstances. His spectacles troubled him, his position was crowded and uncomfortable, and, in short, nothing had been done which ought to have been done to render the performance of this great duty either dignified in its effect or, physically speaking, easy for the President.

The great crowd in the grounds behaved very well, but manifested little or no enthusiasm, and at one point in the speech Mr. Lincoln was thrown completely off his balance for a moment by a crash not far in front of him among the people, followed by something which for an instant looked like a struggle. I was not undisturbed myself, nor were those who were immediately about me; but it appeared directly that nothing more serious had happened than the fall from a breaking bough of a spectator who had clambered up into one of the trees.

Mr. Lincoln's agitation was remarked, and I have no doubt must have been caused by the impressions which the alarmists have been trying so sedulously to make on his mind, and which the exaggerated preparations of General Scott to-day are but too likely to have deepened.

—Rice, ed., "The Diary of a Public Man"

7. "WE ARE NOT ENEMIES BUT FRIENDS"

In his eloquent and moving Inaugural Address, Lincoln insisted that the Union is perpetual and secession unconstitutional and void, and asserted that the government was determined to maintain its authority. At the same time he argued the physical impossibility of separation and urged the Southern people to return to their old place in the American household. The moving final paragraph was probably Seward's contribution.

THAT there are persons in one section or another who seek to destroy the Union at all events and are glad of any pretext to do it, I will neither affirm nor deny; but if there be such, I need address no word to them. To those, however, who really love the Union may I not speak?

Before entering upon so grave a matter as the destruction of our national fabric, with all its benefits, its memories, and its hopes, would it not be wise to ascertain precisely why we do it? Will you hazard so desperate a step while there is any possibility that any portion of the ills you fly from have no real existence? Will you, while the certain ills you fly to are greater than all the real ones you fly from—will you risk the commission of so fearful a mistake? . . .

Physically speaking, we cannot separate. We cannot remove our respective sections from each other, nor build an impassable wall between them. A husband and wife may be divorced and go out of the presence and beyond the reach of each other, but the different parts of our country cannot do this. They cannot but remain face to face, and intercourse, either amicable or hostile, must continue between them. Is it possible, then, to make that intercourse more advantageous or more satisfactory after separation than before? Can aliens make treaties easier than friends can make laws? Can treaties be more faithfully enforced between aliens than laws can among friends? Suppose you go to war, you cannot fight always; and when, after much loss on both sides, and no gain on either, you cease fighting, the identical old questions as to terms of intercourse are again upon you.

This country, with its institutions, belongs to the people who inhabit it. Whenever they shall grow weary of the existing government, they can exercise their constitutional right of amending it or their revolutionary right to dismember or overthrow it. . . .

Why should there not be a patient confidence in the ultimate justice of the people? Is there any better or equal hope in the world? In our present differences is either party without faith of being in the right? If the Almighty Ruler of nations, with His eternal truth and justice, be on your side of the North, or on yours of the South, that truth and that justice will surely prevail by the judgment of this great tribunal of the American people.

By the frame of the government under which we live, this same people have wisely given their public servants but little power for mischief; and have, with equal wisdom, provided for the return of that little to their own hands at very short intervals. While the people retain their virtue and vigilance, no administration, by any extreme of wickedness or folly, can very seriously injure the government in the short space of four years.

My countrymen, one and all, think calmly and well upon this whole subject. Nothing valuable can be lost by taking time. If there be an object to hurry any of you in hot haste to a step which you would never take deliberately, that object will be frustrated by taking time; but no good object can be frustrated by it. Such of you as are now dissatisfied still have the old Constitution unimpaired, and, on the sensitive point, the laws of your own framing under it, while the new administration will have no immediate power, if it would, to change either. If it were admitted that you who are dissatisfied hold the right side in the dispute, there still is no single good reason for precipitate action. Intelligence, patriotism, Christianity, and a firm reliance on Him who has never yet forsaken this favored land, are still competent to adjust in the best way all our present difficulty.

In your hands, my dissatisfied fellow countrymen, and not in mine, is the momentous issue of civil war. The government will not assail you. You can have no conflict without being yourselves the aggressors. You have no oath registered in heaven to destroy the government, while I shall have the most solemn one to "preserve, protect, and defend" it.

I am loath to close. We are not enemies, but friends. We must not be enemies. Though passion may have strained, it must not break, our bonds of affection. The mystic cords of memory, stretching from every battlefield and patriot grave to every living heart and hearthstone all over this broad land, will yet swell the chorus of the Union when again touched, as surely they will be, by the better angels of our nature.

—LINCOLN, "First Inaugural Address"

8. MR. LINCOLN HAMMERS OUT A CABINET

Because Lincoln was the first President elected by the Republican party, he faced peculiar difficulties in making up his Cabinet. It seemed wise to unite the party by giving places to as many of the principal Republican leaders as possible, whether their views agreed with his or not. He therefore selected two former Democrats, Salmon P. Chase of Ohio and Gideon Welles of Connecticut, and three former Whigs, the radical antislavery leader, William H. Seward of New York, a moderate Missourian, Edward Bates, and Caleb Smith of Indiana. The weakest appointment, as time proved, was a practical politician whose political affiliations had been varied—Simon Cameron of Pennsylvania.

Thurlow Weed, who here describes Lincoln's troubles, was editor of the Albany Evening Journal *and a political boss who, Henry Adams thought, was a "model of political management and patient address."*

MR. LINCOLN remarked, smiling, that he supposed I had had some experience in cabinet-making; that he had a job on hand, and as he had never learned that trade, he was disposed to avail himself of the suggestions of friends. Taking up his figure, I replied that though never a boss cabinetmaker, I had as a journeyman been occasionally consulted about state cabinets, and that although President Taylor once talked with me about reforming his cabinet, I had never been concerned in or presumed to meddle with the formation of an original Federal cabinet, and that he was the first President elect I had ever seen. The question thus opened became the subject of conversation at intervals during that and the following day. I say at intervals, because many hours were consumed in talking of the public men connected with former administrations, interspersed, illustrated, and seasoned pleasantly with Mr. Lincoln's stories, anecdotes, etc. And here I feel called upon to vindicate Mr. Lincoln, as far as my opportunities and observation go, from the frequent imputation of telling indelicate and ribald stories. I saw much of him during his whole presidential term, with familiar friends and alone, when he talked without restraint, but I never heard him use a profane or indecent word or tell a story that might not be repeated in the presence of ladies.

Mr. Lincoln observed that the making of a cabinet, now that he had it to do, was by no means as easy as he had supposed; that he had, even before the result of the election was known, assuming the probability of success, fixed upon the two leading members of his cabinet, but that in looking about for suitable men to fill the other departments, he had been much embarrassed, partly from his want of acquaintance with the prominent men of the day, and partly, he believed, that while the population of the country had immensely increased, really great men were scarcer than they used to be. He then inquired whether I had any suggestions of a general character affecting the selection of a cabinet to make. I replied that, along with the question of ability, integrity, and experience, he ought, in the selection of his cabinet, to find men whose firmness and courage fitted them for the revolutionary ordeal which was about to test the strength of our government, and that in my judgment it was desirable that at least two members of his cabinet should be selected from slave-holding States. He inquired whether, in the emergency which I so much feared, they could be trusted, adding that he did not quite like to hear Southern journals and Southern speakers insisting that there must be no "coercion"; that while he had no disposition to coerce anybody, yet after he had taken an oath to execute the laws, he should not care to see them violated. I remarked that there were Union men in Maryland, Virginia, North Carolina, and Tennessee, for whose loyalty, under the most trying circumstances and in any event, I would vouch. "Would you rely on such men if their states should secede?" "Yes, sir; the men whom I have in my mind can always be relied on." "Well," said Mr. Lincoln, "let us have the names of your white crows, such ones as you think fit for the cabinet." I then named Henry Winter Davis, of Maryland; John M. Botts, of Virginia; John A. Gilmer, of North Carolina; and Bailey Peyton, of Tennessee.

As the conversation progressed, Mr. Lincoln remarked that he intended to invite Governor Seward to take the State and Governor Chase the Treasury Department, remarking that, aside from their long experience in public affairs and their eminent fitness, they were prominently before the people and the convention as competitors for the Presidency, each having higher claims than his own for the place which he was to occupy. On naming Gideon Welles as the gentleman he thought of as the representative of New England in the cabinet, I remarked that I thought he could find several New England gentlemen whose selection for a place in his cabinet would be more acceptable to the people of New England. "But," said Mr. Lincoln, "we must remember that the Republican party is constituted of two elements, and that we must have men of Democratic as well as of Whig antecedents in the cabinet."

Acquiescing in this view, the subject was passed over. And then Mr. Lincoln remarked that Judge Blair had been suggested. I inquired, "What Judge Blair?" and was answered, "Judge Montgomery Blair." "Has he been suggested by any one except his father, Francis P. Blair, Sr.?" "Your question," said Mr. Lincoln, "reminds me of a story," and he proceeded with infinite humor to tell a story, which I would repeat if I did not fear that its spirit and effect would be lost. I finally remarked that if we were legislating on the question, I should move to strike out the name of Montgomery Blair and insert that of Henry Winter Davis. Mr. Lincoln laughingly replied, "Davis has been posting you up on this question. He came from Maryland

and has got Davis on the brain. Maryland must, I think, be like New Hampshire, a good state to move from." And then he told a story of a witness in a neighboring county, who, on being asked his age, replied, "Sixty." Being satisfied that he was much older, the judge repeated the question, and on receiving the same answer, admonished the witness, saying that the court knew him to be much older than sixty. "Oh," said the witness, "you're thinking about that fifteen year that I lived down on the eastern shore of Maryland; that was so much lost time, and don't count." This story, I perceived, was thrown in to give the conversation a new direction. It was very evident that the selection of Montgomery Blair was a fixed fact, and although I subsequently ascertained the reasons and influences that controlled the selection of other members of the cabinet, I never did find out how Mr. Blair got there.

—*The Autobiography of Thurlow Weed*

9. SEWARD TRIES TO TAKE CHARGE OF THE LINCOLN ADMINISTRATION

Like William Pitt, a century earlier, Seward was convinced that only he could save his country. As Gideon Welles observed, "Seward liked to be called premier." His "Thoughts for the President's Consideration" were intended to establish his dominance over Lincoln. Seward's proposal to substitute a series of foreign wars for a domestic one revealed, however, a lack of judgment that has never been satisfactorily explained. Lincoln's reply was a masterly rebuke, but one which did not alienate the self-confident secretary. It made clear, however, that Lincoln was going to run his own administration.

A. MEMORANDUM FROM SECRETARY SEWARD
APRIL 1, 1861

Some Thoughts for the President's Consideration

First. We are at the end of a month's administration, and yet without a policy either domestic or foreign.

Second. This, however, is not culpable, and it has even been unavoidable. The presence of the Senate, with the need to meet applications for patronage, have prevented attention to other and more grave matters.

Third. But further delay to adopt and prosecute our policies for both domestic and foreign affairs would not only bring scandal on the administration, but danger upon the country.

Fourth. To do this we must dismiss the applicants for office. But how? I suggest that we make the local appointments forthwith, leaving foreign or general ones for ulterior and occasional action.

Fifth. The policy at home. I am aware that my views are singular, and perhaps not sufficiently explained. My system is built upon this idea as a ruling one, namely, that we must

CHANGE THE QUESTION BEFORE THE PUBLIC FROM ONE UPON SLAVERY, OR
ABOUT SLAVERY, for a question upon UNION OR DISUNION:

In other words, from what would be regarded as a party question, to one
of patriotism or union.

The occupation or evacuation of Fort Sumter, although not in fact a
slavery or a party question, is so regarded. Witness the temper manifested
by the Republicans in the free States, and even by the Union men in the
South.

I would therefore terminate it as a safe means for changing the issue. I
deem it fortunate that the last administration created the necessity.

For the rest, I would simultaneously defend and reinforce all the ports in
the gulf, and have the navy recalled from foreign stations to be prepared for a
blockade. Put the island of Key West under martial law.

This will raise distinctly the question of union or disunion. I would maintain every fort and possession in the South.

FOR FOREIGN NATIONS

I would demand explanations from Spain and France, categorically, at
once.

I would seek explanations from Great Britain and Russia, and send agents
into Canada, Mexico, and Central America to rouse a vigorous continental
spirit of independence on this continent against European intervention.

And, if satisfactory explanations are not received from Spain and France,
Would convene Congress and declare war against them.

But whatever policy we adopt, there must be an energetic prosecution of
it.

For this purpose it must be somebody's business to pursue and direct it
incessantly.

Either the President must do it himself, and be all the while active in it, or

Devolve it on some member of his cabinet. Once adopted, debates on it
must end, and all agree and abide.

It is not in my especial province;

But I neither seek to evade nor assume responsibility.

B. REPLY TO SECRETARY SEWARD'S MEMORANDUM

Executive Mansion, April 1, 1861

My dear Sir: Since parting with you I have been considering your paper
dated this day, and entitled "Some Thoughts for the President's Consideration." The first proposition in it is, "*First,* We are at the end of a month's
administration, and yet without a policy either domestic or foreign."

At the beginning of that month, in the inaugural, I said: "The power
confided to me will be used to hold, occupy, and possess the property and
places belonging to the government, and to collect the duties and imposts."
This had your distinct approval at the time; and, taken in connection with the
order I immediately gave General Scott, directing him to employ every

means in his power to strengthen and hold the forts, comprises the exact domestic policy you now urge, with the single exception that it does not propose to abandon Fort Sumter.

Again, I do not perceive how the reinforcement of Fort Sumter would be done on a slavery or a party issue, while that of Fort Pickens would be on a more national and patriotic one.

The news received yesterday in regard to St. Domingo certainly brings a new item within the range of our foreign policy; but up to that time we have been preparing circulars and instructions to ministers and the like, all in perfect harmony, without even a suggestion that we had no foreign policy.

Upon your closing propositions—that "whatever policy we adopt, there must be an energetic prosecution of it.

"For this purpose it must be somebody's business to pursue and direct it incessantly.

"Either the President must do it himself, and be all the while active in it, or

"Devolve it on some member of his cabinet. Once adopted, debates on it must end, and all agree and abide"—I remark that if this must be done, I must do it. When a general line of policy is adopted, I apprehend there is no danger of its being changed without good reason, or continuing to be a subject of unnecessary debate; still, upon points arising in its progress I wish, and suppose I am entitled to have, the advice of all the cabinet.

Your obedient servant,

A. LINCOLN.

—*Complete Works of Abraham Lincoln*

10. THE CONFEDERACY ORGANIZES AT MONTGOMERY

On February 4, 1861, a convention, with representatives from six Southern states, met at Montgomery, Alabama, to organize the government of the Confederacy. This convention drew up a Constitution, chose a provisional President and Vice-President, and acted as a legislature pending the election of a regular Congress.

Thomas Cooper DeLeon, who here describes the political atmosphere of the temporary capital, was a litterateur of some prominence in his day who served in the Confederate Army throughout the war; his brother, David C. DeLeon, was Surgeon General of the Confederacy.

MONTGOMERY, like Rome, sits on seven hills. The city is picturesque in perch upon bold, high bluffs, which, on the city side, cut sheer down to the Alabama river; here, seemingly scarce more than a biscuit-toss across. From the opposite bank spread great flat stretches of marsh and meadow land, while on the other side, behind the town, the formation swells and undulates with gentle rise. As in most southern inland towns, its one great artery, Main street, runs from the river bluffs to the Capitol, perched on a high hill a full mile away. This street, wide and sandy, was in the cradle days badly paved, but rather closely built up.

Nor was the Capitol a peculiarly stately pile, either in size or architectural effect. Still it dominated the lesser structures, as it stared down the street with quite a Roman rigor. The staff upon its dome bore the flag of the new nation, run up there shortly after the Congress met by the hands of a noted daughter of Virginia. Miss Letitia Tyler was not only a representative of proud Old Dominion blood, but was also granddaughter of the ex-President of the United States, whose eldest son, Robert, lived in the new Capital. All Montgomery had flocked to Capitol Hill in holiday attire; bells rang and cannon boomed, and the throng—including all members of the government—stood bareheaded as the fair Virginian threw that flag to the breeze. Then a poet-priest—who later added the sword to the quill—spoke a solemn benediction on the people, their flag and their cause; and a shout went up from every throat that told they meant to honor and strive for it; if need be, to die for it. . . .

On the whole, the effect of Montgomery upon the newly arrived was rather pleasing, with a something rather provincial, quite in keeping with its location inland. Streets, various in length, uncertain in direction and impractical as to pavement, ran into Main street at many points; and most of them were closely built with pretty houses, all of them surrounded by gardens and many by handsome grounds. Equidistant from the end of Main street and from each other, stood, in these cradle days, the two hotels of which the Capital could boast. Montgomery Hall, of bitter memory—like the much-sung "Raven of Zurich," for uncleanliness of nest and length of bill—had been the resort of country merchants, horse and cattle-men; but now the Solon of the hour dwelt therein, with the possible hero of many a field. The Exchange—of rather more pretentions and vastly more comfort—was at that time in the hands of a northern firm, who "could keep a hotel." The latter was political headquarters—the President, the Cabinet and a swarm of the possible great residing there.

Montgomery was Washington over again; only on a smaller scale, and with the avidity and agility in pursuit of the spoils somewhat enhanced by the freshness of scent.

"The President is at this house?" I queried of the ex-member of Congress next me at dinner. "But he does not appear, I suppose?"

"Oh, yes; he's waiting here till his house is made ready. But he doesn't have a private table; takes his meals like an everyday mortal, at the ladies' ordinary."

He had scarcely spoken when Mr. Davis entered by a side door and took his seat, with only an occasional stare of earnest, but not disrespectful, curiosity from the more recent arrivals.

Even in the few weeks since I had seen him there was a great change. He looked worn and thinner; and the set expression of the somewhat stern features gave a grim hardness not natural to their lines. With scarcely a glance around, he returned the general salutations, sat down absently and was soon absorbed in conversation with General Cooper, who had recently resigned the adjutant-generalship of the United States army and accepted a similar post and a brigadier's commission from Mr. Davis. . . .

Little ceremony, or form, hedged the incubating government; and perfect simplicity marked every detail about Mr. Davis. His office, for the moment, was one of the parlors of the hotel. Members of the Cabinet and high officials came in and out without ceremony, to ask questions and receive very brief replies; or for whispered consultation with the President's private secretary, whose desk was in the same room. Casual visitors were simply announced by an usher, and were received whenever business did not prevent. Mr. Davis' manner was unvarying in its quiet and courtesy, drawing out all that one had to tell, and indicating by brief answer, or criticism, that he had extracted the pith from it. At that moment he was the very idol of the people; the grand embodiment to them of their grand cause; and they gave him their hands unquestioning, to applaud any move soever he might make. And equally unthinking as this popular manisfestation of early hero-worship was the clamor that later floated into Richmond on every wind, blaming the government—and especially its head—for every untoward detail of the facile descent to destruction.

A better acquaintance with the Confederate Capital impressed one still more with its likeness to Washington toward the end of the session; but many features of that likeness were salient ones, which had marred and debased the older city. The government just organizing, endless places of profit, of trust, or of honor, were to be filled; and for each and every one of them was a rush of justling and almost rapid claimants. The skeleton of the regular army had just been articulated by Congress, but the bare bones would soon have swelled to more than Falstaffian proportions, had one in every twenty of the ardent aspirants been applied as matter and muscle. The first "gazette" was watched for with straining eyes, and naturally would follow aching hearts; for disappointment here first sowed the dragon's teeth that were to spring into armed opponents of the unappreciative power.

The whole country was new. Everything was to be done—to be made; and who was so capable for both, in their own conceit, as that swarm of worn-out lobbymen and contractors who, having thoroughly exploited "the old concern," now gathered to gorge upon the new. And by the hundred flocked hither those unclean birds, blinking bleared eyes at any chance bit, whetting foul bills to peck at carrion from the departmental sewer. Busy and active at all hours, the lobby of the exchange, when the crowd and the noise rose to the flood at night, smacked no little of pandemonium. Every knot of men had its grievance; every flag in the pavement was a rostrum. Slowness of organization, the weakness of Congress, secession of the border states, personnel of the Cabinet and especially the latest army appointments—these and kindred subjects were canvassed with heat equaled only by ignorance. Men from every section of the South defended their own people in highest of keys and no little temper; startling measures for public safety were offered and state secrets openly discussed in this curbstone congress; while a rank growth of newspaper correspondents, with "the very latest," swelled the hum into a veritable Babel. And the most incomprehensible of all was the diametric opposition of men from the same neighborhood, in their views of the same subject. Often it would be a vital one, of doctrine, or of policy; and yet these neighbors would antagonize more bitterly than would men from opposite parts of the confederation.

—DeLeon, *Four Years in Rebel Capitals*

11. A WAR CLERK DESCRIBES DAVIS AND HIS CABINET

Some of the appointments to the Confederate Cabinet posts excited a good deal of surprise; even more astonishment was excited by the failure of Davis to invite to his official family men like Robert Barnwell Rhett of South Carolina and William L. Yancey of Alabama—men who for more than a decade had been leaders in the secession movement.

John Beauchamp Jones, who has been called the "Confederate Pepys," was an author and journalist of some note who obtained a position as clerk in the War Department in order to keep "a diary of the transactions of the government."

May 17th, 1861.—Was introduced to the President today. He was overwhelmed with papers and retained a number in his left hand, probably of more importance than the rest. He received me with urbanity, and while he read the papers I had given him, as I had never seen him before, I endeavored to scrutinize his features, as one would naturally do, for the purpose of forming a vague estimate of the character and capabilities of the man destined to perform the leading part in a revolution which must occupy a large space in the world's history. His stature is tall, nearly six feet; his frame is very slight and seemingly frail, but when he throws back his shoulders he is as straight as an Indian chief. The features of his face are distinctly marked with character, and no one gazing at his profile would doubt for a moment that he beheld more than an ordinary man. His face is handsome, and [on] his thin lip often basks a pleasant smile. There is nothing sinister or repulsive in his manners or appearance, and if there are no special indications of great grasp of intellectual power on his forehead and on his sharply-defined nose and chin, neither is there any evidence of weakness or that he could be easily moved from any settled purpose. I think he has a clear perception of matters demanding his cognizance, and a nice discrimination of details. As a politician he attaches the utmost importance to *consistency*—and here I differ with him. I think that to be consistent as a politician is to change with the circumstances of the case. When Calhoun and Webster first met in Congress, the first advocated a protective tariff and the last opposed it. This was told me by Mr. Webster himself, in 1842, when he was Secretary of State; and it was confirmed by Mr. Calhoun in 1844, then Secretary of State himself. Statesmen are the physicians of the public weal, and what doctor hesitates to vary his remedies with the new phases of disease?

When the President had completed the reading of my papers, and during the perusal I observed him make several emphatic nods, he asked me what I wanted. I told him I wanted employment with my pen, perhaps only temporary employment. I thought the correspondence of the Secretary of War would increase in volume, and another assistant besides Major Tyler would be required in his office. He smiled and shook his head, saying that such work would be only temporary indeed; which I construed to mean that even he did not then suppose the war to assume colossal proportions.

May 20th.—Mr. Walker, the Secretary of War, is some forty-seven or -eight years of age, tall, thin, and a little bent, not by age, but by study and bad health. He was a successful lawyer and, having never been in governmental employment, is fast working himself down. He has not yet learned how to avoid unnecessary labor, being a man of the finest sensibilities, and exacting with the utmost nicety all due deference to the dignity of his official position. He stands somewhat on ceremony with his brother officials and accords and exacts the etiquette natural to a sensitive gentleman who has never been broken on the wheel of office. I predict for him a short career. The only hope for his continuance in office is unconditional submission to the President, who, being once Secretary of War of the United States, is familiar with all the wheels of the department. But soon, if I err not, the President will be too much absorbed in the fluctuations of momentous campaigns to give much of his attention to any one of the departments. Nevertheless Mr. Walker, if he be an apt scholar, may learn much before that day; and Congress may simplify his duties by enacting a uniform mode of filling the offices in the field. The applications now give the greatest trouble, and the disappointed class give rise to many vexations.

May 21st.—Being in the same room with the Secretary and seen by all his visitors, I am necessarily making many new acquaintances; and quite a number recognize me by my books which they have read. Among this class is Mr. Benjamin, the Minister of Justice. . . . Mr. Benjamin is of course a Jew, of French lineage, born I believe in Louisiana, a lawyer and politician. His age may be sixty, and yet one might suppose him to be less than forty. His hair and eyes are black, his forehead capacious, his face round and as intellectual as one of that shape can be; and Mr. Benjamin is certainly a man of intellect, education, and extensive reading, combined with natural abilities of a tolerably high order. Upon his lip there seems to bask an eternal smile; but if it be studied, it is not a smile—yet it bears no unpleasing aspect.

May 22nd.—Today I had, in our office, a specimen of Mr. Memminger's oratory. He was pleading for an installment of the claims of South Carolina on the Confederacy; and Mr. Walker, always hesitating, argued the other side, merely for delay. Both are fine speakers, with most distinct enunciation and musical voices. The demand was audited and paid, amounting to, I believe, several hundred thousand dollars.

And I heard and saw Mr. Toombs today, the Secretary of State. He is a portly gentleman, but with the pale face of the student and the marks of a deep thinker. To gaze at him in repose, the casual spectator would suppose, from his neglect of dress, that he was a planter in moderate circumstances and of course not gifted with extraordinary powers of intellect; but let him open his mouth, and the delusion vanishes. At the time alluded to he was surrounded by the rest of the cabinet, in our office, and the topic was the policy of the war. He was for taking the initiative and carrying the war into the enemy's country. And as he warmed with the subject, the man seemed to vanish, and the genius alone was visible. . . . These little discussions were of frequent occurrence; and it soon became apparent that the Secretary of War was destined to be the most important man among the cabinet ministers. His position afforded the best prospect of future distinction—always provided he should be equal to the position and his administration attended with success. I felt convinced that Toombs would not be long chafing in the cabinet but that he would seize the first opportunity to repair to the field.

—JONES, *A Rebel War Clerk's Diary at the Confederate States Capital*

12. A STATE AGENT CALLS ON THE CONFEDERATE LEADERS

One of the best descriptions of Confederate leaders comes from the graceful pen of John Peyton, agent from North Carolina to England. Born and educated in Virginia, Peyton had lived for some time in Illinois and was unalterably opposed to secession, which he regarded as not only unwise but unconstitutional. When Virginia seceded, however, he went with his state, raising a regiment largely at his own expense. Kept from active military service by poor health, he served his country in England, and after the war stayed on in the Island of Guernsey for many years.

I CALLED at the Navy Department the morning after my arrival. I found the Honourable Stephen R. Mallory, Secretary of State for the Admiralty, occupying a small room in the second storey of a brick building, north of the capitol square, a house which in former times had been used for some purpose in connection with the Fire Companies of Richmond. He was a short, fat man, with a solid neck, a big head, much strong grizzled hair, a leaden eye, and a heavy countenance. His arms, legs, and neck were very short, and his clothes tightly fitting—so tight, indeed, that, to use an American phrase in a literal sense, which is commonly used metaphorically to express a different idea, he seemed "too big for his breeches." His ideas seemed to be confused, and the right word never to be had at the right moment. What he did say was commonplace. In the first five minutes of my conversation, I found myself forgetting my business, while I wondered what could be Mr. Mallory's peculiar fitness for his position—what secret faculty he possessed for creating an armament and piloting it through the storms of a civil war. . . .

As I passed out of the office of the Secretary of the Navy, expressing a hope that he might enjoy his repast, and digest it satisfactorily, which I doubted, from the character of the provisions then in the Richmond market, I encountered in the hall a lean, yellow, care-worn man, his back bent forward almost into a hump, his chest bowed inward, one shoulder higher than the other, small arms and wasted legs, hands, and fingers long and bony—dress loose and wrinkled, and of shabby gray—looking damp and mouldy. His face was bony and emaciated, withered and twitching, his scanty hair fell on his shoulders in disorder. His chin was smooth and beardless, his breath short, while his restless eyes blazed with excitement. His voice, as he addressed such acquaintances as he met, was sharp, shrill, and squeaky, and his whole appearance faded, anxious, disappointed, extraordinary—so much so that he passed no one who did not turn and take a second gaze. I thought I had never seen so singular an object, and inquired of my nearest neighbor what apparition it was. Imagine my surprise when I was informed that it was Mr. Alexander H. Stephens, the eloquent Georgian orator, the Conservative statesman and energetic Vice-President of the Confederate States. . . .

During the week I had given myself to remain in Richmond I determined to ascertain as much as possible of the views and the policy of the Confederate leaders, and accordingly called from time to time, during leisure hours, upon the President and the members of the cabinet, several of whom I had for years known.

I generally saw Mr. Davis in his office in the United States Custom House, situated not far from the War and Navy departments, on the west side of the capitol square. In this building he occupied a small room, as an office for the transaction of public business and the reception of friends, before the door of which office paced a single sentinel in the gray Confederate uniform. Mr. Davis was thin, gaunt, sallow, terribly worn by the cares and anxieties of his position, but in as high spirits as even Mr. Mallory, as to the prospects of the future.

In person Mr. Davis is tall and slender—what is termed in American parlance "a raw-boned man"—with a small, fine head, blue eyes, one of which is defective, in consequence of a wound he received at the battle of Buena Vista, an aquiline contour, high narrow forehead, leonine cast of mouth, deeply marked by high spirit, strong sense, and no small experience of grim care. He had an easy, dignified manner. . . .

Mr. Davis always impressed me as a man of abilities, but engaged in an enterprise, the foundation of an empire, far too arduous for any energies he possessed; as a man by no means stamped by nature with power and genius, such as his situation and the great crisis demanded. His whole manner and bearing was that of one almost stunned by what was passing before his astonished vision, and incapable of safely controlling and directing the vessel of state, amidst the winds and waves of the tempest. He did not appear to be guiding his conduct by the sober deductions of cool reason, but to be acting without any of that far-seeing sagacity which conciliates enemies and retains friends. . . .

In a back room on the ground floor of an old red brick building, formerly used as the office of an auctioneer, and situated on the same street with the United States Custom House, the Secretary of State, R. M. T. Hunter, was generally found dreaming the day away, in the absence of official duties to occupy his time. Over the front door was a small board inscribed "State Department." I occasionally dropped in to see "Run Mad Tom," as he was called in earlier days, on account of his extreme radical views on the subject of State rights.

However mad he may have been once, he was decidedly sober and soporific then, tame rather than wild, and he illustrated how impossible it is to prevent what is "bred in the bone" from "coming out in the flesh." He was now, as when younger, the most uncompromising of Secessionists, and, as Pitt said on a memorable occasion to Horace Walpole, "ignorant in spite of experience." He professed to see nothing to weaken the force of his sanguine views as to Southern success, in the determination of the Federal Government to maintain the Union at every hazard; nothing in Negro slavery, but its Divine origin and its incalculable blessings for white and black, and nothing better for the South than to labour for its indefinite extension and perpetuity. The logic of passing events did not disturb his dreams, and he indulged in that kind of delusion which professed to believe the success of the South already secured, though the North was giving daily evidences of a determination to bring every energy of its richer, more highly developed country and greater population to bear upon the contest. . . .

Very near the offices of Mr. Mallory were those of Judah P. Benjamin, the acting Secretary of War, who was a short, stout, jaunty gentleman, with a sparkling black eye and a jovial Judaical physiognomy. He was not handsome, but his appearance was prepossessing, and his manners were natural. He was frank and open, with what might be termed a careless flow of spirits. He said a great many witty and pleasant things, and seemed in a short time to appreciate the characters of those with whom he associated. He was a distinguished jurist and statesman, and it was not difficult for even a casual acquaintance to trace in him the characteristics of both professions. He was long one of the leading lawyers of New Orleans, and at the commencement of the civil war, or rather the secession of South Carolina, was, as he had been for several years previous, a United States senator from Louisiana. He was regarded by many as the ablest of the President's cabinet council, and was one of the few persons connected with the Government, who had believed from the first that Secession would lead to a long and bloody war.

—PEYTON, *The American Crisis*

II

The Conflict Precipitated

WHY did the Montgomery government permit the bombardment of Fort Sumter? It is almost a principle of American history that the "other side" must strike the first blow, and that Americans must fight only in defense of their nation and their principles. That was why Polk was so concerned to prove that "American blood had been shed on American soil." Yet at Sumter the South struck the first blow, thus forfeiting, in some part at least, the moral advantage of being the defender rather than the aggressor. From the Confederate point of view, to be sure, the North had already taken the offensive by the occupation of Sumter and by the effort to reprovision it, but this point of view was a bit astigmatic. Clearly the attack on the old flag would arouse and unite the North as would nothing else, and clearly, too, it would precipitate war.

There was, however, one consideration that the Confederates could not afford to overlook. Two days before the bombardment of Sumter Roger Pryor, of Virginia, had put the matter succinctly. "I tell you, gentlemen, what will put Virginia in the Southern Confederacy in less than an hour by Shrewsbury clock—strike a blow." His timing was a bit off, but his argument was sound. Only by striking a blow could the Confederacy be sure of bringing in Virginia—and other wavering states.

Once the war was on, North and South rallied to their causes and their flags. At first unity seemed to obtain, on both sides; only after it became clear that the war would not be over in three months did dissatisfaction appear. There was, in fact, little real unity on either side, and far less real enthusiasm for war than patriotic orators pretended, or than some historians have recorded. Large segments of opinion in the North were opposed to holding the Union together by coercion. Large segments in the South still cherished the old Union and looked upon the war as a slaveholders' fight. Antiwar and disunion sentiment was to be found almost everywhere in the North, but more strongly in the Middle West than in New England; antiwar and Unionist sentiment in the South was controlled largely by geography: the western counties of Virginia seceded from the state and joined the Union, Maryland, Kentucky and Missouri stayed in the Union, and eastern Tennessee was predominantly Unionist in sentiment.

We shall see, later, something of the consequences of antiwar and Copperhead sentiment in the North, of Unionism and State rights in the South. An appreciation of the importance of these attitudes should not, however, blind

30

us to the fact that the majority, in both sections, believed passionately in and fought loyally for their cause.

1. MRS. CHESNUT WATCHES THE ATTACK ON FORT SUMTER

When South Carolina seceded, Major Robert Anderson, commanding the Federal forces in Charleston, secretly moved his garrison from Fort Moultrie to Fort Sumter. The question whether his little force should be withdrawn or supported agitated the closing weeks of the Buchanan and the opening weeks of the Lincoln administration. While the fate of Fort Sumter was being discussed, the Confederacy took over all but four of the forts, arsenals, and military posts in the South. Against the advice of some members of his Cabinet, Lincoln finally decided not to reinforce but to provision the fort, and this decision precipitated the crisis, and the war. On April 11 General Beauregard, who was in command of Confederate forces in Charleston, acting on somewhat ambiguous instructions from Montgomery, demanded an immediate surrender of the fort; when this was refused Confederate batteries opened fire on the Stars and Stripes at dawn of the twelfth, and the war was on.

Mary Boykin Chesnut, whose Diary gives us a lively account of life in the Confederacy, was the wife of ex-Senator Chesnut of South Carolina. She tells us here* of the excitement in Charleston when Sumter was attacked.

April 8th, 1861.—Allen Green came up to speak to me at dinner in all his soldier's toggery. It sent a shiver through me. Tried to read Margaret Fuller Ossoli, but could not. The air too full of war news, and we are all so restless.

Went to see Miss Pinckney, one of the last of the old-world Pinckneys. Governor Manning walked in, bowed gravely, and seated himself by me. Again he bowed low in mock-heroic style and with a grand wave of his hand said, "Madam, your country is invaded." When I had breath to speak I asked, "What does he mean?" He meant this: There are six men-of-war outside the bar. Talbot and Chew have come to say that hostilities are to begin. Governor Pickens and Beauregard are holding a council of war. Mr. Chesnut then came in and confirmed the story. Wigfall next entered in boisterous spirits and said, "There was a sound of revelry by night." In any stir of confusion my heart is apt to beat so painfully. Now the agony was so stifling I could hardly see or hear. The men went off almost immediately. And I crept silently to my room, where I sat down to a good cry.

Mrs. Wigfall came in, and we had it out on the subject of civil war. We solaced ourselves with dwelling on all its known horrors, and then we added what we had a right to expect with Yankees in front and Negroes in the rear. "The slaveowners must expect a servile insurrection, of course," said Mrs. Wigfall, to make sure that we were unhappy enough. Suddenly loud

---

* From: *A Diary from Dixie* by Mary B. Chesnut. Copyright, 1905, D. Appleton & Company. Reprinted by permission of the publishers, Appleton-Century-Crofts, Inc.

shouting was heard. We ran out. Cannon after cannon roared. We met Mrs. Allen Green in the passageway, with blanched cheeks and streaming eyes. Governor Means rushed out of his room in his dressing gown and begged us to be calm. "Governor Pickens," said he, "has ordered, in the plenitude of his wisdom, seven cannon to be fired as a signal to the Seventh Regiment. Anderson will hear as well as the Seventh Regiment. Now you go back and be quiet; fighting in the streets has not begun yet."

So we retired. Doctor Gibbes calls Mrs. Allen Green, Dame Placid. There was no placidity today, with cannon bursting and Allen on the island. No sleep for anybody last night. The streets were alive with soldiers, men shouting, marching, singing. Wigfall, the stormy petrel, is in his glory, the only thoroughly happy person I see. Today things seem to have settled down a little. One can but hope still. Lincoln or Seward has made such silly advances and then far sillier drawings back. There may be a chance for peace after all. Things are happening so fast. My husband has been made an aide-de-camp to General Beauregard.

Three hours ago we were quickly packing to go home. The convention has adjourned. Now he tells me the attack on Fort Sumter may begin tonight; depends upon Anderson and the fleet outside. . . .

Mrs. Hayne called. She had, she said, but one feeling—pity for those who are not here. Jack Preston, Willie Alston, "the take-life-easys," as they are called, with John Green, "the big brave," have gone down to the islands—volunteered as privates. Seven hundred men were sent over. Ammunition wagons were rumbling along the streets all night. Anderson is burning blue lights, signs and signals for the fleet outside, I suppose.

Today at dinner there was no allusion to things as they stand in Charleston harbor. There was an undercurrent of intense excitement. There could not have been a more brilliant circle. In addition to our usual quartet, Judge Withers, Langdon Cheves, and Trescott, our two ex-governors dined with us, Means and Manning. These men all talked so delightfully. For once in my life I listened. That over, business began in earnest. Governor Means has rummaged a sword and red sash from somewhere and brought it for Colonel Chesnut, who had gone to demand the surrender of Fort Sumter. And now, patience—we must wait.

Why did that green goose Anderson go into Fort Sumter? Then everything began to go wrong. Now they have intercepted a letter from him, urging them to let him surrender. He paints the horrors likely to ensue if they will not. He ought to have thought of all that before he put his head in the hole.

12th.—Anderson will not capitulate. Yesterday's was the merriest, maddest dinner we have had yet. Men were audaciously wise and witty. We had an unspoken foreboding that it was to be our last pleasant meeting. Mr. Miles dined with us today. Mrs. Henry King rushed in saying: "The news, I come for the latest news! All the men of the King family are on the island," of which fact she seemed proud.

While she was here our peace negotiator or envoy came in—that is, Mr.

Chesnut returned. His interview with Colonel Anderson had been deeply interesting, but Mr. Chesnut was not inclined to be communicative. He wanted his dinner. He felt for Anderson and had telegraphed to President Davis for instructions—what answer to give Anderson, etc. He has now gone back to Fort Sumter with additional instructions. When they were about to leave the wharf, A. H. Boykin sprang into the boat in great excitement. He thought himself ill-used, with a likelihood of fighting and he to be left behind!

I do not pretend to go to sleep. How can I? If Anderson does not accept terms at four, the orders are he shall be fired upon. I count four, St. Michael's bells chime out, and I begin to hope. At half past four the heavy booming of a cannon. I sprang out of bed, and on my knees prostrate I prayed as I never prayed before.

There was a sound of stir all over the house, pattering of feet in the corridors. All seemed hurrying one way. I put on my double gown and a shawl and went too. It was to the housetop. The shells were bursting. In the dark I heard a man say, "Waste of ammunition." I knew my husband was rowing a boat somewhere in that dark bay. If Anderson was obstinate, Colonel Chesnut was to order the fort on one side to open fire. Certainly fire had begun. The regular roar of the cannon, there it was. And who could tell what each volley accomplished of death and destruction?

The women were wild there on the housetop. Prayers came from the women and imprecations from the men. And then a shell would light up the scene. Tonight they say the forces are to attempt to land. We watched up there, and everybody wondered that Fort Sumter did not fire a shot. . . .

We hear nothing, can listen to nothing; boom, boom, goes the cannon all the time. The nervous strain is awful, alone in this darkened room. "Richmond and Washington ablaze," say the papers—blazing with excitement. Why not? To us these last days' events seem frightfully great. We were all women on that iron balcony. Men are only seen at a distance now. Stark Means was leaning over and looking with tearful eyes, when an unknown creature asked, "Why did he take his hat off?" Mrs. Means stood straight up and said, "He did that in honor of his mother; he saw me." She is a proud mother and at the same time most unhappy. Her lovely daughter Emma is dying in there, before her eyes, of consumption. At that moment I am sure Mrs. Means had a spasm of the heart.

13th.—Nobody has been hurt after all. How gay we were last night! Reaction after the dread of all the slaughter we thought those dreadful cannon were making. Not even a battery the worse for wear. Fort Sumter has been on fire. Anderson has not yet silenced any of our guns. So the aides, still with swords and red sashes by way of uniform, tell us. But the sound of those guns makes regular meals impossible. None of us goes to table. Tea trays pervade the corridors, going everywhere. Some of the anxious hearts lie on their beds and moan in solitary misery. Mrs. Wigfall and I solace ourselves with tea in my room. These women have all a satisfying faith. "God is on our side," they say. When we are shut in Mrs. Wigfall

THE CIVIL WAR 1861-65

and I ask, "Why?" "Of course, He hates the Yankees," we are told, "You'll think that well of Him."

Not by one word or look can we detect any change in the demeanor of these Negro servants. Lawrence sits at our door, sleepy and respectful, and profoundly indifferent. So are they all, but they carry it too far. You could not tell that they even heard the awful roar going on in the bay, though it has been dinning in their ears night and day. People talk before them as if they were chairs and tables. They make no sign. Are they stolidly stupid? or wiser than we are; silent and strong, biding their time? . . .

15th.—I did not know that one could live such days of excitement. Some one called: "Come out! There is a crowd coming." A mob it was, indeed, but it was headed by Colonels Chesnut and Manning. The crowd was shouting and showing these two as messengers of good news. They were escorted to Beauregard's headquarters. For Sumter had surrendered! Those upon the housetops shouted to us, "The fort is on fire." That had been the story once or twice before.

When we had calmed down, Colonel Chesnut, who had taken it all quietly enough, if anything more unruffled than usual in his serenity, told us how the surrender came about. Wigfall was with them on Morris Island when they saw the fire in the fort; he jumped in a little boat and, with his handkerchief as a white flag, rowed over. Wigfall went in through a porthole. When Colonel Chesnut arrived shortly after and was received at the regular entrance, Colonel Anderson told him he had need to pick his way warily, for the place was all mined. As far as I can make out the fort surrendered to Wigfall. But it is all confusion. Our flag is flying there. Fire engines have been sent for to put out the fire. Everybody tells you half of something and then rushes off to tell something else or to hear the last news.

In the afternoon Mrs. Preston, Mrs. Joe Heyward, and I drove out around the battery. We were in an open carriage. What a changed scene—the very liveliest crowd I think I ever saw, everybody talking at once. All glasses were still turned on the grim old fort.

—CHESNUT, *A Diary from Dixie*

2. ABNER DOUBLEDAY DEFENDS FORT SUMTER

A New Yorker by birth and a West Point graduate who had fought in the Mexican War, Captain Abner Doubleday was second in command at Fort Sumter when it was captured by the Confederates in 1861. He served gallantly throughout the rest of the war, fighting at Antietam, at Fredericksburg, at Chancellorsville, and at Gettysburg, and rose to the rank of major general. His other claim to fame is as the "father" of baseball.

ABOUT 4 A.M. on the 12th I was awakened by some one groping about my room in the dark and calling out my name. It proved to be Anderson, who came to announce to me that he had just received a dispatch from Beauregard, dated 3:20 A.M., to the effect that he should open fire upon us in an hour. Finding it was determined not to return the fire until after breakfast, I remained in bed. As we had no lights, we could in fact do nothing before that time except to wander around in the darkness and fire without an accurate view of the enemy's works.

As soon as the outline of our fort could be distinguished, the enemy carried out their program. It had been arranged, as a special compliment to the venerable Edmund Ruffin, who might almost be called the father of secession, that he should fire the first shot against us from the Stevens battery on Cummings Point. Almost immediately afterward a ball from Cummings Point lodged in the magazine wall and by the sound seemed to bury itself in the masonry about a foot from my head, in very unpleasant proximity to my right ear. This is the one that probably came with Mr. Ruffin's compliments. In a moment the firing burst forth in one continuous roar, and large patches of both the exterior and interior masonry began to crumble and fall in all directions. The place where I was had been used for the manufacture of cartridges, and there was still a good deal of powder there, some packed and some loose. A shell soon struck near the ventilator, and a puff of dense smoke entered the room, giving me a strong impression that there would be an immediate explosion. Fortunately, no sparks had penetrated inside.

Nineteen batteries were now hammering at us, and the balls and shells from the ten-inch columbiads, accompanied by shells from the thirteen-inch mortars which constantly bombarded us, made us feel as if the war had commenced in earnest.

When it was broad daylight, I went down to breakfast. I found the officers already assembled at one of the long tables in the mess hall. Our party were calm and even somewhat merry. We had retained one colored man to wait on us. He was a spruce-looking mulatto from Charleston, very active and efficient on ordinary occasions, but now completely demoralized by the thunder of the guns and crashing of the shot around us. He leaned back against the wall, almost white with fear, his eyes closed, and his whole expression one of perfect despair. Our meal was not very sumptuous. It consisted of pork and water, but Doctor Crawford triumphantly brought forth a little farina which he had found in a corner of the hospital.

When this frugal repast was over, my company was told off in three details for firing purposes, to be relieved afterward by Seymour's company. As I was the ranking officer, I took the first detachment and marched them to the casemates which looked out upon the powerful ironclad battery of Cummings Point.

In aiming the first gun fired against the rebellion I had no feeling of self-reproach, for I fully believed that the contest was inevitable and was not of our seeking. . . .

Our firing now became regular and was answered from the rebel guns which encircled us on the four sides of the pentagon upon which the fort was built. The other side faced the open sea. Showers of balls from ten-inch columbiads and forty-two-pounders and shells from thirteen-inch mortars poured into the fort in one incessant stream, causing great flakes of masonry to fall in all directions. When the immense mortar shells, after sailing high in the air, came down in a vertical direction and buried themselves in the parade ground, their explosion shook the fort like an earthquake. . . .

The firing continued all day without any special incident of importance and without our making much impression on the enemy's works. They had a great advantage over us as their fire was concentrated on the fort which was in the center of the circle, while ours was diffused over the circumference. Their missiles were exceedingly destructive to the upper exposed portion of the work, but no essential injury was done to the lower casemates which sheltered us. . . .

From 4 to 6:30 A.M. [April 13] the enemy's fire was very spirited. From 7 to 8 A.M. a rainstorm came on, and there was a lull in the cannonading. About 8 A.M. the officers' quarters were ignited by one of Ripley's incendiary shells or by shot heated in the furnaces at Fort Moultrie. The fire was put out, but at 10 A.M. a mortar shell passed through the roof and lodged in the flooring of the second story, where it burst and started the flames afresh. This too was extinguished, but the hot shot soon followed each other so rapidly that it was impossible for us to contend with them any longer. It became evident that the entire block, being built with wooden partitions, floors, and roofing, must be consumed, and that the magazine, containing three hundred barrels of powder, would be endangered; for even after closing the metallic door sparks might penetrate through the ventilator. The floor was covered with loose powder where a detail of men had been at work manufacturing cartridge bags out of old shirts, woolen blankets, etc.

While the officers exerted themselves with axes to tear down and cut away all the woodwork in the vicinity, the soldiers were rolling barrels of powder out to more sheltered spots and were covering them with wet blankets. The labor was accelerated by the shells which were bursting around us, for Ripley had redoubled his activity at the first signs of a conflagration. We only succeeded in getting out some ninety-six barrels of powder, and then we were obliged to close the massive copper door and await the result. A shot soon after passed through the intervening shield, struck the door, and bent the lock in such a way that it could not be opened again. We were thus cut off from our supply of ammunition but still had some piled up in the vicinity of the guns. Anderson officially reported only four barrels and three cartridges as on hand when we left.

By 11 A.M. the conflagration was terrible and disastrous. One fifth of the fort was on fire, and the wind drove the smoke in dense masses into the angle where we had all taken refuge. It seemed impossible to escape suffocation. Some lay down close to the ground, with handkerchiefs over their mouths, and others posted themselves near the embrasures, where the smoke was somewhat lessened by the draught of air. Every one suffered severely. I crawled out of one of these openings and sat on the outer edge, but Ripley made it lively for me there with his case shot which spattered all around. Had not a slight change of wind taken place, the result might have been fatal to most of us.

Our firing having ceased and the enemy being very jubilant, I thought it would be as well to show them that we were not all dead yet, and ordered the gunners to fire a few rounds more. I heard afterward that the enemy loudly cheered Anderson for his persistency under such adverse circumstances.

The scene at this time was really terrific. The roaring and crackling of the flames, the dense masses of whirling smoke, the bursting of the enemy's shells and our own which were exploding in the burning rooms, the crashing of the shot, and the sound of masonry falling in every direction, made the fort a pandemonium. When at last nothing was left of the building but the blackened walls and smoldering embers, it became painfully evident that an immense amount of damage had been done. There was a tower at each angle of the fort. One of these, containing great quantities of shells upon which we had relied, was almost completely shattered by successive explosions. The massive wooden gates studded with iron nails were burned, and the wall built behind them was now a mere heap of debris, so that the main entrance was wide open for an assaulting party. The sally ports were in a similar condition, and the numerous windows on the gorge side which had been planked up had now become all open entrances.

About 12:48 P.M. the end of the flagstaff was shot down and the flag fell. . . .

About 2 P.M. Senator Wigfall, in company with W. Gourdin Young, of

Charleston, unexpectedly made his appearance at one of the embrasures, having crossed over from Morris Island in a small boat rowed by Negroes. He had seen the flag come down, and supposed that we had surrendered in consequence of the burning of the quarters. An artilleryman serving his gun was very much astonished to see a man's face at the entrance and asked him what he was doing there. Wigfall replied that he wished to see Major Anderson. The man, however, refused to allow him to enter until he had surrendered himself as a prisoner and given up his sword. . . . Wigfall, in Beauregard's name, offered Anderson his own terms, which were the evacuation of the fort, with permission to salute our flag and to march out with the honors of war with our arms and private baggage, leaving all other war material behind. As soon as this matter was arranged, Wigfall returned to Cummings Point.

All of the preliminaries having been duly adjusted, it was decided that the evacuation should take place the next morning. Our arrangements were few and simple, but the rebels made extensive preparations for the event in order to give it the greatest éclat and gain from it as much prestige as possible. The population of the surrounding country poured into Charleston in vast multitudes to witness the humiliation of the United States flag. We slept soundly that night for the first time, after all the fatigue and excitement of the two preceding days.

The next morning, Sunday, the 14th, we were up early, packing our baggage in readiness to go on board the transport. The time having arrived, I made preparations, by order of Major Anderson, to fire a national salute to the flag. . . .

The salute being over, the Confederate troops marched in to occupy the fort. The Palmetto Guard, Captain Cuthbert's company, detailed by Colonel De Saussure, and Captain Hollinquist's Company B, of the regulars, detailed by Colonel Ripley, constituted the new garrison under Ripley. Anderson directed me to form the men on the parade ground, assume command, and march them on board the transport. I told him I should prefer to leave the fort with the flag flying and the drums beating "Yankee Doodle," and he authorized me to do so. As soon as our tattered flag came down and the silken banner made by the ladies of Charleston was run up, tremendous shouts of applause were heard from the vast multitude of spectators; and all the vessels and steamers, with one accord, made for the fort.

—DOUBLEDAY, *Reminiscences of Forts Sumter and Moultrie*

3. MAJOR ANDERSON SURRENDERS FORT SUMTER

It was characteristic of the confusion of loyalties at the time that Major Anderson, who defended Fort Sumter heroically for thirty-four hours, was by birth a Kentuckian, of Virginia ancestry, and married to a Georgia girl. Doubleday asserts that he had been given command in Charleston harbor by Buchanan's Secretary of War Floyd precisely for this reason—that Floyd thought he would co-operate with the Confederacy. Anderson proved, how-

ever, loyal to the Union. He was subsequently promoted to brigadier general and was temporarily in charge of Union forces in Kentucky.

Steamship Baltic, off Sandy Hook, April 18 (1861)—10:30 A.M.—via New York—Having defended Fort Sumter for thirty-four hours, until the quarters were entirely burned, the main gates destroyed by fire, the gorge walls seriously injured, the magazine surrounded by flames, and its door closed from the effects of heat, four barrels and three cartridges of powder only being available, and no provisions remaining but pork, I accepted terms of evacuation offered by General Beauregard, being the same offered by him on the 11th instant, prior to the commencement of hostilities, and marched out of the fort Sunday afternoon, the 14th instant, with colors flying and drums beating, bringing away company and private property, and saluting my flag with fifty guns.

ROBERT ANDERSON
Major, First Artillery, Commanding.
—"Reports of Major Anderson . . ."

4. "THE HEATHER IS ON FIRE"

Before the attack on Fort Sumter there had been a strong current of opinion in the North which urged that the "erring sisters" be allowed to "depart in peace." When Beauregard fired on the flag the whole North was aroused and, for the moment, appeared to be unified in its determination to put down rebellion.

The four excerpts given here describe the response of the North as seen and interpreted by an Indiana farm boy, a Boston scholar, a Philadelphia lawyer, and a New York girl.

A. AN INDIANA FARM BOY HEARS THE NEWS

April, 1861

Father and I were husking out some corn. We could not finish before it wintered up. When William Cory came across the field (he had been down after the Mail) he was excited and said, "Jonathan the Rebs have fired upon and taken Fort Sumpter." Father got white and couldn't say a word.

William said, "The President will soon fix them. He has called for 75,000 men and is going to blocade their ports, and just as soon as those fellows find out that the North means business they will get down off thier high horse."

Father said little. We did not finish the corn and drove to the barn. Father left me to unload and put out the team and went to the house. After I had finished I went in to dinner. Mother said, "What is the matter with Father?" He had gone right upstairs. I told her what we had heard. She went to him. After a while they came down. Father looked ten years older.

We sat down to the table. Grandma wanted to know what was the trouble. Father told her and she began to cry. "Oh my poor children in the South! Now they will suffer! God knows how they will suffer! I knew it would come! Jonathan I told you it would come!"

"They can come here and stay," said Father.

"No they will not do that. There is thier home. There they will stay. Oh to think that I should have lived to see the day when Brother should rise against Brother."

She and Mother were crying and I lit out for the barn. I do hate to see women cry.

We had another meeting at the school house last night; we are raising money to take care of the families of those who enlist. A good many gave money, others subscribed. The Hulper boys have enlisted and Steve Lampman and some others. I said I would go but they laughed at me and said they wanted men not boys for this job; that it would all be over soon; that those fellows down South are big bluffers and would rather talk than fight. I am not so sure about that. I know the Hale boys would fight with thier fists at any rate and I believe they would fight with guns too if needs be. I remember how Charlie would get on our Dick and ride on a galop across our south field cutting mullin heads with his wooden sword playing they were Indians or Mexicans (his Father was in the Mexican War), and he looked fine. To be sure there was no danger but I feel pretty certain he could fight. May be it won't be such a picnic as some say it will. There has been a fight down in Virginia at Big Bethel. Al Beechers Nephew was in it and wrote to his Uncle and he read the letter in his store. I could not make out which side whipped but from the papers I think the Rebels had the best of it. Mother had a letter from the Hales. Charlie and his Father are in thier army and Dayton wanted to go but was too young. I wonder if I were in our army and they should meet me would they shoot me. I suppose they would.

—WINTHER, ed., *Journal of Theodore Upson*

B. "THERE NEVER WAS ANYTHING LIKE IT"

To Sir Edmund Head.

Boston, April 21, 1861

My dear Head,—I sent you by yesterday's express a parcel, about which the two papers I enclose will give you all the information you will need. The Danish books, I think, will be all you will want for some time.

But there are other things to talk about now. The heather is on fire. I never before knew what a popular excitement can be. Holiday enthusiasm I have seen often enough, and anxious crowds I remember during the war of 1812-15, but never anything like this. Indeed, here at the North, at least, there never was anything like it; for if the feeling were as deep and stern in 1775, it was by no means so intelligent or unanimous; and the masses to be moved were as a handful compared to our dense population now.

The whole people, in fact, has come to a perception that the question is, whether we shall have anarchy or no. The sovereign—for the people is the only sovereign in this country—has begun to exercise his sovereign functions. Business is susbstantially suspended. Men think, wisely or unwisely, of the state of affairs, and not of much else. The whole population, men, women, and children, seem to be in the streets with Union favors and flags; walking about uneasily, because their anxiety and nervous excitement will not permit them to stay at home, where all ordinary occupation has become unsavory. Public meetings are held everywhere, in the small towns and villages as much as in the cities; considerable sums of money are voted to sustain the movement and take care of the families of those who are mustered into service; and still larger sums are given by individuals. Nobody holds back. Civil war is freely accepted everywhere; by some with alacrity, as the only means of settling a controversy based on long-cherished hatreds; by others as something sent as a judgment from Heaven, like a flood or an earthquake; by all as inevitable, by all as the least of the evils among which we are permitted to choose, anarchy being the obvious, and perhaps the only alternative.

Here in Boston the people are constantly gathering about the State House—which you know is in front of my windows—and about Faneuil Hall, where the troops chiefly assemble or halt on their way through town. When soldiers march by there is grave shouting; nothing like the common cheering. There is an earnestness such as I never witnessed before in any popular movement.

—Ticknor and Hillard, eds., *Life, Letters, and Journals of George Ticknor*

C. "There Is but One Thought—The Stars and Stripes"

Horace Binney to Sir J. T. Coleridge.

Philadelphia, 27 May, 1861

. . . The assault upon Fort Sumter started us all to our feet, as one man; all political division ceased among us from that very moment. Private relations with the South have been put aside, no doubt with great regret. There is among us but one thought, one object, one end, one symbol,—the Stars and Stripes. We are to a great degree at present, and will shortly be throughout, an armed nation. We have the whole naval power of the country. We have nearly all its money at command. We know that we shall be both degraded and ruined unless this government is maintained; and we are not so much embittered at this time (as we hope we shall continue) as to be unable to make the combat as respectable in point of humanity as war between public belligerents can be.

Most of the seceded slave States are much divided. Eastern Tennessee, Northern Alabama, Western Virginia, are wholly in favour of the Union. Kentucky has expressly refused to go out. Tennessee is still balancing; Missouri cannot go. Maryland, now that her mob has been suppressed, speaks and acts the language of Union, and she is encouraged to it by the presence of Pennsylvania forces in Baltimore and overhanging her western counties, which at the same time are known to be faithful, thoroughly Union. It is the slave-selling and slave-working parts of the South that have alone desired to break away,—by no means all of these, nor any considerable part of them but through delusion, venality, or terror. How can the North and West withhold their effort to suppress the terror which has enchained so many? It is their sacred duty under the Constitution. We have, therefore, both duty and right to confirm us in the effort. It will, I have no doubt whatever, be strenuously made. We have no reason to doubt, from either the purposes we entertain, or the motives which actuate us, or the means we shall apply, that God will help us.

Some of the writers for the English press have but an imperfect knowledge of the necessities of the free States when they argue that the slave States should be allowed to depart and make another nation. We are large enough, they say,—and that is true enough, though nothing to the purpose. The North and West cannot conquer them. That also may be true, and yet nothing to the purpose. They will conquer the North and West and destroy the Union, if they can bring about what these writers recommend. Consider, Louisiana and Florida were purchased to make the union of the West with the Atlantic States possible. They hold the Gulf of Mexico and the river Mississippi under their control, if they are left as they claim to be. Texas bounds us and turns us in to the South on the western side of the Gulf. Our intercourse with the Pacific States, all faithful to the Union, lies over the Isthmus of Darien. How can any part of the West continue in union with the North, or the Pacific be united to the Atlantic States, if an independent power holds this control?

The question for negotiation is, Which shall be the master of the gates of entrance and exit to the North and West? Was such a question ever settled by negotiation? The States on the Mississippi and the Gulf must be in union with the North and West, or be commanded by them, or the West must fly from the North. This is an old question. I heard it argued in 1797, when we had Spain to deal with in regard to these waters; and not a man South or North but held the opinion I express. It was from our weakness then that we did not conquer them; and to this single end—of maintaining our Union—we bought them afterwards, which was better; but their importance to the Union of North and West is just what it was. Great Britain knew what their value to the Union was, when her forces endeavoured to seize New Orleans in 1815.

In fine, my dear sir, I do not say we can conquer. I do say that mere conquest would be an absurdity in our relations if we could achieve it; for the Southern States would become Territories again, if anything, and go into the old connection, to go into revolt a second time. But we may subdue the revolutionary violence which has got the upper hand; we may hearten the friends of the Union in those parts to vindicate their own rights in the Union; and if we cannot do this, we may detach Louisiana, Florida, and the river portions of Mississippi, and Arkansas. If we do not, then I admit our dream of union and our national existence in its present form is gone. And such a shame, dishonour, degradation, in the sight of all the world! God forbid that we should live to see it! Three hundred and fifty thousand masters of slaves—not more—breaking down the power and hopes of twenty millions of freemen, for the most part the descendants of Englishmen! You recollect Cowley's burst, in regard to Cromwell's usurpation:

"Come the eleventh plague, rather than this should be,
Come sink us rather in the sea.
* * * * * * * *
In all the chains we ever bore,
We griev'd, we sigh'd, we wept, we never blush'd before."

This has been a long ramble, my dear sir. I have no time to make it shorter, for I am deep in a commission to provide for the poor families of the mechanics who have become volunteers.

—BINNEY, *The Life of Horace Binney*

D. "ONE GREAT EAGLE SCREAM"

Jane Stuart Woolsey to a Friend in Paris.
8 Brevoort Place, Friday, May 10, 1861

I am sure you will like to hear what we are all about in these times of terrible excitement, though it seems almost impertinent to write just now. Everything is either too big or too little to put in a letter. . . . So it will be best perhaps not to try to give you any of my own "views" except, indeed, such views of war as one may get out of a parlor window. Not, in passing, that I haven't any! We all have views now, men, women and little boys,

"Children with drums
Strapped round them by the fond paternal ass,
Peripatetics with a blade of grass
Betwixt their thumbs,"—

from the modestly patriotic citizen who wears a postage stamp on his hat to the woman who walks in Broadway in that fearful object of contemplation, a "Union bonnet," composed of alternate layers of red, white and blue, with streaming ribbons "of the first." We all have our views of the war question and our plans of the coming campaign. An acquaintance the other day took her little child on some charitable errand through a dingy alley into a dirty, noisy, squalid tenement house. "Mamma," said he, "isn't this South Carolina?"

Inside the parlor windows the atmosphere has been very fluffy, since Sumter, with lint-making and the tearing of endless lengths of flannel and cotton bandages and cutting out of innumerable garments. How long it is since Sumter! I suppose it is because so much intense emotion has been crowded into the last two or three weeks, that the "time before Sumter" seems to belong to some dim antiquity. It seems as if we never were alive till now; never had a country till now. How could we ever have laughed at Fourth-of-Julys? Outside the parlor windows the city is gay and brilliant with excited crowds, the incessant movement and music of marching regiments and all the thousands of flags, big and little, which suddenly came fluttering out of every window and door and leaped from every church tower, house-top, staff and ship-mast. It seemed as if everyone had in mind to try and make some amends to it for those late grievous and bitter insults. You have heard how the enthusiasm has been deepening and widening from that time.

A friend asked an Ohio man the other day how the West was taking it. "The West?" he said, "the West is all one great Eagle-scream!" A New England man told us that at Concord the bells were rung and the President's call read aloud on the village common. On the day but one after that reading, the Concord Regiment was marching into Fanueil Hall. Somebody in Washington asked a Massachusetts soldier: "How many more men of your state are coming?" "All of us," was the answer. One of the wounded Lowell men crawled into a machine shop in Baltimore. An "anti-Gorilla" citizen, seeing how young he was, asked, "What brought you here fighting, so far away from your home, my poor boy?" "It was the stars and stripes," the dying voice said. Hundreds of such stories are told. Everybody knows one. You read many of them in the papers. In our own little circle of friends one mother has sent away an idolized son; another, two; another, four. One boy, just getting over diphtheria, jumps out of bed and buckles his knapsack on. One throws up his passage to Europe and takes up his "enfield." One sweet young wife is packing a regulation valise for her husband today, and doesn't let him see her cry. Another young wife is looking fearfully for news from Harper's Ferry, where her husband is ordered. He told me a month ago, *before Sumter,* that no Northman could be found to fight against the South. One or two of our soldier friends are surgeons or officers, but most of them are in the ranks, and think no work too hard or too mean, so it is for The Flag. Captain Schuyler Hamilton was an aid of General Scott's in Mexico, and saw service there, but he shouldered his musket and marched as a private with the Seventh. They wanted an officer when he got down there, and took him out of the ranks, but it was all the same to him; and so on, indefinitely.

The color is all taken out of the "Italian Question." Garibaldi indeed! "Deliverer of Italy!" Every mother's son of us is a "Deliverer." We women regretfully "sit at home at ease" and only appease ourselves by doing the little we can with sewing machines and patent bandage-rollers. Georgy, Miss Sarah Woolsey and half a dozen other friends earnestly wish to join the Nurse Corps, but are under the required age. The rules are stringent, no doubt wisely so, and society just now presents the unprecedented spectacle of many women trying to make it believed that they are over thirty!

The Vermont boys passed through this morning, with the "strength of the hills" in their marching and the green sprigs in their button-holes. The other day I saw some companies they told me were from Maine. They looked like it—sun-browned swingers of great axes, horn-handed "breakers of the glebe," used to wintering in the woods and getting frost-bitten and having their feet chopped off and conveying huge fleets of logs down spring-tide rivers in the snow and in the floods.—The sound of the drum is never out of our ears.

Never fancy that we are fearful or gloomy. We think we feel thoroughly that war is dreadful, especially war with the excitement off and the chill on, but there are so many worse things than gun-shot wounds! And among the worst is a hateful and hollow peace with such a crew as the "Montgomery mutineers." There was a dark time just after the Baltimore murders, when communication with Washington was cut off and the people in power seemed to be doing nothing to re-establish it. It cleared up, however, in a few days, and now we don't feel that the "social fabric"—I believe that is what it is called—is "falling to pieces" at all, but that it is getting gloriously mended. So, "Republicanism will wash"—*is* washed already in the water and the fire of this fresh baptism, "clothed in white samite, mystic, wonderful," and has a new name, which is *Patriotism*.

—BACON AND HOWLAND, eds., *Letters of a Family During the War*

5. "THE SPIRIT OF VIRGINIA CANNOT BE CRUSHED"

Virginia, where the tradition of nationalism was strong, hesitated to join the seceding states, but the attack on Fort Sumter and Lincoln's proclamation calling for 75,000 troops—together with geographical necessity—finally drew her into the Confederacy. On April 17, 1861, a convention voted for secession, 103 to 46, and this vote was ratified a month later by a popular vote of 96,750 to 32,134. Most of the minority vote came from the western counties, which shortly seceded and established the state of West Virginia.

The hopes and fears of Virginians are well illustrated by former President Tyler who, as President of the Peace Convention, labored for compromise but who, like Lee, went with his state when the die was cast. Mrs. Tyler, his second wife, was from New York.

John Tyler to Mrs. Tyler.

Richmond, April 17 [18], 1861

Well, my dearest one, Virginia has severed her connection with the Northern hive of abolitionists, and takes her stand as a sovereign and independent State. By a large vote she decided on yesterday, at about three o'clock, to resume the powers she had granted to the Federal government, and to stand before the world clothed in the full vestments of sovereignty. The die is thus cast, and her future in the hands of the god of battle. The contest into which we enter is one full of peril, but there is a spirit abroad in Virginia which cannot be crushed until the life of the last man is trampled out. The numbers opposed to us are immense; but twelve thousand Grecians conquered the whole power of Xerxes at Marathon, and our fathers, a mere handful, overcame the enormous power of Great Britain.

The North seems to be thoroughly united against us. The *Herald* and the *Express* both give way and rally the hosts against us. Things have gone to that point in Philadelphia that no one is safe in the expression of a Southern sentiment. . . . At Washington a system of martial law must have been established. The report is that persons are not permitted to pass through the city to the South. . . .

Two expeditions are on foot—the one directed against the Navy Yard at Gosport, the other Harper's Ferry. Several ships are up the river at the Navy Yard, and immense supplies of guns and powder; but there is no competent leader, and they have delayed it so long that the government has now a very strong force there. The hope is that Pickens will send two thousand men to aid in capturing it. From Harper's Ferry nothing is heard. The city is full of all sorts of rumors. To-morrow night is now fixed for the great procession; flags are raised all about town.

Your devoted,

J. TYLER.

Mrs. John Tyler to her mother.

Richmond, June 16, 1861

I rejoice in an opportunity to write you through the kindness of a gentleman who has some means of communication with Baltimore. The convention met again on the 12th, and I accompanied the President up. Shall return home on Tuesday. In the meantime the children left behind are in good hands. Mrs. R. Tyler and family of four children are at Sherwood. Gardie is with me here enjoying the military excitement, and Julia is at Mrs. Pegram's. All are well.

You have heard of the battle in the vicinity of Hampton and Bethel (that is around the location of Bethel church). The fight on the Southern side was more wonderful than the taking of Sumter—only 1,100 troops (eleven hundred) were there, eight hundred of whom were engaged against a force of Northern troops amounting to four or five thousand; but *one* killed and four slightly wounded on the Southern side; loss larger on the other. How can it be otherwise than that? The hand of Providence should assist this holy Southern cause. The Northern papers give garbled accounts, but *this* is the true statement. Hampton and vicinity have suffered all sorts of depredations from Lincoln's army—inoffensive people, and their private residences have been disturbed in every possible way; but the Villa I hear has been treated with more respect as yet.

More and more we have the *realization* of war; from day to day the people, the entire people, are making up their minds to it, until every family of high and low degree are seeing their male members don the soldier's dress and shoulder their musket to go forth for the protection of their invaded firesides. It makes the heart beat and the eyes fill to witness such noble resolution and bravery on the part of all, but in particular on the part of those who, bred in ease and luxury, still cheerfully accept every and any hardship that comes with a soldier's life, whether as officers or in the ranks, for the latter are thick with accomplished gentlemen, than permit the unresisted invasion of their dearest rights. The men have become heroes—*all*, from youths of seventeen to those far advanced in years; but one common feeling swells their bosoms, deep indignation against those who should have been their best friends, and not their worst enemies. An unlawful war has been waged against them, and if the possession of every warrior trait will enable them to "conquer a peace," there will soon be one for us. Every way I turn I see an acquaintance and friend, either in the flannel shirt of a private, or in the braided jacket of the zouave, or the plumed cap of the cavalry officer. It is women and children only that are not in arms *all ready* for a moment's notice. A large body of noble, brave Marylanders have found it impossible to *wait*, and have resigned with a feeling of relief their homes to *fight* side by side with their Southern brethren. By all sorts of stratagems they are slipping over fully armed, and joining their companions without delay.

Subjugate or *bring to terms* such a people! Little do you *dream* at the North of what stuff they are made. Why, even Gardie and Alex, mourn that they cannot at once be of them; they are *fired up* with enthusiasm for what they consider such a sacred cause as the defense of their soil from the wicked and cruel invader. It is a thrilling, melting sight to see the entrances into the city of troops by the trains from all parts of the Southern country, coming as they appear to feel, to the *rescue of old Virginia*. The fatigue of travel makes no impression upon them, and they joyfully march off to their encampments, apparently congratulating themselves they are so near the scene of action. "Still they come."

At church to-day Gen. Davis was introduced to me. He mentioned that Mrs. D. and himself would be to see me to-morrow. He is a splendid man, fine manners, and the bearing of one good and great. Gen. Lee called upon us after church; rather grayer than when I last met him, some years ago, but still the elegant officer, looking animated and full of vigor. He spoke very calmly and indifferently of the desecration of his home at Arlington, and the flight of his invalid wife. She has moved out of the way of the enemy twice, and now she says *they will have to take her*—she will move no more. The General laughed, as he repeated what she said, but added, as her health was much affected by rheumatism, it was quite a trial to her to be deprived of her home.

And now adieu, dear Mamma. Continue perfectly at ease about me. All I ask is, take care of yourself, and don't get sick.

Your affectionate daughter,

JULIA.

—TYLER, *Letters and Times of the Tylers*

6. "I AM FILLED WITH HORROR AT THE CONDITION OF OUR COUNTRY"

Nowhere in the Confederacy was Union sentiment stronger than in North Carolina, which was the last state to secede. The despair of Southern Union-

ists, faced as they were with hostility from both sides, can be read in the correspondence of Jonathan Worth, later governor of his state.

Jonathan Worth to Dr. C. W. Woolen.

Asheboro, May 17, 1861

I am filled with horror at the condition of our country. According to my notions of Government, there is much that is wrong on both sides. The Abolitionists of the Free States ought not to have agitated the slavery question at all, even conceding that their feeling is right. It only tends to make the treatment of slaves more vigorous and to encourage bitterness between the two sections. When it was seized upon as a party question it was easy to see it must soon become sectional. . . .

I have always regarded the dissolution of the Union as the greatest misfortune which could befall the whole nation and the whole human race. Hence I have abhorred the agitation of the slavery question as tending to this result. Acting on that conviction I have used all the efforts in my power to stay what I regarded as the madness of both sections, and in the immediate sphere of my influence have impressed my views upon others. My immediate constituents sustained me with greater unanimity than did the constituents of any other representative. I was the first public man in the State to call on the people to vote down the Convention on the 28th Feb., on the ground that the calling of it would tend to a dissolution of the Union. Everybody attributed to me a larger share of the credit or discredit of defeating the call of a Convention than to any other man in the State. I regarded the result in N. C. and Tenn. as arresting the march of madness. Union men had gained strength up to the proclamation of Lincoln. If he had withdrawn the garrison of Fort Sumter on the principle of a military necessity and in obedience in what seemed to be the will of Congress in refusing to pass the force bill, this State and Tenn. and the other slave States which had not passed the ordinance of Secession, would have stood up for the Union. In the feverish state of the popular mind, if he be a man of good sense, he knew he would crush the Union men in the Slave States by the policy he adopted. All of us who had stood by the Union, felt that he had abandoned us and surrendered us to the tender mercies of Democracy & the Devil. He must have known that he was letting loose on us a torrent to which we could oppose no resistance.

It may be said, theoretically, that this should not have been the effect. Statesmen should have common sense. All sensible men knew it would be the effect. We are still at a loss to determine whether he is an old goose, as well as each of his advisers, thinking to preserve the Union by his course, or whether he became apprehensive that the Union men were about to gain strength enough in the South to stay Secession and he desired to drive us all into rebellion, in order to make a crusade against slavery and desolate our section. In the former case he is a fool: in the latter—a devil. He could have adopted no policy so effectual to destroy the Union. Since the issue of that great proclamation, it is unsafe for a Union man in even N. C. to own he is for the Union. The feeling is to resist to the death. Union men feel that just as they had got so they could stand on their legs, Lincoln had heartlessly turned them over to the mercy of their enemies. We feel that his co-operation with the Secessionists left us no alternative but to take arms against our neighbors, or to defend ourself against his aggression.

I am still a Union man, but for military resistance to Lincoln, believing that Lincoln and his cabinet have acted on their mistaken impression that their policy was the best for the preservation of the Union, and that they do not intend to proclaim servile insurrection. If the latter is the design the South can be conquered only by extermination. If his purpose be, as he says, to respect property and discountenance rebellion or insurrection among our servile population, and our people become satisfied of this, many of our people will not willingly take arms.

I see no hope of any good and stable government except in the United government we are pulling down. It can not be united by war. If peace be immediately made, it will soon re-unite, with an anti-secession clause.

Write me again soon. The Quakers here will not believe your statements as to your Quakers volunteering and the floating of the Stars and Stripes over a Quaker Church.

—HAMILTON, ed., *The Correspondence of Jonathan Worth*

7. A NORTHERN DEMOCRAT URGES PEACEFUL SEPARATION

Peace sentiment was to be found in the North as well as in the South; many whose loyalty to the Union was beyond question were nevertheless in favor of letting the seceding states go in peace. Much of the antiwar sentiment, however, was inspired by distaste for Lincoln and for "black Republicanism." The attitude here expressed took extreme form in copperheadism, or in the activities of such organizations as the Knights of the Golden Circle.

John L. O'Sullivan was a distinguished lawyer, editor and journalist who is credited with the authorship of the phrase "manifest destiny"; he had been appointed Minister to Portugal by President Pierce and after his term ran out lingered on in Lisbon, Paris and London. Tilden was a leading Northern Democrat and, in 1876, candidate for the Presidency.

J. L. O'Sullivan to S. J. Tilden.

Lisbon, May 6, 1861

My Dear Tilden,—The heart-breaking news has just reached us here, first of the attack and capture of Sumter, for which the signal was so madly and so wickedly given by the administration (dominated, evidently, by the war portion of that party) in its despatch of reinforcements; and, secondly, of Lincoln's declaration of war by his proclamation for 75,000 volunteers for the recapture of all the Southern forts, that is, for the invasion of the South— an act followed of course, by secession of Virginia, and soon to be followed,

I have no doubt, by that of all or nearly all the border States. Also the telegraph tells of a Massachusetts regiment resisted in an (insane) attempt to force a passage through Baltimore. Gracious God, that we should have lived to see such things! You can better judge, than I could describe, my affliction. At first it drew from me convulsions of tears. . . .

What doom is sufficient for the mad authors of all this! By that I mean, for 9/10 of the crime, the ultra portion of the Republican party. The papers say that there is a common enthusiasm of all parties at the North for the support of the admn. I may stand alone, but I do not share this. I am extremely anxious to hear from you. Do write me your views. I chafe terribly under the impossibilities which alone prevent my hastening home. Not only have I not the means, but I cannot leave my debts here, when a short, prolonged stay will probably assure me the means of paying them. Then I shall come, to do my best in the fight at home for *peaceful* separation if reunion has become indeed impossible.

What will New York do? I trust devoutly that if any troops march from our State southward they may consist only of Republicans. My hope now is that the North will at last realize the mad horror of the whole thing, and that a cloud of witnesses will arise to protest against its being carried further. Thus far the country has drifted along, both sides standing obstinate to the consistency of their opposite *theories*. But surely all should now agree to pause and hold back! But the Republican leaders, I fear, will now move heaven and hell to push and drag the North to sustain them in the position to which they have brought things. And I fear much from the fighting character of our people. I dread the next news. If Maryland goes with Virginia, there will probably be dreadful fighting for the possession of Washington, unless the wise and patriotic like you can stop it.

We are exemplifying the fable of the dispute between the head and the tail of the snake for the right to lead. The Democratic party is the natural and the only possible government of our Democratic confederation. It alone has ever understood the idea of State rights. The tail has taken its turn of leadership and you see to what a pass it has brought the country.

Were it not for the immediate question of fighting to grow out of the question of the possession of Washington, I should say it were best that the border States should now all go at once, so as to make the North feel the absurdity of further prosecution of war. But reunion is now, I fear, scarcely to be hoped for!

Ever yours,

J. L. O'SULLIVAN.

—BIGELOW, ed., *Letters and Literary Memorials of Samuel J. Tilden*

8. "THE RACE OF PHILIP SIDNEYS IS NOT EXTINCT"

From his diplomatic post in Vienna the historian Motley watched with mounting anxiety the progress of the war. This letter to his old friend Dr. Holmes suggests something of the pride of the Boston aristocracy whose sons fought for the Union as the aristocrats of Virginia and South Carolina fought for independence.

The Wendell Holmes who had been wounded at Ball's Bluff was the later Justice of the U. S. Supreme Court, who said, "The generation that carried on the war has been set apart by its experience. Through our great good fortune our hearts were touched with fire."

John Lothrop Motley to Dr. O. W. Holmes.

Vienna, November 14th, 1861

My Dear Holmes,—Your letter of October 8th awaited me here. I need not tell you with what delight I read it, and with what gratitude I found you so faithful to the promises which we exchanged on board the *Europa*. . . . As soon as I read your letter I sat down to reply, but I had scarcely written two lines when I received the first telegram of the Ball's Bluff affair. I instantly remembered what you had told me—that Wendell "was on the right of the advance on the Upper Potomac, the post of honour and danger," and it was of course impossible for me to write to you till I had learned more, and you may easily conceive our intense anxiety. The bare brutal telegram announcing a disaster arrives always four days before any details can possibly be brought. Well, after the four days came my London paper; but, as ill-luck would have it, my American ones had not begun to arrive. At last, day before yesterday, I got a New York *Evening Post*, which contained Frank Palfrey's telegram. Then our hearts were saddened enough by reading, "Willie Putnam, killed; Lee, Revere, and George Perry, captured;" but they were relieved of an immense anxiety by the words, "O. W. Holmes, jun., slightly wounded."

Poor Mrs. Putnam! I wish you would tell Lowell (for to the mother or father I do not dare to write) to express the deep sympathy which I feel for their bereavement, that there were many tears shed in our little household in this distant place for the fate of his gallant, gentle-hearted, brave-spirited nephew. I did not know him much—not at all as grown man; but the name of Willie Putnam was a familiar sound to us six years ago on the banks of the Arno, for we had the pleasure of passing a winter in Florence at the same time with the Putnams, and I knew that that studious youth promised to be all which his name and his blood and the influences under which he was growing up entitled him to become. We often talked of American politics—I mean his father and mother and ourselves—and I believe that we thoroughly sympathized in our views and hopes. Alas, they could not then foresee that that fair-haired boy was after so short a time destined to lay down his young life on the Potomac, in one of the opening struggles for freedom and law with the accursed institution of slavery! Well, it is a beautiful death—the most beautiful that man can die. Young as he was, he had gained name and fame, and his image can never be associated in the memory of the hearts which mourn for him except with ideas of honor, beauty, and purity of manhood.

After we had read the New York newspaper, the next day came a batch of Boston dailies and a letter from my dear little Mary. I seized it with avidity and began to read it aloud, and before I had finished the first page it dropped from my hand and we all three burst into floods of tears. Mary wrote that Harry Higginson, of the 2nd, had visited the camp of the 20th, and that Wendell Holmes was shot through the lungs and not likely to recover. It seemed too cruel, just as we had been informed that he was but slightly wounded. After the paroxysm was over, I picked up the letter and read a rather important concluding phrase of Mary's statement, viz., "But this, thank God, has proved to be a mistake." I think if you could have been clairvoyant, and looked in upon our dark little sitting-room of the Archduke Charles Hotel, fourth storey, at that moment, you could have had proof enough, if you needed any fresh ones, of the strong hold that you and yours have on all our affections. There are very many youths in that army of freedom whose career we watch with intense interest; but Wendell Holmes is ever in our thoughts side by side with those of our own name and blood.

I renounce all attempt to paint my anxiety about our affairs. I do not regret that Wendell is with the army. It is a noble and healthy symptom that brilliant, intellectual, poetical spirits like his spring to arms when a noble cause like ours inspires them. The race of Philip Sidneys is not yet extinct, and I honestly believe that as much genuine chivalry exists in our Free States at this moment as there is or ever was in any part of the world, from the Crusaders down. I did not say a word when I was at home to Lewis Stackpole about his plans—but I was very glad when he wrote to me that he had accepted a captaincy in Stevenson's regiment. I suppose by this time that they are in the field. . . .

Nobody on this side the Atlantic has the faintest conception of our affairs. Let me hear from time to time, as often as you can, how you are impressed by the current events, and give me details of such things as immediately interest you. Tell me all about Wendell. How does your wife stand her trials? Give my love to her and beg her to keep a brave heart. *Haec olim meminisse juvabit.* And how will those youths who stay at home "account themselves accursed they were not there," when the great work has been done, as done it will be! Of that I am as sure as that there is a God in heaven.

—Curtis, ed., *The Correspondence of John Lothrop Motley*

9. A YOUNG POET EXPLAINS THE SIGNIFICANCE OF THE WAR

Edmund Clarence Stedman was working on the New York World *when the war broke out. He hastened at once to Washington, went to the front as a war correspondent, and reported the First Battle of Bull Run. He took some pride in the fact that he had been the first to use the army telegraph—in June 1861. Later Stedman worked in the Attorney General's office and subsequently made a minor fortune in a brokerage office and a minor reputation as a poet.*

This letter was in answer to maternal arguments against the war. It is perhaps worth adding that, though Stedman was only twenty-seven when war came, he did not enlist in the army.

Edmund Clarence Stedman to his mother.

Oct. 16, 1861 (Near Baker's Camp, Poolesville, Md.)

Pardon me for saying that I have attentively studied your and Mary's echoes of the family oracle's views on the war question, and think you do not have the slightest appreciation of the real points at issue. You need not take my notions for anything more than they are worth, but I am going, contrary to my usual habit, to give you some reasons for what you call my "enthusiasm." Premise that I am angry with myself for doing so, since first what is the use? Why trouble one's self with writing and arguing when no bread-and-butter are to be gained thereby? Why should I care what you think about it? and second, is it possible in a few lines, to make the issue to your mind? I think not; yet will make a few statements ... from which your own judgment may reason out the whole.

I have enlisted all my humble energies in this cause, then, for two reasons: First, one of selfishness—the necessity for personal shaking-up and *rejuvenating*—the old, *healthy* love *action* rising in me, as described in the first part of the "Flood Tide"; the credit and reputation to be derived, and the subsistence earned, by my present occupation—the love of adventure, etc. Second, one of principle. I am really surprised to find myself sometimes forgetting self, and feeling human love and heartthrobs and patriotism. I think the War right and noble. For the first time the hackneyed stars-and-stripes have to me a significance. With the half-million noble and more simple-hearted men who are fighting for their country, I think that the "individual lessens and the cause is more and more." For eight years I have cared *nothing* for politics—have been disgusted with American life and doings. Now, for the first time, I am proud of my country and my grand heroic brethren. The greatness of the crisis, the Homeric grandeur of the contest, surrounds and elevates us all. See what it is:

1. *A complete revolution and renovation of all the customs and constitution of Americans North and South. A.* One million of the late emasculate Americans are put under magnificent hygienic training. Strong men and noble will henceforth inherit the land. *B.* The base passions attendant upon scheming and money-grubbing are laid aside for simple, chivalric, national love and hate, and henceforth the sentimental and poetic will fuse with the intellectual to dignify and elevate our race. The pride, pomp and *circumstance* of glorious war, and the big contests, *do* make ambition, virtue; and all *here, on the spot, see* that even bloodshed doeth its own good work. Men, that we once despised as small politicians, loafers, traders and what-not, are having all the good and heroic in them developed—are brightly transformed amid these altered scenes and nobler motives. *C.* Thousands of men of real talent, *born soldiers,* for whom in this country there has been no use hitherto, and who have consequently been "black sheep," gamblers, vagabonds, and

loafers, are now finding their legitimate calling—shooting back into their natural spheres. Suppose, there was no such thing as literature—what would fellows like myself do but be vagabonds and proletarians? Just so with your late fillibusters.

2. *The War is a duty on the part of the North.* It is not waged by abolitionists, it is *not* the result of abolitionism. We are not sure but that slavery is a very good thing in the Cotton states. In other latitudes I see for myself that it is good enough for the Negroes, but ruinous to the whites. There is a theory, that the Virginia and Kentucky gentry own slaves; this is false: I have seen for myself that the *niggars own the gentry*. Now I wish to make you and Mary understand that, although we see that this War will probably settle the slavery question, and possibly forever limit slavery to the Cotton States, *yet we are not fighting the Negro's cause.* Slavery has been the cause of the war in no sense other than that it has added another distinctness to the line betwixt North and South which climate and race had already drawn. The real cause of the War is a bitter and criminal hatred, entertained by the South against the North, and based on other than slave interests.

For fifty years the *character* of Southerners has become daily more domineering, insolent, irrational, haughty, scornful of justice. They have so long cracked their whips over Negroes that they now assume a certain inherent right to crack them over *white men;* assume the positive rights of a superior race; and have taken advantage of the North's desire for quiet and peace to impose upon us without stint. For years the tone of their actions and speeches, in Congress and society has expressed this sentiment and determination. Even Southern students at College, when I was at Yale, adopted the same tactics. One hundred of them—poor scholars, but blustering with rum and bowie knives—lorded it over four hundred studious New Englanders, simply because the latter *were* studious and desired to attain the objects aimed at in a collegiate course. At length the thing became degrading, and we arose one day and kicked them all out.

For fifty years the same plan has been practised on a larger scale in our national affairs. The South, assisted by Northern merchants whom it has governed, has been true enough to the Union, so long as every election gave *it* the power, and as foreign missions, army and navy commissions, presidencies, etc. were held in its own hands. But the census of 1850 shewed that the enterprising and industrious North was getting the balance of power. Then the South began to rebel and would have seceded had not the Clay compromise taken away *its sole pretext.* Now the census of 1860, and the Lincoln election have revived *both the desire and* the pretext, and it *has* seceded. . . .

3. *Right, power, and noble sentiments being on our side, it is our duty to carry on the War.* The South took active part in last Fall's election, thereby pledging itself to acquiesce in the result, and now *breaks* its pledge. The South has attacked the North; the South commenced the War; the South proceeded from domineering in Congress to actual hostilities, and I say that the North ignored the necessity of fighting for a period that became

almost degrading. You would perhaps like to have Northerners turn themselves into spittoons at once. Why, I was so indignant at the *too* long-suffering of the North that I seriously thought of disowning my own country and going to Canada or England to live. Tell your husband that if the Union is to be shattered at the will of a minority, we might as well give up the idea of nationality at once, disown patriotism and let all go to pieces. That nation is noblest which is the most sensitive about its own integrity, and will shed the most blood for a *principle*, and noble nations make noble individual men.

For such reasons I think the War of 1861 a benefit to both North and South, a duty on the part of the North, and please God, it shall be pushed to the true end. For one I have no objection to let the South go, and hope they will; but the dignity of right must first be sustained, and the injury to the republic avenged, and *they must ask to go in the proper way*. They might easily have effected a peaceful separation, by petition and vote, years ago. But that course would not have elevated Davis and the other ambitious men, now deluding their brave but senseless followers. And if we should now make peace, without proving our determination, power and heroism, we should forever hereafter be the world's laughing stock and the white slaves of our Southern neighbors.

You have lived so long away, and remained as it were, stationary in knowledge, of our affairs, that the whole character of America has whirled ten years by you and become transformed into necessities and emotions that you fail to comprehend.

Now don't say anything more against the War without first reading over this letter and seeing if I have now answered it.

—STEDMAN AND GOULD, *Life and Letters of Edmund Clarence Stedman*

10. THE SUPREME COURT UPHOLDS THE CONSTITUTION

Was the rebellion a war? Could the President proclaim a blockade, raise troops, and exercise, generally, war powers, without a recognition of a state of war by the Congress? These questions were not entirely in the realm of speculation. Alleging that only Congress could declare war, that there had been no such declaration or even recognition of war by Congress, that a blockade is an instrument of war, and that the Presidential proclamation of the blockade was therefore illegal, a group of owners of ships seized as prizes for trying to run the blockade sued for recovery of their property.

Justice Grier, in his decision in the so-called Prize Cases, recognized the existence of a state of war, sustained the blockade, and denounced the illegality of secession. But it was a close thing. Astonishing as it seems, today, four judges dissented.

Mr. Justice Grier:

Let us inquire whether, at the time this blockade was instituted, a state of war existed which would justify a resort to these means of subduing the hostile force.

War has been well defined to be, "That state in which a nation prosecutes its right by force."

The parties belligerent in a public war are independent nations. But it is not necessary, to constitute war, that both parties should be acknowledged as independent nations or sovereign States. A war may exist where one of the belligerents claims sovereign rights as against the other.

Insurrection against a government may or may not culminate in an organized rebellion, but a civil war always begins by insurrection against the lawful authority of the government. A civil war is never solemnly declared; it becomes such by its accidents—the number, power, and organization of the persons who originate and carry it on. When the party in rebellion occupy and hold in a hostile manner a certain portion of territory; have declared their independence; have cast off their allegiance; have organized armies; have commenced hostilities against their former Sovereign, the world acknowledges them as belligerents, and the contest a war. They claim to be in arms to establish their liberty and independence, in order to become a sovereign State, while the sovereign party treats them as insurgents and rebels who owe allegiance, and who should be punished with death for their treason. . . .

As a civil war is never publicly proclaimed, *eo nomine* against insurgents, its actual existence is a fact in our domestic history which the court is bound to notice and to know. . . .

This greatest of civil wars was not gradually developed by popular commotion, tumultuous assemblies, or local unorganized insurrections. However long may have been its previous conception, it nevertheless sprung forth suddenly from the parent brain, a Minerva in the full panoply of war. The President was bound to meet it in the shape it presented itself, without waiting for Congress to baptize it with a name; and no name given to it by him or them could change the fact.

It is not the less a civil war, with belligerent parties in hostile array, because it may be called an "insurrection" by one side, and the insurgents be considered as rebels or traitors. It is not necessary that the independence of the revolted province or State be acknowledged in order to constitute it a party belligerent in a war according to the law of nations. Foreign nations acknowledge it as war by a declaration of neutrality. The condition of neutrality cannot exist unless there be two belligerent parties. . . .

After such an official recognition by the sovereign, a citizen of a foreign State is estopped to deny the existence of a war, with all its consequences, as regards neutrals. They cannot ask a court to affect a technical ignorance of the existence of a war, which all the world acknowledges to be the greatest civil war known in the history of the human race, and thus cripple the arm of the government and paralyze its power by subtile definitions and ingenious sophisms.

The law of nations is also called the law of nature; it is founded on the common consent as well as the common sense of the world. It contains no such anomalous doctrine as that which this court are now for the first time desired to pronounce, to wit: That insurgents who have risen in rebellion

Frank Leslie's Illustrated Newspaper

Lincoln's First Inauguration

Harper's Weekly

The House Tops in Charleston During the Bombardment
of Fort Sumter

against their sovereign, expelled her courts, established a revolutionary government, organized armies, and commenced hostilities, are not enemies because they are traitors; and a war levied on the government by traitors, in order to dismember and destroy it, is not a war because it is an "insurrection."

—*Prize Cases*, 67 United States Supreme Court Reports 635 (1863)

III

The Gathering of the Hosts

LOOKING *back on four years of war Lincoln said, in his memorable Second Inaugural Address, "Neither party expected for the war the magnitude or the duration which it has already attained. . . . Each looked for an easier triumph, and a result less fundamental and astounding."*

Certainly neither side was prepared for a long war or even for a hard one. Northerners could hardly believe that the South would actually fight; Southerners deluded themselves that Yankee traders and workingmen were unwilling to fight. The North had a regular army of some 16,000, but with secession many of these resigned to go with their states; the South had no army, though as early as February 28 the President had been authorized to accept such state troops as were offered.

The firing on Fort Sumter inspired widespread enthusiasm in the South; in the North it inspired not so much enthusiasm as sober loyalty to the flag and the Union. Everywhere, North and South, boys and men rallied to the colors; everywhere great crowds assembled to see the new recruits march off to some near-by camp, proud of their improvised uniforms, happily unaware of what lay ahead.

> *North and South they assembled, one cry and the other cry.*
> *And both are ghosts to us now, old drums hung up on a wall,*
> *But they were the first hot wave of youth too-ready to die,*
> *And they went to war with an air, as if they went to a ball.*
>
> *Dress-uniform boys who rubbed their buttons brighter than gold,*
> *And gave them to girls for flowers and raspberry-lemonade,*
> *Unused to the sick fatigue, the route-march made in the cold,*
> *The stink of the fever camps, the tarnish rotting the blade.**

By act of March 8, 1861, the Confederate Congress created an army of seven regiments with enlistments for from three to five years. Two months later the President was authorized to accept the services of all volunteers who presented themselves. For the most part, however, the Confederacy raised its army through the states; some states even provided for conscription, on their own. As volunteering proved inadequate, the Confederate government

---

* From *John Brown's Body* in *The Selected Works of Stephen Vincent Benét*, published by Rinehart and Company, Inc. Copyright 1927, 1928 by Stephen Vincent Benét.

adopted conscription; an act of April 16, 1862, made all men between the ages of 18 and 35 subject to draft, and these age limits were later broadened to embrace all between 17 and 50.

On April 15, 1861, Lincoln called for 75,000 three-months volunteers, assigning quotas to each state and Territory. The method of raising companies was left pretty much to the states and localities. The initiative was usually taken by local leaders who undertook to recruit companies—and get themselves elected to captaincies or lieutenancies. When an appropriate number of volunteers had been pledged (many deserted to other companies), the governor of the state would enroll the company in the state militia and assume appropriate expenses. Such matters as providing uniforms, arms, equipment, even provisions, were handled haphazardly; sometimes these things were provided by rich men who raised the companies, sometimes by community effort, but usually by the states.

The first call for troops proved inadequate and on May 3 the President called for an additional 500,000; actually 700,000 were raised under this call. Thereafter came a series of calls for varying numbers and for varying periods of service. Altogether the states were required to raise 2,763,670 troops, and furnished 2,772,408, but this figure includes re-enlistments. Perhaps two thirds of these actually served in the army.

This is as good a place as any to deal with the vexatious question of numbers in the Union and Confederate armies. Let it be said at once that the statistics for the Union armies are confusing and unreliable, and that there are no satisfactory statistics whatever for the Confederate armies. A number of considerations enter into even the most elementary computations. There is, for example, the problem of differing periods of service. In both armies service varied from three months to three years, or the duration of the war: obviously a soldier in for four years counts more than one in for three or six months. There is the difficult question of desertion, or failure to report (which was technical desertion); this ran as high as ten per cent in both armies. There is the problem of re-enlistment, and of bounty jumping. There is the problem of the wounded and the sick; these were in the army, but were of course ineffectives.

Frederick Phisterer, statistician of the Union armies, gives a total of 2,772,408 furnished by the states and Territories, or credited to them; reducing this to a three-years-service standard he arrives at the figure 2,320,272. Thomas Livermore, whose Numbers and Losses *is perhaps more reliable, estimates total enlistments of 2,898,304 of whom some 230,000 failed to serve, for one reason or another. Reducing this figure to a three-years-service equivalent—and taking into account desertion—he gives a total of 1,556,678 for the Union armies. Estimates of the numbers in the Confederate Army run all the way from a low of 600,000 to a high of 1,500,000. Livermore's estimate of the number equivalent to three-years service is 1,082,119—perhaps as good as any.*

Far more illuminating are the numbers actually on the rolls at any one time: this gives a much truer index of relative numbers. The simplest thing here is to reproduce the table which Livermore worked out from the Official Records:

	UNION	CONFEDERATE
July 1861	186,751	112,040
Jan. 1862	575,917	351,418
Mar. 1862	637,126	401,395
Jan. 1863	918,121	446,622
Jan. 1864	860,737	481,180
Jan. 1865	959,460	445,203

Two conclusions emerge from these figures. First that a relatively much higher proportion of Southern than Northern men served in the army. Second that, given the requirements of offensive warfare, of invasion, and of maintaining long lines of communication, the North had far less effective numerical superiority than the bare figures would suggest.

1. "OUR PEOPLE ARE ALL UNITED"

A member of a great Huguenot family of South Carolina, Henry William Ravenel is remembered for his career as one of the leading American botanists and for his charming and illuminating Journal, *from which this account of the impact of the war is taken.*

[April 18, 1861] . . . This morning Mr. Cornish called to see us. One of the remarkable features of the times is that men of all classes & conditions, of all occupations & professions are of one mind. We have students of Divinity & ministers of the Gospel in the ranks with musket on their shoulders doing battle for their country. Some have gone as chaplains & followed their companies into camp. All give us their prayers & cheer us onward with words of approval. The ablest vindication of our institution of domestic slavery has only lately been published in New York from the pen of Dr. Seabury, a distinguished minister of the Prot. Epis. Church. The war feeling has been nourished & stimulated at the North by the intense hatred of disappointed politicans & mad fanatics, who would consummate their hellish purposes upon us through a sea of blood if possible. The collision which has just taken place, from their determined purpose to hold a fort in our waters & thus subject us to a humiliating position, will probably raise a fury of excitement & bring over many to their side, who think their Govt. should be sustained in war, right or wrong;—but we have great numbers of staunch friends, who will be heard in time, as soon as the first paroxysm is over. Old memories of former party attachments, personal intercourse with Southerners, connections by friendships & blood, & above all, self interest will bring about a reaction & sober second thought will give them time for consideration, & to mature a public feeling there, which even those who are thirsting for our blood, will have to respect. . . .

Th. 25. . . . The New York Herald speaks of raising 500000 men & speedily conquering a peace. Easier said than done. We can do the same if necessary & fighting for our liberty & our homes, we have no doubt of the issue. All good men should ardently desire a return of peace, but it must be upon terms honorable to us & our rights. I fear the Northern people have an impression that we are unable to cope with them, from inferiority in numbers, want of necessary means; & that our slave population is an element of weakness. It may be necessary therefore that they should be disabused of such impressions, & learn to appreciate & understand us better. If we *must* pass through the terrible ordeal of War to teach them this lesson, so be it. It may be best in the end. We put our trust in the God of battles & the impartial Dispenser of Justice, & are willing to abide the issue. Our people are all united & stand up as one man in defence of their country. Our Negroes are contented & loyal. The old & the infirm who have not yet gone out to battle are ready to take their places in the ranks when their services are needed. Our women & children all enthusiastic for the common defence, 'Can such a population be subjugated?' . . .

M. 29. . . . We have never sought to assail the Northern people in any way—we have only asked to be let alone. We have been satisfied, in the sight of God & of our approving conscience, that our institutions were sanctioned by justice & religion, that mutual benefits were secured to both races inhabiting our Southern states—that our very existence as a people was staked upon its preservation;—& that it has the sanction of natural, as well as revealed religion. They have refused to permit us to remain in peace with them, & now that we have decided as a last effort of self preservation to establish a govert. for ourselves, they insolently threaten us with subjugation. We have desired to separate from them in peace, & have offered to negotiate on friendly terms the manner of separation. They have rejected all our overtures & have answered us with insult & defiance. They appeal to arms. We will meet them, putting our trust in Him who is the father of us all & in whose hands are the destinies of his people.

—CHILDS, ed., *The Private Journal of Henry William Ravenel*

2. SOUTHERN LADIES SEND THEIR MEN OFF TO WAR

Here is an unpretentious recollection of the impact of secession and war on a Georgia community. The enthusiasm of the women of the South for the war was remarked by countless contemporaries and has served as a theme for countless novels and stories. What Mrs. Ward says of the situation in Rome might have been said with equal truth about almost every other Southern community—"if the Southern men had not been willing to go I reckon they would have been made to go by the women."

Mrs. Ward was a Georgia matron of twenty when the war came; these recollections were given verbally to a Congressional committee investigating labor relations in the South. Douglas Freeman calls them "one of the most remarkable of all the women's commentaries on the war."

WELL, it was pretty hard for any one in private life, especially for a lady, to realize or appreciate the imminent danger that existed up to the very breaking out of the war, up to the time that the troops were ordered out. Discussions about the state of the country and about the condition of public affairs and the causes for war were frequent, of course, and I think I may safely say that in those discussions the women of the South without exception all took the secession side. There were a great many men in the Southern homes that were disposed to be more conservative and to regret the threatened disruption of the Union, but the ladies were all enthusiastically in favor of secession. Their idea was to let war come if it must, but to have the matter precipitated and get through with it, because this feeling of apprehension and this political wrangling had been continued for many years previous, and we felt that we in the South were strong in our own resources, and in fact we knew very little of the resources of the North compared with those of the South. My mother was a Northern woman and she always regarded the threat of war with the greatest apprehension and fear, because, as she said, she knew more about the resources of the North than others did, more than I did, for instance, or the other people of my age. But the women of the South generally were altogether in favor of secession and of the war, if there had to be a war, and if the Southern men had not been willing to go I reckon they would have been made to go by the women.

The day that Georgia was declared out of the Union was a day of the wildest excitement in Rome. There was no order or prearrangement about it at all, but the people met each other and shook hands and exchanged congratulations over it and manifested the utmost enthusiasm. Of course a great many of the older and wiser heads looked on with a great deal of foreboding at these rejoicings and evidences of delight, but the general feeling was one of excitement and joy.

Then we began preparing our soldiers for the war. The ladies were all summoned to public places, to halls and lecture-rooms, and sometimes to churches, and everybody who had sewing-machines was invited to send them; they were never demanded because the mere suggestion was all-sufficient. The sewing-machines were sent to these places and ladies that were known to be experts in cutting out garments were engaged in that part of the work, and every lady in town was turned into a seamstress and worked as hard as anybody could work; and the ladies not only worked themselves but they brought colored seamstresses to these places, and these halls and public places would be just filled with busy women all day long.

But even while we were doing all these things in this enthusiastic manner, of course there was a great deal of the pathetic manifested in connection with this enthusiasm, because we knew that the war meant the separation of our soldiers from their friends and families and the possibility of their not coming back. Still, while we spoke of these things we really did not think that there was going to be actual war. We had an idea that when our soldiers got upon the ground and showed, unmistakably that they were really ready and willing to fight—an idea that then, by some sort of hocus-pocus, we didn't know what, the whole trouble would be declared at an end. Of course we were not fully conscious of that feeling at the time, but that the feeling existed was beyond doubt from the great disappointment that showed itself afterwards when things turned out differently. We got our soldiers ready for the field, and the Governor of Georgia called out the troops and they were ordered out, five companies from Floyd County and three from Rome. They were ordered to Virginia under the command of General Joseph E. Johnston. The young men carried dress suits with them and any quantity of fine linen. . . .

Every soldier, nearly, had a servant with him, and a whole lot of spoons and forks, so as to live comfortably and elegantly in camp, and finally to make a splurge in Washington when they should arrive there, which they expected would be very soon indeed. That is really the way they went off; and their sweethearts gave them embroidered slippers and pin-cushions and needle-books, and all sorts of such little et ceteras, and they finally got off, after having a very eloquent discourse preached to them at the Presbyterian church, by the Presbyterian minister, Rev. John A. Jones. I remember his text very well. It was, "Be strong and quit yourselves like men." I don't know that I have had occasion to think of that sermon for years, but although this occurred more than twenty years ago, I remember it very distinctly at this moment. Then the choir played music of the most mournful character—"Farewell," and "Good Bye," and all that, and there was just one convulsive sob from one end of the church to the other, for the congregation was composed of the mothers and wives and sisters and daughters of the soldiers who were marching away.

The captain of the Light Guards, the most prominent company, a company composed of the *élite* of the town, had been married on the Thursday evening before this night of which I am speaking. He was a young Virginian. His wife came of very patriotic parents, and was a very brave woman herself. She came into the church that day with her husband, and walked up the aisle with him. She had on a brown traveling-dress, and a broad scarf crossed on her dress, and, I think, on it was inscribed, "The Rome Light Guards," and there was a pistol on one side and a dagger on the other. This lady went to the war with her husband, and staid there through the whole struggle, and never came home until the war was over.

—Testimony of Mrs. Mary A. Ward

3. TWO ENGLISH VISITORS DESCRIBE THE CONFEDERATE ARMY

How remarkable the American volunteer armies really were has never been appreciated by Americans themselves. It is foreigners who note the difference between American and European armies. The American Civil War attracted a large number of foreign observers, and most of them seemed to find their way into the Confederacy. A substantial number of them went home to write articles about their experiences.

Here we have two English views of the Confederate armies and soldiers. As neither of them is signed, it is difficult to know just when these visitors got their glimpse of the Confederacy, but it was clearly in 1861 and 1862.

A. "THE PERSONNEL OF THE ARMY IS VERY VARIED"

THE appearance which a regiment presents on parade is remarkable to the eye of a European. Many are composed of companies who have uniforms of different colours; but in these cases there is always some distinctive badge by which their particular corps can be easily told. This defect, consequent upon the companies being raised in different neighbourhoods, is being quickly remedied, and we saw numerous regiments which had lately arrived, whose dress was all that the Horse Guards could desire.

The *personnel* of the army is very varied. For instance, in the Louisiana regiments are seen the bronzed and fiery-eyed French creoles mingled with many Irish and native Americans from New Orleans. The Alabamans, proud of their gallant 4th, their flying artillery, and other regiments, may be known by their strong frames, gay manners, and devil-may-care air. The South Carolinians, sallow in complexion, tall in stature, seldom need the Palmetto to tell the stranger the State from which they come; but in all regiments it is easy to perceive differences in manner and bearing, indicative of the various classes of which the army is composed.

Numbers of wealthy planters serve as privates side by side with the professional man, the shopkeeper, the clerk, the labourer; and all go through the ordinary fatigue duties incident to camp-life. We saw a poor Negro servant actually shedding tears because his master, on being told off to dig a trench round a battery, would not allow him "to lend a hand."

" 'Twill nebber do, massa," he said; "I go 'tarnal mad wid dem darn'd Yankees."

One day we heard a lad boasting to one of a different regiment of the number of gentlemen in his company who had thousands of dollars at their command. The latter replied, "Oh, of course they fight; but we have some in ours who have not got a cent!" The Washington artillery, comprising many batteries is composed of the best blood in New Orleans. The gunners, dressed in light-blue uniforms, are all men of independent means. General Beauregard's son, for instance, left his father's staff, and entered as a private. The drivers are regularly enlisted into the army, and paid by the regiment; so here is a force which does not cost the country a single farthing. Their efficiency is undoubted, and the execution which they did at Bull's Run has led to their material augmentation, and the formation of others on similar principles. From the same city comes a very different regiment, called the New Orleans "Zouaves," dressed in red caps, blue braided jackets, and trousers striped with light grey and red. These men look like pirates—bearded, fierce-looking fellows. . . . As they marched past the General with a long swinging step, singing a wild martial air, we thought they were as formidable a body of men as we should care to see.

The drill of the army is the same as the French, the step even quicker than the Zouaves, and a good deal longer than that of the English infantry. Movements are executed with considerable precision, and as rapidly as in English light-infantry battalions.

From the reports we had heard in the North, we expected to find ragged and half-clad regiments; instead of which we failed, during many rides through the various camps, to see one man who was not clad in serviceable attire. It was expected that winter clothing would be served out before the 1st of November, and that dress would then become more uniform.

But the point to which the chief attention of officers and men is directed is the arms. Besides the Enfield rifle, most of the privates in the army carry at least one revolver and a bowie-knife: these are invariably kept bright and in good condition; and the early training which all Southerners undergo in shooting squirrels as soon as they are able to handle a gun, gives them a facility of using their weapons and a correctness of aim that renders their fire unusually formidable.

—Anonymous, "A Month with the 'Rebels' "

B. "The High Standards of Intelligence"

The Confederate soldier at first sight certainly presented a somewhat uncouth and even sorry appearance: about his person any kind of coat, or more commonly nothing beyond shirt and pantaloons; on his head, as the case might be, a cap, a straw hat, a slouch hat, or no hat at all. A closer scrutiny, however, showed that essentials were well provided. Besides his musket and cartridge-box, every man had a canteen, most men a blanket and a haversack. A more suitable equipment for summer service in Virginia could hardly have been devised.

What gives peculiar interest to the Confederate soldier's dress is the individual history which attaches to each separate article. From the blanket he sleeps on to the cartridge he shoots with, almost everything has been appropriated from the enemy at one time or another. This rifle was exchanged for the old flint-lock on the field of Manassas; that canteen was taken at Shiloh; the grey mare yonder, with M'Clellan's saddle, was captured in the cavalry charge at Williamsburg; these boots were taken out of the Yankee stores at Winchester. The Negro who is following with the saucepan and the extra blanket, being wiser than his master, has consulted comfort rather than prejudice, and prevailed upon himself to wear a Yankee uniform, in consideration that the former proprietor was a full colonel.

Entire batteries pass down the road, with "U. S." in prominent white letters on the caissons. It is no exaggeration to say that a great part of the Confederate army has been equipped at the expense of the United States. Flint-locks and fowling-pieces have been exchanged for good Minie rifles. There was, however, still so great a want of small-arms, that a considerable part of the army were armed with smooth-bore of home manufacture, loaded with a ball and three buckshot. This deficiency has, perhaps, not been altogether a disadvantage, inasmuch as the necessity of getting to close quarters, in order to put themselves on an equality with their opponents, has in no small degree produced among the Confederates that habit of closing with the enemy which has proved so inconvenient to the Northern troops. It seems inconceivable until witnessed, that the same men who have been marching, or rather carelessly lounging, along the road in loose and slovenly array, should, at the sound of the first shell that whistles overhead, form up at the words of their officers, with ease and rapidity, into a line so close and compact, that the sight of it would give joy to a martinet's heart. The soldiers of the Southern army were scrambled together in a few months, and the greater part of them never have gone through any regular course of drill, and are, therefore, wanting in the smartness and precision which distinguish good troops in Europe. Men take off their hats instead of saluting; orders are given in a loose conversational tone, and the gunner in a battery will suggest an opinion to the captain. But though, for these reasons, the troops might not be presentable on parade, a year's hard service has rendered them efficient for the field.

The very high standard of individual intelligence, moreover, supplies the want of order in a great measure. Things which, in other armies, if not done on strict rule, would be altogether neglected, somehow "get themselves done" in this volunteer army. . . .

The great strength and power of the Southern army lies in the individual resolution of the men. Every private feels a determination, not only to carry his regiment through the fight, but to see his country through the war. Boys of fifteen may be seen by the side of grey-haired men. Men who could not obtain arms have been known to fall in with the rear rank, and go into action on the chance of picking up a musket on the first opportunity. It has been described how, at the commencement of the war, all the wealthiest men crowded into the ranks: there has been time for the first enthusiasm to wear away, and yet there are no signs of any flinching from the contest. Scores of names could be mentioned of men who, after having served out their first term of enlistment (twelve months), spent a week with their relations, and then returned to volunteer for three years or for the war. Indeed, no man who shrank from the war could ever again venture to address a lady.

Such was the condition and such the material of the army under General Lee, who, after having for weeks awaited an onward move to Richmond on the part of the Federal army, was now about to take the initiative.

—Anonymous, "Ten Days in Richmond"

4. THE NORTH BUILDS A VAST ARMY OVERNIGHT

The United States was notoriously unprepared for war, and the temper of the people—in the North even more than in the South—was pacific. Many foreign critics doubted that a nation without military traditions or a military caste could organize for war. Edward Dicey, a liberal English journalist and scholar, spent six months in the United States in the midst of the Civil

War and, after his return, hastened to publish a book giving his countrymen a better appreciation of the Union cause. Another Englishman, the novelist Anthony Trollope, who visited the United States during these years, was similarly impressed by the might of the North.

S URELY no nation in the world has gone through such a baptism of war as the people of the United States underwent in one short year's time. With the men of the Revolution the memories of the revolutionary wars had died out. Two generations had passed away to whom war was little more than a name. The Mexican campaign was rather a military demonstration than an actual war, and the sixteen years which had elapsed since its termination form a long period in the life of a nation whose whole existence has not completed its first century. Twenty months ago there were not more than 12,000 soldiers in a country of 31,000,000. A soldier was as rare an object throughout America as in one of our country hamlets. I recollect a Northern lady telling me that, till within a year before, she could not recall the name of a single person whom she had ever known in the army, and that now she had sixty friends and relatives who were serving in the war; and her case was by no means an uncommon one.

Once in four years, on the fourth of March, two or three thousand troops were collected in Washington to add to the pomp of the Presidential inauguration; and this was the one military pageant the country had to boast of. Almost in a day this state of things passed away. Our English critics were so fond of repeating what the North could not do—how it could not fight, nor raise money, nor conquer the South—that they omitted to mention what the North *had* done. There was no need to go farther than my windows at Washington to see the immensity of the war. It was curious to me to watch the troops as they came marching past. Whether they were regulars or volunteers, it was hard for the unprofessional critic to discern; for all were clad alike, in the same dull, grey-blue overcoats, and most of the few regular regiments were filled with such raw recruits that the difference between volunteer and regular was not a marked one.

Of course it was easy enough to pick faults in the aspect of such troops. As each regiment marched, or rather waded through the dense slush and mud which covered the roads, you could observe many inaccuracies of military attire. One man would have his trousers rolled up almost to his knees; another would wear them tucked inside his boots; and a third would appear with one leg of his trousers hanging down, and the other gathered tightly up. It was not unfrequent, too, to see an officer with his epaulettes sewed on to a common plain frock-coat. Then there was a slouching gait about the men, not soldierlike to English eyes. They used to turn their heads round when on parade, with an indifference to rule which would drive an old drill-sergeant out of his senses. There was an absence, also, of precision in the march. The men kept in step; but I always was at a loss to discover how they ever managed to do so. The system of march, it is true, was copied rather from the French than the English or Austrian fashion; but still it was something very different from the orderly disorder of a Zouave march. That all these, and a score of similar irregularities, are faults, no one—an American least of all—would deny. But there are two sides to the picture.

One thing is certain, that there is no physical degeneracy about a race which could produce such regiments as those which formed the army of the Potomac. Men of high stature and burly frames were rare, except in the Kentucky troops; but, on the other hand, small, stunted men were almost unknown. I have seen the armies of most European countries; and I have no hesitation in saying that, as far as the average raw material of the rank and file is concerned, the American army is the finest.

The officers are, undoubtedly, the weak point of the system. They have not the military air, the self-possession which long habit of command alone can give; while the footing of equality on which they inevitably stand with the volunteer privates, deprives them of the esprit de corps belonging to a ruling class. Still they are active, energetic, and constantly with their troops.

Wonderfully well equipped too, at this period of the war, were both officers and men. Their clothing was substantial and fitted easily, their arms were good, and the military arrangements were as perfect as money alone could make them.

It was remarkable to me how rapidly the new recruits fell into the habits of military service. I have seen a Pennsylvanian regiment, raised chiefly from the mechanics of Philadelphia, which, six weeks after its formation, was, in my eyes, equal to the average of our best-trained volunteer corps, as far as marching and drill-exercise went. Indeed, I often asked myself what it was that made the Northern volunteer troops look, as a rule, so much more soldier-like than our own. I suppose the reason is, that across the Atlantic there was actual war, and that at home there was at most only a parade. I have no doubt that, in the event of civil war or invasion, England would raise a million volunteers as rapidly as America has done—more rapidly she could not; and that, when fighting had once begun, there would only be too much of grim earnestness about our soldiering; but it is not want of patriotism to say that the American volunteers looked to me more business-like than our own. At the scene of war itself there was no playing at soldier-ing. No gaudy uniforms or crack companies, no distinction of classes. From every part of the North; from the ports of New York and Boston; from the homesteads of New England; from the mines of Pennsylvania and the fac-tories of Pittsburgh; from the shores of the great lakes; from the Mississippi valley; and from the far-away Texan prairies, these men had come to fight for the Union. It is idle to talk of their being attracted by the pay alone. Large as it is, the pay of thirteen dollars a month is only two dollars more than the ordinary pay of privates in the Federal army during peace times. Thirteen shillings a week is poor pay for a labouring man in America, even with board, especially during this war, when the wages of unskilled labour amounted to from twenty to thirty shillings a week. . . .

The bulk of the native volunteers consisted of men who had given up good situations in order to enlist, and who had families to support at home;

and for such men the additional pay was not an adequate inducement to incur the dangers and hardships of war. Of course, wherever there is an army, the scum of the population will always be gathered together; but the average morale and character of the couple of hundred thousand troops collected round Washington was extremely good. There was very little outward drunkenness, and less brawling about the streets than if half a dozen English militia regiments had been quartered there. The number of papers purchased daily by the common soldiers, and the amount of letters which they sent through the military post, was astonishing to a foreigner, though less strange when you considered that every man in that army, with the exception of a few recent immigrants, could both read and write. The ministers, also, of the different sects, who went out on the Sundays to preach to the troops, found no difficulty in obtaining large and attentive audiences.

—DICEY, *Six Months in the Federal States*

5. NORTHERN BOYS JOIN THE RANKS

We have here four brief accounts of the process of recruiting companies. Warren Goss of the 2nd Massachusetts Artillery contributes the first; he fought through most of the campaigns in the East, was twice captured and exchanged, and lived to write a number of lively books on the war.

Josiah Favill, who got himself a commission as a lieutenant, rose to be brevet colonel before the end of the war; his diary is one of the better accounts of the war in the East.

Sergeant—later Captain—John Adams enlisted in the 1st Battalion of Rifles, part of the 19th Massachusetts Infantry; his major, Ben: Perley Poore, was a famous journalist and historian whose experience in the war was of the briefest.

The fourth, and the most realistic of them all, is from the pen of Michael Fitch, of the 6th (later the 21st) Wisconsin Volunteers; Fitch was brevetted out as a colonel at the end of the war.

A. WARREN GOSS ENLISTS IN THE UNION ARMY

BEFORE the war had really begun I enlisted. I had read the papers, and attended flag-raisings, and heard orators declaim of "undying devotion to the Union." One speaker to whom I listened declared that "human life must be cheapened," but I never learned that he helped on the work experimentally. When men by the hundred walked soberly and deliberately to the front and signed the enlistment papers, he didn't show any inclination that way. As I came out of the hall with conflicting emotions, feeling as though I should have to go finally or forfeit my birthright as an American citizen, one of the orators who stood at the door, glowing with enthusiasm and patriotism, and shaking hands effusively with those who enlisted, said to me:

"Did you enlist?"

"No," I said, "Did you?"

"No; they won't take me. I have got a lame leg and a widowed mother to take care of."

Another enthusiast I remember, who was eager to enlist—others. He declared the family of no man who went to the front should suffer. After the war he was prominent among those in our town who at town meeting voted to refund the money to such as had expended it to procure substitutes during the war. He has, morever, been fierce and uncompromising toward the ex-Confederates since the war closed, and I have heard him repeatedly express the wish that all the civil and general officers of the late Confederacy might be court-martialled and shot.

I was young, but not unobserving, and did not believe, from the first, in a sixty days' war; nor did I consider ten dollars a month and the promised glory, large pay for the services of an able-bodied young man. Enlistment scenes are usually pictured as entirely heroic, but truth compels me to acknowledge that my feelings were mixed. At this moment I cannot repress a smile of amusement and pity for that young recruit—myself.

It was the news that the Sixth Massachusetts Regiment had been mobbed by roughs on their passage through Baltimore which gave me the war fever. When I read Governor Andrews' pathetic telegram to have the hero martyrs "preserved in ice and tenderly sent forward," somehow, though I felt the pathos of it, I could not reconcile myself to the ice. Ice in connection with patriotism did not give me agreeable impressions of the war, and when I came to think of it, the stoning of the heroic "sixth" didn't suit me; it detracted from my desire to die a soldier's death. I lay awake all night thinking it over, with the "ice" and "brickbats" before my mind. However, the fever culminated that night, and I resolved to enlist.

"Cold chills" ran up and down my back as I got out of bed after the sleepless night, and shaved, preparatory to other desperate deeds of valor. I was twenty years of age, and when anything unusual was to be done, like fighting or courting, I shaved. With a nervous tremor convulsing my whole system, and my heart thumping like muffled drum-beats, I stood before the door of the recruiting office and, before turning the knob to enter, read and re-read the advertisement for recruits posted thereon, until I knew all its peculiarities. The promised chances for "travel and promotion" seemed good, and I thought I might have made a mistake in considering war so serious after all. "Chances for travel." I must confess now, after four years of soldiering, that the "chances for travel" were no myth. But "promotion" was a little uncertain and slow.

I was in no hurry to open the door. Though determined to enlist I was half inclined to put it off awhile; I had a fluctuation of desires; I was faint-hearted and brave; I wanted to enlist,—and yet—— Here I turned the knob, and was relieved. I had been more prompt, with all my hesitation, than the officer in his duty; he wasn't in.

Finally he came and said: "What do you want, my boy?"

"I want to enlist," I responded, blushing deeply with upwelling patriotism and bashfulness. Then the surgeon came to strip and examine me. In justice to myself, it must be stated that I signed the rolls without a tremor. It is common to the most of humanity, I believe, that when confronted with actual danger, men have less fear than in its contemplation.

My first uniform was a bad fit; my trousers were too long by three or four inches; the flannel shirt was coarse and unpleasant, too large at the neck and too short elsewhere. The forage cap was an ungainly bag with pasteboard top and leather visor; the blouse was the only part which seemed decent; while the overcoat made me feel like a little nib of corn amid a preponderance of husk. Nothing except "Virginia mud" ever took down my ideas of military pomp quite so low.

After enlisting I didn't seem of so much consequence as I expected. There was not so much excitement on account of my military appearance as I deemed justly my due. I was taught my facings, and at the time I thought the drill-master needlessly fussy about shouldering, ordering, and presenting arms. At this time men were often drilled in company and regimental evolutions long before they learned the manual of arms, because of the difficulty of obtaining muskets. These we obtained at an early day, but we would willingly have resigned them after carrying them for a few hours. The musket, after an hour's drill, seemed heavier and less ornamental than it had looked to be. The first day I went out to drill, getting tired of doing the same things over and over, I said to the drill-sergeant: "Let's stop this fooling and go over to the grocery."

His only reply was addressed to the corporal: "Corporal, take this man out and drill him like hell."; and the corporal did. I found that suggestions were not as well appreciated in the army as in private life, and that no wisdom was equal to a drill-master's. "Right face," "Left wheel," and "Right, oblique, march."

It takes a raw recruit some time to learn that he is not to think or suggest, but obey. Some never do learn. I acquired it at last, in humility and mud, but it was tough. Yet I doubt if my patriotism, during my first three weeks' drill, was quite knee high. Drilling looks easy to a spectator, but it isn't. . . . After a time I cut down my uniform so that I could see out of it, and conquered the drill sufficiently to see through it. Then the word came: On to Washington! . . .

We bad adieu to our friends with heavy hearts, for lightly as I may seem to treat the subject, it was no light thing for a boy of twenty to start out for three years into the unknown dangers of a civil war. Our mothers—God bless them!—had brought us something good to eat,—pies, cakes, doughnuts, and jellies. . . . Our young ladies, (sisters, of course) brought an invention, generally made of leather or cloth, containing needles, pins, thread, buttons, and scissors, so that nearly every recruit had an embryo tailor's shop—with the goose outside. One old lady, in the innocence of her heart, brought her son an umbrella. We did not see anything particularly laughable about it at the time, but our old drill-sergeant did.

—Goss, *Recollections of a Private*

B. Lieutenant Favill Raises a Company and Gets a Commission

As soon as I was mustered out of service with the Seventy-first regiment I lost no time in seeking for a commission, fully determined to return to the field, but not as a private soldier. I soon found that commissions were to be obtained only by securing a certain number of men to enlist, and so after applying to various organizations in every state of formation, all with the same results, in connection with an ex-Danish officer, Julius Ericcson, living in Brooklyn, I set to work to raise the requisite number of men to secure the prize.

New York and Brooklyn were transformed into immense recruiting camps. In all the public squares and parks hundreds of tents were erected, covered with flags and immense colored bills, on which the advantage of the various branches of the service were fully stated. There were bands of music and scores of public speakers, all engaged by patriotic citizens, to stimulate the military ardor of the other fellow, and get him to enlist for three years.

We soon found a great change had come over the spirit of the people since the departure of the military regiments in April. Then, everybody wanted to go; now, apparently, most people wanted to stay at home. We put up a wall tent in the New York City Hall Park, and another at the junction of the Atlantic and Flatbush Avenues, Brooklyn, in an open lot. The captain and I took turns in attendance in New York, while John Ericcson, the captain's eldest son, who was to go out as orderly sergeant, was put in charge of the Brooklyn tent. We got some immense posters printed, and among other inducements offered by our company was the experience of the future officers, one gained in a foreign service, the other on the field of Bull Run. Notwithstanding these seeming advantages, our best efforts, and the prodigious enthusiasm of the times, recruiting proved very slow. I coaxed one man into enlisting, through my knowledge of the Crimean War, one Stuart, a fine six-foot Englishman who had served in the Crimean War and had been a soldier in the British army almost all his life. He took hold with a will, and we put him in charge of the tent as second sergeant.

As the recruiting proved so slow at home, it was decided to send me, at the expense of the State, to Oswego, N. Y., and there I promptly repaired; advertised in both the daily papers, setting forth the advantages of a metropolitan regiment. While there I enjoyed the brief distinction of being the only man in town who had been at Bull Run, and in consequence, was feted and honored as an exceptional personage.

With the assistance of a young man named Hamilton, native there, I actually obtained some twenty-nine or thirty men, and was just upon the point of starting with them to New York, when they deserted in a body, and went over to one of the local organizations. Disgusted, I returned immediately, and in a few days afterwards went to Poughkeepsie, and remained there for two weeks, but succeeded in getting only about half a dozen men, mostly from Wappingers Falls. I was taken, while in that place, with a severe attack of fever and ague and was almost shaken to pieces.

Considering the ground no longer profitable I returned home, and found we had already got more than the number required by the State, to muster us into its service, with a captain and first lieutenant; and so, on the 23rd of September, 1861, we marched our company of recruits to the state arsenal on Elm Street, where they were stripped naked, examined by a surgeon, and all of them passed as able bodied men. Then the mustering officer called the roll, and every man in succession stepped one pace to the front, took the oath of allegiance to the State, and swore to serve as a soldier for three years, or during the war. Immediately afterwards, in compliance with the state law a very perfunctory election of officers took place, in the presence of the mustering officer; and Julius Ericcson was declared duly elected captain and I the first lieutenant of the new company. The muster roll was made out, signed by the mustering officer, and we were at last in the service of the State; legally held for duty, and under pay. Before leaving the arsenal, the company was furnished with uniforms, underclothing, haversacks, canteens, and blankets, and at once divested themselves of their citizen garb, and emerged from the arsenal, looking something like real soldiers.

—FAVILL, *The Diary of a Young Officer*

C. RECRUITING A BATTALION OF "SAVAGES"

It was my good fortune to enlist April 19th, 1861, in Company A, 1st Battalion of Rifles. The old battalion was commanded by Major Ben: Perley Poore, and was called "The Savages." Our uniform was dark green, trimmed with light green, and I was the greenest thing in the whole outfit. We were armed with Windsor rifles, with sabre bayonets; our drill, as I remember it, was running around the old Town Hall in West Newbury, yelling like devils, and firing at an imaginary foe. We drilled in these tactics some three months, and were then ordered to Lynnfield, forming a part of the 19th Massachusetts Infantry, and when placed under an experienced drill-master, found that it would have been better not to have drilled at all. Before being mustered into the service of the United States, we elected the members of the company, and were, therefore, picked men.

One day while in camp at Lynnfield, an Irishman came into the company street. He looked the company over carefully, then went to the captain's tent. Taking off his hat, he said: "Captain, I am an Irishman, born in the old country, but an adopted citizen of the United States. The prosperity of this country is my prosperity, its life is in danger and I feel that I ought to enlist to save it. Will you take me in your company?"

After dress parade, his name was proposed and he was elected. We soon found we had made no mistake. Mike was a true son of Erin, and was at once a favorite with the men. One night at Camp Benton, Mike was on guard. It had rained hard and he was wet to the skin. His post was at Headquarters, in front of the colonel's tent. In the morning Colonel Hincks came out. Mike saw him and said: "Pardon me, Colonel, but I would like to speak a word with you." "What is it?" said the colonel. "Well," said Mike, "I wish you believed as you did before the war." "Don't I?" said the colonel. "I think not," said Mike. "You used to run a paper, and your motto was 'Put none but Americans on guard;' and here I am, an Irishman, wet to the skin, while the Americans are sleeping in their tents." Colonel Hincks had, before the war, edited a "Know-nothing" paper, and the motto was, "Put none but Americans on guard." . . .

Another man who joined the company at Lynnfield was Benjamin F. Falls. He had been a sailor and said that having sailed under the old flag for years, he would like a job to follow it on land. He was a grand old man, and was soon called "Uncle Ben." He brought his palm needle and thread with him, and was in constant demand as a tent mender. Colonel Hincks had known Uncle Ben in Lynn, and would often send for him to repair his tent. Ben would send the orderly back to know if it was a wet job or a dry one. If wet, he would take Mike with him to hold the tent, and they would return from their work in a happy condition.

Our company was made up of young men from the country, and was sometimes called "Merritt's Sabbath School children," on account of their goodness, but at Harper's Ferry, as is often the case, these good men fell. Captain Merritt as provost marshal, captured six barrels and a ten gallon keg of whiskey. The keg was lost in transit and could not be accounted for. We were quartered in a deserted house, and the captain came to inform me (I being at the time first sergeant) that we were to march to Bolivar Heights to join the regiment. He soon saw that the missing keg must have been found, for the men were in every stage of intoxication, from the moderate drinker to the gutter drunkard. As we were going through the rooms, we met Uncle Ben perfectly sober. The captain, feeling sad that the company had gone wrong, said,—"Ben, I am sorry." Ben said,—"It is not my fault, Captain. I have been on guard and have not found the stuff, but as soon as I do, will catch up and be just as drunk as the best of them."

At the battle of White Oak Swamp, a shot struck Ben's musket as he was going into the fight at right shoulder shift. It took the lock off, and all thought Ben severely wounded. In a few minutes, we were again moving forward and up came Ben with another gun. "Wasn't you wounded, Ben?" said the captain. "No, only winged, I am all right now."

—ADAMS, "Sunshine and Shadows of Army Life"

D. "WE THOUGHT THE REBELLION WOULD BE OVER BEFORE OUR CHANCE WOULD COME"

The region in northwestern Wisconsin, bounded on the west and northwest by the Mississippi and the St. Croix rivers, and contiguous thereto, in 1861 was sparsely settled. There was no railroad. Transportation was made either by steamboat on the water or by horses on the land. These factors made the raising of a volunteer company for service, an arduous task. When

Mr. Lincoln made the first call for seventy-five thousand volunteers, the quota of Wisconsin was one regiment. At least, only one regiment of three months' men left the state under that call. That regiment, I believe, was largely made up of militia companies that had been previously organized and equipped. Yet active recruiting commenced at once all over the state in the latter part of April, 1861. I presume every company that was recruited in any part of the state at that time, made effort to get into that three months' regiment. The sentiment then was quite universal that three months would close the war. Hence, whoever failed to become a part of the first regiment would see no service and receive no military glory.

A mass meeting was held at once in our town, Prescott, Pierce County. Several addresses were made. Patriotism was effervescent, and thirty young men signed the roll of the Prescott Guards. We at once notified the Governor that we would like to be a part of the troops about to be called. But at that time, as we were informed, enough companies had been offered to fill four regiments. As only one regiment was called for three months, our little squad out on the northwestern border had very little show. This did not discourage this little patriotic band. They began drilling every day, studied the tactics, erected a liberty pole mounted by a bayonet, pointing south, with the stars and stripes floating from its top. The fiery spirit of '76, as we understood it, was thoroughly aroused. By April 30th, a full company was enlisted.

Daniel J. Dill, a prominent merchant who had military tastes and who afterwards became captain of the company, went up the river to Hastings, Minnesota, and down the river to various towns, in pursuit of recruits. Rollin P. Converse and myself took a pair of horses and a buggy and started into the back country. That ride across the prairie and through the woods for several days, was novel and exceedingly interesting. We visited, not only the towns, but every farm. At one town, I think River Falls, we met recruiting officers from Hudson, the county seat of the adjoining county of St. Croix, on the same errand. We held a joint meeting at night at which several addresses were made.

We found western pioneer hospitality everywhere. Every rugged backwoodsman, whether American, German or Norwegian, was full of patriotism. Indignation at the firing on Fort Sumter was genuine and universal. The roads, especially through the woods, were in a wretched condition. It rained, and the mud was frightful. One evening in a lonely spot in the primeval forest, a singletree of the buggy broke. But there stood, by the side of the road, a sturdy pioneer with an axe on his shoulder. In five minutes he had cut a hickory withe, twisted it into a pliable rope, tied it around the broken tree in the most skilful manner, and sent us on our way rejoicing, with a buggy stronger than it was before. Wherever we stopped over night the host would refuse pay for our entertainment. The mother and daughters would look after our comfort, even drying our apparel when wet with rain. Everywhere we were bidden Godspeed in our patriotic efforts.

How many recruits we procured on this trip, I have now forgotten. But some walked to Prescott for miles to enlist. The muster rolls of the company show that almost every township in Pierce County was represented among its members. There were no better soldiers in the army than many of these backwoods farmer boys. A number of them never returned. We had some enlistments from far up the St. Croix River among the lumbermen and loggers. Captain Dill was successful in getting recruits from Hastings, Menominee and other towns. A. C. Ellis, a bright-eyed boy with curly black hair brought quite a number from Menominee.

Before the first of May, between ninety and one hundred had taken the oath of service and allegiance to the United States. I administered the oath to each one who signed the enlistment. D. J. Dill was elected captain. Two alleged Mexican war veterans were made lieutenants. I was appointed first sergeant. The Governor was notified that we were ready for service. But, not only the first, but the second, third, fourth and fifth regiments of volunteer infantry were organized at Madison without our company being assigned. There was great uncertainty for some time after this about being called into service. The men went back to their homes, and some of them enlisted in other companies. We thought the rebellion would be over before our chance would come. However, by May 10th, we were informed that we were the sixth company in the sixth regiment.

—FITCH, *Echoes of the Civil War*

6. THE REVEREND JAMES T. AYERS RECRUITS NEGRO SOLDIERS IN TENNESSEE

Although many Northern Negroes offered to enlist in the Union ranks, President Lincoln was at first opposed to using them as soldiers. Several Union officers—Butler and Hunter for example—attempted to use "contrabands" for semimilitary purposes, but were repudiated by the administration. In October 1861 came a modification of this no-Negro policy, and the next year General Hunter raised a Negro regiment in South Carolina, only to disband it when Congress refused to provide pay or maintenance. With Congressional authorization for Negro recruiting in July 1862, a number of Negro regiments were raised. The next year saw a vast expansion of Negro recruiting. Altogether a total of 186,000 Negroes fought in the Union Army, of which over 100,000 were recruited in Confederate territory. Negro troops were, however, consistently discriminated against, both in pay and promotions.

James T. Ayers was a Methodist minister from Illinois who was assigned to Federal recruiting headquarters at Nashville—one of 237 Federal agents. After the war he enlisted as chaplain with the 104th Regiment of Colored Troops.

Huntsville May 6th 64.

Just been to Dinner. Eat harty, had Salit   Asparagrass, turnip top greens, good fryed ham   Corn and wheat bread and buttermilk for Dinner. I am Boarding with or Rather hiring them to Board me now 2 black women and am Living fine for A soaldier. My health Never better than now, but what of all this. Oh I am So loansome way down here. Soaldiers nearly all gon no one to Associate with, nothing to do but Eat and grow fat, set at my window and watch the Rebs, as they geather in groups at the Corners to plot Deviltry and Hatch Secession and for those geatherings Bully Corner Acrosst the Street North of my office is the most fruitful. They rally here soon in the morning and a Crowd there mostly all day. Once and a while I pitch in among them and try to Raise A dust but they have give me over Long since for A hard Job boath Men and women. A few days since I came in Contact with three women. I had just took one of there nigger men and he had deserted me and Missus had him hid. This happened in Trianna A Little vilage on the Tennessee River 14 miles from here. I went to Missus house and was searching for Cuffy and out comes Missus Russeling in Silk and Curls with two other women, Ladys I suppose they call them-selves and says Missus "What on earth, sir, are you hunting here? Is Any thing missing?"

"Yes mam my nigger man. Just a few minutes since Run in at this gate and is missing, and I am hunting for him. Have you seen him?"

"Why no sir, your nigger man who is he?"

"Why, mam, he is one I just now presst up at the incampment for to make A soldier of."

"What is his name, Mister," says she.

"Sam he calls himself."

"I dont know anything of him" said she.

"Dont you live here, mam" said I.

"Yes sir" was the Reply.

"Well, mam, not five minutes ago this niger Come in at that gate, and he cant get out of here only at the same place without being helped for I have stood in sight of the gate ever since he entered. He told me he wanted to get his coat and would come Strait back. I waited but he haint Come." This Lot was fenced in with Boards Eight or nine foot high nailed on end-wise A kind of nigger Jail or pen with several Houses in and one verry fine House where this woman Stayed. "Well," said I "aint this fellow your niger?" The niger had toald me his missus Lived there as we Came from incampment.

"Well I gess he is Likely."

"And do you say, mam, you haint seen him within the Last Five minutes?"

"Why dear me I told you once I had not seen him."

"Well now look here, mam, I always want to be kind to Ladys, but you must Excuse me when I tell you you Could not help seeing him and you did see him and have him now hid Away." Thare was A black Boy with me that belonged to the Capt thare he had sent with me. Said I "Joe stand at this gate and watch while I search. I am bound to have this fellow dead or Alive."

Said the oald lady, "what did you say you wanted him for, A soaldier?"

"Yes mam."

"Why he wont make A soaldier" says she.

"Well," said I, "thats my business not yours."

"Well do you not think it is wicket to take our Slaves from us?"

"No mam."

"Why I am A widow woman and have no one else to Chop and hawl wood and see to my affairs but this nigger."

"Why dont you keep [*him*] at home then?"

"Why dear me I do," says she.

"You do, why, Mam, the Colonel out yonder toald me he had been sneaking Round the camps for two months past stealing hard tacks and sow belly, for himself and you, till he was tired of him, and hoped I would take him Away, and now you say you keep him at home. Come tell me whare he is. I am determined to have him."

"Do you take them whether they are willing or not?"

"Not generally, but in cases Like this I do, whare they are Loafing round stealing for themselves and there masters two."

"Well do you think slaverry is wrong?" says she.

"I dont think it is write," said I.

"Well the Bible is full of slaverry."

"Oh yes Mam and so is it full of war and blood shead. Do you think war and bloodshead is write mam?"

"No sir."

"Well I dont think so Either so thare we Agree."

"May I not ask Aint you A minister?"

"Sometimes pass for one, Mam."

"I thought so."

Now up steps Paul pry or who Ever she was and Rather Likely at that had she not been Reb. Say she "and you are A minister then are you?"

"They say so, yes mam."

"Well do you sir feel you are doing write in the sight of God and man to Come here Among us peacible citizens and take our slaves Away? They are our money, beside this one you are after now belongs to this widowed Lady. What on Earth will she do if you take him Away?"

"Send and get her son home out of the Rebel Army. He is there now plotting with others how to Cut the throats of yanks as you Call us." This was A Jolter and choked my Little fair faiced new comer for A while but she Rallyed Again.

"Well if you are a preacher I suppose you believe the bible."

"Well, yes, mam, I profess to, to some extent At least."

"Well, sir, I am prepaired to show you Clearly and plainly that slaverry is A bible doctrine. Why sir from first of Genesis to Last of Revelation the Bible is full of slaverry, and the best of men owned slaves, why Abraham Isaac Jacob and all the oald fathers and christians owned there slaves."

"Oh, yes mam, we will not fall out here by no means but Dear woman did you Ever for one Moment Reflect that the verry same Bible gives A historical Account all Along through as much or more Even, how men used to have wives. Why Solomon had three hundred, and not satisfyed with them took seven hundred concubines. David had several wives and was still Dissatisfyed, kiled Uriah and took his wife. And now, siss," says I, "in all good Continence how would you like the thousand wife sistom Revived? Would you like to be one of seven hundred Concubines all the darlings of one man or even the two hundred and 99th Lovely darling who was called wife of one man or would you be willing some one should kill your man Just for the sake of putting you Among his herd of wives. I guess not, you would say give me My Uriah, Ill be satisfyed. I think it is wrong men should have so many wives. Well thease are Historical Accounts of former usages and Customs Among the People which the Bible from some cause keeps silent only in Davids Case who the Bible says was sorely punished. And now Ladys I have A good way to go yet this afternoon. Sorry I haint the time to Discuss this subject longer. Hope Ill see you again and have more Leisure   will be pleased to talk with you. You seem like women of inteligence and are disposed to treat me Courteously for which I thank you Ladys. I am Aware of the prejudices you southerners have in favour of the institution of slavery and am prepared on my part to mak Allowances in that direction."

"Well," said the oald Lady, "I Really like to hear you talk. You talk Reasonable and Jentlemanly. You must call Again."

"Thank you," said I.

"Well now," said this Little bewitching yong Blue Eyed fairskined widow tidy Enough for one to eat, "you will Leave Aunts nigger wont you?" Well I leave you to guess whether I did or know. I made A Low Bow with A promise to call Again hoped, they might enjoy happyer days when this war was over and so I left fully intending if ever convenient to Call Again and see them Blue eyes that wore by that little Angel widow. When I had Rode Awhile why said I "that Little woman has Caused me to forget my nigger. Well let him go," so I joged on Humming Away some oald tune to kill time.

And this is only one Case. Those cases for some two months or more ware nearly of every day occurrence and sometimes two or three times A day only the Blue eyed widow seldom do I meet her Eaquals anywhere. She is A Splendid Little Piece of Humanity in Shape of A Female, and gained her Point, and saved the nigger. God bless the Little widow, them Blue Eyes that Little plump Rosy Cheek   them Delicate Lilly white hands that Lady Like Smile   that well Seasoned Christian Like spirit. Man would be A monster Could he Deny such an Angel as this. So my Cannon being Spiked I Rode off, threatening A return at A Convenient season.

Jas. T. Ayers.

—Franklin, ed., *The Diary of James T. Ayers*

7. BALTIMORE MOBS ATTACK THE SIXTH MASSACHUSETTS

Massachusetts, which had been preparing since January, was the first state to respond to the President's call to arms. On April 16 the state militia began to muster at Boston, and on the following day the famous 6th Massachusetts started its historic trip to Washington. There was no through railroad connection to the capital at that time; the 6th, which reached Baltimore on the morning of April 19 had to ride on horsecars, or walk, from the Philadelphia, Wilmington and Baltimore Railroad station to the Baltimore and Ohio Railroad station. Seven companies managed to get through on horse cars; then a mob of Southern sympathizers erected street barricades to block the passage of the remaining four. The militia fought its way through, but at the cost of four killed and 36 wounded; the mob casualties are unknown.

"The excitement is fearful," the Governor of Maryland wired the President. "Send no more troops here." To avoid a repetition of the riot the Maryland authorities burned down the railroad bridges connecting Baltimore with Philadelphia and Harrisburg.

This Baltimore fracas excited, among other things, "Maryland! My Maryland!"

EARLY on the morning of April 19th, 1861, a train of thirty-five cars left the Broad and Washington avenue depot, Philadelphia, having on board twelve hundred troops from Boston, Lowell, and Acton, Massachusetts, and known as the Sixth Massachusetts Regiment, under the command of Colonel Edward F. Jones, a gallant soldier and courteous gentleman; and a regiment, one thousand strong, from Philadelphia, under the command of Colonel William F. Small. Nothing was known in Baltimore of their departure from Philadelphia, but about eleven o'clock it became noised abroad that a large force of Federal soldiers had arrived at President street depot. This depot is in the southeastern portion of the city, and is connected with the Baltimore and Ohio depot, which is situated in the southwestern section, by a line of rail along Pratt street—a leading thoroughfare—and some minor streets. It was necessary for the troops, on disembarking at President street depot, either to march to the Baltimore and Ohio depot or to be drawn thither in the cars by horses. The news of the arrival of the troops spread like wildfire, and in a comparatively short time an immense crowd gathered on Pratt street, with the intention of preventing the passage of the troops. While waiting for the appearance of the soldiers the crowd kept itself up to the requisite pitch of indignation and enthusiasm by "groaning" for Lincoln, Hicks, and the Federal Government, and by cheering Jefferson Davis and the Southern Confederacy.

The first intimation had by the city authorities that the troops were about to enter the city was received by Mayor Brown about ten o'clock. Mr. Brown at once repaired to the office of the Police Commissioners, but found that the Marshal of Police had already gone to Camden station, where he had concentrated his men by request of the railroad authorities. The Mayor at once followed him to Camden station, and on arriving there found him posted with his men prepared to put down any attack. Unfortunately the mob had gathered not at Camden station but on Pratt street, at a point a short distance west of the depot where the troops were disembarking. Pratt street is a narrow thoroughfare, and easily capable of defense. The strategical position of the mob was excellent as they proceeded to fortify it.

About half-past eleven o'clock a car drawn by horses was seen approaching, and was greeted by the mob with cheers for the South. The car, and eight others which followed, were, however, permitted to pass without any molestation, except the usual taunts and gibes at the occupants. A trivial accident, which happened to the tenth car, let loose all the elements of disorder in the mob, and precipitated the fatal conflict. As this car neared Commerce street the brake was accidentally thrown out of gear, and the car stopped. The crowd took advantage of the mishap at once, and began to attack the occupants with stones. Windows were broken, and a few of the soldiers were hurt, but not seriously. Finally the driver of the car became frightened, lost his head, and, having attached his team to the other end of the car, started to haul it back to the depot. The mob followed the car, stoning it all the while, but the driver having urged the horses to a run, succeeded in distancing them. A large portion of the mob, however, followed it into the depot.

The section of the mob which remained at the bridge on Pratt street then, under the advice of their leaders, many of whom, as I have said, were well known citizens of Baltimore, began to build a barricade, Paris fashion. They commenced by digging up the paving stones and the railroad track for a distance of some fifty yards. The stones were piled up with the iron rails, the bridges over the gutters were torn up, and eight large anchors which were found on the wharf near by were placed on the barricade. A car loaded with sand attempted to pass, but was seized by the rioters, who backed it up to the barricade, and emptied the sand on the pile of stones and anchors. A large number of Negroes were working on the wharves at the time. These were ordered to quit work, which they did with alacrity, and were directed by the rioters to assist them on the barricade. . . .

In the meantime, the commander of the Massachusetts troops, finding that the cars would not be permitted to pass through, decided to disembark his men and force a passage on foot through the mob. When this determination was announced, some confederates of the Pratt street rioters at once communicated the news to them. It was also rumored that the troops had decided to go by a different route to Camden station. A portion of the rioters at once started to head them off, while the main body maintained its position on Pratt street. A large crowd assembled at the depot during the disembarkation of the troops, and here several exciting, but not very sanguinary, encounters occurred between Unionists and secessionists in the crowd. As the troops descended from the cars they were hooted, jeered, and twitted. They succeeded, however, in forcing their way to the footway, which extends for several hundred yards along the outer edge of the depot, where they formed in double file and awaited the orders of their officers.

At this point a man appeared bearing a Confederate flag at the head of about one hundred rioters. His appearance was the signal for wild cheering. A rush for the flag was made by several Northern sympathizers in the crowd, and the flag-staff was broken. One of these men was caught by the flag-bearer who, with his companions, throttled, and would have killed him, but for the interference of the police, who succeeded in bearing him away. The shreds of the flag were caught up and tied to the flag-staff. On being raised again they were saluted with an outburst of cheering.

The men surrounding the flag then began to taunt the troops, and declared that they would be forced to march behind it to the Camden depot. Colonel Jones gave the order to march, and the troops started. The men surrounding the flag, however, planted themselves directly in front of the soldiers and refused to yield an inch. The troops wheeled about, but found themselves surrounded on all sides, and were unable to move in any direction. Several of the soldiers were hustled away from their comrades, and would have been roughly used by the crowd but for the police, who succeeded, with great difficulty, in rescuing them. The troops again endeavored to force a passage, and this time, with the assistance of the police, they succeeded. As they started, however, the Confederate flag was borne to the front, and they were compelled to march for several squares behind this flag. Too much praise cannot be given to the commander or men for their admirable self-control during this trying episode.

The presence of the Confederate flag was the immediate cause of the sanguinary street fight and loss of life which followed. Several Northern sympathizers in the mob, exasperated at the triumph of the flag-bearer and his friends, made another dash for the flag, but were defeated and pursued. Some of them took refuge in the ranks of the soldiers. This exasperated the citizens against the soldiers, and a savage attack upon the latter was made with stones and other missiles. One of the soldiers, William Patch, was struck in the back with a large paving-stone, and fell to the ground. His musket was seized, and the poor wretch was brutally beaten by the rioters before the police could rescue him. When Patch was seen to fall Colonel Jones gave the order "double quick" to his men, and the whole column started off at a run, ducking and dipping to avoid the stones. At this the crowd set up a yell of derision and started after them full tilt. Two soldiers were knocked down, while running, but managed to make their escape—one of them with the assistance of the police.

While the foregoing events were transpiring in and near President street depot, an immense concourse of people had gathered at the barricade. When the troops appeared in full run a great shout was raised, and the head of the column was greeted with a shower of paving-stones. The troops faltered, and finally, in the face of a second shower of stones, came to a dead halt. The patience of their commander was at last exhausted. He cried out in a voice, which was heard even above the yells of the mob, "Fire!" The soldiers leveled their pieces and the mob seemed to pause, as if to take breath. The soldiers fired. A young man, named F. X. Ward, now a well-known lawyer of this city, fell pierced by a ball. A hoarse yell of fear and rage went up from the mob, but it did not give way. The troops fired again and again, and the crowd wavering, they rushed upon them with fixed bayonets and forced a passage over the barricade.

A scene of bloody confusion followed. As the troops retreated, firing, the rioters rushed upon them only to be repulsed by the line of bayonets. Some of the rioters fought like madmen. Finally, the mob, exasperated by their failure to prevent the passage of the troops, made a desperate rush upon them, and one young man, who was in the front rank of the rioters, was forced close upon the soldiery. One of the soldiers raised his gun, took deliberate aim at the rioter and fired. The cap exploded, but the gun failed to go off. The rioter rushed forward, seized the gun, wrested it by an almost super-human effort from the soldier's grasp, and plunged the bayonet through the man's shoulder.

During the firing a number of the rioters fell, killed and wounded. At the intersection of Charles and Pratt streets, Andrew Robbins, a soldier from Stoneham, Massachusetts, was shot in the neck by a rioter. He was carried into a drug store near by, and was protected from the mob. At Howard street a strong force of rioters from Camden station met the troops and refused to yield. The soldiers fired again and the mob gave way. The soldiers again started at the double quick and reached Camden station without further trouble. Thirteen cars were drawn out, and the soldiers left the depot amid the hisses and groans of the multitude.

One of the most remarkable features of the riot was the persistency and courage with which the mob hung on to the troops, in spite of the continued firing. Another remarkable feature was the extraordinary coolness and for-bearance of the troops.

—FREDERIC EMORY, "The Baltimore Riots"

8. HOW THE SEVENTH REGIMENT GOT FROM NEW YORK TO WASHINGTON

Because the Maryland authorities had burned the railroad bridges leading from Philadelphia to Baltimore, the New York 7th and the Massachusetts 8th were transported by water up Chesapeake Bay to Annapolis, whence they marched to Annapolis Junction and then entrained for the capital.

The story of this famous march can be read in Theodore Winthrop's article in the Atlantic Monthly *for June 1861; it is told here by the gifted poet, dramatist and journalist Fitz-James O'Brien who was decorated for gallantry in action at Bloomery Gap and paid with his life for his devotion to the Union.*

The Capitol, Washington, Saturday, April 27, 1861

We are here. Those three words sum up as much as Napier's "Peccavi," when he took Scinde, and we all feel somewhat as Mr. Caesar Augustus must have felt when he had crossed the Rubicon.

It is almost unnecessary for me to detail to you the events of the day on which we left New York....

At 3 o'clock, P.M., we mustered at the Armory, against which there beat a surge of human beings like waves against a rock. Within, all was commotion.

Fitting of belts, wild lamentations over uniforms expected but not arrived. Hearty exchanges of comradeships between members of different companies, who felt that they were about to depart on a mission which might end in death. Here and there flickered Spring bonnets, which inclosed charming faces, as the calyx enfolds the flower; and, let me tell you, that on the faces of many of those dear blossoms there hung drops of mournful dew. At last the regiment was formed in companies, and we marched. Was there ever such an ovation? . . .

The faces of the buildings were so thick with people, that it seemed as if an army of black ants were marching, after their resistless fashion, through the city, and had scaled the houses. Handkerchiefs fluttered in the air like myriads of white butterflies. An avenue of brave, honest faces smiled upon us as we passed, and sent a sunshine into our hearts that lives there still. In a prominent position stood Major Anderson, who saluted us, and was welcomed as such a man should be welcomed. And so on to the ferry.

Swift through New Jersey—against which no sneer be uttered evermore. All along the track shouting crowds, hoarse and valorous, sent to us, as we passed, their hopes and wishes. When we stopped at the different stations, rough hands came in through the windows, apparently unconnected with any one in particular until you shook them, and then the subtle magnetic thrill told that there were bold hearts beating at the end. This continued until night closed, and, indeed, until after midnight. . . .

Our arrival at Philadelphia took place at 4 o'clock. We slept in the cars, awaiting orders from our Colonel, but at daylight hunger—and it may be thirst—becoming imperious, we sallied out, and roamed about the cheerless neighborhood that surrounds the depot. Close by there was a small wooden shanty—let us say an Irish palace—which was presently filled by arid soldiers. The prog in the larder of this sumptuous residence was, I regret to say, limited. I did not even see the traditional pig about, although heaven knows he would have been appropriate enough.

Finding that we were likely to remain for some time in the city—although under the impression that we were to go straight through to Baltimore—we wandered away from the Desert of the Depot and descended on civilized quarters. The superintendent of the Deaf and Dumb Asylum was a man for the emergency. He provided a handsome breakfast for all such members of the Seventh as chose to partake of it, and we commanded beefsteak on our fingers, and ordered tea by sign-manual. Great numbers of our regiment, being luxurious dogs, went down to the Continental and Girard hotels, where they campaigned on marble floors, and bivouacked on velvet couches. They are such delicate fellows, the Seventh Regiment! Further on you will see what those delicate hands have done. . . .

There was one peculiar difference that I noticed existing between the Massachusetts regiments that we met in Philadelphia and our men. The Massachusetts men—to whom all honor be given for the splendid manner in which they afterwards acted in a most trying situation—presented a singular moral contrast to the members of the Seventh. They were earnest, grim, determined. Badly equipped, haggard, unshorn, they yet had a manhood in their look that hardships could not kill. They were evidently thinking all the time of the contest into which they were about to enter. Their gray, eager eyes seemed to be looking for the heights of Virginia. With us, it was somewhat different. Our men were gay and careless, confident of being at any moment capable of performing, and more than performing, their duty. They looked battle in the face with a smile, and were ready to hobnob with an enemy and kill him afterwards. The one was courage in the rough; the other was courage burnished. The steel was the same in both, but the last was a little more polished.

On April 20, at 4:20 P.M., we left the Philadelphia dock, on board the steamer *Boston*. The regiment was in entire ignorance of its destination. Some said we were going back to New York, at which suggestion there was a howl of indignation. Others presumed that we were going to steam up the Potomac—a course which was not much approved of, inasmuch that we were cooped up in a kind of river steamer that a shot from the fort at Alexandria might sink at any moment. We, however—to make use of a familiar expression—"went it blind," and the faces did not smile the less because our object was unknown. . . .

I regret to say that all was not rose-colored. The steamer that the Colonel chartered had to get ready at three or four hours' notice, he having changed his plans, in consequence of the tearing up of the rails around Baltimore. The result was that she was imperfectly provisioned. As the appetites of the men began to develop, the resources of the vessel began to appear. In the first place, she was far too small to accommodate a thousand men, and we were obliged to sleep in all sorts of impossible attitudes. There is an ingenious device known to carpenters as "dove-tailing," and we were so thick that we had positively to dove-tail, only that there was very little of the dove about it; for when perambulating soldiers stepped on the faces and stomachs of the sleepers, as they lay on the deck, the greeting that they received had but little flavor of the olive branch.

Notwithstanding that we found very soon that the commissariat was in a bad way, the men were as jolly as sandboys. I never saw a more good-humored set of men in my life. Fellows who would at Delmonico's have sent back a *turban de volaille aux truffes* because the truffles were tough, here cheerfully took their places in file between decks, tin plates and tin cups in hand, in order to get an insufficient piece of beef and a vision of coffee. But it was all merrily done. The scant fare was seasoned with hilarity; and here I say to those people in New York who have sneered at the Seventh Regiment as being dandies, and guilty of the unpardonable crimes of cleanliness and kid gloves, that they would cease to scoff and remain to bless, had they beheld the square, honest, genial way in which these military Brummells roughed it. . . .

On the afternoon of the 22d we landed at the Annapolis dock. . . . For the first time in his life your correspondent was put to work to roll flour-barrels. He was entrusted with the honorable and onerous duty of transporting stores from the steamer to the dock. Later still he descended to the position of mess servant, when, in company with gentlemen well known in Broadway for immaculate kids, he had the honor of attending on his company with buckets of cooked meat and crackers. The only difference between him and Co. and the ordinary waiter being, that the former were civil. . . .

We were quartered in the buildings belonging to the Naval School at Annapolis. I had a bunking-place in what is there called a fort, which is a rickety structure, that a lucifer match would set on fire, but furnished with imposing guns. I suppose it was merely built to practice the cadets, because as a defence it is worthless. The same evening boats were sent off from the yard, and towards nightfall the Massachusetts men landed, fagged, hungry, thirsty, but indomitable. At an early hour there was a universal snore through the Naval School of Annapolis. . . .

On the morning of the 24th of April we started on what afterwards proved to be one of the hardest marches on record. The Secessionists of Annapolis and the surrounding district had threatened to cut us off in our march, and even went so far as to say that they would attack our quarters. This, of course, was the drunken Southern ebullition. A civilian told me that he met in the streets of Annapolis two cavalry soldiers who came to cut our throats without delay, but as each brave warrior was endeavoring to hold the other up, my friend did not apprehend much danger.

A curious revulsion of feeling took place at Annapolis, and indeed all through Maryland, after our arrival.

The admirable good conduct which characterizes the regiment, the open liberality which it displays in all pecuniary transactions, and the courteous demeanor which it exhibits to all classes, took the narrow-minded population of this excessively wretched town by surprise. They were prepared for pillage. They thought we were going to sack the place. They found, instead, that we were prepared and willing to pay liberal prices for everything, and that even patriotic presentations were steadily refused. While we were in the Navy School, of course all sorts of rumors as to our operations were floating about. It surprised me that no one suggested that we were to go off in a balloon; however, all surmises were put to an end by our receiving orders, the evening of the 23d, to assemble in marching order next morning. The dawn saw us up. Knapsacks, with our blankets and overcoats strapped on them, were piled on the green. A brief and insufficient breakfast was taken, our canteens filled with vinegar and water, cartridges distributed to each man, and after mustering and loading, we started on our first march through a hostile country. . . .

The tracks had been torn up between Annapolis and the Junction, and here it was that the wonderful qualities of the Massachusetts Eighth Regiment came out. The locomotives had been taken to pieces by the inhabitants, in order to prevent our travel. In steps a Massachusetts volunteer, looks at the piecemeal engine, takes up a flange, and says coolly, "I made this engine, and I can put it together again." Engineers were wanted when the engine was ready. Nineteen stepped out of the ranks. The rails were torn up. Practical railroad makers out of the regiment laid them again, and all this, mind you, without care or food. These brave boys, I say, were starving while they were doing this good work. What their Colonel was doing, I can't say. As we marched along the track that they had laid, they greeted us with ranks of smiling but hungry faces. One boy told me, with a laugh on his young lips, that he had not eaten any thing for thirty hours. There was not, thank God, a haversack in our regiment that was not emptied into the hands of these ill-treated heroes, nor a flask that was not at their disposal. I am glad to pay them tribute here, and mentally doff my cap. . . .

After marching about eight miles, during which time several men caved in from exhaustion, and one young gentleman was sunstruck and sent back to New York, we halted, and instantly, with the Divine instinct which characterizes the hungry soldier, proceeded to forage. The worst of it was there was no foraging to be done. The only house within reach was inhabited by a lethargic person, who, like most Southern men, had no idea of gaining money by labor. We offered him extravagant prices to get us fresh water, and it was with the utmost reluctance we could get him to obtain us a few pailfuls. Over the mantel-piece of his miserable shanty I saw—a curious coincidence—the portrait of Col. Duryea, of our regiment.

After a brief rest of about an hour, we again commenced our march; a march which lasted until the next morning—a march than which in history, nothing but those marches in which defeated troops have fled from the enemy, can equal. Our Colonel, it seems, determined to march by railroad, in preference to the common road, inasmuch as he had obtained such secret information as led him to suppose that we were waited for on the latter route. Events justified his judgment. There were cavalry troops posted in defiles to cut us off. They could not have done it, of course, but they could have harassed us severely. As we went along the railroad we threw out skirmishing parties from the Second and Sixth companies, to keep the road clear.

I know not if I can describe that night's march. I have dim recollections of deep cuts through which we passed, gloomy and treacherous-looking, with the moon shining full on our muskets, while the banks were wrapped in shade, and each moment expecting to see the flash and hear the crack of the rifle of the Southern guerilla. The tree frogs and lizards made a mournful music as we passed. The soil on which we travelled was soft and heavy. The sleepers lying at intervals across the track made the march terribly fatiguing. On all sides dark, lonely pine woods stretched away, and high over the hooting of owls or the plaintive petition of the whip-poor-will rose the bass commands of Halt! Forward, march!—and when we came to a ticklish spot, the word would run from the head of the column along the line, "Holes," "Bridge, pass it along," &c.

As the night wore on the monotony of the march became oppressive. Owing to our having to explore every inch of the way, we did not make more than a mile or a mile and a half an hour. We ran out of stimulants, and almost out of water. Most of us had not slept for four nights, and as the night advanced our march was almost a stagger. This was not so much fatigue as want of excitement. Our fellows were spoiling for a fight, and when a dropping shot was heard in the distance, it was wonderful to see how the languid legs straightened, and the column braced itself for action. If we had had even the smallest kind of a skirmish the men would have been able to walk to Washington. As it was, we went sleepily on. I myself fell asleep walking in the ranks. Numbers, I find, followed my example; but never before was there shown such indomitable pluck and perseverance as the Seventh showed in the march of twenty miles. The country that we passed through seemed to have been entirely deserted. The inhabitants, who were going to kill us when they thought we daren't come through, now vamosed their respective ranches, and we saw them not. Houses were empty. The population retired into the interior, burying their money, and carrying their families along with them. They, it seems, were under the impression that we came to ravage and pillage, and they fled as the Gauls must have fled when Attila and his Huns came down on them from the North. As we did at Annapolis, we did in Maryland State. We left an impression that cannot be forgotten. Every thing was paid for. No discourtesy was offered to any inhabitant, and the sobriety of the regiment should be an example to others.

I have now to finish without bringing our journey up to here. But let that rest for my next letter. I wish, however, before I conclude, to state that nothing could have been more effective or energetic than the movements of the Engineer Corps, to whom we were indebted for the rebuilding of a bridge in an incredibly short space of time.

—O'BRIEN, in the *New York Times*

9. FRANK WILKESON GOES SOUTH WITH BLACKGUARDS, THIEVES, AND BOUNTY JUMPERS

Joining the army and entraining for the battle front was not all a matter of cheers and flag-waving. As the going got tougher and the government resorted increasingly to bounties, a regular system of bounty jumping sprang up, and the army had to take drastic measures to see to it that men who enlisted for bounties actually stayed in the army.

Frank Wilkeson, who found himself in the bad company which he here describes so graphically, was a Buffalo boy who later became lieutenant in the 4th United States Artillery and, after the war, worked on the staffs of the New York Sun *and the* New York Times.

THE war fever seized me in 1863. All the summer and fall I had fretted and burned to be off. That winter, and before I was sixteen years old, I ran away from my father's high-lying Hudson River valley farm. I went to Albany and enlisted in the Eleventh New York Battery, then at the front in Virginia, and was promptly sent out to the penitentiary building.

There, to my utter astonishment, I found eight hundred or one thousand ruffians, closely guarded by heavy lines of sentinels, who paced to and fro,

March of New York 7th Regiment Down Broadway

A. J. Volck

The Battle in the Streets of Baltimore, April 19, 1861

day and night, rifle in hand, to keep them from running away. When I entered the barracks these recruits gathered around me and asked, "How much bounty did you get?" "How many times have you jumped the bounty?" I answered that I had not bargained for any bounty, that I had never jumped a bounty, and that I had enlisted to go to the front and fight. I was instantly assailed with abuse. Irreclaimable blackguards, thieves, and ruffians gathered in a boisterous circle around me and called me foul names. I was robbed while in these barracks of all I possessed—a pipe, a piece of tobacco, and a knife.

I remained in this nasty prison for a month. I became thoroughly acquainted with my comrades. A recruit's social standing in the barracks was determined by the acts of villainy he had performed, supplemented by the number of times he had jumped the bounty. The social standing of a hard-faced, crafty pick-pocket, who had jumped the bounty in say half a dozen cities, was assured. He shamelessly boasted of his rascally agility. Less active bounty-jumpers looked up to him as to a leader. He commanded their profound respect. When he talked, men gathered around him in crowds and listened attentively to words of wisdom concerning bounty-jumping that dropped from his tobacco-stained lips. His right to occupy the most desirable bunk, or to stand at the head of the column when we prepared to march to the kitchen for our rations, was undisputed.

If there was a man in all that shameless crew who had enlisted from patriotic motives, I did not see him. There was not a man of them who was not eager to run away. Not a man who did not quake when he thought of the front. Almost to a man they were bullies and cowards, and almost to a man they belonged to the criminal classes. . . .

On my urgent solicitation Major Van Rensselaer promised to ship me with the first detachment of recruits going to the front. One cold afternoon, directly after the ice had gone out of the Hudson River, we were ordered out of the barracks. We were formed into ranks, and stood in a long, curved line 1,000 rascals strong. We were counted, as was the daily custom, to see if any of the patriots had escaped. Then, after telling us to step four paces to the front as our names were called, the names of the men who were to form the detachment were shouted by a sergeant, and we stepped to the front, one after another, until 600 of us stood in ranks. We were marched to the barracks, and told to pack our knapsacks as we were to march at once.

The 400 recruits who had not been selected were carefully guarded on the ground, so as to prevent their mingling with us. If that had happened, some of the recruits who had been chosen would have failed to appear at the proper time. The idea was that if we were kept separate, all the men in the barracks, all outside of the men grouped under guard, would have to go. Before I left the barracks I saw the guards roughly haul straw-littered, dust-coated men out of mattresses, which they had cut open and crawled into to hide. Other men were jerked out of the water-closets. Still others were drawn by the feet from beneath bunks. One man, who had burrowed into the contents of a water-tight swill-box, which stood in the hall and into which we threw our waste food and coffee slops, was fished out, covered with coffee grounds and bits of bread and shreds of meat, and kicked down stairs and out of the building. Ever after I thought of that soldier as the hero of the swill-tub.

Cuffed, prodded with bayonets, and heartily cursed, we fell into line in front of the barracks. An officer stepped in front of us and said in a loud voice that any man who attempted to escape would be shot. A double line of guards quickly took their proper positions around us. We were faced to the right and marched through a room, where the men were paid their bounties. Some men received $500, others less; but I heard of no man who received less than $400. I got nothing.

As the men passed through the room they were formed into column by fours. When all the recruits had been paid, and the column formed, we started to march into Albany, guarded by a double line of sentinels. Long before we arrived at State Street three recruits attempted to escape. They dropped their knapsacks and fled wildly. Crack! crack! crack! a dozen rifles rang out, and what had been three men swiftly running were three bloody corpses. The dead patriots lay by the roadside as we marched by. We marched down State Street, turned to the right at Broadway, and marched down that street to the steamboat landing.

Previous to my enlistment I had imagined that the population of Albany would line the sidewalks to see the defenders of the nation march proudly by, bound for the front, and that we would be cheered, and would unbend sufficiently to accept floral offerings from beautiful maidens. How was it? No exultant cheers arose from the column. The people who saw us did not cheer. The faces of the recruits plainly expressed the profound disgust they felt at the disastrous outcome of what had promised to be a remunerative financial enterprise. Small boys derided us. Mud balls were thrown at us. One small lad, who was greatly excited by the unwonted spectacle, rushed to a street corner, and after placing his hands to his mouth, yelled to a distant and loved comrade: "Hi, Johnnie, come see de bounty-jumpers!" He was promptly joined by an exasperating, red-headed, sharp-tongued little wretch, whom I desired to destroy long before we arrived at the steamboat landing. Men and women openly laughed at us. Fingers, indicative of derision, were pointed at us. Yes, a large portion of the populace of Albany gathered together to see us; but they were mostly young males, called gutter-snipes. They jeered us, and were exceedingly loth to leave us. It was as though the congress of American wonders were parading in the streets preparatory to aërial flights under tented canvas.

Once on the steamboat; we were herded on the lower deck, where freight is usually carried, like cattle. No one dared to take off his knapsack for fear it would be stolen. Armed sentinels stood at the openings in the vessel's sides out of which gangplanks were thrust. Others were stationed in the bows; others in the dark, narrow passage-ways where the shaft turns; still others were on the decks. We were hemmed in by a wall of glistening steel. "Stand back, stand back, damn you!" was the only remark the alert-eyed, stern-faced sentinels uttered, and the necessity of obeying that command was impressed on us by menacing bayonets. Whiskey, guard-eluding whiskey, got in. Bottles, flasks, canteens, full of whiskey, circulated freely among us, and many men got drunk. There was an orgie on the North River steamer that night, but comparatively a decent one.

In spite of the almost certain death sure to ensue if a man attempted to escape, two men jumped overboard. I saw one of these take off his knapsack, loosen his overcoat and then sit down on his knapsack. He drew a whiskey flask from an inner pocket and repeatedly stimulated his courage. He watched the guards who stood by the opening in the vessel's side intently. At last they turned their heads for an instant. The man sprang to his feet, dropped his overcoat and ran to the opening and jumped far out into the cold waters of the river. Above us, in front of us, at our sides, behind us, wherever guards were stationed, there rifles cracked. But it was exceeding dark on the water, and I believe that the deserter escaped safely. Early in the morning, before it was light, I again heard firing. I was told that another recruit had jumped overboard and had been killed.

—WILKESON, *Recollections of a Private Soldier*

10. SUPPLYING THE CONFEDERACY WITH ARMS AND AMMUNITION

The industrial development of the South was in its infancy at the time of secession, and the Confederacy experienced greatest difficulty in supplying itself with the munitions for modern warfare. Edward P. Alexander, from whose entrancing Memoirs *this passage is taken, had been an instructor at West Point where he perfected the system of military signals used by both armies during the war. President Davis appointed him Chief of Ordnance of the Army of Northern Virginia, and he served later as chief artillerist in Longstreet's corps.*

ON the day after Bull Run I was appointed Chief of Ordnance of Beauregard's corps, and within a few days Johnston extended my office over the whole army, which, about this period, took the name ever afterwards used,—"The Army of Northern Virginia." The enemy, about the same time, adopted their equally well-known title, "The Army of the Potomac."

My new duties largely absorbed my time, but I remained in charge of the signal service, the work being now confined to sending instructed parties to all parts of the Confederacy where they might be of use. During the fall a "Department of Signals" was organized in Richmond, and the charge of it, with the rank of colonel, was offered me, but declined, as I was unwilling to leave the field. As head of a department I was soon made Major, and, later, Lieutenant-Colonel of Artillery. Col. William Norris of Baltimore became Chief Signal Officer.

Briefly, my duties embraced the supply of arms and ammunition to all troops in the field,—infantry, artillery, and cavalry. I organized the department, with an ordnance officer or sergeant in every regiment, from whom I received weekly statements showing the arms and ammunition on hand in cartridge boxes and regimental wagons. Reserve storehouses were provided at the nearest railroad points, and reserve trains for brigades and divisions, to run between the storehouses and the troops. For emergency, under my own control was held a train of ammunition and battery wagons equipped with tools and expert mechanics for all sorts of repairs from a broken mainspring to a spiked fieldpiece. I was fortunate in securing for superintendent of this train, Maj. George Duffy, an expert from Alexandria, who became an institution in the army, and remained with it throughout the war.

In its early stages we had great trouble with the endless variety of arms and calibres in use, scarcely ten per cent of them being the muzzle-loading rifle musket, calibre .58, which was then the regulation arm for United States infantry. There were several breech-loading small-arms manufactured at the North, but none had secured the approval of the United States Ordnance Department, although many of them would have made more formidable weapons than any muzzle-loaders.

The old idea was still widely entertained that, because the percentage of hits is always small, the fire of infantry should not be rapid, lest the men waste too much ammunition. After a year or two some of the best breech-loaders got admission among cavalry regiments, and common sense and experience gradually forced a recognition of the value of a heavy fire. By 1864, the Spencer breech-loading carbine had been adopted as the regulation arm for the Federal cavalry, and by the fall of that year brigades of infantry began to appear with it. . . .

There is reason to believe that had the Federal infantry been armed from the first with even the breech-loaders available in 1861 the war would have been terminated within a year.

The old smooth-bore musket, calibre .69, made up the bulk of the Confederate armament at the beginning, some of the guns, even all through 1862, being old flint-locks. But every effort was made to replace them by rifled muskets captured in battle, brought through the blockade from Europe, or manufactured at a few small arsenals which we gradually fitted up. Not until after the battle of Gettysburg was the whole army in Virginia equipped with the rifled musket. In 1864 we captured some Spencer breech-loaders, but we could never use them for lack of proper cartridges.

Our artillery equipment at the beginning was even more inadequate than our small-arms. Our guns were principally smooth-bore 6-Prs. and 12-Prs. howitzers, and their ammunition was afflicted with very unreliable fuses. Our arsenals soon began to manufacture rifled guns, but they always lacked the copper and brass, and the mechanical skill necessary to turn out first-class ammunition. Gradually we captured Federal guns to supply most of our needs, but we were handicapped by our own ammunition until the close of the war.

No department of our government deserves more credit than our Ordnance Bureau in Richmond under Gen. Josiah Gorgas, for its success in supplying the enormous amount of ordnance material consumed during the war. Although always economical of ammunition, yet we never lost any action from the lack of it. We were, however, finally very near the end of our resources, in the supply of one indispensable article. To make percussion caps nitric acid, mercury, and copper were required. Our Nitre and Mining Bureau had learned to make saltpetre from caves, and the earth under old barns and smoke houses, and from all kinds of nitrogenous waste material. From the saltpetre our chemists could make nitric acid. Our quicksilver came from Mexico, but after the fall of Vicksburg we were cut off from it, and about the same time our supply of sheet copper was exhausted. The chemists found out a mixture of chlorate of potash and sulphuret of antimony which they could use in place of fulminate of mercury; and we collected all the turpentine and apple-brandy stills in the country and sent them to Richmond to be cut up and rerolled into copper strips.

From this copper and the above chemical mixture all the caps were made which we used during the last year of the war, but at its close the copper stills were exhausted. It is hard to imagine what we would then have done had not the surrender at Appomattox relieved the quandary.

—ALEXANDER, *Military Memoirs of a Confederate*

11. HOW THE ARMY OF NORTHERN VIRGINIA GOT ITS ORDNANCE

Almost wholly without industries, and cut off from Europe by the blockade, the Confederacy had to get its arms and equipment as best it could. Some ordnance was seized when the Confederate states seceded; some was imported before the blockade became effective; some was smuggled in from the North; substantial quantities were captured from the enemy or "gleaned" on the battlefield.

Colonel William Allan, from whose reminiscences this excerpt is taken, was Chief of Ordnance of the Second Army Corps and author of an invaluable history of the campaign in the Shenandoah Valley and of the Army of Northern Virginia.

THE troops at this time [1863] were armed in a heterogeneous fashion. Many of the men had smooth bore muskets, calibre .69. Others had rifled muskets, calibre .54; and others still had Springfield muskets, calibre .58. There were some other arms, as, for instance, some Belgian rifles, calibre .70, but the three kinds I have mentioned were the principal kinds in the hands of the infantry in January, 1863. We were all anxious to replace the smooth bores with rifles, and especially with calibre .58, which was the model the Confederate as well as the Federal Government had adopted. The battlefields of the preceding summer had enabled many commands to exchange their smooth bores for Springfield muskets, but as nine-tenths of the arms in the Confederacy at the beginning of the war had been smooth bore muskets, it required time and patience to effect a complete re-arming. This was finally done in the Second corps at Chancellorsville, but in the winter of 1862-'63, there was often found in the same brigade the three kinds of arms above enumerated, and the same wagon often carried the three kinds of ammunition required. During this winter it was found difficult to obtain arms as fast as we needed them for the new men, and of course we were very glad to take what the department could furnish. Between the first of January and the first of May, General Jackson's corps grew from about twenty-three thousand muskets to thirty-three thousand. These ten thousand arms we obtained from Richmond in small quantities, and they were of different calibres, but the corps was fully armed when it went to Chancellorsville. After that battle the men all had muskets, calibre .58, and henceforth but one sort of ammunition was needed.

Our artillery armament was even more heterogeneous. Six-pounder guns, howitzers, some Napoleons, three-inch rifles, ten-pounder Parrotts, and a few twenty-pounder Parrotts were in our corps, besides, probably, some other odd pieces. I remember a Blakely gun or two and a Whitworth, the latter used both at Chancellorsville and Gettysburg. Our batteries had been greatly improved by a number of guns captured from the enemy. We especially valued the three-inch rifles, which became the favorite field piece. During the winter of 1862-'63, the artillery was first thoroughly organized under General Pendleton as chief. Batteries were detached from brigades, and were organized into battalions, containing four batteries, usually of four guns each. A number of these battalions were assigned to each corps under the chief of artillery of that corps, while a number of others constituted the general reserve, of which General Pendleton took immediate oversight. All that our supplies admitted was done to thoroughly equip these batteries during the winter, and they were ready for action when the campaign opened. A train of wagons was organized to carry the reserve ammunition for the artillery, and this was placed in charge of the artillery ordnance officer of the corps, and, besides this, there was a reserve train for the army under the direct orders of the chief ordnance officer of the army. . . .

Gleaning the battlefields was one of the important duties of the field ordnance officers. They were directed to save everything which could be made of use. Of course they took care of the good arms and good ammunition, but they had to preserve no less carefully all damaged arms, gun barrels, wasted ammunition, of which the lead was the valuable consideration, bayonets, cartridge-boxes, &c. After Chancellorsville and the gathering which had been done during the battle, an ordnance officer of the Second corps was sent to the field with power to call upon a neighboring brigade for as large details as he wished, and he spent a week in gathering the débris of the battle and sending it to Guiney's Station or Hamilton's Crossing, whence it was shipped to Richmond. My recollection is that over twenty thousand stand of damaged arms were sent in this way to the arsenal, besides a considerable quantity of lead, &c. After the first day at Gettysburg the battlefield was gleaned, and such material as we had transportation for sent back. . . .

In the winter of 1864 it was impossible to obtain an adequate quantity of horseshoes and nails from the ordnance department. The cavalry, which had been with General Early during that fall, had seen severe service, and it was absolutely necessary, in reference to the future, to procure in some way a supply of horseshoes and nails during the winter. We had to depend upon ourselves. I determined to establish, if possible, twenty forges in Waynes-boro', Augusta county, Virginia, and have blacksmiths detailed from the army to make shoes and nails. We sent through the country and got such blacksmith tools as we were able to find. I think I got some, too, from Richmond, from the ordnance department. There was no difficulty in getting good blacksmiths out of the army. A number of men were put to work, and horseshoes and nails began to accumulate. We soon ran out of iron, however, and found that the department at Richmond could not fully supply our wants. There was a fine lot of iron at Columbia furnace, near Mount Jackson, which was at this time in the debatable ground between the two armies. This iron was of fine quality, suitable for casting cannon as well as any other purpose. The commander of the arsenal informed me that if I could manage to get this to Richmond he would give me back in bars as much as I needed for horseshoes and nails. Trains of wagons were sent after it from Staunton, and these trains were protected by cavalry, which General Early sent for the purpose, and they returned in safety with the iron, which was promptly shipped to Richmond.

From this time forward our forges were fully supplied, and I think when Sheridan overhauled and dispersed our forces at Waynesboro', at the beginning of March, 1865, we had manufactured some twenty thousand pounds of horseshoes and nails. They were loaded upon the cars, which were gotten through the tunnel, but were captured by some of Sheridan's people at or near Greenwood depot.

—ALLAN, "Reminiscences of Field Ordnance Service"

12. THE TREDEGAR IRON WORKS SERVE THE CONFEDERATE ARMIES

Aside from the foundries at Selma, Alabama, the Tredegar Iron Works was almost the only source for the supply of Confederate arms; it was the existence of these works outside Richmond which imperatively demanded the defense of Richmond and influenced the choice of that city as permanent capital of the Confederacy. During the war the Tredegar works expanded to include rolling mills, machine shops, forges, coal mines, sawmills, and even a blockade-runner, employed some 2,500 men, and produced some 1,100 cannon for the Confederacy.

We have met Thomas Cooper DeLeon before.

GAMBLE'S hill, a pretty but steep slope, cuts the river west of the bridge. Rising above its curves, from the Capitol view-point, are the slate-roofed Tredegar Works; their tall chimneys puffing endless black smoke against the sunshine, which reflects it, a livid green, upon the white foam of the rapids.

So potent a factor in the aggressive power of the Confederacy was this foundry that it overtopped the regular government agencies. When the war began, this was the only rolling-mill of great capacity, of which the South could boast; the only one, indeed, capable of casting heavy guns. Almost the first decisive act of Virginia was to prevent, by seizure, the delivery to United States officers of some guns cast for them by the Tredegar Works; and, from that day, there were no more earnest and energetic workers for the cause of southern independence than the firm of Jos. R. Anderson & Co.

It was said, at this time that the firm was in financial straits. But it thrived so well on government patronage—spite of sundry boards to consider if army and navy work was not paid for at ruinously low rates—that it greatly increased in size; added to its utility by importations of costly machinery, through the blockade; stood loss of one-third of its buildings, by fire; used a ship of its own for importation; and, at the close of the struggle, was in better condition than at the commencement. The senior partner was, for a time, in the field at head of his brigade; but affairs were so well managed, in the interval, by the Messrs. Tanner—father and son, who were partners with General Anderson—that his absence was not appreciable in the work.

It was at the Tredegar Works that the famous "Brooke gun"—a rifled 7-inch—was cast, tested and perfected. Here the plates for the iron-clads, in almost all southern waters, were rolled or made ready for use. Here heavy ordnance for the forts was cast, together with shells and shot; and here the torpedoes—sometimes so effective, and usually so useless—were contrived and made. Indeed, the Tredegar Works so greatly aided the Confederacy, that the lengthening of the war may be, in large measure, attributed to their capacity, and to the able zeal with which they were managed.

So great and effective an agent could not fail to receive, from the Richmond government, every aid in obtainance of supplies, labor and transportation. "The Works" had mines, mills and pork packeries in various sections of the South; thus obtaining coal and metals, as well as food—at reduced rates, within reach of their wages—for an army of employés. So great was the necessary number of these—whites, skilled in labor—that even closest conscription left the junior of the firm a full battalion of infantry. This, drilled and equipped from his own shops, Major Tanner led in person, when raids or other straits made their soldiering paramount to other occupation. And—even when greatest scarcity of provisions came—the agents of "the Works" proceeded with those of the commissary of the Confederacy, *pari passu.*

An odd incident, coming to mind just here, will point the general estimate of the importance of the Tredegar Works. A special train was crossing the bridge, en route for Petersburg, at a time when transportation was rare. A huge Negro, blacker than the soot upon his face, sat placidly on the platform of the rear car.

"What are you doing here?" was asked by the officer in charge.

"Rid'n' t' Petesbug," was the placid reply.

"Have you paid your fare?"

"Don' got non t' pay, boss. Rides onner pass, I does!"

"Work for the government?"—this rather impatiently.

Ebo rolled his eyes, with expression of deep disgust, as he responded grandly:

"No—*sah!* Fur t'uther consarn!"

· —DeLeon, *Four Years in Rebel Capitals*

13. SECRETARY BENJAMIN RECALLS THE MISTAKES OF THE CONFEDERATE CONGRESS

The Confederate government was no more ready for war than was the Union government, and confusion and mismanagement attended the beginnings of that conflict on both sides. More serious even than incompetence and shortsightedness, as events were to prove, was that jealousy between state and federal governments to which Secretary Benjamin here refers.

Benjamin himself, whom we have already met in the pages of Jones's Diary and Peyton's visit to Richmond, was successively Attorney General, Secretary of War, and Secretary of State of the Confederacy, and probably the ablest and most trusted of President Davis' advisers. This letter was written after the war to Charles Marshall, an aide-de-camp of Lee.

AS soon as war became certain, every possible effort was made by the President and his advisers to induce Congress to raise an army enlisted "for the war." The fatal effects of enlistments for short terms, shown by the history of the War of Independence against England, were invoked as furnishing a lesson for our guidance. It was all in vain. The people as we were informed by the members would not volunteer for the war, but they would rise in mass as volunteers for twelve months. We did not wish them to rise in mass nor in great numbers for any such short term, for the reason that *we could not arm them*, and their term of service would expire before we could equip them. I speak from memory as to numbers, but only a moderate force was raised (all that we could provide with arms) for twelve months service, and thus a *provisional* army was formed, but the fatal effect of the short term of service, combined with the painful deficiency of supplies, were felt long before the end of the year. While the Northern States after the Battle of Manassas were vigorously engaged in preparing for an overwhelming descent upon Virginia, our own army was falling to pieces. . . .

The representatives of the people could not be persuaded to pass measures unpalatable to the people; and the unthinking multitude upon whose *voluntary* enlistments Congress forced us to depend were unable to foresee or appreciate the dangers of the policy against which we protested. It was only the imminent danger of being left without *any* army by the return home in mass of the first levy of twelve-month volunteers that drove Congress into passing a law for enlistments for the war, and in order to induce the soldiers under arms to re-enlist we were driven to the fatal expedient of granting them not only bounties but furloughs to return from Virginia to their homes in the far South, and if our actual condition had been at all suspected by the enemy they might have marched through Virginia with but the faintest show of resistance.

As to supplies of munitions I will give a single instance of the straits to which we were reduced. I was Secretary of War *ad interim* for a few months, during which Roanoke Island, commanded by General Wise, fell into the hands of the enemy. The report of that General shows that the capture was due in great measure to the persistent disregard by the Secretary of War of his urgent demands for munitions and supplies. Congress appointed a committee to investigate the conduct of the Secretary. I consulted the President whether it was best for the country that I should submit to unmerited censure or reveal to a Congressional Committee our poverty and my utter inability to supply the requisitions of General Wise, and thus run the risk that the fact should become known to some of the spies of the enemy of whose activity we were well assured. It was thought best for the public service that I should suffer the blame in silence and a report of censure on me was accordingly made by the Committee of Congress.

The *dearth* even of powder was so great that during the descent of the enemy on Roanoke, General Wise having sent me a despatch that he was in instant need of ammunition, I ordered by telegraph General Huger at Norfolk to send an immediate supply; this was done but accompanied by a despatch from General Huger protesting against this exhausting of his small store, and saying that it was insufficient to defend Norfolk for a day. General Lee was therefore ordered to send a part of his very scanty supply to Norfolk, General Lee being in his turn aided by a small cargo of powder which had just run into one of the inlets on the coast of Florida.

Another terrible source of trouble, disorganisation and inefficiency was the incurable jealousy in many states of the General Government. Each State has its own mode of appointing officers, generally by election. Until disaster forced Congress to pass the Conscription law, all that we could do was to get laws passed calling for certain quotas of troops from the states, and in order to prevent attempts made to create officers of higher rank than the Confederate officers, who would thus have been placed under the orders of raw militia generals, we resorted to the expedient of refusing to receive any higher organisation than a regiment. But the troops being State troops officered by the State officers, the army was constantly scandalized by electioneering to replace regimental officers, and Confederate Commanders were without means of enforcing discipline and efficiency except through the cumbrous and most objectionable expedient of Courts Martial. Another fatal defect was that we had no power to consolidate regiments, battalions, and companies. If a company was reduced to five men or a regiment to fifty, we had no power to remedy this. The message of the President of the 12th of August, 1862, showed the fatal effects of our military system, and a perusal of that message will shed a flood of light on the actual position of things and the hopeless helplessness to which the Executive was reduced by the legislation of Congress, and the restrictions imposed on his power to act efficiently for military success by the jealousy of Congress and the States. When I look back on it all, I am lost in amazement that the struggle could have been so prolonged, and one of the main, if not the main source of strength and encouragement to the Executive was the genius, ability, constancy, fidelity, and firmness of General Lee.

—Sir Frederick Maurice, ed., *An Aide-de-Camp of Lee*

14. NORTHERN ORDNANCE

The North, with its highly developed arms industries, and with easy access to Britain, had no difficulty supplying its armies with whatever weapons were needed, yet the supply of small arms did not meet requirements until the war was a year old. Altogether some four million muskets were issued to Union soldiers, but less than eight thousand cannon.

The Comte de Paris, from whose compendious history of the Civil War this extract is taken, served, with his brother the Duc de Chartres, on Mc-Clellan's staff, fighting at Yorktown and Gaines' Mill.

THE task of supplying the Federal troops with arms and ammunition, which devolved upon the ordnance department, was the most difficult of all. In fact, both the government armories and private manufactories were insufficient to meet the demand, and it required time to establish additional ones. The wonderful machines by which the most complicated rifles now in use throughout Europe are constructed almost without the aid of man are of American invention, and have given a well-deserved reputation to the expansion rifles manufactured at the government armory in Springfield. But this establishment had only capacity for producing from ten to twelve thousand yearly, and the supply could not be increased except by constructing new machines. The private workshops were equally insufficient; the Federal factory at Harper's Ferry had been destroyed by fire, and the dépôts were empty. It was important, however, to supply the most pressing of all the wants of the soldier, that of having a weapon in his hands.

During the first year of the war the ordnance department succeeded in furnishing the various armies in the field, not counting what was left at the dépôts, one million two hundred and seventy-six thousand six hundred and eighty-six portable firearms (muskets, carbines, and pistols), one thousand nine hundred and twenty-six field- or siege-guns, twelve hundred pieces for batteries in position, and two hundred and fourteen million cartridges for small-arms and for cannon. But it was obliged to apply to Europe for muskets and ammunition; this was the only war commodity that America procured in considerable quantities from the Old World, and it was this supply which proved to be the most defective. Agents without either experience or credit, and sometimes unscrupulous, bought in every part of Europe, on account of the Federal government, all the muskets they could pick up, without any regard to their quality or price. The English and Belgian manufactories not being able to satisfy their demands fast enough, they procured from the little German states all their old-fashioned arms, which those states hastened to get rid of at a price which enabled them to replace them with needle-guns. In short, the refuse of all Europe passed into the hands of the American volunteers.

A portion of the muskets being unfit for use, the few that were serviceable had to be kept for the soldiers doing guard duty in each company. The calibres were all mixed up; conical balls were issued for the large German smooth-bore muskets, while the old American cartridge, containing one ball and four buckshot, was given to those who had the good fortune to possess a minie rifle. The defective armament of the infantry would have been sufficient to delay the opening of the campaign for several months. In order to remedy this it was found necessary, in the first instance, to classify the calibres of the muskets by regiments, then gradually to throw aside the most worthless. After a while the American factories, both national and private, were able to furnish a sufficient quantity of new arms to justify this process.

While willing to encourage private enterprise to a great extent, the Federal government determined to control it; and in order to avoid being at its mercy, it largely extended its own establishments. Thus, in 1862, the Springfield manufactory delivered two hundred thousand rifles, while in the year 1863, during which there were manufactured two hundred and fifty thousand there, the importation of arms from Europe by the Northern States ceased altogether. The rifle which bore the name of the Federal manufactory had the advantage of not requiring heavy charges, of giving a great precision of aim at a distance of from six to seven hundred metres, and of being easily loaded and managed. It was therefore introduced throughout the army as fast as the ordnance department was able to meet the demands that were made for that arm from every quarter.

But, at the same time, a great number of new inventions were tried upon a scale which enabled the authorities to test their merits. Some were even adopted by whole regiments of cavalry; and the practice of breech-loading, which was common to all the systems, contributed greatly to their efficiency in the numerous engagements in which those regiments had to fight on foot. With the exception of this mode of loading, they differed greatly in their construction; it would be impossible for us to describe all, for there were no less than eleven of the first class. We shall only mention two belonging to the class called repeating-rifles—that is to say, arms which fire a certain number of shots without being reloaded. The Colt rifle is a long-barrelled revolver with five or six chambers, and the ball is forced into seven grooves forming a spiral which grows more and more contracted. This heavy weapon was formidable in practiced hands, but it required considerable time to reload it. The second was the Spencer rifle, an excellent arm, the use of which became more and more extended in the Federal army. The butt is pierced, in the direction of the length, by a tube containing seven cartridges, which are deposited successively, after each fire, in the chamber, replacing in turn those which, when discharged, are thrown out by a very simple mechanism. This magazine, entirely protected, is very easily recharged. Many extraordinary instances have been cited of successful personal defence due to the rapidity with which this arm can be fired, and some Federal regiments of infantry which made a trial of it were highly pleased with the result. Most of these rifles were of two models—one for the use of the infantry, the other, lighter and shorter, for the cavalry.

The *matériel* of the artillery, which had to be created, was as extensive as the armament of the infantry, and its construction was also new to American manufactories. Nevertheless, the great workshops for smelting iron and steel were so rapidly transformed into cannon foundries that the ordnance department was not obliged to depend on Europe for a supply.

At the time when the war broke out none of the systems of rifle cannon invented a few years before had ever been adopted, or even seriously experimented upon, by the officers of the regular army. But the latter, while adhering to the brass smooth-bore cannon, had studied these different inventions, and did not conceal their preference for the rifled system, by which the ball, like the minie bullet, inserted through the mouth of the cannon, is driven into the grooves under the pressure of the gases which propel it forward. The impression obtained from these inquiries in common was never forgotten by the officers who were placed in positions of command in the two hostile armies; and notwithstanding the diversity of details, the guns of those two armies always bore a strong family resemblance. But nothing could limit the fertility of inventors stimulated by the war.

—COMTE DE PARIS, *History of the Civil War in America*

IV

Bull Run and the Peninsular Campaign

AFTER the attack on Fort Sumter and the secession of Virginia, both sides marked time. Neither was eager to assume the offensive, and neither was prepared to do so.

Conscious that it could never hope to muster the numerical or material strength of the North, the Confederacy preferred to exploit the great advantages of defensive operations and of interior lines of communication. Nor was there, from the larger political or diplomatic point of view, anything to be gained by invading the North. The Confederacy was merely asking to be let alone. It wanted to go its way in peace; if the North would not permit this it was prepared to fight. But it rested its hopes of victory not in conquest of the North but in wearing down the Northern will to fight, and in foreign intervention.

The North, on the other hand, could not escape the offensive. Its military task was to invade and conquer the South. This required an altogether more elaborate military organization than it was possible to create in a few months. It meant not only a large army—one necessarily much larger than the Confederate—but a permanent one; three-months militiamen would be worse than useless for an invasion. It meant building up immense quantities of war matériel, developing and maintaining long lines of communication, imposing a blockade on the South, wresting major ports and rivers from Southern control. It meant, in short, a military effort on a scale unprecedented in modern history.

General Scott's original plan was to make the major offensive down the Mississippi—a plan which had much to commend it. Circumstances, however—the proximity of the two capitals to each other, and of the first armies that were organized—dictated that Virginia should be the first and for long the major theater of the war. It is important therefore that we get clearly in mind the geography of that theater in so far as it controlled military operations.

Just a hundred miles separated the two capitals, Washington and Richmond. Between them lay four great rivers—the James, the York, the Rappahannock, and the Potomac—and many lesser streams such as the Chickahominy, the North and South Anna, and Bull Run. The ground between these two cities, and particularly from the Rappahannock to the James, was low, swampy, covered with woods and underbrush; the roads were deep in mud in winter and spring. To the west lay a series of hills and mountains, notably the Blue Ridge and the Shenandoah. The great Valley *between these ranges ran northeast and southwest. Its mouth came out on the Potomac, that is to say on the Baltimore and Ohio Railroad and the Chesapeake and Ohio Canal—just fifty miles from Washington, and opened up into the rich Maryland and Pennsylvania country just across the Potomac. Thus the Confederates could use the Valley for striking into the heart of the North, cutting communications with Washington, and threatening that city. But to the Federals the Valley was of little value. If they succeeded in fighting their way up it to Staunton they were as far from Richmond as ever.*

Thus while Washington was vulnerable to attack from both south and west, an attack on Richmond presented formidable difficulties. There were two possible approaches to Richmond: the direct approach by land, southward through Fredericksburg; the approach by sea to the Peninsula and up the Peninsula to the capital city. There was a variation on these, or a combination of them, that Grant finally used: a movement southward by land, across the James, and to Petersburg, and an attack on the rear of the city.

During May both governments tried to organize armies chiefly for defensive purposes. By the beginning of June Davis had one army of about 22,000 men under Beauregard at Manassas Junction, an important railroad center some 25 miles southwest of Washington; and a smaller force of about 11,000 under Joseph E. Johnston at Winchester, in the Valley. General Scott, the aged veteran of the War of 1812 and the Mexican War, had assembled a force of some 35,000, under McDowell, in and around Centerville, Virginia, and a force of about 12,000 under the veteran General Patterson at Harpers Ferry. Here at once we see the advantages that the Confederacy enjoyed in its interior lines. Johnston and Beauregard were only a few hours apart, by rail; Patterson and McDowell were days apart.

Scott had no intention of launching an offensive with his three-months militia, but public opinion called loudly for action. On June 24, McDowell submitted his plan for an offensive; it was approved and early in July he began to move on Beauregard. Meantime, however, everything depended on Patterson holding Johnston in the Valley. This he failed to do, with results that were disastrous for the Union cause. The result was the defeat at First Bull Run.

That story and its sequel are told in the following accounts. The direct overland approach having failed, McClellan tried the approach by sea and up the Peninsula. That, too, failed, but whether through the incompetence of the Federal commander, or the interference in his plans by the administration, or the genius of Lee will ever remain a subject of debate.

1. A CONFEDERATE DOCTOR DESCRIBES THE VICTORY AT FIRST BULL RUN

The first major engagement of the war came when public opinion forced an advance on Richmond before the raw Union army was ready for fighting. Union troops, under McDowell, outnumbered the Confederates under

Beauregard, but the success of the Union advance depended on the ability of General Patterson to prevent the Confederate General J. E. Johnston from bringing a force of some 9,000 men from the Shenandoah Valley. In this Patterson failed, and on July 20 the vanguard of Johnston's forces began to arrive at Manassas Junction. Before dawn on Sunday, July 21, 1861, Mc-Dowell attacked and by three o'clock that afternoon seemed to have carried the day. Then additional Confederate reinforcements threw themselves on the weary Federals and drove them back across the Bull Run. Soon the reverse became a disorderly retreat. Bull Run—or First Manassas as it is known in the South—proved a costly victory, for it created a sense of overconfidence in the South while it spurred the North on to more determined efforts.

Richmond, July 23, 1861

Dear Harleston: I have seen the great and glorious battle of Manassas, which brought a nation into existence, and the scene was grand and impressive beyond the power of language. We foresaw the action several days ahead—the enemy were known to be advancing in immense masses from Arlington towards Fairfax, and the master stroke was at once made, to order Johnston down from Winchester, by forced marches, before Patterson could get down on the other side. Johnston's troops marched all twenty-six miles, then crowded into the railroad, came down in successive trains, without sleeping or eating, (15,000,) and arrived, many of them, while the battle was raging.

I got to Manassas the morning of the day previous to the fight; and knowing well both Generals Beauregard and Johnston, and their staff officers, I went immediately to headquarters. . . . General Beauregard determined to attack them in several columns at once the next morning, so as to cut them up before Patterson could arrive—but our scouts came early in the morning, informing the generals that the enemy had been in motion since two hours before day, which settled the question as to their intention to make the attack. Beauregard, who had studied the whole ground around—knew every hill, ravine, and pathway—had made all the necessary arrangements and planned the battle. Not knowing at what point of a semicircle of ten miles around Manassas the enemy would attack, his forces had to be scattered in such a way as to guard all points, prevent a flank movement on either side, and guard his intrenchments and supplies in the centre.

We got up in the morning at daylight, took a cup of coffee and remained quietly laughing and talking at head-quarters, while the scouts were passing in and out bringing news from the enemy. At a quarter past six in the still, bright morning, we heard the first deep-toned sound of cannon on the centre of our line, about three miles off. We waited till nine for further information, and at nine the generals ordered to horse, and away we dashed to the hill overlooking the point at which cannon, like minute guns, had continued slowly to fire. The enemy could not see any of our troops, but were firing at the dust kicked up along the road, which they saw above the low trees. We were for some time at the point they were firing at, and some twenty or thirty balls of their rifled cannons whizzed through the air above us, and I felt very forcibly the remark of Cuddy to his mother Mause, that "a straggling bullet has nae discretion" and might take my head off as well as that of anybody else.

The firing at this point kept up slowly from a quarter past six till eleven, when we heard a gun fire on the extreme left of the semicircle, and we were then satisfied that the firing in front was a mere feint. In a few minutes the cannon firing came in rapid succession, as if one battery was answering another. The generals then ordered "to horse" again, and away we rode to the seat of battle, about three miles off. When we arrived on the top of a hill, in an old field, we could get glimpses of the fight through the woods. The cannons were roaring and the musketry sounded like a large bundle of fire crackers, and the constant roaring of the big guns, the sharp sound of rifled cannons, Minié rifles and muskets, with the bursting of shells, made one feel that death was doing his work with fearful rapidity.

The enemy had concentrated all his forces on this one point while ours were scattered around a half circle of ten miles, and the few regiments who received the first onset were most terribly cut up. It was far greater odds than human nature could stand, the regiments were torn to pieces, driven back, and so overwhelmed by numbers that I feared the day was lost. At this stage of the game the enemy was telegraphing to Washington that the battle had been won, and secession was about to be crushed. My heart failed me as I saw load after load of our poor wounded and dying soldiers brought and strewed on the ground, along the ravine where I was at work. Dr. Fanthray, who belonged to General Johnston's staff, and myself were just getting fully to work, when an old surgeon, whom I do not know, came to us and said the enemy were carrying every thing before them, and ordered us to fall back to another point with the wounded, as they were turning our flank, and the battle would soon be upon us. Accordingly the wounded were taken up and we fell back, but after following the ambulances for a mile, we found that they were to be taken all the way to Manassas—about four miles— where there were hospitals and surgeons to receive them, and we returned to our position near the battle.

At this juncture I saw our reinforcements pouring in with the rapidity and eagerness of a fox chase, and was satisfied that they would drive every thing before them. No one can imagine such a grand, glorious picture as these patriots presented, rushing to the field through the masses of wounded bodies which strewed the roadside as they passed along. For half a mile behind me the road passed down a gradual slope, and through an old field, as I looked back, I could see a regiment of infantry coming in a trot, with their bright muskets glittering in the sun; then would come a battery of artillery, each gun carriage crowded with men and drawn by four horses in full gallop. Next came troops of cavalry, dashing with the speed of Murat; after these followed, with almost equal speed, wagons loaded with ammunition, &c., screaming all the while, "push ahead boys," "pitch into the d—d Yankees," "drive them into the Potomac."

This kept up from about mid-day till dark, and I felt as if the Alps themselves could not withstand such a rush. The cannon and small-arms were roaring like a thunder storm as they rushed to the battle-field. One regiment, which had been driven back by overwhelming numbers, was now supported and I soon perceived that the firing was getting further off, as I had expected, and I knew that the "pet lambs" now could only be saved by their superior heels. About this time, too, the last of General Johnston's command arrived on the cars, opposite the battle-ground, to the number of some three or four thousand, and although they had been two nights without sleep, they jumped from the cars and cut across to the field.

By this time we had collected about 15,000 against their 35,000, and, from all accounts, no red fox ever made tracks, so fast as did these cowardly wretches. They were all fresh and better accoutred in every respect than our men, one half or more of whom had to make forced marches to get at them. They had selected their position coolly and deliberately in the morning, while ours were scattered over ten miles and had to run through the midday sunshine. If our men had been equally fresh they would have gone straight into their intrenchments at Arlington.

But I will not speculate on the future and weary you with details which really will reach you through print long before this.

—Letter of Dr. J. C. Nott

2. "BULL RUN RUSSELL" REPORTS THE ROUT OF THE FEDERALS

The English journalist William Howard Russell arrived in America in 1861 with a great and merited reputation as war correspondent, and soon began sending the London Times *shrewd and outspoken accounts of American men and affairs. His description of the Federal demoralization after First Bull Run aroused a good deal of criticism, but all the evidence shows that it was by no means exaggerated.*

July 20th, 1861.—The great battle which is to arrest rebellion or to make it a power in the land is no longer distant or doubtful. McDowell has completed his reconnaissance of the country in front of the enemy, and General Scott anticipates that he will be in possession of Manassas tomorrow night. . . .

Some senators and many congressmen have already gone to join McDowell's army or to follow in its wake in the hope of seeing the Lord deliver the Philistines into his hands. . . . Every carriage, gig, wagon, and hack has been engaged by people going out to see the fight. The price is enhanced by mysterious communications respecting the horrible slaughter in the skirmishes at Bull Run. The French cooks and hotelkeepers, by some occult process of reasoning, have arrived at the conclusion that they must treble the prices of their wines and of the hampers of provisions which the Washington people are ordering to comfort themselves at their bloody Derby. . . .

It was a strange scene before us. From the hill a densely wooded country,

THE FIRST BATTLE OF BULL RUN

dotted at intervals with green fields and cleared lands, spread five or six miles in front, bounded by a line of blue and purple ridges, terminating abruptly in escarpments toward the left front and swelling gradually towards the right into the lower spines of an offshoot from the Blue Ridge Mountains. On our left the view was circumscribed by a forest which clothed the side of the ridge on which we stood and covered its shoulder far down into the plain. A gap in the nearest chain of the hills in our front was pointed out by the by-standers as the Pass of Manassas by which the railway from the West is carried into the plain, and still nearer at hand before us is the junction of that rail with the line from Alexandria and with the railway leading south-ward to Richmond. The intervening space was not a dead level; undulating lines of forest marked the course of the streams which intersected it and gave by their variety of color and shading an additional charm to the landscape which, inclosed in a framework of blue and purple hills, softened into violet in the extreme distance, presented one of the most agreeable displays of simple pastoral woodland scenery that could be conceived.

But the sounds which came upon the breeze and the sights which met our eyes were in terrible variance with the tranquil character of the land-scape. The woods far and near echoed to the roar of cannon, and thin, frayed lines of blue smoke marked the spots whence came the muttering sound of rolling musketry; the white puffs of smoke burst high above the treetops, and the gunners' rings from shell and howitzer marked the fire of the artillery.

Clouds of dust shifted and moved through the forest, and through the wavering mists of light blue smoke and the thicker masses which rose com-mingling from the feet of men and the mouths of cannon, I could see the gleam of arms and the twinkling of bayonets.

On the hill beside me there was a crowd of civilians on horseback and in all sorts of vehicles, with a few of the fairer, if not gentler, sex. A few officers and some soldiers, who had straggled from the regiments in reserve, moved about among the spectators and pretended to explain the movements of the troops below, of which they were profoundly ignorant. ...

The spectators were all excited, and a lady with an opera glass who was near me was quite beside herself when an unusually heavy discharge roused the current of her blood—"That is splendid. Oh, my! Is not that first-rate? I guess we will be in Richmond this time tomorrow." These, mingled with coarser exclamations, burst from the politicians who had come out to see the triumph of the Union arms. ...

Loud cheers suddenly burst from the spectators as a man dressed in the uniform of an officer, whom I had seen riding violently across the plain in an open space below, galloped along the front, waving his cap and shouting at the top of his voice. He was brought up, by the press of people round his horse, close to where I stood. "We've whipped them on all points," he cried. "We have taken all their batteries. They are retreating as fast as they can, and we are after them." Such cheers as rent the welkin! The congressmen shook hands with each other and cried out: "Bully for us! Bravo! Didn't I tell you so?" The Germans uttered their martial cheers, and the Irish hurrahed wildly. At this moment my horse was brought up the hill and I mounted and turned toward the road to the front. . . .

I had ridden between three and a half and four miles, as well as I could judge, when I was obliged to turn for the third and fourth time into the road by a considerable stream which was spanned by a bridge, toward which I was threading my way, when my attention was attracted by loud shouts in advance and I perceived several wagons coming from the direction of the battlefield, the drivers of which were endeavoring to force their horses past the ammunition carts going in the contrary direction near the bridge; a thick cloud of dust rose behind them, and running by the side of the waggons were a number of men in uniform whom I supposed to be the guard. My first impression was that the waggons were returning for fresh supplies of ammunition. But every moment the crowd increased; drivers and men cried out with the most vehement gestures: "Turn back! Turn back! We are whipped." They seized the heads of the horses and swore at the opposing drivers. Emerging from the crowd, a breathless man in the uniform of an officer, with an empty scabbard dangling by his side, was cut off by getting between my horse and a cart for a moment. "What is the matter, sir? What is all this about?" "Why, it means we are pretty badly whipped, that's the truth," he gasped, and continued.

By this time the confusion had been communicating itself through the line of waggons toward the rear, and the drivers endeavored to turn round their vehicles in the narrow road, which caused the usual amount of imprecations from the men and plunging and kicking from the horses.

The crowd from the front continually increased, the heat, the uproar, and the dust were beyond description, and these were augmented when some cavalry soldiers, flourishing their sabers and preceded by an officer, who cried out, "Make way there—make way there for the General," attempted to force a covered waggon, in which was seated a man with a bloody handkerchief round his head, through the press.

I had succeeded in getting across the bridge, with great difficulty, before the waggon came up, and I saw the crowd on the road was still gathering thicker and thicker. Again I asked an officer, who was on foot with his sword under his arm, "What is all this for?" "We are whipped, sir. We are all in retreat. You are all to go back." "Can you tell me where I can find General McDowell?" "No! nor can any one else. . . ."

In a few seconds a crowd of men rushed out of the wood down toward the guns, and the artillerymen near me seized the trail of a piece and were wheeling it round to fire when an officer or sergeant called out: "Stop! stop! They are our own men"; and in two or three minutes the whole battalion came sweeping past the guns at the double and in the utmost disorder. Some of the artillerymen dragged the horses out of the tumbrils, and for a moment the confusion was so great I could not understand what had taken place; but a soldier whom I stopped said, "We are pursued by their cavalry; they have cut us all to pieces."

Murat himself would not have dared to move a squadron on such ground. However, it could not be doubted that something serious was taking place; and at that moment a shell burst in front of the house, scattering the soldiers near it, which was followed by another that bounded along the road; and in a few minutes more out came another regiment from the wood, almost as broken as the first. The scene on the road had now assumed an aspect which has not a parallel in any description I have ever read. Infantry soldiers on mules and draft horses with the harness clinging to their heels, as much frightened as their riders; Negro servants on their masters' chargers; ambulances crowded with unwounded soldiers; waggons swarming with men who threw out the contents in the road to make room, grinding through a shouting, screaming mass of men on foot who were literally yelling with rage at every halt and shrieking out: "Here are the cavalry! Will you get on?" This portion of the force was evidently in discord.

There was nothing left for it but to go with the current one could not stem. I turned round my horse. . . . I was unwillingly approaching Centerville in the midst of heat, dust, confusion, imprecations inconceivable. On arriving at the place where a small rivulet crossed the road the throng increased still more. The ground over which I had passed going out was now covered with arms, clothing of all kinds, accouterments thrown off and left to be trampled in the dust under the hoofs of men and horses. The runaways ran alongside the waggons, striving to force themselves in among the occupants, who resisted tooth and nail. The drivers spurred and whipped and urged the horses to the utmost of their bent. I felt an inclination to laugh which was overcome by disgust and by that vague sense of something extraordinary taking place which is experienced when a man sees a number of people acting as if driven by some unknown terror. As I rode in the crowd, with men clinging to the stirrup leathers or holding on by anything they could lay hands on, so that I had some apprehension of being pulled off, I spoke to the men and asked them over and over again not to be in such a hurry. "There's no enemy to pursue you. All the cavalry in the world could not get at you." But I might as well have talked to the stones. . . .

It never occurred to me that this was a grand debacle. All along I believed the mass of the army was not broken and that all I saw around was the result of confusion created in a crude organization by a forced retreat, and knowing the reserves were at Centerville and beyond, I said to myself, "Let us see how this will be when we get to the hill." . . .

I was trotting quietly down the hill road beyond Centerville when suddenly the guns on the other side or from a battery very near opened fire, and a fresh outburst of artillery sounded through the woods. In an instant the mass of vehicles and retreating soldiers, teamsters, and civilians, as if agonized by an electric shock, quivered throughout the tortuous line. With dreadful shouts and cursings the drivers lashed their maddened horses and, leaping from the carts, left them to their fate and ran on foot. Artillerymen and foot soldiers and Negroes, mounted on gun horses with the chain traces and loose trappings trailing in the dust, spurred and flogged their steeds down the road or by the side paths. The firing continued and seemed to approach the hill, and at every report the agitated body of horsemen and waggons was seized, as it were, with a fresh convulsion.

Once more the dreaded cry: "The cavalry! cavalry are coming!" rang through the crowd, and looking back to Centerville, I perceived coming down the hill, between me and the sky, a number of mounted men who might at a hasty glance be taken for horsemen in the act of sabering the fugitives. In reality they were soldiers and civilians, with, I regret to say, some officers among them, who were whipping and striking their horses with sticks or whatever else they could lay hands on. I called out to the men who were frantic with terror beside me, "They are not cavalry at all; they're your own men"—but they did not heed me. A fellow who was shouting out, "Run! run!" as loud as he could beside me, seemed to take delight in creating alarm; and as he was perfectly collected as far as I could judge, I said: "What on earth are you running for? What are you afraid of?" He was in the roadside below me and, at once turning on me and exclaiming, "I'm not afraid of you," presented his piece and pulled the trigger so instantaneously that had it gone off I could not have swerved from the ball. As the scoundrel deliberately drew up to examine the nipple, I judged it best not to give him another chance and spurred on through the crowd, where any man could have shot as many as he pleased without interruption. The only conclusion I came to was that he was mad or drunken. When I was passing by the line of the bivouacs a battalion of men came tumbling down the bank from the field into the road with fixed bayonets, and as some fell in the road and others tumbled on top of them, there must have been a few ingloriously wounded.

22d.—I awoke from a deep sleep this morning about six o'clock. The rain was falling in torrents and beat with a dull, thudding sound on the leads outside my window; but louder than all came a strange sound as if of the tread of men, a confused tramp and splashing and a murmuring of voices. I got up and ran to the front room, the windows of which looked on the street, and there, to my intense surprise, I saw a steady stream of men covered with mud, soaked through with rain, who were pouring irregularly, without any semblance of order, up Pennsylvania Avenue toward the Capitol. A dense stream of vapor rose from the multitude, but looking closely at the men, I perceived they belonged to different regiments, New Yorkers, Michiganders, Rhode Islanders, Massachusetters, Minnesotans, mingled pellmell together. Many of them were without knapsacks, crossbelts, and firelocks. Some had neither greatcoats nor shoes; others were covered with blankets. Hastily putting on my clothes, I ran downstairs and asked an officer who was passing by, a pale young man who looked exhausted to death and who had lost his sword, for the empty sheath dangled at his side, where the men were coming from. "Where from? Well, sir, I guess we're all coming out of Virginny as far as we can, and pretty well whipped too." "What! the whole army, sir?" "That's more than I know. They may stay that like. I know I'm going home. I've had enough of fighting to last my lifetime."

The news seemed incredible. But there before my eyes were the jaded, dispirited, broken remnants of regiments passing onward, where and for what I knew not, and it was evident enough that the mass of the grand army of the Potomac was placing that river between it and the enemy as rapidly as possible. "Is there any pursuit?" I asked of several men. Some were too surly to reply; others said, "They're coming as fast as they can after us"; others, "I guess they've stopped it now—the rain is too much for them." A few said they did not know and looked as if they did not care. . . .

The rain has abated a little, and the pavements are densely packed with men in uniforms, some with, others without, arms, on whom the shopkeepers are looking with evident alarm. They seem to be in possession of all the spirit houses. Now and then shots are heard down the street or in the distance, and cries and shouting, as if a scuffle or a difficulty were occurring. Willard's is turned into a barrack for officers and presents such a scene in the hall as could only be witnessed in a city occupied by a demoralized army. There is no provost guard, no patrol, no authority visible in the streets. General Scott is quite overwhelmed by the affair and is unable to stir. General McDowell has not yet arrived. The Secretary of War knows not what to do, Mr. Lincoln is equally helpless, and Mr. Seward, who retains some calmness, is, notwithstanding his military rank and militia experience, without resource or expedient. There are a good many troops hanging on about the camps and forts on the other side of the river, it is said; but they are thoroughly disorganized and will run away if the enemy comes in sight without a shot, and then the capital must fall at once. Why Beauregard does not come I know not, nor can I well guess. I have been expecting every hour since noon to hear his cannon. Here is a golden opportunity. If the Confederates do not grasp that which will never come again on such terms, it stamps them with mediocrity.

—RUSSELL, *My Diary North and South*

3. HOW THE WOMEN TOOK THE NEWS OF BULL RUN

The fortitude and gallantry of the women of the South is a thrice-told tale. It was they, in the words of Stephen Benét,

> *That mended the broken gentlemen*
> *And sent them out to the war again . . .*
> *Made courage from terror and bread from bran*
> *And propped the South on a swansdown fan. . . .* *

Susan Blackford, whose letter is reproduced here,† was the wife of Charles Minor Blackford of the 2nd Virginia Cavalry, and sister-in-law to Colonel W. W. Blackford, whose War Years with Jeb Stuart *is one of the minor classics of the war.*

* From *John Brown's Body* in *The Selected Works of Stephen Vincent Benét*, published by Rinehart and Company, Inc. Copyright 1927, 1928 by Stephen Vincent Benét.
† Reprinted from *Letters from Lee's Army* by Susan Lee Blackford; copyright 1947 by Charles Scribner's Sons; used by permission of the publishers.

[July 1861. From Lynchburg]

The sound of the cannon were distinctly heard on the hills of Lynchburg, and we well knew that a great battle was being fought from early morn until sunset, and that not only the fate of our country and our homes was at stake, but that each boom which stirred the air might be fraught with the dying sigh of those we loved best. Mrs. Robert C. Saunders, whose husband was in the battle, stood all day on one of the hills near her home in Campbell and listened in agony to every gun. Other ladies whom I knew did the same thing near Pedlar Mills in Amherst County. Mrs. Saunders was all of one hundred and seventy miles from the battlefield. A large number of people came into town Sunday evening from the surrounding country to hear the news of the result, and many stayed long enough to hear sad tidings the next day of those for whom their hearts beat with such nervous strain; amongst the latter was Mrs. Winston Radford, of Bedford, whose husband was killed by a shell from a battery of the enemy commanded by a Captain Arnald.

The next day the rain poured in torrents. Mrs. Robert C. Saunders came up from her home to Father Blackford's to hear tidings of her husband. We could hear nothing Sunday night except that a great battle had been fought. I remained at Father's with Betty Colston and the children waiting and trembling, at one time on my knees praying for my husband's safety and at another trying to prepare myself for the worse news should it come.

This Monday morning was a time of terrible strain on us all. Father and Mother Blackford were very nervous, and he could not go down to his business, but walked about trying to take comfort from every circumstance mentioned. He had prayers in which we all joined. He and Mother had three sons in the battle, and Mrs. Saunders and myself our respective husbands. Old Dr. Thomas Blackford came up and sat with us. He, too, had one or more sons in the fight and was very nervous. My dear little children seemed to understand the trouble which cast its dark shadow over us all and little Nannie clung to me and whispered words of hope in my ear. Father at last went down town to hear what could be heard, while we waited with growing impatience and terror for his return.

At last we heard his footsteps on the front porch, and our hearts stopped beating, but the hurried way in which he opened the front door and the elasticity of his step announced the good news to my eager ear. With one bound we rushed to meet him, and sent out a shout of grateful joy when he caught his breath enough to say, with choking voice, "All safe"! We all gathered around Mother's bed where she was lying, some of us sobbing for joy, while Father offered up thanks to God for having spared our loved ones.

The telegrams which came were from my husband to me, which was the first which had come through, and one from Eugene and William which soon followed. Mr. Blackford's also told that none of his men were hurt, and my first impulse was to rush out and tell the wives and mothers of his men. It was such a happy day! I never shall forget it.

—BLACKFORD, ed., *Letters from Lee's Army*

4. STONEWALL JACKSON CREDITS GOD WITH
THE VICTORY

First Bull Run gave the Confederacy one of its greatest heroes. When on the morning of that battle the bluecoats were driving the Confederates back across the Warrenton turnpike, Thomas J. Jackson's brigade stood firm. "Look at Jackson," cried General Bee to his troops. "There he stands like a stonewall." Courage was common enough in the Confederate command; Jackson was soon to reveal other military qualities of a high order. His letter to his wife, written two days after the battle, shows that devoutness which was just as characteristic of the man as was courage.

Manassas, July 23d [1861]

My Precious Pet,—Yesterday we fought a great battle and gained a great victory, for which all the glory is due to *God alone*. Although under a heavy fire for several continuous hours, I received only one wound, the breaking of the longest finger of my left hand; but the doctor says the finger can be saved. It was broken about midway between the hand and knuckle, the ball passing on the side next the forefinger. Had it struck the centre, I should have lost the finger. My horse was wounded, but not killed. Your coat got an ugly wound near the hip, but my servant, who is very handy, has so far repaired it that it doesn't show very much. My preservation was entirely due, as was the glorious victory, to our God, to whom be all the honor, praise and glory. The battle was the hardest that I have ever been in, but not near so hot in its fire. I commanded the centre more particularly, though one of my regiments extended to the right for some distance. There were other commanders on my right and left. Whilst great credit is due to other parts of our gallant army, God made my brigade more instrumental than any other in repulsing the main attack. This is for your information only—say nothing about it. Let others speak praise, not myself.

—M. JACKSON, *Life and Letters of General Thomas J. Jackson*

5. "THE CAPTURE OF WASHINGTON SEEMS INEVITABLE"

After Bull Run the Confederates could have advanced on Washington; had they moved promptly they could probably have taken the city. But political and diplomatic considerations suggested that such an offensive would be inadvisable. The people of Washington, however, were for a time a-tremble for their safety.

Edwin M. Stanton—who had the jitters easily—had been Attorney General under Buchanan and was shortly to be appointed Secretary of War by Lincoln.

Washington, July 26, 1861

Dear Sir: ... The dreadful disaster of Sunday can scarcely be mentioned. The imbecility of this Administration culminated in that catastrophe—an irretrievable misfortune and national disgrace never to be forgotten are to be added to the ruin of all peaceful pursuits and national bankruptcy as the result of Lincoln's "running the machine" for five months. You perceive that Bennett is for a change of the Cabinet, and proposes for one of the new Cabinet Mr. Holt. . . . It is not unlikely that some change in the War and Navy Departments may take place, but none beyond these two departments until Jefferson Davis turns out the whole concern.

The capture of Washington seems now to be inevitable—during the whole of Monday and Tuesday it might have been taken without any resistance. The rout, overthrow, and utter demoralization of the whole army is complete. Even now I doubt whether any serious opposition to the entrance of the Confederate forces could be offered. While Lincoln, Scott, and the Cabinet are disputing who is to blame, the city is unguarded and the enemy at hand. General McClellan reached here last evening. But, if he had the ability of Caesar, Alexander, or Napoleon, what can he accomplish? Will not Scott's jealousy, Cabinet intrigues, Republican interference, thwart him at every step? While hoping for the best, I can not shut my eyes against the dangers that beset the Government, and especially this city. It is certain that Davis was in the field on Sunday, and the Secessionists here assert that he headed in person the last victorious charge. General Dix is in Baltimore. After three weeks' neglect and insult he was sent there. The warm debate between Douglas's friend Richardson and Kentucky Burnett has attracted some interest, but has been attended with no bellicose result.

Since this note was commenced, the morning paper has come in, and I see that McClellan did *not* arrive last night, as I was informed he had. General Lee was after him, but will have to wait awhile before they can meet.

Yours truly,
Edwin M. Stanton.

His Excellency, James Buchanan

—Rice, ed., "A Page of Political Correspondence"

6. THE YANKEES SUFFER DISASTER AT BALL'S BLUFF

After Bull Run, McClellan was appointed commander of all land forces around Washington and, in a short time, replaced the aged Scott as commander in chief of the United States Army. Meantime, as the Union soldiers drilled and the Confederates strengthened their position, all was quiet along the Potomac. On October 21, however, General Stone crossed the river at Leesburg, just above Washington, to attack what he thought was a handful of defenders. The Confederates got wind of the attack and turned it into a rout. Colonel Baker, Senator from Oregon and Lincoln's friend, was killed; young Lieutenant Oliver Wendell Holmes was badly wounded. The disaster at Ball's Bluff led to the creation of the ill-omened Congressional Committee on the Conduct of the War.

Randolph Abbott Shotwell, from whose autobiography this account is taken, was a Virginia-born boy of seventeen studying in Pennsylvania when the war broke out. He promptly headed south, joined the first regiment he found—the 8th Virginia—and fought through the war until his capture at Cold Harbor. After the war he was long prominent in North Carolina politics and journalism.

Oct. 21, '61—General Evans decided to advance and meet McCall, taking post at the "burned bridge" over Goose Creek, three miles southeast of Leesburg. This stream, notwithstanding its euphonious title, is no duck-pond outlet; but, with its wooded bluffs, forms quite a good line of defense against an enemy approaching from the east. . . . During the afternoon a scouting party returned with information that General McCall's corps, after marching up as far as Dranesville, had then, like the king of France, "marched down again." So the morning's flurry was a false alarm. But hold!—here is a dispatch, captured on a Federal courier, which bears the address "To General Stone, in Leesburg." Other intimations reveal the whole plot. Meantime, Gen. Stone, watching from the Maryland heights, rubs his hands in glee on seeing Evans' four regiments filing down the turnpike towards Dranesville. Orders were hastily issued for Colonel Devens to cross into Virginia and push forward to Leesburg; while other troops are to follow as fast as they can cross the Potomac.

Colonel Devens, with five companies, landed upon Harrison's Island shortly after midnight; and while a portion of the command were transporting the boats across the island, the remainder were employed in digging rifle pits to command the passage. . . . Opposite the island, the Virginia shore rises abruptly; in many places directly from the water's edge, in cliffs or bluffs, now historic as "Ball's Bluff." These cliffs, while favorable to the secrecy of the Federal advance, in the end proved a source of fearful disaster. . . .

Colonel Devens drew up his battalion along the brow of Ball's Bluff about 2:30 A.M. on the morning of October 21st, and began to advance in skirmish order toward Leesburg. The citizens of that town had retired early, fatigued by the excitements of the day, and blissfully unconscious of impending peril. All the troops were miles away, except one company of Mississippians, under Captain Duff, which had been left as a camp-guard. Morning brought a startling apparition to these men, as they rubbed their eyes, and yawned for breakfast. Over the green-clad hills toward the northeast, within musket-shot of town, came a long line of blue-coated skirmishers, their polished musket-barrels gleaming in the sunlight, and the "red, white, and blue" fluttering in vivid contrast with the dark foliage of the cedar copse. It was Devens' battalion, advancing from the Potomac! But Captain Duff was no "duffer"; he speedily trotted his men to the nearest fence in the path of the invaders and opened a scorching fire, killing six and wounding twenty before he lost a man, owing to the advantage of shelter and his defensive attitude.

Colonel Devens, seeing a section of artillery coming into town, fell back a short distance into a skirt of timber, to await instructions and reinforcements. He was now joined by Colonel Lee, with four companies; but about the same time two strong companies of Mississippians came to the rescue of Captain Duff, taking Devens on the flank and compelling him to retire nearer Ball's Bluff. Meanwhile General Stone, with the Nineteenth Massachusetts and other troops, had crossed the Potomac at Edwards' ferry, just above the mouth of Goose Creek; his apparent design being to seize the bridge over the turnpike one mile above and oppose Evans' return from Dranesville. Finding, however, the Thirteenth Mississippi, a strong regiment (which he supposed a full brigade), confronting him at the ferry, he hastened to send the main body of his army to cross at Harrison's, two and a half miles above. This column, which he styled "the right wing," was now given into command of Colonel E. D. Baker. It was composed of the Fifteenth and Twentieth Massachusetts, the First California, the "Tammany" (New York) Regiment, and some "unattached" companies, with four mountain howitzers and one 6-pound rifled-gun. Intelligence of these proceedings reached General Evans at an early hour, and Colonel Eppa Hunton with the Eighth Virginia, was sent at a rapid trot three miles across the fields to drive back Devens.

Colonel Hunton, having deployed his men along a little ridge, advanced and engaged the Federals a few minutes after 1:00 P.M. Sharp musketry firing ensued and continued during the next two hours. Here was the fatal mistake of the day on the Federal side. In the long-range duello the Confederates had all the advantage. So thin was their line that nearly every man could have the shelter of a tree or stump; whereas their own shots could hardly miss the dense line of blue coats. The Virginians and Mississippians being accustomed to the rifle, most of them old hunters, rarely missed their man. Climbing into the tops of trees, creeping through the tall grass, or concealed in the gullies, they plied their weapons with murderous havoc especially among the Federal officers. It was very poor management to allow this to go on. Had Baker ordered a couple of regiments to sweep the woods he would have cleared his path of all those death-stinging hornets and marched into Leesburg. The Federal position at this time was upon the plateau of the bluff, some 700 yards in front of the river, where there was a cleared field of ten or twelve acres, with a shallow ravine or hollow, running through the middle of it. The artillery was planted to sweep this clearing in front, while the flanks were measurably protected by a series of steep little hills and rocky ravines, overgrown with scrubby, stunted pines.

By 4:00 P.M. the last of the Federal troops had crossed and were drawn up in horseshoe shape, with the point of the shoe fronting the ten-acre cleared lot, 600 yards from the bluff. But the loss in officers had greatly crippled the effectiveness of the force. Lieutenant-Colonel Wistar, of the First California, had been killed, and his regiment much shattered. Furthermore, the Confederates had been reinforced by the remainder of the Seventeenth Mississippi, perhaps 600 muskets, and the Eighteenth Mississippi was within one mile, advancing rapidly. *Per contra* the Virginia regiment had exhausted its ammunition, and no one knew where the wagon trains could be found; war was a new business at that date. Men could be seen crawling about, searching the boxes of the dead or borrowing cartridges of their comrades—to get one more shot. Colonel Hunton dispatched his adjutant to say to General Evans: "My powder is out; what shall I do?" "Fix bayonets and run 'em into the river!" quoth "Old Shanks" (his regular army *sobriquet*) who had just taken a liquid reinforcement, equivalent to 10,000 men. It was time for some decisive measure, for Colonel Baker had ordered his right wing to advance and flank the little ridge whence came the rebel bullets.

Fortunately for the Confederates, at the moment this movement began, there was heard the pattering footsteps and jingling canteens of the Eighteenth Mississippi double quicking through the brush, then a wild, terror striking yell; then the simultaneous crash of 1,000 muskets, each hurling its leaden contents along the Federal left and centre! The effect was electric. The roar of this sudden, blinding, raking volley was like the crack of doom to the already demoralized Federals, most of whom were under fire for the first time! A strange report ran along the lines that General Joe Johnston, with 10,000 fresh men, had just arrived. Colonel Baker, himself, remarked to an aide that he had seen Johnston, mounted on a white horse, riding in advance. Baker, Colonel Cogswell, Major Harvey and others were at the time working the small howitzers, which had been crippled several times, being plainly exposed to the fire of the concealed sharp-shooters. The rifled six-pounder could not be used.

Seeing that the crisis was come—as the Confederates were assuming the offensive and closing upon him from three sides, with the river at his back—Colonel Baker turned to the bayonet as the last hope. Calling to the nearest battalions, he shouted, ordered, and entreated them to advance, to charge! His voice, ringing above the murderous crack of the rifle, could be heard even in the Confederate ranks, urging his men to charge and save the day for themselves. Thus incited they began to move, but in a wavering irresolution—a sure precursor of failure. Baker ran forward and at once received a stinging wound. But without pausing he gallantly rushed onward and was at the head of his men, when a beardless youth emptied five barrels of his revolver into him, at twenty paces. Four of the balls took effect, the first passing through his brain!

At this moment the hostile lines were within stone's throw, and both advancing. The Federals, seeing the fall of their leader, halted. Some soldiers seized Baker's body and ran with it rearward. This started the rest, and a general retreat took place, though several brave fellows moved so slowly that hand-to-hand fights raged along the whole line during the next ten minutes. Many of the Southerners also stopped at the cannon, which they wheeled around and endeavored to fire upon their late owners, but could not succeed. Subsequently one of the guns was found to have the ball put in before the powder—a very good reason for its refusal to explode. The temporary failure to pursue enabled Colonel Cogswell—now in command—to rally a portion of the survivors on the brow of a bluff, but he himself bleeding from a wound; Colonel Devens was in like condition; all regimental order was lost, and the huddling of the men on the hill rendered the Confederate fire, which was rapidly closing in on all sides, so much the more fatal. Suddenly the Seventeenth Mississippi closed in on the flank with a terrific volley and ended the battle.

Then ensued an awful spectacle! A kind of shiver ran through the huddled mass upon the brow of the cliff; it gave way; rushed a few steps; then, in one wild, panic-stricken herd, rolled, leaped, tumbled over the precipice! The descent is nearly perpendicular, with ragged, jutting crags, and a water laved base. Screams of pain and terror filled the air. Men seemed suddenly bereft of reason; they leaped over the bluff with muskets still in their clutch, threw themselves into the river without divesting themselves of their heavy accoutrements, hence went to the bottom like lead. Others sprang down upon the heads and bayonets of those below. A gray-haired private of the First California was found with his head mashed between two rocks by the heavy boots of a ponderous "Tammany" man, who had broken his own neck by the fall! The side of the bluff was worn smooth by the number sliding down.

From the beginning of the battle a steady stream of wounded men had been trickling down the zig-zag path leading to the narrow beach, whence the boats were to convey them to the Island. As it happened, the two larger bateaux were just starting with an overload when the torrent of terror-stricken fugitives rolled down the bluffs—upon them. Both boats were instantly submerged, and their cargoes of helpless human beings (crippled by wounds) were swept away to unknown graves! The whole surface of the river seemed filled with heads, struggling, screaming, fighting, dying! Man clutched at man, and the strong, who might have escaped, were dragged down by the weaker. Voices that strove to shout for help were stifled by the turbid, sullen waters of the swollen river and died away in gurgles. It is strange how persons about to drown turn to their fellows for strength; they may be in mid-ocean, with no hope for any, yet will they grasp one another and sink in pairs. Captain Otter, of the First California, (an apposite name for a swimmer,) was found a few days later with two men of his company clutching his neckband. Had he attempted to save them, or had they seized him and dragged him down? One officer was found with $126 in gold in his pocket; it had cost his life.

—SHOTWELL, "Three Years in Battle"

7. McCLELLAN OPENS THE PENINSULAR CAMPAIGN

George B. McClellan is doubtless the most controversial military figure of the Civil War. We meet him first as he embarks on the campaign that is to reduce Richmond, destroy Johnston's army, and end the war; we shall meet him again. With an army almost twice as strong as Johnston's, he was reluctant to take the offensive, and while the North clamored for action, he stayed in and around Washington. Finally on January 27, 1862, President Lincoln issued War Order No. 1 positively ordering an advance on or before February 22, but McClellan ignored this as well as subsequent orders. Early in March McClellan decided to shift his army to Urbana, on the south bank of the Rappahannock, but when Johnston moved his forces south of the Rappahannock this shift of base became pointless. On March 17 McClellan embarked his army for Fortress Monroe, and on April 4 began a snaillike advance up the Peninsula toward Yorktown, investing the ground as he went. Johnston withdrew from Yorktown to Williamsburg, and there, on May 5, the blue and the gray locked in battle. Although McClellan claimed a victory, his losses were 50 per cent higher than Johnston's. This letter to his wife reveals his characteristic self-confidence and vanity.

Williamsburg, May 6, 1862—

I telegraphed you this morning that we had gained a battle. Every hour its importance is proved to be greater. On Sunday I sent Stoneman in pursuit with the cavalry and four batteries of horse-artillery. He was supported by the divisions of Hooker, Smith, Couch, Casey, and Kearny, most of which arrived on the ground only yesterday. Unfortunately I did not go with the advance myself, being obliged to remain to get Franklin and Sedgwick started up the river for West Point. Yesterday I received pressing messages from Smith and others begging me to go to the front. I started with half a dozen aides and some fifteen orderlies, and found things in a bad state. Hancock was engaged with a vastly inferior force some two miles from any support. Hooker fought nearly all day without assistance, and the mass of the troops were crowded together where they were useless. I found everybody discouraged, officers and men; our troops in wrong positions, on the wrong side of the woods; no system, no co-operation, no orders given, roads blocked up.

As soon as I came upon the field the men cheered like fiends, and I saw at once that I could save the day. I immediately reinforced Hancock and arranged to support Hooker, advanced the whole line across the woods, filled up the gaps, and got everything in hand for whatever might occur. The result was that the enemy saw that he was gone if he remained in his position, and scampered during the night. His works were very strong, but his loss was very heavy. The roads are in such condition that it is impossible to pursue except with a few cavalry.

It is with the utmost difficulty that I can feed the men, many of whom have had nothing to eat for twenty-four hours and more. I had no dinner yesterday, no supper; a cracker for breakfast, and no dinner yet. I have no baggage; was out in the rain all day and until late at night; slept in my clothes and boots, and could not even wash my face and hands. I, however, expect my ambulance up pretty soon, when I hope for better things. I have been through the hospitals, where are many of our own men and of the rebels. One Virginian sent for me this morning and told me that I was the only general from whom they expected any humanity. I corrected this mistake.

This is a beautiful little town; several very old houses and churches, pretty gardens. I have taken possession of a very fine house which Joe Johnston occupied as his headquarters. It has a lovely flower-garden and conservatory. If you were here I should be much inclined to spend some weeks here.

THE PENINSULAR CAMPAIGN

G. W. was one of the whipped community, also Joe Johnston, Cadmus Wilcox, A. P. Hill, D. H. Hill, Longstreet, Jeb Stuart, Early (badly wounded); and many others that we know. We have all their wounded; eight guns so far. In short, we have given them a tremendous thrashing, and I am not at all ashamed of the conduct of the Army of the Potomac.

—Letter to his wife, in *McClellan's Own Story*

8. GENERAL WOOL TAKES NORFOLK

Johnston's withdrawal from Yorktown exposed Norfolk to capture, and on May 9 the Confederates blew up the crippled Merrimac *and abandoned the city which they had held since the beginning of the war. General Wool who "captured" Norfolk had been a major in the War of 1812 and a general in the Mexican War, and was 77 at the outbreak of the Civil War. The happily named Egbert Ludovicus Viele was a brigadier general of volunteers; after the war he projected a plan for subways for New York City and served as commissioner of parks.*

NO time was lost on the following morning in re-embarking the troops for the purpose of marching on Norfolk by the rear. At the last moment General Wool, with much emotion begged the Secretary (Chase) to allow him to command the troops. The Secretary had decided to relieve him of the command of the expedition on account of his advanced age, but finally reversed his decision with the remark that he could not inflict sorrow upon gray hairs. . . .

Starting at once to the front with our escort, we had not gone very far before it became evident that a great deal of confusion existed in the command—in fact, that there was no organization, and an utter absence of definite instructions or orders of any kind. Overtaking a regiment that was scattered along the road—most of the men lying down wherever any shade could be found, as the day was intensely warm—Mr. Chase inquired of the colonel to whose command he belonged and what his orders were. He replied that he had no idea who was his commander, that some said Weber and some said Mansfield. He had received no orders except that when he landed he was told to take a certain road, and he thought he would wait to see what was to be done next. Overtaking another regiment a mile or two beyond, the Secretary received the same answers. Going on still farther, we came upon General Mansfield and his staff, who had dismounted in the shade near a spring of cool water. Farther still, another straggling regiment was found; yet no one had any orders or instructions. Suddenly the booming of cannon was heard immediately in front, and as no artillery had been landed by us, it was evident that the firing proceeded from the enemy. Straggling soldiers now came running toward us with exaggerated rumors of the enemy being in force, burning the bridges, and contesting with artillery the passage of the streams that crossed the road. The ridiculousness of the situation would have been amusing if it had not been for the serious aspect that it was gradually assuming. Two regiments of cavalry had been embarked and two batteries of artillery; yet not a horse or a gun had been sent to the front. Four regiments of infantry were marching along, uncertain what road to take and unassigned to any brigade; two brigadier generals and their staffs, without orders and without commands, were sitting by the roadside waiting for something to turn up. This was the situation with the enemy firing in front.

Secretary Chase took it all in at a glance and rose at once to the necessities of the occasion. Tearing some leaves from his memorandum book, he directed me to send one of our escort back to General Wool with a written requisition for artillery and cavalry. This brought the general to the front with two pieces of artillery and some mounted troops. As he rode up, Mr. Chase expressed to him in very strong language his astonishment at the con-dition of things. General Wool replied by saying that he presumed General Mansfield had felt some delicacy in assuming command over General Weber and that General Weber had hesitated to act while General Mansfield was so near.

"Talk of delicacy," exclaimed the Secretary, "with the enemy firing in front! What absurdity! Let General Mansfield go to the rear and bring up reinforcements, and that will settle all questions of delicacy." This brought about a prolonged discussion between Generals Wool and Mansfield, which was carried on at a short distance from the rear under the shade of a large sycamore tree. Losing all patience, the Secretary exclaimed, "Two cackling hens!" and turning to me with a voice and manner that would have become Wellington or Soult, he said: "Sir! I order you in the name of the President of the United States to take command of these troops and march them upon Norfolk."

An infantry regiment was deployed at double-quick as skirmishers in advance, and the other regiments were soon moving rapidly down the Norfolk road. They had proceeded some distance before General Wool was aware of the movement. He was not long in overtaking us, however, and on his demand for an explanation from me Mr. Chase assumed the responsibility, after which we proceeded harmoniously toward our destination. At the extreme limits of the city and before the formidable line of intrenched works was reached, a large deputation headed by the mayor and municipal councils made its appearance with a flag of truce and performed a most skillful ruse to gain time for the Confederates to secure their retreat from the city. The mayor, with all the formality of a medieval warden, appeared with a bunch of rusty keys and a formidable roll of papers which he proceeded to read with the utmost deliberation previous to delivering the "keys of the city." The reading of the documents—which embraced a large portion of the history of Virginia, the causes that led to the war, the peculiar position of the good citizens of Norfolk, and in short a little of everything that could have the remotest bearing upon the subject and exhaust the longest possible space of time in reading—was protracted until nearly dark.

In the meantime the Confederates were hurrying with their artillery and stores over the ferry to Portsmouth, cutting the water pipes and flooding the public buildings, setting fire to the navy yard, and having their own way generally, while our General was listening in the most innocent and complacent manner to the long rigmarole so ingeniously prepared by the mayor and skillfully interlarded with fulsome personal eulogium upon himself. . . .

And now another well-devised plan presented itself in the shape of a number of carriages which the mayor particularly desired should be used by the officers in taking possession of the city, the troops in the meanwhile to remain where they were. Falling readily into this second little trap, the General accepted and we were driven to the city hall, where some more rusty keys were produced and more formal speeches were made. A collection of several thousand people, some of them in butternut and gray, assembled in front of the building. While the General and mayor were going through their high formalities, Mr. Chase asked for a pen and a piece of paper and wrote an order assigning the command of the city to myself as military governor, which General Wool signed at his direction. Then, bidding me goodbye, he took the General by the arm and departed, leaving me the solitary occupant of the city hall, without a soldier within two miles and with not even an aide-de-camp to assist me. Fortunately an enterprising newspaper correspondent had followed the carriages on foot, and him I appointed an aide and dispatched for the troops. By the time the troops arrived the moon had risen, and by its light they were placed in position. A regiment dispatched to the navy yard was too late to rescue it from almost complete destruction, but it cut off the *Merrimac* from any supplies from either side of the river.

It was long after midnight before the final disposition of troops was made, and this had hardly been accomplished when, with a shock that shook the city and with an ominous sound that could not be mistaken, the magazine of the *Merrimac* was exploded, the vessel having been cut off from supplies and deserted by the crew; and thus this most formidable engine of destruction that had so long been a terror not only to Hampton Roads but to the Atlantic coast went to her doom.

—VIELE, "A Trip with Lincoln, Chase and Stanton"

9. THE ARMY OF THE POTOMAC MARCHES TO MEET McCLELLAN

By the end of May McClellan had worked his way slowly and painfully up the Peninsula, and was within sight—and sound—of Richmond. The Federals outnumbered the Confederates probably by a ratio of five to three, but as new regiments and companies swarmed in to the defense of the beleaguered capital the opposing forces became more nearly equal. At this time the Confederate army north of Richmond was called the Army of the Potomac; this is not to be confused with the Federal army of the same name.

Sallie Putnam, from whose delightful reminiscences of Richmond during the war this excerpt is taken, was one of the Virginia gentry who stayed on in the city throughout the war.

THE day of the passage of the Army of the Potomac through Richmond will long be remembered by those who were in the city. It was known that they were on their way to the Peninsula, and for days they had been expected to march through the streets of the capital. The greatest interest and excitement prevailed. The morning was bright and beautiful in the early spring, balmy with the odors of the violet and the hyacinth, and the flaunting narcissus, the jonquil, and myriads of spring flowers threw on their particolored garments to welcome the army of veterans as they passed.

From an early hour until the sun went down in the West the steady tramp of the soldier was heard on the streets. Continuous cheers went up from thousands of voices; from every window fair heads were thrust, fair hands waved snowy handkerchiefs, and bright eyes beamed "Welcome!" Bands of spirit-stirring music discoursed the favorite airs,—Dixie's Land, My Maryland, the Bonny Blue Flag, and other popular tunes—and as the last regiments were passing we heard the strains of "Good-Bye," and tears were allowed to flow, and tender hearts ached as they listened to the significant tune. Soldiers left the ranks to grasp the hands of friends in passing, to receive some grateful refreshment, a small bouquet, or a whispered congratulation. Officers on horseback raised their hats, and some of the more gallant ventured to waft kisses to the fair ones at the doors and windows. We shall never forget the appearance of General Longstreet, the sturdy fighter, the obstinate warrior, as he dashed down Main Street surrounded by his splendid staff.

Through other streets poured our cavalry, under their gallant chieftain, the pink of Southern chivalry,—the gay, rollicking, yet bold, daring and venturous "Jeb." Stuart. As we saw him then, sitting easily on his saddle, as though he was born to it, he seemed every inch the cavalier. His stout yet lithe figure, his graceful bearing, his broad, well-formed chest and shoulders, on which was gracefully poised his splendid head, his bright, beaming countenance, lighted up with a smile as pleasant as a woman's, his dark red hair and flowing beard, with his lower limbs encased in heavy cavalry boots, made up the *tout ensemble* of this brave son of Maryland. His genial temperament made him the idol and companion of the most humble of his men, and his deeds of daring and heroic courage made him respected as their leader.

As they swept through our streets on that beautiful morning, with their horses in good order, their own spirits buoyant and cheerful, many of them wearing in their caps bouquets of the golden daffodils of early spring, cheered on by the ringing sounds of the bugle, we thought never to see them pass again with worn-out horses and weary, listless spirits, as they spurred on their broken-down steeds; but so it was. . . .

—[Sallie Putnam], *Richmond during the War*

10. R. E. LEE TAKES COMMAND

After First Bull Run Joseph E. Johnston was assigned to command the Confederate armies in northern Virginia, and in July 1861 appointed gen-

*eral—fourth in rank in the whole Confederacy. When McClellan got himself
entangled in the swamps of the Chickahominy, Johnston moved out to meet
him. The Battle of Seven Pines, or Fair Oaks, which came on May 31 and
June 1, was, in Freeman's phrase, "a battle of strange errors." Badly fought
on both sides, it was at best indecisive. Though Confederate losses ran to
almost eight thousand, and Union to less than six thousand, the Confederates
claimed a victory. General Johnston was severely wounded on the battle-
field and Davis turned to Lee—who then held the ambiguous position of
"general in charge of military operations under the direction of the President" and assigned him the command. That very day he baptized the army
by the name it was to make immortal, "The Army of Northern Virginia."*

*General Evander M. Law, who tells us here how Lee appeared when he
took command during the Battle of Seven Pines, was a South Carolinian who
was teaching at an Alabama military academy when the war broke out. He
raised a company from his own school and took it to Virginia. He served all
through the war in the East until wounded at Cold Harbor.*

DURING the months of April, May, and the early part of June, while
Jackson in the Valley was conducting a series of the most brilliant operations of the war, successively defeating Milroy, Banks, Shields, and Fremont,
and while McDowell was oscillating like an eccentric pendulum between the
Rappahannock and the Valley, General McClellan's army had been transferred by water to the lower Peninsula, and was moving upon Richmond
from the southeast. His advance was met by General Magruder, who, with
his small command of eleven thousand men, took up a short and strong defensive line extending from Yorktown on his left to the James River on his
right, a portion of his front being covered by the Warwick River.

In the meantime General Johnston was rapidly transferring his army from
Centreville and the posts on the lower Potomac, where it had wintered, to
unite with Magruder on the lines at Yorktown. Johnston held the line established by Magruder until the 4th of May, when he evacuated Yorktown and
slowly retired up the Peninsula. McClellan followed promptly, and coming
up with the Confederate rear on the 6th, the battle of Williamsburg was
fought. Another smaller affair occurred on the 7th at Eltham's Landing, at
the head of York River, where a portion of Whiting's division attacked and
drove back to the river a Federal force under General Franklin, which had
been pushed up by water to fall upon the flank of the Confederate army as it
retired. The Federal advance was thenceforward much more cautious, and
it was not until the 24th of May that McClellan's army was in position along
the east bank of the Chickahominy and the struggle for Richmond itself
began.

The Federal army, holding the line of the Chickahominy from Mechanicsville to Bottom's bridge, at once commenced the construction of military
bridges between those points, and before the end of May McClellan's left
wing was advanced by throwing the two corps of Heintzelman and Keyes
across the river. The latter took position and entrenched on a line running

BATTLEFIELDS OF THE SEVEN DAYS

in front of "Seven Pines" on the Williamsburg road, with its right extending across the York River Railroad in front of Fair Oaks station. Heintzelman was placed in supporting distance in the rear, near Savage's station. Mc-Clellan's outposts were now within five miles of Richmond. Almost near enough to realize President Lincoln's suggestion, when he inquired by telegraph on May 26th, "Can you get near enough to throw shells into the city?" This amiable desire was not destined to be gratified, for during the afternoon and night of the 30th of May a heavy rain-storm occurred, flooding the low grounds of the Chickahominy and threatening the destruction of the military bridges constructed by the Federal army. The two wings were to a certain extent isolated, and General Johnston took advantage of this condition of affairs to attack Keyes' corps near Seven Pines on the 31st of May. This corps was assailed by D. H. Hill's division and thoroughly routed. Heintzelman came to its support, but by this time the divisions of Longstreet and G. W. Smith had united in the attack with D. H. Hill, and this corps fared little better than that of Keyes. By the most strenuous exertions Sumner's Federal corps was thrown across the almost ruined bridges, during the afternoon and night of the 31st, and this timely reinforcement, together with the intervention of night, saved the left wing of McClellan's army from destruction.

The tardy movements of some of the Confederate commanders on the extreme right delayed the attack several hours beyond the time when it should have been made, and this delay was fatal to the complete success of General Johnston's plans. While G. W. Smith's division, to which I was attached, was warmly engaged near the junction of the "Nine Mile" road and the York River Railroad, General Johnston rode up and gave me an order as to the movements of my command. Night was rapidly approaching, and he seemed anxious to urge forward the attack with all possible speed so as to clear the field of the enemy before night. He was moving with the troops and personally directing the advance, when he received a severe wound in the shoulder and was compelled to relinquish the command. The Confederates had been checked on their left wing by the arrival of Sumner's corps, and the fighting ceased just after dark. It was renewed on our right wing on the morning of the 1st of June without advantage to either side, and by 2 o'clock P.M. the battle was over, without having accomplished the purpose for which it was fought.

General G. W. Smith, an officer of acknowledged ability, succeeded General Johnston in command of the Confederate army on the night of the 31st of May. But during the afternoon of the next day, June 1st, he in turn relinquished the command to General Lee, under orders from President Davis. Our right wing was at once withdrawn from its advanced position, and Smith's division on the left followed the next day. As I was standing near the Nine Mile road a day or two after the battle, General Lee passed along the road accompanied by two staff officers. I had never seen him before, and he was pointed out by some one near me. I observed the new commander of the "Army of Northern Virginia" very closely and with a great deal of interest. General Johnston was universally beloved and pos-

sessed the unbounded confidence of the army, and the commander who succeeded him must be "every inch a man" and a soldier to fill his place in their
confidence and affection. General Lee had up to this time accomplished
nothing to warrant the belief in his future greatness as a commander. He
had made an unsuccessful campaign in Western Virginia the year before,
and since that time had been on duty first at Charleston and then in Richmond. There was naturally a great deal of speculation among the soldiers
as to how he would "pan out." The general tone, however, was one of confidence, which was invariably strengthened by a sight of the man himself.
Calm, dignified, and commanding in his bearing, a countenance strikingly
benevolent and self-possessed, a clear, honest eye that could look friend or
enemy in the face; clean-shaven, except a closely-trimmed mustache which
gave a touch of firmness to the well-shaped mouth; simply and neatly dressed
in the uniform of his rank, felt hat, and top boots reaching to the knee; sitting
his horse as if his home was in the saddle; such was Robert E. Lee as he appeared when he assumed command of the army of "Northern Virginia" in
the early days of June, 1862, never to relinquish it for a day, until its colors
were furled for ever at Appomattox.

—LAW, "The Fight for Richmond"

11. "BEAUTY" STUART RIDES AROUND McCLELLAN'S ARMY

*Although heavily outnumbered Lee planned to seize the offensive and
destroy McClellan's army or drive it off the Peninsula. In preparation for the
offensive he sent J. E. B. (Beauty) Stuart out to reconnoiter the Federal
position, especially between the Chickahominy and the Totopotomy. Stuart
set out on June 12 with some 1,000 cavalrymen, made the called-for reconnaissance, and then, instead of turning back, decided to ride 150 miles around
McClellan's whole army.*

*This account of the last part of the ride is by the famous Virginia novelist
and historian who fought all through the war with Stuart, John Esten Cooke.*

THE gayest portion of the raid now began. From this moment it was
neck or nothing, do or die. We had one chance of escape against ten of
capture or destruction.

Stuart had decided upon his course with that rapidity, good judgment,
and decision, which were the real secrets of his splendid efficiency as a leader
of cavalry, in which capacity I believe that he has never been surpassed, either
in the late war or any other. He was now in the very heart of the enemy's
citadel, with their enormous masses upon every side. He had driven in their
advanced force, passed within sight of the white tents of General McClellan's
headquarters, burned their camps, and ascertained all that he wished. How
was he to return? He could not cross the Pamunkey, and make a circuit
back; he had no pontoons. He could not return over the route by which
he had advanced. As events afterward showed, the alarm had been given,
and an overpowering force of infantry, cavalry, and artillery had been rapidly

moved in that direction to intercept the daring raider. Capture stared him in the face, on both of these routes—across the Pamunkey, or back as he came; he must find some other loophole of escape.

Such was the dangerous posture of affairs, and such was the important problem which Stuart decided in five minutes. He determined to make the complete circuit of McClellan's army; and crossing the Chickahominy below Long Bridge, re-enter the Confederate lines from Charles City. If on his way he encountered cavalry he intended to fight it; if a heavy force of infantry barred his way he would elude, or cut a path through it; if driven to the wall and debarred from escape he did not mean to surrender. A few days afterward I said to him:

"That was a tight place at the river, General. If the enemy had come down on us, you would have been compelled to have surrendered."

"No," was his reply; "one other course was left."

"What was that?"

"To *die game*."

And I know that such was his intention. When a commander means to die game rather than surrender he is a dangerous adversary. . . .

Everywhere the ride was crowded with incident. The scouting and flanking parties constantly picked up stragglers, and overhauled unsuspecting wagons filled with the most tempting stores. In this manner a wagon, stocked with champagne and every variety of wines, belonging to a General of the Federal army, fell a prey to the thirsty gray-backs. Still they pressed on. Every moment an attack was expected in front or rear. Colonel Will. T. Martin commanded the latter. "Tell Colonel Martin," Stuart said to me, "to have his artillery ready, and look out for an attack at any moment." I had delivered the message and was riding to the front again, when suddenly a loud cry arose of "Yankees in the rear!" Every sabre flashed, fours were formed, the men wheeled about, when all at once a stunning roar of laughter ran along the line; it was a *canard*. The column moved up again with its flanking parties well out. The men composing the latter were, many of them, from the region, and for the first time for months saw their mothers and sisters. These went quite wild at sight of their sons and brothers. . . .

The column was now skirting the Pamunkey, and a detachment hurried off to seize and burn two or three transports lying in the river. Soon a dense cloud rose from them, the flames soared up, and the column pushed on. Everywhere were seen the traces of flight—for the alarm of "hornets in the hive" was given. Wagons had turned over, and were abandoned—from others the excellent army stores had been hastily thrown. This writer got a fine red blanket, and an excellent pair of cavalry pantaloons, for which he still owes the United States. Other things lay about in tempting array, but we were approaching Tunstall's, where the column would doubtless make a charge; and to load down a weary horse was injudicious. The advance guard was now in sight of the railroad. There was no question about the affair before us. The column must cut through, whatever force guarded the railroad; to reach the lower Chickahominy the guard here must be overpowered. Now was the time to use the artillery, and every effort was made to hurry it forward. But alas! it had got into a tremendous mudhole, and the wheels were buried to the axle. The horses were lashed, and jumped, almost breaking the traces; the drivers swore; the harness cracked—but the guns did not move.

"Gat! Lieutenant," said a sergeant of Dutch origin to the brave Lieutenant McGregor, "it can't be done. But just put that keg on the gun, Lieutenant," pointing, as he spoke, to a keg of whiskey in an ambulance, the spoil of the Federal camp, "and tell the men they can have it if they pull through!"

McGregor laughed, and the keg was quickly perched on the gun. Then took place an exhibition of herculean muscularity which would have delighted Guy Livingston. With eyes fixed ardently upon the keg, the powerful cannoneers waded into the mudhole up to their knees, seized the wheels of gun and caisson loaded down with ammunition, and just simply lifted the whole out, and put them on firm ground. The piece whirled on—the keg had been dismounted—the cannoneers revelled in the spoils they had earned.

Tunstall's was now nearly in sight, and that good fellow Captain Frayser, afterward Stuart's signal officer, came back and reported one or two companies of infantry at the railroad. Their commander had politely beckoned to him as he reconnoitred, exclaiming in wheedling accents, full of Teutonic blandishment, "Koom yay!" But this cordial invitation was disregarded; Frayser galloped back and reported, and the ringing voice of Stuart ordered "Form platoons! draw sabre! charge!" At the word the sabres flashed, a thundering shout arose, and sweeping on in column of platoons, the gray people fell upon their blue adversaries, gobbling them up, almost without a shot. . . .

The men swarmed upon the railroad. Quick axes were applied to the telegraph poles, which crashed down, and Redmond Burke went in command of a detachment to burn a small bridge on the railroad near. Suddenly in the midst of the tumult was heard the shrill whistle of a train coming from the direction of the Chickahominy. Stuart quickly drew up his men in a line on the side of the road, and he had no sooner done so than the train came slowly round a wooded bend, and bore down. When within two hundred yards it was ordered to halt, but the command was not obeyed. The engineer crowded on all steam; the train rushed on, and then a thundering volley was opened upon the "flats" containing officers and men. The engineer was shot by Captain Farley, of Stuart's staff, and a number of the soldiers were wounded. The rest threw themselves upon their faces; the train rushed headlong by like some frightened monster bent upon escape, and in an instant it had disappeared.

Stuart then reflected for a single moment. The question was, should he go back and attack the White House, where enormous stores were piled up? It was tempting, and he afterwards told me he could scarcely resist it. But a considerable force of infantry was posted there; the firing had doubtless given them the alarm; and the attempt was too hazardous. The best thing for that gray column was to set their faces toward home, and "keep moving," well closed up both day and night, for the lower Chickahominy. Beyond the railroad appeared a world of wagons, loaded with grain and coffee—standing in the road abandoned. Quick work was made of them. They were all set on fire, and their contents destroyed. From the horse-trough of one I rescued a small volume bearing on the fly-leaf the name of a young lady of Williamsburg. I think it was a volume of poems—poetic wagon-drivers!

These wagons were only the "vaunt couriers"—the advance guard—of the main body. In a field beyond the stream thirty acres were covered with them. They were all burned. The roar of the soaring flames was like the sound of a forest on fire. How they roared and crackled! The sky over-head, when night had descended, was bloody-looking in the glare. . . .

Pushing on by large hospitals which were not interfered with, we reached at midnight the three or four houses known as Talleysville; and here a halt was ordered to rest men and horses, and permit the artillery to come up. This pause was fatal to a sutler's store from which the owners had fled. It was remorselessly ransacked and the edibles consumed. This historian ate in succession figs, beef-tongue, pickle, candy, tomato catsup, preserves, lemons, cakes, sausages, molasses, crackers, and canned meats. In presence of these attractive commodities, the spirits of many rose. Those who in the morning had made me laugh by saying, "General Stuart is going to get his command destroyed—this movement is mad," now regarded Stuart as the first of men; the raid was a feat of splendour and judicious daring which could not fail in terminating successfully. Such is the difference in the views of the military machine, unfed and fed. . . .

The column . . . began to move on the road to Forge Bridge. The highway lay before us, white in the unclouded splendour of the moon. The critical moment was yet to come. Our safety was to turn apparently on a throw of the dice, rattled in the hand of Chance. The exhaustion of the march now began to tell on the men. Whole companies went to sleep in the saddle, and Stuart himself was no exception. He had thrown one knee over the pommel of his saddle, folded his arms, dropped the bridle, and—chin on breast, his plumed hat drooping over his forehead—was sound asleep. His sure-footed horse moved steadily, but the form of the General tottered from side to side, and for miles I held him erect by the arm. The column thus moved on during the remainder of the night, the wary advance guard en-countering no enemies and giving no alarm. At the first streak of dawn the Chickahominy was in sight, and Stuart was spurring forward *to the ford*.

It was impassable! The heavy rains had so swollen the waters that the crossing was utterly impracticable! Here we were within a few miles of McClellan's army, with an enraged enemy rushing on our track to make us rue the day we had "circumvented" them, and inflicted on them such injury and insult; here we were with a swollen and impassable stream directly in our front—the angry waters roaring around the half-submerged trunks of the trees—and expecting every instant to hear the crack of carbines from the rear-guard indicating the enemy's approach! The "situation" was not pleasing. I certainly thought that the enemy would be upon us in about an hour, and death or capture would be the sure alternative. This view was general. I found that cool and resolute officer, Colonel William H. F. Lee, on the river's bank. He had just attempted to swim the river, and nearly drowned his horse among the tangled roots and snags. I said to him:

"What do you think of the situation, Colonel?"

"Well, Captain," was the reply, in the speaker's habitual tone of cheerful courtesy, "I think we are caught."

The men evidently shared this sentiment. The scene upon the river's bank was curious. The men lay about in every attitude, half-overcome with sleep, but holding their bridles, and ready to mount at the first alarm. Others sat their horses asleep, with drooping shoulders. Some gnawed crackers; others ate figs, or smoked, or yawned. Things looked "blue," and the colour was figuratively spread over every countenance. When this writer assumed a gay expression of countenance, laughed, and told the men it was "all right," they looked at him as sane men regard a lunatic! The general conviction evidently was that "all right" was the very last phrase by which to describe the situation.

There was only one man who never desponded, or bated one "jot or tittle of the heart of hope." That was Stuart. . . . He said a few words to Colonel Lee, found the ford impassable, and then ordering his column to move on, galloped down the stream to a spot where an old bridge had formerly stood. Reaching this point, a strong rear-guard was thrown out, the artillery placed in position, and Stuart set to work vigorously to rebuild the bridge, determined to bring out his guns or die trying.

The bridge had been destroyed, but the stone abutments remained some thirty or forty feet only apart, for the river here ran deep and narrow between steep banks. Between these stone sentinels, facing each other, was an "aching void" which it was necessary to fill. Stuart gave his personal superintendence to the work, he and his staff labouring with the men. A skiff was procured; this was affixed by a rope to a tree, in the mid-current just above the abutments, and thus a movable pier was secured in the middle of the stream. An old barn was then hastily torn to pieces and robbed of its timbers; these were stretched down to the boat, and up to the opposite abutment, and a foot-bridge was thus ready. Large numbers of the men immediately unsaddled their horses, took their equipments over, and then returning, drove or rode their horses into the stream, and swam them over. In this manner a considerable number crossed; but the process was much too slow. There, besides, was the artillery, which Stuart had no intention of leaving. A regular bridge must be built without a moment's delay, and to this work Stuart now applied himself with ardour.

Heavier blows resounded from the old barn; huge timbers approached, borne on brawny shoulders, and descending into the boat anchored in the middle of the stream, the men lifted them across. They were just long enough; the ends rested on the abutments, and immediately thick planks were hurried forward and laid crosswise, forming a secure footway for the cavalry and artillery horses. Standing in the boat beneath, Stuart worked with the men, and as the planks thundered down, and the bridge steadily advanced, the gay voice of the General was heard humming a song. He was singing carelessly, although at every instant an overpowering force of the enemy was looked for, and a heavy attack upon the disordered cavalry.

At last the bridge was finished; the artillery crossed amid hurrahs from the men, and then Stuart slowly moved his cavalry across the shaky footway. . . . The hoofs clattered on the hasty structure, the head of the column was turned toward the ford beyond, the last squadron had just passed, and the bridge was being destroyed, when shots resounded on the opposite bank of the stream, and Colonel Rush thundered down with his "lancers" to the bank. He was exactly ten minutes too late. Stuart was over with his artillery, and the swollen stream barred the way, even if Colonel Rush thought it prudent to "knock up against" the one thousand five hundred crack cavalry of Stuart. His men banged away at Colonel Lee, and a parting salute whizzed through the trees as the gray column slowly disappeared. . . .

—COOKE, *Wearing of the Gray*

12. PRESIDENT DAVIS VISITS THE BATTLEFIELD AT MECHANICSVILLE

With the information which Stuart was able to bring him, with large reinforcements from Georgia and the Carolinas, and with the aid of Jackson, who had just concluded his whirlwind campaign in the Valley, Lee was now prepared to initiate his campaign against the Federals. Summoning Jackson from the Valley, Lee planned to concentrate most of his forces north of the Chickahominy and roll up the Union flank. Jackson was unaccountably late, but the attack came off, almost as planned, on June 26—the first of the famous Seven Days battles.

President Davis, who could never forget that he had been colonel of the Mississippi Riflemen and Secretary of War, fancied himself as a military leader and tended constantly to intervene in the military conduct of the war. His visits to the battlefields—one of which is here described by the famous social leader Constance Harrison—were wholly in character, as was General Lee's courteous but firm handling of the situation.

DURING all this time President Davis was a familiar and picturesque figure on the streets, walking through the Capitol square from his residence to the executive office in the morning, not to return until late in the afternoon, or riding just before nightfall to visit one or another of the encampments near the city. He was tall, erect, slender, and of a dignified and soldierly bearing, with clear-cut and high-bred features, and of a demeanor of stately courtesy to all. He was clad always in Confederate gray cloth, and wore a soft felt hat with wide brim. Afoot, his step was brisk and firm; in the saddle he rode admirably and with a martial aspect.

His early life had been spent in the Military Academy at West Point and upon the then north-western frontier in the Black Hawk War, and he afterward greatly distinguished himself at Monterey and Buena Vista in Mexico; at the time when we knew him, everything in his appearance and manner was suggestive of such a training. He was reported to feel quite out of place in the office of President, with executive and administrative duties, in the midst of such a war; General Lee always spoke of him as the best of military advisers; his own inclination was to be with the army, and at the first tidings of sound of a gun, anywhere within reach of Richmond, he' was in the saddle and off for the spot—to the dismay of his staff-officers, who were expected to act as an escort on such occasions, and who never knew at what hour of the night or of the next day they should get back to bed or to a meal.

The stories we were told of his adventures on such excursions were many, and sometimes amusing. For instance, when General Lee had crossed the Chickahominy, President Davis, with several staff-officers, overtook the column, and, with the Secretary of War and a few other non-combatants, forded the river just as the battle of Mechanicsville began. General Lee, surrounded by members of his own staff and other officers, was found a few hundred yards north of the bridge, in the middle of the broad road, mounted and busily engaged in directing the attack then about to be made by a brigade sweeping in the line over the fields to the east of the road and toward Ellerson's Mill, where in a few minutes a hot engagement commenced. Shot, from the enemy's guns out of sight, went whizzing overhead in quick succession, striking every moment nearer the group of horsemen in the road as the gunners improved their range.

General Lee observed the President's approach, and was evidently annoyed at what he considered a foolhardy expedition of needless exposure of the head of the Government, whose duties were elsewhere. He turned his back for a moment, until Colonel Chilton had been dispatched at a gallop with the last direction to the commander of the attacking brigade; then, facing the cavalcade and looking like the god of war indignant, he exchanged with the President a salute, with the most frigid reserve of anything like welcome or cordiality.

In an instant, and without allowance of opportunity for a word from the President, the general, looking not at him but at the assemblage at large, asked in a tone of irritation: "Who are all this army of people, and what are they doing here?"

No one moved or spoke, but all eyes were upon the President; everybody perfectly understood that this was only an order for him to retire to a place of safety, and the roar of the guns, the rattling fire of musketry, and the bustle of a battle in progress, with troops continually arriving across the bridge to go into action, went on. The President twisted in his saddle, quite taken aback at such a greeting—the general regarding him now with glances of growing severity. After a painful pause the President said, deprecatingly: "It is not my army, General."

"It certainly is not *my* army, Mr. President," was the prompt reply, "and this is no place for it"—in an accent of command.

Such a rebuff was a stunner to Mr. Davis, who, however, soon regained his serenity and answered: "Well, General, if I withdraw, perhaps they will follow," and, raising his hat in another cold salute, he turned his horse's head to ride slowly toward the bridge—seeing, as he turned, a man killed immediately before him by a shot from a gun which at that moment got the range of the road. The President's own staff-officers followed him, as did various others; but he presently drew rein in a stream, where the high bank and the bushes concealed him from General Lee's repelling observation, and there remained while the battle raged. The Secretary of War had also made a show of withdrawing, but improved the opportunity afforded by rather a deep ditch on the roadside to attempt to conceal himself and his horse there for a time from General Lee, who at that moment was more to be dreaded than the enemy's guns.

—HARRISON, "Richmond Scenes in '62"

13. THE FIGHTING AT GAINES' MILL

After his initial attack at Mechanicsville, Lee struck eastward to Gaines' Mill, in the second of the Seven Days battles. Although McClellan's forces greatly outnumbered Lee's, so faulty were the Union general's tactics that Lee was able to throw some 57,000 troops against scarcely half that number under the unfortunate Fitz-John Porter. Porter put up a magnificent resistance, but by sundown of June 27 the Federal ranks were broken and the Federals retreated across the Chickahominy.

The two selections here given describe the fighting as seen by the ordinary soldier of both armies. J. B. Polley, the author of the first selection, was a private in the 4th Texas Regiment of Hood's Texas Brigade. His vivacious letters to his "charming Nellie"—whom he did not meet personally until the close of the war—are entertaining, but not wholly reliable. Oliver Norton, who answered Lincoln's first call for volunteers, fought through the entire war, first as a private in the 83rd Regiment, Pennsylvania Volunteers, then as a first lieutenant of the 80th United States Colored Troops. He participated in as many as 26 battles and skirmishes. He here describes how he was wounded three times within a few moments.

A. HOOD'S TEXANS CAPTURE A BATTERY AT GAINES' MILL

Camp Near Richmond, July 12, 1862

Friday morning, June 27, we again advanced. The Yankees fell back until they reached a strong, almost impregnable position on the ground in the vicinity of Gaines' Mill. They occupied a ridge overlooking the Chickahominy and between us and that stream, their artillery being massed behind three lines of breastworks so constructed along the side of the ridge next to us that firing from one could be done over the heads of the troops in the other. All the force of the enemy on our side of the Chickahominy was concentrated to check the advance of Jackson. The Confederates began their assaults on this position about noon, but were constantly beaten back. Brigade after brigade had been ordered to charge. They had charged and met repulse before Whiting's division—which consists, you know, of Law's brigade and ours—reached the scene of action at 4 o'clock in the evening.

Said General Whiting to General Hood, pointing to a battery that was doing tremendous execution in the Confederate rank, "That battery ought to be taken, General."

"Then why has it not been done?" asked Hood.

"Because the position is too strong," answered Whiting. "My brigade is composed of veterans, but they can do nothing with it."

"I have a regiment that will capture it," said Hood; and, galloping to the Fourth Texas, dismounted and called it to attention. Then marching it by the flank to an open field, he gave the orders to bring it into line of battle, and shouted, "Forward!"

Shot and shell began to come thick and fast as, surmounting the rise of the hill, we arrived in plain view of the Yankees, and half way across the field men began to drop, wounded or dead, from the ranks. We passed over two regiments—said to have been Virginians—who, protected by a depression of the ground, were lying down, apparently afraid either to advance or retreat. At the crest of the hill Hood shouted rapidly the orders, "Fix bayonets! Make ready! Aim! Fire! Charge!" The timber between us and the enemy hid them from view, but we pulled triggers nevertheless, and rushed down the hill into and across the branch, at the Yankees in the first line of breastworks. They waited not for the onset, but fled like a flock of sheep, carrying with them their supports in the second and third lines. Reaching the road which ran along the summit of the hill beyond the branch, and looking to our left, we could see large bodies of the enemy in full retreat, but they were so far behind us that, mistaken for our own troops, not a shot was fired at them. . . .

The regiment had more work to do, and gallantly did it. Hood formed the remnant of the command in an old apple orchard while exposed to a terrific fire from the batteries, and once more gave the order to charge. Lieutenant-Colonel Warwick sprang to the front, shouting, "Wait, General, until I get ahead of them," and fifty yards farther fell mortally wounded. The Fourth rushed down into a ravine and up the steep bank to find that instead of one battery, there were three so disposed as to attack from the front and on the flank. The enemy made no stand at the first, but supporting the second were eight companies of the Second United States Cavalry—among them the very company in which Hood had served as a lieutenant. A squadron of this command charged upon the Fourth, but more than half of it were killed and wounded, and the balance forced to retire in disorder. This was the last organized resistance, the third battery being easily captured and the enemy driven a mile beyond it. Then night came on and human slaughter ceased. . . .

After the fighting I was surprised to learn how little of it I had really seen and participated in. It is only the General, who stands back in the rear and directs the movements of an army, who is able to take note of all that occurs. We privates look only to our immediate front, right, and left, and are not permitted to stand on eminences which overlook the whole field of battle. Therefore you must bear in mind that much of what I relate comes from the lips of others. Caesar could say, "*Veni, vidi, vici*," but the privates of his army had to speak in the first person plural, and say, "*We* came, *we* saw, *we* conquered."

General Hood kept the promise made to us when he was promoted to be brigadier-general, and commanded the Fourth in its first fight. He exposed himself most recklessly, but was not harmed. The Veteran said to me yesterday. "I tell you what, Joe, I got mighty nervous and shaky while we were forming in the apple orchard to make that last desperate charge on the batteries. But when I looked behind me and saw old Hood resting on one foot, his arm raised above his head, his hand grasping the limb of a tree, looking as unconcerned as if we were on dress parade, I just determined that if he could stand it, I would."

—POLLEY, *A Soldier's Letters to Charming Nellie*

B. Oliver Norton Fights Like a Madman at Gaines' Mill

Camp near James River, July 4, 1862

Dear Friends at Home:—

I sent a few words to you yesterday just to relieve your suspense, and to-day I will write a little more, though, in the present condition of my mind and body, worn out by fatigue and exposure, you cannot expect much but a disconnected letter. The papers will have told you of the strategic movement of McClellan's army, its causes and its complete success. All that remains for me to write, and all that I can be expected to know is where the Eighty-third went and what it did.

The fight on the right began on Thursday, the 26th of June, and we took all on our backs and went out that afternoon but did no fighting. Friday morning at daylight we fell back to a position on a stream near Gaines' Mill. The rebels soon followed, feeling their way along, and at about 2 o'clock the fighting became general along the whole line. Our brigade formed the left flank of the line and lay nearest the river. The Eighty-third was posted in a deep gully, wooded, and with the stream I mentioned running in front of us. We built a little breastwork of logs and had a good position. On the hill behind us the Forty-fourth and Twelfth New York and the Sixteenth Michigan were posted. When the rebels made the first attack, we could not fire a shot, the hill concealing them from us, and so we lay still while the bullets of two opposing lines whistled over our heads. They were repulsed, but only to pour in new troops with greater vigor than before.

Suddenly I saw two men on the bank in front of us gesticulating violently and pointing to our rear, but the roar of battle drowned their voices. The order was given to face about. We did so and tried to form in line, but while the line was forming, a bullet laid low the head, the stay, the trust of our regiment—our brave colonel, and before we knew what had happened the major shared his fate. We were then without a field officer, but the boys bore up bravely. They rallied round the flag and we advanced up the hill to find ourselves alone. It appears that the enemy broke through our lines off on our right, and word was sent to us on the left to fall back. Those in the rear of us received the order but the aide sent to us was shot before he reached us and so we got no orders. Henry and Denison were shot about the same time as the colonel. I left them together under a tree.

I returned to the fight, and our boys were dropping on all sides of me. I was blazing away at the rascals not ten rods off when a ball struck my gun just above the lower band as I was capping it, and cut it in two. The ball flew in pieces and part went by my head to the right and three pieces struck just below my left collar bone. The deepest one was not over half an inch, and stopping to open my coat I pulled them out and snatched a gun from Ames in Company H as he fell dead. Before I had fired this at all a ball clipped off a piece of the stock, and an instant after, another struck the seam of my canteen and entered my left groin. I pulled it out, and, more maddened than ever, I rushed in again. A few minutes after, another ball took six inches off the muzzle of this gun. I snatched another from a wounded man under a tree, and, as I was loading kneeling by the side of the road, a ball cut my rammer in two as I was turning it over my head. Another gun was easier got than a rammer so I threw that away and picked up a fourth one. Here in the road a buckshot struck me in the left eyebrow, making the third slight scratch I received in the action. It exceeded all I ever dreamed of, it was almost a miracle.

Then came the retreat across the river; rebels on three sides of us left no choice but to run or be killed or be taken prisoners. We left our all in the hollow by the creek and crossed the river to Smith's division. The bridge was torn up and when I came to the river I threw my cartridge box on my shoulder and waded through. It was a little more than waist deep. I stayed that night with some Sherman boys in Elder Drake's company in the Forty-ninth New York.

Sunday night we lay in a cornfield in the rain, without tent or blanket. Monday we went down on the James river, lying behind batteries to support them. Tuesday the same—six days exposed to a constant fire of shot and shell, till almost night, when we went to the front and engaged in another fierce conflict with the enemy. Going on to the field, I picked up a tent and slung it across my shoulder. The folds of that stopped a ball that would have passed through me. I picked it out, put it in my pocket, and, after firing sixty rounds of my own and a number of a wounded comrade's cartridges, I came off the field unhurt, and ready, but not anxious, for another fight.

—Norton, *Army Letters*

14. THE END OF SEVEN DAYS

Lee's success at Gaines' Mill forced McClellan to shift his base from White House on the Pamunkey to Harrison's Landing on the James—a shift which he made with great skill. As soon as Lee discovered that his opponent was heading for the James, he set his troops the task of turning the retreat into a rout. In this he was, however, unsuccessful. The Confederate attacks at Savage's Station and Frayser's Farm, on June 29 and 30, were unco-ordinated and without strategic value. During the night of the twenty-ninth Mc-Clellan retreated across the White Oak Swamp, a swampy tributary of the Chickahominy. Longstreet and A. P. Hill attacked him there, on the thirtieth, but Jackson failed to get into the fight; once more it was inconclusive and the Federals managed to get away to the heights of Malvern Hill.

The final attack at Malvern Hill, on July 1, was likewise a failure—again chiefly because of Lee's failure to bring all his available troops into battle. While Confederate losses in the Seven Days campaign were heavier than the Union, the campaign must be accounted a Confederate success because it achieved its object of relieving pressure on Richmond and persuaded the administration to abandon the Peninsula.

Thomas Livermore, from whose fascinating wartime reminiscences these excerpts are taken, was a boy of seventeen when the war broke out, studying at Lombard College, Illinois. He hurried east to get into the fighting, found the 1st New Hampshire Infantry encamped in Maryland, and enlisted; he ended the war as colonel of the 18th New Hampshire Volunteers.

A. THE FEDERALS ARE FORCED BACK AT WHITE OAK SWAMP

THE sun rose and darted his fiery rays upon us, and as most of us had eaten, we stuck our rifles up by the bayonets, fastened our blankets in the locks, and lay down in their shade to shun the scorching rays, and sleep. The dust of the barren plain was a sweet couch, and the stifling heat which enveloped us could not prevent profound sleep. A few, perhaps, bestirred themselves to complete the breakfasts which had been begun at our first halt when we had crossed the bridge, but there seemed to be a soothing quiet around us, and we could praise the economy of Nature which made the pleasure of sleep so intense as to requite us almost for our labors and deprivations before. What I thought or dreamed of I do not know, but suddenly, whatever visions of peace hovered around me were dispelled by the thunders of artillery, the shriek of shells, and the horrid humming of their fragments. Hell seemed to have opened upon us. In a twinkling every man was on his feet, the blankets were slung over our shoulders, and the men were in their places, shrinking under the storm, perhaps, but steady and prepared for action. The rebels had planted a large number of cannon on the other side of the swamp, and having pointed them at the host which lay on the plain had fired them all at once.

And what a scene it was! As far as the eye could see the tired troops were springing to arms; batteries were whirling into position or hurrying out of reach with horses on the gallop; wagons drawn by teams of frightened mules, driven by frantic drivers, rattled away to the woods; the teams of six mules which belonged to a pontoon train which were surprised watering at the swamp, fled up the hill and away, leaving their boats; stragglers and non-combatants of all kinds fled in all directions from the fire; while the air was filled with clouds of dust and wreaths of smoke which spread out from the fierce clouds, breathing fire of bursting shells, and the ear was dimmed with explosions, shouts, and a storm of other noises.

The —— New York Volunteers was said to have run away when the first shell burst in front of it, and —— battery, also of New York, I think, disgraced itself in like manner. But the rest of the troops quickly formed lines of battle, and when we in a very few minutes had reached our position and lain down in line with our faces to the enemy, order had come out of chaos. Near us, in front and rear and right, the troops of our own division lay in parallel lines; on other parts of the plain Smith's division and Naglee's brigade were in similar order, and a few rods in front the welcome sight of Hazzard's battery of our corps, firing with rapidity at the enemy, greeted our eyes. The enemy's fire was unremitting, and from noon until nearly dark we endured the slow torture of seeing our comrades killed, mangled, and torn around us, while we could not fire a shot, as our business was to lie and wait to repel attacks and protect our batteries. With every discharge of the enemy's guns, the shells would scream over our heads and bury themselves in the woods beyond, burst over us and deal death in the ranks, or ricochet over the plain, killing whenever they struck a line.

The —— New York Volunteers in changing position either attempted to escape to the rear or mistook its colonel's orders and retreated right down toward us. General Caldwell, who was near, galloped to our rear and cried out, "5th New Hampshire, rise up!" and we rose, leveled our bayonets, and received the —— at their points. This was a decisive barrier to further retreating, and after a little confusion they went back and behaved themselves. We were pleased to have rebuked this cowardice, but were sorry for Colonel ——, who was a brave man.

The shot hit some of our men and scattered their vitals and brains upon the ground, and we hugged the earth to escape this horrible fate, but nothing could save a few who fell victims there. I saw a shot strike in the 2d Delaware, a new regiment with us, which threw a man's head perhaps twenty feet into the air, and the bleeding trunk fell over toward us. The men seemed paralyzed for a moment, but presently gathered up the poor fellow's body in a blanket and carried it away. I do not know that I have ever feared artillery as I did then, and I can recollect very well how close I lay to the ground while the messengers of death, each one seemingly coming right into us, whistled over us. . . .

I had just reached my place, when the order was given to rise up and face about. A cannon shot came quicker than the wind through my company, and close by me. Tibbetts fell and Nichols fell. We reached the line designated with a few hasty steps, and resumed our line with faces to the front. Nichols got up, and came back to the captain and said, "Captain, I am wounded and want to go to the rear." The poor fellow held up one arm with the other hand, for it dangled only by a strip of flesh. Some men went forward and hastily gathered up Tibbetts in a blanket and bore him away; the shot had gone through his body. We felt a little safer now. Hazzard's battery withdrew, cut to pieces, and with Captain Hazzard mortally wounded; and for a short time it seemed as if the rebels would fire unmolested, but Pettit galloped up with his battery of 10-pounder Parrotts and went into action, and then iron *did* fly, and the rebels had their hands full. Captain Keller sat up on a knapsack in front of us and gave warning when the shells were coming, and perhaps saved lives by it; anyhow it was a brave thing to do.

It was not a long time before we perceived that Captain Pettit's fire was getting too hot for the rebels, and they only fired at intervals; and at last Pettit would hold up until they fired, when he would fire his whole battery at them, and as his shells went screaming over the tops of the trees to where the smoke was seen, our hearts bounded, for we perceived that their range was almost perfect; the rebels grew timid, and finally toward night they ceased firing, and we felt grateful to Pettit for it.

Once during the afternoon we saw a battery heavily engaged on our side close to the swamp on the right, and I think that we heard in that direction the rattle of musketry, perhaps where the rebels were attempting a crossing. The portion of the pontoon train which was left on the plain was set fire to in the afternoon, and the smoke and flames added to the infernal aspect of affairs. If ever stillness and rest were appreciated, I think it was on the verge of that evening, and even the dusty plain must have assumed a lovely hue when it was no longer disturbed by ricocheting shot.

—LIVERMORE, *Days and Events*

B. CAPTAIN LIVERMORE FIGHTS AT MALVERN HILL

This was the morning of July 1, and we were on Malvern Hill. The army had retreated during the day before and that night, and on this morning were placed in position to meet the advancing enemy again, and I have an indistinct recollection of seeing General McClellan on the field that morning, but he went on board a gunboat soon after and stayed until late in the day. The sun rose as hot as ever and again prostrated some of the men.

Presently a battery appeared in our front and opened fire on us at the distance of perhaps three quarters of a mile. As we lay directly on the crest of the hill, we presented a fair mark and our quarters were decidedly uncomfortable.

Ammunition was sent to us, and I was ordered to distribute it. As I was performing the work, or about that time, a cannon shot took off the foot of a man lying near by, and I was glad when I could lie down again.

The slow hours dragged along until the middle of the afternoon, when the battle opened in earnest on our left far down in front. Cannon and muskets roared and rattled, the blue smoke made the air heavy, and cheers and yells made the heavens ring. We did not remain long in suspense; an order came to move, and setting our faces to the fighting ground, we shook from our feet the dust of that ground where we were fired at without the privilege of a return fire. We moved down the hill, in front of the woods, and into a road, and marched toward the left flank. On our right was a wheatfield and beyond it another field. Through this last one, as we passed it, the shot came whirling over and through our ranks, spending their force in the woods, where they cracked and crashed through limbs, trunks, and foliage. Our men in the line of battle cheered and cheered again, and our hearts bounded to think that we had met with a success. A color sergeant, with his colors all torn, came by us and reported victory. We filed into the field on our right and moved forward. But I must not omit to mention that while we marched by the flank a shot crashed through the ranks of the 61st New York which led us. Captain —— fell and cried out in mortal agony, "One man! two men! three men! carry me off the field!" The pitying men sprang forward and raised him up gently to find that the shot had only taken off his coat-tail.

As I have said, we formed line on our right and moved forward. At this time Colonel Barlow, of the 61st New York, was with General Caldwell, and seemed to be maneuvering the brigade for him and in a very cool manner. We moved forward, and as we neared the fight could see our men crouching behind the fences and hedges, firing with a will. The rest of the brigade moved away from us, where I knew not, and we halted behind what was, I think, West's house by the Quaker road. Here we lay down for a few minutes in peace, but very soon a rebel battery close in front opened on us with fury. Some of our officers had got into an outbuilding just in front of us for shelter, but a shell came right in among them and they left. General Howe, a fine-looking man, whose command was near by, rode up and ordered Captain Sturtevant to move over to the right and support one of our batteries. In order to do this the quickest way, we had to move directly in front of the rebel battery within not more than four hundred yards, over an open plain with no obstacle between us.

The general rode away, and Captain Sturtevant, who was honest and brave, but a little wanting in decision, got up and, beginning scratching his leg, said, "There! I am ordered to go and support that battery. If I go clear out of range I shall be too long, and if I go across we shall go right into the fire of the rebels; I don't know what to do!"

Perhaps my boldness arose from having been placed in command of "I" Company that day, its officers being absent; but whatever might be the cause, I said to him, "Well, Captain, we might just as well go across under fire as to lie here, for we shall get killed here; so let us go!"

"That's so," said he; "rise up, men! Forward, march!"—and away we went on the double-quick; and then how the rebel battery did pepper us!

Shells flew all around us, and the wonder was that more were not hurt. I turned my head to the left and saw the battery and the gunners, springing to their work amid the smoke. I saw one pull the string, saw the flash of the piece, heard the roar, and the whiz of the shell, heard it burst, heard the humming of the fragments, and wondered if I was to be hit, and quicker than a flash something stung my leg on the calf, and I limped out of the ranks, a wounded man. My first impulse was to go to the rear, but the plain for a quarter of a mile was dotted with dust raised by the flying pieces and ricocheting shot, and I concluded that if I could, 't were better to stay at the front than to be killed going to the rear. So I stooped down, opened the ragged hole in my trousers leg, and saw no blood, but the form of a piece of shell two or three inches long, printed in a cruel bruise on my leg; then I limped to the regiment, which had halted and lain down. I took my place, and was so vexed with pain that I swore at a Frenchman in my company roundly for being out of his place, and then commenced behaving myself. The same shell wounded two or three others, I believe.

We lay just behind the crest of a gentle slope and in front of some trees. In front of us first came the open field and then some woods. The rebel battery had been silenced somehow, but sharpshooters in the farther woods shot at us with uncomfortable precision. The battery on our left threw shell into the woods and I imagine made hot quarters for the sharpshooters. In the course of an hour my leg had swelled badly, and my lameness was such that I could hardly step otherwise than on my toes. It was a matter of honor and pride with me to stay with the regiment as long as I could, but Captain Sturtevant and Captain Cross both urged me to go to the hospital, for (they said) we were liable to move on the enemy at any moment, and as I seemed to grow lamer, I might be in such a plight that I should give out in a bad place and lose my life or be taken prisoner. The force of these arguments was evident, and at length I hobbled away. I passed some of the Third Corps in a field where the wheat was stacked in many piles, and reached the road on which we had marched down, and then climbed the hill and searched for the hospital. I met a good-looking Negro man in my wanderings, and with an eye to business engaged him as a servant, his former employer, a captain in our army, having been killed that day, he said.

At length I found a building which looked like a church, in the darkness which had now settled on the field, around which great numbers of our wounded lay among the trees, groaning and complaining bitterly, and it was a scene of utter misery. I groped around carefully among the prostrate men, who were agonized if any one stepped too close to them, and sat down by a tree. Beside me a groaning man proved to be Second Lieutenant Lawrence, of our regiment, who dolefully informed me that he was very badly wounded in the ankle, but who really, as I learned afterwards, had nothing but a contusion. He was the color sergeant who was promoted to second lieutenant at Camp California, and never rejoined the regiment for duty. How it transpired I do not recollect, but I found our own regimental hospital wagon in the woods, and got my leg bound up, and then lay down in company with some of our men to sleep.

—LIVERMORE, *Days and Events*

15. RICHARD AUCHMUTY REVIEWS THE PENINSULAR CAMPAIGN

A member of one of the most distinguished of New York families, Richard Auchmuty was practicing architecture in New York, in the office of the famous Renwick, when the war broke out. He was commissioned a captain in the V Corps of the Army of the Potomac, and fought gallantly through all the campaigns in Virginia to Gettysburg. Invalided out he took work in the War Department, and participated in the defense of Washington at the time of Early's raid in 1864. After the war Auchmuty devoted himself to architecture and philanthropy.

Harrison's Landing, James River, Saturday, July 5, 1862

My Dear Mother,—

I sincerely thank God that I have passed unhurt through the horrors of the last ten days. I am, of course, worn out with fatigue, but am otherwise well.

I see by the *Times* of the 4th, that you are still but slightly informed of what has been going on here. The correspondents mostly wrote from the steamboats on the Pamunkey.

The army is too immense for one person to have a clear idea of what is going on all along the line. I will confine myself to the right wing, which was supposed to be sufficient to protect the rear.

McClellan undoubtedly meant to swing the army around until it rested on the James; but the fate of war had, in the end, more to do with it than he. On Thursday [June 26], about five o'clock, while enjoying a dinner of lamb and green peas, an order came to send a brigade to assist McCall near Mechanicsville. Butterfield's brigade was on an expedition to the rear, Martindale's somewhere else, and Griffin's (he had taken command that day of the Second) alone remained. We went with them about four miles, and got in a very heavy cannonading, the rebels having crossed the Chickahominy at that point. This lasted until about 9 P.M. The cannonading was the loudest I have heard, batteries being planted for nearly a mile; and after dark it became more terrible than by day. The Fourth Michigan came to close quarters with the Fourteenth Louisiana and Sixty-sixth Virginia, losing fifty men. The rest of our division suffered but slightly. At eight o'clock Morrell left me with Weedon and went to look after Martindale. I lay on one of the gun-carriages and got a nap of two hours.

At 2 A.M., an order came to fall back to our old camp near Gaines' Mills (Camp New Bridge); I went after Griffin, and by daylight we were on our way back, the rebels shelling the road. At Gaines' Mills we had breakfast, and heard that our camp was to be abandoned for a better position. Most of the supplies had been sent over the Chickahominy during the night; those remaining were burned.

At 9 A.M., on Friday, the 27th, we crossed the mill-dam and broke down the bridge, the rebel scouts coming in sight. The men were posted in order of battle, and lay down to rest. The sun was extremely hot. Morrell's division was posted along a wooded ravine, with an open field rising behind them. In the ravine ran a creek, draining the mill-dam. I did not see the position of the right of the line. Behind us, in reserve, was McCall's division.

About twelve, the artillery commenced, and the skirmishers, who were in a field beyond the ravine, returned. Musketry began on the right, and gradually worked down to us. About one o'clock hell itself seemed to break loose on our division. First Martindale's, then Griffin's, and then Butterfield's brigades, caught a storm of shot, shell, and musketry, which made the trees wave like a hurricane. The enemy would bring a large number of guns to bear on one point, and then advance a whole brigade on one of our regiments. Three times they did this, each attack lasting about half an hour. After each attack, reënforcements went in, but our men still formed the front line. At six came the fourth attack, more fearful than any. The right wing had gradually fallen back, until our line was thus: ━━━━━━━━━━━━

Suddenly a rush of men, horses, and guns passed over the field, the line was broken, the battle was lost. A line was attempted further back, but it broke at once and all moved towards the bridge. A line of fresh troops being formed near the bridge, the men halted, and the officers tried to collect the regiments, or even the brigades, together. Darkness coming on, the firing ceased, and the men were sent over the bridge in good order. The last passed about 6 A.M., destroying it after them.

I got a cup of coffee, and slept on the ground for two or three hours at daylight. At one o'clock we were told to move to Savage Station, about three miles, but marched eight miles to White Oak Swamp. There we had a beautiful camp and a good night's rest. We were around the house of a Mr. Brilton. The next morning McClellan and his staff took breakfast with us. Everything looked so pretty and peaceful there, that I left my horse that had been shot at Gaines' Mills with him, but the next day the whole army swept over his place and destroyed everything. The rear guard was attacked, a fight took place, and his house was burned to the ground.

That day (Sunday) we were posted ready for an attack, and at night commenced to make for the James River. The night was an awful one, as dark as pitch, with constant alarms that the cavalry were upon us, when all would be confusion. To add to our troubles, it was found that our corps had gone by the wrong road, which made it 10 A.M. before we reached the James.

We lay down in a wheat field till one o'clock (on Monday), when heavy firing began, and we were sent to the front. The enemy shelled us from the woods without doing much harm. In the meantime McCall and Heintzelman suffered terribly and fell back to our line.

We were encamped at a lovely place—an old picturesque brick house, surrounded by splendid white oak trees, on a terrace as fine as Hyde Park, overlooking the river. This terrace, instead of following the river, came abruptly around at right angles to it, overlooking the fields and woods, which were humming and crashing under the shells from the gunboats. Towards the enemy the ground sloped gradually down, rising again in wooded hills, first occupied by Heintzelmann and now by the enemy.

The men slept that night in order of battle. I got about an hour, on the floor of the old house. At daybreak things were gotten ready, and at 8 A.M. the enemy opened. The day was clear and cool. The Second Brigade was posted around two sides of the front. At 5 P.M. the enemy advanced in great force on the Fourteenth New York and Sixty-second Pennsylvania, and much the same scene as at Gaines' Mills was gone through, excepting that the men stood like heroes.

At 6.30 things looked very black. Then up came Porter, who took command in person, with Meagher's Irish brigade. As they passed to the front, Colonel Cass, of the Ninth Massachusetts, was being brought back, his jaw shattered by a ball. As they recognized a fellow-countryman, they gave a yell that drowned the noise of the guns. They moved to the front, and Porter sent for a battery of thirty-two-pounders, something very unusual in a field fight. This turned the enemy back. They said they lay down trembling with fright as the immense shells roared through the woods. At nine the firing ceased on our side, the rebels having stopped about an hour before.

We had repulsed their attack, and remained masters of the field, but, great God! what a field it was. To the surprise of all came the order to retreat. The troops could not stand another such attack, no reënforcements having come.

I took part of the Second Brigade with me, and after showing them the way, went back for our light wagon, which I got in a battery, and rushed through, riding in it myself. This retreat was a regular stampede, each man going off on his own hook, guns in the road at full gallop, teams on one side in the fields, infantry on the other in the woods. At daybreak came rain in torrents, and the ground was ankle deep in mud. This was Wednesday. I found shelter in a quartermaster's tent, and lay down to rest.

Your affectionate son,

R. T. A.

—E. S. A., ed., *Letters of Richard Tylden Auchmuty*

V

Stonewall Jackson and the Valley Campaign

JACKSON'S *Valley campaign has long been regarded as one of the most brilliant in the history of modern warfare; perhaps no other in American warfare, unless it is Lee's campaign at Second Manassas or Grant's below Vicksburg, has been so assiduously studied abroad. The grand strategy of the Valley campaign was Lee's and, to some extent, Joe Johnston's; but the tactics were Jackson's—and the resolute spirit that gave them meaning. The strategy of the Valley campaign was essentially simple, though the campaign itself is one of the most confusing, in detail, in the history of the war. That strategy was to prevent McDowell from joining McClellan on the Peninsula, to frighten Washington into scattering its effective forces on offensive-defensive operations, and to defend Richmond from the west. All these purposes it attained.*

After his brilliant performance at Bull Run Jackson had been made a major general and assigned command in the Shenandoah Valley. Only a familiarity with the geography of the Valley will make clear the details of the campaign, and that requires a careful study of the map. It is sufficient to note here that the Valley between the Blue Ridge and the Shenandoah mountains was divided by the Massanutten range, thus making in effect two valleys—the Luray to the east and the Shenandoah to the west. At the head, or southern end, of the Valley was Staunton, connected by railroad with Richmond; midway down the Valley was Strasburg on the Manassas Gap Railroad which also connected with Richmond; at the mouth, or northern end, was Harpers Ferry. Jackson knew the Valley intimately, had a small and mobile force, and interior lines of communication. The Valley campaign, as he conducted it, was a military chess game; his objective not so much to defeat the enemy as to distract, confuse, check, and eventually checkmate them.

Altogether, even with the forces of Ewell and Edward Johnson that were added to his command, Jackson had only some 18,000 men. Against these were Frémont, in the west with 15,000, and Banks, at Winchester with over 20,000, while McDowell on the Rappahannock stood ready to send reinforcements if needed. Jackson knew that he could not defeat all these forces, but he hoped to prevent them from combining, and to hold them in the Valley while Johnston and Lee dealt with McClellan.

In March 1862 Banks advanced from Harpers Ferry to Winchester. Jackson fell back, to Strasburg and then to Mount Jackson on the western edge of the Massanuttens. Supposing that he had driven Jackson from the Valley Banks prepared to move east to McDowell. This was what Jackson had to prevent. First he sent his cavalry leader Ashby to strike Shields at Winchester; then he himself moved down to Kernstown to join in the attack. Banks brought up his full forces, repulsed Jackson, and threw him back to Mount Jackson. It was a defeat, but it served its purpose. Banks was back in the Valley in full strength; McDowell was held on the Rappahannock ready to go to his aid. Moving swiftly up the Valley Jackson crossed over westward at Staunton, surprised and defeated Frémont at the Battle of McDowell, then hurried back down the Valley and burst on the astonished Banks at Front Royal (May 23). Banks retreated to Winchester where Jackson struck and scattered his forces. Panic-stricken, Washington detached 20,000 from McDowell's command and hurried them to the Valley.

Jackson meantime doubled on his tracks and retired up the Valley to Port Republic. His plan was to hold Frémont at Cross Keys with Ewell's division while he dealt with Shields. The plan worked out, and with the twin battles of Cross Keys and Port Republic the Valley campaign came to an end. A week later Jackson was on his way east to join Lee in the Peninsular campaign. In three months he had immobilized a good part of the Union army, defeated Milroy, Banks, Shields and Frémont, and proved the value of the Valley as a threat to Washington and the North.

1. STONEWALL JACKSON BREAKS THE SABBATH

"An iron sabre vowed to an iron Lord," Stephen Vincent Benét calls Jackson, and the phrase suggests something of that Covenanter quality which Jackson, more than any other Civil War general, indubitably had. Both of his wives were daughters of Presbyterian ministers, and he himself was so devout that he would neither march nor fight on the Sabbath if he could avoid it. He regarded himself as an instrument of the Lord, and to the Lord he gave credit for every victory.

His letters to his wife are filled with pious admonitions and with protestations of devotion and humility.

April 11th [1862]. I am very much concerned at having no letter this week, but my trust is in the Almighty. How precious is the consolation flowing from the Christian's assurance that "all things work together for good to them that love God!" . . . God gave us a glorious victory in the Southwest (at Shiloh), but the loss of the great Albert Sidney Johnston is to be mourned. I do not remember having ever felt so sad at the death of a man whom I had never seen. . . .

Although I was repulsed in the attempt to recover Winchester, yet the enemy's loss appears to have been three times that of ours. In addition to this, the great object which required me to follow up the enemy, as he fell back from Strasburg, seems to have been accomplished very thoroughly. I am well satisfied with the result. Congress has passed a vote of thanks, and General Johnston has issued a very gratifying order upon the subject, one which will have a fine effect upon my command. The great object to be acquired by the battle demanded time to make known its accomplishments. Time has shown that while the field is in possession of the enemy, the most essential fruits of the battle are ours. For this and all of our Heavenly Father's blessings, I wish I could be ten thousand times more thankful. Should any report be published, my views and object in fighting and its fruits will then become known.

You appear much concerned at my attacking *on Sunday.* I was greatly concerned, too; but I felt it my duty to do it, in consideration of the ruinous effects that might result from postponing the battle until morning. So far as I can see, my course was a wise one; the best that I could do under the circumstances, though very distasteful to my feelings; and I hope and pray to our Heavenly Father that I may never again be circumstanced as on that day. I believed that so far as our troops were concerned, necessity and mercy both called for the battle.

I do hope the war will soon be over, and that I shall never again have to take the field. Arms is a profession that, if its principles are adhered to for success, requires an officer to do what he fears may be wrong, and yet, according to military experience, must be done, if success is to be attained. And this fact of its being necessary to success, and being accompanied with success, and that a departure from it is accompanied with disaster, suggests that it must be right. Had I fought the battle on Monday instead of Sunday, I fear our cause would have suffered; whereas, as things turned out, I consider our cause gained much from the engagement.

—M. Jackson, *Life and Letters of General Thomas J. Jackson*

2. DICK TAYLOR CAMPAIGNS WITH JACKSON IN THE VALLEY

Richard Taylor, from whose recollections this and the following selection are taken, was the son of President Zachary Taylor, and a Louisiana planter and politician of wealth and prominence. Commissioned colonel of the 9th Louisiana Infantry, Taylor fought through the whole of the war—in the Valley, at Seven Days, on the Red River, and in Hood's Tennessee campaign, rising to the rank of lieutenant general. He was a man of unusual intellectual attainments—he had studied at Edinburgh and Paris as well as at Harvard and Yale—and his volume of reminiscences is one of the most enchanting of all Civil War books. His account of the Valley campaign during May and June of 1862 tells the story in sufficient detail.

E WELL'S division reached the western base of Swift Run Gap on a lovely spring evening, April 30, 1862, and in crossing the Blue Ridge seemed to have left winter and its rigors behind. Jackson, whom we moved to join, had suddenly that morning marched toward McDowell, some eighty miles west, where, after uniting with a force under General Edward Johnson, he defeated the Federal general Milroy. Some days later he as suddenly returned. Meanwhile we were ordered to remain in camp on the Shenandoah near Conrad's store, at which place a bridge spanned the stream.

The great Valley of Virginia was before us in all its beauty. Fields of wheat spread far and wide, interspersed with woodlands, bright in their robes of tender green. Wherever appropriate sites existed, quaint old mills, with turning wheels, were busily grinding the previous year's harvest; and grove and eminence showed comfortable homesteads. The soft vernal influence shed a languid grace over the scene. The theatre of war in this region was from Staunton to the Potomac, one hundred and twenty miles, with an average width of some twenty-five miles; and the Blue Ridge and Alleghanies bounded it east and west. Drained by the Shenandoah with its numerous affluents, the surface was nowhere flat, but a succession of graceful swells, occasionally rising into abrupt hills. . . . Frequent passes or gaps in the mountains, through which wagon roads had been constructed, afforded easy access from east and west; and pikes were excellent, though unmetaled roads became heavy after rains.

But the glory of the Valley is Massanutten. Rising abruptly from the plain near Harrisonburg, twenty-five miles north of Staunton, this lovely mountain extends fifty miles, and as suddenly ends near Strasburg. Parallel with the Blue Ridge, and of equal height, its sharp peaks have a bolder and more picturesque aspect, while the abruptness of its slopes gives the appearance of greater altitude. Midway of Massanutten, a gap with good road affords communication between Newmarket and Luray. The eastern or Luray valley, much narrower than the one west of Massanutten, is drained by the east branch of the Shenandoah, which is joined at Front Royal, near the northern end of the mountain, by its western affluent, whence the united waters flow north, at the base of the Blue Ridge, to meet the Potomac at Harper's Ferry.

The inhabitants of this favored region were worthy of their inheritance. The north and south were peopled by scions of old colonial families, and the proud names of the "Old Dominion" abounded. In the central counties of Rockingham and Shenandoah were many descendants of German Settlers. These were thrifty, substantial Farmers, and, like their kinsmen of Pennsylvania, expressed their opulence in huge barns and fat cattle. The devotion of all to the Southern cause was wonderful. Jackson, a Valley man by reason of his residence at Lexington, south of Staunton, was their hero and idol. The women sent husbands, sons, lovers, to battle as cheerfully as to marriage feasts. No oppression, no destitution could abate their zeal. Upon a march I was accosted by two elderly sisters, who told me they had secreted a large quantity of bacon in a well on their estate, hard by. Federals had been in possession of the country, and, fearing the indiscretion of their slaves, they had done the work at night with their own hands, and now desired to *give* the meat to their people. Wives and daughters of millers, whose husbands and brothers were in arms, worked the mills night and day to furnish flour

THE VALLEY OF VIRGINIA

The Stampede from Bull Run

Illustrated London News

Malvern Hill

to their soldiers. To the last, women would go distances to carry the modicum of food between themselves and starvation to a suffering Confederate. . . .

While in camp near Conrad's store, the 7th Louisiana, Colonel Hays, a crack regiment, on picket down stream, had a spirited affair, in which the enemy was driven with the loss of a score of prisoners. Shortly after, for convenience of supplies, I was directed to cross the river and camp some miles to the southwest. The command was in superb condition, and a four-gun battery from Bedford county, Virginia, Captain Bowyer, had recently been added to it. The four regiments, 6th, 7th, 8th, and 9th Louisiana, would average above eight hundred bayonets. . . . The 6th, Colonel Seymour, recruited in New Orleans, was composed of Irishmen, stout, hardy fellows, turbulent in camp and requiring a strong hand, but responding to kindness and justice, and ready to follow their officers to the death. The 9th, Colonel Stafford, was from North Louisiana. Planters or sons of planters, many of them men of fortune, soldiering was a hard task to which they only became reconciled by reflecting that it was "niddering" in gentlemen to assume voluntarily the discharge of duties and then shirk. The 8th, Colonel Kelly, was from the Attakapas— "Acadians," the race of which Longfellow sings in "Evangeline." A homeloving, simple people, few spoke English, fewer still had ever before moved ten miles from their natal *cabanas;* and the war to them was "a liberal education," as was the society of the lady of quality to honest Dick Steele. They had all the light gayety of the Gaul, and, after the manner of their ancestors, were born cooks. A capital regimental band accompanied them, and whenever weather and ground permitted, even after long marches, they would waltz and "polk" in couples with as much zest as if their arms encircled the supple waists of the Célestines and Mélazies of their native Teche. The Valley soldiers were largely of the Presbyterian faith, and of a solemn, pious demeanor, and looked askant at the caperings of my Creoles, holding them to be "devices and snares." . . .

At nightfall of the second day in this camp, an order came from General Jackson to join him at Newmarket, twenty odd miles north; and it was stated that my division commander, Ewell, had been apprised of the order. Our position was near a pike leading south of west to Harrisonburg, whence, to gain Newmarket, the great Valley pike ran due north. . . . Early dawn saw us in motion, with lovely weather, a fairish road, and men in high health and spirits.

Later in the day a mounted officer was dispatched to report our approach and select a camp, which proved to be beyond Jackson's forces, then lying in the fields on both sides of the pike. Over three thousand strong, neat in fresh clothing of gray with white gaiters, bands playing at the head of their regiments, not a straggler, but every man in his place, stepping jauntily as on parade, though it had marched twenty miles and more, in open column with arms at "right shoulder shift," and rays of the declining sun flaming on polished bayonets, the brigade moved down the broad, smooth pike, and wheeled on to its camping ground. Jackson's men, by thousands, had gathered on either side of the road to see us pass. Indeed, it was a martial sight, and no man with a spark of sacred fire in his heart but would have striven hard to prove worthy of such a command.

After attending to necessary camp details, I sought Jackson, whom I had never met. . . . The mounted officer who had been sent on in advance pointed out a figure perched on the topmost rail of a fence overlooking the road and field, and said it was Jackson. Approaching, I saluted and declared my name and rank, then waited for a response. Before this came I had time to see a pair of cavalry boots covering feet of gigantic size, a mangy cap with visor drawn low, a heavy, dark beard, and weary eyes—eyes I afterward saw filled with intense but never brilliant light. A low, gentle voice inquired the road and distance marched that day.

"Keazletown road, six and twenty miles."

"You seem to have no stragglers."

"Never allow straggling."

"You must teach my people; they straggle badly." A bow in reply. Just then my creoles started their band and a waltz. After a contemplative suck at a lemon, "Thoughtless fellows for serious work" came forth. I expressed a hope that the work would not be less well done because of the gayety. A return to the lemon gave me the opportunity to retire. Where Jackson got his lemons "no fellow could find out," but he was rarely without one. To have lived twelve miles from that fruit would have disturbed him as much as it did the witty Dean.

Quite late that night General Jackson came to my camp fire, where he stayed some hours. He said we would move at dawn, asked a few questions about the marching of my men, which seemed to have impressed him, and then remained silent. If silence be golden, he was a "bonanza." He sucked lemons, ate hard-tack, and drank water, and praying and fighting appeared to be his idea of the "whole duty of man."

In the gray of the morning, as I was forming my column on the pike, Jackson appeared and gave the route—north—which, from the situation of its camp, put my brigade in advance of the army. After moving a short distance in this direction, the head of the column was turned to the east and took the road over Massanutten gap to Luray. Scarce a word was spoken on the march, as Jackson rode with me. From time to time a courier would gallop up, report, and return toward Luray. An ungraceful horseman, mounted on a sorry chestnut with a shambling gait, his huge feet with out-turned toes thrust into his stirrups, and such parts of his countenance as the low visor of his shocking cap failed to conceal wearing a wooden look, our new commander was not prepossessing. That night we crossed the east branch of the Shenandoah by a bridge, and camped on the stream, near Luray. Here, after three long marches, we were but a short distance below Conrad's store, a point we had left several days before. I began to think that Jackson was an unconscious poet, and, as an ardent lover of nature, desired to give strangers an opportunity to admire the beauties of his Valley. It seemed hard lines to be wandering like sentimental travelers about the country, instead of gaining "kudos" on the Peninsula.

Off the next morning, my command still in advance, and Jackson riding with me. The road led north between the east bank of the river and the western base of the Blue Ridge. Rain had fallen and softened it, so as to delay the wagon trains in rear. Past midday we reached a wood extending from the mountain to the river, when a mounted officer from the rear called Jackson's attention, who rode back with him. A moment later, there rushed out of the wood to meet us a young, rather well-looking woman, afterward widely known as Belle Boyd. Breathless with speed and agitation, some time elapsed before she found her voice. Then, with much volubility, she said we were near Front Royal, beyond the wood; that the town was filled with Federals, whose camp was on the west side of the river, where they had guns in position to cover the wagon bridge, but none bearing on the railway bridge below the former; that they believed Jackson to be west of Massanutten, near Harrisonburg; that General Banks, the Federal commander, was at Winchester, twenty miles northwest of Front Royal, where he was slowly concentrating his widely scattered forces to meet Jackson's advance, which was expected some days later.

All this she told with the precision of a staff officer making a report, and it was true to the letter. Jackson was possessed of these facts before he left Newmarket, and based his movements upon them; but, as he never told anything, it was news to me, and gave me an idea of the strategic value of Massanutten—pointed out, indeed by Washington before the Revolution. There also dawned on me quite another view of our leader than the one from which I had been regarding him for two days past.

Convinced of the correctness of the woman's statements, I hurried forward at "a double," hoping to surprise the enemy's idlers in the town, or swarm over the wagon bridge with them and secure it. Doubtless this was rash, but I felt immensely "cocky" about my brigade, and believed that it would prove equal to any demand. Before we had cleared the wood Jackson came galloping from the rear, followed by a company of horse. He ordered me to deploy my leading regiment as skirmishers on both sides of the road and continue the advance, then passed on. We speedily came in sight of Front Royal, but the enemy had taken the alarm, and his men were scurrying over the bridge to their camp, where troops could be seen forming.

The situation of the village is surpassingly beautiful. It lies near the east bank of the Shenandoah, which just below unites all its waters, and looks directly on the northern peaks of Massanutten. The Blue Ridge, with Manassas Gap, through which passes the railway, overhangs it on the east; distant Alleghany bounds the horizon to the west; and down the Shenandoah, the eye ranges over a fertile, well-farmed country. Two bridges spanned the river—a wagon bridge above, a railway bridge some yards lower. A good pike led to Winchester, twenty miles, and another followed the river north, whence many cross-roads united with the Valley pike near Winchester. The river, swollen by rain, was deep and turbulent, with a strong current. The Federals were posted on the west bank, here somewhat higher than the opposite, and a short distance above the junction of waters, with batteries bearing more especially on the upper bridge.

Under instructions, my brigade was drawn up in line, a little retired from the river, but overlooking it—the Federals and their guns in full view. So far, not a shot had been fired. I rode down to the river's brink to get a better look at the enemy through a field-glass, when my horse, heated by the march, stepped into the water to drink. Instantly a brisk fire was opened on me, bullets striking all around and raising a little shower-bath. Like many a foolish fellow, I found it easier to get into than out of a difficulty. I had not yet led my command into action, and, remembering that one must "strut" one's little part to the best advantage, sat my horse with all the composure I could muster. A provident camel, on the eve of a desert journey, would not have laid in a greater supply of water than did my thoughtless beast. At last he raised his head, looked placidly around, turned, and walked up the bank.

This little incident was not without value, for my men welcomed me with a cheer; upon which, as if in response, the enemy's guns opened, and, having the range, inflicted some loss on my line. We had no guns to reply, and, in advance as has been mentioned, had outmarched the troops behind us. Motionless as a statue, Jackson sat his horse some few yards away, and seemed lost in thought. Perhaps the circumstances mentioned some pages back had obscured his star; but if so, a few short hours swept away the cloud, and it blazed, Sirius-like, over the land. I approached him with the suggestion that the railway bridge might be passed by stepping on the cross-ties, as the enemy's guns bore less directly on it than on the upper bridge. He nodded approval.

The 8th regiment was on the right of my line, near at hand; and dismounting, Colonel Kelly led it across under a sharp musketry fire. Several men fell to disappear in the dark water beneath; but the movement continued with great rapidity, considering the difficulty of walking on ties, and Kelly with his leading files gained the opposite shore. Thereupon the enemy fired combustibles previously placed near the center of the wagon bridge. The loss of this structure would have seriously delayed us, as the railway bridge was not floored, and I looked at Jackson, who, near by, was watching Kelly's progress. Again he nodded, and my command rushed at the bridge. Concealed by the cloud of smoke, the suddenness of the movement saved us from much loss; but it was rather a near thing. My horse and clothing were scorched, and many men burned their hands severely while throwing brands into the river. We were soon over, and the enemy in full flight to Winchester, with loss of camp, guns, and prisoners.

Just as I emerged from flames and smoke, Jackson was by my side. How he got there was a mystery, as the bridge was thronged with my men going at full speed; but smoke and fire had decidedly freshened up his costume. . . .

Late in the night Jackson came out of the darkness and seated himself by my camp fire. He mentioned that I would move with him in the morning, then relapsed into silence. I fancied he looked at me kindly, and interpreted it into an approval of the conduct of the brigade. The events of the day, anticipations of the morrow, . . . drove away sleep, and I watched Jackson. For hours he sat silent and motionless, with eyes fixed on the fire. I took up the idea that he was inwardly praying, and he remained through the night.

Off in the morning, Jackson leading the way, my brigade, a small body of horse, and a section of the Rockbridge (Virginia) artillery forming the column. Major Wheat, with his battalion of "Tigers," was directed to keep close to the guns. Sturdy marchers, they trotted along with the horse and artillery at Jackson's heels, and after several hours were some distance in advance of the brigade, with which I remained.

A volley in front, followed by wild cheers, stirred us up to a "double," and we speedily came upon a moving spectacle. Jackson had struck the Valley pike at Middletown, twelve miles south of Winchester, along which a large body of Federal horse, with many wagons, was hastening north. He had attacked at once with his handful of men, overwhelmed resistance, and captured prisoners and wagons. The gentle Tigers were looting right merrily, diving in and out of wagons with the activity of rabbits in a warren; but this occupation was abandoned on my approach, and in a moment they were in line, looking as solemn and virtuous as deacons at a funeral. Prisoners and spoil were promptly secured. . . .

At dusk we overtook Jackson, pushing the enemy with his little mounted force, himself in advance of all. I rode with him, and we kept on through the darkness. There was not resistance enough to deploy infantry. A flash, a report, and a whistling bullet from some covert met us, but there were few casualties. I quite remember thinking at the time that Jackson was invulnerable, and that persons near him shared that quality. An officer, riding hard, overtook us, who proved to be the chief quartermaster of the army. He reported the wagon trains far behind, impeded by a bad road in Luray Valley.

"The ammunition wagons?" sternly.

"All right, sir. They were in advance, and I doubled teams on them and brought them through."

"Ah!" in a tone of relief.

To give countenance to this quartermaster, if such can be given of a dark night, I remarked jocosely: "Never mind the wagons. There are quantities of store in Winchester, and the General has invited me to breakfast there to-morrow."

Jackson, who had no more capacity for jests than a Scotchman, took this seriously, and reached out to touch me on the arm. In fact, he was of Scotch-Irish descent, and his unconsciousness of jokes was *de race*. Without physical wants himself, he forgot that others were differently constituted, and paid little heed to commissariat; but woe to the man who failed to bring up ammunition! In advance, his trains were left far behind. In retreat, he would fight for a wheelbarrow.

Some time after midnight, by roads more direct from Front Royal, other troops came on the pike, and I halted my jaded people by the roadside, where they built fires and took a turn at their haversacks.

Moving with the first light of morning, we came to Kernstown, three miles from Winchester, and the place of Jackson's fight with Shields. Here heavy and sustained firing, artillery and small arms, was heard. A staff officer approached at full speed to summon me to Jackson's presence and move up my command. A gallop of a mile or more brought me to him. Winchester was in sight, a mile to the north. To the east Ewell with a large part of the army was fighting briskly and driving the enemy on to the town. On the west a high ridge, overlooking the country to the south and southeast, was occupied by a heavy mass of Federals with guns in position. Jackson was on the pike, and near him were several regiments lying down for shelter, as the fire from the ridge was heavy and searching. A Virginian battery, Rockbridge artillery, was fighting at a great disadvantage, and already much cut up. Poetic authority asserts that "Old Virginny never tires," and the conduct of this battery justified the assertion of the muses. With scarce a leg or wheel for man and horse, gun or caisson, to stand on, it continued to hammer away at the crushing fire above.

Jackson, impassive as ever, pointed to the ridge and said, "You must carry it." I replied that my command would be up by the time I could inspect the ground, and rode to the left for that purpose. A small stream, Abraham's creek, flowed from the west through the little vale at the southern base of the ridge, the ascent of which was steep, though nowhere abrupt. At one point a broad, shallow, trough-like depression broke the surface, which was further interrupted by some low copse, outcropping stone, and two fences. On the summit the Federal lines were posted behind a stone wall, along a road coming west from the pike. Worn somewhat into the soil, this road served as a countersink and strengthened the position. Further west, there was a break in the ridge, which was occupied by a body of horse, the extreme right of the enemy's line.

There was scarce time to mark these features before the head of my column appeared, when it was filed to the left, close to the base of the ridge, for protection from the plunging fire. Meanwhile, the Rockbridge battery held on manfully and engaged the enemy's attention. Riding on the flank of my column, between it and the hostile line, I saw Jackson beside me. This was not the place for the commander of the army, and I ventured to tell him so; but he paid no attention to the remark. We reached the shallow depression spoken of, where the enemy could depress his guns, and his fire became close and fatal. Many men fell, and the whistling of shot and shell occasioned much ducking of heads in the column. This annoyed me no little, as it was but child's play to the work immediately in hand. Always an admirer of delightful "Uncle Toby," I had contracted the most villainous habit of his beloved army in Flanders, and, forgetting Jackson's presence, ripped out, "What the h— are you dodging for? If there is any more of it, you will be halted under this fire for an hour."

The sharp tones of a familiar voice produced the desired effect, and the men looked as if they had swallowed ramrods; but I shall never forget the reproachful surprise expressed in Jackson's face. He placed his hand on my shoulder, said in a gentle voice, "I am afraid you are a wicked fellow," turned, and rode back to the pike.

The proper ground gained, the column faced to the front and began the ascent. At the moment the sun rose over the Blue Ridge, without cloud or mist to obscure his rays. It was a lovely Sabbath morning, the 25th of May, 1862. The clear, pure atmosphere brought the Blue Ridge and Alleghany and Massanutten almost overhead. Even the cloud of murderous smoke from the guns above made beautiful spirals in the air, and the broad fields of luxuriant wheat glistened with dew. . . .

As we mounted we came in full view of both armies, whose efforts in other quarters had been slackened to await the result of our movement. I felt an anxiety amounting to pain for the brigade to acquit itself handsomely; and this feeling was shared by every man in it. About half way up, the enemy's horse from his right charged; and to meet it, I directed Lieutenant-Colonel Nicholls, whose regiment, the 8th, was on the left, to withhold slightly his two flank companies. By one volley, which emptied some saddles, Nicholls drove off the horse, but was soon after severely wounded. Progress was not stayed by this incident. Closing the many gaps made by the fierce fire, steadied the rather by it, and preserving an alignment that would have been creditable on parade, the brigade, with cadenced step and eyes on the foe, swept grandly over copse and ledge and fence, to crown the heights from which the enemy had melted away. Loud cheers went up from our army, prolonged to the east, where warm-hearted Ewell cheered himself hoarse, and led forward his men with renewed energy. In truth, it was a gallant feat of arms, worthy of the pen of him who immortalized the charge of the "Buffs" at Albuera.

Breaking into column, we pursued closely. Jackson came up and grasped my hand, worth a thousand words from another, and we were soon in the streets of Winchester, a quaint old town of some five thousand inhabitants. There was a little fighting in the streets, but the people were all abroad—certainly all the women and babies. They were frantic with delight, only regretting that so many "Yankees" had escaped, and seriously impeded our movements.

A buxom, comely dame of some five and thirty summers, with bright eyes and tight ankles, and conscious of these advantages, was especially demonstrative, exclaiming, "Oh! you are too late—too late!"

Whereupon, a tall creole from the Teche sprang from the ranks of the 8th regiment, just passing, clasped her in his arms, and imprinted a sounding kiss on her ripe lips, with *"Madame! je n'arrive jamais trop tard."* A loud laugh followed, and the dame, with a rosy face but merry twinkle in her eye, escaped.

—TAYLOR, *Destruction and Reconstruction*

3. TAYLOR'S IRISHMEN CAPTURE A BATTERY AT PORT REPUBLIC

The climax of the Valley campaign came on June 8 and 9 with the battles of Cross Keys on the north and Port Republic on the south bank of the Shenandoah. Confronted by two armies—one under Frémont, the other under

Shields—Jackson, instead of retreating, struck each of them separately. At Cross Keys, on June 8, Ewell checked Frémont while on the following day Ewell and Taylor broke the strongly entrenched Union line at Port Republic, and forced the enemy back to Conrad's Store, some five miles down the river. It was, as Jackson said, a "delightful excitement."

EWELL, in immediate charge at Cross Keys, was ready early in the morning of the 8th, when Fremont attacked. The ground was undulating, with much wood, and no extended view could be had. In my front the attack, if such it could be called, was feeble in the extreme—an affair of skirmishers, in which the enemy yielded to the slightest pressure.

A staff officer of Jackson's, in hot haste, came with orders from his chief to march my brigade double-quick to Port Republic. Elzey's brigade, in second line to the rear, was asked to take my place and relieve my skirmishers; then, advising the staff officer to notify Ewell, whom he had not seen, we started on the run, for such a message from Jackson meant business. Two of the intervening miles were quickly passed, when another officer appeared with orders to halt.

In half an hour, during which the sound of battle at Cross Keys thickened, Jackson came. . . . He had passed the night in the village, with his staff and escort. Up as usual at dawn, he started alone to recross the bridge, leaving his people to follow. The bridge was a few yards below the last house in the village, and some mist overhung the river. Under cover of this a small body of horse, with one gun, from Shields's forces, had reached the east end of the bridge and trained the gun on it. Jackson was within an ace of capture. As he spurred across, the gun was fired on him, but without effect, and the sound brought up staff and escort, when the horse retired north. This incident occasioned the order to me. After relating it (all save his own danger), Jackson passed on to Ewell. Thither I followed, to remain in reserve until the general forward movement in the afternoon, by which Fremont was driven back with loss of prisoners. We did not persist far, as Shields's force was near upon us.

From Ewell I learned that there had been some pretty fighting in the morning, though less than might have been expected from Fremont's numbers. I know not if the presence of this commander had a benumbing influence on his troops, but certainly his advanced cavalry and infantry had proved bold and enterprising.

In the evening we moved to the river and camped. Winder's and other brigades crossed the bridge, and during the night Ewell, with most of the army, drew near, leaving Trimble's brigade and the horse at Cross Keys. No one apprehended another advance by Fremont. The following morning, Sunday, June 9, my command passed the bridge, moved several hundred yards down the road, and halted. Our trains had gone east over the Blue Ridge. The sun appeared above the mountain while the men were quietly breakfasting. Suddenly, from below, was heard the din of battle, loud and sustained, artillery and small arms. The men sprang into ranks, formed column, and marched, and I galloped forward a short mile to see the following scene:

From the mountain, clothed to its base with undergrowth and timber, a level—clear, open, and smooth—extended to the river. This plain was some thousand yards in width. Half a mile north, a gorge, through which flowed a small stream, cut the mountain at a right angle. The northern shoulder of this gorge projected farther into the plain than the southern, and on an elevated plateau of the shoulder were placed six guns, sweeping every inch of the plain to the south. Federal lines, their right touching the river, were advancing steadily, with banners flying and arms gleaming in the sun. A gallant show, they came on. Winder's and another brigade, with a battery, opposed them. This small force was suffering cruelly, and its skirmishers were driven in on their thin supporting line. As my Irishmen predicted, "Shields's boys were after fighting." Below, Ewell was hurrying his men over the bridge, but it looked as if we should be doubled up on him ere he could cross and develop much strength.

Jackson was on the road, a little in advance of his line, where the fire was hottest, with reins on his horse's neck, seemingly in prayer. Attracted by my approach, he said, in his usual voice, "Delightful excitement." I replied that it was pleasant to learn he was enjoying himself, but thought he might have an indigestion of such fun if the six-gun battery was not silenced. He summoned a young officer from his staff, and pointed up the mountain.

The head of my approaching column was turned short up the slope, and speedily came to a path running parallel with the river. We took this path, the guide leading the way. From him I learned that the plateau occupied by the battery had been used for a charcoal kiln, and the path we were following, made by the burners in hauling wood, came upon the gorge opposite the battery. Moving briskly, we reached the hither side a few yards from the guns. Infantry was posted near, and riflemen were in the undergrowth on the slope above. Our approach, masked by timber, was unexpected. The battery was firing rapidly, enabled from elevation to fire over the advancing lines. The head of my column began to deploy under cover for attack, when the sounds of battle to our rear appeared to recede, and a loud Federal cheer was heard, proving Jackson to be hard pressed.

It was rather an anxious moment, demanding instant action. Leaving a staff officer to direct my rear regiment—the 7th, Colonel Hays—to form in the wood as a reserve, I ordered the attack, though the deployment was not completed, and our rapid march by a narrow path had occasioned some disorder. With a rush and shout the gorge was passed and we were in the battery. Surprise had aided us, but the enemy's infantry rallied in a moment and drove us out. We returned, to be driven a second time. The riflemen on the slope worried us no little, and two companies of the 9th regiment were sent up the gorge to gain ground above and dislodge them, which was accomplished. The fighting in and around the battery was hand to hand, and many fell from bayonet wounds. Even the artillerymen used their rammers in a way not laid down in the Manual, and died at their guns. As Conan said to the devil, " 'Twas claw for claw." I called for Hays, but he, the promptest of men, and his splendid regiment, could not be found. Something unexpected had occurred, but there was no time for speculation. With a desperate rally, in which I believe the drummer-boys shared, we carried the battery for the third time, and held it.

Infantry and riflemen had been driven off, and we began to feel a little comfortable, when the enemy, arrested in his advance by our attack, appeared. He had countermarched, and, with left near the river, came into full view of our situation. Wheeling to the right, with colors advanced, like a solid wall he marched straight upon us. There seemed nothing left but to set our backs to the mountain and die hard. At the instant, crashing through the underwood, came Ewell, outriding staff and escort. He produced the effect of a reenforcement, and was welcomed with cheers. The line before us halted and threw forward skirmishers. A moment later, a shell came shrieking along it, loud Confederate cheers reached our delighted ears, and Jackson, freed from his toils, rushed up like a whirlwind, the enemy in rapid retreat. We turned the captured guns on them as they passed, Ewell serving as a gunner.

Though rapid, the retreat never became a rout. Fortune had refused her smiles, but Shields's brave "boys" preserved their organization and were formidable to the last; and had Shields himself, with his whole command, been on the field, we should have had tough work indeed.

Jackson came up, with intense light in his eyes, grasped my hand, and said the brigade should have the captured battery. I thought the men would go mad with cheering, especially the Irishmen. A huge fellow, with one eye closed and half his whiskers burned by powder, was riding cock-horse on a gun, and, catching my attention, yelled out, "We told you to bet on your boys."

—TAYLOR, *Destruction and Reconstruction*

4. GENERAL LAW DESCRIBES JACKSON AT SEVEN DAYS

As soon as Jackson had achieved the purpose of the Valley campaign—holding strong Federal forces in the Valley and preventing the reinforcement of McClellan—he hastened to join Lee to take part in the battles that were to drive McClellan from Richmond.

General Law, who here gives us a vivid picture of "Stonewall" at the height of his popularity, we have met before.

HERE, too, I saw General Jackson for the first time since I had seen him in the heat of the fight at the battle of Manassas. He passed our division on the march, and for a time no one seemed to know who he was. As soon as he was recognized, however, a general shout was raised for "Old Stonewall," which continued as long as he was in sight. He was mounted on a very ordinary sorrel horse, whose appearance indicated rather short rations. His uniform was well-worn, faded, and covered with the yellow dust which was plentiful along the line of march. His cap, originally blue, but now faded and dusty, was of the style then known as the "Beauregard," the crown falling forward upon the visor which nearly touched the point of his nose. He certainly needed the new uniform presented to him shortly afterward by the ladies of Richmond. An ordinary saber with an iron scabbard completed his equipment. He was not a graceful rider, and sat his horse carelessly. He looked neither to the right nor to the left, but straight forward, as if that was the one direction in which he cared to think or move. The square and massive lower jaw, covered with a short, thick beard, the firm, set lips, and the preoccupied expression of his whole face were forcibly suggestive of his *nom de guerre*, "Stonewall," in their firmness as well as inscrutability.

A few days later, June 26th, as we were approaching McClellan's lines in rear of Mechanicsville, I went to report to General Whiting the result of a *reconnoissance* that had been ordered on our left flank as we advanced. I found him at the edge of the field near the road, in company with General Jackson. Jackson was leaning carelessly against a fence which separated the field from the adjacent woods. They were both perfectly silent, not a word passing between them, and, so far as I could judge from their attitudes, had been so from the time I came in sight. When I had made my report, Jackson asked a question or two and again relapsed into silence, which was unbroken by a word until I left them. But this plain, silent soldier, as he appeared on the march, was not always the same. At the first sounds of approaching battle, his whole appearance changed; his movements became quick and energetic; his eyes seemed to gleam with a fierce joy, and every muscle became tense with the fire that burned within. And when he led a regiment or a brigade to the charge, which he sometimes did, he became the very incarnation of battle. He was "a man of iron and fire," enthusiastically admired by his men, almost invariably successful in his undertakings, and one of the very few Confederate commanders who knew how to improve a victory.

—LAW, "The Fight for Richmond"

5. COLONEL WOLSELEY VISITS STONEWALL JACKSON

Fresh from campaigns in the Crimea, India and China, Colonel Garnet Wolseley—later Lord Wolseley—was ordered to Canada as quartermaster general in December 1861. In August of the next year he applied for leave of absence and, without the approval of his superiors, made his way into the Confederate States and visited scenes of recent battles, and the headquarters of Lee and Jackson. Already favorable to the Confederate cause, his enthusiasm was confirmed by what he saw. His account of his month's visit to Confederate Headquarters, which appeared anonymously in Blackwood's Magazine, *aroused widespread interest in Britain and America.*

UPON leaving, we drove to Bunker's Hill, six miles nearer Martinsburg, at which place Stonewall Jackson, now of world-wide celebrity, had his headquarters. With him we spent a most pleasant hour, and were agreeably surprised to find him very affable, having been led to expect that he was silent and almost morose. Dressed in his grey uniform, he looks the hero that he is; and his thin compressed lips and calm glance, which meets yours un-flinchingly, give evidence of that firmness and decision of character for which he is so famous. He has a broad open forehead, from which the hair is well brushed back; a shapely nose, straight, and rather long; thin colourless cheeks, with only a very small allowance of whisker; a cleanly-shaven upper lip and chin; and a pair of fine greyish-blue eyes, rather sunken, with over-hanging brows, which intensify the keenness of his gaze, but without impart-ing any fierceness to it. Such are the general characteristics of his face; and I have only to add, that a smile seems always lurking about his mouth when he speaks; and that though his voice partakes slightly of that harshness which Europeans unjustly attribute to *all* Americans, there is much unmistakable cordiality in his manner: and to us he talked most affectionately of England, and of his brief but enjoyable sojourn there.

The religious element seems strongly developed in him; and though his conversation is perfectly free from all puritanical cant, it is evident that he is a person who never loses sight of the fact that there is an omnipresent Deity ever presiding over the minutest occurrences of life, as well as over the most important.

Altogether, as one of his soldiers said to me in talking of him, "he is a glorious fellow!" and, after I left him, I felt that I had at last solved the mystery of Stonewall Bridge, and discovered why it was that it had accom-plished such almost miraculous feats. With such a leader men would go any-where, and face any amount of difficulties; and for myself, I believe that, inspired by the presence of such a man, I should be perfectly insensible to fatigue, and reckon upon success as a moral certainty.

Whilst General Lee is regarded in the light of infallible Jove, a man to be reverenced, Jackson is loved and adored with all that childlike and trustful affection which the ancients are said to have lavished upon the particular deity presiding over their affairs. The feeling of the soldiers for General Lee resembles that which Wellington's troops entertained for him—namely, a fixed and unshakable faith in all he did, and a calm confidence of victory when serving under him. But Jackson, like Napoleon, is idolised with that intense fervour which, consisting of mingled personal attachment and de-voted loyalty, causes them to meet death for his sake, and bless him when dying.

—[WOLSELEY], "A Month's Visit to Confederate Headquarters"

6. STONEWALL JACKSON GETS A NEW UNIFORM

Heros von Borcke, who gives us this delightful anecdote of Jackson and his new uniform, was one of the most picturesque figures in the Confederate Army. A Prussian nobleman and professional soldier, he obtained leave of absence from the staff of the Prince of Prussia, ran the blockade, and was

*promptly made Stuart's chief of staff. Gigantic in stature, lusty, gay, reck-
less, yet withal a good soldier, he was known in the South as "Major Band-
box." Stuart wanted Von Borcke to succeed to his own command, but
instead the Confederacy sent him, in 1864, on a futile mission to England. His*
Memoirs of the Confederate War *are hard to beat for color and excitement.
This episode occurred in September 1862.*

FROM a long rest, after the dissipations of the past night, I was roused
about noon by General Stuart, with orders to ride, upon some little matters of duty, to the camp of General Jackson. I was also honoured with the
pleasing mission of presenting to old Stonewall, as a slight token of Stuart's
high regard, a new and very "stunning" uniform coat, which had just arrived
from the hands of a Richmond tailor. The garment, neatly wrapped up, was
borne on the pommel of his saddle by one of our couriers who accompanied
me; and starting at once I reached the simple tent of our great general just
in time for dinner. I found him in his old weather-stained coat, from which
all the buttons had been clipped long since by the fair hands of patriotic
ladies, and which, from exposure to sun and rain and powder-smoke, and by
reason of many rents and patches, was in a very unseemly condition.

When I had despatched more important matters, I produced General
Stuart's present, in all its magnificence of gilt buttons and sheeny facings and
gold lace, and I was heartily amused at the modest confusion with which
the hero of many battles regarded the fine uniform from many points of
view, scarcely daring to touch it, and at the quiet way in which, at last, he
folded it up carefully, and deposited it in his portmanteau, saying to me,
"Give Stuart my best thanks my dear Major—the coat is much too handsome
for me, but I shall take the best care of it, and shall prize it highly as a
souvenir. And now let us have some dinner." But I protested energetically
against this summary disposition of the matter of the coat, deeming my mission, indeed, but half executed, and remarked that Stuart would certainly
ask me how the uniform fitted its owner, and that I should, therefore, take it
as a personal favour if he would put it on.

To this he readily assented with a smile, and having donned the garment,
he escorted me outside the tent to the table where dinner had been served in
the open air. The whole of the Staff were in a perfect ecstasy at their chief's
brilliant appearance, and the old Negro servant, who was bearing the roast-
turkey from the fire to the board, stopped in mid-career with a most bewildered expression, and gazed in wonderment at his master as if he had been
transfigured before him. Meanwhile, the rumour of the change ran like
electricity through the neighboring camps, and the soldiers came running by
hundreds to the spot, desirous of seeing their beloved Stonewall in his new
attire; and the first wearing of a fresh robe by Louis XIV., at whose morning
toilet all the world was accustomed to assemble, never created half the sensation at Versailles, that was made in the woods of Virginia by the investment
of Jackson in this new regulation uniform.

—VON BORCKE, *Memoirs of the Confederate War for Independence*

7. HENRY KYD DOUGLAS REMEMBERS
STONEWALL JACKSON

Henry Kyd Douglas, whose reminiscences give us the liveliest and fullest picture of Jackson that we have from any contemporary, was practicing law in St. Louis when the war broke out. Hastening home he enlisted as a private in the 2nd Virginia Regiment—part of the Stonewall Brigade. He was later aide-de-camp to Jackson, and fought with him until his death at Chancellorsville. Douglas rose to be brigadier general—the youngest in either army, it is said—and his brigade fired the last shot and was the last to surrender at Appomattox.

IN face and figure Jackson was not striking. Above the average height, with a frame angular, muscular, and fleshless, he was, in all his movements from riding a horse to handling a pen, the most awkward man in the army. His expression was thoughtful, and, as a result I fancy of his long ill health, was generally clouded with an air of fatigue. His eye was small, blue, and in repose as gentle as a young girl's. With high, broad, forehead, small sharp nose, thin, pallid lips generally tightly shut, deep-set eyes, dark, rusty beard, he was certainly not a handsome man. His face in tent or parlor, softened by his sweet smile, was as different from itself on the battlefield as a little lake in summer noon differs from the same lake when frozen. Walking or riding the General was ungainly: his main object was to get over the ground. He rode boldly and well, but not with grace or ease; and "Little Sorrel" was as little like a Pegasus as he was like an Apollo. He was not a man of style. General Lee, on horseback or off, was the handsomest man I ever saw. It was said of Wade Hampton that he looked as knightly when mounted as if he had stepped out from an old canvas, horse and all. John C. Breckinridge was a model of manly beauty, John B. Gordon, a picture for the sculptor, and Joe Johnston looked every inch a soldier. None of these things could be said of Jackson.

The enemy believed he never slept. In fact he slept a great deal. Give him five minutes to rest, he could sleep three of them. Whenever he had nothing else to do he went to sleep, especially in church. He could sleep in any position, in a chair, under fire, or on horseback. Being a silent man, he gave to sleep many moments which other men gave to conversation. And yet he was never caught "napping."

He was quiet, not morose. He often smiled, rarely laughed. He never told a joke but rather liked to hear one, now and then. He did not live apart from his personal staff, although they were nearly all young; he liked to have them about, especially at table. He encouraged the liveliness of their conversation at meals, although he took little part in it. His own words seemed to embarrass him, unless he could follow his language by action. As he never told his plans, he never discussed them. He didn't offer advice to his superiors, nor ask it of his subordinates. Reticent and self-reliant he believed "he walks with speed who walks alone." The officer next in command often and very justly complained of this risky reticence; but Jackson is reported to have said, "If my coat knew what I intended to do, I'd take it off and throw it away." Such reticence at times was neither judicious nor defensible; but luck saved him from evil consequences. . . .

On the battlefield where Longstreet's doughty men were confronting a stubborn foe and A. P. Hill, as usual, was doing his share of the fighting, soldiers heard the cannonade and were encouraged in their hot work. Soon came to them a sharper and more earnest clamor, and there was such a rattle and roar of musketry as I never heard before or after. A staff officer dashed along Longstreet's wearied lines, crying out, "Stonewall's at them!" and was answered with yell after yell of joy, which added a strange sound to the din of battle. The battle was on in earnest; skirmishing died away and was succeeded by the crash of line meeting line.

General Jackson mounted his gaunt sorrel (not "Little Sorrel") and leaving his position moved more to the front. At that moment someone handed him a lemon—a fruit of which he was specially fond. Immediately a small piece was bitten out of it and slowly and unsparingly he began to extract its flavor and its juice. From that moment until darkness ended the battle, that lemon scarcely left his lips except to be used as a baton to emphasize an order. He listened to Yankee shout or Rebel yell, to the sound of musketry advancing or receding, to all the signs of promise or apprehension, but he never for an instant lost his interest in that lemon and even spoke of its excellence. His face, nevertheless, was calm and granite-like. His blue eye was restful and cold, except when now and then it gave, for a moment, an ominous flash. His right hand lay open and flat on his thigh, but now and then was raised into the air as was his habit—a gesture which the troops learned to believe was as significant as the extended arm of Aaron. But the lemon was not abandoned.

The moment came when it was taken from his mouth with an impatient jerk. A wild yell came from the battlefield which attracted his attention. Pendleton came up and said it was from the Stonewall Brigade, for he had just seen Winder taking them in. He drew the lemon away abruptly and said, "We shall soon have good news from that charge. Yes, they are driving the enemy!" and he lifted up his yellow banner, as if in triumph. When I last saw that lemon, it was torn open and exhausted and thrown away, but the day was over and the battle was won. . . .

The 6th of July [1862] was a very warm day. The General had returned from his morning ride to the front and was trying to make himself comfortable. Headquarters were in bivouac. He seated himself at the foot of a large tree to take a nap—he could always go to sleeep when he had nothing else to do. After a very short rest he aroused himself and asked me if I had a novel. I did not have one, nor did any of the staff, as all books had been left in the vicinity of Mechanicsville with the wagons. He said he had not read a novel for a long time before the war. Hugh McGuire, a clerk at Headquarters, afterwards Captain in T. L. Rosser's Cavalry Brigade, handed me a yellow-back novel of the sensational type, saying he had picked it up on the battle-field. It looked like literary trash, and it was—sensational and full of wood cuts. I handed it to the General, who looked at it with a smile, seated himself again at the foot of the tree, and began to read it. He gave his whole attention to it, as if it was a duty not to give it up, and waded on through it. Now and then his features would relax and smile, but he did not take his eyes from the book. He did not speak a word but kept on until he had finished it; fortunately, it was a small paper volume of large print. He then returned it with thanks, saying it had been a long time since he had read a novel and it would be a long time until he read another. This was the only book not strictly military or religious that I ever saw him attempt to read in the army.

On the 8th of July [1862] the Army of Northern Virginia began to move back to the vicinity of Richmond. When Jackson's command started he and his staff remained behind until some time after the rest of the army had gone. It was after dark when he started and about midnight when he reached his Headquarters. He was riding along at ten or eleven o'clock with his drowsy staff, nodding on "Little Sorrel," as was his custom, and trusting to that intelligent beast not to give him a fall. More than once did we see his head nod and drop on his breast and his body sway a little to one side or the other, expecting to see him get a tumble; but he never got it. On this occasion our sleepy cavalcade at different times passed small squads of soldiers in fence corners before blazing fires, roasting green corn and eating it. Passing one of these, our staggering leader was observed by one of those thirsty stragglers, who was evidently delighted at the sight of a drunken cavalry-man. Perhaps encouraged with the hope of a drink ahead, the ragged Reb jumped up from his fire and, brandishing a roasting-ear in his hand, sprang into the road and to the head of the General's horse, with, "Hello! I say, old fellow, where the devil did you get your licker?"

The General suddenly woke up and said, "Dr. McGuire, did you speak to me? Captain Pendleton, did you? Somebody did," and reined up his horse.

The soldier got a look at him and took in the situation; he saw whom he had thus spoken to. "Good God! it's Old Jack!" he cried, and with several bounds and a flying leap he had cleared the road, was over the fence, and disappeared in the dark.

As soon as the staff could recover from their laughter, McGuire explained the situation to the General, who was much amused. He immediately rode up to the fence, dismounted, and took half an hour's nap. Then he roused himself, said he felt better, and we went on to Headquarters. . . .

Under orders from General Leee, General Jackson left his camp at Richmond for Gordonsville about the 14th of July. General John Pope, Commander of the Army of Virginia, was gathering his forces for an advance from the vicinity of Washington. He had settled himself "in the saddle" and from that contracted Headquarters had fulminated his celebrated proclamation in the shape of a general order, for which he was afterward ridiculed by the pen and punished by the sword. Believing that Jackson was not likely to be scared by so much military fustian, General Lee sent him to look after his advancing Hannibal. The General went on in advance and we were soon far ahead of troops and wagon trains on the road to Ashland.

About sundown of the first day, we were driven temporarily into a blacksmith shop for shelter from a rain storm, and from there sent out to seek shelter for the night. We found it in a most hospitable house where a plentiful supper, good rooms, and pleasant beds were made doubly enjoyable by the easy and sincere hospitality of host and hostess. The next morning we were in Ashland early and had sundry invitations to breakfast. The General seemed in excellent humor and unusually talkative. While waiting for breakfast he sat in the parlor, amused himself and others as well by his attempts to be playful with a prattling little girl who was running about the room, and then again listened with most respectful attention to a young lady who was at the piano, giving us such songs and instrumental music as she thought to our taste. Now the General had the least possible knowledge of music and, as was said of him, he had so little of it in his soul, that he was necessarily "fit for treason, strategy and spoils." Still it was a matter of amazement to his staff, when he said with much politeness to the young lady, "Miss ——, won't you play a piece of music they call 'Dixie'? I heard it a few days ago and it was, I thought, very beautiful."

The young lady was nonplussed and answered, "Why, General, I just sang it a few minutes ago—it is about our oldest war song."

"Ah, indeed, I didn't know it."

He had heard it a thousand times. Perhaps he thought he would startle the young lady with his knowledge of music; if so, he succeeded. . . .

One night, after the middle of it, General Stuart came riding into our Headquarters, accompanied by his artillery pet, Captain John Pelham, the "boy Major," as he was afterwards called, or "the gallant Pelham," as General Lee named him at Fredericksburg. . . . Everyone had gone to rest. Stuart went directly to General Jackson's tent; Pelham came into mine. The General was asleep and the cavalry chief threw himself down by his side, taking off nothing but his sabre. As the night became chilly, so did he, and unconsciously he began to take possession of blankets and got between the sheets. There he discovered himself in the early morn in the full panoply of war, and he got out of it. After a while, when a lot of us were standing by a blazing log-fire before the General's tent, he came out for his ablutions.

"Good morning, General Jackson," said Stuart, "how are you?"

Old Jack passed his hands through his thin and uncombed hair and then in tones as nearly comic as he could muster he said, "General Stuart, I'm always glad to see you here. You might select better hours sometimes, but I'm always glad to have you. But, General"—as he stooped and rubbed himself along the legs—"you must not get into my bed with your boots and spurs on and ride me around like a cavalry horse all night!"

—DOUGLAS, *I Rode with Stonewall*

VI
Second Bull Run and Antietam

THE *Peninsular campaign was indecisive. Lee had saved Richmond, but at heavy cost, and McClellan was at Harrison's Landing preparing to renew the contest. But Lincoln and Halleck, who in July had been appointed Military Adviser to the President, had different plans. They had lost confidence in McClellan and wanted to try a different commander; they decided that the scattered armies in Virginia ought to be consolidated into one great fighting force. First the armies of the Valley were consolidated under John Pope, who had won a somewhat dubious reputation in the West; then Burnside was ordered north from Fortress Monroe to Falmouth; finally McClellan was directed to bring his great army to Alexandria and unite with Pope.*

There was only one serious flaw in this plan: it ignored Lee and the Army of Northern Virginia. While the Union commanders were carrying through these complicated operations, Lee determined to strike. His forces were so small that he could not hope to contest with a united Federal army, but he could strike the scattered armies singly. And for this he had the great advantage of interior lines of communication.

Leaving only a few brigades to protect Richmond Lee started his army toward the Valley. There was a sharp fight at Cedar Mountain near Culpeper Court House, where Jackson inflicted heavy losses on the hapless Banks. Then while Pope was trying to concentrate his forces along the Rapidan, Jackson swung around his rear and on August 26 destroyed Pope's headquarters and supply depots at Manassas Junction. Pope fatuously supposed that he had Jackson in a trap and hurried to close it. Jackson marched west to Groveton and invited the attack of Pope's forces. On August 29 Pope finally caught up with Stonewall and all day long wore out his army in desperate assaults on Jackson's iron lines. Meanwhile Longstreet was hurrying up the valley between the Blue Ridge and the Bull Run Mountains. On the twenty-ninth he turned east, forced Thoroughfare Gap—which Pope had left practically undefended—and the next day struck Pope's left flank, rolled it up, and sent the whole army reeling toward Bull Run.

The battle ended in a cloud of recriminations, and no wonder. Porter's corps had stood idle the whole afternoon of the twenty-ninth; Banks's 6,500 men had taken no part in the fight; McClellan, at near-by Alexandria, had failed to get any part of his large army to Pope in time to do any good. Porter was later made the scapegoat for all this tragedy of errors, but the real failure was Pope's and McClellan's.

On August 3 Pope withdrew to the defenses of Washington, and two days later McClellan supplanted him as commander of the Army of the

Potomac. Lee now determined to carry the war to the North. He knew that his army was in no condition to wage an aggressive campaign, but he hoped that an invasion of the North might be effected without any major battle and that it might accomplish many things. He hoped to cut the B. & O. and possibly the Pennsylvania Railroad, thus temporarily isolating Washington; to reprovision his troops—many of them without shoes; to relieve pressure on Virginia; to bring foreign recognition.

In the first week of September, then, Lee's butternuts were splashing across the fords of the Potomac onto the shores of Maryland. "Virginia shall not call in vain," James Randall had written in the song that every Southerner was singing, but it did: Lee lost more soldiers by straggling and desertion than he gained. His ultimate objective was probably Harrisburg and he planned originally to move his army north between the Catoctin and South Mountains into Pennsylvania. To make sure of his communications he detached half his force under Jackson to take Harpers Ferry. Thus by September 13 his meager force—some 50,000 at most—was badly scattered.

At this juncture fate intervened. Lee's famous Order 191 detailing the entire plan of the campaign fell into McClellan's hands. That general moved with what was for him admirable rapidity. He was convinced that Lee had an army of 120,000 men, so he observed his customary caution, but at least he did go forward. The first clashes came on September 14 at South Mountain and Crampton's Gap. Both were Federal victories, but they did not come in time to save Harpers Ferry, which fell on the morning of the fifteenth, the Confederates bagging 11,000 prisoners and an immense body of equipment.

With his rear safe Lee moved back to Sharpsburg, entrenching his army along the little Antietam creek, his flanks resting on two bends of the Potomac. He had only 18,000 men, McClellan was hot on his trail with 70,000, and prudence would have dictated a retreat. But McClellan did not attack, and the next day Jackson came up, raising Lee's forces to about 40,000: A. P. Hill was still at Harpers Ferry. The great battle came the next day and was, perhaps, the most hotly contested of the whole war. All day long the mighty hosts in blue hurled themselves on the thin gray lines, first on Jackson on the left; then on Hill at the center; then on Longstreet on the right. Again and again it seemed as if the Confederates would be overwhelmed and destroyed, but each time they managed to hang on and to inflict such losses that the final blow was suspended. When night fell McClellan still had not used his reserves, Lee had held his lines, and the battle could fairly be called a draw. Federal losses in killed and wounded were 14,000, Confederate over 11,000.

1. "WHO COULD NOT CONQUER WITH SUCH TROOPS AS THESE?"

Reinforced by A. P. Hill's division, Jackson started toward the Valley on August 7. On the ninth he reached Cedar Mountain, south of Culpeper, and there ran into Banks. Banks attacked, won some initial success, and was then thrown back and overwhelmed by superior numbers. Finding the whole of Pope's army in front of him, on the Rapidan line, Jackson fell back toward Gordonsville. After some maneuvering for position, Lee decided to send Jackson around Pope's army, and it is one phase of this great swinging movement that Robert Dabney here describes.

A distinguished clergyman and college professor, Dabney was a major on Jackson's staff and later wrote a biography of his idolized hero.

WHILE the enemy was thus deluded with the belief that the race up the Rappahannock was ended, and that he now had nothing more to do than to hold its northern bank at this place, General Jackson was preparing, under the instructions of the Commander-in-Chief, for the most adventurous and brilliant of his exploits. This was no less than to separate himself from the support of the remainder of the army, pass around Pope to the westward, and place his *corps* between him and Washington City, at Manassa's Junction. To effect this, the Rappahannock must be passed on the upper part of its course, and two forced marches made through the western quarters of the county of Fauquier, which lie between the Blue Ridge and the subsidiary range of the Bull Run Mountains. Having made a hasty and imperfect issue of rations, Jackson disembarrassed himself of all his trains, save the ambulances and the carriages for the ammunition, and left Jeffersonton early on the morning of August 25th. Marching first westward, he crossed the two branches of the Rappahannock, passed the hamlet of Orlean, and paused at night, after a march of twenty-five miles, near Salem, a village upon the Manassa's Gap Railroad. His troops had been constantly marching and fighting since the 20th; many of them had no rations, and subsisted upon the green corn gathered along the route; yet their indomitable enthusiasm and devotion knew no flagging. As the weary column approached the end of the day's march, they found Jackson, who had ridden forward, dismounted, and standing upon a great stone by the road-side.

His sun-burned cap was lifted from his brow, and he was gazing toward the west, where the splendid August sun was about to kiss the distant crest of the Blue Ridge, which stretched far away, bathed in azure and gold; and his blue eye, beaming with martial pride, returned the rays of the evening with almost equal brightness. His men burst forth into their accustomed cheers, forgetting all their fatigue at his inspiring presence; but, deprecating the tribute by a gesture, he sent an officer to request that there should be no cheering, inasmuch as it might betray their presence to the enemy. They at once repressed their applause, and passed the word down the column to their comrades: "No cheering, boys; the General requests it." But as they passed him, their eyes and gestures, eloquent with suppressed affection, silently declared what their lips were forbidden to utter. Jackson turned to his Staff, his face beaming with delight, and said: "Who could not conquer, with such troops as these?" . . .

On the morning of the 26th, he turned eastward, and passing through the

Bull Run Mountains, at Thoroughfare Gap, proceeded to Bristoe Station, on the Orange Railroad, by another equally arduous march. At Gainsville, he was joined by Stuart, with his cavalry, who now assumed the duty of guarding his right flank, and watching the main army of Pope, about Warrenton. As the Confederates approached Bristoe Station, about sunset, the roar of a railroad train proceeding eastward, was heard, and dispositions were made to arrest it, by placing the brigade of Hays, under Colonel Forno, across the track. The first train broke through the obstructions placed before it, and escaped. Two others which followed it were captured, but were found to contain nothing.

The *corps* of Jackson, had now marched fifty miles in two days. The whole army of Pope was interposed between it and its friends. They had no supplies whatever, save those which they might capture from the enemy. But they were between that enemy and his capital, and were cheered by the hope of inflicting a vital blow upon him before he escaped. This movement would be pronounced wrong, if judged by a formal and common-place application of the maxims of the military art. But it is the very prerogative of true genius to know how to modify the application of those rules according to circumstances. It might have been objected, that such a division of the Confederate army into two parts, subjected it to the risk of being beaten in detail; that while the Federal commander detained and amused one by a detachment, he would turn upon the other with the chief weight of his forces, and crush it into fragments. Had Pope been a Jackson, this danger would have been real; but because Pope was but Pope, and General Lee had a Jackson to execute the bold conception, and a Stuart to mask his movement during its progress, the risk was too small to forbid the attempt. The promptitude of General Stuart in seizing the only signal station whence the line of march could possibly be perceived, and the secrecy and rapidity of General Jackson in pursuing it, with the energy of his action when he had reached his goal, ensured the success of the movement.

—DABNEY, *Life and Campaigns of Lt. Gen. Thomas J. Jackson*

2. JACKSON OUTSMARTS AND OUTFIGHTS POPE AT MANASSAS

Jackson's plans worked out to perfection. While Pope's forces were scattered over a wide area between the Catharpin and the Cedar Run rivers, Jackson circled around through Thoroughfare Gap, captured Pope's headquarters at Manassas Junction, swung northward to Groveton and westward to Gainesville. Pope ordered his forces to concentrate at Manassas, then set out in pursuit of the elusive Jackson, wearying his men with marches and countermarches and his commanders with orders that were confusing and contradictory. On August 29 Pope's army finally converged on Jackson between Groveton and Sudley Springs and exhausted itself in savage piecemeal attacks on Stonewall's line. Meantime Longstreet was swinging through Thoroughfare Gap ready to pounce on Pope's flank.

The "rebel lieutenant" of this narrative is John Hampden Chamberlayne, a young graduate of the University of Virginia who fought through the whole war to Petersburg, then made his way west hoping to find an army that would continue the fighting.

Frederick City, Md., Saturday, Sept. 6 [1862]

My Dear Mother:

I am brimful of matter as an egg of meat. Let me try to outline our progress since my last letter—date not remembered—from Raccoon Ford—you bearing in mind that I am in A. P. Hill's division, in Jackson's corps—that corps consisting of Jackson's own division, Ewell's and Hill's. You will not think me egotistical for speaking of this corps and of the corps of Hill's division, for of them I know most, and in truth their share was, to me at least, the most memorable in the almost incredible campaign of the last fortnight.

Crossing Raccoon Ford, Jackson in front—remember, Jackson, so used, includes Hill, Ewell, and the Stonewall division—General Lee, without much opposition, reached Rappahannock River, a few miles above Rappahannock station, where a part of Longstreet's troops had a sharp fight. On Friday Evening, August twenty-second, Jackson bivouacked in Culpeper, opposite Warrenton Springs, and the same evening threw over two of Ewell's brigades. The river rose and destroyed the bridge. Saturday the bridge was rebuilt, and that night the two brigades, after some sharp fighting, were withdrawn.

On Monday morning the enemy appeared in heavy force, and the batteries of Hill's division were put in position and shelled their infantry. They retired the infantry, and bringing up a large number of batteries, threw a storm of shot and shell at us—we not replying. They must have exploded several thousand rounds, and in all, so well sheltered were we, our killed did not reach twenty. That evening Jackson's whole force moved up to Jefferson, in Culpeper County, Longstreet close to him. The enemy was completely deceived, and concluded that we had given the thing up.

Now comes the great wonder. Starting up the bank of the river on Monday, the twenty-fifth, we marched through Amosville, in Rappahannock County—still further up, crossed the Rappahannock within ten miles of the Blue Ridge, marched across open fields, by strange country paths and comfortable homesteads, by a little town in Fauquier, called Orleans, on and on, as if we would never cease—to Salem, on the Manassas Gap Railroad, reaching there after midnight. Up again by day-dawn, and still on, along the Manassas Gap road, meeting crowds—all welcoming, cheering, staring with blank amazement. So all day Tuesday, through White Plains, Haymarket, Thoroughfare Gap, in Bull Run Mountains, Gainesville, to Bristow station, on the Orange and Alexandria Railroad—making the difference from Amosville to Bristow (between forty-five and fifty miles) within the forty-eight hours. We burned up at Bristow two or three railway-trains, and moved up to Manassas Junction on Wednesday, taking our prisoners with us. Ewell's division brought up the rear, fighting all the way a force Pope had sent up from Warrenton, supposing us a cavalry party.

Upon reaching Manassas Junction, we met a brigade—the First New-Jersey—which had been sent from Alexandria on the same supposition. They were fools enough to send a flag demanding our surrender at once. Of course we scattered the brigade, killing and wounding many, and among them the Brigadier-General (Taylor,) who has since died. At the Junction was a large dépôt of stores, five or six pieces of artillery, two trains containing probably two hundred large cars loaded down with many millions of quarter-master and commissary stores. Beside these, there were very large sutlers' dépôts, full of every thing; in short, there was collected there, in the space of a square mile, an amount and variety of property such as I had never conceived of, (I speak soberly.) 'Twas a curious sight to see our ragged and famished men helping themselves to every imaginable article of luxury or necessity, whether of clothing, food, or what not. For my part, I got a tooth-brush, a box of candles, a quantity of lobster salad, a barrel of coffee, and other things which I forget. But I must hurry on, for I have not time to tell the hundredth part, and the scene utterly beggars description.

A part of us hunted that New-Jersey brigade like scattered partridges over the hills just to the right of the battle-field of the eighteenth of July, 1861, while the rest were partly plundering, partly fighting the forces coming on us from Warrenton. Our men had been living on roasted corn since crossing the Rappahannock, and we had brought no wagons, so we could carry little away of the riches before us. But the men could eat for one meal at least. So they were marched up, and as much of every thing eatable served out as they could carry. To see a starving man eating lobster-salad and drinking Rhine wine, barefooted and in tatters, was curious; the whole thing was incredible.

Our situation now was very critical. We were between Alexandria and Warrenton—between the hosts of McClellan and Pope with over eighteen thousand jaded men, for the corps had not more than that. At nightfall, fire was set to the dépôt, storehouses, the loaded trains, several, empty trains, sutlers' houses, restaurants, every thing. As the magnificent conflagration began to subside, the Stonewall or First division of Jackson's corps moved off toward the battlefield of Manassas, the other two divisions to Centreville, six miles distant.

As day broke, we came in sight of Centreville, rested a few hours, and toward evening the rear-guard of the corps crossed Bull Run at Stone Bridge—the scene of the great slaughter of last year—closely pursued by the enemy. A part of the force came up the Warrenton turnpike, and in a furious action of two hours—the last two daylight hours of Thursday, August twenty-eighth—disputed the possession of a ridge running from Sudley Church Ford to the Warrenton turnpike. We drove them off, and on Friday morning we held the ridge, in front of which runs an incomplete railroad-cut and embankment. Now, we had made a circuit from the Gap in Bull Run Mountains around to the Junction and Centerville, breaking up the railroad and destroying their stores, and returned to within six miles of the Gap, through which Longstreet must come. The enemy disputed his passage and delayed him till late in the day, and, meanwhile, they threw against our corps, all day long, vast masses of troops—Sigel's, Banks's, and Pope's own division. We got out of ammunition; we collected more from cartridge-boxes of fallen friend and foe; that gave out, and we charged with never-failing yell and steel. All day long they threw their masses on us; all day they fell back shattered and shrieking. When the sun went down, their dead were heaped in front of the incomplete railway, and we sighed with relief, for Longstreet could be seen coming into position on our right. The crisis was over; Longstreet never failed yet; but the sun went down so slowly. . . .

I am proud to have borne my humble part in these great operations—to have helped, even so little, to consummate the grand plan, whose history will be a text-book to all young soldiers, and whose magnificent success places Lee at the side of the greatest captains, Hannibal, Caesar, Eugene, Napoleon. I hope you have preserved my letters in which I have spoken of my faith in Lee. He and his round-table of generals are worthy the immortality of Napoleon and his Marshals. He moves his agencies like a god—secret, complicated, vast, resistless, complete.

—[CHAMBERLAYNE], "Narrative by a Rebel Lieutenant"

3. POPE WASTES HIS STRENGTH ON JACKSON

Had Pope been able to employ all of his available forces, or had he employed what he had properly, he might have driven Jackson from the field on August 29, or overwhelmed him. But Porter's corps, near Bristoe, failed for some reason to get into the fight; Sigel, Reynolds, Heintzelman and Reno attacked separately, McDowell came late. The result was a repulse for the Federals. Pope should have realized that Longstreet was coming up on his flank, and retired to some defensive position where he could have awaited help from McClellan. Instead he elected to renew the battle on the following day.

This account of the fighting on the twenty-ninth is from the pen of David Strother, a Virginia littérateur who went with the Union, served on the staffs of Banks, McClellan, Pope and Hunter, and ended the war with a brigadier generalship. While his account is in diary form, there is some doubt that it was actually written up from day to day, and some of his statements are probably inaccurate.

August 29, Friday.—Clear and warm. At three o'clock this morning I was aroused by Colonel Ruggles in person to carry written orders to General Fitz-John Porter, supposed to be lying at Manassas Junction, or alternatively at Bristoe. . . . Porter's orders are to move his Corps on Centreville without delay.

I started with an orderly. It was pitchy dark—so dark that I couldn't see my horse's ears—and I presently found I had wandered from the road. The orderly knew nothing, or was stupid from sleepiness, so that in endeavoring to retrieve I found myself entangled in thickets, and then wandering through the half-decayed villages of log-huts built by the rebels during their first occupation. As I got out of one of these desolate encampments I fell into another, and began to suspect I was wandering in circles, which frequently happens to people bewildered or benighted. I at length dismounted, and feeling the road got out into the open plain, where the still smouldering fires of the recent destruction served to guide me. I found no troops here, and it was broad daylight when I reached Porter's quarters at Bristoe. Entering his tent I found the handsome General lying on his cot, covered with a blanket of imitation leopard skin.

At his request I lit a candle and read the message, then handed it to him. While he coolly read it over I noted the time by his watch, which marked five o'clock and twenty minutes precisely. He then proceeded to dress himself, and continued to question me in regard to the location of the different commands and the general situation. As I was but imperfectly informed myself I could only give vague and general replies to his queries. We believed Jackson separated from the main army of Lee by a day's march at least; and General Pope desired to throw all his disposable force upon him and crush him before Lee came up. The troops were immediately ordered to cook breakfast and prepare for the march.

Meanwhile the head-quarters breakfast had been served, and I sat down with the Staff officers to partake. The General, who was busy writing dispatches on the corner of the same table, looked up and asked, How do you spell "chaos?" I spelled the word letter by letter c-h-a-o-s. He thanked me, and observed, smiling, that, by a singular lapse of memory, he often forgot the spelling of the most familiar words. . . .

I immediately took leave and started back to general head-quarters. The road was now lined with wagons, stragglers, and droves of cattle, all moving northward. From time to time at long intervals the cannon sounded, but no heavy firing yet. Arrived at Bull Run I found our camp broken up; but meeting with Lieutenant-Colonel Myers I was informed that the enemy had developed in great force near Centreville, and I must seek the General in that direction. Riding rapidly forward I found the General and Staff grouped around a house on the heights of Centreville, observing a fight which was going on some five or six miles distant in the direction of the old Bull Run battlefield. The fight was evidently thickening and extending, as could be seen by the white cumulus clouds hanging over the batteries, and the long lines of thinner smoke rising above the tree-tops.

We could furthermore see the moving dust-clouds, indicating the march of supporting columns all converging toward the centre of action. The line of the Bull Run Mountains was visible beyond and from Thoroughfare Gap, which appeared to the right of the battle-cloud. We could see the dust and reciprocal artillery-fire of our retreating and the enemy's advancing forces. Between eleven and twelve o'clock I was standing with Colonel Beckwith and commenting on these movements, when I learned that this was probably Longstreet's command forcing back Ricketts's Division from the Gap, which he had attempted to hold. I was afterward informed it was an artillery duel between the cavalry forces of Stuart and Buford. . . .

As we approached the field the pounding of the guns was tremendous, but as we were ascending the last hill that rose between us and the magnificent drama, and just beginning to snuff the sulphurous breath of battle, a Staff officer from Sigel (I think) rode up to General Pope and reported that the ammunition was failing. Immediately the General turned to me: "Captain, ride back to Centreville and hurry up all the ammunition you can find there!" I felt for a moment disgusted and mutinous, but I could not dispute the importance of my mission, so I sullenly drew rein and galloped back over the hot and dusty road. Amidst the vast accumulation of vehicles and baggage-trains at Centreville I should have had great difficulty in finding the wagons I was in search of, had I not fortunately fallen in with Lieutenant-Colonel Myers, of M'Dowell's Corps, who seemed to be always on hand in an emergency. With his assistance in a marvelously short time I got between twenty-five and thirty wagons started in the proper direction: and then, by his invitation, stopped to swallow a cup of coffee and a hasty lunch. Observing a considerable body of well-equipped troops lying here apparently idle, I expressed astonishment, and inquired the cause of it. The answer was expressed evasively, but with some bitterness: "There are officers here to-day who would be doing themselves far more credit by marching to the battle-field than by lying idle and exciting disaffection by doubts, sneering criticism, and open abuse of the Commander-in-Chief."

I followed my wagons until I had got them clear of Centreville and in a full trot down the turnpike; I then dug spurs into my mare's flanks, and in the shortest time possible returned to the great centre of interest. I found the General and Staff grouped around a large pine-tree which stood solitary on the crest of an open hill, overlooking our whole line of battle. The summit immediately in our front was occupied by a line of batteries, some thirty or forty pieces, blazing and fuming like furnaces. Behind these a fine brigade of Reno's command lay resting on their arms. To their right stood Heintzelman, with the divisions of Hooker and Kearney, whose musketry kept up a continuous roar. Supporting the left of this line of guns was Sigel, also sharply engaged with small-arms. On an open bluff still further to the left, and on the opposite side of the valley traversed by the Warrenton turnpike, lay Schenck's Division, which had been a good deal cut up, and was not actively engaged at this moment. The dry grass which covered the hill he occupied had taken fire, and was burning rapidly, occasionally obscuring that portion of the field with its smoke. Beyond him, on the extreme left of our line, General Reynolds, with the Pennsylvania Reserves, lay masked from the enemy by a wood. The enemy's position can only be known by the smoke of his guns, for all his troops and batteries are concealed by the wood. He occupies strong lines on a plateau and along an unfinished railroad embankment, which is equal to a regularly intrenched line. He fights stubbornly, and has thus far resisted all our efforts to dislodge him. The General relies on the advance of M'Dowell and Porter to crush him, and we are in momentary expectation of hearing their guns. The shot and shells of the enemy directed at the batteries in our front render this position rather uncomfortable, as they are continually screeching over our heads, or plowing the gravelly surface with an ugly rasping whir, that makes one's flesh creep. . . .

Our efforts to carry the wood in front having thus far failed, I was sent to General Reno with orders that he should throw forward the division lying in reserve to support the attack of Heintzelman's troops. The order was promptly and gallantly executed, the troops moving in beautiful order and with admirable spirit. I accompanied the advance until they passed our guns beyond the summit, and remained there admiring until the troops, moving down a fine open slope, reached the edge of the wood. The enemy was pelting away industriously from his wooded strong-hold, and the air was lively with singing bullets. For half an hour or more the roar of musketry was unceasing. At length Reno in person reported to the General, and stated that he had failed to carry the wood. Simultaneously with his return our position was so sharply raked with shot and shell that the General withdrew a short distance to the right, establishing himself on the verge of a wood. . . .

It was now about four o'clock when General Phil Kearney came in and received orders to attack and carry the disputed position at all hazards. He rode off promising to do so. While he was forming his troops for the advance it was thought necessary to pound the position with artillery. Reno, who was riding beside the Commanding General, remarked, "The wood is filled with the wounded of both armies." The Commander replied, "And yet the safety of this army and the nation demands their sacrifice, and the lives of thousands yet unwounded." After a moment's hesitation the necessity of the order was acquiesced in, and forty guns were opened upon the fatal wood. The artillerymen worked with a fiendish activity, and the sulphurous clouds which hung over the field were tinged with a hot coppery hue by the rays of the declining sun. Meanwhile Kearney had gone in, and the incessant roar of musketry resembled the noise of a cataract.

An hour later Kearney again appeared, and informed the General that the coveted position was carried. I stood beside him as he gave in his report, and while elated with the tidings he communicated, admired the man as the finest specimen of the fighting soldier I had ever seen. With his small head surmounted by the regulation forage-cap, his thin face with its energetic beck, his colorless eyes, glaring as it were with a white heat, his erect figure with the empty coat-sleeve pinned across his breast, down to the very point of his sabre, whose ragged leathern scabbard stuck out like a gaff, he looked the game-cock all over. His very voice had the resolute guttural cluck which characterizes that gallant fowl. . . .

Meanwhile M'Dowell in person arrived on the field, and reported the approach of his command. It is a relief to see him here, although it is too late for him to accomplish any thing decisive. While exchanging greetings with me M'Dowell looked toward the west, where the radiance of a rich golden sunset was breaking through the grim battle-clouds, illuminating the mingled glories and horrors of the hard-fought field. "Look," said he, "what a dramatic and magnificent picture! How tame are all Vernet's boasted battle-pieces in comparison with such a scene as this! Indeed, if an artist could successfully represent that effect it would be criticised as unreal and extravagant."

I warmed toward a man who amidst the dangers and responsibilities of the occasion could mark its passing beauties and sublimities. At this point the two Generals, with their aids and escort, rode to the front to inspect the situation. . . . The battery was still working rapidly, and the enemy fighting back with equal spirit, when one of the guns burst, throwing off a heavy fragment of the muzzle, which described an arc immediately over the heads of the line of officers and fell with a thud, just clearing the last man and horse; two feet lower and it would have swept off the whole party. I had remarked since we came over that the ammunition used seemed miserably and dangerously defective; nearly all the shells bursting prematurely, and several so close to the muzzles of the pieces as to endanger the artillerymen. . . .

We remained on this hill until after sunset, when the firing gradually ceased. When it became quite dark there was a beautiful pyrotechnical display about a mile distant on our left, and near the Warrenton turnpike, occasioned by a collision of King's Division of M'Dowell's Corps with the enemy's right. The sparkling lines of musketry shone in the darkness like fire-flies in a meadow, while the more brilliant flashes of artillery might have been mistaken for swamp meteors. This show continued for an hour, the advancing and receding fires indicating distinctly the surging of the battle tide; and all this time not the slightest sound either of small-arms or artillery was perceptible. It seemed at length that the fire of the enemy's line began to extend and thicken, while ours wavered and fell back, but still continued the contest. Between eight and nine o'clock it ceased entirely, and we returned to our head-quarters station, where we picketed our horses and prepared to pass the night beside a camp-fire.

—STROTHER, "Personal Recollections of the War"

4. GENERAL GREGG EXHORTS HIS MEN TO DIE IN THEIR TRACKS

Perhaps the hottest fighting of the twenty-ninth came on the extreme left of the Confederate line where Gregg's South Carolinians held a little knoll commanding the Sudley Springs road. If the Federals succeeded in overrunning this point they could turn Jackson's flank and roll him up in defeat. All afternoon Kearny hurled his men against Gregg's thin line; when Hill inquired whether he could hold out he made the famous answer that his ammunition was almost gone but he could hold with the bayonet.

Edward McCrady, who tells the story of Gregg's brigade, was a lieuten-

ant colonel of the 1st South Carolina Volunteers who later distinguished himself as the historian of his state.

TEN hours of actual conflict had exhausted all the romance of the battle. It was business; it was work, wearisome work, in the face of death we were doing. Our feet were worn and weary, and our arms were nerveless. Our ears were deadened with the continuous roar of the battle, and our eyes were dimmed with the smoke. Ah! we too needed rest. The rest Schurz's men were having yonder, over the hill in their rear. But Kearney was pitiless. It mattered not to him that we were tired, and that our ammunition was gone. On, on he came, pouring into us his deadly volleys, and then the rush. Our men fell fast around us. The Thirteenth and the First after having held our position all day, at last were pushed back. The enemy pressed on, crossed the cut, and slowly but steadily compelled us, step by step, to yield the long coveted position—the position, on the extreme left, a little in advance of Hill's line, with which, early in the morning, our brigade had been entrusted, and which we had maintained all day. But we would not give it up without a desperate struggle. Now again the same hand to hand fight we had with Grover, we renewed with Kearney—we were not, however, entirely without help. General Branch came to our assistance with one of his regiments, and, literally, with coat off, personally took part in the affray. With his aid we made a stand on the top of the knoll, and there, over the bodies of our dead and wounded comrades, we struggled on. On our left, too, the Rifles were still contending for the cornfield, and there that gallant soldier, Colonel J. Foster Marshall, and his Lieutenant-Colonel, D. A. Leadbetter, were both killed, with many other good men of that devoted regiment, but the enemy attacking them was again repulsed, and those who had pressed the rest of us back to the top of the hill, now hesitated and commenced to yield. We pressed them in our turn. They broke and fell back in disorder.

I recollect that as they did so, they left a mule which, notwithstanding all the turmoil, was quietly cropping a green blade, here and there, in the blood-stained grass around him. His singular appearance attracted our attention even in that terrible moment, and I was looking at him, wondering, when some one exclaimed, "Why, he has a mountain howitzer behind him!" Sure enough, there it was. Amidst the roar of musketry and the din of arms we had not noticed this instrument of destruction which, in a few yards of us, had been mowing down our men with canister. Probably it was one of the same that Sigel had sent to Krzyzanowski and which Gordon tells us were "happily placed" in his skirmish line in the first attack in the morning.

But Stevens, who was supporting Kearney, was on hand to make one more last effort of the day. We heard the cheers of his men as he ordered them in—telling us that our work was not yet done.

It was at this time that an officer rode up to Gregg, with a message from General Hill, asking if he could hold the position any longer; and then was his famous reply, that his ammunition was exhausted, but "he thought he could still hold his position with the bayonet."

And this was absolutely true. The ammunition we had carried into action had been expended for some time; and it was one of the cruelties of our position, that before the Infirmary corps were allowed to help a wounded man, before his wound was looked at, he must be stripped of his accoutrements, and his ammunition distributed among his comrades. This economy, and the ammunition we got from the dead and wounded of our assailants, had enabled us to carry on the fight.

I have always wished that the scene which followed General Gregg's message could be painted by some great artist able to do it justice. Having sent word to Hill that he had no ammunition, but would hold the position with the bayonet, General Gregg drew up the remnants of his five regiments, now reduced to a mere handful in two lines, the Twelfth, Thirteenth and Fourteenth in one line, in front, under Lieutenant-Colonel Simpson, of the Fourteenth, and the First and Rifles under my command, as a second line, behind the First. All the other field officers, except Lieutenant-Colonel Jones, of the Twelfth, had by this time been killed or wounded. We were upon the top of the hill, the point to which we had been driven back by Kearney, some two or three hundred yards from the railroad excavation. Here General Gregg formed us to await the assault of the enemy, whose cheers we heard as they were ordered forward.

I can see him now, as with his drawn sword, that old Revolutionary scimitar we all knew so well, he walked up and down the line, and hear him as he appealed to us to stand by him and die there. "Let us die here, my men, let us die here." And I do not think that I exaggerate when I say that our little band responded to his appeal, and were ready to die, at bay, there if necessary.

The moment was, indeed, a trying one—a trying one to men who had shown themselves no cowards that day. We could hear the enemy advancing, and had not a round with which to greet them, but must wait the onslaught with only our bayonets. On they came. They had nearly reached the railroad, and were about to cross to the charge when a shout behind paralyzed us with dread. Was all the glorious fight we had made that livelong day to end in our capture by an unseen movement to our rear? Terror stricken we turned, when lo! there were our friends coming to our assistance, and not the enemy to our attack. Field, with his Virginians, and Pender, with his North Carolinians, relieved by Early and Forno, of Ewell's division, came rushing up, comparatively fresh for the work, and cheering us as they advanced on either side of our little band, waited not the assault, as we were doing perforce, but with a wild Confederate yell, rushed upon Stevens as he was in the confusion of crossing to our attack. The Federals halted, turned and fled, our friends crossing the railroad and pursuing them.

—McCrady, "Gregg's Brigade in the Second Battle of Manassas"

5. LONGSTREET OVERWHELMS POPE AT MANASSAS

Both Jackson and Pope were exhausted on the evening of the twenty-
ninth. Jackson, however, knew that Longstreet was at hand; Pope merely

hoped that Franklin and Sumner were on the way from Alexandria. But Pope had deluded himself that Jackson was whipped and in full retreat, he had finally brought up Porter's corps, and he refused to credit the information that Longstreet was through Thoroughfare Gap and on the battlefield. He therefore determined to renew the fight the next day. Later he gave a somewhat different explanation. "I felt it my duty," he said, "notwithstanding the desperate condition of my command from great fatigue, from want of provisions and forage, and from the small hope I had of any effective assistance from Alexandria, to hold my position at all hazards and under all privations." The battle was renewed early on the afternoon of the thirtieth, Porter assaulting Jackson furiously. Just when this fighting was at its height Longstreet, whose forces were stretched out at almost a right angle to Jackson's, moved forward with his whole line and overwhelmed Porter and Reynolds.

The story is told here by Alexander Hunter, a private in the 17th Virginia—part of Hood's division. That division had made an initial thrust at the Federal lines on the night of the twenty-ninth, and on the thirtieth it led the attack.

THE rapid pounding of the artillery caused us to hurry through the morning meal, almost before the sun rose above the hill, and we pushed for Thoroughfare Gap to rejoin the regiment. We knew by instinct that there would be a battle that day; for there was blood upon the moon. . . . Never had life seemed more worth living than on a morning such as this; never existence sweeter; never Death so loath the dying.

Long streams of soldiers were wending their way to the front. The troops seemed everywhere; they filled the railroad track as far as the eye could reach; they emerged from the narrow gap in the mountain and spread out over the fields and meadows; they wound along the base of the hills, and marched in a steady tramp over the dusty highways; following a dozen different routes, but each face turned directly or obliquely northward. Ordnance wagons were being pushed rapidly ahead; batteries were taking position, staff officers were riding at a gallop, as if seconds and minutes were golden. In short, all fighting material was pushing to the van and all the peacefully inclined were valiantly seeking the rear. By a law as fixed as that which bound the Stoics, as unalterable as those which govern the affinities of the chemical world, this separation of the two types ever occurred on the eve of battle. An instant sifting of wheat from the tares took place quietly but surely in every company, and the mass of men so lately mingled became as incapable of mixture as oil and water.

The great receding tide at full ebb sank back toward the Gap; the mighty army of the backsliders whom naught could hinder, non-combatants, camp darkies, shirking soldiers playing possum, and camp followers. Warm work was expected and all this genus, like war-horses, "sniffed danger from afar." . . .

It was this crowd belonging to the wagon-train or detailed for work such as blacksmithing, using every artifice to avoid the marching and fighting, which hung on the army like barnacles on a staunch ship's bottom, impeding its course and weighting it down. It was the impedimenta that flocked to the battle-field as soon as the shot and shell ceased firing, and despoiled and stripped friend and foe alike, dead or wounded, it mattered not, though they never killed or illtreated the injured or maimed.

Reaching the Gap we found that the brigade had passed through. Fol-

A. J. Volck

Prayer in Stonewall Jackson's Camp

Alonzo Chappel

The Fight at Burnside's Bridge, Antietam

lowing hard upon the track, our little squad after an hour's march caught up and took its place in rank.

The men were in a fearful humor, grumbling at their luck and cursing the commissary. They had ample cause; not a single ration had been issued to the troops for several days and the soldiers were savage from hunger. . . .

The forenoon had passed and the sound of hostile cannon was breaking the silence in our front while a battle was being fought on our left. . . .

"Fall in!" the officers shouted, and the men sprang to their feet, the line was dressed, and the brigade headed to the front to take position. On the way we were halted, and every soldier was compelled to strip for the fight by discarding his blanket,—if he had one, which was not often—oilcloth or overcoat. All these were deposited in a large pile, and guards set over them, looking very much as if we did not intend to retreat. Cartridge-boxes were filled with forty rounds, and in our haversacks we carried twenty more, making sixty rounds per man.

Soon the crack of the skirmisher's rifles were heard, then the artillery opened, and the purple-colored smoke drifted like mist from lowland marshes, across the valley.

"Forward! Guide to the colors! March!"

Across that level plateau the First Brigade moved, the flower of Virginia in its ranks, the warm blood rushing in its veins as it did in warrior ancestors centuries ago. It was a glorious and magnificent display, the line keeping perfect time, the colors showing red against the azure sky. There was no cheering, only the rattling of the equipments and the steady footfalls of the men who trod the earth with regular beat. As the brigade swept across the plain it was stopped by a high Virginia snake fence; hundreds of willing hands caught the rails, tossed them aside, and then instinctively touching each other's elbows, the ranks were dressed as if by magic.

The first shell now shrieked over us. Another burst not ten feet from the ground directly over the heads of our forces. The long chain kept intact, though close to the spot where the explosion occurred; the links vibrated and oscillated for a moment, then grew firm again and pressed onward.

How the shells rained upon us now; a Yankee six-gun battery, on a hill about half a mile off, turned its undivided attention upon us and essayed to shatter the advancing line. It did knock a gap here and there, but the break was mended almost as soon as broken, and the living wall kept on. Shells were bursting everywhere, until it seemed as if we were walking on torpedoes. They crackled, split and exploded all around, throwing dirt and ejecting little spirts of smoke that for a moment dimmed the sky.

Colonel Marye dismounted, drew his sword from the scabbard, and looking the beau ideal of a splendid soldier, placed himself at the head of his men. He stopped for a moment and pointed his sword with an eloquent and vivid gesture toward the battery on the hill. A cheer answered him, and the line instinctively quickened its pace. Though the shells were tearing through the ranks, the men did not falter. One man's resonant voice was sounding above the din, exercising a magical influence; one man's figure strode on in front and where he led, his men kept close behind. We followed unwaveringly our colonel over the hill, down the declivity, up the slope, straight across the plain toward the battery, with even ranks, though the balls were tearing a way through flesh and blood. The brigade stretched out for several hundred yards, forming, as they marched, a bow with concave toward the enemy. The Seventeenth was on the right of the line, and the other regiments dressed by our colors as we bore right oblique toward the battery, which was now hidden by a volleying fume that settled upon the crest.

Still the advance was not stayed nor the ranks broken. We neared the Chinn House, when suddenly a long line of the enemy rose from behind an old stone wall and poured straight in our breasts a withering volley at point-blank distance. It was so unexpected, this attack, that it struck the long line of men like an electric shock. Many were falling killed or wounded, and but for the intrepid coolness of its colonel, the Seventeenth would have retired from the field in disorder. His clear, ringing voice was heard, and the wavering line reformed. A rattling volley answered the foe, and for a minute or two the contest was fiercely waged. Then the colonel fell with his knee frightfully shattered by a Minie-ball. Once down, the calm, reassuring tones heard no longer, the line broke. Now individual bravery made up for the disaster. The officers surged ahead with their swords waving in the air, cheering on the men, who kept close to their heels, loading and firing as they ran. The line of blue was not fifty yards distant and every man took a sure, close aim before his finger pressed the trigger. It was a decisive fight of about ten minutes, and both sides stood up gamely to their work. Our foes were a Western regiment from Ohio, who gave and received and asked no odds. The left of our brigade having struck the enemy's right and doubled it up, now sent one volley into their flank.

In a moment the blue line quivered and then went to pieces. Officers and men broke for the rear, one regimental colors captured by Jim Coleman, of the Seventeenth. In a few moments there were none left except the dead and wounded.

There was hardly a breathing spell, only time indeed to take a full draught from the canteen, transfer the cartridges from the haversacks to the cartridge-box, and the enemy was upon us with a fresh line.

We were now loading and firing at the swiftly approaching enemy, who were about two hundred yards distant, advancing straight towards us and shouting with their steady hurrah, so different from the Rebel yell. It was a trying moment and proved the metal of the individual man. Some ran, or white with fear cowered behind the Chinn House, while others hid in a long gulley near by; others yet stood in an irregular form and loaded and fired, unmindful of the dust and noise of the hurtling shell and screaming shot. . . .

The brigade was scattered everywhere now. For an hour they had fired as fast as the cartridges could be rammed home. When the Union troops came up to retake the Chinn House, our men began to give ground. On came the Yankees in splendid style, with the Stars and Stripes waving and their line capitally dressed. It was a perfect advance, and some of us forgot to fire our muskets while watching them. In their front line was a little drummer beating a *pas de charge*, the only time we ever heard the inspiriting sound on the battle-field. The dauntless little fellow was handling his sticks lustily, too, for the roll of the drum was heard above the noise of the guns.

It was high time to be leaving, we thought, and now our men were turning to fire one good shot before heeling it to the rear, when right behind us there came with a rush and a vim a fresh Rebel brigade aiming straight for the Yankees. They ran over us and we joined their lines. Not a shot was fired by them in response to the fusilade of musketry that was raining lead all around. Every man with his head bent sideways and down, like people breasting a hailstorm, for soldiers always charge so, and the Gray and the Blue met with a mighty shock. A tremendous sheet of flame burst from our line; the weaker side went to the ground in a flash, and with a wild yell the Gray swept on toward the six-gun battery that had been sending forth a stream of death for the past hour. We could only see the flashes of light through the dense smoke.

The line stopped a moment at the foot of the hill to allow itself to catch up. It was late in the evening and the battle was raging in all its deadliest fury. On our right, on our left, in the front, in the rear, from all directions came the warring sound of cannon and musketry. We could see nothing but smoke, breathe nothing except the fumes of burning powder, feel nothing save the earth jarred by the concussion of the guns, hear nothing but the dire, tremendous clamor and blare of sound swelling up into a vast volume of fire. How hot it was! The clothes damp with perspiration, the canteens empty, throats parched with thirst, faces blackened by powder, the men mad with excitement.

The left of the line came up and then some one asked:

"Whose brigade is this?"

"Hood's," was the answer.

Then burst a ringing cry, "Forward, Texans!"

The line sprang like a tightly-bent bow suddenly loosened, and rushed up the hill in a wild, eager dash—a frenzied, maddening onset up the hill through the smoke, nearer and nearer to the guns.

When about a hundred yards from them the dense veil lifted, floated upward and softly aside, and discovered to us that the battery had ceased firing. We could see the muzzles of the guns, their sullen black mouths pointing at us, and behind them the gunners, while from the center of the battery was a flag that lay drooping upon its staff. It was for a second only, like the rising of the curtain for a moment on a hideous tableau, only to be dropped as the eye took in the scene in all its horrors, yet it impressed itself, that vivid picture, brief as it was, upon mind, heart and brain.

At once came a noise like a thunder shock, that seemed as if an earthquake had riven the place. The ground trembled with the concussion. The appalling sound was heard of iron grapeshot tearing its way through space and through bodies of bone, flesh and blood.

Mercifully for us, but not intended by our foes, the guns were elevated too high, or it would have been simply annihilation; for when those six guns poured their volley into the charging lines they were loaded to the muzzle with grape, and the distance was only about pistol shot. Of course the execution was fearful, and for a second the line was stupefied and nearly senseless from the blow. The ground was covered with victims and the screams of the wounded rose high above the din and were awful to hear.

The advance was not stayed long.

"Forward, boys! Don't stop now! Forward, Texans!" and with a cry from every throat the Southerners kept on, officers and men together without form or order, the swiftest runners ahead, the slowest behind, 'tis true, but struggling desperately to better their time. Up! Still up! until we reached the crest! As the Yankees pulled the lanyards of the loaded pieces our men were among them. A terrific shock. A lane of dead in front. Those standing before the muzzles were blown to pieces like captured Sepoy rebels. I had my hand on the wheel of one cannon just as it fired, and I fell like one dead, from the concussion. There was a frenzied struggle in the semi-darkness around the guns, so violent and tempestuous, so mad and brain-reeling that to recall it is like fixing the memory of a horrible, blood-curdling dream. Every one was wild with uncontrollable delirium.

Then the mists dissolved and the panting, gasping soldiers could see the picture as it was. The battery had been captured by the Texans and every man at the pieces taken prisoner. Many were killed by a volley that we had poured into them when only a few paces distant, and a large proportion wounded. The few who escaped unhurt stood in a group, so blackened with powder that they ceased to look like white men. These soldiers had nobly worked their guns and had nothing to be ashamed of. All that men could do they had done. . . .

Just as the day was drawing to a close a mighty yell arose, a cry from twice ten thousand throats, as the Rebel reserves, fresh from the rear, rushed resistlessly to the front. Never did mortal eyes behold a grander sight; not even when MacDonald put his columns in motion at Wagram or Ney charged the Russian center at Borodino.

It was an extended line, reaching as far as the eye could see, crescent in form, and composed of many thousand men. It was, in fact, a greater part of Longstreet's corps. The onset was thrilling in the extreme, as the men swept grandly forward, the little battle-flags with the Southern cross in the center fluttering saucily and jauntily aloft, while the setting sun made of each bayonet and musket-barrel a literal gleam of fire that ran along the chain of steel in a scintillating flame. As they swept over the plain they took up all the scattered fighting material, and nothing was left but the wounded which had sifted through, and the dead.

Then ensued the death struggle, a last fearful grappling in mortal combat. The enemy threw forward all their reserves to meet the shock, and for the space of fifteen minutes the commotion was terrible. Bursts of sound surpassed everything that was ever heard or could be conceived. The baleful flashes of the cannon, darting out against the dusky horizon, played on the surface of the evening clouds like sharp, vivid lightning. Long lines of musketry vomited through the plain their furious volleys of pestilential lead, sweeping scores of brave soldiers into the valley of the Shadow of Death. . . .

At last the enemy staggered, wavered, broke and fled in utter rout. Where Longstreet was dealing his heavy blows, they were throwing away their knapsacks and rushing madly for the rear. Only one final stand was made by a brigade in the woods close by; but as the long gray line closed in on each flank they threw down their arms and surrendered with but few exceptions; those few, as they ran, turned and fired.

On the hill, which had been occupied by the Washington Artillery of eighteen guns in the earlier part of the day, the eye took in a dim and fast-fading yet extended view of the whole surrounding country. A vast panorama stretched out on an open plain with patches of wood here and there on its surface, and with but two or three hills in the whole range of sight to break the expanded level. It was unutterably grand. Jackson could be seen swinging his left on his right as a pivot, and Longstreet with his entire corps in the reverse method. The whole Yankee army was in retreat, and certainly nothing but darkness prevented it from becoming *une affaire flambée.*

—HUNTER, *Johnny Reb and Billy Yank*

6. STEVENS AND KEARNY ARE KILLED AT CHANTILLY

After his defeat at Bull Run Pope withdrew to Centreville, some twenty miles from Washington, where he was joined by the corps of Franklin and Sumner. Stuart swung northward, and down the Little River Turnpike, to cut his communications, and Jackson hurried on after Stuart. To meet this threat Pope sent two brigades of infantry under General Isaac Stevens toward the threatened turnpike. The opponents met at the little village of Chantilly; just as Jackson was forcing the outnumbered Federals back, Kearny arrived with his division and succeeded in stemming the enemy advance until darkness fell. The delay was purchased at a high price: both Stevens and Kearny were killed.

General Stevens had been colonel of the mutinous 79th New York; it is gratifying to find that regiment fighting so courageously at Chantilly. Kearny was one of the most romantic figures in the Union Army, and one of its most promising officers. Distinguished in appearance and in family, and distinguished, too, by his great wealth, he had early dedicated himself to a military career. He had seen service on the frontier, in Algiers, lost an arm in the Mexican War, and fought with the French army in Italy. On the outbreak of the war he was appointed brigadier general of the 1st New Jersey Brigade. His superiors admired him, his men loved him, and his death was a serious blow to the Union cause.

EARLY on the morning of September 1, a beautiful morning, Jackson moved slowly forward on the Little-River turnpike, reaching Chantilly about noon, while Longstreet was pressing forward to join him. Owing, probably, both to the extreme weariness of his troops and a desire to have Longstreet within close supporting distance, Jackson's three divisions moved from Chantilly up the turnpike slowly and well in hand. . . . The infantry moved in two columns, one on each side of the road, with the artillery in the road.

The Union army, at a terrible disadvantage in the broken-down condition of its cavalry, was unaware of the strength of the Confederate movement until nearly noon of Monday, September 1. . . .

It is probable that General Pope was informed of Jackson's flanking movement by stragglers from the late battle-field, or by some fortunate accident. . . .

At 12 o'clock Gen. Pope ordered McDowell to hasten with his corps to Fairfax Court-House, take command of the two brigades there, and occupy Germantown with his whole force, so *as to cover the turnpike from Centreville to Alexandria* (in other words, keep open his line of retreat). . . .

McDowell acted with great vigor; and, at once putting his troops in motion, hastened towards Fairfax Court-House. Fortunately meeting Gen. Patrick's brigade, . . . and who, after observations from the hill-tops, seeing no signs of the enemy, were on the return march to Centreville, Gen. McDowell at once diverted them into the old intrenchments across the Little-River turnpike near Germantown. This brigade was posted with two guns bearing upon the turnpike before 4 o'clock in the afternoon, just in time, in conjunction with some of Buford's cavalry and Gen. Ricketts's (Second) division of the Third Corps, to receive and repulse Stuart's cavalry. . . .

To aid in securing time to get his army to the new position near Fairfax Court-House, Gen. Pope, early in the afternoon, sent Reno's command . . . (which was then under Gen. Stevens's command, as Gen. Reno, commander of the Second Division and the ranking officer, was sick and off active duty) to march at once across the fields to the Little-River turnpike, take a position across it, and hold in check a Confederate force said to be advancing by that road towards Fairfax Court-House. These men were under orders to accompany Gen. Stevens as guides on the march, and did so. As they rode with Capt. Stevens, in advance of the division, they informed him that, while foraging down the Little-River pike that morning, they had seen a large body of Confederate infantry moving east, had ridden back at once and informed Gen. Pope, and had then been directed by him to guide Gen. Stevens to a point on the turnpike some distance in advance of the place where they had noticed the head of the Confederate column.

Getting his command under arms with all possible haste Gen. Stevens moved rapidly towards the indicated point, his division (the First) having the lead, followed shortly by the Second Brigade of the Second (Reno's) Division. . . .

Meanwhile, Stevens's approach having been noticed, Jackson was hurrying Branch's and Brockenbrough's brigades into position to strike him.

Gen. Stevens, who was watching the development of affairs from a wooded knoll near the old railroad, as his skirmishers began to come in set to work to throw his division of six regiments into a column of attack. . . .

General Stevens had formed his men for the attack with great rapidity, and his column was ready to move as soon as his skirmishers had come in. At about half-past 4 o'clock he gave the order to advance, first sending Capt. Belcher, provost-marshal on the division staff, back to the Warrenton pike, to report that his division was engaged with a heavy force of the enemy, and must have support, with orders to give the message to Gen. Pope, if he could find him at once, if not, to every corps and division commander that he could find until support was furnished.

Dismounting from his horse the General had taken post in the centre of the charging column, and, to aid in holding the men to their work and driving the charge home with all possible vigor, had assigned a member of his staff to each of his regiments; his Adjutant-General (his son, Capt. Hazard Stevens) being assigned to the Seventy-ninth New York, of which regiment the General had formerly been Colonel. The column moved forward across the open land, with the left skirting through the cornfield, some hundreds of yards, steadily and in silence, without a shot being fired, until they came to within 75 yards of a rail fence on the edge of the woods bordering the fields; then, from Branch's brigade of five North Carolina and Brocken-brough's of three Virginia regiments, a terrific fire of musketry was opened from the cover of the fence, and the Seventy-ninth and Twenty-eighth, suffering terribly, came to a halt.

To be checked there in the open ground was to be lost; the colors of the Seventy-ninth were down, and the column wavered. Passing by his son, who had fallen wounded in the hip and arm, Gen. Stevens seized the flag of the Seventy-ninth, and ran in front of the column, shouting, "Follow me, my Highlanders!" The wavering column moved on again with resistless force; surging up to the fence, they threw it over and gained the edge of the woods, breaking Branch's brigade, and forcing back Brockenbrough; but Gen. Stevens, their devoted leader, was now lying dead upon the broken fence, a rebel bullet through his brain, with the colors of his Highlanders still held firmly in his grasp. . . .

The rain had now ceased, and, although it could hardly have been later than half-past 6 o'clock in the evening, the atmosphere was thick, and the sky still so heavily overcast, that night coming on prematurely made it impossible to distinguish any object clearly more than a few rods away. As the shattered Twenty-first Massachusetts regiment emerged from the woods, Gen. Kearny, who had just arrived upon the field, and was searching for troops to cover Birney's right flank, rode full upon us, and in fierce haste ordered the regiment to move on the run to take post on Birney's right, the position of whose line was indicated only by the flashes of their muskets.

When Gen. Kearny came upon us there was hardly a musket in our line that could be fired, as our disastrous fight in the woods had occurred in the midst of the terrific thunder-storm which had soon rendered the guns unserviceable. The officer in command of the regiment at the time begged the General to allow them a few moments to draw the wet charges from the guns, but was refused, with a hot sneer at our cowardice, and the threat that unless the regiment moved instantly, as ordered, he would turn a battery upon us, emphasizing his threat by riding from us directly towards Randolph's battery, posted a few rods in our rear, and which was then firing with solid shot (its only ammunition) into the woods across the cornfield. The General, fearful for Birney's right, and perhaps, also, somewhat unduly excited by the reply provoked by his imputation upon the valor of the regiment, at once sent an officer from the battery to us, with his compliments, coupled with the assurance that it would play upon us unless the order given was instantly obeyed.

Luckily two of our companies, which had been detached in the woods to cover our flanks, had escaped the ambuscade into which the others had fallen, and had now joined us with serviceable guns, and the regiment, about two hundred strong, moved across the open ground towards the cornfield and the front of Birney's right, deploying a thin skirmish line to cover our right and front as we advanced.

As our skirmishers came up to the rail fence of the cornfield they were fired on by Thomas's skirmishers, whose brigade, with two of Pender's regiments, was in the cornfield and coming from the woods, well on Birney's right. Crossing the line of the fence we soon halted in the corn, under a dropping fire from the enemy.

Gen. Kearny was following us up closely, and as we came to a halt fiercely tried to force us forward, saying that we were firing on our own men, and that there were no rebels near us. We had the proof in two prisoners—an officer and private of a Georgia regiment—brought in by our skirmishers, beside the warning cries of "Surrender!" coming both from our right and front; but, unfortunately, Kearny's judgment seemed unable to appreciate the existence of the peril which his military instinct had caused him to guard against. Lieut. Walcott, of the brigade staff, took our prisoners to him, saying, "General, if you don't believe there are rebels in the corn, here are two prisoners from the Forty-ninth Georgia, just taken in our front."

Crying out fiercely, "—— —— you and your prisoners!" the General, entirely alone, apparently in uncontrollable rage at our disregard of his peremptory orders to advance, forced his horse through the deep, sticky mud of the cornfield past the left of the regiment, passing within a few feet of where I was standing. I watched him moving in the murky twilight through the corn, and, when less than twenty yards away, saw his horse suddenly rear and turn, and half-a-dozen muskets flash around him: so died the intrepid soldier, Gen. Philip Kearny!

—GENERAL CHARLES F. WALCOTT, "The Battle of Chantilly"

7. "LITTLE MAC" IS REAPPOINTED TO COMMAND

Pretty clearly neither the army nor public opinion would tolerate Pope after the fiasco of Second Bull Run. On September 5 Lincoln relieved him of command and, over vigorous opposition from his Cabinet, reappointed McClellan to command of the now reunited Army of the Potomac.

McClellan is the most controversial military figure of the Civil War and, after ninety years, the controversy still rages. Lee was supposed to have characterized him as the ablest of his opponents, but it is highly doubtful that he ever did so, and if he did the characterization was palpable nonsense. That McClellan was an able organizer, a close student of war, and beloved by his troops, few will deny. On the other hand his timidity, vacillation, procrastination and sensitiveness, his persecution mania, his arrogance toward Lincoln, and his monumental egotism, suggest a psychopathic personality. To an almost total want of real military ability he united a vaulting ambition; discredited on the field of battle he sought compensation in politics, and his career is a standing warning against the mixture of the military and the civil.

The three following selections present varying views of McClellan. The first is from the acid but honest pen of Gideon Welles; the second from General Sherman; and the third the same Norton whose account of the Seven Days fighting we have already read. It is important to note the dates of the observations. Welles wrote just after Pope's debacle and just before McClellan was reappointed to command; Sherman two years after McClellan's final dismissal; Norton at the height of McClellan's popularity.

A. "To Fight Is Not His Forte"

September 3, 1862

McClellan is an intelligent engineer and officer, but not a commander to lead a great army in the field. To attack or advance with energy and power is not in him; to fight is not his forte. I sometimes fear his heart is not earnest in the cause; yet I do not entertain the thought that he is unfaithful. The study of military operations interests and amuses him. It flatters him to have on his staff French princes and men of wealth and position; he likes show, parade, and power. Wishes to outgeneral the Rebels, but not to kill and destroy them. In a conversation which I had with him in May last at Cumberland on the Pamunkey, he said he desired of all things to capture Charleston; he would demolish and annihilate the city. He detested, he said, both South Carolina and Massachusetts, and should rejoice to see both States extinguished. Both were and always had been ultra and mischievous, and he could not tell which he hated most. These were the remarks of the General-in-Chief at the head of our armies then in the field, and when as large a proportion of his troops were from Massachusetts as from any State in the Union. . . .

I cannot relieve my mind from the belief that to him, in a great degree, and to his example, influence, and conduct, are to be attributed some portion of our late reverses, more than to any other person on either side. His reluctance to move or to have others move, his inactivity, his detention of Franklin, his omission to send forward supplies unless Pope would send a cavalry escort from the battle-field, and the tone of his conversation and dispatches, all show a moody state of feeling. The slight upon him and the generals associated with him, in the selection of Pope, was injudicious, impolitic, wrong perhaps, but is no justification for their withholding one tithe of strength in a great emergency, where the lives of their countrymen and the welfare of the country were in danger. The soldiers whom McClellan has commanded are doubtless attached to him. They have been trained to it, and he has kindly cared for them while under him. With partiality for him they have imbibed his prejudices, and some of the officers have, I fear, a spirit more factious and personal than patriotic.

—*Diary of Gideon Welles*

B. General Sherman Explains Why He Cannot Like McClellan

To his wife.*

Gaylesville, Ala., October 27, 1864

You ask my opinion of McClellan. I have been much amused at similar inquiries of John and others in answer to a news paragraph that I pledged ninety-nine votes of the hundred to McClellan. Of course this is the invention of some knave. I never said such thing. I will vote for nobody, because I am not entitled to vote. Of the two, with the inferences to be drawn at home and abroad, I would prefer Lincoln, though I know that McClellan, Vallandigham or even Jeff Davis if President of the U. S. would prosecute the war, and no one with more vigor than the latter.

But at the time the howl was raised against McClellan I knew it was in a measure unjust, for he was charged with delinquencies that the American people are chargeable for. Thus, how unjust to blame me for any misfortune now when all the authorities and people are conspiring to break up the Army till the election is over. Our armies vanish before our eyes and it is useless to complain because the election is more important than the war. Our armies are merely paper armies. I have 40,000 Cavalry on paper but less than 5,000 in fact. A like measure runs through the whole, and so it was with McClellan. He had to fight partly with figures.

Still I admit he never manifested the simple courage and manliness of Grant, and he had too much staff, too many toadies, and looked too much to No. 1. When I was in Kentucky he would not heed my counsels, and never wrote me once, but since I have gained some notoriety at Atlanta and the papers announced, as usually falsely, that I was for him, he has written me twice and that has depreciated him more in my estimation than all else. He cannot be elected. Mr. Lincoln will be, but I hope it will be done quick, that voters may come to their regiments and not give the Rebels the advantage they know so well to take.

I believe McClellan to be an honest man as to money, of good habits, decent, and of far more than average intelligence, and therefore I never have joined in the hue and cry against him. In revolutions men fall and rise. Long before this war is over, much as you hear me praised now, you may hear me

* Reprinted from *Home Letters of General Sherman* edited by M. A. De Wolfe Howe; copyright 1909 by Charles Scribner's Sons, 1937 by M. A. De Wolfe Howe; used by permission of the publishers.

cursed and insulted. Read history, read Coriolanus, and you will see the true measure of popular applause. Grant, Sheridan and I are now the popular favorites, but neither of us will survive this war. Some other must rise greater than either of us, and he has not yet manifested himself.

—Howe, ed., *Home Letters of General Sherman*

C. "Little Mac's A-Coming"

Harrison's Landing, James River, Va., Sunday, July 13, 1862
Dear Brother and Sister:—

We had a review by moonlight a few nights ago. "Old Abe" was down here to see the army, and he did not get round to us till 9 o'clock at night, but it was beautiful moonlight, and as he went galloping past, riding beside "Little Mac," everyone could tell him by his "stovepipe hat" and his unmilitary acknowledgment of the cheers which everywhere greeted him. His riding I can compare to nothing else than a pair of tongs on a chair back, but notwithstanding his grotesque appearance, he has the respect of the army.

But the man in the army is "Little Mac." No general could ask for greater love and more unbounded confidence than he receives from his men, and the confidence is mutual. He feels that he has an army he can depend on to do all that the same number of men can do anywhere. He is everywhere among "his boys," as he calls them, and everywhere he is received with the most unbounded enthusiasm.

He was here yesterday about noon. The boys were getting dinner or lounging about under the trees, smoking, reading or writing, when we heard a roar of distant cheers away down the road a mile or more. "Little Mac's a-coming" was on every tongue. "Turn out the guard—General McClellan," called the sentry on the road. The guard paraded and the men flocked to the roadside. He came riding along on his "Dan Webster," by the way as splendid a horse as you ever saw. He rode slowly, looking as jovial and hearty as if he could not be more happy. Up go the caps, and three rousing cheers that make the old woods ring, greet the beloved leader of the Army of the Potomac. He raises his cap in graceful acknowledgement of the compliment, and so he passes along. Those cheers always give notice of his approach. He speaks an occasional encouraging word, and the men return to their occupations more and more devoted to the flag and their leader.

But what have they to say to the men who have been using their influence to prevent his being reinforced, to secure his defeat, and in some way to so prolong the war as to make the abolition of slavery a military necessity? Curses loud and deep are heaped on such men. Old Greeley would not live twenty-four hours if he should come here among the army. I used to be something of an abolitionist myself, but I've got so lately that I don't believe it is policy to sacrifice everything to the nigger. Such a policy as Greeley advocates, of letting this army be defeated for the purpose of making the people see that slavery must be abolished before we could end the war, I tell you is "played out." Ten thousand men have been sacrificed to that idea now, and the remainder demand that some other policy be adopted henceforth.

We want that three hundred thousand men raised and sent down here immediately. We want them drafted if they won't volunteer. We want the men who have property to furnish the government with the means to carry on the war. We want such a force sent here that the whole thing can be finished up by fall. We've been fooling about this thing long enough, and now we want a change. No more playing at cross purposes by jealous generals, no more incompetent or traitorous officials. The army demands and the people demand such a vigorous prosecution of the war as shall give some hope of ending it some time or other. McClellan must be reinforced sufficiently to enable him to do something more than keep at bay three times his force. That will never conquer the South. We must take the offensive and destroy their army and take their capital. When this is done, the clouds will begin to break.

–NORTON, *Army Letters*

8. McCLELLAN "SAVES HIS COUNTRY" TWICE

But let McClellan speak for himself. We give here excerpts from his letters to his wife. These letters, it will be seen, begin with the Peninsular campaign and carry through the Antietam campaign to McClellan's dismissal from the command of the Army of the Potomac. As they are valuable primarily for their reflection of McClellan's character rather than for their analysis of military operations, we print them as a unit even though this violates chronolgy.

April 8, 1862, 8 A.M.—

I have raised an awful row about McDowell's corps. The President very coolly telegraphed me yesterday that he thought I had better break the enemy's lines at once. I was much tempted to reply that he had better come and do it himself.

April 11, 1862—

Don't worry about the wretches; they have done nearly their worst, and can't do much more. I am sure that I will win in the end, in spite of all their rascality. History will present a sad record of these traitors who are willing to sacrifice the country and its army for personal spite and personal aims. The people will soon understand the whole matter.

May 12, 1862, Monday P.M.—

I hope that the result in front of Richmond will cause still greater satisfaction to the country. I still hope that the God who has been so good to me will continue to smile upon our cause, and enable me to bring this war to a speedy close, so that I may at last have the rest I want so much. . . . I do need rest. You know I have had but little in my life. But the will of God be done! What is given me to do I will try to do with all my might. . . .

I think one more battle here will finish the work. I expect a great one, but feel that confidence in my men and that trust in God which makes me very sanguine as to the result. They will fight me in front of Richmond, I am confident. Defeat there is certain destruction to them, and I think will prove the ruin of their wretched cause. They are concentrating everything for the last death-struggle. My government, alas! is not giving me any aid. But I will do the best I can with what I have, and trust to God's mercy and the courage of my men for the result. . . .

We march in the morning to Cumberland, gradually drawing nearer to Richmond.

July 17, 1862, A.M.—

You do not feel one bit more bitterly towards those people than I do. I do not say much about it, but I fear they have done all that cowardice and folly can do to ruin our poor country, and the blind people seem not to see it. It makes my blood boil when I think of it. I cannot resign so long as the fate of the Army of the Potomac is entrusted to my care. I owe a great duty to this noble set of men, and that is the only feeling that retains me. I fear that my day of usefulness to the country is past—at least under this administration. I hope and trust that God will watch over, guide, and protect me. I accept most resignedly all He has brought upon me. Perhaps I have really brought it on myself; for while striving conscientiously to do my best, it may well be that I have made great mistakes that my vanity does not permit me to perceive. When I see so much self-blindness around me I cannot arrogate to myself greater clearness of vision and self-examination.

I *did* have a terrible time during that week [the Seven Days], for I stood alone, without any one to help me. I felt that on me rested everything, and I felt how weak a thing poor, mortal, erring man is! I felt it sincerely, and shall never, I trust, forget the lesson; it will last me to my dying days. . . . I am very well now, perfectly well, and ready for any amount of fatigue that can be imagined.

July 18, 1862, 9:00 P.M.—

I am inclined now to think that the President will make Halleck commander of the army, and that the first pretext will be seized to supersede me in command of this army. Their game seems to be to withhold reinforcements, and then to relieve me for not advancing, well knowing that I have not the means to do so. If they supersede me in the command of the Army of the Potomac I will resign my commission at once. If they appoint Halleck commanding general I will remain in command of this army as long as they will allow me to, provided the army is in danger and likely to play an active part. I cannot remain as a subordinate in the army I once commanded any longer than the interests of my own Army of the Potomac require. I owe no gratitude to any but my own soldiers here; none to the government or to the country. I have done my best for the country; I expect nothing in return; they are my debtors, not I theirs. . . .

If things come to pass as I anticipate I shall leave the service with a sad heart for my country, but a light one for myself. But one thing keeps me at my work—love for my country and my army. Surely no general had ever better cause to love his men than I have to love mine.

July 20, 1862, P.M.—

Which despatch of mine to Stanton do you allude to? The telegraphic one in which I told him that if I saved the army I owed no thanks to any one in Washington, and that he had done his best to sacrifice my army? It was pretty frank and quite true. Of course they will never forgive me for that. I knew it when I wrote it; but as I thought it possible that it might be the last I ever wrote, it seemed better to have it exactly true. The President, of course, has not replied to my letter, and never will. His reply may be, however, to avail himself of the first opportunity to cut my head off. I see it reported in this evening's paper that Halleck is to be the new general-in-chief. Now let them take the next step and relieve me, and I shall once more be a free man. . . .

Later.—I believe it is now certain that Halleck is commander-in-chief. . . . I am content. I have not disgraced my name, nor will my child be ashamed of her father. Thank God for that! I shall try to get something to do which will make you comfortable; and it will be most pleasant and in the best taste for me that we should lead hereafter a rather quiet and retired life. It will not do to parade the tattered remnants of my departed honors to the gaze of the world. Let us try to live for each other and our child, and to prepare for the great change that sooner or later must overtake us all.

I have had enough of earthly honors and place. I believe I can give up all and retire to privacy once more, a better man than when we gave up our dear little home with wild ideas of serving the country. I feel that I have paid all that I owe her. I am sick and weary of all this business. I am tired of serving fools. God help my country! He alone can save it. It is grating to have to serve under the orders of a man whom I know by experience to be my inferior. But so let it be. God's will be done! All will turn out for the best. My trust is in God, and I cheerfully submit to His will.

August 10, 1862, 4 P.M.—

The absurdity of Halleck's course in ordering the army away from here is that it cannot possibly reach Washington in time to do any good, but will necessarily be too late. I am sorry to say that I am forced to the conclusion that H. is very dull and very incompetent. Alas, poor country! I hope to be ready tomorrow afternoon to move forward in the direction of Richmond. I will try to catch or thrash Longstreet, and then, if the chance offers, follow in to Richmond while they are lamming away at Pope. It is in some respects a desperate step, but it is the best I can do for the nation just now, and I would rather even be defeated than retreat without an effort to relieve Washington in the only way at all possible. If I fail, why well and good. I will fall back. If I win I shall have saved my country, and will then gracefully retire to private life. . . .

I half apprehend that they will be too quick for me in Washington, and relieve me before I have the chance of making the dash. If so, well and good. I am satisfied that the dolts in Washington are bent on my destruction, if it is possible for them to accomplish it.

August 22, 1862, 10 A.M. (Fort Monroe)—

I think they are all pretty well scared in Washington, and probably with good reason. I am confident that the disposition to be made of me will depend entirely upon the state of their nerves in Washington. If they feel safe there I will, no doubt, be shelved; perhaps placed in command here *vice* Gen. Dix. I don't care what they do; would not object to being kept here for a while, because I could soon get things in such condition that I could have you here with me. . . .

Their sending for me to go to Washington only indicates a temporary alarm. If they are at all reassured you will see that they will soon get rid of me. I shall be only too happy to get back to quiet life again; for I am truly and heartily sick of the troubles I have had, and am not fond of being a target for the abuse and slander of all the rascals in the country. Well, we will continue to trust in God and feel certain that all is for the best. It is often difficult to understand the ways of Providence; but I have faith enough to believe that nothing is done without some great purpose.

September 2, 1862, 12:30 P.M.—

I was surprised this morning, when at breakfast, by a visit from the President and Halleck, in which the former expressed the opinion that the troubles now impending could be overcome better by me than by any one else. Pope is ordered to fall back upon Washington, and, as he re-enters, everything is to come under my command again! A terrible and thankless task. Yet I will do my best, with God's blessing, to perform it. God knows I need His help. I am too busy to write any more now. Pray that God will help me in the great task now imposed upon me. I assume it reluctantly, with a full knowledge of all its difficulties and of the immensity of the responsibility. I only consent to take it for my country's sake and with the humble hope that God has called me to it; how I pray that He may support me! . . . Don't be worried; my conscience is clear, and I trust in God.

September 5, 1862, 11 A.M.—

Again I have been called upon to save the country. The case is desperate, but with God's help I will try unselfishly to do my best, and, if He wills it, accomplish the salvation of the nation. My men are true and will stand by me till the last. I still hope for success, and will leave nothing undone to gain it. . . . How weary I am of this struggle against adversity! But one thing sustains me—that is, my trust in God. I know that the interests at stake are so great as to justify His interference; not for me, but for the innocent thousands, millions rather, who have been plunged in misery by no fault of theirs. It is probable that our communications will be cut off in a day or two, but don't be worried. You may rest assured that I am doing all I can for my country, and that no shame shall rest upon you, wilfully brought upon you by me. . . . My hands are full, so is my heart.

September 8, 1862, camp near Rockville—

You don't know what a task has been imposed upon me! I have been obliged to do the best I could with the broken and discouraged fragments of two armies defeated by no fault of mine. Nothing but a desire to do my duty could have induced me to accept the command under such circumstances. Not feeling at all sure that I could do anything, I felt that under the circumstances no one else *could* save the country, and I have not shrunk from the terrible task.

McDowell's own men would have killed him had he made his appearance among them; even his staff did not dare to go among his men. I can afford to forgive and forget him. I saw Pope and McDowell for a few moments at Upton's Hill when I rode out to meet the troops and assume command. I have not seen them since; I hope never to lay eyes on them again. Between them they are responsible for the lives of many of my best and bravest men. They have done all they could (unintentionally, I hope) to ruin and destroy the country. I can never forgive them that. Pope has been foolish enough to try to throw the blame of his defeat on the Army of the Potomac. He would have been wiser to have accepted his defeat without complaint.

I will probably move some four or five miles further to the front tomorrow, as I have ordered the whole army forward. I expect to fight a great battle and to do my best at it. I do not think secesh will catch me very badly.

September 20, 1862, 9 A.M., camp near Sharpsburg—

The battle of Wednesday *was* a terrible one. I presume the loss will prove not less than 10,000 on each side. Our victory was complete, and the disorganized rebel army has rapidly returned to Virginia, its dreams of "invading Pennsylvania" dissipated for ever. I feel some little pride in having, with a beaten and demoralized army, defeated Lee so utterly and saved the North so completely. Well, one of these days history will, I trust, do me justice in deciding that it was not my fault that the campaign of the Peninsula was not successful. . . .

Since I left Washington, Stanton has again asserted that *I*, not Pope, lost the battle of Manassas No. 2! . . . I am tired of fighting such disadvantages, and feel that it is now time for the country to come to my help and remove these difficulties from my path. If my countrymen will not open their eyes and assist themselves they must pardon me if I decline longer to pursue the thankless avocation of serving them.

September 20, 1862, 9 P.M., camp near Sharpsburg—

I feel that I have done all that can be asked in twice saving the country. If I continue in its service I have at least the right to demand a guarantee that I shall not be interfered with. I know I cannot have that assurance so long as Stanton continues in the position of Secretary of War and Halleck as general-in-chief. . . . I can retire from the service for sufficient reasons without leaving any stain upon my reputation. I feel now that this last short campaign is a sufficient legacy for our child, so far as honor is concerned. . . .

You should see my soldiers *now!* You never saw anything like their enthusiasm. It surpasses anything you ever imagined. . . . My tent is filled quite to overflowing with trophies in the way of captured secesh battle-flags. We have more than have been taken in all battles put together, and all sorts of inscriptions on them.

November 7, 1862, 11:30 P.M. (camp near Rectorton)—

Another interruption—this time more important. It was in the shape of Burnside, accompanied by Gen. Buckingham, the secretary's adjutant-general. They brought with them the order relieving me from the command of the Army of the Potomac, and assigning Burnside to the command. No cause is given. I am ordered to turn over the command immediately and repair to Trenton, N. J., and on my arrival there to report by telegraph for further orders. . . .

Of course I was much surprised; but as I read the order in the presence of Gen. Buckingham I am sure that not the slightest expression of feeling was visible on my face, which he watched closely. . . .

They have made a great mistake. Alas for my poor country! I know in my inmost heart she never had a truer servant. I have informally turned over the command to Burnside, but shall go to-morrow to Warrenton with him, and perhaps remain a day or two there in order to give him all the information in my power. . . .

Do not be at all worried—I am not. I have done the best I could for my country; to the last I have done my duty as I understand it. That I must have made many mistakes I cannot deny. I do not see any great blunders; but no one can judge of himself. Our consolation must be that we have tried to do what was right; if we have failed it was not our fault.

—Letters of McClellan to his wife, in *McClellan's Own Story*

9. McCLELLAN FINDS THE LOST ORDER

Almost before Pope had carried out his retirement to Washington, Lee had started his army northward into Maryland. There were large strategic, and even political, purposes in this campaign, but there were practical purposes too—a chance to get food for soldiers and forage for animals. McClellan learned almost at once of Lee's advance, but did not know what his ultimate objectives would be. When news came that Lee was across the Potomac McClellan edged ahead to head him off, reaching Frederick, Maryland, on the twelfth. The next day he had the great good fortune to learn the whole of Lee's plans.

Mystery still surrounds the loss of Special Order 191. That it was picked up at Frederick, Maryland, by Private Mitchell of the 27th Indiana on September 13 and delivered promptly to McClellan's headquarters is clear, but who was responsible for its loss is not known. Lee learned that the Order was in McClellan's hands sometime the next day. To what extent the disclosure of his plans forced Lee to change them is not wholly clear. According to Colonel Allan, historian of the Army of Northern Virginia, Lee said in 1868 that "had the Lost Dispatch not been lost . . . I would have had all my troops reconcentrated on Md. side, stragglers up, men rested, and intended then to attack McClellan hoping the best results from state of my troops and those of the enemy."

ON the 13th an order fell into my hands, issued by General Lee, which fully disclosed his plans, and I immediately gave orders for a rapid and vigorous forward movement.

The following is a copy of the order referred to:

"SPECIAL ORDERS No. 191.
"Headquarters Army of Northern Virginia,
"September 9, 1862.

"The army will resume its march to-morrow, taking the Hagerstown road. General Jackson's command will form the advance, and, after passing Middletown, with such portions as he may select, take the route towards Sharpsburg, cross the Potomac at the most convenient point, and, by Friday night, take possession of the Baltimore and Ohio railroad, capture such of the enemy as may be at Martinsburg, and intercept such as may attempt to escape from Harper's Ferry.

"General Longstreet's command will pursue the same road as far as Boonsboro', where it will halt with the reserve, supply and baggage trains of the army.

"General McLaws, with his own division and that of General R. H. Anderson, will follow General Longstreet; on reaching Middletown, he will take the route to Harper's Ferry, and, by Friday morning, possess himself of the Maryland heights, and endeavor to capture the enemy at Harper's Ferry and vicinity.

"General Walker, with his division, after accomplishing the object in which he is now engaged, will cross the Potomac at Cheek's ford, ascend its right bank to Lovettsville, take possession of Loudon heights, if practicable, by Friday morning; Keys's ford on his left, and the road between the end of the mountain and the Potomac on his right. He will, as far as practicable, co-operate with General McLaws and General Jackson in intercepting the retreat of the enemy.

"General D. H. Hill's division will form the rear guard of the army, pursuing the road taken by the main body. The reserve artillery, ordnance and supply trains, &c., will precede General Hill.

"General Stuart will detach a squadron of cavalry to accompany the commands of Generals Longstreet and McLaws, and, with the main body of the cavalry, will cover the route of the army, and bring up all stragglers that may have been left behind.

"The commands of Generals Jackson, McLaws, and Walker, after accomplishing the objects for which they have been detached, will join the main body of the army at Boonsboro' or Hagerstown.

"Each regiment on the march will habitually carry its axes in the regimental ordnance wagons, for use of the men at their encampments, to procure wood, &c.

"By command of General R. E. Lee.

"R. H. Chilton,

"Assistant Adjutant General."

—*Letter of the Secretary of War*

10. McCLELLAN FORCES TURNER'S GAP AND CRAMPTON'S GAP

As the Lost Order tells, Lee divided his little army, sending Jackson with some 25,000 men to seize Harpers Ferry. Alive to the danger of being cut off from Jackson, now that McClellan knew his plans, Lee turned westward toward Sharpsburg, leaving only token forces to hold back the Federals. Moving with unwonted celerity McClellan pushed after the Confederates. The armies were separated by two low-lying ranges, South Mountain and Elk's Ridge; the easiest roads through these were at Turner's Gap and Crampton's Gap. The Confederates put up a stiff resistance at both places, but were brushed aside.

Here is David Strother, whom we have already met at Manassas, telling how these fights looked from McClellan's headquarters. His comments on Maryland's reaction to the invasion are especially perspicacious.

September 13, Saturday.—Fair and pleasant. Making an early start we entered Frederick City about ten o'clock A.M., and were welcomed with a spontaneous ovation that stirred every soul to its depths. The whole city was fluttering with national flags; while the streets through which we passed, from the sidewalks to the house-tops, shone with happy human faces. It seemed as if the whole population had turned out, wild with joy. Handkerchiefs fluttered and flowers showered upon the moving troops; and when the Commander and Staff appeared the crowd became so demonstrative that we were forcibly brought to a halt. The officers of the Staff received their due share of the floral honors, but the General and horse were absolutely covered with wreaths and bouquets; while old men, women, and children crowded around, anxious to touch his hand, or by some word or act to testify their enthusiasm for the leader of the National power.

As soon as the General could release himself from this pleasing but rather embarrassing position he rode to Burnside's head-quarters on the Baltimore turnpike, and then dismounting entered the General's tent. While waiting outside I fell into conversation with a cavalry officer, who narrated the following incident of the occupation which took place on yesterday: Our advanced cavalry met that of the enemy in the streets and drove them through the town. Being reinforced the enemy returned, driving our men back as

rapidly as they had advanced. Meanwhile a section of artillery had been unlimbered and posted to support the cavalry, the guns charged with canister
and the gunners with the lanyards taut, ready to open at command. As our
squadrons rushed back in disordered flight a stupid trooper rode between the
gunner and the piece, thus drawing the friction primer and discharging the
gun full in the faces of our men, killing two outright and wounding half a
dozen. Our infantry having arrived in the mean time, the rebels abandoned
the town, retiring westward by the Hagerstown road. While the Commander
tarried with General Burnside I rode into the city again, accompanied by
some young Staff officers, and hoping to meet some former acquaintance
among the citizens. . . .

Lee entered Maryland evidently indulging in the belief that the State
would rise and welcome the Southern army. His proclamation was plausibly
framed to engage the good-will of the inhabitants, and the conduct of his
troops as constrainedly regular as was possible under the circumstances.
The observation of a few days was sufficient to disenchant him. In the districts which he visited the mass of the population was of undoubted and uncompromising loyalty. Yet the open defiance and hatred of this class was
not so discouraging as the coldness and even terror with which the Maryland
secessionists regarded their ragged and needy liberators. In truth, the spirit
of rebellion which had boiled over scalding hot in April, 1861, had by this
time simmered down to a tepid sentimentalism which manifested itself in
weak social snobbery, silly songs, intriguing, speculating, and blockade-running. There were, indeed, some more daring spirits left, who, in spite of the
Federal martial law, would on occasions drink themselves drunk to the success of "the good cause," and hurrah for Jeff Davis at the risk of a night in
the guard-house. But that living, practical faith which is willing to undergo
hard knocks for opinion's sake, and take pay in Confederate promises, is
totally lacking in Maryland. In brief, except a few young Hotspurs attracted
by the love of adventure, and a few cock-eyed politicians who have com-
promised themselves unwittingly, rebel Maryland seems to prefer the side-
board to the field, and from all accounts Lee will lose two by desertion where
he gains one by recruiting. . . .

September 14, Sunday.—Pleasant. On rising this morning I heard cannon
sounding to the westward, and evidently nearer to us than Harper's Ferry. I
also observed our columns moving in the same direction, and winding over
the Catoctin Ridge, which divides Frederick from the Middletown Valley.
We were presently in the saddle; and on arriving at the summit of the mountain with one accord drew rein to admire the scene which presented itself.
The Valley of the Catoctin, which lay beneath us like a map unrolled, is one
of the most fertile and best improved districts in Maryland. As far as the eye
can reach, north and southward, it is dotted with handsome farm-houses, and
pretty thriving villages, and checkered with cultivated fields and scraps of
woodland, enlivened by silvery streams and traversed by fine public roads.
The western horizon is limited by a mountain range which rises abruptly to
the height of a thousand feet. This ridge, about four miles distant, is a con-

tinuation of the Great Blue Ridge of Virginia, here called the South Mountain, and within sight is crossed by two great highways—the national turnpike passing over Turner's Gap immediately in front of us, and a less important road passing at Crampton's Gap opposite Burkittsville, about five miles to the southward and leading directly to Maryland Heights and Harper's Ferry. From both these passes we could hear the sullen booming of the guns, and see the white wreaths of smoke rolling up the blue face of the mountain. Across the lovely valley, by every road and pathway, our columns of horse, foot, and artillery were moving, all centring toward the defiant batteries.

Comprehending the beauty and thrilling interest of the scene at a glance, the Commander rode rapidly forward to Middletown, where he stopped at Burnside's quarters, located in an orchard at the eastern end of the village. . . .

About two o'clock P.M. it was ascertained that the passage of South Mountain would cost us a battle; and following the Commander through Middletown we rode forward about two miles, and ascending a spur of the mountain took a position between two of our batteries. From this point we had as comprehensive a view of the position as could be conveniently obtained. The windings of the main turnpike through cleared fields were visible from the valley to the summit; but the flanking roads and positions to the right and left of the turnpike were a good deal obscured by forest which covered the ridge continuously. By both these flanking roads our columns were already ascending to the attack—that on the left commanded by Reno, while Hooker led the forces on the right. At the same time Gibbon's Brigade was advanced on the national turnpike in the centre to amuse the enemy with a feint attack. Generals Cox and Wilcox with their brigades had already made a lodgment on the left summit, and the continuous peals of musketry from that quarter showed that they were stoutly resisted. Sturgis was ordered forward to support them; and as his glittering column was seen ascending the steep road Reno, who had been riding with McClellan, started forward, saying, "I must see to this matter in person."

There is nothing like the master's eye "when work is to be done," and for an hour after Reno's departure the redoubled roar of musketry proved the truth of the proverb. In time the sounds waxed fainter and fainter, the line of white smoke disappeared over the crest, and then news came that the position was carried and the enemy retreating.

Simultaneously with this action the column under Hooker, supported by Meade, was seen crawling up the rocky and difficult ascent on the right. Slowly trailing across the open ground, now entering a piece of wood, and again emerging on the upper side, winding over spurs and up ravines, the march resembled the course of a black serpent with glittering scales stealing upon its prey.

At length we had a glimpse of Hooker's command in some open ground on the summit, moving in column of companies, and heading in toward the Gap. They presently disappeared in the wood, and then came the distant muttering of musketry, which continued with little intermission until after dark, and always approaching the Gap. As Hooker moved in from the exterior position on the right, we could discern a dense and continuous column of the enemy moving to meet him by a road diverging from the National turnpike at the Summit House. This we ascertained was Longstreet's reinforcing column, and it seemed a heavy one; but after a short time it was seen retiring by the same route. All the while the batteries posted on the different eminences were unremitting in their activity, but so broken and densely wooded was the field that comparatively little artillery was used, and that probably with but little effect.

From the position of the Staff we also had a good view of Franklin's operations at Burkittsville and Crampton's Gap, between three and four miles distant, and as matters in our immediate proximity seemed to promise a fortunate conclusion, we found leisure at intervals to turn our glasses in that direction. From the summit the enemy's guns were working industriously, no batteries replying from our side, but the line of musketry smoke was evidently advancing up the ascent, and that indicated a victory there.

About sunset it was understood that both our flanking columns had established themselves solidly in positions commanding the main pass. The enemy had contested the ground with the greatest obstinacy, making repeated and determined efforts to recover what they had lost, but all in vain. As they still maintained a defiant attitude, Gibbon was ordered to advance on the centre, and carry the main road. This he did in gallant style, deploying his lines on either side of the turnpike, and moving a section of artillery on the road. His advance was difficult and slow, as the enemy had greatly the advantage of position, and disputed every step with bitter tenacity. This fight took place after dark, and the General-in-Chief, riding to an adjacent knoll, continued to overlook the sparkling combat until after nine o'clock. About that time the fires died away, Gibbon having advanced apparently about half-way up the mountain. . . .

General McClellan occupied a room in which was a table, two or three chairs, and a couple of tallow-candles, without other furniture or embellishment. Here, surrounded by the officers of his Staff and the chiefs of the army, he discussed the events of the day. We had carried all our points, and inflicted heavy loss on the enemy, capturing between one and two thousand prisoners. . . .

It seems that we have spent the day manœuvring and studying the ground. I don't like the delay. We should have attacked on sight, Monday evening, or this morning at all risks. We might then have got Lee at a disadvantage. But while we take time to concentrate he will do the same or escape. If he is here to-morrow it will be because he feels quite confident of his game. We are entirely too methodical.

—STROTHER, "Personal Recollections of the War"

11. THE BLOODIEST DAY OF THE WAR

With the loss of the passes through South Mountain and the major part of his army still tied down at Harpers Ferry, Lee decided to recross the

Potomac and stand on the defensive. Then on September 15 he got word that Harpers Ferry had fallen and that Jackson was on his way. Lee decided to go ahead with his original plan; by the night of the fifteenth he had three of his divisions in place along the Antietam, and next day Jackson came up and took place alongside them. That day, too, McClellan brought up his mighty host—twice the force that Lee commanded—but did not offer battle.

A word about the terrain and the disposition of the contending forces. Sharpsburg stands in a great bend in the Potomac; the little Antietam flows below the town, winding through woods, orchards and fields of grain. Lee ranged his divisions between the Antietam and the town, Jackson on the left, D. H. Hill at the center, Longstreet on the right, Walker's division in reserve. It was, strategically, about as bad a position as an army could take. Both flanks were vulnerable, and if McClellan could roll up the right flank he would interpose his army between Lee and Virginia. McClellan's forces straddled the Antietam, Hooker, Sumner and Franklin on the right, across the stream, and Burnside on the left, east of the stream, with Porter in reserve.

The battle itself was a piecemeal affair, fought not by armies or even by corps, but by divisions and brigades. At no time did McClellan launch a concerted assault on the Confederate line or use his reserves; instead he wasted his superior strength in a series of fragmentary attacks. While there was some fighting all along the line most of the day, there were in fact three major and separate battles: first, Hooker's attack on the Confederate left; second, Sumner's drive on the Confederate center; third, Burnside's struggle to get across the river and his assault on the Confederate right. All three were partially successful, none was followed through to that complete success which would have destroyed Lee's army and might have spelled the end of the Confederacy.

Antietam was not a decisive battle—but it might have been. A signal victory by Lee would not have altered the military situation, for the Confederate commander could not have followed up victory. But a victory by McClellan would have cut Lee off from his base, or destroyed him and exposed Richmond to imminent capture. McClellan, to be sure, claimed a victory but, as the historian Major Steele observes, "it is hard to say which should reflect least credit upon the Union commander, not to have defeated Lee's army, or not to have destroyed it if he defeated it. Truth to tell, McClellan did neither."

We begin our story of the battle with a general view—a sort of headquarters view—by Colonel Strother, who had the confidence of McClellan.

September 17, Wednesday. . . . At Newcomer's I found the Commander-in-Chief, surrounded by a number of subordinate generals, planning and receiving orders. Thus far the great argument had been opened and conducted solely by those stately and bombastic orators—the cannon. The dispute presently assumed a closer and more conversational tone as the angry chattering of the musketry prevailed. About half past seven o'clock this had swelled to an ominous roar, accompanied by repeated and triumphant cheers. The General-in-Chief, followed by all his attendants, hurried to a bluff just behind the house, whence they had a splendid view of Hooker's advance driving the enemy before them in rapid and disordered flight.

Horses were forthwith ordered, and we rode rapidly across to a commanding knoll on the eastern side of the Sharpsburg turnpike, about the centre of our line of battle, and nearly opposite the town of Sharpsburg, whose locality was indicated by the belfry of a small church which peered above the opposite hill. This was the same point from which the General reconnoitred the enemy on Monday afternoon, and afforded the most comprehensive view of the field that could be had from any single point.

Our order of battle, as detailed to me by McClellan on yesterday afternoon, was as follows: Our right wing under Sumner was established across the Antietam, and would swing round, closing in upon the enemy's left and forcing it back upon the centre, thus cutting off the roads to Hagerstown and Williamsport. Our left, under Burnside, was ordered to force the passage of the Antietam at a stone bridge a mile below the central turnpike, and driving the enemy's right back on Sharpsburg, would bar his retreat toward Antietam Ford on the Potomac and Harper's Ferry, thus (to use the General's own words) pinching him up in a vice. Our centre was refused, and lay behind the stream ready to act as circumstances might require. . . .

The enemy's lines, occupying the ridge which conceals Sharpsburg from us, and thence westward along the Hagerstown pike and the wood behind the Dunker church, are only indicated by the smoke of his guns and an occasional horseman showing himself over the summit to reconnoitre. Meanwhile Sumner had crossed and taken full possession of the position in front of the Dunker church, driving the enemy back into the wood. Several brigades, which I understood to be Richardson's Division, advanced to a position still nearer the centre, confronting the enemy between the Dunker church and the town. To meet them the enemy's lines moved out into the open ground and opened fire, when a portion of our troops broke in confusion and ran down the road toward the central bridge. In a few moments, however, they were rallied, and returned to their positions, showing great steadiness for the rest of the day. The rebel line also stood as straight and firm as a stone-wall, although under a heavy fire both of artillery and musketry. I saw the shells strike them frequently, and when there appeared symptoms of wavering I could see the officers collaring the men and forcing them back to their places.

Our troops fought splendidly, and made several advances at a run, but the force seemed entirely too light and too much isolated to effect any decisive purpose. They did their part, however, and gave their *vis-à-vis* full occupation. A portion of Sumner's advance had pushed forward nearly to the line of fence in front of the Dunker church; but they seemed to be so cut up and reduced in numbers that they took shelter behind a slope in the field, and only kept up a light skirmishing against the wood.

During these operations the clamor of the artillery along the whole line of battle (several miles in extent) was incessant. We could hear the distant muttering of musketry from the flanks, but Sumner's movement had evidently come to a stand. This produced a lull in the battle within our sight, and I had leisure to remark upon the head-quarters group immediately about me. In the midst was a small redan built of fence-rails, behind which sat General Fitz John Porter, who, with a telescope resting on the top rail, studied the field with unremitting attention, scarcely leaving his post during the whole day. His observations he communicated to the commander by nods, signs, or in words so low-toned and brief that the nearest by-standers had but little benefit from them. When not engaged with Porter, McClellan stood in a soldierly attitude intently watching the battle and smoking with the utmost apparent calmness; conversing with surrounding officers and giving his orders in the most quiet under-tones. General Marcy, his Chief of Staff, was always near him, and through him orders were usually given to the aides-de-camp to be transmitted to distant points of the field. Several foreign officers of the French, Prussian, and Sardinian service were present. Every thing was as quiet and punctilious as a drawing-room ceremony.

While the activity of the infantry within sight seemed to have been temporarily suspended, the thunder of between two and three hundred pieces of artillery still kept up the continuity of the battle. The shells had set fire to several barns, which were in full blaze, while at intervals I recognized from among the enemy's guns the sudden spring of that tall mushroom-shaped cloud which indicates the explosion of a caisson or ammunition-wagon, showing that our artillery was doing good work.

Franklin's Corps having arrived on the field he is ordered to fill a gap between Sumner and Hooker, occasioned by the rapid advance of the latter doubling back the enemy's left. Shortly after this order was sent I observed a sudden movement from the line of wood behind the Dunker church, and in a moment, as it appeared, the whole field in front was covered with masses of the enemy, formed in columns of grand divisions, advancing at a run, with arms at right shoulder shift, and yelling like demons. I could see the heads of four columns, which seemed to be composed of a brigade each; but the extreme left of the movement was masked by a wood and the smoke of a burning farm-house. The attack was evidently made to recover the wood and position from which they had been driven by Hooker at the commencement of the fight.

The rush of this fiery avalanche swept away the feeble remnant of Sumner's command as the flame of a torch scatters the swarms of blue flies from the shambles. As these, in their disordered and more rapid flight, unmasked the front of the rebel advance there was a swell in the chorus of the battle so vast and voluminous that it seemed as if heaven and earth vibrated with the stunning roar. Cannon and musketry mingled in a tonic outpouring that exceeded in grandeur all sounds I ever heard, except, perhaps, Niagara. The check of pulsation produced by this sudden apparition was relieved by an officer, who whispered: "That's Franklin. Hear him!"

The rebel columns had swept on, disappearing entirely in the dust raised by their own movement through the trampled field, the rolling smoke of the burning houses, and the sulphurous cloud which rose like a snowy mountain over the assailed position. We could distinctly see Sumner's débris rallying behind the wood, forming in line, and returning to the combat. Higher and higher rolled the white clouds, steady and unbroken; the roar of ordnance continued for twenty minutes or more, when, emerging from the smoke, flying in the wildest disorder, thinned and scattered, we saw the enemy returning to the wood from which he had advanced. Shot and shell followed with vengeful rapidity, and anon our ordered lines were seen sweeping over the disputed field to resume their position in front of the Dunker church. As the smoke and dust disappeared I was astonished to observe our troops moving along the front and passing over what appeared to be a long, heavy column of the enemy without paying it any attention whatever. I borrowed a glass from an officer, and discovered this to be actually a column of the enemy's dead and wounded lying along a hollow road—afterward known as Bloody Lane. Among the prostrate mass I could easily distinguish the movements of those endeavoring to crawl away from the ground; hands waving as if calling for assistance, and others struggling as if in the agonies of death.

I was standing beside General McClellan during the progress and conclusion of this attack. The studied calmness of his manner scarcely concealed the underlying excitement, and when it was over he exclaimed: "By George, this is a magnificent field, and if we win this fight it will cover all our errors and misfortunes forever!"

"General," I said, "fortune favors the bold; hurl all our power upon them at once, and we will make a glorious finish of the campaign and the war."

"Colonel," said he, "ride forward to Pleasonton and tell him to throw a couple of squadrons forward on the Sharpsburg road, as far as they can go, to find out what is there."

I surmise, from this order, the General had suspected the enemy's line immediately in front of our centre was weak. I rode down the turnpike, leaving Porterstown to the left, and near the central bridge found General Pleasonton, to whom I delivered the message. He responded promptly by throwing forward two horse-batteries, which took position across the Antietam on either side of the turnpike.

Thus far we had heard nothing and seen no results from Burnside's wing. The General was impatient, and frequently asked: "What is Burnside about? Why do we not hear from him?" During the morning he sent several messengers to hasten his movements; but we only heard vaguely that he had not yet effected a crossing and could not carry the bridge.

Meanwhile the news from the right showed that matters were taking an unfavorable turn there. Hooker was wounded and withdrawn from the field. Mansfield was killed, and a number of other valuable general officers *hors de combat*. Our right wing seemed to have spent its aggressive power, and held its ground because the enemy was equally incapable of aggression.

About one o'clock we had news that Burnside had carried the bridge; but there seemed to be a lull in the battle along the whole line from right to left. An aid was wanted to carry another urgent message to Burnside. General

Marcy asked me if I was ready for the service. I promptly led up my mare, but the General observing that she was sweltering from my recent ride, called Colonel Key, whose horse was fresh, and asked him to ride over to General Burnside's position and ascertain what was the cause of the delay. I was extremely anxious to see what was going on there, and begged to be permitted to carry the message, but Key would not yield. He returned with the information that Burnside had effected a crossing and thought he could hold the bridge.

The Commander-in-Chief replied, "He should be able to do that with five thousand men; if he can do no more I must take the remainder of his troops and use them elsewhere in the field." . . .

As the afternoon wore away, and while the Commanding General was absent, the fires of death were rekindled along the whole line. Since the overwhelming repulse by Franklin of the enemy's powerful attacking column he seemed to have yielded the contested ground on the right, and to have fallen back to a more sheltered line between the Dunker church and the town. Yet, though his infantry was less demonstrative, his artillery appeared to be stronger and more active than during the forenoon. About this time we witnessed one of the handsomest exhibitions of gallantry which occurred during the day. A battery of ours was seen entering the field in the vicinity of Richardson's Division; moving at a walk and taking position, apparently in advance of our line, it opened fire at short range, and maintained its ground for half an hour under the concentrated fire of at least forty guns of the enemy. As they moved in with the utmost deliberation I saw a number of shells strike and overthrow men and horses, and during the combat the battery sometimes appeared covered with the smoke and dust of the enemy's bursting shells. Unable to sustain the unequal contest they at length withdrew to shelter, and then we saw parties returning to the ground to bring off the wounded in blankets and to remove the limbers of two guns the horses of which had been killed. This, I afterward ascertained, was Graham's Battery United States Artillery, and I was further informed by Lieutenant Elder, who commanded a section in the action, that in half an hour they lost eleven men and seventeen horses. The affair was observed from head-quarters with the greatest interest, and elicited the warmest commendation, especially from the foreign officers on the ground.

At length, about four o'clock in the afternoon, the cumulating thunder on the left announced that Burnside's advance had at last commenced (three hours too late). The advance was distinctly visible from our position, and the movement of the dark columns, with arms and banners glittering in the sun, following the double line of skirmishers, dashing forward at a trot, loading and firing alternately as they moved, was one of the most brilliant and exciting exhibitions of the day. As this splendid advance seemed to be carrying every thing before it our attention was withdrawn to the right by the appearance of large bodies of the enemy with glittering arms and banners moving up the Hagerstown road toward the Dunker church with the apparent intention of renewing the attack in that direction. In a short time, however, this menacing cloud was dispelled by the concentrated fire of forty-two guns which Franklin had in position.

Meanwhile Burnside's attack had carried the height overlooking Sharpsburg on the left, having driven the enemy and captured the guns; but a counter attack on his troops, exhausted with their victory, sent them streaming down the hill again, and the last rays of the setting sun shone upon the bayonets of the enemy crowning the hill from which ours had just been driven. At this crisis the General, followed by his whole retinue, rode forward to a bluff nearer the scene of action. It was nearly dark when we reached the point, yet the sullen boom of an occasional gun, and the sparkling lines of musketry on a line about midway between Sharpsburg and the Antietam, showed that ours still held on to a portion of the field they had wrested from the enemy. About this time Burnside's messenger, asking for reinforcements, arrived. It was too late to repair errors or initiate any new movement, and they were not sent.

By eight o'clock the wailing cries of the wounded and the glare of the burning buildings alone interrupted the silence and darkness which reigned over the field of the great battle. The General then led us back to the headquarters camp, established in the rear of Keedysville, where, forgetting the events of the day for the time, we supped heartily and slept profoundly.

—STROTHER, "Personal Recollections of the War"

12. HOOKER HAMMERS THE CONFEDERATE LEFT—IN VAIN

The Federal attack was launched at sunrise as Doubleday and Ricketts, of Hooker's corps, moved with great élan on Jackson's line stretching at almost a right angle from the Dunker Church through the West Woods toward the Potomac. Stuart opened with artillery; Jackson moved Lawton's Georgians into a field of corn, head-high; and the lines held. Hooker sent in reserves, and Jackson called on Hood to go to the rescue. The fighting raged for an hour; then Hood sent his famous message, "Tell General Jackson unless I get reinforcements I must be forced back, but I am going on while I can." Reinforcements came—from Early and finally from McLaws, who had come up just that morning. But the Federal attack, too, was reinforced. Mansfield's corps—now under Williams—entered the battle, drove the Confederates back through the savage cornfield, and captured the Dunker Church. A counterattack by McLaws recaptured it. By nine o'clock both sides were exhausted, and the fighting on the left died down. When a brother officer asked Hood, "Where is your division?" he answered, "Dead on the field."

Those who actually participated in fighting of this kind could give only their own experience and that of their company or regiment. Here are a Federal and a Confederate account of the fighting through the cornfield and for the Dunker Church. Major Rufus R. Dawes was with the 6th Wisconsin; James Graham a captain in the 27th North Carolina—one of the regiments that was rushed to the rescue of Hood. A third item, from Longstreet himself, fills out the story that Graham has to tell.

A. Wisconsin Boys Are Slaughtered in the Cornfield

OUR lines on the left now came sweeping forward through the corn and the open fields beyond. I ordered my men up to join in the advance, and commanded: "Forward—guide left—march!" We swung away from the turnpike, and I sent the sergeant-major to Captain Kellogg, commanding the companies on the turnpike, with this order: "If it is practicable, move forward the right companies, aligning with the left wing." Captain Kellogg said: "Please give Major Dawes my compliments, and say it is impracticable; the fire is murderous."

As we were getting separated, I directed Sergeant Huntington to tell Captain Kellogg that he could get cover in the corn, and to join us, if possible. Huntington was struck by a bullet, but delivered the order. Kellogg ordered his men up, but so many were shot that he ordered them down again at once. While this took place on the turnpike, our companies were marching forward through the thick corn, on the right of a long line of battle. Closely following was a second line. At the front edge of the cornfield was a low Virginia rail fence. Before the corn were open fields, beyond which was a strip of woods surrounding a little church, the Dunkard church. As we appeared at the edge of the corn, a long line of men in butternut and gray rose up from the ground. Simultaneously, the hostile battle lines opened a tremendous fire upon each other. Men, I can not say fell; they were knocked out of the ranks by dozens. But we jumped over the fence, and pushed on, loading, firing, and shouting as we advanced. There was, on the part of the men, great hysterical excitement, eagerness to go forward, and a reckless disregard of life, of every thing but victory. Captain Kellogg brought his companies up abreast of us on the turnpike.

The Fourteenth Brooklyn Regiment, red legged Zouaves, came into our line, closing the awful gaps. Now is the pinch. Men and officers of New York and Wisconsin are fused into a common mass, in the frantic struggle to shoot fast. Every body tears cartridges, loads, passes guns, or shoots. Men are falling in their places or running back into the corn. The soldier who is shooting is furious in his energy. The soldier who is shot looks around for help with an imploring agony of death on his face. After a few rods of advance, the line stopped and, by common impulse, fell back to the edge of the corn and lay down on the ground behind the low rail fence.

Another line of our men came up through the corn. We all joined together, jumped over the fence, and again pushed out into the open field. There is a rattling fusilade and loud cheers. "Forward" is the word. The men are loading and firing with demoniacal fury and shouting and laughing hysterically, and the whole field before us is covered with rebels fleeing for life, into the woods. Great numbers of them are shot while climbing over the high post and rail fences along the turnpike. We push on over the open fields half way to the little church. The powder is bad, and the guns have become very dirty. It takes hard pounding to get the bullets down, and our

ANTIETAM

firing is becoming slow. A long and steady line of rebel gray, unbroken by the fugitives who fly before us, comes sweeping down through the woods around the church. They raise the yell and fire. It is like a scythe running through our line. "Now, save, who can." It is a race for life that each man runs for the cornfield. A sharp cut, as of a switch, stings the calf of my leg as I run. Back to the corn, and back through the corn, the headlong flight continues.

At the bottom of the hill, I took the blue color of the state of Wisconsin, and waving it, called a rally of Wisconsin men. Two hundred men gathered around the flag of the Badger state. Across the turnpike just in front of the haystacks, two guns of Battery "B," 4th U. S. artillery were in action. The pursuing rebels were upon them. General John Gibbon, our brigade commander, who in regular service was captain of this battery, grimed and black with powder smoke in himself sighting these guns of his old battery, comes running to me, "Here, major, move your men over, we must save these guns."

I commanded "Right face, forward march," and started ahead with the colors in my hand into the open field, the men following. As I entered the field, a report as of a thunderclap in my ear fairly stunned me. This was Gibbon's last shot at the advancing rebels. The cannon was double charged with canister. The rails of the fence flew high in the air.

A line of union blue charged swiftly forward from our right across the field in front of the battery, and into the corn-field. They drove back the rebels who were firing upon us. It was our own gallant 19th Indiana, and here fell dead their leader, Lieutenant Colonel A. F. Bachman; but the youngest captain in their line, William W. Dudley, stepped forward and led on the charge.

I gathered my men on the turnpike, reorganized them, and reported to General Doubleday, who was himself there. He ordered me to move back to the next woods in the rear, to remain and await instruction. Bullets, shot, and shell, fired by the enemy in the corn-field, were still flying thickly around us, striking the trees in this woods, and cutting off the limbs. I placed my men under the best shelter I could find, and here we figured up, as nearly as we could, our dreadful losses in the battle. Three hundred and fourteen officers and men had marched with us into battle. There had been killed and wounded, one hundred and fifty-two. Company "C" under Captain Hooe, thirty-five men, was not in the fight in front of the corn-field. That company was on skirmish duty farther to our right. In this service they lost two men. Of two hundred and eighty men who were at the corn-field and turnpike, one hundred and fifty were killed or wounded. This was the most dreadful slaughter to which our regiment was subjected in the war. We were joined in the woods by Captain Ely, who reported to me, as the senior officer present, with the colors and eighteen men of the second Wisconsin. They represented what remained for duty of that gallant regiment.

—DAWES, *Service with the Sixth Wisconsin Volunteers*

B. McLAWS TO THE RESCUE OF HOOD

Before day on the morning of 17 September, 1862, we were moved and placed in line of battle on the extreme right of the Confederate lines, our left resting upon the yard of a man whose name I did not learn, who, to prevent our getting water, broke off his pump-handle and destroyed his pump, so that we were compelled to fill our canteens from a mud hole in his stable lot or do without water. Most of us filled from this mud-hole, and I can testify that, while not as fresh and sweet as some I have seen, yet in the heat and strife of that day its filth was almost forgotten and it served very well to quench thirst. We remained in this position till about 8:30 o'clock A.M., when we were ordered to the left centre. After double-quicking one and a half or two miles we were placed in line about one mile to the left of the town of Sharpsburg.

The Twenty-seventh North Carolina infantry, Colonel John R. Cooke, and the Third Arkansas, Captain Ready commanding, were detached from the rest of the division and fought as a little brigade by themselves under the command of Colonel Cooke of the Twenty-seventh North Carolina; Colquitt's Georgia Brigade being some 500 yards to our right, and the rest of our division about the same distance to our left. Forming in a corn field we advanced under a heavy fire of grape and canister at a quick step, up a little rise, and halted at a rail fence, our right considerably advanced. Captain Greenough's battery, attached to General Kershaw's Brigade was placed on our left, but was soon withdrawn. After holding this position for half an hour or more our front was changed; the left retiring about ten steps and the right thrown back considerably, so as to be upon a line with the other troops.

In the meantime we had suffered heavily and, I think inflicted equally as much damage upon the enemy. The Yankees getting possession of a piece of woods upon our left, Companies F, K, and G, the three left companies of the Twenty-seventh, were directed to center their fire upon that point; and right well did they do their work, as it appeared upon an examination of the field next day that the enemy were piled two or three deep in some places. About 1 o'clock P.M., the enemy having retired behind the hill upon which they were posted, and none appearing within range in our front, Colonel Cooke ordered us to fall back some twenty steps in the corn field and lie down, so as to draw them on; he in the meantime, regardless of personal danger from sharpshooters, remained at the fence beside a small hickory tree.

After remaining there some twenty minutes the enemy attempted to sneak up a section of artillery to the little woods on our left. Colonel Cooke, watching the movement, ordered the four left companies of the Twenty-seventh North Carolina up to the fence and directed them to fire upon this artillery. At the first fire, before they had gotten into position, nearly every horse and more than half the men fell, and the infantry line which had moved up to support them showed evident signs of wavering. Colonel Cooke seeing this, and having received orders to charge if opportunity offered, ordered a charge. Without waiting a second word of command both regiments leaped the fence and "went at them" and soon we had captured these guns and had the troops in front of us in full retreat. A battery posted near a little brick church upon a hill (the Dunkard church, so often referred to in accounts of this battle, which was situated on the "Hagerstown Pike" and just to our left and front), was playing sad havoc with us, but thinking that would be taken by the troops upon our left, who we supposed were charging with us, we still pursued the flying foe. Numbers of them surrendered to us and they were ordered to the rear. Two or three hundred took shelter behind a lot of haystacks, and fastening white handkerchiefs to their muskets and bayonets, held them out offering to surrender.

We pushed on, and soon wheeling to the right drove down their line, giving them an enfilade fire, and succeeded in breaking six regiments, which fled in confusion. Only one Federal regiment, that I saw, left the field in anything like good order. After pushing on in this way, we found ourselves opposed by a body of the enemy behind a stone wall in a corn field. Stopping to contend with these we found that we were almost out of ammunition; the cartridges which we had captured on the field, and of these there was a large quantity, not fitting our guns.

Colonel Cooke, learning this fact, and seeing that we were not supported in our charge, ordered us to fall back to our original position. This, of course, was done at double-quick. As we returned we experienced the perfidy of those who had previously surrendered to us and whom we had not taken time to disarm. They, seeing that we were not supported, attempted to form a line in our rear and in a few minutes would have done so. As it was, we had to pass between two fires, a part of the troops having been thrown back to oppose our movement on their flank and these supposed prisoners having formed on the other side. A bloody lane indeed it proved to us. Many a brave man lost his life in that retreat. At some points the lines were not sixty yards distant on either side of us. Arriving at our original position both regiments halted and were soon reformed.

In this retreat we were very materially aided and protected by Cobb's Brigade, then commanded by Colonel William MacRae, of the Fifteenth North Carolina Regiment. . . .

As soon as the regiments could reform behind their rail fence, they opened fire with the few cartridges they had left and soon checked the advance of the enemy who did not come beyond the line which they had occupied in the morning. In a short while all our ammunition was exhausted, Colonel Cooke sent courier after courier for ammunition, but still none was sent. Four or five times during the afternoon General Longstreet sent couriers telling Colonel Cooke to hold the position at all hazards, that "it was the key to the whole line." Colonel Cooke's reply was always, "Tell General Longstreet to send me some ammunition. I have not a cartridge in my command, but will hold my position at the point of the bayonet."

The rail fence, which was our only protection, was riddled with bullets and torn with shot and shell and our men were falling fast, but still the Twenty-seventh North Carolina and the Third Arkansas flinched not. Imbued with the courage of their commander, they stood firm to their post.

For about two hours and a half they held the position literally without a cartridge. . . . Between 4 and 5 o'clock in the afternoon we were relieved (I think by the Third North Carolina and a Louisiana regiment), and were moved about a mile to the rear to get ammunition and fresh water. After resting about half an hour we were marched again to the front and placed in position just behind and in support of the troops who had relieved us. Here we were subjected to a severe shelling, but had no chance to return the fire. The day had been a long one, but the evening seemed longer; the sun seemed almost to go backwards, and it appeared as if night would never come. As soon as it became dark we were moved to the left, rejoined our division, and with them bivouacked upon the battlefield.

The regiment entered the battle with 325 officers and men and lost in killed and wounded 203, about 63 per cent. One company (G) went in 30 strong and had but five left at the end of the day. Another (Company E), with an average company and a full complement of officers, lost its Captain, First Lieutenant and Second Lieutenant killed, and two-thirds of its men killed or wounded.

—GRAHAM, "Twenty Seventh Regiment"

C. LONGSTREET TURNS A BATTERY ON THE FEDERALS

We were under the crest of a hill occupying a position that ought to have been held by from four to six brigades. The only troops there were Cooke's regiment of North Carolina infantry, and they were without a cartridge. As I rode along the line with my staff I saw two pieces of the Washington Artillery (Miller's battery), but there were not enough men to man them. The gunners had been either killed or wounded. This was a fearful situation for the Confederate center. I put my staff-officers to the guns while I held their horses. It was easy to see that if the Federals broke through our line there, the Confederate army would be cut in two and probably destroyed, for we were already badly whipped and were only holding our ground by sheer force of desperation. Cooke sent me word that his ammunition was out. I replied that he must hold his position as long as he had a man left. He responded that he would show his colors as long as there was a man alive to hold them up. We loaded up our little guns with canister and sent a rattle of hail into the Federals as they came up over the crest of the hill.

That little battery shot harder and faster, with a sort of human energy, as though it realized that it was to hold the thousands of Federals at bay or the battle was lost. So warm was the reception we gave them that they dodged back behind the crest of the hill. We sought to make them believe we had many batteries before them. As the Federals would come up they would see the colors of the North Carolina regiment waving placidly and then would receive a shower of canister. We made it lively while it lasted. In the meantime General Chilton, General Lee's chief of staff, made his way to me and asked, "Where are the troops you are holding your line with?" I pointed to my two pieces and to Cooke's regiment, and replied, "There they are; but that regiment hasn't a cartridge."

Chilton's eyes popped as though they would come out of his head; he struck spurs to his horse and away he went to General Lee. I suppose he made some remarkable report, although I did not see General Lee again until night. After a little a shot came across the Federal front, plowing the ground in a parallel line. Another and another, each nearer and nearer their line. This enfilade fire, so distressing to soldiers, was from a battery on D. H. Hill's line, and it soon beat back the attacking column.

Meanwhile, R. H. Anderson and Hood came to our support and gave us more confidence. It was a little while only until another assault was made against D. H. Hill, and extending far over toward our left, where McLaws and Walker were supporting Jackson. In this desperate effort the lines seemed to swing back and forth for many minutes, but at last they settled down to their respective positions, the Confederates holding with a desperation which seemed to say, "We are here to die."

—LONGSTREET, "The Invasion of Maryland"

13. THE DESPERATE FIGHTING ALONG BLOODY LANE

The second part of the battle came at the Confederate center, and almost by accident. About nine in the morning Sumner's corps had moved out to support Hooker. French's division went astray, and struck at the Confederate line as it curved eastward from the Dunker Church. Here D. H. Hill stood behind a sunken lane that was that day to be rebaptized "bloody." French was shortly joined by Richardson's division. Outnumbered, Hill put up a savage resistance. "The combat that took place," writes the historian Ropes, "was beyond question one of the most sanguinary and desperate in the whole war." When the Federals succeeded in enfilading the lane, the Confederates withdrew, leaving a yawning hole between the left and the center. It was a crucial moment for the Confederacy; General Alexander later wrote that "Lee's army was ruined and the end of the Confederacy was in sight." Now was the moment for McClellan to hurl in his reserves—Franklin's VI Corps, which had scarcely seen action, and Porter's V. McClellan did nothing. The attack ebbed away, the Confederates rallied, and the line held.

We have included two accounts of this fight at the center. The first is from Thomas Livermore of the 18th New Hampshire; we have met him before and he needs no further introduction. The second is by the famous John B. Gordon, who rose to be lieutenant general by the end of the war and was subsequently Senator from Georgia and commander in chief of the Confederate Veterans.

A. THOMAS LIVERMORE PUTS ON HIS WAR PAINT

THE events of a battle in which the troops maneuver a good deal are almost always confused in one's memory, and I am not exactly certain of the order in which I place events, nor of the duration of the various struggles here, but they are related as now pictured on my mind. I believe that while we fired by file a little before we advanced across the road, yet that we did not meet with great opposition here, probably because the Irish regiment we relieved had done considerable toward using up the line we first dealt with. At any rate, we swept forward, and as we were advancing (either now or previously across the sward) I heard old General Richardson cry out, "Where's General ——?" I looked over my right shoulder and saw that gallant old fellow advancing on the right of our line, almost alone, afoot and with his bare sword in his hand, and his face was as black as a thunder cloud; and well it might be, for some of our own men, turning their heads toward him, cried out, "Behind the haystack!" and he roared out, "God damn the field officers!" I shall never cease to admire that magnificent fighting general who advanced with his front line, with his sword bare and ready for use, and his swarthy face, burning eye, and square jaw, though long since lifeless dust, are dear to me.

We swept on over the road into the cornfield, taking prisoner the broken remnants of the line which had opposed, now crouching in the corn before us, and down into a ravine, to the foot of the slope on which the rebel batteries stood, and not more than two hundred yards from them; all the time being pelted with canister from the battery in our front, which hurtled through and tore down even the slender cornstalks. . . . The rebels then attempted to send a line of battle down the slope to meet us under cover of the artillery fire, but by this time we had advanced beyond the range of the batteries on the right, and my impression is that either on account of the depth of the ravine we were in or because of the advancing rebel line being in the way, the pieces of the battery in our front were not depressed enough to hurt us, and we gave our undivided attention to this advancing line. We were fresh, and opened a withering, *literally* withering, fire on the rebels; for although they may have started in regular order, yet before they got to the foot of the slope there was no semblance of a line, and the individuals of what had been the line, either by reason of invincible bravery, or for the purpose of gaining shelter, ran forward scatteringly in the face of our fire, with heads down as if before a storm, to a fence which was a few yards in front of us, but did not form a line which annoyed us, that I recollect.

In my opinion here was a glorious chance to win the victory. We seemed to have penetrated to the right flank of the enemy, no infantry appeared to turn our left flank at this juncture, and no battery opened on our left front, and the line which the rebels sent down in our front was broken by a regiment of 300 men or less. Of course, I don't know what troops there were in reserve behind the rebel line at this point, but from all that I have learned I see no reason to doubt that if the prolongation of our line to the left, which we ended, had been continued by one division, we should have turned the right of the left wing of this rebel army.

But, however triumphant our advance had been, it seems that Colonel Cross found that he was not only in advance of the line on his right, but that there was an interval between his right and its left on the same alignment; so to avoid the catastrophe which such a position might bring upon us, he moved us to the right and rear until at length we found ourselves in the vicinity of the sunken road again with our line intact. The rebels followed this movement closely with an advance of a formidable line of battle, which we met with a rapid fire, but the rebels now attempted a maneuver, which was the very one I have suggested we might have accomplished, that is, the flanking of our left. We were very busily engaged in the corn when some one on the left detected this movement of the enemy around our left, which was concealed from the most of us by the corn. Colonel Cross convinced himself that this was the case when he in some way changed our front "to the left and rear" so as to confront the rebel line squarely. . . .

And then we filed to the left . . . and outflanking the rebel line in turn poured such a fire into it as to drive it off. As I was near the right of the line I did not see how much the rebels outflanked us, nor did I see how much we outflanked them, and was very busily occupied with the rebels in my own front.

At this time we were subjected to a most terrible fire of artillery, and I recollect one shell or case shot which burst in the middle of "G," the color company, and killed and wounded eight men and tore a great hole in one of our flags, and our regiment, already weakened, was fast losing men from its ranks. At this trying time the rebel infantry advanced for the third time against us, when the colonel moved us into the sunken road and there we planted ourselves for the last struggle.

On looking around me I found that we were in the old, sunken road mentioned several times before, and that the bed of it lay from one to three feet below the surface of the crest along which it ran. In this road there lay so many dead rebels that they formed a line which one might have walked upon as far as I could see, many of whom had been killed by the most horrible wounds of shot and shell, and they lay just as they had been killed apparently, amid the blood which was soaking the earth. It was on this ghastly flooring that we kneeled for the last struggle. The rebels advanced through the corn, firing, the artillery played upon us without mercy, and now we were harder pressed than ever before, with no help at hand from the reserves which we could see. The battle still raged on our right, and it seemed useless to expect aid from that quarter; this is retrospective, however, and I am not aware that we thought of or prayed for help.

As the rebel advance became apparent, we plied the line with musketry with all our power, and no doubt with terrible effect, but they still advanced. A color-bearer came forward within fifteen yards of our line, and with the utmost desperation waved a rebel flag in front of him. Our men fairly roared, "Shoot the man with the flag!" and he went down in a twinkling and the flag was not raised in sight again. As the fight grew furious, the colonel cried out, "Put on the war paint"; and looking around I saw the glorious man standing erect, with a red handkerchief, a conspicuous mark, tied around his bare head and the blood from some wounds on his forehead streaming over his face, which was blackened with powder. Taking the cue somehow we rubbed the torn end of the cartridges over our faces, streaking them with powder like a pack of Indians, and the colonel, to complete the similarity, cried out, "Give 'em the war whoop!" and all of us joined him in the Indian war whoop until it must have rung out above all the thunder of the ordnance. I have sometimes thought it helped to repel the enemy by alarming him to see this devilish-looking line of faces, and to hear the horrid whoop; and at any rate, it reanimated us and let him know we were unterrified.

Added to the inspiration of these devices, a stream of shouts, curses, and appeals to "Fire! Fire! Fire faster!" came from our mouths, and while with our first advance into the cornfield my contemplation of death in the abstract had given place to inflicting it in reality, at this time my spirits became fairly boisterous between firing, shouts, and the smell of powder smoke and all. The dead rebel whom I knelt on held in his hands a "Belgian rifle" (a poor enough arm, but worth something in a pinch like this), and although it was my duty to tend solely to my men's behavior, yet as they were each one of them doing their best, and the cap on this rifle denoted that it was loaded, I took it out of his hands, and discharged it at his living comrades, and liking the work I looked around for another piece to discharge, when Colonel Cross, who was omnipresent, omniscient, and omnipotent in the fight, cried out sharply, "Mr. Livermore, tend to your company!" and I quenched my aspirations and thenceforward watched my men. . . .

Among the incidents I remember on this day were these. I saw a private of the 61st New York, who was mounted for some reason, with a brilliant red shirt on, riding to and fro along the infantry line when the musketry was hottest, and he being the only mounted man in his vicinity was especially conspicuous, and I learned that he was doing his best to encourage the men. I was told, too, that a woman, who followed the Irish Brigade as laundress or nurse, went up with it, and standing with it in the fight, swung her bonnet around and cheered on the men; and that Colonel Barlow, of the 61st New York, tired of seeing his drummers shrink from their duty, tied them to his waist with his sash and led them under fire. A rebel in flying before our advance was killed as he was climbing over a fence and remained fixed upon it, and through mistake or rage our men had shot or bayoneted him many times.

—LIVERMORE, *Days and Events*

B. GENERAL GORDON IS WOUNDED FIVE TIMES AT ANTIETAM

Vigorously following up the success achieved at South Mountain, McClellan, on the 16th day of September, 1862, marshalled his veteran legions on the eastern hills bordering the Antietam. On the opposite slopes, near the picturesque village of Sharpsburg, stood the embattled lines of Lee. As these vast American Armies, the one clad in blue and the other in gray, stood contemplating each other from the adjacent hills, flaunting their defiant banners, they presented an array of martial splendor that was not equalled, perhaps, on any other field. It was in marked contrast with other battle-grounds. On the open plain, where stood these hostile hosts in long lines, listening in silence for the signal summoning them to battle, there were no breastworks, no abatis, no intervening woodlands, nor abrupt hills, nor hiding-places, nor impassable streams. The space over which the assaulting columns were to march, and on which was soon to occur the tremendous struggle, consisted of smooth and gentle undulations and a narrow valley covered with green grass and growing corn. From the position assigned me near the centre of Lee's lines, both armies and the entire field were in view. . . .

On the elevated points beyond the narrow valley the Union batteries were rolled into position, and the Confederate heavy guns unlimbered to answer them. For one or more seconds, and before the first sounds reached us, we saw the great volumes of white smoke rolling from the mouths of McClellan's artillery. The next second brought the roar of the heavy discharges and the loud explosions of hostile shells in the midst of our lines, inaugurating the great battle. The Confederate batteries promptly responded; and while the artillery of both armies thundered, McClellan's compact columns of infantry fell upon the left of Lee's lines with the crushing weight of a land-slide. The Confederate battle line was too weak to withstand the momentum of such a charge. Pressed back, but neither hopelessly broken nor dismayed, the Southern troops, enthused by Lee's presence, reformed their lines, and, with a shout as piercing as the blast of a thousand bugles, rushed in counter-charge upon the exulting Federals, hurled them back in confusion, and recovered all the ground that had been lost. Again and again, hour after hour, by charges and counter-charges, this portion of the field was lost and recovered, until the green corn that grew upon it looked as if it had been struck by a storm of bloody hail.

Up to this hour not a shot had been fired in my front. There was an ominous lull on the left. From sheer exhaustion, both sides, like battered and bleeding athletes, seemed willing to rest. General Lee took advantage of the respite and rode along his lines on the right and centre. He was accompanied by Division Commander General D. H. Hill. With that wonderful power which he possessed of divining the plans and purposes of his antagonist, General Lee had decided that the Union commander's next heavy blow would fall upon our centre, and those of us who held that important position were notified of this conclusion. We were cautioned to be prepared for a determined assault and urged to hold that centre at any sacrifice, as a break at that point would endanger his entire army. My troops held the most advanced position on this part of the field, and there was no supporting line behind us. It was evident, therefore, that my small force was to receive the first impact of the expected charge and to be subjected to the deadliest fire. To comfort General Lee and General Hill, and especially to make, if possible, my men still more resolute of purpose, I called aloud to these officers as they rode away: "These men are going to stay here, General, till the sun goes down or victory is won." Alas! many of the brave fellows are there now.

General Lee had scarcely reached his left before the predicted assault came. The day was clear and beautiful, with scarcely a cloud in the sky. The men in blue filed down the opposite slope, crossed the little stream (Antietam), and formed in my front, an assaulting column four lines deep. The front line came to a "charge bayonets," the other lines to a "right shoulder shift." The brave Union commander, superbly mounted, placed himself in front, while his band in rear cheered them with martial music. It was a thrilling spectacle. The entire force, I concluded, was composed of fresh troops from Washington or some camp of instruction. So far as I could see, every soldier wore white gaiters around his ankles. The banners above them had apparently never been discolored by the smoke and dust of battle. Their gleaming bayonets flashed like burnished silver in the sunlight. With the precision of step and perfect alignment of a holiday parade, this magnificent array moved to the charge, every step keeping time to the tap of the deep-sounding drum. As we stood looking upon that brilliant pageant, I thought, if I did not say, "What a pity to spoil with bullets such a scene of martial beauty!" But there was nothing else to do. . . .

My extraordinary escapes from wounds in all the previous battles had made a deep impression upon my comrades as well as upon my own mind. So many had fallen at my side, so often had balls and shells pierced and torn my clothing, grazing my body without drawing a drop of blood, that a sort of blind faith possessed my men that I was not to be killed in battle. This belief was evidenced by their constantly repeated expressions: "They can't hurt him." "He's as safe one place as another." "He's got a charmed life."

If I had allowed these expressions of my men to have any effect upon my mind the impression was quickly dissipated when the Sharpsburg storm came and the whizzing Miniés, one after another, began to pierce my body.

The first volley from the Union lines in my front sent a ball through the brain of the chivalric Colonel Tew, of North Carolina, to whom I was talking, and another ball through the calf of my right leg. On the right and the left my men were falling under the death-dealing crossfire like trees in a hurricane. The persistent Federals, who had lost so heavily from repeated repulses, seemed now determined to kill enough Confederates to make the debits and credits of the battle's balance-sheet more nearly even. Both sides stood in the open at short range and without the semblance of breastworks, and the firing was doing a deadly work. Higher up in the same leg I was again shot; but still no bone was broken. I was able to walk along the line and give encouragement to my resolute riflemen, who were firing with the coolness and steadiness of peace soldiers in target practice. When later in the day the third ball pierced my left arm, tearing asunder the tendons and mangling the flesh, they caught sight of the blood running down my fingers, and these devoted and big-hearted men, while still loading their guns, pleaded with me to leave them and go to the rear, pledging me that they would stay there and fight to the last. I could not consent to leave them in such a crisis. The surgeons were all busy at the field-hospitals in the rear, and there was no way, therefore, of stanching the blood, but I had a vigorous constitution, and this was doing me good service.

A fourth ball ripped through my shoulder, leaving its base and a wad of clothing in its track. I could still stand and walk, although the shocks and loss of blood had left but little of my normal strength. I remembered the pledge to the commander that we would stay there till the battle ended or night came. I looked at the sun. It moved very slowly; in fact, it seemed to stand still.

I thought I saw some wavering in my line, near the extreme right, and Private Vickers, of Alabama, volunteered to carry any orders I might wish to send. I directed him to go quickly and remind the men of the pledge to General Lee, and to say to them that I was still on the field and intended to stay there. He bounded away like an Olympic racer; but he had gone less than fifty yards when he fell, instantly killed by a ball through his head. I then attempted to go myself, although I was bloody and faint, and my legs did not bear me steadily. I had gone but a short distance when I was shot down by a fifth ball, which struck me squarely in the face, and passed out, barely missing the jugular vein. I fell forward and lay unconscious with my face in my cap; and it would seem that I might have been smothered by the blood running into my cap from this last wound but for the act of some Yankee, who, as if to save my life, had at a previous hour during the battle, shot a hole through the cap, which let the blood out.

I was borne on a litter to the rear, and recall nothing more till revived by stimulants at a late hour of the night.

—GORDON, *Reminiscences of the Civil War*

14. "THE WHOLE LANDSCAPE TURNS RED" AT ANTIETAM

The third, and what should have been the most important, battle came on the Confederate right. Burnside was massed east of the Antietam; a thin line of Confederates under Longstreet were ranged on the hills along the western side of the stream. The first efforts to get across what came to be known as Burnside's Bridge were repulsed by Toombs. Not until one o'clock was the bridge carried; not until almost four did Burnside finally launch a full-scale attack. It was irresistible. The Federals swept up the hill, pushed the butter-nuts back onto the Cemetery and into Sharpsburg, and threatened disaster to the whole Confederate army.

Then came one of the dramatic moments of the war. Jackson had left A. P. Hill at Harpers Ferry with about 2,500 men. Early on the seventeenth Hill had started for Sharpsburg, a 15-mile hike which involved fording the Potomac. Just as Burnside broke the Confederate line, Hill's men came up on the double-quick from Shepardstown, and sounding the rebel yell burst on the triumphant Federals, hurled them back down the hill, and saved the day. That was the end. The next day Lee stood his ground; then he slipped away, across the Potomac and into Virginia.

David Thompson, who here recalls the fighting across the Burnside Bridge, was a member of the 9th New York Volunteers.

ABOUT noon the battle began afresh. This must have been Franklin's men of the Sixth Corps, for the firing was nearer, and they came up behind the center. Suddenly a stir beginning far up on the right, and running like a wave along the line, brought the regiment to its feet. A silence fell on every one at once, for each felt that the momentous "now" had come. Just as we started I saw, with a little shock, a line-officer take out his watch to note the hour, as though the affair beyond the creek were a business appointment which he was going to keep.

When we reached the brow of the hill the fringe of trees along the creek screened the fighting entirely, and we were deployed as skirmishers under their cover. We sat there two hours. All that time the rest of the corps had been moving over the stone bridge and going into position on the other side of the creek. Then we were ordered over at a ford which had been found below the bridge, where the water was waist-deep. One man was shot in mid-stream. At the foot of the slope on the opposite side the line was formed and we moved up through the thin woods. Reaching the level we lay down behind a battery which seemed to have been disabled. There, if anywhere, I should have remembered that I was soaking wet from my waist down. So great was the excitement, however, that I have never been able to recall it. Here some of the men, going to the rear for water, discovered in the ashes of some hay-ricks which had been fired by our shells the charred remains of several Confederates. After long waiting it became noised along the line that we were to take a battery that was at work several hundred yards ahead on the top of a hill. This narrowed the field and brought us to consider the work before us more attentively.

Right across our front, two hundred feet or so away, ran a country road bordered on each side by a snake fence. Beyond this road stretched a plowed field several hundred feet in length, sloping up to the battery, which was hidden in a cornfield. A stone fence, breast-high, inclosed the field on the left, and behind it lay a regiment of Confederates, who would be directly on our flank if we should attempt the slope. The prospect was far from encouraging, but the order came to get ready for the attempt.

Our knapsacks were left on the ground behind us. At the word a rush was made for the fences. The line was so disordered by the time the second fence was passed that we hurried forward to a shallow undulation a few feet ahead, and lay down among the furrows to re-form, doing so by crawling up into line. A hundred feet or so ahead was a similar undulation to which we ran for a second shelter. The battery, which at first had not seemed to notice us, now, apprised of its danger, opened fire upon us. We were getting ready now for the charge proper, but were still lying on our faces. Lieutenant-Colonel Kimball was ramping up and down the line. The discreet regiment behind the fence was silent. Now and then a bullet from them cut the air over our heads, but generally they were reserving their fire for that better shot which they knew they would get in a few minutes. The battery, however, whose shots at first went over our heads, had depressed its guns so as to shave the surface of the ground. Its fire was beginning to tell. I remember looking behind and seeing an officer riding diagonally across the field—a most inviting target—instinctively bending his head down over his horse's neck, as though he were riding through driving rain. While my eye was on him I saw, between me and him, a rolled overcoat with its straps on bound into the air and fall among the furrows. One of the enemy's grape-shot had plowed a groove in the skull of a young fellow and had cut his overcoat from his shoulders. He never stirred from his position, but lay there face downward—a dreadful spectacle. A moment after, I heard a man cursing a comrade for lying on him heavily. He was cursing a dying man.

As the range grew better, the firing became more rapid, the situation desperate and exasperating to the last degree. Human nature was on the rack, and there burst forth from it the most vehement, terrible swearing I have ever heard. Certainly the joy of conflict was not ours that day. The suspense was only for a moment, however, for the order to charge came just after. Whether the regiment was thrown into disorder or not, I never knew. I only remember that as we rose and started all the fire that had been held back so long was loosed. In a second the air was full of the hiss of bullets and the hurtle of grape-shot. The mental strain was so great that I saw at that moment the singular effect mentioned, I think, in the life of Goethe on a similar occasion—the whole landscape for an instant turned slightly red. I see again, as I saw it then in a flash, a man just in front of me drop his musket and throw up his hands, stung into vigorous swearing by a bullet behind the ear. Many men fell going up the hill, but it seemed to be all over in a moment, and I found myself passing a hollow where a dozen wounded men lay—among them our sergeant-major, who was calling me to come down. He had caught sight of the blanket rolled across my back, and called me to unroll it and help to carry from the field one of our wounded lieutenants.

When I returned from obeying this summons the regiment (?) was not to be seen. It had gone in on the run, what there was left of it, and had disappeared in the corn-field about the battery. There was nothing to do but lie there and await developments. Nearly all the men in the hollow were wounded, one man—a recruit named Devlin, I think—frightfully so, his arm being cut short off. He lived a few minutes only. All were calling for water, of course, but none was to be had.

We lay there till dusk, perhaps an hour, when the fighting ceased. During that hour, while the bullets snipped the leaves from a young locust-tree growing at the edge of the hollow and powdered us with the fragments, we had time to speculate on many things—among others, on the impatience with which men clamor, in dull times, to be led into a fight. We heard all through the war that the army "was eager to be led against the enemy." It must have been so, for truthful correspondents said so, and editors confirmed it. But when you came to hunt for this particular itch, it was always the next regiment that had it. The truth is, when bullets are whacking against tree-trunks and solid shot are cracking skulls like egg-shells, the consuming passion in the breast of the average man is to get out of the way. Between the physical fear of going forward and the moral fear of turning back, there is a predicament of exceptional awkwardness from which a hidden hole in the ground would be a wonderfully welcome outlet.

Night fell, preventing further struggle. Of 600 men of the regiment who crossed the creek at 3 o'clock that afternoon, 45 were killed and 176 wounded. The Confederates held possession of that part of the field over which we had moved, and just after dusk they sent out detachments to collect arms and bring in prisoners. When they came to our hollow all the unwounded and slightly wounded there were marched to the rear—prisoners of the 15th Georgia. We slept on the ground that night without protection of any kind; for, with a recklessness quite common throughout the war, we had thrown away every incumbrance on going into the fight.

—THOMPSON, "With Burnside at Antietam"

VII

Fredericksburg and Chancellorsville

McCLELLAN had won a technical victory at Antietam, and Lincoln took advantage of it to issue his preliminary Emancipation Proclamation. But once again "Little Mac" had the slows. On October 6 Halleck ordered him "to cross the Potomac and give battle to the enemy," but McClellan procrastinated. While he delayed Stuart rode with impunity around his army. Finally, on November 2, McClellan succeeded in getting his army across the Potomac; five days later Lincoln relieved him from command and appointed General Ambrose Burnside—who gave his name to sideburns—to his place. A second-rate officer with little to recommend him, Burnside was ambitious to succeed where so many had failed. Noting that Lee's forces were widely scattered, he proposed to drive south through Fredericksburg to Richmond before Lee could collect an army to oppose him. Moving with laudable celerity Burnside concentrated his "Grand Divisions" at Falmouth, just north of Fredericksburg on the Rappahannock. But alas there were no pontoons, and while the army marked time Jackson joined Lee at Fredericksburg and the Confederates dug in.

Properly defended, Fredericksburg was well-nigh impregnable, and with Lee in command of over 75,000 men and 306 guns there was no doubt that it would be properly defended. The town lay on a bend of the broad Rappahannock; behind it were a series of low-lying hills from Marye's Heights southward to Prospect Hill, along the base of which ran the tiny Massapomax River. It was along these heights that the Confederates were entrenched, Jackson commanding the left, on Marye's Heights, and Longstreet the right. In front of Marye's Heights ran a drainage ditch, and at the base of Marye's Hill—a knoll at the southern end of the Heights—was a sunken road with a stone retaining wall which offered almost perfect protection to infantry. It was against this position that Burnside hurled his army, in vain.

Fredericksburg ended in a bloody repulse. Burnside blamed his subordinates, and demanded that the President dismiss them or him. Lincoln dismissed him, and—somewhat reluctantly, as his letter reveals—appointed in his place "Fighting Joe" Hooker, whom Burnside had declared to be "unfit to hold an important commission during a crisis like the present." It was, perhaps, the one time when Burnside's judgment proved sound.

Hooker took command of an army that had been defeated but was far from demoralized, and that was far larger than Lee's; when Longstreet was sent south of the James to find provisions and forage for men and horses, Hooker outnumbered Lee by at least two to one.

Hooker's strategy was admirable. Leaving Sedgwick with 40,000 men at Fredericksburg, he planned to move up the Rappahannock, cross over through the Wilderness, catch Lee in a giant pincers movement, and overwhelm him. If Lee chose to stand and fight at Fredericksburg, Hooker could strike him from the rear; if he moved into the Wilderness to grapple with Hooker, Sedgwick could sweep down on Richmond. By the end of April Hooker had completed the reorganization and rebuilding of his army, and on the twenty-seventh his advance guard began fording the Rappahannock. By the thirtieth the whole army, except for a reserve corps, was across and prepared to move on Lee.

But once again, as we shall see, Lee outgeneraled and outfought his adversary, using on Hooker the strategy that Hooker had planned to use on him. Instead of being himself caught in a pincers, he caught Hooker in a pincers, rolled him up on both flanks, and pushed him back to the edge of the river; then he turned on the hapless Sedgwick and sent him, too, hurtling back across the river. It was a great victory, in some ways the most spectacular of Lee's career, but it was bought at a great price: Jackson.

1. LINCOLN URGES McCLELLAN TO ADVANCE

McClellan's conduct of the Antietam campaign seemed to vindicate his reappointment to the command of the armies. Once that battle was over, however, he fell back into his old habits of delay. On October 1 Lincoln went personally to view the situation and on his return to Washington formally ordered McClellan "to cross the Potomac and give battle to the enemy." Even this categorical demand was disregarded. The following letter, characteristically patient and reasonable, was sent a week later. McClellan met it with the plea that his cavalry was broken down—a reply which drew from Lincoln the memorable retort, "Will you pardon me for asking what the horses of your army have done since the battle of Antietam that fatigues anything?" Finally on October 26 McClellan got under way, but when he permitted Lee to interpose his army between Richmond and the Federal forces, Lincoln removed him.

Few generals, it is safe to say, ever did more to merit dismissal. The Democrats sought to make a martyr out of McClellan, nominating him for the Presidency in 1864 on a platform which called the war a failure and demanded a cessation of hostilities. McClellan repudiated this plank in the platform but accepted the nomination; fortunately for the Union he was defeated that November.

To General G. B. McClellan.

Executive Mansion, Washington, October 13, 1862

My Dear Sir:—You remember my speaking to you of what I called your over-cautiousness. Are you not over-cautious when you assume that you cannot do what the enemy is constantly doing? Should you not claim to be at least his equal in prowess, and act upon the claim?

As I understand, you telegraphed General Halleck that you cannot subsist your army at Winchester unless the railroad from Harper's Ferry to that point be put in working order. But the enemy does now subsist his army at Winchester, at a distance nearly twice as great from railroad transportation as you would have to do, without the railroad last named. He now wagons from Culpepper Court-House, which is just about twice as far as you would have to do from Harper's Ferry. He is certainly not more than half as well provided with wagons as you are. I certainly should be pleased for you to have the advantage of the railroad from Harper's Ferry to Winchester; but it wastes all the remainder of autumn to give it to you, and, in fact, ignores the question of *time*, which cannot and must not be ignored.

Again, one of the standard maxims of war, as you know, is "to operate upon the enemy's communications as much as possible, without exposing your own." You seem to act as if this applies *against* you, but cannot apply in your *favor*. Change positions with the enemy, and think you not he would break your communication with Richmond within the next twenty-four hours? You dread his going into Pennsylvania. But if he does so in full force, he gives up his communications to you absolutely, and you have nothing to do but to follow and ruin him; if he does so with less than full force, fall upon and beat what is left behind all the easier.

Exclusive of the water line, you are now nearer to Richmond than the enemy is, by the route that you *can* and he *must* take. Why can you not reach there before him, unless you admit that he is more than your equal on a march? His route is the arc of a circle, while yours is the chord. The roads are as good on yours as on his.

You know I desired, but did not order, you to cross the Potomac below instead of above the Shenandoah and Blue Ridge. My idea was, that this would at once menace the enemy's communications, which I would seize if he would permit. If he should move northward, I would follow him closely, holding his communications. If he should prevent our seizing his communications, and move toward Richmond, I would press closely to him, fight him if a favorable opportunity should present, and at least try to beat him to Richmond on the inside track. I say "try;" if we never try, we shall never succeed. If he makes a stand at Winchester, moving neither north or south, I would fight him there, on the idea that if we cannot beat him when he bears the wastage of coming to us, we never can when we bear the wastage of going to him. This proposition is a simple truth, and is too important to be lost sight of for a moment. In coming to us he tenders us an advantage which we should not waive. We should not so operate as to merely drive him away. As we must beat him somewhere or fail finally, we can do it, if at all, easier near to us than far away. If we cannot beat the enemy where he now is, we never can, he again being within the intrenchments of Richmond. . . .

It is all easy if our troops march as well as the enemy, and it is unmanly to say they cannot do it. This letter is in no sense an order.

Yours truly,

A. LINCOLN.

—War of the Rebellion . . . Official Records

2. A DAY OF REBEL RULE IN CHAMBERSBURG

While the President—and the nation—was waiting impatiently for Mc-Clellan to take up the pursuit of Lee after Antietam, the Confederates seized the initiative. On October 10 General Stuart, acting under instructions from Lee, began his second "ride around the army." Crossing the Potomac with some 1,800 cavalry he rode into Chambersburg, destroyed some stores, and, before any intercepting force could be organized, turned east to Cashtown and thence down the Emmitsburg road and across the Potomac to rejoin Lee. Aside from the destruction of stores the raid was of little value, but as the total cost to Stuart was one man wounded, it was doubtless worth while. The courtesy and restraint which characterized Confederate conduct was in accordance with Lee's specific orders.

Colonel McClure, who here describes rebel rule in Chambersburg, was owner and editor of the local newspaper and a power in the Republican party.

Chambersburgh, Pa., October ——, 1862

Our people were confounded with astonishment at the brilliant audacity of the rebels penetrating twenty miles in Gen. McClellan's rear; but, however reckless or well devised on their part, the fact and the rebels were both staring our people in the face. The rain was pouring down in torrents, and in a little time citizens were seen running to and fro with their muskets; but there was no organization, and no time to effect one. Col. Kennedy attempted to improvise mounted pickets for the several roads on which they might enter, but he had scarcely got his forces mounted until the clattering of hoofs was heard on the western pike, and in a few minutes the rebel advance was in the centre of the town. They stated that they bore a flag of truce, and wished to be taken to the commandant of the post. . . .

I went up town to meet the flag of truce, and found a clever-looking "butternut," dripping wet, without any mark of rank, bearing a dirty white cloth on a little stick. He politely stated that he sought the commander or authorities of the town, and in the name of the general commanding the confederate forces, he demanded the surrender of the village. He refused to give his name, or the name of the general commanding, and he could not state on what terms they would accept a surrender. As I had no command other than the scattered and bewildered home guards—all brave enough, but entirely without drill or organization—and about three hundred wounded men in hospitals, I acted with the citizens as one of them; and it did not require a protracted council to determine that we could not successfully resist cavalry and artillery. So we concluded that the venerable village had to be consigned over to rebel keeping. . . .

General Hampton . . . assured us that he would scrupulously protect citizens—would allow no soldiers to enter public or private houses unless under command of an officer upon legitimate business—that he would take such private property as he needed for his government or troops, but that he would allow no wanton destruction, and who would give receipts for the same, if desired, so that claim might be made therefor against the United States Government. All property belonging to or used by the United States, he stated, he would use or destroy at his pleasure, and the wounded in hospitals would be paroled. . . .

The committee went through the form of a grave but brief consultation, somewhat expedited, perhaps, by the rain, and we then solemnly and formally surrendered the town upon the terms proposed. . . . So rebel rule began at Chambersburgh. They marched in very orderly, and most of their force started out different roads to procure horses, forage, and provisions.

I started in advance of them for my house, but not in time to save the horses. I confidently expected to be overrun by them, and to find the place one scene of desolation in the morning. I resolved, however, that things should be done soberly, if possible, and I had just time to destroy all the liquors about the house. As their pickets were all around me, I could not get it off. A barrel of best old rye, which Senator Finney had sent me to prove the superiority of the Crawford County article over that of Franklin, was quietly rolled out of a cellar side-door, and a good-sized hole bored into it. A keg of Oberholtzer's best, sent me several years ago, but never tapped, followed Finney's testimonial to Crawford County distillation; and a couple cases of Presbury's best Girard House importation had the necks of the bottles taken off summarily, and the contents given to the angry storm. I finished just in time, for they were soon out upon me in force, and every horse in the barn—ten in all—was promptly equipped and mounted by a rebel cavalryman. They passed on towards Shippensburgh, leaving a picket-force on the road.

In an hour they returned with all the horses they could find, and dismounted to spend the night on the turnpike in front of my door. It was now midnight, and I sat on the porch observing their movements. They had my best corn-field beside them, and their horses fared well. In a little while, one entered the yard, came up to me, and, after a profound bow, politely asked for a few coals to start a fire. I supplied him, and informed him as blandly as possible where he would find wood conveniently, as I had dim visions of camp-fires made of my palings. I was thanked in return, and the mild-mannered villain proceeded at once to strip the fence and kindle fires. Soon after, a squad came and asked permission to get some water. I piloted them to the pump, and again received a profusion of thanks.

Communication having thus been opened between us, squads followed each other closely for water, but each called and asked permission before getting it, and promptly left the yard. I was somewhat bewildered at this uniform courtesy, and supposed it but a prelude to a general movement upon every thing eatable in the morning. . . .

About one o'clock, half a dozen officers came to the door and asked to have some coffee made for them, offering to pay liberally for it in confederate scrip. After concluding a treaty with them on behalf of the colored servants, coffee was promised them, and they then asked for a little bread with it. They were wet and shivering, and seeing a bright, open wood-fire in the library, they asked permission to enter and warm themselves until their coffee should be ready, assuring me that under no circumstances should any thing in the house be disturbed by their men. I had no alternative but to accept them as my guests until it might please them to depart, and I did so with as good grace as possible.

Once seated around the fire, all reserve seemed to be forgotten on their part, and they opened a general conversation on politics, the war, the different battles, the merits of generals in both armies, etc. They spoke with entire freedom upon every subject but their movement into Chambersburgh. Most of them were men of more than ordinary intelligence and culture, and their demeanor was in all respects eminently courteous. I took a cup of coffee with them, and have seldom seen any thing more keenly relished. They said they had not tasted coffee for weeks before, and then they had paid from six dollars to ten dollars per pound for it. When they were through, they asked whether there was any coffee left, and finding that there was some, they proposed to bring some more officers and a few privates who were prostrated by exposure to get what was left. They were, of course, as welcome as those present, and on they came in squads of five or more, until every grain of browned coffee was exhausted. They then asked for tea, and that was served to some twenty more.

In the mean time, a subordinate officer had begged of me a little bread for himself and few men, and he was supplied in the kitchen. He was followed by others in turn, until nearly an hundred had been supplied with something to eat or drink. All, however, politely asked permission to enter the house, and behaved with entire propriety. They did not make a single rude or profane remark, even to the servants. In the mean time, the officers, who had first entered the house, had filled their pipes from the box of Killickinick on the mantel—after being assured that smoking was not offensive—and we had another hour of free talk on matters generally. When told that I was a decided Republican, they thanked me for being candid. . . .

At four o'clock in the morning the welcome blast of the bugle was heard, and they rose hurriedly to depart. Thanking me for the hospitality they had received, we parted mutually expressing the hope that should we ever meet again, it would be under more pleasant circumstances. In a few minutes, they were mounted and moved into Chambersburgh. About seven o'clock I went into town, and found that the First brigade, under General Hampton, had gone toward Gettysburg. Gen. Stuart sat on his horse in the centre of the town, surrounded by his staff, and his command was coming from the country in large squads, leading their old horses and riding the new ones they had found in the stables hereabouts. General Stuart is of medium size, has a keen eye, and wears immense sandy whiskers and moustache. His demeanor to our people was that of a humane soldier. In several instances his men commenced to take private property from stores, but they were arrested by General Stuart's provost-guard. In a single instance only, that I have heard of, did they enter a store by intimidating the proprietor. All our shops and stores were closed, and, with a very few exceptions, were not disturbed.

There were considerable Government stores here—some two hundred pairs of shoes, a few boxes of clothing, and a large quantity of ammunition captured recently from General Longstreet. It was stored in the warehouses of Wunderlich & Nead. About eleven o'clock their rear-guard was ready to leave, and they notified the citizens residing near the warehouses to remove their families, as they were going to burn all public property. The railroad station-house, machine-shops, round house, and the warehouses, filled with ammunition, were then fired, and the last of the rebels fled the town. In a little time a terrific explosion told that the flames had reached the powder, and for hours shells were exploding with great rapidity. The fire companies came out as soon as the rebels left, but could not save any of the buildings fired because of the shells. They saved all others, however.

So ended a day of rebel rule in Chambersburgh. They took some eight hundred horses from our people, and destroyed, perhaps, one hundred thousand dollars' worth of property for the Cumberland Valley Railroad Company, probably five thousand dollars for Wunderlich & Nead, and one hundred and fifty thousand dollars for the Government. Our people generally feel that, bad as they are, they are not so bad as they might be. . . .

Hoping that I shall never again be called upon to entertain a circle of rebels around my fireside, believe me, truly thine,

A. K. McCLURE.

—McCLURE, "The Invasion of Pennsylvania"

3. BURNSIDE BLUNDERS AT FREDERICKSBURG

We have here two accounts of Fredericksburg—a Confederate and a Union. Each tells its own story, and it is unnecessary to recapitulate that story here, but we may give something of the setting of the battle. It was on December 10 that Burnside began laying five pontoon bridges across the Rappahannock. Confederate sharpshooters interfered effectively with this undertaking and Burnside attempted to drive them out first by a heavy bombardment of the town itself, then by sending four companies of Federal sharpshooters across in boats to hold down the Confederate fire. By the twelfth two of the "Grand Divisions" were across the river—Sumner's in Fredericksburg itself and Franklin's to the south. On the morning of the thirteenth the attack began, all along the line.

The first account here is by one of the defenders, William Owen of the Washington Artillery of New Orleans. Few of those who have left us records had a more varied experience than this Louisianian who fought in the Virginia

campaigns to *1863, then went west, took part in the Chickamauga-Chatta-
nooga campaign, and then returned east to fight in the Wilderness and at
Petersburg. The second account is taken from the* Cincinnati Commercial.

A. THE YANKEES ATTACK MARYE'S HEIGHTS

ON the night of the 10th of December [1862] we, of the New Orleans
Washington Artillery, sat up late in our camp on Marye's Heights, entertaining some visitors in an improvised theater, smoking our pipes, and
talking of home. A final punch having been brewed and disposed of, everybody crept under the blankets and was soon in the land of Nod.

In an hour or two we were aroused by the report of a heavy gun. I was
up in an instant, for if there should be another it would be the signal that
the enemy was preparing to cross the river. Mr. Florence, a civilian in the
bivouac, bounced as if he had a concealed spring under his blanket, and cried
out, "Wake up! wake up! what's that?"

The deep roar of the second gun was heard, and we knew what we had
to do. It was 4 o'clock. Our orders were that upon the firing of these signal
guns we should at once take our places in the redoubts prepared for us on
Marye's Hill, and await developments. "Boots and saddles" was sounded, and
the camp was instantly astir, and in the gray of the morning we were on the
Plank road leading up the hill. The positions reached, . . . without delay the
men made the redoubts as snug as possible, and finding the epaulements not
to their liking, went to work with pick and shovel throwing the dirt a little
higher, and fashioning embrasures to fire through. The engineers objected,
and said they were "ruining the works," but the cannoneers said, "We have
to fight here, not you; we will arrange them to suit ourselves." And General
Longstreet approvingly said, "If you save the finger of a man's hand, that
does some good." A dense fog covered the country, and we could not discern what was going on in the town.

The morning of the 12th was also foggy, and it was not until 2 P.M. that
it cleared off, and then we could see the Stafford Heights, across the river,
densely packed with troops. At 3 P.M. a heavy column moved down toward
one of the bridges near the gas-works, and we opened upon it, making some
splendid practice and apparently stirring them up prodigiously, for they soon
sought cooler localities. While our guns were firing, the enemy's long range
batteries on the Stafford Heights opened upon us, as much as to say, "What
are you about over there?" We paid no attention to their inquiry, as our guns
could not reach them.

At dawn the next morning, December 13th, in the fresh and nipping air,
I stepped upon the gallery overlooking the heights back of the little old-
fashioned town of Fredericksburg. Heavy fog and mist hid the whole plain
between the heights and the Rappahannock, but under cover of that fog and
within easy cannon-shot lay Burnside's army. Along the heights, to the right
and left of where I was standing, extending a length of nearly five miles, lay
Lee's army.

BATTLE
OF
FREDERICKSBURG
Dec 10-16. 1862

The bugles and the drum corps of the respective armies were now sounding reveille, and the troops were preparing for their early meal. All knew we should have a battle to-day and a great one, for the enemy had crossed the river in immense force, upon his pontoons during the night. On the Confederate side all was ready, and the shock was awaited with stubborn resolution. Last night we had spread our blankets upon the bare floor in the parlor of Marye's house, and now our breakfast was being prepared in its fire-place, and we were impatient to have it over. After hastily dispatching this light meal of bacon and corn-bread, the colonel, chief bugler, and I (the adjutant of the battalion) mounted our horses and rode out to inspect our lines . . . and found everything ready for instant action. . . .

At 12 o'clock the fog had cleared, and while we were sitting in Marye's yard smoking our pipes, after a lunch of hard crackers, a courier came to Colonel Walton, bearing a dispatch from General Longstreet for General Cobb, but, for our information as well, to be read and then given to him. It was as follows: "Should General Anderson, on your left, be compelled to fall back to the second line of heights, you must conform to his movements." Descending the hill into the sunken road, I made my way through the troops, to a little house where General Cobb had his headquarters, and handed him the dispatch. He read it carefully, and said, "Well! if they wait for me to fall back, they will wait a long time."

Hardly had he spoken, when a brisk skirmish fire was heard in front, toward the town, and looking over the stone-wall we saw our skirmishers falling back, firing as they came; at the same time the head of a Federal column was seen emerging from one of the streets of the town. They came on at the double-quick, with loud cries of "Hi! Hi! Hi!" which we could distinctly hear. Their arms were carried at "right shoulder shift," and their colors were aslant the shoulders of the color-sergeants. They crossed the canal at the bridge, and getting behind the bank to the low ground to deploy, were almost concealed from our sight. It was 12:30 P.M., and it was evident that we were now going to have it hot and heavy.

The enemy, having deployed, now showed himself above the crest of the ridge and advanced in columns of brigades, and at once our guns began their deadly work with shell and solid shot. How beautifully they came on! Their bright bayonets glistening in the sunlight made the line look like a huge serpent of blue and steel. The very force of their onset leveled the broad fences bounding the small fields and gardens that interspersed the plain. We could see our shells bursting in their ranks, making great gaps; but on they came, as though they would go straight through and over us. Now we gave them canister, and that staggered them. A few more paces onward and the Georgians in the road below us rose up, and, glancing an instant along their rifle barrels, let loose a storm of lead into the faces of the advance brigade. This was too much; the column hesitated, and then, turning, took refuge behind the bank.

But another line appeared from behind the crest and advanced gallantly, and again we opened our guns upon them, and through the smoke we could discern the red breeches of the "Zouaves," and hammered away at them especially. But this advance, like the preceding one, although passing the point reached by the first column, and doing and daring all that brave men could do, recoiled under our canister and the bullets of the infantry in the road, and fell back in great confusion. Spotting the fields in our front, we could detect little patches of blue—the dead and wounded of the Federal infantry who had fallen facing the very muzzles of our guns.

Cooke's brigade of Ransom's division was now placed in the sunken road with Cobb's men. At 2 P.M. other columns of the enemy left the crest and advanced to the attack; it appeared to us that there was no end of them. On they came in beautiful array and seemingly more determined to hold the plain than before; but our fire was murderous, and no troops on earth could stand the *feu d'enfer* we were giving them. In the foremost line we distinguished the green flag with the golden harp of old Ireland, and we knew it to be Meagher's Irish brigade. The gunners of the two rifle-pieces, Corporals Payne and Hardie, were directed to turn their guns against this column; but the gallant enemy pushed on beyond all former charges, and fought and left their dead within five and twenty paces of the sunken road.

Our position on the hill was now a hot one, and three regiments of Ransom's brigade were ordered up to reënforce the infantry in the road. We watched them as they came marching in line of battle from the rear, where they had been lying in reserve. They passed through our works and rushed down the hill with loud yells, and then stood shoulder to shoulder with the Georgians. The 25th North Carolina regiment, crossing Miller's guns, halted upon the crest of the hill, dressed its line, and fired a deadly volley at the enemy at close range, and then at the command "Forward!" dashed down the hill. It left dead men on Miller's redoubt, and he had to drag them away from the muzzles of his guns.

At this time General Cobb fell mortally wounded, and General Cooke was borne from the field, also wounded. Among other missiles a 3-inch rifle-ball came crashing through the works and fell at our feet. Kursheedt picked it up and said, "Boys, let's send this back to them again"; and into the gun it went, and was sped back into the dense ranks of the enemy.

General Kershaw now advanced from the rear with two regiments of his infantry, to reënforce the men in the sunken road, who were running short of ammunition, and to take command.

The sharp-shooters having got range of our embrasures, we began to suffer. Corporal Ruggles fell mortally wounded, and Perry, who seized the rammer as it fell from Ruggles's hand, received a bullet in the arm. Rodd was holding "vent," and away went his "crazy bone." In quick succession Everett, Rossiter, and Kursheedt were wounded. Falconer in passing in rear of the guns was struck behind the ear and fell dead. We were now so short-handed that every one was in the work, officers and men putting their shoulders to the wheels and running up the guns after each recoil. The frozen ground had given way and was all slush and mud. We were compelled to call upon the infantry to help us at the guns. Eshleman crossed over from the right to report his guns nearly out of ammunition; the other officers reported the same. They were reduced to a few solid shot only. It was now 5 o'clock, P.M., and there was a lull in the storm. The enemy did not seem inclined to renew his efforts, so our guns were withdrawn one by one, and the batteries of Woolfolk and Moody were substituted.

The little whitewashed brick-house to the right of the redoubt we were in was so battered with bullets during the four hours and a half engagement that at the close it was transformed to a bright brick-dust red. An old cast-iron stove lay against the house, and as the bullets would strike it it would give forth the sound of "bing! bing!" with different tones and variations. During the hottest of the firing old Mr. Florence, our non-combatant friend, was peering around the end of the house (in which, by the way, our wounded took refuge), looking out to see if his son, who was at the gun, was all right. A cannon-ball struck the top of the work, scattering dirt all over us and profusely down our necks, and, striking the end of the house, carried away a cart-load of bricks, just where Mr. Florence had been looking an instant before. We thought surely he had met his fate, but in a moment we were pleased to see his gray head "bob up serenely," determined to see "what was the gage of the battle."

After withdrawing from the hill the command was placed in bivouac, and the men threw themselves upon the ground to take a much-needed rest. We had been under the hottest fire men ever experienced for four hours and a half, and our loss had been three killed and twenty-four wounded. Among them was Sergeant John Wood, our leading spirit in camp theatricals, who was severely injured and never returned to duty. One gun was slightly disabled, and we had exhausted all of our canister, shell and case shot, and nearly every solid shot in our chests. At 5:30 another attack was made by the enemy, but it was easily repulsed, and the battle of Fredericksburg was over, and Burnside was baffled and defeated.

—OWEN, "A Hot Day on Marye's Heights"

B. "FREDERICKSBURG WAS A TRAP"

Falmouth, December 17, 1862

On Friday morning [Dec. 12, 1862] those of us not fully posted, and not conversant with all the mysteries of "strategy," expected a battle. But the morning passed quietly, the smoke veiling all distant objects from observation. Our troops were crossing into Fredericksburgh. . . . The town, in the afternoon, literally swarmed with troops. The enemy's batteries were ominously silent. If the rebel general had any particular objections to the presence of our troops in the town, why did he not open upon them from his batteries? What was to prevent the enemy from shelling the town, as we had done? I asked several military gentlemen the question, for the situation appeared to me to be one of the deepest peril. One said: "The enemy had not ammunition to spare." Another: "Oh! a bombardment don't amount to any thing any how." Another: "They don't care about bombing us, it is an inconsequential sort of business. We threw four thousand shells yesterday, and it amounted to nothing." Another: "They're afraid of our siege-guns on this side." Another: "General Lee thinks he will have a big thing on us about the bombardment of this town. He proposes to rouse the indignation of the civilized world, as they call it. You'll see he won't throw a shell into it. He is playing for the sympathies of Europe." Another thought the enemy were skedaddling, and spoke of the laugh that would be raised at Burnside's expense in that case. But I think a private soldier came nearer the mark than any one else. He said, with the usual expletives: "They want us to get in. Getting out won't be quite so smart and easy. You'll see if it will." . . .

At night I crossed into the town. . . . The streets were full of soldiers lounging and smoking about their fires, or wrapped in their blankets and sleeping, their muskets stacked, in numbers that indicated the immense mass of troops that occupied the place. The sky was clear, and thickly as the stars sparkled overhead the camp-fires blazed along the Rappahannock, lighting up the front of the shattered city, and gleaming far and wide to the north. Behind the dark and gloomy hills compassing the town on the enemy's side, there was a wide glare of many fires, like an aurora borealis, marking the presence of the rebel army of Virginia. Returning to the north side of the river, the roads were choked with batteries of field-artillery, and ammunition and supply-trains, rumbling and creaking forward. . . .

It was after eleven o'clock before the contest deepened into earnest, desperate battle. Then our columns were visible along the slope leading to the second terrace, and as they advanced, battery after battery of the rebels, quiet through all the bombardment, opened. It was evident that without artillery to support them, our troops would be overpowered by the withering cannonade of the enemy. I had been told the day before, by an officer who ought to have been well informed, that when the battle begun we would open a battery of heavy rifled guns upon the rebels, and make them glad to stop their artillery, and rely on musket and bayonet and the natural advantages of their position. I waited and watched for the opening of this battery, which was to astonish the rebels, with a sharp interest and anxiety that it would be impossible to express. Our long columns of noble fellows pushed on, and the weight of the enemy's artillery-fire continued every minute to increase.

Our batteries upon the left augmented their fire, and the guns of which I had been led to hope so much opened. I saw with horror that at least half the shells were bursting behind our own men, and that they were certainly killing more of them than the enemy. Gen. Burnside, I have since learned, sent orders to the battery to cease firing, and it did so. Then for dreadful hours the rebel artillerists had it all their own way. They had, at one time, seven batteries in full blast upon our devoted columns. Several of their guns were very heavy ones. One seven-inch rifle was heard loud and often over the roar of other arms in the engagement. I shall always have a profound remembrance of the keen, terrific report of that gun. Every shot made the hills quiver, and the number of times it spoke during the day was surprising. It seemed that the reports of that piece, like the movements of a pendulum, divided the time into periods—that the wicked emphasis of its utterances must be taken to note the passage of time and mark the progress of the fight.

It became perfectly apparent to all observers of any reasonable degree of intelligence, as the din of rebel artillery and the rage of the musketry increased, and as the big rebel rifle spoke through the gloom of the conflict, as appeared the very voice of doom, that the fortunes of the day on our side were desperate. It was manifestly absolutely impossible for our columns of unsupported infantry to carry the terrible heights. Our only hope then was in Franklin. It might be possible that he would do something grand on the left, break the enemy's line, turn his position, and come sweeping along the crest, from which the murderous artillery "volleyed and thundered." But it was drearily evident that Franklin's progress was slow. We could hear the grumbling of his guns, and see, in the distance, the battle-cloud that swelled from the combat, but alas, that cloud did not advance by perceptible degrees. The sound of the guns came no more distinctly. Clearly enough, there was hard work and slow progress on the left. . . .

While our artillery was silent, and that of the enemy was jarring the earth and filling the valley of the Rappahannock with crashing reverberations, our noble infantry maintained, for hours, a line of fire across the field, the smoke rolling from the play of their muskets in long fleecy clouds. Presently some batteries of our field-artillery got to work, and for a while the action did not look so one-sided. Flash answered flash, as gun responded to gun, but it was our field-guns to their siege-guns; and their batteries, with advantages of position and number of pieces, as well as weight of metal, and after a gallant contest our guns were silenced. It was impossible the result should be otherwise, as the converging fire of the enemy was plainly crushing. When the enemy charged upon our men they met their masters, and were invariably beaten back, terribly damaged. But their bellowing batteries, the smoke of which rushed from nearly every clump of pines—batteries opened out here and there, as occasion offered, as if the country were literally full of them— and the swarm of sharp-shooters, secure in rifle-pits and behind a stone wall, and in a sunken road, . . . were too much for the naked valor of our infantry. No troops in the world would have won a victory if placed in the position ours were. Few armies, however renowned, would have stood as well as ours did. It can hardly be in human nature for men to show more valor, or generals to manifest less judgment, than were perceptible on our side that day.

It was with a deep sense of relief that I saw the sun go down, and felt that in a little while darkness would put an end to the unequal combat. But for a time the fury of the fire on both sides redoubled as the discovery was made by the combatants that their day's work was about done. For half an hour, the din was awful, and the smoke drifted through the streets, as sometimes in a city, when there is a high wind and a great dust. There was severe fighting even after dark, and the sparkle of musketry made a fine display. Then the big rebel rifled cannon ceased to mark time, the sputter and crackle of small arms ceased on the centre, Franklin and Jackson's guns throbbed heavily a few times on the left; and all was still on the north side of the river, save the rumble of army-wagons, which are probably intimately connected with Bryant's "innumerable caravan, that moves for ever through the gate of death." . . .

It was not possible for any one who had witnessed the fight, and was candid with himself, to dispute the fact that we had had the worst of it. We had started out to take the enemy's batteries on the hills. That we had done no such thing was painfully apparent. . . . The city of Fredericksburgh was a trap, and we had plunged into it. The policy of permitting us to "occupy and possess" it under commanding batteries, was clear enough. The blunder stood revealed.

—*Cincinnati Commercial*

4. THE ASSAULT ON MARYE'S HILL

It was the attack on the Confederate left, on Marye's Hill, that proved most costly to the Union army. All through that deadly afternoon of December 13 Burnside hurled his men against the sunken road and the stone walls and the artillery of the Confederates, and when in the end darkness fell upon the battlefield Union losses had mounted to over 6,000.

Here are a Confederate and a Union account of the assaults on the Hill. The first is from the pen of the effervescent J. B. Polley, who fought with Hood's Texans—and whose figures are dramatic rather than accurate; the second by Corporal—later Captain—John McCrillis of the 5th New Hampshire Volunteers, one of the regiments that suffered most heavily in the attack on Marye's Hill.

A. The Irish Brigade Is Repulsed on Marye's Hill

Camp near Fredericksburg, Va., Dec. 20, 1862

At nine o'clock on the morning . . . the battle began in earnest. On the top of the hill, and close to the edge of the bluff, there was a battery, and behind the stone fence crouched Cobb's brigade of Georgians—one of the regiments being the gallant Eighteenth, which, when in our brigade, complimented us by its willingness to be known as the Third Texas. . . . To assault this position was a desperate undertaking. . . . Even Irish hearts had to be tempered for the ordeal, and to this end it was necessary not only to appeal to their love for "ould Ireland" but to imbue them with a supplemental fictitious courage. Only when a sprig of arbor vitae, stolen from the deserted yards of the town, was pinned upon their caps to remind them of the shamrock of their native Isle, their throats moistened liberally and their canteens filled with liquor, did they become ready to move forward as an initiatory forlorn hope. . . .

Between the last houses of the town proper and the stone fence stretched a piece of level open ground about two hundred yards wide. Entering this, the Federals halted a second or two to reform their lines; and then, some shouting "Erin go bragh," and others the Yankee huzzah, they rushed impetuously forward against a storm of grape and canister that, as long as the guns on the hilltop could be sufficiently depressed, tore great gaps in their ranks. But, wavering not, they closed together and rushed onward until within fifty yards of the stone fence, when in one grand, simultaneous burst of light, sound, and death, came the blinding flash, the deafening roar, the murderous destruction of two thousand well-aimed rifles, the wild, weird, blood-curdling Confederate yell, and two thousand Irishmen sank down wounded or dead, and a cowed and demoralized remnant sought safety in inglorious flight.

Seven assaults were made on the stone fence during the day, and five thousand men were sent to eternity before Burnside convinced himself that the position was impregnable. Only two regiments of our division were engaged in any undertaking that might be called a battle. These were the Fifty-seventh and Fifty-fourth North Carolina regiments composed of conscripts—young men under twenty and old men—all dressed in homespun, and presenting to the fastidious eyes of us veterans a very unsoldierly appearance. But we judged hastily. Ordered to drive the enemy back, they not only charged with surprising recklessness, but kept on charging until, to save them from certain capture, General Hood peremptorily recalled them. As they passed our brigade on their return, one old fellow halted, wiped the powder grime from his weather-beaten face with the sleeve of his coat, and wrathfully exclaimed, "Durn ole Hood, anyhow! He jes' didn't have no bus'ness ter stop us when we'uns was a-whippin' the durn blue-bellies ter h-ll an' back, an' eff we'uns hadder bin you Texicans, he'd never o' did it."

—POLLEY, *A Soldier's Letters to Charming Nellie*

B. The 5th New Hampshire to the Rescue

On the 13th at 12:30 P.M., the order was given for the Second Corps to assault the rebel position. In less than thirty minutes French's Division was driven back, shattered and broken with a loss of about one-half its number killed and wounded. The brigades of Zook and Meagher advance and are broken, and lose more than one-half their men.

At this time, and during the operations of the Irish Brigade, General Hancock sat upon his horse in our immediate front, cool and collected. All at once his voice is heard above the cannon's roar. How well I remember the precise words; they have been ringing in my ears ever since: 'General Caldwell, you will forward your brigade at once; the Irish Brigade is suffering severely.' Then comes the quick and impetuous command of Colonel Cross: 'Attention! Every man is expected to do his duty to-day. If I fall never mind me. Fix bayonets! No man to fire a shot until he is inside the rebel lines. Shoulder arms! Trail arms! Forward, march!' Each man firmly grasps his musket, and the lines move forward into that rain of death, and the last march of many, this side of the eternal camping-ground, begins.

The artillery fire seemed to increase, shells bursting overhead and in the ranks, the solid shot crashing through that on-sweeping line of blue, opening large gaps which were quickly closed up again to have, the next moment, that crimson swath again cut through. Now we are in range of their infantry behind a stone wall, when a stream of fire and a shower of leaden hail causes the line to disappear like dew before a morning sun. 'Close in on the colors!' is the order heard above the din of battle. 'Steady! Forward!' rose in trumpet tones from lips that were the next moment hushed in death. The colors go down, only to be again upborne by some brave spirit who in his turn slept the sleep that knows no waking.

The line has now reached the brick house. Every man belonging to the color guard of the Fifth is dead or wounded. Colonel Cross is severely wounded; no man dares to leave the ranks to assist him. Major Sturtevant, Captains Perry, Murray and Moore, Lieutenants Ballou, Nettleton and Little are killed. Beyond the brick house extends a close board fence, parallel to the stone wall. We have now reached the fence, the point beyond which no previous line had been able to go. The dead and dying lay in a windrow along this fence. With the butts of our muskets we knocked the boards off in several places. Sergeant George S. Gove of Company K, with the colors, dashed on toward the rebel line.

At the fence all formation of the line of battle was lost. Beyond this point we saw no officers, neither did we receive any orders. At about twenty-five yards from the stone wall, Gove halted. I was the first man on his left; next on my left was Foss of Company E. Gove and Foss were the only two men standing. All the others, who were not shot down, fell down of their own accord. I asked them to lay down. Gove made no reply, while Foss said he would stand up until he was hit. Hardly had Foss said this before he was shot through the hip. At the same instant I heard Gove call my name. I looked, and he was down. I started to go to him when I was struck with a piece of shell in the left arm above the elbow, cutting a piece out of my overcoat, blouse and shirt, rendering my arm useless. I managed to get to Gove. He told me that he was shot through, and that I must save the colors and not mind anything about him. I rolled him over as carefully as I could, and gathered the tattered folds about the staff.

The fire of the enemy had slackened considerably. At this time there was no one in sight to my right or left, except the dead or wounded. Fixing my eye on an opening in the fence, I made a break for the rear, out to the brick house, where there were hundreds of men huddled. A shell dropped in their midst, killing and wounding a great many. I decided to go on to the rear. Arriving at the place where we came into line near the canal, I found a few of our own regiment and one officer. By his orders we fell back into the city.

Of the 5,500 men of Hancock's Division, 2,000 were killed and wounded. The Fifth went into action with 249 officers and men. Out of nineteen commissioned officers, seven were killed and ten wounded. Total loss, killed and wounded, 180.

—McCRILLIS in CHILD, *A History of the Fifth New Hampshire Volunteers*

5. THE GALLANT PELHAM AT FREDERICKSBURG

The Confederate artillery took a heavy toll of the Federals at Fredericksburg, and much of the credit for its performance went to "the gallant Pelham." This "boy major," as he was known, was one of the most romantic figures in the Army of Northern Virginia. Resigning from West Point in 1861 he entered the Confederate Army as a lieutenant, was assigned to the horse artillery, fought effectively in the Seven Days campaign, at Second Manassas and Antietam, and was promoted to a majority in 1862, at the age of twenty-one. Handsome, chivalrous, and courageous, he was one of the most widely admired officers in the army. Stuart named his daughter "Virginia Pelham," Lee characterized him as "the gallant Pelham" and recommended his promotion to a lieutenant colonelcy. When he was killed at Kelly's Ford, in March 1863, the whole South mourned.

This account is from the pen of the romantic novelist, John Esten Cooke.

HE was ever by the guns which were under the hottest fire; and, when the enemy shifted their fire to other portions of the field, he proceeded thither, riding at full speed, and directed the fresh batteries in person. His men will remember how cheering and inspiring was his presence with them—how his coolness steadied them in the most exciting moments—and his brave cheerful voice was the herald of success. "He was the bravest human being I ever saw in my life," said one of his officers whom I conversed with recently; and all who have seen him under fire will bear similar testimony. His coolness had something heroic in it. It never deserted him, or was affected by those chances of battle which excite the bravest. He saw guns shattered and dismounted, or men torn to pieces, without exhibiting any signs of emotion. His nature seemed strung and every muscle braced to a pitch which made him rock; and the ghastliest spectacle of blood and death left his soul unmoved—his stern will unbent.

That unbending will had been tested often, and never had failed him yet. At Manassas, Williamsburg, Cold Harbour, Groveton, Oxhill, Sharpsburg, Shepherdstown, Kearneysville, Aldie, Union, Upperville, Markham, Barbee's, Hazel River, and Fredericksburg—at these and many other places he fought his horse artillery, and handled it with heroic coolness. One day when I led him to speak of his career, he counted up something like a hundred actions which he had been in—and in every one he had borne a prominent part. Talk with the associates of the young leader in those hard-fought battles, and they will tell you a hundred instances of his dauntless courage. At Manassas he took position in a place so dangerous that an officer, who had followed him up to that moment, rode away with the declaration that "if Pelham was fool enough to stay there, *he was not.*"

But General Jackson thanked him, as he thanked him at Cold Harbour, when the brave young soldier came back covered with dust from fighting his Napoleon—the light of victory in his eyes. At Markham, while he was fighting the enemy in front, they made a circuit and charged him in the rear;

but he turned his guns about, and fought them as before, with his "Napoleon detachment" singing the loud, triumphant *Marseillaise*, as that same Napoleon gun, captured at Seven Pines, and used at Fredericksburg, drove them back. All that whole great movement was a marvel of hard fighting, however, and Pelham was the hero of the stout, close struggle. Any other chief of artillery might have sent his men in at Fredericksburg and elsewhere, leaving the direction of the guns to such officers as the brave Captain Henry; but this did not suit the young chieftain. He must go himself with the one gun sent forward, and beside that piece he remained until it was ordered back— directing his men to lie down, but sitting his own horse, and intent solely upon the movements and designs of the enemy, wholly careless of the "fire of hell" hurled against him. . . .

The work done by Pelham on the great day of Fredericksburg is a part of history now. All know how stubbornly he stood on that day—what laurels encircled his young brow when night at last came. This was the climax of his fame—the event with which his name will be inseparably connected. With one Napoleon gun, he opened the battle on the right, and instantly drew upon himself the fire, at close range, of three or four batteries in front, and a heavy enfilading fire from thirty-pound Parrots across the river. But this moved him little. That Napoleon gun was the same which he had used at the battle of Cold Harbour—it was taken from the enemy at Seven Pines—and, in the hands of the young officer, it had won a fame which must not be tarnished by defeat! Its grim voice must roar, however great the odds; its reverberating defiance must roll over the plain, until the bronze war-dog was silenced.

So it roared on steadily with Pelham beside it, blowing up caissons, and continuing to tear the enemy's ranks. General Lee was watching it from the hill above, and exclaimed, with eyes filled with admiration, "It is glorious to see such courage in one so young!" It was glorious indeed to see that one gun, placed in an important position, hold its ground with a firmness so unflinching. Not until his last round of ammunition was shot away did Pelham retire; and then only after a peremptory order sent to him. He afterwards took command of the entire artillery on the right, and fought it until night with a skill and courage which were admirable. He advanced his guns steadily, and at nightfall was thundering on the flank of the retreating enemy, who no longer replied. No answering roar came back from those batteries he had fought with his Napoleon so long; he had triumphed. That triumph was complete, and placed for ever upon record when the great Commander-in-Chief, whom he loved and admired so ardently, gave him the name in his report of "the gallant Pelham."

—Cooke, *Wearing of the Gray*

6. NIGHT ON THE FIELD OF FREDERICKSBURG

Here is a description of the dreadful night of December 13-14, from the pen of one of the most gifted of all the chroniclers of the war, General Joshua

L. Chamberlain, colonel of the 20th Maine Volunteers. A professor at Bowdoin College, Chamberlain enlisted in 1862, received the Congressional Medal of Honor for his defense of Little Round Top, was promoted to brevet major general, was six times wounded, and was selected to receive the surrender of the Confederates at Appomattox. Later he was four times governor of Maine, and president of Bowdoin College. We shall meet him again—at Gettysburg and at Appomattox.

THE desperate charge was over. We had not reached the enemy's fortifications, but only that fatal crest where we had seen five lines of battle mount but to be cut to earth as by a sword-swoop of fire. We had that costly honor which sometimes falls to the "reserve"—to go in when all is havoc and confusion, through storm and slaughter, to cover the broken and depleted ranks of comrades and take the battle from their hands. Thus we had replaced the gallant few still struggling on the crest, and received that withering fire, which nothing could withstand, by throwing ourselves flat in a slight hollow of the ground, within pistol shot of the enemy's works; and, mingled with the dead and dying that strewed the field, we returned the fire till it reddened into night, and at last fell away through darkness into silence.

But out of that silence from the battle's crash and roar rose new sounds more appalling still; rose or fell, you knew not which, or whether from the earth or air; a strange ventriloquism, of which you could not locate the source, a smothered moan that seemed to come from distances beyond reach of the natural sense, a wail so far and deep and wide, as if a thousand discords were flowing together into a key-note weird, unearthly, terrible to hear and bear, yet startling with its nearness; the writhing concord broken by cries for help, pierced by shrieks of paroxysm; some begging for a drop of water; some calling on God for pity; and some on friendly hands to finish what the enemy had so horribly begun; some with delirious, dreamy voices murmuring loved names, as if the dearest were bending over them; some gathering their last strength to fire a musket to call attention to them where they lay helpless and deserted; and underneath, all the time, that deep bass note from closed lips too hopeless or too heroic to articulate their agony.

Who could sleep, or who would? Our position was isolated and exposed. Officers must be on the alert with their command. But the human took the mastery of the official; sympathy of soldiership. Command could be devolved; but pity, not. So with a staff officer I sallied forth to see what we could do where the helpers seemed so few. Taking some observations in order not to lose the bearing of our own position, we guided our steps by the most piteous of the cries. Our part was but little; to relieve a painful posture; to give a cooling draught to fevered lips; to compress a severed artery, as we had learned to do, though in bungling fashion; to apply a rude bandage, which yet might prolong the life to saving; to take a token or farewell message for some stricken home; it was but little, yet it was an endless task. We had moved towards the right and rear of our own position—the part of the field immediately above the city. The farther we went the more the need deepened, and the calls multiplied. Numbers half wakening from the lethargy of death, or of despair, by sounds of succor, begged us to take them quickly to a surgeon; and when we could not do that, imploring us to do the next most merciful service and give them quick dispatch out of their misery. Right glad were we when, after midnight, the shadowy ambulances came gliding along, and the kindly hospital stewards, with stretchers and soothing appliances, let us feel that we might return to our proper duty.

And now we were aware of other figures wandering, ghostlike, over the field. Some on errands like our own, drawn by compelling appeals; some seeking a lost comrade, with uncertain steps amidst the unknown, and ever and anon bending down to scan the pale visage closer, or, it may be, by the light of a brief match, whose blue, flickering flame scarcely can give the features a more recognizable or more human look; some man, desperately wounded, yet seeking, with faltering step, before his fast ebbing blood shall have left him too weak to move, some quiet or sheltered spot out of sound of the terrible appeals he could neither answer nor endure, or out of reach of the raging battle coming with the morning; one creeping, yet scarcely moving, from one lifeless form to another, if, perchance, he might find a swallow of water in the canteen still swung from the dead soldier's side; or another, as with just returning or just remaining consciousness, vainly striving to rise from a mangled heap, that he may not be buried with them while yet alive; or some man, yet sound of body, but pacing feverishly his ground because in such a bivouac his spirit could not sleep. And so we picked our way back, amidst the stark, upturned faces, to our little living line.

The night chill had now woven a misty veil over the field. Fortunately, a picket fence we had encountered in our charge from the town had compelled us to abandon our horses, and so had saved our lives on the crest; but our overcoats had been strapped to the saddles, and we missed them now. Most of the men, however, had their overcoats or blankets—we were glad of that. Except the few sentries along the front, the men had fallen asleep—the living with the dead. At last, outwearied and depressed with the desolate scene, my own strength sunk, and I moved two dead men a little and lay down between them, making a pillow of the breast of a third. The skirt of his overcoat drawn over my face helped also to shield me from the bleak winds. There was some comfort even in this companionship. But it was broken sleep. The deepening chill drove many forth to take the garments of those who could no longer need them, that they might keep themselves alive. More than once I was startled from my unrest by some one turning back the coat-skirt from my face, peering, half vampire-like, to my fancy, through the darkness, to discover if it too were of the silent and unresisting; turning away more disconcerted at my living word than if a voice had spoken from the dead.

Having held our places all the night, we had to keep to them all the more closely the next day, for it would be certain death to attempt to move away. As it was, it was only by making breastworks and barricades of the dead men that covered the field that we saved any alive. We did what we could

Edwin Forbes

A Cavalry Charge

A. C. Redwood

Cobb's and Kershaw's Troops Behind the Stone Wall at Fredericksburg

THE SEAT OF THE WAR IN VIRGINIA

to take a record of these men. A testament that had fallen from the breast pocket of the soldier who had been my pillow, I sent soon after to his home—he was not of my command—and it proved to be the only clue his parents ever had to his fate.

The next midnight, after thirty-six hours of this harrowing work, we were bidden to withdraw into the town for refreshment and rest. But neither rest nor motion was to be thought of till we had paid fitting honor to our dead. We laid them on the spot which they had won, on the sheltered edge of the crest, and committed their noble forms to the earth, and their story to their country's keeping.

> We buried them darkly, at dead of night,
> The sod with our bayonets turning.

Splinters of boards torn by shot and shell from the fences we had crossed served as headstones, each name hurriedly carved under brief match lights, anxiously hidden from the foe. It was a strange scene around that silent and shadowy sepulture. "We will give them a starlight burial," it was said; but heaven ordained a more sublime illumination. As we bore them in dark and sad procession, their own loved North took up the escort and lifting all her glorious lights led the triumphal march over the bridge that spans the worlds—an aurora borealis of marvelous majesty! fiery lances and banners of blood and flame, columns of pearly light, garlands and wreaths of gold, all pointing upward and beckoning on. Who would not pass on as they did, dead for their country's life, and lighted to burial by the meteor splendors of their native sky?

—CHAMBERLAIN, "Night on the Field of Fredericksburg"

7. LINCOLN APPOINTS HOOKER TO THE COMMAND OF THE ARMY

After Fredericksburg Burnside prepared an order dismissing Hooker and three other general officers, and relieving Franklin and four other officers from duty. This he laid before Lincoln with the choice of accepting it or dismissing him. Inevitably Lincoln relieved Burnside from command and—less inevitably—appointed Hooker to his place. A West Pointer, with experience in the Florida campaign and the Mexican War, Hooker had been appointed brigadier general of volunteers in 1861 and had fought in the Peninsular and the Antietam campaigns. Like Pope he was given to boasting. "My plans are perfect," he said shortly after his appointment to the top command. "May God have mercy on General Lee for I will have none." Lincoln, as this famous letter reveals, was not so sure.

Executive Mansion, Washington, D. C.
Major-General Hooker: January 26, 1863
General:

I have placed you at the head of the Army of the Potomac. Of course I have done this upon what appears to me to be sufficient reasons, and yet I think it best for you to know that there are some things in regard to which I am not quite satisfied with you. I believe you to be a brave and skillful soldier, which, of course, I like. I also believe you do not mix politics with your profession, in which you are right. You have confidence in yourself, which is a valuable, if not an indispensable, quality. You are ambitious, which, within reasonable bounds, does good rather than harm; but I think that during General Burnside's command of the army you have taken counsel of your ambition, and thwarted him as much as you could, in which you did a great wrong to the country and to a most meritorious and honorable brother officer. I have heard, in such a way as to believe it, of your recently saying that both the Army and the Government needed a dictator. Of course, it was not for this, but in spite of it, that I have given you the command. Only those generals who gain successes can set up dictators. What I now ask of you is military success, and I will risk the dictatorship. The Government will support you to the utmost of its ability, which is neither more nor less than it has done or will do for all commanders. I much fear that the spirit which you have aided to infuse into the army, of criticizing their commander and withholding confidence from him, will now turn upon you. I shall assist you as far as I can to put it down. Neither you nor Napoleon, if he were alive again, could get any good out of an army while such a spirit prevails in it. And now beware of rashness. Beware of rashness, but with energy and sleepless vigilance go forward and give us victories.

Yours, very truly,

A. LINCOLN.

—War of the Rebellion . . . Official Records

8. LEE WHIPS HOOKER AT CHANCELLORSVILLE

By the end of April Hooker had what he called "the finest army on the planet." Certainly it was the largest and best equipped that had ever been seen in America. Against Hooker's force of some 130,000 men Lee could muster less than 60,000, for Longstreet's corps was south of the James. No wonder Hooker was sure of victory. "The enemy must either ingloriously fly, or come out from behind his defenses and give us battle on our own ground where certain destruction awaits him," he said in an order to his troops. First he sent Stoneman off on a raid designed to disorganize Lee's communications and threaten Richmond. Then, leaving Sedgwick at Fredericksburg, he moved the rest of his vast army up the Rappahannock and Rapidan, crossed at Kelly's Ford, and on April 30 reached Chancellorsville in the heart of the Wilderness. He failed however to catch Lee by surprise and when Slocum's corps moved down the Plank Road toward Fredericksburg, the next day, it ran into the well-entrenched Confederates. Instead of joining battle Hooker mysteriously withdrew his forces to Chancellorsville, giving the initiative over to Lee, who promptly seized and exploited it.

We begin with a general account of the battle. Charles Morse here recounts the errors of judgment that led to Federal defeat. A colonel of the 2nd Massachusetts Infantry, Morse fought in Virginia through the first two years of the war, then in Tennessee and the Carolinas.

Stafford C. H., May 7, 1863

I am going to give you without any introduction, a history of this last campaign against Richmond by the army under the great Joe Hooker. I believe I have seen it and judged it fairly.

On Monday, April 27th, our corps broke camp early in the morning and marched to Hartwood Church, ten miles; there it went into camp for the night. The Eleventh and Fifth Corps also came up there and camped in our vicinity; next morning, we all moved and camped that night near Kelly's Ford. A pontoon bridge was thrown across and the Eleventh was over before daylight Wednesday; the other corps followed rapidly and the advance began towards the Rapidan. The Eleventh and Twelfth marched on the road to Germana Ford, the Fifth on the road to Ely's Ford; all three of the corps were under command of General Slocum. I was detailed, the morning of the advance, as Aide to General Slocum, and another officer was made Acting Provost Marshal. All the companies of the Second Massachusetts were sent to the Regiment. We skirmished all the way to Germana Ford; there we met quite a determined resistance; our cavalry was drawn in and the Second Massachusetts and the Third Wisconsin sent forward to clear the way; they drove everything before them and, by their heavy fire, forced the rebels at the Ford to surrender (about one hundred officers and men). We lost in this skirmish about a dozen killed and wounded.

General Slocum now determined to cross the Rapidan, though there was no bridge and the ford was almost impassable. . . . At about noon [April 30], we arrived at Chancellorsville, and found the Fifth Corps already there. We had a small cavalry skirmish, . . . but besides that, nothing of importance occurred during that day; the troops were formed in line of battle, but were not attacked. Up to this time you see everything had gone well and success seemed certain.

Towards night [April 30], General Hooker arrived with his staff, and we heard of the crossing at the U. S. Ford of the Second, Third and First Corps. All the headquarters were in the vicinity of the Chancellor House, a large, fine brick mansion. General Hooker took supper with General Slocum; he didn't seem to be able to express his gratification at the success of General Slocum in bringing the three corps up so rapidly. Then, in the most extravagant, vehement terms, he went on to say how he had got the rebels, how he was going to crush them, annihilate them, etc.

The next morning at ten, the Fifth and Twelfth Corps advanced in order of battle on two parallel roads; we soon met the enemy and skirmished for about two miles, when they appeared in considerable force and the battle began. We were in a splendid position and were driving the enemy when an order came to General Slocum to retire his command to its former position. No one could believe that the order was genuine, but almost immediately, another of General Hooker's staff brought the same order again. Now, perhaps, you don't know that to retire an army in the face of an enemy when you are engaged is one of the most difficult operations in war; this we had to do. I carried the order to General Geary to retire his division in echelon by brigades, and stayed with him till the movement was nearly completed. It was a delicate job; each brigade would successively bear the brunt of the enemy's attack. Before the last brigades of the Fifth and Twelfth Corps were in position, the enemy made a furious attack on the Chancellor House; luckily we had considerable artillery concentrated there and they were driven back. The next attack was on our corps, but the enemy was severely repulsed. This about ended the fighting on Friday; we lost, I suppose, about five hundred men.

During the night, the men were kept at work digging trenches and throwing up breastworks of logs. Our headquarters were at Fairview, an open piece of ground rising into quite a crest in the centre. Skirmishing began at daylight next morning [May 2] and continued without much result to either side, till afternoon, when the enemy began to move, in large force, towards our right, opposite General Howard, Eleventh Corps. This corps was in a fine position in intrenchments, with almost open country in front of them, the right resting on Hunting Creek. At about four P.M. the Third Corps, General Sickles, was moved out to the right of the Twelfth and advanced towards Fredericksburgh. The order then came to General Slocum that the enemy were in full retreat, and to advance his whole line to capture all he could of prisoners, wagons, etc. Our right, General Williams' Division, advanced without much trouble, driving the enemy before it, but the Second Division had hardly got out of the trenches before it was attacked with great determination, yet it steadily retained its position.

At about five P.M. a tremendous and unceasing musketry fire began in the direction of the Eleventh Corps. As it was necessary to know what was going on there in order to regulate the movements of the Twelfth Corps, General Slocum and the rest of us rode for our lives towards this new scene of action. What was our surprise when we found that instead of a fight, it was a complete Bull Run rout. Men, horses, mules, rebel prisoners, wagons, guns, etc. etc. were coming down the road in terrible confusion, behind them an unceasing roar of musketry. We rode until we got into a mighty hot fire, and found that no one was attempting to make a stand, but every one running for his life. Then General Slocum dispatched me to General Hooker to explain the state of affairs, and three other staff officers to find General Williams and order him back to his trenches with all haste.

I found General Hooker sitting alone on his horse in front of the Chancellor House, and delivered my message; he merely said, "Very good, sir." I rode back and found the Eleventh Corps still surging up the road and still this terrible roar behind them. Up to this time, the rebels had received no check, but now troops began to march out on the plank road and form across it, and Captain Best, Chief of Artillery of our corps, had on his own responsibility gathered together all the batteries he could get hold of, had put them in position (forty-six guns in all) on Fairview, and had begun firing at the rate of about one hundred guns a minute, into the rebels. This, in my opinion, saved our army from destruction. . . .

The artillery men were hard at work all night, throwing up traverses to protect their guns, and about two in the morning we all lay down on the ground and slept until about four, when daylight [May 3] began to appear. Our right was now formed by the Third, Fifth and First Corps, about five hundred yards in the rear of our first position. The rebels began the attack as soon as there was light enough, from the left of our First Division to about the right of the Third Corps. General Birney's Division of the Third Corps was out in front of General Williams; his men behaved badly, and after a slight resistance, fell back into our lines, losing a battery.

The rebels now charged down our First Division, but were met with such a deadly fire that they were almost annihilated. Their second line was then sent in, but met the same fate, and their third and last line advanced. Our men now had fired more than forty rounds of cartridges and were getting exhausted. General Slocum sent almost every one of his staff officers to General Hooker, stating his position and begging for support; Hooker's answer was, "I can't make men or ammunition for General Slocum."

Meantime, Sickles' Corps was holding its own on the right of ours, but it was rapidly getting into the same condition as the Twelfth. The rebels were driven back every time they advanced, and we were taking large numbers of prisoners and colors. All this time while our infantry was fighting so gallantly in front, our battery of forty-six guns was firing incessantly. The rebels had used no artillery until they captured the battery from Birney, when they turned that on us, making terrible destruction in General Geary's line. General Meade, Fifth Corps, now went to Hooker and entreated that he might be allowed to throw his corps on the rebel flank, but General Hooker said, "No, he was wanted in his own position." On his own responsibility General Meade sent out one brigade, which passed out in the rear of the enemy's right, recaptured a battery, three hundred of our men who were prisoners, and four hundred of the rebels, and took them safely back to their corps.

It was now after seven o'clock. Our men had fired their sixty rounds of cartridges and were still holding their position; everything that brave men could do, these men had done, but now nothing was left but to order them to fall back and give up their position to the enemy. This was done in good order and they marched off under a heavy fire to the rear of our batteries. The rebels, seeing us retreating, rushed forward their artillery and began a fearful fire. I found I could be useful to Captain Best, commanding our artillery, so I stayed with him. I never before saw anything so fine as the attack on that battery; the air was full of missiles, solid shot, shells, and musket balls. I saw one solid shot kill three horses and a man, another took a leg off one of the captains of the batteries. Lieutenant Crosby of the Fourth Artillery was shot through the heart with a musket ball; he was a particular friend of Bob Shaw and myself; he lived just long enough to say to Captain Best, "Tell father I die happy."

The rebels came up to the attack in solid masses and got within three hundred yards, but they were slaughtered by the hundreds by the case-shot and canister, and were driven back to the woods. Still not an infantry man was sent to the support of the guns. More than half the horses were killed or wounded; one caisson had blown up, another had been knocked to pieces; in ten minutes more the guns would have been isolated. They, too, therefore, were ordered to retire, which they did without losing a gun. You see, now our centre was broken, everything was being retired to our second line, the rebel artillery was in position, their line of battle steadily advancing across our old ground. This fire of the batteries was concentrated on the Chancellor House, Hooker's original headquarters, and it was torn almost to pieces by solid shot and was finally set on fire by a shell.

The army was now put in position in the second line; the centre was on a rising piece of ground and protected by a battery of forty or fifty guns. . . . You can easily see that, if the enemy once forced our right or left, our communications would at once be cut and all possibility of retreat prevented. Late that night we lay down close beside the Rappahannock. By three o'clock next morning we were awakened by a heavy artillery fire and shells bursting over us. Our guns replied and kept at it for about an hour, when the enemy's batteries were silenced. We now mounted our horses and rode along the lines to look at our position; we found that it was a very strong one and capable of being made very much more so. . . .

I doubt if ever in the history of this war, another chance will be given us to fight the enemy with such odds in our favor as we had last Sunday, and that chance has been worse than lost to us. I don't believe any men ever fought better than our Twelfth Corps, especially the First Division; for two hours, they held their ground without any support, against the repeated assaults of the enemy; they fired their sixty rounds of cartridges and held their line with empty muskets until ordered to fall back. The old Second, of course, did splendidly, and lost heavily. . . . Our colors got thirty holes in them and the staff (the third one) was smashed to pieces.

—MORSE, *Letters Written During the Civil War*

9. PLEASONTON STOPS THE CONFEDERATES AT HAZEL GROVE

Early on May 2 Lee sent Jackson with the bulk of the army along the Plank Road and through the Wilderness to Hooker's rear. Although Hooker was repeatedly warned of this movement, he fatuously insisted that the Confederates were retreating, and took no precautions. On the afternoon of the second Jackson swept out of the woods and fell on Howard's corps and on Sickles. Pleasonton hurried up his cavalry, collected scattered elements of infantry and artillery, and made a stand that may have saved the army from destruction.

General Pleasonton was a West Pointer with long military experience in the Mexican, Sioux and Seminole wars, who commanded the Union cavalry at Gettysburg and was later transferred to the Trans-Mississippi theater.

O N arriving at Hazel Grove, about one mile from Chancellorsville, I found that General Sickles was moving two of the divisions of the Third Corps in the direction of Catherine Furnace, and shortly after he became engaged there with a strong rear-guard. Hazel Grove was the highest ground in the neighborhood and was the key of our position, and I saw that if Lee's forces gained it the Army of the Potomac would be worsted.

General Sickles wanted some cavalry to protect his flanks, and I gave him the 6th New York. This left me with only the 8th and 17th Pennsylvania regiments and Martin's New York battery of horse artillery. I posted this command at the extreme west of the clearing, about two hundred yards from the woods in which the Eleventh Corps was encamped. This position at Hazel Grove was about a quarter of a mile in extent, running nearly north-east and south-west, but was in no place farther than two hundred yards from the woods, and on the south and east it sloped off into a marsh and a creek. It commanded the position of the army at Fairview and Chancellorsville and enfiladed our line. The moving out to the Furnace of the two divisions of the Third Corps left a gap of about a mile from Hazel Grove to the right of the Twelfth Corps. Shortly after General Sickles had been engaged at the Furnace, he sent me word that the enemy were giving way and cavalry could be used to advantage in pursuit. Before moving my command I rode out to the Furnace to comprehend the situation. It was no place for cavalry to operate, and as I could hear spattering shots going more and more toward the north-west, I was satisfied that the enemy were not retreating.

I hastened back to my command at Hazel Grove; when I reached it, the Eleventh Corps to our rear and our right was in full flight, panic-stricken beyond description. We faced about, having then the marsh behind us. It was an ugly marsh, about fifty yards wide, and in the stampede of the Eleventh Corps, beef cattle, ambulances, mules, artillery, wagons, and horses became stuck in the mud, and others coming on crushed them down, so that when the fight was over the pile of débris in the marsh was many feet high. I saw that something had to be done, and that very quickly, or the Army of the Potomac would receive a crushing defeat. The two cavalry regiments were in the saddle, and as I rode forward Major Keenan of the 8th Pennsylvania came out to meet me, when I ordered him to take the regiment, charge into the woods, which, as we had previously stood, were to our rear, and hold the enemy in check until I could get some guns into position. He replied, with a smile at the size of the task, that he would do it, and started off immediately. Thirty men, including Major Keenan, Captain Arrowsmith, and Adjutant Haddock, never came back.

I then directed Captain Martin to bring his guns into battery, load with double charges of canister, and aim them so that the shot would hit the ground half-way between the guns and the woods. I also stated that I would give the order to fire. Just then a handsome young lieutenant of the 4th U. S. Artillery, Frank B. Crosby (son of a distinguished lawyer of New York City), who was killed the next day, galloped up and said, "General, I have a battery of six guns; where shall I go? what shall I do?" I told him to place his battery in line on the right of Martin's battery, and gave him the same instructions I had given Martin as to how I wanted him to serve his guns. These 2 batteries gave me 12 guns, and to obtain more I then charged 3 squadrons of the 17th Pennsylvania Cavalry on the stragglers of the Eleventh Corps to clear the ground, and with the assistance of the rest of the regiment succeeded in placing 10 more pieces of artillery in line. The line was then ready for Stonewall Jackson's onset. It was dusk when his men swarmed out of the woods for a quarter of a mile in our front (our rear ten minutes before). They came on in line five and six deep, with but one flag—a Union flag dropped by the Eleventh Corps.

I suspected deception and was ready for it. They called out not to shoot, they were friends; at the same time they gave us a volley from at least five thousand muskets. As soon as I saw the flash I gave the command to fire, and the whole line of artillery was discharged at once. It fairly swept them from the earth; before they could recover themselves the line of artillery had been loaded and was ready for a second attack. After the second discharge, suspecting that they might play the trick of having their men lie down, draw the fire of the artillery, then jump up and charge before the pieces could be reloaded, I poured in the canister for about twenty minutes, and the affair was over. . . .

For half an hour General Jackson had the Army of the Potomac at his mercy. That he halted to re-form his troops in the woods, instead of forging ahead into the clearing, where he could reform his troops more rapidly, and where he could have seen that he was master of the situation, turned out to be one of those fatalities by which the most brilliant prospects are sacrificed. When he advanced upon the artillery at Hazel Grove Jackson had another opportunity to win, if his infantry had been properly handled. The fire of his infantry was so high it did no harm; they should have been ordered to fire so low as to disable the cannoneers at the guns. Had his infantry fire been as effective as that of our artillery, Jackson would have carried the position. The artillery fire was effective because I applied to it that principle of dynamics in which the angle of incidence is equal to the angle of reflection,— that is to say, if the muzzle of a gun is three feet from the ground and it is discharged so that the shot will strike the ground at a distance of one hundred yards, it will glance from the earth at the same angle at which it struck it, and in another one hundred yards will be three feet from the ground. I knew my first volley must be a crushing one, or Jackson, with his superior numbers, would charge across the short distance which separated us and capture the artillery before the guns could be reloaded.

—PLEASONTON, "The Successes and Failures of Chancellorsville"

10. CAPTAIN LIVERMORE HOLDS THE LINES
AGAINST JACKSON

After the smart engagement at Hazel Grove Jackson circled around through the Wilderness to the rear of Hooker's army. Toward sundown he fell like a thunderbolt on Hooker's exposed right flank. The impact of his impetuous charge scattered the Federals and threatened, for the moment, to turn the whole flank. The XI Corps retreated in disorder, but elements from the corps of Reynolds, Couch and Sickles hurried to the rescue. "Through the surging rout of the XI Corps," writes John Bigelow, "these sterling organizations forged their way, unchecked and unshaken, towards the mass of yelling and firing assailants."

Livermore we already know as an officer—later colonel—of the 18th New Hampshire Volunteers and as the author of the invaluable study, Numbers and Losses of the Civil War.

NOW, at about sunset [May 2, 1863] there was a rattling of musketry all along our southern and western fronts, but nothing severe enough to cause us any anxiety. I think the fight on our right flank had dwindled to a skirmish and things did not to me look like hot work before next day. We were resting easily with our arms beside us or stacked, and I suppose about eating our evening rations. There seemed to us to have been nothing serious against us, and no one of us in the companies had reason to suppose we should be otherwise than successful, that I am aware of. We could see the situation of the troops on our right; saw the evidences of a large force of our men on the west and north fronts; knew that General Hooker was at the Chancellorsville house close by; and could see parties of the reserves who lay to the east of us; but further than this we were ignorant, at least I was, and I did not know that any rebels had been marching along our western front; did not know anything of the contact of the Twelfth Corps with the rear of his column; of Barlow's movements; of the position of the Eleventh Corps, nor in fact anything more than I saw, and I suppose the most of the army were just as ignorant.

While resting satisfied in this blissful state of ignorance, and facing the foe on the south with placidity and waiting his next advance, our astonished ears were greeted with a sudden outburst of the most tremendous musketry and cannonade directly in our rear on the north front, accompanied with all the yells and confused noises of a bloody engagement. We sprang to our feet and looked with anxious hearts across the plain to the north. The noise continued for some minutes, and then suddenly wagons, ambulances, men, artillery, and everything that makes an army, came rushing out of the woods on the north into the plain and across it and down the turnpike, and after a short interval a flying, confused, panic-stricken mass of soldiers in the direst confusion, to the number of thousands, running for life, and alas! our own men.

When this contest broke out, the presence of the enemy in an attacking force on our north front seemed so improbable that we offered ourselves every explanation but the right one. The most plausible story was that General Stoneman, who was known to have gone off in the enemy's rear, or some one else, had now come up in the rear of a body of the enemy and was driving them toward us. I was so elated with the news that I behaved quite extravagantly with cheering and "cutting up" generally, and the shells which came sailing over from the northwest high in the air, which we could distinguish by their burning fuses in the twilight now come, actually added to the delusion, since I thought with the rest that they were those of our forces advancing in the rear of the enemy. When the truth dawned upon my mind, I kept up my cheerfulness for the sake of appearances, that the men might not learn the truth, and there was need of every precaution, for in less time than it has taken to write this page, after the first group of soldiers appeared running out of the woods, the plain was swarming with them, flying with all speed, and in such bodies and so blindly terrified that neither natural obstacles nor the well-ordered array of lines arrested their flight; and some, escaping through the south front, actually ran clear to our skirmish line and through it to or toward the enemy on the south. The musketry kept crashing away in the woods as long as there were men to fire at, and the shells screamed through the air trailing fire like shooting stars clear over to the Chancellorsville house.

It was a trying time. No one could fail to see that our north front was broken, and it was uncertain how short a time would elapse before the victorious enemy might be upon our backs, and the flying Dutchmen, for they proved to be the Eleventh Corps, actually endangered our formation; but we made our men lie flat on the ground facing south and then each officer with drawn sword paced in rear of his company and drove back every Dutchman. Our men behaved admirably. Neither the dangers nor the panic affected them, but they lay calmly in their places, aided no doubt by their contempt for the Dutch who were running away. Some idea of the numbers who endangered us may be found when I say that about sixty Dutchmen were captured by my regiment. They were kept in our ranks and some were killed on the next day, I believe. One general came rushing over to Colonel Cross, who was lying down. The colonel arose and with infuriated looks and drawn saber rushed upon him. He fled to the shelter of a ditch, crying, "Sare, you do not know who I am! I am a Prigadier Gineral!" To which the colonel replied, "You are n't, you're a damned coward!"

At last the torrent of fugitives ceased, and astonishing to relate the enemy did not advance across the plain. But a tremendous artillery fire which had been opened by some batteries of ours on the north side of the plain had undoubtedly prevented his advancing farther. When order was secure, I stood a little back of my company, where I could see across the plain, and watched for developments on the north side. The firing had nearly ceased, and an ominous stillness prevailed. Peering through the not impenetrable darkness now lighted by the moon, I saw moving into position in the plain facing north two or three lines of troops numbering several thousand, whose dark bodies in serried ranks holding grim silence were exceedingly majestic. I had no doubt they were our own men of some other corps who were to restore our broken lines, and presently they moved forward slowly and in beautiful order apparently with a brigade front. Their advance was pursued in silence close up to the woods, when a sheet of flame like a most brilliant flash of lightning burst out from their front, followed instantly by the tremendous crash of a volley, and moving forward still they maintained their position, and in some measure, I do not know how far, restored our lines. This, I think, was Wood's division of the Third Corps.

The events of the few hours of this afternoon and evening are imprinted on my memory in a grand picture. I can now, and probably always shall be able to again bring before my eyes the dusty plain bounded by long lines of men on all sides; the smoke of musketry and batteries, whose thunders still reverberate in my ears; the gradual diminishing of the battle, and then the sudden rush of fugitives accompanied by the roar of muskets and cannon; the dire confusion of the panic; the curves of fire described in the sky by the shrieking shells; then darkness, the deliberate movements of the dark masses who constituted our attacking force, and the sheet of flame which burst out as they approached the woods; and can still hear the tumult of the battle.

—LIVERMORE, *Days and Events*

11. STUART AND ANDERSON LINK UP
AT CHANCELLORSVILLE

The timely employment of artillery, the coming of darkness, and the death of Jackson combined to save the Federals on the second day. Early next morning Lee renewed the attack on both flanks, Stuart on the right, Anderson at the center, and McLaws on the left. Stuart quickly seized Hazel Grove and pushed on ahead to take Chancellorsville itself; at about noon his line linked up with Anderson's, and the Federals were hemmed in on three sides. Hooker had been injured that morning by a falling brick; perhaps that is why he failed to put in his reserves or to get Sedgwick's attack under way in time to afford any effective relief. Sedgwick had, to be sure, swept the thin Confederate line off Marye's Heights, but when Lee sent McLaws to Early's aid Sedgwick found himself encircled just as Hooker was encircled, and retired across the Rappahannock. The Federals, still twice as strong as Lee, stood their ground on May 4, but next day withdrew across the river.

Heros von Borcke, the jolly Prussian whom we have met before, here tells the story of the third day.

THE enemy, fully three times our number, occupied a piece of wood extending about two miles from our immediate front towards the plateau and open fields round Chancellorsville, a village consisting of only a few houses. The Federals had made good use of their time, having thrown up in the wood during the night three successive lines of breastworks, constructed of strong timber, and on the plateau itself, occupied by their reserves, had erected a regular line of redoubts, mounted by their numerous artillery, forty pieces of which were playing on the narrow plank-road. . . .

All our divisions now moving forward, the battle soon became general, and the musketry sounded in one continued roll along the lines. Nearly a hundred hostile guns opening fire at the same time, the forest seemed alive with shot, shell, and bullets, and the plank-road, upon which, as was before mentioned, the fire of forty pieces was concentrated, was soon enveloped in a cloud of smoke from the bursting of shells and the explosion of caissons. This road being our principal line of communication, and crowded therefore with ambulances, ammunition-trains, and artillery, the loss of life soon became fearful, and dead and dying men and animals were strewing every part of it. How General Stuart, and those few staff-officers with him who had to gallop to and fro so frequently through this *feu infernal*, escaped unhurt, seems to me quite miraculous. . . .

Stuart was all activity, and wherever the danger was greatest there was he to be found, urging the men forward, and animating them by the force of his example. The shower of missiles that hissed through the air passed round him unheeded; and in the midst of the hottest fire I heard him, to an old melody, hum the words, "Old Joe Hooker get out of the Wilderness."

After a raging conflict, protracted for several hours, during which the tide of battle ebbed and flowed on either side, we succeeded in taking the advanced works, and driving the enemy upon their third line of intrenchments, of a still stronger character than those before it. This partial success was only gained with a sad sacrifice of life, while countless numbers were seen limping and crawling to the rear. The woods had caught fire in several places from the explosion of shells—the flames spreading principally, however, over a space of several acres in extent where the ground was thickly covered with dry leaves; and here the conflagration progressed with the rapidity of a prairie-fire, and a large number of Confederate and Federal wounded thickly scattered in the vicinity, and too badly hurt to crawl out of the way, met a terrible death. The heartrending cries of the poor victims, as the flames advanced, entreating to be rescued from their impending fate— entreaties which it was impossible to heed in the crisis of the battle, and amidst duties on which the lives of many others depended—seem still in my ears.

Among the heart-sickening scenes of this terrible conflict which are still vivid in my memory, is one no lapse of time can ever efface, and in contemplating which I scarcely could check the tears from starting to my eyes. Riding to the front, I was hailed by a young soldier, whose boyish looks and merry songs on the march had frequently attracted my attention and excited my interest, and who was now leaning against a tree, the life-blood streaming down his side from a mortal wound, and his face white with the pallor of approaching death. "Major," said the poor lad, "I am dying, and I shall never see my regiment again; but I ask you to tell my comrades that the

Yankees have killed but not conquered me." When I passed the place again half an hour afterwards I found him a corpse. Such was the universal spirit of our men, and in this lay the secret of many of our wonderful achievements.

The enemy had in the meanwhile been strongly reinforced, and now poured forth from their third line of intrenchments a fire so terrible upon our advancing troops that the first two divisions staggered, and, after several unsuccessful efforts to press onward, fell back in considerable confusion. In vain was it that our officers used every effort to bring them forward once more; in vain even was it that Stuart, snatching the battle-flag of one of our brigades from the hands of the colour-bearer and waving it over his head, called on them as he rode forward to follow him. Nothing could induce them again to face that tempest of bullets, and that devastating hurricane of grape and canister vomited at close range from more than sixty pieces of artillery, and the advantages so dearly gained seemed about to be lost. At this critical moment, we suddenly heard the yell of Rodes's division behind us, and saw these gallant troops, led by their heroic general, charge over the front lines, and fall upon the enemy with such impetus that in a few minutes their works were taken, and they were driven in rapid flight from the woods to their redoubts on the hills of Chancellorsville.

A slight pause now intervened in the conflict, both sides, after the terrible work of the last few hours, being equally willing to draw breath awhile; and this gave us an opportunity to re-form our lines and close up our decimated ranks. The contest, meanwhile, was sustained by the artillery alone, which kept up a heavy cannonade; and the nature of the ground being now more favourable, most of our batteries had been brought into action, while from a hill on our extreme right, which had only been abandoned by the enemy after the charge of Rodes's division, twenty 12-pounder Napoleons played with a well-directed flank-fire upon the enemy's works, producing a terrible effect upon their dense masses.

About half-past ten we had news from General Lee, informing us that, having been pressing steadily forward the entire morning, he had now, with Anderson's and M'Laws's divisions, reached our right wing. I was at once despatched by Stuart to the Commander-in-Chief to report the state of affairs, and obtain his orders for further proceedings. I found him with our twenty-gun battery, looking as calm and dignified as ever, and perfectly regardless of the shells bursting round him, and the solid shot ploughing up the ground in all directions. General Lee expressed himself much satisfied with our operations, and intrusted me with orders for Stuart, directing a general attack with his whole force, which was to be supported by a charge of Anderson's division on the left flank of the enemy.

With renewed courage and confidence our three divisions now moved forward upon the enemy's strong position on the hills, encountering, as we emerged from the forest into the open opposite the plateau of Chancellorsville, such a storm of canister and bullets, that for a while it seemed an impossibility to take the heights in the face of it. Suddenly we heard to our right, piercing the roar and tumult of the battle, the yell of Anderson's men, whom we presently beheld hurled forward in a brilliant charge, sweeping everything before them. Short work was now made of the Federals, who, in a few minutes, were driven from their redoubts, which they abandoned in disorderly flight, leaving behind them cannons, small-arms, tents, and baggage in large quantities, besides a host of prisoners, of whom we took 360 in one redoubt.

A more magnificent spectacle can hardly be imagined than that which greeted me when I reached the crest of the plateau, and beheld on this side the long lines of our swiftly advancing troops stretching as far as the eye could reach, their red flags fluttering in the breeze, and their arms glittering in the morning sun; and farther on, dense and huddled masses of the Federals flying in utter rout towards the United States Ford, whilst high over our heads flew the shells which our artillery were dropping amidst the crowd of the retreating foe. The Chancellorsville House had caught fire, and was now enveloped in flames, so that it was with difficulty that we could save some portion of the Federal wounded lying there, to the number of several hundreds, the majority of whom perished. . . . The flight and pursuit took the direction of United States Ford, as far as about a mile beyond Chancellorsville, where another strong line of intrenchments offered their protection to the fugitives, and heavy reserves of fresh troops opposed our further advance.

—Von Borcke, *Memoirs of the Confederate War for Independence*

12. LEE LOSES HIS RIGHT ARM

Chancellorsville was a dearly bought victory; Confederate casualties were 13,156, of whom almost eleven thousand were killed and wounded. Irreparable was the loss of Stonewall Jackson, wounded by his own men. To Chaplain Lacy Lee said, "Give him my affectionate regards, and tell him to make haste and get well and come back to me as soon as he can. He has lost his left arm; but I have lost my right arm." But pneumonia and other complications set in and the mighty Stonewall "passed over the river."

The Reverend James Power Smith, who here describes the wounding of Jackson, was Jackson's aide-de-camp.

WHEN Jackson had reached the point where his line now crossed the turnpike, scarcely a mile west of Chancellorsville, and not half a mile from a line of Federal troops, he had found his front line unfit for the farther and vigorous advance he desired, by reason of the irregular character of the fighting, now right, now left, and because of the dense thickets, through which it was impossible to preserve alignment. Division commanders found it more and more difficult as the twilight deepened to hold their broken brigades in hand. Regretting the necessity of relieving the troops in front, General Jackson had ordered A. P. Hill's division, his third and reserve line, to be placed in front.

While this change was being effected, impatient and anxious, the general rode forward on the turnpike, followed by two or three of his staff and a number of couriers and signal sergeants. He passed the swampy depression and began the ascent of the hill toward Chancellorsville, when he came upon a line of the Federal infantry lying on their arms. Fired at by one or two muskets (two musket-balls from the enemy whistled over my head as I came to the front), he turned and came back toward his line, upon the side of the road to his left.

As he rode near to the Confederate troops, just placed in position and ignorant that he was in the front, the left company began firing to the front, and two of his party fell from their saddles dead—Captain Boswell, of the Engineers, and Sergeant Cunliffe, of the Signal Corps. Spurring his horse across the road to his right, he was met by a second volley from the right company of Pender's North Carolina brigade. Under this volley, when not two rods from the troops, the general received three balls at the same instant. One penetrated the palm of his right hand and was cut out that night from the back of his hand. A second passed around the wrist of the left arm and out through the left hand. A third ball passed through the left arm half-way from shoulder to elbow. The large bone of the upper arm was splintered to the elbow-joint, and the wound bled freely. His horse turned quickly from the fire, through the thick bushes which swept the cap from the general's head, and scratched his forehead, leaving drops of blood to stain his face.

As he lost his hold upon the bridle-rein, he reeled from the saddle, and was caught by the arms of Captain Wilbourn, of the Signal Corps. Laid upon the ground, there came at once to his succor General A. P. Hill and members of his staff. The writer reached his side a minute after, to find General Hill holding the head and shoulders of the wounded chief. Cutting open the coat-sleeve from wrist to shoulder, I found the wound in the upper arm, and with my handkerchief I bound the arm above the wound to stem the flow of blood. Couriers were sent for Dr. Hunter McGuire, the surgeon of the corps and the general's trusted friend, and for an ambulance. Being outside of our lines, it was urgent that he should be moved at once. With difficulty litter-bearers were brought from the line near by, and the general was placed upon the litter and carefully raised to the shoulder, I myself bearing one corner.

A moment after, artillery from the Federal side was opened upon us; great broadsides thundered over the woods; hissing shells searched the dark thickets through, and shrapnels swept the road along which we moved. Two or three steps farther, and the litter-bearer at my side was struck and fell, but, as the litter turned, Major Watkins Leigh, of Hill's staff, happily caught it. But the fright of the men was so great that we were obliged to lay the litter and its burden down upon the road. As the litter-bearers ran to the cover of the trees, I threw myself by the general's side and held him firmly to the ground as he attempted to rise. Over us swept the rapid fire of shot and shell—grape-shot striking fire upon the flinty rock of the road all around us, and sweeping from their feet horses and men of the artillery just moved to the front.

Soon the firing veered to the other side of the road, and I sprang to my feet, assisted the general to rise, passed my arm around him, and with the wounded man's weight thrown heavily upon me, we forsook the road. Entering the woods, he sank to the ground from exhaustion, but the litter was soon brought, and again rallying a few men, we essayed to carry him farther, when a second bearer fell at my side. This time, with none to assist, the litter careened, and the general fell to the ground, with a groan of deep pain. Greatly alarmed, I sprang to his head, and, lifting his head as a stray beam of moonlight came through clouds and leaves, he opened his eyes and wearily said: "Never mind me, Captain, never mind me." Raising him again to his feet, he was accosted by Brigadier-General Pender: "Oh, General, I hope you are not seriously wounded. I will have to retire my troops to re-form them, they are so much broken by this fire." But Jackson, rallying his strength, with firm voice said: "You must hold your ground, General Pender; you must hold your ground, sir!" and so uttered his last command on the field.

Again we resorted to the litter, and with difficulty bore it through the bush, and then under a hot fire along the road. Soon an ambulance was reached, and stopping to seek some stimulant at Chancellor's (Dowdall's Tavern), we were found by Dr. McGuire, who at once took charge of the wounded man. Passing back over the battle-field of the afternoon, we reached the Wilderness store, and then, in a field on the north, the field-hospital of our corps under Dr. Harvey Black. Here we found a tent prepared, and after midnight the left arm was amputated near the shoulder, and a ball taken from the right hand.

All night long it was mine to watch by the sufferer, and keep him warmly wrapped and undisturbed in his sleep. At 9 A.M., on the next day, when he aroused, cannon firing again filled the air, and all the Sunday through the fierce battle raged, General J. E. B. Stuart commanding the Confederates in Jackson's place. A dispatch was sent to the commanding general to announce formally his disability,—tidings General Lee had received during the the night with profound grief. There came back the following note:

"GENERAL: I have just received your note, informing me that you were wounded. I cannot express my regret at the occurrence. Could I have directed events, I should have chosen, for the good of the country, to have been disabled in your stead. I congratulate you upon the victory which is due to your skill and energy. Most truly yours, R. E. LEE, GENERAL."

When this dispatch was handed to me at the tent, and I read it aloud, General Jackson turned his face away and said, "General Lee is very kind, but he should give the praise to God."

The long day was passed with bright hopes for the wounded general, with tidings of success on the battle-field, with sad news of losses, and messages to and from other wounded officers brought to the same infirmary.

On Monday the general was carried in an ambulance, by way of Spotsylvania Court House, to most comfortable lodging at Chandler's, near Guinea's

Station, on the Richmond, Fredericksburg and Potomac railroad. And here, against our hopes, notwithstanding the skill and care of wise and watchful surgeons, attended day and night by wife and friends, amid the prayers and tears of all the Southern land, thinking not of himself, but of the cause he loved, and for the troops who had followed him so well and given him so great a name, our chief sank, day by day, with symptoms of pneumonia and some pains of pleurisy, until, at 3:15 P.M. on the quiet of the Sabbath afternoon, May 10th, 1863, he raised himself from his bed, saying, "No, no, let us pass over the river, and rest under the shade of the trees"; and, falling again to his pillow, he passed away, "over the river, where, in a land where warfare is not known or feared, he rests forever 'under the trees.' "

—SMITH, "Stonewall Jackson's Last Battle"

VIII

How the Soldiers Lived: Eastern Front

THE *Union and Confederate armies were haphazardly raised, badly organ-*
ized, poorly trained, inadequately fed, clothed and housed, and almost wholly
without comforts, sports, entertainments or proper medical care. Whether a
regiment was well or badly trained, disciplined, and cared for depended
largely on its officers, and to some extent on the initiative and enterprise of
the men themselves. Regiments camped where they could, foraged for fuel
and often for food, and depended on their own resources, on the sutlers, and
on friends and relatives, for amusement and for luxuries. The Civil War
armies were youthful, high-spirited, sentimental, and for the most part moral.
They endured what seem to us wholly unnecessary hardships—heavy woolen
clothing in the summertime, for example, or leaky tents or maggoty food—but
they managed to enjoy themselves, indulged in rough sports and horseplay,
fixed up their winter quarters with "all the comforts of home," sang romantic
songs, enjoyed religious services and revivals, and generally acted like civilians
on a picnic—when the enemy permitted!

Most of these items tell their own story; few need explanatory introduc-
tions. The first 11 describe various aspects of camp life—clothing, housing,
marching, work and play. The others deal more specifically with the ever-
lasting problem of food, with religion, politics, red tape, corruption, and
morale. Some of them are by men who for one reason or another distin-
guished themselves—in soldiering, in literature, in politics—or merely by
writing a memorable memoir. Others are by men whom it has not been
possible to rescue from obscurity. The notes will serve as introductions to
the writers rather than to the subjects—which explain themselves.

1. THEODORE WINTHROP RECALLS A TYPICAL DAY AT CAMP CAMERON

Lawyer, novelist, and professional traveler, Theodore Winthrop is prob-
ably best remembered for his two volumes of sketches: The Canoe and the
Saddle *and* Life in the Open Air; *his novels,* Cecil Dreeme *and* John Brent,
are universally unread. At the beginning of the war he enlisted in the 7th
New York, and his account of its journey to Washington has already been
mentioned. He was killed in a charge at the Battle of Great Bethel, June 1861.

BOOM! I would rather not believe it; but it is—yes, it is—the morning gun,
uttering its surly "Hullo!" to sunrise. Yes,—and, to confirm my suspicions, here rattle in the drums and pipe in the fifes, wooing us to get up,
get up, with music too peremptory to be harmonious.

I rise up *sur mon séant* and glance about me. I, Private W., chance, by reason of sundry chances, to be a member of a company recently largely recruited and bestowed all together in a big marquee. As I lift myself up, I see others lift themselves up on those straw bags we kindly call our mattresses. The tallest man of the regiment, Sergeant K., is on one side of me. On the other side I am separated from two of the fattest men of the regiment by Sergeant M., another excellent fellow, prime cook and prime forager.

We are all presently on our pins,—K. on those lengthy continuations of his, and the two stout gentlemen on their stout supporters. The deep sleepers are pulled up from those abysses of slumber where they had been choking, gurgling, strangling, death-rattling all night. There is for a moment a sound of legs rushing into pantaloons and arms plunging into jackets.

Then, as the drums and fifes whine and clatter their last notes, at the flap of our tent appears our orderly, and fierce in the morning sunshine gleams his moustache,—one month's growth this blessed day. "Fall in, for roll-call!" he cries, in a ringing voice. The orderly can speak sharp, if need be.

We obey. Not "Walk in!" "March in!" "Stand in!" is the order; but "Fall in!" as sleepy men must. Then the orderly calls off our hundred. There are several boyish voices which reply, several comic voices, a few mean voices, and some so earnest and manly and alert that one says to himself, "Those are the men for me, when work is to be done!" I read the character of my comrades every morning in each fellow's monosyllable "Here!"

When the orderly is satisfied that not one of us has run away and accepted a Colonelcy from the Confederate States since last roll-call, he notifies those unfortunates who are to be on guard for the next twenty-four hours of the honor and responsibility placed upon their shoulders. Next he tells us what are to be the drills of the day. Then, "Right face! Dismissed! Break ranks! March!"

With ardor we instantly seize tin basins, soap, and towels, and invade a lovely oak-grove at the rear and left of our camp. Here is a delicious spring into which we have fitted a pump. The sylvan scene becomes peopled with "National Guards Washing,"—a scene meriting the notice of Art as much as any "Diana and her Nymphs." But we have no Poussin to paint us in the dewy sunlit grove. Few of us, indeed, know how picturesque we are at all times and seasons.

After this *beau idéal* of a morning toilet comes the ante-prandial drill. Lieutenant W. arrives, and gives us a little appetizing exercise in "Carry arms!" "Support arms!" "By the right flank, march!" "Double quick!"

Breakfast follows. My company messes somewhat helter-skelter in a big tent. We have very tolerable rations. Sometimes luxuries ·appear of potted meats and hermetical vegetables, sent us by the fond New-Yorkers. Each little knot of fellows, too, cooks something savory. Our table-furniture is not elegant, our plates are tin, there is no silver in our forks; but *à la guerre, comme à la guerre*. Let the scrubs growl! Lucky fellows, if they suffer no worse hardships than this!

By and by, after breakfast, come company drills, bayonet practice, battalion drills, and the heavy work of the day. Our handsome Colonel, on a nice black nag, manoeuvres his thousand men of the line-companies on the parade for two or three hours. Two thousand legs step off accurately together. Two thousand pipe-clayed cross-belts—whitened with infinite pains and waste of time, and offering a most inviting mark to a foe—restrain the beating bosoms of a thousand braves, as they—the braves, not the belts—go through the most intricate evolutions unerringly. Watching these battalion movements, Private W., perhaps, goes off and inscribes in his journal—"Any clever, prompt man, with a mechanical turn, an eye for distance, a notion of time, and a voice of command, can be a tactician. It is pure pedantry to claim that the manoeuvring of troops is difficult; it is not difficult, if the troops are quick and steady. But to be a general, with patience and purpose and initiative,—ah!" thinks Private W., "for that purpose you must have the man of genius; and in this war he already begins to appear out of Massachusetts and elsewhere."

Private W. avows without fear that about noon, at Camp Cameron, he takes a hearty dinner, and with satisfaction. Private W. has had his feasts in cot and chateau in Old World and New. It is the conviction of said private that nowhere and no-when has he expected his ration with more interest, and remembered it with more affection, than here.

In the middle hours of the day, it is in order to get a pass to go to Washington, or to visit some of the camps, which now, in the middle of May, begin to form a cordon around the city. . . . Our capital seems arranged by nature to be protected by fortified camps on the circuit of its hills. It may be made almost a Verona, if need be. Our brother regiments have posts nearly as charming as our own, in these fair groves and on these fair slopes on either side of us.

In the afternoon comes target practice, skirmishing-drill, more company- or recruit-drill, and at half past five our evening parade. Let me not forget tent-inspection, at four, by the officer of the day, when our band plays deliciously.

At evening parade all Washington appears. A regiment of ladies, rather indisposed to beauty, observe us. Sometimes the Dons arrive,—Secretaries of State, of War, of Navy,—or military Dons, bestriding prancing steeds, but bestriding them as if " 'twas *not* their habit often of an afternoon." All which,—the bad teeth, pallid skins, and rustic toilets of the fair, and the very moderate horsemanship of the brave,—privates, standing at ease in the ranks, take note of, not cynically, but as men of the world.

Wondrous gymnasts are some of the Seventh, and after evening parade they often give exhibitions of their prowess to circles of admirers. Muscle has not gone out, nor nerve, nor activity, if these athletes are to be taken as the types or even as the leaders of the young city-bred men of our time. All the feats of strength and grace of the gymnasiums are to be seen here, and show to double advantage in the open air.

Then comes sweet evening. The moon rises. It seems always full moon at Camp Cameron. Every tent becomes a little illuminated pyramid. Cooking-fires burn bright along the alleys. The boys lark, sing, shout, do all these merry things that make the entertainment of volunteer service. The gentle moon looks on, mild and amused, the fairest lady of all that visit us.

At last when the songs have been sung and the hundred rumors of the day discussed, at ten the intrusive drums and scolding fifes get together and stir up a concert, always premature, called tattoo. The Seventh Regiment begins to peel for bed; at all events, Private W. does; for said W. takes, when he can, precious good care of his cuticle, and never yields to the lazy and unwholesome habit of soldiers,—sleeping in the clothes. At taps—half past ten—out go the lights. If they do not, presently comes the sentry's peremptory command to put them out. Then, and until the dawn of another day, a cordon of snorers inside of a cordon of sentries surrounds our national capital. The outer cordon sounds its "All's well"; and the inner cordon, slumbering, echoes it.

And that is the history of any day at Camp Cameron. It is monotonous, it is not monotonous, it is laborious, it is lazy, it is a bore, it is a lark, it is half war, half peace, and totally attractive, and not to be dispensed with from one's experience in the nineteenth century.

—WINTHROP, *Life in the Open Air, and Other Papers*

2. DAILY LIFE IN CAMP MILLINGTON

Lawrence Van Alstyne was a young Hudson Valley boy who enlisted in August 1862 in the 128th New York Volunteers—popularly called "Bostwick's Tigers." He trained for a short time at Camp Hudson, and then at Camp Millington, outside Baltimore, before sailing to the Gulf region. His account of daily life in the camp, in diary form, is one of the most authentic that has come down to us.

September 17, 1862. Maybe I have described our life here before, but as no one description can do it justice I am going to try again. We are in a field of 100 acres, as near as I can judge, on the side of a hill, near the top. The ground is newly seeded and wets up quickly, as such ground usually does. We sleep in pairs, and a blanket spread on the ground is our bed while another spread over us is our covering. A narrow strip of muslin, drawn over a pole about three feet from the ground, open at both ends, the wind and rain, if it does rain, beating in upon us, and water running under and about us; this, with all manner of bugs and creeping things crawling over us, and all the while great hungry mosquitoes biting every uncovered inch of us, is not an overdrawn picture of that part of a soldier's life, set apart for the rest and repose necessary to enable him to endure several hours of right down hard work at drill, in a hot sun with heavy woollen clothes on, every button of which must be tight-buttoned, and by the time the officers are tired watching us, we come back to camp wet through with perspiration and too tired to make another move.

Before morning our wet clothes chill us to the marrow of our bones, and why we live and apparently thrive under it, is something I cannot understand. But we do, and the next day are ready for more of it. Very few even take cold. It is part of the contract, and while we grumble and growl among ourselves, we don't really mean it, for we are learning what we will be glad to know at some future time.

Now I am about it, and nothing better to do, I will say something about our kitchen, dining room and cooking arrangements. Some get mad and cuss the cooks, and the whole war department, but that is usually when our stomachs are full. When we are hungry we swallow anything that comes and are thankful for it. The cook's house is simply a portion of the field we are in. A couple of crotches hold up a pole on which the camp kettles are hung, and under which a fire is built. Each company has one, and as far as I know they are all alike. The camp kettles are large sheet-iron pails, one larger than the other so one can be put inside the other when moving. If we have meat and potatoes, meat is put in one, and potatoes in the other. The one that gets cooked first is emptied into mess pans, which are large sheet-iron pans with flaring sides, so one can be packed in another. Then the coffee is put in the empty kettle and boiled. The bread is cut into thick slices, and the breakfast call sounds. We grab our plates and cups, and wait for no second invitation. We each get a piece of meat and a potato, a chunk of bread and a cup of coffee with a spoonful of brown sugar in it. Milk and butter we buy, or go without. We settle down, generally in groups, and the meal is soon over. Then we wash our dishes, and put them back in our haversacks. We make quick work of washing dishes. We save a piece of bread for the last, with which we wipe up everything, and then eat the dish rag. Dinner and breakfast are alike, only sometimes the meat and potatoes are cut up and cooked together, which makes a really delicious stew. Supper is the same, minus the meat and potatoes.

The cooks are men detailed from the ranks for that purpose. Every one smokes or chews tobacco here, so we find no fault because the cooks do both. Boxes or barrels are used as kitchen tables, and are used for seats between meals. The meat and bread are cut on them, and if a scrap is left on the table the flies go right at it and we have so many the less to crawl over us. They are never washed, but are sometimes scraped off and made to look real clean. I never yet saw the cooks wash their hands, but presume they do when they go to the brook for water.

—Van Alstyne, *Diary of an Enlisted Man*

3. ABNER SMALL PAINTS A PORTRAIT OF A PRIVATE IN THE ARMY OF THE POTOMAC

Abner Small, whose diary, The Road to Richmond, *is one of the best of Civil War sources, enlisted as a private in the 16th Maine Volunteers, fought through all the campaigns until 1864, was captured at Petersburg and imprisoned in Libby prison. He was later appointed historian of his regiment.*

PORTRAIT *of a private.*—The ideal picture of a soldier makes a veteran smile. Be a man never so much a man, his importance and conceit dwindle when he crawls into an unteaseled shirt, trousers too short and very baggy behind, coat too long at both ends, shoes with soles like firkin covers, and a cap as shapeless as a feed bag. Let me recall how our private looked to me in the army, in the ranks, a position he chose from pure patriotism. I can see him exactly as I saw him then. He is just in front of me trying to keep his balance and his temper, as he spews from a dry mouth the infernally fine soil of Virginia, and with his hands—he hasn't a handkerchief—wipes the streaks of dirty sweat that make furrows down his unshaven face. No friend of civilian days would recognize him in this most unattractive and disreputable-looking fellow, bowed under fifty-eight pounds of army essentials, and trying to suck a TD.

His suit is a model one, cut after the regulation pattern, fifty thousand at a time, and of just two sizes. If he is a small man, God pity him; and if he is a big man, God pity him still more; for he is an object of ridicule. His forage cap, with its leather visor, when dry curls up, when wet hangs down, and usually covers one or both ears. His army brogans, nothing can ever make shine or even black. Perhaps the coat of muddy blue can be buttoned in front, and it might be lapped and buttoned behind. The tailor never bushels army suits, and he doesn't crease trousers, although he is always generous in reënforcing them with the regulation patch.

The knapsack (which is cut to fit, in the engraving) is an unwieldy burden with its rough, coarse contents of flannel and sole leather and sometimes twenty rounds of ammunition extra. Mixed in with these regulation essentials, like beatitudes, are photographs, cards, huswife, Testament, pens, ink, paper, and oftentimes stolen truck enough to load a mule. All this is crowned with a double wool blanket and half a shelter tent rolled in a rubber blanket. One shoulder and the hips support the "commissary department"—an odorous haversack, which often stinks with its mixture of bacon, pork, salt junk, sugar, coffee, tea, desiccated vegetables, rice, bits of yesterday's dinner, and old scraps husbanded with miserly care against a day of want sure to come.

Loaded down, in addition, with a canteen, full cartridge-box, belt, cross belt, and musket, and tramping twenty miles in a hurry on a hot day, our private was a soldier, but not just then a praiser of the soldier's life. I saw him multiplied by thousands. A photograph of any one of them, covered with yellow dust or mosaics of mud, would have served any relation, North or South, and ornamented a mantel, as a true picture of "Our Boy." . . .

Beans.—Long, weary marches were patiently endured if in the distant perspective could be seen the company bean-hole, and no well-disciplined New England regiment would be in camp thirty minutes without the requisite number. When we went into bivouac, every cook would have one dug and a fire over it before the companies broke to the rear and stacked arms. In the early morning I would hang around a particular hole, and ask Ben to just h'ist the cover and let me get a sniff for an appetizer; and how

Ben would roll his orbs, till only the whites were visible, and say, "Golly, Adjutant, dem yalla-eyes don' got dere kivers off yet; you'll just natchely have to wait a while!" But many's the time we would have to "git up and git," eating our beans half-cooked, and then would come an internal disturbance—not that infernal demon, dyspepsia, of civil life, but an almighty bellyache that would double a man up and send him into line at "Surgeon's Call."

Desiccated vegetables.—Too many beans with salt junk demanded an antiscorbutic, so the government advertised proposals for some kind of vegetable compound in portable form, and it came—tons of it—in sheets like pressed hops. I suppose it was healthful, for there was variety enough in its composition to satisfy any condition of stomach and bowels. What in Heaven's name it was composed of, none of us ever discovered. It was called simply "desiccated vegetables." Ben once brought in just before dinner a piece with a big horn button on it, and wanted to know "if dat 'ere was celery or cabbage?" I doubt our men have ever forgotten how a cook would break off a piece as large as a boot top, put it in a kettle of water, and stir it with the handle of a hospital broom. When the stuff was fully dissolved, the water would remind one of a dirty brook with all the dead leaves floating around promiscuously. Still, it was a substitute for food. We ate it, and we liked it, too.

—SMALL, *The Road to Richmond*

4. LIFE WITH THE THIRTEENTH MASSACHUSETTS

The 13th Massachusetts was organized in Boston shortly after the attack on Fort Sumter and, after brief training at Fort Independence, left for New York in July 1861. The story of the march southward to the fields of battle is told in these pages of diaries put together by the regimental historian, Charles E. Davis. The regiment fought in the Valley campaign, at Antietam, Chancellorsville, Gettysburg, and Petersburg. Davis himself was wounded and imprisoned at Manassas. It is no exaggeration to say that this is on the whole the most interesting of all the many regimental histories.

1861. Thursday, Aug. 1, Hagerstown: After tents were pitched some of the men turned in and went to sleep, though the novelty of the thing was too great for most of us, who straggled back into town. During the day one of the boys brought in a Virginia paper in which it was stated that one "Southerner could lick five Northern mudsills." It was not so very comforting to feel that we were to be killed off in blocks of five. Nothing was said to us on the 16th of July, the date of our muster-in, about this wholesale slaughter. There was a kind of airy confidence as well as contemptuousness about the statement that made our enlistment look a little less like a picnic than when we marched down Broadway. It was hard to realize that we had come so far from home merely to solve a problem in mathematics, yet so it seemed to the writer of that philippic.

Some time during the night an alarm was sounded by the beating of the "long roll," and we were ordered into line to drive the terrible foe, who was thought, even then, to be in our midst. Immediately everything was excitement and confusion. We can afford to laugh now, but then it was terribly serious, and no doubt we did some silly things; but it should be borne in mind that this was very early in the war. When it was discovered, as it shortly was, that all this excitement was caused by a pig who strolled into camp and was mistaken by the officer of the guard for the rebel army, many of us were imbued with a courage we hardly felt before. There was little sleep during the balance of the night, as the matter had to be discussed and talked about, as most things were in the rank and file of the Thirteenth, particularly when it related to the foolishness of an officer.

Although orders awaited us, on our arrival in Hagerstown, to march to Harper's Ferry, we were delayed on account of the bad condition of the roads from recent rains. This kind of consideration went out of fashion very soon after, we are sorry to say.

About sunset we struck tents and marched to Boonesboro', fourteen miles, arriving there at the witching hour of night when it is said church-yards yawn. We were led into an empty corral, lately occupied by mules, to bivouac for the night.

Ordinarily a mule-yard would not be considered a desirable place in which to spend the night, but it was midnight, and we were weary with marching, and worn out with excitement and loss of sleep. This was our fifth night from home. The first night was spent on a Sound steamer, the second on our way to Philadelphia, the third *en route* to Hagerstown, and the fourth in driving pigs out of camp, so that this old mule-yard, as far as we could see it, appeared the most delightful place in the world. At eighteen to twenty years of age little time is wasted in seeking sleep. It comes quickly and takes entire possession of your soul and body, and all we did was to drop in our tracks, making no inquiries about camp or picket guard, but let Morpheus lead us to the land of pleasant dreams. This being our first bivouac, occurrences made a deeper impression than at any time afterward. When reveille was sounded, and our eyes opened to the bright sunlight, we looked about to see where we were and who were near us. The bright red blankets of the regiment made the place look attractive. Many of the boys were still stretching themselves into activity, while others were examining their bed to account for sundry pains in the body from neglect to brush the stones aside when they laid down. How we all laughed when we saw where we were! Many and many a time while sitting round a camp fire have we recalled this night in the mule-yard.

Saturday, Aug. 3: A very hot day. Shortly after breakfast we left for Pleasant Valley, sixteen miles, where we arrived in the afternoon, and where we bivouacked for the night. A good many of the men were overcome by the heat, and didn't reach camp until after dark. The size of the knapsack was too heavy for men unused to carrying such a weight. It must be reduced, and there were no more Bibles. Just what to throw away it was difficult to decide, as many of the articles we carried were connected by association with those we held most dear. Some of the boys had dressing-cases among their luxuries. They hated to dispense with them, but it had to be done.

Among the articles provided us by the State were "havelocks," commonly used in hot countries by the English army. The havelock was named after Sir Henry Havelock, a distinguished English general. It is made of white linen, to be worn on the head as a protection from the rays of the sun. As it was made sufficiently large to cover the neck and shoulders, the effect, when properly adjusted, was to deprive the wearer of any air he might otherwise enjoy. An Englishman would melt in his boots before he would give up a custom enjoyed by his grandfather. Not so a Yankee. The motive which prompted the State to supply them was a good one, as was also the suggestion that prompted their immediate transfer to the plebeian uses of a dish-cloth or a coffee-strainer, which suggestion was universally adopted,—a dish-cloth or coffee-strainer being the only things in the world, apparently, we were unprovided with.

Friday, Aug. 23: While at Sandy Hook we received the hats and uniform coats issued to us by the State, and which were forwarded by express. The coat was much too heavy, with the thermometer in the eighties. It was made with long skirts, and when fitting the wearer was not a bad-appearing garment; but as very few of them did fit, our personal appearance was not improved. They were made large in front, to meet an abnormal expansion of chest. Until we grew to them, it was a handy place to stow some of the contents of our knapsack.

The hats were neither useful nor ornamental. They were made of black felt, high-crowned, with a wide rim turned up on one side, and fastened to the crown by a brass shield representing an eagle with extended wings, apparently screaming with holy horror at so base an employment. On the front of the crown was a brass bugle containing the figure 13. Now it so happened that the person who selected the sizes was under the impression that every man from Massachusetts had a head like Daniel Webster—a mistake that caused most of us much trouble, inasmuch as newspapers were in great demand to lessen the diameter of the crown. Those of us who failed to procure newspapers made use of our ears to prevent its falling on our shoulders. As will be seen later on, they mysteriously disappeared. . . .

September 13: A man in one of the Connecticut regiments was shot to-day for sleeping on guard. It was not pleasant to feel that a quiet nap, on picket, might be followed by death, so we swore off sleeping while on guard.

It was at Darnestown that we were first made acquainted with an article of food called "desiccated" vegetables. For the convenience of handling, it was made in to large, round cakes about two inches thick. When cooked, it tasted like herb tea. From the flow of language which followed, we suspected it contained powerful stimulating properties. It became universally known in the army as "desecrated" vegetables, and the aptness of this term would be appreciated by the dullest comprehension after one mouthful of the abominable compound. It is possible that the chaplain, who overheard some of the remarks, may have urged its discontinuance as a ration, inasmuch as we rarely, if ever, had it again.

[1862]. Wednesday, March 12: The rattle of drums and the sweet singing of birds announced that morn was here. The army was to move on Winchester at once, so we hastily cooked our coffee, and as quickly as possible ate our breakfast. There was no time to spare, as orders to "fall in" were heard in every direction. Orders were received for the Thirteenth to take the advance of the column as skirmishers. Winchester was four miles away, occupied by 25,000 troops under Stonewall Jackson, and well-fortified by earthworks. As soon as we were out of the woods the regiment was deployed as skirmishers, and marched in that order in quick time across fields, over fences and stone walls, fording brooks or creeks, preserving distances and line as well as we could under such disadvantages.

The sensations we experienced on this bright, beautiful morning are not likely to be forgotten. It was very warm, and the march a hard one, because the line was irregularly obstructed. That is to say, while one part would be marching on the smooth surface of the ground, another part might be climbing a fence or wading a brook. To keep the line tolerably straight under such exasperating circumstances was very trying and perspiring work. In addition to this we were, for the first time, in line of battle, and in plain sight of the rest of the division, who were watching our movements as they followed in close column.

Situated as we were, there was no opportunity for obeying, without disgrace, those instincts of discretion which are said to be the better part of valor, and which prompt human nature to seek safety in flight. Those of us who omitted to sneak away before the line was formed, but who afterward showed such ingenuity and skill in escaping the dangers of battle, found no chance open for skulking on this occasion. Yes! like other regiments, we had our percentage of men who dared to run away, that they might live to fight some other, far distant day.

We saw those dreaded earthworks a long time before we reached them, and wondered at the enemy's silence, but concluded they were reserving their fire until we should be close enough for the greatest execution. Whatever the boys felt, there was no faltering or wavering. Within a short distance of the earthworks we formed in close order, and with a yell and a rush we bounded over them to find, after all our fears and anticipations, they were empty. We were soon formed in line, and marched, in columns of companies, into town, being the first Union regiment that entered Winchester. We felt proud enough at our bloodless victory.

We had hardly entered the main street of the town when General Jackson and Colonel Ashby were discovered on horseback, in front of the Taylor House, waving an adieu with their hats. An order was immediately given to fire, but we were not quick enough to do them harm or retard their flight. This was a daring thing to do, though common enough with such men as Jackson and Ashby.

We marched down the main street, the band playing patriotic airs, while the people scanned our appearance to see what a Yankee looked like. Some who were prepared to scoff could get no farther than "How fat they are!"

After the companies were assigned to quarters the officers met at the Taylor House, and dined on the meal provided for Jackson and his staff.

Tuesday, July 22: In passing through towns and villages, and even on the high-roads, we naturally attracted a good deal of attention. We frequently noticed among the crowds so gathered, the scowling faces of women, who, upon learning we were from Massachusetts, saluted us as "Nigger-lovers," and other opprobrious epithets, while it occasionally happened that by grimaces only could they express the intensity of their feelings. . . .

The remarks we heard from the bystanders as we marched along often became by-words in the regiment. We were no exception to the generality of mankind, of liking to see a pretty face, even if it did belong to a woman of "secesh" sentiments. When the boys at the head of the column discovered a pretty girl, if she was on the right side of the road, *"guide right"* would be passed along the line; and *"guide left"* if on the left side of the road. By this ingenious device we were enabled to direct our eyes where we would receive the largest return for our admiration. . . .

Various were the devices adopted by the boys to relieve the monotony of weary marches. On these occasions, as conversation was allowed, stories were told, gossip repeated, discussions carried on, and criticisms made on the acts of public men, as well as on the merits of our commanders. An occasional silence would be broken by the starting of a familiar song, and very soon the whole regiment would join in the singing. Sometimes it would be a whistling chorus, when all would be whistling. Toward the end of a day, however, so tired we were all, that it was difficult to muster courage for these diversions, then our only reliance for music would be the band. When a temporary halt was granted, it was curious to see how quickly the boys would dump themselves over on their backs at the side of the road as soon as the word was given, looking like so many dead men. There was one thing we were thankful to the colonel for, and that was his freedom from nonsense on such occasions. No "right-facing," no "right-dressing," no "stacking arms," to waste valuable minutes, but "get all the rest you can, boys," and when the order was given to "forward," each man took his place in line without confusion or delay. . . .

It would often occur, when we were tired and dusty from a long day's march, "Old Festive" would ride by, when suddenly you would hear sung:

"Saw my leg off,
Saw my leg off,
Saw my leg off—
SHORT!!!"

There was another man in the regiment who contributed a large share of fun for the amusement of others, and that was the "Medicine man"—the man who honored the doctor's sight-drafts for salts, castor-oil, etc., delicacies intended for the sick, but greatly in demand by those who wished to rid themselves of unpleasant duties. He was the *basso profundo* of the glee club, and could gaze without a tremor at the misery of a man struggling with castor-oil, while at the same time encouraging him to show his gratitude at the generosity of the Government by drinking the last drop. "Down with it, my boy, the more you take the less I carry."

Saturday, Aug. 9: The last place to look for a stock company would be among a regiment of soldiers. After being deprived of camp kettles, mess pans, etc., each man was obliged to do his own cooking, as already stated, in his tin dipper, which held about a pint. Whether it was coffee, beans, pork, or anything depending on the services of a fire to make it palatable, it was accomplished by the aid of the dipper only. Therefore any utensil like a frying-pan was of incalculable service in preparing a meal. There were so few of these in the regiment, that only men of large means, men who could raise a dollar thirty days after a paymaster's visit, could afford such a luxury.

In one instance the difficulty was overcome by the formation of a joint-stock company, composed of five stockholders, each paying the sum of twenty cents toward the purchase of a frying-pan, which cost the sum of one dollar. The par value of each share was therefore twenty cents. It was understood that each stockholder should take his turn at carrying the frying-pan when on a march, which responsibility entitled him to its first use in halting for the night. While in camp, it passed from one to the other each day in order of turn. It was frequently loaned for a consideration, thereby affording means for an occasional dividend among the stockholders. The stock advanced in value until it reached as high as forty cents per share, so that a stockholder in the "Joint Stock Frying Pan Company" was looked upon as a man of consequence. Being treated with kindness and civility by his comrades, life assumed a roseate hue to the shareholders in this great company, in spite of their deprivations. It was flattering to hear one's self mentioned in terms of praise by some impecunious comrade who wished to occupy one side of it while you were cooking.

On this particular morning, when we started out, expecting shortly to be in a fight, the stock went rapidly down, until it could be bought for almost nothing. As the day progressed, however, there was a slight rise, though the market was not strong. When the order was given to leave knapsacks, it necessarily included this utensil, and so the "Joint Stock Frying Pan Company" was wiped out.

—DAVIS, *Three Years in the Army*

5. MINUTIAE OF SOLDIER LIFE IN THE ARMY OF NORTHERN VIRGINIA

To an extraordinary degree—or what to us now seems an extraordinary degree—the Civil War soldier, North and South, was on his own. He often supplied his own uniform and his own arms; often he had to depend upon his own ingenuity, or that of his company, for food. He depended almost wholly upon himself for entertainment. He was—like American soldiers in all wars—an individualist. He regarded all regulations with distaste, avoided regimentation, tried to live his own life as much as he could.

Of all the many accounts of life in the Confederate armies, that of Carlton McCarthy is the best—the best because the most detailed. McCarthy was a private in the famous Richmond Howitzers.

THE volunteer of 1861 made extensive preparations for the field. Boots, he thought, were an absolute necessity, and the heavier the soles and longer the tops the better. His pants were stuffed inside the tops of his boots, of course. A double-breasted coat, heavily wadded, with two rows of big brass buttons and a long skirt, was considered comfortable. A small stiff cap, with a narrow brim, took the place of the comfortable "felt," or the shining and towering tile worn in civil life.

Then over all was a huge overcoat, long and heavy, with a cape reaching nearly to the waist. On his back he strapped a knapsack containing a full stock of underwear, soap, towels, comb, brush, looking-glass, tooth-brush, paper and envelopes, pens, ink, pencils, blacking, photographs, smoking and chewing tobacco, pipes, twine string, and cotton strips for wounds and other emergencies, needles and thread, buttons, knife, fork, and spoon, and many other things as each man's idea of what he was to encounter varied. On the outside of the knapsack, solidly folded, were two great blankets and a rubber or oil-cloth. This knapsack, etc., weighed from fifteen to twenty-five pounds, sometimes more. All seemed to think it was impossible to have on too heavy clothes, or to have too many conveniences, and each had an idea that to be a good soldier he must be provided against every possible emergency.

In addition to the knapsack, each man had a haversack, more or less costly, some of cloth and some of fine morocco, and stored with provisions always, as though he expected any moment to receive orders to march across the Great Desert, and supply his own wants on the way. A canteen was considered indispensable, and at the outset it was thought prudent to keep it full of water. Many, expecting terrific hand-to-hand encounters, carried revolvers, and even bowie-knives. Merino shirts (and flannel) were thought to be the right thing, but experience demonstrated the contrary. Gloves were also thought to be very necessary and good things to have in winter time, the favorite style being buck gauntlets with long cuffs.

In addition to each man's private luggage, each mess, generally composed of from five to ten men, drawn together by similar tastes and associations, had *its* outfit, consisting of a large camp chest containing skillet, frying pan, coffee boiler, bucket for lard, coffee box, salt box, meal box, flour box, knives, forks, spoons, plates, cups, etc., etc. These chests were so large that eight or ten of them filled up an army wagon, and were so heavy that two strong men had all they could do to get one of them into the wagon. In addition to the chest each mess owned an axe, water bucket, and bread tray. Then the tents of each company, and little sheet-iron stoves, and stove pipe, and the trunks and valises of the company officers, made an immense pile of stuff, so that each company had a small wagon train of its own.

All thought money to be absolutely necessary, and for a while rations were disdained and the mess supplied with the best that could be bought with the mess fund. Quite a large number had a "boy" along to do the cooking and washing. Think of it! a Confederate soldier with a body servant all his own, to bring him a drink of water, black his boots, dust his clothes, cook his corn bread and bacon, and put wood on his fire. Never was there fonder admiration than these darkies displayed for their masters. Their chief delight and glory was to praise the courage and good looks of "Mahse Tom," and prophesy great things about his future. Many a ringing laugh and shout of fun originated in the queer remarks, shining countenance, and glistening teeth of this now forever departed character.

It is amusing to think of the follies of the early part of the war, as illustrated by the outfits of the volunteers. They were so heavily clad, and so burdened with all manner of things, that a march was torture, and the wagon trains were so immense in proportion to the number of troops, that it would have been impossible to guard them in an enemy's country. Subordinate officers thought themselves entitled to transportation for trunks, mattresses, and folding bedsteads, and the privates were as ridiculous in their demands.

Thus much by way of introduction. The change came rapidly, and stayed not until the transformation was complete. Nor was this change attributable alone to the orders of the general officers. The men soon learned the inconvenience and danger of so much luggage, and, as they became more experienced, they vied with each other in reducing themselves to light-marching trim.

Experience soon demonstrated that boots were not agreeable on a long march. They were heavy and irksome, and when the heels were worn a little one-sided, the wearer would find his ankle twisted nearly out of joint by every unevenness of the road. When thoroughly wet, it was a laborious undertaking to get them off, and worse to get them on in time to answer the morning roll-call. And so, good, strong brogues or brogans, with broad bottoms and big, flat heels, succeeded the boots, and were found much more comfortable and agreeable, easier put on and off, and altogether the more sensible.

A short-waisted and single-breasted jacket usurped the place of the long-tailed coat, and became universal. The enemy noticed this peculiarity, and called the Confederates gray jackets, which name was immediately transferred to those lively creatures which were the constant admirers and inseparable companions of the Boys in Gray and in Blue.

Caps were destined to hold out longer than some other uncomfortable things, but they finally yielded to the demands of comfort and common sense, and a good soft felt hat was worn instead. A man who has never been a soldier does not know, nor indeed can know, the amount of comfort there is in a good soft hat in camp, and how utterly useless is a "soldier hat" as they are generally made. Why the Prussians, with all their experience, wear

The Army of the Potomac on the Move, January 1863

A. R. Waud

General Stuart's Headquarters on the Rapidan

Commissary Department of the 6th Massachusetts

their heavy, unyielding helmets, and the French their little caps, is a mystery to a Confederate who has enjoyed the comfort of an old slouch.

Overcoats an inexperienced man would think an absolute necessity for men exposed to the rigors of a northern Virginia winter, but they grew scarcer and scarcer; they were found to be a great inconvenience. The men came to the conclusion that the trouble of carrying them on hot days outweighed the comfort of having them when the cold day arrived. Besides they found that life in the open air hardened them to such an extent that changes in the temperature were not felt to any degree. Some clung to their overcoats to the last, but the majority got tired lugging them around, and either discarded them altogether, or trusted to capturing one about the time it would be needed. Nearly every overcoat in the army in the latter years was one of Uncle Sam's captured from his boys.

The knapsack vanished early in the struggle. It was inconvenient to "change" the underwear too often, and the disposition not to change grew, as the knapsack was found to gall the back and shoulders, and weary the man before half the march was accomplished. The better way was to dress out and out, and wear that outfit until the enemy's knapsacks, or the folks at home supplied a change. Certainly it did not pay to carry around clean clothes while waiting for the time to use them.

Very little washing was done, as a matter of course. Clothes once given up were parted with forever. There were good reasons for this: cold water would not cleanse them or destroy the vermin, and hot water was not always to be had. One blanket to each man was found to be as much as could be carried, and amply sufficient for the severest weather. This was carried generally by rolling it lengthwise, with the rubber cloth outside, tying the ends of the roll together, and throwing the loop thus made over the left shoulder with the ends fastened together hanging under the right arm.

The haversack held its own to the last, and was found practical and useful. It very seldom, however, contained rations, but was used to carry all the articles generally carried in the knapsack; of course the stock was small. Somehow or other, many men managed to do without the haversack, and carried absolutely nothing but what they wore and had in their pockets.

The infantry threw away their heavy cap boxes and cartridge boxes, and carried their caps and cartridges in their pockets. Canteens were very useful at times, but they were as a general thing discarded. They were not much used to carry water, but were found useful when the men were driven to the necessity of foraging, for conveying buttermilk, cider, sorghum, etc., to camp. A good strong tin cup was found better than a canteen, as it was easier to fill at a well or spring, and was serviceable as a boiler for making coffee when the column halted for the night.

Revolvers were found to be about as useless and heavy lumber as a private soldier could carry, and early in the war were sent home to be used by the women and children in protecting themselves from insult and violence at the hands of the ruffians who prowled about the country shirking duty.

Strong cotton was adopted in place of flannel and merino, for two reasons: first, because easier to wash; and second, because the vermin did not propagate so rapidly in cotton as in wool. Common white cotton shirts and drawers proved the best that could be used by the private soldier.

Gloves to any but a mounted man were found useless, worse than useless. With the gloves on, it was impossible to handle an axe, buckle harness, load a musket, or handle a rammer at the piece. Wearing them was found to be simply a habit, and so, on the principle that the less luggage the less labor, *they* were discarded.

The camp-chest soon vanished. The brigadiers and major-generals, even, found them too troublesome, and soon they were left entirely to the quarter-masters and commissaries. One skillet and a couple of frying pans, a bag for flour or meal, another bag for salt, sugar, and coffee, divided by a knot tied between served the purpose as well. The skillet passed from mess to mess. Each mess generally owned a frying pan, but often one served a company. The oil-cloth was found to be as good as the wooden tray for making up the dough. The water bucket held its own to the last!

Tents were *rarely seen*. All the poetry about the *"tented field"* died. Two men slept together, each having a blanket and an oil-cloth; one oil-cloth went next to the ground. The two laid on this, covered themselves with two blankets, protected from the rain with the second oil-cloth on top, and slept very comfortably through rain, snow or hail, as it might be.

Very little money was seen in camp. The men did not expect, did not care for, or often get any pay, and they were not willing to deprive the old folks at home of their little supply, so they learned to do without any money.

When rations got short and were getting shorter, it became necessary to dismiss the darkey servants. Some, however, became company servants, instead of private institutions, and held out faithfully to the end, cooking the rations away in the rear, and at the risk of life carrying them to the line of battle to their "young mahsters."

Reduced to the minimum, the private soldier consisted of one man, one hat, one jacket, one shirt, one pair of pants, one pair of drawers, one pair of shoes, and one pair of socks. His baggage was one blanket, one rubber blanket, and one haversack. The haversack generally contained smoking tobacco and a pipe, and a small piece of soap, with temporary additions of apples, persimmons, blackberries, and such other commodities as he could pick up on the march.

The company property consisted of two or three skillets and frying pans, which were sometimes carried in the wagon, but oftener in the hands of the soldiers. The infantry-men generally preferred to stick the handle of the frying pan in the barrel of a musket, and so carry it.

The wagon trains were devoted entirely to the transportation of ammunition and commissary and quartermaster's stores, which had not been issued. Rations which had become company property, and the baggage of the men, when they had any, was carried by the men themselves. If, as was sometimes the case, three days' rations were issued at one time and the troops ordered to cook them, and be prepared to march, they did cook them, *and eat them if possible*, so as to avoid the labor of carrying them. It was not such an undertaking either, to eat three days' rations in one, as frequently none had been issued for more than a day, and when issued were cut down one half.

The infantry found out that bayonets were not of much use, and did not hesitate to throw them, with the scabbard, away.

The artillerymen, who started out with heavy sabres hanging to their belts, stuck them up in the mud as they marched, and left them for the ordnance officers to pick up and turn over to the cavalry.

The cavalrymen found sabres very tiresome when swung to the belt, and adopted the plan of fastening them to the saddle on the left side, with the hilt in front and in reach of the hand. Finally sabres got very scarce even among the cavalrymen, who relied more and more on their short rifles.

No soldiers ever marched with less to encumber them, and none marched faster or held out longer.

The courage and devotion of the men rose equal to every hardship and privation, and the very intensity of their sufferings became a source of merriment. Instead of growling and deserting, they laughed at their own bare feet, ragged clothes and pinched faces; and weak, hungry, cold, wet, worried with vermin and itch, dirty, with no hope of reward or rest, marched cheerfully to meet the well-fed and warmly clad hosts of the enemy.

—McCarthy, *Detailed Minutiae of Soldier Life in the Army of Northern Virginia*

6. GETTING A HAIRCUT IN THE ARMY

Here is another example of what now would seem to be the primitive conditions of warfare in the sixties. There was no organized barber service; the soldiers arranged for their own haircuts and shaves—or went without. The popularity of beards actually antedated the Civil War by a year or two— witness Lincoln's growing a beard after his nomination—but the exigencies of wartime service helped make beards fashionable.

William Dame was a Maryland Confederate, a student of theology who entered the ministry after the war. His volume of memoirs is particularly valuable for its pictures of daily life in the army.

THERE was only one man in the Battery who could cut hair—Sergeant Van McCreery—and he had the only pair of scissors that could cut hair. So every aspirant to this fashionable cut tried to make interest with Van to fix him up; and Van, who was very good natured, would, as he had time and opportunity, accommodate the applicant, and trim him close.

Several of us had gone under the transforming hands of this tonsorial artist, when Bob McIntosh got his turn. Bob was a handsome boy with a luxuriant growth of hair. He had raven black, kinky hair that stuck up from his head in a bushy mass, and he hadn't had his hair cut for a good while, and it was very long and seemed longer than it was because it stuck out so from his head. Now, it was all to go, and a crowd of the boys gathered 'round to see the fun. The modus operandi was simple, but sufficient. The candidate sat on a stump with a towel tied 'round his neck, and he held up the corners making a receptacle to catch the hair as it was cut. Why this—I don't know; force of habit I reckon. . . .

Van stood behind Bob and began over his right ear. He took the hair off clean, as he went, working from right to left over his head; the crowd around—jeering the victim and making comments on his ever-changing appearance as the scissors progressed, making a clean sweep at every cut. We were thus making much noise with our fun at Bob's expense, until the shears had moved up to the top of his head, leaving the whole right half of the head as clean of hair as the palm of your hand, while the other half was still covered with this long, kinky, jet black hair, which in the absence of the departed locks looked twice as long as before—and Bob did present a spectacle that would make a dog laugh. It was just as funny as it could be.

Just at that moment, in the midst of all this hilarity, suddenly we heard a man yell out something as he came running down the hill from the guns. We could not hear what he said. The next moment, he burst excitedly into our midst, and shouted out, "For God's sake, men, get your guns. The Yankees are across the river and making for the guns. They will capture them before you get there, if you don't hurry up."

This was a bolt out of a clear sky—but we jumped to the call. Everybody instantly forgot everything else and raced for the guns. I saw McCreery running with the scissors in his hand; he forgot that he had them—but it was funny to see a soldier going to war with a pair of scissors! I found myself running beside Bob McIntosh, with his hat off, his head half shaved and that towel, still tied round his neck, streaming out behind him in the wind.

Just before we got to the guns, Bob suddenly halted and said, "Good Heavens, Billy, it has just come to me what a devil of a fix I am in with my head in this condition. I tell you now that if the Yankees get too close to the guns, I am going to run. If they got me, or found me dead, they would say that General Lee was bringing up the convicts from the Penitentiary in Richmond to fight them. I wouldn't be caught dead with my head looking like this. . . ."

In the meantime, the enemy guns across the river opened on us and the shells were flying about us in lively fashion. It was rather a sudden transition from peace to war, but we had been at this busines before; the sound of the shells was not unfamiliar—so we were not unduly disturbed. We quickly got the guns loaded, and opened on that Infantry, advancing up the hill. We worked rapidly, for the case was urgent, and we made it as lively for those fellows as we possibly could. In a few minutes a pretty neat little battle was making the welkin ring. . . .

The battle ceased, the picket line was restored along the river bank, and all was quiet again. Bob McIntosh was more put out by all this business than anybody else—it had interrupted his hair cut. When we first got the guns into action, everybody was too busy to notice Bob's head. After we got settled down to work, I caught sight of that half-shaved head and it was the funniest object you ever saw. Bob was No. 1 at his gun, which was next to mine, and had to swab and ram the gun. This necessitated his constantly turning from side to side, displaying first this, and then the other side of his head. One side was perfectly white and bare; the other side covered by a mop of kinky, jet black hair; but when you caught sight of his front elevation, the effect was indescribable. While Bob was unconsciously making this absurd exhibition, it was too much to stand, even in a fight. I said to the boys around my gun, "Look at Bob." They looked and they could hardly work the gun for laughing.

Of course, when the fight was over McCreery lost that pair of scissors, or *said* he did. There was not another pair in camp, so Bob had to go about with his head in that condition for about a week—and he wearied of life. One day in his desperation, he said he wanted to get some of that hair off his head so much that he would resort to any means. He had tried to cut some off with his knife. One of the boys, Hunter Dupuy, was standing by chopping on the level top of a stump with a hatchet. Hunter said, "All right, Bob, put your head on this stump and I'll chop off some of your hair." The blade was dull, and it only forced a quantity of the hair down into the wood, where it stuck, and held Bob's hair fast to the stump, besides pulling out a lot by the roots, and hurting Bob very much. He tried to pull loose and couldn't. Then he began to call Hunter all the names he could think of, and threatened what he was going to do to him when he got loose. Hunter, much hurt by such ungracious return for what he had done at Bob's request, said, "Why, Bob, you couldn't expect me to cut your hair with a hatchet without hurting some"—which semed reasonable. We made Bob promise to keep the peace, on pain of leaving him tied to the stump—then we cut him loose with our knives.

After some days, when we had had our fun, Van found the scissors and trimmed off the other side of his head to match—Bob was happy.

—DAME, *From the Rapidan to Richmond*

7. INVENTIONS AND GADGETS USED BY THE SOLDIERS

Civil War soldiers, like their successors in the First and Second World Wars, were endlessly resourceful. They had to be. Their resourcefulness appeared not only in such contrivances as those here described, but in the creation of new weapons and new techniques of warfare.

John D. Billings, whose Hardtack and Coffee *is one of the most entertaining of all Civil War books, was a member of the 10th Massachusetts battery of light artillery.*

ONE of the first products of their genius which I recall was a combination *knife-fork-and-spoon* arrangement, which was peddled through the state camping-grounds in great numbers and variety. Of course every man must have one. So much convenience in so small a compass must be taken advantage of. It was a sort of soldier's trinity, which they all thought that they understood and appreciated. But I doubt whether this invention, on the average, ever got beyond the first camp in active service.

I still have in my possession the remnants of a *water-filterer* in which I invested after enlistment. There was a metallic mouth-piece at one end of a small gutta-percha tube, which latter was about fifteen inches long. At the other end of the tube was a suction-chamber, an inch long by a half-inch in diameter, with the end perforated, and containing a piece of bocking as a filter. Midway of the tubing was an air-chamber. The tubing long since dried and crumbled away from the metal. It is possible that I used this instrument half a dozen times, though I do not recall a single instance, and on breaking camp just before the Gettysburg Campaign, I sent it, with some other effects, northward.

I remember another filterer, somewhat simpler. It consisted of the same kind of mouth-piece, with rubber tubing attached to a small conical piece of pumice stone, through which the water was filtered. Neither of these was ever of any practical value.

There was another invention that must have been sufficiently popular to have paid the manufacturer a fair rate on his investment, and that was the steel-armor enterprise. There were a good many men who were anxious to be heroes, but they were particular. They preferred to be *live* heroes. They were willing to go to war and fight as never man fought before, if they could only be insured against bodily harm. They were not willing to assume all the risks which an enlistment involved, without securing something in the shape of a drawback.

Well, the iron tailors saw and appreciated the situation and sufferings of this class of men, and came to the rescue with a vest of steel armor, worth, as I remember it, about a dozen dollars, and greaves. The latter, I think, did not find so ready a market as the vests, which were comparatively common. These ironclad warriors admitted that when panoplied for the fight their sensations were much as they might be if they were dressed up in an old-fashioned air-tight stove; still, with all the discomforts of this casing, they felt a little safer with it on than off in battle, and they reasoned that it was the right and duty of every man to adopt all honorable measures to assure his safety in the line of duty.

This seemed solid reasoning, surely; but, in spite of it all, a large number of these vests never saw Rebeldom. Their owners were subjected to such a storm of ridicule that they could not bear up under it. It was a stale yet common joke to remind them that in action these vests must be worn behind. Then, too, the ownership of one of them was taken as evidence of faint-heartedness. Of this the owner was often reminded; so that when it came to the packing of the knapsack for departure, the vest, taking as it did considerable space, and adding no small weight to his already too heavy burden, was in many cases left behind. The officers, whose opportunity to take baggage along was greater, clung to them longest; but I think that they were quite generally abandoned with the first important reduction made in the luggage. . . .

Then there were fancy patent-leather haversacks, with two or three compartments for the assortment of rations, which Uncle Sam was expected to furnish. But those who invested in them were somewhat disgusted at a little later stage of their service, when they were ordered to throw away all such "high-toned" trappings and adopt the regulation pattern of painted cloth. This was a bag about a foot square, with a broad strap for the shoulder, into which soldiers soon learned to bundle all their food and table furniture, which . . . after a day's hard march were always found in such a delightful hodge-podge. . . .

The Turkish fez, with pendent tassel, was seen on the heads of some soldiers. Zouave regiments wore them. They did very well to lie around camp in, and in a degree marked their owner as a somewhat conspicuous man among his fellows, but they were not tolerated on line; few of them ever survived the first three months' campaigning.

And this recalls the large number of the soldiers of '62 who did not wear the forage cap furnished by the government. They bought the "McClellan cap," so called, at the hatters' instead, which in most cases faded out in a month. This the government caps did not do, with all their awkward appearance. They may have been coarse and unfashionable to the eye, but the colors would stand. Nearly every man embellished his cap with the number or letter of his company and regiment and the appropriate emblem. For infantry this emblem is a bugle, for artillery two crossed cannons, and for cavalry two crossed sabres.

—Billings, Hardtack and Coffee

8. SHOEMAKING AND TAILORING IN WINTER QUARTERS

Here is another account of the ingenuity of the American soldier. McHenry Howard, who gives us this fascinating insight into the domestic economy of a Southern army in winter quarters, was a Marylander who, at the outbreak of the war, hurried south and joined Johnston's army at Bull Run. Subsequently he fought through the whole war, serving as a staff officer to Jackson and Lee. He was taken by the Federals and held for a time on Johnson's Island in Lake Erie.

A NUMBER of shoemakers in the different regiments, seventeen I think, were encouraged to send home—and in some instances were given leave to go—for their tools, and were put to work repairing shoes, being exempted from guard and other routine camp duty, but ready to fall in with their commands on any call to arms. The shoe-shops were a separate camp of tents, near brigade headquarters and under our immediate supervision, guarded by sentinels, and no person was allowed to visit them or to carry his shoes to be mended without a pass and order from his company and regimental commanders, approved by the adjutant or inspector general. A careful estimate

and report of the saving of the issue of shoes to our brigade during the winter
was made to the higher authorities at one time, but I am afraid to say from
memory what the saving was confidently stated to have been, certainly several hundred pairs; besides, the men's feet were kept in better condition by
the correction of ill fitting shoes. On the march back from Gettysburg in the
summer before, the "barefooted" men of the division—not literally that except in the case of some, but those whose shoes were worn out or whose feet
were sore from wearing bad shoes or other causes—were organized into a
separate command, under officers, to pick their way on the grassy roadside
and by easy stages on each day's march. My recollection is that this barefooted and sorefooted command sometimes numbered a fourth of the division.

Having taken a sort of census of the whole brigade, we knew exactly
where to look at any time for skilled workmen in different occupations. The
37th Virginia, from the mountains of the south-western part of the State, we
found to furnish a greater proportion of mechanics—or at least men who
were used to doing jobs of handywork—the other regiments being more
largely composed of men from the farming class or from sections where
there were regular artizans and stores convenient. Wheelwrights were detailed to put the ambulances (this under the zealous charge of Surgeon
Henkel of that regiment, senior surgeon or medical director), and transportation generally in good order. I think log shelters were made for the horses
and they were carefully looked after. General Steuart had also detailed, or
meditated detailing, tinners to mend canteens, cups and other tinwork.
Drummers or tanners were given a few days leave to go to their homes or
places not far distant on condition of bringing back dog skins for drum
heads, and although the animal's integument was tanned in a marvellously
short time, it was found to answer very well.

The General was especially desirous of establishing "tailor shops" to patch
and mend clothing, on a like scale with the shoe shops, or greater, and sent
up urgent applications for waste odds and ends of cloth and thread at the
government factories, but had received no response when the opening of
the Spring campaign put a check to these and many other schemes.

In short, recognizing the straits that the Confederacy was now put to in
the furnishing of supplies, we aimed to save and eke out issues in every
possible way.

—HOWARD, *Recollections of a Maryland Confederate Soldier*

9. HOW THE SOLDIERS MARCHED

*No hardships were harder than those of the march, if we are to trust the
voluminous testimony of the foot soldiers. The roads were dusty in the
summer, muddy in the winter; the soldier was dressed in heavy woolens,
loaded down with fifty or sixty pounds of equipment, often without food
for long stretches of the day. It is no wonder that straggling was almost*

universal, or that literally thousands of men fell out of line and got lost. It is difficult to know whether the Confederate or the Federal soldiers suffered most from marching. More Confederates than Federals were country bred, and therefore more accustomed to cross-country hiking; on the other hand the Confederacy was low on shoes, and there are any number of stories of Southern soldiers marching barefoot, even in the winter months.

Joel Cook, who here describes some of the techniques of the seasoned marcher, was a correspondent of the Philadelphia Press *who was with Mc-Clellan during the Peninsular campaign.*

IN the army of the Potomac there were two species of marching employed,—in "heavy marching-order," and in "light marching-order." The former meant that the troops were to carry all they possessed with them; the other was to march with only the musket, ammunition, haversack, and canteen, thus being in trim for working or fighting. Every order to march specified one or the other manner. For heavy marches, two or three hours' notice were usually given, so that time might be had for preparation; light marches, unless to picket, were generally to be commenced on the instant. Another style of order, always implying light marching-order, was sometimes made. This was "to be held in readiness to march at five minutes' notice." Such an order as this was given when an engagement was in progress or anticipated, and the soldiers stood in line behind their musket-stacks until the order was rescinded or they were marched off in accordance with it.

In a heavy march to a new camp, the generals of division and brigade would first arrange the order of the brigades and artillery on the line of march, and next the order of the regiments of each brigade. This would all be specified in the official order commanding the march, and every part of the whole would be able to, and usually did, fall into its proper place in the line, without confusion. The division general and staff preceded the division, and each brigadier and staff rode at the head of his brigade. Artillery rolled along in regular order—cannon, caisson, forge and ammunition wagon—to the end of their line. A regiment marched in the following manner: first the adjutant; then the pioneers; then the band and drum-corps; then the colonel and lieutenant-colonel; then the regiment, each man with his knapsack, haversack, canteen, and arms; and, bringing up the rear, the major, chaplain, and two surgeons, and, on foot, the hospital-knapsack-carrier. The colonel and adjutant sometimes exchanged places, however.

When these marches commenced, the men would be in regular military order, four abreast; but the first half-mile usually broke up all regularity. The men before they had walked that distance would become dispersed all over the road, some walking along the banks and others in the ditches: a squad straggling along the centre would be all the orderly part of the regiment. Some ran down into gullies to search for water, and others started off to see curiosities. Many on long marches became exhausted by fatigue, and lay down under the trees to rest. In warm weather these marches—if prolonged to six or eight miles—were most trying. The suffering for water was usually the greatest trouble,—men carrying such heavy burdens as the soldiers requiring a great deal, and good water in any quantity being rarely discovered. Several halts of an hour or half-hour each were made in these marches, to allow the men to unsling knapsacks and rest or search for water, and to give the stragglers time to come up. The wagon-trains of each regiment followed at the rear of the division in the same order as the regiments marched. Each regimental quartermaster and quartermaster-sergeant attended the teams of his regiment.

A march to battle would be made in light marching-order, the men four abreast, and generally on the double quick. The men were held under strict discipline during such marches. The march from the field, however, was far different. If a victory had been gained, the men would cheer and talk, and the officers imposed no restraint. If a defeat had been suffered, angry arguments about its cause would foreshadow the disaster long before they reached the camp. A march to picket was in light marching order, and at common or quick time, and, when the picket tour was approached, it was conducted with great care and quietness. Homeward it was the same.

A march to chop wood or build roads and bridges would also be in light marching-order, at common or quick time, and—if the place to which the troops were going was not a dangerous one—without arms. Upon reaching the scene of labor, the command was usually given to an officer of engineers, who, through their company officers, directed the movements of the men. The march back to camp was as the one from it.

The general conduct of the troops upon these marches was such as could scarcely be found fault with. The burdens carried in heavy marches, and the discipline exercised in light ones, usually kept them to the road,—though, of course, in the former some would stray and visit the deserted houses in the fields. The inmates of every Negro-hut were besought for "hoecakes;" and when the amazed woman would naturally say, "Why, bress de Lord! how can I gub one cake to all o' you?—dar, ye see dat I hab but one!"—some oily customer's reply would come, "Give it to me, aunty; I asked you first." Plaguing the Negroes for "hoecakes" was usually the greatest extent of lawlessness when the troops were marching. No rapine or wanton destruction disgraced the marches of the army of the Potomac.

—Cook, *The Siege of Richmond*

10. HARDTACK AND COFFEE

Here is the invaluable John Billings again, giving us what appears to be a wholly faithful account of eating—and not eating—in the Army of the Potomac.

I WILL now give a complete list of the rations served out to the rank and file, as I remember them. They were salt pork, fresh beef, salt beef, rarely ham or bacon, hard bread, soft bread, potatoes, an occasional onion, flour, beans, split pease, rice, dried apples, dried peaches, desiccated vegetables, coffee, tea, sugar, molasses, vinegar, candles, soap, pepper, and salt.

It is scarcely necessary to state that these were not all served out at one time. There was but one kind of meat served at once, and this ... was usually pork. When it was hard bread, it wasn't *soft* bread or flour, and when it was pease or beans it wasn't rice.

Here is just what a single ration comprised, that is, what a soldier was entitled to have in one day. He should have had twelve ounces of pork or bacon, *or* one pound four ounces of salt or fresh beef; one pound six ounces of soft bread or flour, *or* one pound of hard bread, *or* one pound four ounces of corn meal. With every hundred such rations there should have been distributed one peck of beans or pease; ten pounds of rice or hominy; ten pounds of green coffee, *or* eight pounds of roasted and ground, *or* one pound eight ounces of tea; fifteen pounds of sugar; one pound four ounces of candles; four pounds of soap; two quarts of salt; four quarts of vinegar; four ounces of pepper; a half bushel of potatoes when practicable, and one quart of molasses. Desiccated potatoes or desiccated compressed vegetables might be substituted for the beans, pease, rice, hominy, or fresh potatoes. Vegetables, the dried fruits, pickles, and pickled cabbage were occasionally issued to prevent scurvy, but in small quantities.

But the ration thus indicated was a camp ration. Here is the *marching* ration: one pound of hard bread; three-fourths of a pound of salt pork, or one and one-fourth pounds of fresh meat; sugar, coffee, and salt. The beans, rice, soap, candles, etc., were not issued to the soldier when on the march, as he could not carry them; but, singularly enough, as it seems to me, unless the troops went into camp before the end of the month, where a regular depot of supplies might be established from which the other parts of the rations could be issued, they were *forfeited*, and *reverted to the government*— an injustice to the rank and file, who, through no fault of their own, were thus cut off from a part of their allowance at the time when they were giving most liberally of their strength and perhaps of their very heart's blood. ...

I will speak of the rations more in detail, beginning with the hard bread, or, to use the name by which it was known in the Army of the Potomac, *Hardtack*. What was hardtack? It was a plain flour-and-water biscuit. Two which I have in my possession as mementos measure three and one-eighth by two and seven-eighths inches, and are nearly half an inch thick. Although these biscuits were furnished to organizations by weight, they were dealt out to the men by number, nine constituting a ration in some regiments, and ten in others; but there were usually enough for those who wanted more, as some men would not draw them. While hardtack was nutritious, yet a hungry man could eat his ten in a short time and still be hungry. ...

For some weeks before the battle of Wilson's Creek, Mo., where the lamented Lyon fell, the First Iowa Regiment had been supplied with a very poor quality of hard bread (they were not then [1861] called hard*tack*). During this period of hardship to the regiment, so the story goes, one of its members was inspired to produce the following touching lamentation:—

> Let us close our game of poker,
> Take our tin cups in our hand,
> While we gather round the cook's tent door,
> Where dry mummies of hard crackers
> Are given to each man;
> O hard crackers, come again no more!

Chorus:

> 'Tis the song and sigh of the hungry,
> "Hard crackers, hard crackers, come again no more!
> Many days have you lingered upon our stomachs sore,
> O hard crackers, come again no more!"

> There's a hungry, thirsty soldier
> Who wears his life away,
> With torn clothes, whose better days are o'er;
> He is sighing now for whiskey,
> And, with throat as dry as hay,
> Sings, "Hard crackers, come again no more!"
>   Chorus.

> 'Tis the song that is uttered
> In camp by night and day,
> 'Tis the wail that is mingled with each snore,
> 'Tis the sighing of the soul
> For spring chickens far away,
> "O hard crackers, come again no more!"
>   Chorus.

When General Lyon heard the men singing these stanzas in their tents, he is said to have been moved by them to the extent of ordering the cook to serve up corn-meal mush, for a change, when the song received the following alteration:—

> But to groans and to murmurs
> There has come a sudden hush,
> Our frail forms are fainting at the door;
> We are starving now on horse-feed
> That the cooks call mush,
> O hard crackers, come again once more!

Chorus:

> It is the dying wail of the starving,
> Hard crackers, hard crackers, come again once more;
> You were old and very wormy, but we pass your failing o'er.
> O hard crackers, come again once more!

The name hardtack seems not to have been in general use among the men in the Western armies.

But I now pass to consider the other bread ration—the *loaf* or *soft bread*. Early in the war the ration of flour was served out to the men uncooked; but as the eighteen ounces allowed by the government more than met the needs of the troops, who at that time obtained much of their living from outside sources . . . it was allowed, as they innocently supposed, to be sold for the benefit of the Company Fund, already referred to. Some organizations drew, on the requisition, ovens, semi-cylindrical in form, which were properly set in stone, and in these regimental cooks or bakers baked bread for the regiment. But all of this was in the tentative period of the war. As rapidly as the needs of the troops pressed home to the government, they were met with such despatch and efficiency as circumstances would permit. For a time, in 1861, the vaults under the broad terrace on the western front of the Capitol were converted into bakeries, where sixteen thousand loaves of bread were baked daily. The chimneys from the ovens pierced the terrace where now the freestone pavement joins the grassy slope, and for months smoke poured out of these in dense black volumes. The greater part of the loaves supplied to the Army of the Potomac up to the summer of 1864 were baked in Washington, Alexandria, and at Fort Monroe, Virginia. The ovens of the latter place had a capacity of thirty thousand loaves a day. But even with all these sources worked to their uttermost, brigade commissaries were obliged to set up ovens near their respective depots, to eke out enough bread to fill orders. These were erected on the sheltered side of a hill or woods, then enclosed in a stockade, and the whole covered with old canvas. . . .

I began my description of the rations with the bread as being the most important one to the soldier. Some old veterans may be disposed to question the judgment which gives it this rank, and claim that *coffee*, of which I shall speak next, should take first place in importance. . . .

It would have interested a civilian to observe the manner in which this ration was served out when the army was in active service. It was usually brought to camp in an oat-sack, a regimental quartermaster receiving and apportioning his among the ten companies, and the quartermaster-sergeant of a battery apportioning his to the four or six detachments. Then the orderly-sergeant of a company or the sergeant of a detachment must devote himself to dividing it. One method of accomplishing this purpose was to spread a rubber blanket on the ground—more than one if the company was large,—and upon it were put as many piles of the coffee as there were men to receive rations; and the care taken to make the piles of the same size to the eye, and to keep the men from growling, would remind one of a country physician making his powders, taking a little from one pile and adding to another. The sugar which always accompanied the coffee was spooned out at the same time on another blanket. When both were ready, they were given out, each man taking a pile, or, in some companies, to prevent any charge of unfairness or injustice, the sergeant would turn his back on the rations, and take out his roll of the company. Then, by request, some one else would point to a pile and ask, "Who shall have this?" and the sergeant, without turning, would call a name from his list of the company or detachment, and the person thus called would appropriate the pile specified. This process would be continued until the last pile was disposed of. There were other plans for distributing the rations; but I have described this one because of its being quite common.

The manner in which each man disposed of his coffee and sugar ration after receiving it is worth noting. Every soldier of a month's experience in campaigning was provided with some sort of bag into which he spooned his coffee; but the *kind* of bag he used indicated pretty accurately, in a general way, the length of time he had been in the service. For example, a raw recruit just arrived would take it up in a paper, and stow it away in that well known receptacle for all eatables, the soldier's haversack, only to find it a part of a general mixture of hardtack, salt pork, pepper, salt, knife, fork, spoon, sugar, and coffee by the time the next halt was made. A recruit of longer standing, who had been through this experience and had begun to feel his wisdom-teeth coming, would take his up in a bag made of a scrap of rubber blanket or a *poncho;* but after a few days carrying the rubber would peel off or the paint of the *poncho* would rub off from contact with the greasy pork or boiled meat ration which was its travelling companion, and make a black, dirty mess, besides leaving the coffee-bag unfit for further use. Now and then some young soldier, a little starchier than his fellows, would bring out an oil-skin bag lined with cloth, which his mother had made and sent him; but even oil-silk couldn't stand everything, certainly not the peculiar inside furnishings of the average soldier's haversack, so it too was not long in yielding. But your plain, straightforward old veteran, who had shed all his poetry and romance, if he had ever possessed any, who had roughed it up and down "Old Virginny," man and boy, for many months, and who had tried all plans under all circumstances, took out an oblong plain cloth bag, which looked as immaculate as the every-day shirt of a coal-heaver, and into it scooped without ceremony both his sugar and coffee, and stirred them thoroughly together. . . .

The coffee ration was most heartily appreciated by the soldier. When tired and foot-sore, he would drop out of the marching column, build his little camp-fire, cook his mess of coffee, take a nap behind the nearest shelter, and when he woke, hurry on to overtake his company. Such men were sometimes called stragglers; but it could, obviously, have no offensive meaning when applied to them. Tea was served so rarely that it does not merit any particular description. In the latter part of the war, it was rarely seen outside of hospitals.

One of the most interesting scenes presented in army life took place at night when the army was on the point of bivouacking. As soon as this fact became known along the column, each man would seize a rail from the nearest fence, and with this additional arm on the shoulder would enter the proposed camping-ground. In no more time than it takes to tell the story, the little camp-fires, rapidly increasing to hundreds in number, would shoot up along the hills and plains, and as if by magic acres of territory would be luminous with them. Soon they would be surrounded by the soldiers, who made it an almost invariable rule to cook their coffee first, after which a large number, tired out with the toils of the day, would make their supper of hardtack and coffee, and roll up in their blankets for the night. If a march was ordered at midnight, unless a surprise was intended, it must be preceded by a pot of coffee; if a halt was ordered in mid-forenoon or afternoon, the same dish was inevitable, with hardtack accompaniment usually. It was coffee *at* meals and *between* meals; and men going on guard or coming off guard drank it at all hours of the night, and to-day the old soldiers who can stand it are the hardest coffee-drinkers in the community, through the schooling which they received in the service.

—BILLINGS, *Hardtack and Coffee*

11. "STARVATION, RAGS, DIRT, AND VERMIN"

At school in Pennsylvania when the war broke out, Randolph Shotwell left at once for his native Virginia, determined to join the first Confederate outfit that he found. He served through the whole of the war, until 1864, when he was captured; we shall read later his bitter description of conditions in Federal prisons. After the war he went into journalism in North Carolina, and was active, for a time, in the Ku Klux Klan and in politics. The conditions which he describes so vividly were not characteristic of the whole of the Confederate Army, but were doubtless to be found quite commonly toward the end of the war when the whole economic machinery of the South seemed to be breaking down.

OUR Quarter Master's department . . . really did a great deal more to break down the army than to keep it up. I mean that their shortcomings, their negligence, improvidence, and lack of energy counterbalanced their services. It is a well-known fact, and a most disgraceful one, that when General Lee crossed the Potomac fully *ten thousand* of his men were *barefooted, blanketless,* and *hatless!* The roads were lined with stragglers limping on swollen and blistered feet, shivering all night, (for despite the heat of the day the nights were chilly), for want of blankets; and utterly devoid of underclothes—if indeed they possessed so much as one shirt!

And the lack of proper equipment gradually made itself felt on the *morale* of the men. In the earlier stages of the war when our men were well dressed and cleanly—every company having its wagon for extra baggage—enabling the private soldier to have a change of clothing and necessary toilet articles—the men retained much of their individuality as *citizen*-soldiers, volunteering to undergo for a time, the privations and perils of army life, but never forgetting that they were *citizens* and *gentlemen*, with a good name and reputation for gentlemanliness to maintain. Hence, when in battle array, these gallant fellows, *each had a pride in bearing himself bravely;* and when the hour of conflict arrived they rushed upon the foe with an impetuosity and fearlessness that amazed the old army officers; and caused foreign military men to declare them the best fighters in the world. After a while the spirit of the men became broken. Constant marching and fighting were sufficient of themselves to gradually wear out the army; but it was more undermined by the continual neglect and ill-provision to which the men were subjected.

Months on months they were without a change of underclothing, or a chance to wash that they had worn so long, hence it became actually coated with grease and dust, moistened with daily perspiration under the broiling sun.

Pestiferous vermin swarmed in every camp, and on the march—an indescribable annoyance to every well-raised man yet seemingly uneradicable. Nothing would destroy the little pests but *hours of steady boiling,* and of course, we had neither kettles, nor the time to boil them, if we had been provided with ample means.

As to purchasing clothes, the private soldiers did not have an opportunity of so doing once in six months, as their miserable pittance of $12 per month was generally withheld that length of time, or longer—(I only drew pay *three* times in *four years,* and after the first year, I could not have bought a *couple of shirts* with a *whole month's pay.*) Naturally fastidious in tastes, and habituated to the strictest personal cleanliness and neatness, I chafed from morning till night at the insuperable obstacles to decency by which I was surrounded, and as a consequence there was not one time in the whole four years of the war that I could not have blushed with mortification at meeting with any of my old friends.

It is impossible for such a state of things to continue for years without breaking down one's self-respect, wounding his *amour propre,* stirring his deepest discontent, and very materially impairing his efficiency as a soldier.

Starvation, rags, dirt, and vermin may be borne *for a time* by the neatest of gentlemen; but when he has become habituated to them, he is no longer a gentleman. The personal pride which made many a man act the *hero* during the first year of the war was gradually worn out, and undermined by the open, palpable neglect, stupidity, and indifference of the authorities until during the last year of the war, the hero became a "shirker," and finally a "deserter."

—Shotwell, "Three Years in Battle"

12. VOTING IN THE FIELD

The problem of the soldier vote agitated the Civil War as it did World War II. The Republican party was particularly eager to provide opportunity for soldiers to go home to vote or machinery for voting in the field. Both methods were widely used in the state elections of 1863 and the Presidential election of 1864. The Wisconsin soldier vote—which James Leonard describes—was decisive in the election of a chief justice. That the soldier vote was decisive in the 1864 election, too, is generally conceded—and this notwithstanding such support for McClellan as is revealed by George Breck, of Rochester, New York. Thousands of soldiers were furloughed home at voting time. Lincoln wrote to Sherman, for example, that it might be well to let Indiana's soldiers "or any part of them go home and vote at the state elections," and so enthusiastically did Sherman act on the suggestion that the 19th Vermont Volunteers found themselves voting in the Indiana elections—which the Republicans carried. Some states—New York, for example, and Ohio— arranged for voting in the field, and the overwhelming majority of these votes went to Lincoln. The most careful student of the subject concludes that "without the soldiers' vote in six crucial states, Lincoln would have lost the election."

A. Electioneering in the Camps

Camp near White Oak Church, May 14, 1863

Let me state a simple instance as regards myself and the late election that took place in Co. A for Chief Justice of Wisconsin The morning of election day the Captain and Lieutenants asked me and the Orderly our opinion in regard to holding an election, The Captain was rather against it, fearing that very few of the boys would vote as was the case last fall, I almost sided with him but I and the Orderly both advised to open a poll, and take what votes could be got, He finally consented to commence on the condition that I would act as runner and speak to, or rather electioneer the boys in the company, I declined at first, advising the selection of some one who as I thought had more influence than myself Finally however I consented just to satisfy the Captain and Lieutenant but satisfied in my own mind that I could accomplish but little I went to work and first brought up all those whom I knew to be sure and then I set at those who were a little wavering or careless and by some talking got them up, then I went at those who are true Union men but still cling to party, all that was needed with them, was to satisfy them that Mr. Cothren was a Copperhead and we had the papers to do that The result was that 53 votes were polled every man in the company voting who was old enough, save one before the polls were opened I would not have believed that 30 votes could be obtained unless he set some one to work who had more influence than me, I wish though that I could have more influence in the temperance cause here Whiskey rations are occasionally dealt out now and I am the only one in our Co who does not use his ration, it is rather embarrassing to be thus the odd member of a family with the rest joking you on the matter, but I have withstood these temptations thus far and I hope by the sustaining grace of God to hold out firm to the end.

—James A. Leonard, "Letters of a Fifth Wis. Volunteer"

B. President Lincoln Needs the Soldier Vote

To General W. T. Sherman.

Executive Mansion, Washington, September 19, 1864

Major-General Sherman:

The State election of Indiana occurs on the 11th of October, and the loss of it, to the friends of the Government would go far toward losing the whole Union cause. The bad effect upon the November election, and especially the giving the State government to those who will oppose the war in every possible way, are too much to risk if it can be avoided. The draft proceeds, notwithstanding its strong tendency to lose us the State. Indiana is the only important State voting in October whose soldiers cannot vote in the field. Anything you can safely do to let her soldiers, or any part of them, go home and vote at the State election will be greatly in point. They need not remain for the Presidential election, but may return to you at once. This is in no sense an order, but is merely intended to impress you with the importance to the Army itself of your doing all you safely can, yourself being the judge of what you can safely do.

Yours truly,

A. LINCOLN.

—*The Complete Works of Abraham Lincoln*

C. VOTING FOR MCCLELLAN

"Fort Keen," Va., Oct. 23, 1864

My dear Ellen

It seems a long time since I have written home, and so it is indeed, nearly three weeks, if I mistake not. You have, perhaps, thought I must be sick, but no, I have enjoyed the best of health. I have been very, very busy, however, with company matters, and with politics also. Last week was devoted, or a good share of it, evenings principally, to the polling of votes from the company and from outside commands. Battery L. cast 108 votes, 61 for McClellan and 47 for Lincoln. Quite a strong vote was cast for Lincoln in consequence of a number of new recruits, between thirty and forty, having joined the Battery very recently, one year men, from the strong Republican district of St. Lawrence Co., men who got $1000 to $1300 bounty each. Nearly all the old men voted for McClellan. I shall send my vote home by Lieut. Anderson to give to Father to poll. Quite a form has to be gone through by New York soldiers who vote, giving power of attorney to some legal voter where they reside to cast their votes for them, taking an oath that they are legal voters etc. all of which requires a good deal of writing. The affidavits are administered by some commanding officer, and I being such, I have administered something in the neighborhood of 500 oaths. About that number of votes have been polled by Lieut. Anderson and I for "Little Mac," which would never have been cast, had we not interested ourselves in the matter. Such mean, contemptible favoritism or partisanship as has been and is shown for Lincoln, by many officers in the army, representatives of the Sanitary and Christian Commissions, etc., you little imagine. Hundreds of soldiers have been literally proscribed from voting for McClellan by their officers, and they have been obliged to get McClellan ballots from other sources and to get other officers to administer the necessary oath to them. I think I shall have to write a letter to the *Union* about the matter, which I think would tell for *our* side, and it might tell in such a manner as to eject me from the army. . . .

—"George Breck's Civil War Letters"

13. RED TAPE, NORTH AND SOUTH

It is the complaint of soldiers and civilians alike that every war is cursed by red tape. The Civil War was no exception; indeed, in some respects, it was the worst administered of all American wars.

Samuel Fiske—or Dunn Browne as he was known—was a Massachusetts clergyman who enlisted in the 14th Connecticut Volunteers, became a captain, fought at Chancellorsville and Gettysburg, spent two weeks in Libby prison, was exchanged, and killed in the Wilderness. During the war he contributed a series of letters to the Springfield Republican; *these were published posthumously as* Dunn Browne's Experiences in the Army. *It is interesting to note that Randolph Shotwell's complaints about red-tapism in the Confederacy parallel those of Samuel Fiske.*

A. Dunn Browne Has Trouble with the War Department

JUDGE of this other case I will relate: about a fair specimen of my experience. An errand at the adjutant-general's office. Went up at ten o'clock. Found a fat doorkeeper. Asked him if I could see any of the assistant adjutant-generals or their clerks. No: couldn't see anybody on business till eleven o'clock. Departed. Came back at eleven. Found a long string of people passing in slowly to one of the rooms. Took my turn. Got a word at last with the clerk. Found it wasn't his specialty to answer questions of the sort I asked him. Was referred by him to another clerk who perhaps could. Went to another room. Stopped by a doorkeeper. At last, permitted to enter, after some other people had come out. Stated my case to the clerk at the desk: "Pay of certain officers of my regiment stopped by order from your office near four months since. No reason assigned. No notice given. Come to you for reason."

"Why don't you send up your request through the proper military channels, sir?"

"Request was so sent up eight weeks ago, enclosing a precise copy of the order issued from your own office to the paymaster. Instead of looking in your own office to find the reason of your own order, you sent our request over to the paymaster-general, asking him why the order was issued. He sent it back indorsed with the statement, that no such order of stoppage was recorded in the pay-department. This you sent back to us 'through the regular channel' as eminently satisfactory. So it would be, only the paymaster, having your positive order not to pay us, and no order countermanding it, refuses to come down with the greenbacks. Another paper came up to you from us several weeks ago, and has not been heard from. This is the progress of eight weeks through the regular channel."

"Why don't you ask the paymaster to find out about the matter?"

"We have done so. He says he has been repeatedly to your office, which, of course, is the only place where information can be obtained, and is unable to get any satisfactory reply."

"Why don't you go to the ordnance and quartermasters departments, and see if your accounts are all right there?"

"We have done so, and find it a reasonable certainty that no stoppages against us have been ordered there. Moreover, they would not stop through your department. The order came from you. You had a precise copy of it sent you with our application. Where could we apply for information as to the reason of your acts save to you?"

"Very well: we'll try to look it up."

"But, sir, if you would let a clerk look at your orders of that date, and answer us to-day, we can perhaps get our pay; otherwise we shall not have access to the paymaster again for two or three months."

The clerk, utterly disgusted at such pertinacity, dismisses us with an appointment to call again at two o'clock. He will see what he can do for us. Call again at two o'clock. Doorkeeper refuses to let us in. No person seen on business after two o'clock. Finally work our way through with the plea of the special appointment. Find, of course, that nothing has been done. "What shall be our next course?"

"Oh! send up another paper through the regular channel."

—[SAMUEL FISKE], *Mr. Dunn Browne's Experiences in the Army*

B. A CONFEDERATE LIEUTENANT COMPLAINS THAT RED-TAPEISM WILL LOSE THE WAR

Red Tapeism at Richmond threatens to work our everlasting ruin! Some of our junior officers say that anyone under the rank of Brigadier-General can rarely gain so much as access to the Departments, and even the Brigadiers got but little attention if they happen to be out of favor with the "parlour Cabinet" at the Executive Mansion. The President now has *six* aides, ranking as colonels, and decked in all the bravery of gold lace, and feathers, to someone of whom the "commoner," or "common soldier" must make the "*grande salaam*," and have his plea for audience first "*vised*" by the popinjay before he may approach the "magic circle" within which is his Supreme Excellency—"clothed with the divinity which doth hedge" a "*servant of the people.*"

All members of this noble Court are beginning to "feel their dignity" in the same manner. Secretary of the Treasury Memminger, (said to be a born *Hessian*) whose chief duties consist in writing his autograph upon unlimited quantities of half-worthless "bank-notes" "so-called," has adopted a set of rules governing all applicants for permission to interview his Royalty. A favorite clerk named Jacques —— is posted in the ante-chamber to scrutinize all callers, and *vise* the talismanic bit of cardboard which shall be your "Open Sesame," to audience with his secretaryship. *Some* gentlemen are not willing to be catechized by Jacques as to their business, wishes, etc., consequently retire enraged at the Royal customs of our not too firmly established *Republic*.

Oh! that Mr. Davis could see and realize, the fallacy of undermining our cause by wearying the people with red tape regulations, and nice points of etiquette, instead of showing common fraternity and sympathy with one and all, the poorest and most tiresome citizen as well as the epauletted Major General.

General Winder rules Richmond like a military Camp; nay, not like a well-disciplined camp, for his rule gives annoyance merely to honest men and faithful soldiers, while permitting the city to be over-run by rogues, spies, speculators, foreigners, blockade runners, and fellows of that ilk. His police force is mainly composed of ex-"Plugs" and "Roughs" from Baltimore and Washington, who care little for the cause, and less for honesty, so that it is a matter of common notoriety that any one who has a hundred or two hundred in greenbacks, or a less sum in specie, can not only travel over the whole South—spying out the weakness of the land—but pass through the "underground road" to the North whenever so minded.

Whereas veteran soldiers—armed with furlough, or special order from their general—must lose a day or two—at their own expense—kicking their heels at the doors of the Pass Port Bureau, awaiting the convenience of some dandified clerk within. Is it any wonder that the veteran grows *soured*, and in telling his family, or his comrades in camp how he had been treated sows the seeds for discontent, and ultimate desertion?

How sad to see the enthusiasm and energies of a great people gradually relaxing under the ill-shaped, negligent, insensate policy of the appointed agents for the administration of the government!

I verily believe if we shall ultimately fail in our efforts to secure independence (which God forbid!) the causes of such failure will be found in the fact that all our great military and civil leaders have become infatuated with the idea that success is assured, and that they can conduct the war as if we were an old established nation, or as France and England would conduct it. They do not seem at all aware that if once the spirit and faith of *the people* is broken all will be lost.

Instances of mismanagement by the Red Tape-ists are coming to light by every mail. The great "Flour Contract" of Secretary Randolph, giving Crenshaw, Haxall, and Company, an exclusive monopoly of the flour furnishing business is causing much comment. Aside from the reports of undue influences in the execution of the original contract, it is evident that the monopoly thus created is working injury to the people. Flour is now $40, a barrel in Richmond, and cornmeal $3.50 a bushel, and no doubt these prices will be considered *cheap* before spring.

"Crenshaw Mills," by the terms of the contract are allowed the preference in the use of the railways in the shipment of grain, so that while the depots are full of goods and flour only $8.00 per barrel in the upper valley, the people of Richmond must pay four times that amount or starve!

The Government seems to have less discretion and good judgment than would be found in "an old field school" debating society. Thus, for instance, when we lay at Manassas and Centreville last year, and could easily have drawn supplies from the rich regions of Loudon, Farquier, Warren, and from the valley, via the Manassas and Strasburg Railroad—all our rations and stock-provender was hauled all the way from Richmond—to which it must first have been hauled—merely because Red-Tapeism had its "system" and wanted a "regular issue," and to have things done "through proper channels," and as the result the fine resources of the region referred to, were left untouched to be gathered by the marauders of Pope, Fremont, Banks and Sigel, while that portion of Virginia which should have been reserved to feed the besieged city nine months later, was drained of its provisions to ship to an army surrounded by adjacent supplies! . . .

I haven't a doubt of Mr. Davis' patriotism, or his intention to do *right*, but he is dreadfully mistaken in his selection of Cabinet officers, and in his whole civil policy of administration. . . . I am more and more convinced that our chief chance of success lies in a short, sharp, aggressive warfare.

—SHOTWELL, "Three Years in Battle"

14. THE CONFEDERATES GET RELIGION

The generation that fought the war, North and South alike, was a deeply religious one. Chaplains were customarily attached to regiments of both armies, and numerous preachers visited the troops with or without official status. One of the most interesting features of the history of the Confederacy was the series of revivals that swept the armies, both East and West, throughout the war. There were a few revivals in the winter of 1861-62, but the "great revival" came in the Army of Northern Virginia in the winter and spring of 1863 and spread to the armies of the West. The Reverend John W. Jones, whose Christ in the Camp *is perhaps the best history of this great revival, estimates that no less than 150,000 soldiers "got religion" that year. What is equally interesting is that the religious revival affected the leaders of the Confederacy as well as the rank and file. It was at this time that Jefferson Davis, Generals Bragg, Ewell, Hood, Hardee, and Joseph E. Johnston all entered the church. It is entirely possible that General Lee's deep piety played a role here.*

The two brief excerpts given here describe the great revival of 1863 in the Army of Northern Virginia. Benjamin W. Jones was a private in the 3rd Virginia Infantry Regiment; John Dooley a Virginia boy who left Georgetown College in 1862 to enlist in the famous 1st Virginia Infantry—a regiment whose history dated from 1661. We shall meet him again.

A. RELIGION IN THE CONFEDERATE ARMY

Camp Roper, Va., Feby. 20, 1863

My dear Friend:

I hear that a great religious spirit and revival is spreading throughout Lee's army, and some of the other armies of the South, and there are some evidences of it here, and in other camps about Richmond. Old professors that had become lukewarm in their zeal, are arousing to a sense of their duty, and many of the openly sinful are growing more temperate and reverent in their conversation and regard for religious things. There is less of cursing and profligacy, and much less of card playing in our Company now than formerly. The voice of prayer is often heard in camp among the men, and many commands now have regular, or at least, occasional, preaching. Many ministers have gone out as evangelists to the armies, and some have gone into the ranks as private soldiers, or have become regular chaplains in some command. Their example and teaching are exerting a wide-spread and salutary influence. Rev. J. W. Ward, of Isle of Wight, has preached to our Company once recently, and other ministers hold meetings near us occasionally.

Almost nightly now, before the tattoo is sounded, we hear the voice of song in our camp, religious and revival songs and hymns. There are several men here who sing well, and these assemble together and pass an hour or two together at night very pleasantly. Sergeant N. B. Pond's tent is headquarters for these exercises, and doubtless, to some extent, this method of praise and prayer is doing good here and toning down some of the rougher vices of the men. May it lead finally to a great outpouring of the Holy Spirit upon all the armies, and all the people of all the South. A soldier may fight and be a religious and God-fearing man, too.

But let me tell you of a little incident that has really taken place in our camp lately—one of the little comedies, not altogether innocent, but wholly harmless, that are occasionally happening and which serve as safety-valves to let off the superfluous steam engendered by the life of confinement and idleness in camp.

One of the songs that were being sung quite frequently, almost nightly in fact, by our religious choir was that somewhat eccentric refrain:

> "Scotland's burning! Scotland's burning!
> Cast on water! Cast on water!"

and so some of the prankish set among our boys conceived the idea of turning a little joke on the men in Sergeant Pond's tent. As a few of the tents had been fixed up with rude dirt chimneys for fireplaces, and Sergeant Pond's was one of these, it gave the boys a fine chance to play their game. And so, one night, one of the smallest among the men, with a bucket of water in hand, was lifted up by a big, strong fellow to the top of the little stick chimney. And just as the choir rang out the alarm,

> "Scotland's burning!
> Cast on water!"

the little fellow on the chimney cast his bucket of water down upon the fire inside, which deluged the whole fireplace, put out the fire, and scattered the embers in every direction.

Of course, too, it put a sudden stop to the song, and sent the men quickly out of the tent after the offenders. But not in time to discover who they were. Before they were fairly out of the tent, the boys had gained their own bunks, and were enjoying the fun at a distance.

The choir soon saw the joke, and, as they could do no more, submitted quietly. But it is presumed that nothing more will be heard of "Scotland's burning" for some time.

With a prayer for your continued safety and welfare at home, I remain,

Your friend, B.

—Jones, *Under the Stars and Bars*

B. John Dooley Describes Prayer Meetings

Perhaps this is the night for prayer meeting, for the parsons, taking advantage of this period of calm, are indefatigable in their efforts to draw the soldiers together to sing psalms and assist at prayer. Hundreds and thousands respond to their call and the woods resound for miles around with the unscientific but earnest music of the rough veterans of Lee's army. In doleful contrast to the more enlivening notes of the initiated, the chorus of the 'Mourners' may often be recognized; for conversions among the non-religious members of the army of Lee are of daily occurrence, and when they establish themselves upon the 'Mourners'' Bench, it is evident to all how deep and loud is their repentance. There is something very solemn in these immense choruses of earnest voices, and there are, I am sure, hundreds of these honest soldiers truly sincere in believing that they are offering their most acceptable service to God.

Some of the parsons or chaplains are very zealous and persevering in assembling the soldiers to prayer; especially the chaplain of the eleventh Va. and the seventh. The latter is held in high esteem by all, whether members of religion or not; for, they say, in times of action, he is as bold as the bravest and is to be seen in the first and fiercest battles, consoling and assisting the wounded. 'Florence McCarthy' of Richmond, chaplain of the 7th inf., is also distinguished for his preaching and zeal among the soldiers. They say he told his congregation the other day that when they heard the doors and windows of the church slamming while the minister of God was preaching, they might be sure that the devil was at work trying to hinder the faithful from listening to the divine word. Some might very naturally presume from this that his Satanic Majesty was most at large during the blustering month of March than at any other time in the year.

—Durkin, ed., *John Dooley, Confederate Soldier*

IX

Incidents of Army Life: Eastern Front

THE war was not all fighting, and the fighting was not all in the pitched battles that have been commemorated in history. Judge Oliver Wendell Holmes liked to say that war was an organized bore, but it was Holmes, too, who observed that "accidents may call up the events of the war. You see a battery of guns go by at a trot and for a moment you are back at the White Oak Swamps, or Antietam, or on the Jerusalem Road. You hear a few shots fired in the distance, and for an instant your heart stops as you say to yourself, The Skirmishers are at it, and listen for the long roll of fire from the main line." For most of the soldiers, boys from farms and villages who had lived quietly and simply, the war was exciting enough, and most of the veterans came to look back on the war with pride and nostalgia—witness the enthusiastic reunions of the GAR and the Confederate Veterans. It was filled with minor adventures—scouting, foraging, the picket line, the forced march; it was memorable for good fellowship and lasting friendship; it had humor as well as pathos and tragedy; it was a microcosm of life.

What we have here is a series of incidents, episodes and experiences that illustrate the vicissitudes of fighting. Some of the circumstances here set forth were peculiar, but that, too, was typical: it was not only (as Winston Churchill said of World War I) a "very dangerous war," it was, in many respects, a very odd war—a war where enemies fraternized between battles, where newspapers kept correspondents in enemy capitals, where the line between regulars and guerillas was tenuous; where foreigners with strange names were always turning up as observers, or sometimes in uniform; where soldiers were expected to take care of themselves and to exercise their ingenuity; where there was opportunity for play and high jinks as well as for fighting.

No collection of excerpts can describe the whole of these varied experiences; all we can hope to do is to submit some that are illustrative and that suggest the dangers and adventures and vicissitudes of the war. There is little continuity in this series of incidents, and we shall content ourselves with notes on the authors and on those episodes which may have some more general significance.

1. HOW IT FEELS TO BE UNDER FIRE

It must not be forgotten that both Federal and Confederate armies were made up largely of volunteers who had never before had experience in battle,

*and that only a small proportion even of the Regular Army had ever been
under fire. Frank Holsinger, who here recalls what it was like to be under
fire, was a captain of the 19th U. S. Colored Infantry who was given brevet
rank of major at the end of his service, and settled later in Kansas.*

THE influence of a courageous man is most helpful in battle. Thus at
Antietam, when surprised by the Sixth Georgia Regiment, lying immediately behind the fence at the celebrated cornfield, allowing our regiment
to approach within thirty feet, and then pouring in a volley that decimated
our ranks fully one-half; the regiment was demoralized. I was worse—I was
stampeded. I did not expect to stop this side of the Pennsylvania line. I met
a tall, thin young soldier, very boyish in manner, but cool as a cucumber, his
hat off, which he was lustily swinging, who yelled: "Rally, boys, rally! Die
like men; don't run like dogs!" Instantly all fear vanished. "Why can I not
stand and take what this boy can?" I commenced loading and firing, and
from this on I was as comfortable as I had been in more pleasant places.

How natural it is for a man to suppose that if a gun is discharged, he or
some one is sure to be hit. He soon finds, however, that the only damage
done, in ninety-nine cases out of a hundred, the only thing killed is the
powder! It is not infrequently that a whole line of battle (this among raw
troops) will fire upon an advancing line, and no perceptible damage ensue.
They wonder how men can stand such treatment, when really they have
done no damage save the terrific noise incident to the discharge. To undertake to say how many discharges are necessary to the death of a soldier in
battle would be presumptuous, but I have frequently heard the remark that
it took a man's weight in lead to kill him.

In presentiments of death I have no confidence. While I have seen men
go into battle predicting truthfully their own death, yet I believe it is the
belief of nine out of ten who go into battle that that is their last. I have never
gone into battle that I did not expect to be killed. I have seen those who had
no thought of death coming to them killed outright. Thus Corporal George
Horton, wounded at South Mountain, wrapped his handkerchief around his
wounded arm and carried the colors of our regiment to Antietam. Being
asked why he did not make the best of it and go to the hospital, that he was
liable to be killed, he answered, "The bullet has not been moulded to kill
me." Alas! he was killed the next day.

My sensations at Antietam were a contradiction. When we were in line
"closed *en masse,*" passing to the front through the wood at "half distance,"
the boom of cannon and the hurtling shell as it crashed through the trees or
exploding found its lodgment in human flesh; the minies sizzing and savagely
spotting the trees; the deathlike silence save the "steady men" of our officers.
The shock to the nerves were indefinable—one stands, as it were, on the brink
of eternity as he goes into action. One man alone steps from the ranks and
cowers behind a large tree, his nerves gone; he could go no farther. General
Meade sees him, and, calling a sergeant, says, "Get that man in ranks." The
sergeant responds, the man refuses; General Meads rushes up with, "I'll

move him!" Whipping out his saber, he deals the man a blow, he falls—who he was, I do not know. The general has no time to tarry or make inquiries. A lesson to those witnessing the scene. The whole transaction was like that of a panorama. I felt at the time the action was cruel and needless on the part of the general. I changed my mind when I became an officer, when with sword and pistol drawn to enforce discipline by keeping my men in place when going into the conflict.

When the nerves are thus unstrung, I have known relief by a silly remark. Thus at Antietam, when in line of battle in front of the wood and exposed to a galling fire from the cornfield, standing waiting expectant with "What next?" the minies zipping by occasionally, one making the awful *thud* as it struck some unfortunate. As we thus stood listlessly, breathing a silent prayer, our hearts having ceased to pulsate or our minds on home and loved ones, expecting soon to be mangled or perhaps killed, some one makes an idiotic remark; thus at this time it is Mangle, in a high nasal twang, with "D——d sharp skirmishing in front." There is a laugh, it is infectious, and we are once more called back to life.

The battle when it goes your way is a different proposition. Thus having reached the east wood, each man sought a tree from behind which he not only sought protection, but dealt death to our antagonists. They halt, also seeking protection behind trees. They soon begin to retire, falling back into the corn-field. We now rush forward. We cheer; we are in ecstasies. While shells and canister are still resonant and minies sizzing spitefully, yet I think this one of the supreme moments of my existence. . . .

The worst condition to endure is when you fall wounded upon the field. Now you are helpless. No longer are you filled with the enthusiasm of battle. You are helpless—the bullets still fly over and about you—you no longer are able to shift your position or seek shelter. Every bullet as it strikes near you is a new terror. Perchance you are enabled to take out your handkerchief, which you raise in supplication to the enemy to not fire in your direction and to your friends of your helplessness. This is a trying moment. How slowly times flies! Oh, the agony to the poor wounded man, who alone can ever know its horrors! Thus at Bermuda Hundreds, November 28th, being in charge of the picket-line, we were attacked, which we repulsed and were rejoiced, yet the firing is maintained. I am struck in the left forearm, though not disabled; soon I am struck in the right shoulder by an explosive bullet, which is imbedded in my shoulder-strap. We still maintain a spiteful fire. About 12 M. I am struck again in my right forearm, which is broken and the main artery cut; soon we improvise a tourniquet by using a canteen-strap, and with a bayonet the same is twisted until blood ceases to flow. To retire is impossible, and for nine weary hours, or until late in the night, I remain on the line. I am alone with my thoughts; I think of home, of the seriousness of my condition; I see myself a cripple for life—perchance I may not recover; and all the time shells are shrieking and minie bullets whistling over and about me. The tongue becomes parched, there is no water to quench it; you cry, "Water! water!" and pray for night, that you can be carried off the field and to the hospital, and there the surgeons' care—maimed, crippled for life, perchance die. These are your reflections. Who can portray the horrors coming to the wounded?

The experiences of a man under fire differ materially between his first and subsequent engagements. Why? Because of discipline. "Familiarity with death begets contempt" is an old and true saying. With the new troops, they have not been called on to train or restrain their nerves. They are not only nervous, but they blanch at the thought of danger. They want education. What to them, on joining the service, was a terrible mental strain, is soon transformed into indifference. It is brought about by discipline.

—HOLSINGER, "How Does One Feel Under Fire?"

2. THE THIRD OHIO IS FLOODED OUT IN WEST VIRGINIA

At the beginning of the war the Federals planned to attack the Confederacy across the Ohio in western Virginia—a mountainous region which had already seceded from Virginia and set up as the independent state of West Virginia. Here both McClellan and Lee saw their first Civil War fighting; though that fighting was inconclusive McClellan emerged with reputation enhanced, Lee—from whom so much had been expected—with reputation somewhat clouded.

Colonel John Beatty, who here recalls some of the hardships of campaigning in this difficult country, was an Ohio banker and politician who had been appointed lieutenant colonel of the 3rd Ohio Volunteer Infantry on its organization in April 1861. He fought through most of the war in the West, was promoted to a brigadier generalship, and later served in Congress. We shall meet him again.

August 20 [1861]. These mountain streams are unreliable. We had come to regard the one on which we had encamped as a quiet, orderly little river that would be good enough to notify us when it proposed to swell out and overflow the adjacent country. In fact we had bragged about it, made all sorts of complimentary mention of it, put our tents on its margin, and allowed it to encircle our sick and wounded; but we have now lost all confidence in it. Yesterday, about noon, it began to rise. It had been raining, and we thought it natural that the waters should increase a little. At four o'clock it had swelled very considerably, but still kept within its bed of rock and gravel, and we admired it all the more for the energy displayed in hurrying along branches, logs, and sometimes whole trees. At six o'clock we found it was rising at the rate of one foot per hour and that the water had now crept to within a few feet of the hospital tent, in which lay two wounded and a dozen or more of sick. Dr. McMeens became alarmed and called for help. Thirty or more boys stripped, swam to the island, and removed the hospital to higher ground—to the highest ground, in fact, that the island afforded. The boys returned, and we felt safe.

At seven o'clock, however, we found the river still rising rapidly. It covered nearly the whole island. Logs, brush, green trees, and all manner of drift went sweeping by at a tremendous speed, and the water rushed over land that had been dry half an hour before, with apparently as strong a current as that in the channel. We knew then that the sick and wounded were in danger. How to rescue them was now the question. A raft was suggested; but a raft could not be controlled in such a current, and if it went to pieces or was hurried away, the wounded must drown. Fortunately a better way was suggested; getting into a wagon, I ordered the driver to go above some distance, so that we could move with the current, and then ford the stream. After many difficulties, occasioned mainly by floating logs and driftwood, and swimming the horses part of the way, we succeeded in getting over.

I saw it was impossible to carry the sick back and that there was but one way to render them secure. I had the horses unhitched and told the driver to swim them back and bring over two or three more wagons. Two more finally reached me, and one team, in attempting to cross, was carried downstream and drowned. I had the three wagons placed on the highest point I could find, then chained together and staked securely to the ground. Over the boxes of two of these we rolled the hospital tent, and on this placed the sick and wounded, just as the water was creeping upon us. On the third wagon we put the hospital stores. It was now quite dark. Not more than four feet square of dry land remained of all our beautiful island; and the river was still rising. We watched the water with much anxiety. At ten o'clock it reached the wagon hubs and covered every foot of the ground; but soon after we were pleased to see that it had gone down a little. Those of us who could not get into the wagons climbed the trees. At one o'clock it commenced to rain again, when we managed to hoist a tent over the sick. At two o'clock the long roll, the signal for battle, was beaten in camp and we could just hear, above the roar of the water, the noise made by the men as they hurriedly turned out and fell into line.

It will not do, however, to conclude that this was altogether a night of terrors. It was, in fact, not so very disagreeable after all. There was a byplay going on much of the time, which served to illuminate the thick darkness and divert our minds from the gloomier aspects of the scene. Smith, the teamster who brought me across, had returned to the mainland with the horses, and then swam back to the island. By midnight he had become very drunk. One of the hospital attendants was very far gone in his cups also. These two gentlemen did not seem to get along amicably; in fact they kept up a fusillade of words all night, and so kept us awake. The teamster insisted that the hospital attendant should address him as Mr. Smith. The Smith family, he argued, was of the highest respectability, and being an honored member of that family, he would permit no man under the rank of a major-general to call him Jake. George McClellan sometimes addressed him by his Christian name; but then George and he were Cincinnatians, old neighbors and intimate personal friends and, of course, took liberties with each other. This could not justify one who carried out pukes and slop buckets from a field hospital in calling him Jake, or even Jacob.

Mr. Smith's allusions to the hospital attendant were not received by that gentleman in the most amiable spirit. He grew profane and insisted he was not only as good a man as Smith but a much better one, and he dared the bloviating mule scrubber to get down off his perch and stand up before him like a man. But Jake's temper remained unruffled, and along toward morning, in a voice more remarkable for strength than melody, he favored us with a song:

> Ho! gif ghlass uf goodt lauger du me;
> Du mine fadter, mine modter, mine vife;
> Der day's vork vas done, undt we'll see
> Vot bleasures der vos un dis life.

> Undt ve sit us aroundt mit der table
> Undt ve speak of der oldt, oldt time,
> Ven ve lif un dot house mit der gable,
> Un der vine-cladt banks uf der Rhine;
>
> . . . . .
>
> So libft up your ghlass, mine modter,
> Und libft up yours, Gretchen, my dear,
> Undt lift up your lauger, mine fadter,
> Und drink du long life and good cheer.

—BEATTY, *The Citizen-Soldier*

3. FITZ JOHN PORTER VIEWS THE CONFEDERATES FROM A BALLOON

The use of balloons for observation dates back to the 1790s, but the Civil War was the first war in which they were generally used for military purposes. At the outbreak of the war Thaddeus Lowe was authorized to create an aeronautic service; he built five balloons which were used during the Peninsular and later campaigns. Lowe was the first person in America to take photographs from a balloon. Fitz John Porter, whose ascent is here described, is the general whose career was ruined by charges of disobedience at Second Bull Run; his long struggle to win vindication ended favorably in 1886.

ON the 11th of April [1862] at five o'clock, an event at once amusing and thrilling occurred at our quarters. The commander-in-chief had appointed his personal and confidential friend, General Fitz John Porter, to conduct the siege of Yorktown. Porter was a polite, soldierly gentleman, and a native of New Hampshire, who had been in the regular army since early manhood. He fought gallantly in the Mexican war, being thrice promoted and once seriously wounded, and he was now forty years of age,—handsome, enthusiastic, ambitious, and popular. He made frequent ascensions with Lowe, and learned to go aloft alone. One day he ascended thrice, and finally seemed as cosily at home in the firmament as upon the solid earth. It is needless to say that he grew careless, and on this particular morning leaped into the car and demanded the cables to be let out with all speed. I saw with some surprise that the flurried assistants were sending up the great straining canvas with a single rope attached. The enormous bag was only partially inflated, and the loose folds opened and shut with a crack like that of a musket. Noisily, fitfully, the yellow mass rose into the sky, the basket rocking like a feather in the zephyr; and just as I turned aside to speak to a comrade, a sound came from overhead, like the explosion of a shell, and something striking me across the face laid me flat upon the ground.

Half blind and stunned, I staggered to my feet, but the air seemed full of cries and curses. Opening my eyes ruefully, I saw all faces turned upwards, and when I looked above,—the balloon was adrift.

The treacherous cable, rotted with vitriol, had snapped in twain; one fragment had been the cause of my downfall, and the other trailed, like a great entrail, from the receding car, where Fitz John Porter was bounding upward upon a Pegasus that he could neither check nor direct.

The whole army was agitated by the unwonted occurrence. From battery No. 1, on the brink of the York, to the mouth of Warwick river, every soldier and officer was absorbed. Far within the Confederate lines the confusion extended. We heard the enemy's alarm-guns, and directly the signal flags were waving up and down our front.

The General appeared directly over the edge of the car. He was tossing his hands frightenedly, and shouting something that we could not comprehend.

"O—pen—the—valve!" called Lowe, in his shrill tones; "climb—to—the—netting—and—reach—the—valve—rope."

"The valve!—the valve!" repeated a multitude of tongues, and all gazed with thrilling interest at the retreating hulk that still kept straight upward, swerving neither to the east nor the west.

It was a weird spectacle,—that frail, fading oval, gliding against the sky, floating in the serene azure, the little vessel swinging silently beneath, and a hundred thousand martial men watching the loss of their brother in arms, but powerless to relieve or recover him. Had Fitz John Porter been drifting down the rapids of Niagara, he could not have been so far from human assistance. But we saw him directly, no bigger than a child's toy, clambering up the netting and reaching for the cord.

"He can't do it," muttered a man beside me; "the wind blows the valve-rope to and fro, and only a spry, cool-headed fellow can catch it."

We saw the General descend, and appearing again over the edge of the basket, he seemed to be motioning to the breathless hordes below, the story of his failure. Then he dropped out of sight, and when we next saw him, he was reconnoitring the Confederate works through a long black spy-glass. A great laugh went up and down the lines as this cool procedure was observed, and then a cheer of applause ran from group to group. For a moment it was doubtful that the balloon would float in either direction; it seemed to falter, like an irresolute being, and moved reluctantly southeastward, towards Fortress Monroe. A huzza, half uttered, quivered on every lip. All eyes glistened, and some were dim with tears of joy. But the wayward canvas now turned due westward, and was blown rapidly toward the Confederate works. Its course was fitfully direct, and the wind seemed to veer often, as if contrary currents, conscious of the opportunity, were struggling for the possession of the daring navigator. The south wind held mastery for awhile, and the balloon passed the Federal front amid a howl of despair from the soldiery. It kept right on, over sharpshooters, rifle-pits, and outworks, and finally passed, as if to deliver up its freight, directly over the heights of Yorktown.

The cool courage, either of heroism or despair, had seized upon Fitz John Porter. He turned his black glass upon the ramparts and masked cannon below, upon the remote camps, upon the beleaguered town, upon the guns of Gloucester Point, and upon distant Norfolk. Had he been reconnoitring from a secure perch at the tip of the moon, he could not have been more vigilant, and the Confederates probably thought this some Yankee device to peer into their sanctuary in despite of ball or shell. None of their great guns could be brought to bear upon the balloon; but there were some discharges of musketry that appeared to have no effect, and finally even these demonstrations ceased. Both armies in solemn silence were gazing aloft, while the imperturbable mariner continued to spy out the land.

The sun was now rising behind us, and roseate rays struggled up to the zenith, like the arcs made by showery bombs. They threw a hazy atmosphere upon the balloon, and the light shone through the network like the sun through the ribs of the skeleton ship in the *Ancient Mariner*. Then, as all looked agape, the air-craft "plunged, and tacked, and veered," and drifted rapidly toward the Federal lines again.

The allelujah that now went up shook the spheres, and when he had regained our camp limits, the General was seen clambering up again to clutch the valve-rope. This time he was successful, and the balloon fell like a stone, so that all hearts once more leaped up, and the cheers were hushed. Cavalry rode pell-mell from several directions, to reach the place of descent, and the General's personal staff galloped past me like the wind, to be the first at his debarkation. I followed the throng of soldiery with due haste, and came up to the horsemen in a few minutes. The balloon had struck a canvas tent with great violence, felling it as by a bolt, and the General, unharmed, had disentangled himself from innumerable folds of oiled canvas, and was now the cynosure of an immense group of people. While the officers shook his hands, the rabble bawled their satisfaction in hurrahs, and a band of music marching up directly, the throng on foot and horse gave him a vociferous escort to his quarters.

—TOWNSEND, *Campaigns of a Non-Combatant*

4. STUART'S BALL IS INTERRUPTED BY THE YANKEES

We have met both Von Borcke and Stuart before and know that they are good company. Von Borcke's Memoirs first appeared in Blackwood's Magazine and did much to popularize the Southern cause and leaders in Britain.

The Memoirs *give us, with* John Esten Cooke's Wearing of the Gray, *the best of all pictures of "Beauty" Stuart.*

WE were indulging in the dreamy sentiment natural to the hour, when the gay voice of Stuart broke in—"Major, what a capital place for us to give a ball in honour of our arrival in Maryland! don't you think we could manage it?" To this there was a unanimous response in the affirmative, which was especially hearty on the part of the ladies. It was at once agreed that the ball should be given. I undertook to make all necessary arrangements for the illumination and decoration of the hall, the issuing of the cards of invitation, &c., leaving to Stuart the matter of the music, which he gladly consented to provide.

A soldier's life is so uncertain, and his time is so little at his own disposal, that in affairs of this sort delays are always to be avoided; and so we determined on our way home, to the great joy of our fair companions, that the ball should come off on the following evening.

There was great stir of preparation at headquarters on the morning of the 8th. Invitations to the ball were sent out to all the families in Urbana and its neighbourhood, and to the officers of Hampton's brigade. The large halls of the Academy were aired and swept and festooned with roses, and decorated with battle flags borrowed from the different regiments. At seven in the evening all was complete, and already the broad avenue was filled with our fair guests, proceeding to the scene of festivity according to their social rank and fortune—some on foot, others in simple light "rockaways," others again in stately family coaches, driven by fat Negro coachmen who sat upon the box with great dignity. Very soon the sound of distant bugles announced the coming of the band of the 18th Mississippi Infantry, the Colonel and Staff of the regiment, who had been invited as an act of courtesy, leading the way, and the band playing in excellent style, the well-known air of Dixie. Amid the loud applause of the numerous invited and uninvited guests, we now made our grand *entrée* into the large hall, which was brilliantly lighted with tallow candles.

As master of the ceremonies, it was my office to arrange the order of the different dances, and I had decided upon a polka as the best for an animated beginning. I had selected the New York Rebel as the queen of the festival, and had expected to open the ball with her as my partner, and my surprise was great indeed when my fair friend gracefully eluded my extended arms, and with some confusion explained that she did not join in round dances, thus making me uncomfortably acquainted for the first time with the fact that in America, and especially in the South, young ladies rarely waltz except with brothers or first cousins, and indulge only in reels and contredances with strangers.

Not to be baffled, however, I at once ordered the time of the music to be changed, and had soon forgotten my disappointment as to the polka in a very lively quadrille. Louder and louder sounded the instruments, quicker and quicker moved the dancers, and the whole crowded room, with its many exceedingly pretty women and its martial figures of officers in their best uniforms, presented a most striking spectacle of gaiety and enjoyment.

Suddenly enters an orderly covered with dust, and reports in a loud voice to General Stuart that the enemy have surprised and driven in our pickets and are attacking our camp in force, while at the same moment the sound of shots in rapid succession is distinctly borne to us on the midnight air.

The excitement which followed this announcement I cannot undertake to describe. The music crashed into a *concordia discors*. The officers rushed to their weapons and called for their horses, panic-stricken fathers and mothers endeavoured in a frantic way to collect around them their bewildered children, while the young ladies ran to and fro in most admired despair. General Stuart maintained his accustomed coolness and composure. Our horses were immediately saddled, and in less than five minutes we were in rapid gallop to the front. Upon arriving there we found, as is usually the case in such sudden alarms, that things were by no means so desperate as they had been represented.

Colonel Baker, with the splendid 1st North Carolina regiment, had arrested the bold forward movement of the Yankees. Pelham, with his guns in favourable position, was soon pouring a rapid fire upon their columns. The other regiments of the command were speedily in the saddle. The line of battle having been formed, Stuart gave the order for a general attack, and with great rage and fury we precipitated ourselves upon the foe, who paid, with the loss of many killed and wounded, and a considerable number of prisoners for their unmannerly interruption of our social amusement. They were pursued in their headlong flight for several miles by the 1st North Carolina, until, a little past midnight, they got quite out of reach, and all was quiet again.

It was about one o'clock in the morning when we got back to the Academy, where we found a great many of our fair guests still assembled, awaiting with breathless anxiety the result of the conflict. As the musicians had never dispersed, General Stuart ordered them again to strike up; many of our pretty fugitives were brought back by young officers who eagerly volunteered for that commendable purpose; and as everybody was determined that the Yankees should not boast of having completely broken up our party, the dancing was resumed in less than half an hour, and kept up till the first glimmer of dawn. At this time the ambulances laden with the wounded of last night's engagement were slowly approaching the Academy, as the only building at Urbana that was at all suited to the purposes of an hospital. Of course the music was immediately stopped and the dancing ceased, and our lovely partners in the quadrille at once became "ministering angels" to the sufferers.

—Von Borcke, *Memoirs of the Confederate War for Independence*

5. MAJOR R—— WHIPS THE YANKEES SINGLEHANDED

John Esten Cooke, whom we have met before, was another of Stuart's happy band, and his Major R—— might be Von Borcke himself. Member of a distinguished Virginia family, Cooke early turned from the law, to which he was trained, to literature, and even before the outbreak of the war had become the Virginia Cooper or Sims. An ardent secessionist he fought all through the war; after Appomattox he retired to the Valley and devoted himself to celebrating the heroes of the great conflict and to historical novels. He had already written a biography of Stonewall Jackson; after the war came a biography of Lee, a volume of military essays, Hammer and Rapier, *and the delightful and authentic* Wearing of the Gray *from which this rollicking excerpt is taken.*

A WORD first of the doughty sabreur who figured as hero on the occasion, my friend, Major R——, of the C. S. A.

The Major is stout, rosy, of a portly figure, and from his appearance you would not take him for a very active or dangerous personage. But he is both. No man delights more in movement, adventure, and combat. No man sits a horse with more of the true cavalry ease. You may see from the manner in which he handles his sabre that he is master of that weapon; and in the charge he is a perfect thunderbolt. He fingers his pistol and makes the barrels revolve with admirable grace; his salute with the sabre is simply perfection; his air, as he listens to an order from his superior officer, says plainly, "All I wish is to know what you want me to do, General—if it can be done it will be done." This air does not deceive. It is well known to the Major's friends that his motto is, "Neck or nothing." At Mine Run, when General Meade confronted the Southern lines, the worthy said to me, "A soldier's duty is to obey his orders; and if General Stuart told me to charge the Yankee army by myself, I would do it. *He* would be responsible."

It will be seen from the above sketch of the gallant Major, that he is a thorough soldier. In fact he loves his profession, and is not satisfied with performing routine duty. He is fond of volunteering on forlorn hopes, and in desperate emergencies—when he cannot get at the blue-coats for any length of time—he pines.

This mood came to him in the fall of 1862. Quiet had reigned along the lines so long, that he grew melancholy. His appetite did not fail, as far as his friends could perceive, but something obviously rested on his mind. He was rusting, and was conscious of the process. "Why don't they come out and fight?" the Major seemed to ask with his calm, sad eyes. They were in Virginia for the purpose of "crushing the rebellion,"—why didn't they set about the work?

These questions meeting with no satisfactory response, Major R—— determined himself to take the initiative, and see if he could not bring on a little fight, all on his private account. He would thus relieve his bosom of the perilous stuff which preyed upon his heart. It had, indeed, become absolutely necessary to his peace of mind to come into collision with his friends across the way, and he set about devising the best plan for arriving at his object.

The Southern cavalry to which the Major was attached, at that time occupied the county of Culpepper, and picketed along the Rappahannock.

So did the enemy's horsemen, and the Federal pickets were stationed on the southern bank at every ford. This was the case at Warrenton Springs, where a bridge, afterwards destroyed, spanned the Rappahannock; and at this point Major R—— determined to bring on the little affair which had become so necessary to his happiness. He intended to combine pleasure with business by visiting some young ladies at a hospitable mansion not far from the bridge; and having thus laid out his programme he proceeded to execute it, and "all alone by himself" attack the picket guard of some twenty of the enemy.

Behold the Major now in warlike panoply—that is to say, in fine gray dress coat with burnished buttons (for the eyes of Venus after the conflict with Mars); pistol carefully loaded, in holster on his right side; and sabre in excellent order, jingling against his top boots. It was a saying of the worthy, that he "generally kept his arms in good order," and on this occasion nothing was left to be desired. His pistol revolved at the touch, with a clear ringing click; and you could see your face in his sabre blade. Thus accoutred, and mounted on a good, active horse, he set off from Hazel river, and making a detour around Jeffersonton, came to an elevation in rear of Mr. ——'s house, where he stopped to reconnoitre.

The Federal picket—of nineteen men, as he afterwards discovered—was at the bridge; and in the yard of the mansion were two videttes, with their horses tied to the trees under which they were lying. Whether he could succeed in "driving in" the whole picket was problematical, but the videttes were pretty sure game. He would either run them off or capture them.

With the Major execution followed conception rapidly. Pushing boldly over the crest from behind which he had made his reconnoissance, he charged across the field at a thundering gallop, whirling his burnished sabre around his head, yelling in a manner that was truly awful; and shouting as he rode to a suppositious squadron:

"Charge! charge! cut down every man!"

So portentous was the reverberating shout of onset from the lips of the Major, that the videttes started to their feet, and clutched the bridles of their horses instantly. As the warlike figure, surrounded by the brilliant lightning of the flashing sabre, swept on, the videttes probably saw at least a squadron of "Rebel cavalry" in the dust which rose behind; and hastily mounting, darted away, pursued by the triumphant Major, whose yells were now more tremendous than ever.

Across the broad field, past the house, on toward the bridge, galloped the furious assailant, bent on striking terror to the enemy's hearts, and successfully completing his adventure. Before him fled the frightened videttes—their movements accelerated by several balls, which issued from the Major's pistol, and whistled by their ears. On toward the bridge, and into the midst of the picket fled the videttes; and as the Major's shouts, and vociferous orders to his cavalry to charge, and let no one escape, resounded nearer, the pickets, too, mounted in hot haste, and clattered across the bridge, pursued by the Major's pistol shots.

In vain did the officer in charge of the picket-post shout to his men: "Halt! halt! Shoot down the rascal! Shoot him down, I say! There's only one of them!"

His voice was unheard or his order unheeded. The picket was composed of stuff less soldierly than their officer, and would not obey him. Before their vivid imaginations rose at least a squadron of Confederate cavalry, sweeping on to ride over them, sword in hand.

The result was that Major R—— in ten minutes had possession of the bridge, and sat his horse defiantly in the middle of it. He then amused himself by sending a few parting shots after the demoralized picket, and having performed this agreeable duty rode back to the house of Mr. ——, laughing low in his peculiar way; his breast completely lightened of the oppressive weight which had so long weighed upon it.

At Mr. ——'s he met with a triumphant reception; was greeted with a perfect ovation. The young ladies of the mansion were crazy almost with delight at the manner in which they had been delivered from the presence of their enemies; and when the hero of the occasion made his appearance they met him as women only can meet their deliverers—with smiles such as shine rarely for the poor "civilian." After all it is something to be a soldier. The trade is hard, but the feminine eye has a peculiar brightness when it rests on the sons of Mars!—of Mars, proverbially the favourite of Venus!

The Major was an old soldier, and in no hurry to depart. He counted on the extent of the "scare" he had given the enemy, and quietly enjoyed himself in the charming society of his hostesses. He had once more become "excellent company." The smile had returned to his lips, the light to his eyes. That melancholy which had made his friends uneasy had quite disappeared, and the Major was "himself again"—that is to say, the gayest and most delightful of companions.

When, rising slowly and carelessly, he bade his friendly entertainers good-bye, he was again happy. He came back to camp, smiling, amiable, the soul of sweetness and cheerfulness. I saw him. He was absolutely radiant. His eloquent eye beamed brightly; his countenance was charming; his movements energetic and elastic; the fullest satisfaction was apparent in every lineament of his face. His gay and friendly smile seemed to say, "I went at nineteen of them; ran them off; held the bridge against them; had an excellent supper, a delightful talk—I am happy!"

—Cooke, *Wearing of the Gray*

6. FOREIGNERS FIGHT IN THE NORTHERN ARMY

The Civil War, like the Revolution, attracted soldiers of fortune and ardent partisans from abroad. Literally dozens of more or less distinguished foreigners served in the Confederate ranks; somewhat fewer were attracted to the Union cause. Most of the visiting warriors preferred to stay in the East, in the armies of Northern Virginia or of the Potomac. Many foreign visitors—the Comte de Paris, Fremantle, Wolseley, Estvan, Trobiand, and others—wrote up their wartime experiences, and we have drawn on these from time to time. This account is taken from McClellan's Own Story.

THE most entertaining of my duties were those which sometimes led me to Blenker's camp, whither Franklin was always glad to accompany me to see the "circus," or "opera," as he usually called the performance. As soon as we were sighted, Blenker would have the "officer's call" blown to assemble his polyglot collection, with their uniform as varied and brilliant as the colors of the rainbow. Wrapped in his scarlet-lined cloak, his group of officers ranged around him, he would receive us with the most formal and polished courtesy. Being a very handsome and soldierly-looking man himself, and there being many equally so among his surroundings, the tableau was always very effective, and presented a striking contrast to the matter-of-fact way in which things were managed in the other divisions.

In a few minutes he would shout, *"Ordinanz numero eins!"* whereupon champagne would be brought in great profusion, the bands would play, sometimes songs be sung. It was said, I know not how truly, that Blenker had been a non-commissioned officer in the German contingent serving under King Otho of Greece.

His division was very peculiar. So far as "the pride, pomp, and circumstance of glorious war" were concerned, it certainly outshone all the others. Their drill and bearing were also excellent; for all the officers, and probably all the men, had served in Europe. I have always regretted that the division was finally taken from me and sent to Fremont. The officers and men were all strongly attached to me; I could control them as no one else could, and they would have done good service had they remained in Sumner's corps. The regiments were all foreign and mostly of Germans; but the most remarkable of all was the Garibaldi regiment. Its colonel, D'Utassy, was a Hungarian, and was said to have been a rider in Franconi's Circus, and terminated his public American career in the Albany Penitentiary. His men were from all known and unknown lands, from all possible and impossible armies: Zouaves from Algiers, men of the "Foreign Legion," Zephyrs, Cossacks, Garibaldians of the deepest dye, English deserters, Sepoys, Turcos, Croats, Swiss, beer-drinkers from Bavaria, stout men from North Germany, and no doubt Chinese, Esquimaux, and detachments from the army of the Grand Duchess of Gerolstein.

Such a mixture was probably never before seen under any flag, unless, perhaps, in such bands as Holk's Jagers of the Thirty Years' War, or the free lances of the middle ages.

I well remember that in returning one night from beyond the picket-lines I encountered an outpost of the Garibaldians. In reply to their challenge I tried English, French, Spanish, Italian, German, Indian, a little Russian and Turkish; all in vain, for nothing at my disposal made the slightest impression upon them, and I inferred that they were perhaps gypsies or Esquimaux or Chinese.

Mr. Seward's policy of making ours "a people's war," as he expressed it, by drumming up officers from all parts of the world, sometimes produced strange results and brought us rare specimens of the class vulgarly known as "hard cases." Most of the officers thus obtained had left their own armies for the armies' good, although there were admirable and honorable exceptions, such as Stahl, Willich, Rosencranz, Cesnola, and some others. Few were of the slightest use to us, and I think the reason why the German regiments so seldom turned out well was that their officers were so often men without character.

Soon after General Scott retired I received a letter from the Hungarian Klapka informing me that he had been approached by some of Mr. Seward's agents to get him into our army, and saying that he thought it best to come to a direct understanding with myself as to terms, etc. He said that he would require a bonus of $100,000 in cash and a salary of $25,000 per annum; that on his first arrival he would consent to serve as my chief of staff for a short time until he acquired the language, and that he would then take my place of general commanding-in-chief. He failed to state what provision he would make for me, that probably to depend upon the impression I made upon him.

I immediately took the letter to Mr. Lincoln, who was made very angry by it, and, taking possession of the letter, said that he would see that I should not be troubled in that way again.

Cluseret—afterwards Minister of War under the Commune—brought me a letter of introduction from Garibaldi, recommending him in the highest terms as a soldier, man of honor, etc. I did not like his appearance and declined his services; but without my knowledge or consent Stanton appointed him a colonel on my staff. I still declined to have anything to do with him, and he was sent to the Mountain Department, as chief of staff, I think. . . .

Of a different order were the French princes who formed part of my military family from September 20, 1861, to the close of the Seven Days. They served as captains, declining any higher rank, though they had fully earned promotion before the close of their connection with the army. They served precisely as the other aides, taking their full share of all duty, whether agreeable or disagreeable, dangerous or the reverse. They were fine young fellows and good soldiers, and deserved high credit in every way.

Their uncle, the Prince de Joinville, who accompanied them as a mentor, held no official position, but our relations were always confidential and most agreeable. The Duc de Chartres had received a military education at the military school at Turin; the Comte de Paris had only received instruction in military matters from his tutors. They had their separate establishment, being accompanied by a physician and a captain of *chasseurs-à-pied*. The latter was an immense man, who could never, under any circumstances, be persuaded to mount a horse: he always made the march on foot.

Their little establishment was usually the jolliest in camp, and it was often a great relief to me, when burdened with care, to listen to the laughter and gayety that resounded from their tents. They managed their affairs so well that they were respected and liked by all with whom they came in contact. The Prince de Joinville sketched admirably and possessed a most keen sense of the ridiculous, so that his sketch-book was an inexhaustible source of amusement, because everything ludicrous that struck his fancy on the march was sure to find a place there. He was a man of far more than ordinary ability and of excellent judgment. His deafness was, of course, a disadvantage to him, but his admirable qualities were so marked that I became warmly attached to him, as, in fact, I did to all the three, and I have good reason to know that the feeling was mutual.

Whatever may have been the peculiarities of Louis Philippe during his later life, it is very certain that in his youth, as the Duc de Chartres, he was a brave, dashing, and excellent soldier. His sons, especially the Ducs d'Orléans, d'Aumale, Montpensier, and the Prince de Joinville, showed the same characteristics in Algiers and elsewhere; and I may be permitted to say that my personal experience with the three members of the family who served with me was such that there could be no doubt as to their courage, energy, and military spirit. The course pursued by the Prince de Joinville and the Duc de Chartres during the fatal invasion of France by the Germans was in perfect harmony with this. Both sought service, under assumed names, in the darkest and most dangerous hours of their country's trial. The duc served for some months as Capt. Robert le Fort, and under that name, his identity being known to few if any beyond his closest personal friends, gained promotion and distinction by his gallantry and intelligence.

—McClellan's Own Story

7. THE MUD CAMPAIGN

After the stunning defeat at Fredericksburg, on December 13, 1862, Burnside withdrew his forces across the Rappahannock and marked time while he planned another assault. None of his division commanders, however, supported this plan. For over a month the two armies watched each other across the swollen Rappahannock. Then on the nineteenth of January Burnside prepared to move northward along the river, possibly with a view to crossing at Banks' Ford. The next day a violent storm came up, turning the Virginia roads to mud; horses and artillery bogged down, pontoons could not be moved; the grand movement of the army became, instead, a "mud march," and on the twenty-fifth Burnside was relieved from command.

The querulous Dunn Browne we have met before.

Jan. 23, 1863

The army has tried to move, and been prevented by reasons over which man has no control. The order came to advance again across the Rappahannock, and meet the enemy. Tuesday morning, camps were broken up, tents struck, knapsacks packed; and soon long lines of troops were in motion over hill and dale all around us. The roads for miles were choked with supply-wagons, ammunition-trains and rumbling batteries. All was noise, confusion, and utmost activity. Trumpets sounded, drums beat, whips cracked, mules squealed, and teamsters cursed. In short, all things showed that a vast army was on the move. Excitement took the place of the quiet that had reigned in our midst for a month. Hearts beat high with hope and patriotic ardor, and spirits sank in dismay at the thought of approaching danger, wounds, and death. Some left couches of sickness, roused to new strength at the call to arms. Some, who had been perfectly well, paled into sudden sickness at the same prospect, and came sneaking round the surgeons' tents, and crawling into hospitals.

For ourselves, under orders to be ready for instant march, our regiment waited through the livelong day, with three days' cooked rations in their haversacks, and sixty rounds of ball-cartridge disposed about their persons; blankets, shelter-tents, &c., rolled up, and guns at hand to march in a moment; all constituting a fair mule's load, and what is, in military phrase, facetiously termed "light marching order,"—waited all day, watching the troops, that rolled like a river unceasingly by us, and wondering when we should be emptied into the stream; but waited, most fortunately for us, in vain. For the clouds gathered all day thicker and darker, and night ushered in a storm of wind and pouring rain, harder for that moving army to encounter than a hundred thousand enemies; a driving rain that drenched and chilled the poor shelterless men and horses, and that poached the ground into mud deeper than the New-England mind can conceive of, and stickier than—well, I am at a loss for a similitude. Pitch, for cohesive attraction, is but as sand compared with it.

So the artillery and the wagons stuck fast on Wednesday; the pontoons couldn't go on wheels; and, though the rain continued in floods, there wasn't quite enough to carry them by water: and so the river rose, and couldn't be crossed; and so every thing got mixed up, and all our fine arrangements spoiled; and we experienced the uncertainty that attends human events, and especially a winter campaign in Virginia. And so our noble Burnside goes up to report his disappointment at Washington; and the army comes dragging back, in the deep mud and drizzling rain, to its old quarters. All yesterday and today, the bedraggled and tired regiments are passing us; and all the roads and streams are full of dead horses and mules (I presume fifty are in sight from the top of the hill back of my tent), and pieces of wagons, and the way obstructed with caissons, and pieces of artillery, and pontoons, and all sorts of vehicles, fast in the mud.

We must wait till the earth is dried up a little from the effects of this storm, and then try it again, running the same risks. And I suppose poor Burnside must take all the blame of failures now; whereas I am disposed to look back to the man who kept us two months in inactivity, after the battle of Antietam, in the most beautiful and precious time of the whole year, to find the shoulders on which to lay the blame. However, finding fault now isn't going to help the past. Something must be done even now, as you and the whole North tell us. Only you must consider what a winter's campaign in these regions really means, when you make up your judgment of us and our doings. It means to the soldiers wet feet every day of the march, the cold ground to lie upon, and insufficient food for them to eat. It means coughs, colds, consumptions, rheumatism, and fevers; a row of unmarked graves all along the track of the army, and desolation and mourning to thousands of pleasant homes. It means the pain of seeing in every company brave fellows sinking right down to death before your eyes, with no possibility of helping them, or even doing much to soothe their last hours.

It means, if battle comes, the wounded left to freeze in the severity of the nights, or to mingle their blood with the deep mud on which they lie. It means every possible form of human suffering, privation, and hardship. Make all allowances for us, then, and pray for our strength, endurance, and success; and drop a tear over the brave fellows who are sacrificed, not merely to the demon of battle, but to the more dreaded severities of the winter season.

—[SAMUEL FISKE], *Mr. Dunn Browne's Experiences in the Army*

8. WITH "EXTRA BILLY" SMITH AT YORK

After Chancellorsville Lee planned once again to move into Pennsylvania, in part to bring the war home to the North, in part to find food for his soldiers and forage for his horses. Early in June the Army of Northern Virginia was on the move, Ewell's corps swinging through the Valley and crossing the upper Potomac near Sharpsburg. Ewell had been authorized by Lee, not only to find flour and horses but, if possible, to capture Harrisburg. On June 27 he reached Carlisle; the same day Early moved out from Gettysburg to York, levying a $28,000 contribution on that town.

It was here that Stiles—whose Four Years is a minor classic—heard "Extra Billy" Smith haranguing the natives. This "Extra Billy" was one of the fabulous characters of the Confederacy. He had received this curious name a generation earlier when, as local postmaster, he collected so much "extra" money for deliveries. Later he was elected Governor of Virginia; went out to California where he took a prominent part in Democratic politics; returned to Virginia and served as Congressman for the decade before the war; and at the age of sixty-five offered his services to the Confederacy. Appointed brigadier general, he refused that rank and took, instead, the colonelcy of the 49th Virginia Infantry. Serving with distinction, and with reckless daring, he was promoted to major general but resigned in 1864 to accept once again the Governorship of his state.

Robert Stiles was a major of the famous Richmond Howitzers.

THINGS were not likely to be dull when our old friend "Extra Billy" was about; . . . in fact there was apt to be "music in the air" whenever he was in charge. On the occasion below described, the old Governor seemed to be rather specially concerned about the musical part of the performance.

We were about entering the beautiful Pennsylvania town of York, General Smith's brigade in the lead. Under these conditions, feeling sure there was likely to be a breeze stirring about the head of the column, I rode forward so as to be near the General and not miss the fun. As we approached, the population seemed to be very generally in the streets, and I saw at a glance that the old Governor had blood in his eye. Turning to Fred, his aide,—who was also his son, and about the strongest marked case of second edition I ever saw,—he told him to "go back and look up those tooting fellows," as he called the brigade band, "and tell them first to be sure their drums and horns are all right, and then to come up here to the front and march into town tooting 'Yankee Doodle' in their very best style."

Fred was off in a jiffy, and soon here came the band, their instruments looking bright and smart and glistening in the June sunlight—playing, however, not "Yankee Doodle," but "*Dixie*," the musicians appearing to think it important to be entirely impartial in rendering these national airs, and therefore giving us "Dixie" by way of prelude to "Yankee Doodle."

When they got to the head of the column and struck up "Yankee Doodle," and the Governor, riding alone and bareheaded in front of his staff, began bowing and saluting first one side and then the other, especially every pretty girl he saw, with that manly, hearty smile which no man or woman ever doubted or resisted—the Yorkers seemed at first astounded, then pleased. Finally, by the time we reached the public square they had reached the point of ebullition, and broke into enthusiastic cheers as they crowded about the head of the column actually embarrassing its progress, till the old Governor,— the "Governor-General," we might call him,—nothing loth, acceded to the half suggestion and called a halt, his brigade stacking arms and constituting, if not formally organizing, themselves and the people of York into a political meeting.

It was a rare scene—the vanguard of an invading army and the invaded and hostile population hobnobbing on the public green in an enthusiastic public gathering. The General did not dismount, but from the saddle he made a rattling, humorous speech which both the Pennsylvanians and his own brigade applauded to the echo. He said substantially:

"My friends, how do you like this way of coming back into the Union? I hope you like it; I have been in favor of it for a good while. But don't misunderstand us. We are not here with any hostile intent—unless the conduct of your side shall render hostilities unavoidable. You can see for yourselves we are not conducting ourselves like enemies today. We are not burning your houses or butchering your children. On the contrary, we are behaving ourselves like Christian gentlemen, as we are.

"You see, it was getting a little warm down our way. We needed a summer outing and thought we would take it at the North, instead of patronizing the Virginia springs, as we generally do. We are sorry, and apologize that we are not in better guise for a visit of courtesy, but we regret to say our trunks haven't gotten up yet; we were in such a hurry to see you that we could not wait for them. You must really excuse us.

"What we all need, on both sides, is to mingle more with each other, so that we shall learn to know and appreciate each other. Now here's my brigade—I wish you knew them as I do. They are such a hospitable, wholehearted, fascinating lot of gentlemen! Why, just think of it—of course this part of Pennsylvania is ours to-day; we've got it, we hold it, we can destroy it, or do what we please with it. Yet we sincerely and heartily invite you to stay. You are quite welcome to remain here and to make yourselves entirely at home—so long as you behave yourselves pleasantly and agreeably as you are doing now. Are we not a fine set of fellows? You must admit that we are."

At this point my attention was called to a volley of very heated profanity poured forth in a piping, querulous treble, coming up from the rear, and being mounted and located where I commanded a view of the road I saw that the second brigade in column, which had been some distance in the rear, had caught up and was now held up by our public meeting, which filled and obstructed the entire street. Old Jube (Early), who had ridden forward to ascertain the cause of the deadlock, was fairly blistering the air about him and making furious but for the time futile efforts to get at Extra Billy, who in plain sight and not far off, yet blissfully unconscious of the presence of the major-general and of his agreeable observations and comments, was still holding forth with great fluency and acceptability.

The jam was solid and impervious. As D. H. Hill's report phrased it, "Not a dog, no, not even a sneaking exempt, could have made his way through," and at first and for some time Old Jube couldn't do it, and no one would help him. But at last officers and men were compelled to recognize the division commander, and he made his way so far that, by leaning forward, a long stretch, and a frantic grab, he managed to catch General Smith by the back of his coat collar. Even Jube did not dare curse the old General in an offensive way, but he did jerk him back and around pretty vigorously and half screamed:

"General Smith, what the devil are you about! stopping the head of this column in the cursed town?"

With unruffled composure the old fellow replied:

"Having a little fun, General, which is good for all of us, and at the same time teaching these people something that will be good for them and won't do us any harm."

Suffice it to say the matter was amicably arranged and the brigade and its unique commander moved on, leaving the honest burghers of York wondering what manner of men we were. I should add that General Early had the greatest regard and admiration for General Smith, which indeed he could not well avoid, in view of his intense patriotic devotion and his other sterling and heroic qualities. I have seldom heard him speak of any other officer or soldier in the service, save of course Lee and Jackson, in such exalted terms as of the old "Governor-General."

—STILES, *Four Years Under Marse Robert*

9. BLUE AND GRAY FRATERNIZE ON THE PICKET LINE

The bitterness which characterizes any civil war was ameliorated by friendliness among the soldiers on opposite sides. This friendliness was found among the officers, many of whom belonged to the West Point fraternity or had fought together in Mexican and Indian wars; it was found, no less pervasively, among the rank and file, who, for the most part, respected each other and fought without animosity. Civil War narratives are filled with examples of fraternization across picket lines, the exchange of tobacco and food, acts of courtesy and friendliness.

Alexander Hunter, whose Johnny Reb *and* Billy Yank *is one of the liveliest of descriptions of life in the ranks, was a college boy who joined the 17th Virginia Regiment at the outbreak of the war.*

IT was the latter part of August [1863]; orders were given to be prepared to go on picket early in the morning; and until a late hour the men were busy cooking rations and cleaning equipments.

Before the mists had been chased by the rising sun, the company in close column of fours marched down the road. Men and animals were in perfect condition, brimful of mettle and in buoyant spirits.

The route lay along the banks of the river, upon the winding course of which, after several hours' riding, the regiment reached its destination and relieved the various pickets. A sergeant and squad of men were left at each post, the company being spread out several miles on the river banks to act as videttes, whose duty it was to watch the enemy on the other side of the Rappahannock.

The next day our squad, Sergeant Joe Reid in command, sauntered down the bank, but seeing no one we lay at length under the spreading trees, smoking as solemnly and meditatively as the redoubtable Wilhelmus Kraft and all the Dutch Council, over the affairs of state.

The Rappahannock, which was at this place about two hundred yards wide, flowing slowly oceanward, its bosom reflecting the roseate-hued morn, was as lovely a body of water as the sun ever shone upon. The sound of the gentle ripple of its waves upon the sand was broken by a faint "halloo" which came from the other side.

"Johnny Reb; I say, J-o-h-n-n-y R-e-b, don't shoot!"

Joe Reid shouted back, "All right!"

"What command are you?"

The spoken words floated clear and distinct across the water, "The Black Horse Cavalry. Who are you?"

"The Second Michigan Cavalry."

"Come out on the bank," said our spokesman, "and show yourselves; we won't fire."

"On your honor, Johnny Reb?"

"On our honor, Billy Yank."

In a second a large squad of blue-coats across the way advanced to the water's brink. The Southerners did the same; then the former put the query.

"Have you any tobacco?"

"Plenty of it," went out our reply.

"Any sugar and coffee?" they questioned.

"Not a taste nor a smell."

"Let's trade," was shouted with eagerness.

"Very well," was the reply. "We have not much with us, but we will send to Fredericksburg for more, so meet us here this evening."

"All right," they answered; then added, "Say, Johnny, want some news-papers?"

"Y-e-s!"

"Then look out, we are going to send you some."

"How are you going to do it?"

"Wait and see."

The Rebs watched the group upon the other side curiously, wondering how even Yankee ingenuity could devise a way for sending a batch of papers across the river two hundred yards wide, and in the meantime each man had his own opinion.

"They will shoot arrows over," said Martin.

"Arrows, the devil!" replied the sergeant; "there never was a bow bent which could cast an arrow across this river."

"Maybe they will wrap them around a cannon ball and shoot them across; we'd better get away from here," hastily answered a tall, slim six-footer, who was rather afraid of big shots.

A roar of laughter followed this suggestion, but the originator was too intent on his own awakened fears to let the slightest movement of the enemy pass unscanned. Eagerly he watched while the others were having all the fun at his expense. Presently he shouted:

"Here they come!" and then in a tone of intense admiration, "I'll be dog-goned if these Yanks are not the smartest people in the world."

On the other side were several miniature boats and ships—such as school-boys delight in—with sails set; the gentle breeze impelled the little crafts across the river, each freighted with a couple of newspapers. Slowly, but surely, they headed for the opposite bank as if some spirit Oberon or Puck sat at the tiller; and in a few minutes had accomplished their voyage and were drawn up to await a favorable wind to waft them back.

Drawing lots, Joe Boteler, who found luck against him, started to town, with a muttered curse, to buy tobacco, leaving his comrades to seek some shady spot, and with pipes in our mouths sink deep in the latest war news from the enemy's standpoint, always interesting reading.

It was a cloudless day,—a day to dream,—and with a lazy *sans souci* man-ner and half-shut eyes, enjoy to the soul the deep loveliness of the scene which lay around us like some fair creation of the fancy, listening the while to the trills of the blue-bird which sat on the top of a lofty tree industriously practicing his notes like a prima donna getting a new opera by heart.

Joe returned in the evening with a box of plug tobacco about a foot square; but how to get it across was the question. The miniature boats could not carry it, and we shouted over to the Yanks that we had about twenty pounds of cut plug, and asked them what we must do? They hallooed back to let one of us swim across, and declared that it was perfectly safe. We held a council of war, and it was found that none of the Black Horse could swim beyond a few rods. Then I volunteered. Having lived on the banks of the Potomac most of my life, I was necessarily a swimmer.

Sergeant Reid went to a house not far off and borrowed a bread trough, and placing it on a plank, the box of tobacco was shipped, and disrobing I started, pushing my queer craft in front of me. As I approached the shore the news of my coming had reached camp, and nearly all the Second Michigan were lined up along the bank.

I felt a little queer, but I had perfect faith in their promise and kept on without missing a stroke until my miniature scow grounded on the beach. The blue-coats crowded around me and gave me a hearty welcome, and relieving the trough of its load, heaped the craft with offerings of sugar, coffee, lemons, and even candy, till I cried out that they would sink my transport. I am sure they would have filled a rowboat to the gunwhale had I brought one.

There was no chaffing or banter, only roistering welcomes.

Bidding my friends the enemy good-by, I swam back with the precious cargo, and we had a feast that night.

—HUNTER, *Johnny Reb and Billy Yank*

10. LIFE WITH THE MOSBY GUERRILLAS

There is a Robin Hood quality about the Mosby Guerrillas. Mosby himself had served as cavalryman under Stuart in the Peninsular campaign, at Manassas and Antietam, but in January 1863 he set up on his own with a band of some three hundred free spirits, harrying the Federals north of the Rappahannock and, later, in the Valley. While the Federals regarded Mosby's men as outlaws, they operated under a Confederate "partisan ranger" law which made them subject to the same regulations as other soldiers, but permitted them almost complete freedom of action. When, on one occasion, Sheridan executed some of his men, Mosby hung seven prisoners in reprisal. At the close of the war the Mosby Guerrillas consisted of eight companies, well mounted and equipped; Mosby himself had been promoted to a colonelcy.

John Munson, from whose recollections this excerpt has been taken, was himself one of the Mosby Guerrillas.

THE life led by Mosby's men was entirely different from that of any other body of soldiers during the war. His men had no camps nor fixed quarters, and never slept in tents. They did not even know anything about pitching a tent. The idea of making coffee, frying bacon, or soaking hardtack was never entertained. When we wanted to eat we stopped at a friendly farm house, or went into some little town and bought what we wanted. Every man in the Command had some special farm he could call his home.

The people in that part of the state which was designated "Mosby's Confederacy," embracing in a general way the counties of Fauquier and Loudoun, were loyal to the South, though frequently outside the lines of the Southern army, and they were glad to have Mosby's men among them, not only to show their sympathy with the South, but also to have the protection which the presence of the Partisans afforded them.

During the war all local government in that country was suspended. There were no courts nor court officers. The people looked to Mosby to make the necessary laws and to enforce them, and no country before, during or since the war was ever better governed. Mosby would not permit any man to commit a crime, or even a misdemeanor, in his domain. One of our men, in a spirit of deviltry, once turned over an old Quaker farmer's milk cans, and when Mosby heard of it he ordered me to take the man over to the army, which was then near Winchester, and turn him over to General Early, with the message that such a man was not fitted to be a Guerrilla.

As a Command we had no knowledge of the first principles of cavalry drill, and could not have formed in a straight line had there ever been any need for our doing so. We did not know the bugle-calls, and very rarely had roll-call. Our dress was not uniform in make or color; we did not address our officers, except Mosby, by their titles; in fact, we did not practice anything usually required of a soldier; and yet withal there was not another body of men in the army under better or more willing control of their leader. Two things were impressed upon us well, however; to obey orders, and to fight. . . .

Each of Mosby's men was armed with two muzzle-loading Colt's army revolvers of forty-four caliber. They were worn in belt holsters. Some few who could afford it, or who had succeeded in capturing extra pistols or who wanted to gratify a sort of vanity, wore an extra pair in their saddle-holsters or stuck into their boot legs. These weapons were extremely deadly and effective in the hand-to-hand engagements in which our men indulged. Long and frequent practice had made every man in the Command a good shot, and each was as sure with his revolver as every cow-boy is with his six-shooter. As a general thing our real fights were fast and furious and quickly over, one or the other side withdrawing at a dead run when the pistols were empty. . . .

"Something gray" was the one requisite of our dress and the cost of it mattered little. Much of it was paid for by Uncle Sam out of the money we got from him directly and indirectly. Like gamblers we took chances with fate. We had ups and downs; but after our successful raids we were the best dressed, best equipped, and best mounted Command in the Confederate army. There were meek and lowly privates among us, of whom it might truly be said that Solomon in all his glory was not arrayed as one of these. Union army sutlers supplied us with a varied assortment of luxuries, and I cannot recall an instance when we rejected what they had on hand on over-hauling their stock, or when we threatened to take our trade to some competitor. . . .

Some of the Command were extremely fastidious in the matter of dress and affected gold braid, buff trimmings, and ostrich plumes in their hats. After the "greenback raid" when we captured General Sheridan's paymasters with a hundred and seventy thousand dollars in crisp new Government notes, each man received as his share more than twenty-one hundred dollars. The result was that all had clothes and accoutrements such as had never gladdened their hearts before. At all times, whether things went well or ill, the Guerrillas were as vain a lot of dandies as one would wish to see; blithe in the face of danger, full of song and story, indifferent to the events of tomorrow, and keyed up to a high pitch of anticipation; mingled with this was the pride that goes hand in hand with repeated victories and the possession of spoils. . . .

Whenever we made a successful raid, we made it a point to repay the farmers and country people whose bounty we enjoyed, in live stock and supplies. The return from a sutler's raid was a holiday occasion, for everybody got something. On one occasion we captured about two hundred and fifty fat cattle from General Sheridan's supply train, and we gave our country friends half of them, dividing them among all the people living within range.

On one occasion, we got into some sutler's stores at Duffield depot on the Baltimore & Ohio Railroad and the goods were so tempting that I concluded to carry an assortment back to our lady hostess and her household. I loaded up a sack with all sorts of useful and ornamental goods, and fastened it to my saddle securely. Then, going back into the store and looking around, I spied some hoop-skirts which the sutler had no doubt bought for some special order from an army officer's wife. I took these and strapped them to my saddle. Then I made another and final round of the store, and began stuffing my many pockets with notions, such as buttons, hair pins, thread, hooks and eyes, and the like; finally I found a lot of papers of needles, and I thrust a handful of these into my trousers' pocket.

Just then some one poked his head into the door and cried: "The Yankees are coming."

We made a break for our horses and galloped away with our plunder, and our prisoners; keeping up a pretty fast gait for some miles for fear our burdens would slacken the usual speed we practiced when we were retreating. I had not gone a mile before my papers of needles began to come undone in my pocket, and at every jump of my horse a newly released needle would remind me that I had captured it, until at the end of our run I had dozens of needle marks on my anatomy, and two or three points were left inside, to work upward or downward, or out, as they severally saw fit.

I recollect that I delivered all my presents safely to my kind friends, except needles, and I made no reference to these in my account of the raid. In all my later raids on sutler's stores I contented myself with things that were not likely to prove troublesome, or stick into me, such as boots, and gloves, and furnishing goods; but I ignored needles.

—Munson, *Reminiscences of a Mosby Guerrilla*

11. THOMAS WENTWORTH HIGGINSON CELEBRATES LIFE IN A BLACK REGIMENT

Colonel Higginson is one of the romantic figures of the war. A Massachusetts aristocrat, he had early thrown in his lot with the poor and the op-

pressed, had championed such causes as abolition and woman's rights, taken part in the attempted rescue of Anthony Burns, and gone to Kansas for the Emigrant Aid Society. A Unitarian clergyman in Worcester at the outbreak of the war, he had raised and drilled a company when he was offered the colonelcy of the first colored regiment—the famous 1st South Carolina. He joined his regiment at Beaufort, sailed with it to Florida, where he raided up the St. John's River and temporarily occupied Jacksonville. Bad health and a wound forced Higginson to resign his commission in '64 and return to the North.

After the war he had a long and distinguished career in literature, writing novels, short stories, critical essays, biographies of notable literary figures, and some charming reminiscences, Cheerful Yesterdays. *It is no exaggeration to say that the best of all his many literary productions is this classic* Army Life in a Black Regiment.

Camp Saxton, near Beaufort, S. C., November 27, 1862

Thanksgiving-Day; it is the first moment I have had for writing during these three days, which have installed me into a new mode of life so thoroughly that they seem three years. Scarcely pausing in New York or in Beaufort, there seems to have been for me but one step from the camp of a Massachusetts regiment to this, and that step over leagues of waves.

It is a holiday wherever General Saxton's proclamation reaches. The chilly sunshine and the pale blue river seem like New England, but those alone. The air is full of noisy drumming, and of gunshots; for the prize-shooting is our great celebration of the day, and the drumming is chronic. My young barbarians are all at play. I look out from the broken windows of this forlorn plantation house, through avenues of great live-oaks, with their hard, shining leaves, and their branches hung with a universal drapery of soft, long moss, like fringe-trees struck with grayness. Below, the sandy soil, scantly covered with coarse grass, bristles with sharp palmettos and aloes; all the vegetation is stiff, shining, semi-tropical, with nothing soft or delicate in its texture. Numerous plantation-buildings totter around, all slovenly and unattractive, while the interspaces are filled with all manner of wreck and refuse, pigs, fowls, dogs, and omnipresent Ethiopian infancy. All this is the universal Southern panorama; but five minutes' walk beyond the hovels and the live-oaks will bring one to something so un-Southern that the whole Southern coast at this moment trembles at the suggestion of such a thing,—the camp of a regiment of freed slaves.

One adapts one's self so readily to new surroundings that already the full zest of the novelty seems passing away from my perceptions, and I write these lines in an eager effort to retain all I can. Already I am growing used to the experience, at first so novel, of living among five hundred men, and scarce a white face to be seen,—of seeing them go through all their daily processes, eating, frolicking, talking, just as if they were white. Each day at dress-parade I stand with the customary folding of the arms before a regimental line of countenances so black that I can hardly tell whether the men stand steadily or not; black is every hand which moves in ready cadences as I vociferate, "Battalion! Shoulder arms!" nor is it till the line of white officers moves forward, as parade is dismissed, that I am reminded that my own face is not the color of coal. . . .

It needs but a few days to show the absurdity of distrusting the military availability of these people. They have quite as much average comprehension as whites of the need of the thing, as much courage (I doubt not), as much previous knowledge of the gun, and, above all, a readiness of ear and of imitation, which, for purposes of drill, counterbalances any defect of mental training. To learn the drill, one does not want a set of college professors; one wants a squad of eager, active, pliant school-boys; and the more childlike these pupils are the better. There is no trouble about the drill; they will surpass whites in that. As to camp-life, they have little to sacrifice; they are better fed, housed, and clothed than ever in their lives before, and they appear to have few inconvenient vices. They are simple, docile, and affectionate almost to the point of absurdity. The same men who stood fire in open field with perfect coolness, on the late expedition, have come to me blubbering in the most irresistibly ludicrous manner on being transferred from one company in the regiment to another.

In noticing the squad-drills I perceive that the men learn less laboriously than whites that "double, double, toil and trouble," which is the elementary vexation of the drill-master,—that they more rarely mistake their left for their right,—and are more grave and sedate while under instruction. The extremes of jollity and sobriety, being greater with them, are less liable to be intermingled; these companies can be driven with a looser rein than my former one, for they restrain themselves; but the moment they are dismissed from drill every tongue is relaxed and every ivory tooth visible. This morning I wandered about where the different companies were target-shooting, and their glee was contagious. Such exulting shouts of "Ki! ole man," when some steady old turkey-shooter brought his gun down for an instant's aim, and then unerringly hit the mark; and then, when some unwary youth fired his piece into the ground at half-cock, such infinite guffawing and delight, such rolling over and over on the grass, such dances of ecstasy, as made the "Ethiopian minstrelsy" of the stage appear a feeble imitation.

December 3, 1862—7 P.M.

What a life is this I lead! It is a dark, mild, drizzling evening, and as the foggy air breeds sand-flies, so it calls out melodies and strange antics from this mysterious race of grown-up children with whom my lot is cast. All over the camp the lights glimmer in the tents, and as I sit at my desk in the open doorway, there come mingled sounds of stir and glee. Boys laugh and shout,—a feeble flute stirs somewhere in some tent, not an officer's—a drum throbs far away in another,—wild kildeer-plover flit and wail above us, like the haunting souls of dead slave-masters,—and from a neighboring cook-fire comes the monotonous sound of that strange festival, half pow-wow, half prayer-meeting, which they know only as a "shout." These fires are usually enclosed in a little booth, made neatly of palm-leaves and covered in at top, a regular native African hut, in short, such as is pictured in books, and such as I once got up from dried palm-leaves for a fair at home.

This hut is now crammed with men, singing at the top of their voices, in one of their quaint, monotonous, endless, Negro-Methodist chants, with obscure syllables recurring constantly, and slight variations interwoven, all accompanied with a regular drumming of the feet and clapping of the hands, like castanets. Then the excitement spreads: inside and outside the enclosure men begin to quiver and dance, others join, a circle forms; some "heel and toe" tumultuously, others merely tremble and stagger on, others stoop and rise, others whirl, others caper sideways, all keep steadily circling like dervishes; spectators applaud special strokes of skill; my approach only enlivens the scene; the circle enlarges, louder grows the singing, rousing shouts of encouragement come in, half bacchanalian, half devout, "Wake 'em, brudder!" "Stan' up to 'em, brudder!"—and still the ceaseless drumming and clapping, in perfect cadence, goes steadily on. Suddenly there comes a sort of *snap*, and the spell breaks, amid general singing and laughter. And this not rarely and occasionally, but night after night, while in other parts of the camp the soberest prayers and exhortations are proceeding sedately.

A simple and lovable people, whose graces seem to come by nature, and whose vices by training. Some of the best superintendents confirm the first tales of innocence, and Dr. Zachos told me last night that on his plantation, a sequestered one, "they had absolutely no vices." Nor have these men of mine yet shown any worth mentioning; since I took command I have heard of no man intoxicated, and there has been but one small quarrel. I suppose that scarcely a white regiment in the army shows so little swearing. . . . If camp regulations are violated, it seems to be usually through heedlessness. They love passionately three things besides their spiritual incantations; namely, sugar, home, and tobacco. This last affection brings tears to their eyes, almost, when they speak of their urgent need of pay; they speak of their last-remembered quid as if it were some deceased relative, too early lost, and to be mourned forever. As for sugar, no white man can drink coffee after they have sweetened it to their liking.

I see that the pride which military life creates may cause the plantation trickeries to diminish. For instance, these men make the most admirable sentinels. It is far harder to pass the camp lines at night than in the camp from which I came; and I have seen none of that disposition to connive at the offences of members of one's own company which is so troublesome among white soldiers. Nor are they lazy, either about work or drill; in all respects they seem better material for soldiers than I had dared to hope.

December 5, 1862

This evening, after working themselves up to the highest pitch, a party suddenly rushed off, got a barrel, and mounted some man upon it, who said, "Gib anoder song, boys, and I'se gib you a speech." After some hesitation and sundry shouts of "Rise de sing, somebody," and "Stan' up for Jesus, brudder," irreverently put in by the juveniles, they got upon the John Brown song, always a favorite, adding a jubilant verse which I had never before heard,—"We'll beat Beauregard on de clare battle-field." Then came the promised speech, and then no less than seven other speeches by as many men, on a variety of barrels, each orator being affectionately tugged to the pedestal and set on end by his special constituency. Every speech was good, without exception; with the queerest oddities of phrase and pronunciation, there was an invariable enthusiasm, a pungency of statement, and an understanding of the points at issue, which made them all rather thrilling. . . .

The most eloquent, perhaps, was Corporal Prince Lambkin, just arrived from Fernandina, who evidently had a previous reputation among them. His historical references were very interesting. He reminded them that he had predicted this war ever since Fremont's time, to which some of the crowd assented; he gave a very intelligent account of that Presidential campaign, and then described most impressively the secret anxiety of the slaves in Florida to know all about President Lincoln's election, and told how they all refused to work on the fourth of March, expecting their freedom to date from that day. He finally brought out one of the few really impressive appeals for the American flag that I have ever heard.

January 1, 1863 (evening)

A happy New Year to civilized people,—mere white folks. Our festival has come and gone, with perfect success, and our good General has been altogether satisfied. Last night the great fires were kept smouldering in the pit, and the beeves were cooked more or less, chiefly more,—during which time they had to be carefully watched, and the great spits turned by main force. Happy were the merry fellows who were permitted to sit up all night, and watch the glimmering flames that threw a thousand fantastic shadows among the great gnarled oaks. And such a chattering as I was sure to hear whenever I awoke that night!

My first greeting to-day was from one of the most stylish sergeants, who approached me with the following little speech, evidently the result of some elaboration:—

"I tink myself happy, dis New Year's Day, for salute my own Cunnel. Dis day las' year I was servant to a Cunnel ob Secesh; but now I hab de privilege for salute my own Cunnel."

That officer, with the utmost sincerity, reciprocated the sentiment.

About ten o'clock the people began to collect by land, and also by water,—in steamers sent by General Saxton for the purpose; and from that time all the avenues of approach were thronged. The multitude were chiefly colored women, with gay handkerchiefs on their heads, and a sprinkling of men, with that peculiarly respectable look which these people always have on Sundays and holidays. There were many white visitors also,—ladies on horseback, and in carriages, superintendents and teachers, officers, and cavalry-men. Our companies were marched to the neighborhood of the platform, and allowed to sit or stand, as at the Sunday services; the platform was occupied by ladies and dignitaries, and by the band of the Eighth Maine, which kindly volunteered for the occasion; the colored people filled up all the vacant openings in the beautiful grove around, and there was a cordon of mounted visitors beyond. Above, the great live-oak branches and their trailing moss; beyond the people, a glimpse of the blue river.

The services began at halfpast eleven o'clock, with prayer by our chaplain, Mr. Fowler, who is always, on such occasions, simple, reverential, and impressive. Then the President's Proclamation was read by Dr. W. H. Brisbane, a thing infinitely appropriate; a South Carolinian addressing South Carolinians; for he was reared among these very islands, and here long since emancipated his own slaves. Then the colors were presented to us by the Rev. Mr. French, a chaplain who brought them from the donors in New York. All this was according to the programme. Then followed an incident so simple, so touching, so utterly unexpected and startling, that I can scarcely believe it on recalling, though it gave the key-note to the whole day. The very moment the speaker had ceased, and just as I took and waved the flag, which now for the first time meant anything to these poor people, there suddenly arose, close beside the platform, a strong male voice (but rather cracked and elderly), into which two women's voices instantly blended, singing, as if by an impulse that could no more be repressed than the morning note of the song-sparrow.—

> "My Country, 't is of thee,
> Sweet land of liberty,
> Of thee I sing!"

People looked at each other, and then at us on the platform, to see whence came this interruption, not set down in the bills. Firmly and irrepressibly the quavering voices sang on, verse after verse; others of the colored people joined in; some whites on the platform began, but I motioned them to silence. I never saw anything so electric; it made all other words cheap; it seemed the choked voice of a race at last unloosed. Nothing could be more wonderfully unconscious; art could not have dreamed of a tribute to the day of jubilee that should be so affecting; history will not believe it; and when I came to speak of it, after it was ended, tears were everywhere. If you could have heard how quaint and innocent it was! Old Tiff and his children might have sung it; and close before me was a little slave-boy, almost white, who seemed to belong to the party, and even he must join in. Just think of it!—the first day they had ever had a country, the first flag they had ever seen which promised anything to their people, and here, while mere spectators stood in silence, waiting for my stupid words, these simple souls burst out in their lay, as if they were by their own hearths at home! When they stopped, there was nothing to do for it but to speak, and I went on; but the life of the whole day was in those unknown people's song.

—Higginson, *Army Life in a Black Regiment*

12. REBEL AND YANKEE YELLS

We hear a great deal about the Rebel Yell, though no two people seem agreed on just what it was, or even on its origin. It has been variously described as "more overpowering than the cannon's roar" and "a mingling of Indian whoop and wolf-howl"; it was probably born of the hunting field. There is far less information on the Yankee Yell; this was undoubtedly something that varied greatly from army to army.

Harvie Dew was a member of the 9th Virginia Cavalry, attached to Stuart.

THAT there existed a marked difference between the yells of the opposing armies during our late war was a recognized fact, and a frequent source of comment. The notes and tones peculiar to each of them were well defined, and led to their designation as the "Yankee" and the "Rebel" yells. . . .

The Federal, or "Yankee," yell, compared with that of the Confederate, lacked in vocal breadth, pitch, and resonance. This was unquestionably attributable to the fact that the soldiery of the North was drawn and recruited chiefly from large cities and towns, from factory districts, and from the more densely settled portions of the country.

Their surroundings, their circumstances of life and employment, had the effect of molding the character and temperament of the people, and at the same time of restraining their vocal development. People living and working in close proximity to one another have no absolute need for loud or strained vocal efforts, and any screaming or prolonged calling becomes seriously annoying to neighbors. Consequently, all such liberties or inconsiderate indulgences in cities, towns, etc., have long ago been discouraged by common consent. . . .

To afford some idea of the difference between these "yells," I will relate an incident which occurred in battle on the plains at Brandy Station, Virginia, in the fall of 1863. Our command was in full pursuit of a portion of Kilpatrick's cavalry. We soon approached their reserves (ours some distance behind), and found ourselves facing a battery of artillery with a regiment of cavalry drawn up on each side. A point of woods projected to the left of their position. We were ordered to move by the right flank till the woods protected us from the battery, and then, in open field, within a few hundred yards of the enemy, we were ordered to halt and right dress.

In a moment more one of the Federal regiments was ordered to charge, and down they came upon us in a body two or three times outnumbering ours. Then was heard their peculiar characteristic yell—"Hoo-ray! Hoo-ray! Hoo-ray!" etc. (This yell was called by the Federals a "cheer," and was intended for the word "hurrah," but that pronunciation I never heard in a charge. The sound was as though the first syllable, if heard at all, was "hoo," uttered with an exceedingly short, low, and indistinct tone, and the second was "ray," yelled with a long and high tone slightly deflecting at its termination. In many instances the yell seemed to be the simple interjection "heigh," rendered with the same tone which was given to "ray.")

Our command was alone in the field, and it seemed impossible for us to withstand the coming shock; but our commander, as brave an officer as ever drew a saber, frequently repeated, as the charging column approached us, his precautionary orders, to "Keep steady, boys! Keep steady!" and so we remained till the Federals were within a hundred yards of us. Then, waving his sword in air, he gave the final order, loud enough to be heard the field over: "Now is your time, boys! Give them the saber! Charge them, men! Charge!"

In an instant every voice with one accord vigorously shouted that "Rebel yell," which was so often heard on the field of battle. "Woh-who-ey! who-ey! who-ey! Woh-who-ey! who-ey!" etc. (The best illustration of this "true yell" which can be given the reader is by spelling it as above, with directions to sound the first syllable "woh" short and low, and the second "who" with a very high and prolonged note deflecting upon the third syllable "ey.")

A moment or two later the Federal column wavered and broke. In pursuit we chased them to within twenty feet of their battery, which had already begun to retreat. The second regiment to the right and rear of the battery then charged upon us, and for a moment we were forced back; but by that time our reserves were up, and we swept the field.

—Dew, "The Yankee and Rebel Yells"

13. DEATH ON THE BATTLEFIELD

There are many descriptions of death in battle, but few more graphic than this from the pen of Henry Blake describing the aftermath of the minor Battle of Williamsburg, on the Peninsula. Blake was a captain in the 11th Massachusetts Volunteers who served all through the war from First Bull Run to the Wilderness.

THE storm continued after the deadly struggle was ended; but it was not heeded by those who had battled from morning till night. In these hours of rest for the wearied, the non-combatants of the army, the members of the supply departments and ambulance corps, clerks, teamsters, musicians, and stragglers, who remain in the rear in time of action, visited the field, plundered the dead of both armies, and rifled the knapsacks of those who had fought while they were asleep. The sun rose in a cloudless sky upon the 6th [May]; but the enemy, having saved their trains had fled; and Williamsburg was occupied without opposition. Seven cannon had been abandoned, because the horses could not extricate them from the mud; and shot and shell were scattered in the road. The guns had been spiked; dishes, pans, kettles, and Dutch ovens, were demolished in the camps and redoubts; and packs of playing cards had been thrown into the streets of the town.

The soldiers visited every portion of the field to search for wounded or dead comrades, and witnessed without emotion scenes which lost their horror on account of their frequency; and, in many cases in which the death had been instantaneous, the attitude of the slain indicated the last act of their lives. The adjutant of a New-Jersey regiment was shot while he was resting upon one knee, and glancing towards the advancing line of the enemy through a field glass; but his limbs had not relaxed. Many hands, in every motion of loading and firing, clutched with the firm hand of death the rammer, gun, or cartridge. I noticed that a number of the dead of the Union army had been mutilated by bowie-knives, made of large, coarse files which the rebels carried in their sheaths; and gashes disfigured the heads and faces. The brief experience of a single engagement satisfied men of the uselessness of revolvers or dirks for the purposes of war, and they disappeared from both armies. Nearly one hundred of the enemy, in one part of the woods, had been killed while they were lying upon the ground; and the bullets had penetrated their foreheads. Some, who had lived a few hours after they were wounded, grasped photographs or letters, upon which their dying eyes rested when the thoughts of cherished and happy homes banished suffering.

Some of the cartridges used by the foe contained no bullet, but consisted of twelve buckshot. The pockets of friend and enemy had been turned inside out by the army thieves . . . and the buttons of the uniforms of every traitor had been removed. "I wish there was a battle every week," one of those miscreants remarked, in speaking of the amount he had stolen.

In wandering over the field, a corporal found in the pocket of a rebel a piece of tobacco upon which the blood had been coagulated, and the professional army thief had not touched it; but he washed the article, took a "chaw," and reserved the rest for future consumption. Head-boards were erected over the graves of the Union soldiers by their comrades, and the corpses of the enemy were buried by fatigue-parties; and the spot upon which they died was their last resting-place upon the earth. Details interred the horses, large numbers of which had been killed. The woods and abattis upon the battle-field were burned for sanitary reasons; and the unexploded shells which had been thrown during the conflict were continually bursting in the flames. A surgeon ordered the pioneers to dig the grave for an unconscious and wounded rebel, who was supposed to be dying; but the general sent him to the hospital, and he lived.

—BLAKE, *Three Years in the Army of the Potomac*

X

From Fort Donelson to Stones River

WHILE *the war in the East surged back and forth between Washington and Richmond, the Chesapeake Bay and the Valley, the war in the West raged and burned over an enormous territory, from Missouri to the Gulf, from the Alleghenies to the Mississippi, with great outcroppings in Missouri, Arkansas, Louisiana, and even in Texas and New Mexico. Nor is it to be forgotten that the heaviest blows of the war in the East were directed, in the end, from the Western theater, Sherman carrying the war to Georgia and the Carolinas.*

Not only were the geographical circumstances of the war in the West profoundly different from those in the East, the strategic objectives, too, were different. The objectives of fighting in Virginia and Maryland were the capture of the rival capitals and the destruction of the rival armies. The war in the West was of necessity directed to different ends. There was, first, the control of the belt of border states—Kentucky and Missouri—and of eastern Tennessee, heavily Unionist in sentiment and commanding the approaches to the East and the South. There was, second, control of the great arteries of commerce: the Mississippi, the Cumberland, Tennessee, and Red rivers, and the railroads which connected the deep South with the Atlantic coast, the border states with the Gulf. The greatest strategical objective was, of course, control of the Mississippi River, and the separation of the Trans-Mississippi West from the rest of the Confederacy. Almost all the major battles of the Western theater involved some strategic point on some river or railroad: Fort Donelson, Island No. 10, Shiloh, Murfreesboro, Vicksburg, Port Hudson, Chattanooga, and others. The otherwise confusing cavalry raids, too, fall into a logical pattern when we see them against the background of lines of communication; and the cavalry leaders of the Western armies— men like Forrest and Morgan and Grierson—played a very different role from Eastern cavalry leaders like Stuart and Buford.

Most of the campaigns of the West involved control of rivers or railroads. There was one prolonged campaign for the control of the Mississippi—a campaign that began with the minor Battle of Belmont and was concluded with the fall of Port Hudson. A second was directed to the first Confederate line of defense—the line stretching from Columbus to Forts Henry and Donelson and to Bowling Green. A third was directed to the second Confederate line of defense—Memphis to Corinth to Chattanooga. The fourth major campaign—that of Chickamauga and Chattanooga—was for the gateway to Georgia, and was followed by the fifth—the campaign for Atlanta and the march from Atlanta to the sea. There were, to be sure, other campaigns, for different objectives. The confused series of campaigns for Kentucky and eastern Tennessee were directed as much to political as to military or economic ends; the fighting in the Trans-Mississippi area, too, was for the allegiance of that area.

The struggle in the West began at St. Louis and the region to the south. If the Confederates could win Missouri, and above all St. Louis, they could strike into the very heart of the Union—through Illinois and Indiana. As early as July 1861 General Hardee ordered Pillow to reinforce New Madrid on the Missouri side of the Mississippi and Columbus on the Kentucky side; if these could be held it would be easy to mount an offensive toward Cairo at the southern tip of Illinois. Frémont, then in command in Missouri, promptly ordered Brigadier General Grant to go to Cape Girardeau, take command of all the troops in the vicinity of the mouth of the Ohio, strengthen Cairo, and drive the Confederates away from the river. It was a big order. For meantime Pillow had built up a force of almost 15,000 men at Columbus, and was preparing to move either across the river into Missouri or up the river toward Illinois. And meantime, too, the Confederates had built up their defenses at Forts Henry and Donelson on the Tennessee and Cumberland rivers, and General Albert Sidney Johnston had sent Buckner to Bowling Green, threatening Louisville. The Confederates had established their first line of defense; could the Federals break it?

1. U. S. GRANT APPLIES FOR A JOB

Grant was working in his father's store in Galena, Illinois, when the war broke out. A West Pointer, he had made a good record in the Mexican War, and then seen service on distant frontier posts until, in 1854, he had resigned from the army, probably under pressure. With the outbreak of the war he applied for appointments from the Governor of Illinois and probably from the Governor of Ohio, tried to get an appointment under McClellan, who ignored him, and worked in the state adjutant general's office. His application to the adjutant general at Washington was ignored. Finally, in June, Governor Yates appointed him colonel of an unruly regiment, the 21st Illinois. Two months later, somewhat to his surprise, he was made brigadier general.

Galena, Illinois, May 24, 1861

Col. L. Thomas
Adjt. Gen. U. S. A.

Sir:—Having served for fifteen years in the regular army, including four years at West Point, and feeling it the duty of every one who has been educated at the Government expense to offer their services for the support of that Government, I have the honor, very respectfully, to tender my services, until the close of the war, in such capacity as may be offered. I would say, in view of my present age and length of service, I feel myself competent to command a regiment, if the President, in his judgment, should see fit to intrust one to me.

Since the first call of the President I have been serving on the staff of the Governor of this State, rendering such aid as I could in the organization of our State militia, and am still engaged in that capacity. A letter addressed to me at Springfield, Illinois, will reach me.

I am very respectfully,

Your obt. svt.,

U. S. GRANT.

—Personal Memoirs of U. S. Grant

2. GRANT WINS HIS SPURS AT BELMONT

After whipping his regiment into shape Grant took it to Missouri, then under the command of John C. Frémont, whose only claim to military ability was his record as an explorer. Frémont was trying, with no great success, to hold Missouri for the Union. Meantime Pillow had built up a strong force at Columbus, just south of Cairo; from Columbus he could not only block the Mississippi but threaten Paducah at the mouth of the Tennessee, Cairo at the junction of the Ohio and the Mississippi, or advance into Missouri to support the Confederates there. To forestall these moves Grant fortified Cairo, then pounced on Paducah; then he asked and obtained permission to make a demonstration against Columbus. Lacking strength for a direct attack he selected instead the little village of Belmont, opposite the great fort, where Pillow had a force of some 2,500 men. Belmont was a minor affair, and it was not very clearly a victory, but it brought Grant recognition.

AUTUMN glided away; the leaves were dropping along the banks of the Potomac and the Ohio; the fairest season of the year would soon be gone. It was a period of disaster and inaction. . . . Grant meantime was busily employed in drilling new troops at Cairo, and probably in wondering why they were not made use of. He always believed that where both sides are equally undisciplined the most active would be the most successful. He saw Columbus grow into an impregnable fortress under the care of Pillow and Polk; he heard that the Tennessee and the Cumberland were to be closed by new fortifications; and he asked his superior officer at St. Louis, Fremont, to be allowed to take Columbus (September 10) while it was yet assailable. At length (November 1, 1861) he received orders to make a demonstration against the fortress, to prevent the enemy from sending reinforcements to their general, Price, in Missouri. Grant resolved finally to turn the movement into an actual attack on Belmont.

Columbus rises on a high bluff above the Mississippi on the Kentucky shore. It was now so strongly fortified as to be quite impregnable; armies might have wasted their strength against its lofty bluff for months without result; its long range of heavy cannon closed up the navigation of the river; and a large force of the enemy filled its walls. But it was Belmont, a post on

The Campaigns in Tennessee and Kentucky

the opposite side of the Mississippi, under the guns of Columbus, that Grant meant to threaten or assail. Here a considerable force of rebels had formed their camp, defended by rough lines of felled trees and the fire of Columbus; and it was here that the reinforcements were chiefly ferried over the river to aid Price in Missouri. Grant's aim was to destroy their camp, disperse their troops, and then return to Cairo. He would thus practice his new levies, and at the same time alarm the enemy.

No sooner did the brave Western soldiers at Cairo learn that a real attack was to be made than all was exultation and excitement. They rejoiced to be relieved from the dull monotony of camp-life, and to test their courage in the fierce trial of actual combat. Grant ordered General Smith from Paducah to make a demonstration against Columbus, to employ the enemy's attention on that side of the river, while he himself set out for Missouri. His troops, it should be remembered, were all untried men. His two chief commanders, Logan and M'Clernand, had never heard a shot fired in actual battle, and Grant stood alone in the midst of a brave but inexperienced army. His force numbered about thirty-one hundred men.

After several feints he landed his troops from transports at Hunter's Point, in Missouri, and marched at once against Belmont, about three miles below. The enemy were soon found, and the brave troops, advancing as skirmishers, threw themselves against the rude defenses; the officers behaved like veterans, always in the front of the battle; the soldiers climbed, crept, or sprang over the strong abatis; the enemy were slowly driven back to the shore. Pillow, who had crossed over with reinforcements from Columbus, was forced to give way, and the disordered and broken force, larger in numbers than the assailants, took refuge under the river bank and the fire of Columbus.

A strange scene followed. Grant's troops, carried away by the joy of the moment, having taken several hundred prisoners and the enemy's camp, broke into disorder. Speeches were delivered by excited orators; the captured camp was plundered; in the midst of their enemies the inexperienced soldiers believed themselves secure. Grant ordered the camp to be set on fire to drive the troops to their ranks, and suddenly the heavy guns of Columbus opened upon the Union army. Meanwhile large bodies of rebels had crossed the river, and with the aid of Pillow's men had surrounded their late victors.

A startled aid-de-camp, riding up to Grant, exclaimed in alarm, "General, we are surrounded!"

"Well," said he, "we must cut our way out as we cut our way in."

His calmness reassured his little army, and with Grant, M'Clernand, and Logan at their head, they broke through the enemy's line and passed in good order to the landing. Here the whole force was safely embarked, with but slight loss. Grant acted as his own rear-guard, was the last man on the shore, and at one time found himself not more than one hundred and fifty feet from a line of the enemy. He paused a moment to survey them, then turned his horse's head, rode slowly away, and finally broke into a gallop as he approached the river. He made his way with difficulty upon one of the transports, and then the little flotilla moved on under a heavy fire of musketry from the shore. By five o'clock the last vessel was beyond reach of the enemy, and the successful expedition arrived safely at Cairo.

—EUGENE LAWRENCE, "Grant on the Battle-Field"

3. U. S. GRANT BECOMES UNCONDITIONAL SURRENDER GRANT

Grant had already forestalled a Confederate advance down the Tennessee to the Ohio by seizing Paducah. Now he proposed to General Halleck, who had succeeded the incompetent Frémont, an attack on the bastions of Forts Henry and Donelson. The reduction of these forts would not only clear two great rivers, the Tennessee and the Cumberland, but cut the Confederate line of defense from Columbus to Bowling Green, Kentucky, and force the Confederates to retire from Kentucky to Tennessee. After a good deal of prodding Halleck authorized a joint attack on the forts by Grant and Commodore Foote, the latter to blast the forts from his gunboats. Early in February 1862 Grant's army of 17,000 men advanced on Fort Henry. Meantime the gunboats had already reached the fort, which was promptly abandoned, its small defending force marching overland to the much larger and stronger Fort Donelson.

Here is Grant's own story of how he forced the surrender of this fort. As he makes clear, the surrender was quite unnecessary; the Confederates could have withstood a long siege, or they could have fought their way out— as Forrest did. The capture of these two forts, coming on the heels of the Belmont affair, gave Grant a national reputation and brought him a major generalship.

I WAS very impatient to get to Fort Donelson because I knew the importance of the place to the enemy and supposed he would reinforce it rapidly. I felt that 15,000 men on the 8th would be more effective than 50,000 a month later. I asked Flag-officer Foote, therefore, to order his gunboats still about Cairo to proceed up the Cumberland River and not to wait for those gone to Eastport and Florence; but the others got back in time and we started on the 12th [February 1862]. I had moved McClernand out a few miles the night before so as to leave the road as free as possible. . . .

I started from Fort Henry with 15,000 men, including eight batteries and part of a regiment of cavalry, and, meeting with no obstruction to detain us, the advance arrived in front of the enemy by noon. That afternoon and the next day were spent in taking up ground to make the investment as complete as possible. General Smith had been directed to leave a portion of his division behind to guard forts Henry and Heiman. He left General Lew. Wallace with 2,500 men. With the remainder of his division he occupied our left, extending to Hickman creek. McClernand was on the right and covered the roads running south and south-west from Dover. His right extended to the backwater up the ravine opening into the [Cumberland] south of the village. The troops were not intrenched, but the nature of the ground was such that they were just as well protected from the fire of the enemy as if rifle-pits had been thrown up. Our line was generally along the crest of ridges. The artillery was protected by being sunk in the ground. The men who were not serving the guns were perfectly covered from fire on taking position a little back from the crest. The greatest suffering was from want of shelter. It was midwinter and during the siege we had rain and snow, thawing and freezing alternately. It would not do to allow camp-fires except far down the hill out of sight of the enemy, and it would not do to allow many of the troops to remain there at the same time. In the march over from Fort Henry numbers of the men had thrown away their blankets and overcoats. There was therefore much discomfort and absolute suffering.

During the 12th and 13th, and until the arrival of Wallace and Thayer on the 14th, the National forces, composed of but 15,000 men, without intrenchments, confronted an intrenched army of 21,000 without conflict further than what was brought on by ourselves. Only one gunboat had arrived. There was a little skirmishing each day, brought on by the movement of our troops in securing commanding positions; but there was no actual fighting during this time except once, on the 13th, in front of McClernand's command. That general had undertaken to capture a battery of the enemy which was annoying his men. Without orders or authority he sent three regiments to make the assault. The battery was in the main line of the enemy, which was defended by his whole army present. Of course the assault was a failure, and of course the loss on our side was great for the number of men engaged. In this assault Colonel William Morrison fell badly wounded. Up to this time the surgeons with the army had no difficulty in finding room in the houses near our line for all the sick and wounded; but now hospitals were overcrowded. Owing, however, to the energy and skill of the surgeons the suffering was not so great as it might have been. The hospital arrangements at Fort Donelson were as complete as it was possible to make them, considering the inclemency of the weather and the lack of tents, in a sparsely settled country where the houses were generally of but one or two rooms.

On the return of Captain Walke to Fort Henry on the 10th, I had requested him to take the vessels that had accompanied him on his expedition up the Tennessee, and get possession of the Cumberland as far up towards Donelson as possible. He started without delay, taking, however, only his own gunboat, the *Carondelet*, towed by the steamer *Alps*. Captain Walke arrived a few miles below Donelson on the 12th, a little after noon. About the time the advance of troops reached a point within gunshot of the fort on the land side, he engaged the water batteries at long range. On the 13th I informed him of my arrival the day before and of the establishment of most of our batteries, requesting him at the same time to attack that day so that I might take advantage of any diversion. The attack was made and many shots fell within the fort, creating some consternation, as we now know. The investment on the land side was made as complete as the number of troops engaged would admit of. . . .

Confederate Camp in Virginia

Edwin Forbes

Pulling Artillery into Position, Army of the Potomac

The plan was for the troops to hold the enemy within his lines, while the gunboats should attack the water-batteries at close quarters and silence his guns if possible. Some of the gunboats were to run the batteries, get above the fort and above the village of Dover. I had ordered a reconnaissance made with the view of getting troops to the river above Dover in case they should be needed there. That position attained by the gunboats it would have been but a question of time—and a very short time, too—when the garrison would have been compelled to surrender.

By three in the afternoon of the 14th Flag-officer Foote was ready, and advanced upon the water batteries with his entire fleet. After coming in range of the batteries of the enemy the advance was slow, but a constant fire was delivered from every gun that could be brought to bear upon the fort. I occupied a position on shore from which I could see the advancing navy. The leading boat got within a very short distance of the water battery, not further off I think than two hundred yards, and I soon saw one and then another of them dropping down the river, visibly disabled. Then the whole fleet followed and the engagement was closed for the day. The gunboat which Flag-officer Foote was on, besides having been hit about sixty times, several of the shots passing through near the water-line, had a shot enter the pilot-house which killed the pilot, carried away the wheel, and wounded the flag-officer himself. The tiller-ropes of another vessel were carried away, and she, too, dropped helplessly back. Two others had their pilot-houses so injured that they scarcely formed a protection to the men at the wheel.

The enemy had evidently been much demoralized by the assault, but they were jubilant when they saw the disabled vessels dropping down the river entirely out of the control of the men on board. Of course I only witnessed the falling back of our gunboats and felt sad enough at the time over the repulse. Subsequent reports, now published, show that the enemy telegraphed a great victory to Richmond. The sun went down on the night of the 14th of February, 1862, leaving the army confronting Fort Donelson anything but comforted over the prospects. The weather had turned intensely cold; the men were without tents and could not keep up fires where most of them had to stay; and, as previously stated, many had thrown away their overcoats and blankets. Two of the strongest of our gunboats had been disabled, presumably beyond the possibility of rendering any present assistance. I retired this night not knowing but that I would have to intrench my position, and bring up tents for the men or build huts under the cover of the hills.

On the morning of the 15th, before it was yet broad day, a messenger from Flag-officer Foote handed me a note, expressing a desire to see me on the flag-ship and saying that he had been injured the day before so much that he could not come himself to me. I at once made my preparations for starting. . . .

When I reached the fleet I found the flag-ship was anchored out in the stream. A small boat, however, awaited my arrival and I was soon on board with the flag-officer. He explained to me in short the condition in which he was left by the engagement of the evening before, and suggested that I should intrench while he returned to Mound City with his disabled boats, expressing at the time the belief that he could have the necessary repairs made and be back in ten days. I saw the absolute necessity of his gunboats going into hospital, and did not know but I should be forced to the alternative of going through a siege. But the enemy relieved me from this necessity.

When I left the National line to visit Flag-officer Foote I had no idea that there would be any engagement on land unless I brought it on myself. The conditions for battle were much more favorable to us than they had been for the first two days of the investment. From the 12th to the 14th we had but 15,000 men of all arms and no gunboats. Now we had been reinforced by a fleet of six naval vessels, a large division of troops under General L. Wallace and 2,500 men brought over from Fort Henry belonging to the division of C. F. Smith. The enemy, however, had taken the initiative. Just as I landed I met Captain Hillyer of my staff, white with fear, not for his personal safety, but for the safety of the National troops. He said the enemy had come out of his lines in full force and attacked and scattered Mc-Clernand's division, which was in full retreat. The roads, as I have said, were unfit for making fast time, but I got to my command as soon as possible. The attack had been made on the National right. I was some four or five miles north of our left. The line was about three miles long. In reaching the point where the disaster had occurred I had to pass the divisions of Smith and Wallace. I saw no sign of excitement on the portion of the line held by Smith; Wallace was nearer the scene of conflict and had taken part in it. He had, at an opportune time, sent Thayer's brigade to the support of Mc-Clernand and thereby contributed to hold the enemy within his lines.

I saw everything favorable for us along the line of our left and center. When I came to the right appearances were different. The enemy had come out in full force to cut his way out and make his escape. McClernand's division had to bear the brunt of the attack from this combined force. His men had stood up gallantly until the ammunition in their cartridge-boxes gave out. There was abundance of ammunition near by lying on the ground in boxes, but at that stage of the war it was not all of our commanders of regiments, brigades, or even divisions, who had been educated up to the point of seeing that their men were constantly supplied with ammunition during an engagement. When the men found themselves without ammunition they could not stand up against troops who seemed to have plenty of it. The division broke and a portion fled, but most of the men, as they were not pursued, only fell back out of range of the fire of the enemy. It must have been about this time that Thayer pushed his brigade in between the enemy and those of our troops that were without ammunition. At all events, the enemy fell back within his intrenchments and was there when I got on the field.

I saw the men standing in knots talking in the most excited manner. No officer seemed to be giving any directions. The soldiers had their muskets, but no ammunition, while there were tons of it close at hand. I heard some of the men say that the enemy had come out with knapsacks, and haversacks filled with rations. They seemed to think this indicated a determination on his part to stay out and fight just as long as the provisions held out. I turned to Colonel J. D. Webster, of my staff, who was with me, and said: "Some of our men are pretty badly demoralized, but the enemy must be more so, for he has attempted to force his way out, but has fallen back: the one who attacks first now will be victorious and the enemy will have to be in a hurry if he gets ahead of me." I determined to make the assault at once on our left. It was clear to my mind that the enemy had started to march out with his entire force, except a few pickets, and if our attack could be made on the left before the enemy could redistribute his forces along the line, we would find little opposition except from the intervening abatis. I directed Colonel Webster to ride with me and call out to the men as we passed: "Fill your cartridge-boxes, quick, and get into line; the enemy is trying to escape, and he must not be permitted to do so." This acted like a charm. The men only wanted someone to give them a command. We rode rapidly to Smith's quarters, when I explained the situation to him and directed him to charge the enemy's works in his front with his whole division, saying at the same time that he would find nothing but a very thin line to contend with. The general was off in an incredibly short time, going in advance himself to keep his men from firing while they were working their way through the abatis intervening between them and the enemy. The outer line of rifle-pits was passed, and the night of the 15th General Smith, with much of his division, bivouacked within the lines of the enemy. There was now no doubt but that the Confederates must surrender or be captured the next day. . . .

A council of war was held by the enemy at which all agreed that it would be impossible to hold out longer. General Buckner, who was third in rank in the garrison but much the most capable soldier, seems to have regarded it a duty to hold the fort until the general commanding the department, A. S. Johnston, should get back to his headquarters at Nashville. Buckner's report shows, however, that he considered Donelson lost and that any attempt to hold the place longer would be at the sacrifice of the command. Being assured that Johnston was already in Nashville, Buckner too agreed that surrender was the proper thing. Floyd turned over the command to Pillow, who declined it. It then devolved upon Buckner, who accepted the responsibility of the position. Floyd and Pillow took possession of all the river transports at Dover and before morning both were on their way to Nashville, with the brigade formerly commanded by Floyd and some other troops, in all about 3,000. Some marched up the east bank of the Cumberland; others went on the steamers. During the night Forrest also, with his cavalry and some other troops, about a thousand in all, made their way out, passing between our right and the river. They had to ford or swim over the back-water in the little creek just south of Dover.

Before daylight General Smith brought to me the following letter from General Buckner:

Headquarters, Fort Donelson,
February 16, 1862.

Sir:—In consideration of all the circumstances governing the present situation of affairs at this station, I propose to the Commanding Officer of the Federal forces the appointment of Commissioners to agree upon terms of capitulation of the forces and fort under my command, and in that view suggest an armistice until 12 o'clock to-day.

I am, sir, very respectfully,

Your ob't se'v't,
S. B. BUCKNER
Brig. Gen. C. S. A.

To this I responded as follows:

Headquarters Army in the Field,
Camp near Donelson,
February 16, 1862.

General S. B. Buckner,
Confederate Army.

Sir:—Yours of this date, proposing armistice and appointment of Commissioners to settle terms of capitulation, is just received. No terms except an unconditional and immediate surrender can be accepted. I propose to move immediately upon your works.

I am, sir, very respectfully,

Your ob't se'v't,
U. S. GRANT
Brig. Gen.

To this I received the following reply:

Headquarters, Dover, Tennessee,
February 16, 1862.

To Brig. Gen'l U. S. Grant,
U. S. Army.

Sir:—The distribution of the forces under my command, incident to an unexpected change of commanders, and the overwhelming force under your command, compel me, notwithstanding the brilliant success of the Confederate arms yesterday, to accept the ungenerous and unchivalrous terms which you propose.

I am, sir,

Your very ob't se'v't,
S. B. BUCKNER
Brig. Gen. C. S. A.

. . . I had been at West Point three years with Buckner and afterwards served with him in the army, so that we were quite well acquainted. In the course of our conversation, which was very friendly, he said to me that if he had been in command I would not have got up to Donelson as easily as I did. I told him that if he had been in command I should not have tried in the way I did: I had invested their lines with a smaller force than they had to defend them, and at the same time had sent a brigade full 5,000 strong, around by water; I had relied very much upon their commander to allow me to come safely up to the outside of their works.

—Personal Memoirs of U. S. Grant

4. GENERAL POPE CAPTURES NEW MADRID

The fall of Forts Henry and Donelson forced the Confederates back on their second line of defense. Johnston withdrew to Murfreesboro, in Tennessee, and prepared to fall back to Corinth. Polk gave up Columbus but was ordered to hold on to New Madrid and Island No. 10 in the great bend of the Mississippi at the juncture of Missouri, Arkansas, Kentucky and Tennessee. New Madrid was vulnerable from land, but Island No. 10 was almost impregnable.

On March 3 General Pope advanced on New Madrid with 20,000 men; by cutting off access to it he succeeded in starving it into submission in ten days. There was some sharp fighting in the final assault, but the battle was a minor affair.

Far more spectacular was the reduction of Island No. 10. As there was no direct approach to the island by land, Pope cut a channel through the great bend north of the island and ferried his army to Point Pleasant below Island No. 10. Meantime Commodore Foote's gunboats, Commander Walke's Carondelet in the lead, ran the batteries of the island. Isolated, the Confederates tried to evacuate their forts, but were cut off and forced to surrender 7,000 men and 123 heavy guns on April 7. These two victories gave Pope a reputation which he shortly lost in the East.

Colonel Gilbert, who here describes the Battle of New Madrid, was a Cincinnati engineeer who helped organize the 39th Ohio Volunteers.

In Camp New Madrid (Mo.)
March 14 1862

My dear Wife

"Glory to God in the highest & on earth peace & good will to men—glory to God for the signal & complete victory that has crowned our arms in the recent conflict with rebellious villains at New Madrid & peace & good will to men which I do hope is soon to follow such successes all over our country. On yesterday morning we arose at 2 oclk & prepared breakfast & at 4 oclk we passed from our Camp into the outer darkness on our way to the battle ground. This time I *knew* we were going into the fight & certainly felt as if it were possible that I might never get back alive. On this occasion I had to part from our good Dr Nixon; I had always had him with me before on all occasions & now he would no more be by my side.

Before daylight we arrived on the ground selected for the battle & in the grey morning took silently our respective positions in order of battle.

The night previous the sappers & miners were engaged all night in placing the heavy guns intended to silence the Gunboats as well as the guns of the Fort. The battery was placed so quietly by our men that the pickets of the enemy stationed within less than three hundred yards were not aware of its being done & when our regiments came up to their positions to support the battery we were fired upon & it was then the grey of the morning & the guns of our battery replied much doubtless to the consternation of said pickets. We took them completely by surprize, the gun boats had no steam up & it was some time before they got into position.

The 39th was given the position of honor & of greatest danger being on the extreme right, that is in the advance of all & our boys behaved splendidly. Gen Pope & all the generals under him paid us the highest compliments. We were under fire of shot & shell for twelve mortal hours & wonderful to say only one man in our whole regiment was wounded & he only a slight round shot. I suppose 300 or 400 shot & large shells passed within thirty to forty feet of our men during the day. The cannonading & bursting of bombs was like continuous peals of thunder. The whizzing of the balls & shell was very peculiar & caused involuntary dodging all around &, notwithstanding the real danger we were constantly in, it was a constant source of amusement & merriment amongst the men. . . . Our business was to lay perfectly still in the position in which we were placed & be ready at any time to repel an attack upon the battery & in consequence our men *lay* on the ground the whole day, none being allowed to rise except for reasonable purposes.

The hair breadth escapes were very numerous. I can only say that a large round shell took off a mans haversack & bent his bayonet hanging by his side without touching the man; another man laying on the ground with his knapsack strapped to his back had a 32 lb shot pop right on his back & bounce off without doing more than knock his breath out of his body *for a time*—the ball of course was nearly spent. A 24 lb shot passed within 18 inches of my head & ploughed into the ground 20 ft beyond me. I was sitting down at the time. The large & small balls bounced about just as if some of the great powers were playing a game of foot ball & the bombs burst over & around us until we really got to regard them more as if it was a pyrotechnic display, than if they were instruments of death, sent from a malignant & treacherous enemy. The enemy got our range very correctly & fired all day right to our position, but we were wonderfully preserved.

I got at one time upon a high stump & with my glass commenced looking all along the levee some 1200 yards off for the position of the gun boats & had not more than got down on the ground than bang bang went the heavy guns from one of the gun boats & the shot & shell came whirling right over head & some 20 shots were fired right in our direction showing that I had been seen by the enemy with their glasses.

A large shot came bounding along the ground in the early part of the day & passing us went right in to the ranks of the 27 Ohio who were on our left & took off the legs of three men & stopped right there as if tired. Another large 32 lb shot struck a large log behind which an officer had just dodged &

bounced up in the air about fifty feet looking like a great foot ball. At times the shot could be distinctly seen as they came along and easily dodged.

When night came on we were ordered to remain on the field in just the same position with the strictest injunctions against either sleeping or allowing a single man to sleep & we prepared to pass the night as best we could. I sent my man to camp for my rubber blanket & buffalo & stood up against a tree most of the night. At about 12 oclk a most terrific rain & thunder storm came on & Heavens artillery outdid in noise that of the day. It was a singular sight to see by the glare of the lightning which was very bright to see two thousand men standing up with their blankets on being thoroughly drenchd in the rain.

At daylight we were relieved & marchd back to camp where we had hardly arrived when we heard loud & continuous cheering in the direction of the Fort & after a while we learned that the enemy had evacuated the place leaving a large amt of stores, tents, 500 head of horses & mules, some 20 or 30 large guns besides many stores in the levee & ample supplies of ammunition—everything in fact was abandoned last night in the greatest confusion & we found we had done them terrible damage yesterday. One or two gun boats very much disabled, guns in the fort badly knocked about & there is no doubt they were terribly frightened at seeing us remain on the field of battle all night lest we should storm their works. They must have had 11000 men. . . . They left tents sufficient for 10,000 men & everything else in proportion.

It is one of the most thorough & complete victories we have had & with very little loss of life. The generalship displayed by Genl Pope is entitled to all praise. I am very tired. Good night

ALFRED

—COLONEL A. W. GILBERT, Letter to His Wife

5. HENRY STANLEY FIGHTS WITH THE DIXIE GRAYS AT SHILOH

After the debacle in Kentucky, the Confederates formed a line of defense stretching from Memphis through Corinth to Chattanooga. Johnston collected some 40,000 troops here, and awaited the arrival of Van Dorn with another 20,000 from the west. Halleck, now in command of the entire Western theater, directed Grant and Buell to advance to Savannah on the Tennessee River about 30 miles northeast of Corinth. Grant's army began to arrive at Savannah on March 11, and within a week he had some 35,000 men at and around Savannah and Pittsburg Landing, a few miles below on the western side of the river. Buell, however, made a leisurely advance from Nashville, taking 22 days to cover 135 miles.

All unsuspecting of danger, Grant's army was scattered over a large irregular quadrangle bounded on the east by the Tennessee, on the north by Owl Creek and on the south by Lick Creek; the land was mostly wooded and cut by many gullies and ravines. Early on the morning of April 6

Johnston struck the Federal outposts, drove them in, and pushed on to the main attack. Although taken by surprise the Federals rallied and fought back with great courage and pertinacity. The fighting raged for over 12 hours, the Confederates steadily pushing back the Union right flank and driving toward Pittsburg Landing on the left flank.

During the afternoon, when the situation looked desperate for the Federals, advance detachments of Lew Wallace's division and of Buell's reached the field of battle, and the gunboats joined in the fray. By nightfall victory rested with the Confederates, but they had succeeded neither in destroying Grant's army nor in capturing Pittsburg Landing, and they had lost their leader, the brilliant and beloved Albert Sidney Johnston. By the next day the whole situation was reversed. Grant had 25,000 fresh men to throw into the battle; the Confederates were exhausted, and on the defensive. There was some sharp fighting on the seventh, but the Confederates withdrew and Grant failed to pursue. By the time he did get ready to pursue, the Confederate army had retired to Corinth. Shiloh was, with Antietam, the bloodiest day of the war, and the hardest fought. Union losses were over 13,000—of whom some 2,500 were prisoners; Confederate losses over 10,500.

Our first account of Shiloh is by young Henry M. Stanley, later the world-famous Sir Henry Stanley. Born in Wales as John Rowlands 19 years earlier, he had shipped as a cabin boy to Louisiana, where he was adopted by a New Orleans merchant, Henry Morton Stanley, whose name he took. In 1861 he enlisted in the Dixie Grays. Captured at Shiloh he endured the discomforts of Camp Douglas prison, enlisted briefly in the Federal artillery, was discharged, and returned to England, only to come back to the United States and enlist in the Union Navy. Later he returned to England and to an illustrious career in journalism and exploration. The Autobiography, from which this account of Shiloh is taken, was written many years after the war; though authentic enough in general, the circumstantial details must be put down to skillful journalism.

O N April 2, 1862, we received orders to prepare three days' cooked rations. Through some misunderstanding, we did not set out until the 4th; and, on the morning of that day, the 6th Arkansas Regiment of Hindman's brigade, Hardee's corps, marched from Corinth to take part in one of the bloodiest battles of the West. We left our knapsacks and tents behind us. After two days of marching, and two nights of bivouacking and living on cold rations, our spirits were not buoyant at dawn of Sunday, the 6th April, as they ought to have been for the serious task before us. . . .

At four o'clock in the morning, we rose from our damp bivouac, and, after a hasty refreshment, were formed into line. We stood in rank for half an hour or so, while the military dispositions were being completed along the three-mile front. Our brigade formed the centre; Cleburne's and Gladden's brigades were on our respective flanks.

Day broke with every promise of a fine day. Next to me, on my right, was a boy of seventeen, Henry Parker. I remember it because, while we stood-at-ease, he drew my attention to some violets at his feet, and said, "It would be a good idea to put a few into my cap. Perhaps the Yanks won't shoot me if they see me wearing such flowers, for they are a sign of peace."

"Capital," said I, "I will do the same."

We plucked a bunch, and arranged the violets in our caps. The men in the ranks laughed at our proceedings, and had not the enemy been so near, their merry mood might have been communicated to the army.

We loaded our muskets, and arranged our cartridge-pouches ready for use. Our weapons were the obsolete flint-locks, and the ammunition was rolled in cartridge-paper, which contained powder, a round ball, and three buckshot. When we loaded we had to tear the paper with our teeth, empty a little powder into the pan, lock it, empty the rest of the powder into the barrel, press paper and ball into the muzzle, and ram home. Then the Orderly-sergeant called the roll, and we knew that the Dixie Greys were present to a man. . . .

Before we had gone five hundred paces, our serenity was disturbed by some desultory firing in front. It was then a quarter-past five. "They are at it already," we whispered to each other. "Stand by, gentlemen,"—for we were all gentlemen volunteers at this time,—said our Captain L. G. Smith. Our steps became unconsciously brisker, and alertness was noticeable in everybody. The firing continued at intervals, deliberate and scattered, as at target practice. We drew nearer to the firing, and soon a sharper rattling of musketry was heard. "That is the enemy waking up," we said. Within a few minutes, there was another explosive burst of musketry, the air was pierced by many missiles, which hummed and pinged sharply by our ears, pattered through the treetops, and brought twigs and leaves down on us. "Those are bullets," Henry whispered with awe.

At two hundred yards further, a dreadful roar of musketry broke out from a regiment adjoining ours. It was followed by another further off, and the sound had scarcely died away when regiment after regiment blazed away and made a continuous roll of sound. "We are in for it now," said Henry. . . .

"Forward, gentlemen, make ready!" urged Captain Smith. In response, we surged forward, for the first time marring the alignment. We trampled recklessly over the grass and young sprouts. Beams of sunlight stole athwart our course. . . . Nothing now stood between us and the enemy.

"There they are!" was no sooner uttered, than we cracked into them with levelled muskets. "Aim low, men!" commanded Captain Smith. I tried hard to see some living thing to shoot at, for it appeared absurd to be blazing away at shadows. But, still advancing, firing as we moved, I, at last, saw a row of little globes of pearly smoke streaked with crimson, breaking-out with spurtive quickness, from a long line of blue figures in front; and simultaneously, there broke upon our ears an appalling crash of sound, the series of fusillades following one another with startling suddenness, which suggested to my somewhat moidered sense a mountain upheaved, with huge rocks tumbling and thundering down a slope, and the echoes rumbling and receding through space. Again and again, these loud and quick explosions were repeated, seemingly with increased violence, until they rose to the highest pitch of fury, and in unbroken continuity. All the world seemed involved in one tremendous ruin! . . .

Though one's senses were preternaturally acute, and engaged with their impressions, we plied our arms, loaded, and fired, with such nervous haste as though it depended on each of us how soon this fiendish uproar would be hushed. My nerves tingled, my pulses beat double-quick, my heart throbbed loudly, and almost painfully; but, amid all the excitement, my thoughts, swift as the flash of lightning, took all sound, and sight, and self, into their purview. I listened to the battle raging far away on the flanks, to the thunder in front, to the various sounds made by the leaden storm. I was angry with my rear rank, because he made my eyes smart with the powder of his musket; and I felt like cuffing him for deafening my ears! I knew how Captain Smith and Lieutenant Mason looked, how bravely the Dixie Greys' banner ruffled over Newton Story's head, and that all hands were behaving as though they knew how long all this would last. Back to myself my thoughts came, and, with the whirring bullet, they fled to the blue-bloused ranks afront. They dwelt on their movements, and read their temper, as I should read time by a clock. Through the lurid haze the contours of their pink faces could not been seen, but their gappy, hesitating, incoherent, and sensitive line revealed their mood clearly.

We continued advancing, step by step, loading and firing as we went. To every forward step, they took a backward move, loading and firing, as they slowly withdrew. Twenty thousand muskets were being fired at this stage, but, though accuracy of aim was impossible, owing to our labouring hearts, and the jarring and excitement, many bullets found their destined billets on both sides.

After a steady exchange of musketry, which lasted some time, we heard the order: "Fix Bayonets! On the double-quick!" in tones that thrilled us. There was a simultaneous bound forward, each soul doing his best for the emergency. The Federals appeared inclined to await us; but, at this juncture, our men raised a yell, thousands responded to it, and burst out into the wildest yelling it has ever been my lot to hear. It drove all sanity and order from among us. It served the double purpose of relieving pent-up feelings, and transmitting encouragement along the attacking line. I rejoiced in the shouting like the rest. It reminded me that there were about four hundred companies like the Dixie Greys, who shared our feelings. Most of us, engrossed with the musket-work, had forgotten the fact; but the wave after wave of human voices, louder than all other battle-sounds together, penetrated to every sense, and stimulated our energies to the utmost.

"They fly!" was echoed from lip to lip. It accelerated our pace, and filled us with a noble rage. Then I knew what the Berserker passion was! It deluged us with rapture, and transfigured each Southerner into an exulting victor. At such a moment, nothing could have halted us.

Those savage yells, and the sight of thousands of racing figures coming towards them, discomfited the blue-coats; and when we arrived upon the placè where they had stood, they had vanished. Then we caught sight of their beautiful array of tents, before which they had made their stand, after being roused from their Sunday-morning sleep, and huddled into line, at hearing their pickets challenge our skirmishers. The half-dressed dead and wounded showed what a surprise our attack had been. We drew up in the enemy's camp, panting and breathing hard. Some precious minutes were thus lost in recovering our breaths, indulging our curiosity, and reforming our line. Signs of a hasty rouse to the battle were abundant. Military equipments, uniform-coats, half-packed knapsacks, bedding, of a new and superior quality, littered the company streets.

Meantime, a series of other camps lay behind the first array of tents. The resistance we had met, though comparatively brief, enabled the brigades in rear of the advance camp to recover from the shock of the surprise; but our delay had not been long enough to give them time to form in proper order of battle. There were wide gaps between their divisions, into which the quick-flowing tide of elated Southerners entered, and compelled them to fall back lest they should be surrounded. Prentiss's brigade, despite their most desperate efforts, were thus hemmed in on all sides, and were made prisoners.

I had a momentary impression that, with the capture of the first camp, the battle was well-nigh over; but, in fact, it was only a brief prologue of the long and exhaustive series of struggles which took place that day.

Continuing our advance, we came in view of the tops of another mass of white tents, and almost at the same time, were met by a furious storm of bullets, poured on us from a long line of blue-coats, whose attitude of assurance proved to us that we should have tough work here. But we were so much heartened by our first success that it would have required a good deal to have halted our advance for long. Their opportunity for making a full impression on us came with terrific suddenness. The world seemed bursting into fragments. Cannon and musket, shell and bullet, lent their several intensities to the distracting uproar. If I had not a fraction of an ear, and an eye inclined towards my Captain and Company, I had been spell-bound by the energies now opposed to us. I likened the cannon, with their deep bass, to the roaring of a great herd of lions; the ripping, cracking musketry, to the incessant yapping of terriers; the windy whisk of shells, and zipping of minie bullets, to the swoop of eagles, and the buzz of angry wasps. All the opposing armies of Grey and Blue fiercely blazed at each other.

After being exposed for a few seconds to this fearful downpour, we heard the order to "Lie down, men, and continue your firing!" Before me was a prostrate tree, about fifteen inches in diameter, with a narrow strip of light between it and the ground. Behind this shelter a dozen of us flung ourselves. The security it appeared to offer restored me to my individuality. We could fight, and think, and observe, better than out in the open. But it was a terrible period! How the cannon bellowed, and their shells plunged and bounded, and flew with screeching hisses over us! Their sharp rending explosions and hurtling fragments made us shrink and cower, despite our utmost efforts to be cool and collected. I marvelled, as I heard the unintermitting patter, snip, thud, and hum of the bullets, how anyone could live under this raining death. I could hear the balls beating a merciless tattoo on the outer surface of the log, pinging it vivaciously as they flew off at a tangent from it, and thudding into something or other, at the rate of a hundred a second. One, here and there, found its way under the log, and buried itself in a comrade's body. One man raised his chest, as if to yawn, and jostled me. I turned to him, and saw that a bullet had gored his whole face, and penetrated into his chest. Another ball struck a man a deadly rap on the head, and he turned on his back and showed his ghastly white face to the sky.

"It is getting too warm, boys!" cried a soldier, and he uttered a vehement curse upon keeping soldiers hugging the ground until every ounce of courage was chilled. He lifted his head a little too high, and a bullet skimmed over the top of the log and hit him fairly in the centre of his forehead, and he fell heavily on his face. But his thought had been instantaneously general; and the officers, with one voice, ordered the charge; and cries of "Forward, forward!" raised us, as with a spring, to our feet, and changed the complexion of our feelings. The pulse of action beat feverishly once more; and, though overhead was crowded with peril, we were unable to give it so much attention as when we lay stretched on the ground. . . .

Our progress was not so continuously rapid as we desired, for the blues were obdurate; but at this moment we were gladdened at the sight of a battery galloping to our assistance. It was time for the nerve-shaking cannon to speak. After two rounds of shell and canister, we felt the pressure on us slightly relaxed; but we were still somewhat sluggish in disposition, though the officers' voices rang out imperiously. Newton Story at this juncture strode forward rapidly with the Dixies' banner, until he was quite sixty yards ahead of the foremost. Finding himself alone, he halted; and turning to us smilingly said, "Why don't you come on, boys? You see there is no danger!" His smile and words acted on us like magic. We raised the yell, and sprang lightly and hopefully towards him. "Let's give them hell, boys!" said one. "Plug them plum-centre, every time!"

It was all very encouraging, for the yelling and shouting were taken up by thousands. "Forward, forward; don't give them breathing time!" was cried. We instinctively obeyed, and soon came in clear view of the bluecoats, who were scornfully unconcerned at first; but, seeing the leaping tide of men coming on at a tremendous pace, their front dissolved, and they fled in double-quick retreat. Again we felt the "glorious joy of heroes." It carried us on exultantly, rejoicing in the spirit which recognises nothing but the prey. We were no longer an army of soldiers, but so many school-boys racing, in which length of legs, wind, and condition tell.

We gained the second line of camps, continued the rush through them, and clean beyond. It was now about ten o'clock. My physical powers were quite exhausted, and, to add to my discomfiture, something struck me on my belt-clasp, and tumbled me headlong to the ground. I could not have been many minutes prostrated before I recovered from the shock of the blow and fall, to find my clasp deeply dented and cracked. My company was not in sight. I was grateful for the rest, and crawled feebly to a tree, and plunging my hand into my haversack, ate ravenously. Within half an hour, feeling renovated, I struck north in the direction which my regiment had taken, over a ground strewn with bodies and the débris of war.

The desperate character of this day's battle was now brought home to my mind in all its awful reality. While in the tumultuous advance, and occupied with a myriad of exciting incidents, it was only at brief intervals that I was conscious of wounds being given and received; but now, in the trail of pursuers and pursued, the ghastly relics appalled every sense. I felt curious as to who the fallen Greys were, and moved to one stretched straight out. It was the body of a stout English Sergeant of a neighbouring company, the members of which hailed principally from the Washita Valley. . . .

Close by him was a young Lieutenant, who, judging by the new gloss on his uniform, must have been some father's darling. A clean bullet-hole through the centre of his forehead had instantly ended his career. A little further were some twenty bodies, lying in various postures, each by its own pool of viscous blood, which emitted a peculiar scent, which was new to me, but which I have since learned is inseparable from a battle-field. Beyond these, a still larger group lay, body overlying body, knees crooked, arms erect, or wide-stretched and rigid according as the last spasm overtook them. The company opposed to them must have shot straight. . . .

It was the first Field of Glory I had seen in my May of life, and the first time that Glory sickened me with its repulsive aspect, and made me suspect it was all a glittering lie. . . . Under a flag of truce, I saw the bearers pick up the dead from the field, and lay them in long rows beside a wide trench; I saw them laid, one by one, close together at the bottom. . . .

I overtook my regiment about one o'clock. . . . The enemy resolutely maintained their ground, and our side was preparing for another assault. The firing was alternately brisk and slack. We lay down, and availed ourselves of trees, logs, and hollows, and annoyed their upstanding ranks; battery pounded battery, and meanwhile we hugged our resting-places closely. Of a sudden, we rose and raced towards the position, and took it by sheer weight and impetuosity. About three o'clock, the battle grew very hot. The enemy appeared to be more concentrated, and immovably sullen. Both sides fired better as they grew more accustomed to the din; but, with assistance from the reserves, we were continually pressing them towards the river Tennessee, without ever retreating an inch.

About this time, the enemy were assisted by the gun-boats, which hurled their enormous projectiles far beyond us; but, though they made great havoc among the trees, and created terror, they did comparatively little damage to those in close touch with the enemy.

The screaming of the big shells, when they first began to sail over our heads, had the effect of reducing our fire; for they were as fascinating as they were distracting. But we became used to them. . . .

As it drew near four o'clock . . . several of our company lagged wearily behind, and the remainder showed, by their drawn faces, the effects of their efforts. Yet, after a short rest, they were able to make splendid spurts. As for myself, I had only one wish, and that was for repose. The long-continued excitement, the successive tautening and relaxing of the nerves, the quenchless thirst, made more intense by the fumes of sulphurous powder, and the caking grime on the lips caused by tearing the paper cartridges, and a ravening hunger, all combined, had reduced me to a walking automaton, and I earnestly wished that night would come. . . .

Finally, about five o'clock, we assaulted and captured a large camp; after driving the enemy well away from it; the front line was as thin as that of a skirmishing body, and we were ordered to retire to the tents. . . .

An hour before dawn, I awoke and, after a hearty replenishment of my vitals with biscuit and molasses, I conceived myself to be fresher than on Sunday morning. While awaiting day-break, I gathered from other early risers their ideas in regard to the events of yesterday. They were under the impression that we had gained a great victory, though we had not, as we had anticipated, reached the Tennessee River. Van Dorn, with his expected reinforcements for us, was not likely to make his appearance for many days yet; and, if General Buell, with his 20,000 troops, had joined the enemy during the night, we had a bad day's work before us. We were short of provisions and ammunition, General Sidney Johnston, our chief Commander, had been killed; but Beauregard was safe and unhurt, and, if Buell was absent, we would win the day.

At daylight I fell in with my Company, but there were only about fifty of the Dixies present. . . . Regiments were hurried into line, but, even to my inexperienced eyes, the troops were in ill-condition for repeating the efforts of Sunday. . . . In consequence of our pickets being driven in on us, we were moved forward in skirmishing order. With my musket on the trail I found myself in active motion, more active than otherwise I would have been, perhaps, because Captain Smith had said, "Now, Mr. Stanley, if you please, step briskly forward!" This singling-out of me wounded my *amour-propre*, and sent me forward like a rocket. In a short time, we met our opponents in the same formation as ourselves, and advancing most resolutely. We threw ourselves behind such trees as were near us, fired, loaded, and darted forward to another shelter. Presently, I found myself in an open grassy space, with no convenient tree or stump near; but, seeing a shallow hollow some twenty paces ahead, I made a dash for it, and plied my musket with haste.

I became so absorbed with some blue figures in front of me, that I did not pay sufficient heed to my companion greys. . . . Seeing my blues in about the same proportion, I assumed that the greys were keeping their position, and never once thought of retreat. However, as, despite our firing, the blues were coming uncomfortably near, I rose from my hollow; but, to my speechless amazement, I found myself a solitary grey, in a line of blue skirmishers! My companions had retreated! The next I heard was, "Down with that gun, Secesh, or I'll drill a hole through you! Drop it, quick!"

Half a dozen of the enemy were covering me at the same instant, and I dropped my weapon, incontinently. Two men sprang at my collar, and marched me, unresisting, into the ranks of the terrible Yankees. *I was a prisoner!*

—*The Autobiography of Sir Henry Morton Stanley*

6. AN ILLINOIS PRIVATE FIGHTS AT THE HORNET'S NEST

The hottest fighting in the Battle of Shiloh—and some of the hottest of the whole war—was at the so-called Hornet's Nest, at the center of the Union line. Here Hulbert, W. H. L. Wallace, and Prentiss held out for hours against a series of savage attacks. In the end Wallace was killed, and only a fragment of his regiments succeeded in fighting their way out.

Leander Stillwell, who here tells us how thrilling it was to see the battle flags of the 36th Indiana come on the field, was an Illinois boy who enlisted at St. Louis in 1862, fought at Shiloh, Corinth, and Vicksburg, and later in Arkansas and Tennessee. His recollections, though written years after the war, are based on letters and diaries.

[April 6, 1862]

We had "turned out" about sunup, answered to roll-call, and had cooked and eaten our breakfast. We had then gone to work, preparing for the regular Sunday morning inspection, which would take place at nine o'clock. The boys were scattered around the company streets and in front of the company parade grounds, engaged in polishing and brightening their muskets, and brushing up and cleaning their shoes, jackets, trousers, and clothing generally.

It was a most beautiful morning. The sun was shining brightly through the trees, and there was not a cloud in the sky. It really seemed like Sunday in the country at home. During week days there was a continual stream of army wagons going to and from the landing, and the clucking of their wheels, the yells and oaths of the drivers, the cracking of whips, mingled with the braying of mules, the neighing of the horses, the commands of the officers engaged in drilling the men, the incessant hum and buzz of the camps, the blare of bugles, and the roll of drums,—all these made up a prodigious volume of sound that lasted from the coming-up to the going-down of the sun. But this morning was strangely still. The wagons were silent, the mules were peacefully munching their hay, and the army teamsters were giving us a rest. I listened with delight to the plaintive, mournful tones of a turtle-dove in the woods close by, while on a dead limb of a tall tree right in the camp a wood-pecker was sounding his "long roll" just as I had heard it beaten by his Northern brothers a thousand times on the trees in the Otter Creek bottom at home.

Suddenly, away off on the right, in the direction of Shiloh church, came a dull, heavy "Pum!" then another, and still another. Every man sprung to his feet as if struck by an electric shock, and we looked inquiringly into one another's faces. "What is that?" asked every one but no one answered.

PLAN OF THE

BATTLE OF SHILOH
April 6th & 7th 1862

Those heavy booms then came thicker and faster, and just a few seconds after we heard that first dull, ominous growl off to the southwest, came a low, sullen, continuous roar. There was no mistaking that sound. That was not a squad of pickets emptying their guns on being relieved from duty; it was the continuous roll of thousands of muskets, and told us that a battle was on.

What I have been describing just now occurred during a few seconds only, and with the roar of musketry the long roll began to beat in our camp. Then ensued a scene of desperate haste, the like of which I certainly had never seen before, nor ever saw again. I remember that in the midst of this terrible uproar and confusion, while the boys were buckling on their cartridge boxes, and before even the companies had been formed, a mounted staff officer came galloping wildly down the line from the right. He checked and whirled his horse sharply around right in our company street, the iron-bound hoofs of his steed crashing among the tin plates lying in a little pile where my mess had eaten its breakfast that morning. The horse was flecked with foam and its eyes and nostrils were red as blood. The officer cast one hurried glance around him, and exclaimed: "My God! this regiment not in line yet! They have been fighting on the right over an hour!" And wheeling his horse, he disappeared in the direction of the colonel's tent. . . .

Well, the companies were formed, we marched out on the regimental parade ground, and the regiment was formed in line. The command was given: "Load at will; load!" We had anticipated this, however, as the most of us had instinctively loaded our guns before we had formed company. All this time the roar on the right was getting nearer and louder. Our old colonel rode up close to us, opposite the center of the regimental line, and called out, "Attention, battalion!" We fixed our eyes on him to hear what was coming. It turned out to be the old man's battle harangue.

"Gentlemen," said he, in a voice that every man in the regiment heard, "remember your State, and do your duty today like brave men."

That was all. . . . Immediately after the colonel had given us his brief exhortation, the regiment was marched across the little field I have before mentioned, and we took our place in line of battle, the woods in front of us, and the open field in our rear. We "dressed on" the colors, ordered arms, and stood awaiting the attack. By this time the roar on the right had become terrific. The Rebel army was unfolding its front, and the battle was steadily advancing in our direction. We could begin to see the blue rings of smoke curling upward among the trees off to the right, and the pungent smell of burning gun-powder filled the air. As the roar came travelling down the line from the right it reminded me (only it was a million times louder) of the sweep of a thunder-shower in summer-time over the hard ground of a stubble-field.

And there we stood, in the edge of the woods, so still, waiting for the storm to break on us. . . .

The time we thus stood, waiting the attack, could not have exceeded five minutes. Suddenly, obliquely to our right, there was a long, wavy flash of bright light, then another, and another! It was the sunlight shining on gun barrels and bayonets—and—there they were at last! A long brown line, with muskets at a right shoulder shift, in excellent order, right through the woods they came.

We began firing at once. From one end of the regiment to the other leaped a sheet of red flame, and the roar that went up from the edge of that old field doubtless advised General Prentiss of the fact that the Rebels had at last struck the extreme left of his line. We had fired but two or three rounds when, for some reason,—I never knew what,—we were ordered to fall back across the field, and did so. The whole line, so far as I could see to the right, went back. We halted on the other side of the field, in the edge of the woods, in front of our tents, and again began firing. The Rebels, of course, had moved up and occupied the line we had just abandoned. And here we did our first hard fighting during the day. Our officers said, after the battle was over, that we held this line an hour and ten minutes. How long it was I do not know. I "took no note of time."

We retreated from this position as our officers afterward said, because the troops on our right had given way, and we were flanked. Possibly those boys on our right would give the same excuse for their leaving, and probably truly, too. Still, I think we did not fall back a minute too soon. As I rose from the comfortable log from behind which a bunch of us had been firing, I saw men in gray and brown clothes, with trailed muskets, running through the camp on our right, and I saw something else, too, that sent a chill all through me. It was a kind of flag I had never seen before. It was a gaudy sort of thing, with red bars. It flashed over me in a second that that thing was a Rebel flag. It was not more than sixty yards to the right. The smoke around it was low and dense and kept me from seeing the man who was carrying it, but I plainly saw the banner. It was going fast, with a jerky motion, which told me that the bearer was on a double-quick. About that time we left. We observed no kind of order in leaving; the main thing was to get out of there as quick as we could. I ran down our company street, and in passing the big Sibley tent of our mess I thought of my knapsack with all my traps and belongings, including that precious little packet of letters from home. I said to myself, "I will save my knapsack, anyhow;" but one quick backward glance over my left shoulder made me change my mind, and I went on. I never saw my knapsack or any of its contents afterwards.

Our broken forces halted and re-formed about half a mile to the rear of our camp on the summit of a gentle ridge, covered with thick brush. I recognized our regiment by the little gray pony the old colonel rode, and hurried to my place in the ranks. Standing there with our faces once more to the front, I saw a seemingly endless column of men in blue, marching by the flank, who were filing off to the right through the woods, and I heard our old German adjutant, Cramer, say to the colonel, "Dose are de troops of Sheneral Hurlbut. He is forming a new line dere in de bush." I exclaimed to myself from the bottom of my heart, "Bully for General Hurlbut and the new line in the bush! Maybe we'll whip 'em yet." I shall never forget my feelings about this time. I was astonished at our first retreat in the morning across the field back to our camp, but it occurred to me that maybe that was only "strategy" and all done on purpose; but when we had to give up our camp, and actually turn our backs and run half a mile, it seemed to me that we were forever disgraced, and I kept thinking to myself: "What will they say about this at home?"

I was very dry for a drink, and as we were doing nothing, just then, I slipped out of ranks and ran down to the little hollow in our rear, in search of water. Finding a little pool, I threw myself on the ground and took a copious draught. As I rose to my feet, I observed an officer about a rod above me also quenching his thirst, holding his horse meanwhile by the bridle. As he rose I saw it was our old adjutant. At no other time would I have dared accost him unless in the line of duty, but the situation made me bold.

"Adjutant," I said, "What does this mean—our having to run this way? Ain't we whipped?"

He blew the water from his mustache, and quickly answered in a careless way: "Oh, no; dat is all ride. We yoost fall back to form on the reserve. Sheneral Buell vas now crossing der river mit 50,000 men, and vill be here pooty quick; and Sheneral Lew Vallace is coming up from Crump's Landing mit 15,000 more. Ve vips 'em; ve vips 'em. Go to your gompany." . . . But as the long hours wore on that day, and still Buell and Wallace did not come, my faith in the adjutant's veracity became considerably shaken.

It was at this point that my regiment was detached from Prentiss' division and served with it no more that day. We were sent some distance to the right to support a battery, the name of which I never learned. It was occupying the summit of a slope, and was actively engaged when we reached it. We were put in position of about twenty rods in the rear of the battery, and ordered to lie flat on the ground. The ground sloped gently down in our direction, so that by hugging it close, the rebel shot and shell went over us.

It was here, at about ten o'clock in the morning, that I first saw Grant that day. He was on horseback, of course, accompanied by his staff, and was evidently making a personal examination of his lines. He went by us in a gallop, riding between us and the battery, at the head of his staff. The battery was then hotly engaged; shot and shell were whizzing overhead, and cutting off the limbs of trees, but Grant rode through the storm with perfect indifference, seemingly paying no more attention to the missiles than if they had been paper wads.

We remained in support of this battery until about 2 o'clock in the afternoon. We were then put in motion by the right flank, filed to the left, crossed the left-hand Corinth road; then we were thrown into the line by the command: "By the left flank, march." We crossed a little ravine and up a slope, and relieved a regiment on the left of Hurlbut's line. This line was desperately engaged, and had been at this point, as we afterwards learned, for fully four hours. I remember as we went up the slope and began firing, about the first thing that met my gaze was what out West we would call a "windrow" of dead men in blue; some doubled up face downward, others with their white faces upturned to the sky, brave boys who had been shot to death in "holding the line." Here we stayed until our last cartridge was shot away. We were then relieved by another regiment. We filled our cartridge boxes again and went back to the support of our battery. The boys laid down and talked in low tones. Many of our comrades alive and well an hour ago, we had left dead on that bloody ridge. And still the battle raged. From right to left, everywhere, it was one never-ending, terrible roar, with no prospect of stopping.

Somewhere between 4 and 5 o'clock, as near as I can tell, everything became ominously quiet. Our battery ceased firing; the gunners leaned against the pieces and talked and laughed. Suddenly a staff officer rode up and said something in a low tone to the commander of the battery, then rode to our colonel and said something to him. The battery horses were at once brought up from a ravine in the rear, and the battery limbered up and moved off through the woods diagonally to the left and rear. We were put in motion by the flank and followed it. Everything kept so still, the loudest noise I heard was the clucking of the wheels of the gun-carriages and caissons as they wound through the woods. We emerged from the woods and entered a little old field. I then saw at our right and front lines of men in blue moving in the same direction we were, and it was evident that we were falling back.

All at once, on the right, the left, and from our recent front, came one tremendous roar, and the bullets fell like hail. The lines took the double-quick towards the rear. For awhile the attempt was made to fall back in order, and then everything went to pieces. My heart failed me utterly. I thought the day was lost. A confused mass of men and guns, caissons, army wagons, ambulances, and all the debris of a beaten army surged and crowded along the narrow dirt road to the landing, while that pitiless storm of leaden hail came crashing on us from the rear. It was undoubtedly at this crisis in our affairs that the division of General Prentiss was captured. . . .

It must have been when we were less than half a mile from the landing on our disorderly retreat before mentioned, that we saw standing in line of battle, at ordered arms, extending from both sides of the road until lost to sight in the woods, a long well-ordered line of men in blue. What did that mean? and where had they come from? I was walking by the side of Enoch Wallace, the orderly sergeant of my company. . . . Even he, in the face of this seemingly appalling state of things, had evidently lost heart.

I said to him: "Enoch, what are those men there for?"

He answered in a low tone: "I guess they are put there to hold the Rebels in check till the army can get across the river."

And doubtless that was the thought of every intelligent soldier in our beaten column. And yet it goes to show how little the common soldier knew of the actual situation. We did not know then that this line was the last line of battle of the "Fighting Fourth Division" under General Hurlbut; that on its right was the division of McClernand, the Fort Donelson boys; that on its right, at right angles to it, and, as it were, the refused wing of the army, was glorious old Sherman, hanging on with a bulldog grip to the road across Snake Creek from Crump's Landing by which Lew Wallace was coming with 5,000 men. In other words, we still had an unbroken line confronting the enemy, made up of men who were not yet ready, by any manner of means, to give up that they were whipped. . . .

Well, we filed through Hurlbut's line, halted, re-formed, and faced to the front once more. We were put in place a short distance in the rear of Hurlbut, as a support to some heavy guns. It must have been about five o'clock now. Suddenly, on the extreme left, and just a little above the landing, came a deafening explosion that fairly shook the ground beneath our feet, followed by others in quick and regular succession. The look of wonder and inquiry that the soldiers' faces wore for a moment disappeared for one of joy and exultation as it flashed across our minds that the gunboats had at last joined hands in the dance, and were pitching big twenty-pound Parrott shells up the ravine in front of Hurlbut, to the terror and discomfiture of our adversaries.

The last place my regiment assumed was close to the road coming up from the landing. As we were lying there I heard the strains of martial music and saw a body of men marching by the flank up the road. I slipped out of ranks and walked out to the side of the road to see what troops they were. Their band was playing "Dixie's Land," and playing it well. The men were marching at a quick step, carrying their guns, cartridge-boxes, haversacks, canteens, and blanket-rolls. I saw that they had not been in the fight, for there was no powder-smoke on their faces. "What regiment is this?" I asked of a young sergeant marching on the flank. Back came the answer in a quick, cheery tone. "The 36th Indiana, the advance guard of Buell's army."

I did not, on hearing this, throw my cap into the air and yell. That would have given those Indiana fellows a chance to chaff and guy me, and possibly make sarcastic remarks, which I did not care to provoke. I gave one big, gasping swallow and stood still, but the blood thumped in the veins of my throat and my heart fairly pounded against my little infantry jacket in the joyous rapture of this glorious intelligence. Soldiers need not be told of the thrill of unspeakable exultation they have all felt at the sight of armed friends in danger's darkest hour. Speaking for myself alone, I can only say, in the most heart-felt sincerity, that in all my obscure military career, never to me was the sight of reinforcing legions so precious and so welcome as on that Sunday evening when the rays of the descending sun were flashed back from the bayonets of Buell's advance column as it deployed on the bluffs of Pittsburg Landing.

—STILLWELL, *The Story of a Common Soldier of Army Life in the Civil War*

7. ROSECRANS WHIPS VAN DORN AT CORINTH

After Shiloh Halleck took personal command of the vast Federal army of over 100,000 men. Instead of advancing boldly on the exhausted army of Beauregard—who had temporarily succeeded Johnston—he inched forward in a series of "siege" operations, reaching Corinth on May 30. Then he proceeded to break up his own army, sending Buell off toward Chattanooga—

which he did not reach—and detaching another 20,000 men to guard railroad communications. By this imbecility he reduced his grand army to less than 40,000, and the initiative passed to Bragg, who had superseded Beauregard. Bragg hurried off to Chattanooga, leaving Van Dorn and Price with about 40,000 men to oppose Grant, who commanded an equal number. Grant, however, was expected to protect the whole of western Tennessee: he had 7,000 men at Memphis, 12,000 at Bolivar, 6,000 at Jackson, and 23,000 at Corinth, under Rosecrans. It was this latter force that Van Dorn planned to attack; his hope was to turn the whole Union flank all the way up to Fort Donelson.

The battle was joined on October 3; by sunset the Confederates had driven the Federals into the town of Corinth; the next morning, however, the Federals counterattacked and threw Van Dorn back in confusion. This minor battle had some important consequences. It saved the Federal line from Memphis to Corinth; it made Rosecrans' reputation; and it persuaded President Davis to supplant Van Dorn by General Pemberton, who later lost Vicksburg.

Oscar Jackson, who here tells the story, was a twenty-two-year-old captain of the 63rd Ohio Volunteers who later marched to the sea with Sherman; after the war he had a minor political career in Pennsylvania.

O N the first appearance of dawn, the rebels threw out a cloud of skirmishers that annoyed us seriously, as every few minutes someone was hit and this was annoying. Details were made from the line to go out and drive them off. Five were called for from my company. I asked for volunteers and the whole company offered to go on this specially dangerous detail. I took the five I thought had spoken first. They started out and had a regular Indian fight, giving the enemy their fill of bushwhacking, and driving them back to their main force. I was out to see them and shot a time or two, or more, at a "butternut" who returned the fire, the balls going "zip" quite close to my ear. . . .

About ten o'clock the rebels began pouring out of the timber and forming storming columns. All the firing ceased and everything was silent as the grave. They formed one column of perhaps two thousand men in plain view, then another, and crowding out of the woods another, and so on. I thought they would never stop coming out of the timber. While they were forming, the men were considerable distance from us but in plain sight and as soon as they were ready they started at us with a firm, slow, steady step.

> "Firm paced and slow a fearful front they form,
> Still as the breeze but dreadful as the storm."

So it seemed to us. In my campaigning I had never seen anything so hard to stand as that slow, steady tramp. Not a sound was heard but they looked as if they intended to walk over us. I afterwards stood a bayonet charge when the enemy came at us on the double-quick with a yell and it was not so trying on the nerves as that steady, solemn advance.

I could see that my men were affected by it. They were in line and I knew that they would stand fire but this was a strong test. I noticed one man examining his gun to see if it was clean, another to see if his was primed right; a third would stand a while on one foot then on the other; whilst others were pulling at their blouses, feeling if their cartridge boxes or cap-pouches were all right, and so on, but all the time steadily watching the advancing foe. It is customary in engagements to have some motto or battle cry given by some commander, such as "Fire low," "Stick to your company," "Remember some battle," (naming it). To draw the attention of my company while the charge was advancing I said: "Boys, I guess we are going to have a fight." This is always a doubtful question to an old soldier until he sees it, but they all believed it this time. "I have two things I want you to remember today. One is, we own all the ground behind us. The enemy may go over us but all the rebels yonder can't drive Company H back. The other is, if the butternuts come close enough, remember you have good bayonets on your rifles and use them." And well did they remember what I said.

When the enemy had advanced about one-third of the distance toward us, we got orders to lie down, and then, when the enemy got close enough, we were to fire by companies. The unevenness of the ground now screened us from their view and the second line of infantry, some distance to the rear, appeared to the rebels to be the first they would have to fight, and when they came upon us it was a surprise to them. My company being on the left of the regiment, and our regiment on the left of the brigade, I was among the nearest to the enemy.

The enemy had to come over a bluffish bank a few yards in front of me and as soon as I saw their heads, still coming slowly, I jumped up and said: "Company H, get up." The column was then in full view and only about thirty yards distant. Captain Smith of our regiment thought only about twenty-five yards. Just in front of me was a bush three or four feet high with sear leaves on it. Hitting this with my sword, I said: "Boys, give them a volley just over this. Ready! aim! (and jumping around my company to get from in front of their guns) fire!" In a few seconds the fire was continued along the whole line.

It seems to me that the fire of my company had cut down the head of the column that struck us as deep back as my company was long. As the smoke cleared away, there was apparently ten yards square of a mass of struggling bodies and butternut clothes. Their column appeared to reel like a rope shaken at the end. I had heard this idea advanced and here I saw it plainly. The enemy were stopped, but deploying their column, returned the fire, and, a fine thing for us, fired too low, striking the ground, knocking the dirt and chips all over us, wounding a very few, not one in my company. We got ahead of them with the next volley which we delivered right in their faces. (The guns were all muzzle-loading). At this close distance we fought for perhaps five minutes, when the enemy gave back in confusion. The leafy bush I struck with my sword, on giving the first command to fire, was stripped almost clean. The boys made a fine volley. The enemy came at us in fine order, moving handsomely, but in retreating, every fellow went as suited him, and it appeared to suit all to go fast.

The column that fought us was led by General Rodgers of Texas who fell dead but a few feet from me. When I saw the enemy retreating in such confusion, I remarked to a comrade that we would not have to fight those men any more today, as I thought it would be impossible to rally them again, but strange to say, in some forty minutes I saw them reformed and coming at us again with that slow, steady step, but they made a change in their tactics, for as they came over the bank, or rather out of ravine in front of us, they came at us with a yell on the double-quick. Our men stood firm with loaded guns and fixed bayonets and gave them a volley that threw them somewhat into confusion, slaughtering them fearfully, but pressing on, and firing at us rapidly, they dashed themselves against us like water against a rock and were a second time repulsed and gave back.

Colonel Sprague had all the while been in the thickest of the fight. I think I see him now rush to where the line wavered and with sabre sweeping the air, exclaim, "What does this mean, men? Company ——, close up!" He then spoke and said, "Men, it is your time to cheer now," and with a hearty good will did they respond.

Some distance to the left and front of me were a pair of parrot guns, that we called Battery Robinett in distinction from the small fort of the same name a short distance in the rear of them. Captain Brown and his Company A supported these guns immediately, that is, were between me and them. He was almost annihilated by the first two charges and between me and the guns was clear ground.

Colonel Sprague gave me this order: "Captain Jackson, move your company up to those guns and hold them."

Saluting, I replied, "I will do it," and turning to my command I added, "Left face, forward march." It was like moving into dead men's shoes, for I had seen one company carried away from there on litters, but without a moment's hesitation we moved up.

I had scarce posted my men in rear of the guns when I saw that the enemy were again coming at us, and that a detachment was moving from the main column toward my guns. I knew what they wanted and, as the guns were not for close action, I moved my men in front of them and waited their approach. On they came, formed in their favorite manner, namely, in a solid square or column. I now had but twenty-four men in line formed in two ranks, but even the detachment of the enemy which veered off towards me were formed in a square. As I afterwards learned, they were dismounted Texan rangers and very few of their guns had bayonets. I am told Colonel Sprague asked permission to move the regiment up to my support, but permission was denied.

The rebel officer in command of the Texans was marching at the left of his men and when he came nigh us he turned and walked backwards and said to his men, "Boys, when you charge, give a good yell." I heard his command distinctly and it almost made the hair stand up on my head. The next instant the Texans began yelling like savages and rushed at us without firing. The ground in front of us was about like that where we stood previously and at the proper moment I gave them a volley that halted them, cutting down their entire front. I saw they meant to overwhelm us and drive us from the guns, as they out-numbered us. I estimated their force at one hundred men. My men began loading at will and the Texan, by a dexterous movement, was putting his bayonets to the front, doing the thing among and literally over his dead and wounded comrades. I saw that he would strike us before we could get another volley at them and I gave the command, "Don't load, boys; they are too close on you; let them have the bayonet." In a second every bayonet was brought down to a charge. I have never lived through moments of such intense excitement. Events happened quicker than I can record them. The rebels rushed toward us and just before they struck us, I yelled, "Charge!" in order to give my men momentum to meet the shock. My men sprang at the enemy as one man. It reminded me of a man cutting heavy grain, striking at a thick place. The hostile guns clashed. For an instant we parried like boxers, when the enemy gave back, firing at us now for the first [time] as they retired.

Never have I felt so proud of anything as I was of my men. I thought that no such company was in that army. Hand to hand we fought them. A few of the enemy rushed around my left to my rear to get at the guns and two rebels were killed in rear of my line in single-handed combat. Corporal Selby, then a private, killed a rebel with his bayonet there, which is a remarkable thing in a battle and was spoken of in the official report. Selby called on the Texan to surrender, but he replied, "We'll see who surrenders," and made a lunge at Selby with his bayonet. Selby's skill in the bayonet exercise, in which they had been well drilled, gave him the advantage and he parried the stroke and plunged his own bayonet through the body of the Texan, who fell dead with Selby's bayonet sticking in his body. Thomas Lady also killed a man with his bayonet. Lady was mortally wounded. During this time, terrible fighting was being done along the whole line.

My company was fearfully cut up in this last charge. I had but eleven men standing when I thought the enemy was repulsed, but just as they went into the ravine, one of the rebels turned toward us and fired. I was at the head of my command and a little in front. I saw the fire was aimed at me and tried to avoid it but fate willed otherwise and I fell right backwards, indeed "with my back to the field and my feet to the foe." I was struck in the face. I felt as if I had been hit with a piece of timber, so terrible was the concussion and a stunning pain went through my head. I thought I was killed. It was my impression that I would never rise, but I was not alarmed or distressd by the thought that I was dying; it seemed a matter of indifference to me. In a little while I tried to rise and found I could do so. I got up and tried to walk to the rear. There was no one wounded in my company after I fell. Just at that time our supports charged and pursued the retreating foe, and the battle closed. The victory was ours.

When I got on my feet I walked to the rear a few yards till I came to the trunk of a fallen tree. I was too weak to cross it, but I observed Private Frank Ingmire standing on the tree trunk and I said "Ingmire, help me over."

"Yes," he replied, "let me help you across," and gave me his left hand.

I then noticed that his right arm was dangling at his side, his hand dripping blood. His wrist had been shattered by a ball. He helped me over the log and I took hold of his left arm with both my hands to support myself, saying, "Ingmire, don't leave me," but I only walked a short distance till I felt my hands slipping off his arm, my knees doubling under me, and I sank to the ground unconscious, and knew nothing more until I came to, in the field hospital two days later.

—JACKSON, *The Colonel's Diary*

8. THE ORPHAN BRIGADE IS SHATTERED AT STONES RIVER

After Shiloh Braxton Bragg was appointed to command the Army of Tennessee. When Halleck detached Buell for an advance on Chattanooga, Bragg took some 40,000 men and got there before him. From September through December 1862 there was confused marching and countermarching through central Kentucky and Tennessee. One detachment of Bragg's army, under Kirby Smith, reached Frankfort, Kentucky, and inaugurated a secession government in that state. Buell advanced on the Confederates there, and on October 8 struck them at Perryville; the battle was a draw but the Confederates retired into East Tennessee and then to Murfreesboro, on the Stones River, not far from Nashville. Meantime Rosecrans had supplanted Buell in command of the newly organized Army of the Cumberland. He built up supplies at Nashville and, when he was ready, moved out to fight Bragg.

The two armies met December 31, outside Murfreesboro, and one of the most bitterly contested battles of the war ensued. It was, in a sense, another Shiloh. Bragg got the jump on Rosecrans, smashed his right flank, and rolled him up against Stones River. Just as disaster threatened the whole Federal army Thomas turned his artillery on the enemy and held him in check. The next day the Confederates renewed the battle, but the most desperate effort came on the third day, January 2, when the misguided Bragg ordered Breckinridge to attack the Union left.

Lieutenant L. D. Young of the 4th Kentucky "Orphan Brigade" tells the story of the futile attack.

CAPTAIN Bramblett with two of his lieutenants, myself one of them, crawled through the weeds a distance of several hundred yards to a prominent point of observation from which through his field glass and even the naked eye we could see the enemy's concentrated forces near and above the lower ford on the opposite side of the river, his artillery being thrown forward and nearest to the river. His artillery appeared to be close together and covering quite a space of ground; we could not tell how many guns, but there was quite a number. The infantry was seemingly in large force and extended farther down toward the ford.

Captain Bramblett was a man of no mean order of military genius and information, and after looking at, and studying the situation in silence for some minutes, he said to us boys, "that he believed Rosecrans was setting a trap for Bragg." Continuing, he said, "If he means to attack us on this side, why does he not reinforce on this side? Why concentrate so much artillery on the bluff yonder? He must be expecting us to attack that force yonder, pointing to Beatty's position on the hill North of us, and if we do, he will use that artillery on us as we move to the attack." At another time during the afternoon I heard him while discussing the situation with other officers of the regiment use substantially the same argument. I accompanied Captain Bramblett to General Breckinridge's headquarters and heard him make substantially in detail a report containing the facts above recited. . . .

General Breckinridge, to thoroughly and unmistakably understand the situation and satisfy himself, in company with one or two of his staff examined the situation as best he could and I presume reached the same conclusion, and when he (Breckinridge) repaired to Bragg's headquarters and vouchsafed this information and suggested the presumptive plan of the enemy, Bragg said: "Sir, my information is different. I have given the order to attack the enemy in your front and expect it to be obeyed."

What was General Breckinridge to do but attempt to carry out his orders, though in carrying out this unwise and ill-conceived order it should cost in one hour and ten minutes 1,700 of as brave and chivalrous soldiers as the world ever saw. What a terrible blunder, what a bloody and useless sacrifice! . . .

How was this wicked and useless sacrifice brought about? "That subordinate must always obey his superior"—is the military law. In furtherance of Bragg's order we were assembled about three o'clock on the afternoon of January 2, 1863 (Friday, a day of ill luck) in a line North of and to the right of Swain's hill, confronting Beatty's and Growes' brigades, with a battery or two of artillery as support. They being intended for the bait that had been thrown across the river at the lower ford, and now occupied an eminence some three-quarters of a mile to the right-front of the Orphan's position on Swain's hill.

This was the force, small as it was that Bragg was so anxious to dislodge. Between the attacking line and federal position was a considerable scope of open ground, fields and pastures, with here and there a clump of bushes or briars, but the entire space was in full view of and covered by the enemy's batteries to the left of the line on the opposite side of the river previously referred to. If the reader will only carry these positions in his eye, he can readily discover the jaws of the trap in this murderous scheme.

A more imposing and thoroughly disciplined line of soldiers never moved to the attack of an enemy than responded to the signal gun stationed immediately in our rear, which was fired exactly at four o'clock. Every man vieing with his fellowman, in steadiness of step and correct alignment, with the officers giving low and cautionary commands, many knowing that it was their last hour on earth, but without hesitating moved forward to their inevitable doom and defeat. We had gotten only fairly started, when the great jaws of the trap on the bluff from the opposite side of the river were sprung, and bursting shells that completely drowned the voice of man were plunging and tearing through our columns, ploughing up the earth at our feet in front and behind, everywhere. But with steadiness of step we moved on. Two companies of the Fourth regiment, my own and adjoining company, encountered a pond, and with a dexterous movement known to the skilled officer and soldier was cleared in a manner that was perfectly charming, obliquing to the right and left into line as soon as passed.

By reason of the shorter line held by the enemy, our line, which was much longer and the colors of each of our battalions being directed against this shorter line, caused our lines to interlap, making it necessary, in order to prevent confusion and crowding, that some of the regiments halt, until the others had passed forward out of the way. When thus halted they would lie down in order to shield themselves from the enemy infantry fire in front, who had by this time opened a lively fusillade from behind their temporary works.

While lying on the ground momentarily . . . a shell exploded right in the middle of the company, almost literally tearing it to pieces. When I recovered from the shock the sight I witnessed was appalling. Some eighteen or twenty men hurled in every direction, including my dear friend, Lieut. George Burnley of Frankfort. But these circumstances were occurring every minute now while the battle was raging all around and about us. Men moved intuitively—the voice being silenced by the whizzing and bursting shells. On we moved, Beatty's and Growes' lines giving way seemingly to allow the jaws of the trap to press with more and ever increasing vigor upon its unfortunate and discomfited victims. But, on we moved, until the survivors of the decoy had passed the river and over the lines stationed on the other side of the river, when their new line of infantry opened on our confused and disordered columns another destructive and ruinous fire.

Coupled with this condition and correlative to it, a battery of Growes and a part of their infantry had been cut off from the ford and seeing our confused condition, rallied, reformed and opened fire on our advanced right now along the river bank. Confronted in front by their infantry, with the river intervening; swept by their artillery from the left and now attacked by both infantry and artillery by an oblique fire from the right, we found ourselves in a helpless condition, from which it looked like an impossibility to escape; and but for the fact that two or three batteries had been ordered into position to check the threatened advance of the enemy and thereby distract their attention, we doubtless would have fared still worse.

We rallied some distance to the right of where we started and found that many, very many, of our noblest, truest and best had fallen. Some of them were left on the field, among whom was my military preceptor, advisor and dear friend, Captain Bramblett, who fell into the hands of the enemy and who died a few days after in Nashville. I shall never forget our parting, a moment or two before he received his wound—never forget the last quick glance and the circumstances that called it forth. He was a splendid soldier and his loss grieved me very much. Many another gallant Kentuckian, some of our finest line and field officers, were left on the field, a sacrifice to stupidity and revenge. Thirty-seven per cent in one hour and ten minutes—some say one hour—was the frightful summary. Among the first of these was the gallant and illustrious Hanson, whose coolness and bearing was unsurpassed and whose loss was irreparable. He with Breckinridge, understood and was fully sensible of—as indicated by the very seriousness of his countenance—the unwisdom of this move and as shown in their protest to Bragg. What a pity that a strict observance of military rule compelled it to be obeyed against his mature military mind and judgment, causing the loss of such a magnificent soldier and gentleman—uselessly and foolishly.

Comtemplating this awful sacrifice, as he rode by the dead and dying in the rear of our lines, General Breckinridge, with tears falling from his eyes, was heard to say in tones of anguish, "My poor Orphans! My poor Orphans!" little thinking that he was dedicating to them a name that will live throughout the annals of time and crown the history of that dear little band with everlasting immortality.

—YOUNG, *Reminiscences of a Soldier in the Orphan Brigade*

XI

The Struggle for Missouri and the West

THE *war in the Trans-Mississippi West has been unjustly neglected by historians. The outcome of the war was decided, to be sure, in the East—at Gettysburg and Vicksburg, at Chattanooga and Atlanta and the Wilderness—yet the fighting in the West profoundly influenced the course of these Eastern campaigns, and some of these campaigns, in turn, were directed to the severance of the Confederacy along the Mississippi River.*

It was Missouri that was crucial. Had that state gone with the Confederacy the consequences would have been grave and might have been decisive. It outflanked Illinois and the Northwest; controlled the Mississippi; conditioned the fighting in Kentucky and Tennessee. And there was, from the beginning, a likely chance that Missouri would throw in its lot with the Confederacy, or yield to Confederate invasion. It was a slave state; a substantial part of its population was of Southern origin; its government was in the hands of Confederate sympathizers. Fortunately northern Missouri and the large German population were pro-Union; fortunately, too, the powerful Blair family was unalterably opposed to secession.

But at the beginning it was touch and go, and indeed it remained that until the war was well under way. Prompt action saved the St. Louis arsenal for the Union; prompt action, too, prevented Governor Jackson from using Camp Jackson as a rallying center for a secession movement. Meantime the Confederate forces grew apace, and in the fighting of the first year the Confederates had the best of it. Not until the Battle of Pea Ridge, in Arkansas, was Missouri safe for the Union, and even after that Sterling Price and Ben McCulloch, the bold Confederate leaders, tried one invasion after another. Even as late as summer of 1864 there was a major battle along the Missouri-Kansas boundary line at Westport, the "Gettysburg of the West." Meantime Missouri was the scene of the most desperate guerrilla and partisan fighting of the war: no other theater of the war could confess anything like the Lawrence and Baxter Springs massacres.

Much of the fighting in Arkansas was part of the Missouri campaign, and Arkansas, too, saw bitter guerrilla warfare. The campaigns along the Red River were part of the larger campaign for the control of the Mississippi. As the Federals closed both the lower and the upper portions of the Mississippi, the only major route from the West to the eastern Confederacy was the Red River, and the Confederate forces in Louisiana threatened New Orleans,

Baton Rouge, and even the Vicksburg expedition, from the Red River valley. There was, as we shall see, a good deal of marching and some fighting in the Bayou Teche country west of New Orleans.

Even the Far West boasted its campaigns. The Confederacy obtained substantial supplies through Mexico, and in the fall and winter of 1863 Banks had occupied Brownsville at the mouth of the Rio Grande and a number of harbors along the coast to Corpus Christi. In distant New Mexico, too, there was a campaign which ended disastrously for Confederate arms.

In a sense all the miscellaneous fighting over this vast area constitutes one great campaign for the control of the West and of the supplies and men that might come from the West to the East. At the risk therefore of cutting across or violating chronology, we present the various segments of the Trans-Mississippi fighting geographically rather than chronologically.

1. HOW THE ARMS WERE TAKEN FROM
THE ST. LOUIS ARSENAL

Nowhere was opinion more sharply—or evenly—divided than in Missouri; Governor Jackson went so far as to characterize Lincoln's call for troops as "illegal, unconstitutional, revolutionary, inhuman and diabolical." Although a state convention had voted against secession, Southern sympathizers planned to swing the state into the Confederacy. The first step in this plan was to seize the Federal arsenal at St. Louis, with 60,000 stand of arms. To forestall this plan Governor Yates of Illinois and Nathaniel Lyon, hero of the Union cause in Missouri, removed the arms to Illinois.

Here is the story of that early and decisive gambit in the chess game of Missouri politics and war.

CAPTAIN James H. Stokes, of Chicago, late of the regular army, volunteered to undertake the perilous mission, and Governor Yates placed in his hands the requisition of the Secretary of War for 10,000 muskets. Captain Stokes went to St. Louis, and made his way as rapidly as possible to the arsenal. He found it surrounded by an immense mob, and the postern gates all closed. His utmost efforts to penetrate the crowd were for a long time unavailing. The requisition was shown. Captain Lyon doubted the possibility of executing it. He said the arsenal was surrounded by a thousand spies, and every movement was watched and reported to the headquarters of the Secessionists, who could throw an overpowering force upon them at any moment. Captain Stokes represented that every hour's delay was rendering the capture of the arsenal more certain, and the arms must be moved to Illinois now or never. Major Callender agreed with him, and told him to take them at his own time and in his own way. This was Wednesday night, 24th April (1861).

Captain Stokes had a spy in the camp, whom he met at intervals in a certain place in the city. On Thursday, he received information that Gov. Jackson had ordered two thousand armed men from Jefferson city, whose movements could only contemplate a seizure of the arsenal, by occupying the heights around it, and planting batteries thereon. The job would have been an easy one. They had already planted one battery on the St. Louis levee, and another at Powder Point, a short distance below the arsenal. Capt. Stokes immediately telegraphed to Alton to have the steamer *City of Alton* drop down to the arsenal landing about midnight. He then returned to the arsenal, and commenced moving the boxes of guns, weighing some three hundred pounds each, down to the lower floor.

About 700 men were employed in the work. He then took 500 Kentucky flint-lock muskets, which had been sent there to be altered, and sent them to be placed on a steamer as a blind to cover his real movements. The Secessionists nabbed them at once, and raised a perfect Bedlam over the capture. A large portion of the outside crowd left the arsenal when this movement was executed; and Capt. Lyon took the remainder, who were lying around as spies, and locked them up in the guard-house. About 11 o'clock the steamer *City of Alton* came alongside, planks were shoved out from the windows to the main deck, and the boxes slid down. When the 10,000 were safely on board, Capt. Stokes went to Capt. Lyon and Major Callender, and urged them, by the most pressing appeals, to let him empty the arsenal. They told him to go ahead and take whatever he wanted. Accordingly, he took 10,000 more muskets, 500 new rifle carbines, 500 revolvers, 110,000 musket cartridges, to say nothing of the cannon and a large quantity of miscellaneous accoutrements, leaving only 7,000 muskets in the arsenal to arm the St. Louis volunteers.

When the whole were on board, about 2 o'clock on Friday morning the order was given by the captain of the steamer to cast off. Judge of the consternation of all hands when it was found that she would not move. The arms had been piled in great quantities around the engines to protect them against the battery on the levee, and the great weight had fastened the bows of the boat firmly on a rock, which was tearing a hole through the bottom at every turn of the wheels. A man of less nerve than Capt. Stokes would have gone crazy on the spot. He called the arsenal men on board, and commenced moving the boxes to the stern.

Fortunately, when about two hundred boxes had been shifted, the boat fell away from the shore, and floated in deep water. "Which way?" said Captain Mitchell, of the steamer. "Straight to Alton, in the regular channel," replied Captain Stokes. "What if we are attacked?" said Captain Mitchell. "Then we will fight," said Captain Stokes. "What if we are overpowered?" said Captain Mitchell. "Run her to the deepest part of the river, and sink her," replied Captain Stokes. "I'll do it," was the heroic answer of Capt. Mitchell; and away they went past the secession battery, past the entire St. Louis levee, and on to Alton, in the regular channel, where they arrived at five o'clock in the morning.

When the boat touched the landing, Capt. Stokes, fearing pursuit by some two or three of the Secession military companies by which the city of St. Louis is disgraced, ran to the market-house and rang the fire-bell. The citi-

Pickets Trading Tobacco and Coffee Across the Rappahannock

J. O. Casler

Edwin Forbes

Checking Confederate Advance at Shiloh

zens came flocking pell-mell to the river, in all sorts of habiliments. Capt. Stokes informed them of the situation of things, and pointed out the freight cars. Instantly, men, women, and children boarded the steamer, seized the freight, and clambered up the levees to the cars. Rich and poor tugged together with might and main for two hours, when the cargo was all deposited in the cars, and the train moved off, amid their enthusiastic cheers, for Springfield.

—Chicago Tribune, April 29, 1861

2. COTTON IS KING AT THE BATTLE OF LEXINGTON

On June 12, 1861, Governor Jackson abandoned his pretense of neutrality and declared openly for the Confederacy, calling for 50,000 volunteers to defend the state against the Federal invaders. Not that many were forthcoming, but Sterling Price gathered an army of perhaps 10,000, and was shortly reinforced from Arkansas by Ben McCulloch, a famous Texas Ranger. Nathaniel Lyon moved speedily to get control of the state capital, Jefferson City, then sent General Franz Sigel after Price. The two small armies met at Carthage, on the edge of the Ozarks, and Sigel was roundly beaten. Lyon himself came up to take command, followed the Confederates to Wilson's Creek, and—though outnumbered almost two to one—attacked them, August 10, 1861. The gallant Lyon was killed, and his beaten army fell back on Rolla, which had direct railroad connections with St. Louis. The Confederates marched north to the Missouri, by-passed Jefferson City, and attacked a small force of Federals at Lexington. It was another Confederate victory. After that the incompetent Frémont was removed from command in the West, and the Union organized its strength to drive the Confederates out of Missouri.

This story of the Battle of Lexington is told by an Englishman, Samuel P. Day, correspondent for the London Morning Herald.

THE Union forces, under Colonel Mulligan . . . had for some time previous occupied the town of Lexington, around which they had erected defences. On the night of the 11th September [1861] the attack was initiated by an advance party of Confederate troops, who appeared in front of the Federal entrenchments, when a sharp action took place. Four cannons were planted, so as to command the different points, including the entire semi-circle of the Federal position, and a falling fire was kept up in addition to an incessant discharge of musketry. The Confederates rendered themselves almost invisible, being concealed in the adjacent corn-fields and woods; so the attacked party had no other means of doing execution among them, than by firing in the neighbourhood of the localities designated by the cannon smoke, and now and again taking aim at the sharp-shooters who had ventured out of ambush. . . .

On the morning of Wednesday the 17th, the Confederates, under General Price, opened fire from all their batteries, and kept pouring in a shower of iron hail the entire day upon the enemy's entrenchments; while the practice of the sharp-shooters was excellent, as has been acknowledged by the enemy himself. Some time after the siege had commenced, with a praiseworthy humanity General Price sent a flag of truce to Colonel Mulligan, demanding a surrender, and informing him, that as the force he commanded was so superior as to render it useless for him to contend, he had no desire to fight for the sake of shedding blood. He proposed, moreover, to allow the Federal forces to march out of the town under arms, taking their property and baggage with them. All that General Price required was the position; and, this yielded, General Mulligan was free to go with his command wherever he pleased. Half-way between the lines both Generals met, attended by their respective Staff-officers. General Mulligan was obstinate, and would not accept the liberal proposition made to him. They separated, however, in a seemingly friendly manner, and with mutual expressions of regret that the fortunes of war had made their interest so antagonistic and deadly.

During the afternoon of the 18th a hand-to-hand conflict took place, which was but of short duration, when the Confederate troops attacked and carried a portion of the works. Advancing in a strong and steady line up a slope, after slight opposition they caused the Montgomery Guards to break from their entrenchments and retire in disorder before their approach. A murderous volley was then poured into the dispersed ranks, inflicting the heaviest loss that had been experienced since the opening of the siege. Colonel Mulligan endeavoured to rally his men for a charge, but few of them responded to his call.

Hot shot and shell kept pouring into the town, one ball having fired the College building, in which the Federal provisions had been collected. Nevertheless, the troops succeeded in saving the stores and extinguishing the conflagration. From eight o'clock until midnight was occupied by both belligerents in burying their dead. When the truce had expired, the cannonade opened again with additional vigour on the Confederate side, which the enemy did not reply to until the morning. So soon as daybreak had revealed localities sufficiently to afford correct aim, the cannonading became more furious still. The firing on both sides was continuous and furious, and nothing could be heard save the heavy boom of artillery and the sharp clank of musketry.

The ingenuity of the Southerners was conspicuously manifested by the invention of a moving breast-work of cotton bales, which received the Federal shot harmlessly, and completely protected the troops from injury. The effect created by this novel appliance of warfare may be estimated by the following account furnished by the Correspondent of a Northern journal:—

"At this juncture our men discovered, with no little dismay, an engine of war, which was being brought to bear upon them, threatening the very consequences which they dreaded most—a safe approach for the enemy, and an ultimate charge in force over the entrenchments. The rebels presented a strong breast-work of hemp-bales, which appeared like a moving barrier, impenetrable to bullets or cannon shot, and swarming with men in the rear. It was about twenty rods in length, and the height of two bales of hemp. The bales were placed with the ends facing our fortifications, affording a thickness of about six feet. This immense breast-work commenced moving forward, not by detachments or singly, but in one vast body, unbroken and steady, as though it slid along the ground at its own volition. It advanced steadily over the smooth surface, parting to pass trees, and closing up again, as impenetrable as a rock. Behind it were hundreds of men pushing and urging with levers, while others held the bales steadily to their places, and others still, whose numbers were almost indefinite, firing between the crevices and over the top at our soldiers.

"Our men looked at the moving monster in astonishment. It lay like a large serpent, winding over the hills and hollows, apparently motionless, yet moving broadside on, to envelop and destroy them in its vast folds. In vain the cannon were turned upon it. The heavy bales absorbed the shot harmlessly, or quietly resumed the positions from which they were displaced, seemingly moving without hands, but in reality controlled by strong arms, which were unseen. In vain the musket bullets rained upon it in unremitting showers. The thousands that it concealed were safe from such puny assaults, and slowly gliding along, they waited with eagerness the time when their position should warrant them in bursting through its walls and storming up to the intrenchments. Our brave soldiers could only watch it with keen anxiety, and wait for the fearful result."

After having been desperately attacked upon various sides, and finding it useless to resist, about four o'clock on the afternoon of Wednesday, Major Becker, who commanded the Home Guards, crawled out to an advanced breast-work, and ran up a white flag.

The Home Guards deserted their trenches at the order of Major Becker, and rushed into the inner fortification, where they again raised the white flag, and kept it flying. Immediately upon this the Confederates ceased firing, and the garrison was thrown into the greatest confusion. Word was passed around that a surrender had been made, and the men left their entrenchments in disorder to ascertain the truth. Consternation reigned in all directions—Colonel Mulligan, it is said, being on the opposite side, and nobody present to assume control. Word was sent to him, and he ordered the flag down; but the Captains, who by this time realized their true position, and saw nothing but death or surrender before them, implored him to save the men.

Meanwhile the hemp breast-works had moved up under cover of the general confusion, until they had got within a few yards of the Federal entrenchments. The Confederate forces advanced, and everything indicated that the moment had arrived when the crowning assault was to be attempted. In this emergency Colonel Mulligan ordered his men to lay down their arms, and an officer was dispatched to General Price with a flag of truce.

—DAY, *Down South*

3. GUERRILLA WARFARE IN MISSOURI

This long succession of Confederate victories heartened Southern sympathizers not only in Missouri but in Kansas and Arkansas as well. Guerrilla bands harried Union sympathizers everywhere, and some of them were not too careful whom they attacked; from Kansas came the Jay Hawkers—a term applied indiscriminately to Unionists and Confederates—to join in the civil war.

We have here two accounts of guerrilla warfare after Wilson's Creek and Lexington. The first is from the pen of young William Gulick of the 1st Iowa Cavalry, who fought through the campaigns in Missouri and Arkansas until his death, in September 1864; the fighting he describes was in Bates County, on the border of Kansas. The second comes from Colonel Monks and describes conditions in Ozark County, on the Arkansas border, in 1862.

A. "The Contemptable Jay Hawkers"

Butler, Bates Co. Mo. June 1 [1862]

Dear Sister Cynthia.

The 29th the wind blew hard & the Tents as well as every thing else was a cloud of dust. Next day I was on Guard, & yesterday I just comencd this letter when a messenger came from Johnstown with foaming stead stating that a small party with baggage train from here to Osceola had been attacked by a larger party of Rebel J[ay] H[awkers]. I volunteered with two other of our Co. & as many from each of the six Cos here to go to the rescue. In less than twenty minutes we were on the raod. Our Horses were let out to Fourteen miles an hour all hands expecting for once to have some fighting. But it turned out as usual we were to late, for about Fifteen minutes after the engagement commenced a party of Co. L. came up. They were on their way from Clinton to this place. The rebels took to the brush.

Our boys followed them but the brush is so thick at this season of the year that they all escaped. One or two of there men were wounded. Our loss was one horse killed. One man shot in the foot. One through his coat collar, another through the hat.

The contemptable J. H.s have the advantage of us now & they use it too. It is folly to even *attempt* to hunt them in the brush. They lay in ambush & shoot a Soldier where ever they can. Not long since Three of our men were killed & one severely wounded while out after Forage. The rebels fired at them while watering at a creek. One escaped to give the alarm. the killed were bruitaly stabed and heads nearly mashed in the ground also Robed of every thing they had even boots. The men killed were from Cos C. & D.— Last week Three men were killed at Osceola in nearly the same manner. . . . A man was also shot from Co. I. Three or Four days ago near this place. as yet we have only succeeded in killing one of the miscreants. But now a special order has been issued to shoot Two of the prisoners we have in our prison for every soldier that is shot. I think this order will be carried out. We have some hard cases in prison here & about Forty of them too. nearly every night some of our Pickets are fired at, or fire to some one. I am one of the unfortunate ones I can never get a shot or scarcely ever have an occasion to shoot. I go on nearly every scout but cannot shoot a secesh. They say we will not scout much more here. I hope then we will leave this miserable God forsaken country where we will have something to do. I observe those that lay around camp the most are the most sickly. There is a lot in every Co. that is never ready for duty, never go a scouting or scarcely anything else, *except to their rations,* and they are always behind. they think *so much gained.* But they mistake for it is an injury to their health. Our Co. is Generally healthy. as for myself I weigh One hundred Fifty Eight lbs. never better in my life.

Truly Yours
WM O. GULICK

—GUYER, ed., "Journal and Letters of Corporal William O. Gulick"

B. THE DISPLACED PERSONS OF SOUTHERN MISSOURI

THE rebels being encouraged by the late victory, determined to rid the country of all Union men at once. About that time about 350 men, mostly from Oregon county, commanded by two very prominent men, made a scout into Ozark county, Mo. On reaching the North Fork of White River they went into camp at what was known as Jesse James' mill. The owner, a man of about 55 or 60 years of age, as good a man as resided in Ozark county, was charged with grinding corn for Union men and their families; at the time he and a man by the name of Brown were cutting saw logs about two miles from home in the pinery. They went out and arrested them, arrested an old man by the name of Russell and several others, carried them to a man's house, who was a Union man, and had fled to prevent arrest. They took Brown and James about 300 yards from the house, procured a rope, hunted a long limb of a tree, rolled a big rock up to the tree where the first rope was tied to the limb, placed the noose about James' neck, stood him on the rock, rolled the rock out from under him and left him swinging, rolled the rock to the next rope, stood Brown on it, placed the noose around his neck, rolled the rock out and left Brown swinging in the air, went to the third rope, placed Russell on the rock, and just as they aimed to adjust the noose, word came that the home guards and Federals were right upon them in considerable force. They fled, leaving Russell standing upon the rock and both Brown and James dangling in the air.

Every Union man now having fled in fear of his life, the next day the wives of Brown and James, with the help of a few other women, buried them as best they could. They dug graves underneath the swinging bodies, laid bed clothing in the graves and cut them loose. The bodies fell into the coffinless graves and the earth was replaced. So the author is satisfied that the bones of these men still remain in the lonely earth underneath where they met their untimely death with no charge against them except that they had

INDIANA

Wabash River

White River

Ohio

KENTUCKY

Cumberland Riv.

Tennessee Riv.

Fort Donelson

Fort Henry

TENNESSEE

Cairo
Paducah
Columbus
Belmont

ILLINOIS

St. Louis

Mississippi River

New Madrid

MISSOURI

Rolla

Jefferson City

Booneville

Missouri River

Lexington

OZARK MOUNTAINS

Springfield

Wilson's Creek

Carthage

Cassville

Pea Ridge

Fayetteville

ARKANSAS

THE STRATEGIC POSITION OF MISSOURI

been feeding Union men, with no one to bury them but their wives and a few other women who aided. . . .

A short time after this hanging there was a man by the name of Rhodes, who resided at the head of Bennett's Bayou in Howell County. He was about eighty years of age and had been a soldier under General Jackson. His head was perfectly white and he was very feeble. When he heard of the hanging of Brown and James he said openly that there was no civil war in that, and that the men who did it were guilty of murder.

Some two weeks from the date of the hanging of Brown and James, about twenty-five men, hearing of what he had said, organized themselves and commanded by Dr. Nunly and William Sapp, proceeded to the house of Rhodes, where he and his aged wife resided alone, calling him out and told him they wanted him to go with them. His aged wife came out, and being acquainted with a part of the men, and knowing that they had participated in the hanging and shooting of a number of Union men, talked with them and asked: "You are not going to hurt my old man?" They said: "We just want him to go a piece with us over here." Ordering the old man to come along, they went over to a point about a quarter of a mile from the house and informed him of what he had said. There they shot him, cut his ears off and his heart out. Dr. Nunly remarked that he was going to take the heart home with him, pickle it and keep it so people could see how a black Republican's heart looked.

In the meantime, Rhodes not having returned home, and not a single Union man left in the country that Mrs. Rhodes could get to look after him, and having heard when they reached Joseph Spears' that the old man was not with them, although very feeble, she still continued the search; on the second day, about fifty yards from the road and about a quarter of a mile from home, she heard hogs squealing and grunting as though they were eating something. She proceeded to the place and found the hogs were just about to commence eating the remains of her husband. The Union men having fled, she notified some of the neighbors, and the women came in and helped dress the body and buried him the best they could.

There never was a man arrested by the Confederate authorities, or a single word of condemnation uttered, but as far as could be heard there was general approval. It was said that the means were desperate, but that was the only way to get rid of the men and strike terror to them so they could neither give aid nor countenance to the lop-eared Dutch. . . .

After they had hung, shot, and captured and driven from the country all of the Union men, they called a public meeting for the purpose of taking into consideration what should be done with the families of the Union men, which meeting had a number of preachers in it. After discussing the premises, they arrived at the conclusion that if they let the families of the Union men, who had escaped and gone into the Federal lines, remain, they would return and bring in the lop-eared Dutch. They didn't believe that both parties could ever live together, and as they now had the country completely rid of the Union men, they would force their families to leave. They at once appointed men, among whom were several preachers, to go to each one of the Union families and notify them that they would not be allowed to remain; because if they let them stay, their men would be trying to come back, and they didn't believe both parties could live together. They stated at the same time that they were really sorry for the women and children, but nobody was to blame but their husbands and sons, who had cast their lot with the lop-eared Dutch. Also, as they had taken up arms against the Confederate States, all the property they had, both real and personal, was subject to confiscation and belonged to the Confederate authorities; but they would allow them to take enough of their property to carry them inside of the lines of the lop-eared Dutch, where they supposed their men were and where they could care for them.

They said they might have a reasonable time to make preparations to leave the country, and if they didn't leave, they would be forced to do so, if they had to arrest them and carry them out.

The wildest excitement then prevailed among the women and children. They had no men to transact their business and make preparations to leave. Little had they thought, while they were chasing, arresting, hanging and shooting their men, that they, too, would become victims of the rebel hatred and be forced to leave house and home, not knowing where their men were or whether they were dead or alive. All they knew of their whereabouts was, that those who escaped arrest had left their homes, aiming to reach the nearest Federal lines.

Women were at once dispatched to reach the nearest Federal lines, if possible, and inform them of the Confederate order, and procure help to take them out. Their homes and houses were being continually raided by small bands of Confederates roaming over the country, claiming that they were hunting Union men, taking all classes of property that they might see proper to take, without any restraint whatever.

The suffering that followed the women and children is indescribable. They had to drive their own teams, take care of the little ones, travel through the storms, exposed to it all without a man to help them, nor could they hear a single word of comfort spoken by husband, son or friend. On reaching the Federal lines, all vacant houses and places of shelter were soon filled, and they were known and styled as refugees. Many of them went into soldier huts, where the soldiers had wintered and covered the tops of their huts with earth. They had to leave home with a small amount of rations, and on the road the rebels would stop them and make them divide up the little they had started with, and reaching the Federal lines they would be almost destitute of food and many of them very scantily clothed.

—Monks, "A History of Southern Missouri and Northern Arkansas"

4. THE TIDE TURNS AT PEA RIDGE

Halleck was now in command in the West. In December he sent Pope out with greatly strengthened forces to restore Union control of northern and central Missouri. Price had retreated to Springfield; he now moved south-ward to Arkansas where he was joined by Ben McCulloch with a force that included some 5,000 Indians from the Five Civilized Nations. Their com-bined force numbered over 20,000, and was under the command of General Van Dorn. After him went General Samuel Curtis. The two armies met at Pea Ridge, Arkansas, at the southernmost tip of the Ozarks. With almost a two-to-one superiority Van Dorn thought it safe to divide his army and try an attack from front and rear. The attempt miscarried. While the Con-federate left flank was successful, the right under McCulloch was thrown back with heavy loss. The next day, March 8, 1862, Curtis extended his line around both Confederate flanks, enfiladed the Confederates with artillery fire, and forced them to retreat. It was a decisive victory; thereafter Missouri was safe for the Union.

Curtis was one of the ablest—and most neglected—officers in the Union Army. A graduate of West Point he served as colonel of the 3rd Ohio in the Mexican War, became chief engineer of St. Louis, joined the Republican party and served as Congressman from Iowa from 1858 to 1861. Appointed brigadier general he was sent west and commanded the troops at Pea Ridge; later he was in command at the important Battle of Westport.

General Franz Sigel, who tells this story, was one of the noble band of '48ers who had fought for liberalism in Germany. He fled to Switzerland and later to England, and came to the United States in 1852. The outbreak of the war found him director of public schools of St. Louis; he was appointed gen-eral of the 2nd Missouri Brigade, fought at Pea Ridge, and went with Pope to Virginia. After the war Sigel moved to New York City, where he had a long and distinguished career as editor.

IT was a little after 6 o'clock in the morning [March 8] when I sent out Colonel Osterhaus with Captain Asmussen of my staff to reconnoiter the ground on which I intended to deploy, and to find the nearest road leading to it. The 44th Illinois followed the two officers for the purpose of marking the right of the position to be taken, but with orders to keep concealed as much as possible, and not to enter into an engagement unless attacked. Half an hour later, I was standing in front of my tent, ready to mount, and anx-iously awaiting the return of the staff-officers, when suddenly a few cannon-shots in our front, from Davidson's Union battery, announced the conflict. At this moment General Curtis, to whom I had sent word during the night where my two divisions were assembling, and that they would be ready for action in the morning, rode toward me from the direction where the firing had begun, and, somewhat excitedly, said: "General, I have opened the bat-tle; it will be a hard fight; Davis is already there. Please bring your troops in line as quickly as possible."

I confess that I did not understand the reason why a cannonade was com-menced on our side when we were not ready to meet a counter-attack of the enemy with a good chance of success, the more so, as I had been out in our front before General Curtis met me, and had found that our line was weak, stretched out in an open field, the Telegraph road obstructed by artillery, ammunition-wagons, and other vehicles, and that there was no room to deploy my divisions, except behind the first line and masked by it; nor on the left, unless immediately exposed to and raked by the fire of the enemy, whose batteries were supposed to be posted in the margin of the woods, whence they could reach my troops at point-blank range. I explained this to General Curtis, made him acquainted with the object in view, told him that I expected Colonel Osterhaus and Captain Asmussen back every moment, and finally asked him to give me ten minutes' time to wait for them, when I would move immediately to the position selected and commence the attack. Even if our troops on the right should be compelled to yield, it could only be momentarily, as the enemy would have to direct his whole attention to my attack on his flank and rear. I never felt more relieved than when General Curtis, evidently encouraged by this proposition, said: "Well, General, do what you propose." I must add here that I had not seen General Curtis during the night and before I met him near my tent; he could, therefore, not have been fully aware of what I had experienced in my position away from him on the left, and what my intention was to do in the morning, although I had sent Captain Asmussen to his headquarters to report to him, receiving, however, no orders from him in return. After our conversation, which lasted only a few minutes, the two officers came back in all haste, and reported that they had found an excellent position; that no enemy was in sight, and that Colonel Knobelsdorff, with his regiment, was posted as directed. General Curtis declared himself satisfied and rode off, but scarcely had he left me when the cannonade in front became very brisk, some of the hostile missiles bursting over our heads.

I mounted, told Colonel Osterhaus to take charge of our column and move it to the position to be occupied; then, accompanied by Captain Asmussen, I rode to the front, where Davis's division had formed into line, to see what was going on. I found one of our batteries hotly engaged, but compelled to withdraw, which exposed the infantry on the right to an enfilading fire, and also forced it to change its position. One of the regiments—I think it was the 22d or the 8th Indiana—was thrown into momentary disorder by this surprise, and the men fell back toward an eminence on the right of the road on which I was halting. I assisted their brave commander to rally them, which did not take long, and spoke a few words to them, saying that if the right could hold out for half an hour, assistance would come, and all would be well. Meanwhile another regiment had formed on the left, the battery had taken position again and was supported by four other guns (of White's brigade), farther to the left, diverting the enemy's fire.

The line stood firm, and as no hostile infantry appeared, I took leave of the commander of the "Indiana boys," and hastened to my own troops. I reached the head of the column when it was just debouching from the woods, and the first battery that arrived took position on the left of the 44th Illinois, which was kneeling behind a fence. In about 15 minutes the First Division (Osterhaus's) was formed into line, with the artillery in the intervals between the infantry, the Second Division in reserve, about 250 paces behind our right, with General Asboth at its head, who, in spite of his wound received on the 7th, was again in the saddle. Our position, in full view of the open fields, which sloped gently down toward the long skirt of woods, where the enemy's artillery and infantry were posted, was excellent, and allowed the full development of our forces. The enemy's batteries received us well, but many of their shots were either aimed too high, or struck the ground and were buried a short distance in front of us. When well in action, we advanced slowly from position to position, at the same time contracting our line, the infantry following, rising quickly, and as soon as they had reached a new position lying down again. . . .

It was now a little after 11 o'clock; most of the enemy's batteries (about fifty guns) were silenced one after another, by our concentric fire; his infantry, not venturing out of the woods into the open fields, was now treated with a shower of shell and shrapnel. Opposite our extreme left, however, near Elkhorn Tavern, Van Dorn made a determined effort to hold the high spur of hills, the top of which was crowned and protected by rocks and bowlders. Some of Price's infantry had already taken possession of it, and a battery was being placed in position, when Hoffmann's and Elbert's batteries were ordered to direct their fire against them chiefly with solid shot. Not more than fifteen minutes elapsed before the enemy evacuated this last stronghold, while our infantry on the left—the 36th Illinois, and the 2d, 3d, and 17th Missouri—rushed up the steep hill and forced the remnants of the enemy's troops down into Cross Timber Hollow. Almost simultaneously the 12th Missouri, the 25th and the 44th Illinois advanced in double-quick from the center and right into the woods, engaged the enemy's infantry, drove it back, and one of our regiments (the 12th Missouri) captured the "Dallas Battery." On the extreme right, where General Curtis had directed the movements of the troops, Davis's division and a part of Carr's, assisted by Hayden's and Jones's batteries (the latter commanded by Lieutenant David), pushed forward against the left wing of the enemy and forced it to leave the field. The army of Van Dorn and Price, including about two-thirds of McCulloch's troops under Churchill and Greer, and one-third of Pike's Indian Brigade, all of whom had joined Price during the night, were now in precipitate retreat in all directions, pursued by the First and Second Divisions as far as Keetsville, 9 miles to the north, and by a cavalry force under Colonel Bussey with 2 mountain howitzers to the south-west beyond Bentonville. So ended the battle of Pea Ridge, and our little army, instead of being "beaten and compelled to surrender," had gained a decisive victory.

—SIGEL, "The Pea Ridge Campaign"

5. THE CONFEDERATES SCATTER AFTER PEA RIDGE

Confederate losses at Pea Ridge had been shattering; the losses on the retreat were doubtless as heavy. Alarmed at the situation in western Tennessee and in Mississippi, the Confederate government ordered Van Dorn to

transfer his army to Memphis. This put an effective end to the formal fight-
ing in Arkansas; guerrilla warfare continued.

William Watson, who here tells us something of the retreat and disin-
tegration of Confederate forces after Pea Ridge, was a Scotsman engaged in
business at Baton Rouge. He enlisted in the Confederate Army; fought in
the Missouri and Arkansas campaigns and at Corinth; was mustered out and
re-enlisted; was captured and exchanged. Later he was active in blockade-
running. His Life in the Confederate Army *is one of the liveliest accounts*
of the nonmilitary aspects of the war in the West.

WE had now the march before us, and we must undertake it, without provisions, without tents or cooking utensils, without blankets or over-coats, and our thin clothing now worn and ragged. I have never seen or read either in newspaper or history any details of this miniature Moscow retreat. It was, perhaps, one of those black or blurred pages in history that is un-readable, and is best to be torn out.

We proceeded to scramble along the best way we could, wading through creeks and rivers and scrambling over rocks and through brushwood. At night we kindled large fires and took off our wet clothes, wrung the water out of them, and dried them the best way we could. Occasionally we passed a small settlement from which the inhabitants had fled, but everything had been carried away by Price's army. In the gardens we sometimes found the remains of some turnips or onions, which were eagerly dug out of the ground with our sabres and eaten raw. Everything like military order of march was at an end, but the battalions and companies kept in their places, and dis-cipline was still maintained, although to leave the line in search of something to eat could no longer be strictly forbidden. Several times it was found that we had taken the wrong road and had to turn back. Sometimes we passed through rather better tracts of country which had been settled, but the few settlers had all fled from their homes and the houses were deserted, and every-thing in the shape of food had been taken by Price's troops. . . .

About the seventh night we halted on the sloping banks of a creek which ran at the bottom of a pretty deep valley. On the near side of the creek there was abundance of dry grass, making a fine place to bivouac; and, what was better, the weather had suddenly changed, and the afternoon and eve-ning were warm and sultry. We expected to get some sleep to-night if the pangs of hunger would allow us. How the other companies were faring we were not sure, but supposed they had just their little chances same as ourselves.

Notwithstanding the wretchedness of our condition, there was through-out the whole of this trying campaign still kept up a continual animation by light merry-making. Joking was always the order of the day. The most dis-agreeable and trying privations were alleviated and smoothed over by turning them into a cause for laughter. If some became sullen and desponding, there were always some spirits who could by some comical expressions raise the merry laugh and incite good humour, and put animation into the men. . . .

When daylight came, and we were about to proceed on our march, we found we were in something of a fix.

Our line of march was across the creek, and we had not followed the rules, which was that a creek should always be crossed and the troops to bivouac on the far side. This rule had been departed from at this time, because on the far side of the creek there was not for some distance any suitable place for bivouacing, besides creeks here were so plentiful, and had to be crossed so often, that if we got on the far side we were not far from the near side of another. However, in this case the meaning or object of the rule was very well demonstrated.

The creek, by the sudden storm, was swollen to a great extent, so that it was impossible to cross, and we could not proceed; and if the enemy had been harassing our rear we would have been in the same position as the Israelites at the Red Sea. What was now to be done? No other route was possible; we were pressed by starvation, and no food was to be obtained in the neighbourhood. It would be at least two days before the creek was passable, and if more rain fell it was quite uncertain when we might get across. There was only the remnant or wreck of the 2nd brigade here, but who was in command of it, or whether it had any commander, we did not know, every regiment seeming to act for itself, and every company to act for itself.

After a consultation among the officers of our regiment, it was agreed that the regiment should separate and each company act for itself, and get along the best way they could to Van Buren, and there join again.

Each company then started to shift for itself as they best could. The novelty of the thing was pleasing, as they were now comparatively free. Our company, amounting in the aggregate to 32, proceeded by itself. We had two axes which we carried along for cutting wood for fires, etc., but that was all the company property we had beyond our arms. We proceeded along the creek to see if there was any possibility of finding a place where we might effect a crossing by felling trees so as to fall across it.

We had some splendid fellows for such an emergency, who could handle the axe as well as the rifle, one of whom we called Canada, as he was a native of that country.

Some gigantic trees grew along the edge of the creek in some places, and soon one of them fell across the stream, but it went whirling away with the roaring torrent as if it had been chips. Another and another was cut, but all were carried away.

At length we came to a place where the creek was narrow and the banks high, but there did not seem to be any tree large enough and sufficiently near the bank to fall across, and at this narrow part all were eagerly looking for a tree that would, if felled, span the creek.

"Here, sergeant! here, sergeant," cried Tim D., in great ecstasy, "here is a fine one."

I hastened to where he was. "Where is it?" said I.

"Over yonder," said he, pointing to a tree on the opposite side of the creek, "if we could only manage to get over to cut it."

"You confounded fool," said I, "if we could only manage to get over to it, it would be of no use to us, because we would not want it."

"What is that?" cried some one.

"Oh, it is one of Tim's bulls," said I. "He proposes that we cross the river first, and then cut a tree on the other side."

"Throw him in the river!" cried two or three of the boys.

"Well, now, that was not what I said at all," cried Tim. "I said, There is a fine tree over there, and if some of yees would go over and cut it, we would all get over; and if you would just come and see the tree, you would say yourself that it was a splendid one."

"Then, go over and cut it;" cried two or three of the boys.

At that time Lieutenant G. and Canada, the axe-man, came up; we looked across at the tree and pondered. "Well, certainly, if any one was on that side to cut that tree it would just fall across and make a splendid bridge. I wonder if there could be no means of getting one man across to cut it."

There was a place a little farther down, where the stream ran through a narrow chasm, where the banks were high on each side, and not quite 30 feet from bank to bank, but there were no trees near the place. It was suggested that we might get one of the tall ash trees, which grew higher up the bank, and carry it down, and raise it on end and let it fall across, and if it did not break it would be strong enough for some active fellow to straddle over upon, and then we could throw him over the axe to cut the tree.

"The very thing!" cried Canada, "and I will volunteer to cross on it." And he was off at once to select a suitable ash tree.

One was soon cut down and trimmed, and all hands carried it to the place, and a hole was dug in the ground with our sabres to put the thick end into, while the men got about it, and with the aid of long forked sticks got it raised to the perpendicular; and it was thrown across, and landed successfully on the other side.

The roaring torrent below looked rather trying to the nerves.

"Here, Tim," cried some of the boys, "go over now and cut the tree."

Tim said he would go, but, as he was no axe-man, he could not cut the tree.

"Then stand aside, you useless bog-trotter."

The end of the tree was firmly bedded, and held tight to keep it from rolling, while Canada straddled across, like Blondin, crossing Niagara Falls on the tight rope. He landed safely on the other side, amidst the cheers of the boys; while another immediately crossed after him, and we threw them over the two axes. Of course, they cried back in a joke, pretending to bid us goodbye, as they were going to proceed on and leave us, but we could not hear them for the roaring of the torrent.

They both set to work with a will and the tree, a very large one, soon fell across the creek, forming an excellent bridge, and in a few minutes all had scrambled over.

We ascended the banks on the opposite side, where we looked back and saw some of the other companies along on the banks, vainly searching for a place to cross. We gave a loud cheer to attract their attention. There was soon a commotion among them, and a cry of—"Hilloa, the rifles are over!"

We pointed in the direction of where we had crossed, that they might see our bridge and make use of it, and we proceeded on our way.

"Now, don't yees see," said Tim D., "that I was right after all; you talk about bulls and bog-trotters, but if it had not been for me you would all have been left behind."

"Why, what did you do?"

"Well, it was my tree that was the right tree, and if it had not been the right tree you might all have been drowned in the river, and then you would have said that I had been right." . . .

We now got on to the regular road, and the track of an army was now only too plainly visible—every house was deserted, and everything in the shape of food or forage was carried away, and a good deal of property seemed to have been wantonly destroyed.

We saw some stragglers on the road before us, and we hastened to overtake them, thinking that they might be a part of our regiment, or perhaps Lieutenant G.'s party. When we overtook them we found them to be mostly of our regiment, but not more than a dozen in all, and among them were two of our company, from Lieutenant G.'s party.

Upon inquiring how it was with the party, and why they were separated from it, they said that Lieutenant G. had heard something about some of the missing from our company, and that our 2nd lieutenant, B., was lying very ill somewhere, and some others were also in distress, and he was going to try to render them assistance; and that he had told these two to go and see if they could meet with our party, and tell us not to wait for them, but to push on to Van Buren.

The effects of an army passing over a country distracted by war were now clearly to be seen. Be that army friend or foe, it passes along like a withering scourge, leaving only ruin and desolation behind.

We found it needless to attempt to procure anything like food on the way, and it was only a loss of time and strength going off the road to look for it. We therefore resolved to push on and reach Van Buren as soon as possible, as the road was now plain before us.

At length we drew near to the place. The poor fellows were brightened up with hope, but they were in a sorry plight. They were actually staggering from want and fatigue. Their shoes were worn off their feet, from passing over rocks and boulders, and through creeks. Their clothes were in rags from scrambling through the woods and briars, and burnt in holes from crouching too close to the camp fires in their broken slumbers. Their eyes were bleared and bloodshot, from want of sleep and the smoke of the wood-fires, and their bodies were emaciated by hunger. But now their difficulties were overcome, and their privations supposed to be at an end for the time at least.

It was about three o'clock in the afternoon when we entered Van Buren.

—WATSON, *Life in the Confederate Army*

6. QUANTRILL AND HIS GUERRILLAS SACK LAWRENCE

William C. Quantrill is probably the most unsavory figure of the Civil War. Born in Ohio, he moved to Kansas in 1857, where he lived something of a Jekyll-Hyde life, teaching school as William Quantrill, gambling and stealing—and perhaps murdering—as Charley Hart. With the outbreak of the war he raised an irregular band of Confederate sympathizers in the border country of Kansas and Missouri, fought at Lexington, and then embarked upon a career of guerrilla warfare. The Federal government declared him an outlaw, but the Confederates mustered him into service and commissioned him captain. In August 1863 he rode into Lawrence, Kansas, at the head of some 450 men, killed upward of 150 men, women, and children, pillaged the town and left it in ashes. Two months later he repeated this exploit at Baxter Springs, Missouri. All efforts to capture him were vain; in 1865 he appeared in Kentucky, but there he was surprised and fatally wounded.

This story of the infamous Lawrence massacre is by one of the few men who escaped, Gurdon Grovenor.

THE raid occurred on the morning of Aug. 21st, 1863. It was a clear, warm, still morning, in the midst of one of the hot, dry, dusty spells of weather common in Kansas in the month of August. The guerrillas reached Lawrence just before sunrise after an all night's ride from the border of Missouri. Myself and family were yet in bed and asleep. They passed directly by our house, and we were awakened by their yelling and shouting.

I thought at first that the noise came from a company of colored recruits who were camped just west of our house; thought that they had got to quarrelling among themselves. I got up and went to the window to see what was the matter, and as I drew aside the curtain the sight that met my eyes was one of terror—one that I never shall forget. The bushwhackers were just passing by my house. There were 350 of them, all mounted and heavily armed; they were grim and dirty from their night's ride over the dusty roads and were a reckless and bloodthirsty set of men. It was a sight we had somewhat anticipated, felt that it might come, and one that we had dreaded ever since the commencement of the war. I turned to my wife and said: "The bushwhackers are here."

They first made for the main street, passing up as far as the Eldridge House to see if they were going to meet with any opposition, and when they found none they scattered out all over town, killing, stealing and burning. We hastily dressed ourselves and closed up the house tightly as possible and began to talk over what was best to do. My first thought was to get away to some hiding place, but on looking out there seemed no possibility of that as the enemy were everywhere, and I had a feeling that I ought not to leave my family, a young wife and two children, one a babe of three months old, and so we sat down and awaited developments. We saw men shot down and fires shooting up in all directions.

Just on the north of our house, a half a block away and in full view was a camp of recruits twenty-two in all, not yet mustered into service and unarmed. They were awakened by the noise, got up and started to run but were all shot down but five. I saw this wholesale shooting from my window, and it was a sight to strike terror to a stouter heart than mine. But we had not long to wait before our time came. Three of the guerrillas came to the house, stepped up on the front porch, and with the butt of a musket smashed in one of the front windows; my wife opened the door and let them in. They ransacked the house, talked and swore and threatened a good deal, but offered no violence. They set the house on fire above and below, took such things as they fancied, and left. After they had gone I put the fire out below, but above it had got too strong a hold, and I could not put it out.

Not long after a single man rode up to the front gate; he was a villainous looking fellow, and was doubly villainous from too much whiskey. He saw me standing back in the hall of the house, and with a terrible oath he ordered me to come out. I stepped out on the piazza, and he leveled his pistol at me and said; "Are you union or secesh?"

It was my time of trial; my wife with her little one in her arms, and our little boy clinging to her side, was standing just a little ways from me. My life seemingly hung on my answer, my position may be imagined but it cannot be described. The thought ran through me like an electric shock, that I could not say that I was a secessionist, and deny my loyalty to my country; that I would rather die than to live and face that disgrace; and so I answered that I was a union man. He snapped his pistol but it failed to fire. I stepped back into the house and he rode around to the north door and met me there, and snapped his pistol at me again, and this time it failed. Was there a providence in this?

Just then a party of a half dozen of the raiders came riding towards the house from the north, and seeing my enemy, hallooed to him "Don't shoot that man." They rode up to the gate and told me to come there; I did so and my would be murderer came up to me and placed the muzzle of his revolver in my ear. It was not a pleasant place to be in, but the leader of the new crowd told him not to shoot, but to let me alone until he could inquire about me, so he asked me if I had ever been down in Missouri stealing niggers or horses; I told him "No that I never had been in Missouri, except to cross the state going and coming from the east." This seemed to be satisfactory so he told my old enemy to let me alone and not to kill me. This seemed to make him very angry, and he cursed me terribly, but I ventured to put my hand up and push away his revolver. The leader of the party then told me if I did not expect to get killed, I must get out of sight, that they were all getting drunk, and would kill everybody they saw; I told him that that was what I had wanted to do all the morning, but I could not; "Well," he says, "you must hide or get killed." And they all rode away.

After they had gone I told my wife that I would go into the cellar, and stay until the fire reached me, and if any more of the raiders inquired for me to tell them that I had been taken a prisoner and carried off. Some years ago

I read an article in the Sunday School Times, saying that a lie under any circumstances was a sin. I thought then that I should like to see that writer try my experiences at the time of the raid and see what he would think then; I did not feel my lie a sin then and never have since.

The cellar of my house was under the ell and the fire was in the front and in the upper story. There was an outside bulk-head door, where I knew I could get out after the fire had reached the floor above me. I had not been in the cellar long before my wife came and said they had just killed my neighbor across the street.

Soon after the notorious Bill Anderson, passing by the house, saw my wife standing in the yard, stopped and commenced talking with her; told her how many men he had killed that morning, and inquiring where her husband was; she told him that he had been taken prisoner and carried away—was it my wife's duty to tell him the truth, tell him where I was and let him come and shoot me as he would a dog, which he would have done? Awhile after my wife came and said she thought the raiders had all gone, and so I came out of my prison just as the fire was eating through the floor over my head, thankful that I had passed through that dreadful ordeal and was safe.

Such was my experience during those four or five terrible hours. Our home and its contents was in ashes, but so thankful were we that my life was spared that we thought but little of our pecuniary loss. After the raiders had left and the people could get out on the street, a most desolate and sickening sight met their view. The whole business part of the town, except two stores, was in ashes. The bodies of dead men, some of them partly burned away, were laying in all directions. A large number of dwellings were burned to the ground, and the moaning of the grief stricken people was heard from all sides. Gen. Lane, who was in the city at the time, told me that he had been over the battleground of Gettysburg a few days before, but the sight was not so sickening as the one which the burned and sacked city of Lawrence presented. The exact number killed was never known, but it was about 150, many of them of the best citizens.

—GROVENOR in *Quantrill and the Border Wars*

7. COLONEL BAILEY DAMS THE RED RIVER

Early in 1864 General Halleck projected an elaborate plan for crushing remaining Confederate resistance in Arkansas and Louisiana. Banks was ordered to move up the Red River to Alexandria, where we would be joined by General Steele, coming down from Arkansas. Together they were to advance on Shreveport and crush the Confederate forces under Kirby Smith and Taylor. The whole expedition was to be supported by a flotilla of gunboats and transports.

From the beginning things went wrong. Taylor dug in at Mansfield, and repulsed a Federal attack with heavy loss. Taylor in turn advanced, only to be repulsed. But Banks decided to retreat to Alexandria. Meantime however the spring floods had not materialized and the Red River, already low, threatened to fall so low that the fleet would be isolated.

At this juncture Colonel Bailey, chief engineer for the defenses of New Orleans and in the Port Hudson campaign, saved the day by constructing a series of wing dams which got the boats over the falls at Alexandria. For this service Bailey was promoted to a brigadier generalship. After the war he went to Missouri, was elected sheriff of his county, and was murdered by two bushwhackers whom he had arrested.

The story of this exploit is here told by Admiral Porter in a report to Secretary of the Navy Gideon Welles.

MISSISSIPPI SQUADRON, FLAGSHIP BLACK HAWK,
MOUTH RED RIVER, MAY 16TH, 1864.

Sir: I have the honor to inform you that the vessels lately caught by low water above the falls at Alexandria, have been released from their unpleasant position. The water had fallen so low that I had no hope or expectation of getting the vessels out this season, and, as the army had made arrangement to evacuate the country, I saw nothing before me but the destruction of the best part of the Mississippi squadron.

There seems to have been an especial Providence looking out for us in providing a man equal to the emergency. Lieut.-Col. Bailey, Acting Engineer of the 19th Army Corps, proposed a plan of building a series of dams across the rocks at the falls, and raising the water high enough to let the vessels pass over. This proposition looked like madness, and the best engineers ridiculed it; but Col. Bailey was so sanguine of success that I requested to have it done, and he entered heartily into the work. Provisions were short and forage was almost out, and the dam was promised to be finished in ten days or the army would have to leave us. I was doubtful about the time, but I had no doubt about the ultimate success, if time would only permit. Gen. Banks placed at the disposal of Col. Bailey all the forces he required, consisting of some three thousand men and two or three hundred wagons. All the neighboring stream-mills were torn down for material; two or three regiments of Maine men were set to work felling trees, and on the second day after my arrival in Alexandria, from Grand Ecore, the work had fairly begun.

Trees were falling with great rapidity, teams were moving in all directions, bringing in brick and stone; quarries were opened; flat-boats were built to bring stone down from above, and every man seemed to be working with a vigor I have seldom seen equalled, while perhaps not one in fifty believed in the undertaking. These falls are about a mile in length, filled with rugged rocks, over which at the present stage of water it seemed to be impossible to make a channel.

The work was commenced by running out from the left bank of the river a tree dam, made of the bodies of very large trees, brush, brick, and stone, cross-tied with heavy timber, and strengthened in every way which ingenuity could devise. This was run out about three hundred feet into the river; four large coal barges were then filled with brick and sunk at the end of it. From the right bank of the river, cribs filled with stone were built out to meet the barges, all of which were successfully accomplished, notwithstanding there was a current running of nine miles an hour, which threatened to sweep every thing before it.

It will take too much time to enter into the details of this truly wonderful work; suffice it to say that the dam had nearly reached completion in eight days' working time, and the water had risen sufficiently on the upper falls to allow the *Fort Hindman, Osage,* and *Neosho,* to get down and be ready to pass the dam. In another day it would have been high enough to enable all the other vessels to pass the upper falls. Unfortunately, on the morning of the 9th inst., the pressure of water became so great that it swept away two of the stone-barges which swung in below the dam on one side. Seeing this unfortunate accident, I jumped on a horse and rode up to where the upper vessels were anchored, and ordered the *Lexington* to pass the upper falls if possible, and immediately attempt to go through the dam. I thought I might be able to save the four vessels below, not knowing whether the persons employed on the work would ever have the heart to renew the enterprise.

The *Lexington* succeeded in getting over the upper falls just in time, the water rapidly falling as she was passing over. She then steered directly for the opening in the dam, through which the water was rushing so furiously that it seemed as if nothing but destruction awaited her. Thousands of beating hearts looked on anxious for the result.

The silence was so great as the *Lexington* approached the dam that a pin might almost have been heard to fall. She entered the gap with a full head of steam on, pitched down the roaring torrent, made two or three spasmodic rolls, hung for a moment on the rocks below, was then swept into deep water by the currents, and rounded to safely into the bank.

Thirty thousand voices rose in one deafening cheer, and universal joy seemed to pervade the face of every man present. The *Neosho* followed next—all her hatches battened down, and every precaution taken against accident. She did not fare as well as the *Lexington,* her pilot having become frightened as he approached the abyss, and stopped her engine when I particularly ordered a full head of steam to be carried. The result was that for a moment her hull disappeared from sight, under the water. Every one thought she was lost. She rose, however, swept along over the rocks with the current, and fortunately escaped with only one hole in her bottom, which was stopped in the course of an hour. The *Hindman* and *Osage* both came through beautifully without touching a thing, and I thought if I was only fortunate enough to get my large vessels as well over the falls my fleet once more would do good service on the Mississippi.

The accident to the dam, instead of disheartening Col. Bailey, only induced him to renew his exertions, after he had seen the success of getting four vessels through. The noble-hearted soldiers, seeing their labor of the last eight days swept away in a moment, cheerfully went to work to repair damages, being confident now that all the gunboats would be finally brought over. The men had been working for eight days and nights, up to their necks in water, in the broiling sun, cutting trees and wheeling bricks, and nothing but good humor prevailed among them. On the whole, it was very fortunate the dam was carried away, as the two barges that were swept away from the centre swung around against some rocks on the left and made a fine cushion for the vessels, and prevented them, as it afterward appeared, from running on certain destruction.

The force of the water and the current being too great to construct a continuous dam of six hundred feet across the river in so short a time, Col. Bailey determined to leave a gap of fifty-five feet in the dam, and build a series of wing dams on the upper falls. This was accomplished in three days' time, and on the 11th instant the *Mound City*, the *Carondelet*, and *Pittsburgh* came over the upper falls, a good deal of labor having been expended in hauling them through, the channel being very crooked, scarcely wide enough for them. Next day the *Ozark, Louisville, Chillicothe*, and two tugs also succeeded in crossing the upper falls.

Immediately afterward the *Mound City, Carondelet*, and *Pittsburgh* started in succession to pass the dam, all their hatches battened down and every precaution taken to prevent accident.

The passage of these vessels was a most beautiful sight, only to be realized when seen. They passed over without an accident except the unshipping of one or two rudders. This was witnessed by all the troops, and the vessels were heartily cheered when they passed over. Next morning at ten o'clock, the *Louisville, Chillicothe, Ozark*, and two tugs passed over without any accident except the loss of a man, who was swept off the deck of one of the tugs. By three o'clock that afternoon, the vessels were all coaled, ammunition replaced, and all steamed down the river with the convoy of transports in company. A good deal of difficulty was anticipated in getting over the bars in lower Red River—depth of water reported only five feet; gunboats were drawing six. Providentially, we had a rise from the back-water of the Mississippi—that river being very high at that time—the back water extending to Alexandria, one hundred and fifty miles distant, enabling it to pass all the bars and obstructions with safety.

Words are inadequate to express the admiration I feel for the ability of Lieut.-Col. Bailey. This is without doubt the best engineering feat ever performed. . . .

I have the honor to be, very respectfully, your obedient servant,

DAVID D. PORTER, Rear-Admiral.

—Letter from David D. Porter to Gideon Welles

8. DEFEAT AND RETREAT ON THE RED RIVER

After Pea Ridge the Confederates were never able to establish a strong force in Arkansas or Missouri; they contented themselves with occasional raids. Curtis had advanced to Batesville; later the forces in northern Arkansas

*were transferred to Union General Frederick Steele, who in August 1863
advanced on Little Rock and captured that capital. The next spring General
Banks was directed to advance up the Red River toward Shreveport, Confederate headquarters for the Southwest. The plan was for Banks to drive up
from the south, Steele to come down from Little Rock, and the two armies
to converge on Kirby Smith and destroy him. Like so many plans in which
Banks was involved, this one miscarried. Banks took Alexandria and moved
north on Shreveport but was stopped by General Taylor at Mansfield. At
the Battle of Sabine Crossing, April 8, 1864, Banks was repulsed, and retreated.
We have seen how he—or Colonel Bailey—got the fleet over the falls of the
Red River. Banks continued his retreat toward the Mississippi, harassed by
Kirby Smith, while Steele fell back on Little Rock.*

Lawrence Van Alstyne here tells the story of Banks's repulse and retreat.

May 18, 1864. *Wednesday.* The rear guard was just coming in sight this
morning when we heard firing at the rear. Soon aides came riding down the
line, halting some and turning others out of the way. They raced across the
bridge and in a little while troops were hurrying back across the bridge from
the front.

It beat all how soon the scene was changed. The firing in the rear kept
increasing and grew plainer to hear. The 90th stood at attention on the bank,
which overlooked the whole plain where the trouble seemed to be centering.
Unless the bridge was attacked we had only to look on, and it was a sight
worth a lifetime to see. The ground, except where worn down by the passing army, was covered with weeds and bushes, which hid the skirmish line
from our view until they rose up and fired almost in each others' faces.
Smoke soon hid the battleground. There was no wind and the smoke rose
up like a cloud instead of spreading. The smoke came nearer and it began
to look as if our turn would soon come, but by and by it stood still and then
began to move back. By noon it was plain to see that the fight was ours, for
the smoke cloud went faster and the firing grew less. By 4 P.M. it was over
and the troops began recrossing toward the front.

The surgeons had their shop under a big tree near the bridge. I heard
one of them say to another that he had never seen so few slight wounds
among so many. Most of those that were hit were either killed outright or
mortally wounded. Only a few legs or arms were cut off. The saddest sight
I saw was the killing of a boy, son of a colonel somebody, whose name or
regiment I could not get. I had often seen the boy while at Alexandria and
wondered why such a child should be in such a place. He rode a handsome
bay pony and wore the infantry uniform, even to a little sword. When the
fight began he was somewhere in the advance, and came riding back at the
head of his regiment by the side of his father. They went into the cloud of
smoke and in a few minutes a man came leading the pony back with the little
fellow stretched across the saddle, his hands and feet hanging down on either
side. He was taken back toward the front and I suppose his body will be
sent home. . . .

May 19, *Tuesday.* Our dead were picked up and brought to the bayou where they were laid in rows on the ground. Those that were identified were buried in separate graves, and the others put crosswise in a wide ditch, with blankets spread under and over them. Our loss was estimated at 500 and that of the Rebs at 800. That must mean killed and wounded, for no such number was buried. The rebel dead were buried in the field, I suppose, for none of them were brought in.

Later. A couple of our men are sick and Dr. Warren called in another doctor to look at them. They called it smallpox, and the men were put in a wagon and carted off right away. When the team came back the driver said they were put in the first house they came to, and a man who has had the disease was left to give them medicine. By night everything but the rear guard was across the bridge, and we had orders to be ready to march. We settled down to get some sleep if we could, but the long roll soon sounded and we sprang to our places. No enemy appearing, we built fires and made coffee, and then sat round nodding our sleepy heads until 4 o'clock in the morning.

May 20, *Friday.* By 4 A.M. the troops were across and the pontoons loaded. We marched at quick time and at 6 o'clock were at Simmsport, where we stopped for breakfast of hard-tack and coffee. While at it a man rode in saying the Rebs were already bridging Yellow Bayou. Simmsport is on the Atchafalaya River, and the same Colonel who planned the dam at Alexandria had built a bridge of boats for us to cross over. Twenty-four steamboats were lashed together side and side, and reached from shore to shore. Across the bows of these the artillery, cavalry and wagons were passing in a continuous stream, and infantry was crossing through and among them as best they could. Other boats were busy ferrying the troops, and such getting across a river I never saw. The *Liberty* took us across and we marched down the opposite side for an hour, and halted for the line to straighten out.

And so the whole day went, first starting and then stopping again, but expecting every minute to set out for good. The time we were waiting, if all put together, would have given us a good rest, and the marching we did would have been good exercise. But as it was, we had a hard day of it. It was pitch dark when we finally started. We came to woods and the darkness could be felt. The train got stalled in the narrow road and then another wait. I was so dead sleepy that twice I fell flat on the ground as I was walking along. The fall woke me up each time and I kept going some way. Men had given out and were sleeping all along beside the road like dead men. Daylight never seemed so long coming. We got through the woods and could see much better. My naps as we walked along, and the falls I had in consequence of them, helped to drive off the dreadful drowsiness and by daylight I was wide awake.

May 21, *Saturday.* When daylight came we were passing the mouth of the Atchafalaya and were again on the banks of the Red River. About sunrise we halted. Lieutenant Moody and I sat down and began to figure up how long we had been awake, when we both tumbled over on the ground and were fast asleep. The next thing I knew Moody was shaking me and asking if I was hurt. His face was bloody and I supposed he had been shot. But we soon found that a horse had run over us, his hoofs striking between our heads and scraping the skin off Moody's forehead as he picked them up.

We soon started again, and at 8 o'clock stopped for breakfast, after which we took a livelier gait than ever. The day was hot. The horses and mules showed the strain as well as the men, and it was impossible to rouse them from the deathlike sleep that had overtaken them. There was nothing to do but pull them out of the road and leave them, for every horse and vehicle was loaded with all it could carry. No stop was made for dinner. On we went, and by 6 o'clock the men were lying all along by the roadsides. Teams gave out and were left panting, their sides showing how cruelly they had been whipped to get the very last effort out of them. My feet were blistered, I knew by the feeling, though I had no time to see or attend to them. The pain each step gave me was, I think, the only thing that kept me awake and going.

About sundown we passed a little village and turned from the road across the country, which was said to be the nearest way to the Mississippi. It was a beautiful country, much like the Teche country, which is sometimes called the "Garden of Louisiana." There were some cattle, and a drove of them was gathered and driven along for our supper. . . .

At 9 P.M. we reached the Mississippi at Morgan's Bend or Morganzia. The cattle had been shot and were lying as they fell. It was everyone for himself. Chunks were cut out and were being eaten before the animal was done kicking. A pack of wolves never acted more ravenous and bloodthirsty. I managed to get my hand between the ribs of one and hold of the liver. I couldn't pull my hand out without straightening the fingers and so got only shreds, but I kept it up until I had taken the edge off my appetite and then lay over on my back and was sound asleep. I suppose a hundred men stepped over me and maybe on me, but nothing disturbed my slumbers. I slept like a dead man.

—VAN ALSTYNE, *Diary of an Enlisted Man*

9. PRICE INVADES THE NORTH AND IS DEFEATED AT WESTPORT

As Banks moved toward the Mississippi, Steele retired on Little Rock. Swollen rivers delayed his retreat, and at the end of April 1864 the forces of Price and Kirby Smith caught up with him at Jenkins's Ferry on the Saline River. The Confederates were repulsed, and Steele made good his retirement. Emboldened by their success, however, the Confederates decided to launch another offensive into Missouri.

Wiley Britton of the 6th Kansas Cavalry—later the historian of the fight-

*ing in the Trans-Mississippi area—here tells the story of the confused fighting
of the last six months, culminating in the smashing Union victory at Westport.*

AFTER the battle of Jenkins's Ferry [April 30, 1864], instead of making
preparations to attack the Federal forces at Little Rock and Fort Smith,
Price commenced organizing his forces for an expedition into Missouri, to
be led by him in person. The Confederate troops under Cooper, Maxey, and
Gano, in the Indian Territory and western Arkansas, were to make demonstrations against Fort Smith and Fort Gibson, and the line of communication
between those points and Kansas, while another part of the Confederate army
was to threaten Little Rock. Price's army for the invasion of Missouri numbered some 15,000 men and 20 pieces of artillery before crossing the Arkansas
River, and consisted of three divisions, commanded by Generals Fagan,
Marmaduke, and Shelby. These troops were mostly veterans, having been
in active service since the first year of the war.

About the 1st of September, while strong demonstrations were being
made against Fort Smith and Little Rock, Price, with his army, crossed the
Arkansas River about half-way between those points at Dardanelle, and
marched to the northern part of the State without opposition, and, in fact,
without his movements being definitely known to General Rosecrans, who
then commanded the Department of the Missouri at St. Louis. When the
Confederate forces entered Missouri they were met by detachments of the
State militia, who captured several Confederate prisoners, from whom it was
ascertained that the invading force was much larger than had been supposed,
and that Price was marching direct for St. Louis. Rosecrans at once commenced collecting his forces to meet and check the enemy. General Thomas
Ewing, Jr., was in command of the District of South-east Missouri. Pilot
Knob, near Iron Mountain, was a post of importance, with fortifications of
considerable strength, and was on Price's direct line of march to St. Louis,
which was only eighty-six miles distant.

Finding that General Price was certainly advancing toward St. Louis,
Ewing, in order to defend Pilot Knob, drew in the detachments of his command stationed at different points in south-east Missouri. As the Federal
forces around and in the vicinity of St. Louis were considered inadequate to
defend the city against the reported strength of Price's veteran army, on
the request of Rosecrans General A. J. Smith's veteran division of the Army
of the Tennessee, 4500 strong, passing up the Mississippi River to join Sherman's army, was detained at Cairo to assist in checking the advance of the
Confederate army.

Price arrived before Pilot Knob in the afternoon of September 26th, and
skirmished until night with detachments of Federal cavalry, which had been
thrown out to meet his advance. Ewing had 1051 men at that post, which
were only enough to man the works. Having got his troops and artillery all
up, Price opened the attack on the fort at daylight on the 27th, and kept it
up all day with great resolution. But Ewing's well-served artillery of eleven

pieces and his thousand small-arms repulsed every assault made by the Confederates. When night came, however, Ewing was satisfied that he could not hold out another day against the superior attacking force, and he determined to evacuate the fort. Shortly after midnight his troops marched out, and a few moments later his magazine was blown up, and the ammunition which could not be taken along was destroyed. Ewing then marched with his force and joined the troops engaged in the defense of St. Louis and of Jefferson City. On hearing the explosion of the magazine, Price suspected the retreat of the garrison, and immediately ordered his generals to start in pursuit. Continuing his march north with his army he came up and attacked the defenses of St. Louis some miles south of the city, but was repulsed by General A. J. Smith's veterans and other troops, and then changed his line of march and moved westward toward Jefferson City, the State capital.

While Price's plans were not definitely known, his movements indicated that he would endeavor to take Jefferson City. But Rosecrans determined not to allow the State capital to fall into the hands of the invader, and not only called out the enrolled militia of central Missouri for its defense, but also ordered General John B. Sanborn, commanding the District of Southwest Missouri at Springfield, and General John McNeil, commanding the District of Rolla, to march to its defense with their available forces, with the least possible delay. General E. B. Brown and General Clinton B. Fisk, commanding districts in central and north Missouri, were also directed to bring forward to Jefferson City all the State militia that could be spared from their respective districts. General Price moved forward and attacked the capital, but as he was closely pursued by the Federal forces from St. Louis he was soon driven off, and continued his march westward up the south side of the Missouri River.

His next objects were understood to be the capture of Kansas City, and Fort Leavenworth, Kansas, and more particularly the invasion and desolation of Kansas. He conscripted and pressed into service every man and youth found at home able to bear arms. Major-General S. R. Curtis, commanding the Department of Kansas and the Indian Territory, the moment he was advised of the approaching storm, began collecting all his forces along the eastern border of the State south of Kansas City, and urged Governor Carney, of Kansas, to call out the militia to coöperate with the volunteers in resisting the threatened invasion. In response to the governor's call, twenty-four regiments of militia were hastily organized, and took position along the eastern line of the State. Early in these preparatory operations for the defense of the border, Major-General George Sykes, commanding the District of South Kansas, was, at his own request, relieved, and Major-General James G. Blunt was placed in command. As soon as information was received that Price had been driven from Jefferson City and was moving westward, Curtis and Blunt took the field in person to direct the operations of their forces in defense of the border. Blunt took the available force of the volunteers and several sections of artillery, and moved down to Lexington, some forty miles, to meet and hold the enemy as long as possible, so that Rosecrans's forces in pursuit from St. Louis and Jefferson City, under Generals Alfred Pleasonton and A. J. Smith, could come up and attack Price in the rear.

On the afternoon of October 20th Price's advance under Shelby came within sight of Lexington on the south side of the city. Sharp fighting at once commenced between the opposing forces, and lasted until night, when Blunt, having ascertained the strength of the enemy, fell back to Little Blue River, a few miles east of Independence, to form a new line of battle. As this stream was fordable at different points above and below where the Independence and Lexington road crossed it, Blunt's forces, under Colonel Thomas Moonlight, were obliged, on the 21st, to abandon the position taken up behind it after an engagement with Shelby's division, lasting several hours, and fall back behind the Big Blue River, a few miles west of Independence. Here a new line of battle was formed with all Curtis's available troops, including most of the Kansas State militia, who had consented to cross the State line into Missouri. Curtis and Blunt determined to hold Price's army east of the Big Blue as long as practicable in the hope of receiving assistance from Rosecrans, who, it was thought, was following close upon the rear of the Confederate army.

While Curtis's forces were thus fighting and skirmishing with the enemy over nearly every foot of the ground from Lexington to Big Blue, Pleasonton's provisional cavalry division of Rosecrans's army was marching day and night from Jefferson City to overtake the invading force. On the 22d, just as Curtis's troops were being driven from the line of the Big Blue back upon the State line and Kansas City, Pleasonton's cavalry came up and attacked the rear of Price's army, east of Independence, and routed it and drove it in great disorder through the town. Pleasonton at once sent a messenger to Curtis, announcing his presence upon the field. The night of the 22d Price's army encamped on the west side of the Big Blue, just south of Westport. Pleasonton's cavalry encamped that night around and in the neighborhood of Independence, east of the Big Blue. Curtis's forces were encamped from Kansas City to Westport and along the State line west of Westport.

At daylight on the 23d the columns of Pleasonton began to move west, and those of Curtis to move south, and in a short time afterward they became warmly engaged with the Confederates, who were drawn up in the line of battle two and a half miles south of Westport. The opposing armies fought over an area of five or six square miles, and at some points the fighting was furious. At times there were as many as forty or fifty guns throwing shot and shell and grape and canister. About the middle of the afternoon Price's lines began to give way, and by sundown the entire Confederate army was in full retreat southward along the State line, closely pursued by the victorious Federal forces. . . .

The "Price raid," as it was called in the West, was the last military operation of much consequence that took place in Missouri and Arkansas. It is certain that Price lost more than he gained in war material and that the raid did not tend to strengthen the Confederate cause in the West.

—BRITTON, "Resumé of Military Operations in Arkansas and Missouri"

10. THE CONFEDERATES WIN AN EMPTY VICTORY AT GLORIETTA PASS

Even distant New Mexico saw some fighting. In July 1861 the Confederate government authorized General Sibley to organize a brigade for the conquest of New Mexico, and that November Sibley moved out from San Antonio with a force of almost 3,700. The Union forces were under the command of Colonel Canby, a West Pointer who happened to be stationed at Fort Defiance, New Mexico. In January 1862 Sibley advanced up the Rio Grande to Valverde, Canby moved out to meet him, there was a fierce fight in which the Confederates gained the upper hand, and Canby retired to the defenses of Fort Craig. Sibley advanced on Albuquerque and Santa Fe and captured that capital, its defenders retiring to Fort Union in the northeastern corner of the territory. Meantime the Federals had been reinforced by Colonel Slough with the 1st Colorado Volunteers.

The opposing forces met in the rugged Apache Cañon, on the Pecos River, and there ensued the Battle of Apache Cañon or Glorietta Pass which is here described by Colonel Scurry, the Confederate commander. Glorietta was technically a Confederate victory, but it was a barren one. As Canby came up to join Slough, the Confederates started their retreat—a harrowing trek through 200 miles of desert country. Sibley had started out with 3,700 men; he returned with less than 2,000.

Although this campaign took place early in 1862 it was an isolated affair and is placed here to avoid interrupting the continuity of the story of the fighting in Missouri and Arkansas.

Santa Fe, New Mexico, March 31, 1862

To Major A. M. Jackson,
    A. A. General, Army New Mexico.

Major: Late on the afternoon of the 26th, while encamped at Galistoe, an express from Major Pyron arrived with the information that the major was engaged in a sharp conflict with a greatly superior force of the enemy, about sixteen miles distant, and urging me to hasten to his relief.

The critical condition of Major Pyron and his gallant comrades was made known to the command, and in ten minutes the column was formed, and the order to march given. Our baggage train was sent forward under a guard of one hundred men, under the command of Lieut. Taylor, of the 7th regiment, to a point some six miles in the rear of Major Pyron's position; the main command marching directly across the mountains to the scene of conflict. It is due to the brave men making this cold night march to state, that where the road over the mountain was too steep for the horses to drag the artillery, they were unharnessed, and the men cheerfully pulled it over the difficulties of the way by hand. About three o'clock in the morning we reached Major Pyron's encampment at Johnson's ranche in *canon* Cito. There had been an agreed cessation of hostilities until eight o'clock the next morning. Too much praise cannot be bestowed upon the courage of the officers and men engaged in the affair of the 26th.

As soon as daylight enabled me, I made a thorough examination of the ground, and so formed the troops as to command every approach to the position we occupied, which was naturally a very strong one. The disposition of the troops was soon completed, and by 8 o'clock were ready to receive the expected attack. In this position we remained until the next morning. The enemy still not making their appearance, I concluded to march forward and attack them. Leaving a small wagon guard, I marched in their direction with portions of nine companies of the 4th regiment. . . . From details and other causes they were reduced, until, all combined, they did not number over six hundred men fit for duty. At about six miles from our camp the advance guard gave notice that the enemy were near, in force. I hastened in front to examine their position, and found they were about one mile west of "Pigeon's Ranche," in *canon Glorietta*.

The mounted men who were marching in front were ordered to retire slowly to the rear, dismount, and come into the action on foot. The artillery was pushed forward to a slight elevation in the *canon*, and immediately to open fire. The infantry were rapidly deployed into line, extending across the *canon* from a fence on our left up into the pine forest on our right.

About the time these dispositions were made, the enemy rapidly advanced in separate columns, both upon our right and left. I dispatched Major Pyron to the right to check them in that direction, and placing the centre in command of Major Ragnet, I hastened with the remainder of the command to the left.

A large body of infantry, availing themselves of a gulch that ran up the centre of an inclosed field to our left, were moving under its cover past our left flank to the rear of our position.

Crossing the fence on foot, we advanced over the clearing some two hundred yards under a heavy fire from the foe, and dashed into the gulch in their midst, pistol and knife in hand. For a few moments a most desperate and deadly hand to hand conflict raged along the gulch, when they broke before the steady courage of our men, and fled in the wildest disorder and confusion. . . .

Sending to the rear to have two of the guns brought back to the field, a pause was made to reunite our forces, which had become somewhat scattered in the last rencontre. When we were ready to advance, the enemy had taken cover, and it was impossible to tell whether their main body was stationed behind a long adobe wall that ran nearly across the *canon*, or had taken position behind a large ledge of rocks in the rear. . . .

I took command of the right and immediately attacked the enemy, who were at the ranche. Majors Ragnet and Pyron opened a galling fire upon their left from the rock on the mountain side, and the centre charging down the road, the foe were driven from the ranche to the ledge of rocks before alluded to, where they made their final and most desperate stand. At this point three batteries of eight guns opened a furious fire of grape, canister, and shell upon our advancing troops.

Our brave soldiers, heedless of the storm, pressed on, determined, if possible, to take their battery. A heavy body of infantry, twice our number, interposed to save their guns. Here the conflict was terrible. Our men and officers, alike inspired with the unalterable determination to overcome every obstacle to the attainment of their object, dashed among them. The right and centre had united on the left. The intrepid Ragnet, and the cool, calm, courageous Pyron, had pushed forward among the rocks, until the muzzle of the opposing forces' guns passed each other. Inch by inch was the ground disputed, until the artillery of the enemy had time to escape with a number of their wagons. The infantry also broke ranks and fled from the field. So precipitate was their flight, that they cut loose their teams and set fire to two of their wagons. The pursuit was kept up until forced to halt from the extreme exhaustion of the men, who had been engaged for six hours in the hardest contested fight it had ever been my lot to witness. The enemy is now known to have numbered fourteen hundred men, Pike's Peak miners and regulars, the flower of the United States army.

During the action, a part of the army succeeded in reaching our rear, surprising the wagon guard, and burning our wagons, taking at the same time some sixteen prisoners. About this time a party of prisoners, whom I had sent to the rear, reached there, and informed them how the fight was going in front, whereupon they beat a hasty retreat, not, however, until the perpetration of two acts which the most barbarous savage of the plains would blush to own. One was the shooting and dangerously wounding the Rev. L. H. Jones, chaplain of the 4th regiment, with a white flag in his hand; the other an order that the prisoners they had taken be shot in case they were attacked on their retreat. These instances go to prove that they have lost all sense of humanity, in the insane hatred they bear to the citizens of the Confederacy, who have the manliness to arm in defence of their country's independence.

W. R. SCURRY,
Colonel commanding A. N. M.
—SCURRY, "Report of the Battle of Glorietta"

XII

How the Soldiers Lived : Western Front

ON THE *whole Americans were the same, East and West, the Army of Tennessee much like the Army of Northern Virginia, the Army of the Cumberland much like the Army of the Potomac. Not only this but the troops were, in fact, very mixed; Illinois and Minnesota, Texas and Alabama regiments fought in Virginia. But the Western armies were made up, almost wholly, from the region west of the Alleghenies, though this was less true of the Confederate than of the Union armies. There were, however, minor differences.*

There was probably a larger proportion of foreign-born soldiers in the Union armies in the West—Germans and Scandinavians particularly. The war in this theater was somewhat more of a real civil war: in Missouri and Arkansas, in Kentucky and particularly in Tennessee, the division of Union and Confederate sentiment ran right through society. In the East only Maryland had regiments in both armies; but the Army of the Tennessee (Union) included a "1st Alabama" cavalry brigade, while there were many Kentucky and Missouri regiments in the Confederate ranks.

A third difference was imposed by geography and grand strategy. The Western armies fought over an enormous territory, and it is suggestive that there are half a dozen accounts of the hardships of long marches from the West for every one from the East. Cavalry played, perhaps, a larger role—not the cavalry charge but the long raids and the harassment of lines of communication. Climate and geography permitted more winter campaigns. The necessity of co-operating with the navy for control of the Mississippi, the Tennessee and the Cumberland, and the Red rivers made operations more nearly a joint affair, and there are examples even of amphibious operations.

Yet on the whole the excerpts we give here need little elaboration. Life in camp; the forced march; religion and play; relations with civilians; the roles of the commissary and of the sutler—these things were pretty much the same East as West, and North as South. It will be sufficient to introduce some of the chroniclers themselves.

1. JOHN CHIPMAN GRAY VIEWS THE WESTERN SOLDIER

Member of a distinguished Massachusetts family, and graduate of the Harvard Law School, Gray enlisted in the 41st Massachusetts Volunteers in 1862 and fought for a year in the Valley and the Peninsular campaigns. In

1863 he was appointed assistant judge advocate and the following year judge advocate, assigned to the Department of the South. All through the war he corresponded with his law school friend, John Codman Ropes—future historian of the Civil War—and this letter, so Eastern in its point of view, is part of that correspondence.

On Board Steamboat 'Bostona No. 2'
White River, Arkansas, July 24, 1864

My Dear John,—

With regard to the general appearance of the Westerners, it is not so different from our own as I had supposed, but certain it is that discipline is most astonishingly lax. We came up from New Orleans to Memphis with veterans of the 49th Indiana Regiment going home on furlough. They were on terms of great familiarity with their officers, eating, drinking and playing cards with them; yet I must say a finer, cleaner, more orderly and well behaved set of men I never saw; the bar was open all the time and was always filled with men and officers, but I did not see an officer or man drunk and indeed in all my boating on these rivers, I have seen but two men at all affected by liquor, though this may be in some measure due to the exceeding weakness of the tipple concocted at the bar. Other western troops that I have seen have not been so clean and good looking as these Indiana men, but the same lack of discipline exists in all. This is carried to so great an extent that General Gordon, whom you will not suppose to be lax in this respect, says he thinks it very doubtful whether it would be worth while to attempt to impart a severer discipline to troops who have been brought up as these have for more than three years. In Memphis there was a sentry whom I had to pass daily, he was always seated in an arm-chair, his gun rested on the wall near his side, he was often reading, and had another chair by him for the convenience of any friend who might like to stop and chat a while. This is no solitary instance, I might tell you of a dozen things as strange.

Our white troops manage to get along though indifferently, on account of the individual character of the men, but I cannot conceive that the Negro troops commanded by officers taken from the ranks of white regiments, and with men taken from the lowest state of degradation can be anything but a burden to the Government and all the Negro troops I have seen in the West (not many to be sure) have been squalid and miserable in the extreme, very different in look from some of the fine Massachusetts and Maryland Regiments that I have seen in the Department of the South.

The run of officers and citizens that one meets in the towns and on the boats is much less rough than I had anticipated, and I have never seen officials more civil and accommodating than the Captains and Clerks of the river boats. My prejudices against the West have been materially lessened by the experience I have had.

There has been and is undoubtedly an immense deal of contraband cotton dealing and other trading, and almost every commanding officer is accused of having a hand in it. The army accuse the navy and the navy accuse

the army. The profligacy too in all the large towns in this region is great. Partly from natural causes and partly from want of the means of life, the prostitution in all this region is astonishing. General Steele at Little Rock lives quite like an Eastern Prince with his harem, wines, dogs, horses, equipages and everything in great style. There is something almost romantic in the existence of all these appliances of luxury and civilization in a little town in the midst of a howling wilderness of bloodthirsty enemies.
—Ford, ed., *War Letters of John Chipman Gray and John Codman Ropes*

2. A WISCONSIN BOY COMPLAINS OF THE HARDSHIPS OF TRAINING

A farm boy from the Wisconsin frontier, Chauncey Cooke was barely sixteen when he went to La Crosse to enlist in the 25th Wisconsin Infantry. He was with Pope in the abortive Sioux campaign of 1862; then in the following year his regiment was sent south, where it fought through the Vicksburg and subsequent campaigns. His letters home have an unpretentious and authentic quality that commends them to the historian of the war. This letter—not the last that we shall read—describes training at a camp outside Madison.

Madison, Wis. Dec. 25th, 1862
Co. G., 25th Regt.

Dear Mother:

You see my paper don't have the regulation picture on it of Soldiers in file or in battle array. I am tired of such flummery. The meaning of the whole thing is to make money for the inventor and not for the soldier. We are told that the life of the Nation is at stake, and every fellow that enlists offers himself as a martyr to save his country. I was thinking these things over last, about 2 P.M. in the morning when I was nearly froze and the relief guard came around and I was off duty to go to my tent and get some sleep. It seems like foolery to the common soldier that for two hours we must stand in a temperature of 30 or 40 degrees when we are a thousand miles from the enemy. I had to walk and walk to keep from freezing. The mercury was down near 40 below zero and the guard house where we sat down between reliefs or lay down was little better than out of doors.

The health of our Regiment is none too good. One man dies on an average every day. As I write this letter the drum is beating. The food we get is to blame for our bad health. The boys threaten a riot every day for the bad beef and spoilt bread issued to us and all this in our home state of Wisconsin.

I went to meeting yesterday both morning and evening. In the morning at the Baptist, in the evening at the Episcopal church. The preacher discussed the state of the Union. I thot he talked a bit like a traitor. He was sorry the states should go to war over the question of slavery. He hoped the Union would be preserved and he thot Uncle Tom's Cabin was much to blame for the war. Capt. Dorwin said the preacher ought to live in South Carolina.

There is talk that we will get pay tomorrow. I have sent a record of our company home. Hope you got it. I shall send you a lot of clothing just before we leave.

From your son,
CHAUNCEY

—COOKE, "Letters of a Badger Boy in Blue"

3. AN OFFICER'S QUARTERS IN CAMP CURTIS

Life in camp could be pleasant enough, especially for an officer. William W. Orme—he was commissioned brigadier general the day this letter was written—was colonel of the 94th Illinois Volunteers. An Illinois lawyer, and a friend of Lincoln's, he had been commissioned at the outbreak of the war, fought in Missouri and Tennessee and at Vicksburg, and was later in command at Camp Douglas.

Camp Curtis—Mo. Nov. 29, 1862

Dearest wife—

It is now half past seven o'clock Saturday night. The band is now playing the regular evening tattoo, and everything has the sound of martial life; but it is nothing unusual.

By the way did you know that in our camp life we move by the music of the band. We rise in the morning by the tune the band plays at Reveille, and we go to bed by the martial music at tattoo and taps.

There are some things delightfully pleasant in camp life, and some things terribly monotonous. . . .

You ask me about myself; well! I'll tell you how I live now. I go to bed when I feel like it; sometimes at 7, sometimes at 9, sometimes later. There being no limit to the hours of an officer. My bed consists of my cot laid on the ground flat for purposes of warmth; it being warmer on the ground than if raised on the legs. I have two blankets and my buffalo robe under me, and three blankets over me. If the night is very cold I throw my overcoat over my feet. I sleep very soundly—I am not troubled with much undressing or dressing as I only take off my coat, vest, and boots. I rise in the morning at various hours from 6 to 8 o'clock. Ike (or Zach, is his proper name— Zachariah Lawson) comes into my tent about daylight and starts a fire in my little camp stove—brings me water to wash in, blacks my boots &c. My camp stove is a little round sheet iron drum, set flat on the ground with a little stove pipe running out of the side of the tent. Ike has spread a piece of bagging by the side of my cot for a carpet. So you see I live in fine style. Breakfast is announced at about 8 o'clock, Dinner about 1, and supper about 6. Sometimes we have plenty to eat and sometimes we dont. Tonight we had mush and milk. The ordinary routine of camp duties, such as business drill &c. occupies the day; & so day after day whiles away—while we wonder each succeeding day when and where we'll march. I take a ride every day; pay my respects to the general, trot around the camp &c. & back to my quarters.

It is now after 8 O'clock. I am getting sleepy. We are all well and hearty. There is nothing new. Kiss the dear ones. Tell me if Willy & Berry read their letters themselves. My love to all at home. And as for yourself you possess me entirely my constant love & thoughts.

As ever devotedly yours,
Wm.

—"Civil War Letters of Brigadier General William Ward Orme"

4. RELIGION AND PLAY IN THE ARMY OF THE TENNESSEE

There is nothing dramatic or stirring about this simple chronicle of daily life in camp. Jenkin Jones was another of the many Wisconsin boys who fought in the Army of the Tennessee. Born in Wales he had been brought to this country as a baby; enlisted, at nineteen, in the 6th Wisconsin Battery; fought at Corinth, Vicksburg, Chattanooga, and in Georgia. After the war Jones became a prominent Unitarian preacher and editor. His diary is one of the most revealing about soldier life in the Western theater.

Huntsville [Alabama], Sunday, Jan 17, 1864. A pleasant day. Meeting was announced to be had at 2 P.M. in the Presbyterian Church. Obtained permission and went down, but found none, it being held at 6 P.M. Walked over town. Visited the waterworks of the city, which is the largest of the kind South, with the exception of one at Columbia, S. C. A large stream gushes out of the solid rock under the courthouse, which is dammed about four feet and propels a large water wheel which works a powerful force pump that forces water all over the city, furnishing a hydrant at every corner. Pump is enclosed in a neat stone house. Returned to camp for supper and evening roll-call, then we walked back again. The church was very neat and filled with soldiers, but one woman in the audience. Chaplain of 18th Wisconsin officiated, of the Calvinistic school, and but ill agreed with my views, but it seemed good to be once more listening to an earnest speaker and hear the old-fashioned tunes swell in the bass voices that filled the room. Returned to camp, if not better, a more thoughtful man. It was the second sermon I have listened to since leaving home, and in common with all soldiers, I have acquired a careless and light way of passing time.

Sunday, Feb. 7. Rough night for the guard. Rainy and cold. The countersign "Vicksburg" which gave rise to musings which aided in forgetting time. Relieved at 9 A.M. Attended church in company with Griff, E. W. and D. J. D. Service was held in the Methodist, Presbyterian and Epsicopal churches at the same hour (10 A.M.) Curiosity prompted to attend the latter, an elegant furnished church of unique construction, Gothic style, poorly arranged for sound. The civilians were apparently of the aristocratic class, mostly women, equalling the military in numbers. The white-robed minister was a young intelligent Irishman, I should judge. A good choir with the deep-toned organ opened the service with fitting music, after which prayers were read and ceremonies performed for nearly an hour and a half, which to me was mere mockery of religion, reading their desires to God from an established formula, but careful always to omit the prayer for the President of the U. S. A. It was not worship. Ah no! the heart was cold. It was but Phariseeical affectations. A short sermon on charity was read at the close. Very good, the effect of which was tested by passing the plates which were returned well laden with "soldier greenbacks." The money of that government they will not pray for is very acceptable.

I returned to camp, although not pleased with the exercise, yet I trust, benefited. The solemn notes of the organ had awakened feelings that are too apt to lie dormant in the soldier's breast, those that raise the mind above the din of common life, and look to a future of immortality, purity, which all hope to obtain ere long. "Heaven is my home."

Saturday, Feb. 20. As soon as breakfast was over I hitched a new team and drove out to a confiscated fence, a mile off, for a load of lumber, as the two Hungerfords were desirous of coming in with us, and we must build a larger one [hut]. After we were all loaded, a guard commanded us to unload, but after some talk allowed us to leave in quiet with our lumber. Tore down our "humble cot" and six of us went to work in earnest to erect a more commodious one. Had no tent. Built it entirely of lumber. Had it almost completed by night. Was quite tired, with a settled cold on my lungs, almost sick.

Friday, March 4. Evie Evans and myself went to the city on pass. Visited the Christian Commission rooms. Bought stamps. Also went to the colored school under charge of Chaplain of 17th Colored. Had school-teachers, being volunteers from the ranks, teaching the little wooly-heads their "A. B. C.'s." One class of youngsters was taught by a large Negro. A class of young ladies was reading in the *Second Reader*. All seemed attentive and anxious to receive the instruction but poorly imparted to them. Harnesses were opened and distributed to the platoons. I was given one set. No horses.

Sunday, March 13. A delightful Sabbath morning. T. J. Hungerford very sick, heavy fever and hard breathing. Afraid he is going to have a fever. Bathed him, towels kept around him, and all we can do for him is done gladly. After inspection 8 A.M. attended Sabbath school and meeting at the Methodist Church. . . . The minister preached from the 35th and 36th verses of the fourth chapter of St. John, a discourse filled with hell fire and eternal misery, with but little consolation to the many bereaved mothers and sisters present who had lost their all in the Confederate army. Although enemies, I could but feel for their distressing sobs, that were audible all over the room. In the afternoon the day was so cheering that I could not resist the temptation of another walk to town, where in a crowded house of soldiers and citizens I listened to an excellent practical sermon on the ten virgins, wise and foolish.

Tuesday, March 29. Our camp was visited to-day by Mother Bickerdyke with four mule teams loaded with good things from the North for the soldiers. Left us three barrels of potatoes, turnips, carrots, etc., one barrel of sourkraut with one of dried apples. *Noble woman*. I still remember with gratitude the motherly interest she took in my welfare while lying in the hospital at Corinth. Here again she comes with that which she has gathered by her own labor in the North, not leaving it to be wholly absorbed by surgeons, directors and officers, as is too often the case with sanitary goods. She comes along in a mule wagon and delivers it herself to the "good boys" as she terms us, without seeking the officers. She drew a large crowd around her soon. Her glowing, welcoming face, filled with cordiality, had a magnetic influence upon the hearts of all, such a contrast to the haughty, disdainful looks we are accustomed to receive from women in general. May God bless her noble, self-sacrificing spirit, is the soldier's prayer.

Monday, April 4. A cloudy rainy day. Orders given us at 8 A.M. to put our tents in order preparatory to an inspection by medical director. All filth to be removed. Dirty clothes were washed, etc. In the evening the artillery boys listened to a stirring speech on the parade ground by Rev. Collins, chaplain 57th Illinois, a spicy and able speaker. Kept the crowd laughing much of the time, at the same time encouraging and instructing each one in the duty of the hour, and had a good effect. Sold several tracts.

Monday, April 11. Spent the day in the usual way. Two hours' gun drill in the morning, then game of ball; an hour company drill in the afternoon; a game or two of chess, then parade 4 P.M.; reading, writing, the remainder of the time till retreat at 8 P.M. when I made down my cot. In the quiet of alone I lay down, a few yearning thoughts of home, mother, etc. and all is oblivion till reveille calls me forth from the land of nod. A little after noon we were startled by a terrible explosion near the depot. A caisson of the Illinois Battery had exploded while returning from drill, killing six cannoneers instantly and wounding two. A very sad affair. Bodies torn to shreds.

Sunday, April 17. A beautiful and holy Sabbath morning. Warmed even the coldest heart to softness and filled the thoughtful mind with piety, though to many imperceptibly. Knapsack inspection at 8 A.M. Afterwards D. J. D. Griff and myself attended Sabbath school taught by a chaplain. The presiding elder of the Methodist church was sick, and to my astonishment the Yankee chaplain was invited to preach, which he did very fittingly, delivering an excellent sermon from Romans 8th chapter, XV verse. Went down in the afternoon to witness the baptizing at the Methodist church, but we were too late. Visited the new font that is going up, and caught in heavy rain storm before we got back.

Sunday, April 24. Awoke to hear the rain pattering thick and fast on the pine boards overhead. At first I was dissatisfied with the anticipation of a wet day with mud—very blue, but at the thought of yesterday's dusty ordeal I could but say "blessed be the rain that clears the atmosphere and makes all nature look more pleasing when it ceases." Cleared off into a most delightful day by 9 A.M., and I listened to a thorough scientific sermon from Dr. Ross upon technical points, existence of evil. His arguments were very concise and binding. Although differing in opinion I received many new ideas. He is one of the leading Southern clergy and formerly a rabid secessionist, and to-day he touched upon the war, but so nicely that it could not displease any of his audience which was composed of the two extremes, viz: Yankee soldiers and secesh women. He sat way up, he said, upon his faith in God, "looking down upon the struggle with as much composure as though they were but the convulsions of so many pigmies—God would do it right." Just found it out I suppose.

Monday, May 2. A cold, windy day for this time of the year. At night a fire was very comfortable. Expect to move camp nearer to town soon so as to shorten the picket line. The left wing of the 16th Corps under Dodge was moving in all day. Stood on the roadside most of the afternoon, the first time we were ever permitted to see a moving column without ourselves forming a part of it. 26th Wisconsin passed. Many of our boys found acquaintances and friends. In the same Brigade was a regiment of Yanks all the way from Jersey, regular blue-blooded Yankees. Made a strange appearance in their leggins and yellow tassels. Physically made a poor comparison by the side of our sturdy Western boys.

Tuesday, May 10. . . . All the Negroes in town pressed in and put to work. Twenty of us detailed with Corporal Ferris to load a train with 3 by 8 stuff for gun platforms to obtain which we had to tear down an old machine shop. Returned and unloaded by noon.

All the details marched up in line to McBride's headquarters, where whiskey rations were freely issued to all that wanted, many of the most greedy drinking in several different details. After this issue the Captain mounted a table and read a dispatch from Sherman by telegraph, of glorious news from Grant. Whips Lee and in full pursuit. Butler in Petersburg within ten miles of Richmond. The news and whiskey brought forth thundering acclamations from the soldiers. After stating the importance of the immediate completion of the works, we were dismissed for dinner and started home. Deplorable sight. The intemperate indulgence by those but little used to the poison, caused a large portion of them to be beastly drunk, and our march through town was filled with demoniac yells, tumbling in the mud and mire. I felt ashamed to be seen in the crowd. Such mistaken kindness tends to demoralize the army as well as to increase the hatred of our enemy. Many of the boys had to be carried to their tents, and were unable to return to the work in the afternoon. Rained heavy all the afternoon. Worked hard. After night a terrible thunder storm deluged our camp, water standing in one of the tents eighteen inches deep. Our floor was all afloat, and we had to climb into our bunks to keep dry. Dry land could not be seen. Much noise and fun in order to forget the disagreeable in the humorous.

—Jones, *An Artilleryman's Diary*

5. THE GREAT REVIVAL IN THE ARMY OF TENNESSEE

In 1863 and 1864 the Army of Tennessee, like the Army of Northern Virginia, was swept by a "great revival." Officers and men alike were bap-

tized, and piety spread—perhaps with despair. These letters are from the Reverend T. J. Stokes, a member—probably chaplain—of the 10th Texas. Mrs. Gay, who reproduces them in her charming Life in Dixie, *lived in Decatur, Georgia.*

Near Dalton, April 5th, 1864.—We have had for some weeks back very unsettled weather, which has rendered it very disagreeable, though we haven't suffered; we have an old tent which affords a good deal of protection from the weather. It has also interfered some with our meetings, though there is preaching nearly every night that there is not rain. Brother Hughes came up and preached for us last Friday night and seemed to give general satisfaction. He was plain and practical, which is the only kind of preaching that does good in the army. He promised to come back again. I like him very much. Another old brother, named Campbell, whom I heard when I was a boy, preached for us on Sabbath evening. There was much feeling, and at the close of the services he invited mourners to the anxious seat, and I shall never forget that blessed half-hour that followed; from every part of that great congregation they came, many with streaming eyes; and, as they gave that old patriarch their hands, asked that God's people would pray for them. Yes, men who never shrank in battle from any responsibility, came forward weeping. Such is the power of the Gospel of Christ when preached in its purity. Oh, that all ministers of Christ could, or would, realize the great responsibility resting upon them as His ambassadors. . . .

Since my return we have established a prayer-meeting in our company, or, rather, a kind of family service, every night after roll call. There is one other company which has prayer every night. Captain F. is very zealous. There are four in our company who pray in public—one sergeant, a private, Captain F. and myself. We take it time about. We have cleared up a space, fixed a stand and seats, and have a regular preaching place. I have never seen such a spirit as there is now in the army. Religion is the theme. Everywhere, you hear around the camp-fires at night the sweet songs of Zion. This spirit pervades the whole army. God is doing a glorious work, and I believe it is but the beautiful prelude to peace. I feel confident that if the enemy should attempt to advance, that God will fight our battles for us, and the boastful foe be scattered and severely rebuked.

I witnessed a scene the other evening, which did my heart good—the baptism of three men in the creek near the encampment. To see those hardy soldiers taking up their cross and following their Master in His ordinance, being buried with Him in baptism, was indeed a beautiful sight. I really believe, Missouri, that there is more religion now in the army than among the thousands of skulkers, exempts and speculators at home. There are but few now but who will talk freely with you upon the subject of their soul's salvation. What a change, what a change! when one year ago card playing and profane language seemed to be the order of the day. Now, what is the cause of this change? Manifestly the working of God's spirit. He has chastened His people, and this manifestation of His love seems to be an earnest of the good things in store for us in not a far away future. "Whom the Lord loveth He chasteneth, and scourgeth every son whom He receiveth." Let all the people at home now, in unison with the army, humbly bow, acknowledge the afflicting hand of the Almighty, ask Him to remove the curse upon His own terms, and soon we will hear, so far as our Nation is concerned, "Glory to God in the highest, on earth peace, good will toward men!"

Your affectionate brother,

T. J. STOKES.

In Camp, Near Dalton, Ga., April 18, 1864,—

The good work still goes on here. Thirty-one men were baptized at the creek below our brigade yesterday, and I have heard from several other brigades in which the proportion is equally large (though the thirty-one were not all members of this brigade). Taking the proportion in the whole army as heard from (and I have only heard from a part of one corps), there must have been baptized yesterday 150 persons—maybe 200. This revival spirit is not confined to a part only, but pervades the whole army. . . . Brother Hughes was with us the other night, but left again the next morning. The old man seemed to have much more influence in the army than young men. I have preached twice since writing to you, and the Spirit seemed to be with me. . . . Many presented themselves, and I could hear many among them, with sobs and groans, imploring God to have mercy upon them; and I think the Lord did have mercy upon them, for when we opened the door of the church six united with us. Every Sabbath you may see the multitude wending their way to the creek to see the solemn ordinance typical of the death, burial and resurrection of our Savior. . . .

If this state of things should continue for any considerable length of time, we will have in the Army of Tennessee an army of believers. Does the history of the world record anywhere the like? Even Cromwell's time sinks into insignificance. A revival so vast in its proportions, and under all the difficulties attending camp life, the bad weather this spring, and innumerable difficulties, is certainly an earnest of better, brighter times not far in the future.

Near Dalton, May 5th, 1864.

The great revival is going on with widening and deepening interest. Last Sabbath I saw eighty-three immersed at the creek below our brigade. Four were sprinkled at the stand before going down to the creek, and two down there, making an aggregate within this vicinity of eighty-nine, while the same proportion, I suppose, are turning to God in other parts of the army, making the grand aggregate of many hundreds. Yesterday I saw sixty-five more baptized, forty more who were to have been there failing to come because of an order to be ready to move at any moment. They belong to a more distant brigade. . . . If we do not move before Monday, Sabbath will be a day long to be remembered—"the water will," indeed, "be troubled." Should we remain three weeks longer, the glad tidings may go forth that the Army of Tennessee is the army of the Lord. But He knoweth best what is for our good, and if he sees proper can so order His providence as to keep us here. His will be done.

—GAY, *Life in Dixie during the War*

6. FROM REVEILLE TO TAPS

Most of the accounts of marching emphasize its hardships. Here is a simple factual account of how an army on the march spends its day. The auspices were, of course, favorable, for this is Sherman's army marching through Georgia. A young man of twenty-four or five when he joined the army, George Ward Nichols had already lived a busy life. Born in Maine and educated in Boston, he had worked as a journalist, taken part in the struggle for free Kansas, studied art in France, and become art editor on the New York Evening Post. Shortly after the outbreak of the war he joined Frémont's staff; then went as provost marshal to Wisconsin; and ended up as aide-de-camp to General Sherman. His Story of the Great March *from which this excerpt is taken was one of the most popular of all postwar books, published in England and translated into many European languages. After the war Nichols had a long and distinguished career promoting art and music in Cincinnati.*

AMONG the most characteristic features of the soldier's life is the important step of breaking camp, which is at once the close of a season of monotonous inactivity and the preliminary stage of a phase of exciting adventure. The same general details are on such occasions observed throughout the entire army, differing slightly in some of the corps, when the division which was in the centre or rear marches first, taking the place of the division which was in advance the day before.

The order of march is issued by the army commanders the preceding night, from them to the corps commanders, and then passed along until every soldier, teamster, and camp-follower knows that an early start is to be made. "The second division will be on the Milledgeville road promptly at five o'clock" reads an order, by way of instance.

At three o'clock the watch-fires are burning dimly, and, but for the occasional neighing of horses, all is so silent that it is difficult to imagine that twenty thousand men are within a radius of a few miles. The ripple of the brook can be distinctly heard as it breaks over the pebbles, or winds petulantly about the gnarled roots. The wind sweeping gently through the tall pines overhead only serves to lull to deeper repose the slumbering soldier, who in his tent is dreaming of his far-off Northern home.

But in an instant all is changed. From some commanding elevation the clear-toned bugle sounds out the *reveillé*, and another and another responds, until the startled echoes double and treble the clarion calls. Intermingled with this comes the beating of drums, often rattling and jarring on unwilling ears. In a few moments the peaceful quiet is replaced by noise and tumult, arising from hill and dale, from field and forest. Camp-fires, hitherto extinct or smouldering in dull gray ashes, awaken to new life and brilliancy, and send forth their sparks high into the morning air. Although no gleam of sunrise blushes in the east, the harmless flames on every side light up the scene, so that there is no disorder or confusion.

The æsthetic aspects of this sudden change do not, however, occupy much of the soldier's time. He is more practically engaged in getting his breakfast ready. The potatoes are frying nicely in the well-larded pan; the chicken is roasting delicately on the red-hot coals, and grateful fumes from steaming coffee-pots delight the nostrils. The animals are not less busy. An ample supply of corn and huge piles of fodder are greedily devoured by these faithful friends of the boys in blue, and any neglect is quickly made known by the pawing of neighing horses and the fearful braying of the mules. Amid all is the busy clatter of tongues and tools—a Babel of sound, forming a contrast to the quiet of the previous hour as marked as that between peace and war.

Then the animals are hitched into the traces, and the droves of cattle relieved from the night's confinement in the corral. Knapsacks are strapped, men seize their trusty weapons, and as again the bugles sound the note of command, the soldiers fall into line and file out upon the road, to make another stage of their journey—it may be to win fresh laurels in another victory, or perhaps to find a rest which shall only be broken by the *reveillé* of the last trump.

A day's march varies according to the country to be traversed or the opposition encountered. If the map indicates a stream crossing the path, probably the strong party of mounted infantry or of cavalry which has been sent forward the day before has found the bridges burned, and then the pontoons are pushed on to the front. If a battle is anticipated, the trains are shifted to the rear of the centre. Under any circumstances, the divisions having the lead move unencumbered by wagons, and in close fighting trim. The ambulances following in the rear of the division are in such close proximity as to be available if needed. In the rear of each regiment follow the pack-mules, laden with every kind of camp baggage, including blankets, pots, pans, kettles, and all the kitchen-ware needed for cooking. Here will be found the led horses, and with them the Negro servants, who form an important feature of the *ménage*.

Having placed the column upon the road, let us now follow that long line of muskets gleaming in the rays of the morning sunlight, and ride, heedless of the crack of the rifles, to the head of the column. The advance are driving a squad of Rebel cavalry before them so fast that the march is not in the least impeded. The flankers spread out, on a line parallel to the leading troops, for several hundred yards, more or less, as the occasion may require. They search through the swamps and forests, ready for any concealed foe, and anxiously looking out for any line of works which may have been thrown up by the enemy to check our progress. Here the General of the division, if a fighting man, is most likely to be found; his experienced eye noting that there is no serious opposition, he orders up a brigade or another regiment, who, in soldier's phraseology, send the Rebel rascals "kiting," and the column moves on. A large plantation appears by the road-side. If the "bummers" have been ahead, the chances are that it has been visited, in which event the interior is apt to show evidences of confusion; but the barns are full of corn and fodder, and parties are at once detailed to secure and convey the prize to the road-side. As the wagons pass along they are not allowed to halt, but the grain or fodder is stuffed into the front and rear of the vehicles as they pass, the unhandy operation affording much amusement to the soldiers, and not unfrequently giving them a poor excuse for swearing as well as laughing.

When the treasure-trove of grain, and poultry, and vegetables has been secured, one man is detailed to guard it until the proper wagon comes along. Numbers of these details will be met, who, with proper authority, have started off early in the morning, and have struck out miles away from the flank of the column. They sit upon some cross-road, surrounded with their spoils—chickens, turkeys, geese, ducks, pigs, hogs, sheep, calves, nicely-dressed hams, buckets full of honey, and pots of fresh white lard. . . .

There is a halt in the column. The officer in charge of the pioneer corps, which follows the advance guard, has discovered an ugly place in the road, which must be "corduroyed" at once, before the wagons can pass. The pioneers quickly tear down the fence near by and bridge over the treacherous place, perhaps at the rate of a quarter of a mile in fifteen minutes. If rails are not near, pine saplings and split logs supply their place. Meanwhile the bugles have sounded, and the column has halted. The soldiers, during the temporary halt, drop out of line on the road-side, lying upon their backs, supported by their still unstrapped knapsacks. If the halt is a long one, the different regiments march by file right, one behind the other, into the fields, stacking their muskets, and taking their rest at ease, released from their knapsack.

These short halts are of great benefit to the soldier. He gains a breathing-spell, has a chance to wipe the perspiration from his brow and the dust out of his eyes, or pulls off his shoes and stockings to cool his swollen, heated feet, though old campaigners do not feel the need of this. He munches his bit of hard bread, or pulls out a book from his pocket, or oftener a pipe, to indulge in that greatest of luxuries to the soldier, a soothing, refreshing smoke. Here may be seen one group at a brook-side, bathing their heads and drinking; and another, crowded round an old song-book, are making very fair music. One venturesome fellow has kindled a fire, and is brewing a cup of coffee. All are happy and jolly; but when the bugle sounds "fall in," "attention," and "forward," in an instant every temporary occupation is dropped, and they are on the road again.

This massing of brigades and wagons during a halt is a proper and most admirable arrangement. It keeps the column well closed up; and if a brigade or division has by some means been delayed, it has the opportunity to overtake the others. The 20th Corps manage this thing to perfection.

A great many of the mounted officers ride through the fields, on either side of the line of march, so as not to interfere with the troops. General Sherman always takes to the fields, dashing through thickets or plunging into the swamps, and, when forced to take the road, never breaks into a regiment or brigade, but waits until it passes, and then falls in. He says that they, and not he, have the right to the road.

Sometimes a little creek crosses the path, and at once a foot-bridge is made upon one side of the way for those who wish to keep dry-shod; many, however, with a shout of derision, will dash through the water at a run, and then they all shout the more when some unsteady comrade misses his footing and tumbles in at full length. The unlucky wight, however, takes the fun at his expense in the best of humor. Indeed, as a general rule, soldiers are good-humored and kind-hearted to the last degree. I have seen a soldier stand at a spring of water for ten minutes, giving thirsty comers cool draughts, although it would delay him so that he would have to run a quarter of a mile or more to overtake his company. The troops, by the way, kept their ranks admirably during this Georgia campaign. Occasionally, however, they would rush for a drink of water, or for a bee-hive which they would despoil of its sweets with a total disregard of the swarm of bees buzzing about their ears, but which, strange to say, rarely stung.

But the sun has long since passed the zenith, the droves of cattle which have been driven through the swamps and fields are lowing and wandering in search of a corral, the soldiers are beginning to lag a little, the teamsters are obliged to apply the whip oftener, ten or fifteen miles have been traversed, and the designated halting-place for the night is near. The column must now be got into camp.

Officers ride on in advance to select the ground for each brigade, giving the preference to slopes in the vicinity of wood and water. Soon the troops file out into the woods and fields, the leading division pitching tents first, those in the rear marching on yet farther, ready to take their turn in the advance the next day.

As soon as the arms are stacked, the boys attack the fences and rail-piles, and with incredible swiftness their little shelter-tents spring up all over the ground. The fires are kindled with equal celerity, and the luxurious repast prepared, while "good digestion waits on appetite, and health on both." After this is heard the music of dancing or singing, the pleasant buzz of conversation, and the measured sound of reading. The wagons are meanwhile parked and the animals fed. If there has been a fight during the day, the incidents of success or failure are recounted; the poor fellow who lies wounded in "the anguish-laden ambulance" is not forgotten, and the brave comrade who fell in the strife is remembered with words of loving praise.

By-and-by the tattoo rings out on the night air. Its familiar sound is understood. "Go to rest, go to rest," it says, as plainly as organs of human speech.

Shortly after follows the peremptory command of "Taps." "Out lights, out lights, out lights!" The soldier gradually disappears from the camp-fire. Rolled snugly in his blanket, the soldier dreams again of home, or revisits in imagination the battle-fields he has trod. The animals, with dull instinct, lie down to rest, and with dim gropings of consciousness ruminate over "fresh fields and pastures new." The fires, neglected by the sleeping men, go out, gradually flickering and smouldering, as if unwilling to die.

All is quiet. The army is asleep. Perhaps there is a brief interruption to the silence as some trooper goes clattering down the road on an errand of speed, or some uneasy sleeper turns over to find an easier position. And around the slumbering host the picket-guards keep quiet watch, while constant, faithful hearts in Northern and Western homes pray that the angels of the Lord may encamp around the sleeping army.

—NICHOLS, *The Story of the Great March*

7. FORCED MARCHES IN THE TECHE COUNTRY

There was no more difficult marching or fighting country than the Teche country stretching west of New Orleans. An alluvial region filled with lakes and swamps, almost impassable, and cursed by heat and mosquitoes in the summer, it presented very real difficulties to Northern boys.

John De Forest, who here describes the cruel hardships of a forced march through the Teche country in the spring of 1863, was an historian and novelist who returned from Europe, on the outbreak of the war, to recruit a company for the 12th Connecticut Volunteers. He served with Banks in the Southwest and later in the Shenandoah Valley. His essays on the war, contributed to Harper's *and* The Galaxy, *were later collected as* A Volunteer's Adventures; *of his many novels the best known is* Miss Ravenel's Conversion from Secession to Loyalty, *one of the earliest forays into realism.*

SLING blankets and shoulder arms was the order now, and we set off on our long chase to Alexandria [Louisiana]. Mouton had gained five or six hours the start of us, and Texans on horseback can travel faster than Yankees on foot, so that, although we marched furiously that hot day, making twenty-four miles before nightfall, Grover had finished his battle long before we reached him. Unacquainted with the country and ordered to the wrong place, he had gone to the wrong place. He had posted himself on one of two parallel roads, instead of where the two met in one, affording him a chance to fight decisively. The consequence was a sidelong battle, both sides suffering, but the enemy escaping.

Forward at full speed the next day and the day after, scurrying and popping of cavalry in the front, as our van skirmished with their rear. At times a great distant dust, showing how close we were upon the Rebel flight. It is a solemn and menacing phenomenon, the dust of a marching enemy, but more particularly so, of course, when it is advancing upon you. The smoke of burning cotton streaked the day, and the flare of it luridly starred the night; for even in his haste Mouton was determined that no fraction of the financial king should fall to the Yankees. Stragglers in grey and butternut dropped back among us with pacific waving of caps and handkerchiefs; for although we could not catch the Texan horsemen, we were marching the Louisiana infantry to tatters. It seemed like meeting old friends to come across the fellows of the Crescent regiment, whom we had encountered six months before at Labadieville, or Georgia Landing. Shouts of recognition took place, gayer on our side than on theirs. They told us that their officers were driving the men on with drawn sabres, or the whole force would have gone to pieces under the exhaustion of the retreat. Mightily encouraged by these statements, we blistered our soles with renewed energy.

Oh, the horrors of marching on blistered feet! It is an incesant bastinado applied by one's own self, from morning to night. I do not mean a single blister, as big as a pea, but a series of blisters, each as large as a dollar, or, to judge by one's sensations, as large as a cartwheel. I have had them one under the other, on the heel, behind the heel, on the ball of the foot, on every toe, a network, a labyrinth, an archipelago of agony. Heat, hunger, thirst, and fatigue are nothing compared with this torment. When you stand, you seem to be on red-hot iron plates; when you walk, you make grimaces at every step. In the morning the whole regiment starts limping, and by noon the best soldiers become nearly mutinous with suffering. They snarl and swear at each other; they curse the general for ordering such marching; they curse the enemy for running away instead of fighting; they fling themselves down in the dust, refusing to move a step further. Fevered with fatigue and pain, they are actually not themselves. Meantime, the company officers, as sore-footed as anyone, must run about from straggler to straggler, coaxing, arguing, ordering, and, perhaps, using the flat of the sabre. Instead of marching in front of my company, I followed immediately in the rear, so that I could see and at once pounce upon everyone who fell out.

It was curious to note how cheerful everyone became if cannon in front told of the proximity of the enemy. We were ready to fight the bloodiest of combats rather than march a mile further. We filed into line of battle delighted, and then resumed our pursuit heartsick.

It will be asked, perhaps, whether I, an officer and claiming, of course, to to be a patriot, preserved my staunchness under these trials. I must confess, and I do it without great shame, conscious of being no more than human, that in my inmost soul I was as insubordinate as the worst men were in speech and behavior. In my unspeakable heart I groaned and raved. I wished the bridges would break down—I wished the regiment would refuse to take another step—it seemed to me that I should have been silent in the face of mutiny. But nothing of all this passed my lips, and none could suspect it from my actions.

When we bivouacked at night came the severest trial. Our regiment was on the left of the brigade, and as we always slept in line of battle, this threw us half a mile from the bayou, along which we marched, and which was our only source of water. It was necessary to order a squad of the blistered and bloody-footed men to bring water for the company's coffee. The first sergeant takes out his book and reads off the fatigue detail: "Corporal Smith,

Privates Brown, Jones, Robinson, and Brown second, fall in with canteens to get water."

Now ensues a piteous groaning, pleading, and showing of bloody heels or blistered soles, on the part of the most fagged or least manly of the victims of rotation in labor. The first sergeant feels that he has no discretion in the matter, and he knows, moreover, that the other men are fully as incapable of marching as these. He stands firm on his detail, and the opposition grumblingly yields. Slowly and sadly Messrs. Brown, Jones, Robinson, and Brown second take up the canteens of the company, each backing six or eight, and limp away to the river, returning, an hour later, wet, muddy, dragged out, and savage.

Somewhat similar scenes happened on the march. Aides passed down the length of the trailing column with the order, "Water half a mile in front; details will be sent forward with canteens." Under these circumstances, roguish soldiers would sometimes use the chance to forage, falling in an hour later with a load of chickens as well as of fluid.

Having tried various alleviations for the hardships of marching, without much benefit, I conclude that man was not made to foot it at the rate of thirty miles a day. Soaping the inside of the stockings does some good, by diminishing the friction and, as a consequence, the blistering. It is also advisable to wash the feet before starting, always providing you have sufficient time and water. Beware of washing them at night; it cracks the heated skin and increases the misery. Beware, too, of trying to march on the strength of whiskey; you go better for a few minutes, and then you are worse off than ever. Opium is far superior as a temporary tonic, if I may judge by a single day's experience. I started out sick, took four grains of opium, marched better and better every hour, and at the end of twenty-two miles came in as fresh as a lark.

It must be understood by the non-military reader that company officers of infantry are not permitted to mount horses, whether by borrowing or stealing, but must foot it alongside of their men, for the double purpose of keeping them in order and of setting them an example of hardihood. On this march, General Banks impounded, at a certain point on the road, more than a dozen infantry officers who were found astride of animals, causing each to rejoin his command as it passed, placing some under arrest and summarily dismissing one from the service. They looked exceedingly crestfallen as they stood there, cooped up in a barnyard under charge of the provost guard. The passing soldiers grinned at them, hooted a little, and marched on, much cheered by the spectacle.

If it had not been for the counter irritant of blistered feet, we should have heard a mutinous deal of grumbling on account of thirst. A man strapped up as a soldier is, and weighted with forty rounds of ammunition, knapsack, three days' rations, canteen containing three pints, and rifle, perspires profusely. I have seen the sweat standing on the woolly fibres of their flannel sacks like dew. To supply this waste of moisture they pour down the warm water of their canteens, and are soon begging for leave to fall out of the ranks in search of incredibly situated springs and rivulets. It will not do to accede to the request, for if one man goes, all have a right to go, and, moreover, the absence would probably terminate in a course of foraging or pillaging. Mindful of his duty and the orders of his superiors, the captain grimly responds, "Keep your place, sir," and trudges sufferingly on, cursing inwardly the heat, the dust, the pace and, perhaps, the orders. He knows that if his fellows are caught a mile to the rear wringing the necks of chickens, he may be sent after them; and, in view of his blisters and the fifteen miles already marched and the indefinite miles yet to go, he has no fancy for such an expedition. . . .

In describing the miseries of marching, I must not forget the dust. The movement of so many thousands of feet throws up such dense and prodigious clouds that one who has not witnessed the phenomenon will find it difficult to imagine it in all its vastness and nuisance. The officers dodge from side to side of the road to escape the pulverous suffocation; and the men, bound to their fours, choke desperately along in the midst of it. The faces become grimed out of all human semblance; the eyelashes are loaded, the hair discolored, and the uniform turns to the color of the earth. It frequently happens that you cannot see the length of your regiment, and it has occurred to me that I have been unable to see the length of my own company of perhaps twenty files. Of course, this annoyance varies greatly in magnitude, according to the nature of the earth.

Rain is good or bad, according to circumstances. In hot weather it cools the skin, invigorates the muscles, and is a positive comfort, except in so far as it spoils the footing. On the second day of this advance we had a pelting shower, which soaked everybody, including General Banks—which last circumstance was a source of unmixed satisfaction to the soldiers. Enlisted men like to see officers bear their share of the troubles of war; and, moreover, our fellows held the general responsible for the tearing speed at which we were going. But rain, although pleasant to the skin in warm weather, will reach the earth and make puddles; and to infantry in march a puddle in the road is a greater nuisance than people in carriages would imagine. No man, however wet he may be, wants to step into it; he crowds his next comrade, and so gets into a growling bout; or he hangs back, and so checks the succeeding files. A large puddle always produces a tailing-off of the regiment, which must be made up presently by double-quicking, much to the fatigue and wrath of the rearmost. Oh, miserable left of the column! how many times a day it has to run in order to catch up with the right! and how heartily it hates the right in consequence! Put a regiment or a brigade "left in front," and see how it will go. The men who usually march in the rear are now in the lead, and they are sure to give the fellows at the other end of the line a race. This opening out of the column of march is a constant evil, and one which officers soon learn to struggle against with incessant watchfulness. I believe that I used to shout, "Close up, men," at least a hundred times a day, in every conceivable tone of authority, impatience, and entreaty.

But are there no comforts, no pleasures, in forced marching? Just one:

stopping it. Yes, compared with the incessant anguish of going, there was a keen luxury in the act of throwing one's self at full length and remaining motionless. It was a beast's heaven; but it was better than beast's hell—insupportable fatigue and pain. The march done, the fevered feet bare to the evening breeze, the aching limbs outstretched, the head laid on the blanket roll which had been such a burden through the day, the pipe in mouth, nature revived a little and found that life retained some sweetness. Delicious dreams, too—dreams wonderfully distinct and consecutive—made slumber a conscious pleasure. All night I was at home surrounded by loving faces. No visions of war or troubles; no calling up of the sufferings of the day, nor anticipation of those of the morrow; nothing but home, peace, and friends. I do not know why this should be, but I have always found it so when quite worn out with fatigue, and I have heard others say that it was their experience.

I have already said that we were *en bivouac*. Shelter tents were as yet unknown in the Department of the Gulf, and our wall tents, as well as every other article of not absolutely essential baggage, had been left at Brashear City. For cover, our servants made hasty wigwams or lean-tos of rails, over which we threw our rubber blankets to keep out the "heft" of the showers. If it rained we sat up with our overcoats over our heads, or perhaps slept through it without minding. Not until August, more than three months later, did we again enjoy the shelter of a tent; and during that time we had only two brief opportunities for providing ourselves with board shanties. Meantime we became as dirty and ragged as beggars, and eventually as lousy.

For some time I supposed that what I ate was the free gift of the colored population, and rejoiced in the gratitude of the emancipated slaves who shared their food with their deliverers. My man George, a sly and slippery darkey, brought in sheep, chickens and corn-dodgers, saying that they had been given to him. Given they were, but by the providence of war, and not by the willing hands of emancipated men and brethren. George, representative of hungry Mars, entered whatever dwelling came handiest, whether of white or black, and took therefrom whatever was good to eat without offering to pay or consulting the inclination of the proprietor. I soon discovered this, but I had not the stomach to stop it. To march without food was impossible, and to buy without money was equally out of the question.

Let me suggest, in passing, that the irregular payments of the army were a fruitful source of demoralization. The officer cannot draw rations, and if his money is withheld from for six or eight or twelve months, as was frequently the case, he must allow his servant to forage for him, or he must starve. If he forages, the men will follow the example, although not driven by the same necessity, inasmuch as they are provided with food and clothing. The result is widespread straggling and often atrocious plundering. . . .

At Opelousas our pursuit of Mouton ceased for a few days. Even to this moment I am grateful for that halt and smile with pleasure over the recollection of it. Our provisions were out, and we thanked heaven for it, seeing starvation on the morrow to be pleasanter than marching today. So, until the Teche could be cleared of sunken gunboats, and the transports could come up with additional salt beef and hardtack, we rested in the green Opelousas. Oh, rest! oh, sleep! Three days and nights of solid sleep! It was better than kingdoms and the glory thereof. Except when I was on duty, or eating, I did little but lie folded in slumber. The hard ground was miraculously softened, and fitted my weary limbs like down. No one can imagine the luxury of rest to the utterly weary; it is like the first draught of water to one who has pined with thirst; it must be proven to be comprehended.

For one poor fellow of my company there was no repose, even now. Sick at Brashear City, he had voluntarily left hospital for the sake of fighting; had behaved nobly at Camp Beaseland, but failed rapidly under the severities of the pursuit. During this last day he staggered along between men detailed to support him, agonized with fever and half delirious, moaning: "We never rest! Oh, when shall we ever rest?" Now, with no bedding but his blanket, he lay on the ground, quite out of his head and muttering constantly, "Fall in!" as if he were still on the march. Ambulances we had none in the army, but he was sent in a country cart to hospital, and, after a long sickness, recovered.

On the arrival of the regiment it had been placed on picket, two miles north of the town; and when, next day, an order came to relieve it, men and officers begged to be allowed to remain undisturbed. Watching and the chance of fighting were trifles compared with even two miles of marching on those unhealed blisters. The petition was granted, and the Twelfth continued its picket duty, looking contentedly out over the great bare plain which led northward. No one would have wondered at our choice who had seen the plight in which the regiment reached this blessed bivouac. Seventy-five men and officers dragged along with the colors, while four hundred others lay gasping by the roadside for miles rearward, fagged nigh unto death with speed and the scorching rays of the Louisiana sun. In the whole history of the Twelfth, before and after, there never was such another falling out—not even when it was following Early up the Shenandoah, under cavalry Sheridan. The truth is that Banks was the most merciless marcher of men that I ever knew.

Our blisters had scarcely well hardened to callosities when orders reached Weitzel's brigade to break camp, overtake Dwight, who was five miles ahead, and push the enemy as rapidly as possible to Alexandria. I was at this time on a court-martial at Opelousas, and we might, I suspect, have remained on that duty, and so have escaped the three days of misery which followed; but, anticipating a battle, we enthusiastically deemed it our duty to adjourn to the General's headquarters and beg leave to join the column.

Starting at five in the afternoon, we reached a broken bridge about seven, made it passable by dint of several hours of labor, and then pushed on until three in the morning. Next to the stupidity and fruitless worry of night fighting comes the stupidity and fruitless worry of night marching. Except under extraordinary circumstances, the results which it achieves do not half compensate for the mischief which it works on the discipline of an army, and the morale and physique of the individual soldier. The officer cannot see his men, and they straggle in spite of him. There is constant falling, stumbling, and unrewarded waste of strength, accompanied by irritation, quarrelling, and disorderliness. Every molehill seems a mountain; every unusual darkness in the path shows like an abyss; the line is continually opening and must be closed up by laborious double-quicking. The men stagger against each other, and slumber marching. At every halt to rest, some fall asleep and are left behind in the darkness. When we bivouacked at three in the morning, ten hours from our starting point, we had made only sixteen miles, and were as exhausted as if we had gone thirty. My company was immediately sent out on picket, and this duty kept me moving and watching until sunrise. After a breakfast of hardtack and coffee, I dozed a few minutes while the fall-in call was beating, and then set off on a day's march of twenty-seven miles, coming in after nightfall well blistered.

The next day, bivouacked on rolling turf by the side of a lovely stream, we bathed and rested. Before dawn on the third morning, having as yet had less than ten hours' sleep since leaving Opelousas, I commenced the hardest day's work of my life. Starting lame, and improving from hour to hour, like foundered horses, we accomplished twenty-four miles by three in the afternoon. As usual, we had halted ten minutes in every hour, closing up, coming to a front, dressing the line, stacking arms, and dropping down by the side of the road to rest. The men had kept well together; such few as had fallen out had come up during the long pause which took place at three; and we were, so far, proud of our march and rather pleased at having done so much. But this sentiment was based on the expectation that we would presently go into bivouac. When, therefore, General Banks joined the column, and some one heard him say that we must reach Alexandria that night, and the horrible tale passed down along the line of stacks, our hearts were suddenly full of despair and growling.

For the next ten miles it was a fight against nature. Every effort was made to cheer the men onward and beguile them from a sense of their miseries. The staggering drummers were forced to beat the march for the staggering regiments. Some of the field officers dismounted and walked at the head of their commands. At one halt, Lieutenant Colonel Van Petten ran foot races in his big boots with a private, to make the soldiers laugh at the unusual buffoonery. Staff officers rode up and down the line, giving orders to yell and setting the example of uproar. The company officers carried the rifles of tottering men, and hastened from straggler to straggler, cheering, ordering, and threatening, but, I think, never striking; for no one could find it in his heart to maltreat poor fellows who were almost at the last gasp with pain and fatigue. We reeled, crawled, and almost rolled toward Alexandria.

As night fell, the pace increased, and the whooping became continuous, and we seemed like a column of maniacs. But in the last two miles, in the pitchy darkness between eight and nine of the evening, a silence of despair descended upon us, and then the regiments melted like frost in sunshine. I could not see who fell out of my company, and I did not care. My whole official sentiment of honor was concentrated, under the flame of intense physical suffering, into the one little idea of getting myself to Alexandria with the colors, no matter who else dropped by the way. The few men remaining in the organization reeled on speechlessly. If they passed a dying artillery horse, they no longer shouted, with savage defiance, "Fresh horses! bring on your horses!" They had stopped muttering curses against Banks and the Confederates—those two enemies. They were at the point, morally, of unspeakable desperation and, physically, of mere movement in one direction, without a thought or a sentiment beyond what was necessary to put one foot before the other, and to lean toward Alexandria.

If the enemy had been there we could not have fought him nor run away from him. But, fortunately, there was no enemy within twenty miles of us, as there had been none from the hour we started. God alone knows why we marched thus; our commander has probably forgotten. We had nothing more to boast of than that we had accomplished thirty-four miles in one day, and eighty-seven miles in the whole burst of seventy-six hours, to which Company D of the Twelfth Connecticut had added five miles by a nocturnal foraging expedition. About one third of the regiment stacked arms in the little wood where we bivouacked, and nearly all the remainder straggled in before morning. That night I was too tired to eat, and went contentedly to sleep without supper. . . .

Longer and more rapid forced marches than this of ours have been made, but I am glad that I was not called upon to assist at the performance. We should not have suffered so much as we did, had it not been for the heat, which not only wore out our muscular forces, but greatly increased the blistering of our feet.

Perhaps it is worth while to mention that, after two or three days of repose, we were excessively proud of our thirty-four miles in a day, and were ready to march with any other brigade in the army for a wager.

—De Forest, "Forced Marches"

8. AN INDIANA BOY REASSURES HIS MOTHER ABOUT MORALS IN THE ARMY

Theodore Upson was barely seventeen when he enlisted in the 100th Regiment of Indiana Volunteers. Brought up in a strict Presbyterian household, he was much concerned to reassure his parents about such matters as drinking, swearing, and gambling. On the whole the morals of both armies were remarkably good. There was comparatively little drunkenness and, by modern standards, little gambling. While there was a great deal of pillaging, especially among the invaders, crimes against persons were rare and sex offenses almost unknown. Young Upson fought at Vicksburg and Chattanooga and was with Sherman in his March to the Sea.

Bellefont, Ala., April 2, 1864

Dear Mother—

I have had several letters from the home people asking me about drinking in the Army, and Father has written me saying he hopes I am not getting to be a d[r]unkard as he hears many of the soldiers are. I think you good people at home must imagine we keep a barell of whisky on tap all of the time. Now for the truth about this and other things that are told about our boys. There is some drinking in the Army, I am sorry to say, but it is the exception rather than the rule. Some of our officers may take a social glass when they get together at times but few if any of them drink to excess, and I think drinking among the officers is less now than ever before. Good officers know that when wine is in, wit is out. They know too that the men distrust and have no confidence in an intemperate officer, in fact will make fun of him. And an officer whose men make fun of him had better resign as some *have done*, for his usefulness is at an end. I know what I am talking about for I have been around Hd Quarters enough to have learned the habits of our Generals. Grant does not drink at all; Sherman but little, if any; I don't think any. Howard never; McPherson, I think, never; Logan is no tippler; and in our Division and Brigade officers all, or nearly all, are total abstainers.

As to the rank and file hardly a man is a drinker. It is not so easy for a soldier to get liquor as most people seem to think. First, he has to have an order from a commissioned officer. Not so easy to get as the officers do not want thier men to drink. Next, it takes money which the men are often without. Another thing, good hard experience has taught them that liquour is no good, that they need clear heads and sound bodies to stand the strain and hardships of Army life. A soldier must be above all temperate in all things.

As to profanity a good many of the boys do use swear words, some liberaly, some not at all. But this is a strenuous life. Men will do here what they would not do at home and I know this. Profanity is not deep nor vicious. Let a Chaplain come along who the men respect and the most of them will be gaurded in thier talk. Why? Because all the time thier better selves are lying dormant and under different conditions would assert themselves. We have a good many men, Uncle Aaron Woflord, for instance, who set a good quiet example which is respected, to say the least, by the roughest.

As to gambling, there is very little of it. The men play cards a good deal, it is true, sometimes for small stakes, but it is for amusement alone. No gambling about it. A real gambler would not be held in any respect by the men.

As to other vices, I think I am safe in saying that you might search the world over and not find as clean a lot of men as comprise the Army today. I do not say it has always been so, but the men who compose the great Army to which I have the honor to belong have passed through the trials and temptations of the soldiers life and now are like gold—cleared of its dross. And when this war is ended and what are left of this Army return to civil life, you will see that they will be accepted as among the best and highest of ideal American citizens. All the roughness will fall away and they will be shining lights in thier chosen walks of life. As for myself, I am too proud to dabble in mud and mire. So do not worry, Father mine, I am not going to the dogs; neither are any of the other boys you know.

I have at one time mentioned our excellent Chaplain, Rev John A Brouse, father of Captain Charles Brouse, who was so teribly wounded at Mission Ridge. Chaplain Brouse is a valient soldier, not only of the Cross, but also of this war. He never seems to think of himself and was right on the firing line helping care for the wounded and saying words of comfort to the dying. A noble man is Chaplain Brouse and the boys love him as a Father. There is also a Chaplain of the 90 Ill, a Catholic Preist, who is greatly loved and respected by all of the men of his and other Regiments. So you see this war is breaking down the barriers between beliefs and creeds as well as doing many other things you may think more or less desirable. And another thing I know you will find it hard to understand, money has but little value with the boys now. They all seem to think the pittance paid them by the Government is an incident of the service, that they are giving this part of thier lives for a principle and do not expect to gain any personal profit from it in any way.

—WINTHER, ed., *Journal of Theodore Upson*

9. AN ILLINOIS PRIVATE COMPLAINS OF BAD COOKING

The food provided for the Union soldiers was adequate quantitatively, but that is about all that can be said for it. The normal ration consisted of a pound of hardtack, or its equivalent, three-quarters pound of bacon or salt pork or a pound of beef, plus coffee, sugar and salt. By modern dietary standards this diet was calculated to break down the strongest constitutions. Not only was it badly planned, and monotonous, but it was generally badly cooked. Cooking was commonly assigned not to trained cooks but to soldiers detailed for brief periods to that unpleasant job. Fortunately many of the soldiers supplemented their regular rations by setting up their own messes, by boxes from home, or—more commonly in the West—by foraging.

We have met Leander Stillwell before, in the midst of battle.

I RETAIN a vivid recollection of the kind of army cooking we had for the first few months in Tennessee. At Camp Carrolton and Benton Barracks we had company cooks who prepared the food for the entire company. They were merely enlisted men, detailed for that purpose, and while their cooking was nothing to brag about, it was vastly superior to what now ensued. We divided up into messes, of four, eight, or twelve men, or thereabouts, to the mess, and generally would take turns in the culinary line. Very few of us knew anything whatever about cooking, and our exploits in that regard would have been comical if the effects had not been so pernicious. Flour was issued to us after our arrival at Pittsburg Landing, but we had no utensils in which we could cook biscuits, or loaves. So we would make a batter out of flour, water, grease, and salt, and cook it in a mess pan, the product being the army "flapjack." It invariably was tough as a mule's ear, about as heavy as lead, and very indigestible. Later we learned to construct ovens of wood, daubed with mud, or of stone, and in them, in the course of time, we acquired the knack of baking good bread. But with us in the west the hardtack was generally our standard bread diet, and nothing could beat it.

And for some time our cooking of "Yankee beans," as we called them, was simply atrocious. As you know, beans should be cooked until they are thoroughly done; otherwise they are decidedly harmful. Well, we would not cook them much more than half enough, the result being a sloppy, slimy mess, its looks alone being well-nigh sufficient to extinguish one's appetite. And as for the rice—the horrible messes we would make of that defy description. I know that one consequence with me was I contracted such an aversion to rice that for many years afterwards, while in civil life, I just couldn't eat it in any form, no matter how temptingly it was prepared.

Owing to improperly cooked food, change of climate and of water, and neglect of proper sanitation measures in the camps, camp diarrhea became epidemic at Pittsburg Landing, especially among the "green" regiments like ours. And for about six weeks everybody suffered, more or less, the difference being only in degree. The fact is, the condition of the troops in that quarter during the prevalence of that disorder was simply so bad and repulsive that any detailed description thereof will be passed over. I never saw the like before, and never have seen it since. I always thought that one thing which aggravated this trouble was the inordinate quantity of sugar some of the men would consume. They would not only use it to excess in their coffee and rice, but would frequently eat it raw, by handfuls.

I happen to think, right now, of an incident that illustrates the unnatural appetite of some of the men for sugar. It occurred in camp one rainy day during the siege of Corinth. Jake Hill, of my company, had covered the top of a big army hardtack with sugar in a cone-like form, piling it on as long as the tack would hold a grain. Then he seated himself on his knapsack and proceeded to gnaw away at his feast, by a system of "regular approaches." He was even then suffering from the epidemic before mentioned, and was so weak he could hardly walk.

Some one said to him, "Jake, that sugar ain't good for you in your condition."

He looked up with an aggrieved air and responded in a tone of cruelly injured innocence, "Haven't I the right to eat my r-a-a-tion?"

Strange to say, Jake got well, and served throughout the war. He was a good soldier, too. . . .

In consequence of the conditions at Pittsburg Landing that have been alluded to, men died by the score like rotten sheep. And a great many more were discharged for disability and thereby were lost to the service. It is true that some of these discharged men, especially the younger ones, subsequently re-enlisted, and made good soldiers. But this loss to the Union armies in Tennessee in the spring of '62 by disease would undoubtedly surpass the casualties of a great battle, but, unlike a battle, there was no resulting compensation whatever.

—STILLWELL, *The Story of a Common Soldier of Army Life in the Civil War*

10. HOW TO MAKE MONEY IN THE ARMY

There were fraud and chicanery in American business a-plenty in the sixties, and inevitably they made their appearance in the armies, North and South. As Federal soldiers had more money to spend—and more things to spend it on—there was more of the sort of thing described here in the North than in the South.

E. W. Locke, who here recalls the various methods of preying on the soldiers, was a professional singer, author of such popular songs as "Down by the Sea" and "I Feel I'm Growing Old, Lizzie," and temperance lecturer who "attached" himself to General Abercrombie's division.

FOR a time, peddling watches in the camps was a great business; they were made almost expressly for the Army, showy, cheap as possible, and if they would only run for a short time, it mattered little whether they would keep time or not. But will the soldier, who in the first year of the war gets but eleven dollars a month, spend twenty dollars for a watch, and especially without knowing whether it is good or worthless? Those only who are ignorant of the tastes of young people will ask this question. Of course he will, unless he thinks he wants something else more. . . .

Watch-peddling was a business in the Army not to be sneered at. One Jew, who has been dodging in and out of the tents of one regiment all day, has sold twenty-seven before sundown, and he will sell many more before tattoo. They are all of one pattern, and very taking to the eye. They may run a month or a year, and they may keep tolerably correct time. But they were made more for sale than service, and they sell. . . .

Among the most useful of the camp-followers were the picture-makers. This business continued in the camp, with short intervals of exclusion, to the end of the war; and the number was small, indeed, who did not send home likenesses. If the friends at home have not seen the boy in soldier-clothes, he is anxious to show them how he looks. If he has been promoted to a Corporal, with two stripes on his arm, or a Sergeant, with three, or an Orderly, with stripes and a square, the picture sent home will tell the story better than a letter. Jealous neighbors cannot gainsay the ambrotype. The Lieutenant, the Captain, the Major, the Colonel, all must go to the artist as soon as they receive the insignia of their promotion. It is not necessary to write that a Lieutenant has become a Captain, those two bars on that shoulder-strap tell the news.

Some of the artists made considerable money, but they earned all they received. It sometimes happened that a shell, or other missile, would come whizzing along, while the operator was adjusting the lenses. Squinting at his man, through the camera, suddenly his apparatus is *non est.*

Often the picture taken in camp is the last and most precious memento the home-circle has of him who sleeps they know not where. These mementos exist in every town and hamlet in our country.

Another most useful class of camp-followers were the soldiers' memorial agents. We see these significant lithographs hanging in many a house. When my eye catches one of them in a stranger's house, I know at once that family had a near friend in the war. There is one name on that paper, perhaps more, very precious to them. . . . The day will come when they will be to many families precious as a coat of arms. A hundred years hence, and they will be shown with pride, and exultant men will say, "That was my grandfather's brother, or that was my great-uncle. He died for the flag."

Every one has seen these memorials; but all do not know how they were prepared. A lithographer executed the design on stone, leaving blank space for printing in the names, company, regiment, and other items of interest, such as time of enlistment, discharge, or death. The lithograph, as it comes from the stone, is as good for one regiment as another. Agents visit the camp, and obtain all the necessary items for printing, take orders, at perhaps a dollar and a half each, return to have the printing done, and, in due time, probably soon after pay-day, reappear in camp to furnish the subscribers with the coveted memorial. If a battle has occurred in the agent's absence, many of his orders are worthless. "Fell in battle." An asterisk at their names directs to these fearful words. At one time this was a largely-paying business.

Taking butter to the Army was, at times, a profitable speculation. If the trader was shrewd, he would time his shipment so that it would reach the camp about pay-day. I do not remember, however, to have met any one who made a fortune in this business.

Many made considerable money in purchasing the hides of the slaughtered cattle. But there were rings in the Army, as there are out; and if you were not in the ring, you could not purchase hides.

An enterprising, but not very shrewd Yankee, visited Chatanooga, in the winter of '64, and seeing the great number of hides that were daily accumulating, endeavored to buy them; but some were ahead of him, or were in the ring, while our Yankee was out. He would then purchase the tallow. "O, yes; he could have the tallow;" for as yet there was no tallow-ring, and speedily there is a large candle-factory in operation, not in Chatanooga, Murfreesboro', or Nashville, but in the brain of the speculator. He has learned the price of candles, and is not long in coming to the conclusion, that with tallow at two, and candles at twelve cents per pound, there is a moderate fortune in the business. Hurrying to Nashville for a quantity of moulds, some large kettles, and one or two experts to assist in the new speculation, he soon has his plans well matured. But it requires time to make the moulds, and before the army candle-factory is completed, the short evenings have come, the Army is ready to move, and the anticipated fortune vanishes.

While the Army lay in winter quarters, it was a good field for theatrical and minstrel troupes. I know one man who made thirty thousand dollars in two seasons, in this line. Just how he did it, I am not able to say; but this I know, he went there with nothing, and came away at the end of the second winter with that amount of money.

Many made a great deal of money by circulating bills of worthless banks.

I met one man who had a thousand dollars in notes of the Bank of Tecumseh, Michigan. They, of course, were worthless at home; but I doubt not they brought him their face in whatever he wished to buy. Notes of broken banks were sent to the Army, and sold to shrewd, unscrupulous men, as counterfeit money is sold, and the dealers made small fortunes. "But how could this be done to any extent?" If one had a nominal thousand dollars in these notes, he could easily sell them at half price, it answering as well as good money to purchase anything the Southern people or Negroes had to sell. For a year after greenbacks were issued, the Southern people preferred notes of State banks, whether good or not, to them. It sometimes happened that our troops would advance on a place, as, for example, Winchester, hold it a short time, retire for a season, and then reoccupy. If they had distributed greenbacks at the first occupation, at the second there was an opportunity to gather them in exchange for State bills. Then was the time for the dealer in notes of broken banks.

The most cruel swindles were perpetrated on the Southern people and Negroes, after the issue of facsimile Confederate notes. These could be bought for a trifle. At times the Negroes made quite a business of washing, baking hoe-cakes, picking cherries, and other fruit, and bringing sweet potatoes to camp. It was cruel to pretend to pay them for their hard toil in this worthless stuff, yet the quantity thus disposed of no doubt amounted to a million of dollars. . . .

If I knew the mysteries of cotton-buying, I could make this chapter intensely interesting. I saw it brought in by ten, twenty and fifty bales, but never a pound sold. Here was a ring that only the favored few could enter. Expeditions failed through the avarice of the leading officers. Men preferred making five hundred thousand dollars to gaining a victory.

I always noticed when cotton was brought in, that some of the officers connected with the Provost-Marshal's Department took special interest in it. I noticed, furthermore, that when a citizen of the North came to the Army with funds, and the hope of buying this article, there was always something in the way. The authorities at Washington were not granting permits, or the Army was to advance shortly, or it would be extremely hazardous to attempt to move it. I was told by one of these citizens that he was informed by one of the officers who stood very near the General commanding, that he could not only obtain a permit to buy cotton, but have the exclusive privilege of the department, by furnishing the requisite capital, taking all risks, and dividing the profits. . . .

Many persons made money by smuggling quinine, and other articles which brought a great price. In taking my trunk to the depot at Louisville one morning, I noticed a woman of middle age, dressed in black, standing by . her trunk, waiting, as we all were, to have our baggage carefully inspected, before it could be taken aboard the train for Nashville. Inspecting the articles in due order, the officer comes to the lady's trunk, which she has already opened, and proceeds to examine dresses, skirts, and other articles of female apparel, which, having done to his satisfaction, he locks the trunk, and politely hands her the key. Turning it on end to mark it, his suspicions are aroused, and he demands the key again, opening it, running his cane down inside, then measuring to the floor, he sees that the trunk has a false bottom. The articles are removed, the thin board split out with his cane, and there are needles enough to supply a good sized town for a year; neither she nor her trunk went to Nashville on that train. The last I saw of her she was turning a corner with an officer, who was escorting her to the office of the Provost-Marshal. How she expected to get these needles through the lines, and how much profit there would have been on the sales had her enterprise been successful, I know not.

Judging from what I saw of the people where we went, I should think needles were the last things to smuggle. The articles most needed were wheat and soap.

—Locke, *Three Years in Camp and Hospital*

11. GRAFT AND CORRUPTION IN THE CONFEDERATE COMMISSARY

Complaints against the commissary were ardent, on both sides. The simple fact was that there was no such organization of the commissary department, during the Civil War, as we are familiar with from the First and Second World Wars. Nor was there any adequate check on the food and drink that went through the commissary, or on the activities of the sutlers.

This picture of graft in the Confederate commissary is doubtless accurate enough for Watson's particular outfit, but it is by no means a faithful picture of conditions generally in the Confederate armies. We have already met the irrepressible Watson on the retreat from Pea Ridge.

THE army was furnished, through the quarter master's department, with quarters, whether houses or tents, camp equipage, arms, ammunition, accoutrements, and clothing, and all means of transport. These the department obtained from contractors, and the shocking quality of the materials furnished showed corruption to a great extent. The soldier, of course, knew nothing about the contracts, and in the South they had always the excuse that good materials were not to be got; but the things which mostly affected the soldier personally were shoes and clothing, and these, to a great extent, they managed to provide for themselves, or they were sent to them by their friends at home.

The system pursued by the commissaries, even making allowance for the difficulties they were subject to, were simply disgraceful. I do not exaggerate when I say that on an average from every requisition of rations said to be issued to the troops, the commissary took off one-third and sold it, putting the proceeds in his pocket. The cause of this peculation lay greatly in the system of management. I might say that the system, as it then existed, was such that even a man of the most sterling integrity, and of honest and upright principles, if appointed commissary of a regiment on active service could hardly, after six months, remain an honest man. If so, he would deserve the greatest credit for it.

The system was this: The commissary received a supply of provisions from the depot. He got with it an invoice detailing quantity and price. From these he issued to the non-commissioned officers and soldiers, on requisitions signed by the orderly-sergeants and captains of companies. He sold for money to all officers and men pertaining to the army. He had to account for the amount of the consignment (losses and casualties excepted) by money and requisitions. The practice was this: An orderly sergeant made out a requisition for his company—say for 100 men for one day—flour, 100 lb.; beef, pork, or bacon, 75 lb.; coffee, seven lb.; sugar, 14 lb.; rice or pease, six lb.; soap, two lb.; salt, pepper, vinegar, etc. This requisition was signed by the captain, and men were detailed to go to the commissary store to draw these rations. The commissary takes the requisition and calls his assistant, and says to the men, "Well, you can get three-quarter ration of flour, half ration of pork, half ration of coffee, and half ration of sugar, and that is all." The men would grumble and say, "We only got half rations yesterday." "Can't help it, I am short of provisions, and there are other companies to serve as well as you, and all must get their share." He then sticks the requisition on the file, and his assistant weighs out the rations. "Will we get the back rations when the supplies come up?" some mischievous young rascal would say as he dodged behind a barrel. The commissary would put his hand on his revolver, but restrain himself, and pretend to take no notice of a thing so absurd, and buries his face in his book, while he credits himself with full rations issued to 100 men as per requisition, while his assistant and the men would laugh at the audacity of the offender, "no back rations" being the commissary's watchword, and, what was more strange, no requisition would be received unless it was made out for the full amount.

Thus the commissary had a voucher for and was credited with supplying a full requisition when he had only supplied a small part of it, and he had the rest to sell for his own benefit. I have frequently known instances of a company, after giving the full requisition and being supplied with half rations on the grounds that provisions were scarce, getting one of the army waggon drivers, and giving him money to go to the commissary store and purchase four or five pounds of coffee, or other necessaries, which had been kept off them, which he would obtain for money without the least trouble, and this system was carried on quite openly. I more than once nearly got into serious difficulty by insisting on marking on the requisition the actual quantity of provisions delivered.

In the post-commissaries and depots there was another system of peculation.

In these depots there were immense stocks of provisions stored for army use. These were periodically inspected by officers, generally of the sinecure kind appointed through favour for such purposes, and there was always a considerable quantity marked "condemned" as being unfit for use. The ceremony of inspecting was generally done in this way: The inspecting officers would come to the depot, where they would be met by the post-commissary, who would receive them in the most friendly manner, and conduct them into the large stores. On each side along the wall would be piled up on the top of each other with their ends exposed, a great many barrels of beef, pork, flour, biscuit, etc.

"These," says the commissary, "are what I have myself picked out as being bad. Those on this side are good, but you can inspect for yourself. Cooper, open one or two of these barrels." The cooper opens a barrel which of course had been already selected. The unsavoury brine spurts out. The officers stand back to save their handsome uniforms. Other barrels are examined of flour, biscuit, etc., similarly selected. Then all on that side, the bulk of which were probably the best provisions, are ordered to be marked condemned. The officers would take a list of the numbers to make their report, and then go and inspect the hospital stores of wines, brandies, etc., of which they would acknowledge they were better judges. A few days' notice would then be given of a sale of "condemned army stores" and they would be auctioned off for a mere trifle. The commissary of course has an agent present who knew what lots to purchase.

Thus it was said large quantities of the very best stores were often marked "Condemned" and sold off at a mere trifle, the commissary having an agent on the ground to buy them in.

—WATSON, *Life in the Confederate Army*

12. THE SOLDIERS GET PAID AND THE SUTLER GETS THE MONEY

By European standards the United States paid its soldiers well; by American standards the pay was shockingly low. At the beginning of the war it was 11 dollars a month for privates, plus a clothing allowance; this was raised to 13 and then to 16 dollars, but the depreciation of money meant that the purchasing value of this pay actually declined during the war. It should be remembered, however, that soldiers' pay was supplemented by Federal and state bounties. The pay of Confederate soldiers was even lower, and the rapid depreciation of Confederate currency meant that most soldiers were fighting without pay.

Not only was Civil War pay low, but soldiers were expected to supply most of the services and comforts that the government furnished in later wars. Thus they had to do their own wash, or find some camp hanger-on to do it; they supplemented their food by private purchases; they even bought their own stoves. Sutlers, who supplied luxuries to the soldiers—tobacco, fruit, cheese, and sometimes liquor—held a semiofficial position. In an effort to regulate them, Congress provided that a board of officers should fix the prices charged, and that no sutler might take a lien on more than one sixth of a soldier's pay in any one month, but these provisions were generally ignored.

AT intervals, various in duration, we were visited by the paymaster, who paid us what was coming from the Government. A paymaster had the rank of Major in the regular army. To us in the field he always came with his "strong box" conveyed in an ambulance, or army wagon, and well guarded by a troop of cavalry with loaded carbines in their hands. Reaching a particular regiment he would go over the amount due each man, as reported by the Adjutant, and, if this was found correct, the specified sum would be put in a pay envelope; then the men would be formed in line, and when the name of a given soldier was called he would step forward and receive his money, which was always in currency or "greenbacks." Even small fractional amounts were paid in paper money, as neither gold, silver, nor even copper was in circulation.

The paymaster always had on a bright, new uniform, his linen was immaculate, and his boots never failed to be glossy black. In all this he presented a striking contrast to the other officers in active service in the field.

The more thrifty among the soldiers sent, by far, the greater part of their pay home. In most instances this was done through express companies which followed us in the field, and were new institutions to practically all of us. The prudent soldier, if so disposed, had opportunity to lay by substantially all his wages, which, in the early part of the war, was for the private soldier $13 per month, but later was advanced to $16. The ration furnished by the Government was ample, and so was the clothing allowed each man. Indeed, some of the more thrifty did not use all that was allowed in this way, and consequently received commutation in the way of small, but by no means, intangible amounts of money.

As said above, a few men sent their pay home to almost the last cent. In contrast to these of the more thrifty there was a pitiful minority who had squandered their last farthing in a few hours after being paid off. How? Some of them in gambling with cards, some of them at dice, and others by indulging in what was called "chuck-a-luck." This last was a game of chance, with the *chances* very greatly against the poor soldier victim on the outside.

Not a few "blew-in" all they had received from the paymaster at the Sutler's tent. The Sutler was the recognized regimental merchant. After securing the consent of the commanding officer the Sutler proceeded to lay in a stock of such things as he thought the men would need in the field, and in amount about what could be loaded in a wagon.

His stock included such articles as tobacco, cigars, lemons, oranges, apples, candy, raisins, soda crackers, cakes, canned fruits of various kinds, loaf sugar, mackerel, salt fish, bacon, ginger ale, "pop" and other "soft" drinks. Nearly all these articles were outside the soldier's rations, and were hence, by him, regarded as luxuries which the more provident refused to buy.

Arrived in camp the Sutler transferred his goods to a strong tent of proper size, which through the day, was open in front and, at which, was a wide transverse board which served the double purpose of counter and showcase. The sides of the tent came well down and were securely fastened. The Sutler always slept in his tent and in the midst of his stock. However, sometimes a thief would take advantage of the darkness to rip a hole in the sides of the tent and make a hasty dash for whatever he might be able to lay his hands on.

That the Sutler's prices were always high, and sometimes even exorbitant, can well be imagined. But to make a good profit he had to mark his goods high, for he necessarily incurred great risk. In the field he was in danger of capture. Then, when the regiment had orders to move on short notice, he had to pack his stock hurriedly and often put it "pell-mell" in a wagon for transfer to the next camping place. Furthermore, unless quickly turned some of his goods would grow stale on his hands. One article of this nature was butter, which not infrequently became so rancid as to be wholly unusable.

As to the Sutler himself, he might be long or short. He might be a blonde or brunette. He might be a native or foreigner. But one thing he was always sure to be, namely, "on the make." At the time the average regiment was organized those who joined it were actuated by motives more or less mixed in character. But with the Sutler it was different, for his sole motive was gain.

An "easy-mark" for the Sutler was the financial "tenderfoot," the "live-to-day-and-starve-to-morrow" man who was in every regiment, in every company, and indeed, in practically every squad. And no sooner had this "come-easy-go-easy" specimen received his pay than he forthwith went to the Sutler's tent and proceeded to get "outside" a good deal that, for the man's good, had far better have been left on the shelves.

But not only would these "easy-goers" get rid of their money, but oftentimes the stuff they ate would make them sick. Indeed, in every regiment more than one death could primarily be attributed to certain articles in the Sutler's tent.

—CHARLES BENEULYN JOHNSON, *Muskets and Medicine*

13. SONG AND PLAY IN THE ARMY OF TENNESSEE

The period which Bromfield Ridley here describes was toward the end of the war, when things looked blackest for the Confederacy. By that time Johnston's army had been driven out of South Carolina and into North Carolina. In the midst of this scene of disaster Ridley took the opportunity to recall some of the more cheerful aspects of army life. What he recorded is of interest alike to students of social history and of the American language. Ridley was a first lieutenant, attached to the staff of General A. P. Stewart.

ONE night, one of Colonel McLemore's captains formed a line of battle by saying: "Boys, you can't see me, but dress up on my voice." Colonel Anderson would say, "Dress up on my friend Brit." These things got to be by-words in those commands. Instead of "Blow the Bugle," it was "Toot the Dinner Horn." That takes me to some of our greenhorns in the drill. When we first started, a fellow in East Tennessee began drilling his company thus: "Men, tangle in fours! By move forward! Put! Wheel into line! By turn around! Git!" A Middle Tennessee captain, wanting his company to cross a creek on a log, said: "Attention, company! In one rank to walk a log! Walk a log! March!"

It carried you back to old times to hear the guards around a regiment halloo out, "T-w-e-l-v-e o'-c-l-o-c-k and a-l-l-'s well!" The rude and untrained soldier would play on that and say: "T-w-e-l-v-e o'-c-l-o-c-k, and sleepy as h—l!" When a soldier goes out foraging it is called going on a "lark;" when he goes stealing, it is "impressing it into service;" when a Quartermaster wants to shield his rascality, he has a favorite abstract called "L," which is used, and means "Lost in the service;" when a squad runs from the enemy, it is "Skedadling;" the ricochetting of a cannon ball is "Ski-ugling"—words whose origin began with the war. Let a stranger or soldier enter camp and call for a certain company—say, Company F. Some soldier will say, "Here's Company F!" By the time he can get there, another will cry out at the far part of the regiment, "Here's Company F!" Then the whole command will take up the refrain, until the poor fellow in vexation will sulk away. Let an old soldier recognize a passing friend, and say, "How are you Jim?" a marching division will keep it up, with "How are you, Jim?" until the poor fellow swoons.

In the army we have some of the finest mimics in the world. Let one cackle like a hen, and the monotony of camp is broken by the encore of "S-h-o-o!" Then other cacklers take it up, until it sounds like a poultry yard stirred up over a mink or a weasel. Let one bray like an ass, others take it up until the whole regiment will personate the sound, seemingly like a fair ground of asses. As mimics they are perfect; as musicians, also. I met one once who said, "If you will give me a jigger, I'll give you some chin music." He put his hands to his chin, and with his teeth made a sound like rattling bones, keeping time to his pat and song. Some of the finest singers I ever heard were soldiers and some of the best acting I ever saw was done by them. In camp it is so delightful to hear the brass band dispensing music in the sweetest strains. Near Atlanta, a Dutch battery entertained us every fifteen minutes, and whilst we kept our eyes open to the music of the shells from far away would beat upon our ears the music of the enemy's brass bands; our bands would tune up and make us oblivious to the roar of that old battery. I tried once in the progress of the battle to assimilate it to music. The sound of the minnie ball—Zip! Zip!—I dubbed the soprano; the roar of the musketry, the alto; the lingering sound of battle, the tenor; the artillery, the basso. Now, intersperse it with the interlude of an old Rebel yell, and you've got it.

As to wit and sarcasm you hear in camp, I'd defy the world to beat it. Anyone attempting to be consequential, or unnatural, is the character to work on, and the gravest of the Chaplains cannot look upon their ridicule without smiling. A psalm-singing soldier one day gave out a distich for song, to sing to the long meter hymn of St. Thomas. Some blasphemous fellow changed it to

C. Parsons

Gun and Mortar Boats on the Mississippi

Confederate Sharpshooters Attacking Mortar Boats

"The possum am a cunning fowl,
  He climbs upon a tree."

The regiment broke out with the chorus.

"Rye-straw! Rye-straw! Rye-straw!"
"And when he wraps his tail 'round a limb,
  He turn and looks at me."
"Rye-straw! Rye-straw! Rye-straw! Rye-straw!"

This is shocking to us now, but when you reflect upon the idea that in their daily walk the soldiers had no way of entertainment, it was excusable to find some means of pastime and of keeping cheerful, if sacrilege is pardonable.

Some of the parodies on our Southern songs should be remembered. I copy a verse to the tune of "My Maryland." (If you know the tune, sing it.)

Old Stonewall Jackson's in the field,
Here's your mule, Oh, here's your mule!
And he has the boys that will not yield,
Here's your mule, Oh, here's your mule!
And when you hear the old man pray,
You may be sure that on next day,
The very Devil will be to pay—
Here's your mule, Oh, here's your mule!

And now since my native place is Old Jefferson, Tennessee, within a stone's throw of the battlefield of Murfreesboro (Stone's river), I think of the devastation and desolation created there by war. I will give a verse of my parody that I used to sing, as I rode along in Ward's regiment, Morgan's cavalry.

Also to enjoy it sing it as you read.

The Yankee's heel is on the street,
  Jefferson, Old Jefferson!
I hear the tramp of the vandal's feet,
  Jefferson, Old Jefferson!
Hark! I hear a rooster squall,
  The vandal takes them hen and all,
And makes the men and women bawl,
  Jefferson, Old Jefferson!

One more on the Happy Land of Canaan, and I am done. (If you know the tune sing it.)

I will sing you a song, as the ladies pass along,
All about the times we are gaining; aha!
I will sing it in rhymes, and suit it to the times,
And we'll call it the "Happy Land of Canaan."—CHORUS.

Oh me! Oh my! The pride of our Southern boys am coming; aha!
So it's never mind the weather, but get over double trouble,
For I'm bound for the Happy Land of Canaan.

In the Harper's Ferry section, there was an insurrection,
Old John Brown thought the niggers would sustain him, aha!
But old Governor Wise put his specks upon his eyes,
And sent him to the Happy Land of Canaan.—CHORUS.

Old John Brown is dead, and the last words he said,
"Don't keep me here a long time remaining;" aha!
So we led him up a slope, and hung him on a rope,
And sent him to the Happy Land of Canaan.—CHORUS.

—RIDLEY, *Battles and Sketches of the Army of Tennessee*

XIII

Incidents of Army Life : Western Front

FUNDAMENTALLY, *as we have already observed, the war in the East and in the West was pretty much the same. The same soldiers fought, the same officers commanded; the same weapons and techniques were used. Differences were imposed by considerations of geography rather than by social or psychological considerations. Thus warfare in the West was more mobile, more fluid. Armies fought over vast areas and army corps and divisions were shifted back and forth from Missouri to Mississippi to Tennessee. Occasionally—as with Rosecrans' army at Murfreesboro, between Stones River and the Tullahoma campaigns—the Western armies did stay put for some length of time, but normally they were on the move. The soldiers got a chance to see more varied types of society and economy than in the fighting in Virginia.*

There was another difference—in degree rather than in kind, to be sure. As has been mentioned, the fighting in the West was more nearly a civil war than was the fighting in the East. Family fought against family, brother against brother. The pillaging was about as bad in the East as in the West, but there was nothing in the East so savage as the guerrilla warfare in Missouri, nor was there anything like the bitterness in West Virginia that was found in eastern Tennessee.

Because of these circumstances of geography and history there is, about the fighting in the West, a more personal and perhaps a more casual character than is to be found elsewhere. Thus Mark Twain tells us how uncertain he and his friends were whether they were Confederates or Unionists. Thus there seemed to be—perhaps it is an illusion—a more personal quality about the cavalry fighting; Forrest and Morgan roamed pretty much where they would; Grierson seemed to be on his own; Wilson raised his cavalry his own way.

It is perhaps not too bold a generalization to say that the warfare in Virginia approached more nearly the traditional warfare of the Old World, while the warfare in the West kept a bit more its casual independence and almost its frontier character.

1. MARK TWAIN RECALLS A CAMPAIGN THAT FAILED

As a young man of twenty-two Mark Twain was apprenticed to a river pilot—the most glorious of all professions, he thought—and four years on the river gave him the material for Life on the Mississippi. *The Civil War closed*

*the river to ordinary steamboat traffic, and he returned to his boyhood town,
Hannibal, Missouri. There he joined a volunteer company of a dozen or so,
which, according to his own story, was ready to fight on either side. "Out
West," he wrote, "there was a good deal of confusion in men's minds during
the first months of the great trouble. . . . It was hard for us to get our bear-
ings." His campaign came to an inglorious end when he sprained an ankle
falling out of a barn hayloft. One of the "Marion Rangers," Absalom Grimes,
later became a famous Confederate scout. As Mark Twain himself says, this
is not an unfair picture of what went on in the border states during the early
months of the war.*

YOU have heard from a great many people who did something in the war;
is it not fair and right that you listen a little moment to one who started
out to do something in it, but didn't? Thousands entered the war, got just a
taste of it, and then stepped out again, permanently. These, by their very
numbers, are respectable, and are therefore entitled to a sort of voice,—not a
loud one, but a modest one; not a boastful one, but an apologetic one. They
ought not to be allowed much space among better people—people who did
something—I grant that; but they ought at least to be allowed to state why
they didn't do anything, and also to explain the process by which they
didn't do anything. Surely this kind of light must have a sort of value.

Out West there was a good deal of confusion in men's minds during the
first months of the great trouble—a good deal of unsettledness, of leaning first
this way, then that, then the other way. It was hard for us to get our bear-
ings. I call to mind an instance of this. I was piloting on the Mississippi when
the news came that South Carolina had gone out of the Union on the 20th
of December, 1860. My pilot-mate was a New Yorker. He was strong for
the Union; so was I. But he would not listen to me with any patience; my
loyalty was smirched, to his eye, because my father had owned slaves. I said,
in palliation of this dark fact, that I had heard my father say, some years
before he died, that slavery was a great wrong, and that he would free the
solitary Negro he then owned if he could think it right to give away the
property of the family when he was so straitened in means. My mate re-
torted that a mere impulse was nothing—anybody could pretend to a good
impulse; and went on decrying my Unionism and libeling my ancestry. A
month later the secession atmosphere had considerably thickened on the
Lower Mississippi, and I became a rebel; so did he. We were together in
New Orleans, the 26th of January, when Louisiana went out of the Union.
He did his full share of the rebel shouting, but was bitterly opposed to
letting me do mine. He said that I came of bad stock—of a father who had
been willing to set slaves free. In the following summer he was piloting a
Federal gun-boat and shouting for the Union again, and I was in the Confederate army. I held his note for some borrowed money. He was one of
the most upright men I ever knew; but he repudiated that note without
hesitation, because I was a rebel, and the son of a man who owned slaves.

In that summer—of 1861—the first wash of the wave of war broke upon the shores of Missouri. Our State was invaded by the Union forces. They took possession of St. Louis, Jefferson Barracks, and some other points. The Governor, Claib Jackson, issued his proclamation calling out fifty thousand militia to repel the invader.

I was visiting in the small town where my boyhood had been spent—Hannibal, Marion County. Several of us got together in a secret place by night and formed ourselves into a military company. One Tom Lyman, a young fellow of a good deal of spirit but of no military experience, was made captain; I was made second lieutenant. We had no first lieutenant; I do not know why; it was long ago. There were fifteen of us. By the advice of an innocent connected with the organization, we called ourselves the Marion Rangers. I do not remember that any one found fault with the name. I did not; I thought it sounded quite well. The young fellow who proposed this title was perhaps a fair sample of the kind of stuff we were made of. He was young, ignorant, good-natured, well-meaning, trivial, full of romance, and given to reading chivalric novels and singing forlorn love-ditties. He had some pathetic little nickel-plated aristocratic instincts, and detested his name, which was Dunlap; detested it, partly because it was nearly as common in that region as Smith, but mainly because it had a plebeian sound to his ear. So he tried to ennoble it by writing it in this way: *d'Unlap.* That contented his eye, but left his ear unsatisfied, for people gave the new name the same old pronunciation—emphasis on the front end of it. He then did the bravest thing that can be imagined,—a thing to make one shiver when one remembers how the world is given to resenting shams and affectations; he began to write his name so: *d'Un Lap.* And he waited patiently through the long storm of mud that was flung at this work of art, and he had his reward at last; for he lived to see that name accepted, and the emphasis put where he wanted it, by people who had known him all his life, and to whom the tribe of Dunlaps had been as familiar as the rain and the sunshine for forty years. . . .

That is one sample of us. Another was Ed Stevens, son of the town jeweler,—trim-built, handsome, graceful, neat as a cat; bright, educated, but given over entirely to fun. There was nothing serious in life to him. As far as he was concerned, this military expedition of ours was simply a holiday. I should say that about half of us looked upon it in the same way; not consciously, perhaps, but unconsciously. We did not think; we were not capable of it. As for myself, I was full of unreasoning joy to be done with turning out of bed at midnight and four in the morning, for a while; grateful to have a change, new scenes, new occupations, a new interest. In my thoughts that was as far as I went; I did not go into the details; as a rule one doesn't at twenty-four. . . .

These samples will answer—and they are quite fair ones. Well, this herd of cattle started for the war. What could you expect of them? They did as well as they knew how, but really what was justly to be expected of them? Nothing, I should say. That is what they did.

We waited for a dark night, for caution and secrecy were necessary; then, toward midnight, we stole in couples and from various directions to the Griffith place, beyond the town; from that point we set out together on foot. Hannibal lies at the extreme south-eastern corner of Marion County, on the Mississippi River; our objective point was the hamlet of New London, ten miles away, in Ralls County.

The first hour was all fun, all idle nonsense and laughter. But that could not be kept up. The steady trudging came to be like work; the play had somehow oozed out of it; the stillness of the woods and the somberness of the night began to throw a depressing influence over the spirits of the boys, and presently the talking died out and each person shut himself up in his own thoughts. During the last half of the second hour nobody said a word.

Now we approached a log farm-house where, according to report, there was a guard of five Union soldiers. Lyman called a halt; and there, in the deep gloom of the overhanging branches, he began to whisper a plan of assault upon that house, which made the gloom more depressing than it was before. It was a crucial moment; we realized, with a cold suddenness, that here was no jest—we were standing face to face with actual war. We were equal to the occasion. In our response there was no hesitation, no indecision: we said that if Lyman wanted to meddle with those soldiers, he could go ahead and do it; but if he waited for us to follow him, he would wait a long time.

Lyman urged, pleaded, tried to shame us, but it had no effect. Our course was plain, our minds were made up: we would flank the farm-house—go out around. And that is what we did.

We struck into the woods and entered upon a rough time, stumbling over roots, getting tangled in vines, and torn by briers. At last we reached an open place in a safe region, and sat down, blown and hot, to cool off and nurse our scratches and bruises. Lyman was annoyed, but the rest of us were cheerful; we had flanked the farm-house, we had made our first military movement, and it was a success; we had nothing to fret about, we were feeling just the other way. Horse-play and laughing began again; the expedition was become a holiday frolic once more.

Then we had two more hours of dull trudging and ultimate silence and depression; then, about dawn, we straggled into New London, soiled, heel-blistered, fagged with our little march, and all of us except Stevens in a sour and raspy humor and privately down on the war. We stacked our shabby old shot-guns in Colonel Ralls's barn, and then went in a body and breakfasted with that veteran of the Mexican war. Afterwards he took us to a distant meadow, and there in the shade of a tree we listened to an old-fashioned speech from him, full of gunpowder and glory, full of that adjective-piling, mixed metaphor, and windy declamation which was regarded as eloquence in that ancient time and that remote region; and then he swore us on the Bible to be faithful to the State of Missouri and drive all invaders from her soil, no matter whence they might come or under what flag they might march. This mixed us considerably, and we could not make out just what service we were embarked in; but Colonel Ralls, the practiced politician and phrase-juggler, was not similarly in doubt; he knew quite clearly that he had invested us in the cause of the Southern Confederacy. He closed the solemnities by belting around me the sword which his neighbor, Colonel Brown, had worn at Buena Vista and Molino del Rey; and he accompanied this act with another impressive blast.

Then we formed in line of battle and marched four miles to a shady and pleasant piece of woods on the border of the far-reaching expanses of a flowery prairie. It was an enchanting region for war—our kind of war.

We pierced the forest about half a mile, and took up a strong position, with some low, rocky, and wooded hills behind us, and a purling, limpid creek in front. Straightway half the command were in swimming, and the other half fishing. The ass with the French name gave this position a romantic title, but it was too long, so the boys shortened and simplified it to Camp Ralls.

We occupied an old maple-sugar camp, whose half-rotted troughs were still propped against the trees. A long corn-crib served for sleeping quarters for the battalion. On our left, half a mile away, was Mason's farm and house; and he was a friend to the cause. Shortly after noon the farmers began to arrive from several directions, with mules and horses for our use, and these they lent us for as long as the war might last, which they judged would be about three months. The animals were of all sizes, all colors, and all breeds. They were mainly young and frisky, and nobody in the command could stay on them long at a time; for we were town boys, and ignorant of horsemanship. The creature that fell to my share was a very small mule, and yet so quick and active that it could throw me without difficulty; and it did this whenever I got on it. Then it would bray—stretching its neck out, laying its ears back, and spreading its jaws till you could see down to its works. It was a disagreeable animal, in every way. If I took it by the bridle and tried to lead it off the grounds, it would sit down and brace back, and no one could budge it. However, I was not entirely destitute of military resources, and I did presently manage to spoil this game; for I had seen many a steamboat aground in my time, and knew a trick or two which even a grounded mule would be obliged to respect. There was a well by the corn-crib; so I substituted thirty fathom of rope for the bridle, and fetched him home with the windlass.

I will anticipate here sufficiently to say that we did learn to ride, after some days' practice, but never well. We could not learn to like our animals; they were not choice ones, and most of them had annoying peculiarities of one kind or another. Stevens's horse would carry him, when he was not noticing, under the huge excrescences which form on the trunks of oak-trees, and wipe him out of the saddle; in this way Stevens got several bad hurts. Sergeant Bowers's horse was very large and tall, with slim, long legs, and looked like a railroad bridge. His size enabled him to reach all about, and as far as he wanted to, with his head; so he was always biting Bowers's legs. On the march, in the sun, Bowers slept a good deal; and as soon as the horse recognized that he was asleep he would reach around and bite him on the leg.

His legs were black and blue with bites. This was the only thing that could ever make him swear, but this always did; whenever the horse bit him he always swore, and of course Stevens, who laughed at everything, laughed at this, and would even get into such convulsions over it as to lose his balance and fall off his horse; and then Bowers, already irritated by the pain of the horse-bite, would resent the laughter with hard language, and there would be a quarrel; so that horse made no end of trouble and bad blood in the command.

However, I will get back to where I was—our first afternoon in the sugar-camp. The sugar-troughs came very handy as horse-troughs, and we had plenty of corn to fill them with. I ordered Sergeant Bowers to feed my mule; but he said that if I reckoned he went to war to be dry-nurse to a mule, it wouldn't take me very long to find out my mistake. I believed that this was insubordination, but I was full of uncertainties about everything military, and so I let the thing pass, and went and ordered Smith, the blacksmith's apprentice, to feed the mule; but he merely gave me a large, cold, sarcastic grin, such as an ostensibly seven-year-old horse gives you when you lift his lip and find he is fourteen, and turned his back on me. I then went to the captain, and asked if it was not right and proper and military for me to have an orderly. He said it was, but as there was only one orderly in the corps, it was but right that he himself should have Bowers on his staff. Bowers said he wouldn't serve on anybody's staff; and if anybody thought he could make him, let him try it. So, of course, the thing had to be dropped; there was no other way.

Next, nobody would cook; it was considered a degradation; so we had no dinner. We lazied the rest of the pleasant afternoon away, some dozing under the trees, some smoking cob-pipes and talking sweethearts and war, some playing games. By late suppertime all hands were famished; and to meet the difficulty all hands turned to, on an equal footing, and gathered wood, built fires, and cooked the meal. Afterward everything was smooth for a while; then trouble broke out between the corporal and the sergeant, each claiming to rank the other. Nobody knew which was the higher office; so Lyman had to settle the matter by making the rank of both officers equal. The commander of an ignorant crew like that has many troubles and vexations which probably do not occur in the regular army at all. However, with the song-singing and yarn-spinning around the camp-fire, everything presently became serene again; and by and by we raked the corn down level in one end of the crib, and all went to bed on it, tying a horse to the door, so that he would neigh if any one tried to get in.

We had some horsemanship drill every forenoon; then, afternoons, we rode off here and there in squads a few miles, and visited the farmers' girls, and had a youthful good time, and got an honest good dinner or supper, and then home again to camp, happy and content.

For a time, life was idly delicious, it was perfect; there was nothing to mar it. Then came some farmers with an alarm one day. They said it was rumored that the enemy were advancing in our direction, from over Hyde's prairie. The result was a sharp stir among us, and general consternation. It was a rude awakening from our pleasant trance. The rumor was but a rumor—nothing definite about it; so, in the confusion, we did not know which way to retreat. Lyman was for not retreating at all, in these uncertain circumstances; but he found that if he tried to maintain that attitude he would fare badly, for the command were in no humor to put up with insubordination. So he yielded the point and called a council of war—to consist of himself and the three other officers; but the privates made such a fuss about being left out, that we had to allow them to be present. I mean we had to allow them to remain, for they were already present, and doing the most of the talking too. The question was, which way to retreat; but all were so flurried that nobody seemed to have even a guess to offer. Except Lyman. He explained in a few calm words, that inasmuch as the enemy were approaching from over Hyde's prairie, our course was simple: all we had to do was not to retreat *toward* him; any other direction would answer our needs perfectly. Everybody saw in a moment how true this was, and how wise; so Lyman got a great many compliments. It was now decided that we should fall back on Mason's farm.

It was after dark by this time, and as we could not know how soon the enemy might arrive, it did not seem best to try to take the horses and things with us; so we only took the guns and ammunition, and started at once. The route was very rough and hilly and rocky, and presently the night grew very black and rain began to fall; so we had a troublesome time of it, struggling and stumbling along in the dark; and soon some person slipped and fell, and then the next person behind stumbled over him and fell, and so did the rest, one after the other; and then Bowers came with the keg of powder in his arms, whilst the command were all mixed together, arms and legs, on the muddy slope; and so he fell, of course, with the keg, and this started the whole detachment down the hill in a body, and they landed in the brook at the bottom in a pile, and each that was undermost pulling the hair and scratching and biting those that were on top of him; and those that were being scratched and bitten scratching and biting the rest in their turn, and all saying they would die before they would ever go to war again if they ever got out of this brook this time, and the invader might rot for all they cared, and the country along with him—and all such talk as that, which was dismal to hear and take part in, in such smothered, low voices, and such a grisly dark place and so wet, and the enemy may be coming any moment.

The keg of powder was lost, and the guns too; so the growling and complaining continued straight along whilst the brigade pawed around the pasty hillside and slopped around in the brook hunting for these things; consequently we lost considerable time at this; and then we heard a sound, and held our breath and listened, and it seemed to be the enemy coming, though it could have been a cow, for it had a cough like a cow; but we did not wait, but left a couple of guns behind and struck out for Mason's again as briskly as we could scramble along in the dark. But we got lost presently among the rugged little ravines, and wasted a deal of time finding the way again, so it was after nine when we reached Mason's stile at last; and then before we could open our mouths to give the countersign, several dogs came bounding over the fence, with great riot and noise, and each of them took a soldier by the slack of his trousers and began to back away with him. We could not shoot the dogs without endangering the persons they were attached to; so we had to look on, helpless, at what was perhaps the most mortifying spectacle of the civil war. There was light enough, and to spare, for the Masons had now run out on the porch with candles in their hands. The old man and his son came and undid the dogs without difficulty, all but Bowers's; but they couldn't undo his dog, they didn't know his combination; he was of the bull kind, and seemed to be set with a Yale time-lock; but they got him loose at last with some scalding water, of which Bowers got his share and returned thanks. Peterson Dunlap afterwards made up a fine name for this engagement, and also for the night march which preceded it, but both have long ago faded out of my memory.

We now went into the house, and they began to ask us a world of questions, whereby it presently came out that we did not know anything concerning who or what we were running from; so the old gentleman made himself very frank, and said we were a curious breed of soldiers, and guessed we could be depended on to end up the war in time, because no government could stand the expense of the shoe-leather we should cost it trying to follow us around. "Marion *Rangers!* good name, b'gosh!" said he. And wanted to know why we hadn't had a picket-guard at the place where the road entered the prairie, and why we hadn't sent out a scouting party to spy out the enemy and bring us an account of his strength, and so on, before jumping up and stampeding out of a strong position upon a mere vague rumor—and so on and so forth, till he made us all feel shabbier than the dogs had done, not half so enthusiastically welcome. So we went to bed shamed and low-spirited; except Stevens. Soon Stevens began to devise a garment for Bowers which could be made to automatically display his battle-scars to the grateful, or conceal them from the envious, according to his occasions; but Bowers was in no humor for this, so there was a fight, and when it was over Stevens had some battle-scars of hs own to think about.

Then we got a little sleep. But after all we had gone through, our activities were not over for the night; for about two o'clock in the morning we heard a shout of warning from down the lane, accompanied by a chorus from all the dogs, and in a moment everybody was up and flying around to find out what the alarm was about. The alarmist was a horseman who gave notice that a detachment of Union soldiers was on its way from Hannibal with orders to capture and hang any bands like ours which it could find, and said we had no time to lose. Farmer Mason was in a flurry this time, himself. He hurried us out of the house with all haste, and sent one of his Negroes with us to show us where to hide ourselves and our tell-tale guns among the ravines half a mile away. It was raining heavily.

We struck down the lane, then across some rocky pasture-land which offered good advantages for stumbling; consequently we were down in the mud most of the time, and every time a man went down he blackguarded the war, and the people that started it, and everybody connected with it, and gave himself the master dose of all for being so foolish as to go into it. At last we reached the wooded mouth of a ravine, and there we huddled ourselves under the streaming trees, and sent the Negro back home. It was a dismal and heart-breaking time. We were like to be drowned with the rain, deafened with the howling wind and the booming thunder, and blinded by the lightning. It was indeed a wild night. The drenching we were getting was misery enough, but a deeper misery still was the reflection that the halter might end us before we were a day older. A death of this shameful sort had not occurred to us as being among the possibilities of war. It took the romance all out of the campaign, and turned our dreams of glory into a repulsive nightmare. As for doubting that so barbarous an order had been given, not one of us did that.

The long night wore itself out at last, and then the Negro came to us with the news that the alarm had manifestly been a false one, and that breakfast would soon be ready. Straightway we were lighted-hearted again, and the world was bright, and life as full of hope and promise as ever—for we were young then. . . .

The mongrel child of philology named the night's refuge Camp Devastation, and no soul objected. The Masons gave us a Missouri country breakfast, in Missourian abundance, and we needed it: hot biscuits; hot "wheat bread" prettily criss-crossed in a lattice pattern on top; hot corn pone; fried chicken; bacon, coffee, eggs, milk, buttermilk, etc.;—and the world may be confidently challenged to furnish the equal to such a breakfast, as it is cooked in the South.

We staid several days at Mason's. . . . At last it was with something very like joy that we received news that the enemy were on our track again. With a new birth of the old warrior spirit, we sprang to our places in line of battle and fell back on Camp Ralls.

Captain Lyman had taken a hint from Mason's talk, and he now gave orders that our camp should be guarded against surprise by the posting of pickets. I was ordered to place a picket at the forks of the road in Hyde's prairie. Night shut down black and threatening. I told Sergeant Bowers to go out to that place and stay till midnight; and, just as I was expecting, he said he wouldn't do it. I tried to get others to go, but all refused. Some excused themselves on account of the weather; but the rest were frank enough to say they wouldn't go in any kind of weather. This kind of thing sounds odd now, and impossible, but there was no surprise in it at the time. On the contrary, it seemed a perfectly natural thing to do. There were scores of little camps scattered over Missouri where the same thing was happening. These camps were composed of young men who had been born and reared to a sturdy independence, and who did not know what it meant to be ordered around by Tom, Dick, and Harry, whom they had known familiarly all their lives, in the village or on the farm. It is quite within the probabilities that this same thing was happening all over the South. . . .

It was quite the natural thing. One might justly imagine that we were hopeless material for war. And so we seemed, in our ignorant state; but there were those among us who afterward learned the grim trade; learned to obey like machines; became valuable soldiers; fought all through the war, and came out at the end with excellent records. One of the very boys who refused to go out on picket duty that night, and called me an ass for thinking he would expose himself to danger in such a foolhardy way, had become distinguished for intrepidity before he was a year older.

I did secure my picket that night—not by authority, but by diplomacy. I got Bowers to go, by agreeing to exchange ranks with him for the time being, and go along and stand the watch with him as his subordinate. We staid out there a couple of dreary hours in the pitchy darkness and the rain, with nothing to modify the dreariness but Bowers's monotonous growlings at the war and the weather; then we began to nod, and presently found it next to impossible to stay in the saddle; so we gave up the tedious job, and went back to the camp without waiting for the relief guard. We rode into camp without interruption or objection from anybody, and the enemy could have done the same, for there were no sentries. Everybody was asleep; at midnight there was nobody to send out another picket, so none was sent. We never tried to establish a watch at night again, as far as I remember, but we generally kept a picket out in the daytime.

In that camp the whole command slept on the corn in the big corn-crib; and there was usually a general row before morning, for the place was full of rats, and they would scramble over the boys' bodies and faces, annoying and irritating everybody; and now and then they would bite some one's toe, and the person who owned the toe would start up and magnify his English and begin to throw corn in the dark. The ears were half as heavy as bricks, and when they struck they hurt. The persons struck would respond, and inside of five minutes every man would be locked in a death-grip with his neighbor. There was a grievous deal of blood shed in the corn-crib, but this was all that was spilt while I was in the war. . . .

The rest of my war experience was of a piece with what I have already told of it. We kept monotonously falling back upon one camp or another, and eating up the country. I marvel now at the patience of the farmers and their families. They ought to have shot us; on the contrary, they were as hospitably kind and courteous to us as if we had deserved it. In one of these camps we found Ab Grimes, an Upper Mississippi pilot, who afterwards became famous as a dare-devil rebel spy, whose career bristled with desperate adventures. The look and style of his comrades suggested that they had not come into the war to play, and their deeds made good the conjecture later. They were fine horsemen and good revolver-shots; but their favorite arm was the lasso. Each had one at his pommel, and could snatch a man out of the saddle with it every time, on a full gallop, at any reasonable distance.

In another camp the chief was a fierce and profane old blacksmith of sixty, and he had furnished his twenty recruits with gigantic home-made bowie-knives, to be swung with the two hands, like the *machetes* of the Isthmus. It was a grisly spectacle to see that earnest band practicing their murderous cuts and slashes under the eye of that remorseless old fanatic.

The last camp which we fell back upon was in a hollow near the village of Florida, where I was born—in Monroe County. Here we were warned, one day, that a Union colonel was sweeping down on us with a whole regiment at his heels. This looked decidedly serious. Our boys went apart and consulted; then we went back and told the other companies present that the war was a disappointment to us and we were going to disband. They were getting ready, themselves, to fall back on some place or other, and were only waiting for General Tom Harris, who was expected to arrive at any moment; so they tried to persuade us to wait a little while, but the majority of us said no, we were accustomed to falling back, and didn't need any of Tom Harris's help; we could get along perfectly well without him—and save time too. So about half of our fifteen, including myself, mounted and left on the instant; the others yielded to persuasion and staid—staid through the war.

An hour later we met General Harris on the road, with two or three people in his company—his staff, probably, but we could not tell; none of them were in uniform; uniforms had not come into vogue among us yet. Harris ordered us back; but we told him there was a Union colonel coming with a whole regiment in his wake, and it looked as if there was going to be a disturbance; so we had concluded to go home. He raged a little, but it was of no use; our minds were made up. We had done our share; had killed one man, exterminated one army, such as it was; let him go and kill the rest, and that would end the war. I did not see that brisk young general again until last year; then he was wearing white hair and whiskers.

In time I came to know that Union colonel whose coming frightened me out of the war and crippled the Southern cause to that extent—General Grant. I came within a few hours of seeing him when he was as unknown as I was myself; at a time when anybody could have said, "Grant?—Ulysses S. Grant? I do not remember hearing the name before." It seems difficult to realize that there was once a time when such a remark could be rationally made; but there *was*, and I was within a few miles of the place and the occasion too, though proceeding in the other direction.

The thoughtful will not throw this war-paper of mine lightly aside as being valueless. It has this value: it is a not unfair picture of what went on in many and many a militia camp in the first months of the rebellion, when the green recruits were without discipline, without the steadying and heartening influence of trained leaders; when all their circumstances were new and strange, and charged with exaggerated terrors, and before the invaluable experience of actual collision in the field had turned them from rabbits into soldiers. If this side of the picture of that early day has not before been put into history, then history has been to that degree incomplete, for it had and has its rightful place there. There was more Bull Run material scattered through the early camps of this country than exhibited itself at Bull Run. And yet it learned its trade presently, and helped to fight the great battles later. I could have become a soldier myself, if I had waited. I had got part of it learned; I knew more about retreating than the man that invented retreating.

—MARK TWAIN, "The Private History of a Campaign That Failed"

2. MAJOR CONNOLLY LOSES FAITH IN THE CHIVALRY OF THE SOUTH

One of the best of all Civil War commentators, Major James A. Connolly was an Illinois lawyer who in 1862 raised a company which promptly elected him captain. Later he was made major in the 123rd Illinois Infantry and at the end of the war had been promoted to lieutenant colonel. After Chickamauga he was assigned as division inspector in the XIV Army Corps, and went with Sherman to the sea and beyond. He wrote of his Civil War diary that "like an old army ambrotype it may not be a delight, but it is a true picture just as it was taken in the stirring days." We shall turn to him again for lively pictures of the battlefield. After the war Connolly was U. S. Attorney for the Southern District of Illinois and a member of Congress. He tells us here of a holiday trip from Cairo up the Ohio and the Cumberland to Fort Donelson shortly after its capture.

March 10th, '62

Dear ——:

The Cumberland was on a regular bender. We passed several small villages, completely inundated; some of the houses floating off and others stationary with nothing but the chimneys visible.

In the villages built higher up on the bluffs everything appeared like a Sunday; no smoke visible, except from an occasional chimney—no doors open—no signs of life—no citizens except occasionally a solitary butternut as the soldiers called them. Most of the farm houses along the river are built of logs in very primitive style, and nearly every one we saw was surrounded by water, so that their occupants had to go around the premises in rude canoes made of logs. It is probable that I am prejudiced, but I certainly thought I never saw such miserable looking creatures as inhabit the banks of the Cumberland, and their habitations looked more wretched than themselves. We frequently sailed so close to farm houses that we could easily hold conversation with the occupants, and wherever a man appeared the soldiers invariably made him swing his hat, the boys consoling themselves with the idea that the swinging of the hat was an evidence of respect for the Union and for "Yankee" soldiers. One instance I recollect, where we must have sailed through the door yard of a cabin (if cabins have such things in Dixie,) the inmates were assembled on the rude porch, five dirty children, three dirty, tangle haired, parchment faced women, sans crinoline, sans shoes, sans stockings,—half a dozen dogs of low degree, and one middle-aged, lantern jawed, long haired butternut clad concern such as they called a man in Dixie.

As we neared the cabin the soldier boys called out "swing your hat and hurrah for the Union, old butternut;" no response from butternut who leans lazily against his porch, and throws a sullen, defiant look toward the passing steamer; that don't suit the boys; they never pass a native without making him do some reverence toward the Union, so they hail him again, still he is silent; then the boys clamor to have the boat stopped; they want to "clean him out," "set his cabin adrift," "take him in out of the wet," and all such expressions are heard amongst the soldiers, but one cool fellow picks up his musket as the boat is just opposite the cabin, and pointing it at the butternut, takes aim at him; butternut darts within the cabin door amid the shouts of the soldiers, and the women follow him; in an instant out comes a woman with a dirty white rag which she swings lustily, and after a swing or two of the rag out comes the man again, and swinging his slouch hat vigorously, gives three rousing yells; the boys conclude they have converted him—made a Union man of him, so they gave him three such cheers as a regiment of Western boys can give when they are in good humor, and they sail on satisfied, to produce similar conversions on all refractory butternuts they meet. The last I saw of the cabin, as we turned a bend in the river, the man was swinging his hat and the women white rags at a steamer loaded with soldiers just behind us.

We passed several double log houses that were probably the residences of well to do farmers, judging alone from the number of "niggers" around. In every instance the blacks would manifest the most extravagant delight; jumping up and down, clapping their hands, the little nigs rolling and tumbling on the ground, performing as many antics as so many monkeys. We passed several large iron works surrounded by the little cabins of the operatives, and generally one large fine brick mansion—the residence, probably of the manager. But all was silent—no smoke curling from the chimneys—sounds of machinery hushed—the operatives scattered on battle fields, within prison walls, and in rude graves, the children of these iron villages orphaned and with the taint of treason on their lives—the mothers widowed and the proprietors ruined. The banks of the Cumberland are desolated, not by "Yankee invaders" but by the mad folly of the inhabitants; they had been traitors all the way up the river, and their new born respect for the Union was only begotten by the thunder of Grant's guns at Fort Donelson. My faith in the superior chivalry of the South is gone. It is mere gasconade. They boast of their chivalry and courage, but so did Don Quixote and the renowned Jack Falstaff. Their boasted chivalry will in the end avail no more than the chivalry of Lilliput in the grasp of Gulliver. Many of them no doubt had been Union men at the commencement of the struggle, but the slow progress of the Union army led them to believe rebellion would triumph and so their want of faith in the old Union led them to embrace the rebel cause.

They thought they won the race at "Bull Run," but that proved only to be "false start." We steamed on up the river, the same appearance of desolation on every hand, the same sport with the soldiers and "butternuts" on the banks, the same deserted villages and jubilant darkies, until the word passed around, "Three miles to Fort Donelson." Then came a scene of excitement, all crowding to the bow of the boat, every eye strained to catch the first glimpse of the rebel stronghold. We turn a bend in the river and the fort is in view, the stars and stripes floating over it. A cheer bursts from the soldiers on board, the band strikes up the "Star Spangled Banner" and we sail gaily over the same waters that our gunboats breasted a few days before in a murderous hail of rebel shot and shell. We passed the batteries and went up the river about half a mile to the landing at the village of Dover. I was soon ashore and wandering through the city of tents, in search of my home company. I found it in about an hour, and was soon surrounded by the company answering inquiries about home, the wounded, etc. They had supper before I found them, but a fire was soon lighted, some coffee made, some fat pork fried, and with the ground for my table and seat, a tin pan full of fried pork, a tin cup full of coffee and plenty of "hard tack," I ate a hearty supper. . . .

The battle was fought in dense timber, on very high hills and deep ravines, and nearly the whole of the fighting was done by the enemy outside of their entrenchments. The lines of the battle extended over a space of three or four miles, and the whole distance is thickly strewn with the pits of the dead. . . .

I saw a great many taken up. I saw one pit containing five opened and the dead taken out to be sent home. They lay there side by side, with uniform and cartridge box on, just as they fell, covered over with blankets and the dirt thrown in on them. From the best estimate I could make I should say there were 500 of our men buried on the field and at least an equal number of rebels; and I should think there were 1,500 of our men wounded so as to be obliged to go into hospital, and probably 500 more who were wounded, but not seriously enough to go into hospital. A very small proportion of our wounded, however, will, for most of their wounds are from buckshot and are not very serious. . . . A great many horses were lying on the field, just where they fell, scattered all over the field, singly, by twos, threes and fours. Frozen pools of blood were visible on every hand, and I picked up over twenty hats with bullet holes in them and pieces of skull, hair and blood sticking to them inside.

The ground was strewn with hats, caps, coats, pants, canteens, cartridge boxes, bayonet scabbards, knapsacks, rebel haversacks filled with biscuits of their own making, raw pork, broken guns, broken bayonets, dismounted cannon, pieces of exploded shells, six and twelve-pound balls, and indeed all sorts of things that are found in an army. There was such a profusion of everything that I scarcely could determine what to take as a memento of that terrible field, which is probably the only one I shall ever have a chance to see. You can form no conception of what a battlefield looks like. No pen and ink description can give you anything like a true idea of it. The dead were buried from two to two and a half feet deep; the rebels didn't bury that deep and some had their feet protruding from the graves. . . .

The ignorance of many of the rebels surprised me and I should not have believed it had I not talked with them myself. Some of them told me, and they seemed to be honest in it, that they thought they had been fighting for the Union; others told me they thought our army was coming down there to carry off all the "niggers;" they told me they thought none but abolitionists were in our army, and that they were surprised when they found there were more Democrats than abolitionists in it. An amusing incident occurred at the Fort in a conversation between an Illinoisan and a Mississippi captain. The Mississippian remarked that they could whip the New England Yankees every time, and went on to speak of the New England Yankee as a dried up, bloodless specimen of humanity, without courage or physical power, and without a single idea higher than money. The Illinoisan heard him through and then pointing to a Federal captain standing in sight, about 6 feet 3 in height and weighing at least two hundred pounds, remarked: "There is a New England Yankee, born and raised in the state of Maine, and he was among the first men who climbed over your breastworks and ran over your guns." The Mississippian changed the topic of conversation speedily.

—"Major Connolly's Letters to His Wife"

3. THE GREAT LOCOMOTIVE CHASE IN GEORGIA

General Ormsby McK. Mitchel, who organized this locomotive raid, was one of the most remarkable minor figures of the war. Born in Kentucky and a graduate of West Point, Mitchel was a combination engineer, philosopher, and astronomer—chief engineer for the Little Miami Railroad, professor of philosophy and astronomy at Cincinnati College with the largest telescope on the continent. Appointed brigadier at the outbreak of the war he served in the Department of Ohio and later under Buell in Tennessee and Alabama. Quarreling with Buell he resigned late in 1862 but was transferred, instead, to Hilton Head, South Carolina, where he contracted yellow fever and died.

The locomotive raid was designed to disrupt Confederate communications far behind the lines. William Pittenger of the 2nd Ohio Volunteers was a member of the "Andrews Raiders" who carried out this assignment. Twenty-two of the raiders were captured and of these eight were hanged and eight escaped. Pittenger later became a Methodist minister.

THE railroad raid to Georgia, in the spring of 1862, has always been considered to rank high among the striking and novel incidents of the civil war. At that time General O. M. Mitchel, under whose authority it was organized, commanded Union forces in middle Tennessee, consisting of a division of Buell's army. The Confederates were concentrating at Corinth, Mississippi, and Grant and Buell were advancing by different routes toward that point. Mitchel's orders required him to protect Nashville and the country around, but allowed him great latitude in the disposition of his division, which, with detachments and garrisons, numbered nearly seventeen thousand men. His attention had long been strongly turned toward the liberation of east Tennessee, which he knew that President Lincoln also earnestly desired, and which would, if achieved, strike a most damaging blow at the resources of the rebellion. . . . He determined, therefore, to press into the heart of the enemy's country as far as possible, occupying strategical points before they were adequately defended and assured of speedy and powerful reinforcement. To this end his measures were vigorous and well chosen.

On the 8th of April, 1862, ... he marched swiftly southward from Shelbyville, and seized Huntsville in Alabama on the 11th of April, and then sent a detachment westward over the Memphis and Charleston Railroad to open railway communication with the Union army at Pittsburg Landing. Another detachment, commanded by Mitchel in person, advanced on the same day seventy miles by rail directly into the enemy's territory, arriving unchecked with two thousand men within thirty miles of Chattanooga,—in two hours' time he could now reach that point,—the most important position in the West. Why did he not go on? The story of the railroad raid is the answer. The night before breaking camp at Shelbyville, Mitchel sent an expedition secretly into the heart of Georgia to cut the railroad communications of Chattanooga to the south and east. The fortune of this attempt had a most important bearing upon his movements, and will now be narrated.

In the employ of General Buell was a spy named James J. Andrews, who had rendered valuable services in the first year of the war, and had secured the full confidence of the Union commanders. In March, 1862, Buell had sent him secretly with eight men to burn the bridges west of Chattanooga; but the failure of expected coöperation defeated the plan, and Andrews, after visiting Atlanta, and inspecting the whole of the enemy's lines in that vicinity and northward, had returned, ambitious to make another attempt. His plans for the second raid were submitted to Mitchel, and on the eve of the movement from Shelbyville to Huntsville Mitchel authorized him to take twenty-four men, secretly enter the enemy's territory, and, by means of capturing a train, burn the bridges on the northern part of the Georgia State Railroad, and also one on the East Tennessee Railroad where it approaches the Georgia State line, thus completely isolating Chattanooga, which was virtually ungarrisoned.

The soldiers for this expedition, of whom the writer was one, were selected from the three Ohio regiments belonging to General J. W. Sill's brigade, being simply told that they were wanted for secret and very dangerous service. So far as known, not a man chosen declined the perilous honor. Our uniforms were exchanged for ordinary Southern dress, and all arms except revolvers were left in camp. On the 7th of April, by the roadside about a mile east of Shelbyville, in the late evening twilight, we met our leader. Taking us a little way from the road, he quietly placed before us the outlines of the romantic and adventurous plan, which was: to break into small detachments of three or four, journey eastward into the Cumberland Mountains, then work southward, traveling by rail after we were well within the Confederate lines, and finally, the evening of the third day after the start, meet Andrews at Marietta, Georgia, more than two hundred miles away. When questioned, we were to profess ourselves Kentuckians going to join the Southern army.

On the journey we were a good deal annoyed by the swollen streams and the muddy roads consequent on three days of almost ceaseless rain. Andrews was led to believe that Mitchel's column would be inevitably delayed; and as we were expected to destroy the bridges the very day that Huntsville was entered, he took the responsibility of sending word to our different groups that our attempt would be postponed one day—from Friday to Saturday, April 12. This was a natural but a most lamentable error of judgment.

One of the men detailed was belated, and did not join us at all. Two others were very soon captured by the enemy; and though their true character was not detected, they were forced into the Southern army, and two reached Marietta, but failed to report at the rendezvous. Thus, when we assembled very early in the morning in Andrews's room at the Marietta Hotel for final consultation before the blow was struck we were but twenty, including our leader. All preliminary difficulties had been easily overcome, and we were in good spirits. But some serious obstacles had been revealed on our ride from Chattanooga to Marietta the previous evening. The railroad was found to be crowded with trains, and many soldiers were among the passengers. Then the station—Big Shanty—at which the capture was to be effected had recently been made a Confederate camp.

To succeed in our enterprise it would be necessary first to capture the engine in a guarded camp with soldiers standing around as spectators, and then to run it from one to two hundred miles through the enemy's country, and to deceive or overpower all trains that should be met—a large contract for twenty men. Some of our party thought the chances of success so slight, under existing circumstances, that they urged the abandonment of the whole enterprise. But Andrews declared his purpose to succeed or die, offering to each man, however, the privilege of withdrawing from the attempt—an offer no one was in the least disposed to accept. Final instructions were then given, and we hurried to the ticket-office in time for the northward-bound mail-train, and purchased tickets for different stations along the line in the direction of Chattanooga.

Our ride, as passengers, was but eight miles. We swept swiftly around the base of Kenesaw Mountain, and soon saw the tents of the Confederate forces camped at Big Shanty gleam white in the morning mist. Here we were to stop for breakfast, and attempt the seizure of the train. The morning was raw and gloomy, and a rain, which fell all day, had already begun. It was a painfully thrilling moment. We were but twenty, with an army about us, and a long and difficult road before us, crowded with enemies. In an instant we were to throw off the disguise which had been our only protection, and trust to our leader's genius and our own efforts for safety and success. Fortunately we had no time for giving way to reflections and conjectures which could only unfit us for the stern task ahead.

When we stopped, the conductor, the engineer, and many of the passengers hurried to breakfast, leaving the train unguarded. Now was the moment of action. Ascertaining that there was nothing to prevent a rapid start, Andrews, our two engineers, Brown and Knight, and the firemen hurried forward, uncoupling a section of the train consisting of three empty baggage or box-cars, the locomotive, and the tender. The engineers and the firemen sprang into the cab of the engine, while Andrews, with hand on the rail and foot on the step, waited to see that the remainder of the party had gained entrance into the rear box-car. This seemed difficult and slow, though it really consumed but a few seconds, for the car stood on a considerable bank, and the first who came were pitched in by their comrades, while these in turn dragged in the others, and the door was instantly closed. A sentinel, with musket in hand, stood not a dozen feet from the engine, watching the whole proceeding; but before he or any of the soldiers or guards around could make up their minds to interfere all was done, and Andrews, with a nod to his engineer, stepped on board. The valve was pulled wide open, and for a moment the wheels slipped round in rapid, ineffective revolutions; then, with a bound that jerked the soldiers in the box-car from their feet, the little train darted away, leaving the camp and the station in the wildest uproar and confusion. The first step of the enterprise was triumphantly accomplished.

According to the time-table, of which Andrews had secured a copy, there were two trains to be met. These presented no serious hindrance to our attaining high speed, for we could tell just where to expect them. There was also a local freight not down on the time-table, but which could not be far distant. Any danger of collision with it could be avoided by running according to the schedule of the captured train until it was passed; then at the highest possible speed we could run to the Oostenaula and Chickamauga bridges, lay them in ashes, and pass on through Chattanooga to Mitchel at Huntsville, or wherever eastward of that point he might be found, arriving long before the close of the day. It was a brilliant prospect, and so far as human estimates can determine it would have been realized had the day been Friday instead of Saturday. On Friday every train had been on time, the day dry, and the road in perfect order. Now the road was in disorder, every train far behind time, and two "extras" were approaching us. But of these unfavorable conditions we knew nothing, and pressed confidently forward.

We stopped frequently, and at one point tore up the track, cut telegraph wires, and loaded on cross-ties to be used in bridge-burning. Wood and water were taken without difficulty, Andrews very coolly telling the story to which he adhered throughout the run—namely, that he was one of General Beauregard's officers, running an impressed powder-train through to that commander at Corinth. We had no good instruments for track-raising, as we had intended rather to depend upon fire; but the amount of time spent in taking up a rail was not material at this stage of our journey, as we easily kept on the time of our captured train. There was a wonderful exhilaration in passing swiftly by towns and stations through the heart of an enemy's country in this manner. It possessed just enough of the spice of danger, in this part of the run, to render it thoroughly enjoyable. The slightest accident to our engine, however, or a miscarriage in any part of our program, would have completely changed the conditions.

At Etowah we found the "Yonah," an old locomotive owned by an iron company, standing with steam up; but not wishing to alarm the enemy till the local freight had been safely met, we left it unharmed. Kingston, thirty miles from the starting-point, was safely reached. A train from Rome, Georgia, on a branch road, had just arrived and was waiting for the morning mail—our train. We learned that the local freight would soon come also, and, taking the side-track, waited for it. When it arrived, however, Andrews saw, to his surprise and chagrin, that it bore a red flag, indicating another train not far behind. Stepping over to the conductor, he boldly asked: "What does it mean that the road is blocked in this manner when I have orders to take this powder to Beauregard without a minute's delay?" The answer was interesting, but not reassuring: "Mitchel has captured Huntsville, and is said to be coming to Chattanooga, and we are getting everything out of there." He was asked by Andrews to pull his train a long way down the track out of the way, and promptly obeyed.

It seemed an exceedingly long time before the expected "extra" arrived, and when it did come it bore another red flag. The reason given was that the "local," being too great for one engine, had been made up in two sections, and the second section would doubtless be along in a short time. This was terribly vexatious; yet there seemed nothing to do but to wait. To start out between the sections of an extra train would be to court destruction. There were already three trains around us, and their many passengers and others were all growing very curious about the mysterious train, manned by strangers, which had arrived on the time of the morning mail. For an hour and five minutes from the time of arrival at Kingston we remained in this most critical position. The sixteen of us who were shut up tightly in a box-car,—personating Beauregard's ammunition,—hearing sounds outside, but unable to distinguish words, had perhaps the most trying position. Andrews sent us, by one of the engineers, a cautious warning to be ready to fight in case the uneasiness of the crowd around led them to make any investigation, while he himself kept near the station to prevent the sending off of any alarming telegram. So intolerable was our suspense, that the order for a deadly conflict would have been felt as a relief. But the assurance of Andrews quieted the crowd until the whistle of the expected train from the north was heard; then as it glided up to the depot, past the end of our side-track, we were off without more words.

But unexpected danger had arisen behind us. Out of the panic at Big Shanty two men emerged, determined, if possible, to foil the unknown captors of their train. There was no telegraph station, and no locomotive at hand with which to follow; but the conductor of the train, W. A. Fuller, and Anthony Murphy, foreman of the Atlanta railway machine-shops, who happened to be on board of Fuller's train, started on foot after us as hard as they could run. Finding a hand-car they mounted it and pushed forward till they neared Etowah, where they ran on the break we had made in the road, and were precipitated down the embankment into the ditch. Continuing with more caution, they reached Etowah and found the "Yonah," which was at once pressed into service, loaded with soldiers who were at hand, and hurried with flying wheels toward Kingston. Fuller prepared to fight at that point, for he knew of the tangle of extra trains, and of the lateness of the regular trains, and did not think we should be able to pass.

We had been gone only four minutes when he arrived and found himself stopped by three long, heavy trains of cars, headed in the wrong direction. To move them out of the way so as to pass would cause a delay he was little inclined to afford—would, indeed, have almost certainly given us the victory. So, abandoning his engine, he with Murphy ran across to the Rome train, and, uncoupling the engine and one car, pushed forward with about forty armed men. As the Rome branch connected with the main road above the depot, he encountered no hindrance, and it was now a fair race. We were not many minutes ahead.

Four miles from Kingston we again stopped and cut the telegraph. While trying to take up a rail at this point we were greatly startled. One end of the rail was loosened, and eight of us were pulling at it, when in the distance we distinctly heard the whistle of a pursuing engine. With a frantic effort we broke the rail, and all tumbled over the embankment with the effort. We moved on, and at Adairsville we found a mixed train (freight and passenger) waiting, but there was an express on the road that had not yet arrived. We could afford no more delay, and set out for the next station, Calhoun, at terrible speed, hoping to reach that point before the express, which was behind time, should arrive. The nine miles which we had to travel were left behind in less than the same number of minutes. The express was just pulling out, but, hearing our whistle, backed before us until we were able to take the side-track. It stopped, however, in such a manner as completely to close up the other end of the switch. The two trains, side by side, almost touched each other, and our precipitate arrival caused natural suspicion. Many searching questions were asked, which had to be answered before we could get the opportunity of proceeding. We in the box-car could hear the altercation, and were almost sure that a fight would be necessary before the conductor would consent to "pull up" in order to let us out. Here again our position was most critical, for the pursuers were rapidly approaching.

Fuller and Murphy saw the obstruction of the broken rail in time, by reversing their engine, to prevent wreck, but the hindrance was for the present insuperable. Leaving all their men behind, they started for a second foot-race. Before they had gone far they met the train we had passed at Adairsville, and turned it back after us. At Adairsville they dropped the cars, and with locomotive and tender loaded with armed men, they drove forward at the highest speed possible. They knew that we were not many minutes ahead, and trusted to overhaul us before the express train could be safely passed.

But Andrews had told the powder story again with all his skill, and added a direct request in peremptory form to have the way opened before him, which the Confederate conductor did not see fit to resist; and just before the pursuers arrived at Calhoun we were again under way. Stopping once more to cut wires and tear up the track, we felt a thrill of exhilaration to which we had long been strangers. The track was now clear before us to

Chattanooga; and even west of that city we had good reason to believe that we should find no other train in the way till we had reached Mitchel's lines. If one rail could now be lifted we would be in a few minutes at the Oostenaula bridge; and that burned, the rest of the task would be little more than simple manual labor, with the enemy absolutely powerless. We worked with a will.

But in a moment the tables were turned. Not far behind we heard the scream of a locomotive bearing down upon us at lightning speed. The men on board were in plain sight and well armed. Two minutes—perhaps one— would have removed the rail at which we were toiling; then the game would have been in our own hands, for there was no other locomotive beyond that could be turned back after us. But the most desperate efforts were in vain. The rail was simply bent, and we hurried to our engine and darted away, while remorselessly after us thundered the enemy.

Now the contestants were in clear view, and a race followed unparalleled in the annals of war. Wishing to gain a little time for the burning of the Oostenaula bridge, we dropped one car, and, shortly after, another; but they were "picked up" and pushed ahead to Resaca. We were obliged to run over the high trestles and covered bridge at that point without a pause. This was the first failure in the work assigned us.

The Confederates could not overtake and stop us on the road; but their aim was to keep close behind, so that we might not be able to damage the road or take in wood or water. In the former they succeeded, but not in the latter. Both engines were put at the highest rate of speed. We were obliged to cut the wire after every station passed, in order that an alarm might not be sent ahead; and we constantly strove to throw our pursuers off the track, or to obstruct the road permanently in some way, so that we might be able to burn the Chickamauga bridges, still ahead. The chances seemed good that Fuller and Murphy would be wrecked. We broke out the end of our last box-car and dropped cross-ties on the track as we ran, thus checking their progress and getting far enough ahead to take in wood and water at two separate stations. Several times we almost lifted a rail, but each time the coming of the Confederates within rifle-range compelled us to desist and speed on. Our worst hindrance was the rain. The previous day (Friday) had been clear, with a high wind, and on such a day fire would have been easily and tremendously effective. But to-day a bridge could be burned only with abundance of fuel and careful nursing.

Thus we sped on, mile after mile, in this fearful chase, round curves and past stations in seemingly endless perspective. Whenever we lost sight of the enemy beyond a curve, we hoped that some of our obstructions had been effective in throwing him from the track, and that we should see him no more; but at each long reach backward the smoke was again seen, and the shrill whistle was like the scream of a bird of prey. The time could not have been so very long, for the terrible speed was rapidly devouring the distance; but with our nerves strained to the highest tension each minute seemed an hour. On several occasions the escape of the enemy from wreck was little less than miraculous. At one point a rail was placed across the track on a curve so skilfully that it was not seen till the train ran upon it at full speed. Fuller says that they were terribly jolted, and seemed to bounce altogether from the track, but lighted on the rails in safety. Some of the Confederates wished to leave a train which was driven at such a reckless rate, but their wishes were not gratified.

Before reaching Dalton we urged Andrews to turn and attack the enemy, laying an ambush so as to get into close quarters, that our revolvers might be on equal terms with their guns. I have little doubt that if this had been carried out it would have succeeded. But either because he thought the chance of wrecking or obstructing the enemy still good, or feared that the country ahead had been alarmed by a telegram around the Confederacy by the way of Richmond, Andrews merely gave the plan his sanction without making any attempt to carry it into execution.

Dalton was passed without difficulty, and beyond we stopped again to cut wires and to obstruct the track. It happened that a regiment was encamped not a hundred yards away, but they did not molest us. Fuller had written a despatch to Chattanooga, and dropped a man with orders to have it forwarded instantly, while he pushed on to save the bridges. Part of the message got through and created a wild panic in Chattanooga, although it did not materially influence our fortunes. Our supply of fuel was now very short, and without getting rid of our pursuers long enough to take in more, it was evident that we could not run as far as Chattanooga.

While cutting the wire we made an attempt to get up another rail; but the enemy, as usual, were too quick for us. We had no tool for this purpose except a wedge-pointed iron bar. Two or three bent iron claws for pulling out spikes would have given us such incontestable superiority that, down to almost the last of our run, we should have been able to escape and even to burn all the Chickamauga bridges. But it had not been our intention to rely on this mode of obstruction—an emergency only rendered necessary by our unexpected delay and the pouring rain.

We made no attempt to damage the long tunnel north of Dalton, as our enemies had greatly dreaded. The last hope of the raid was now staked upon an effort of a kind different from any that we had yet made, but which, if successful, would still enable us to destroy the bridges nearest Chattanooga. But, on the other hand, its failure would terminate the chase. Life and success were put upon one throw.

A few more obstructions were dropped on the track, and our own speed increased so that we soon forged a considerable distance ahead. The side and end boards of the last car were torn into shreds, all available fuel was piled upon it, and blazing brands were brought back from the engine. By the time we approached a long, covered bridge a fire in the car was fairly started. We uncoupled it in the middle of the bridge, and with painful suspense waited the issue. Oh for a few minutes till the work of conflagration was fairly begun! There was still steam pressure enough in our boiler to carry us to the next wood-yard, where we could have replenished our fuel by force, if necessary, so as to run as near to Chattanooga as was deemed prudent. We did not know of the telegraph message which the pursuers had sent ahead. But, alas! the minutes were not given. Before the bridge was extensively fired the enemy was upon us, and we moved slowly onward, looking back to see what they would do next. We had not long to conjecture. The Confederates pushed right into the smoke, and drove the burning car before them to the next side-track.

With no car left, and no fuel, the last scrap having been thrown into the engine or upon the burning car, and with no obstruction to drop on the track, our situation was indeed desperate. A few minutes only remained until our steed of iron which had so well served us would be powerless.

But it might still be possible to save ourselves. If we left the train in a body, and, taking a direct course toward the Union lines, hurried over the mountains at right angles with their course, we could not, from the nature of the country, be followed by cavalry, and could easily travel—athletic young men as we were, and fleeing for life—as rapidly as any pursuers. There was no telegraph in the mountainous districts west and northwest of us, and the prospect of reaching the Union lines seemed to me then, and has always since seemed, very fair. Confederate pursuers with whom I have since conversed freely have agreed on two points—that we could have escaped in the manner here pointed out, and that an attack on the pursuing train would likely have been successful. But Andrews thought otherwise, at least in relation to the former plan, and ordered us to jump from the locomotive one by one, and, dispersing in the woods, each endeavor to save himself. Thus ended the Andrews railroad raid.

It is easy now to understand why Mitchel paused thirty miles west of Chattanooga. The Andrews raiders had been forced to stop eighteen miles south of the same town, and no flying train met him with the expected tidings that all railroad communications of Chattanooga were destroyed, and that the town was in a panic and undefended. He dared advance no farther without heavy reinforcements from Pittsburg Landing or the north; and he probably believed to the day of his death, six months later, that the whole Andrews party had perished without accomplishing anything.

A few words will give the sequel to this remarkable enterprise. There was great excitement in Chattanooga and in the whole of the surrounding Confederate territory for scores of miles. The hunt for the fugitive raiders was prompt, energetic, and completely successful. Ignorant of the country, disorganized, and far from the Union lines, they strove in vain to escape. Several were captured the same day on which they left the cars, and all but two within a week. Even these two were overtaken and brought back when they supposed that they were virtually out of danger. Two of those who had failed to be on the train were identified and added to the band of prisoners.

Now follows the saddest part of the story. Being in citizens' dress within an enemy's lines, the whole party were held as spies, and closely and vigorously guarded. A court-martial was convened, and the leader and seven others out of the twenty-two were condemned and executed. The remainder were never brought to trial, probably because of the advance of Union forces, and the consequent confusion into which the affairs of the departments of east Tennessee and Georgia were thrown. Of the remaining fourteen, eight succeeded by a bold effort—attacking their guard in broad daylight—in making their escape from Atlanta, Georgia, and ultimately in reaching the North. The other six who shared in this effort, but were recaptured, remained prisoners until the latter part of March, 1863, when they were exchanged through a special arrangement made with Secretary Stanton. All the survivors of this expedition received medals and promotion. The pursuers also received expressions of gratitude from their fellow-Confederates, notably from the governor and the legislature of Georgia.

—Pittenger, "The Locomotive Chase in Georgia"

4. CAPTAIN CANFIELD TRIES TO FREE SLAVES

The attitude of the Union government and the Union Army toward slaves was, from the beginning, anomalous. On the one hand the war was actually over slavery, and a large segment of Northern opinion took for granted that it was a war to end slavery. Not only this but in so far as slaves performed essential labor, they contributed to Confederate military strength. On the other hand the official position of Congress and of the President was that the Federal government had no power over slavery in the states, and that the war was one for the restoration of the Union. Very early in the war slaves began pouring into the Union armies, and as these armies advanced into the South the problem of disposing of the Negroes became acute. Generals Frémont and Hunter proclaimed emancipation, on their own, and were repudiated by Lincoln. General Butler tried to solve the problem by declaring slaves "contraband of war" and the term "contrabands" stuck.

Not until July 1862 did Congress try to deal with the problem in a general fashion. An act of that month provided that slaves of persons engaged in or contributing to the rebellion were forfeited, and that all slaves of persons in rebellion were to be free on entering Union lines. What this meant was that claimants of fugitive slaves were required to prove their loyalty. The administration of the act varied greatly from commander to commander. As Captain Canfield's account—written partly in the third person—makes clear, a commanding officer hostile to emancipation—and there were many of these—could in effect nullify the act. Canfield was a captain in the 21st Ohio Volunteers.

WHILE at Athens the black calaboose of the south nearly terminated the usefulness of our regiment. Slaves came to us bringing information of the enemy far south of our lines, and expecting protection and freedom, to be greatly disappointed.

Individual members of the regiment often secreted them or steered them on to the north, but they were usually surrendered to their masters, who came boldly after them.

In one case at least, a slave was not allowed to enter our lines, but was detained at the outpost, and surrendered to his master for ten dollars; and it was a republican who took the money. This was reported at regimental headquarters, but nothing was done about it. Lieutenant Colonel Neibling was a pronounced pro-slavery man, and did not hesitate to voluntarily detain slaves in the county jail until their masters came for them.

Slaves were often surrendered, to be taken south beyond the lines of our army, in violation of orders of the Secretary of War.

The fore part of August, Captain Canfield and Lieutenants Wicker and Patterson, each employed a colored servant. About the middle of the month Lieutenant Colonel Niebling went to Co. K's quarters, and thus ordered Lieutenant Wickers servant: "Van! come out of there and go with your master," whereupon the Lieutenant Colonel and Lieutenant Patterson had some harsh words passed between them.

This, and what was termed rebel influence had now provoked much indignation, and the men of Company K declared if another man came into camp hunting slaves, they would throw him into a slop hole.

On the 23d a planter came near camp, and meeting Captain Canfield, said he heard his servant was in his (Canfield's) camp, and asked the captain if he had any objection to his going to see. "Oh no," said the captain, "not in the least;" but seeing several groups of men casting significant glances toward the stranger, he added, "You will not consider me responsible for anything that happens."

Hearing this the stranger turned back. Shortly after the Lieutenant Colonel's orderly came with an order dated and directed to Captain Canfield, saying:

> HEADQUARTERS 21ST, O. V. I.
> Athens, Ala., Aug. 23d, 1862.

Negro boy Pat in your company is the property of ——. You will deliver him outside camp lines to his master. Signed,

> J. M. NIEBLING.
> *Lieut. Col. Comdg. Regt.*

Captain Canfield wrote in answer, acknowledging the receipt of the order, and added, "I respectfully decline to obey it," signed it officially, as Captain Commanding Company, and kept a copy of the correspondence. Nothing further was said or done about this, however.

Matters were in this condition, when for the first time in two months I was detailed as officer of the day, a duty I should often have performed before. I received my order in the evening, and that night I made up my mind that when I went on duty the next morning, I would break up the slave trade in the regiment for twenty-four hours at least; and my success surprised me. The county jail was full of prisoners, chiefly fugitive slaves, who were not turned over to me, but one of my sentinels was posted there, and I assumed whatever authority I lacked to investigate the reason of their detention. I knew very well there were no charges against the black men. After my guard was fully posted and every duty performed, I took a non-commissioned officer and file of men for escort, and reported to Lieutenant Colonel Niebling for any orders he might be pleased to give me. I found him sitting in the shade of a public house near the depot, surrounded by a number of gentlemen of the town. After informing me that there were no new orders for me, I was turning away to leave him, when he called out to me, "Where are you going with that guard?" to which I answered, "I am going down to release the prisoners in the jail, against whom there are no charges."

He answered, "Sir, I order you not to do it."

I then said with deference of manner, "Colonel, will you be so good as to have charges preferred against them."

He replied in a towering rage, it was none of my damned business, and that I should go to my quarters in arrest. Of course I obeyed the order of arrest, and quite crestfallen, went to my tent, followed by the boisterous laughter and jeers of Colonel Niebling's companions, who were sitting about him and heard all that was said.

I had up to this time been considered a severe disciplinarian, and had incurred the displeasure of many officers and men of the regiment on that account, and their judgment at first was, that I was served just right. But before sundown that day, all the slaves were relieved by Colonel Niebling himself, and the regiment was in rebellion against its commanding officer, and my arrest was made the pretext for the mutiny.

That night a meeting of officers was held in the court house, and an address prepared, wherein they told Colonel Niebling of his sins, which was presented to him next day. A committee of which Captain Silas S. Canfield was chairman, was appointed to prefer charges against him, and eight counts were agreed upon, provided he did not resign his commission at once.

Yet the outcome of it all was, that the slave trade was abolished effectually, and while there was no doubt that grave charges could have been sustained against Colonel Niebling, none were ever preferred. It was understood that General Buell, who commanded the army at that time, approved of his course in surrendering fugitive slaves, and nothing could have saved the officers concerned in that address, but he never referred it. I was released from arrest without any explanation whatever, and returned to the command of my company.

—CANFIELD, *History of the 21st Regiment Ohio Volunteer Infantry*

5. A BADGER BOY MEETS THE ORIGINALS OF
UNCLE TOM'S CABIN

Here is our old friend Chauncey Cooke again—the Wisconsin boy who enlisted at sixteen, fought the Sioux Indians, and then was sent to Kentucky to take part in the campaign against Bragg. It is not to be supposed that all Union soldiers saw the Negroes through the eyes of Harriet Beecher Stowe;

many of them—like Colonel Niebling—were bitterly hostile to emancipation.

Columbus, Ky., March 5th, 1863
25th Wis. Vol. Infantry

Dear Folks at Home:

I sent you a letter a day or two ago and maybe I will hear from you soon. I hope I shall. I am well and we are hearing and seeing things and the days are not so heavy as at Madison. The weather is fine—most of the time warm and clear.

We drill every day, do police work, cleaning round the camp, and take a stroll now and then back in the country, far as the pickets will let us. We are really in the "Sunny South." The slaves, contrabands, we call them, are flocking into Columbus by the hundred. General Thomas of the regular army is here enlisting them for war. All the old buildings on the edge of the town are more than full. You never meet one but he jerks his hat off and bows and shows the whitest teeth. I never saw a bunch of them together, but I could pick out an Uncle Tom, a Quimbo, a Sambo, a Chloe, an Eliza, or any other character in *Uncle Tom's Cabin*. The women take in a lot of dimes washing for the soldiers, and the men around picking up odd jobs. I like to talk with them. They are funny enough, and the stories they tell of slave life are stories never to be forgotten. Ask any of them how he feels and the answer nearly always will be, "Sah, I feels might good, sah," or "God bress you, massa, I'se so proud I'se a free man." Some are leaving daily on up-river boats for Cairo and up the Ohio River. The Ohio has always been the river Jordan to the slave. It has been the dream of his life even to look upon the Ohio River.

The government transports returning from down river points where they had been with troops or supplies would pick up free men on every landing and deliver them free of charge at places along the Ohio and upper Mississippi points.

The slaves are not all black as we in the North are apt to suppose. Some of them are quite light. Those used as house servants seem to have some education and don't talk so broad. A real pretty yellow girl about 18 was delivering some washing to the boys yesterday. She left her master and mistress in December and came to Columbus. In answer to the questions of the boys she said she left home because her mistress was cross to her and all other servants since Lincoln's emancipation. She said her mother came with her. One of the boys asked her why her father did not come with her. She said, "My father hain't no colored man, he's a white man." When the boys began to laugh she picked up her two-bushel basket of clothes, balanced it on her head, and went her way. That girl must have made fifty stops among the tents leaving her basket of clothes. I wonder if she heard the same dirty talk in each of them. The talk wasn't clean, but some of us who tho't so just let it pass and kept still. . . .

Your son,
CHAUNCEY

Columbus, Ky., March 21st., 1863
25th Wisconsin Vol.

Dear Mother:

After drill went out in the edge of the woods. Its more peaceful and homelike than the racket of the camp. I can see the picket guard beyond me slowly pacing his beat. There is no enemy about but the discipline and regulations are just as rigid as they are in Georgia. No white man can come within the picket line except he has the password. A Negro is allowed to come in. We are afraid that the whites may be spies, we know the blacks are our friends.

The health of the regiment is good save a few cases of bowel trouble. The boys call it the Kentucky quickstep. There is more sickness among the poor lazy blacks. They are filling all the vacant houses and even sleeping under the trees, so anxious are they to get near "de Lincoln soldiers." They live on scraps and whatever they can pick up in camp and they will shine our shoes or do any camp work for an old shirt or cast-off coat. They had a revival meeting at the foot of the bluff last night and such shouting and singing and moaning. It was Massa Lincoln was a savior that came after two hundred years of tribulation in the cotton fields and cane. They had long known that something was going to happen because so many times their massa had visitors and they would tell the servants to stay in their cabins and not come to the "big house" until they were called. Then some of the house servants would creep round under the windows and hear the white folks talking about war and that the slaves were going to be free. And when the one that was sent to listen would come back and tell the others, they would get down on their knees and pray in whispers and give thanks to the Lord. Everything with the darkies is Lord, Lord. Their faith that the Lord will help them has held out more than 200 years.

I sometimes wonder if the Lord is not partial to the white race and rather puts it onto the black race because they are black. We sometimes get terribly confused when we try to think of the law of Providence. This black race for instance, they can't talk ten words about slavery and old Massa and old Missus, but they get in something about "de blessed Lord and de lovely Jesus" and yet in this land of Washington, God has permitted them to be bought and sold like our cattle and our hogs in the stockyards for more than 200 years.

I listened for two hours this morning to the stories of a toothless old slave with one blind eye who had come up the river from near Memphis. He told me a lot of stuff. He said his master sold his wife and children to a cotton planter in Alabama to pay his gambling debts, and when he told his master he couldn't stand it, he was tied to the whipping post stripped and given 40 lashes. The next night he ran to the swamps. The bloodhounds were put on his track and caught him and pulled him down. They bit him in the face and put out his eye and crushed one of his hands so he could not use it. He stripped down his pants and showed me a gash on one of his hips where one of the hounds hung unto him until he nearly bled to death.

This happened in sight of Nashville, the capitol of Tennessee. I told this to some of the boys and they said it was all bosh, that the niggers were lying to me. But this story was just like the ones in Uncle Tom's Cabin, and I believe them. And father knows of things very much like this that are true.

I will write you again soon,

Your son

CHAUNCEY

—COOKE, "Letters of a Badger Boy in Blue"

6. INCIDENTS OF THE PICKET LINE AT CHATTANOOGA

We have met the vivacious Joseph Polley before. His Texas Brigade was sent west with Longstreet to support Bragg at Chickamauga, and it was in that fierce battle that its leader, Hood, lost his leg. After Chickamauga Bragg's forces moved onto the heights above Chattanooga where they hoped to starve Rosecrans out. The incidents which Polley recalls here are from the short period of watchful waiting between the two great battles.

Chattanooga, Tenn. Oct. 1, 1863

I was lucky enough to be on picket duty a few nights ago with my friends Will Burges and John West, of Companies D and E of the Fourth, each of whom is not only a good soldier, but a most entertaining companion. As the night advanced, it became cold enough to make a fire very acceptable, and, appropriating a whole one to ourselves, we had wandered from a discussion of the war and of this particular campaign that was little flattering to General Bragg, into pleasant reminiscences of our homes and loved ones, when someone on horseback said, "Good evening, gentlemen." Looking hastily up, we discovered that the intruder was General Jenkins, alone and unattended by either aide or orderly, and were about to rise and salute in approved military style, when, with a smile plainly perceptible in the bright moonlight, he said, "No, don't trouble yourselves," and, letting the reins drop on his horse's neck, threw one leg around the pommel of his saddle and entered into conversation with us.

Had you been listening for the next half hour or so, Charming Nellie, you would never have been able to guess which of us was the General, for, ignoring his rank as completely as we careless Texans forgot it, he became at once as private a soldier as either of us, and talked and laughed as merrily and unconcernedly as if it were not war times. I offered him the use of my pipe and smoking tobacco, Burges was equally generous with the plug he kept for chewing, and West was even polite enough to regret that the whisky he was in the habit of carrying as a preventive against snake bites was just out; in short, we were beginning to believe General Jenkins of South Carolina the only real general in the Confederate service, when, to our surprise and dismay, he straightened himself up on his saddle, and climbing from "gay to grave, from lively to severe," announced that at midnight the picket line would be expected to advance and drive the Yankees to the other side of the creek.

We might easily have forgiven him for being the bearer of this discomforting intelligence had that been the sum total of his offending; but it was not; he rode away without expressing the least pleasure at having made our acquaintance, or even offering to shake hands with us—the necessary and inevitable consequence of such discourtesy being that he descended at once in our estimation to the level of any other general.

But midnight was too near at hand to waste time in nursing indignation. Instant action was imperative, and resolving ourselves into a council of war with plenary powers, it was unanimously decided by the three privates there assembled that our recent guest was an upstart wholly undeserving of confidence; that the contemplated movement was not only foolish and impracticable, but bound to be dangerous; and that, if a single shot were fired at us by the enemy, we three would just lie down and let General Jenkins of South Carolina do his own advancing and driving. Being veterans, we knew far better than he how easy it was at night for opposing lines to intermingle with each other and men to mistake friends for enemies, and we did not propose to sanction the taking of such chances.

All too soon the dreaded and fateful hour arrived; all too soon the whispered order "Forward" was passed from man to man down the long line, and, like spectral forms in the ghastly moonlight, the Confederate pickets moved slowly out into the open field in their front, every moment expecting to see the flash of a gun and hear or feel its messenger of death, and all awed by the fear the bravest men feel when confronting unknown danger. Not ten minutes before, the shadowy forms of the enemy had been seen by our videttes, and if the line of the creek was worth capturing by us, it surely was worth holding by the Yankees. But all was silent and still; no sight of foe, no tread of stealthy footstep, no sharp click of gunlock—not even the rustling of a leaf or the snap of a twig came out of the darkness to relieve our suspense and quiet the expectant throbbing of our hearts.

Under these circumstances, West, Burges, and your humble servant, like the brave and true men they are, held themselves erect and advanced side by side with their gallant comrades until the terra incognita and impenetrability of the narrow but timbered valley of the stream suggested ambush and the advisability of rifle-pits. Working at these with a will born of emergency, we managed to complete them just as the day dawned, and jumping into them with a sigh of inexpressible relief—our courage rising as the night fled— waited for hostilities to begin. But the Yankees had outwitted us, their withdrawal, by some strange coincidence, having been practically simultaneous with our advance—they taking just enough start, however, to keep well out of our sight and hearing. West remarked next morning, "It's better to be born lucky than rich," but whether he referred to our narrow escape, or to that of the Yankees, he refused to say. . . . Soon afterward a truce along the picket lines in front of the Texans was arranged; that is, there was to be no more shooting at each other's pickets—the little killing and wounding done by

The Hut Picket

In the Hut

Edwin Forbes

"Fall in for Soup"

the practice never compensating for the powder and shot expended, and the discomfort of being always on the alert, night and day.

But the South Carolinians, whose picket line began at our left, their first rifle-pit being within fifty feet of the last one of the First Texas, could make no terms, whatever. The Federals charge them with being the instigators and beginners of the war, and, as I am informed, always exclude them from the benefit of truces between the pickets. It is certainly an odd spectacle to see the Carolinians hiding in their rifle pits and not daring to show their heads, while, not fifty feet away, the Texans sit on the ground playing poker, in plain view and within a hundred yards of the Yankees. Worse than all, the palmetto fellows are not even permitted to visit us in daylight, except in disguise—their new uniforms of gray always betraying them wherever they go. One of them who is not only very fond of, but successful at, the game of poker, concluded the other day to risk being shot for the chance of winning the money of the First Texas, and, divesting himself of his coat, slipped over to the Texas pit an hour before daylight, and by sunrise was giving his whole mind to the noble pastime.

An hour later a keen-sighted Yankee sang out, "Say, you Texas Johnnies! ain't that fellow playing cards, with his back to a sapling, one of them d——d South Carolina secessionists? Seems to me his breeches are newer 'n they ought to be." This direct appeal for information placed the Texans between the horns of a dilemma; hospitality demanded the protection of their guest—prudence, the observance of good faith toward the Yankees. The delay in answering obviated the necessity for it by confirming the inquirer's suspicions, and, exclaiming, "D—n him, I just know it is!" he raised his gun quickly and fired. The South Carolinian was too active, though; at the very first movement of the Yankee, he sprang ten feet and disappeared into a gulch that protected him from further assault. . . .

Jack Smith, of Company D, is sui generis. A brave and gallant soldier he is yet an inveterate straggler, and is therefore, not always on hand when the battle is raging, but at Chickamauga he was, and, singularly enough, counted for two.

Another member of Company D is constitutionally opposed to offering his body for sacrifice on the altar of his country, and, when he cannot get on a detail which will keep him out of danger, is sure to fall alarmingly sick. Jack determined to put a stop to this shirking, so early on the morning of the 19th, he took the fellow under his own protecting and stimulating care, and, attacking him in the most vulnerable point, to the surprise of everybody, carried him into and through the fight of that day.

"Come right along with me, Fred, and don't be scared a particle," Jack was heard to say in his coaxing, mellifluous voice as we began to advance on the enemy, "for I'll shoot the head off the first man who points a gun in front of you, and I'll watch out for your carcass, and after we have whipped the Yanks you an' me'll finish them bitters in my haversack."

"But I don't like bitters," protested Fred in a trembling voice.

"I know that, ole feller, an' I don't generally like 'em myself, but these are made on the old nigger's plan—the least mite in the world of cherry bark, still less of dogwood, and then fill up the bottle with whisky."

Needless to say that after the battle was over and Jack had brought his protege safely through its perils, quite a number of comrades looked longingly at the bottle. In vain, however; Jack was loyal to his promise and he and Fred were the merriest men in Company D that night.

—POLLEY, *A Soldier's Letters to Charming Nellie*

7. THE CONFEDERATES ESCAPE IN THE TECHE COUNTRY

Before he could support Grant in the Vicksburg-Port Hudson campaign General Banks, who had replaced Butler in New Orleans, felt that he had to dispose of the Confederate forces in the Teche country west of the city, a country of bayous, lakes, and swamps. In January 1863 Banks organized the first of his expeditions against General Taylor's miscellaneous forces, but this petered out. A second advance took place in April and met with some success. It is this advance that is recorded here. Later that summer General Taylor, whom we have already met in the Valley campaign, and his subordinate Mouton struck back, recovering the whole Teche country up to the gates of New Orleans. The fall of Port Hudson released large forces for a counterattack, however, and Taylor retreated to the Red River country.

It is, once more, the novelist De Forest who tells the story.

THE Teche country was to the war in Louisiana what the Shenandoah Valley was to the war in Virginia. It was a sort of back alley, parallel to the main street wherein the heavy fighting must go on; and one side or the other was always running up or down the Teche with the other side in full chase after it. There the resemblance ends, for the Teche country is a long flat, hemmed in by marshes and bayous, which, as everybody but a blind man can see, is a very different thing from a rolling valley bordered by mountains. . . .

My first adventure in this region was in January, 1863. Weitzel dashed up to the confluence of the Teche and Atchafalaya with five or six regiments, scared Mouton out of his position there, smashed the Confederates' new ironclad gunboat *Cotton*, and returned next morning. Although pestered with cold and hunger, our march homeward was as hilarious as a bacchanal procession. It was delightful to have beaten the enemy, and it was delightful to be on the way back to our comfortable quarters. The expedition was thus brief because it had fulfilled its object, which was to weaken the Confederate naval power on the Teche, and thus enable Banks to take the back alley in his proposed advance on Port Hudson.

But why should he go by the back alley of the Teche instead of by the main street of the Mississippi? Because it was necessary to destroy the army of Mouton, or, at least, to drive it northward as far as possible, in order to incapacitate it from attacking New Orleans while we should be engaged with the fortress of the bluffs. The story ran in our brigade that this sensible plan originated in the head of our own commandant, Weitzel. I believed it then, and I have learned no better since, although I can affirm nothing. The reader will please to remember that there is a great deal of uncertainty in war, not only before but after.

About the middle of April, 1863, I was once more at the confluence of the Teche and the Atchafalaya. This time Mouton was there in strong force, posted behind entrenchments which seemed to me half a mile in length, with an impassable swamp on his right and armored gunboats on his left. Banks's army was far superior in numbers and, supported as it was by a sufficient fleet of gunboats, could doubtless have carried the position; but the desirable thing to do was of course, not so much to beat Mouton as to bag him, and so finish the war in this part of Louisiana. Accordingly, by mysterious waterways of which I know nothing, Grover's division was transported to Irish Bend, in Mouton's rear, while Emory's and Weitzel's divisions should amuse him in front.

And here I am tempted . . . to describe this same amusement. The first part of the joke was to push up Weitzel's brigade to draw the enemy's fire. In a single long line, stretching from the wood on the left well toward the river on the right, the brigade advanced directly toward the enemy's works, prostrating or climbing fences, and struggling amid horrible labyrinths of tangled sugar cane. Rush through a mile of Indian corn, taking the furrows diagonally, then imagine yourself three times as tired and breathless as you are, and you will form some conception of what it is to move in line through a canefield. At first you valiantly push aside the tough green obstacles; then you ignominiously dodge under or around them; at last you fall down with your tongue out. The ranks are broken; the regiment tails off into strings, the strongest leading; the ground is strewn with panting soldiers; the organization disappears.

The cane once passed, stragglers began to come up and find their places; the ranks counted off anew while advancing, and we had once more a regiment. Now we obtained a full view of the field of projected amusement. Before us lay a long and comparatively narrow plain, bounded by forests rising out of swamps, and decorated by a long low earthwork, a third of a mile ahead of us, and barely visible to the naked eye. Away to our right were two half-demolished brick sugar-houses, near which there was a scurrying of dust to and fro, bespeaking a skirmishing of cavalry. Otherwise the scene was one of perfect quietness and silence and desertion.

Of a sudden *bang, bang, bang*, roared an unseen battery, and *jiz, jiz, jiz*, screeched the shells over our heads. Evidently the enemy was too much amused to keep his mouth shut. Then our own batteries joined in with their *bang, bang, bang, jiz, jiz, jiz*, and for twenty minutes or more it was as disgusting as a Fourth of July. The shelling did not hurt us a bit, and consequently did not scare us much, for we were already accustomed to this kind of racket, and only took it hard when it was mingled with the cries of the wounded. I never assisted, as the French phrase it, at a noisier or a more harmless bout of cannonading. Not a man in my regiment was injured, although the shells hummed and cracked and fought each other in flights over our heads, dotting the sky with the little globes of smoke which marked their explosions, and sending buzzing fragments in all directions.

Meantime our point was gained; the enemy had defined his position. There was a battery in the swampy wood on his right, which would enfilade an attacking column, while on his left the same business would be performed by his armored gunboats in the Teche. Now came an order to take the brigade to the rear. A greenhorn of an aide, shrieking with excitement, galloped up to our commander and yelled: "Colonel, double-quick your men out of range. Double-quick!"

I remember the wrath with which I heard this order. Run? Be shot if I would run or let a man of my company run. The regiment, hearing the command, had faced about and was going to the rear at a pace which threatened confusion and panic. I rushed through the ranks, drew my sword, ordered, threatened, and brought my own company from a double-quick down to the ordinary marching step. Every other officer, from the colonel downward, instinctively did the same; and the regiment moved off in a style which we considered proper for the Twelfth Connecticut.

That night we bivouacked with mosquitoes, who drew more blood than the cannonade of the afternoon. Next morning the heavy guns of the opposing gunboats opened a game of long bowls, in which the Parrotts of the Twenty-first Indiana took a part, sending loud-whispering shells into the farthest retreats of the enemy. At ten, the whole army, three lines deep and stretching across the river—a fine martial spectacle—advanced slowly through the canefields toward the entrenchments. Marching in my preferred position, in the front rank of my company and next to the regimental colors, I felt myself to be an undesirably conspicuous person, as we came out upon the open ground in view of the enemy, and received the first discharge of their artillery. It is a grand thing to take the lead in battle, but all the same it is uncomfortable. The first cannon shot which I noticed struck the ground sixty or eighty feet in front of our color guard, threw up the ploughed soil in a little cloud, leaped a hundred feet behind the regiment, and went bounding off to the rear.

"That's bad for the fellows behind us," I said to my men, with that smile which a hero puts on when he makes the best he can of battle, meantime wishing himself at home.

The next shot struck within thirty feet of the line, and also went jumping and whistling rearward. They were evidently aiming at the colors, and that was nearly equivalent to aiming at me.

"You'll fetch him next time," I thought, grimly; and so, doubtless, thought hundreds of others, each for himself.

But at this moment one of our own batteries opened with great violence and evidently shook the nerves of the enemy's gunners, for their next shot screeched over the colors and first struck the ground far in rear of the regiment, and thereafter they never recovered their at first dangerously accurate range. Now came an order to the infantry to halt and lie down, and no veteran will need to be told that we obeyed it promptly. I never knew that order to be disregarded on a field of battle, not even by the most inexperienced and insubordinate of troops, unless, indeed, they were already running.

The battle of Camp Beaseland was an artillery duel of fifteen or twenty pieces on a side, lasting hotly from eleven in the morning till six in the evening, with a dash of infantry charging and heavy musketry on either flank, and a dribble of skirmishing along the whole line. Where we were, it was all artillery and skirmishing, noisy and lively enough, but by no means murderous. Bainbridge's regular battery on our right pitched into a Louisiana battery on our left front, and a little beyond it a battery of the Twenty-first Indiana pounded away at the Confederate gunboats and at an advanced earthwork. The loud metallic spang of the brass howitzers, the dull thud of the iron Parrotts, and the shrieking and cracking of the enemy's shells made up a *charivari* long to be remembered.

Meantime, companies moved out here and there from the line of infantry, deployed as skirmishers, advanced to within two or three hundred yards of the breastworks, and opened fire. This drew the Rebel musketry and made things hotter than ever. The order to lie low passed along, and we did the best we could with the cane-hills, wishing that they were bigger. As I lay on my side behind one of these six-inch fortifications, chewing the hardtack which was my only present creature comfort, several balls cut the low weeds which overhung me. Yet, notwithstanding the stunning racket and the quantity of lead and iron flying about, our loss was very small.

Nor could the enemy have suffered more severely, except on our left. There the Seventy-fifth and 114th New York, drawn up in the swampy wood which at that point separated the two armies, repulsed with a close volley of musketry a swarm of Texans who attempted to ford the morass and turn our flank. There, too, the heaviest fire of our batteries was concentrated and made havoc, as I afterward heard, of the enemy's artillery. An officer of one of our skirmishing companies, whose position enabled him to see this part of the enemy's line, assured me, with a jocose exaggeration founded on fact, that "the air was full of horses' tails and bits of harness." But, in a general way, there was very little slaughter for the amount of powder expended. We were not fighting our hardest; we were merely amusing the enemy. The only serious work done was to smash one or two of his gunboats. Meanwhile, it was hoped that Grover was gaining Mouton's rear and so posting himself as to render escape impossible.

An officer, major of a Texas regiment, as I was told by prisoners, attracted the notice of both armies by riding from left to right of the enemy's position in full view of our line. He was behind the entrenchment, it is true, but that was little more than a rifle pit and hardly concealed the legs of his horse. He was undoubtedly a staff officer engaged in carrying orders to the battery in the wood. As he came back on his perilous mission every skirmisher fired at him, and many men in the line of battle added their bullets to the deadly flight which sought his life, while all our brigade watched him with breathless interest. Directly in front of me the horse reared; the rider dismounted and seemed to examine him; then, remounting, cantered a few yards; then leaned backwards and slid to the ground. Away went the horse, wildly, leaving his gallant master dead.

About five o'clock an order arrived to move out of range of fire. The skirmishers came in; the men rose and took their places in line; and we marched slowly back to our position of the morning. During the night we fought mosquitoes, not with the idea of amusing them, but in deadly earnest. During the night, also, the colonel in charge of the pickets, a greenhorn of some nine-months' regiment, distinguished himself by an exhibition of the minimum of native military genius. Early in the morning he reported to Weitzel that the enemy had vacated their position.

"How do you know?" demanded the startled general.

"I heard their artillery going off about two o'clock."

"Good God, sir! why didn't you inform me of it immediately?"

"Why, General, I thought you wanted them to clear out; and I didn't like to disturb you after such a hard day's work."

Thus collapsed the plan by which we were to stick like a burr to the enemy and pitch into his rear whenever he should attempt to force his way through Grover.

—De Forest, "Forced Marches"

8. FORREST'S CAVALRYMEN CAPTURE A COLT

The cavalry, Union and Confederate, always needed horses, and in a region like Middle Tennessee, which had been fought over and pillaged over for three years, the need was acute. Here Private John Milton Hubbard of Forrest's cavalry corps—the 7th Tennessee—tells how the brave raiders captured "Sal's colt."

THAT a little fun can be mixed up with the horrors of war was illustrated on this trip somewhere over in the hills of Wayne. James E. Wood's little chestnut sorrel, the horse which had been tendered by his owner to Captain Tate, as related in the account of the fight at Ripley, and from which that gallant officer was shot, struck the frog of one foot against a stone and was rendered unserviceable. Austin Statler and Tom Joyner set about the task of helping their fellow-soldier to a remount. This was difficult to do in a country which had been stripped of all the good stock. The only animal available appeared to be a three-year-old, standing in an enclosure near an humble cottage. Statler, in his blandest manner, explained the situation to the mistress of the cottage, and alluded in earnest words to the fine points of the lame horse, which needed only a few days' rest to restore him to his former condition of usefulness. No, no; the old lady couldn't see it in the light in which it had been so earnestly presented. There were seven stout daughters standing by ready to assist their mother, who averred that the animal was "Sal's colt," and he couldn't have it upon any terms whatever. Statler persisted until high words resulted, and the soldiers advanced towards "Sal's colt." Thoroughly aroused, and reinforced by her mother and sisters,

Sal herself, a buxom lassie, now came to the rescue, cleared the fence at a bound, and sat astride of the bridleless colt.

Victory now seemed to perch upon the banner of the females, but the soldiers, who had no idea of seeing their comrade hotfoot it along the roads of Wayne, moved to the assault, determined to capture the colt, but anxious to inflict no bruises upon their adversaries, who fought like wildcats. The contest was fast and furious, but in a class entirely by itself. There were blood and hair in evidence, but no mortal casualties. There were pinching and twisting, wrenching and wringing, clutching and hugging, yes, hugging, till the female side had mostly lost its wind and Sal, grasping the mane of the colt with the grip of despair, while she planted her heels in its sides, was gently lifted from her position by the gallant trio. "It was all over but the shouting." The bit was forced and the girth was buckled. "Sal's colt" had changed its politics and been mustered into the service of the Confederacy.

The old lady intimated that "men folks" were at hand and ready to avenge all her wrongs. Statler, as a precautionary measure, rode out in the direction indicated by her and saw three armed citizens approaching. With cocked gun and ready pistol he commanded them, with assumed bravado, to lead the way to the cottage, while he assured them that he, too, had "a whole gang in reach." Tableau vivant: An elderly man "breathing out threatening and slaughter" and declaring that he would have satisfaction before the sun went down; two lusty young men with guns and in the poise of interested spectators; six bouncing young girls well distributed in the ensemble and joining in a chorus of abuse; an elderly woman standing in the kitchen door and wiping the sweat from her neck and ears with her checked apron, beaten but not conquered; Sal perched upon the top rail of the front fence in the attitude of a show girl about to dance a horn pipe, and gazing at three vanishing cavaliers just then turning a corner and making time to overtake the command; lastly, the abandoned warhorse, which had heard the guns at Tishomingo, stripped of his trappings and "turned out to grass," was standing meekly by and looking as if he might be thinking he had no friends at all.

—Hubbard, *Notes of a Private*

9. GENERAL WILSON RAISES HIS CAVALRY THE HARD WAY

This entertaining episode is from the closing chapter of the war in the West. After Sherman launched his March to the Sea he sent General Thomas to Nashville to collect an army that would hold Tennessee against Hood. The troubles General Wilson had getting horses for his cavalry suggest how that army was improvised.

We will meet James Harrison Wilson again and need not pause here for a lengthy introduction. Only twenty-four when the war broke out, he had a meteoric rise, ending the war with the rank of major general. He was, by general agreement, with Sheridan the most brilliant cavalry commander in the Union armies.

WHILE Hood was advancing from the Tennessee and I had nominally six divisions of cavalry, my actual force with the colors in front of Hood did not exceed five thousand fighting men. Until the movement began I remained at Nashville, engaged night and day in perfecting the paper work, in gathering horses, arms, and equipments, and in making ready for the campaign which was soon to burst upon us. Generally, the supply departments responded promptly to my call, but horses, our greatest want, were scarce, and with the higher requirements and closer inspections I had myself prescribed a few months before, and the advance in price which had naturally followed the advance in quality, the western horse contractors found it impossible to supply our demands. The War Department itself seemed to despair, and while Stanton appeared willing to do what he could, he finally lost patience and his good sense besides, and telegraphed Thomas that if he waited for Wilson to remount his cavalry he would wait "till the crack of doom." But as this was after I had asked and he had granted permission to impress horses from the people wherever they could be found south of the Ohio River, his pessimistic assertion was shortly shown to be both unjust and unfounded.

This arbitrary measure was entirely without precedent within our lines, but it was carried ruthlessly into effect while the contending armies were facing each other in front of Nashville. Within seven days after the Secretary's authority came to hand seven thousand horses were obtained in middle and western Kentucky and our mounted force was thereby increased to twelve thousand, nine thousand of which were actually assembled at Edgefield or within supporting distance. The quartermasters to whom this duty was assigned gave vouchers in proper form for every horse taken and it is believed that no permanent loss or injury was inflicted upon the loyal people.

Every horse and mare that could be used was taken. All street-car and livery stable horses, and private carriage- and saddle-horses, were seized. Even Andrew Johnson, the vice-president-elect, was forced to give up his pair. A circus then at Nashville lost everything except its ponies; even the old white trick horse was taken but it is alleged that the young and handsome equestrienne, who claimed him, succeeded in convincing my adjutant general that the horse was unfit for cavalry service. Be this as it may, a clean sweep was made of every animal that could carry a cavalry-man and the result is shown by the fact that although two brigades of three thousand men were sent to Kentucky in pursuit of Lyon's Confederate cavalry, about ten thousand well mounted men crossed the Cumberland on the night of December 12 [1864] and marched out against the enemy on the morning of the 15th, as soon as the thaw made it possible to move at all.

The great victory which resulted from turning the enemy's flank shows how important the measure was in making the cavalry the tremendous factor it became, not only in that battle but in the campaign which wound up the war.

—WILSON, *Under the Old Flag*

XIV

The Problem of Discipline

WHY *should discipline have been a problem in the Civil War? There are a number of reasons for this, and not all of them are discreditable. Americans had never taken kindly to discipline, either in peace or in war. In civil life every man thought himself as good as his neighbor—even if that neighbor happened to be a merchant or a physician, a mayor or a Congressman—and this attitude was carried over into the armies. There was no military tradition in America, and little understanding of the value of rules and of discipline. This was the first major war in which Americans had ever been engaged, and it was the first to levy on the whole population. From 3,500,000 to 4,000,000 men fought, at one time or another, in Union or Confederate armies—an astonishingly high percentage of the total population of 31,000,000—and all but a handful of these were wholly without previous military experience.*

These considerations suggest that the problem of discipline would have been difficult in the best of circumstances; it was aggravated by the policies of Federal and Confederate governments. There was, for example, no trained officer class, and neither government did anything effective either to use such material as was available or to train officers. At the outbreak of the war the Regular Army consisted of 16,367 officers and men; there were, in addition, a number of graduates of West Point or of the Citadel and the Virginia Military Institute who were available. This nucleus of Regular Army and veterans might have been sufficient to provide officers for the volunteers of 1861 and 1862; by the time of the draft the war had produced a crop of competent officers. But the government did not follow the policy of breaking up the Regular Army, nor did the Confederacy use its officer material to best advantage. Most of the field and many of the general officers were appointed by state governors, usually on political grounds; a great many of these, especially in the North, earned their appointments by raising their own regiments or companies. Lower officers were customarily elected by the rank and file. Most of the officers were totally ignorant of the rules of warfare, of military tactics, and of the requirements of discipline. Some learned quickly; others never learned.

One result of this situation was widespread insubordination, downright disobedience, and a staggeringly high rate of desertion. It was not that the typical American was either disorderly or disobedient; it was rather that while willing enough to fight, he saw no reason for observing discipline when there was no fighting at hand. He had little respect for officers, as such, and many

481

of these were not deserving of respect. He was unfamiliar with the require-ments of camp sanitation; saw no harm in straggling; was inclined to regard most regulations as something between a joke and a nuisance. Circumstances, as well as the inevitable opportunities and temptations of war, encouraged him to foraging and pillaging.

Punishment for insubordination varied greatly from army to army, from regiment to regiment, and from time to time. Many officers were lax dis-ciplinarians because they curried favor with their men; in the long run the men respected more the strict disciplinarians. Military courts—often drum-head courts—dealt with more serious cases. The penalty for desertion, or for sleeping on sentry duty, was death, but this extreme penalty was rarely in-flicted. Statistics for the Confederacy are wholly wanting; those for the Union are inadequate and misleading. While there are numerous accounts of execu-tions and numerous accounts, too, of last-minute reprieves, the surgeon gen-eral's office gives total executions as 121; when we recall that there were well over 200,000 desertions from the Union Army, and that some 75,000 of these were arrested during the last two years of the war, we realize how feeble was the machinery of enforcement and discipline.

The excerpts which follow are designed to show some of the varied aspects of the problem of discipline: the causes of soldier discontent, the manifestations of that discontent in insubordination and desertion, the ravages of pillaging, the methods of punishment, and the impression that the conduct and misconduct of the Civil War soldiers made on thoughtful observers.

1. THOMAS WENTWORTH HIGGINSON EXPLAINS THE VALUE OF TRAINED OFFICERS

Higginson himself was an amateur—a Unitarian clergyman who had helped raise and train a Massachusetts regiment and then found himself colonel of the 1st South Carolina colored regiment, where his chief problems were in the realm of training, discipline, sanitation, the commissary, and so forth. This essay on the problem of command—one of the very best in our literature—appeared within a few months of Higginson's retirement from the army.

NOW that three years have abolished many surmises, and turned many others into established facts, it must be owned that the total value of the professional training has proved far greater, and that of the general prepara-tion far less, than many intelligent observers predicted. The relation between officer and soldier is something so different in kind from anything which civil life has to offer, that it has proved almost impossible to transfer methods or maxims from the one to the other. If a regiment is merely a caucus, and the colonel the chairman,—or merely a fire-company, and the colonel the fore-man,—or merely a prayer-meeting, and the colonel the moderator,—or merely a bar-room, and the colonel the landlord,—then the failure of the whole thing is a foregone conclusion.

War is not the highest of human pursuits, certainly; but an army comes very near to being the completest of human organizations, and he alone succeeds in it who readily accepts its inevitable laws, and applies them. An army is an aristocracy, on a three-years' lease, supposing that the period of enlistment. No mortal skill can make military power effective on democratic principles. A democratic people can perhaps carry on a war longer and better than any other; because no other can so well comprehend the object, raise the means, or bear the sacrifices. But these sacrifices include the surrender, for the time being, of the essential principle of the government. Personal independence in the soldier, like personal liberty in the civilian, must be waived for the preservation of the nation. With shipwreck staring men in the face, the choice lies between despotism and anarchy, trusting to the common sense of those concerned, when the danger is over, to revert to the old safeguards. It is precisely because democracy is an advanced stage in human society, that war, which belongs to a less advanced stage, is peculiarly inconsistent with its habits. Thus the undemocratic character, so often lamented in West Point and Annapolis, is in reality their strong point. Granted that they are no more appropriate to our stage of society than are revolvers and bowie-knives, that is precisely what makes them all serviceable in time of war. War being exceptional, the institutions which train its officers must be exceptional likewise.

The first essential for military authority lies in the power of command,—a power which it is useless to analyze, for it is felt instinctively, and it is seen in its results. It is hardly too much to say, that, in military service, if one has this power, all else becomes secondary; and it is perfectly safe to say that without it all other gifts are useless. Now for the exercise of power there is no preparation like power, and nowhere is this preparation to be found, in this community, except in regular army-training. Nothing but great personal qualities can give a man by nature what is easily acquired by young men of very average ability who are systematically trained to command.

The criticism habitually made upon our army by foreign observers at the beginning of the war continues still to be made, though in a rather less degree,—that the soldiers are relatively superior to the officers, so that the officers lead, perhaps, but do not command them. The reason is plain. Three years are not long enough to overcome the settled habits of twenty years. The weak point of our volunteer service invariably lies here, that the soldier, in nine cases out of ten, utterly detests being commanded, while the officer, in his turn, equally shrinks from commanding. War, to both, is an episode in life, not a profession, and therefore military subordination, which needs for its efficiency to be fixed and absolute, is, by common consent, reduced to a minimum. The white American soldier, being, doubtless, the most intelligent in the world, is more ready than any other to comply with a reasonable order, but he does it because it is reasonable, not because it is an order. With advancing experience his compliance increases, but it is still because he better and better comprehends the reason. Give him an order that looks utterly unreasonable,—and this is sometimes necessary,—or give him one which looks trifling, under which head all sanitary precautions are yet to apt to rank, and you may, perhaps, find that you still have a free and independent citizen to deal with, not a soldier. *Implicit* obedience must be admitted still to be a rare quality in our army; nor can we wonder at it.

In many cases there is really no more difference between officers and men, in education or in breeding, than if the one class were chosen by lot from the other; all are from the same neighborhood, all will return to the same civil pursuits side by side; every officer knows that in a little while each soldier will again become his client or his customer, his constituent or his rival. Shall he risk offending him for life in order to carry out some hobby of stricter discipline? If this difficulty exist in the case of commissioned officers, it is still more the case with the non-commissioned, those essential intermediate links in the chain of authority. Hence the discipline of our soldiers has been generally that of a town-meeting or of an engine-company, rather than that of an army; and it shows the extraordinary quality of the individual men, that so much has been accomplished with such a formidable defect in the organization. Even granting that there has been a great and constant improvement, the evil is still vast enough. And every young man trained at West Point enters the service with at least this advantage, that he has been brought up to command, and has not that task to learn.

He has this further advantage, that he is brought up with some respect for the army-organization as it is, with its existing rules, methods, and proprieties, and is not, like the newly commissioned civilian, desposed in his secret soul to set aside all its proprieties as mere "pipe-clay," its methods as "old-fogyism," and its rules as "red-tape." How many good volunteer officers will admit, if they speak candidly, that on entering the service they half believed the "Army Regulations" to be a mass of old-time rubbish, which they would gladly reëdit, under contract, with immense improvements, in a month or two,—and that they finally left the service with the conviction that the same book was a mine of wisdom, as yet but half explored!

Certainly, when one thinks for what a handful of an army our present military system was devised, and with what an admirable elasticity it has borne this sudden and stupendous expansion, it must be admitted to have most admirably stood the test. Of course, there has been much amendment and alteration needed, nor is the work done yet; but it has mainly touched the details, not the general principles. The system is wonderfully complete for its own ends, and the more one studies it the less one sneers. Many a form which at first seems to the volunteer officer merely cumbrous and trivial he learns to prize at last as almost essential to good discipline; he seldom attempts a short cut without finding it the longest way, and rarely enters on that heroic measure of cutting red-tape without finding at last that he has entangled his own fingers in the process.

More thorough training tells in another way. It is hard to appreciate, without the actual experience, how much of military life is a matter of mere detail. The maiden at home fancies her lover charging at the head of his company, when in reality he is at that precise moment endeavoring to convince his company-cooks that salt-junk needs five hours' boiling, or is anxiously deciding which pair of worn-out trousers shall be ejected from a drummer-boy's knapsack. Courage is, no doubt, a good quality in a soldier, and luckily not often wanting; but, in the long run, courage depends largely on the haversack. Men are naturally brave, and when the crisis comes, almost all men will fight well, if well commanded. As Sir Philip Sidney said, an army of stags led by a lion is more formidable than an army of lions led by a stag. Courage is cheap; the main duty of an officer is to take good care of his men, so that every one of them shall be ready, at a moment's notice, for any reasonable demand.

A soldier's life usually implies weeks and months of waiting, and then one glorious hour; and if the interval of leisure has been wasted, there is nothing but a wasted heroism at the end, and perhaps not even that. The penalty for misused weeks, the reward for laborious months, may be determined within ten minutes.

Without discipline an army is a mob, and the larger the worse; without rations the men are empty uniforms; without ammunition they might as well have no guns; without shoes they might almost as well have no legs. And it is in the practical appreciation of all these matters that the superiority of the regular officer is apt to be shown. . . .

Military glory may depend on a thousand things,—the accident of local position, the jealousy of a rival, the whim of a superior. But the merit of having done one's whole duty to the men whose lives are in one's keeping, and to the nation whose life is staked with theirs,—of having held one's command in such a state, that, if at any given moment it was not performing the most brilliant achievement, it might have been,—this is the substantial triumph which every faithful officer has always within reach.

Now will any one but a newspaper flatterer venture to say that this is the habitual standard in our volunteer service? Take as a test the manner in which official inspections are usually regarded by a regimental commander. These occasions are to him what examinations by the School Committee are to a public-school teacher. He may either deprecate and dodge them, or he may manfully welcome them as the very best means of improvement for all under his care. Which is the more common view? What sight more pitiable than to behold an officer begging off from inspection because he has just come in from picket, or is just going out on picket, or has just removed camp, or was a day too late with his last requisition for cartridges?

No doubt it is a trying ordeal to have some young regular-army lieutenant ride up to your tent at an hour's notice, and leisurely devote a day to probing every weak spot in your command,—to stand by while he smells at every camp-kettle, detects every delinquent gun-sling, ferrets out old shoes from behind the mess-bunks, spies out every tent-pole not labelled with the sergeant's name, asks to see the cash-balance of each company-fund, and perplexes your best captain on forming from two ranks into one by the left flank. Yet it is just such unpleasant processes as these which are the salvation of an army; these petty mortifications are the fulcrum by which you can lift your whole regiment to a first-class rank, if you have only the sense to use them. So long as no inspecting officer needs twice to remind you of the same thing, you have no need to blush. But though you be the bravest of the brave, though you know a thousand things of which he is utterly ignorant, yet so long as he can tell you one thing which you ought to know, he is master of the situation. He may be the most conceited little popinjay who ever strutted in uniform; no matter; it is more for your interest to learn than for his to teach. Let our volunteer officers, as a body, once resolve to act on this principle, and we shall have such an army as the world never saw. But nothing costs the nation a price so fearful, in money or in men, as the false pride which shrinks from these necessary surgical operations, or regards the surgeon as a foe. . . .

In those unfortunate early days, when it seemed to most of our Governors to make little difference whom they commissioned, since all were alike untried, and of two evils it was natural to choose that which would produce the more agreeable consequences at the next election-time,—in those days of darkness many very poor officers saw the light. Many of these have since been happily discharged or judiciously shelved. The trouble is, that those who remain are among the senior officers in our volunteer army, in their respective grades. They command posts, brigades, divisions. They preside at court-martials. Beneath the shadow of their notorious incompetency all minor evils may lurk undetected. To crown all, they are, in many cases, sincere and well-meaning men, utterly obtuse as to their own deficiencies, and manifesting (to employ a witticism coeval with themselves) all the Christian virtues except that of resignation.

The present writer has beheld the spectacle of an officer of high rank, previously eminent in civil life, who could only vindicate himself before a court-martial from the ruinous charge of false muster by summoning a staff-officer to prove that it was his custom to sign all military papers without looking at them. He has seen a lieutenant tried for neglect of duty in allowing a soldier under his command, at an important picket-post, to be found by the field-officer of the day with two inches of sand in the bottom of his gun,—and pleading, in mitigation of sentence, that it had never been the practice in his regiment to make any inspection of men detailed for such duty. That such instances of negligence should be tolerated for six months in any regiment of regulars is a thing almost inconceivable, and yet in these cases the regiments and the officers had been nearly three years in service. . . .

The glaring defect of most of our volunteer regiments, from the beginning to this day, has lain in slovenliness and remissness as to every department of military duty, except the actual fighting and dying. When it comes to that ultimate test, our men usually endure it so magnificently that one is tempted to overlook all deficiencies on intermediate points. But they must not be overlooked, because they create a fearful discount on the usefulness of our troops, when tried by the standard of regular armies. I do not now refer to the niceties of dress-parade or the courtesies of salutation: it has long since been tacitly admitted that a white American soldier will not present arms to any number of rows of buttons, if he can by any ingenuity evade it; and to shoulder arms on passing an officer is something to which only Ethiopia or the regular army can attain. Grant, if you please, (though I do not grant,) that these are merely points of foolish punctilio. But there are many things which are more than punctilio, though they may be less than fighting.

The efficiency of a body of troops depends, after all, not so much on its bravery as on the condition of its sick-list. A regiment which does picket-duty faithfully will often avoid the need of duties more terrible. Yet I have ridden by night along a chain of ten sentinels, every one of whom should have taken my life rather than permit me to give the countersign without dismounting, and have been required to dismount by only four, while two did not ask me for the countersign at all, and two others were asleep. I have ridden through a regimental camp whose utterly filthy condition seemed enough to send malaria through a whole military department, and have been asked by the colonel, almost with tears in his eyes, to explain to him why his men were dying at the rate of one a day. The latter was a regiment nearly a year old, and the former one of almost two years' service, and just from the old Army of the Potomac.

The fault was, of course, in the officers. The officer makes the command, as surely as, in educational matters, the teacher makes the school. There is not a regiment in the army so good that it could not be utterly spoiled in three months by a poor commander, nor so poor that it could not be altogether transformed in six by a good one. The difference in material is nothing,— white or black, German or Irish; so potent is military machinery that an officer who knows his business can make good soldiers out of almost anything, give him but a fair chance. The difference between the present Army of the Potomac and any previous one,—the reason why we do not daily hear, as in the early campaigns, of irresistible surprises, overwhelming numbers, and masked batteries,—the reason why the present movements are a tide and not a wave,—is not that the men are veterans, but that the officers are. There is an immense amount of perfectly raw material in General Grant's force, besides the colored regiments, which in that army are all raw, but in which the Copperhead critics have such faith they would gladly select them for dangers fit for Napoleon's Old Guard. But the newest recruit soon grows steady with a steady corporal at his elbow, a well-trained sergeant behind him, and a captain or a colonel whose voice means something to give commands.

—HIGGINSON, "Regular and Volunteer Officers"

2. THE NEW YORK SEVENTY-NINTH MUTINIES

Mutiny was in fact very rare; when it occurred, as it did with the 79th New York and a few other regiments, it attracted a great deal of attention. The trouble here seems to have been twofold: misunderstanding about the term of enlistment, and incompetent officers. There was a good deal of drunkenness in the regiment, and over a hundred desertions. When the regiment was ordered to Virginia it refused to march. Firm action on the part of

Colonel Andrew Porter and General Isaac Stevens restored order, and eventually the regiment earned back its colors and its good name, and at Chantilly, as we have seen, it fought gallantly.

Captain William Lusk, who tells the story, was a Yale graduate who returned from medical studies abroad to enlist in this Highland Regiment, was commended for gallantry in action, and helped put down the draft riots in New York. After the war he became one of the nation's leading obstetricians.

Maryland, Camp Causten, Aug. 17th, 1861

My dear Mother:

This has been a busy and painful week for the officers of the Highland Regiment. You have seen various accounts of our troubles in the papers, but they contain nothing authentic, although perhaps about as much as an outsider can understand. The mutiny of Thursday is only the legacy of a quarrel begun among the officers before the Regiment left for the seat of war. The quarrel ended after the battle of Bull Run, in the resignation of several of the officers whose ambition was disappointed as to governing the affairs of the Regiment. . . . Since the battle, owing to the loss through resignations or deaths, of our Colonel, Major and 9 of the 10 Captains, besides that of many of the Lieutenants, we were left in a condition peculiarly unfavorable to discipline; and this much is to be said that the companies of Captain Ellis (my own) and that of Captain Elliot, which were provided with officers, obeyed their orders, and refused to join the mutineers.

The mutiny commenced in the morning by the men's refusing to strike their tents as commanded. They were to have been struck at 5 A.M. and the Regiment was to move at 6 o'clock. Col. Stevens repeated the orders, but they were still silently and sullenly neglected. He then went among the men and used all his powers of persuasion, but they had been told that they had the law on their side, and if they only persevered, they would be able to return home as a militia regiment. Col. Stevens next sent to each company singly and read the articles of war, appending to them such remarks as would enforce in the men the danger of their course; but by this time, the camp, left without sentry, became exposed to the whiskey dealers who made good use of their opportunities.

Soon a scene of the wildest confusion took place. The soldiers, throwing off all authority, presented the hideous and disgusting spectacle of a debauched and drunken Helotry. It was a time trying to one's nerves—more trying far than the musketry or cannonading of Bull Run. The Colonel ordered the officers to strike the tents themselves. This we did amid the jeers, the taunts, and the insults of an infuriated mob. One man brought me his gun, cocked it, showed me it was capped, and reminded me it was intended for one officer at least to die, should our release be attempted. Still we worked quietly on, obeying our orders. Some of the Lieutenants were allowed to take down the tents undisturbed, but on leaving them a moment, they were again pitched by the men. Everywhere we were threatened, and it became equally necessary to show neither fear of the men, nor, on the other hand, to allow ourselves any act of violence which would precipitate bloodshed.

Luckily for us, when the men were most maddened by drink, an old country quarrel broke out among them, viz:—the feud between the Orangemen and the Ribandmen, which we only know of through English novels, and history. We were not, however, altogether forgotten. Names neither poetical, decent, or complimentary were bestowed upon us.

Finally afternoon advanced, and nothing was gained. The Colonel called on the men for the last time to render obedience. Soberness and reflection had begun their work upon a few. These fell into their places, and were stationed around the Camp as a guard over the others. Still, though thus yielding, their sympathies were either extended to their mutinous comrades, or else they were too fearful to render much assistance. It was necessary for the officers to be everywhere, and I confess I was quite exhausted when a body of cavalry and a line of infantry appeared, coming toward us. This was a great relief. The mutineers, all unconscious, were surrounded, and, when it was too late to resist, obeyed the orders issued, a death penalty being promised to those who wavered. You have seen in the papers the punishment awarded to the Regiment—the taking of our colors and the disgrace from which we are suffering.

Dear Mother, I feel heartsick and much depressed. I begin to repent bitterly of having cast my lot with a foreign Regiment. Our men have not the feelings of Americans, and cannot, when a reverse comes, be inspired to renewed efforts by enthusiasm for the cause. I am eager for another battle in order that we may have an opportunity to regain our colors, yet dread to risk it now that our men are much demoralized. I wish old Connecticut had a place for me.

Goodbye, dear mother.
Love to sisters and all.
Affec'y.,
W. T. Lusk.
—*War Letters of William Thompson Lusk*

3. "IT DOES NOT SUIT OUR FELLOWS TO BE COMMANDED MUCH"

The major difficulty in discipline was with the officers. Captains and lieutenants were customarily elected by the men; as this letter tells, they could be dismissed by the men, too.

Charles Johnson was a Swedish-born boy who enlisted in the Hawkins Zouaves—a New York regiment—and fought through the Peninsular, the Roanoke, and the Antietam campaigns. This letter was written from Fort Clark, near Hampton, Virginia.

Monday, October 28th [1861]
Our Company seems to be not only unfortunate in the choice of officers, but in the officers chosen for us as well. Captain Coppault, certainly a splendid drillmaster and with every outward appearance of a soldier, turns out a failure in the field, and has resigned. Lieutenant Russell is not much better, and perhaps ought to resign. Flemming is the best of men, but too good a

fellow for a disciplinarian, and our First Sergeant is so ridiculously boyish that all his discipline loses its effect. Second Sergeant Peret, the slave of a clique which runs the Company, dares not say his soul is his own, and not an intelligent officer in our tribe, except it be Corporal Davis of the Color Guard, and he, being an artist who cares nothing for this military business except for the subjects it furnishes his pencil, is neither appreciated nor understood. And now we are to have one Barnard for our Captain. This man, for shooting a subordinate in the First New York Volunteers, had to fly for his life, but instead of resigning, he was transferred to this Regiment. Colonel Hawkins refused to recognize him, however, and he is, in consequence thereof, under arrest. Lieutenant-Colonel Betts has assigned Barnard to our Company to fill the vacancy caused by the resignation of Captain Coppault.

It does not suit the temper of our fellows to be commanded much, anyway; and for one of our own Regiment even, unless he carried a pretty strong hand, it might be an unpleasant task to take hold of Company I, and that being the case, the feeling of the Company as a whole can easily be imagined. The idea of being controlled by a man for whom most of us felt an abhorrence, seemed entirely intolerable. This feeling, sharpened by the notion that we would be submitting to another indignity put upon us, assisted by the contemptuous opinion we held of Barnard as to his bravery, combined to give the Captain a reception such as perhaps no other officer had ever before had from his subordinates. A variety of insults were heaped upon him openly, the moment he entered our quarters, and last Thursday, when he came out to take command, the Company refused to a man to obey his orders. And this, too, after he had made a speech to the effect that the insulting remarks he had heard must be stopped, and that he would shoot another man under the same circumstances, etc.; but all in vain—our boys insisted that they did not know him and would not obey, and he was obliged to retire, leaving the command to Lieutenant Russell.

During that day he was burned in effigy, a caricature was made on his tent, and a variety of greater indignities suggested, should he ever attempt to take command. On Dress Parade, a general order was read assigning him to our Company with every circumstance of name and rank, which only served to exasperate our men the more. Russell did all he could in a few remarks, laying down the law, but his little speech was instantly followed by three cheers for Russell and three groans for Barnard, and that night the Company's quarters seemed a perfect bedlam, so that the poor man dared not step out of his tent. This was the last of Captain Barnard. In the morning, the Major sent in a request that the Company cease their demonstrations, as Captain Barnard had already sent in his resignation.

—Johnson, *The Long Roll*

4. GRIPING IN THE UNION ARMY

Griping is a prerogative of all soldiers; it was probably indulged in more wholeheartedly during the Civil War than in any other American war, and with more justification. What we have constantly to keep in mind is that the nation was wholly unprepared for war, approached it with reluctance and timidity, and looked to its early conclusion.

Nothing is more revealing of this situation than the reluctance with which Lincoln prepared to create an army. With a Regular Army of less than 16,000—many officers and soldiers had gone over to the Confederacy—Lincoln relied on the states to furnish such troops as might be necessary to put down the rebellion. Not until mid-April 1861 did Lincoln call for 75,000 militia—to serve for three months! This, to be sure, was in accordance with the Acts of 1795 and 1803, and as Congress was not in session there appeared to be no authority for raising a volunteer army. There was a rush to the colors—that is to state regiments. Most of those who enlisted expected that they would be permitted to return in three months. After Bull Run it became clear that the war would be a long one, and the Secretary of War called on the state governors to extend the three-months service to three years or the duration of the war. For the most part the volunteers fell in with this arrangement, but in many regiments there was sharp discontent—discontent aggravated by the breakdown of supplies, incompetent officers, delays in pay, and other untoward considerations.

Samuel Partridge here describes some of the causes for discontent in the 13th New York Volunteers, a regiment recruited from around Elmira, New York.

Fort Bennet Virginia, Tuesday Aug. 14, 1861

My dear Mac,

A tent with a wet bottom—and one which sways from side to side and whose skirts flap like sails taken aback with every gust is by no means the most comfortable apartment in which to write. A wet backside and a candle flickering with every gust which soughs through my princely abode are no very great aids. A heavy overcoat does not assist materially in chirographic movements—and two or three hundred bitterly disappointed men— by a continual volley of double distilled profanity which completely silences the storm, and fairly dissipates the heavy fog do not assist to any great degree one's facility of composition or clearness of expression or the beauty of one's style. Amid all these drawbacks I am about to give you a statement of the present condition of the regiment—and to set at rest the conflicting rumors and newspaper reports which I know have reached you ere this does.

What I now write will be but introductory to and explanatory of what I shall probably write tomorrow. Tomorrow, the 14th, completes the three months for which the 13th Regiment of New York Volunteers were sworn into the United States service, and the time at which they fully expected to be mustered out.

First—concerning the promises made them. The mustering officer at Elmira told many of them that they would not be held beyond the time, but would have an opportunity to re-enlist if they chose. Rifles were promised them by the state; the state tried hard to break its word, but by the herculean efforts of our Noble Colonel—the arms were furnished us on the eve of an action.

The state promised us camp and garrison equipage—medical stores and uniforms. The former are now and ever have been very incomplete and uncomfortable. The medical and commissary departments have been with difficulty kept supplied—though much honor is due to the Regimental officers in charge of those departments. Our uniforms were of shoddy—of different shades and of Anakite size—and are now so completely worn out that no two men are dressed alike—and when the Regiment is in line it looks like un-uniformed militia on training day, or rather like a mob or rabble—dozens of men appear in shirts and drawers, many have no shoes or stockings, the pants of those so fortunate as to have any are worn to tatters so as to excuse their nakedness—and some, the seats of whose baggy breeches are gone, have gathered the tattered edges together and bound them with a few straws into a rope as you would fasten the mouth of a bag.

Many of us are gentlemen and this style of dress goes hard with them—but having only been paid as yet to the First of June they have not the means to clothe themselves.

After the dreadful affair of July 21—came a severe rain in which most of the men were obliged to sleep uncovered by the roadside, numbers thereby incurring incurable diseases—many became ruptured on the battle field where the hardest work was entrusted to the 13th Volunteers—Gentleman soldiers instead of the rough regulars.

We were promised a discharge—Gen. Sherman refused to grant applications for furloughs or leaves of absence, saying "You will all *probably* go home in a few days." or—"I am *almost positive though not quite certain* that your regiment will be discharged"—his "uncertainty" leaving him a hole to creep out of.

General McClellan told us verbally—"You shall go home in a few days." These things raised the expectations of the men to the highest pitch—but Secretary Seward dashed the cup of joy from our lips on Sunday afternoon by telling us that we *must* remain two years in accordance with a requisition on Gov. Morgan and a subsequent turning over.

Lieut. Col. [Carl] Stephan and Major [Oliver L.] Terry yesterday called on the Secretary of War—to ascertain the facts. We are to be held because other regiments in the same circumstances would press their own claims based on ours as a precedent, if we were permitted to leave. They make us fair promises—they will arm and equip us as well as any regiment in the service—will allow us to remove to a more salubrious climate. We can choose our own place—

The 13th have been victimized for three months by fair promises—and can not and will not put any more faith in them—nor can I blame them for feeling doubts.

Again I cannot blame them for wishing a discharge—cut up in battle—broken up in health and greatly reduced in numbers—a small regiment at first too—and a valiant one under the deadly fire of the enemy—and not now worth one single dime. You have heard greatly exaggerated reports of their condition heretofore—but now no report can be too bad to be true. We have no discipline whatever. Though the oldest volunteer regiment now in Virginia we are the most demoralized most deplorably so—and if thus impressed into service never will be of any use whatever. I am not writing this in a spirit of discontent. I am satisfied and happy to remain and shall be so if discipline can be maintained. Otherwise you can imagine that I shall [be] somewhat unhappily situated in a body of dissatisfied discontented and mutinous men.

—McKELVEY, ed., "Civil War Letters of Samuel S. Partridge"

5. A CAMP OF SKULKERS AT CEDAR MOUNTAIN

There were various kinds and degrees of desertion: failure to report for the draft, bounty jumping, outright desertion, and skulking and straggling to avoid battle.

George Alfred Townsend, whom we have met once before, here describes a camp of skulkers hiding in the woods during the Battle of Cedar Mountain—or, as it is sometimes called, Slaughter Mountain—of August 9, 1862. This was one of the minor engagements preceding the Second Manassas campaign; partly because Banks and McDowell were unable to bring up their full forces, it was a victory for Jackson.

BEYOND this the way was comparatively clear; but as I knew that other guards held the road further on, I passed to the right, and with the hope of finding a rill of water, went across some grass fields, keeping toward the low places. The fields were very still, and I heard only the subdued noises wafted from the road; but suddenly I found myself surrounded by men. They were lying in groups in the tall grass, and started up suddenly, like the clansmen of Roderick Dhu. At first I thought myself a prisoner, and these some cunning Confederates, who had lain in wait. But, to my surprise, they were Federal uniforms, and were simply skulkers from various regiments, who had been hiding here during the hours of battle. Some of these miserable wretches asked me the particulars of the fight, and when told of the defeat, muttered that they were not to be hood-winked and slaughtered.

"I was sick, anyway," said one fellow, "and felt like droppin' on the road."

"I didn't trust my colonel," said another; "he ain't no soldier."

"I'm tired of the war, anyhow," said a third, "and my time's up soon; so I shan't have my head blown off."

As I progressed, dozens of these men appeared; the fields were strewn with them; a true man would rather have been lying with the dead on the field of carnage, than here, among the craven and base. I came to a spring at last, and the stragglers surrounded it in levies. One of them gave me a cup to dip some of the crystal, and a prayerful feeling came over me as the cooling draught fell over my dry palate and parched throat. Regaining the road, I encountered reinforcements coming rapidly out of Culpepper, and among them was the 9th New York. My friend, Lieutenant Draper, recognized me, and called out that he should see me on the morrow, if he was not killed meantime. Culpepper was filling with fugitives when I passed up the main street, and they were sprinkled along the sidewalks, gossiping with each other. The wounded were being carried into some of the dwellings, and when I reached the Virginia Hotel, many of them lay upon the porch. I placed my blanket on a clean place, threw myself down exhaustedly, and dropped to sleep directly.

—TOWNSEND, *Campaigns of a Non-Combatant*

6. "THE ARMY IS BECOMING AWFULLY DEPRAVED"

Away from home, in the enemy's country, and without any inbred sense of discipline or firm officers, many of the soldiers were, indeed, "awfully depraved." Depravity ran the gamut from drunkenness and profanity to theft, pillaging, and murder.

Charles Wills, whose moral sense was deeply affronted by what he saw, was an Illinois boy of twenty-one when he enlisted as a private in the 8th Illinois Infantry. Before the end of the war he had been promoted to lieutenant colonel. He fought in Missouri, Tennessee, and Alabama, and was with Sherman in the March to the Sea. His letters are filled with accounts of immorality and pillaging in the army.

Provost Marshal's Office, Waterford, Miss., December 12, '62

From captain of the provost guard I have been changed to provost marshal. I had charge of two companies, doing the guard duty for the provost of our division until yesterday; the division was ordered forward to Oxford, except our regiment, which was left to guard the railroad between this point and the Tallahatchie river. Headquarters being here, Colonel Dickerman appointed me provost and sent my company to guard a bridge one and one-half miles south of this place. My business is to attend to all prisoners, deal with citizens (administer oaths, take paroles, etc.), give all passes for citizens and soldiers leaving, have charge of all soldiers straggling from their regiments, issue permits to sutlers, etc., and overlook the cotton trade. Altogether, quite enough for any one man to attend to.

The little advantage of having a comfortable house to live in, etc., is worth something; but I kind o' feel as if I would rather be with my company. Another regiment came in to-night, 12th Indiana, and we may possibly be relieved to-morrow. Shall be glad if we can only get with our division again. General Lanman has again taken command of our division, and although we know nothing against McKean, yet we know so much good of Lanman, that we're much pleased. Eight of our companies are guarding bridges, so we only have two here. Confound this railroad guarding; I'm down on it. 'Tis more dangerous than regular soldiering, harder work, and no shadow of a chance for glory. There's a smart chance of fun in my present business, particularly in the citizens branch thereof.

It would have furnished you with amusement enough for a month, could you have heard an old lady talk who visited me to-day. She was a F. F. and blooded, O Lord! We let all come within the lines; but before they can pass out, an oath or parole is required of them. How they squirm! Rebels, though they are, 'tis shocking and enough to make one's blood boil to see the manner in which some of our folks have treated them. Trunks have been knocked to pieces with muskets when the women stood by, offering the keys, bureau drawers drawn out, the contents turned on the floor, and the drawer thrown through the window, bed clothing and ladies' clothing carried off and all manner of deviltry imaginable perpetrated. Of course the scoundrels who do this kind of work would be severely punished if caught, but the latter is almost impossible. Most of the mischief is done by the advance of the army, though, God knows, the infantry is bad enough. The d—d thieves even steal from the Negroes (which is lower business than I ever thought it possible for a white man to be guilty of) and many of them are learning to hate the Yankees as much as our "Southern Brethern" do.

The army is becoming awfully depraved. How the civilized home folks will ever be able to live with them after the war, is, I think, something of a question. If we don't degenerate into a nation of thieves, 'twill not be for lack of the example set by a fair sized portion of our army. Do you remember that I used to write that a man would no sooner lose his morality in the army than at home? I now respectfully beg to recall the remark.

Scottsboro, Ala., January 5, 1864

It's all over now, the mounting part has "played" and that string will not probably be harped on again for this brigade to dance to. I think that today, Sherman, Logan or Ewing would not trust a detachment of this brigade on sorebacked mules if they had only three legs. This little squad of 500 men in the two months they have been mounted have committed more devilment than two divisions of regular cavalry could in five years. Everything you can think of, from shooting Negroes, or marrying these simple country women, down to stealing babies' diapers. From taking $2,700.00 in gold, to snatching a brass ring off the finger of the woman who handed a drink of water. From taking the last "old mar'" the widow had to carry her grist to mill, to robbing the bed of its cord, for halters, and taking the clothes line and bedclothing "to boot." I'll venture that before we were dismounted, not a wellrope, tracechain, or piece of cord of any kind strong enough to hold a horse could be found in the districts through which we have foraged.

I want you to understand that my command is not responsible for the heavy devilment. I have steadily discountenanced it, and watched my men carefully. I am willing to be responsible for all they did, and will probably have a chance, as I understand a board of inquiry sits on the subject shortly. Some of the officers will, I think, have cause to wish they were never mounted; and to think that "Mission Ridge" would have been preferable to the duty they have been on.

—WILLS, *Army Life of an Illinois Soldier*

7. ROBERT GOULD SHAW COMPLAINS THAT WAR IS A DIRTY BUSINESS

Robert Gould Shaw, member of a prominent Massachusetts merchant family, was a lieutenant in the 2nd Massachusetts Volunteers when the famous 54th Massachusetts colored regiment was formed; he volunteered for service and was appointed colonel. His regiment saw duty off the coast of Florida and Georgia and then in the heroic attack on Battery Wagner, where Shaw lost his life. Although only a minor figure in the war he has had raised to him two noble memorials—St. Gaudens' great Shaw Memorial overlooking Boston Common, and William Vaughn Moody's "Ode in Time of Hesitation."

St. Simon's Island [Georgia], June 9th, 1863

We arrived at the southern point of this island at six this morning. I went ashore to report to Colonel Montgomery, and was ordered to proceed with my regiment to a place called Pike's Bluff, on the inner coast of the island, and encamp. We came up here in another steamer, the *Sentinel*, as the *De Molay* is too large for the inner waters, and took possession of a plantation formerly owned by Mr. Gould. . . .

On Wednesday, a steamboat appeared off our wharf, and Colonel Montgomery hailed me from the deck with, "How soon can you get ready to start on an expedition?"

I said, "In a half an hour," and it was not long before we were on board, with eight companies, leaving two for camp-guard.

We steamed down by his camp, where two other steamers, with five companies from his regiment, with two sections of Rhode Island artillery, joined us. A little below there we ran aground and had to wait until midnight for flood-tide, when we got away once more.

At 8 A.M. we were at the mouth of the Altamaha river, and immediately made for Darien. We wound in and out through the creeks, twisting and turning continually, often heading in directly the opposite direction from that which we intended to, and often running aground, thereby losing much time. Besides our three vessels, we were followed by the gunboat *Paul Jones*.

On the way up, [Colonel] Montgomery threw several shells among the plantations, in what seemed to me a very brutal way, for he didn't know how many women and children there might be.

About noon, we came in sight of Darien, a beautiful little town. Our artillery peppered it a little, as we came up, and then our three boats made fast to the wharves, and we landed the troops. The town was deserted, with exception of two white women and two Negroes.

Montgomery ordered all the furniture and movable property to be taken on board the boats. This occupied some time; and, after the town was pretty thoroughly disembowelled, he said to me, "I shall burn this town." He speaks always in a very low tone, and has quite a sweet smile when addressing you. I told him "I did not want the responsibility of it;" and he was only too happy to take it all on his shoulders. So the pretty little place was burnt to the ground, and not a shed remained standing—Montgomery firing the last buildings with his own hand. One of my companions assisted in it, because he ordered them out, and I had to obey. You must bear in mind, that not a shot had been fired at us from this place, and that there were evidently very few men left in it. All the inhabitants (principally women and children) had fled on our approach, and were, no doubt, watching the scene from a distance. Some of our grapeshot tore the skirt of one of the women whom I saw. Montgomery told her that her house and property should be spared; but it went down with the rest.

The reasons he gave me for destroying Darien were, that the Southerners must be made to feel that this was a real war, and that they were to be swept away by the hand of God, like the Jews of old. In theory, it may seem all right to some, but when it comes to being made the instrument of the Lord's vengeance, I myself don't like it. Then he says "We are outlawed, and, therefore, not bound by the rules of regular warfare." But that makes it none the less revolting to wreak our vengeance on the innocent and defenceless.

By the time we had finished this dirty piece of business, it was too dark to go far down the narrow river, where our boat sometimes touched both sides at once: so we lay at anchor until daylight, occasionally dropping a shell at a stray house. The *Paul Jones* fired a few guns as well as we.

I reached camp at about 2 P.M., to-day, after as abominable a job as I ever had a share in.

Remember not to breathe a word of what I have written about this raid, for I have not yet made up my mind what I ought to do. Besides my own distaste for this barbarous sort of warfare, I am not sure that it will not harm very much the reputation of black troops and of those connected with them. For myself, I have gone through the war so far without dishonor, and I do not like to degenerate into a plunderer and robber—and the same applies to every officer in my regiment. . . .

All I complain of is wanton destruction. After going through the hard campaigning and hard fighting in Virginia, this makes me very much ashamed of myself, Montgomery, from what I have seen of him, is a conscientious man, and really believes what he says, "that he is doing his duty to the best of his knowledge and ability." There are two courses only for me to pursue: to obey orders and say nothing, or to refuse to go on any more such expeditions, and be put under arrest, probably court-martialed, which is a serious thing.

—Post, ed., *Soldiers' Letters from Camp, Battle-Field and Prison*

8. THE YANKEE INVADERS PILLAGE AND BURN

With the exception of Lee's two invasions north of the Potomac, Morgan's abortive raid into Indiana, Early's thrust toward Washington, and the fight-

ing in Missouri, the war was fought entirely in the South. This meant not only the devastation and ruin that inevitably accompany the bombardment of cities, pitched battles, the encampment and marching of hostile armies, but destruction and pillaging. Pillaging is to be distinguished from organized and systematic destruction such as that carried out by Sheridan and Hunter in the Valley of Virginia and by Sherman in his March to the Sea; the first was an expression of individual lawlessness, the second systematic and authorized. From the point of view of the victims, to be sure, it made little difference whether their houses were sacked out of motives of high strategy or of wantonness: the result was the same. Pillaging was sometimes inspired by greed, sometimes by the kind of brutal destructiveness familiar to us from the Second World War, sometimes by bitterness and hatred. Some officers made sincere efforts to prevent or at least to control pillaging; others appear to have connived at it. That it was a violation of the rules of war and destructive of discipline is too obvious for emphasis.

The four excerpts which follow speak for themselves, and it will be sufficient to say a word about the circumstances and the authors.

David Cronin—who called himself "Major Eyland"—was a New York artist who returned from studies abroad to join the Union army in April 1861; he fought at Harpers Ferry, in southeastern Virginia, and in the Peninsular campaign, where he was an artist for Harper's Weekly. *It is from his account of that campaign that we have taken this appalling picture of the wanton sacking of the Governor John Page mansion and the destruction of one of the most valuable libraries in the South.*

Francis Pierce, who describes the looting of Fredericksburg—already battered by artillery—was a member of the 108th New York Volunteers.

Sarah Morgan we shall meet again; her lively description of the sacking of the Judge Thomas Gibbes Morgan house in Baton Rouge, Louisiana, is something of a classic.

General Grierson's great raid of 1863, commemorated elsewhere, was merely one of a series by that dashing cavalry officer; the intrepid Elizabeth Beach gives us an incident from one of his raids of the following year.

A. The Yankees Sack the Page House in Williamsburg

NEARLY all the residences in town, that had not been entirely deserted by their inhabitants after the battle of Williamsburg, were unmolested by our troops. The presence of even one servant would almost certainly save a dwelling from hostile visitation, and we all know how strict McClellan was in protecting private property; but those that were entirely abandoned had been more or less despoiled. This was notably the case with the ancient mansion of Governor John Page, situated on the Bowling Green, near the remains of the colonial palace of Lord Dunmore. It had been a stately, handsomely furnished relic of the pre-Revolutionary period and in its parlors Washington had executed a minuet and La Fayette had saluted a partner in the dance. It had contained a library scarcely surpassed in value by any other private library then in the United States. Page, who belonged to the Revolutionary epoch, was at one time Governor of Virginia; a personal friend of Washington; a school-mate and intimate associate of Jefferson; a true patriot and one of the ruling political spirits of his age and country. He seems to have been the confidential friend and adviser of many of the more active progenitors of the Revolution.

I was told that the occupants of the Page mansion were at dinner when the battle of Williamsburg began, and that in their haste to get away, they left the house without even a servant to take charge of the premises, and a portion of costly dining-plate remained upon the table. The invaders ransacked the house from cellar to roof; there was no one to ask McClellan to protect it. I have never looked upon a more deplorable picture of the ravages of war than when standing amid the litter of half-destroyed books, papers and documents on the floor of the Governor's library. Shattered marble busts and statuary, fragments of ornamented book-cases, heaps of old engravings, loose manuscripts, vellum bound volumes, torn files of precious colonial newspapers, bills of lading and commercial correspondence, pieces of window glass and crushed stucco, mixed with straw and mud, on every side. Hundreds of heavy-booted and spurred cavalrymen had played football with everything of value in the house.

When I took command, I placed a guard in front of the house and forbade all intrusion. Upon my first visit I picked up a bound volume of the *Virginia Gazette*, the first Virginia newspaper, containing files of 1776 and 1777; a rare old folio edition of Shakespeare's plays, and a copy of the book written by Captain John Smith, giving a general history of his explorations in Virginia, with a queer map of the territory and water ways, drawn by himself, and published in London in 1624. These relics I carried to head-quarters where they attracted the attention of my numerous visitors—principally officers from the command stationed at Fort Magruder. The files of the *Virginia Gazette* were of great interest and value. I recall a letter they contained from Boston, describing an incident at a theatre during the investment of that place. Some one entered the theatre during a performance and shouted "The Red-coats are coming" and immediately the audience arose in great consternation and left the house without ceremony. These files disappeared from my quarters and a long and close search to discover who had taken them was fruitless. The Shakespeare was given to some officer who fancied it. So was Captain Smith's very rare work. The same copy, or another of the same edition, recently sold in New York for a sum a little above a thousand dollars. I regarded these relics with less value at that time because they could not be carried about, and a soldier must be prepared to move at any moment. Indeed, they could possess but a momentary interest to those who were almost constantly in the saddle and facing death every day. Few of my visitors appreciated their true value.

—[DAVID EDWARD CRONIN], *The Evolution of a Life*

B. "The Soldiers Delight in Destroying Everything"

Fredericsburgh [was] given up to pillage and destruction. Boys came into our place *loaded* with *silver* pitchers, *silver* spoons, silver lamps and castors etc. Great 3 story brick houses furnished magnificently were broken into and their contents scattered over the floors and trampled on by the muddy feet of the soldiers. Splended alabaster vases and pieces of statuary were thrown at 6 and 700 dollar mirrors. Closets of the very finest china ware were broken into and their contents smashed onto the floor and stamped to pieces. Finest cut glass ware goblets were hurled at nice plate glass windows, beautifully embroidered window curtains torn down, rosewood pianoes piled in the street and burned or soldiers would get on top of them and dance and kick the keyboard and internal machinery all to pieces—little table ornaments kicking in every direction—wine cellars broken into and the soldiers drinking all they could and then opening the faucets and let the rest run out—boys go to a barrel of flour and take a pailful and use enough to make one batch of pancakes and then pour the rest in the street—everything turned up side down. The soldiers seemed to delight in destroying everything. Libraries worth thousands of dollars were overhauled and thrown on the floor and in the streets—Ed I can't begin to *describe* the scenes of destruction. It was so throughout the whole city and from its appearance very many wealthy families must have inhabited it.

—McKelvey, ed., "Civil War Letters of Francis Edwin Pierce"

C. The Yankees Sack Sarah Morgan's Home

August 13th, 1862.—I am in despair. Miss Jones, who has just made her escape from town, brings a most dreadful account. She, with seventy-five others, took refuge at Doctor Enders', more than a mile and a half below town, at Hall's. It was there we sent the two trunks containing Father's papers and our clothing and silver. Hearing that guerrillas had been there, the Yankees went down, shelled the house in the night, turning all those women and children out, who barely escaped with their clothing, and let the soldiers loose on it. They destroyed everything they could lay their hands on, if it could not be carried off; broke open armoires, trunks, sacked the house, and left it one scene of devastation and ruin. They even stole Miss Jones's braid! She got here with nothing but the clothes she wore.

This is a dreadful blow to me. Yesterday I thought myself beggared when I heard that our house was probably burnt, remembering all the clothing, books, furniture, etc., that it contained; but I consoled myself with the recollection of a large trunk packed in the most scientific style, containing quantities of nightgowns, skirts, chemises, dresses, cloaks—in short, our very best—which was in safety. Winter had no terrors when I thought of the nice warm clothes; I only wished I had a few of the organdy dresses I had packed up before wearing. And now? It is all gone, silver, Father's law papers, without which we are beggars, and clothing! Nothing left!

August 25th.—About twelve at night.—Sleep is impossible after all that I have heard; so, after vainly endeavoring to follow the example of the rest and sleep like a stoic, I have lighted my candle and take to this to induce drowsiness.

Just after supper, when Anna and I were sitting with Mrs. Carter in her room, I talking as usual of home and saying I would be perfectly happy if Mother would decide to remain in Baton Rouge and brave the occasional shellings, I heard a well-known voice take up some sentence of mine from a dark part of the room; and with a cry of surprise, I was hugging Miriam until she was breathless. Such a forlorn creature!—so dirty, tired, and fatigued as to be hardly recognizable. We thrust her into a chair and made her speak. She had just come with Charlie, who went after them yesterday, and had left Mother and the servants at a kind friend's on the road. I never heard such a story as she told. I was heartsick, but I laughed until Mrs. Badger grew furious with me and the Yankees and abused me for not abusing them.

She says when she entered the house she burst into tears at the desolation. It was one scene of ruin. Libraries emptied, china smashed, sideboards split open with axes, three cedar chests cut open, plundered, and set up on end; all parlor ornaments carried off; her desk lay open with all letters and notes well thumbed and scattered around, while Will's last letter to her was open on the floor, with the Yankee stamp of dirty fingers. Mother's portrait, half cut from its frame, stood on the floor. Margaret, who was present at the sacking, told how she had saved Father's. It seems that those who wrought destruction in our house were all officers. One jumped on the sofa to cut the picture down (Miriam saw the prints of his muddy feet) when Margaret cried: "For God's sake, gentlemen, let it be! I'll help you to anything here. He's dead, and the young ladies would rather see the house burn than lose it!"

"I'll blow your damned brains out," was the "gentleman's" answer as he put a pistol to her head, which a brother officer dashed away, and the picture was abandoned for finer sport. All the others were cut up in shreds.

Upstairs was the finest fun. Mother's beautiful mahogany armoire, whose single door was an extremely fine mirror, was entered by crashing through the glass, when it was emptied of every article and the shelves half split and half thrust back crooked. Letters, labeled by the boys private, were strewn over the floor; they opened every armoire and drawer, collected every rag to be found, and littered the whole house with them, until the wonder was where so many rags had been found. Father's armoire was relieved of everything, Gibbes's handsome Damascus sword with the silver scabbard included. All his clothes, George's, Hal's, Jimmy's, were appropriated. They entered my room, broke that fine mirror for sport, pulled down the rods from the bed, and with them pulverized my toilet set, taking also all Lydia's china ornaments I had packed in the washstand. The debris filled my basin and ornamented my bed. My desk was broken open. Over it were spread all my letters and private papers, a diary I kept when twelve years old, and sundry tokens of dried roses, etc., which must have been very funny, they all being labeled with the donor's name and the occasion. Fool! how I writhe when I think of all they saw; the invitations to buggy rides, concerts, "compliments of," etc.! Lilly's sewing machine had disappeared, but as Mother's was too heavy to move, they merely smashed the needles.

In the pillaging of the armoires they seized a pink flounced muslin of Miriam's, which one officer placed on the end of a bayonet and paraded round with, followed by the others who slashed it with their swords, crying: "I have stuck the damned Secesh! That's the time I cut her!" and continued their sport until the rags could no longer be pierced. One seized my bonnet, with which he decked himself, and ran in the streets. Indeed, all who found such rushed frantically around town, by way of frolicking, with the things on their heads. They say no frenzy could surpass it. Another snatched one of my calico dresses and a pair of vases that Mother had when she was married, and was about to decamp when a Mrs. Jones jerked them away and carried them to her boardinghouse, and returned them to Mother the other day. Blessed be Heaven! I have a calico dress! Our clothes were used for the vilest purposes and spread in every corner, at least those few that were not stolen.

Aunt Barker's Charles tried his best to defend the property. "Ain't you 'shamed to destroy all dis here that belongs to a poor widow lady who's got two daughters to support?" he asked of an officer who was foremost in the destruction.

"Poor? Damn them! I don't know when I have seen a house furnished like this! Look at that furniture! They poor!" was the retort, and thereupon the work went bravely on of making us poor indeed.

It would have fared badly with us had we been there. The servants say they broke into the house, crying: "Where are those damned Secesh women? We know they are hid in here, and we'll make them dance for hiding from federal officers!" And they could not be convinced that we were not there until they had searched the very garret. Wonder what they would have done? Charles caught a Captain Clark in the streets, when the work was almost over, and begged him to put an end to it. The gentleman went readily, but though the devastation was quite evident, no one was to be seen, and he was about to leave when, insisting that there was some one there, Charles drew him into my room, dived under the bed, and drew from thence a Yankee captain by one leg, followed by a lieutenant, each with a bundle of the boys' clothes which they instantly dropped, protesting they were only looking around the house. The gentleman captain carried them off to their superior.

Ours was the most shockingly-treated house in the whole town. We have the misfortune to be equally feared by both sides, because we will blackguard neither. So the Yankees selected the only house in town that sheltered three forlorn women, to wreak their vengeance on. From far and near, strangers and friends flocked in to see the ravages committed. Crowds rushed in before, crowds came in after, Miriam and Mother arrived, all apologizing for the intrusion, but saying they had heard it was a sight never before seen. So they let them examine to their hearts' content, and Miriam says the sympathy of all was extraordinary. A strange gentleman picked up a piece of Mother's mirror, which was as thick as his finger, saying: "Madame, I should like to keep this as a memento. I am about to travel through Mississippi and, having seen what a splendid piece of furniture this was and the state your house is left in, should like to show this as a specimen of Yankee vandalism." . . .

Thursday, August 28th—I am satisfied. I have seen my home again. Tuesday I was up at sunrise, and my few preparations were soon completed, and before any one was awake I walked over to Mr. Elder's, through mud and dew, to meet Charlie. Fortunate was it for me that I started so early, for I found him hastily eating his breakfast and ready to leave. He was very much opposed to my going, and for some time I was afraid he would force me to remain, but at last he consented, perhaps because I did not insist; and with wet feet and without a particle of breakfast, I at length found myself in the buggy on the road home.

Our house could not be reached by the front; so we left the buggy in the back yard, and running through the lot without stopping to examine the storeroom and servants' rooms that opened wide, I went through the alley and entered by the front door.

Fortunate was it for this record that I undertook to describe the sacking only from Miriam's account. If I had waited until now, it would never have been mentioned; for as I looked around, to attempt such a thing seemed absurd. I stood in the parlor in silent amazement, and in answer to Charlie's "Well?" I could only laugh. It was so hard to realize. As I looked for each well-known article, I could hardly believe that Abraham Lincoln's officers had really come so low down as to steal in such a wholesale manner. . . .

Bah! What is the use of describing such a scene? Many suffered along with us, though none so severely. Indeed, the Yankees cursed loudly at those who did not leave anything worth stealing. They cannot complain of us on that score. All our handsome Brussels carpets, together with Lydia's fur, were taken, too. What did they not take? In the garret, in its darkest corner, a whole gilt-edged china set of Lydia's had been overlooked; so I set to work and packed it up, while Charlie packed her furniture in a wagon to send to her father.

—SARAH DAWSON, *A Confederate Girl's Diary*

D. GRIERSON'S RAIDERS ON A RAMPAGE

New Albany Miss. July 29th 1864

Dear Father & Mother

I am seated once more to write to you all. . . . I went up to Mr. Hills in the evening to see Gen Grearson, and asked him to place a guard at my house, told him that his men were searching all over my house and tearing up every thing. Told him that they had already got all I had to eat, that I only asked protection that night, for myself and children. he said certainly he would send me a guard, and if I would treat him right he would protect me untill they left. So he sent one of his body guard, and we rested quietly that night. I treated him very kindly, made him a good pallet in the passage and we were not bothered with any other Yankees that night. They all left next morning, so I thought I had got off tolerably well.

I talked with Greaerson about half an hour. he treated me very politely, but I dont think he has much feeling. You ought to have seen how grand him and his staff looked. There were five of them, him and his adjutant sergeon and two others. They were sitting in Mrs Hills passage *dressed into fits,* with three or four bottles of champaign, and boxes of segars setting around them. They asked me a great many questions about my husband. I told them the truth, told them he had gone off to save his horse, that he had lost four horses by them. he says has he a fine horse now. I told him yes that he could not practice medicine on a sorry one, that good horses were scarce in this country now, and he had got him a good one, and went off to keep them from getting him. Oh! he says he had as well stay at home, we would not bother him nor his horse either. I told him that I knew better than that, that he had been taken once, and his horse every time. . . .

Well next morning Mr Hill got on his horse, came down here and asked Asa to go up and see Luly. They concluded they would then ride up towards Ellistown, and see what the Yankees done up there the night before. They rode up to Mr Hills hitched their horses at the gate, and went in to see the child. Asa put medicine in his pocket for her, and left his saddle bags on his horse, something he very seldom ever does. They had not been in there more than five minutes, before the Yankees came *tearing* down the lane from Langstons right up to Hills house. Mr Hill and Asa broke to run as hard as they could. Mrs. Hill screamed at them to stop they would shoot them. Mr. Hills stopped. They were so close by, but Asa put out and never looked back, untill he was out of hearing. Says he forgot he ever had the rheumatism, he went through the back yard, and horse lot. The Yankees never saw him at all. he did not pretend to go towards his horse. That would have been going right into the Yankees. They were riding round the corner before they knew they wer[e] in ten miles of them. They rode up and took the horses first thing. The one that got Asa's horse says, well I have got a fine horse, rode off saddle-bags, and all. Asa says he would not mind loosing the saddle-bags much, if they had not have had his surgical instruments in them. They cant be replaced. Mr Hill went back in the house and staid untill they left. That was not till next day. They did not bother him.

They staid here all that day, camped in the same place that night, and left next day, but they ruined us all before they left. I cant begin to tell you what they done to other people, it would take so long but will *try* and tell you how they treated us, they came here thicker than they did before if possible. *All day* working like ants, all over the house up stairs and down, in every hole and corner, searching & peeping every where, carried off every irish potatoe beet onion beans, even took time to pick pans of beans took my pillow cases to put them in took towels one new table cloth all my knives but 3 some of my dishes and every pan they could find. Took my shears Asas hatchet. Tore my house all to pieces, it would take me a week to mess it up like they did, pulled all our dirty clothes out of the closets, and examined

R. F. Zogbaum

Questioning a Prisoner

Illustrated London News

Confederate Deserter Coming into Union Lines

Illustrated London News

Punishments in the Federal Camp

them. Took all Asa's clothes they could find. Worked here all day I reckon two hundred had been up stairs looked around and came down I followed after them, untill I was nearly broke down, *scared* nearly to death for fear they would find my things that were hid for I knew that was *my all*, provision clothes bed-clothes blankets and every thing was in there, after awhile about a dozen of the infantry came in, and up stairs they went to searching all about, commenced looking under the floor I had a few things hid under their, they commenced pulling them out, pulled out medicine tobacco cards and other little things, but did not seem to want any thing but the tobacco.

After awhile one *rascal* went up in the corner and in stooping to put his hand under the floor, put it against the planks, and they slipped a little. he pulled them off, and says, by george, boys here is the place, they just ripped the planks off and in they went. One says run down and guard the door, dont let another fellow come up, we'll divide the things amongst us. I had in there, meat, flour sugar, coffee, molasses, lard & salt. All of Asas good clothes, Sarahs mine and the childrens. We all had new shoes in there that we had not worn, in a pillow case. They pulled them all out and looked at them. I stood over them and as they would pull out the shoes & clothes, I would grab them and tell them that they could not have them, but every time they came to anything of Asa's they *would* take it. Took his over coat, a pair of new blue jeans pants, three pair of summer pants all his drawers except the ones he had on, one shirt, a new silk handkerchief. So you know he is very near without clothes. They did not take any of my clothes, except pocket handkerchiefs. Sarah & me both had some new handkerchiefs, they got them all, and would have taken our dresses, if we had not fought over them so, as they pulled them out, I would take them from them, and throw them to Sarah, she would sit down on them, untill she had a large pile under her, she said she would fight over them a long time before they got them. They took two of her dresses, that were left hanging in her room, and Melia's white embroidered dress it was hanging in one of Sarahs. They were taken while we were up stairs *fighting* over the others. We dont know who took them, every room was full at once, we could not watch them all. They were old dresses of Sarahs she hid all her best onces, her pink flounce and dark striped skirt. I hate their taking Melia's, very much, because it came from where it did. I gave Sarah my purple flounce muslin in the place of the one she lost. I have not had it on in three summers. They took one of my best quilts, and three nice blankets but I stole one of them from him after he had got it. he laid it down by him to divide the provision. I slipped up behind him and got it, there was such confusion amongst them he never discovered it.

They left me nothing to eat at all. Took *every solitary* thing I had, except one jar of lard and my salt. There was not even a grain of corn on the place to make hominy after they were gone, and we had enough of every thing to last us till christmas. I hated their taking my chickens and groceries worse than any thing else. I knew we could get meat and bread as soon as they left, but the other things cannot be replaced without sending to Memphis, and we have no cotton. We were living well, but will have to live on meat &

bread after this, and we may not be able to get that all the time. They killed all of Asa's hogs for next years meat, but we happened to save our cows. They killed nearly every bodys cows & calves around here but ours. We have two good cows with young calves. They happened not to come up untill very late. We turned them in the yard and kept them there. My calves were in the orchard. They started to shoot them several times, but I ran after them and begged them not to kill them. Told them they had taken every thing I had to eat, but if they would leave the calves that we could live on milk & bread.

Mr Bond milked fifteen cows. They killed every cow and calf he had he now has no cow at all. They nearly ruined him, burned 40 bags of cotton, and killed all his stock took every thing he had in the house to eat, and *every* Negro he had, went with them. Mrs Bond has all her work to do.

They treated Mr Hill in the same manner took & killed nearly every thing he had. They had a little provision hid that they did not find. Every one of his Negroes went with them there is not a Negro on his place large nor small. Mrs Hill has all her work to do. . . .

Well I will quit writing about the Yankees. I know you are all tired of it. I have not told you half that I could tell you. I must tell you though about their finding Mr Bells money. Mrs Bell heard they were coming, and went and buried the money in the corner of a fence. Not a living soul knew where she put it, they went there and dug it up. They had 25 dollars in gold, 15 in greenback, and 100 Confederate.

I must tell you of another thing too, how bad we were scared, after the Yankees had been gone about five days, the news came here, that they had sent all the Negroes & waggons on to Memphis, and they were coming back burning every house they passed, turning the people out of doors. We heard one evening that they would be here next morning, and burn us out, heard it from several different sources. Every body went to work, bundling up their clothes, to try & save some. We tied up a bundle apiece, to carry of[f] when they set the house on fire, Asa put on his best clothes that were left, took his account books, and left. You would have laughed to seen us next morning. Sarah May Jones me and Kitsy, all had a string of clothes tied under our hoops. Mr Flournoy worked all night carrying things of[f] in the woods, they did not come back though we soon heard it was all false. . . .

You must all write to me as soon as you get this. I would have written sooner, but have not had energy enough to write a letter since the Yankees left untill now. They turned over my molasses, up stairs, spilt all over the house up stairs & down, and I did not have it scoured up in a week, so you see I did not care much for anything. I have got over that now, we are all in good spirits again. . . .

This leaves us all well, children are getting along well and growing fast. Clara's school is broken up, the teacher cant get board. All send love to you

Your affectionate daughter

E. J. BEACH

—SMITH, ed., "The Yankees in New Albany"

9. PUNISHMENTS IN THE UNION AND CONFEDERATE ARMIES

Punishments varied greatly from regiment to regiment and from army to army. Much depended on the character of the commanding officers; much, too, on the circumstances in which the offenses were committed. As might be expected, too, the attitude of the soldiers toward the punishment of their comrades varied considerably. Companies that were badly officered, or that had suffered from a poorly managed commissary, or from other forms of mistreatment and neglect, generally sympathized with the culprits. Sometimes the punishments were brutal; generally they were merely humiliating. Although flogging had been forbidden by law before the Civil War, it is evident that the practice continued in both armies.

We have already met all three of our reporters: Wilder Dwight of the 2nd Massachusetts, who was killed at Antietam; Frank Wilkeson, who went south with bounty jumpers; and the effervescent John Dooley of the 1st Virginia Infantry.

A. Maintaining Discipline in the Army of the Potomac

Pleasant Hill, Camp near Darnestown, September 4, 1861

It is afternoon. You have come to visit the camp of the Massachusetts Second. The General had at once pointed it out last evening. You then admired the regularity of its form. You now admire the neatness and order that you find within.

You go out in front and look over at the opposite hill, where the —— Regiment is in camp. The officer of the day in our camp is administering a punishment. The court-martial had sentenced a drunken and insubordinate fellow to be tied to a tree for one hour three successive days. There he *is tied.* The —— Regiment catch sight of him. At once, in a disorderly mob, they rush to the edge of their hill. They cry out 'Cut him down,' they groan and yell against us. Our guard is called out. Their officers cannot restore order, though they succeed in keeping their men within their lines. The punishment is concluded. Not a man in our lines stirs or speaks. You have contrasted the discipline of the two regiments. You have seen pictures enough, because you want to hear more of this one. Colonel Gordon, as Acting Brigadier, directs the arrest of the ringleaders of the —— Regiment, and their officer of the day. The next morning . . . Colonel —— comes to ask that the man may be tied somewhere where the regiment which he is *commanded by* cannot see him. Colonel Gordon says, No. General Banks, on being consulted by Colonel Gordon, directs him to go on. 'Discipline must be maintained,' says the General. Colonel —— then goes to General Banks, and, by what persuasion we know not, wheedles out of him a recommendation to Colonel Gordon that the punishment be inflicted with less 'publicity.' This recommendation comes just before the time for punishment. General

Banks cannot be found in season to give any explanation of his written recommendation. Colonel Gordon makes up his mind to tie the man in the same place, and in the same way, come what may. It is done without trouble. But the recommendation from headquarters has shaken our confidence.

This illustrates the difficulties under which discipline is maintained. We are the only regiment that attempts it, and even the officers among our neighbors discountenance the severity which alone insures our discipline. But *our men* are getting, every day, a better tone. They pride themselves on the obvious contrast between their regiment and the others. They submit to the rules out of which this contrast comes. But the fact that the other regiments do as they please aggravates our difficulties and endangers our success. We are beginning to long for the direct command of McClellan, who would sustain our system without fear, favor, or affection. A political education does not favor the direct disregard of consequences which belongs to military command. Yet I do not wish to complain of General Banks. I think he means well, but I fear that he lacks a little either of education or confidence to push things through.

I have been working away at the deficiencies of our commissariat. I do not hesitate to say that its condition is disgraceful. No organization, and not even accidental and disproportioned abundance, in any direction. A general short commons. This we hope to remedy. But I do not make much progress. In fact, General Banks's division is not officered in the Quartermaster and Subsistence Departments as it should be.

But enough of this. We are getting on well, and I only grumble because we might do so much better. To-day, again, the man *shall* be tied to the tree.

—Dwight, *Life and Letters of Wilder Dwight*

B. Punishments in the Army of the Potomac

The discipline throughout the Army of the Potomac during the winter of 1863-64 was necessarily severe. The ranks of the original volunteers, the men who sprang to arms at the tap of the northern war-drum had been shot to pieces. Entire platoons had disappeared. Regiments that had entered the great camps of instruction formed around Washington in 1861-62 a thousand men strong, had melted before the heat of Confederate battle-fire till they numbered three hundred, two hundred, and as low as one hundred and fifty men. During the winter of 1863-64 these regiments were being filled with bounty-jumpers, and these men had to be severely disciplined, and that entailed punishment. There was no longer the friendly feeling of cordial comradeship between the enlisted men and their officers, which was one of the distinguishing characteristics of the volunteer troops. The whole army was rapidly assuming the character and bearing of regular troops, and that means mercenaries. The lines drawn between the recruits of 1863-64 and their officers were well marked and they were rigid. The officers were resolute in their intention to make the recruits feel the difference in their rank. Breaches of army discipline were promptly and severely punished. . . .

The punishments inflicted on the enlisted men were various, and some of them were horribly brutal and needlessly severe; but they apparently served their purpose, and the times were cruel, and men had been hardened to bear the suffering of other men without wincing. One punishment much affected in the light artillery was called "tying on the spare wheel." Springing upward and rearward from the centre rail of every caisson was a fifth axle, and on it was a spare wheel. A soldier who had been insubordinate was taken to the spare wheel and forced to step upon it. His legs were drawn apart until they spanned three spokes. His arms were stretched until there were three or four spokes between his hands. Then feet and hands were firmly bound to the felloes of the wheel. If the soldier was to be punished moderately he was left, bound in an upright position on the wheel for five or six hours. If the punishment was to be severe, the ponderous wheel was given a quarter turn after the soldier had been lashed to it, which changed the position of the man being punished from an upright to a horizontal one. Then the prisoner had to exert all his strength to keep his weight from pulling heavily and cuttingly on the cords that bound his upper arm and leg to the wheel. I have frequently seen men faint while undergoing this punishment, and I have known men to endure it for hours without a murmur, but with white faces, and set jaws and blazing eyes. To cry out, to beg for mercy, to protest, ensured additional discomfort in the shape of a gag, a rough stick, being tied into the suffering man's mouth. Tying on the spare wheel was the usual punishment in the artillery service for rather serious offences; and no man wanted to be tied up but once. . . .

To be bucked and gagged? Yes, that was severe, but not dangerous. It was highly disagreeable and painful, too, if prolonged, and at all times calculated to make a man's eyes stick out of his head as lobster's eyes do. And then the appearance of a man while undergoing the punishment was highly discreditable. The soldier about to be bucked and gagged, generally a drunken or noisy soldier, was forced to sit on the ground; his knees were drawn up to his chin, then his hands were drawn forward to his shins, and there they were securely bound together. A long stick was then thrust under his knees and over his arms. A gag was then securely bound in his mouth. The soldier who was bucked and gagged could not hurt himself or any one else. He could not speak, but he could make inarticulate sounds indicative of his suffering, and he invariably made them before he was released.

Daily many men were tied up by the thumbs, and that was far from pleasant. The impudent bounty-jumper who had stood on his toes under a tree for a couple of hours to keep his weight off of his thumbs, which were tied to a limb over his head, was exceedingly apt to heed the words of his officers when next they spoke to him. The bounty-jumper lacked the moral qualities which could be appealed to in an honest endeavor to create a soldier out of a ruffian; but his capacity to suffer physically was unimpaired, and that had to be played upon.

Then there was the utterly useless and shoulder-chafing punishment of carrying a stick of cord-wood. The stick that one picked up so cheerfully, and stepped off with so briskly, and walked up and down before a sentinel with so gayly in the early morning, had an unaccountable property of growing heavier and heavier as the sun rose higher and higher. One morning at ten o'clock I dropped a stick that did not weigh more than twelve pounds at sunrise. I sat down by it and turned it over and over. It had not grown, but I was then willing to swear that it had gained one hundred and eighty pounds in weight during the time I had carried it.

—WILKESON, *Recollections of a Private Soldier*

C. Punishments in the Army of Northern Virginia

I would like to tell you how breakers of discipline are treated. All prisoners of the Regt. are consigned to the guard house and if they prove refractory are liable to be *bucked* or gagged. Some times refractory members of companies are sent to the guard house under condemnation either to be bucked or gagged or perhaps to wear a barrel-shirt.

'Bucking' is making the culprit sit in a doubled up posture, clasping his knees with his hands, and whilst his knees almost touch his chin a long stick is inserted between his arms and underneath his knee joints. 'Gagging' is more severe, and is performed by placing a bayonet in the culprit's mouth and fixing it there by tying behind the head strings or cord attached to either end of the implement of torture. Frequently however a stick is used in place of the bayonet on account of the severity of the former instrument. Should the condemned resist or become very insolent, he is shown no mercy until he evinces some marks of repentance and future subordination. Usually neither of these two punishments lasts more than from an hour to two hours.

The barrel shirt punishment is generally inflicted upon such as have been guilty of some petty or shameful misdemeanors and have been sentenced by a court martial to this ignominious and ludicrous mode of expiation. The barrel shirt is simply a flour barrel minus both head and bottom, with two holes made in the staves. The culprit is clothed with this staving garment, thrusts his arms through the holes, gets his chin over the rim, and has to walk up and down a given space under guard for as many hours during the day as are appointed by his sentence. He finds it quite embarrassing and his legs are at a loss how to proceed. I have never seen any one hung up by the thumbs, which punishment, they say, is very frequent in the Yankee army. I have seen however what may be thought a novel punishment for an offense by no means unusual. Some of the men being caught in the act of straggling from their regiments were brought back and made to march in a circle, like horses working a threshing machine, at the same time having billets of wood tied to their ankles in order to impede their progress. But this novelty I have seen but once. . . .

This evening (March 9, 1863) our Brigade is ordered out to witness a horrible sight. One of the 24th Va. Infantry being tried by court martial for cowardice at the battle of Sharpsburg is condemned to be whipped publicly and then dishonorably dismissed from the service. The brigade is to be present at this degrading punishment.

We are all drawn up in line and the poor man is tied to a pole about fifty yards in front of us. His hands are stretched above his head and his shirt stripped to the waist. The executioner then steps forward and with several heavy switches, the executioner being likewise a criminal who is to earn his release from punishment by inflicting this disgrace on his fellow man.

The word being given, the executioner began his disgusting work, the wretched man wincing and his flesh shrinking neath every blow which one after another were delivered in quick succession until 39 were rec'd. by the culprit. In truth it is a horrid sight, and the executioner was so overcome by his feelings that as soon as his work was done his eyes filled with tears and he wept—he wept! This horrible event transpired without the loss of blood to any one, and the wretched creature (or happy individual, had he truly a craven heart) pockets his dishonorable discharge and leaves for parts unknown.

—DURKIN, ed., *John Dooley, Confederate Soldier*

10. EXECUTING DESERTERS

Desertion was the bane of both Union and Confederate armies. The total number of desertions assumed almost astronomical proportions. There was a total of some 260,000 desertions from the ranks in the Union armies, of whom possibly 60,000 returned to service; in addition there were 160,000 who failed to appear when drafted and qualified technically as deserters. The figures for the Confederate Army are unsatisfactory, but desertion here probably ran to about 10 per cent.

The pattern of desertion varied North and South. A large proportion of Confederate desertions was probably absence without leave—soldiers going home to help get in the crops, or to visit their families. While there was widespread evasion of the draft, in the South, much of this was under the masquerade of legality and was connived at by state authorities. Many Confederate deserters, too, were Union sympathizers who had been pressed into Confederate service: this was particularly true in the border states. There are comparatively few examples of Union soldiers deserting to the enemy; toward the end of the war many Confederates went over to the other side. Yet notwithstanding all the temptations and opportunities to desert, Confederate desertions were proportionately slightly lower than Federal.

The penalty for desertion was death, but this penalty was rarely imposed. Statistics here, too, are unreliable, but it is probable that not one deserter in 500 paid the extreme penalty. Clearly both armies would have been better for more effective punishments here. As executions were in fact rare it is sufficient to confine ourselves to a single witness from each army describing these tragic incidents of war.

A. General Sheridan Executes Two Deserters at Chattanooga

Chattanooga, Tennessee, November 14, 1863

My dear Friend—

This town is suffering severely on account of its rebellious sentiments. Since our army came back from the Chickamauga field the town has been pretty roughly handled by the 'merciless Yankees.' Many of the finest residences, particularly those on the more commanding points have been torn down and 'Yankee forts' erected in their stead. Generally where the buildings have been torn down the owners had gone south among their friends. I think they will be somewhat disappointed when they return and find their beautiful homes among the things that were. But 'the way of the transgressor is hard,' at least it seems so in this case.

I witnessed a painful sight this afternoon—the shooting of two federal soldiers. As it may be of interest I will give you a description of it. The two men belonged to Illinois regiments: one to the 44th and the other to the 88th, both of our division, which as you know is commanded by General Sheridan. The men had been tried for desertion, found guilty and sentenced to be shot. One brigade of the division under arms, with colors flying and band playing formed about noon in nearly a hollow square with one side entirely open. Thousands of soldier spectators gathered about those who stood under arms. About one P.M. a solemn procession composed of two details of infantry, one in front of the prisoners and one in the rear, marched into the inclosure. Behind the first company and immediately in front of the prisoners their coffins were borne each upon the shoulders of four men. In the rear of the doomed men marched the second company with their rifles at the right shoulder shift and bayonets fixed. A band playing a solemn tune marched with slow and measured step in front of the little procession. General Sheridan and staff were present. All were mounted and all in full uniform. The General had a broad yellow sash over his shoulder drawn across his breast and down under his sword belt. He sat motionless upon his big black horse which stood just a little in front of the other horsemen. When the procession arrived at the open side of the square it was halted, the coffins were placed upon the ground, when the prisoners knelt and the chaplain prayed. They then arose, apparently very calm, and sat erect each upon his coffin. A bandage was then bound over the eyes of each. A platoon of soldiers with loaded rifles stood a few paces in front. There was a strange silence for a moment and then the voice of command rang out. "Ready!" "Aim!" "Fire!" And each of the prisoners fell back over his coffin, dead.

It was hard to see men thus killed by their own comrades but you have no idea how many have deserted, encouraged by friends at home to do the disgraceful act. Sad as the scene this afternoon was, it will have a wholesome effect upon the whole division.

Truly yours, W. G.
—"Civil War Letters of Washington Gardner"

B. EXECUTING DESERTERS FROM THE CONFEDERATE ARMY

Camp near Rappahannock River, Va., March 5, 1863

A man was shot near our regiment last Sunday for desertion. It was a very solemn scene. The condemned man was seated on his coffin with his hands tied across his breast. A file of twelve soldiers was brought up to within six feet of him, and at the command a volley was fired right into his breast. He was hit by but one ball, because eleven of the guns were loaded with powder only. This was done so that no man can be certain that he killed him. If he was, the thought of it might always be painful to him. I have seen men marched through the camps under guard with boards on their backs which were labeled, "I am a coward," or "I am a thief," or "I am a shirker from battle," and I saw one man tied hand and foot astride the neck of a cannon and exposed to view for sixteen hours. These severe punishments seem necessary to preserve discipline.

Camp near Orange Court House, Va., September 27, 1863

We had nine more military executions in our division yesterday—one man from Thomas' Brigade, one from Scales' and seven from Lane's. Colonel Hunt was a member of the court-martial which sentenced them, and he tells me that one of the men from Lane's Brigade was a brother of your preacher, and that the two looked very much alike. He said he was a very intelligent man, and gave as his reason for deserting that the editorials in the Raleigh "Standard" had convinced him that Jeff Davis was a tyrant and that the Confederate cause was wrong. I am surprised that the editor of that miserable little journal is allowed to go at large. It is most unfortunate that this thing of shooting men for desertion was not begun sooner. Many lives would have been saved by it, because a great many men will now have to be shot before the trouble can be stopped. . . .

I must close, as a doctor has just come for me to go with him to assist in dissecting two of the men who were shot yesterday.

—WELCH, *A Confederate Surgeon's Letters to his Wife*

11. GENERAL LEE DISCUSSES THE PROBLEM OF DISCIPLINE

Lee was as gentle as any warrior in history, but he was a professional soldier and a firm disciplinarian. From long experience in the Mexican War, on the border, and as Superintendent of the United States Military Academy, he knew that failure to enforce rules or to maintain discipline leads to demoralization and penalizes the innocent instead of the guilty.

In this letter to President Davis Lee discusses the question of amnesty for deserters and touches on one of the problems which most harassed him. It is worth remembering that when he wrote it the Army of Northern Virginia had been reduced to some 70,000 men and was facing Grant's army of almost twice that size; had the Confederate government been able to round up de-

*serters—many of them hiding behind state exemptions and writs of habeas
corpus—he might have brought his army up to a strength sufficient to defeat
Grant.*

HD QRS ARMY N. VA.
13th April 1864

His Excy JEFFERSON DAVIS,
Presdt. Confed. States,
Richmond,
MR. PRESIDENT,

. . . I am satisfied that it would be impolitic and unjust to the rest of the
army to allow previous good conduct alone to atone for an offence most
pernicious to the service, and most dangerous as an example. In this connection, I will lay before your Excellency some facts that will assist you in
forming your judgment, and at the same time, present the opinions I have
formed on the subject of punishment in the army. In reviewing Court
Martial cases, it has been my habit to give the accused the benefit of all
extenuating circumstances that could be allowed to operate in their favor
without injury to the service. In addition to those parties whose sentences I
have remitted altogether or in part, or whom, when capitally convicted, I
have recommended to pardon or commutation of punishment, I have kept a
list during the past winter of certain offenders, whose cases while they could
not be allowed to go unpunished altogether, without injury to the service,
had some extenuating features connected with them. I confirmed the sentences, and all of them have undergone a part of their punishment, but recently I remitted the remainder in the order of which I enclose a copy.

Beyond this, I do not think it prudent to go, unless some reason be presented which will enable me to be lenient without creating a bad precedent,
and encouraging others to become offenders. I have arrived at this conclusion
from experience. It is certain that a relaxation of the sternness of discipline as
a mere act of indulgence, unsupported by good reasons, is followed by an
increase in the number of offenders. The escape of one criminal encourages
others to hope for like impunity, and that encouragement can be given as
well by a repetition of a general act of amnesty or pardon, as by frequent
exercise of clemency towards individuals. If the convicted offenders alone
were concerned, there would be no objection to giving them another trial, as
we should be no worse off if they again deserted than before. But the effect
of the example is the chief thing to be considered, and that it is injurious, I
have no doubt. Many more men would be lost to the service if a pardon be
extended in a large number of cases than would be restored to it by the immediate effects of that action.

The military executions that took place to such an extent last autumn,
had a very beneficial influence, but in my judgment, many of them would
have been avoided had the infliction of punishment in such cases uniformly
followed the commission of the offence. But the failure of courts to convict
or sentence to death, the cases in which pardon or commutation of punish-

ment had been granted upon my recommendation, and the instances in which the same indulgence was extended by your Excellency upon grounds made known to you by others, had somewhat relaxed discipline in this respect, and the consequences became immediately apparent in the increased number of desertions. I think that a return to the current policy would inevitably be attended with like results. Desertion and absence without leave are nearly the only offences ever tried by our Courts. They appear to be almost the only vices in the army. Notwithstanding the executions that have recently taken place, I fear that the number of those who have escaped punishment in some one of the ways above mentioned has had a bad effect already. The returns for the month of March show 5474 men absent without leave, and 322 desertions during the month. There have been 62 desertions within the present month specially reported, but the whole number I fear considerably exceeds that some of the large number absent without leave, are probably sick men who have failed to report, and some of the deserters are probably absent without leave, but the number is sufficiently great to show the necessity of adhering to the only policy that will restrain the evil, and which I am sure will be found truly merciful in the end. Desertions and absence without leave not only weaken the army by the number of offenders not reclaimed, but by the guards that must be kept over those who are arrested. I think therefore that it would not be expedient to pardon & return to duty any of those now under sentence, or release those under charges, except for good cause shown.

I have the honour to be
With great respect
Your obt. servt.
R. E. LEE
Genl.

—FREEMAN, ed., *Lee's Confidential Dispatches*

12. AN ENGLISHMAN PRAISES THE GOOD CONDUCT OF AMERICAN SOLDIERS

After hearing so much about misconduct, it is reassuring to read the testimony of that shrewd observer, Edward Dicey, to the effect that the American soldier was better behaved than the European, as indeed he was. Dicey, whom we have met before, was a distinguished journalist and author whose Six Months in the Federal States, *a report on a visit to America in 1862, is one of the most judicious of foreign views of wartime America.*

THE least creditable incident of the war to the Federal cause was the proclamation of General Butler about the women of New Orleans, which appeared at this period. . . . There was, I admit, much force in the explanation which my Northern friends sought to give of it. It is possible, and I believe true, that General Butler *may* have only meant that the women of New Orleans, who insulted the Federal soldiers, should be imprisoned for the night in the lock-up house allotted to the disorderly women of the town. Whatever the intention may have been, there is no question that the strictest care was taken lest the order should be abused; and it is certain that the Southern ladies were grossly insulting in their behaviour to the Union soldiers, using as they did language and gestures which, in a city occupied by troops of any other nation, would have subjected them, without orders, to the coarsest retaliation.

What is more to the point also—as I can state from my own observation—the rank and file of the American army is the most orderly I have ever seen, a circumstance which is due, probably, to the fact of the privates being mostly married, and all men of some kind of education. There is less brutality about the Federal troops, and more respect for women, than amongst any soldiery we are acquainted with in the Old World.

It once happened to me, I may mention here, to have to escort a party of ladies, after dark, across the long chain-bridge of Washington. For about two-thirds of that weary mile's walk, the whole bridge was crowded with a confused mass of Federal soldiers, who were halting there on their march southwards. The men were excited at the prospect of the approaching campaign, and it was obvious many of them had drunk freely on breaking up their camp at Washington. It was so dark, that no discipline could be maintained, and the men were sitting, sleeping, or singing, as they liked best. We had almost to grope our way through the groups of soldiers scattered along the bridge. The number of gentlemen in our party was so small, we could have afforded but little protection to the ladies under our charge, in case any insult had been offered to them. Having some knowledge of what common soldiers are in other countries under similar circumstances, I own that I felt considerable trepidation as to how far we should be able to extricate ourselves from the melee without annoyance. I can only say that, during the whole of that long passage, no remark whatever was addressed to us. The moment it was seen that there were ladies in our party, the soldiers got up from the planks, on which they were lying, to make way for us; and the songs (many of them loose enough), which the men were singing, were hushed immediately at our approach.

Whether a like journey could have been performed through an European army with like results I leave it to any one acquainted with the subject to say. In truth, the almost morbid sentiment of Americans with regard to women, while it renders them ridiculously susceptible to female influence, protects women in that country from the natural consequences of their own misconduct.

—DICEY, *Six Months in the Federal States*

XV

Great Britain and the American Civil War

THE *Civil War was not fought in isolation; the greatest civil war that the Western world had known could not be a purely domestic affair. The issues that were involved, or that seemed to be involved, deeply affected European peoples and nations, and America, in turn, was affected by European attitudes and policies. Yet Britain and Europe were from the first confused about the Civil War. Was the South fighting for self-determination—or for slavery? Was the North fighting for empire—or for freedom? Official declarations of policy, North and South, did little to clarify the situation. Confusion extended even to the legal realm. Was the war in fact a war, in the legal sense? If so it was entirely proper to recognize the belligerency of the Confederacy. The official Northern position was that the struggle was not a war at all, but a domestic insurrection; yet Lincoln proclaimed a blockade, which is an instrument of war, and recognized in fact, if not in law, the belligerency of the South.*

Just as in the American Revolution the role of France was of crucial importance to those fighting for independence, so in the Civil War the role of Britain was crucial. Southerners were ever conscious of that earlier chapter in American history, and the hopes of the South were fixed, from the beginning, on Britain and on France—which would presumably follow the British lead. It was not merely that Southerners thought that they had a good cause and one that would inevitably appeal to the British who, in the words of Henry Adams, "took naturally to rebellion—when foreign." Nor was it merely that they could count on the sympathy of the British upper classes, whose general social system was far closer to that of the South than to that of the more equalitarian North. There were practical considerations as well. Politically—so it was assumed by Southerners—Britain would prefer to see the United States split into two nations, for the United States was a potential rival, and American democracy a potential threat to the British social and economic system. Economically—again so it was assumed—the British would inevitably favor the creation in America of a nation dedicated to free trade. Finally—and this was the trump card—Cotton was King. English spindles depended on Southern cotton; without it the textile mills would shut down, England would lose her markets, unemployment and political disorder would spread. In sheer self-defense Britain would have to recognize the South and break the blockade.

Breaking the blockade would, almost inevitably, mean war. With England, and doubtless France, as allies how could the Confederacy fail to win! Thus the stakes were high. But Britain, too, knew that the stakes were high. Would she allow the sympathies of her upper classes to dictate her policy? Would she be so affected by the blockade as to intervene in self-defense? Would she risk war with her American cousins—war which would ally her, willy-nilly, with a slave power?

In Britain itself the Civil War divided classes as had no other foreign conflict in her history—not even the French Revolution. On the whole, and with important exceptions, the upper classes were pro-Southern, the middle and working classes pro-Northern. The English aristocracy saw in the American conflict a chance to humiliate an upstart nation whose democratic and equalitarian practices they detested; the middle and working classes saw the struggle as one for the vindication of democracy and—after the Emancipation Proclamation—of freedom. The intellectuals were sharply divided. Some, like Acton, for example, saw the American war as a chapter in the great history of freedom, and supported the South as the champion of self-determination. Others, like Leslie Stephen and John Stuart Mill, saw it, too, as a struggle for freedom, but thought of freedom for the Negro. The most influential spokesmen for the North were, however, liberal statesmen and publicists like Cobden, Bright, and Forster, men who were convinced that the progress of democracy in Britain was intimately bound up with the triumph of the Union.

Both the Union and the Confederate governments made strenuous efforts to win English support: propaganda techniques were as skillfully developed during the Civil War as during the World Wars. Lincoln sent over such spokesmen—and spokeswomen—as Henry Ward Beecher and Harriet Beecher Stowe and the egregious Robert Walker; the Confederacy sent over a number of accredited agents, like James Mason and Pierre Rost and John Peyton, or Captain Bullock, who was to arrange for building ships, or Henry Hotze, who established and edited the Index, *a newspaper devoted to presenting the Southern cause.*

On the whole the official English policy was correct, but the expression of that policy was often discourteous. Thus, though the British position in the Trent *affair was technically correct, the manner of stating that position was arrogant, and the widespread demand for war over what was at worst a minor mistake was unpardonable. Nor were the British themselves guiltless of infractions of international law—witness the subsequent* Alabama *award. Even more deplorable, from the point of view of the future relations of the two great English-speaking peoples, was the persistent expression of sympathy for the South and hostility to the North in such great papers as the* Times *and the* Standard, *and the almost scurrilous attacks on the North in such magazines as the* Edinburgh, Blackwood's, *the* Quarterly, Punch *and the* Saturday Review. *In short the English aristocracy, the press, the Established Church, and even the universities appeared to be pro-Southern. It took a long time for Americans to forget this.*

1. HENRY RAVENEL EXPECTS FOREIGN INTERVENTION

Here is the way the recognition situation looked to a thoughtful Southern observer, and the way it looked to most Southerners.

Ravenel, the reader will recall, was a South Carolina planter who had won distinction as one of the leading American botanists.

M[onday] 8. [April 1861]—The great European powers, as far as we may judge from their leading papers, seem inclined to favour the new Confederacy.

Old prejudices against our misunderstood domestic institution of African servitude (it is the *word* "slavery" that has blinded their eyes) are giving way before the urgent calls of *Self Interest,* & we only need that they should become more intimately acquainted with it, to dissipate their mistaken notions. In addition to their requiring the produce of the Cotton States to keep their manufacturers in motion, & furnish food & employment to their operatives, new complications have arisen which are favourable to their friendly recognition of our independence. The United States have lately increased their Tariff so high on many articles of European manufacture, as to amount almost to prohibition; whilst the Confederate States have lessened theirs from the old standard, & have it in contemplation to reduce still more. The case then stands thus: We furnish what is absolutely essential to their commercial & manufacturing prosperity, & we alone—We offer them a market for their goods on better terms than heretofore. We invite their vessels to do our carrying trade, or at any rate throw open the door of competition to them, which has been hitherto open only to U. S. vessels. On the other hand the United States, now that the Cotton States have seceded, can furnish but little toward supplying their wants with cotton—They have in addition imposed such a tariff, as to cut off trade in a great measure. The U. S. are mainly a manufacturing & commercial nation, & must necessarily come into competition with them. In a word, what the U. S. have lost by our withdrawal from the Union, they have gained. They know too that we are an agricultural people, & will never compete with them in manufactures & commerce, but will always be their best customers.

These various reasons which lie on the surface, & which they already understand, must have their effect. Self Interest is the ruling power among nations, no less than among individuals.

—Childs, ed., *The Private Journal of Henry William Ravenel*

2. *BLACKWOOD'S EDINBURGH MAGAZINE* REJOICES IN THE BREAK-UP OF THE UNION

Most of the English press was implacably hostile to the North. This hostility did not always carry with it friendship to the South. Sometimes it was merely a general hostility to everything American—American republi-

canism, democracy, business, manners, and leaders. Blackwood's Edinburgh Magazine, *which contained some of the best reporting on the war, was from the beginning critical of the Federal government. As was the English practice at the time, the articles are unsigned; this one appeared in October 1861.*

OUR constitution has fulfilled its most important and most delicate office—that of bringing the best of the spirit and intellect of the nation to the service of the state. . . .

It is notorious that this end has not been fulfilled by the American constitution. Nor was it rational to expect that it should be. Statesmanship is born of the collision of great principles or of important interests. No such result can be produced where power is all on one side. When the people have everything, they need no champions. Therefore, in America, patriotism means flattery of the people; party spirit is the spirit of rapine; and debates, instead of eliciting wisdom and truth, are the ignoble squabbles of mediocrities. Where, in American history for the last forty years—that is to say, ever since the impulse of the Revolution died out—are we to look for her great statesmen? Yet in that period there is no great nation in Europe that has not produced men who have secured an enduring fame by their assertion of great principles, or by the influence they have exerted on the destinies of nations. And it is not true, as has been said, and quoted with applause, that the nation is happiest which has no history, for such happiness is stagnation or worse. The spirit that presides over the public life of America has made itself felt over the whole nation. The higher minds stand aloof from politics, as Bayard would turn from a modern prize-ring. The meed for which he had been used to contend with noble knights—the smiles of ladies, the favour of anointed kings, and immortal honour—is now a bag of coin handed to the victor in a pot-house. So the best Americans either betake themselves to other pursuits, or roam disconsolately over the world, where they see their equals winning honour in the field from which they are for ever excluded.

That men of this class should countenance the violent measures of the North is at first sight unaccountable. It is difficult to imagine that intellectual men should either be friendly to a system which extends its theory of equality to intellect, and thus neutralises their natural superiority; or should wish to establish, in its grossest form, the supremacy of a numerical majority, by the forcible subjugation of the great minority which constitutes the South. It is quite possible, however, that, while giving their voice to the North, they may neither be friendly to the Union, nor desirous of seeing the South subjugated. They may wish to see the natural aristocracy to which they belong raised to its proper position in the state. They may consider that, by quiet separation, the Union might, with increased compactness and unanimity, re-recover much of its vitality, and that the system they suffer under might be indefinitely prolonged. And they may view the present convulsion of that system as the necessary preliminary of those political changes which, it is natural to suppose, they must ardently desire. To suppose this is not to impugn their patriotism; for if we have made our views clear in this paper, it is evident that they may look on such a crisis as now exists as necessary for the regeneration of their most important institutions. They may therefore accompany the movement with the expectation of finding an opportunity to control it.

But we do not suppose that any men possessing the powers requisite for statesmanship can really believe that, if by force of arms the reluctant South should be dragged back to the Union, the Union will be thereby restored on its original basis. Successful coercion would be a greater revolution than the acknowledgment of secession—this only lops the branches, while that strikes at the root. Nor do we imagine that any such men as these are to be found in the ranks of the Abolition party. Clever people may belong to that party. Mrs Beecher Stowe is a very clever woman, and has written a very clever novel; but she is, by the success of that novel, committed to sentiments more adapted to fiction than to politics. She evidently looks on the South as a vast confederation of Legrees, keeping millions of virtuous Uncle Toms in horrible subjection; and quotes Mr Wendell Phillipps as if she believed that mischievous monomaniac to be an inspired apostle. But statesmen must ask themselves how the difficulty presented by the condition of the African race would be solved by setting them free. What is to become of the liberated slaves? and how is their labour to be replaced? are questions the very first to be asked, but which we must not expect a crazy Abolitionist to answer. But such considerations do not occur to those enthusiastic philanthropists who testify to their love of the Negro by their hatred of the planter. The destruction of armies, the ravage and ruin of territory, are as nothing, in their heated fancy, compared with the success of their plan. And if secession were accomplished their plan would be at an end, for they would then have no more concern in the liberation of the slaves of the South than in a crusade to set the Georgian and Circassian ladies free from the harems of the Bosphorus. Thus, under present circumstances, their fanaticism has become sanguinary; they are pledged to their course, and will follow it with all the desperate recklessness and tenacity with which weak minds will cling to their only chance of notoriety.

—Anonymous, "Democracy Teaching by Example"

3. YANCEY AND MANN PLEAD THE CONFEDERATE CAUSE

Even before the outbreak of hostilities the Confederate government had sent commissioners to Britain and France. Their primary task was, of course, to represent the government in the somewhat unlikely event of recognition. Failing this they were to drum up support for the Confederacy, win friends and influence people, spread propaganda, try to get supplies through the blockade, and so forth.

John Peyton, whose description of Yancey and Mann is here reproduced, was himself an agent for the state of North Carolina. Born at Montgomery Hall in Virginia, he studied law at the state university, went to France and Austria for the Fillmore administration, moved to Illinois, and then returned to Virginia. Though opposed to secession Peyton went with his state. He sailed from Charleston in October 1861, did what he could for the Confederate cause abroad, and then settled down, after the war, on the Isle of Guernsey.

Yancey was one of the foremost "hotheads" of the South. He had hoped for high office in the Confederacy—perhaps for the Presidency itself; when not even a Cabinet appointment was forthcoming he accepted a foreign mission, but gave up in 1862 and served briefly in the Confederate Congress until his death the following year.

Ambrose Mann was a seasoned diplomat who had served as special commissioner to various German states, to Kossuth's Hungary, and to Switzerland. He spent one year in England; then went to Belgium, where he somewhat pointlessly cultivated the good will of King Leopold under the illusion that that King could influence Queen Victoria and Napoleon III. In 1863-64 he was commissioner to the Vatican. Like Peyton, Mann remained abroad after the war. He died in Paris in 1889.

THE duties of my mission required me to call upon the Confederate Commissioners immediately upon my arrival in London. Two of them only were in town, Mr. Yancey and Colonel Mann. Judge Rost, the third member, was absent in Paris. They were both sanguine of the immediate recognition of the Confederate States; said it might occur at any moment. I saw at once the source of the great confidence manifested in Richmond. These gentlemen were laboriously occupied, as they had been since their arrival, six months before, in the discharge of their official duties, and believed they were now about to have their labours crowned with success. Mr. Yancey had just attended a dinner at the Fishmonger's Hall, to which he had been specially invited, through the instrumentality of Mr. Samuel Isaacs, surviving partner of the firm of S. Isaacs, Campbell, and Co., who was successfully engaged in blockade-running, and in many ways showing his sympathy with the Confederate cause.

Mr. Yancey occupied the seat of honour to the right of the Prime Warden, by whom he was requested to address the meeting, in response to the sixth regular toast. . . .

In answer to the sixth toast, which had reference to the Civil War in America, Mr. Yancey delivered a brief address, which was most favourably received by the Company and the public. . . .

Mr. Yancey availed himself of the first opportunity after my arrival, when I had but imperfectly recovered from the fatigues of the journey, to hold with me a lengthy and earnest conversation upon the line of private conversation and policy which ought to be adopted by all Confederates in Europe, public and private, official and unofficial. He said that he had discovered since arriving in England, that the real cause of a want of sympathy for the South in the beginning, was the existence among us of slavery, and that we ought to feel it our duty to make Europeans understand that the North was not fighting against slavery, but was willing to guarantee it to the South, provided the Confederate people would lay down their arms and re-enter the Union. . . .

As an orator and statesman, Mr. Yancey enjoyed an extended reputation in America, with which I was familiar, as also with the solid foundations upon which it rested, having read many, if not all of his speeches, while he was a representative in Congress from the State of Alabama, and had heard, probably, the ablest of the popular addresses he delivered during the exciting contest which resulted in the election of Lincoln to the Presidency. During the few months we passed in London, in close and intimate friendship, I conceived even a higher opinion than I had previously entertained of his great abilities. Whatever he said bore the genuine marks of creative intellect, and he argued a point with astonishing fertility of genius. He had never indulged in indolent epicureanism, but his life had been one of labour, chiefly devoted to the study and practice of the law. His mind had not, however, been narrowed by the technicalities of the profession; these studies and pursuits had only given a logical precision to his views. He possessed an extended acquaintance with business affairs, financial and commercial. He was methodical and administrative, deducing order from confusion; he used the subtle weapons of casuistry with consummate skill, and always took a comprehensive view of the whole region of political science. To his rare powers he united an umblemished integrity of character, a fervid patriotism, and a benevolence and purity of private life, which enhanced his influence, and made him a delightful companion and friend.

Though he was not admitted to official circles—these were of course reserved for the ministers of actually recognized governments—he had a considerable acquaintance among the chief personages in London society, mainly through the instrumentality of his co-commissioner Colonel Mann, and was never in any company without making a favourable impression, though his manners were plain, and his style of conversation far from the highest. It was only when he had the whole field to himself, and indulged in what might be termed a discourse, that he at all left the conviction that he was a man of ability and power. . . .

Colonel Mann was in many respects the opposite of Mr. Yancey. His early youth had not been given to laborious preparation for a profession, and his after life had not been spent in the confinement of an attorney's office. He had no professional, but a great deal of general knowledge. Bred upon a Virginian plantation, he had early acquired the fine social habits of the hospitable, but often indolent and luxurious planters. His manners and address were frank and easy. The solid parts of an education which he had obtained in his Virginian home, and among those high-bred planters, had gained a European polish. . . .

With excellent tact and knowledge, Colonel Mann had taken his apartments in the desirable quarter of Albemarle Street, within a stone's throw of Cambridge House, the town residence of Lord Palmerston, while Mr. Yancey was lodged further off, in Bury Street. In this central situation, near the Prime Minister (and on the best of terms with his private secretary, the

Hon. Mr. Evelyn), deferred to by his official associates, consulted by all Confederate agents, Colonel Mann was in a position to know everything of moment transpiring at the chief sources of British power, to labour efficiently for his cause, as also to keep the Government on the banks of the James duly informed as to their progress in reaching that desired goal, recognition, always in view, ever near at hand and never reached!

—PEYTON, *The American Crisis*

4. NORTHERNERS INVOKE ENGLISH UNDERSTANDING

The campaign for foreign understanding and sympathy was carried on by private individuals as well as by governments. Here the North doubtless had the best of it, for the intellectual and financial ties between the North and Britain were intimate.

We give here two typical letters; these might be multiplied a hundredfold. The first is from August Belmont of New York, the second from George Ticknor of Boston. Born in Germany, Belmont had early entered the banking house of Rothschild; in his early twenties he had come to New York and, as agent for the Rothschilds, established what was to be one of the great banking houses of the country. He had served as Minister to the Netherlands and made frequent trips abroad to add to his large art collection. A Democrat, Belmont was an ardent Unionist, and in 1861 helped raise and equip the first German regiment from New York City. Throughout the war he pleaded the Union cause in Britain and on the continent, by letter and in person.

Ticknor is so well known that he needs little introduction. He had long been a major figure in the intellectual life of New England and, as author of the notable History of Spanish Literature, *was known everywhere abroad. Like Belmont, and like his friend Charles Sumner, he was indefatigable in presenting the Union cause to his English and European friends.*

A. AUGUST BELMONT WARNS OF BITTER FEELING BETWEEN AMERICA AND ENGLAND

To Baron Lionel de Rothschild, M. P.

New-York, May 21, 1861

Dear Baron: The telegraphic report of Lord John Russell's declaration in Parliament, on the 6th inst., concerning Southern privateers, has created a painful surprise and disappointment throughout the whole North.

In placing them upon the footing of *belligerents,* the English Government takes an initiative step toward recognizing the Southern Confederacy, because the letters of marque of an unauthorized and unrecognized government in rebellion against the constituted authorities can, under the law of nations, only be regarded by every maritime power as pirates, and treated accordingly.

If Ireland or Scotland should revolt against the British crown, or Canada attempt to dissolve her allegiance to the mother country, would the United

States be justified in recognizing the privateers fitted out by the rebels as belligerents? I am sure that our Government would not assume such an unfriendly position, and give so material a support to a rebellious province in endangering the trade of its allies and of the world at large.

With the blockade of the Southern ports, which, before a fortnight can have elapsed, will be an effective one from the Chesapeake to the Rio Grande, the privateers of Jeff. Davis would have soon disappeared from the ocean, even if they ever made their appearance, had the declaration of Lord John not opened to them the British ports in the West Indies, Canada, and Great Britain.

It may be that the British Government will not condemn any prizes brought by the privateers into its ports, but the fact of their being allowed to run in for supplies and coal, and to escape into the many ports and inlets of the West Indies where our ships-of-war cannot follow them, will attract numerous lawless adventurers under the piratical flag of the Southern rebels.

The position which your Government seems inclined to take in the contest is, in my opinion, a very unfortunate one. It will complicate matters, must prolong the struggle, and result in a very bitter feeling between this country and England.

The whole North, without distinction of party, is determined not to allow our Government and our Union to be destroyed, and I am sure the sword will never be laid down until the American flag floats again from Maine to the Mississippi. The people feel that they are fighting for their national existence, and that no sacrifice can be too great in order to maintain and preserve that boon.

What the South claims now is for us to give up every port, from the Chesapeake to the Mississippi, to a foreign power, which has shown sufficiently within the last few months how far public and private property and obligations are to be respected by it.

In the struggle which is before us we had hoped for the sympathy of Europe, and particularly of England. Your statesmen and your press have at all times taken the most violent and uncompromising stand against slavery, and it is more than strange to see the British Government now give its moral countenance to a power which, under the declaration of its Vice-President (Alex. Stephens), is based upon *slavery* as its principal fundamental strength. That basis will most probably require the re-opening of the slave-trade, as soon as England shall have recognized the Confederacy, and should, in that event, the sympathy of the British Cabinet stop short, and not allow the *cotton-growers* to strengthen the foundations of their Government, then Mr. Jeff. Davis will, of course, put an embargo upon the export of cotton, in order to compel England to consent to the nefarious traffic in human flesh. He could certainly not be charged with a want of logic, by reasoning that the same power which induced England to throw her weight into the scale of a rebellious slave power, trying to overthrow our free institutions, would also be sufficiently potent to compel her to consent to the Confederacy drawing its supplies from Africa, of an element which the founders of that Confederacy had openly declared to the civilized world to be the basis of this young creation, claiming rank among the civilized nations of the world. . . .

Lord John Russell draws an analogy of the Southern rebellion to the struggle for independence by Greece, and asserts that, because England recognized Greece then as a belligerent, the South has to be recognized now by her in the same character. Greece was a conquered and enslaved *province* of a semi-barbarous despotism and had never been completely subjugated. It was a Christian people, tyrannized by fanatical Moslemism, and had the warm and active sympathy of the whole civilized world on its side.

The Southern States, who are now in a state of rebellion against the Federal Government, were free and voluntary parties to a compact of union, which was declared to be perpetual. They cannot point to a single right guaranteed to them by the Constitution which has been violated, and the only ground upon which they justify their rebellion is the *fear* that their peculiar institution of slavery may hereafter be interfered with by the party which put Mr. Lincoln into power.

I am free to say that the simile of Lord John is as unfortunate as the position which he has initiated for his Government in this crisis. The British Cabinet will, if this course should be persisted in, commit the fatal error of losing the good will of the party *which in the end must be successful*, in order to gain the friendship of those whose defeat can only be a question of time. We have three times as large a population, as united and brave as theirs; we have a navy, we have money and credit, in which latter they are most sadly and justly deficient.

Already Davis is again in the market with a loan of fifty millions of dollars. Who will loan a dollar to a confederacy of States, of which four have already repudiated their debts, while the remaining five will in less than three months be in default of their semi-annual dividends, unless it be that the name of Jeff. Davis, notwithstanding his advocacy of repudiation in his own State, Mississippi, should have a sweeter sound to European capitalists than I think he will ever acquire? In less than a year the Confederate States will pay their obligations in treasury warrants, which will have the same ultimate value as the French "assignats."

You know that I have never been in favor of the party which is now at the head of our Government, and my convictions on this point have in no way been changed. I am, however, convinced that the whole North to a man will stand by the Administration in the present struggle, and that, *come what may*, the integrity of the Union and the inviolability of our territory will be maintained to the bitter end.

Civil war is now upon us; no human power can prevent it. A vigorous and gigantic effort, on the part of the North, may, and I am confident will, shorten its horrors and disastrous results. An interference or one-sided neutrality, such as is foreshadowed by Lord John Russell's speech, can only prolong the fratricidal war, and entail ruin, not only upon both sections of our country, but upon the material interests and commerce of the world.

—BELMONT, *Letters, Speeches, and Addresses*

B. George Ticknor Explains the War to His English Friends

To Sir Charles Lyell.

Boston, February 11, 1862

My dear Lyell,—No doubt, I ought to have written to you before. But I have had no heart to write to my friends in Europe, since our troubles took their present form and proportions. . . .

You know how I have always thought and felt about the slavery question. I was never an Abolitionist, in the American sense of the word, because I never have believed that any form of emancipation that has been proposed could reach the enormous difficulties of the case, and I am of the same mind now. Slavery is too monstrous an evil, as it exists in the United States, to be reached by the resources of legislation. . . . I have, therefore, always desired to treat the South with the greatest forbearance, not only because the present generation is not responsible for the curse that is laid upon it, but because I have felt that the longer the contest could be postponed, the better for us. I have hoped, too, that in the inevitable conflict with free labor, slavery would go to the wall. I remember writing to you in this sense, more than twenty years ago, and the results thus far have confirmed the hopes I then entertained. The slavery of the South has made the South poor. The free labor of the North has made us rich and strong.

But all such hopes and thoughts were changed by the violent and unjustifiable secession, a year ago; and, since the firing of the first gun on Fort Sumter, we have had, in fact, no choice. We must fight it out. Of the results I have never doubted. We shall beat the South. But what after that? I do not see. It has pleased God that, whether we are to be two nations or one, we should live on the same continent side by side, with no strong natural barrier to keep us asunder; but now separated by hatreds which grow more insane and intense every month, and which generations will hardly extinguish. . . .

Our prosperity has entered largely into the prosperity of the world, and especially into that of England and France. You feel it to have been so. And some persons have been unwise enough to think that your interference in our domestic quarrel can do good to yourselves, and perhaps to us, by attempting to stop this cruel and wicked war. It is, I conceive, a great mistake. I have believed, since last August, that France was urging your government to some sort of intervention,—to break the blockade or to enforce a peace,—but the general opinion here has been that England has been the real mover in the matter, thus engendering a bitter hatred of your people, which the unjustifiable tone of your papers and ours increases and exasperates. All this is wrong, and so far as you are excited by it to intervention, it is most unhappy and portentous. The temptation, no doubt, is strong. It almost always is in the case of civil wars, which, from their very nature, invite interested and neighboring nations to interfere. But how rarely has good come to anybody from such interference. In the present instance I am satisfied that it would only exasperate us, and lead to desperate measures. . . .

As to the present comparative condition of North and South, there can be no question. At Richmond, and elsewhere beyond the Potomac, gold is at forty per cent premium, coffee and tea at four or five prices, salt as dear. . . . Beef and bread they have in abundance, and so resolute and embittered are they, that they seem content with this. But it cannot be. The women, I hear, in a large part of the South, will not speak to men who stay at home from the army without obvious and sufficient cause. But the suffering is great, however the proud spirit may bear up against it, and they must yield, unless, what is all but incredible, they should speedily gain great military success. . . .

At the North the state of things is very different. There is no perceptible increase of poverty. . . . Nor is anybody disheartened. If you were here you would see little change in our modes of life, except that we are all busy and in earnest about the war. . . . This, however, is not to last. The government must either impose taxes heavy enough to sustain its credit, as it ought to have done long ago, and then our incomes will all feel it, or it must rush into a paper currency, and then, of course, prices must rise in proportion, and the whole end in disaster. . . .

A country that has shown the resources and spirit of the North—however they may have been misused, and may continue to be—cannot be ruined by a year or two of adverse fortune, or even more. Changed it will be, how, or how much, I cannot guess, nor do I find anybody worth listening to that can tell me. But we are young and full of life. Diseases that destroy the old are cast off by the vigor of youth; and, though I may not live to see it, we shall again be strong and have an honored place among the nations. For the South I have no vaticinations. The blackness of thick darkness rests upon them, and they deserve all they will suffer. I admit that a portion of the North, and sometimes the whole North, has been very unjust to them. . . . But it is all no justification of civil war. . . . It is the unpardonable sin in a really free State.

You will, perhaps, think me shabby if I stop without saying anything about the Trent affair, and so I may as well make a clean breast of it. Except Everett, all the persons hereabout in whose judgment I place confidence believed from the first that we had no case. I was fully of that mind. . . .

As to the complaint about our closing up harbors, we are not very anxious. It is a harsh measure, but there are precedents enough for it,—more than there ought to be. But two will fully sustain the mere right. By the treaty of Utrecht you stipulated not only for the destruction of the fortifications of Dunkirk, but for filling up the port; and in 1777 (I think it was that year) you destroyed the entrance to Savannah, so that appropriations were made, not many years ago, by our Congress, to remove the obstructions, although the river, there, has cut out itself a new channel. I do not think that we have closed any but the minor and more shallow channels by the blockade. . . . However, if England and France want a pretext for interfering with us, perhaps this will do as well as any other. No doubt the "Times" at least, will be satisfied with it.

—*Life, Letters and Journals of George Ticknor*

5. CAPTAIN WILKES SEIZES MASON AND SLIDELL

It was the Trent *affair that brought the first, and perhaps the major, crisis in Anglo-American affairs during the war. The story itself is fully told in Lieutenant Fairfax's narrative. What Fairfax does not tell is the story of the impact of the* Trent *affair on England, and of the subsequent diplomatic controversy.*

James Mason and John Slidell were, respectively, Confederate commissioners to Britain and France. Learning that they had left Havana for England, Captain Wilkes stopped the Trent *and removed them, without specific instructions from his own government. His act was technically a violation of international law; he should have brought the* Trent *to an American port where a prize court would have adjudicated the whole case. What he did, however, was what the British themselves had done scores of times in the early years of the century. Nor did the British government at first hold Wilkes's act contrary to international law. As early as November 11, 1861, Palmerston had written the editor of the* Times *that "this American cruiser might, by our own principles of International Law, stop the West India packet, search her, and if the Southern men and their despatches and credentials were found on board, either take them out or seize the packet and carry her back to New York for trial." Yet when Wilkes did just this a wave of anger swept over England, and the government itself was moved to threats. The British government demanded that the United States release the prisoners and apologize for Wilkes's action, and insisted on an immediate answer. Fortunately the Prince Consort toned down Lord Russell's first letter, but even after toning down it bore the appearance of an ultimatum. Meantime orders were issued to hold the fleet in readiness for action, and thousands of soldiers were shipped over to Canada, while the export of war munitions to America was for a time stopped.*

Lincoln and Seward were in a dilemma. If they did not satisfy Britain they might find themselves with another war on their hands. If they did public opinion—which had made a hero of Wilkes—would be outraged. With his customary skill Seward found a solution. He did not apologize, but congratulated England on at last adopting the principles of international law for which the United States had long contended; then he had Mason and Slidell shipped off to England. American public opinion was on the whole pleased; the English were satisfied. In the long run the Trent *affair cleared the air; like the Venezuela crisis of Cleveland's administration it led both countries to contemplate war and revealed to both that they did not like the prospect. Yet in the lasting sense of resentment which was planted in America, Britain paid a high price for her insistence on a fine point of law.*

Donald Macneill Fairfax, who here tells the story of the removal of Mason and Slidell, was executive officer of the San Jacinto; he later fought with Farragut at New Orleans, and off Charleston. In 1880 he was named rear admiral.

IN October, 1861, the United States screw-sloop *San Jacinto*, of which Captain Charles Wilkes was commander and the writer was executive officer, on her return from the west coast of Africa, touched at the island of St. Thomas to coal ship. Here for the first time we learned of the presence in those waters of the Confederate cruiser *Sumter* (Captain Raphael Semmes). Captain Wilkes immediately determined to search for the enemy. At Cienfuegos, on the south coast of Cuba, he learned from the United States consul-general at Havana that Messrs. Mason and Slidell, Confederate commissioners to Europe, and their secretaries and families had recently reached that port from Charleston en route to England. He immediately put to sea, October 26th, with the purpose of intercepting the blockade runner which had brought them out. The commissioners . . . had run the Union blockade successfully . . . and had arrived . . . at Havana on the 17th. There we ascertained that their plan was to leave on the 7th of November in the English steamer *Trent* for St. Thomas on their way to England, and readily calculated when and where in the Bahama Channel we might intercept them. Meanwhile . . . Captain Wilkes continued his cruise after the *Sumter* along the north coast of Cuba, also running over to Key West in the hope of finding the *Powhatan* or some other steamer to accompany him to the Bahama Channel. . . . Here, 240 miles from Havana, and 90 miles from Sagua la Grande, where the channel contracts to the width of 15 miles, at noon on the 8th of November the *Trent* was sighted. . . .

It was evident, even at that early day, that the South had the sympathy of nearly all Europe—particularly of England and France. When Captain Wilkes first took me into his confidence, and told me what he purposed to do, I earnestly reminded him of the great risk of a war with these two Governments, supported as they were by powerful navies; and when we reached Key West I suggested that he consult with Judge Marvin, one of the ablest maritime lawyers. I soon saw, however, that he had made up his mind to intercept and capture the *Trent* as well as to take possession of the commissioners, and I therefore ceased to discuss the affair. As the next in rank to Captain Wilkes, I claimed the right to board the mail-packet. Captain Wilkes fully expected that I would tender my services for this "delicate duty," and rather left to me the plan of carrying out his instructions. I was impressed with the gravity of my position, and I made up my mind not to do anything unnecessary in the arrest of these gentlemen, or anything that would irritate the captain of the *Trent*, or any of his passengers, particularly the commissioners—lest it might occur to them to throw the steamer on my hands, which would necessitate my taking her as a prize.

As the *Trent* approached she hoisted English colors; whereupon our ensign was hoisted and a shot was fired across her bow. As she maintained her speed and showed no disposition to heave to, a shell was fired across her bow which brought her to. Captain Wilkes hailed that he intended to send a boat on board, and I then left with the second cutter.

The manner of heaving the *Trent* to evidently was galling to Captain Moir. When he did stop his steamer, he showed how provoked he was by impatiently singing out through his trumpet, "What do you mean by heaving my vessel to in this manner?" I felt that I must in every way conciliate him when I should get on board. Two boats had been equipped ready to lower and the officers and crews detailed to jump into them. These were not employed until later. The boat I took was a third one, and as the sea was smooth, but a few minutes elapsed before we reached the *Trent*. I instructed the boat's crew to remain alongside for orders, and, boarding the vessel, I was escorted by one of her officers to the upper or promenade deck and was introduced to Captain Moir. . . . I immediately asked if I might see his passenger-list, saying that I had information that Messrs. Mason and Slidell were on board. The mention of Mr. Slidell's name caused that gentleman to come up and say, "I am Mr. Slidell; do you want to see me?" Mr. Mason, whom I knew very well, also came up at the same time, thus relieving me from Captain Moir's refusal, which was very polite but very positive, that I could not under such circumstances be shown any list of passengers. . . . In the briefest time . . . I informed Captain Moir that I had been sent by my commander to arrest Mr. Mason and Mr. Slidell and their secretaries, and send them prisoners on board the United States war vessel near by.

As may readily be understood, when it was known why I had boarded the *Trent*, there was an outburst of rage and indignation from the passengers, who numbered nearly one hundred, many of them Southerners. The captain and the four gentlemen bore themselves with great composure, but the irresponsible lookers-on sang out, "Throw the d—— fellow overboard!" I called on Captain Moir to preserve order, but, for the benefit of the excited passengers, I reminded them that our every move was closely observed from the *San Jacinto* by spy-glasses (she was within hailing distance), that a heavy battery was bearing upon them, and that any indignity to any of her officers or crew then on board might lead to dreadful consequences. This, together with Captain Moir's excellent commanding manner, had a quieting effect.

During this uproar among the passengers, the officer in charge of the *San Jacinto's* boat, not knowing what it meant, and fearing some ill-treatment of me, hurried up with six or eight of the crew. Captain Moir was the first to see this body of armed men, and remonstrated with me at their appearance on the promenade-deck among his passengers, there being many ladies and children among them. I immediately directed the officer to return to his boat and await my orders. I assured him, amidst the noise of his passengers, that the men had come contrary to my instructions. I was really pleased to find the captain so tenacious of his command, for my mind was possessed with the idea that Mr. Mason or Mr. Slidell, or both, would urge Captain Moir to relinquish his command, making it necessary for me to assume it, as in such event my instructions left no opening for me to decline it.

After order had been restored, we discussed the affair more generally, Captain Moir, however, scarcely joining in the conversation—always dignified and punctilious. . . . I carefully avoided giving offense, and confined myself strictly to the duty which had taken me on board. I was anxious that Mr. Slidell and Mr. Mason should not leave any of their luggage behind. Mrs. Slidell having asked me who commanded the *San Jacinto*, I replied, "Your old acquaintance, Captain Wilkes"; whereupon she expressed surprise that he should do the very thing the Confederates were hoping for—something to arouse England; ... "Really," she added, "Captain Wilkes is playing into our hands!" ...

After the first uproar had subsided, I sent the boat to Captain Wilkes to say that these gentlemen were all on board, and had objected to being sent to the *San Jacinto*, and that I must use force to accomplish my orders; I asked for a boat to carry them comfortably on board, another for their baggage, and a third to carry stores, which the paymaster's clerk, at Captain Wilkes's order, had already purchased from the steward of the *Trent*, to add to the comfort of the new guests.

When all was ready and the boats were in waiting, I notified both Mr. Mason and Mr. Slidell that the time had come to send them to the *San Jacinto*. They came quietly down to the main-deck, and there repeated that they would not go unless force was used—whereupon two officers, previously instructed, escorted each commissioner to the side, and assisted them into the comfortable cutter sent especially for them. ...

When all was finished I went on board the *San Jacinto* and reported to Captain Wilkes that I had not taken the *Trent* as a prize, as he had instructed me to do, giving certain reasons, which satisfied him; for he replied, "inasmuch as you have not taken her, you will let her go" or "proceed on her voyage." ... The reasons I assigned to Captain Wilkes for my action were: First, that the capture of the *Trent* would make it necessary to put a large prize crew (officers and men) on board, and thus materially weaken our battery for use at Port Royal; secondly, that as there were a large number of women and children and mails and specie bound to various ports, the capture would seriously inconvenience innocent persons and merchants; so that I had determined, before taking her, to lay these matters before him for more serious consideration.

I gave my real reasons some weeks afterward to Secretary Chase, whom I met by chance at the Treasury Department, he having asked me to explain why I had not literally obeyed Captain Wilkes's instructions. I told him that it was because I was impressed with England's sympathy for the South, and felt that she would be glad to have so good a ground to declare war against the United States. Mr. Chase seemed surprised, and exclaimed, "You have certainly relieved the Government from great embarrassment, to say the least."

I returned immediately to the *Trent* and informed Captain Moir that Captain Wilkes would not longer detain him, and he might proceed on his voyage. The steamers soon separated, and thus ended one of the most critical events of our civil war.

—FAIRFAX, "Captain Wilkes's Seizure of Mason and Slidell"

6. "SHALL IT BE LOVE, OR HATE, JOHN?"

Few American poets were better known in England, or more respected, than James Russell Lowell. "Jonathan to John"—one of the famous Biglow

Papers—*was Lowell's criticism of the British reaction to the* Trent *affair, but it covered broad ground. Widely read in America, it long retained its popularity, but needless to say it never achieved a comparable popularity with that people to whom it was directed.*

JONATHAN TO JOHN

It don't seem hardly right, John,
　　When both my hands was full,
To stump me to a fight, John,—
　　Your cousin, tu, John Bull!
　　　Ole Uncle S. sez he, "I guess
　　　We know it now," sez he,
　　"The Lion's paw is all the law,
　　　Accordin' to J. B.,
　　　That's fit for you an' me!"

You wonder why we're hot, John?
　　Your mark wuz on the guns,
The neutral guns, thet shot, John,
　　Our brothers an' our sons:
　　　Ole Uncle S. sez he, "I guess
　　　There's human blood," sez he,
　　"By fits an' starts, in Yankee hearts,
　　　Though 't may surprise J. B.
　　　More 'n it would you an' me." . . .

When your rights was our wrongs, John,
　　You didn't stop for fuss,—
Britanny's trident prongs, John,
　　Was good 'nough law for us.
　　　Ole Uncle S. sez he, "I guess,
　　　Though physic 's good," sez he,
　　"It does n't foller thet he can swaller
　　　Prescriptions signed 'J. B.,'
　　　Put up by you an' me."

We own the ocean, tu, John:
　　You mus'n' take it hard,
Ef we can't think with you, John,
　　It's jest your own back yard.
　　　Ole Uncle S. sez he, "I guess
　　　Ef *thet's* his claim," sez he,
　　"The fencin'-stuff 'll cost enough
　　　To bust up friend J. B.,
　　　Ez wal ez you an' me!" . . .

We give the critters back, John,
   Cos Abram thought 't was right;
It warn't your bullyin' clack, John,
   Provokin' us to fight.
     Ole Uncle S. sez he, "I guess
     We've a hard row," sez he,
"To hoe jest now; but thet, somehow,
     May happen to J. B.,
     Ez wal ez you an' me!"

We ain't so weak an' poor, John,
   With twenty million people,
An' close to every door, John,
   A school-house an' a steeple.
     Ole Uncle S. sez he, "I guess
     It is a fact," sez he,
"The surest plan to make a Man
     Is, think him so, J. B.,
     Ez much ez you or me!" . . .

We know we've got a cause, John,
   Thet's honest, just, an' true;
We thought 't would win applause, John,
   If nowheres else, from you.
     Ole Uncle S. sez he, "I guess
     His love of right," sez he,
"Hangs by a rotton fibre o' cotton:
     There's natur' in J. B.,
     Ez wal ez in you an' me!"

The South says, "*Poor folks down!*" John,
   An' "*All men up!*" say we,—
White, yaller, black, an' brown, John:
   Now which is your idee?
     Ole Uncle S. sez he, "I guess
     John preaches wal," sez he;
"But, sermon thru, an' come to *du*,
     Why, there's the old J. B.
     A-crowdin' you an' me!"

Shall it be love, or hate, John?
   It's you thet's to decide;
Ain't *your* bonds held by Fate, John,
   Like all the world's beside?
     Ole Uncle S. sez he, "I guess
     Wise men forgive," sez he,
"But not forgit; an' some time yit
     Thet truth may strike J. B.,
     Ez wal ez you an' me!"

God means to make this land, John,
Clear thru, from sea to sea,
Believe an' understand, John,
The *wuth* o' bein' free.
Ole Uncle S. sez he, "I guess
God's price is high," sez he;
"But nothin' else than wut he sells
Wears long, an' thet J. B.
May larn, like you an' me!"
—LOWELL, *Poems*

7. COMMONS DEBATES THE RECOGNITION OF THE CONFEDERACY

By two proclamations of April 19 and April 27, 1861, Lincoln had established a blockade of the Confederacy. Was this blockade legally binding? In international law a blockade must be real and effective; a mere "paper" blockade need not be observed. Yet in fact the little United States Navy of 1861 was wholly unable to impose an effective blockade on a dozen or more major ports and several thousand miles of coast line. Britain might, therefore, have taken the position that there was no legal blockade. But to have done so would almost certainly have precipitated war, and Britain neither wanted nor was ready for war. Furthermore Britain was herself a maritime power, dependent on the blockade as an instrument of war; a strict interpretation of blockading might very well redound to her serious disadvantage later on. Lord John Russell, therefore, promptly accepted the blockade.

Southern sympathizers were unwilling to let the matter rest at that. They agitated for a review of the whole blockade question, and for recognition of the Confederacy as a sovereign state. The most prominent of them were Sir John Gregory and William Lindsay. In March 1862 Gregory touched off a debate on the blockade which ended in his total discomfiture. Nothing daunted, Lindsay raised the whole question once again in June 1862. The greatest shipowner in England, Lindsay exercised considerable influence in business circles and, as he was from the Midlands, seemed to speak with peculiar propriety for the starving workingmen of Lancashire. After a trip to Paris and talks with Emperor Napoleon Lindsay returned to London and in June gave notice of a motion to recognize the Confederacy. Then early in July came the news of Lee's victories on the Peninsula and the moment seemed right for pushing the motion to conclusion. The debate ranged over the whole field of relations with the American belligerents. In the end Lindsay was forced to withdraw his motion.

Benjamin Moran, from whose invaluable diary this story is taken, was Secretary of the American Legation in London. His diary is chiefly notable for its acidulous comments on Minister Charles Francis Adams and on his son Henry Adams, as well as on all other Americans who failed to appreciate the merits of Benjamin Moran.

Sat. 19 July, '62. Last evening being the time fixed for the discussion of Lindsay's motion for the recognition of the Rebels, I was sent down to the House by Mr. Adams' direction to observe the feeling and report the proceedings. On going there at about 5 o'clk I found the Commons had adjourned to meet at 6. I went at the appointed hour. There was a very large gathering of strangers extending all through St. Stephen's porch, and filling up nearly the whole of the outside lobby of the House. Among those who were lounging in the hall or corridor leading from the grand central vestibule to the Commons, was Geo. McHenry. This recreant northern man displayed much servility towards the door keepers and policemen, and had a good deal of the mean guilty look of a sheep-stealing dog. He observed me, as I did him, but as I always detested the fellow, I treated him as if I was unaware of his presence. Just as the House again met, the crowd of anxious visitors increased and much confusion followed at the doors. The gate-keepers then increased their already very large stock of insolence and ill-manners, until they became unbearable.

At this time the rebel Mason came up attended by Williams, our late Minister at Constantinople, Geo. McHenry and two or three vulgar looking confederates, whose appearance and manners were not favorable to their modest pretensions to be considered as specimens of the only gentlemen in America. Mason and Williams are both coarse, gross, ponderous, vulgar looking men, and on this occasion they did not show to the best advantage. They were badly dressed. Williams always was a sloven. Last night his shirt front was crumpled and stained with tobacco spit and his trousers were unbuttoned. Mason was impudent—which he mistakes for dignity—and wore a *dress* coat with a black satin vest. Linsey-woolsey don't answer here. The rough boor who keeps the door spoke to them in a loud insolent commanding tone and ordered them back. But while they were parleying Gregory, their champion, came out and in his peculiarly offensive and whining tone said he had orders for the floor for his friend Mr. Mason and suite. The *suite* however being large was not admitted to the privilege he demanded, McHenry and the rest of the mean little rebels being sent into the Speaker's gallery, while Gregory conducted his friends Mason and Williams to seats on the floor under the gallery. I soon followed, and having the privilege of either going into the Diplomatic Gallery or on the floor decided for the floor for the time. Mason sat near the gangway in front and Williams behind.

An ineffectual attempt having been made to induce Lindsay to withdraw his motion, that gentleman rose and began his speech. He opened by striking off every offer of *recognition* and fell back on simple mediation, without referring to hostilities. He is a wretched speaker and soon drove half the members of a very full House away. For years I have entertained great respect for the intelligence and dignity of the English House of Commons, but after hearing the vulgar misrepresentations of Lindsay on the United States last night, welcomed by applause, I can no longer even respect it. His speech, if a blundering utterance of a long tissue of naked falsehoods, can so be called, was simply an insult to intelligence and reason. I thought old Mason was

British Reinforcements for Canada

Illustrated London News

The Cotton Famine, Mottram, near Manchester

ashamed of his advocate. He openly lied about the tariff, and had evidently been crammed by the rebels. After an hour's abuse of us, and his reasons therefore, he wound up by saying that independently of all these, he desired the disruption of the American Union, as every honest Englishman did, because it was too great a Power and England sh'd not let such a power exist on the American continent. Old Mason spat tobacco more furiously at this than ever, and covered the carpet. I thought that if he had a particle of manly feeling left he would blush at the contempt there expressed for him by his champion. For there was in it, a positive declaration that the South was nothing to him, and that he was only trying to array one section against the other for the destruction of both in order to feed the envy of England.

I watched carefully the effect of this speech. At first it was cordially welcomed, but it soon became evident that there was a growing doubt in the House about even *Mediation!* The tories cheered the most. This revealed their policy. I gave Mr. Forster my private telegram giving the denial to the reported capitulation of McClellan & he circulated it. The dates were conclusive, & I began to fear they wouldn't adopt the motion, for after the open abuse of us by Lindsay, and the approval it met by the House, I wanted the resolution passed. It seemed to me that fear of us, and fear alone, was the check to action. There was a lull after Lindsay sat down. Gregory and he, as well as some of the tories went over to Mason. I went up to the Diplomatic Gallery, and Mr. P. Taylor, the new member of Leicester began to speak.

This gentleman was jeered at first, but by perseverance he got a hearing. I observed Palmerston, who seemed to be quietly asleep on the Treasury bench with his hat over his eyes when Lindsay was speaking, but was not, turn and look enquiringly at Taylor. The tories behaved like blackguards. They showed their love of free-speech by trying to put down everybody not of their way of thinking. Mr. Taylor however persevered, and under a great deal of provocation made an eloquent but an indiscreet speech. The popularity, or respect entertained for a speaker, is always evinced in the House by full or empty benches. Mr. Taylor soon brought back the crowd that hobbling Lindsay drove away and he was met both by applause and condemnation. He said the war was between Freedom and Slavery, which was met with loud cries of No, No! and jeers. He also said that mediation was an insult and would lead to war. This was also cried down. And when he mentioned the name of honest Abraham Lincoln, the burst of horse laughter and ridicule that greeted it, was a disgrace to the age. The act itself was bad enough in all conscience, but the manner and tone of the expression were even more offensive. Mr. Taylor was equal to the occasion, and met the guffah of this intelligent assembly of honest and refined English gentlemen with a declaration that shamed them to silence. "Yes," said he "I say honest Abraham Lincoln—a name that will be remembered and honored when all the smooth tongued diplomats and statesmen of the day are forgotten." He also told them that their hostility was hatred of America—that slavery was the cause of the rebellion—and that English advocacy of the rebels was an abandonment of that hostility to slavery that had ever been the characteristic of Englishmen in modern times. The jeers to this were feeble, as the truth it contained was felt. Mr. Taylor quoted most effectually from J. Stuart Mill, and made the most of the point so gained.

Lord A. Vane-Tempest, a dissipated and unprincipled young nobleman spoke next. His manner is that of his class and his speech was like Lindsay's, composed of falsehood and abuse. I thought he was drunk, and so did the House, for he came near falling over the back of the bench in front of him on several occasions. He described the slave-drivers as gentlemen, and the soldiers of the Republic as mercenaries. Went over the old slanders about America insulting England, taking good care to charge to the present Administration all the faults of past cabinets, and wound up with an insult to Mr. Taylor. Vane Tempest is bloated from drink, & would be in the workhouse if he were not a Lord—but being a Lord he is in the English House of Commons. He was a good deal cheered by the tories; and the current of their policy, which until last night they have carefully concealed, was seen to flow with the rebels.

Mr. Forster spoke next. He made a brief but telling speech. Palmerston and Gladstone looked up at him and the tories faintly applauded. I had prepared him with some facts to refute Lindsay, and he used them. He showed that the North had always taxed itself to protect sugar, cotton, tobacco and rice, and that South Carolina never once mentioned tariffs or taxation in her Declaration of Independence. Lindsay had said that odious northern taxation was the cause of the rebellion. But after all, I don't know that it was worth while to notice the fellow. Great respect was paid to Mr. Forster's speech and it did good. By this time the rebel story of McClellan's capitulation had been exploded and their cause was growing palpably weaker.

The tories had however prepared themselves to expound their policy and Mr. Whitesides [Whiteside], the Attorney General for Ireland under Lord Derby in '58, was selected as their mouth-piece. That the proceeding had been pre-arranged is confirmed by the fact that Lord Derby himself came in to hear Mr. Whiteside's speech. Being in the lobby just before Mr. Whitesides began I met the Earl of Derby going into the Commons. D'Israeli usually represents the tories in all great debates in the Lower House, but on this occasion he had evidently declined the task. This fact, and Whiteside's selection, are further proof of prearrangement. He began very deliberately and delivered what was evidently a prepared speech. He is an able eloquent Irish orator and speaks with great force. The tories cheered his references to the supposed failure of Republican institutions loudly, and he belabored us soundly but politely. At times he was severe, but he was never vulgar. One can hear polite slander with a better grace than he can coarse abuse. He was terribly sarcastic at times, but rarely truthful. In fact both classes of the rebel advocates seemed conscious that they could only carry their point by falsehood, and appeals to prejudice. His phillipics at times were savage and were hailed with laughter. Being a tall fine, venerable and powerful man, with considerable action and oratorical force,—rare qualities in England,—

and yet no ranter, he soon had the House with him. He spoke from the floor and therefore had room for movement. His modified Irish accent sounded well when I forgot in my admiration of the orator the subject of his eloquence; but it sent a chill crawling over me when I recollected myself and recalled the fact that its tones were pleading the cause of slavery against freedom. Mr. Forster came up to me while he was speaking and said "You see now where the tories are." I did and was glad of it. They had thrown off the cloak and fixed their position. It was an able speech but altho' well received, its admirers seemed to be more noisy than determined. They were whistling to keep their courage up.

Gregory followed in his insipid way with a lot of platitudes, and expressions of confidence that "this House" would adopt the resolutions; but was not very happy.

There was a pleasant young gentleman whom I did not know in the gallery at my side with whom I had been in conversation during the evening, and who up to this time had thought the vote would be favorable. He however had, like me, been a close observer of the effects of the speeches and the changes in the feeling of the House, and agreed that there would be either no vote or a defeat. I expressed my regret. He knew my sentiments and said he would feel like me if he were a northerner. While we were talking Palmerston, who had nearly all night preserved his sleepy appearance, rose. He was heartily welcomed, and in three minutes settled the matter adversely to the rebels. It was half-past one in the morning, that old man— now 78 years of age—had been for seven hours and a half a listener to the debate, and had heard every word, as all close observers saw, notwithstanding his attitude of sleep, and altho he tottered when he got up, his brain was clear and he delivered the best speech I ever heard from his lips. Silence was accorded him at first—applause and approval at last. His remarks showed that he had watched every action and heard every sentiment of the speakers, and in quoting them he neither misrepresented them nor attributed to any one sentiments that had been uttered by another. He said mediation meant war, and thought the Gov't could manage the affair without going that far, or wounding the feeling of a sensitive, and struggling people. That speech closed the debate, and altho' Fitzgerald spoke afterwards, his remarks amounted to nothing and Lindsay withdrew his motion.

As I came away I met Mason alone, looking sullen and dejected. He has a bad face. In a minute he was joined by Gregory, both evidently disappointed, and putting his arm lovingly round the Irishman's waist the slaveholder and the Briton stalked off to solace their minds and forget their disappointment in the consolations incident to smoking a cigar.

—WALLACE AND GILLESPIE, eds., *The Journal of Benjamin Moran*

8. PALMERSTON AND RUSSELL DISCUSS INTERVENTION

Although the Government had defeated Lindsay's motion, it continued to consider the propriety of an offer of mediation to the American belliger-

ents. By the autumn of 1862 the American situation appeared to justify such a move. McClellan had been defeated on the Peninsula; Lee had whipped Pope at Second Bull Run, and now Lee's victorious hosts were invading the North with every prospect of success. Pressure from Napoleon, too, was mounting. In mid-September 1862 the Prime Minister, the Viscount Palmerston and the Foreign Secretary, Lord John Russell, corresponded about the next move. Both appeared to favor mediation. Then came the news of Antietam—a Union victory after all. Palmerston had sober second thoughts, and the mediation movement died as far as the Government was concerned.

Here are the crucial letters that passed between Palmerston and Russell.

94 Piccadilly: September 14, 1862

My dear Russell,—The detailed accounts given in the 'Observer' to-day of the battles of August 29 and 30 between the Confederates and the Federals show that the latter got a very complete smashing; and it seems not altogether unlikely that still greater disasters await them, and that even Washington or Baltimore may fall into the hands of the Confederates.

If this should happen, would it not be time for us to consider whether in such a state of things England and France might not address the contending parties and recommend an arrangement upon the basis of separation?
—Yours sincerely,

PALMERSTON.

Gotha: September 17, 1862

My dear Palmerston,—Whether the Federal army is destroyed or not, it is clear that it is driven back to Washington, and has made no progress in subduing the insurgent States. Such being the case, I agree with you that the time is come for offering mediation to the United States Government, with a view to the recognition of the independence of the Confederates. I agree further, that, in case of failure, we ought ourselves to recognise the Southern States as an independent State. For the purpose of taking so important a step, I think we must have a meeting of the Cabinet. The 23rd or 30th would suit me for the meeting.

We ought then, if we agree on such a step, to propose it first to France, and then, on the part of England and France, to Russia and other powers, as a measure decided upon by us.

We ought to make ourselves safe in Canada, not by sending more troops there, but by concentrating those we have in a few defensible posts before the winter sets in.

J. RUSSELL

Broadlands: September 23, 1862

My dear Russell,—Your plan of proceedings about the mediation between the Federals and Confederates seems to be excellent. Of course, the offer would be made to both the contending parties at the same time; for, though the offer would be as sure to be accepted by the Southerns as was the proposal of the Prince of Wales by the Danish Princess, yet, in the one case as in the other, there are certain forms which it is decent and proper to go through.

A question would occur whether, if the two parties were to accept the mediation, the fact of our mediating would not of itself be tantamount to an acknowledgment of the Confederates as an independent State.

Might it not be well to ask Russia to join England and France in the offer of mediation? . . .

We should be better without her in the mediation, because she would be too favourable to the North; but on the other hand her participation in the offer might render the North the more willing to accept it.

The after communication to the other European powers would be quite right, although they would be too many for mediation.

As to the time of making the offer, if France and Russia agree,—and France, we know, is quite ready, and only waiting for our concurrence—events may be taking place which might render it desirable that the offer should be made before the middle of October.

It is evident that a great conflict is taking place to the north-west of Washington, and its issue must have a great effect on the state of affairs. If the Federals sustain a great defeat, they may be at once ready for mediation, and the iron should be struck while it is hot. If, on the other hand, they should have the best of it, we may wait awhile and see what may follow.— Yours sincerely,

PALMERSTON.
—WALPOLE, *The Life of Lord John Russell*

October 2

My dear Russell,

I return you Granville's letter which contains much deserving of serious consideration. There is no doubt that the offer of Mediation upon the basis of Separation would be accepted by the South. Why should it not be accepted? It would give the South in principle the points for which they are fighting. The refusal, if refusal there was, would come from the North, who would be unwilling to give up the principle for which they have been fighting so long as they had a reasonable expectation that by going on fighting they could carry their point. The condition of things therefore which would be favourable to an offer of mediation would be great success of the South against the North. That state of things seemed ten days ago to be approaching. Its advance has been lately checked, but we do not yet know the real course of recent events, and still less can we foresee what is about to follow. Ten days or a fortnight more may throw a clearer light upon future prospects.

As regards possible resentment on the part of the Northerns following upon an acknowledgment of the Independence of the South, it is quite true that we should have less to care about that resentment in the spring when communication with Canada was open, and when our naval force could more easily operate upon the American coast, than in winter when we are cut off from Canada and the American coast is not so safe.

But if the acknowledgment were made at one and the same time by England, France and some other Powers, the Yankees would probably not seek a quarrel with us alone, and would not like one against a European Confederation. Such a quarrel would render certain and permanent that Southern Independence the acknowledgment of which would have caused it.

The first communication to be made by England and France to the contending parties might be, not an absolute offer of mediation but a friendly suggestion whether the time was not come when it might be well for the two parties to consider whether the war, however long continued, could lead to any other result than separation; and whether it might not therefore be best to avoid the great evils which must necessarily flow from a prolongation of hostilities by at once coming to an agreement to treat upon that principle of separation which must apparently be the inevitable result of the contest, however long it may last.

The best thing would be that the two parties should settle details by direct negotiation with each other, though perhaps with the rancorous hatred now existing between them this might be difficult. But their quarrels in negotiation would do us no harm if they did not lead to a renewal of war. An armistice, if not accompanied by a cessation of blockades, would be all in favour of the North, especially if New Orleans remained in the hands of the North.

The whole matter is full of difficulty, and can only be cleared up by some more decided events between the contending armies.

PALMERSTON.

—ADAMS, *Great Britain and the American Civil War*

9. "AN ERROR, THE MOST SINGULAR AND PALPABLE"

The great surprise of the diplomatic battle was Gladstone's Newcastle speech of October 7, 1862. By that time the Cabinet had pretty well decided neither to intervene nor to offer mediation. Gladstone was Chancellor of the Exchequer, and presumably supported the Government policy. Yet at Newcastle he said, "Jefferson Davis and other leaders of the South have made an army; they are making, it appears, a navy; and they have made what is more than either, they have made a nation." By British political standards this was clearly an improper speech to make. A few days later the Home Secretary, Sir George Cornwall Lewis, said at Hereford that the Government did not contemplate any change of policy, thus in effect repudiating Gladstone. Gladstone himself later confessed that this speech was one of the great errors of his career. We give his apology, written in July 1896.*

I HAVE yet to record an undoubted error, the most singular and palpable, I may add the least excusable of them all, especially since it was committed so late as in the year 1862, when I had outlived half a century. In the autumn of that year, and in a speech delivered after a public dinner at Newcastle-

* From Morley: *The Life of William Ewart Gladstone*, Vol. II. Copyright 1903 by The Macmillan Company, 1931 by Mary O. Morley, and used with the permission of The Macmillan Company and Mr. Guy E. Morley.

upon-Tyne, I declared in the heat of the American struggle that Jefferson Davis had made a nation, that is to say, that the division of the American Republic by the establishment of a Southern or secession state was an accomplished fact. Strange to say, this declaration, most unwarrantable to be made by a minister of the crown with no authority other than his own, was not due to any feeling of partizanship for the South or hostility to the North. The fortunes of the South were at their zenith. Many who wished well to the Northern cause despaired of its success. The friends of the North in England were beginning to advise that it should give way, for the avoidance of further bloodshed and greater calamity. I weakly supposed that the time had come when respectful suggestions of this kind, founded on the necessity of the case, were required by a spirit of that friendship which, in so many contingencies of life, has to offer sound recommendations with a knowledge that they will not be popular. Not only was this a misjudgment of the case, but even if it had been otherwise, I was not the person to make the declaration. I really, though most strangely, believed that it was an act of friendliness to all America to recognise that the struggle was virtually at an end. I was not one of those who on the ground of British interests desired a division of the American Union. My view was distinctly opposite. I thought that while the Union continued it never could exercise any dangerous pressure upon Canada to estrange it from the empire—our honour, as I thought, rather than our interest forbidding its surrender. But were the Union split, the North, no longer checked by the jealousies of slave-power, would seek a partial compensation for its loss in annexing, or trying to annex, British North America. Lord Palmerston desired the severance as a diminution of a dangerous power, but prudently held his tongue.

That my opinion was founded upon a false estimate of the facts was the very least part of my fault. I did not perceive the gross impropriety of such an utterance from a cabinet minister, of a power allied in blood and language, and bound to loyal neutrality; the case being further exaggerated by the fact that we were already, so to speak, under indictment before the world for not (as was alleged) having strictly enforced the laws of neutrality in the matter of the cruisers. My offence was indeed only a mistake, but one of incredible grossness, and with such consequences of offence and alarm attached to it, that my failing to perceive them justly exposed me to very severe blame. It illustrates vividly that incapacity which my mind so long retained, and perhaps still exhibits, an incapacity of viewing subjects all round, in their extraneous as well as in their internal properties, and thereby of knowing when to be silent and when to speak.

I am the more pained and grieved, because I have for the last five-and-twenty years received from the government and people of America tokens of goodwill which could not fail to arouse my undying gratitude. When we came to the arbitration at Geneva, my words were cited as part of the proof of hostile *animus*. Meantime I had prepared a lengthened statement to show from my abundant declarations on other occasions that there was and could be on my part no such *animus*. I was desirous to present this statement to the arbitrators. My colleagues objected so largely to the proceeding that I desisted. In this I think they probably were wrong. I addressed my paper to the American minister for the information of his government, and Mr. Secretary Fish gave me, so far as intention was concerned, a very handsome acquittal.

And strange to say, *post hoc* though perhaps not *propter hoc*, the United States have been that country of the world in which the most signal marks of public honour have been paid me, and in which my name has been the most popular, the only parallels being Italy, Greece, and the Balkan Peninsula.

—MORLEY, *The Life of William Ewart Gladstone*

10. JOHN BRIGHT DEPLORES THE POLICY OF HIS GOVERNMENT

Cobden, Forster, and Bright were the triumvirate who fought most effectively for the cause of the North, and of the three it was the Quaker Bright whose influence went farthest. Perhaps the greatest figure in the nineteenth-century reform movement in Britain, Bright had fought and triumphed against the Corn Laws, espoused religious, humanitarian, and electoral reform, opposed the Crimean War, and now championed the Union, in and out of Parliament. Henry Adams thought that in the House itself Forster was a more effective advocate of the Union cause, but with the country at large it was Bright's eloquent voice that had greatest influence.

Here is a letter from Bright to his friend Charles Sumner written just three days after Gladstone's "vile" speech.

Llandudno, North Wales, October 10, 1862

DEAR MR. SUMNER,—I was very glad to receive your last letter containing much interesting information on the cotton question. I sent it and the letters, or copies of letters it contained to Mr. Cobden. It is quite clear that your Government was right in not sending an expedition to Texas, when it was a question whether it could keep a footing in Virginia.

I write to you from a feeling of anxiety. You will see what is being said here by public men who speak on your question, and most of all, and worst of all, by your old acquaintance and friend, Mr. Gladstone. He has made a vile speech at Newcastle, full of insulting pity for the North, and of praise and support for the South. He is unstable as water in some things. He is for union and freedom in Italy, and for disunion and bondage in America. A handful of Italians in prison in Naples, without formal trial, shocked his soul so much that he wrote a pamphlet, and has made many speeches upon it; but he has no word of sympathy or of hope for the four millions of the bondsmen of the South! I have known for months past that he talked of an European remonstrance, or mediation, or recognition, or some mischief of that kind, but I did not expect that he would step out openly as the defender and eulogist of Jeff. Davis and his fellow conspirators against God and man. He has spoken, as you will see by the time you receive this, and what he has said will encourage the friends of the South here to encreased exertions to promote something hostile to your Government and people. Palmerston and Russell, I fear, will not need much pressure to induce them to do anything they dare do on behalf of the permanent disruption of your Union.

Now, if I may trouble you again, I want you to write fully and frankly to me, that I may know what is possible and what is likely. If the "proclamation" means anything it means that you will preserve the Union, even tho' it involve a social revolution in the South and the transformation of four millions of slaves into as many laborers and peasants. If you destroy the armed force of the South still you will have a population deeply exasperated and disloyal, and government in their States must be difficult if not impossible. If the black nation can be made a population for the Union, then to hold the South may not be impossible; but without them, I see immeasurable difficulties in your path. Is the North prepared for all the hazards and for all the confusion which for a time such a course may render inevitable; and will the Government be thoroughly supported by all the free States in such a policy? I conclude from the fact that the New York Herald has not dared to condemn the proclamation, that it meets with the support of your people. If the border States should not take fright at it, it seems to me calculated to be a powerful lever in future operations against the revolt. On these points we have, as yet, scarcely received any information, and I look for further tidings with great anxiety.

. . . I talk with men daily, and try to influence opinion in favor of the right; and before long I may have to speak in public on its behalf. I want you to tell me, if you can what I may hope for, and what I may believe, that I may have my faith corrected or strengthened. Will the North persist? Will it grapple with the slavery devil and strangle it? May I believe that your country will be held together?

I begin to believe that another crop of cotton from slave labor will never again be grown on your Northern continent. Terribly as this would make me and mine and multitudes here to suffer, I cannot wish it otherwise. . . .

JOHN BRIGHT

Surely that childish project of removing the black people from America will cease to be talked about. It damages the character of your President and Government.

—Letter from John Bright to Charles Sumner

11. THE ENGLISH PRESS CONDEMNS THE EMANCIPATION PROCLAMATION

It is commonly believed that it was the Emancipation Proclamation that turned the tide of opinion in Britain. There is some truth in this, for that proclamation gave the war a new character. It was no longer a war for Union alone or—as the opposition called it—for Empire. Now it was also a war for Freedom. It is of some interest, however, to note that the immediate reaction of a substantial part of the English press was decidedly hostile to the Proclamation and to the policy which it announced.

We have been able to include here merely two of the many critical editorials on the Proclamation. The first is from the Times, *the most powerful paper in Britain and perhaps in the world; the second from* Blackwood's Edinburgh Magazine.

A. "This Is a Very Sad Document"

IT is rarely that a man can be found to balance accurately mischief to another against advantage to himself. President Lincoln is, as the world says, a good-tempered man, neither better nor worse than the mass of his kind—neither a fool nor a sage, neither a villain nor a saint, but a piece of that common useful clay out of which it delights the American democracy to make great Republican personages. Yet President Lincoln has declared that from the 1st of January next to come every State that is in rebellion shall be, in the eye of Mr. Lincoln, a Free State. After that date Mr. Lincoln proposes to enact that every slave in a rebel State shall be for ever after free, and he promises that neither he, nor his army, nor his navy will do anything to repress *any* efforts which the Negroes in such rebel States may make for the recovery of their freedom.

This means, of course, that Mr. Lincoln will, on the 1st of next January, do his best to excite a servile war in the States which he cannot occupy with his arms. He will run up the rivers in his gunboats; he will seek out the places which are left but slightly guarded, and where the women and children have been trusted to the fidelity of coloured domestics. He will appeal to the black blood of the African; he will whisper of the pleasures of spoil and of the gratification of yet fiercer instincts; and when blood begins to flow and shrieks come piercing through the darkness, Mr. Lincoln will wait till the rising flames tell that all is consummated, and then he will rub his hands and think that revenge is sweet. This is what Mr. Lincoln avows before the world that he is about to do.

Now, we are in Europe thoroughly convinced that the death of slavery must follow as necessarily upon the success of the Confederates in this war as the dispersion of darkness occurs upon the rising of the sun; but sudden and forcible emancipation resulting from "the efforts the Negroes may make for their actual freedom" can only be effected by massacre and utter destruction. Mr. Lincoln avows, therefore, that he proposes to excite the Negroes of the Southern plantations to murder the families of their masters while these are engaged in the war. The conception of such a crime is horrible. The employment of Indians sinks to a level with civilized warfare in comparison with it; the most detestable doctrines of Mazzini are almost less atrocious; even Mr. Lincoln's own recent achievements of burning by gunboats the defenceless villages on the Mississippi are dwarfed by this gigantic wickedness. The single thing to be said for it is that it is a wickedness that holds its head high and scorns hypocrisy. It does not pretend to attack slavery as slavery. It launches this threat of a servile rebellion as a means of war against certain

States, and accompanies it with a declaration of general protection to all other slavery.

Where he has no power Mr. Lincoln will set the Negroes free; where he retains power he will consider them as slaves. "Come to me," he cries to the insurgent planters, "and I will preserve your rights as slaveholders; but set me still at defiance, and I will wrap myself in virtue, and take the sword of freedom in my hand, and, instead of aiding you to oppress, I will champion the rights of humanity. Here are whips for you who are loyal; go forth and flog or sell your black chattels as you please. Here are torches and knives for employment against you who are disloyal; I will press them into every black hand, and teach their use." Little Delaware, with her 2000 slaves, shall still be protected in her loyal tyranny. Maryland, with her 90,000 slaves, shall "freely accept or freely reject" any project for either gradual or immediate abolition; but if Mississippi and South Carolina, where the slaves rather outnumber the masters, do not repent, and receive from Mr. Lincoln a licence to trade in human flesh, that human flesh shall be adopted by Mr. Lincoln as the agent of his vengeance. The position is peculiar for a mere layman. Mr. Lincoln, by this proclamation, constitutes himself a sort of moral American Pope. He claims to sell indulgences to own votaries, and he offers them with full hands to all who will fall down and worship him. It is his to bind, and it is his to loose. His decree of emancipation is to go into remote States, where his temporal power cannot be made manifest, and where no stars and stripes are to be seen; and in those distant swamps he is, by a sort of Yankee excommunication, to lay the land under a slavery interdict. . . .

As a proof of what the leaders of the North, in their passion and their despair, would do if they could, this is a very sad document. As a proof of the hopelessness and recklessness which prompt their actions, it is a very instructive document. We gather from it that Mr. Lincoln has lost all hope of preserving the Union, and is now willing to let any quack try his nostrum. As an act of policy it is, if possible, more contemptible than it is wicked. It may possibly produce some partial risings, for let any armed power publish an exhortation to the labouring class of any community to plunder and murder, and there will be some response. It might happen in London, or Paris, or New York. That Mr. Lincoln's emancipation decrees will have any general effect bearing upon the issue of the war, we do not, however, believe. The Negroes have already abundantly discovered that the tender mercies of the Northerners are cruelties. The freedom which is associated with labour in the trenches, military discipline, and frank avowals of personal abhorrence momentarily repeated does not commend itself to the Negro nature. General Butler could, if he pleased, tell strange stories of the ill success of his tamperings with the Negroes about New Orleans.

We do not think that even now, when Mr. Lincoln plays his last card, it will prove to be a trump. Powerful malignity is a dreadful reality, but impotent malignity is apt to be a very contemptible spectacle. Here is a would-be conqueror and a would-be extirpator who is not quite safe in his seat of government, who is reduced to such straits that he accepts a defeat as a glorious escape, a capitulation of 8000 men as an unimportant event, a drawn battle as a glorious victory, and the retreat of an invading army which retires laden with plunder and rich in stores as a deliverance. Here is a President who has just, against his will, supplied his antagonists with a hundred and twenty guns and millions of stores, and who is trembling for the very ground on which he stands. Yet, if we judged only by his pompous proclamations, we should believe that he had a garrison in every city of the South. This is more like a Chinaman beating his two swords together to frighten his enemy than like an earnest man pressing on his cause in steadfastness and truth.

—*The Times*, October 7, 1862

B. "Monstrous, Reckless, Devilish"

The past month has brought us to the veritable crisis of the great civil war in America. Brought to bay upon their own soil, the Federals in desperation have invoked to their aid the unutterable horrors of a servile war. With their armies baffled and beaten, and with the standards of the rebel army again within sight of Washington, the President has at length owned the impossibility of success in fair warfare, and seeks to paralyse the victorious armies of the South by letting loose upon their hearths and homes the lust and savagery of four million Negroes. The die is cast. Henceforth it is a war of extermination. The North seeks to make of the South a desert—a wilderness of bloodshed and misery; for thus only, now, does it or can it hope to overcome the seceding Confederacy.

Monstrous, reckless, devilish as the project is, we believe it will not succeed. But it at least marks the crisis and turning-point of the war. It shows that the North has shot its last bolt,—the effects of which we do not yet see, but beyond which there is no other. It proves what every one in this country was loth to believe, that rather than let the Southern States be independent, rather than lose their trade and custom, the North would league itself with Beelzebub, and seek to make a hell of half a continent. In return, this atrocious act justifies the South in hoisting the black flag, and in proclaiming a war without quarter against the Yankee hosts. And thus, within the bosom of civilisation, we are called upon to contemplate a war more full of horrors and wickedness than any which stands recorded in the world's history.

When a crisis so manifest and so terrible has been reached in this most melancholy of all civil wars, it is natural that at least something like a crisis should arise amongst the slow-moving minds of her Majesty's Ministers. If they cannot yet agree to act upon their opinions, each member of the Cabinet, we should think, must at least have arrived at some definite opinion of his own. Three weeks ago it was rumoured that before the end of the month Lord Lyons would return to his post at Washington, bearing with him the definite decision of her Majesty's Government. Simultaneously, or immediately in the wake of this rumour, there came Mr Gladstone's speech at Newcastle, where, amid the applause of his audience, he declared that the people of the Southern States were now to be regarded as a NATION. . . .

When Mr Gladstone spoke thus, so plainly and so strongly, it seemed as if the previous rumours were correct, and that before the month was ended the Southern Confederacy would be officially recognised by the British Government as an independent State. But in a few days more, another member of the Cabinet—as is not unusual with that eminently harmonious body—declared himself of an entirely different opinion. . . .

In a moral point of view, there cannot be two opinions in this country as to the President's proclamation. To employ such a means of hostility as a Negro insurrection is simply infamous. In a political point of view we regard it as the greatest mistake which the North has committed. True, the policy of the North has been slowly approximating to this result: it is a natural climax to the mad policy which has animated the North from the beginning. It is the consummation of the mistakes of the North. Union in any shape is now doubly impossible. It remains to be seen, also, whether the temporary accord which the proclamation has established in the North is not on the surface only, and whether the present lull of dissension will not give way ere long to dissensions still more formidable. In the border States of Kentucky, Tennessee, and Missouri, the proclamation cannot fail to excite new and formidable opposition to the Federal Government; while the Confederate States, now menaced with untold horrors, will put forth their whole strength to keep the danger at a distance, and to roll back the war from their frontiers with the fury of desperation.

—*Blackwood's Edinburgh Magazine*, November 1862

12. MANCHESTER WORKINGMEN STAND BY THE UNION

One of the moving and—as it has turned out—one of the historic interchanges of Anglo-American history came when the workingmen of Manchester, most of them thrown out of work by the cotton shortage, addressed a letter to President Lincoln assuring him of their support now that the war was clearly directed to the abolition of slavery. Lincoln's reply was one of his most felicitous efforts.

A. "WE ARE TRULY ONE PEOPLE"

December 31, 1862

To Abraham Lincoln, President of the United States:

As citizens of Manchester, assembled at the Free-Trade Hall, we beg to express our fraternal sentiments toward you and your country. We rejoice in your greatness as an outgrowth of England, whose blood and language you share, whose orderly and legal freedom you have applied to new circumstances, over a region immeasurably greater than our own. We honor your Free States, as a singularly happy abode for the working millions where industry is honored. One thing alone has, in the past, lessened our sympathy with your country and our confidence in it—we mean the ascendency of politicians who not merely maintained Negro slavery, but desired to extend and root it more firmly.

Since we have discerned, however, that the victory of the free North, in the war which has so sorely distressed us as well as afflicted you, will strike off the fetters of the slave, you have attracted our warm and earnest sympathy. We joyfully honor you, as the President, and the Congress with you, for many decisive steps toward practically exemplifying your belief in the words of your great founders: "All men are created free and equal." You have procured the liberation of the slaves in the district around Washington, and thereby made the centre of your Federation visibly free. You have enforced the laws against the slave-trade, and kept up your fleet against it, even while every ship was wanted for service in your terrible war. You have nobly decided to receive ambassadors from the Negro republics of Hayti and Liberia, thus forever renouncing that unworthy prejudice which refuses the rights of humanity to men and women on account of their color. In order more effectually to stop the slave-trade, you have made with our Queen a treaty, which your Senate has ratified, for the right of mutual search. Your Congress has decreed freedom as the law forever in the vast unoccupied or half unsettled Territories which are directly subject to its legislative power. It has offered pecuniary aid to all States which will enact emancipation locally, and has forbidden your Generals to restore fugitive slaves who seek their protection. You have entreated the slave-masters to accept these moderate offers; and after long and patient waiting, you, as Commander-in-Chief of the Army, have appointed to-morrow, the first of January, 1863, as the day of unconditional freedom for the slaves of the rebel States.

Heartily do we congratulate you and your country on this humane and righteous course. We assume that you cannot now stop short of a complete uprooting of slavery. It would not become us to dictate any details, but there are broad principles of humanity which must guide you. If complete emancipation in some States be deferred, though only to a predetermined day, still in the interval, human beings should not be counted chattels. Women must have the rights of chastity and maternity, men the rights of husbands, masters the liberty of manumission. Justice demands for the black, no less than for the white, the protection of law—that his voice be heard in your courts. Nor must any such abomination be tolerated as slave-breeding States, and a slave market—if you are to earn the high reward of all your sacrifices, in the approval of the universal brotherhood and of the Divine Father. It is for your free country to decide whether any thing but immediate and total emancipation can secure the most indispensable rights of humanity against the inveterate wickedness of local laws and local executives.

We implore you, for your own honor and welfare, not to faint in your providential mission. While your enthusiasm is aflame, and the tide of events runs high, let the work be finished effectually. Leave no root of bitterness to spring up and work fresh misery to your children. It is a mighty task, indeed, to reörganize the industry not only of four millions of the colored race, but of five millions of whites. Nevertheless, the vast progress you have made in the short space of twenty months fills us with hope that every stain on your freedom will shortly be removed, and that the erasure of that foul blot upon civilization and Christianity—chattel slavery—during your Presidency will cause the name of Abraham Lincoln to be honored and revered by posterity. We are certain that such a glorious consummation will cement Great Britain to the United States in close and enduring regards. Our interests, moreover, are identified with yours. We are truly one people, though locally separate. And if you have any ill-wishers here, be assured they are chiefly those who oppose liberty at home, and that they will be powerless to stir up quarrels between us, from the very day in which your country becomes, undeniably and without exception, the home of the free.

Accept our high admiration of your firmness in upholding the proclamation of freedom.

—MOORE, ed., *The Rebellion Record*

B. "AN INSTANCE OF SUBLIME CHRISTIAN HEROISM"

January 19, 1863

To the Working-Men of Manchester:

I have the honor to acknowledge the receipt of the address and resolutions which you sent me on the eve of the new year. When I came, on the 4th of March, 1861, through a free and constitutional election to preside in the Government of the United States, the country was found at the verge of civil war. Whatever might have been the cause, or whosoever the fault, one duty, paramount to all others, was before me, namely, to maintain and preserve at once the Constitution and the integrity of the Federal Republic. A conscientious purpose to perform this duty is the key to all the measures of administration which have been and to all which will hereafter be pursued. Under our frame of government and my official oath, I could not depart from this purpose if I would. It is not always in the power of governments to enlarge or restrict the scope of moral results which follow the policies that they may deem it necessary for the public safety from time to time to adopt.

I have understood well that the duty of self-preservation rests solely with the American people; but I have at the same time been aware that favor or disfavor of foreign nations might have a material influence in enlarging or prolonging the struggle with disloyal men in which the country is engaged. A fair examination of history has served to authorize a belief that the past actions and influences of the United States were generally regarded as having been beneficial toward mankind. I have, therefore, reckoned upon the forbearance of nations. Circumstances—to some of which you kindly allude—induce me especially to expect that if justice and good faith should be practised by the United States, they would encounter no hostile influence on the part of Great Britain. It is now a pleasant duty to acknowledge the demonstration you have given of your desire that a spirit of amity and peace toward this country may prevail in the councils of your Queen, who is respected and esteemed in your own country only more than she is by the kindred nation which has its home on this side of the Atlantic.

I know and deeply deplore the sufferings which the working-men at Manchester, and in all Europe, are called to endure in this crisis. It has been often and studiously represented that the attempt to overthrow this government, which was built upon the foundation of human rights, and to substitute for it one which should rest exclusively on the basis of human slavery, was likely to obtain the favor of Europe. Through the action of our disloyal citizens, the working-men of Europe have been subjected to severe trials, for the purpose of forcing their sanction to that attempt. Under the circumstances, I cannot but regard your decisive utterances upon the question as an instance of sublime Christian heroism which has not been surpassed in any age or in any country. It is indeed an energetic and reinspiring assurance of the inherent power of truth and of the ultimate and universal triumph of justice, humanity, and freedom. I do not doubt that the sentiments you have expressed will be sustained by your great nation; and on the other hand, I have no hesitation in assuring you that they will excite admiration, esteem, and the most reciprocal feelings of friendship among the American people. I hail this interchange of sentiment, therefore, as an augury that whatever else may happen, whatever misfortune may befall your country or my own, the peace and friendship which now exist between the two nations will be, as it shall be my desire to make them, perpetual.

ABRAHAM LINCOLN.
—*Complete Works of Abraham Lincoln*

13. "COUNT" GUROWSKI RAGES AGAINST THE ENGLISH

Every student of the Civil War knows the venomous Gurowski Diary, but few use it, for it is highly unreliable. It is, however, reliable enough as a reflection of personal opinion, and it is as such that excerpts from it are included here.

Count Adam Gurowski—the propriety of his title was always a little dubious—was born in the Palatinate of Kaliz in Poland, and by his twentieth year had been expelled for revolutionary activities. He returned to Poland to help organize a revolution against Russia and on the failure of that uprising fled to Paris where he was condemned to death in absentia. He wrote on Polish history, studied at Berlin and Heidelberg, lectured at the University of Berne, and in 1849 came to the United States. During the Civil War he served as a translator in the State Department, and from this unsatisfactory vantage point watched what he considered the mismanagement of the war. He was particularly bitter about British official policy, and in this he reflected faithfully enough a considerable segment of American opinion. The Decembrist to whom Gurowski refers is, of course, Louis Napoleon, who came to power through the coup of December 1851. Gurowski is at his worst in this Diary; he is at his uncertain best in his perceptive America and Europe.

Dec. 7 [1862].—The European wiseacres, the would-be statesmen, whether in or out of power, especially in England, and that opprobrium of our century, the English and the Franco-Bonapartist press, have decided to do all that their clever brains can scheme towards preventing this noble American people from working out its mighty and beneficent destinies, and from elaborating and making more glorious than ever its own already very glorious history. As well might the brainless and heartless conspirators against human progress and human liberty endeavor to arrest the rotation of a planet by the stroke of a pickaxe.

Dec. 30.—Those foreign caterwaulings against Butler. England, in 1848-9, whipped women in Ireland, and how many thousands have been murdered by the *Decembriseur?* And the Russian minister joining in this music. A shame for him and for his government!

Dec. 30.—Poor Greeley looks for intervention, mediation, arbitration; and selects Switzerland for the fitting arbitrator! How little—nay—nothing at all, he knows about Switzerland and the Swiss! Stop! stop! respectable old man!

Jan. 5 [1863].—European rulers, wiseacres, meddlers, humbugs, traitors, demons, diplomats, assert that they must interfere here because European interests suffer by the war. Indeed! You have the whole old continent and Australia to boot, and about nine hundreds millions of population; can you not organise yourself so as not to depend from us? And if by your misrules, etc., our interests were to suffer, you would find very strange any complaint made on our part. Keep aloof with your good wishes, and with your advices, and with your interference. You may burn your noses, and even lose your little scalps. You robbers, murderers, hypocrites, surrounded by your liveried lackeys, you presumptuous, arrogant curses of the human race, stand off, and let these people whose worst criminal is a saint compared to a *Decembriseur*—let this people work out its destinies, be it for good or evil.

January 15.—The noble and lofty voice of the genuine English people, the voice of the working classes, begins to be heard. The people re-echo the key-note struck by a J. S. Mills, by a Bright, a Cobden, and others of like pure mind and noble heart. The voice of the genuine English people resounds altogether differently from the shrill *falsetto* with which turf hunters, rent-roll devourers, lords, lordlings, and all the like shams and whelps try to intimidate the patriotic North, and comfort the traitors, the rebels.

January 16.— ... Sumner will believe that his letters to English old women will change the minds of the English semi-pirates. Sumner is a little afraid of losing ground with the English guardians of civilization. Sumner is full of good wishes, of generous conceptions, and is the man for the millennium. Sumner lacks the keen, sharp, piercing appreciation of common events. And thus Sumner cannot detect that England makes war on our commerce, under the piratic flag of the rebels.

April 2.—Official, lordish, Toryish England, plays treason and infamy right and left. The English money lenders to rebels, the genuine owners of rebel piratical ships, are anxious to destroy the American commerce and to establish over the South an English monopoly. All this because *odiunt dum metuant* the Yankee. You tories, you enemies of freedom, your time of reckoning will come, and it will come at the hands of your own people. You fear the example of America for your oppressions, for your rent-rolls.

April 6.—The people feel how the treason of the English evil wishers slowly extends through its organs. By Butler, Wade, Grimes and others, the people ask for non-intercourse with the English assassin, who surreptitiously, stealthily under cover of darkness, of legal formality, deals, or attempts to deal, a deadly blow. The American sentimentalists strain to the utmost their soft brains, to find excuses for English treason.

English lordlings, scholars, moralists of the Carlyleian mental perversion comment Homer, instead of being clear sighted commentators of what passes under their noses. The English phrase-mongering philanthropists all with joy smacked their bloody lips at the, by them ardently wished and expected downfall of a noble, free and self-governing people. Tigers, hyenas and jackals! clatter your teeth, smack your lips! but you shall not get at the prey.

—Gurowski, *Diary*

14. RICHARD COBDEN REJOICES IN THE EMANCIPATION PROCLAMATION

Cobden, with Bright, was the leader of the English liberals in the mid-nineteenth century. A wealthy manufacturer, he abandoned business to agitate against the Corn Laws and was chiefly instrumental in obtaining their repeal. In Parliament he proved an eloquent spokesman for liberal and humanitarian causes, strongly opposing the Crimean War, intervention in China, and espousing, like Bright, free trade and electoral reform. Twice offered posts in the Cabinet, he twice refused. Worn out with his public labors Cobden died in 1865, but not before he had rendered signal service to the cause of Anglo-American unity; it is not an accident that the Carnegie Endowment has made Cobden's birthplace, Dunford House, an international shrine.

This letter, like Bright's, is addressed to Charles Sumner.

Athenaeum Club, London, 13 Feby., 1863

Private
My dear Sumner.

If I have not written to you before it is not because I have been indifferent to what is passing in your midst. I may say sincerely that my thoughts have run almost as much on American as English politics. But I could do you no service, and shrunk from occupying your overtaxed attention even for a moment. My object in now writing is to speak of a matter which has a practical bearing on your affairs.

You know how much alarmed I was from the first lest our government should interpose in your affairs. The disposition of our ruling class, and the necessities of our cotton trade, pointed to some act of intervention and the indifference of the great mass of our population to your struggle, the object of which they did not foresee and understand, would have made intervention easy indeed popular if you had been a weaker naval power. This state of feeling existed up to the announcement of the President's emancipation Policy. From that moment our old anti-slavery feeling began to arouse itself, and it has been gathering strength ever since. The great rush of the public to all the public meetings called on the subject shows how wide and deep the sympathy for personal freedom still is in the hearts of our people. I know nothing in my political experience so striking as a display of spontaneous public action as that of the vast gathering at Exeter Hall when without one attraction in the form of a popular orator the vast building, its minor rooms and passages and the streets adjoining were crowded with an enthusiastic audience. That meeting has had a powerful effect on our newspapers and politicians. It has closed the mouths of those who have been advocating the side of the South.

And I now write to assure you that any unfriendly act on the part of our government, no matter which of our aristocratic parties is in power, towards your cause is not to be apprehended. If an attempt were made by the government in any way to commit us to the South, a spirit would be instantly aroused which would drive our government from power. This I suppose will be known and felt by the Southern agents in Europe and if communicated to their government must I should think operate as a great discouragement to them. For I *know* that those agents have been incessantly urging in every quarter where they could hope to influence the French and English governments the absolute necessity of *recognition* as a means of putting an end to the war. Recognition of the South, by England, whilst it bases itself on Negro slavery, is an impossibility, unless indeed after the Federal government have recognized the Confederates as a nation.

So much for the influence which your emancipation policy has had on the public opinion of England. But judging from the tone of your press in America it does not seem to have gained the support of your masses. About this however I do not feel competent to offer an opinion. Nor, to confess the truth, do I feel much satisfaction in treating of your politics at all. There appears to me great mismanagement I had almost said incapacity in the management of your affairs, and you seem to be hastening towards financial and economical evils in a manner which fills me with apprehension for the future.

When I met Fremont in Paris two years ago just as you commenced this terrible war I remarked to him that the total abolition of slavery in your northern Continent was the only issue which could justify the war to the civilized world. Every symptom seems to point to this result. But at what a price is the Negro to be emancipated! I confess that if then I had been the arbiter of his fate I should have refused him freedom at the cost of so much white men's blood and women's tears. I do not however blame the North. The South fired the first shot, and on them righteously falls the

malediction that "they who take the sword shall perish by the sword."
    Believe me,

Yours very truly

R. Cobden

—E. L. Pierce, contrib., "Letters of Richard Cobden to Charles Sumner"

15. ENGLISH ARISTOCRATS ORGANIZE FOR SOUTHERN INDEPENDENCE

The mediation crisis of 1862 had been successfully surmounted by An-
tietam, and by the Emancipation Proclamation. Yet the Confederate cause
appeared by no means hopeless, and agitation for some form of intervention
persisted. More and more, however, that agitation took on a class character;
it was supported by the aristocracy and the great shipbuilders and textile
manufacturers. A London Confederate States Aid Association had been or-
ganized in 1862, but had died a lingering death. Early in 1863 it was sup-
planted by a Southern Independence Association, whose Constitution we
reproduce here. The most interesting thing about this otherwise curious
organization is its list of sponsors. It appealed, as the Index *pointed out, to*
"persons of rank and gentlemen of standing." It was this association that
called forth Goldwin Smith's devastating "Letter to a Whig Member," one
of the most powerful of all defenses of the Union cause.

Southern Independence Association of London

Public opinion is becoming enlightened upon the disruption of the late
United States, and upon the character of the war which has been raging on
the American continent for nearly three years. British subjects were at first
hardly able to realize a federation of States each in itself possessed of sovereign attributes; while deriving their views of American history from New
York and New England, they ascribed the secession of the Southern States
to pique at a lost election, and to fear for the continuance of an institution
peculiarly distasteful to Englishmen. Assurances were rife from those quarters that the movement was the conspiracy of a few daring men, and that a
strong Union sentiment existed in the seceding States, which would soon
assert its existence under stress of the war.

Gradually the true causes of the disruption have made themselves more
and more manifest. The long-widening and now insuperable divergence of
character and interests between the two sections of the former Union has
been made palpable by the facts of the gigantic struggle. Their wisdom in
council, their endurance in the field, and the universal self-sacrifice which
has characterized their public and their private life, have won general sympathy for the Confederates as a people worthy of, and who have earned, their
independence.

On the other hand, the favorable judgment which Englishmen had long
cherished as a duty towards that portion of the United States which they

imagined most to resemble the Mother Country has met with many rude shocks from the spectacles which have been revealed in that land of governmental tyranny, corruption in high places, ruthlessness in war, untruthfulness of speech, and causeless animosity towards Great Britain. At the same time the Southerners, who had been very harshly judged in this country, have manifested the highest national characteristics, to the surprise and admiration of all.

Public men are awakening to the truth that it is both useless and mischievous to ignore the gradual settlement of Central North America into groups of States, or consolidated nationalities, each an independent Power. They feel that the present attempt of the North is in manifest opposition to this law of natural progress, and they see that the South can never be reunited with the North except as a conquered and garrisoned dependency; whilst the Northern States, if content to leave their former partners alone, are still in possession of all the elements of great and growing national power and wealth.

Our commercial classes are also beginning to perceive that our best interests will be promoted by creating a direct trade with a people so enterprising as the Confederates, inhabiting a land so wide and so abundant in the richest gifts of Providence, and anxious to place themselves in immediate connection with the manufacturers and consumers of Europe.

In short, the struggle is now felt to be, according to Earl Russell's pregnant expression, one for independence on the part of the South, and for empire on the part of the North; for an independence, on the one hand, which it is equitable for themselves and desirable for the world they should achieve; for an empire, on the other hand, which is only possible at the price of the first principles of Federal Republicanism, and whose establishment by fire and sword, and at a countless cost of human life on both sides, would be the ruin of the Southern States. These, surely, are reasons which invoke the intervention of other Powers, if intervention be possible, in the cause of common humanity.

Therefore, not in enmity to the North, but sympathizing with the Confederates, the Southern Independence Association of London has been formed, to act in concert with that which is so actively and usefully at work in Manchester. . . .

The Association will also devote itself to the cultivation of friendly feelings between the people of Great Britain and of the Confederate States; and it will, in particular, steadily but kindly represent to the Southern States that recognition by Europe must necessarily lead to a revision of the system of servile labor unhappily bequeathed to them by England, in accordance with the spirit of the age, so as to combine the gradual extinction of slavery with the preservation of property, the maintenance of the civil polity, and the true civilization of the Negro race.

> The Most Noble the Marquis of Lothian
> The Most Noble the Marquis of Bath
> The Lord Robert Cecil, M.P.

The Lord Eustace Cecil
The Right Honourable Lord Wharncliffe
The Right Honourable Lord Campbell
The Hon. C. Fitzwilliam, M.P.
The Honourable Robt. Bourke
Edward Akroyd, Esq., Halifax
Colonel Greville, M.P.
W. H. Gregory, Esq. M.P.
T. C. Haliburton, Esq. M.P.
A. J. B. Beresford Hope, Esq.
W. S. Lindsay, Esq. M.P.
Wm. Scholefield, Esq. M.P.
James Spence, Esq., Liverpool
William Vansittart, Esq. M.P.
—GOLDWIN SMITH, *Letter to a Whig Member*

16. MINISTER ADAMS POINTS OUT THAT THIS IS WAR

The last diplomatic crisis between Britain and the United States threatened to be the most serious. As early as 1861 the Confederate government had dispatched Captain Bulloch to England to contract for the construction of commerce-destroyers in British shipyards. English law, and the Proclamation of Neutrality, forbade this, but it was relatively easy to evade the prohibition by juggling the ownership papers.

Thus the Confederates were able to build the Florida and the Alabama in England; the subsequent depredations of these ships laid the basis for the Alabama claims. That the Alabama was being built for the Confederacy was common knowledge, but when Adams protested it, he was met with the assertion that there was no legal proof of Confederate ownership!

Even more serious was the Confederate plan to build ironclad rams in British yards. Contracts for these were placed with the Laird brothers, for delivery in the summer of 1863, and construction was soon under way at Birkenhead. If these should get away the prospects for American commerce were black; there were no United States ships that could stand up to them and, as Captain Gustavus Fox, Assistant Secretary of the Navy, wrote, "it is a question of life and death." Adams took energetic action, laying before Russell evidence of Confederate ownership. Russell was not satisfied, and Adams supplied him with additional evidence, which he found only partly persuasive.

Meantime other influences were more persuasive. One was the Congressional Act of March 1863 authorizing Lincoln to issue letters of marque to merchantmen: the victims would obviously be English vessels. Another was the combination of Gettysburg and Vicksburg.

On September 3 Russell ordered the ironclads to be detained. Adams did not know this, and two days later he sent this famous letter with its somewhat ambiguous threat of war. The letter was not essential, but it helped. In

October the ironclads were seized by the British government, and subsequently purchased and commissioned in the British Navy.

This was the last episode that seriously troubled Anglo-American relations during the war. The combination of Union success on the battlefields and in the coastal waters and of the Emancipation policy persuaded the British government to a far more friendly attitude toward the North. The one thing that continued to exacerbate the relations of the two countries was the ravages of the cruisers Alabama, Shenandoah *and* Florida. *After the war (1872) the* Alabama *Claims Commission found the British government remiss in allowing these ships to escape and required Britain to pay the United States damages of fifteen and one-half million dollars.*

Legation of the United States, London, September 5, 1863

My Lord,

At this moment, when one of the iron-clad war-vessels is on the point of departure from this kingdom on its hostile errand against the United States, I am honoured with the reply of your Lordship to my notes of the 11th, 16th, and 25th of July and of the 14th of August. I trust I need not express how profound is my regret at the conclusion to which Her Majesty's Government have arrived. I can regard it no otherwise than as practically opening to the insurgents free liberty in this kingdom to execute a policy described in one of their late publications in the following language:—

"In the present state of the harbour-defences of New York, Boston, Portland, and smaller Northern cities, such a vessel as the 'Warrior' would have little difficulty in entering any of those ports, and inflicting a vital blow upon the enemy, The destruction of Boston alone would be worth a hundred victories in the field. It would bring such a terror to the 'blue-noses' as to cause them to wish eagerly for peace, despite their overweening love of gain which has been so freely administered to since the opening of this war. Vessels of the 'Warrior' class would promptly raise the blockade of our ports, and would, even in this respect, confer advantages which would soon repay the cost of their construction."

It would be superfluous in me to point out to your Lordship that this is war. No matter what may be the theory adopted of neutrality in a struggle, when this process is carried on in the manner indicated from a territory and with the aid of the subjects of a third party, that third party, to all intents and purposes, ceases to be neutral. Neither is it necessary to show that any Government which suffers it to be done fails in enforcing the essential conditions of international amity towards the country against whom the hostility is directed. In my belief it is impossible that any nation retaining a proper degree of self-respect could tamely submit to a continuance of relations so utterly deficient in reciprocity. I have no idea that Great Britain would do so for a moment.

After a careful examination of the full instructions with which I have been furnished in preparation for such an emergency, I deem it inexpedient for me to attempt any recurrence to arguments for effective interposition in the present case. The fatal objection of impotency which paralyzes Her Majesty's Government seems to present an insuperable barrier against all further reasoning. Under these circumstances I prefer to desist from communicating to your Lordship even such further portions of my existing instructions as are suited to the case, lest I should contribute to aggravate difficulties already far too serious. I therefore content myself with informing your Lordship that I transmit by the present steamer a copy of your note for the consideration of my Government, and shall await the more specific directions that will be contained in the reply.

CHARLES FRANCIS ADAMS
—*State Papers, North America*

XVI

Songs the Soldiers Sang

IT IS *no accident that the motorized armies of the First and Second World Wars inspired so few songs, and sang so few. The Civil War armies were not mechanized; soldiers marched afoot, and as they marched they sang. No other war has provided us with so many songs, or so many that have retained their popularity for so long—marching songs like "Tramp, Tramp, Tramp," inspirational songs like "The Battle Hymn of the Republic," patriotic songs like "Bonnie Blue Flag," humorous songs like "Goober Peas," sentimental songs like "Lorena."*

There was little organized entertainment in the Civil War—the Sanitary Commission had other things to do than entertain soldiers—so the soldiers amused themselves, often by communal singing, and we know that many of these songs were sung around the campfires of Union and Confederate armies. The folks back home sang, too, gathering around the pianos now appearing in increasing numbers in American parlors.

Only a few of these songs—a selection from hundreds—need any explanation. Most of them can be assigned, with some assurance, to particular authors, and sometimes to composers; others are of disputed origin; others still seem to have come spontaneously from the soldiers themselves. Many of them are preserved for us in variant forms.

This selection is designed to suggest what the soldiers, and their families, actually sang. Patriotic poems—the "Barbara Frietchie" and "Little Giffen of Tennessee" type—are omitted. Some songs were popular in particular regions, or with particular armies, or enjoyed only fleeting popularity; others, like "Lorena," seem to have been equally popular North and South, East and West, with soldiers and with civilians.

1. DIXIE

The most famous and most widely sung of all Civil War songs, "Dixie" actually antedated the war by two years. Nor was it, originally, a Southern song. It was composed by an Ohioan, Dan Emmett, and first sung in Mechanics' Hall on Broadway in April 1859. The origin of the name "Dixie" is obscure, but it was used by Emmett himself in another song composed shortly before "Dixie Land." The song caught on at once and, with the coming of secession, swept the South, where numerous other—and supposedly more appropriate—words were attached to it. It was played at Davis' inauguration as provisional President in Montgomery, Alabama, in February 1861. Yet it was never wholly a Southern song; it is worth remembering that when Lincoln was serenaded after the surrender of Lee he came out on a White House balcony and asked the band to play "Dixie"—now once again a national tune.

Daniel Decatur Emmett is remembered as "the father of the Negro Minstrelsy." He had composed "Old Dan Tucker" in 1830, at the age of fifteen, and thereafter poured out a succession of popular songs for his troupe: "Root, Hog, or Die," "Jordan is a Hard Road to Travel," "High Daddy," and many others well known in their day. He wrote both the words and the music for "Dixie."

        I wish I was in de land ob cotton,
        Old times dar am not forgotten,
           Look away, look away, look away, Dixie Land!
        In Dixie Land whar I was born in,
        Early on one frosty mornin',
        Look away, look away, look away, Dixie Land!

        CHORUS—Den I wish I was in Dixie—
               Hooray, hooray!
               In Dixie land I'll take my stan'!
               To lib an' die in Dixie
                   Away, away,
               Away down south in Dixie
                   Away, away,
               Away down south in Dixie.

        Ole Missus marry "Will-de-Weaber,"
        William was a gay deceber
           Look away, look away, look away, Dixie Land!
        But when he put his arm around 'er
        He smiled as fierce as a forty-pounder
        Look away, look away, look away, Dixie Land!—CHORUS

        His face was sharp as a butcher's cleaber,
        But dat did not seem to grieb 'er,
           Look away, look away, look away, Dixie Land!
        Ole Missus acted de foolish part,
        An' died for a man dat broke her heart,
           Look away, look away, look away, Dixie Land!—CHORUS

        Now, here's a health to de next ole Missus,
        An' all de gals dat want to kiss us,
           Look away, look away, look away, Dixie Land!
        But if you want to drive 'way sorrow,
        Come an' hear dis song to-morrow,
           Look away, look away, look away, Dixie Land!—CHORUS

Dar's buckwheat cakes an' Injun batter,
Makes you fat, or a little fatter,
   Look away, look away, look away, Dixie Land!
Den hoe it down and scratch your grabble,
To Dixie's Land I'm bound to trabble,
   Look away, look away, look away, Dixie Land!—CHORUS
           —DANIEL D. EMMETT

2. THE BONNIE BLUE FLAG

"The Bonnie Blue Flag" came out of New Orleans. It was written and first sung by Harry McCarthy, who needed a new song to fill out an act at the Varieties Theatre, in September 1861; the tune was that of an old Irish song, "The Jaunting Car." From New Orleans it spread quickly throughout the South, becoming, in the end, the most popular of Southern marching songs next to "Dixie." When Butler was in command in New Orleans he arrested and fined Blackmar, its publisher, and threatened to fine any one who sang this song 25 dollars. As with so many Civil War songs there are many versions, and many variations in the text.

We are a band of brothers, and native to the soil,
Fighting for the property we gained by honest toil;
And when our rights were threatened, the cry rose near and far:
Hurrah for the bonnie Blue Flag that bears a single star!
   Hurrah! hurrah! for the bonnie Blue Flag
   That bears a single star.

As long as the Union was faithful to her trust,
Like friends and like brothers, kind were we and just;
But now when Northern treachery attempts our rights to mar,
We hoist on high the bonnie Blue Flag that bears a single star.

First, gallant South Carolina nobly made the stand;
Then came Alabama, who took her by the hand;
Next, quickly Mississippi, Georgia, and Florida—
All raised the flag, the bonnie Blue Flag that bears a single star.

Ye men of valor, gather round the banner of the right;
Texas and fair Louisiana join us in the fight.
Davis, our loved President, and Stephens, statesmen are;
Now rally round the bonnie Blue Flag that bears a single star.

And here's to brave Virginia! the Old Dominion State
With the young Confederacy at length has linked her fate.
Impelled by her example, now other States prepare
To hoist on high the bonnie Blue Flag that bears a single star.

Then here's to our Confederacy; strong we are and brave,
Like patriots of old we'll fight, our heritage to save;
And rather than submit to shame, to die we would prefer;
So cheer for the bonnie Blue Flag that bears a single star.

Then cheer, boys, cheer, raise the joyous shout,
For Arkansas and North Carolina now have both gone out;
And let another rousing cheer for Tennessee be given,
The single star of the bonnie Blue Flag has grown to be eleven!
    Hurrah! hurrah! for the bonnie Blue Flag
    That bears a single star.

                       —HARRY McCARTHY

3. JOHN BROWN'S BODY

This, the most widely sung of Federal songs, is apparently a genuine folk song. No one knows its precise origin, or its author. The tune was taken from a Negro melody popular in the Carolina low country, where it was sung to the refrain

        Say, brothers, will you meet us?
        On Canaan's happy shore?

The words have been assigned to Thomas B. Bishop; the adaptation of the words to the familiar tune to James E. Greenleaf of the Boston Light Artillery, and to a Mr. Gilmore who played it before the 12th Massachusetts Volunteers. Perhaps the most popular variation was "We'll Hang Jeff Davis on a Sour Apple Tree."

    John Brown's body lies a-mould'ring in the grave,
    John Brown's body lies a-mould'ring in the grave,
    John Brown's body lies a-mould'ring in the grave,
        His soul is marching on.

      CHORUS: Glory! Glory Hallelujah!
             Glory! Glory Hallelujah!
             Glory! Glory Hallelujah!
             His soul is marching on.

    He's gone to be a soldier in the army of the Lord!
      His soul is marching on.—CHORUS

    John Brown's knapsack is strapped upon his back.
      His soul is marching on.—CHORUS

    His pet lambs will meet him on the way,
      And they'll go marching on.—CHORUS

    They'll hang Jeff Davis on a sour apple tree,
      As they go marching on.—CHORUS

Now for the Union let's give three rousing cheers,
  As we go marching on.
    Hip, Hip, hip, hip, Hurrah!—CHORUS
          —THOMAS B. BISHOP (?)

4. ALL QUIET ALONG THE POTOMAC

Both the author and the composer of this song, so popular with both armies and both peoples, were New Yorkers. Inspired by the oft-repeated headline in the newspapers in 1861, "All Quiet Along the Potomac," with a little notice underneath—"A Picket Shot"—Ethel Lynn Beers composed this poem and published it in Harper's Magazine *in November 1861 under the title "The Picket Guard." Later it was claimed by the fabulous Major Lamar Fontaine of the Confederate Army. The music has been credited to both Henry Coyle and to J. Dayton, both of the 1st Connecticut Artillery, but it seems clearly to have been composed by the famous poet, journalist, and musician, James Hewitt—who at the time was drilling recruits in Richmond, Virginia.*

"All quiet along the Potomac," they say,
  "Except now and then a stray picket
Is shot, as he walks on his beat to and fro,
  By a rifleman hid in the thicket.
'Tis nothing—a private or two now and then
  Will not count in the news of the battle;
Not an officer lost—only one of the men,
  Moaning out, all alone, the death-rattle."

All quiet along the Potomac to-night,
  Where the soldiers lie peacefully dreaming;
Their tents in the rays of the clear autumn moon,
  Or the light of the watch-fire, are gleaming.
A tremulous sigh of the gentle night-wind
  Through the forest leaves softly is creeping;
While stars up above, with their glittering eyes,
  Keep guard, for the army is sleeping.

There's only the sound of the lone sentry's tread,
  As he tramps from the rock to the fountain,
And thinks of the two in the low trundle-bed
  Far away in the cot on the mountain.
His musket falls slack; his face, dark and grim,
  Grows gentle with memories tender,
As he mutters a prayer for the children asleep,
  For their mother; may Heaven defend her!

The moon seems to shine just as brightly as then,
    That night, when the love yet unspoken
Leaped up to his lips—when low-murmured vows
    Were pledged to be ever unbroken.
Then drawing his sleeve roughly over his eyes,
    He dashes off tears that are welling,
And gathers his gun closer up to its place,
    As if to keep down the heart-swelling.

He passes the fountain, the blasted pine-tree,
    The footstep is lagging and weary;
Yet onward he goes, through the broad belt of light,
    Toward the shade of the forest so dreary.
Hark! was it the night-wind that rustled the leaves?
    Was it moonlight so wondrously flashing?
It looked like a rifle . . . "Ha! Mary, good-bye!"
    The red life-blood is ebbing and plashing.

All quiet along the Potomac to-night;
    No sound save the rush of the river;
While soft falls the dew on the face of the dead—
    The picket's off duty forever!
                              —Ethel Lynn Beers

5. MARCHING ALONG

This was a favorite with the soldiers of the Army of the Potomac: the name of the "leader" was changed—pretty frequently as it turned out—to fit the facts. William Bradbury was, in his day, one of the most distinguished of American composers. A student of the great Lowell Mason, he was instrumental in introducing music into the schools, put out a number of singing books, and contributed richly to American psalmody. Among his better known songs are "Just as I Am" and "He Leadeth Me."

The army is gathering from near and from far;
The trumpet is sounding the call for the war;
McClellan's our leader, he's gallant and strong;
We'll gird on our armor and be marching along.

Chorus: Marching along, we are marching along,
            Gird on the armor and be marching along;
            McClellan's our leader, he's gallant and strong;
            For God and our country we are marching along.

The foe is before us in battle array,
But let us not waver, or turn from the way;
The Lord is our strength, and the Union's our song;
With courage and faith we are marching along.—Chorus

Our wives and our children we leave in your care;
We feel you will help them with sorrow to bear:
'Tis hard thus to part, but we hope 't won't be long:
We'll keep up our heart as we're marching along.—Chorus

We sigh for our country, we mourn for our dead;
For them now our last drop of blood we will shed;
Our cause is the right one—our foe's in the wrong;
Then gladly we'll sing as we're marching along.—Chorus

The flag of our country is floating on high;
We'll stand by that flag till we conquer or die;
McClellan's our leader, he's gallant and strong;
We'll gird on our armor and be marching along.—Chorus
              —William Batchelder Bradbury

6. MARYLAND! MY MARYLAND!

This best known of all state songs was written, appropriately enough, by a native of Baltimore. James Ryder Randall had gone to New Orleans in 1859 to clerk in a ship broker's office. The following year he took a position as tutor in English at Poydras College, a Creole school in Pointe Coupee Parish, and he was there when he read the story of the attack on the 6th Massachusetts as it forced its way through Baltimore. That night he wrote "Maryland! My Maryland!" and sent it to the New Orleans Delta, *where it was printed in the issue of April 26. The Misses Cary of Baltimore adapted the words to the familiar music of "O Tannenbaum," and it became one of the favorite marching songs of the Confederacy.*

The despot's heel is on thy shore,
    Maryland!
His torch is at thy temple door,
    Maryland!
Avenge the patriotic gore
That flecked the streets of Baltimore,
And be the battle queen of yore,
    Maryland! My Maryland!

Hark to an exiled son's appeal,
    Maryland!
My mother State! to thee I kneel,
    Maryland!
For life and death, for woe and weal,
Thy peerless chivalry reveal,
And gird thy beauteous limbs with steel,
    Maryland! My Maryland!

Thou wilt not cower in the dust,
 Maryland!
Thy beaming sword shall never rust,
 Maryland!
Remember Carroll's sacred trust,
Remember Howard's warlike thrust,—
And all thy slumberers with the just,
 Maryland! My Maryland!

Come! for thy shield is bright and strong,
 Maryland!
Come! for thy dalliance does thee wrong,
 Maryland!
Come to thine own heroic throng,
Stalking with Liberty along,
And chaunt thy dauntless slogan song,
 Maryland! My Maryland!

Dear Mother! burst the tyrant's chain,
 Maryland!
Virginia should not call in vain,
 Maryland!
She meets her sisters on the plain—
"*Sic semper!*" 'tis the proud refrain
That baffles minions back again,
 Maryland! My Maryland!

I hear the distant thunder-hum,
 Maryland!
The Old Line's bugle, fife, and drum,
 Maryland!
She is not dead, nor deaf, nor dumb—
Huzza! she spurns the Northern scum!
She breathes! she burns! she'll come! she'll come!
 Maryland! My Maryland!
     —James R. Randall

7. YE CAVALIERS OF DIXIE

This song was sung to the tune of "Ye Mariners of England"—a difficult tune which relegated the song largely to the stage.

Ye Cavaliers of Dixie!
Who guard the Southern shores,
Whose standards brave the battle storm
Which o'er our border roars
Your glorious sabers draw once more,

And charge the Northern foe;
And reap their columns deep,
And reap their columns deep,
And reap their columns deep.

CHORUS: Where the raging tempests blow,
Where the raging tempests blow,
And the iron hail in floods descends,
And the bloody torrents flow.

Ye Cavaliers of Dixie!
Though dark the tempest lower,
What arms will wear the tyrant's chains
What dastard heart will cower?
Bright o'er the night a sign shall rise
To lead to victory!
And your swords reap their hordes,
Where the battle tempests blow;
Where the iron hail in floods descends,
And the bloody torrents flow.—CHORUS

The South! she needs no ramparts,
No lofty towers to shield;
Your bosoms are her bulwarks strong,
Breastworks that never yield!
The thunder of your battle blades
Shall sweep the servile foe;
While their gore stains the shore,
Where the battle tempests blow;
Where the iron hail in floods descends,
And the bloody torrents flow.—CHORUS

The battle-flag of Dixie
With crimson field shall flame;
Her azure cross and silver stars
Shall light her sons to fame!
When peace with olive branch returns,
That flag's white folds shall glow
Still bright on every height,
When storm has ceased to blow,
And the battle tempests roar no more;
Nor the bloody torrents flow.—CHORUS
                    —BENJAMIN F. PORTER

8. STONEWALL JACKSON'S WAY

*A whole volume could be compiled of poetic tributes to the great Stone-
wall; if not the best this is certainly the liveliest, and its tune one of the most*

melodious. The author, John W. Palmer, was a Baltimore-born physician who had been in the Gold Rush, sailed to Hawaii, taken part in the Second Burmese War, and settled in New York as journalist, poet and playwright. When the war came Palmer went to Richmond, where, for a time, he was correspondent for the New York Tribune. *Later he served on the staff of General Breckinridge. "Stonewall Jackson's Way" was written at the Battle of Antietam.*

Come, stack arms, men! Pile on the rails,
   Stir up the camp-fire bright;
No matter if the canteen fails,
   We'll make a roaring night.
Here Shenandoah brawls along,
There burly Blue Ridge echoes strong,
To swell the brigade's rousing song
   Of "Stonewall Jackson's Way."

We see him now—the old slouched hat
   Cocked o'er his eye askew,
The shrewd, dry smile, the speech so pat,
   So calm, so blunt, so true.
The "Blue-Light Elder" knows 'em well;
Says he, "That's Banks—he's fond of shell;
Lord save his soul! we'll give him"—well,
   That's "Stonewall Jackson's way."

Silence! ground arms! kneel all! caps off!
   Old Blue-Light's going to pray.
Strangle the fool that dares to scoff!
   Attention! it's his way.
Appealing from his native sod,
In *forma pauperis* to God—
"Lay bare thine arm, stretch forth thy rod!
   Amen!" That's "Stonewall's way."

He's in the saddle now. Fall in!
   Steady! the whole brigade!
Hill's at the ford, cut off—we'll win
   His way out, ball and blade!
What matter if our shoes are worn?
What matter if our feet are torn?
"Quick-step! we're with him before dawn!"
   That's "Stonewall Jackson's way."

The sun's bright lances rout the mists
   Of morning and by George!
Here's Longstreet struggling in the lists,
   Hemmed in an ugly gorge.

Pope and his Yankees, whipped before,
"Bay'nets and grape!" near Stonewall roar;
"Charge, Stuart! Pay off Ashby's score!"
Is "Stonewall Jackson's way."

Ah! maiden, wait and watch and yearn
For news of Stonewall's band!
Ah! widow, read with eyes that burn
That ring upon thy hand.
Ah! wife, sew on, pray on, hope on!
Thy life shall not be all forlorn.
The foe had better ne'er been born
That gets in "Stonewall's way."
—JOHN WILLIAMSON PALMER

9. THE BATTLE HYMN OF THE REPUBLIC

It can hardly be doubted that this is the one great song to come out of the Civil War—the one that transcends that particular conflict and embraces every great moral crusade.

Julia Ward Howe was the daughter of a New York banker and wife of the famous Massachusetts reformer, Samuel Gridley Howe. She early made a name for herself in Boston circles by her essays and poems and by her zealous advocacy of abolition and woman's rights. The following excerpts tell how she came to write the "Battle Hymn," and give a glimpse of the meaning of the song to Union prisoners.

A. WRITING "THE BATTLE HYMN OF THE REPUBLIC"

I DISTINCTLY remember that a feeling of discouragement came over me as I drew near the city of Washington. I thought of the women of my acquaintance whose sons or husbands were fighting our great battle, the women themselves serving in the hospitals, or busying themselves with the work of the Sanitary Commission. My husband was beyond the age of military service, my eldest son but a stripling; my youngest was a child of not more than two years. I could not leave my nursery to follow the march of our armies; neither had I the practical deftness which the preparing and packing of sanitary stores demanded. Something seemed to say to me, "You would be glad to serve, but you cannot help any one; you have nothing to give, and there is nothing for you to do." Yet, because of my sincere desire, a word was given me to say, which did strengthen the hearts of those who fought in the field and of those who languished in the prison.

We were invited one day to attend a review of troops at some distance from the town. While we were engaged in watching the maneuvers, a sudden movement of the enemy necessitated immediate action. The review was discontinued, and we saw a detachment of soldiers gallop to the assistance of a small body of our men who were in imminent danger of being surrounded and cut off from retreat. The regiments remaining on the field were ordered to march to their cantonments. We returned to the city very slowly, of necessity, for the troops nearly filled the road. My dear minister was in the carriage with me, as were several other friends. To beguile the rather tedious drive, we sang from time to time snatches of the army songs so popular at that time, concluding, I think, with:

> John Brown's body lies a-moldering in the ground;
> His soul is marching on.

The soldiers seemed to like this and answered back, "Good for you!" Mr. Clark said, "Mrs. Howe, why do you not write some good words for that stirring tune?" I replied that I had often wished to do this but had not as yet found in my mind any leading toward it.

I went to bed that night as usual and slept, according to my wont, quite soundly. I awoke in the gray of the morning twilight, and as I lay waiting for the dawn, the long lines of the desired poem began to twine themselves in my mind. Having thought out all the stanzas, I said to myself, "I must get up and write these verses down, lest I fall asleep again and forget them." So with a sudden effort I sprang out of bed and found in the dimness an old stump of a pen which I remembered to have used the day before. I scrawled the verses almost without looking at the paper. I had learned to do this when, on previous occasions, attacks of versification had visited me in the night and I feared to have recourse to a light lest I should wake the baby, who slept near me. I was always obliged to decipher my scrawl before another night should intervene, as it was only legible while the matter was fresh in my mind. At this time, having completed my writing, I returned to bed and fell asleep, saying to myself, "I like this better than most things that I have written."

The poem, which was soon after published in the *Atlantic Monthly* [February 1862], was somewhat praised on its appearance, but the vicissitudes of the war so engrossed public attention that small heed was taken of literary matters. I knew and was content to know that the poem soon found its way to the camps, as I heard from time to time of its being sung in chorus by the soldiers.

—HOWE, *Reminiscences*

B. THE BATTLE HYMN OF THE REPUBLIC

Mine eyes have seen the glory of the coming of the Lord:
He is trampling out the vintage where the grapes of wrath are stored;
He hath loosed the fateful lightning of his terrible swift sword:
    His truth is marching on.

I have seen Him in the watch fires of a hundred circling camps;
They have builded Him an altar in the evening dews and damps;
I can read His righteous sentence by the dim and flaring lamps.
    His day is marching on.

I have read a fiery gospel writ in burnished rows of steel:
"As ye deal with my contemners, so with you my grace shall deal;
Let the Hero, born of woman, crush the serpent with his heel,
   Since God is marching on."

He has sounded forth the trumpet that shall never call retreat;
He is sifting out the hearts of men before his judgment seat:
Oh! be swift, my soul, to answer Him! be jubilant, my feet!
   Our God is marching on.

In the beauty of the lilies Christ was born across the sea,
With a glory in His bosom that transfigures you and me:
As He died to make men holy, let us die to make men free,
   While God is marching on.

   —Julia Ward Howe

C. "The Battle Hymn of the Republic" in Libby Prison

Among the singers of the "Battle Hymn" was Chaplain McCabe, the fighting chaplain of the 122d Ohio Volunteer Infantry. He read the poem in the "Atlantic," and was so struck with it that he committed it to memory before rising from his chair. He took it with him to the front, and in due time to Libby Prison, whither he was sent after being captured at Winchester. Here, in the great bare room where hundreds of Northern soldiers were herded together, came one night a rumor of disaster to the Union arms. A great battle, their jailers told them; a great Confederate victory. Sadly the Northern men gathered together in groups, sitting or lying on the floor, talking in low tones, wondering how, where, why. Suddenly, one of the Negroes who brought food for the prisoners stooped in passing and whispered to one of the sorrowful groups. The news was false: there had, indeed, been a great battle, but the Union army had won, the Confederates were defeated and scattered.

Like a flame the word flashed through the prison. Men leaped to their feet, shouted, embraced one another in a frenzy of joy and triumph; and Chaplain McCabe, standing in the middle of the room, lifted up his great voice and sang aloud,—

   "Mine eyes have seen the glory of the coming of the Lord!"

Every voice took up the chorus, and Libby Prison rang with the shout of "Glory, glory, hallelujah!"

The victory was that of Gettysburg. When, some time after, McCabe was released from prison, he told in Washington, before a great audience of loyal people, the story of his war-time experiences; and when he came to that night in Libby Prison, he sang the "Battle Hymn" once more. The effect was magical; people shouted, wept, and sang, all together; and when the song was ended, above the tumult of applause was heard the voice of Abraham Lincoln, exclaiming, while the tears rolled down his cheeks,—

   "Sing it again!"   —Richards and Elliott, *Julia Ward Howe*

10. WE ARE COMING, FATHER ABRAHAM

The losses in the Peninsular campaign were so heavy that Lincoln on July 2, 1862, appealed to the states to raise "three hundred thousand more" soldiers. It was in response to this appeal that James Sloan Gibbons, the New York abolitionist, wrote "We Are Coming, Father Abraham"—an assertion which, as it turned out, was overconfident.

Gibbons was a Philadelphia Quaker who in the thirties moved to New York and simultaneously entered banking and reform, becoming one of the staunchest supporters of the American Anti-Slavery Society. During the draft riots of 1863 his house was sacked. The music for this song was composed by Stephen Foster, then living in poverty and obscurity in New York City.

We are coming, Father Abraham, three hundred thousand more,
From Mississippi's winding stream and from New England's shore;
We leave our ploughs and workshops, our wives and children dear,
With hearts too full for utterance, with but a silent tear;
We dare not look behind us, but steadfastly before:
We are coming, Father Abraham, three hundred thousand more!

If you look across the hill-tops that meet the northern sky,
Long moving lines of rising dust your vision may descry;
And now the wind, an instant, tears the cloudy veil aside,
And floats aloft our spangled flag in glory and in pride,
And bayonets in the sunlight gleam, and bands brave music pour,
We are coming, Father Abraham, three hundred thousand more!

If you look all up our valleys where the growing harvests shine,
You may see our sturdy farmer boys fast forming into line;
And children from their mother's knees are pulling at the weeds,
And learning how to reap and sow against their country's needs;
And a farewell group stands weeping at every cottage door:
We are coming, Father Abraham, three hundred thousand more!

You have called us, and we're coming, by Richmond's bloody tide
To lay us down, for Freedom's sake, our brothers' bones beside,
Or from foul treason's savage grasp to wrench the murderous blade,
And in the face of foreign foes its fragments to parade.
Six hundred thousand loyal men and true have gone before:
We are coming, Father Abraham, three hundred thousand more!

—James Sloan Gibbons

11. THE BATTLE-CRY OF FREEDOM

This song, like "We Are Coming, Father Abraham," was written in response to Lincoln's appeal for troops. George F. Root, who wrote both the

*words and the music, was, with his friend and colleague Henry Clay Work,
the most prolific and successful of Northern Civil War song writers, author
of the ever popular "Tramp, Tramp, Tramp," "The Vacant Chair," "Just
Before the Battle, Mother," and others. He had taught at the Boston Academy
of Music and the New York Normal Institute before going to Chicago, in
1859, to open a music store. "The Battle-Cry of Freedom" was written for a
rally at Court House Square in Chicago; the famous Hutchinson family of
singers carried it throughout the North.*

*There were two versions of this song—the so-called "rallying" version and
the "battle-song" version. The better-known "rallying" song is given here;
the first verse of the "battle-song" is as follows:*

> *We are marching to the field, boys, we're going to the fight,
> Shouting the battle-cry of freedom;
> And we bear the glorious stars for the Union and the right,
> Shouting the battle-cry of freedom.*

*If we are to believe Mrs. Pickett one version of the song was equally
popular in the Confederacy.*

> Yes, We'll rally round the flag,
> Boys, we'll rally once again,
> Shouting the battle-cry of Freedom,
> We will rally from the hillside, we'll gather from the plain,
> Shouting the battle-cry of Freedom.
>
> CHORUS: The Union forever,
> Hurray! boys, Hurrah!
> Down with the traitor, up with the star;
> While we rally round the flag boys, rally once again,
> Shouting the battle-cry of Freedom.
>
> We are springing to the call of our Brothers gone before,
> Shouting the battle-cry of Freedom;
> And we'll fill the vacant ranks with a million freemen more,
> Shouting the battle-cry of Freedom.—CHORUS
>
> We will welcome to our numbers the loyal, true and brave,
> Shouting the battle-cry of Freedom;
> And altho' they may be poor, not a man shall be a slave,
> Shouting the battle-cry of Freedom.—CHORUS
>
> So we're springing to the call from the East and from the West,
> Shouting the battle-cry of Freedom;
> And we'll hurl the rebel crew from the land we love the best,
> Shouting the battle-cry of Freedom.—CHORUS
>
> —GEORGE F. ROOT

12. TRAMP, TRAMP, TRAMP

This song, also by George Root, was even more popular with the soldiers than "The Battle-Cry of Freedom." It is a shining example of the sentimentalism of the Civil War generation, but it is worth noting that it has retained its popularity to this day, largely because of its lively tune.

In the prison cell I sit,
    Thinking, mother dear, of you,
And our bright and happy home so far away,
    And the tears they fill my eyes,
Spite of all that I can do,
    Tho' I try to cheer my comrades and be gay.

CHORUS: Tramp, tramp, tramp, the boys are marching,
            Oh, cheer up, comrades, they will come,
        And beneath the starry flag we shall breath the air again,
            Of freedom in our own beloved home.

In the battle front we stood
    When the fiercest charge they made,
And they swept us off a hundred men or more,
    But before we reached their lines
They were beaten back dismayed,
    And we heard the cry of vict'ry o'er and o'er.—CHORUS

So within the prison cell
    We are waiting for the day
That shall come to open wide the iron door,
    And the hollow eye grows bright,
And the poor heart almost gay,
    As we think of seeing friends and home once more.—CHORUS
                                    —GEORGE F. ROOT

13. JUST BEFORE THE BATTLE, MOTHER

Here is another song from the adept pen of George Root. Better than most songs it lent itself to parody, one of the most widely sung of which ran:

Just before the battle, mother,
I was drinking mountain dew.
When I saw the Rebels marching,
To the rear I quickly flew.

It was widely sung in both armies, but appeared to be more popular in the South than in the North.

Just before the battle, mother,
I am thinking most of you;
While upon the field we are watching,
With the enemy in view.
Comrades brave are 'round me lying,
Filled with thoughts of home and God;
For well they know upon the morrow
Some will sleep beneath the sod.

CHORUS: Farewell, mother, you may never
Press me to your heart again;
But, oh, you'll not forget me, mother,
If I'm numbered with the slain.

Oh! I long to see you, mother,
And the loving ones at home;
But I'll never leave our banner
'Till in honor I can come.
Tell the enemy around you
That their cruel words, we know,
In every battle kill our soldiers
By the help they give the foe.—CHORUS
—GEORGE F. ROOT

14. TENTING TONIGHT

Like so many Civil War songs this one was almost equally popular on both sides. It was written by a New Hampshire singer, Walter Kittredge, who in 1861 had published a compilation of Union songs. Unable to find a publisher for "Tenting Tonight," he sang it himself in the army, and soon, despite its palpable defeatism, it had immense vogue.

We're tenting tonight on the old camp ground,
Give us a song to cheer our weary hearts,
A song of home, and the friends we love so dear.

CHORUS: Many are the hearts that are weary tonight,
Wishing for the war to cease;
Many are the hearts looking for the right
To see the dawn of peace.
Tenting tonight, tenting tonight,
Tenting on the old camp ground.

We've been tenting tonight on the old camp ground,
Thinking of days gone by, of the loved ones at home
That gave us the hand, and the tear that said "good-bye!"—CHORUS

We are tired of war on the old camp ground,
Many are dead and gone, of the brave and true
Who've left their homes, others been wounded long.—CHORUS

We've been fighting today on the old camp ground,
Many are lying near; some are dead
And some are dying, many are in tears.

LAST CHORUS: Many are the hearts that are weary tonight,
Wishing for the war to cease;
Many are the hearts looking for the right,
To see the dawn of peace.
Dying tonight, dying tonight,
Dying on the old camp ground.

—WALTER KITTREDGE

15. WEEPING, SAD AND LONELY

The author of this lachrymose song, Charles Sawyer, wrote a number of sentimental pieces including one tear-jerker, "Who Will Care for Mother Now?" which inspired an equally doleful reply, "Do Not Grieve for Thy Dear Mother." So depressing was "Weeping, Sad and Lonely" that some officers forbade its singing. Yet it was immensely popular on both sides. "There is nothing in this sentimental song," says Charles C. Eggleston, "that enables one to read the riddle of its remarkable popularity. It has no poetic merit; its rhythm is commonplace, and the tune to which it was sung was of the flimsiest musical structure, without even a trick of melody to commend it. Yet the song was more frequently sung, on both sides, than any other, the Southern soldiers inserting 'gray' for 'blue.' . . . Men chanted it on the march, and women sang it to piano accompaniment in all houses."

No introduction is necessary for the three songs that follow this one. They express perfectly the cloying sentimentalism of the Civil War years; they remind us, too, how young were most of the soldiers who fought in the war, and how heavy were the casualties—heavier proportionately than in any other war which the United States has fought.

A. WEEPING, SAD AND LONELY

Dearest love, do you remember
When we last did meet,
How you told me that you loved me,
Kneeling at my feet?
Oh! how proud you stood before me
In your suit of blue,
When you vow'd to me and country
Ever to be true.

CHORUS: Weeping, sad and lonely,
             Hopes and fears how vain!
             Yet praying,
             When this cruel war is over,
             Praying that we meet again.

When the summer breeze is sighing
   Mournfully along;
Or when autumn leaves are falling,
   Sadly breathes the song.
Oft in dreams I see thee lying
   On the battle plain,
Lonely, wounded, even dying,
   Calling, but in vain.—CHORUS

If amid the din of battle,
   Nobly you should fall,
Far away from those who love you,
   None to hear your call—
Who would whisper words of comfort?
   Who would soothe your pain?
Ah! the many cruel fancies
   Ever in my brain.—CHORUS

But our country called you, darling,
   Angels cheer your way:
While our nation's sons are fighting,
   We can only pray.
Nobly strike for God and liberty,
   Let all nations see
How we love the starry banner
   Emblem of the free.—CHORUS
          —CHARLES C. SAWYER

B. THE FADED COAT OF BLUE

My brave lad he sleeps in his faded coat of blue;
In a lonely grave unknown lies the heart that beat so true;
He sank faint and hungry among the famished brave,
And they laid him sad and lonely within his nameless grave.

CHORUS: No more the bugle calls the weary one,
             Rest noble spirit, in thy grave unknown!
             I'll find you and know you, among the good and true,
             When a robe of white is giv'n for the faded coat of blue.

He cried, "Give me water and just a little crumb,
And my mother she will bless you through all the years to come;
Oh! tell my sweet sister, so gentle, good and true,
That I'll meet her up in heaven, in my faded coat of blue."—CHORUS
—J. H. McNaughton

C. The Vacant Chair

We shall meet but we shall miss him,
    There will be one vacant chair;
We shall linger to caress him
    While we breathe our evening prayer.
When a year ago we gathered,
    Joy was in his mild blue eye;
But a golden cord is severed,
    And our hopes in ruins lie.

CHORUS: We shall meet but we shall miss him,
           There will be one vacant chair;
         We shall linger to caress him,
           When we breathe our evening prayer.

At our fireside sad and lonely,
    Often will the bosom swell
At remembrance of the story
    How our noble soldier fell;
How he strove to bear our banner
    Through the thickest of the fight
And uphold our country's honor
    In the strength of manhood's might.—CHORUS
—George F. Root

D. Sleeping for the Flag

When the boys come home in triumph, brother,
With the laurels they shall gain;
When we go to give them welcome, brother,
We shall look for you in vain.
We shall wait for your returning, brother,
You were set forever free;
For your comrades left you sleeping, brother,
Underneath a Southern tree.

CHORUS: Sleeping to waken in this weary world no more;
        Sleeping for your true lov'd country, brother,
        Sleeping for the flag you bore.

You who were the first on duty, brother,
When "to arms" your leader cried,—
You have left the ranks forever,
You have laid your arms aside,
From the awful scenes of battle, brother,
You were set forever free;
When your comrades left you sleeping, brother,
Underneath the Southern tree.—CHORUS
                              —HENRY CLAY WORK

16. MARCHING THROUGH GEORGIA

Few other Civil War songs have had the enduring popularity of this, and probably no other has spread so widely over the globe. The Japanese played it when they entered Port Arthur, the British sang it in India, it was included in a British Soldiers' Songbook in the First World War, and was played and sung by British and Americans alike in the Second World War.

Henry Clay Work was the son of an abolitionist who had suffered imprisonment for his work on the underground railway in Illinois; he himself was active not only in antislavery but in temperance work as well, and among his better-known songs is the memorable "Father, Dear Father, Come Home with Me Now."

Bring the good old bugle, boys, we'll sing another song—
Sing it with a spirit that will start the world along—
Sing it as we used to sing it, fifty thousand strong,
While we were marching through Georgia.

CHORUS: "Hurrah! Hurrah! we bring the jubilee!
         Hurrah! Hurrah! the flag that makes you free!"
         So we sang the chorus from Atlanta to the sea,
         While we were marching through Georgia.

How the darkeys shouted when they heard the joyful sound!
How the turkeys gobbled which our commissary found!
How the sweet potatoes even started from the ground,
While we were marching through Georgia.—CHORUS

Yes, and there were Union men who wept with joyful tears,
When they saw the honored flag they had not seen for years;
Hardly could they be restrained from breaking forth in cheers,
While we were marching through Georgia.—CHORUS

"Sherman's dashing Yankee boys will never reach the coast!"
So the saucy rebels said, and 'twas a handsome boast.
Had they not forgot, alas! to reckon with the host,
While we were marching through Georgia?—CHORUS

So we made a thoroughfare for Freedom and her train,
Sixty miles in latitude—three hundred to the main;
Treason fled before us, for resistance was in vain,
While we were marching through Georgia.—CHORUS
—HENRY CLAY WORK

17. MISTER, HERE'S YOUR MULE

No introduction is needed for this and the following four items. They remind us that Americans of the Civil War generation, for all their sentimentalism, were able to laugh at themselves—and at others. "Mister, Here's Your Mule" was particularly popular in the Western armies. "Do They Miss Me in the Trenches," written by J. W. Naff of the 3rd Louisiana Infantry, is a parody on "Do They Miss Me at Home." The vicissitudes of fighting in the Army of the Potomac inspired the wry "We Are the Boys of Potomac's Ranks," rehearsing the defeat of one Union general after another in the mud and forests of northern Virginia. It was sung to the tune of "When Johnny Comes Marching Home." The "goober peas" of Pender's song are, of course, peanuts. "Grafted into the Army" is something of a take-off both on the draft and on the boys who tried, in vain, to avoid it.

A. MISTER, HERE'S YOUR MULE

A farmer came to camp, one day, with milk and eggs to sell,
Upon a mule who oft would stray to where no one could tell,
The farmer, tired of his tramp, for hours was made a fool
By ev'ryone he met in camp, with "Mister, here's your mule."

CHORUS: Come on, come on, come on, old man, and don't be made a fool,
　　　　I'll tell the truth as best I can,
　　　　John Morgan's got your mule.

His eggs and chickens all were gone before the break of day,
The mule was heard of all along—that's what the soldiers say;
And still he hunted all day long—alas! the witless fool—
While ev'ry man would sing the song, "Mister, here's your mule."—CHORUS

The soldiers now, in laughing mood, on mischief were intent,
They toted muly on their backs, around from tent to tent;
Through this hole and that they pushed his head, and made a rule
To shout with humorous voices all, "Mister, here's your mule."—CHORUS

Alas! one day the mule was missed, ah! who could tell his fate?
The farmer, like a man bereft, searched early and searched late;
And as he passed from camp to camp, with stricken face, the fool
Cried out to ev'ryone he met, "Oh, Mister, where's my mule?"—CHORUS
—AUTHOR UNKNOWN

B. Do They Miss Me in the Trenches?

Do they miss me in the trench, do they miss me
When the shells fly so thickly around?
Do they know that I've run down the hill-side
To look for my hole in the ground?
But the shells exploded so near me,
It seemed best for me to run;
And though some laughed as I crawfished,
I could not discover the fun.

I often get up in the trenches,
When some Yankee is near out of sight,
And fire a round or two at him,
To make the boys think that I'll fight.
But when the Yanks commence shelling,
I run to my home down the hill;
I swear my legs never will stay there,
Though all may stay there who will.

I'll save myself through the dread struggle,
And when the great battle is o'er,
I'll claim my full rations of laurels,
As always I've done heretofore.
I'll say that I've fought them as bravely
As the best of my comrades who fell,
And swear most roundly to all others
That I never had fears of a shell.
—J. W. Naff

C. We Are the Boys of Potomac's Ranks

We are the boys of Potomac's ranks,
 Hurrah! Hurrah!
We are the boys of Potomac's ranks,
We ran with McDowell, retreated with Banks,
And we'll all drink stone blind—
Johnny, fill up the bowl.

We fought with McClellan, the Rebs, shakes, and fever,
 Hurrah! Hurrah!
We fought with McClellan, the Rebs, shakes, and fever,
But Mac joined the navy on reaching James River,
And we'll all drink stone blind—
Johnny, fill up the bowl.

They gave us John Pope, our patience to tax,
   Hurrah! Hurrah!
They gave us John Pope, our patience to tax,
Who said that out West he'd seen naught but *gray backs,*
And we'll all drink stone blind—
Johnny, fill up the bowl.

He said his headquarters were in the saddle,
   Hurrah! Hurrah!
He said his headquarters were in the saddle,
But Stonewall Jackson made him skedaddle—
And we'll all drink stone blind—
Johnny, fill up the bowl.

Then Mac was recalled, but after Antietam,
   Hurrah! Hurrah!
Then Mac was recalled, but after Antietam
Abe gave him a rest, he was too slow to beat 'em,
And we'll all drink stone blind—
Johnny, fill up the bowl.

Oh, Burnside, then he tried his luck,
   Hurrah! Hurrah!
Oh, Burnside, then he tried his luck,
But in the mud so fast got stuck,
And we'll all drink stone blind—
Johnny, fill up the bowl.

Then Hooker was taken to fill the bill,
   Hurrah! Hurrah!
Then Hooker was taken to fill the bill,
But he got a black eye at Chancellorsville,
And we'll all drink stone blind—
Johnny, fill up the bowl.

Next came General Meade, a slow old plug,
   Hurrah! Hurrah!
Next came General Meade, a slow old plug,
For he let them get away at Gettysburg,
And we'll all drink stone blind—
Johnny, fill up the bowl.

             —AUTHOR UNKNOWN

D. GOOBER PEAS

Sitting by the roadside on a summer day,
Chatting with my messmates, passing time away,
Lying in the shadow underneath the trees,
Goodness, how delicious, eating goober peas!

CHORUS: Peas! Peas! Peas! Peas! eating goober peas!
           Goodness, how delicious, eating goober peas!

When a horseman passes, the soldiers have a rule,
To cry out at their loudest, "Mister, here's your mule,"
But another pleasure enchantinger than these,
Is wearing out your grinders, eating goober peas!—CHORUS

Just before the battle the General hears a row,
He says, "The Yanks are coming, I hear their rifles now,"
He turns around in wonder, and what do you think he sees?
The Georgia militia eating goober peas!—CHORUS

I think my song has lasted almost long enough.
The subject's interesting, but the rhymes are mighty rough,
I wish this war was over, when free from rags and fleas,
We'd kiss our wives and sweethearts and gobble goober peas!—CHORUS

                          —A. PENDER

E. GRAFTED INTO THE ARMY

Our Jimmy has gone for to live in a tent,
They have grafted him into the army;
He finally pucker'd up courage and went,
When they grafted him into the army.
I told them the child was too young, alas!
At the captain's fore-quarters, they said he would pass—
They'd train him up well in the infantry class—
So they grafted him into the army.

CHORUS: Oh, Jimmy farewell!
           Your brothers fell
           Way down in Alabarmy;
           I tho't they would spare a lone widder's heir,
           But they grafted him into the army.

Drest up in his unicorn—dear little chap;
They have grafted him into the army;
It seems but a day since he sot in my lap,
But they grafted him into the army.
And these are the trousies he used to wear—
Them very same buttons—the patch and the tear—
But Uncle Sam gave him a bran new pair
When they grafted him into the army.—CHORUS

Now in my provisions I see him revealed—
They have grafted him into the army;
A picket beside the contented field,
They have grafted him into the army.
He looks kinder sickish—begins to cry—
A big volunteer standing right in his eye!
Oh what if the ducky should up and die,
Now they've grafted him into the army?—CHORUS

                                    —HENRY CLAY WORK

18. LORENA

Almost forgotten now, "Lorena" was the most widely sung and the most popular of Civil War songs, and justly so, for, except for some of Stephen Foster's, no song of this decade had a lovelier melody. As with so many Civil War songs, the origin of "Lorena" is obscure. It has been assigned to one H. D. L. Webster, as early as 1850, but John Wyeth, historian of Forrest and author of With Sabre and Scalpel, *gives it a different history:*

"As we passed a home of the Trappist Brotherhood, Lieutenant Frank Brady entertained us by singing Lorena, a war-time poem which had been set to music and was then very popular. He told us that the author of the poem was an inmate of this Trappist home. If this were so, and the self-imprisoned brother heard the sweet voice of the cavalier as he sang 'The Years creep slowly by, Lorena' what sad and tender memories it must have awakened."

The years creep slowly by, Lorena,
The snow is on the grass again;
The sun's low down the sky, Lorena,
The frost gleams where the flowers have been,
But the heart throbs on as warmly now,
As when the summer days were nigh;
Oh, the sun can never dip so low,
Adown affection's cloudless sky.
The sun can never dip so low,
Adown affection's cloudless sky.

A hundred months have passed, Lorena,
Since last I held that hand in mine;
And felt the pulse beat fast, Lorena,
Tho' mine beat faster far than thine.
A hundred months, 'twas flow'ry May,
When up the hilly slope we climbed,
To watch the dying of the day
And hear the distant church bells chime.
To watch the dying of the day
And hear the distant churchbells chime.

We loved each other then, Lorena,
More than we ever dared to tell;
And what we might have been, Lorena,
Had but our lovings prospered well—
But then, 'tis past, the years are gone,
I'll not call up their shadowy forms;
I'll say to them, "lost years, sleep on!
Sleep on! nor heed life's pelting storms."
I'll say to them, "lost years, sleep on!
Sleep on! nor heed life's pelting storms."

The story of that past, Lorena,
Alas! I care not to repeat
The hopes that could not last, Lorena,
They lived, but only lived to cheat.
I would not cause e'en one regret
To rankle in your bosom now;
For "if we *try*, we may forget,"
Were words of thine long years ago.
For "if we *try*, we may forget,"
Were words of thine long years ago.

Yes, these were words of thine, Lorena,
They burn within my memory yet;
They touched some tender chords, Lorena,
Which thrill and tremble with regret.
'Twas not thy woman's heart that spoke;
Thy heart was always true to me;
A duty, stern and pressing, broke
The tie which linked my soul with thee.
A duty, stern and pressing, broke
The tie which linked my soul with thee.

It matters little now, Lorena,
The past is in the eternal Past,
Our heads will soon lie low, Lorena,
Life's tide is ebbing out so fast.
There is a Future! O thank God!
Of life, this is so small a part!
'Tis dust to dust beneath the sod;
But there, *up there*, 'tis heart to heart.
'Tis dust to dust beneath the sod;
But there, *up there*, 'tis heart to heart.

—H. D. L. WEBSTER (?)

19. WHEN JOHNNY COMES MARCHING HOME

This song, more commonly associated with the Spanish-American War, originated in the Civil War, but just when we do not know. It has been assigned to Father Louis Lambert, "the American Newman," who served as chaplain of the 18th Illinois Infantry, but the better claim seems to be that of the extraordinary Patrick Sarsfield Gilmore, Butler's bandmaster in New Orleans and organizer of the gigantic Peace Jubilee of 1869 which employed a chorus of ten thousand and an orchestra of one thousand pieces. The melody itself has entered deeply into American music: Burnet Tuthill wrote a series of variations on it for piano and wind instruments, and Roy Harris composed his American Overture *on its theme.*

When Johnny comes marching home again, hurrah, hurrah!
We'll give him a hearty welcome then, hurrah, hurrah!
The men will cheer, the boys will shout,
The ladies they will all turn out,

CHORUS: And we'll all feel gay when Johnny comes marching home.
                And we'll all feel gay when Johnny comes marching home.

The old church bell will peal with joy, hurrah, hurrah!
To welcome home our darling boy, hurrah, hurrah!
The village lads and lassies say,
With roses they will strew the way,

CHORUS: And we'll all feel gay when Johnny comes marching home.

Get ready for the Jubilee, hurrah, hurrah!
We'll give the hero three times three, hurrah, hurrah!
The laurel wreath is ready now
To place upon his loyal brow,

CHORUS: And we'll all feel gay when Johnny comes marching home.

Let love and friendship on that day, hurrah, hurrah!
Their choicest treasures then display, hurrah, hurrah!
And let each one perform some part,
To fill with joy the warrior's heart,

CHORUS: And we'll all feel gay when Johnny comes marching home.
                And we'll all feel gay when Johnny comes marching home.

—PATRICK S. GILMORE (?)

THE BLUE AND THE GRAY

VOLUME II

General Sheridan's Charge at the Battle of Five Forks

XVII

Gettysburg

THE *Battle of Gettysburg is commonly regarded as the turning point of the war. In a sense it was. Certainly it was high tide for the Confederacy; had Lee won at Gettysburg he might have gone on to Harrisburg, Philadelphia, Baltimore, or Washington, and while it is almost inconceivable that he could have captured and held any of these cities or transferred the theater of the war permanently to the North, a successful invasion might have had far-reaching consequences. It might have brought that foreign recognition so important to the survival of the Confederacy; it might have strengthened the peace party in the North, the Copperheads, and the draft rioters, and created a widespread demand for a negotiated peace. Needless to say all of these possibilities were in Lee's mind, and in the minds of Confederate leaders, in planning the invasion.*

Yet from the strategical point of view Gettysburg was not decisive. It was strategically far less important than Vicksburg, which cleared the Mississippi and cut off the West from the heart of the Confederacy. It is well to remember that there were almost two years of hard fighting ahead, and that in these months the South could still have won the war—won it not by successful invasion or even by overwhelming victories on the battlefield, but by wearing down the Northern will to fight. The draft riots came after Gettysburg; greenbacks and government bonds were lower in 1864 than in 1863; Lincoln thought that he was going to be defeated for re-election in the summer of 1864. It was, after all, the campaigns of 1864 that were decisive— Sherman's capture of Atlanta and the March to the Sea, and the attrition of Lee's forces in the Wilderness.

Yet Gettysburg remains the great battle of the war—the one that everyone knows, the one that has inspired more historical investigation—and more controversy, more fiction and more poetry, than any other; it is wholly appropriate that it gave its name to the most memorable of Lincoln's addresses. The reason is not hard to find. It was the greatest single battle ever fought in North America, both in numbers actually involved and in casualties. It was marked by some of the hardest fighting in the war, and as long as Americans cherish courage such names as Peach Orchard, Little Round Top, and Cemetery Ridge will quicken their pulses. There were other fights as fierce as that for Culp's Hill—the Bloody Angle for instance; there were other charges as gallant as Pickett's—the Union charge up Missionary Ridge or the

Confederate charge at Franklin; there were other battles whose outcome was as uncertain—Shiloh or Antietam; there were other days which exacted heavier casualties than any one day of Gettysburg—Shiloh again. But no other single battle combined so dramatically so many memorable scenes and events.

Gettysburg was, in many respects, a curious battle, but this might be said of most battles. It was, in a sense, an accident: neither Lee nor Hooker wanted to fight at Gettysburg, though once the fighting had begun Meade—who succeeded Hooker—saw the advantages of the Gettysburg terrain for defensive fighting. Neither strategically nor tactically was it a well-fought battle, though Meade, whose task was simpler, appears to better advantage in these matters than Lee. That it was Lee's "worst-fought" battle is generally agreed. He had allowed Stuart to go off on one of his junkets, and was without his eyes. He missed those lieutenants who had brought him victory in the past, especially the incomparable Jackson. Once the battle was joined the Confederates made a series of mistakes—mistakes that in the end proved fateful: the failure to push on and seize Cemetery Hill the first day, to occupy either Big or Little Round Top early on the second day, to attempt a flanking movement around the Union left, the delay in the assault on the third day and the inability to concentrate all available forces for that assault. Meade, too, fought a somewhat disorganized battle. There was confusion on the first day, even in the matter of command; there was a failure to use all potential strength—four of seven Union corps bore the brunt of the battle; there was above all an egregious failure to follow up victory by energetic pursuit.

The literature on Gettysburg is voluminous, and we can only skim its surface. Here are accounts of the preliminary skirmishing in the Valley, the invasion of Maryland and Pennsylvania, the high points of each of the three days of fighting, and the retreat. Wherever possible we have presented Union and Confederate accounts of the same engagements.

1. GENERAL LEE DECIDES TO TAKE THE OFFENSIVE

After Fredericksburg and Chancellorsville, Lee decided once more to carry the war to the North. Many considerations led to this resolution, which he urged successfully on Davis and his Cabinet. He wanted to take his army north of the Potomac where he could find provisions for both men and horses. He wanted to get clear of the Wilderness, to where he could maneuver more effectively against the enemy. He hoped that an invasion of the North would encourage Copperheads and the peace movement in that section and that, if successful, it would hasten foreign recognition.

"I considered the problem in every possible phase," he later recalled, "and to my mind, it resolved itself into a choice of one of two things—either to retire to Richmond and stand a siege, which must ultimately have ended in surrender, or to invade Pennsylvania." We can follow, in his letters, the crystallization of his plans.

(CONFIDENTIAL.) HDQRS. ARMY OF NORTHERN VIRGINIA
June 8, 1863

Hon. JAMES A. SEDDON
Secretary of War, Richmond, Va.:
SIR:
. . . As far as I can judge, there is nothing to be gained by this army remaining quietly on the defensive, which it must do unless it can be re-enforced. I am aware that there is difficulty and hazard in taking the aggressive with so large an army in its front, intrenched behind a river, where it cannot be advantageously attacked. Unless it can be drawn out in a position to be assailed, it will take its own time to prepare and strengthen itself to renew its advance upon Richmond, and force this army back within the intrenchments of that city. This may be the result in any event; still, I think it is worth a trial to prevent such a catastrophe. Still, if the Department thinks it better to remain on the defensive, and guard as far as possible all the avenues of approach, and await the time of the enemy, I am ready to adopt this course. You have, therefore, only to inform me.

R. E. LEE,
General.

HEADQUARTERS ARMY OF NORTHERN VIRGINIA
June 10, 1863

His Excellency JEFFERSON DAVIS, *Richmond:*
MR. PRESIDENT: . . . Conceding to our enemies the superiority claimed by them in numbers, resources, and all the means and appliances for carrying on the war, we have no right to look for exemptions from the military consequences of a vigorous use of these advantages, excepting by such deliverance as the mercy of Heaven may accord to the courage of our soldiers, the justice of our cause, and the constancy and prayers of our people. While making the most we can of the means of resistance we possess, and gratefully accepting the measure of success with which God has blessed our efforts as an earnest of His approval and favor, it is nevertheless the part of wisdom to carefully measure and husband our strength, and not to expect from it more than in the ordinary course of affairs it is capable of accomplishing. We should not, therefore, conceal from ourselves that our resources in men are constantly diminishing, and the disproportion in this respect between us and our enemies, if they continue united in their efforts to subjugate us, is steadily augmenting.

The decrease of the aggregate of this army, as disclosed by the returns, affords an illustration of this fact. Its effective strength varies from time to time, but the falling off in its aggregate shows that its ranks are growing weaker and that its losses are not supplied by recruits.

Under these circumstances, we should neglect no honorable means of dividing and weakening our enemies, that they may feel some of the difficulties experienced by ourselves. It seems to me that the most effectual mode of accomplishing this object, now within our reach, is to give all the encouragement we can, consistently with truth, to the rising peace party of the North.

Nor do I think we should, in this connection, make nice distinction between those who declare for peace unconditionally and those who advocate it as a means of restoring the Union, however much we may prefer the former.

We should bear in mind that the friends of peace at the North must make concessions to the earnest desire that exists in the minds of their countrymen for a restoration of the Union, and that to hold out such a result as an inducement is essential to the success of their party.

Should the belief that peace will bring back the Union become general, the war would no longer be supported, and that, after all, is what we are interested in bringing about. When peace is proposed to us, it will be time enough to discuss its terms, and it is not the part of prudence to spurn the proposition in advance, merely because those who wish to make it believe, or affect to believe, that it will result in bringing us back to the Union. We entertain no such apprehensions, nor doubt that the desire of our people for a distinct and independent national existence will prove as steadfast under the influence of peaceful measures as it has shown itself in the midst of war. . . .

I am, with great respect, your obedient servant,

R. E. LEE,
General.

HEADQUARTERS ARMY OF NORTHERN VIRGINIA

July 31, 1863

GENERAL: I have the honor to submit the following outline of the recent operations, for the information of the Department:

The position occupied by the enemy opposite Fredericksburg being one in which he could not be attacked to advantage, it was determined to draw him from it. The execution of this purpose embraced the relief of the Shenandoah Valley from the troops that had occupied the lower part of it during the winter and spring, and, if practicable, the transfer of the scene of hostilities north of the Potomac. It was thought that the corresponding movements on the part of the enemy to which those contemplated by us would probably give rise, might offer a fair opportunity to strike a blow at the army then commanded by General Hooker, and that in any event that army would be compelled to leave Virginia, and, possibly, to draw to its support troops designed to operate against other parts of the country. In this way it was supposed that the enemy's plan of campaign for the summer would be broken up, and part of the season of active operations be consumed in the formation of new combinations, and the preparation that they would require. In addition to these advantages, it was hoped that other valuable results might be obtained by military success. Actuated by these and other important considerations that may hereafter be presented, the movement began on June 3. McLaws' division, of Longstreet's corps, left Fredericksburg for Culpeper

Court-House, and Hood's division, which was encamped on the Rapidan, marched to the same place. They were followed on the 4th and 5th by Ewell's corps, leaving that of A. P. Hill to occupy our lines at Fredericksburg. . . .

Respectfully submitted,
R. E. LEE,
General

GENERAL S. COOPER,
  Adjutant and Inspector General, Richmond, Va.
  —*War of the Rebellion . . . Official Records*

2. EWELL WHIPS THE FEDERALS AT WINCHESTER

After Chancellorsville both armies marked time for a while. Hooker was too badly hurt to resume the offensive; Lee awaited reinforcement by Longstreet's corps. During May he carried through a reorganization of the command, dividing the army into three corps and appointing A. P. Hill commander of the new corps. Early in June, reinforced by Longstreet and by new recruits and conscripts, he embarked on the most famous of his offensives. Leaving A. P. Hill temporarily at Fredericksburg to tie down Hooker's vast army, Lee began to move his other two corps into the Valley. Hooker, who suspected that something was up, sent his cavalry under Pleasanton to probe out the Confederates; the clash with Stuart at Brandy Station was the largest cavalry engagement of the war, but ended in a draw.

Meantime Ewell was moving down the Valley toward Winchester, which Milroy held with 9,000 men. Warned of the Confederate approach, Milroy decided to stay and fight it out. With an élan reminiscent of Stonewall Jackson, Ewell struck Milroy on June 14, drove him out of Winchester, bagged over 3,300 prisoners, and sent the Federals scurrying toward Harpers Ferry.

John Casler, who tells the story, was a private in the famous Stonewall Brigade.

WE were on the march the next morning, the 13th of June [1863], and soon heard our cavalry skirmishing with the enemy. We moved on to near Winchester when our troops were disposed around in battle order, but there was no engagement of any consequence by our division.

That night our division was marched around to the east of Winchester by Jordon Springs, and came on to the turnpike leading from Winchester north to Martinsburg. We were now at Stephenson's depot, about four miles from Winchester. We were not quite soon enough, for as the head of our column got in sight of the road, we saw the enemy retreating. We were in their rear; and if we had been one hour sooner we would have had our line formed across the road and captured the whole "outfit."

Some had already got through; but it was a running fight as it was. A large number were captured, and others dispersed and demoralized. My old brigade captured six regiments, and got six stands of colors. The Gen. gave one to each regiment and kept one himself.

The Louisiana brigade was running parallel with a brigade of the enemy trying to head them off; but they made such good time that they were about to get away, when they happened to meet about twenty stragglers from our army, who had fallen behind during the night, and who while coming on, seeing the Yankees rushing along at such headlong speed, and knowing that we were in their rear, formed across the road and called on them to halt. The enemy thinking it was another detachment of our infantry, halted and surrendered. But the Louisiana brigade was near by and took them in charge. That was one time stragglers came in good play. The enemy's column would doubtless have escaped had it not been for the stragglers in their front.

Our cavalry were on the flanks and we had none there to follow the retreating enemy. So the infantry gathered up the wagon horses and mules and mounted them, bare-back and in every way, as best they could. They were the hardest looking cavalry regiment I ever saw, with their knapsacks and blankets around their shoulders; with their long rifles and no saddles, and blind bridles, and mounted on mules and horses promiscuously. Away they went down the pike as hard as they could go, yelling and firing, as if it were big fun for an infantry man to be mounted in any shape. They were after the wagon train ahead of the infantry, and made a fine capture.

Hays' Louisiana brigade charged the enemy in their forts around Winchester, driving them out and capturing their guns, and turning them on them. Early's division charged and ran them out of Winchester—our division heading them off and capturing them. Rodes' division was at Berryville to cut off their retreat in that direction, and went from there to Martinsburg and captured a great amount of stores. We followed them on to Harper's Ferry, when they crossed the Potomac and occupied Maryland heights.

—CASLER, *Four Years in the Stonewall Brigade*

3. GENERAL LEE INVADES PENNSYLVANIA

The defeat of Milroy at Winchester and the withdrawal of the Federals from Harpers Ferry to Maryland Heights cleared the Valley; on the seventeenth Ewell forded the Potomac and occupied Hagerstown and Sharpsburg. Meantime Longstreet was swinging up on the east side of the Blue Ridge Mountains while Stuart's cavalry protected the passes on his right. Realizing that Lee had left Richmond practically undefended, Hooker wanted to launch an attack on that city, but was overruled by Lincoln, who insisted that Lee's army and not Richmond was his proper objective. "If the head of Lee's army is at Martinsburg and the tail of it on the plank road between Fredericksburg and Chancellorsville," he wrote, "the animal must be very slim somewhere. Could you not break him?" But by that time it was too late to "break him." Ewell was well into Pennsylvania; Longstreet's corps was splashing across the fords of the Potomac; Stuart had repulsed the Federals in several sharp cavalry engagements—Aldie, Middleburg, and Upperville—and was off on his foraging expedition.

This letter from William Christian reveals something of the spirit of Lee's troops as they invaded the North in that fateful June of 1863.

Camp near Greenwood, Pa., June 28, 1863.—My own darling wife: You can see by the date of this that we are now in Pennsylvania. We crossed the line day before yesterday and are resting today near a little one-horse town on the road to Gettysburg, which we will reach tomorrow. We are paying back these people for some of the damage they have done us, though we are not doing them half as bad as they done us. We are getting up all the horses, etc., and feeding our army with their beef and flour, etc., but there are strict orders about the interruption of any private property by individual soldiers.

Though with these orders, fowls and pigs and eatables don't stand much chance. I felt when I first came here that I would like to revenge myself upon these people for the desolation they have brought upon our own beautiful home, that home where we could have lived so happy, and that we loved so much, from which their vandalism has driven you and my helpless little ones. But though I had such severe wrongs and grievances to redress and such great cause for revenge, yet when I got among these people I could not find it in my heart to molest them. They looked so dreadfully scared and talked so humble that I have invariably endeavored to protect their property and have prevented soldiers from taking chickens, even in the main road; yet there is a good deal of plundering going on, confined principally to the taking of provisions. No houses were searched and robbed, like our houses were done by the Yankees. Pigs, chickens, geese, etc., are finding their way into our camp; it can't be prevented, and I can't think it ought to be. We must show them something of war. I have sent out today to get a good horse; I have no scruples about that, as they have taken mine. We took a lot of Negroes yesterday. I was offered my choice, but as I could not get them back home I would not take them. In fact my humanity revolted at taking the poor devils away from their homes. They were so scared that I turned them all loose.

I dined yesterday with two old maids. They treated me very well and seemed greatly in favor of peace. I have had a great deal of fun since I have been here. The country that we have passed through is beautiful, and everything in the greatest abundance. You never saw such a land of plenty. We could live here mighty well for the next twelve months, but I suppose old Hooker will try to put a stop to us pretty soon. Of course we will have to fight here, and when it comes it will be the biggest on record. Our men feel that there is to be no back-out. A defeat here would be ruinous. This army has never done such fighting as it will do now, and if we can whip the armies that are now gathering to oppose us, we will have everything in our own hands. We must conquer a peace. If we can come out of this country triumphant and victorious, having established a peace, we will bring back to our own land the greatest joy that ever crowned a people. We will show the Yankees this time how we can fight.

Be of good cheer, and write often to your fondly attached husband.

—Letter of William S. Christian

4. THE ARMIES CONVERGE ON GETTYSBURG

"It had not been intended to deliver a general battle so far from our base unless attacked," wrote General Lee later. "But coming unexpectedly upon the whole Federal army, to withdraw through the mountains with our extensive trains would have been difficult and dangerous." This was accurate enough, but not comprehensive. Had Stuart's cavalry been on the job, Lee would have known where the Federal army was, and how widely it was scattered. After being surprised at Brandy Station Stuart was eager to redeem himself and once more suggested riding around the Federal army. On June 22 Lee gave him somewhat ambiguous instructions to "move into Maryland and take position on Ewell's right." This was what Stuart wanted and off he went into Maryland and Pennsylvania. Not until July 1 did he learn that Lee's army was concentrated around Gettysburg.

Meantime Gordon Meade had supplanted Hooker in command of the Army of the Potomac. As General Hunt makes clear, both Hooker and Meade had hoped to fight behind Pipe Creek, in Maryland, and the seven corps of the army were spread out over a wide area south of Gettysburg. Only Buford's cavalry was in the town, and it was Buford who held up Heth when that general, hearing that there was a supply of shoes at Gettysburg, sent Pettigrew's brigade down the Chambersburg Pike on June 30.

General Hunt, who here recalls the beginnings of the great battle, was a veteran of the Mexican War and of the Peninsular, Antietam, and Fredericksburg campaigns. At this time he was chief of artillery of the Army of the Potomac.

HEARING nothing from Stuart, and therefore believing that Hooker was still south of the Potomac, Lee, on the afternoon of the 28th, ordered Longstreet and A. P. Hill to join Ewell at Harrisburg; but late that night one of Longstreet's scouts came in and reported that the Federal army had crossed the river, that Meade had relieved Hooker and was at Frederick. Lee thereupon changed the rendezvous of his army to Cashtown, which place Heth reached on the 29th. Next day Heth sent Pettigrew's brigade on to Gettysburg, nine miles, to procure a supply of shoes. Nearing this place, Pettigrew discovered the advance of a large Federal force and returned to Cashtown. Hill immediately notified Generals Lee and Ewell, informing the latter that he would advance next morning on Gettysburg. Buford, sending Merritt's brigade to Mechanicstown as guard to his trains, had early on the morning of the 29th crossed into and moved up the Cumberland valley via Boonsboro' and Fairfield with those of Gamble and Devin, and on the afternoon of

Tuesday, June 30th, under instructions from Pleasonton, entered Gettysburg, Pettigrew's brigade withdrawing on his approach.

From Gettysburg, near the eastern base of the Green Ridge, and covering all the upper passes into the Cumberland valley, good roads lead to all important points between the Susquehanna and the Potomac. It is therefore an important strategic position. On the west of the town, distant nearly half a mile, there is a somewhat elevated ridge running north and south, on which stands the "Lutheran Seminary." This ridge is covered with open woods through its whole length, and is terminated nearly a mile and a half north of the seminary by a commanding knoll, bare on its southern side, called Oak Hill. From this ridge the ground slopes gradually to the west, and again rising forms another ridge about 500 yards from the first, upon which, nearly opposite the seminary, stand McPherson's farm buildings. The second ridge is wider, smoother, and lower than the first, and Oak Hill, their intersection, has a clear view of the slopes of both ridges and of the valley between them. West of McPherson's ridge Willoughby Run flows south into Marsh Creek. South of the farm buildings and directly opposite the seminary, a wood borders the run for about 300 yards, and stretches back to the summit of McPherson's ridge. From the town two roads run: one south-west to Hagerstown via Fairfield, the other north-westerly to Chambersburg via Cashtown. The seminary is midway between them, about 300 yards from each. Parallel to and 150 yards north of the Chambersburg pike, is the bed of an unfinished railroad, with deep cuttings through the two ridges. Directly north of the town the country is comparatively flat and open; on the east of it, Rock Creek flows south. On the south, and overlooking it, is a ridge of bold, high ground, terminated on the west by Cemetery Hill and on the east by Culp's Hill, which, bending to the south, extends half a mile or more and terminates in low grounds near Spangler's Spring. Culp's Hill is steep toward the east, is well wooded, and its eastern base is washed by Rock Creek.

Impressed by the importance of the position, Buford, expecting the early return of the enemy in force, assigned to Devin's brigade the country north, and to Gamble's that west of the town; sent out scouting parties on all the roads to collect information, and reported the condition of affairs to Reynolds. His pickets extended from below the Fairfield road, along the eastern bank of Willoughby Run, to the railroad cut, then easterly some 1500 yards north of the town, to a wooded hillock near Rock Creek.

On the night of June 30th Meade's headquarters and the Artillery Reserve were at Taneytown; the First Corps at Marsh Run, the Eleventh at Emmitsburg, Third at Bridgeport, Twelfth at Littlestown, Second at Uniontown, Fifth at Union Mills, Sixth and Gregg's cavalry at Manchester, Kilpatrick's at Hanover. A glance at the map will show at what disadvantage Meade's army was now placed. Lee's whole army was nearing Gettysburg, while Meade's was scattered over a wide region to the east and south of that town.

Meade was now convinced that all designs on the Susquehanna had been abandoned; but as Lee's corps were reported as occupying the country from Chambersburg to Carlisle, he ordered, for the next day's moves, the First and

The Seat of the War in Pennsylvania and Maryland

Eleventh corps to Gettysburg, under Reynolds, the Third to Emmitsburg, the Second to Taneytown, the Fifth to Hanover, and the Twelfth to Two Taverns, directing Slocum to take command of the Fifth in addition to his own. The Sixth Corps was left at Manchester, thirty-four miles from Gettysburg, to await orders. But Meade, while conforming to the current of Lee's movement, was not merely drifting. The same afternoon he directed the chiefs of engineers and artillery to select a field of battle on which his army might be concentrated, whatever Lee's lines of approach, whether by Harrisburg or Gettysburg,—indicating the general line of Pipe Creek as a suitable locality. Carefully drawn instructions were sent to the corps commanders as to the occupation of this line, should it be ordered; but it was added that developments might cause the offensive to be assumed from present positions. These orders were afterward cited as indicating General Meade's intention not to fight at Gettysburg. They were, under any circumstances, wise and proper orders, and it would probably have been better had he concentrated his army behind Pipe Creek rather than at Gettysburg; but events finally controlled the actions of both leaders.

At 8 A.M., July 1st, Buford's scouts reported Heth's advance on the Cashtown road, when Gamble's brigade formed on McPherson's Ridge, from the Fairfield road to the railroad cut; one section of Calef's battery A, 2d United States, near the left of his line, the other two across the Chambersburg or Cashtown pike. Devin formed his disposable squadrons from Gamble's right toward Oak Hill, from which he had afterward to transfer them to the north of the town to meet Ewell. As Heth advanced, he threw Archer's brigade to the right, Davis's to the left of the Cashtown pike, with Pettigrew's and Brockenbrough's brigades in support. The Confederates advanced skirmishing heavily with Buford's dismounted troopers. Calef's battery, engaging double the number of its own guns, was served with an efficiency worthy of its former reputation as "Duncan's battery" in the Mexican war, and so enabled the cavalry to hold their long line for two hours. When Buford's report of the enemy's advance reached Reynolds, the latter, ordering Doubleday and Howard to follow, hastened toward Gettysburg with Wadsworth's small division (two brigades, Meredith's and Cutler's) and Hall's 2d Maine battery. As he approached he heard the sound of battle, and directing the troops to cross the fields toward the firing, galloped himself to the seminary, met Buford there, and both rode to the front, where the cavalry, dismounted, were gallantly holding their ground against heavy odds. After viewing the field, he sent back to hasten up Howard, and as the enemy's main line was now advancing to the attack, directed Doubleday, who had arrived in advance of his division, to look to the Fairfield road, sent Cutler with three of his five regiments north of the railroad cut, posted the other two under Colonel Fowler, of the 14th New York, south of the pike, and replaced Calef's battery by Hall's, thus relieving the cavalry. Cutler's line was hardly formed when it was struck by Davis's Confederate brigade on its front and right flank, where upon Wadsworth, to save it, ordered it to fall back to Seminary Ridge. This order not reaching the 147th New York, its gallant major, Harney, held that regiment to its position until, having lost half its numbers, the order to retire was repeated. Hall's battery was now imperiled, and it withdrew by sections, fighting at close canister range and suffering severely. Fowler thereupon changed his front to face Davis's brigade, which held the cut, and with Dawes's 6th Wisconsin—sent by Doubleday to aid the 147th New York—charged and drove Davis from the field. The Confederate brigade suffered severely, losing all its field-officers but two, and a large proportion of its men killed and captured, being disabled for further effective service that day.

—HUNT, "The First Day at Gettysburg"

5. BUFORD AND REYNOLDS HOLD UP THE CONFEDERATE ADVANCE

Lee concentrated his army more rapidly than Meade, Hill pushing on from the west of Gettysburg down the Chambersburg Pike, and Ewell coming down from the north. Only Buford's cavalry division was there to resist the Confederate advance—but that was a formidable force. There was some skirmishing on June 30; the real fighting got under way the next morning when, as we have seen, Buford's cavalrymen, fighting as dismounted troopers, put up a stiff resistance to Heth's and Pender's divisions, giving Reynolds time to hurry up with the I and XI Corps. At about midmorning Wadsworth's division took up position on Seminary Ridge, and from there sallied forth to capture a good part of Arthur's brigade. It was at this time that General Reynolds was killed.

Few officers in the Union Army had longer military experience than John Reynolds. He had served with distinction in the Mexican War and in the Mormon and Indian campaigns of the fifties, and the skill with which he commanded his troops at Fredericksburg and Chancellorsville marked him as one of the coming leaders of the Union forces. He was in command of the left wing of the Union army at Gettysburg, and the rapidity with which he brought up his scattered forces and the discernment which led him to order the occupation of Cemetery Hill contributed largely to ultimate Union victory.

Joseph Rosengarten was a major in the Army of the Potomac.

REYNOLDS knew Buford thoroughly, and knowing him and the value of cavalry under such a leader, sent them through the mountain passes beyond Gettysburg to find and feel the enemy. The old rule would have been to keep them back near the infantry, but Reynolds sent Buford on, and Buford went on, knowing that wherever Reynolds sent him, he was sure to be supported, followed, and secure. It was Buford who first attracted Reynolds' attention to the concentration of roads that gave Gettysburg its strategic importance, and it was Reynolds who first appreciated the strength and value of Cemetery Hill, and the plateau between that point and Round Top, as the stronghold to be secured for the concentration of the scattered corps and as the place where Meade could put his army to meet and overthrow the larger body he was pursuing. Together they found Gettysburg and made it the spot upon which the Union forces won a victory that was bought with his among the precious lives lost there. Buford and Reynolds were soldiers of the same order, and each found in the other just the qualities that were most needed to perfect and complete the task intrusted to them. The brilliant achievement of Buford, with his small body of cavalry, up to that time hardly appreciated as to the right use to be made of them, is but too little considered in the history of the battle of Gettysburg. It was his foresight and energy, his pluck and self-reliance, in thrusting forward his forces and pushing the enemy, and thus inviting, almost compelling their return, that brought on the engagement of the first of July.

Buford counted on Reynolds' support, and he had it fully, faithfully, and energetically. Reynolds counted in turn on having within his reach and at his immediate service at least the three corps that belonged to him, and there can be little question that if they had been up as promptly as he was in answer to Buford's call, the line he had marked out would have been fully manned and firmly held, while Meade's concentration behind Gettysburg would have gone on easily, and the whole of the Army of the Potomac would have done briefly and effectually what was gained only at the end of three days of hard fighting, with varying successes that more than once threatened to turn against us, and the loss on our side would have been so much less that the pursuit of Lee's forces could have been made promptly and irresistibly. It is not, however, given to all men to be of the same spirit, and the three corps that were under Reynolds followed his orders in a very different way from that in which he always did his work. When he got Buford's demand for infantry support on the morning of the first, it was just what Reynolds expected, and with characteristic energy, he went forward, saw Buford, accepted at once the responsibility, and returning to find the leading division of the First Corps (Wadsworth's), took it in hand, brought it to the front, put it in position, renewed his orders for the rest of the corps, assigned the positions for the other divisions, sent for his other corps, urged their coming with the greatest speed, directed the point to be held by the reserve, renewed his report to Meade that Buford had found the place for a battle, and that he had begun it, then calmly and coolly hurried some fresh troops forward to fill a gap in his lengthening lines, and as he returned to find fresh divisions, fell at the first onset.

The suddenness of the shock was in itself, perhaps, a relief to those who were nearest to Reynolds. In the full flush of life and health, vigorously leading on the troops in hand, and energetically summoning up the rest of his command, watching and even leading the attack of a comparatively small body, a glorious picture of the best type of military leader, superbly mounted, and horse and man sharing in the excitement of the shock of battle, Reynolds was, of course, a shining mark to the enemy's sharpshooters. He had taken his troops into a heavy growth of timber on the slope of a hill-side, and, under their regimental and brigade commanders, the men did their work well and promptly. Returning to join the expected divisions, he was struck by a Minnie ball, fired by a sharpshooter hidden in the branches of a tree almost overhead, and killed at once; his horse bore him to the little clump of trees, where a cairn of stones and a rude mark on the bark, now almost overgrown, still tells the fatal spot. The battle went on in varying fortune, and so long as the influence of his orders that had inspired men and officers could still be felt, all went well; but when the command had been changed by the successive arrival of generals who outranked each other, what there was of plan could hardly be made out, and the troops of the First Corps, without reinforcements and worn out and outnumbered, fell back at first with some show of order, and then as best they could, to find shelter in the lines pointed out by Reynolds for the concentration of his fresh troops. Thus even after his death, his military foresight had provided for the temporary defeat, which prepared the way for the great victory.

It is a striking proof of the discipline he had taught his own corps, that the news of the death, although it spread rapidly and that at a time when the inequality of numbers became apparent, produced no ill effect, led to no disorder, changed no disposition that he had directed, and in itself made the men only the more eager to carry out his orders. At the moment that his body was taken to the rear, for his death was instantaneous, two of his most gallant staff officers, Captain Riddle and Captain Wadsworth, in pursuance of his directions, effected a slight movement which made prisoners of Archer's Brigade, so that the rebel prisoners went to the rear almost at the same time, and their respectful conduct was in itself the highest tribute they could pay to him who had thus fallen.

—ROSENGARTEN, "General Reynolds' Last Battle"

6. A BOY CANNONEER DESCRIBES HARD FIGHTING ON THE FIRST DAY

The great battles of the second and third days of Gettysburg have overshadowed the fighting on the first. Had the battle ended with the retreat of the Federals on the afternoon of the first, it would still have gone down in history as one of the hardest fought engagements of the war. The stout resistance of Buford, the charge of Archer's brigade, the sharp fighting along Willoughby's Run, the desperate struggle for the railway cut, the final victorious advance of Pender's and Heth's divisions that hurled the Federals back through Gettysburg to Cemetery and Culp's hills—all these engagements added up to a major battle.

By late afternoon of July 1 the Union front had collapsed, but Schurz and Doubleday managed to retire in good order through Gettysburg and to the hills south of the town. The Confederates had bagged almost 5,000 prisoners and were confidently anticipating another Chancellorsville.

There is no better account of the first day's fighting than that by "cannoneer" Augustus Buell, member of a famous artillery brigade attached to the 1st division of the I Corps of the Army of the Potomac.

A. C. Redwood

The Retreat from Gettysburg

A. J. Volck

Cave Life in Vicksburg

A. J. Volck

The Vicksburg Canal

WE were turned out the next morning about daybreak [July 1, 1863], harnessed up, and, after crossing the creek, halted to let the infantry of Wadsworth's Division file by. There was no mistake now. While we stood there watching these splendid soldiers file by with their long, swinging "route-step," and their muskets glittering in the rays of the rising sun, there came out of the northwest a sullen "boom! boom! boom!" of three guns, followed almost immediately by a prolonged crackling sound, which, at that distance, reminded one very much of the snapping of a dry brush-heap when you first set it on fire. We soon reasoned out the state of affairs up in front. Buford, we calculated, had engaged the leading infantry of Lee's army, and was probably trying to hold them with his cavalry in heavy skirmish line, dismounted, until our infantry could come up. They said that the enemy had not yet developed more than a skirmish line, because if he had shown a heavy formation Buford would be using his artillery, of which he had two or three batteries, whereas we had thus far heard only the three cannon shots mentioned. These apparently trifling incidents show how the men in our Army were in the habit of observing things, and how unerring their judgment was, as a rule, even in matters of military knowledge far beyond their sphere or control.

But my eyes were riveted on the infantry marching by. No one now living will ever again see those two brigades of Wadsworth's Division— Cutler's and the Iron Brigade—file by as they did that morning. The little creek made a depression in the road, with a gentle ascent on either side, so that from our point of view the column, as it came down one slope and up the other, had the effect of huge blue billows of men topped with a spray of shining steel, and the whole spectacle was calculated to give nerve to a man who had none before. Partly because they had served together a long time, and, no doubt, because so many of their men were in our ranks, there was a great affinity between the Battery and the Iron Brigade, which expressed itself in cheers and good-natured chaffing between us as they went by. "Find a good place to camp; be sure and get near a good dry rail fence; tell the Johnnies we will be right along," were the salutations that passed on our part, while the infantry made such responses as "All right; better stay here till we send for you; the climate up there may be unhealthy just now for such delicate creatures as you," and all that sort of thing. It was probably 8 o'clock when the last brigade had passed, and then we got the order to march, moving with Doubleday's Division. As we moved up the road we could see the troops of the next division coming close behind. By this time the leading regiments of Wadsworth's infantry had got on the ground, and the sounds of battle were increasing rapidly. . . .

The sounds of the cavalry fight had been distinct ever since we left Marsh Creek—a fitful crackle—but now we heard fierce, angry crash on crash, rapidly growing in volume and intensity, signifying that our leading infantry—Cutler's and the Iron Brigade—had encountered the "doughboys" of Lee's advance. It is well known that the men of the Iron Brigade always preferred slouch hats (Western fashion), and seldom or never wore caps. At the time this heavy crashing began we were probably half way up from Marsh Creek, and, as the Battery was marching at a walk, most of us were walking along with the guns instead of riding on the limbers. Among the Cannoneers was a man from the 2d Wisconsin (John Holland) who took great pride in the Iron Brigade. So, when that sudden crash! crash! crash! floated over the hills to our ears, John said, with visible enthusiasm, "Hear that, my son! That's the talk! The old slouch hats have got there, you bet!!"

Now the artillery began to play in earnest, and it was evident that the three batteries which had preceded us were closely engaged, while the musketry had grown from the crackling sound of the skirmishing we had heard early in the morning to an almost incessant crash, which betokened the file firing of a main line of battle. Just before reaching the brow of the hill, south of the town, where we could get our first sight of the battle itself, there was a provoking halt of nearly half an hour. We could hear every sound, even the yells of the troops fighting on the ridge beyond Gettysburg, and we could see the smoke mount up and float away lazily to the northeastward; but we could not see the combatants. While halted here Doubleday's Division passed up the road, each regiment breaking into double quick as it reached the top of the hill. The Eleventh Corps also began by this time to arrive from Emmittsburg. Finally, when the last of the Second Brigade of Doubleday's (Stone's) had passed, we got the order to advance again, and in two minutes the whole scene burst upon us like the lifting of the curtain in a grand play. The spectacle was simply stupendous. It is doubtful if there was ever a battle fought elsewhere of which such a complete view was possible from one point as we got of that battle when we reached the top of the hill abreast of Round Top. . . .

Our guns pointed about due west, taking the Cashtown Pike *en echarpe*. The right half-battery was in line with us on the north side of the cut. Its right gun rested on the edge of a little grove, which extended some distance farther to the right, and was full of infantry (the 11th Pennsylvania) supporting us. There was also infantry in our rear, behind the crest and in the Railroad Cut (the 6th Wisconsin). One of our squad volunteered the facetious remark that these infantry "were put there to shoot the recruits if they flinched," for which he was rebuked by Corp'l Packard, who told him to "see that he himself behaved as well as the recruits." As Stewart commanded the right half-battery in person, he did not have much to do with us, directly, during the action that followed.

At this time, which was probably about noon, all the infantry of the First Corps, except that massed immediately about our position, together with Hall's, Reynolds's and one of the cavalry horse-batteries—Calef's—had been struggling desperately in the fields in our front, and for a few moments we had nothing to do but witness the magnificent scene. The enemy had some batteries firing down the pike, but their shot—probably canister—did not reach us. In a few minutes they opened with shell from a battery on a high knoll to the north of us (Oak Hill), and, though at long range, directly enfilading our line. But they sent their shells at the troops who were out in advance. We stood to the guns and watched the infantry combat in our front. Over across the creek (Willoughby's) we could see the gray masses of the Rebel infantry coming along all the roads and deploying in the fields, and it seemed that they were innumerable. At this time some 200 or 300 Rebel prisoners passed by our position on their way to our rear. They were a tough-looking set. Some had bloody rags tied round their limbs or heads, where they had received slight wounds.

In the meantime our infantry out in the field toward the creek was being slowly but surely overpowered, and our lines were being forced in toward the Seminary. It was now considerably past noon. In addition to the struggle going on in our immediate front, the sounds of a heavy attack from the north side were heard, and away out beyond the creek, to the south, a strong force could be seen advancing and overlapping our left. The enemy was coming nearer, both in front and on the north, and stray balls began to zip and whistle around our ears with unpleasant frequency. Then we saw the batteries that had been holding the position in advance of us limber up and fall back toward the Seminary, and the enemy simultaneously advance his batteries down the road. All our infantry out toward the creek on both sides of the pike began to fall back.

The enemy did not press them very closely, but halted for nearly an hour to reform his lines, which had been very much shattered by the battle of the forenoon. At last, having reformed his lines behind the low ridges in front, he made his appearance in grand shape. His line stretched from the railroad grading across the Cashtown Pike, and through the fields south of it half way to the Fairfield Road—nearly a mile in length. First we could see the tips of their color-staffs coming up over the little ridge, then the points of their bayonets, and then the Johnnies themselves, coming on with a steady tramp, tramp, and with loud yells. It was now apparent that the old Battery's turn had come again, and the embattled boys who stood so grimly at their posts felt that another page must be added to the record of Buena Vista and Antietam. The term "boys" is literally true, because of our gun detachment alone, consisting of a Sergeant, two Corporals, seven Cannoneers and six Drivers, only four had hair on their faces, while the other 12 were beardless boys whose ages would not average 19 years, and who, at any other period of our history, would have been at school! The same was more or less true of all the other gun detachments. But if boys in years they were, with one or two exceptions not necessary to name, veterans in battle, and braver or steadier soldiers than they were never faced a foe! A glance along our line at that moment would have been a rare study for an artist. As the day was very hot many of the boys had their jackets off, some with sleeves rolled up, and they exchanged little words of cheer with each other as the gray line came on. In quick, sharp tones, like successive reports of a repeating rifle, came Davison's orders: "Load—Canister—Double!" There was a hustling of Cannoneers, a few thumps of the rammer-heads, and then "Ready!—By piece!—At will!—Fire!!" . . .

Directly in our front—that is to say, on both sides of the pike—the Rebel infantry, whose left lapped the north side of the pike quite up to the line of the railroad grading, had been forced to halt and lie down by the tornado of canister that we had given them from the moment they came in sight over the bank of the creek. But the regiments in the field to their right (south side) of the pike kept on, and kept swinging their right flanks forward as if to take us in reverse or cut us off from the rest of our troops near the Seminary. At this moment Davison, bleeding from two desperate wounds, and so weak that one of the men had to hold him up on his feet (one ankle being totally shattered by a bullet), ordered us to form the half-battery, action left, by wheeling on the left gun as a pivot, so as to bring the half-battery on a line with the Cashtown Pike, muzzles facing south, his object being to rake the front of the Rebel line closing in on us from that side.

Of the four men left at our gun when this order was given two had bloody heads, but they were still "standing by," and Ord. Serg't Mitchell jumped on our off wheels to help us. "This is tough work, boys," he shouted, as we wheeled the gun around, "but we are good for it."

And Pat Wallace, tugging at the near wheel, shouted back: "If we ain't, where'll you find them that is!"

Well, this change of front gave us a clean rake along the Rebel line for a whole brigade length, but it exposed our right flank to the raking volleys of their infantry near the pike, who at that moment began to get up again and come on. Then for seven or eight minutes ensued probably the most desperate fight ever waged between artillery and infantry at close range without a particle of cover on either side. They gave us volley after volley in front and flank, and we gave them double canister as fast as we could load. The 6th Wisconsin and 11th Pennsylvania men crawled up over the bank of the cut or behind the rail fence in rear of Stewart's caissons and joined their musketry to our canister, while from the north side of the cut flashed the chain-lightning of the Old Man's half-battery in one solid streak!

At this time our left half-battery, taking their first line *en echarpe*, swept it so clean with double canister that the Rebels sagged away from the road to get cover from the fences and trees that lined it. From our second round on a gray squirrel could not have crossed the road alive.

How those peerless Cannoneers sprang to their work! Twenty-six years have but softened in memory the picture of "Old Griff" (Wallace), his tough Irish face set in hard lines with the unflinching resolution that filled his soul, while he sponged and loaded under that murderous musketry with the precision of barrack drill; of the burly Corporal, bareheaded, his hair matted with blood from a scalp wound, and wiping the crimson fluid out of his eyes to sight the gun; of the steady Orderly Sergeant, John Mitchell, moving calmly from gun to gun, now and then changing men about as one after another was hit and fell, stooping over a wounded man to help him up, or aiding another to stagger to the rear; of the dauntless Davison on foot among the guns, cheering the men, praising this one and that one, and ever and anon profanely exhorting us to "Feed it to 'em, G— d— em; feed it to 'em!" The very guns became things of life—not implements, but comrades. Every man was doing the work of two or three. At our gun at the finish there were only the Corporal, No. 1 and No. 3, with two drivers fetching ammunition. The water in Pat's bucket was like ink. His face and hands were smeared all over with burnt powder. The thumbstall of No. 3 was burned to a crisp by the hot vent-field. Between the black of the burnt powder and the crimson streaks from his bloody head, Packard looked like a demon from below! Up and down the line men reeling and falling; splinters flying from wheels and axles where bullets hit; in rear, horses tearing and plunging, mad with wounds or terror; drivers yelling, shells bursting, shot shrieking overhead, howling about our ears or throwing up great clouds of dust where they struck; the musketry crashing on three sides of us; bullets hissing, humming and whistling everywhere; cannon roaring; all crash on crash and peal on peal, smoke, dust, splinters, blood, wreck and carnage indescribable; but the brass guns of Old B still bellowed and not a man or boy flinched or faltered! Every man's shirt soaked with sweat and many of them sopped with blood from wounds not severe enough to make such bulldogs "let go"—bareheaded, sleeves rolled up, faces blackened—oh! if such a picture could be spread on canvas to the life! Out in front of us an undulating field, filled almost as far as the eye could reach with a long, low, gray line creeping toward us, fairly fringed with flame! ...

For a few moments the whole Rebel line, clear down to the Fairfield Road, seemed to waver, and we thought that maybe we could repulse them, single-handed as we were. At any rate, about our fifth or sixth round after changing front made their first line south of the pike halt, and many of them sought cover behind trees in the field or ran back to the rail fence parallel to the pike at that point, from which they resumed their musketry. But their second line came steadily on, and as Davison had now succumbed to his wounds Ord. Serg't Mitchell took command and gave the order to limber to the rear, the 6th Wisconsin and the 11th Pennsylvania having begun to fall back down the railroad track toward the town, turning about and firing at will as they retreated.

—BUELL, *"The Cannoneer"*

7. THE STRUGGLE FOR LITTLE ROUND TOP

Gettysburg was won, and lost, on the second day, and the outcome of that day's fighting was determined largely by geography, or by the enterprise of Union commanders in taking advantage of geography. The terrain of the second and third days of the battle is familiar enough. Immediately to the south of Gettysburg lies an irregular string of hills forming, as has often been noted, a giant fishhook almost four miles in length: the eye at Round Top, the shank along Cemetery Ridge, the bend at Cemetery Hill, the barb curving around Culp's Hill. The approach to these hills was everywhere difficult. The slope up to Cemetery Ridge was covered by wheat fields, orchards and patches of woods; the fields in front of the Round Tops, Cemetery and Culp's hills were littered with boulders and underbrush.

On the afternoon of the first Lee, who saw the strategical importance of Cemetery and Culp's hills, ordered Ewell to seize them "if possible." That evening, before Ewell could carry out these instructions, Wadsworth entrenched himself on Culp's Hill and Steinwehr and Schurz took position on Cemetery Hill; Ewell did not find it possible to advance. Longstreet's corps came up during the night, and Lee planned a general assault on the Union lines early the next morning. But Meade, too, had some appreciation of terrain, and as brigade after brigade marched in during the night and next morning—many of them exhausted with long marches—they were assigned positions all along Cemetery Ridge and Culp's Hill. Not until three o'clock in the afternoon did Longstreet's offensive get under way. By that time the Union positions were bristling with guns and men.

Prompt action might still have given victory to the Confederates. For there was an Achilles' heel in the Union position: the Round Tops. Sickles had been ordered to occupy the Round Tops but had chosen, instead, to probe the ground in front of Little Round Top and there—at the Peach Orchard—ran into Longstreet's corps and suffered severe losses. Meantime the Round Tops were all but undefended. Late in the afternoon Hood, who had begged hard to be allowed to swing south of the Federal position and outflank it—a perfectly feasible plan—started for Little Round Top. Just in time General Warren discovered its defenseless position and ordered elements of the V Corps to hurry to its defense. There ensued one of the fiercest fights not only of the battle but of the entire war. It was a touch and go affair, but in the end the Federals held the hill.

We give here four accounts of the struggle for Little Round Top. The first is from the somewhat jaundiced pen of General Hood, who never forgave Longstreet for denying him the chance—and the glory—of outflanking the Union army; this letter—part of the correspondence in a postwar controversy with Longstreet—was written in 1875. The second account is by Captain Porter Farley, a Rochester boy who enlisted in the 140th New York Volunteers, fought through the last years of the war, and later became one of the most distinguished of upstate New York surgeons; it tells how Warren's instant understanding of the importance of Little Round Top came just in time to save the Union position. The third is by William Oates, colonel of the 15th Alabama Infantry and later governor of his state. The fourth is by Theodore Gerrish of the 20th Maine Volunteers—a regiment which bore the brunt of the fighting.

A. GENERAL HOOD WANTS TO OUTFLANK THE UNION LEFT

I ARRIVED with my staff in front of the heights of Gettysburg shortly after daybreak, as I have already stated, on the morning of the 2d of July. My division soon commenced filing into an open field near me, where the troops were allowed to stack arms and rest until further orders. A short distance in advance of this point, and during the early part of that same morning, we were both engaged, in company with Generals Lee and A. P. Hill, in observing the position of the Federals. General Lee—with coat buttoned to the throat, sabre-belt buckled around the waist, and field-glasses pending at his side—walked up and down in the shade of large trees near us, halting now and then to observe the enemy. He seemed full of hope, yet at times, buried in deep thought.

Col. Fremantle, of England, was ensconced in the forks of a tree not far off, with glass in constant use, examining the lofty position of the Federal army.

General Lee was seemingly anxious you should attack that morning. He remarked to me: "The enemy is here, and if we do not whip him he will whip us." You thought it better to await the arrival of Pickett's division—at that time still in the rear—in order to make the attack; and you said to me, subsequently, whilst we were seated together near the trunk of a tree: "The General is a little nervous this morning; he wishes me to attack; I do not wish to do so without Pickett. I never like to go into battle with one boot off."

Thus passed the forenoon of that eventful day, when, in the afternoon—about three o'clock—it was decided to no longer await Pickett's division, but to proceed to our extreme right, and attack up the Emmettsburg road. McLaws moved off, and I followed with my division. In a short time I was ordered to quicken the march of my troops, and pass to the front of McLaws.

This movement was accomplished by throwing out an advanced force to tear down fences and clear the way. The instructions I received were to place my division across the Emmettsburg road, form line of battle, and attack. Before reaching this road, however, I had sent forward some of my picked Texas scouts to ascertain the position of the enemy's extreme left flank. They soon reported to me that it rested upon Round Top mountain; that the country was open and that I could march through an open woodland pasture around Round Top and assault the enemy in flank and rear; that their wagon trains were parked in rear of their line, and were badly exposed to our attack in that direction. As soon as I arrived upon the Emmettsburg road I placed one or two batteries in position and opened fire. A reply from the enemy's guns soon developed his lines. His left rested on or near Round Top, with line bending back and again forward, forming, as it were, a concave line as approached by the Emmettsburg road. A considerable body of troops was posted in front of their main line, between the Emmettsburg road and Round Top mountain. This force was in line of battle upon an eminence near a peach orchard.

I found, that in making the attack according to orders, viz: up the Emmettsburg road, I should have first to encounter and drive off this advanced line of battle; secondly, at the base and along the slope of the mountain, to confront immense boulders of stone, so massed together as to form narrow openings, which would break our ranks and cause the men to scatter whilst climbing up the rocky precipice. I found, moreover, that my division would

MAP of the BATTLE
OF
GETTYSBURG

showing Positions held
JULY 1ST 2D & 3D 1863.

——— Union Lines.
——— Confederate -

Scale of 1 Mile.

be exposed to a heavy fire from the main line of the enemy, in position on the crest of the high range, of which Round Top was the extreme left, and, by reason of the concavity of the enemy's main line, that we would be subject to a destructive fire in flank and rear, as well as in front; and deemed it almost an impossibility to clamber along the boulders up this steep and rugged mountain, and, under this number of cross-fires, put the enemy to flight. I knew that if the feat was accomplished it must be at a most fearful sacrifice of as brave and gallant soldiers as ever engaged in battle.

The reconnoissance by my Texas scouts and the development of the Federal lines were effected in a very short space of time; in truth, shorter than I have taken to recall and jot down these facts, although the scenes and events of that day are as clear to my mind as if the great battle had been fought yesterday. I was in possession of these important facts so shortly after reaching the Emmettsburg road, that I considered it my duty to report to you at once my opinion, that it was unwise to attack up the Emmettsburg road, as ordered, and to urge that you allow me to turn Round Top and attack the enemy in flank and rear. Accordingly, I dispatched a staff officer bearing to you my request to be allowed to make the proposed movement on account of the above-stated reasons. Your reply was quickly received: "Gen'l Lee's orders are to attack up the Emmettsburg road." I sent another officer to say that I feared nothing could be accomplished by such an attack, and renewed my request to turn Round Top. Again your answer was: "Gen'l Lee's orders are to attack up the Emmettsburg road." During this interim I had continued the use of the batteries upon the enemy, and had become more and more convinced that the Federal line extended to Round Top, and that I could not reasonably hope to accomplish much by the attack as ordered. In fact, it seemed to me the enemy occupied a position by nature so strong—I may say impregnable—that, independently of their flank-fire, they could easily repel our attack by merely throwing and rolling stones down the mountain side as we approached.

A third time I dispatched one of my staff to explain fully in regard to the situation, and to suggest that you had better come and look for yourself. I selected, in this instance, my adjutant-general, Colonel Harry Sellers, whom you know to be not only an officer of great courage, but also of marked ability. Colonel Sellers returned with the same message: "Gen'l Lee's orders are to attack up the Emmettsburg road." Almost simultaneously, Col. Fairfax, of your staff, rode up and repeated the above orders.

After this urgent protest against entering into battle at Gettysburg according to instructions—which protest is the first and only one I ever made during my entire military career—I ordered my line to advance and make the assault.

As my troops were moving forward, you rode up in person; a brief conversation passed between us, during which I again expressed the fears above mentioned, and regret at not being allowed to attack in flank around Round Top. You answered to this effect: "We must obey the orders of General Lee." I then rode forward with my line under a heavy fire. In about twenty minutes after reaching the Peach Orchard I was severely wounded in the arm, and borne from the field.

With this wound terminated my participation in this great battle. As I was borne off on a litter to the rear, I could but experience deep distress of mind and heart at the thought of the inevitable fate of my brave fellow-soldiers, who formed one of the grandest divisions of that world-renowned army; and I shall ever believe that had I been permitted to turn Round Top mountain, we would not only have gained that position, but have been able finally to rout the enemy.

—Letter from Hood to Longstreet, June 28, 1875

B. GENERAL WARREN SEIZES LITTLE ROUND TOP

The leading regiments of our brigade were just passing over that slightly elevated ground north of Little Round Top when down its slopes on our left, accompanied by a single mounted officer and an orderly, rode General G. K. Warren, our former brigade commander, then acting as General Meade's chief engineer. Warren came straight toward the head of the regiment, where I was riding with the colonel. He called out to O'Rorke, begining to speak while still some eight or ten rods from us, that he wanted us to come up there, that the enemy were advancing unopposed up the opposite side of the hill, down which he had just come, and he wanted our regiment to meet them. He was evidently greatly excited and spoke in his usual impulsive style.

O'Rorke answered, "General Weed is ahead and expects me to follow him."

"Never mind that," said Warren, "bring your regiment up here and I will take the responsibility."

It was a perplexing situation, but without hesitating O'Rorke turned to the left and followed the officer who had been riding with Warren, while Warren himself rode rapidly down the stony hill, whether in the direction from which we had just come or to overtake the rest of our brigade I cannot say, but evidently to find and order up more troops. . . .

We turned off the road to our left and rushed along the wooded, rocky, eastern slope of Little Round Top, ascending it while at the same time moving toward its southern extremity. It was just here that some of the guns of Hazlett's battery came rapidly up and plunged directly through our ranks, the horses being urged to frantic efforts by the whips of their drivers and the cannoniers assisting at the wheels, so great was the effort necessary to drag the guns and caissons up the ragged hillside.

As we reached the crest a never to be forgotten scene burst upon us. A great basin lay before us full of smoke and fire, and literally swarming with riderless horses and fighting, fleeing and pursuing men. The air was saturated with the sulphurous fumes of battle and was ringing with the shouts and groans of the combatants. The wild cries of charging lines, the rattle of musketry, the booming of artillery and the shrieks of the wounded were the orchestral accompaniments of a scene like very hell itself—as terrific as the warring of Milton's fiends in Pandemonium. The whole of Sickles's corps, and many other troops which had been sent to its support in that ill-chosen hollow, were being slaughtered and driven before the impetuous advance of Longstreet. But fascinating as was this terrible scene we had no time to spend upon it. Bloody work was ready for us at our very feet.

Round Top, a conical hill several hundred feet in height, lay just to the south of us, and was separated from Little Round Top, on whose crest we were now moving, by a broad ravine leading down into the basin where the great fight was raging. Right up this ravine, which offered the easiest place of ascent, a rebel force, outflanking all our troops in the plain below, was advancing at the very moment when we reached the crest of the hill. Vincent's brigade of the First division of our corps, had come up through the woods on the left and were just getting into position, and the right of their line had opened fire in the hollow on our left when the head of our regiment came over the hill. As soon as we reached the crest bullets came flying in among us. We were moving with the right in front and not a musket was loaded, a fact which Warren of course knew nothing about when he rushed us up there. The enemy were coming from our right and to face them would bring our file closers in front. The order, "On the right, by file into line," would have brought us into proper position; but there was no time to execute it, not even time to allow the natural impulse which manifested itself on the part of the men to halt and load the instant we received the enemy's fire.

O'Rorke did not hesitate a moment. "Dismount," said he to me, for the ground before us was too rough to ride over. We sprung from our horses and gave them to the sergeant major. O'Rorke shouted, "Down this way, boys," and following him we rushed down the rocky slope with all the same moral effect upon the rebels, who saw us coming, as if our bayonets had been fixed and we ready to charge upon them. Coming abreast of Vincent's brigade, and taking advantage of such shelter as the huge rocks lying about there afforded, the men loaded and fired, and in less time than it takes to write it the onslaught of the rebels was fairly checked, and in a few minutes the woods in front of us were cleared except for the dead and wounded. Such of the rebels as had approached so near as to make escape almost impossible dropped their guns, threw up their hands, and upon a slight slackening of our fire rushed in upon us and gave themselves up as prisoners, while those not so near took advantage of the chance left them and retreated in disorder.

—FARLEY, "Reminiscences of the 140th New York Volunteers"

C. COLONEL OATES ALMOST CAPTURES LITTLE ROUND TOP

General Law rode up to me as we were advancing, and informed me that I was then on the extreme right of our line and for me to hug the base of Great Round Top and go up the valley between the two mountains, until I found the left of the Union line, to turn it and do all the damage I could, and that Lieutenant-Colonel Bulger would be instructed to keep the Forty-seventh closed to my regiment, and if separated from the brigade he would act under my orders.

Just after we crossed Plum Run we received the first fire from the enemy's infantry. It was Stoughton's Second Regiment United States sharp-shooters, posted behind a fence at or near the southern foot of Great Round Top. They reached that position as we advanced through the old field. No other troops were there nor on that mountain at that time. I did not halt at the first fire, but looked to the rear for the Forty-eighth Alabama, and saw it going, under General Law's order, across the rear of our line to the left, it was said, to reenforce the Texas brigade, which was hotly engaged. That left no one in my rear or on my right to meet this foe. They were in the woods and I did not know the number of them.

I received the second fire. Lieutenant-Colonel Feagin and one or two of the men fell. I knew it would not do to go on and leave that force, I knew not how strong, in our rear with no troops of ours to take care of them; so I gave the command to change direction to the right. The seven companies of the Forty-seventh swung around with the Fifteenth and kept in line with it. The other three companies of that regiment were sent forward as skirmishers before the advance began. The sharp-shooters retreated up the south front of the mountain, pursued by my command.

In places the men had to climb up, catching to the rocks and bushes and crawling over the boulders in the face of the fire of the enemy, who kept retreating, taking shelter and firing down on us from behind the rocks and crags which covered the side of the mountain thicker than grave-stones in a city cemetery. Fortunately they usually over-shot us. We could see our foe only as they dodged back from one boulder to another, hence our fire was scattering. As we advanced up the mountain they ceased firing about half way up, divided, and a battalion went around the mountain on each side. Those who went up to the right fired a few shots at my flank. To meet this I deployed Company A, and moved it by the left flank to protect my right, and continued my rugged ascent until we reached the top.

Some of my men fainted from heat, exhaustion, and thirst. I halted and let them lie down and rest a few minutes. . . . I saw Gettysburg through the foliage of the trees. Saw the smoke and heard the roar of battle which was then raging at the Devil's Den, in the peach orchard, up the Emmitsburg road, and on the west and south of the Little Round Top. I saw from the highest point of rocks that we were then on the most commanding elevation in that neighborhood. I knew that my men were too much exhausted to make a good fight without a few minutes' rest. . . .

When we formed line of battle before the advance began, a detail was made of two men from each of the eleven companies of my regiment to take all the canteens to a well about one hundred yards in our rear and fill them with cool water before we went into the fight. Before this detail could fill the canteens the advance was ordered. It would have been infinitely better to have waited five minutes for those twenty-two men and the canteens of water, but generals never ask a colonel if his regiment is ready to move. The order was given and away we went. The water detail followed with the canteens of water, but when they got into the woods they missed us, walked right into the Yankee lines, and were captured, canteens and all. My men in the ranks, in the intense heat, suffered greatly for water. The loss of those twenty-two men and lack of the water contributed largely to our failure to take Little Round Top a few minutes later. About five minutes after I halted, Captain Terrell, assistant adjutant-general to General Law, rode up by the only pathway on the southeast side of the mountain and inquired why I had halted. I told him. He then informed me that General Hood was wounded, Law was in command of the division, and sent me his compliments, said for me to press on, turn the Union left, and capture Little Round Top, if possible, and to lose no time.

I then called his attention to my position. A precipice on the east and north, right at my feet; a very steep, stony, and wooded mountain-side on the west. The only approach to it by our enemy, a long wooded slope on the northwest. Within half an hour I could convert it into a Gibraltar that I could hold against ten times the number of men that I had, hence in my judgment it should be held and occupied by artillery as soon as possible, as it was higher than the other mountain and would command the entire field. Terrell replied that probably I was right, but that he had no authority to change or originate orders, which I very well knew; but with his sanction I would have remained at that point until I could have heard from Law or some superior in rank. I inquired for Law. Terrell said that as senior brigadier he was commanding the division, and along the line to the left. He then repeated that General Law had sent him to tell me to lose no time, but to press forward and drive everything before me as far as possible. General Meade did not then know the importance of the Round Tops. . . .

Just as the Forty-seventh companies were being driven back, I ordered my regiment to change direction to the left, swing around, and drive the Federals from the ledge of rocks, for the purpose of enfilading their line, relieving the Forty-seventh—gain the enemy's rear, and drive him from the hill. My men obeyed and advanced about half way to the enemy's position, but the fire was so destructive that my line wavered like a man trying to walk against a strong wind, and then slowly, doggedly, gave back a little; then with no one upon the left or right of me, my regiment exposed, while the enemy was still under cover, to stand there and die was sheer folly; either to retreat or advance became a necessity. The Lieutenant-Colonel, I. B. Feagin, had lost his leg at Plum Run; the heroic Captain Ellison had fallen; while Captain Brainard, one of the bravest and best officers in the regiment, in leading his company forward, fell, exclaiming, "O God! that I could see my mother," and instantly expired. Lieutenant John O. Oates, my dear brother, succeeded to the command of the company, but was pierced through by a number of bullets, and fell mortally wounded. Lieutenant Cody fell mortally wounded, Captain Bethune and several other officers were serious wounded, while the carnage in the ranks was appalling.

I again ordered the advance, and knowing the officers and men of that gallant old regiment, I felt sure that they would follow their commander anywhere in the line of duty. I passed through the line waving my sword, shouting, "Forward, men, to the ledge!" and was promptly followed by the command in splendid style. We drove the Federals from their strong defensive position; five times they rallied and charged us, twice coming so near that some of my men had to use the bayonet, but in vain was their effort. It was our time now to deal death and destruction to a gallant foe, and the account was speedily settled. I led this charge and sprang upon the ledge of rock, using my pistol within musket length, when the rush of my men drove the Maine men from the ledge along the line. . . . At this angle and to the southwest of it is where I lost the greatest number of my men. The Twentieth Maine was driven back from this ledge, but not farther than to the next ledge on the mountain-side.

I recall a circumstance which I recollect. I, with my regiment, made a rush forward from the ledge. About forty steps up the slope there is a large boulder about midway the Spur. The Maine regiment charged my line, coming right up in a hand-to-hand encounter. My regimental colors were just a step or two to the right of that boulder, and I was within ten feet. A Maine man reached to grasp the staff of the colors when Ensign Archibald stepped back and Sergeant Pat O'Connor stove his bayonet through the head of the Yankee, who fell dead. I witnessed that incident, which impressed me beyond the point of being forgotten.

There never were harder fighters than the Twentieth Maine men and their gallant Colonel. His skill and persistency and the great bravery of his men saved Little Round Top and the Army of the Potomac from defeat. Great events sometimes turn on comparatively small affairs. My position rapidly became untenable. The Federal infantry were reported to be coming down on my right and certainly were closing in on my rear, while some dismounted cavalry were closing the only avenue of escape on my left rear. I sent my sergeant-major with a request to Colonel Bowles, of the Fourth Alabama, the next in line to the left, to come to my relief. He returned within a minute and reported that none of our troops were in sight, the enemy to be between us and the Fourth Alabama, and swarming the woods south of Little Round Top. The lamented Captain Park, who was afterwards killed at Knoxville, and Captain Hill, killed near Richmond in 1864, came and informed me that the enemy were closing in on our rear. I sent Park to ascertain their number. He soon returned, and reported that two regiments were coming up behind us, and just then I saw them halt behind a fence, some two hundred yards distant, from which they opened fire on us. These, I have since learned from him, were the battalions of Stoughton's sharpshooters, each of which carried a flag, hence the impression that there were two regiments. They had been lost in the woods, but, guided by the firing, came up in our rear. At Balaklava Captain Nolan's six hundred had cannon to the right of them, cannon to the left of them, cannon in front of them, which volleyed and thundered. But at this moment the Fifteenth Alabama had infantry in front of them, to the right of them, dismounted cavalry to the left of them, and infantry in the rear of them. With a withering and deadly fire pouring in upon us from every direction, it seemed that the regiment was doomed to destruction. While one man was shot in the face, his right-hand or left-hand comrade was shot in the side or back. Some were struck simultaneously with two or three balls from different directions. Captains Hill and Park suggested that I should order a retreat; but this seemed impracticable. My dead and wounded were then nearly as great in number as those still on duty. They literally covered the ground. The blood stood in puddles in some places on the rocks; the ground was soaked with the blood of as brave men as ever fell on the red field of battle.

I still hoped for reenforcements or for the tide of success to turn my way. It seemed impossible to retreat and I therefore replied to my captains, "Return to your companies; we will sell out as dearly as possible."

Hill made no reply, but Park smiled pleasantly, gave me the military salute, and said, "All right, sir."

On reflection a few moments later I saw no hope of success and did order a retreat, but did not undertake to retire in order. I sent Sergeant-Major Norris and had the officers and men advised the best I could that when the signal was given that we would not try to retreat in order, but every one should run in the direction from whence we came, and halt on the top of the Big Round Top Mountain. I found the undertaking to capture Little Round Top too great for my regiment unsupported. I waited until the next charge of the Twentieth Maine was repulsed, as it would give my men a better chance to get out unhurt, and then ordered the retreat. . . .

When the signal was given we ran like a herd of wild cattle, right through the line of dismounted cavalrymen. Some of the men as they ran through seized three of the cavalrymen by the collar and carried them out prisoners. As we ran, a man named Keils, of Company H, from Henry County, who was to my right and rear had his throat cut by a bullet, and he ran past me breathing at his throat and the blood spattering. His wind-pipe was entirely severed, but notwithstanding he crossed the mountain and died in the field hospital that night or the next morning.

—OATES, *The War between the Union and the Confederacy*

D. THE 20TH MAINE SAVES LITTLE ROUND TOP

At daylight, on the morning of July 2d, we resumed our march, and in a few hours halted within supporting distance of the left flank of our army, about a mile to the right of Little Round Top. The long forenoon passed away, and to our surprise the enemy made no attack. This was very fortunate for our army, as it enabled our men to strengthen our lines of fortifications, and also to obtain a little rest, of which they were in great need. The rebels were also engaged in throwing up rude lines of defenses, hurrying up reinforcements, and in discussing the line of action they should pursue. . . .

The hour of noon passed, and the sun had measured nearly one-half the distance across the western sky, before the assault was made. Then, as suddenly as a bolt of fire flies from the storm cloud, a hundred pieces of rebel artillery open upon our left flank, and under the thick canopy of screaming, hissing, bursting shells, Longstreet's corps was hurled upon the troops of General Sickles. Instantly our commanders discerned the intention of General Lee. It was to turn and crush our left flank, as he had crushed our right at Chancellorsville. It was a terrible onslaught. The brave sons of the South never displayed more gallant courage than on that fatal afternoon of July 2d. But brave Dan Sickles and the old Third corps were equal to the emergency, and stood as immovable against the surging tides as blocks of granite. But a new and appalling danger suddenly threatened the Union army. Little Round Top was the key to the entire position. Rebel batteries planted on that rocky bluff could shell any portion of our line at their pleasure. For some reason Sickles had not placed any infantry upon this important position. A few batteries were scattered along its ragged side, but they had no infantry support.

Lee saw at a glance that Little Round Top was the prize for which the two armies were contending, and with skillful audacity he determined to wrest it from his opponent. While the terrible charge was being made upon the line of General Sickles, Longstreet threw out a whole division, by extending his line to his right, for the purpose of seizing the coveted prize. The danger was at once seen by our officers, and our brigade was ordered forward, to hold the hill against the assault of the enemy. In a moment all was excitement. Every soldier seemed to understand the situation, and to be inspired by its danger. "Fall in! Fall in! By the right flank! Double-quick! March!" and away we went, under the terrible artillery fire. It was a moment of thrilling interest. Shells were exploding on every side. Sickles' corps was enveloped in sheets of flame, and looked like a vast windrow of fire. But so intense was the excitement that we hardly noticed these surroundings. Up the steep hillside we ran, and reached the crest. "On the right by file into line," was the command, and our regiment had assumed the position to which it had been assigned. We were on the left of our brigade, and consequently on the extreme left of all our line of battle. The ground sloped to our front and left, and was sparsely covered with a growth of oak trees, which were too small to afford us any protection. Shells were crashing through the air above our heads, making so much noise that we could hardly hear the commands of our officers; the air was filled with fragments of exploding shells and splinters torn from mangled trees; but our men appeared to be as cool and deliberate in their movements as if they had been forming a line upon the parade ground in camp.

Our regiment mustered about three hundred and fifty men. Company B, from Piscataquis county, commanded by the gallant Captain Morrill, was ordered to deploy in our front as skirmishers. They boldly advanced down the slope and disappeared from our view. Ten minutes have passed since we formed the line; the skirmishers must have advanced some thirty or forty rods through the rocks and trees, but we have seen no indications of the enemy; "But look!" "Look!" "Look!" exclaimed half a hundred men in our regiment at the same moment; and no wonder, for right in our front, between us and our skirmishers, whom they have probably captured, we see the lines of the enemy. They have paid no attention to the rest of the brigade stationed on our right, but they are rushing on, determined to turn and crush the left of our line. Colonel Chamberlain with rare sagacity understood the movement they were making, and bent back the left flank of our regiment until the line formed almost a right angle with the colors at the point, all these movements requiring a much less space of time than it requires for me to write of them.

How can I describe the scenes that followed? Imagine, if you can, nine small companies of infantry, numbering perhaps three hundred men, in the form of a right angle, on the extreme flank of an army of eighty thousand men, put there to hold the key of the entire position against a force at least ten times their number, and who are desperately determined to succeed in the mission upon which they came. Stand firm, ye boys from Maine, for not once in a century are men permitted to bear such responsibilities for freedom and justice, for God and humanity, as are now placed upon you.

The conflict opens. I know not who gave the first fire, or which line received the first lead. I only know that the carnage began. Our regiment was mantled in fire and smoke. I wish that I could picture with my pen the awful details of that hour,—how rapidly the cartridges were torn from the boxes and stuffed in the smoking muzzles of the guns; how the steel rammers clashed and clanged in the heated barrels; how the men's hands and faces grew grim and black with burning powder; how our little line, baptized with fire, reeled to and fro as it advanced or was pressed back; how our officers bravely encouraged the men to hold on and recklessly exposed themselves to the enemy's fire,—a terrible medley of cries, shouts, cheers, groans, prayers, curses, bursting shells, whizzing rifle bullets and clanging steel. And if that was all, my heart would not be so sad and heavy as I write. But the enemy was pouring a terrible fire upon us, his superior forces giving him a great advantage. Ten to one are fearful odds where men are contending for so great a prize. The air seemed to be alive with lead. The lines at times were so near each other that the hostile gun barrels almost touched. As the contest continued, the rebels grew desperate that so insignificant a force should so long hold them in check. At one time there was a brief lull in the carnage, and our shattered line was closed up, but soon the contest raged again with renewed fierceness. The rebels had been reinforced, and were now determined to sweep our regiment from the crest of Little Round Top.

Many of our companies have suffered fearfully. . . . But there is no relief, and the carnage goes on. Our line is pressed back so far that our dead are within the lines of the enemy. The pressure made by the superior weight of the enemy's line is severely felt. Our ammunition is nearly all gone, and we are using the cartridges from the boxes of our wounded comrades. A critical moment has arrived, and we can remain as we are no longer; we must advance or retreat. It must not be the latter, but how can it be the former? Colonel Chamberlain understands how it can be done. The order is given "Fix bayonets!" and the steel shanks of the bayonets rattle upon the rifle barrels. "Charge bayonets, charge!" Every man understood in a moment that the movement was our only salvation, but there is a limit to human endurance, and I do not dishonor those brave men when I write that for a brief moment the order was not obeyed, and the little line seemed to quail under the fearful fire that was being poured upon it. O for some man reckless of life, and all else save his country's honor and safety, who would rush far out to the front, lead the way, and inspire the hearts of his exhausted comrades!

In that moment of supreme need the want was supplied. Lieut. H. S. Melcher, an officer who had worked his way up from the ranks, and was then in command of Co. F, at that time the color company, saw the situation, and did not hesitate, and for his gallant act deserves as much as any other man the honor of the victory on Round Top. With a cheer, and a flash of his sword, that sent an inspiration along the line, full ten paces to the front he sprang—ten paces—more than half the distance between the hostile lines. "Come on! Come on! Come on, boys!" he shouts. The color sergeant and the brave color guard follow, and with one wild yell of anguish wrung from its tortured heart, the regiment charged.

The rebels were confounded at the movement. We struck them with a fearful shock. They recoil, stagger, break and run, and like avenging demons our men pursue. The rebels rush toward a stone wall, but, to our mutual surprise, two scores of rifle barrels gleam over the rocks, and a murderous volley was poured in upon them at close quarters. A band of men leap over the wall and capture at least a hundred prisoners. Piscataquis has been heard from, and as usual it was a good report. This unlooked-for reinforcement was Company B, whom we supposed were all captured.

Our Colonel's commands were simply to hold the hill, and we did not follow the retreating rebels but a short distance. After dark an order came to advance and capture a hill in our front. Through the trees, among the rocks, up the steep hillside, we made our way, captured the position, and also a number of prisoners.

—GERRISH, *Army Life*

8. EWELL FAILS TO TAKE CULP'S HILL

Lee never succeeded in co-ordinating his attacks on the Union lines at Gettysburg. He had planned a simultaneous advance by Longstreet and Ewell on the afternoon of the second. While Longstreet swept up onto Cemetery Ridge and the Round Tops, Ewell was to strike at Cemetery Hill and Culp's Hill. The importance of Culp's Hill was obvious. Its capture would have flanked the Federals from the east, exposing them to a two-way artillery fire; it would likewise have threatened the Baltimore Pike along which the Federals would have to withdraw if defeated.

But these two hills were heavily defended. The Iron Brigade, decimated on the first day, was moved to Culp's Hill, and speedily reinforced by Slocum's corps. That night and during the next day the defenders threw up

breastworks to supplement the natural defenses afforded by the brawling little
Rock Creek and the boulder-strewed ground, and they brought in artillery.
Not until the evening of July 2 did Ewell launch his attack, and then it was
a disjointed affair. Johnson's division crossed Rock Creek and fought its way
gallantly up the slope of Culp's Hill, but there it was held. Before dawn next
day Ewell sent reinforcements, but they, too, were held by Union artillery
fire. A counterattack by the 2nd Massachusetts exacted a heavy toll and
forced the Confederates to retreat.

We have here a Confederate account of the advance. Randolph McKim
was first lieutenant in Steuart's brigade—the Maryland Brigade—of Johnson's
division. Though written long after the war his "recollections" are based on
diaries and letters and bear the stamp of authenticity.

IT was past six P.M. before our brigade was ordered forward—nearly
twenty-four hours after we had gotten into position. We were to storm
the eastern face of Culp's Hill, a rough and rugged eminence on the southeast
of the town, which formed the key to the enemy's right centre. Passing first
through a small skirt of woods, we advanced rapidly in line of battle across a
corn field which lay between us and the base of the hill, the enemy opening
upon us briskly as soon as we were unmasked. Rock creek, waist-deep in
some places, was waded, and now the whole line, except the First North
Carolina, held in reserve on our left flank, pressed up the steep acclivity
through the darkness, and was soon hotly engaged with the enemy.

After the conflict had been going on for some time, I ventured to urge the
brigadier-general commanding to send forward the First North Carolina to
reinforce their struggling comrades. Receiving orders to that effect, I led the
regiment up the hill, guided only by the flashes of the muskets, until I reached
a position abreast of our line of fire on the right. In front, a hundred yards
or so, I saw another line of fire, but owing to the thick foliage could not determine whether the musket flashes were *up* or *down* the hill. Finding that
bullets were whistling over our heads, I concluded the force in our front must
be the enemy, and seeing, as I thought, an admirable chance of turning their
flank, I urged Colonel Brown to move rapidly forward and fire. When we
reached what I supposed the proper position, I shouted, "Fire on them, boys;
fire on them!"

At that moment Major Parsley, the gallant officer in command of the
Third North Carolina, rushed up and shouted, "They are our own men."

Owing to the din of battle the command to fire had not been heard except
by those nearest to me, and I believe no injury resulted from my mistake. . . .

The position thus so hardly won and at so dear a cost was one of great
importance. It was within a few hundred yards of the Baltimore turnpike,
which I think it commanded. Its capture was a breach in the enemy's lines
through which troops might have been poured and the strong positions of
Cemetery Hill rendered untenable. . . .

It is only in keeping with the haphazard character of the whole battle that
the capture of a point of such strategic importance should not have been

taken advantage of by the Confederates. It remains, however, no less a proud memory for the officers and men of the Third Brigade that their prowess gained for the Confederate general a position where "Meade's entire line might have been taken in reverse."

But if the Confederates did not realize what they had gained, the Federals were fully aware what *they* had lost. Accordingly, they spent the night massing troops and artillery for an effort to regain their works. . . . Through the long hours of the night we heard the rumbling of their guns, and thought they were evacuating the hill. The first streak of daylight revealed our mistake. It was scarcely dawn (the writer of this had just lain down to sleep after a night in the saddle) when their artillery opened upon us, at a range of about 500 yards, a terrific and galling fire, to which we had no means of replying, as our guns could not be dragged up that steep and rugged ascent. Then, a little after sunrise, their infantry moved forward in heavy force to attack us. . . .

They drove in our skirmishers, but could not dislodge us from the works we had captured, although these were commanded in part by the works on the crest of the hill to our right, whence a galling fire was poured into our ranks. Next a strong effort was made to take us in flank, and I well remember that at one time our line resembled three sides of a pentagon, the left side being composed of some other brigade, centre and right composed of our own brigade, which thus occupied the most advanced position toward the crest of the hill. About this time, I think, word came to General Steuart that the men's ammunition was almost exhausted. One of his staff immediately took three men and went on foot to the wagons, distant about a mile and a quarter, and brought up two boxes of cartridges. "We emptied each box into a blanket and swung the blanket on a rail, and so carried it to the front." It was now, I think, about half-past nine, and ever since four o'clock the fire of the enemy had been almost continuous, at times tremendous. . . .

But all the efforts of the enemy failed to dislodge us. Unassisted, the Third Brigade held the position they had won the night before. . . .

Then came General Ewell's order to assume the offensive and assail the crest of Culp's Hill, on our right. My diary says that both General Steuart and General Daniel, who now came up with his brigade to support the movement, strongly disapproved of making the assault. And well might they despair of success in the face of such difficulties. The works to be stormed ran almost at right angles to those we occupied. Moreover, there was a double line of entrenchments, one above the other, and each filled with troops. In moving to the attack we were exposed to enfilading fire from the woods on our left flank, besides the double line of fire which we had to face in front, and a battery of artillery posted on a hill to our left rear opened upon us at short range. What wonder, then, if Steuart was reluctant to lead his men into such a slaughter-pen, from which he saw there could be no issue but death and defeat! But though he remonstrated, he gallantly obeyed without delay the orders he received, giving the command, "Left face," and afterwards, "File right." He made his men leap the breastworks and form in line of battle on the other side at right angles, nearly, to their previous position, galled all the time by a brisk fire from the enemy. Then drawing his sword, he gave the command, "Charge bayonets!" and moved forward on foot with his men into the jaws of death.

On swept the gallant little brigade, the Third North Carolina on the right of the line, next the Second Maryland, then the three Virginia regiments (10th, 23d, and 37th), with the First North Carolina on the extreme left. Its ranks had been sadly thinned, and its energies greatly depleted by those six fearful hours of battle that morning; but its nerve and spirit were undiminished. Soon, however, the left and centre were checked and then repulsed, probably by the severe flank fire from the woods; and the small remnant of the Third North Carolina, with the stronger Second Maryland (I do not recall the banners of any other regiment), were far in advance of the rest of the line. On they pressed to within about twenty or thirty paces of the works—a small but gallant band of heroes daring to attempt what could not be done by flesh and blood.

The end soon came. We were beaten back to the line from which we had advanced with terrible loss, and in much confusion, but the enemy did not make a counter charge. By the strenuous efforts of the officers of the line and of the staff, order was restored, and we re-formed in the breastworks from which we had emerged, there to be again exposed to an artillery fire exceeding in violence that of the early morning. It remains only to say that, like Pickett's men later in the day, this single brigade was hurled unsupported against the enemy's works. Daniel's brigade remained in the breastworks during and after the charge, and neither from that command nor from any other had we any support. Of course it is to be presumed that General Daniel acted in obedience to orders. We remained in this breastwork after the charge about an hour before we finally abandoned the Federal entrenchments and retired to the foot of the hill.

—McKim, *A Soldier's Recollections*

9. HIGH TIDE AT GETTYSBURG

Both Pickett and Stuart had come up during the afternoon of the second. With his army at full strength, and undaunted by the repulses of the second day's fighting, Lee determined to renew the attack the next morning, hurling Longstreet and Hill against the Union center on Cemetery Ridge and Ewell against Culp's Hill. Again ill fortune plagued him. Ewell's attack came off almost as planned, but was thrown back. Longstreet once more had what Lincoln called "the slows," but whether because of natural difficulties of co-ordinating so many forces for attack or because of reluctance to launch an attack which he disapproved is still a subject of controversy.

Meantime two of the greatest artillerists of the war—Alexander and Hunt—made ready. Although the Federals had artillery superiority, Alexander was able to bring over 100 guns to bear on the Union position, while Hunt could not mass more than about 80 on Cemetery Ridge and the Round

Tops. At one o'clock the greatest artillery duel ever seen on the continent begin, and for 40 minutes the roar of cannon shook the earth. Then—with both sides low on artillery ammunition—silence fell over the battlefield.

Now Pickett and Pettigrew were ready for that famous charge which was to live forever in history. "Up men and to your posts!" cried Pickett. "Don't forget today that you are from old Virginia." And Pettigrew called to Colonel Marshall, "Now, Colonel, for the honor of the good Old North State, forward!" Forward they swept, 15,000 men in gray, the colors of 47 regiments fluttering in the breeze, up the long slope of Cemetery Ridge. The Federals, too, were ready, General Gibbon—a Southerner with three brothers in the Confederate ranks—riding up and down encouraging his men to stand firm.

But let our chroniclers tell the great story. They need little introduction. First comes the lionhearted General Alexander, chief of artillery of Longstreet's corps and—as the event proved—a distinguished stylist. Next comes Lee's war horse, James Longstreet, the focal figure in the controversies that raged around Gettysburg for a generation after the battle. We have only one Union historian—but what an historian he is! Frank Haskell had been born in Vermont and educated at Dartmouth; he moved out to Wisconsin and it was there that he joined the famous Iron Brigade, was promoted from lieutenant to colonel, and in time became aide-de-camp to General Gibbon. During the two weeks after the repulse of Pickett's charge he composed a book-length letter to his brother giving a history of the battle. A year later he was killed at Cold Harbor. Haskell's Gettysburg has become a classic of American literature—the only American military account to find its way into the Harvard Classics. Our final account is from the gifted pen of the English observer, Colonel Fremantle, who tells of the aftermath of the charge and gives us an unforgettable picture of Lee at this crisis of his career.

A. Alexander Gives the Signal to Start

BEFORE daylight on the morning of the 3d I received orders to post the artillery for an assault upon the enemy's position, and later I learned that it was to be led by Pickett's division and directed on Cemetery Hill. Some of the batteries had gone back for ammunition and forage, but they were all brought up immediately, and by daylight all then on the field were posted. Dearing's batallion (with Pickett's division) reported sometime during the morning. The enemy fired on our movements and positions occasionally, doing no great damage, and we scarcely returned a shot. The morning was consumed in waiting for Pickett's division, and possibly other movements of infantry. . . .

About 11 A.M. the skirmishers in A. P. Hill's front got to fighting for a barn in between the lines, and the artillery on both sides gradually took part until the whole of Hill's artillery in position, which I think was 63 guns, were heavily engaged with about an equal number of the enemy's guns for over a half hour, but not one of the 75 guns which I then had in line was allowed to fire a shot, as we had at best but a short supply of ammunition for the work laid out. . . .

Gradually the cannonade just referred to died out as it began, and the field became nearly silent, but writers have frequently referred to "the cannonade preceding the assault" as having begun at 11 o'clock and lasted for some hours, being misled by this affair. About 12 M. General Longstreet told me that when Pickett was ready, he would himself give the signal for all our guns to open (which was to be two guns from the Washington Artillery, near the center of our line), and meanwhile he desired me to select a suitable position for observation, and to take with me one of General Pickett's staff, and exercise my judgment in selecting the moment for Pickett's advance to begin. Complying, I selected the advanced salient angle of the wood in which Pickett's line was now formed, just on the left flank of my line of 75 guns. While occupying this position and in conversation with General A. R. Wright, commanding a Georgia brigade in A. P. Hill's corps, who had come out there for an observation of the position, I received a note from General Longstreet, which I copy from the original still in my possession, as follows:

HD. QRS., *July 3rd,* 1863

COLONEL:

If the artillery fire does not have the effect to drive off the enemy or greatly demoralize him so as to make our efforts pretty certain, I would prefer that you should not advise General Pickett to make the charge. I shall rely a great deal on your good judgment to determine the matter, and shall expect you to let General Pickett know when the moment offers.

Respectfully,

J. LONGSTREET, *Lieut.-General.*

To Colonel E. P. ALEXANDER, *Artillery.*

This note at once suggested that there was some alternative to the attack, and placed me on the responsibility of deciding the question. I endeavored to avoid it by giving my views in a note, of which I kept no copy, but of which I have always retained a vivid recollection, having discussed its points with General A. R. Wright as I wrote it. It was expressed very nearly as follows:

GENERAL:

I will only be able to judge of the effect of our fire on the enemy by his return fire, for his infantry is but little exposed to view and the smoke will obscure the whole field. If, as I infer from your note, there is any alternative to this attack, it should be carefully considered before opening our fire, for it will take all the artillery ammunition we have left to test this one thoroughly, and, if the result is unfavorable, we will have none left for another effort. And even if this is entirely successful it can only be so at a very bloody cost.

Very respectfully, &c.,

E. P. ALEXANDER, *Colonel Artillery.*

To this note I soon received the following reply:

COLONEL: HD. QRS., *July 3rd,* 1863

The intention is to advance the infantry if the artillery has the desired effect of driving the enemy's off, or having other effect such as to warrant us in making the attack. When that moment arrives advise General P., and of course advance such artillery as you can use in aiding the attack.

Respectfully,

J. LONGSTREET, *Lieut.-General, Commanding.*

To Colonel ALEXANDER.

This letter again placed the responsibility upon me, and I felt it very deeply, for the day was rapidly advancing (it was about 12 M., or a little later), and whatever was to be done was to be done soon. Meanwhile I had been anxiously discussing the attack with General A. R. Wright, who said that the difficulty was not so much in *reaching* Cemetery Hill, or taking it— that his brigade had carried it the afternoon before—but that the trouble was to hold it, for the whole Federal army was massed in a sort of horse-shoe shape and could rapidly reinforce the point to any extent, while our long, enveloping line could not give prompt enough support. This somewhat re-assured me, as I had heard it said that morning that General Lee had ordered "every brigade in the army to charge Cemetery Hill," and it was at least certain that the question of supports had had his careful attention. Before answering, however, I rode back to converse with General Pickett, whose line was now formed or forming in the wood, and without telling him of the question I had to decide, I found out that he was entirely sanguine of success in the charge, and was only congratulating himself on the oppor-tunity. I was convinced that to make any half-way effort would insure a failure of the campaign, and that if our artillery fire was once opened, after all the time consumed in preparation for the attack, the only hope of success was to follow it up promptly with one supreme effort, concentrating every energy we possessed into it, and my mind was fully made up that *if the artillery opened Pickett must charge.* After the second note from General Longstreet, therefore, and the interview with Pickett, I did not feel justified in making any delay, but to acquaint General Longstreet with my determina-tion. I wrote him a note, which I think I quote verbatim, as follows: "Gen-eral: When our artillery fire is doing its best I shall advise General Pickett to advance." It was my intention, as he had a long distance to traverse, that he should start not later than fifteen minutes after our fire opened. . . .

It was 1 P.M. by my watch when the signal guns were fired, the field at that time being entirely silent, but for light picket firing between the lines, and as suddenly as an organ strikes up in a church, the grand roar followed from all the guns of both armies. The enemy's fire was heavy and severe, and their accounts represent ours as having been equally so, though our rifle guns were comparatively few and had only very defective ammunition. . . .

I had fully intended giving Pickett the order to advance as soon as I saw that our guns had gotten their ranges, say, in ten or fifteen minutes, but the enemy's fire was so severe that when that time had elapsed I could not make up my mind to order the infantry out into a fire which I did not believe they could face, for so long a charge, in such a hot sun, tired as they already were by the march from Chambersburg. I accordingly waited in hopes that our fire would produce some visible effect, or something turn up to make the situation more hopeful; but fifteen minutes more passed without any change in the situation, the fire on neither side slackening for a moment. Even then I could not bring myself to give a peremptory order to Pickett to advance, but feeling that the critical moment would soon pass, I wrote him a note to this effect: "If you are coming at all you must come immediately or I cannot give you proper support; but the enemy's fire has not slackened materially, and at least 18 guns are still firing from the Cemetery itself."

This note (which, though given from memory, I can vouch for as very nearly verbatim) I sent off at 1:30 P.M., consulting my watch. I afterwards heard what followed its receipt from members of the staff of both Generals Pickett and Longstreet, as follows: Pickett on receiving it galloped over to General Longstreet, who was not far off, and showed it to General L. The latter read it and made no reply. (General Longstreet himself, speaking of it afterwards, said that he knew the charge had to be made, but could not bring himself to give the order.) General Pickett then said: "General, shall I advance?" Longstreet turned around in his saddle and would not answer. Pickett immediately saluted, and said: "I am going to lead my division forward, sir," and galloped off to put it in motion; on which General L. left his staff and rode out alone to my position.

Meanwhile, five minutes after I sent the above note to Pickett, the enemy's fire suddenly slackened materially, and the batteries in the Cemetery were limbered up and were withdrawn. As the enemy had such abundance of ammunition and so much better guns than ours that they were not compelled to reserve their artillery for critical moments (as we almost always had to do), I knew that they must have felt the punishment a good deal, and I was a good deal elated by the sight. But to make sure that it was a withdrawal for good, and not a mere change of position or relieving of the batteries by fresh ones, I waited for five minutes more, closely examining the ground with a large glass. At that time I sent my courier to Pickett with a note: "For God's sake come quick; the 18 guns are gone"; and, going to the nearest guns, I sent a lieutenant and a sergeant, one after the other, with other messages to same effect.

A few minutes after this, Pickett still not appearing, General Longstreet rode up alone, having seen Pickett and left his staff as above. I showed him the situation, and said I only feared I could not give Pickett the help I wanted to, my ammunition being very low, and the seven guns under Richardson having been taken off. General Longstreet spoke up promptly: "Go and stop Pickett right where he is, and replenish your ammunition." I answered, that the ordnance wagons had been nearly emptied, replacing expenditures of the day before, and that not over 20 rounds to the gun were left—too little to accomplish much—and that while this was being done the enemy would recover from the effect of the fire we were now giving him. His reply was: "I don't want to make this charge; I don't believe it can succeed. I would stop Pickett now, but that General Lee has ordered it and expects it," and other remarks, showing that he would have been easily induced, even then, to order Pickett to halt.

It was just at this moment that Pickett's line appeared sweeping out of the wood, Garnett's brigade passing over us. I then left General Longstreet and rode a short distance with General Garnett, an old friend, who had been sick, but, buttoned up in an old blue overcoat, in spite of the heat of the day, was riding in front of his line. I then galloped along my line of guns, ordering those that had over 20 rounds left to limber up and follow Pickett, and those that had less to maintain their fire from where they were. I had advanced several batteries or parts of batteries in this way, when Pickett's division appeared on the slope of Cemetery Hill, and a considerable force of the enemy were thrown out, attacking his unprotected right flank. Meanwhile, too, several batteries which had been withdrawn were run out again and were firing on him very heavily. We opened on these troops and batteries with the best we had in the shop, and appeared to do them considerable damage, but meanwhile Pickett's division just seemed to melt away in the blue musketry smoke which now covered the hill. Nothing but stragglers came back. As soon as it was clear that Pickett was "gone up," I ceased firing, saving what little ammunition was left for fear of an advance by the enemy. About this time General Lee came up to our guns alone and remained there a half hour or more, speaking to Pickett's men as they came straggling back, and encouraging them to form again in the first cover they could find.

—Letter from General E. P. Alexander to the Reverend J. Wm. Jones

B. Armistead Falls beside the Enemy's Battery

The signal guns broke the silence, the blaze of the second gun mingling in the smoke of the first, and salvoes rolled to the left and repeated themselves, the enemy's fine metal spreading its fire to the converging lines, plowing the trembling ground, plunging through the line of batteries, and clouding the heavy air. The two or three hundred guns seemed proud of their undivided honors and organized confusion. The Confederates had the benefit of converging fire into the enemy's massed position, but the superior metal of the enemy neutralized the advantage of position. The brave and steady work progressed. . . .

General Pickett rode to confer with Alexander, then to the ground upon which I was resting, where he was soon handed a slip of paper. After reading it he handed it to me. It read:

"If you are coming at all, come at once, or I cannot give you proper support, but the enemy's fire has not slackened at all. At least eighteen guns are still firing from the cemetery itself.

—Alexander"

Pickett said, "General, shall I advance?"

The effort to speak the order failed, and I could only indicate it by an affirmative bow. He accepted the duty, with seeming confidence of success, leaped on his horse, and rode gaily to his command. I mounted and spurred for Alexander's post. He reported that the batteries he had reserved for the charge with the infantry had been spirited away by General Lee's chief of artillery, that the ammunition of the batteries of position was so reduced that he could not use them in proper support of the infantry. He was ordered to stop the march at once and fill up his ammunition chests. But, alas! there was no more ammunition to be had.

The order was imperative. The Confederate commander had fixed his heart upon the work. Just then a number of the enemy's batteries hitched up and hauled off, which gave a glimpse of unexpected hope. Encouraging messages were sent for the columns to hurry on—and they were then on elastic springing step. The officers saluted as they passed, their stern smiles expressing confidence. General Pickett, a graceful horseman, sat lightly in the saddle, his brown locks flowing quite over his shoulders. Pettigrew's division spread their steps and quickly rectified the alignment, and the grand march moved bravely on. As soon as the leading columns opened the way, the supports sprang to their alignments. General Trimble mounted, adjusting his seat and reins with an air and grace as if setting out on a pleasant afternoon ride. When aligned to their places solid march was made down the slope and past our batteries of position.

Confederate batteries put their fire over the heads of the men as they moved down the slope, and continued to draw the fire of the enemy until the smoke lifted and drifted to the rear, when every gun was turned upon the infantry columns. The batteries that had been drawn off were replaced by others that were fresh. Soldiers and officers began to fall, some to rise no more, others to find their way to the hospital tents. Single files were cut here and there; then the gaps increased, and an occasional shot tore wider openings, but, closing the gaps as quickly as made, the march moved on. . . .

Colonel Latrobe was sent to General Trimble to have his men fill the line of the broken brigades, and bravely they repaired the damage. The enemy moved out against the supporting brigade in Pickett's rear. Colonel Sorrel was sent to have that move guarded, and Pickett was drawn back to that contention. McLaws was ordered to press his left forward, but the direct line of infantry and cross fire of artillery was telling fearfully on the front. Colonel Fremantle ran up to offer congratulations on the apparent success, but the big gaps in the ranks grew until the lines were reduced to half their length. I called his attention to the broken, struggling ranks. Trimble mended the battle of the left in handsome style, but on the right the massing of the enemy grew stronger and stronger. Brigadier Garnett was killed; Kemper and Trimble were desperately wounded; Generals Hancock and Gibbon were wounded. General Lane succeeded Trimble and with Pettigrew held the battle of the left in steady ranks.

Pickett's lines being nearer, the impact was heaviest upon them. Most of the field officers were killed or wounded. Colonel Whittle, of Armistead's brigade, who had been shot through the right leg at Williamsburg and lost his left arm at Malvern Hill, was shot through the right arm, then brought down by a shot through his left leg.

General Armistead, of the second line, spread his steps to supply the places of fallen comrades. His colors cut down, with a volley against the bristling line of bayonets, he put his cap on his sword to guide the storm. The enemy's massing, enveloping numbers held the struggle until the noble Armistead fell beside the wheels of the enemy's battery. Pettigrew was wounded but held his command.

General Pickett, finding the battle broken while the enemy was still reinforcing, called the troops off. There was no indication of panic. The broken files marched back in steady step. The effort was nobly made and failed from blows that could not be fended.

—LONGSTREET, *From Manassas to Appomattox*

C. "THE CREST IS SAFE"

Half-past two o'clock, an hour and a half since the commencement, and still the cannonade did not in the least abate; but soon thereafter some signs of weariness and a little slacking of fire began to be apparent upon both sides. . . . All things must end, and the great cannonade was no exception to the general law of earth. In the number of guns active at one time, and in the duration and rapidity of their fire, this artillery engagement, up to this time, must stand alone and pre-eminent in this war. It has not been often, or many times, surpassed in the battles of the world. Two hundred and fifty guns, at least, rapidly fired for two mortal hours. . . .

At three o'clock almost precisely, the last shot hummed, and bounded and fell, and the cannonade was over. The purpose of General Lee in all this fire of his guns—we know it now, we did not at the time so well—was to disable our artillery and break up our infantry upon the position of the Second Corps, so as to render them less an impediment to the sweep of his own brigades and divisions over our crest and through our lines. . . . There was a pause between acts, with the curtain down, soon to rise upon the great final act, and catastrophe of Gettysburg. We have passed by the left of the Second Division, coming from the First; when we crossed the crest the enemy was not in sight, and all was still—we walked slowly along in the rear of the troops, by the ridge cut off now from a view of the enemy on his position, and were returning to the spot where we had left our horses. . . . In a moment afterwards we met Captain Wessels and the orderlies who had our horses; they were on foot leading the horses. Captain Wessels was pale, and he said, excited: "General, they say the enemy's infantry is advancing." We sprang into our saddles, a score of bounds brought us upon the all-seeing crest.

To say that men grew pale and held their breath at what we and they there saw, would not be true. Might not six thousand men be brave and without shade of fear, and yet, before a hostile eighteen thousand, armed, and not five minutes' march away, turn ashy white? None on that crest now need be told that *the enemy is advancing*. Every eye could see his legions, an overwhelming resistless tide of an ocean of armed men sweeping upon us! Regiment after regiment and brigade after brigade moved from the woods and rapidly take their places in the lines forming the assault. Pickett's proud division, with some additional troops, hold their right; Pettigrew's (Worth's) their left. The first line at short interval is followed by a second, and that a third succeeds; and columns between support the lines. More than half a mile their front extends; more than a thousand yards the dull gray masses deploy, man touching man, rank pressing rank, and line supporting line. The red flags wave, their horsemen gallop up and down; the arms of eighteen thousand men, barrel and bayonet, gleam in the sun, a sloping forest of flashing steel. Right on they move, as with one soul, in perfect order, without impediment of ditch, or wall or stream, over ridge and slope, through orchard and meadow, and cornfield, magnificent, grim, irresistible.

All was orderly and still upon our crest; no noise and no confusion. The men had little need of commands, for the survivors of a dozen battles knew well enough what this array in front portended, and, already in their places, they would be prepared to act when the right time should come. The click of the locks as each man raised the hammer to feel with his fingers that the cap was on the nipple; the sharp jar as a musket touched a stone upon the wall when thrust in aiming over it, and the clicking of the iron axles as the guns were rolled up by hand a little further to the front, were quite all the sounds that could be heard. Cap-boxes were slid around to the front of the body; cartridge boxes opened, officers opened their pistol-holsters. Such preparations, little more was needed. The trefoil flags, colors of the brigades and divisions moved to their places in rear; but along the lines in front the grand old ensign that first waved in battle at Saratoga in 1777, and which these people coming would rob of half its stars, stood up, and the west wind kissed it as the sergeants sloped its lance towards the enemy. I believe that not one above whom it then waved but blessed his God that he was loyal to it, and whose heart did not swell with pride towards it, as the emblem of the Republic before that treason's flaunting rag in front.

General Gibbon rode down the lines, cool and calm, and in an unimpassioned voice he said to the men, "Do not hurry, men, and fire too fast, let them come up close before you fire, and then aim low and steadily." The coolness of their General was reflected in the faces of his men. Five minutes has elapsed since first the enemy have emerged from the woods—no great space of time surely, if measured by the usual standard by which men estimate duration—but it was long enough for us to note and weigh some of the elements of mighty moment that surrounded us; the disparity of numbers between the assailants and the assailed; that few as were our numbers we could not be supported or reinforced until support would not be needed or would be too late; that upon the ability of the two trefoil divisions to hold the crest and repel the assault depended not only their own safety or destruction, but also the honor of the Army of the Potomac and defeat or victory at Gettysburg. Should these advancing men pierce our line and become the entering wedge, driven home, that would sever our army asunder, what hope would there be afterwards, and where the blood-earned fruits of yesterday? It was long enough for the Rebel storm to drift across more than half the space that had at first separated it from us. None, or all, of these considerations either depressed or elevated us. They might have done the former, had we been timid; the latter had we been confident and vain. But, we were there waiting, and ready to do our duty—that done, results could not dishonor us.

Our skirmishers open a spattering fire along the front, and, fighting, retire upon the main line—the first drops, the heralds of the storm, sounding on our windows. Then the thunders of our guns, first Arnold's then Cushing's and Woodruff's and the rest, shake and reverberate again through the air, and their sounding shells smite the enemy. . . . All our available guns are now active, and from the fire of shells, as the range grows shorter and shorter, they change to shrapnel, and from shrapnel to canister; but in spite of shells, and shrapnel and canister, without wavering or halt, the hardy lines of the enemy continue to move on. The Rebel guns make no reply to ours, and no charging shout rings out to-day, as is the Rebel wont; but the courage of these silent men amid our shots seems not to need the stimulus of other noise.

The enemy's right flank sweeps near Stannard's bushy crest, and his concealed Vermonters rake it with a well-delivered fire of musketry. The gray lines do not halt or reply, but withdrawing a little from that extreme, they still move on. And so across all that broad open ground they have come, nearer and nearer, nearly half the way, with our guns bellowing in their faces, until now a hundred yards, no more, divide our ready left from their advancing right. The eager men there are impatient to begin. Let them. First, Harrow's breastworks flame; then Hall's; then Webb's. As if our bullets were the fire coals that touched off their muskets, the enemy in front halts, and his countless level barrels blaze back upon us. The Second Division is struggling in battle. The rattling storm soon spreads to the right, and the blue trefoils are vieing with the white. All along each hostile front, a thousand yards, with narrowest space between, the volleys blaze and roll; as thick the sound as when a summer hail-storm pelts the city roofs; as thick the fire as when the incessant lightning fringes a summer cloud.

When the Rebel infantry had opened fire our batteries soon became silent, and this without their fault, for they were foul by long previous use. They were the targets of the concentrated Rebel bullets, and some of them had expended all their canister. But they were not silent before Rhorty was killed, Woodruff had fallen mortally wounded, and Cushing, firing almost his last canister, had dropped dead among his guns shot through the head by a bullet. The conflict is left to the infantry alone. . . .

The conflict was tremendous, but I had seen no wavering in all our line. Wondering how long the Rebel ranks, deep though they were, could stand our sheltered volleys, I had come near my destination, when—great heaven!

were my senses mad? The larger portion of Webb's brigade—my God, it was true—there by the group of trees and the angles of the wall, was breaking from the cover of their works, and, without orders or reason, with no hand lifted to check them, was falling back, a fear-stricken flock of confusion! The fate of Gettysburg hung upon a spider's single thread!

A great magnificent passion came on me at the instant, not one that overpowers and confounds, but one that blanches the face and sublimes every sense and faculty. My sword, that had always hung idle by my side, the sign of rank only in every battle, I drew, bright and gleaming, the symbol of command. Was not that a fit occasion, and these fugitives the men on whom to try the temper of the Solinzen steel? All rules and proprieties were forgotten; all considerations of person, and danger and safety despised; for, as I met the tide of these rabbits, the damned red flags of the rebellion began to thicken and flaunt along the wall they had just deserted, and one was already waving over one of the guns of the dead Cushing. I ordered these men to "halt," and "face about" and "fire," and they heard my voice and gathered my meaning, and obeyed my commands. On some unpatriotic backs of those not quick of comprehension, the flat of my sabre fell not lightly, and at its touch their love of country returned, and, with a look at me as if I were the destroying angel, as I might have become theirs, they again faced the enemy.

General Webb soon came to my assistance. He was on foot, but he was active, and did all that one could do to repair the breach, or to avert its calamity. The men that had fallen back, facing the enemy, soon regained confidence in themselves, and became steady. This portion of the wall was lost to us, and the enemy had gained the cover of the reverse side, where he now stormed with fire. But Webb's men, with their bodies in part protected by the abruptness of the crest, now sent back in the enemies' faces as fierce a storm. Some scores of venturesome Rebels, that in their first push at the wall had dared to cross at the further angle, and those that had desecrated Cushing's guns, were promptly shot down, and speedy death met him who should raise his body to cross it again.

At this point little could be seen of the enemy, by reason of his cover and the smoke, except the flash of his muskets and his waving flags. These red flags were accumulating at the wall every moment, and they maddened us as the same color does the bull. Webb's men are falling fast, and he is among them to direct and encourage; but, however well they may now do, with that walled enemy in front, with more than a dozen flags to Webb's three, it soon becomes apparent that in not many minutes they will be overpowered, or that there will be none alive for the enemy to overpower. Webb, has but three regiments, all small, the 69th, 71st and 72d Pennsylvania—the 106th Pennsylvania, except two companies, is not here to-day—and he must have speedy assistance, or this crest will be lost.

Oh, where is Gibbon? where is Hancock?—some general—anybody with the power and the will to support that wasting, melting line? No general came, and no succor! ... As a last resort I resolved to see if Hall and Harrow could not send some of their commands to reinforce Webb. I galloped to the left in the execution of my purpose, and as I attained the rear of Hall's line, from the nature of the ground and the position of the enemy it was easy to discover the reason and the manner of this gathering of Rebel flags in front of Webb.

The enemy, emboldened by his success in gaining our line by the group of trees and the angle of the wall, was concentrating all his right against and was further pressing that point. There was the stress of his assault; there would he drive his fiery wedge to split our line. In front of Harrow's and Hall's Brigades he had been able to advance no nearer than when he first halted to deliver fire, and these commands had not yielded an inch. To effect the concentration before Webb, the enemy would march the regiment on his extreme right of each of his lines by the left flank to the rear of the troops, still halted and facing to the front, and so continuing to draw in his right, when they were all massed in the position desired, he would again face them to the front, and advance to the storming. This was the way he made the wall before Webb's line blaze red with his battle flags, and such was the purpose there of his thick-crowding battalions.

Not a moment must be lost. Colonel Hall I found just in rear of his line, sword in hand, cool, vigilant, noting all that passed and directing the battle of his brigade. The fire was constantly diminishing now in his front, in the manner and by the movement of the enemy that I have mentioned, drifting to the right.

"How is it going?" Colonel Hall asked me, as I rode up.

"Well, but Webb is hotly pressed and must have support, or he will be overpowered. Can you assist him?"

"Yes."

"You cannot be too quick."

"I will move my brigade at once."

"Good."

He gave the order, and in the briefest time I saw five friendly colors hurrying to the aid of the imperilled three; and each color represented true, battle-tried men, that had not turned back from Rebel fire that day nor yesterday, though their ranks were sadly thinned; to Webb's brigade, pressed back as it had been from the wall, the distance was not great from Hall's right. The regiments marched by the right flank. . . . The movement, as it did, attracting the enemy's fire, and executed in haste, as it must be, was difficult; but in reasonable time, and in order that is serviceable, if not regular, Hall's men are fighting gallantly side by side with Webb's before the all important point.

I did not stop to see all this movement of Hall's, but from him I went at once further to the left, to the 1st brigade. Gen'l Harrow I did not see, but his fighting men would answer my purpose as well. The 19th Me., the 15th Mass., the 32d N. Y. and the shattered old thunderbolt, the 1st Minn.—poor Farrell was dying then upon the ground where he had fallen—all men that I could find I took over to the right at the *double quick*.

A. E. Mathews

The Siege of Vicksburg

Union Prisoners at Salisbury, N. C.

As we were moving to, and near the other brigade of the division, from my position on horseback, I could see that the enemy's right, under Hall's fire, was beginning to stagger and to break. "See," I said to the men, "See the *chivalry!* See the gray-backs run!" The men saw, and as they swept to their places by the side of Hall and opened fire, they roared, and this in a manner that said more plainly than words—for the deaf could have seen it in their faces, and the blind could have heard it in their voices—*the crest is safe!*

The whole Division concentrated, and changes of position, and new phases, as well on our part as on that of the enemy, having as indicated occurred, for the purpose of showing the exact present posture of affairs, some further description is necessary. Before the 2d Division the enemy is massed, the main bulk of his force covered by the ground that slopes to his rear, with his front at the stone wall. Between his front and us extends the very apex of the crest. All there are left of the White Trefoil Division—yesterday morning there were three thousand eight hundred, this morning there were less than three thousand—at this moment there are somewhat over two thousand;—twelve regiments in three brigades are below or behind the crest, in such a position that by the exposure of the head and upper part of the body above the crest they can deliver their fire in the enemy's faces along the top of the wall.

By reason of the disorganization incidental in Webb's brigade to his men's having broken and fallen back, as mentioned, in the two other brigades to their rapid and difficult change of position under fire, and in all the divisions in part to severe and continuous battle, formation of companies and regiments in regular ranks is lost; but commands, companies, regiments and brigades are blended and intermixed—an irregular extended mass—men enough, if in order, to form a line of four or five ranks along the whole front of the division. The twelve flags of the regiments wave defiantly at intervals along the front; at the stone wall, at unequal distances from ours of forty, fifty or sixty yards, stream nearly double this number of the battle flags of the enemy.

These changes accomplished on either side, and the concentration complete, although no cessation or abatement in the general din of conflict since the commencement had at any time been appreciable, now it was as if a new battle, deadlier, stormier than before, had sprung from the body of the old—a young Phoenix of combat, whose eyes stream lightning, shaking his arrowy wings over the yet glowing ashes of his progenitor. The jostling, swaying lines on either side boil, and roar, and dash their flamy spray, two hostile billows of a fiery ocean. Thick flashes stream from the wall, thick volleys answer from the crest. No threats or expostulation now, only example and encouragement. All depths of passion are stirred, and all combatives fire, down to their deep foundations. Individuality is drowned in a sea of clamor, and timid men, breathing the breath of the multitude, are brave. The frequent dead and wounded lie where they stagger and fall—there is no humanity for them now, and none can be spared to care for them. The men do not cheer or shout; they growl, and over that uneasy sea, heard with the roar of musketry, sweeps the muttered thunder of a storm of growls. Webb, Hall, Devereux, Mallon, Abbott among the men where all are heroes, are doing deeds of note.

Now the loyal wave rolls up as if it would overleap its barrier, the crest. Pistols flash with the muskets. My "Forward to the wall" is answered by the Rebel counter-command, "Steady, men!" and the wave swings back. Again it surges, and again it sinks. These men of Pennsylvania, on the soil of their own homesteads, the first and only to flee the wall, must be the first to storm it. . . . "Sergeant, forward with your color. Let the Rebels see it close to their eyes once before they die." The color sergant of the 72d Pa., grasping the stump of the severed lance in both his hands, waved the flag above his head and rushed towards the wall. "Will you see your color storm the wall alone?" One man only starts to follow. Almost half way to the wall, down go color bearer and color to the ground—the gallant sergeant is dead. The line springs—the crest of the solid ground with a great roar, heaves forward its maddened load, men, arms, smoke, fire, a fighting mass. It rolls to the wall—flash meets flash, the wall is crossed—a moment ensues of thrusts, yells, blows, shots, and undistinguishable conflict, followed by a shout universal that makes the welkin ring again, and the last and bloodiest fight of the great battle of Gettysburg is ended and won.

—HASKELL, *The Battle of Gettysburg*

D. "ALL THIS WILL COME RIGHT IN THE END"

July 3d.—The distance between the Confederate guns and the Yankee position—i.e. between the woods crowning the opposite ridges—was at least a mile, quite open, gently undulating, and exposed to artillery the whole distance. This was the ground which had to be crossed in today's attack. Pickett's division, which had just come up, was to bear the brunt in Longstreet's attack, together with Heth and Pettigrew in Hill's corps. Pickett's division was a weak one (under five thousand), owing to the absence of two brigades.

At noon all Longstreet's dispositions were made; his troops for attack were deployed into line and lying down in the woods; his batteries were ready to open. The General then dismounted and went to sleep for a short time. . . .

Finding that to see the actual fighting it was absolutely necessary to go into the thick of the thing, I determined to make my way to General Longstreet. It was then about two-thirty. After passing General Lee and his staff, I rode on through the woods in the direction in which I had left Longstreet. I soon began to meet many wounded men returning from the front; many of them asked in piteous tones the way to a doctor or an ambulance. The farther I got, the greater became the number of the wounded. At last I came to a perfect stream of them flocking through the woods in numbers as great as the crowd in Oxford Street in the middle of the day. Some were walking alone on crutches composed of two rifles, others supported by men less badly wounded than themselves, and others were carried on stretchers by the ambulance corps; but in no case did I see a sound man helping the wounded to the rear unless he carried the red badge of the ambulance corps. They were still under a heavy fire; the shells were continually bringing down great limbs of trees and carrying further destruction amongst this melancholy procession. I saw all this in much less time than it takes to write it, and although astonished to meet such vast numbers of wounded, I had not seen enough to give me any idea of the real extent of the mischief.

When I got close up to General Longstreet, I saw one of his regiments advancing through the woods in good order; so, thinking I was just in time to see the attack, I remarked to the General that "I wouldn't have missed this for anything."

Longstreet was seated at the top of a snake fence at the edge of the wood and looking perfectly calm and unperturbed. He replied, laughing: "The devil you wouldn't! I would like to have missed it very much; we've attacked and been repulsed; look there!"

For the first time I then had a view of the open space between the two positions and saw it covered with Confederates, slowly and sulkily returning toward us in small broken parties, under a heavy fire of artillery. But the fire where we were was not so bad as farther to the rear, for although the air seemed alive with shell, yet the greater number burst behind us. The General told me that Pickett's division had succeeded in carrying the enemy's position and capturing his guns, but after remaining there twenty minutes, it had been forced to retire, on the retreat of Heth and Pettigrew on its left. . . .

Soon afterward I joined General Lee, who had in the meanwhile come to the front on becoming aware of the disaster. If Longstreet's conduct was admirable, that of Lee was perfectly sublime. He was engaged in rallying and in encouraging the broken troops and was riding about a little in front of the wood, quite alone, the whole of his staff being engaged in a similar manner farther to the rear. His face, which is always placid and cheerful, did not show signs of the slightest disappointment, care, or annoyance; and he was addressing to every soldier he met a few words of encouragement, such as: "All this will come right in the end; we'll talk it over afterwards; but in the meantime, all good men must rally. We want all good and true men just now," etc. He spoke to all the wounded men that passed him, and the slightly wounded he exhorted to "bind up their hurts and take up a musket" in this emergency. Very few failed to answer his appeal, and I saw many badly wounded men take off their hats and cheer him.

He said to me, "This has been a sad day for us, Colonel—a sad day; but we can't expect always to gain victories." . . . I saw General Willcox come up to him and explain, almost crying, the state of his brigade. General Lee immediately shook hands with him and said cheerfully: "Never mind, General, all this has been *my* fault—it is I that have lost this fight, and you must help me out of it in the best way you can."

In this way I saw General Lee encourage and reanimate his somewhat dispirited troops and magnanimously take upon his own shoulders the whole weight of the repulse. It was impossible to look at him or to listen to him without feeling the strongest admiration.

—[FREMANTLE], "The Battle of Gettysburg"

10. LEE RETREATS FROM GETTYSBURG

At Gettysburg, as at Antietam, Lee was unwilling to admit defeat, but stood his ground defiantly the next day awaiting a Union attack. Perhaps Meade should have attacked—but he had suffered 25,000 casualties, and an attack on the Confederates entrenched along Seminary Ridge might have led to a bloody repulse. In any event Meade was content to leave Lee alone. On the afternoon of the fourth the Confederates started their ambulance trains and prisoners south across the Potomac. A heavy rain set in, drenching the discouraged Confederates, and Meade's cavalry harassed their rear. The rains had swollen the Potomac, and not until the night of the thirteenth did Lee get his army across to Virginia soil.

Napier Bartlett, who tells the story of the retreat, was attached to the Louisiana Washington Artillery.

DURING the whole of this memorable day, and part of the preceding, the men had nothing to eat, and were very often without water. I succeeded at one time, in satisfying the pangs of hunger, by eating the fruit from a cherry tree, which either hung close to the ground, or whose boughs had been struck off by the bullets and shell. The last bread we tasted was obtained by some of us who, to preserve the strength of the men, were detailed by Capt. Hero to gather food from the dead Federal infantry, whose haversacks were furnished with three day's ration. It was not the kind of food that fastidious stomachs could endure. But a soldier's first motto is to take care of his material wants, and the men who resolutely satisfied the cravings of nature, probably did the best service in marching and fighting, and preserved longest their health.

The day altogether, was productive of different emotions, from any ever experienced on any other battle field. The sight of the dying and wounded, who were lying by the thousand between the two lines, and compelled amid their sufferings, to witness and be exposed to the cannonade of over 200 guns, and later in the day, the reckless charges, and the subsequent destruction or demoralization of Lee's best corps—the fury, tears or savage irony of the commanders—the patient waiting, which would occasionally break out into sardonic laughter at the ruin of our hopes seen everywhere around us, and finally, the decisive moment, when the enemy seemed to be launching his cavalry to sweep the remaining handful of men from the face of the earth: These were all incidents which settled, and will forever remain in the memory. We all remember Gettysburg, though we do not remember and do not care to remember many other of the remaining incidents of the war. . . .

But to return to the battle field, from which at a little distance we bivouacked that night. It is true that many of us shed tears at the way in which our dreams of liberty had ended, and then and there gave them a much more careful burial than most of the dead received; yet when we were permitted at length to lie down under the caissons, or in the fence corners, and realized that we had escaped the death that had snatched away so many others, we felt too well satisfied at our good fortune—in spite of the enemy still near us, not to sleep the soundest sleep it is permitted on earth for mortals to enjoy.

On the following day during a heavy and continuous rain, the army commenced its retreat to the Potomac.

Gen. Imboden was put in the van, in charge of the immense amount of captured plunder, and the many thousand prisoners who had been taken, and our batteries were temporarily assigned to his command. His duty it need not be said, was a very arduous one, as it exposed us constantly to a sudden swooping down of the cavalry. Once they actually dashed down on us, and compelled us to get our pieces unlimbered. Never had the men and horses been so jaded, and stove up. One of our men who dropped at the foot of a tree in a sort of hollow, went to sleep, and continued sleeping until the water rose to his waist. It was only then that he could be awakened with the greatest difficulty. Battery horses would drop down dead. So important was our movement that no halt for bivouac, though we marched scarcely two miles an hour, was made during the route from Gettysburg to Williamsport—a march of over 40 miles. The men and officers on horseback would go to sleep without knowing it, and at one time there was a halt occasioned by all of the drivers—or at least those whose business was to attend to it, being asleep in their saddles. In fact the whole of the army was dozing while marching and moved as if under enchantment or a spell—were asleep and at the same time walking.

Over the rocky turnpike road some of us had to march barefooted, our shoes having been destroyed by the rough Macadamized road, or the heavy mud; and those were especially sufferers whose feet, my own among the number, were inconveniently larger than those of the passing Dutchmen whom we would meet on the road.

Scarcely had we arrived at Williamsport, before we were attacked by Kirkpatrick with a body of Federal cavalry who had already harrassed us at Hagerstown, on our retreat, and captured some of our wagons. At Williamsport, the morning after our arrival, there was a sudden dash and hotly contested fight. These assailants were however, ultimately driven off, with the assistance of the wagoners, who now shouldered the muskets they had been hauling, and fought like Trojans. In this teamsters' fight, the enemy were driven away without doing any serious damage.

Lee's army a few days after reached the Potomac without opposition, and although his pontoons were destroyed, and the Potomac unfordable, a bridge was constructed, and the army on the 13th of July, passed over very quietly— the bridges having been covered with bushes to prevent the rumbling of the wheels. Ewell's corps by this time had managed to ford the river.

—[Napier Bartlett], *A Soldier's Story of the War*

11. GENERAL LEE OFFERS TO RESIGN
AFTER GETTYSBURG

"It is all my fault," said Lee, on the afternoon of the third. History does not agree with that verdict, but it was characteristic of Lee that he should shoulder the blame for the failure of the invasion. On August 8 he sent Davis his offer to resign. In his reply Davis referred finely to those "achievements which will make you and your army the subject of history and object of the world's admiration for generations to come."

CAMP ORANGE, *August 8, 1863*

His Excellency JEFFERSON DAVIS,
    President of the Confederate States:

MR. PRESIDENT: Your letters of July 28 and August 2 have been received, and I have waited for a leisure hour to reply, but I fear that will never come. I am extremely obliged to you for the attention given to the wants of this army, and the efforts made to supply them. Our absentees are returning, and I hope the earnest and beautiful appeal made to the country in your proclamation may stir up the virtue of the whole people, and that they may see their duty and perform it. Nothing is wanted but that their fortitude should equal their bravery to insure the success of our cause. We must expect reverses, even defeats. They are sent to teach us wisdom and prudence, to call forth greater energies, and to prevent our falling into greater disasters. Our people have only to be true and united, to bear manfully the misfortunes incident to war, and all will come right in the end.

I know how prone we are to censure and how ready to blame others for the non-fulfillment of our expectations. This is unbecoming in a generous people, and I grieve to see its expression. The general remedy for the want of success in a military commander is his removal. This is natural, and, in many instances, proper. For, no matter what may be the ability of the officer, if he loses the confidence of his troops disaster must sooner or later ensue.

I have been prompted by these reflections more than once since my return from Pennsylvania to propose to Your Excellency the propriety of selecting another commander for this army. I have seen and heard of expression of discontent in the public journals at the result of the expedition. I do not know how far this feeling extends in the army. My brother officers have been too kind to report it, and so far the troops have been too generous to exhibit it. It is fair, however, to suppose that it does exist, and success is so necessary to us that nothing should be risked to secure it. I therefore, in all sincerity, request Your Excellency to take measures to supply my place. I do this with the more earnestness because no one is more aware than myself of my inability for the duties of my position. I cannot even accomplish what I myself desire. How can I fulfill the expectations of others? In addition I sensibly feel the growing failure of my bodily strength. I have not yet recovered from the attack I experienced the past spring. I am becoming more and more incapable of exertion, and am thus prevented from making the personal examinations and giving the personal supervision to the operations in the field which I feel to be necessary. I am so dull that in making use of the eyes of others I am frequently misled. Everything, therefore, points to the advantages to be derived from a new commander, and I the more anxiously urge the matter upon Your Excellency from my belief that a younger and abler man than myself can readily be attained. I know that he will have as gallant and brave an army as ever existed to second his efforts, and it would be the happiest day of my life to see at its head a worthy leader—one that would accomplish more than I could perform and all that I have wished. I hope Your Excellency will attribute my request to the true reason, the desire to serve my country, and to do all in my power to insure the success of her righteous cause.

I have no complaints to make of any one but myself. I have received nothing but kindness from those above me, and the most considerate attention from my comrades and companions in arms. To Your Excellency I am specially indebted for uniform kindness and consideration. You have done everything in your power to aid me in the work committed to my charge, without omitting anything to promote the general welfare. I pray that your efforts may at length be crowned with success, and that you may long live to enjoy the thanks of a grateful people.

With sentiments of great esteem, I am, very respectfully and truly, yours,

R. E. LEE,

General.

RICHMOND, VA., *August* 11, 1863

General R. E. LEE,

Commanding Army of Northern Virginia:

Yours of 8th instant has been received. I am glad that you concur so entirely with me as to the want of our country in this trying hour, and am happy to add that after the first depression consequent upon our disaster in the west, indications have appeared that our people will exhibit that fortitude which we agree in believing is alone needful to secure ultimate success.

It well became Sidney Johnston, when overwhelmed by a senseless clamor, to admit the rule that success is the test of merit; and yet there has been nothing which I have found to require a greater effort of patience than to bear the criticisms of the ignorant, who pronounce everything a failure which does not equal their expectations or desires, and can see no good result which is not in the line of their own imaginings. I admit the propriety of your conclusions, that an officer who loses the confidence of his troops should have his position changed, whatever may be his ability, but when I read the sentence I was not at all prepared for the application you were about to make. Expressions of discontent in the public journals furnish but little evidence of the sentiment of an army. I wish it were otherwise, even though all the abuse of myself should be accepted as the results of honest observation. I say I wish I could feel that the public journals were not generally partisan nor venal.

Were you capable of stooping to it, you could easily surround yourself with those who would fill the press with your laudations, and seek to exalt you for what you had not done, rather than detract from the achievements which will make you and your army the subject of history and object of the world's admiration for generations to come.

I am truly sorry to know that you still feel the effects of the illness you suffered last spring, and can readily understand the embarrassments you experience in using the eyes of others, having been so much accustomed to make your own reconnaissances. Practice will, however, do much to relieve that embarrassment, and the minute knowledge of the country which you have acquired will render you less dependent for topographical information.

But suppose, my dear friend, that I were to admit, with all their implications, the points which you present, where am I to find that new commander who is to possess the greater ability which you believe to be required? I do not doubt the readiness with which you would give way to one who could accomplish all that you have wished, and you will do me the justice to believe that if Providence should kindly offer such a person for our use, I would not hesitate to avail of his services.

My sight is not sufficiently penetrating to discover such hidden merit, if it exists, and I have but used to you the language of sober earnestness when I have impressed upon you the propriety of avoiding all unnecessary exposure to danger, because I felt our country could not bear to lose you. To ask me to substitute you by some one in my judgment more fit to command, or who would possess more of the confidence of the army, or of the reflecting men of the country, is to demand an impossibility.

It only remains for me to hope that you will take all possible care of yourself, that your health and strength may be entirely restored, and that the Lord will preserve you for the important duties devolved upon you in the struggle of our suffering country for the independence which we have engaged in war to maintain.

As ever, very respectfully and truly, yours,

JEFFERSON DAVIS.
—*War of the Rebellion ... Official Records*

12. "BELLS ARE RINGING WILDLY"

The day after Gettysburg was the greatest Fourth of July since the Declaration. Vicksburg had fallen, Lee had been defeated, the Union was safe! So, at least, thought most Northerners, and the North was swept with enthusiasm and jubilation.

William Lusk tells of the reception of the news in Wilmington.

HEADQUARTERS DELAWARE DEPARTMENT,
WILMINGTON, DEL., July 7th, 1863

Dear, dear Cousin Lou:

I said I would write you so soon as the full purport of the good news was ascertained. And now that it has all broken upon us, although my heels are where my head ought to be, I will try and fulfil my engagement as coherently as possible. We have had the dark hour. The dawn has broken, and the collapsed confederacy has no place where it can hide its head. Bells are ringing wildly all over the city. Citizens grin at one another with fairly idiotic delight. One is on the top of his house frantically swinging a dinner bell, contributing thus his share of patriotic clamor to the general ding-dong. Bully for him! How I envy the heroes of Meade's Army. It would be worth while to die, in order that one's friends might say, "He died at Gettysburg." But to live to hear all the good news, and now to learn that Vicksburg has surrendered, is a little too much happiness for poor mortal men. I can laugh, I can cry with joy. All hysterical nonsense is pardonable now. Manassas, twice repeated, Fredericksburg and Chickahominy! Bless them as the cruel training that has made us learn our duties to our country. Slavery has fallen, and I believe Heaven as well as earth rejoices. Providence has tenderly removed that grand old hero, Jackson, before the blow came, that the one good, earnest, misguided man might be spared the sight of the downfall of a cause fanaticism led him to believe was right. . . . These enthusiastic citizens of Wilmington, not content with bell-ringing, have taken to firing cannon, and the boys, to help matters, are discharging pistols into empty barrels. The people in a little semi-slaveholding State, when not downright traitors, are noisily, obstreperously loyal, to a degree that New England can hardly conceive of. My letter must be short and jubilant, I cannot do anything long to-day.

Just dance through the house for me, and kiss every one you meet. So I feel now. Good-bye.

Affec'y.,

WILL.

—War Letters of William Thompson Lusk

13. "A NEW BIRTH OF FREEDOM"

On July 4 Lincoln had announced to the country the victory of the Army of the Potomac, and invoked "the condolences of all for the many gallant fallen." That November part of the battlefield of Gettysburg was made a permanent cemetery for the soldiers who had fallen there. Edward Everett of Massachusetts delivered the principal oration. The superintendent of the enterprise, David Wills, asked Lincoln to make "a few appropriate remarks" and the result was the most memorable of all American addresses.

FOURSCORE and seven years ago our fathers brought forth on this continent a new nation, conceived in Liberty, and dedicated to the proposition that all men are created equal.

Now we are engaged in a great civil war, testing whether that nation or any nation so conceived and so dedicated can long endure. We are met on a great battlefield of that war. We have come to dedicate a portion of that field as a final resting place for those who here gave their lives that that nation might live. It is altogether fitting and proper that we should do this.

But in a larger sense we cannot dedicate—we cannot consecrate—we cannot hallow—this ground. The brave men, living and dead, who struggled here, have consecrated it, far above our poor power to add or detract. The world will little note nor long remember what we say here, but it can never forget what they did here. It is for us the living, rather, to be dedicated here to the unfinished work which they who fought here have thus far so nobly advanced. It is rather for us to be here dedicated to the great task remaining before us—that from these honored dead we take increased devotion to that cause for which they gave the last full measure of devotion—that we here highly resolve that these dead shall not have died in vain—that this nation, under God, shall have a new birth of freedom—and that government of the people, by the people, for the people, shall not perish from the earth.

—LINCOLN, "The Gettysburg Address"

XVIII

Vicksburg and Port Hudson

THE *Vicksburg campaign, which lasted from November 1862 to July 1863, was the most confused and confusing of all Civil War campaigns. The confusion, however, is in the tactics rather than in the grand strategy. That strategy was simple enough. It was to clear the Mississippi, thus cutting off the Trans-Mississippi West from the rest of the Confederacy, and opening a channel from the Gulf to the North. By midsummer 1862 these grand objectives had been largely achieved. Farragut had taken New Orleans; Columbus had been evacuated; New Madrid and Island No. 10 had fallen; the Confederates had abandoned Fort Pillow and Memphis. In the thousand-mile stretch from the Gulf to the Ohio, only Vicksburg and Port Hudson were still in Confederate hands.*

In June 1862 Farragut had steamed northward toward the gunboat flotilla under Davis; he had been able to run the batteries of Vicksburg, but unable to take the city. Such an operation required a combined land and water attack. Had Halleck moved promptly on Vicksburg after Shiloh he could probably have captured it; he failed to do so and the Confederates, alert to its importance, hastened to reinforce it. As early as October 1862 Grant asked permission to attack Vicksburg, but not until December was that permission granted, and even then it was not clear whether the operation was to be by Grant, Sherman, or McClernand.

The Vicksburg campaign opened in November when Grant established a base at Holly Springs, Mississippi, and prepared to move down the Yazoo on Vicksburg. Forrest attacked Grant's communications and then Van Dorn captured Holly Springs and destroyed his stores, and the plan was abandoned. Late the next month Sherman moved down the Mississippi to the mouth of the Yazoo, and up the Yazoo to Chickasaw Bluffs; on December 29 he attacked the Confederates at the Bluffs and was repulsed.

Thus the first attempt to take Vicksburg from the rear—a joint operation by Grant and Sherman—ended in failure. It was, as events were to prove, the sound approach, and had Grant been properly supported it might have worked. Balked in the attempt to take Vicksburg from Memphis, Grant moved his forces to the west side of the Mississippi and began to probe for a crossing. We cannot follow in detail the long and complex story of the effort to find a crossing below Vicksburg and ferry the great army over for an attack from the south. Eventually Grant moved his army down a series of rivers and bayous west of the Mississippi—Lake Providence, the Bayou

Macon, the Tensas, and the Washita—to Hard Times on the Red River. An attempt to cross at Grand Gulf—about 50 miles below Vicksburg—was frustrated by stiff Confederate opposition. Meantime Porter's gunboats had run the batteries of Vicksburg and steamed south to where Grant's army lay waiting. On April 30 Grant began ferrying his army across the Mississippi at Bruinsburg. Pemberton, now in command at Vicksburg, hurried reinforcements south to Port Gibson, a few miles from Bruinsburg; there was a sharp fight but the Confederates were worsted and retreated. During the next week the whole of Grant's army crossed the river and prepared to move against Vicksburg.

The next two weeks saw a swift development of Grant's campaign, and some of the hottest fighting of the war. Pemberton had some 25,000 men at Vicksburg and along the Vicksburg and Jackson Railway; Joseph E. Johnston had about the same number at and around Jackson. It was Grant's purpose to prevent these two forces from combining, and to defeat them separately. It was a formidable task. He had broken his communications and was forced to live off the country; the terrain—muddy and swampy and with wretched roads—was not favorable to swift movements; if Grant was defeated his army would be lost in enemy territory.

On May 12 Grant moved one wing of his army under McPherson on Jackson, capital of the state and important railroad center. There was a fight at Raymond; the Confederates fell back; and on the fourteenth McPherson defeated Johnston, and seized Jackson. Then the army turned westward to deal with Pemberton. That hapless general, who did everything at the wrong time, had moved out to harry Grant's rear and his nonexistent line of communications. Grant caught him at Champion's Hill on May 15 and defeated him. Pemberton retreated to the Black River, where there was another sharp fight. Once more the Confederates withdrew, this time to the strong works outside Vicksburg. Reluctant to embark on a siege Grant tried, on May 19, to storm the works—and failed. Undaunted he tried another general assault on the twenty-second, only to be repulsed with heavy losses.

Clearly Vicksburg could be taken only by a siege. Methodically Grant collected a large army of some 70,000, over 200 guns, and set about to invest the city. The siege lasted 47 days. Just as Grant was preparing for a final grand attack, Pemberton surrendered. Johnston, who had been preparing to go to Pemberton's aid, fell back with Sherman in pursuit. Port Hudson surrendered on July 9. Once more the Mississippi went unvexed to the sea.

1. SHERMAN FAILS AT CHICKASAW BLUFFS

Grant's first attack on Vicksburg came from the north. On December 8 he instructed Sherman to take command of all the troops at Memphis, move with them down the river to Vicksburg, and, with the co-operation of the gunboat fleet, "proceed to the reduction of that place in such manner as circumstances and your own judgment may dictate." The preparations, writes Sherman, "were necessarily hasty"; as it turned out he had inadequate forces for the task assigned him. His plan was to move on Vicksburg from Cape Bayou, off the Yazoo River, and attack at Chickasaw Bluffs, just north of the town. Here he gives his own account of the failure of that attack.

WE reached Milliken's Bend on Christmas-day, when I detached one brigade, of A. J. Smith's division, to the southwest, to break up the railroad leading from Vicksburg toward Shreveport, Louisiana. Leaving A. J. Smith's division there to await the return of Burbridge, the remaining three divisions proceeded, on the 26th, to the mouth of the Yazoo, and up that river to Johnson's plantation, thirteen miles, and there disembarked. . . . The place of our disembarkation was in fact an island, separated from the high bluff known as Walnut Hills, on which the town of Vicksburg stands, by a broad and shallow bayou—evidently an old channel of the Yazoo. On our right was another wide bayou, known as Old River; and on the left still another, much narrower, but too deep to be forded, known as Chickasaw Bayou. All the island was densely wooded, except Johnson's plantation, immediately on the bank of the Yazoo, and a series of old cotton-fields along Chickasaw Bayou. There was a road from Johnson's plantation directly to Vicksburg, but it crossed numerous bayous and deep swamps by bridges, which had been destroyed; and this road debouched on level ground at the foot of the Vicksburg bluff, opposite strong forts, well prepared and defended by heavy artillery. On this road I directed General A. J. Smith's division, not so much by way of a direct attack as a diversion and threat. . . .

We met light resistance at all points, but skirmished, on the 27th, up to the main bayou, that separated our position from the bluffs of Vicksburg, which were found to be strong by nature and by art, and seemingly well defended. On reconnoitring the front in person, during the 27th and 28th, I became satisfied that General A. J. Smith could not cross the intervening obstacles under the heavy fire of the forts immediately in his front, and that the main bayou was impassable, except at two points—one near the head of Chickasaw Bayou, in front of Morgan, and the other about a mile lower down, in front of M. L. Smith's division. . . .

On the morning of December 29th all the troops were ready and in position. The first step was to make a lodgment on the foot-hills and bluffs abreast of our position, while diversions were made by the navy toward Haines's Bluff, and by the first division directly toward Vicksburg. I estimated the enemy's forces, then strung from Vicksburg to Haines's Bluff, at fifteen thousand men, commanded by the rebel Generals Martin Luther Smith and Stephen D. Lee. Aiming to reach firm ground beyond this bayou, and to leave as little time for our enemy to reënforce as possible, I determined to make a show of attack along the whole front, but to break across the bayou at the two points named, and gave general orders accordingly. I pointed out to General Morgan the place where he could pass the bayou, and he answered, "General, in ten minutes after you give the signal I'll be on those hills." He was to lead his division in person, and was to be supported by Steele's division. The front was very narrow, and immediately opposite, at the base of the hills about three hundred yards from the bayou, was a rebel battery, supported by an infantry force posted on the spurs of the hill behind. To draw attention from this, the real point of attack, I gave instructions to commence the attack at the flanks.

I went in person about a mile to the right rear of Morgan's position, at a place convenient to receive reports from all other parts of the line; and about noon of December 29th gave the orders and signal for the main attack. A heavy artillery-fire opened along our whole line, and was replied to by the rebel batteries, and soon the infantry-fire opened heavily, especially on A. J. Smith's front, and in front of General George W. Morgan. One brigade of Morgan's troops crossed the bayou safely, but took to cover behind the bank, and could not be moved forward. Frank Blair's brigade, of Steele's division, in support, also crossed the bayou, passed over the space of level ground to the foot of the hills; but, being unsupported by Morgan, and meeting a very severe cross-fire of artillery, was staggered and gradually fell back, leaving about five hundred men behind, wounded and prisoners; . . . Meantime the Sixth Missouri Infantry, at heavy loss, had also crossed the bayou at the narrow passage lower down, but could not ascend the steep bank; right over their heads was a rebel battery, whose fire was in a measure kept down by our sharp-shooters posted behind logs, stumps, and trees, on our side of the bayou.

The men of the Sixth Missouri actually scooped out with their hands caves in the bank, which sheltered them against the fire of the enemy, who, right over their heads, held their muskets outside the parapet vertically, and fired down. So critical was the position, that we could not recall the men till after dark, and then one at a time. Our loss had been pretty heavy, and we had accomplished nothing, and had inflicted little loss on our enemy. At first I intended to renew the assault, but soon became satisfied that, the enemy's attention having been drawn to the only two practicable points, it would prove too costly, and accordingly resolved to look elsewhere for a point below Haines's Bluff, or Blake's plantation. That night I conferred with Admiral Porter, who undertook to cover the landing; and the next day (December 30th) the boats were all selected, but so alarmed were the captains and pilots, that we had to place sentinels with loaded muskets to insure their remaining at their posts. Under cover of night, Steele's division, and one brigade of Stuart's, were drawn out of line, and quietly embarked on steamboats in the Yazoo River. The night of December 30th was appointed for this force, under the command of General Fred Steele, to proceed up the Yazoo just below Haines's Bluff, there to disembark about daylight, and make a dash for the hills. Meantime we had strengthened our positions near Chickasaw Bayou, had all our guns in good position with parapets, and had every thing ready to renew our attack as soon as we heard the sound of battle above.

At midnight I left Admiral Porter on his gunboat; he had his fleet ready and the night was propitious. I rode back to camp and gave orders for all to be ready by daybreak; but when daylight came I received a note from General Steele reporting that, before his boats had got up steam, the fog had settled down on the river so thick and impenetrable, that it was simply impossible to move; so the attempt had to be abandoned. The rain, too, began to fall, and the trees bore water-marks ten feet above our heads, so that I became convinced that the part of wisdom was to withdraw. I ordered the stores which had been landed to be reëmbarked on the boats, and preparations made for all the troops to regain their proper boats during the night of the 1st of January, 1863. From our camps at Chickasaw we could hear the whistles of the trains arriving in Vicksburg, could see battalions of men marching up toward Haines's Bluff, and taking post at all points in our front. I was more than convinced that heavy reënforcements were coming to Vicksburg; whether from Pemberton at Grenada, Bragg in Tennessee, or from other sources, I could not tell; but at no point did the enemy assume the offensive; and when we drew off our rear-guard, on the morning of the 2d, they simply followed up the movement, timidly.

—*Memoirs of General William T. Sherman*

2. "ONWARD TO VICKSBURG"

High on a bluff the guns of Vicksburg commanded the Mississippi approaches from both north and south. As Grant feared to run the batteries he decided to move his army to the western side of the river and attack the great fortress city from the south and rear. A long-drawn-out attempt to by-pass Vicksburg by building a canal across the peninsula in the great curve of the Mississippi failed when the Confederates planted batteries below the city and commanding the canal. By the end of April, however, Grant had succeeded in getting his army of some 40,000 down the river system to the west of the Mississippi and across to the east side of the Mississippi at Bruinsburg. Now, as Sergeant Charles Wilcox tells us, the cry was "On to Vicksburg!"

The campaign that followed was one of the most brilliant of the war, both in tactics and in strategy. In three weeks Grant's armies won five victories—Port Gibson, Raymond, Jackson, Champion's Hill, and Big Black River; captured the capital of the state; separated the armies of Johnston and Pemberton; and invested Vicksburg.

Charles Wilcox, whose diary tells something of this story, was a student at Illinois State Normal University when the war opened. He enlisted in the 33rd Illinois Volunteers, fought in Missouri, at Vicksburg, and in Louisiana, and ended up as captain of the 92nd Colored Infantry.

Thursday, [April] 23d [1863]—We are jubilant over the success of our boats (transports) which came past Vicksburg last night. Six transports made the attempt and all got past—this side of the battery (rebel) fartherest down the river when one—the *Tigress*—was sunk, it having sprung a leak from the effect of the enemy's fire; the other five came down past Carthage though one (the *Empire City*) being so disabled it floated all the way from Vicksburg. The other four are somewhat injured but will soon be fitted for

THE VICKSBURG CAMPAIGN

our use. Talked with several of those who came down on the boats. Only three or four out of the crews of the six boats were wounded—none killed—some fatally wounded though. These crews were nearly all soldiers who volunteered their services. . . . The crew of the *Tigress* were all saved. The *Empire City* was under fire one hour and a half; this long time is accounted for by she being totally disabled before she got half way past the batteries.

Some of our baggage came up. Gen. Osterhaus' Division is on transports to go and attack Grand Gulf. Our Brigade is ordered to be ready with 3 days cooked rations to march to the support of Osterhaus' Division.

Sunday, [April] 26th— . . . Weather cloudy—it commenced raining about sunset and still continues. The private news is that we march sometime to-night, and are to make the attack upon Grand Gulf sometime to-morrow. The rebels have been, of late, reinforcing their force at that place. O God, protect us.

Monday, [April] 27th—Got orders about noon to embark immediately, which we very soon prepared to do, but did not succeed in getting aboard the boat (*Forest Queen*, the Flag Boat) till after dark. We leave behind everything save the well men with their knapsacks, guns and accoutrements with 80 rounds of ammunition to the man, three days rations in our haver-sacks, and horses for the main staff officers and their orderlies. Everybody is jolly and each one has a good word of cheer for his friend or comrade—all are in a bustle; every one is confident of victory in the coming contest. It rained in the night and some this forenoon; it is very muddy. . . .

Tuesday, [April] 28th—Did not leave the landing last night as all the boats were not loaded till about eleven o'clock this A.M. Troops are coming in from Milliken's Bend; a part of McPherson's *Corps de Armie* is already here waiting to embark which they will do as soon as the boats can take us down and return. Seven transports and four or five barges, each loaded with a regiment or more, left Perkin's Plantation about noon, we disembark-ing on the Louisiana side, four or five miles above the fortifications at Grand Gulf, about two o'clock P.M. The rebels' position is in plain view. Judging from appearances they have a strong position. We found six of our gun-boats just above Grand Gulf, lying out of reach of the rebels' guns. As the day was closing our gunboats threw three shells into the enemy's position, to learn the range of the guns; the enemy did not reply. The weather is very warm, sky clear. It is said that the ball opens in the morning. The transports and barges are all back after more troops. All of Carr's Division and part of Osterhaus' are here. When we were landing there were some Negroes near by who appeared to be very happy indeed upon seeing us. They clapped their hands in joy, prostrated themselves, shook hands with each other, and thanked the Lord as a Negro only can. 'Twas interesting, affecting, and im-pressive to witness these manifestations of joy. Col. Lippincott, who, until this war has alwas been a proslavery man, seeing them remarked "I was never more tempted to be an abolitionist." I carry a gun, and have no horse to ride while on this expedition.

Wednesday, [April] 29th—The sun arose throwing an impressive splendor upon the exciting scenes of the early morn. Every boat—transport and barge—lies at the landing, about five miles above Grand Gulf, covered till they are black with troops. Every heart here is full of anxiety and emotion; wondering eyes and eyes not altogether tearless, gaze ever and anon upon the *Father of Waters* where lie the formidable fleet of gunboats and rams, transports and barges, the latter heavily loaded with troops whose courage and valor are sufficient when combined with that of the rest of this mighty army, to redeem this lovely valley of the Mississippi from fiends and traitors who are desecrating it.

Now it is 7½ o'clock, A.M. Each gunboat and transport has gotten up full steam. The black smoke curls up from the blacker smoke-pipes, and moves towards the rebels, seeming to tell them of their black deeds and warns them of their portion when we attack them. It is like that which comes from the lower regions, scented with brimstone and issuing as it does from those gunboats, the traitors may well think, as they see it, that that fleet from which it comes has a portion of hell to give them, and that too, ere long, if they do not surrender or run. And now what means that? Every gunboat is steaming up the river. Can it be that the attack is not to be made? Every one is surprised. No; 'tis only the preparation for the attack. They are now "rounding to" and there they go. Thousands of eyes are looking upon. The first gun is fired by the enemy; the *Benton*, I believe, replies. 'Tis 8 o'clock. The contest has fairly begun; every gunboat is engaged. We all know when the enemy fires his heaviest guns as they make a sharper report than any of ours, though we have as large guns as he; this is probably accounted for by ours being on the water.

Eleven o'clock, A.M. Several of the enemy's batteries are silenced. The gunboats ply around and close to his strongest battery which gives them a round every opportunity, but as they near that battery they, one after another, give him broadsides which are terrible and produce a marked effect. The *Benton* "lays off" nearly across the river and just opposite and within good range of this powerful battery; every few minutes she sends an 84 or 64 pounder with nice precision at it; the dust flies and the enemy is quiet for a minute. This boat makes the most of the best shots that are fired. It seems to me that the enemy shoots wildly.

A few minutes after 12 M. The bombardment is over. Every one of the enemy's batteries save one, of three heavy guns are silenced, and we tried in vain to silence it.

The fleet has retired; Gen. Grant who was in a messenger boat during the bombardment, has come ashore. A little while passes and we get orders to start immediately down the levee, past Grand Gulf. The transports are being unloaded. At two P.M. we started for below; all the boats are to run the gauntlet to-night. We are now (evening) three or four miles below the enemy's works, though we only marched about three miles to get from five miles above them. The generals, colonels, and privates all lie down together, one faring no better than another. . . .

Friday, May 1st [1863]—A bright, clear and warm day, with a very slight breeze. This has been a glorious day for the Union, and for the despondent hearts in the North. We have fought a battle and won a complete victory. Having partaken our suppers last evening we again set forth upon our march, the Second Brigade going in the advance on account of our much wearied skirmishers. We came along slowly, carefully feeling our way though the moon shone brightly, and twice dispersing the enemy's pickets, till two o'clock A.M. when we came upon the enemy in force who *saluted* us with several rounds of grape and cannister, though not hurting us very much. . . .

A little after sunrise Major Potter in command of companies A, C, F and G of our regiment was ordered to go out on the road to our left (our line of battle at this time was north and south, facing to the east and hold it till Gen. Osterhaus could relieve him. I asked permission of the Colonel to go with comp. "A," and carry a gun, but was refused so I had to stay with the regiment to be ready to carry and repeat orders. The Major with his pet soldiers had not gone far ere the enemy opened fire upon him with his cannon. This was really the beginning of the battle. Soon the skirmishers in front come in contact and the roar of musketry is heard. . . . We have not *all* got our positions yet, but the battle commences in earnest, the artillery on both sides firing smartly. The enemy has a cross fire upon us and we double quick into line or cover ourselves under the brow of a ridge of land. Our regiment being divided the six companies are ordered to stay back till the other four companies come up.

And now I see Major Potter with his gallant band coming; I tell the fact to Col. Lippincott. He orders me to bring the Major and his command to join the regiment. I go but dear me! how the shells and shot whiz around me. One shell bursts just over me; I shrink and dodge with the flash, but hasten on very soon, and after some difficulty, helping right up capsized caissons and crowding through the excited troops, I find the Major and direct him to the regiment, but on our way the grape, cannister, shells and solid shot drop about us and go over us in storms. I hear a ball whizzing towards me; I fall to the earth for safety and just in time for it to go about three feet over me. It strikes the ground a few yards from me; I dare not turn to look at it, but am up and off.

Now our regiment hastens to its post in the line of battle. Meanwhile the small arms of the other regiments send forth terrible volleys. The line of battle having moved forward it is now just behind the brow of a hill. As our regiment comes up into the line the rebels fire upon it, but our boys pour a deadly fire into them and make them get behind a ridge beyond the one we are on. *"Cease firing"* is ordered; *"Lie down"* follows. Gen. Benton comes along the line and orders us to fix bayonet for he's going to charge. All is quiet for several minutes, and then a few rebel sharpshooters fire at our heads and our flags. When our boys see a rebel they give him a round, the same as they do us.

The 99th Ill, and the 18th and 24th Ind. make a charge; the order don't reach us so we lie quiet. A furious yell is sent up by those who are charging. The rebels break and run but we capture many of them and take two of their cannons. This ends the fight for the forenoon with us, and it is nearly noon now. Osterhaus continues the fight on the left; Hovey's and our Division pursue the rebels that we routed, and we find them, after traveling two miles towards Port Gibson, where they found their reinforcements.

It is a little after noon; again we are thrown into a line of battle, facing as before, to the east, meanwhile the fight is progressing. The enemy masses his troops and try to break our line, but fail. He throws a heavy force upon our right, then centre, and then left. He has but two cannons working upon us and ere night we capture those two. Our artillery fires with powerful effect at them; we have now got a cross fire and an enfilading fire upon them. They have the woods; we have to go over an open field before our musketry can reach them, but there is a ridge, upon which are our cannon, behind which we lie in almost perfect safety. Now we have about 30 pieces of artillery all at work; their booming is not unfamiliar to our ears. With now and then a cessation in firing the battle is thus kept up till night fall when our regiment with some others retires to get a bite to eat, but as soon as we are through eating we return to the field, stack our arms on the line of battle and lie down to sleep, and oh, how thankful we are, for we have slept but about four hours within the last sixty.

We don't know our whole success, but we know this, that we drove the enemy in every close contact.

Sunday, [May] 3d—Reveille at three and was to march at five A.M. but did not get started till nearer seven. Our Division then moved one mile and a half directly towards Grand Gulf when, finding we could not cross Bayou Perre with our artillery as the enemy had burnt the bridges, we about faced and came back to Port Gibson and then came on seven miles from there towards Rocky Spring, having traveled in all ten miles. Saw about 20000 lbs of bacon and shoulders and hams that the enemy had endeavored to secrete. The enemy evacuated Grand Gulf last night, first spiking the cannons and blowing up two of their magazines, our gunboats making it too unpleasant for them to blow up the third. We are bivouaced in line of battle, and live upon what we can forage. The weather was warm—road very dusty. Came through a fine tract of country. Negroes are flocking to our lines with mules, horses, and wagons.

Tuesday, [May] 19th—"Onward to Vicksburg" is the cry. Came up within rifle shot of the enemy's works in rear of Vicksburg. The fight began on our right in the morning. It is stated that Sherman has taken Hanes' Bluff and that we therefore have direct communication with the [Yazoo] river and can get ample supplies. We, too, began the fight at about 2 P.M. and continued it till night closed in upon us. Some of our Regt. were wounded by shell from the enemy. The enemy used his cannon freely upon us. We have now completely invested this place and believe we'll take it with the whole garrison within a day or two. Sherman's Corps is on the right, his right resting on the Yazoo River between Haines' Bluff & Vicksburg, Mc-Pherson's in the center and McClernand's on the left. Our provisions are cooked in our rear and brought up to us. Our (Division) Hospital is a mile and a half directly in our rear and near the railroad. Smith's Division is just to the right of the railroad, ours just to the left and Osterhaus' to the left of us; Hovey is our reserve. Weather warm.

Friday, [May] 22nd—Now that we have tried to take the enemy's works by storm we suffering terribly and doing the enemy but little harm, we are all—generals and privates—content to lay a regular siege to the place. This has been a sad day for the 33d as well as for this whole army. The army's loss to-day will I think exceed 4000 killed and wounded while the enemy has repulsed us his loss, undoubtedly being trifling. At ten we were all ready for the charge and though not very confident of success we put on an air of confidence. Our Brigade filed down the hollow in which we lay last night till it intersected a larger hollow which we followed up to its head, and then, still marching by the flank, we mounted the ridge within 4 rods of the enemy who poured a deadly fire into us till we reached the opposite side of the ridge. To do this we had to run along the brow of the ridge in a direct line of the enemy's fire, for 15 rods.

Here is where our poor boys suffered terribly, the ridge being covered with the dead and wounded. A part of the Brigade halted and lay down in the wagon road which runs along on the ridge; I was among this lot. We lay there about eight minutes and yet it seemed an age to me, for showers of bullets and grape were passing over me and not a foot above me, and on my right and left were my comrades dying and dead as well as living. What an awful eight minutes that was, we having to lay there not allowed to fire a single shot at the enemy who was sending to eternity by scores our brave boys souls! Oh, how my heart palpitated! It seemed to thump the ground (I lay on my face) as hard as the enemy's bullets. The sweat from off my face run in a stream from the tip ends of my whiskers. God only knows all that passed through my mind. Twice I exclaimed aloud, that my comrades might here *"My God, why don't they order us to charge,"* and then I thought perhaps all of our officers were killed and there was no one to order us forward. I thought of dear friends, of home and of heaven, but never wished, as did some who were near me that, *I* had never attempted to charge, and, indeed, wished that I had not become a soldier. Some who were wounded groaned and shrieked, others were calm and resigned. Generally those that were the slightest wounded shrieked the loudest, thinking they were wounded the worst.

One fellow whose performance was the most pleasing thing I saw during the day was wounded slightly just as he got near where I lay. He immediately started to go back, his officers trying in vain to make him stay with us. After stepping a few steps he, it seemed to me, purposely dropped on the ground and then rolled as if the lightning had set him going, clear back into the ravine, a distance of about two and a half rods. Though under such precarious circumstances and in such peril I could not refrain from smiling when seeing the "rolling man."

Receiving orders from Colonel Roe all of our regiment who could arose and made for over the ridge where we could get under cover; meantime Col.

Roe fell just before me, wounded in the leg. The regiment was then divided, all of us who lay down in the road being in one place and the rest in another. The right wing of the 8th Ind. soon coming up our little band joined them and we all charged over the railroad where we were again exposed to an awful fire, though but few were hit as we were exposed but a minute. Here on the south side of the railroad we took a position within three rods of one of the enemy's forts upon which the 77th Ill. had its flag planted, and from which it was taken, by the enemy. Here we lay sharpshooting whenever the enemy showed himself, till after dark when we all fell back without molestation to the position we occupied early in the morning. There were only six companies of the 33d in the charge, (three being out sharpshooting and one on provost guard), about one hundred and fifty men. Out of this number there were 76 killed and wounded. Am wearied and can't tell more of the sad tale. The fragment of the regiment is this evening still a unit and if we are attacked to-night we will be able to give the enemy a warm reception, though our hearts are sad.

   —Erickson, ed., "With Grant at Vicksburg—From the Civil War
   Diary of Captain Charles E. Wilcox"

3. COLONEL GRIERSON DISCOVERS THAT THE CONFEDERACY IS A HOLLOW SHELL

Part of Grant's strategy was to confuse and deceive the Confederates about his intentions below Vicksburg. His own army was strung along the west bank of the Mississippi and its tributary streams, and the Confederates did not know where he would try to cross. To disrupt Confederate plans he sent Colonel Grierson off on a raid through the heart of Mississippi; Grierson's function was to destroy railroads and bridges, capture or destroy supplies, and bewilder the enemy. In all this he succeeded admirably. Leaving LaGrange, Tennessee, on April 17 with a force of 1,700 cavalrymen, he rode 600 miles through enemy country, reaching Baton Rouge on May 2. It was, in some respects, the most spectacular cavalry raid of the war.

Grierson was an Illinois merchant who had enlisted as a private in 1861, was commissioned major of the 6th Illinois Cavalry and promoted to a colonelcy in the spring of 1862. For his "gallant and distinguished service in his great raid through the heart of the so-called Confederacy" he was made major general of volunteers.

HEADQUARTERS FIRST CAVALRY BRIGADE,
Baton Rouge, La., May 5, 1863

Colonel: In accordance with instructions from Maj. Gen. S. A. Hurlbut, received . . . at La Grange, Tenn., I left that place at daylight on the morning of April 17, with the effective force of my command, 1,700 strong. We moved southward without material interruption, crossing the Tallahatchee River on the afternoon of the 18th at three different points. One battalion of the Seventh Illinois, under Major Graham, crossing at New Albany, found the bridge partially torn up, and an attempt was made to fire it. As they approached the bridge they were fired upon, but drove the enemy from their position, repaired the bridge, and crossed. The balance of the Seventh Illinois and the whole of the Sixth crossed at a ford 2 miles above, and the Second Iowa crossed about 4 miles still farther up. After crossing, the Sixth and Seventh Illinois moved south on the Pontotoc road, and encamped for the night on the plantation of Mr. Sloan. The Second Iowa also moved south from their point of crossing, and encamped about 4 miles south of the river. The rain fell in torrents all night.

The next morning, April 19, . . . I moved with the whole force to Pontotoc. Colonel Hatch joined us about noon, reporting having skirmished with about 200 rebels the afternoon before and that morning, killing, wounding, and capturing a number. . . .

The following morning at 6 o'clock I resumed the march southward, and about 8 o'clock came to the road leading southeast to Columbus, Miss. Here I detached Colonel Hatch, with the Second Iowa Cavalry and one gun of the battery, with orders to proceed to the Mobile and Ohio Railroad in the vicinity of West Point, and destroy the road and wires; thence move south, destroying the railroad and all public property as far south, if possible, as Macon; thence across the railroad, making a circuit northward; if practicable, take Columbus and destroy all Government works in that place, and again strike the railroad south of Okolona, and, destroying it, return to La Grange by the most practicable route. . . .

These detachments were intended as diversions, and even should the commanders not have been able to carry out their instructions, yet, by attracting the attention of the enemy in other directions, they assisted us much in the accomplishment of the main object of the expedition.

After having started Colonel Hatch on his way, with the remaining portion of the command, consisting of the Sixth and Seventh Illinois Cavalry, about 950 strong, I continued on my journey southward, still keeping the Starkville road. Arriving at Starkville about 4 P.M., we captured a mail and a quantity of Government property, which we destroyed. From this point we took the direct road to Louisville. We moved out on this road about 4 miles, through a dismal swamp nearly belly-deep in mud, and sometimes swimming our horses to cross streams, when we encamped for the night in the midst of a violent rain. From this point I detached a battalion of the Seventh Illinois Cavalry to proceed about 4 miles, and destroy a large tannery and shoe manufactory in the service of the rebels. They returned safely, having accomplished the work most effectually. They destroyed a large number of boots and shoes and a large quantity of leather and machinery; in all amounting, probably, to $50,000, and captured a rebel quartermaster from Port Hudson, who was there laying in a supply for his command.

We now immediately resumed the march toward Louisville, distant 28 miles, mostly through a dense swamp, the Noxubee River bottom. This was for miles belly-deep in water, so that no road was discernible. The inhabitants through this part of the country generally did not know of our coming, and would not believe us to be anything but Confederates. We arrived at Louisville soon after dark. I sent a battalion of the Sixth Illinois, under Major Starr, in advance, to picket the town and remain until the column had passed, when they were relieved by a battalion of the Seventh Illinois, under Major Graham, who was ordered to remain until we should have been gone an hour, to prevent persons leaving with information of the course we were taking, to drive out stragglers, preserve order, and quiet the fears of the people. They had heard of our coming a short time before we arrived, and many had left, taking only what they could hurriedly move. The column moved quietly through the town without halting, and not a thing was disturbed. Those who remained at home acknowledged that they were surprised. They had expected to be robbed, outraged, and have their houses burned. On the contrary, they were protected in their persons and property.

After leaving the town, we struck another swamp, in which, crossing it, as we were obliged to, in the dark, we lost several animals drowned, and the men narrowly escaped the same fate. Marching until midnight, we halted until daylight at the plantation of Mr. Estes, about 10 miles south of Louisville.

The next morning, April 23, at daylight we took the road for Philadelphia. . . . Here we rested until 10 o'clock at night, when I sent two battalions of the Seventh Illinois Cavalry, under Lieutenant-Colonel Blackburn, to proceed immediately to Decatur, thence to the railroad at Newton Station. With the main force I followed about an hour later. The advance passed through Decatur about daylight, and struck the railroad about 6 A.M. I arrived about an hour afterward with the column. Lieutenant-Colonel Blackburn dashed into the town, took possession of the railroad and telegraph, and succeeded in capturing two trains in less than half an hour after his arrival. One of these, 25 cars, was loaded with ties and machinery, and the other 13 cars were loaded with commissary stores and ammunition, among the latter several thousand loaded shells. These, together with a large quantity of commissary and quartermaster's stores and about five hundred stand of arms stored in the town, were destroyed. Seventy-five prisoners captured at this point were paroled. The locomotives were exploded and other wise rendered completely unserviceable. Here the track was torn up, and a bridge half a mile west of the station destroyed. I detached a battalion of the Sixth Illinois Cavalry, under Major Starr, to proceed eastward and destroy such bridges, &c., as he might find over Chunkey River. Having damaged as much as possible the railroad and telegraph, and destroyed all Government property in the vicinity of Newton, I moved about 4 miles south of the road and fed men and horses. The forced marches which I was compelled to make, in order to reach this point successfully, necessarily very much fatigued and exhausted my command, and rest and food were absolutely necessary for its safety.

From captured mails and information obtained by my scouts, I knew that large forces had been sent out to intercept our return, and having instructions from Major-General Hurlbut and Brigadier General Smith to move in any direction from this point which, in my judgment, would be best for the safety of my command and the success of the expedition, I at once decided tò move south, in order to secure the necessary rest and food for men and horses, and then return to La Grange through Alabama, or make for Baton Rouge, as I might hereafter deem best. Major Starr in the mean time rejoined us, having destroyed most effectually three bridges and several hundred feet of trestle-work, and the telegraph from 8 to 10 miles east of Newton Station.

After resting about three hours, we moved south to Garlandville. At this point we found the citizens, many of them venerable with age, armed with shot-guns and organized to resist our approach. As the advance entered the town, these citizens fired upon them and wounded one of our men. We charged upon them and captured several. After disarming them, we showed them the folly of their actions, and, released them. Without an exception they acknowledged their mistake, and declared that they had been grossly deceived as to our real character. One volunteered his services as guide, and upon leaving us declared that hereafter his prayers should be for the Union Army. I mention this as a sample of the feeling which exists, and the good effect which our presence produced among the people in the country through which we passed. Hundreds who are skulking and hiding out to avoid conscription, only await the presence of our arms to sustain them, when they will rise up and declare their principles; and thousands who have been deceived, upon the vindication of our cause would immediately return to loyalty.

After slight delay at Garlandville, . . . we moved southwest toward Raleigh, making about 12 miles during the afternoon, and halting at dark on the plantation of Dr. Mackadora.

From this point I sent a single scout, disguised as a citizen, to proceed northward to the line of the Southern Railroad, cut the telegraph, and, if possible, fire a bridge or trestle-work. He started on his journey about mid-night, and when within 7 miles of the railroad he came upon a regiment of Southern cavalry from Brandon, Miss., in search of us. He succeeded in mis-directing them as to the place where he had last seen us, and, having seen them well on the wrong road, he immediately retraced his steps to camp with the news. When he first met them they were on the direct road to our camp, and had they not been turned from their course would have come up with us before daylight.

From information received through my scouts and other sources, I found that Jackson and the stations east as far as Lake Station had been re-enforced by infantry and artillery; and hearing that a fight was momentarily expected at Grand Gulf, I decided to make a rapid march, cross Pearl River, and strike the New Orleans, Jackson and Great Northern Railroad at Hazelhurst, and, after destroying as much of the road as possible, endeavor to get upon the flank of the enemy and co-operate with our forces, should they be successful in the attack upon Grand Gulf and Port Gibson.

Having obtained during this day plenty of forage and provisions, and having had one good night's rest, we now again felt ready for any emergency. Accordingly, at 6 o'clock on the morning of the 26th, we crossed Leaf River, burning the bridge behind us to prevent any enemy who might be in pursuit from following; thence through Raleigh, capturing the sheriff of that county, with about $3,000 in Government funds; thence to Westville, reaching this place soon after dark. . . .

At 6 o'clock, . . . April 28, we moved westward. After proceeding a short distance, I detached a battalion of the Seventh Illinois Cavalry, under Captain Trafton, to proceed back to the railroad at Bahala and destroy the road, telegraph, and all Government property he might find. With the rest of the command, I moved southwest toward Union Church. We halted to feed at 2 P.M. on the plantation of Mr. Snyder, about 2 miles northeast of the church. While feeding, our pickets were fired upon by a considerable force. I immediately moved out upon them, skirmished with and drove them through the town, wounding and capturing a number. It proved to be a part of Wirt Adams' (Mississippi) cavalry. After driving them off, we held the town and bivouacked for the night. After accomplishing the object of his expedition, Captain Trafton returned to us about 3 o'clock in the morning of the 29th, having come upon the rear of the main body of Adams' command. The enemy having a battery of artillery, it was his intention to attack us in front and rear at Union Church about daylight in the morning, but the appearance of Captain Trafton with a force in his rear changed his purpose, and, turning to the right, he took the direct road to Port Gibson. From this point I made a strong demonstration toward Fayette, with a view of creating the impression that we were going toward Port Gibson or Natchez, while I quietly took the opposite direction, taking the road leading southeast to Brookhaven, on the railroad.

Before arriving at this place, we ascertained that about 500 citizens and conscripts were organized to resist us. We charged into the town, when they fled, making but little resistance. We captured over 200 prisoners, a large and beautiful camp of instruction, comprising several hundred tents, and a large quantity of quartermaster's and commissary stores, arms, ammunition, &c. After paroling the prisoners and destroying the railroad, telegraph, and all Government property, about dark we moved southward, and encamped at Mr. Gill's plantation, about 8 miles south of Brookhaven.

On the following morning we moved directly south, along the railroad, destroying all bridges and trestle-work to Bongue Chitto Station, where we burned the depot and fifteen freight cars, and captured a very large secession flag. From thence we still moved along the railroad, destroying every bridge, water-tank, &c., as we passed, to Summit, which place we reached soon after noon. Here we destroyed twenty-five freight cars and a large quantity of Government sugar. We found much Union sentiment in this town, and were kindly welcomed and fed by many of the citizens.

Hearing nothing more of our forces at Grand Gulf, I concluded to make for Baton Rouge to recruit my command, after which I could return to La Grange, through Southern Mississippi and Western Alabama; or, crossing the Mississippi River, move through Louisiana and Arkansas. Accordingly, after resting about two hours, we started southwest, on the Liberty road, marched about 15 miles, and halted until daylight on the plantation of Dr. Spurlark.

The next morning we left the road and threatened Magnolia and Osyka, where large forces were concentrated to meet us; but, instead of attacking those points, took a course due south, marching through woods, lanes, and by-roads, and striking the road leading from Clinton to Osyka. Scarcely had we touched this road when we came upon the Ninth Tennessee Cavalry posted in a strong defile, guarding the bridges over Tickfaw River. We captured their pickets, and, attacking them, drove them before us, killing, wounding, and capturing a number. . . .

The enemy were now on our track in earnest. We were in the vicinity of their stronghold, and, from couriers and dispatches which we captured, it was evident they were sending forces in all directions to intercept us. The Amite River, a wide and rapid stream, was to be crossed, and there was but one bridge by which it could be crossed, and this was in exceedingly close proximity to Port Hudson. This I determined upon securing before I halted. We crossed it at midnight, about two hours in advance of a heavy column of infantry and artillery, which had been sent there to intercept us. I moved on to Sandy Creek, where Hughes' cavalry under Lieutenant-Colonel [C. C.] Wilbourn, were encamped, and where there was another main road leading to Port Hudson.

We reached this point at first dawn of day; completely surprised and captured the camp, with a number of prisoners. Having destroyed the camp, consisting of about one hundred and fifty tents, a large quantity of ammunition, guns, public and private stores, books, papers, and public documents, I immediately took the road to Baton Rouge. Arriving at the Comite River, we utterly surprised Stuart's cavalry [Miles' Legion], who were picketing at this point, capturing 40 of them, with their horses, arms, and entire camp. Fording the river, we halted to feed within 4 miles of the town. Major General Augur, in command at Baton Rouge, having now, for the first, heard of our approach, sent two companies of cavalry, under Captain [J. Franklin] Godfrey, to meet us. We marched into the town about 3 P.M., and we were most heartily welcomed by the United States forces at this point. . . .

During the expedition we killed and wounded about 100 of the enemy, captured and paroled over 500 prisoners, many of them officers, destroyed between 50 and 60 miles of railroad and telegraph, captured and destroyed over 3,000 stand of arms, and other army stores and Government property to an immense amount; we also captured 1,000 horses and mules.

Our loss during the entire journey was 3 killed, 7 wounded, 5 left on the route sick; the sergeant-major and surgeon of the Seventh Illinois left with Lieutenant-Colonel Blackburn, and 9 men missing, supposed to have straggled. We marched over 600 miles in less than sixteen days. The last twenty-eight hours we marched 76 miles, had four engagements with the enemy, and forded the Comite River, which was deep enough to swim many of the horses. During this time the men and horses were without food or rest.

Much of the country through which we passed was almost entirely destitute of forage and provisions, and it was but seldom that we obtained over one meal per day. Many of the inhabitants must undoubtedly suffer for want of the necessaries of life, which have reached most fabulous prices.

Two thousand cavalry and mounted infantry were sent from the vicinity of Greenwood and Grenada northeast to intercept us; 1,300 cavalry and several regiments of infantry with artillery were sent from Mobile to Macon, Meridian, and other points on the Mobile and Ohio road; a force was sent from Canton northeast to prevent our crossing Pearl River, and another force of infantry and cavalry was sent from Brookhaven to Monticello, thinking we would cross Pearl River at that point instead of Georgetown. Expeditions were also sent from Vicksburg, Port Gibson, and Port Hudson to intercept us. Many detachments were sent out from my command at various places to mislead the enemy, all of which rejoined us in safety. Colton's pocket map of Mississippi, which, though small, is very correct, was all I had to guide me; but by the capture of their couriers, dispatches, and mails, and the invaluable aid of my scouts, we were always able by rapid marches to evade the enemy when they were too strong and whip them when not too large.

Respectfully, your obedient servant,

B. H. GRIERSON,
Colonel, Commanding Brigade.

Lieut. Col. JOHN A. RAWLINS,
Assistant Adjutant-General.

—War of the Rebellion . . . Official Records

4. A UNION WOMAN SUFFERS THROUGH THE SIEGE OF VICKSBURG

After two futile assaults, May 19 and 22, Grant settled down to reducing Vicksburg by siege. While his batteries hurled shells into the beleaguered city, the gunboats attacked it from the river. Pemberton had failed adequately to provision the city, and its inhabitants were soon enduring near starvation.

This diary by an unknown Union lady, caught in the siege, tells of the hardships and perils that the civilian inhabitants endured.

March 20.—The slow shelling of Vicksburg goes on all the time, and we have grown indifferent. It does not at present interrupt or interfere with daily avocations, but I suspect they are only getting the range of different points; and when they have them all complete, showers of shot will rain on us all at once. Non-combatants have been ordered to leave or prepare accordingly. Those who are to stay are having caves built. Cave-digging has become a regular business; prices range from twenty to fifty dollars, according to size of cave. Two diggers worked at ours a week and charged thirty dollars. It is well made in the hill that slopes just in the rear of the house, and well propped with thick posts, as they all are. It has a shelf also, for holding a light or water. When we went in this evening and sat down, the earthy, suffocating feeling, as of a living tomb, was dreadful to me. I fear I shall risk death outside rather than melt in that dark furnace. The hills are so honey-combed with caves that the streets look like avenues in a cemetery.

The hill called the Sky-parlor has become quite a fashionable resort for the few upper-circle families left here. Some officers are quartered there, and there is a band and a field-glass. Last evening we also climbed the hill to watch the shelling, but found the view not so good as on a quiet hill nearer home. Soon a lady began to talk to one of the officers: "It is such folly for them to waste their ammunition like that. How can they ever take a town that has such advantages for defense and protection as this? We'll just bur-row into these hills and let them batter away as hard as they please." . . .

It is strange I have met no one yet who seems to comprehend an honest difference of opinion, and stranger yet that the ordinary rules of good breed-ing are now so entirely ignored. As the spring comes one has the craving for fresh, green food that a monotonous diet produces. There was a bed of radishes and onions in the garden that were a real blessing. An onion salad, dressed only with salt, vinegar, and pepper, seemed a dish fit for a king; but last night the soldiers quartered near made a raid on the garden and took them all.

April 2.—We have had to move, and thus lost our cave. The owner of the house suddenly returned and notified us that he intended to bring his family back; did n't think there 'd be any siege. The cost of the cave could go for the rent. That means he has got tired of the Confederacy and means to stay here and thus get out of it. . . .

April 28.—I never understood before the full force of those questions— What shall we eat? what shall we drink? and wherewithal shall we be clothed? We have no prophet of the Lord at whose prayer the meal and oil will not waste. Such minute attention must be given the wardrobe to preserve it that I have learned to darn like an artist. Making shoes is now another accomplishment. Mine were in tatters. H. came across a moth-eaten pair that he bought me, giving ten dollars, I think, and they fell into rags when I tried to wear them; but the soles were good, and that has helped me to shoes. A pair of old coat-sleeves saved—nothing is thrown away now—was in my trunk. I cut an exact pattern from my old shoes, laid it on the sleeves, and cut out thus good uppers and sewed them carefully; then soaked the soles and sewed the cloth to them. I am so proud of these home-made shoes, think I'll put them in a glass case when the war is over, as an heirloom. . . .

I have but a dozen pins remaining, so many I gave away. Every time these are used they are straightened and kept from rust. All these curious labors are performed while the shells are leisurely screaming through the air; but as long as we are out of range we don't worry. For many nights we have had but little sleep, because the Federal gunboats have been running past the batteries. The uproar when this is happening is phenomenal. The first night the thundering artillery burst the bars of sleep, we thought it an attack by the river. To get into garments and rush up-stairs was the work of a moment. From the upper gallery we have a fine view of the river, and soon a red glare lit up the scene and showed a small boat, towing two large barges, gliding by.

The Confederates had set fire to a house near the bank. Another night, eight boats ran by, throwing a shower of shot, and two burning houses made the river clear as day. One of the batteries has a remarkable gun they call "Whistling Dick," because of the screeching, whistling sound it gives, and certainly it does sound like a tortured thing. Added to all this is the indescribable Confederate yell, which is a soul-harrowing sound to hear. . . . Yesterday the *Cincinnati* attempted to go by in daylight, but was disabled and sunk. It was a pitiful sight; we could not see the finale, though we saw her rendered helpless.

May 1, 1863.—It is settled at last that we shall spend the time of siege in Vicksburg. Ever since we were deprived of our cave, I had been dreading that H. would suggest sending me to the country, where his relatives lived. As he could not leave his position and go also without being conscripted, and as I felt certain an army would get between us, it was no part of my plan to be obedient. A shell from one of the practising mortars brought the point to an issue yesterday and settled it. Sitting at work as usual, listening to the distant sound of bursting shells, apparently aimed at the court-house, there suddenly came a nearer explosion; the house shook, and a tearing sound was followed by terrified screams from the kitchen. I rushed thither, but met in the hall the cook's little girl America, bleeding from a wound in the forehead, and fairly dancing with fright and pain, while she uttered fearful yells. I stopped to examine the wound, and her mother bounded in, her black face ashy from terror. "Oh! Miss V., my child is killed and the kitchen tore up." Seeing America was too lively to be a killed subject, I consoled Martha and hastened to the kitchen. Evidently a shell had exploded just outside, sending three or four pieces through. When order was restored I endeavored to impress on Martha's mind the necessity for calmness and the uselessness of such excitement. Looking round at the close of the lecture, there stood a group of Confederate soldiers laughing heartily at my sermon and the promising audience I had. They chimed in with a parting chorus:

"Yes, it 's no use hollerin', old lady." . . .

May 17.—Hardly was our scanty breakfast over this morning when a hurried ring drew us both to the door. Mr. J., one of H.'s assistants, stood there in high excitment. "Well, Mr. L., they are upon us; the Yankees will be here by this evening."

"What do you mean?"

"That Pemberton has been whipped at Baker's Creek and Big Black, and his army are running back here as fast as they can come, and the Yanks after them, in such numbers nothing can stop them." . . .

What struck us both was the absence of that concern to be expected, and a sort of relief or suppressed pleasure. After twelve some worn-out-looking men sat down under the window.

"What is the news?" I inquired.

"Ritreat, ritreat!" they said, in broken English—they were Louisiana Acadians.

About three o'clock the rush began. I shall never forget that woeful sight of a beaten, demoralized army that came rushing back,—humanity in the last throes of endurance. Wan, hollow-eyed, ragged, foot-sore, bloody, the men limped along unarmed, but followed by siege-guns, ambulances, gun-carriages, and wagons in aimless confusion. At twilight two or three bands on the court-house hill and other points began playing "Dixie," "Bonnie Blue Flag," and so on, and drums began to beat all about; I suppose they were rallying the scattered army.

May 28.—Since that day the regular siege has continued. We are utterly cut off from the world, surrounded by a circle of fire. Would it be wise like the scorpion to sting ourselves to death? The fiery shower of shells goes on day and night. H.'s occupation, of course, is gone; his office closed. Every man has to carry a pass in his pocket. People do nothing but eat what they can get, sleep when they can, and dodge the shells. There are three intervals when the shelling stops, either for the guns to cool or for the gunners' meals, I suppose,—about eight in the morning, the same in the evening, and at noon. In that time we have both to prepare and eat ours. Clothing cannot be washed or anything else done. On the 19th and 22d, when the assaults were made on the lines, I watched the soldiers cooking on the green opposite. The half-spent balls coming all the way from those lines were flying so thick that they were obliged to dodge at every turn. At all the caves I could see from my high perch, people were sitting, eating their poor suppers at the cave doors, ready to plunge in again. As the first shell again flew they dived, and not a human being was visible. The sharp crackle of the musketry-firing was a strong contrast to the scream of the bombs. I think all the dogs and cats must be killed or starved: we don't see any more pitiful animals prowling around. . . .

The cellar is so damp and musty the bedding has to be carried out and laid in the sun every day, with the forecast that it may be demolished at any moment. The confinement is dreadful. To sit and listen as if waiting for death in a horrible manner would drive me insane. I don't know what others do, but we read when I am not scribbling in this. H. borrowed somewhere a lot of Dickens's novels, and we reread them by the dim light in the cellar. When the shelling abates, H. goes to walk about a little or get the "Daily Citizen," which is still issuing a tiny sheet at twenty-five and fifty cents a copy. It is, of course, but a rehash of speculations which amuses a half hour. To-day he heard while out that expert swimmers are crossing the Mississippi on logs at night to bring and carry news to Johnston.

I am so tired of corn-bread, which I never liked, that I eat it with tears in my eyes. We are lucky to get a quart of milk daily from a family near who have a cow they hourly expect to be killed. I send five dollars to market each morning, and it buys a small piece of mule-meat. Rice and milk is my main food; I can't eat the mule-meat. We boil the rice and eat it cold with milk for supper. Martha runs the gauntlet to buy the meat and milk once a day in a perfect terror. The shells seem to have many different names: I hear the soldiers say, "That's a mortar-shell. There goes a Parrott. That's a rifle-shell." They are all equally terrible. A pair of chimney-swallows have built in the parlor chimney. The concussion of the house often sends down parts of their nest, which they patiently pick up and reascend with.

Friday, June 5. In the cellar. . . . Yesterday morning a note was brought H. from a bachelor uncle out in the trenches, saying he had been taken ill with fever, and could we receive him if he came? H. sent to tell him to come, and I arranged one of the parlors as a dressing-room for him, and laid a pallet that he could move back and forth to the cellar. He did not arrive, however.

It is our custom in the evening to sit in the front room a little while in the dark, with matches and candle held ready in hand, and watch the shells, whose course at night is shown by the fuse. H. was at the window and suddenly sprang up, crying, "Run!"—"Where?"—"*Back!*"

I started through the back room, H. after me. I was just within the door when the crash came that threw me to the floor. It was the most appalling sensation I 'd ever known—worse than an earthquake, which I 've also experienced. Shaken and deafened, I picked myself up; H. had struck a light to find me. I lighted mine, and the smoke guided us to the parlor I had fixed for Uncle J. The candles were useless in the dense smoke, and it was many minutes before we could see. Then we found the entire side of the room torn out. The soldiers who had rushed in said, "This is an eighty-pound Parrott." . . .

June 7. (In the cellar.)—There is one thing I feel especially grateful for, that amid these horrors we have been spared that of suffering for water. The weather has been dry a long time, and we hear of others dipping up the water from ditches and mud-holes. This place has two large underground cisterns of good cool water, and every night in my subterranean dressing-room a tub of cold water is the nerve-calmer that sends me to sleep in spite of the roar. One cistern I had to give up to the soldiers, who swarm about like hungry animals seeking something to devour. Poor fellows! my heart bleeds for them. They have nothing but spoiled, greasy bacon, and bread made of musty pea-flour, and but little of that. The sick ones can't bolt it. They come into the kitchen when Martha puts the pan of corn-bread in the stove, and beg for the bowl she mixed it in. They shake up the scrapings with water, put in their bacon, and boil the mixture into a kind of soup, which is easier to swallow than pea-bread. When I happen in, they look so ashamed of their poor clothes. I know we saved the lives of two by giving a few meals.

To-day one crawled on the gallery to lie in the breeze. He looked as if shells had lost their terrors for his dumb and famished misery. I 've taught Martha to make first-rate corn-meal gruel, because I can eat meal easier that way than in hoe-cake, and I fixed him a saucerful, put milk and sugar and nutmeg—I 've actually got a nutmeg! When he ate it the tears ran from his eyes. "Oh, madam, there was never anything so good! I shall get better."

June 13.—Shell burst just over the roof this morning. Pieces tore through both floors down into the dining-room. The entire ceiling of that room fell in a mass. We had just left it. Every piece of crockery on the table was smashed up. The "Daily Citizen" to-day is a foot and a half long and six inches wide. It has a long letter from a Federal officer, P. P. Hill, who was on the gunboat *Cincinnati*, that was sunk May 27. Says it was found in his floating trunk. The editorial says, "The utmost confidence is felt that we can maintain our position until succor comes from outside. The undaunted Johnston is at hand."

June 18.—To-day the "Citizen" is printed on wallpaper; therefore has grown a little in size. It says, "But a few days more and Johnston will be here"; also that "Kirby Smith has driven Banks from Port Hudson," and that "the enemy are throwing incendiary shells in."

June 21.—I had gone up-stairs to-day during the interregnum to enjoy a rest on my bed, and read the reliable items in the "Citizen," when a shell burst right outside the window in front of me. Pieces flew in, striking all around me, tearing down masses of plaster that came tumbling over me. When H. rushed in I was crawling out of the plaster, digging it out of my eyes and hair. When he picked up a piece as large as a saucer beside my pillow, I realized my narrow escape. The window-frame began to smoke, and we saw the house was on fire. H. ran for a hatchet and I for water, and we put it out. Another [shell] came crashing near, and I snatched up my comb and brush and ran down here. It has taken all the afternoon to get the plaster out of my hair, for my hands were rather shaky.

June 25.—A horrible day. The most horrible yet to me, because I 've lost my nerve. We were all in the cellar, when a shell came tearing through the roof, burst up-stairs, tore up that room, and the pieces coming through both floors down into the cellar, one of them tore open the leg of H.'s pantaloons. This was tangible proof the cellar was no place of protection from them. On the heels of this came Mr. J. to tell us that young Mrs. P. had had her thigh-bone crushed. When Martha went for the milk she came back horror-stricken to tell us the black girl there had her arm taken off by a shell. For the first time I quailed. I do not think people who are physically brave deserve much credit for it; it is a matter of nerves. In this way I am constitutionally brave, and seldom think of danger till it is over; and death has not the terrors for me it has for some others. Every night I had lain down expecting death, and every morning rose to the same prospect, without being unnerved. It was for H. I trembled. But now I first seemed to realize that something worse than death might come: I might be crippled, and not killed. Life, without all one's powers and limbs, was a thought that broke down my courage. I said to H., "You must get me out of this horrible place; I cannot stay; I know I shall be crippled." Now the regret comes that I lost control, because H. is worried, and has lost his composure, because my coolness has broken down.

July 3.—To-day we are down in the cellar again, shells flying as thick as ever; provisions so nearly gone, except the hogshead of sugar, that a few more days will bring us to starvation indeed. Martha says rats are hanging dressed in the market for sale with mule-meat: there is nothing else. The officer at the battery told me he had eaten one yesterday. We have tried to leave this Tophet and failed, and if the siege continues I must summon that higher kind of courage—moral bravery—to subdue my fears of possible mutilation.

July 4.—It is evening. All is still. Silence and night are once more united. I can sit at the table in the parlor and write. Two candles are lighted. I would like a dozen. We have had wheat supper and wheat bread once more. H. is leaning back in the rocking-chair; he says:

"G., it seems to me I can hear the silence, and feel it, too. It wraps me like a soft garment; how else can I express this peace?"

But I must write the history of the last twenty-four hours. About five yesterday afternoon, Mr. J., H.'s assistant, who, having no wife to keep him in, dodges about at every change and brings us the news, came to H. and said:

"Mr. L., you must both come to our cave to-night. I hear that to-night the shelling is to surpass everything yet. An assault will be made in front and rear. You know we have a double cave; there is room for you in mine, and mother and sister will make a place for Mrs. L. Come right up; the ball will open about seven."

We got ready, shut up the house, told Martha to go to the church again if she preferred it to the cellar, and walked up to Mr. J.'s. When supper was eaten, all secure, and ladies in their cave night toilet, it was just six, and we crossed the street to the cave opposite. As I crossed a mighty shell flew screaming right over my head. It was the last thrown into Vicksburg. We lay on our pallets waiting for the expected roar, but no sound came except the chatter from neighboring caves, and at last we dropped asleep. I woke at dawn stiff. A draft from the funnel-shaped opening had been blowing on me all night. Every one was expressing surprise at the quiet. We started for home and met the editor of the "Daily Citizen." H. said:

"This is strangely quiet, Mr. L."

"Ah, sir," shaking his head gloomily, "I'm afraid (?) the last shell has been thrown into Vicksburg."

"Why do you fear so?"

"It is surrender. At six last evening a man went down to the river and blew a truce signal; the shelling stopped at once."

—CABLE, ed., "A Woman's Diary of the Siege of Vicksburg"

5. VICKSBURG SURRENDERS

On May 18, 1863, Johnston had ordered Pemberton to abandon Vicksburg and escape, if possible. Pemberton decided that escape was impossible, and retired behind the formidable works of the city. By the end of June it was clear that he could not hold out much longer, and Grant's army was by that time so large that it appeared unlikely that Johnston could break through to his aid. He therefore decided to surrender. That decision was probably inevitable; what inspired a good deal of criticism was the decision to make the formal surrender on July 4. Altogether over 30,000 Confederates were surrendered at Vicksburg—the largest force, it is alleged, in the history of modern warfare up to that time.

General Grant himself here tells the story of the surrender.

ON July 1st Pemberton, seeing no hope of outside relief, addressed the following letter to each of his four division commanders:

"Unless the siege of Vicksburg is raised, or supplies are thrown in, it will become necessary very shortly to evacuate the place. I see no prospect of the former, and there are many great, if not insuperable, obstacles in the way of the latter. You are, therefore, requested to inform me with as little delay as possible as to the condition of your troops, and their ability to make the marches and undergo the fatigues necessary to accomplish a successful evacuation."

Two of his generals suggested surrender, and the other two practically did the same; they expressed the opinion that an attempt to evacuate would fail. Pemberton had previously got a message to Johnston suggesting that he should try to negotiate with me for a release of the garrison with their arms. Johnston replied that it would be a confession of weakness for him to do so; but he authorized Pemberton to use his name in making such an arrangement.

On the 3d, about 10 o'clock A.M., white flags appeared on a portion of the rebel works. Hostilities along that part of the line ceased at once. Soon two persons were seen coming toward our lines bearing a white flag. They proved to be General Bowen, a division commander, and Colonel Montgomery, aide-de-camp to Pemberton, bearing the following letter to me:

"I have the honor to propose an armistice for —— hours, with the view to arranging terms for the capitulation of Vicksburg. To this end, if agreeable to you, I will appoint three commissioners, to meet a like number to be named by yourself, at such place and hour to-day as you may find convenient. I make this proposition to save the further effusion of blood, which must otherwise be shed to a frightful extent, feeling myself fully able to maintain my position for a yet indefinite period. This communication will be handed you, under a flag of truce, by Major-General John S. Bowen."

It was a glorious sight to officers and soldiers on the line where these white flags were visible, and the news soon spread to all parts of the command. The troops felt that their long and weary marches, hard fighting, ceaseless watching by night and day in a hot climate, exposure to all sorts of weather, to diseases, and, worst of all, to the gibes of many Northern papers that came to them, saying all their suffering was in vain, Vicksburg would never be taken, were at last at an end, and the Union sure to be saved.

Bowen was received by General A. J. Smith, and asked to see me. I had been a neighbor of Bowen's in Missouri, and knew him well and favorably before the war; but his request was refused. He then suggested that I should meet Pemberton. To this I sent a verbal message saying that if Pemberton desired it I would meet him in front of McPherson's corps, at 3 o'clock that afternoon. I also sent the following written reply to Pemberton's letter:

"Your note of this date is just received, proposing an armistice for several hours, for the purpose of arranging terms of capitulation through commissioners to be appointed, etc. The useless effusion of blood you propose stopping by this course can be ended at any time you may choose, by the unconditional surrender of the city and garrison. Men who have shown so much endurance and courage as those now in Vicksburg will always challenge the respect of an adversary, and I can assure you will be treated with all the respect due to prisoners of war. I do not favor the proposition of appointing commissioners to arrange the terms of capitulation, because I have no terms other than those indicated above."

At 3 o'clock Pemberton appeared at the point suggested in my verbal message, accompanied by the same officers who had borne his letter of the morning. Generals Ord, McPherson, Logan, A. J. Smith, and several officers of my staff accompanied me. Our place of meeting was on a hill-side within a few hundred feet of the rebel lines. Near by stood a stunted oak-tree, which was made historical by the event. It was but a short time before the last vestige of its body, root, and limb had disappeared, the fragments being taken as trophies. Since then the same tree has furnished as many cords of wood, in the shape of trophies, as "The True Cross."

Pemberton and I had served in the same division during a part of the Mexican war. I knew him very well, therefore, and greeted him as an old acquaintance. He soon asked what terms I proposed to give his army if it surrendered. My answer was the same as proposed in my reply to his letter. Pemberton then said, rather snappishly, "The conference might as well end," and turned abruptly as if to leave. I said, "Very well." General Bowen, I saw, was very anxious that the surrender should be consummated. His manners and remarks while Pemberton and I were talking showed this. He now proposed that he and one of our generals should have a conference. I had no objection to this, as nothing could be made binding upon me that they might propose. Smith and Bowen accordingly had a conference, during which Pemberton and I, moving some distance away toward the enemy's lines, were in conversation. After a while Bowen suggested that the Confederate army should be allowed to march out, with the honors of war, carrying their small-arms and field-artillery. This was promptly and unceremoniously rejected. The interview here ended, I agreeing, however, to send a letter giving final terms by 10 o'clock that night. I had sent word to Admiral Porter soon after the correspondence with Pemberton had commenced, so that hostilities might be stopped on the part of both army and navy. It was agreed on my parting with Pemberton that they should not be renewed until our correspondence should cease.

When I returned to my headquarters I sent for all the corps and division commanders with the army immediately confronting Vicksburg. (Half the army was from eight to twelve miles off, waiting for Johnston.) I informed them of the contents of Pemberton's letters, of my reply, and the substance of the interview, and was ready to hear any suggestion; but would hold the power of deciding entirely in my own hands. This was the nearest to a "council of war" I ever held. Against the general and almost unanimous judgment of the council I sent the following letter:

"In conformity with agreement of this afternoon I will submit the following proposition for the surrender of the city of Vicksburg, public stores, etc. On your accepting the terms proposed I will march in one division as a guard, and take possession at 8 A.M. to-morrow. As soon as rolls can be made out and paroles be signed by officers and men, you will be allowed to march out of our lines, the officers taking with them their side-arms and clothing; and the field, staff, and cavalry officers one horse each. The rank and file will be allowed all their clothing, but no other property. If these conditions are accepted, any amount of rations you may deem necessary can be taken from the stores you now have, and also the necessary cooking-utensils for preparing them. Thirty wagons also, counting two-horse or mule teams as one, will be allowed to transport such articles as cannot be carried along. The same conditions will be allowed to all sick and wounded officers and soldiers as fast as they become able to travel. The paroles for these latter must be signed, however, whilst officers present are authorized to sign the roll of prisoners."

. . . Late at night I received the following reply to my last letter:

"I have the honor to acknowledge the receipt of your communication of this date, proposing terms of capitulation for this garrison and post. In the main, your terms are accepted; but, in justice both to the honor and spirit of my troops manifested in the defense of Vicksburg, I have to submit the following amendments, which, if acceded to by you, will perfect the agreement between us. At 10 o'clock A.M. to-morrow I propose to evacuate the works in and around Vicksburg, and to surrender the city and garrison under my command, by marching out with my colors and arms, stacking them in front of my present lines, after which you will take possession. Officers to retain their side-arms and personal property, and the rights and property of citizens to be respected."

This was received after midnight; my reply was as follows:

"I have the honor to acknowledge the receipt of your communication of 3d July. The amendment proposed by you cannot be acceded to in full. It will be necessary to furnish every officer and man with a parole signed by himself, which, with the completion of the roll of prisoners, will necessarily take some time. Again, I can make no stipulations with regard to the treatment of citizens and their private property. While I do not propose to cause them any undue annoyance or loss, I cannot consent to leave myself under any restraint by stipulations. The property which officers will be allowed to take with them will be as stated in my proposition of last evening; that is, officers will be allowed their private baggage and side-arms, and mounted officers one horse each. If you mean by your proposition for each brigade to march to the front of the lines now occupied by it, and stack arms at 10 o'clock A.M., and then return to the inside and there remain as prisoners until properly paroled, I will make no objection to it. Should no notification be received of your acceptance of my terms by 9 o'clock A.M., I shall regard them as having been rejected, and shall act accordingly. Should these terms be accepted, white flags should be displayed along your lines to prevent such of my troops as may not have been notified from firing upon your men."

Pemberton promptly accepted these terms.

During the siege there had been a good deal of friendly sparring between the soldiers of the two armies, on picket and where the lines were close together. All rebels were known as "Johnnies"; all Union troops as "Yanks." Often "Johnny" would call, "Well, Yank, when are you coming into town?" The reply was sometimes: "We propose to celebrate the 4th of July there." Sometimes it would be: "We always treat our prisoners with kindness and do not want to hurt them"; or, "We are holding you as prisoners of war while you are feeding yourselves." The garrison, from the commanding general down, undoubtedly expected an assault on the 4th. They knew from the temper of their men it would be successful when made, and that would be a greater humiliation than to surrender. Besides it would be attended with severe loss to them.

The Vicksburg paper, which we received regularly through the courtesy of the rebel pickets, said prior to the 4th, in speaking of the "Yankee" boast that they would take dinner in Vicksburg that day, that the best receipt for cooking rabbit was, "First ketch your rabbit." The paper at this time, and for some time previous, was printed on the plain side of wall paper. The last was issued on the 4th and announced that we had "caught our rabbit."

I have no doubt that Pemberton commenced his correspondence on the 3d for the twofold purpose; first, to avoid an assault, which he knew would be successful, and second, to prevent the capture taking place on the great national holiday,—the anniversary of the Declaration of American Independence. Holding out for better terms, as he did, he defeated his aim in the latter particular.

At the 4th, at the appointed hour, the garrison of Vicksburg marched out of their works, and formed line in front, stacked arms, and marched back in good order. Our whole army present witnessed this scene without cheering. . . .

Pemberton says in his report: "If it should be asked why the 4th of July was selected as the day for surrender, the answer is obvious. I believed that upon that day I should obtain better terms. Well aware of the vanity of our foe, I knew they would attach vast importance to the entrance, on the 4th of July, into the stronghold of the great river, and that, to gratify their national vanity, they would yield then what could not be extorted from them at any other time." This does not support my view of his reasons for selecting the day he did for surrendering. But it must be recollected that his first letter asking terms was received about 10 o'clock, A.M., July 3d. It then could hardly be expected that it would take 24 hours to effect a surrender. He knew that Johnston was in our rear for the purpose of raising the siege, and he naturally would want to hold out as long as he could. He knew his men would not resist an assault, and one was expected on the 4th. In our interview he told me he had rations enough to hold out some time—my recollection is two weeks. It was this statement that induced me to insert in the terms that he was to draw rations for his men from his own supplies. . . .

As soon as our troops took possession of the city, guards were established along the whole line of parapet, from the river above to the river below. The prisoners were allowed to occupy their old camps behind the intrenchments. No restraint was put upon them, except by their own commanders. They were rationed about as our own men, and from our supplies. The men of the two armies fraternized as if they had been fighting for the same cause. When they passed out of the works they had so long and so gallantly defended, between lines of their late antagonists, not a cheer went up, not a remark was made that would give pain. I believe there was a feeling of sadness among the Union soldiers at seeing the dejection of their late antagonists.

—U. S. GRANT, "The Vicksburg Campaign"

6. GENERAL BANKS TAKES PORT HUDSON

Port Hudson, just above Baton Rouge, was the last remaining Confederate fort on the Mississippi. As early as December 1862 Banks had made a demonstration against it, but had not been strong enough to take it. Feeling that he could not undertake a full-scale attack on the fort while the Confederates were in strength in the Bayou Teche and Red River country, Banks undertook several expeditions west of the Mississippi. These were for the most part inconclusive. When Grant succeeded in crossing the river at Bruinsburg, Banks was ordered to co-operate by reducing Port Hudson. He arrived there with some 30,000 men in mid-May. It was the story of Vicksburg over again. Like Grant, Banks launched two futile assaults on the strong works of the fort, then settled down to a siege. By July the defenders of the fort were reduced to eating mules; the surrender of Vicksburg made the Confederate position untenable, and on July 9 General Gardner surrendered.

We have here three accounts of the Port Hudson operations, one from the journal of Lieutenant Root of the 75th New York Volunteers, the other two from the pen of an unknown Confederate officer.

A. BANKS IS REPULSED AT PORT HUDSON

Sunday, June 14, 1863

At about 1 o'clock the regiment was formed and marched about 2 miles to the place of assault; halted and left blankets and overcoats piled so that the men would go in light. Col. Babcock was in command of the skirmishers 12th and 75th and he called the officers together to explain the part we were to perform. He said we were to approach the enemy's works by a covered way, and would come out of the covered road at an angle of the rebel works, here the 75th were to file to the right, in single file and the 12th to the left in like manner, so that the regiments would form a strong line of skirmishers directly under the enemy's works. He cautioned us to take every precaution against making any noise, as it was desirous that we should gain that position without alarming the enemy if possible.

The plan was after we got our position the 91st N. Y. were to come up with hand grenades, and when the main body of the assaulting column came up, they were to deliver their hand grenades and the skirmishers rush over the intrenchments followed by the whole assaulting column. The plan was most miserably followed. In the first place the 12th Conn. did not come up until too late to enable us to get our position before daylight and in fact after waiting some time we started forward without them. Our regt. started into the covered way as it is called, but before we got half way to the breast works, the enemy knew we were coming and fired on us. When we came out in sight of the breast works it was daylight and the rebels fired volley after volley from behind the intrenchments at us, but still we pressed on and I did not stop till I reached the ditch alongside the breast works; there I halted with a few men but we received a volley from about 6 rifles lengthwise of the ditch, which wounded two or three. Seeing that they could rake the ditch the whole length, we fell back over the bank of it, and sought cover partly by the works themselves and partly by the rise in ground. Capt Savery who was in command of the left 4 companies came along and stopped by the side of me. I asked him if we should go over, he said "no, we can't now, haven't men enough." So we lay close to the ground, and fired at a rebel head whenever we saw one raise above the parapet to fire on us.

For about half an hour we lay under the fire of the enemy without support. Our men in coming over a knoll had been mowed down like grass and I expected that our loss would be enormous. I looked around me and saw but 4 men of my company, and about 25 of the regiment. Captain Savery was the only officer with me and we seemed to be separated from the rest of the regiment by a kind of ridge. In a few minutes Lieut. Hosmer, Acting Adjutant, came up and Capt. Savery was wounded in the arm just at my side while aiming a gun at the man who shot him. He jumped up and started towards the rear with the exclamation "O! Christ, Will" and left the field. I did not see how bad his wound was, but I hope it is not serious. Two or three attempts at charging were made without success. A part of the 114th N. Y. tried to charge where I was. They went as far as the ditch and there halted a moment. That moment was death and dismay to their ranks and they hurried back in confusion leaving their colors and part of their number in the ditch. As the day advanced the heat of the sun became very oppressive and it was most heartrending to hear the wounded begging to be moved into the shade, and we unable to do anything for them. More troops were brought in and kept under cover of the ravines, but little was done after 9 o'clock A.M. Further attempts to charge seemed to have been given up. After dark most of the troops were withdrawn and our brigade returned to its old position. My friend Lt. Hutchinson of Co. D was killed early in the morning. Polaski Olmstat my old schoolmate and friend was also killed. Our loss must be very heavy, though I do not hear of any killed in Co. B. . . . Darkness put an end to the scene of conflict and threw a veil over the field whereon lay hundreds of dead and dying.

—Root, ed., "Private Journal of William H. Root"

B. Eating Mules at Port Hudson

The last quarter ration of beef had been given out to the troops on the 29th of June [1863]. On the 1st of July, at the request of many officers, a wounded mule was killed and cut up for experimental eating. All those who partook of it spoke highly of the dish. The flesh of mules is of a darker color than beef, of a finer grain, quite tender and juicy, and has a flavor something between that of beef and venison. There was an immediate demand for this kind of food, and the number of mules killed by the commissariat daily increased. Some horses were also slaughtered, and their flesh was found to be very good eating, but not equal to mule. Rats, of which there were plenty about the deserted camps, were also caught by many officers and men and were found to be quite a luxury—superior, in the opinion of those who eat them, to spring chicken; and if a philosopher of the Celestial Empire could have visited Port Hudson at the time, he would have marveled at the progress of the barbarians there toward the refinements of his own people.

Mule meat was regularly served out in rations to the troops from and after the 4th of July, and there were very few among the garrison whose natural prejudices were so strong as to prevent them from cooking and eating their share. The stock of corn was getting very low, and besides that nothing was left but peas, sugar, and molasses. These peas were the most indigestible and unwholesome articles that were ever given to soldiers to eat, and that such a large quantity was left on hand was probably accounted for by the fact that most of the troops would not have them on any consideration. To save corn they were issued out to horses and mules and killed a great many of these animals. All of the horses and mules which were not needed for hauling or other imperative duties had been turned out to graze, where numbers of them were killed or disabled by the enemy's cannonade and rain of Minie balls and the rest nearly starved to death.

The sugar and molasses were put to good use by the troops in making a weak description of beer which was constantly kept at the lines by the barrelful and drunk by the soldiers in preference to the miserable water with which they were generally supplied. This was a very pleasant and healthful beverage and went far to recompense the men for the lack of almost every other comfort or luxury. In the same way, after the stock of tobacco had given out, they substituted sumac leaves, which grew wild in the woods. It had always been smoked by the Indians under the name of killickinnic and when properly prepared for the pipe is a tolerably good substitute for tobacco.

There was a small proportion of the garrison who could not, however, reconcile themselves so easily to the hardships and dangers of the siege. Some one hundred and fifty or more men, almost entirely foreigners of a low class or ignorant conscripts from western Louisiana, men who were troubled with none of that common feeling usually styled patriotism, deserted us for the better-provided commissariats of the enemy, slinking away by couples and squads during the night time. Their loss was not wept over, nor could the information they carried with them concerning our position enable the enemy to capture it.

—*Port Hudson ... As Sketched from the Diary of an Officer*

C. Blue and Gray Fraternize after the Surrender of Port Hudson

At two o'clock on the morning of the 8th of July [1863] General Gardner sent to General Banks by flag of truce for confirmation of the fall of Vicksburg, which was accorded him. About nine o'clock the same morning he dispatched commissioners to treat for the surrender of the post [Port Hudson]. They did not return until afternoon and then announced that an unconditional surrender of the place and garrison had been agreed upon and that the ceremony would take place at seven o'clock the next morning.

A cessation of hostilities had already taken place, and immediately that it was known that the capitulation had been agreed upon, a singular scene was presented to the observer, particularly upon the extreme right, where the contending parties, almost near enough to clutch each other by the throat, had been engaged in a desperate struggle for the mastery.

Soldiers swarmed from their places of concealment on either side and met each other in the most cordial and fraternal spirit. Here you would see a group of Federal soldiers escorted round our works and shown the effects of their shots and entertained with accounts of such part of the siege operations as they could not have learned before. In the same way our men went into the Federal lines and gazed with curiosity upon the work which had been giving them so much trouble, escorted by Federal soldiers, who vied with each other in courtesy and a display of magnanimous spirit. The subject of the attack and defense seemed to be a tireless one with both sides, and the conversations that ensued between them were of so cheerful and pleasant a character that one could hardly believe it possible these men had just before been fighting with the ferocity of tigers and striving by every art to slaughter the men they were now fraternizing with.

Not a single case occurred in which the enemy, either officers or privates, exhibited a disposition to exult over their victory, but on the contrary, whenever the subject came up in conversation it elicited from them only compliments upon the skill and bravery of the defense. Nor was their conduct limited to mere expressions. They were liberal in making presents of tobacco and other luxuries, asking of the garrison only such articles as they could retain as relics of the siege. One of their surgeons came in during a heavy rainstorm and brought medicines for our sick, repeating his visit the next morning and bringing a large quantity of quinine, which he dosed out to the fever patients. During the afternoon and evening of the 8th a large number of Federals were within our lines visiting at our camps, whither most of our men had repaired to pack up their little stock of clothing preparatory to an expected departure on the morrow.

—Port Hudson ... As Sketched from the Diary of an Officer

7. "THE FATHER OF WATERS AGAIN GOES UNVEXED TO THE SEA"

Lincoln had been invited to address a meeting of Union men at Springfield, Illinois; finding it impossible to leave Washington he sent, instead, a long letter to the chairman of the meeting, James Conkling. Most of the letter argued the necessity of emancipation; the concluding paragraphs—some of the most felicitous words Lincoln ever wrote—discussed some of the implications of the war and of victory.

Executive Mansion, Washington, August 26, 1863

HON. JAMES C. CONKLING

My Dear Sir.

. . . The signs look better. The Father of Waters again goes unvexed to the sea. Thanks to the great Northwest for it. Nor yet wholly to them. Three hundred miles up they met New England, Empire, Keystone, and Jersey, hewing their way right and left. The sunny South, too, in more colors than one, also lent a hand. On the spot, their part of the history was jotted down in black and white. The job was a great national one; and let none be banned who bore an honorable part in it. And while those who have cleared the great river may well be proud, even that is not all. It is hard to say that anything has been more bravely and well done than at Antietam, Murfreesboro', Gettysburg, and on many fields of lesser note. Nor must Uncle Sam's web-feet be forgotten. At all the watery margins they have been present. Not only on the deep sea, the broad bay, and the rapid river, but also up the narrow muddy bayou, and wherever the ground was a little damp, they have been, and made their tracks. Thanks to all. For the great republic—for the principle it lives by, and keeps alive—for man's vast future— thanks to all.

Peace does not appear so distant as it did. I hope it will come soon, and come to stay; and so come as to be worth the keeping in all future time. It will then have been proved that, among free men, there can be no successful appeal from the ballot to the bullet; and that they who take such an appeal are sure to lose their case, and pay the cost. And then, there will be some black men who can remember that, with silent tongue, and clenched teeth, and steady eye, and well-poised bayonet, they have helped mankind on to this great consummation; while, I fear, there will be some white ones, unable to forget that with malignant heart, and deceitful speech, they strove to hinder it.

Still, let us not be over-sanguine of a speedy final triumph. Let us be quite sober. Let us diligently apply the means, never doubting that a just God, in his own good time, will give us the rightful result.

Yours very truly

A. LINCOLN.

—Complete Works of Abraham Lincoln

8. GENERAL MORGAN INVADES THE NORTH

After Stones River (December 31, 1862) General Bragg had fallen back on Tullahoma, and then to Chattanooga. To cover his retreat he ordered General Morgan to raid the railroads in Kentucky and, if possible, threaten Louisville. Morgan wanted to invade Ohio, but to this plan Bragg refused his consent. Starting out on July 2, 1863—just as Pemberton was getting ready to surrender Vicksburg—Morgan swept through Kentucky, crossed the Green River, captured Lebanon, and on July 9 reached the banks of the Ohio. Contrary to orders he then went ahead with his own plan of an invasion— with disastrous results.

Morgan himself was one of the most glamorous figures in the Confederacy. He had fought in the Mexican War and as early as 1857 had organized the Lexington (Kentucky) Rifles. Commissioned captain in 1861 he began the series of raids that were so effective in disrupting Federal communications in the West. By the time of Shiloh he was a colonel, and in June a brigadier. With Forrest and Wheeler he was one of the three great cavalry leaders of the Army of Tennessee. Captured at the end of this raid Morgan was imprisoned in the Ohio State Penitentiary; we will read elsewhere how he escaped. In 1864 he was sent to western Virginia to deal with the attack launched by Averell and Crook, and was killed at Greenville, Tennessee, in September of that year.

We have here two accounts of the Morgan raid. The first, by Colonel Alston, Morgan's chief of staff, carries the story up through July 5, 1863; the second, by Colonel James B. McCreary, continues the story to its end. McCreary was later Governor of Kentucky and served for six terms in Congress.

A. MORGAN'S CAVALRYMEN SWEEP THROUGH KENTUCKY

July 1st, 1863.—On the banks of the Cumberland. The river very high. No boats. General M. obliged to build a number of boats, which he accomplished with very little delay, and commenced crossing at sundown.

July 2d.—Bucksville. He had great difficulty in making the horses swim, but by united and systematic exertion succeeded in getting the entire command of —— regiments over by ten A.M., though the command was very much scattered. At eleven o'clock, scouts came into Bucksville and reported the enemy advancing, and within four miles of the town. It was supposed to be only a scouting party, and a portion of Dick Morgan's command was sent out to make a reconnoissance. The report of the scouts of the enemy advancing proved to be correct, and a message was received from Colonel Ward that he was attacked. Colonel Grigsby was sent to reënforce him, and succeeded in driving the Yankees back in great confusion upon their reënforcements. My regiment lost two mortally wounded and two others slightly. Five of the Yankees were known to be killed and a number wounded, with about fifteen prisoners. No tidings heard of the Second brigade until dark, when they arrived and reported that Colonel Johnson, commanding, had experienced great difficulty in crossing, and that in addition to the precipitous banks and absence of all boats or other means of transportation, the enemy were hovering on the river and harassing him as far as they could. He was, however, quite successful in driving them back. Yesterday a young man, calling himself Charles Rogers, dressed in full confederate uniform, came into our lines and expressed a desire to join our command. I suspicioned him, and, after a few questions, I was convinced that he was a spy. I threatened to shoot him, when he confessed that he had been lying, and that his name was Simon Blitz—in fact he convicted himself of being a spy. I hated to shoot him, although he deserved it.

July 3d.—My regiment behaved very gallantly in yesterday's fight with the enemy, frequently having hand-to-hand encounters. To-day we experienced the same difficulty in getting the artillery on, and had to press a number of oxen for the purpose. After two halts for the column to close up, our advance proceeded to Columbia. They were met by detachments from three regiments said to be under command of Colonel Wolford. A brief engagement followed, in which we drove the enemy in great haste through the town, capturing six prisoners, killing two, among them Captain Carter, and wounding three. Our loss was two killed and two wounded, among them Captain Cassel, a most dashing and daring officer, wounded in the thigh. Our men behaved badly at Columbia, breaking open a store and plundering it. I ordered the men to return the goods, and made all the reparation in my power. These outrages are very disgraceful, and are usually perpetrated by men accompanying the army simply for plunder. They are not worth a ——, and are a disgrace to both armies. Passed through Columbia, and camped six miles from Green River Bridge.

July 4th.—New-Market, Ky. A day of gloom, deep gloom, to our entire command. How many who rose this morning full of enthusiasm and hope now "sleep the sleep that knows no waking." The sun rose bright and beautiful, the air was cool and balmy, all nature wore the appearance of peace and harmony. While riding along, affected by the stillness of all around, Captain Magennis, the Adjutant-General, rode up and remarked how dreadful to reflect that we were marching on to engage in deadly strife, and how many poor fellows would pass into eternity before the setting of yonder sun. I have no doubt the poor fellow was moved to these reflections by one of those unaccountable presentiments which are so often the harbingers of evil. (Before dark he was a corpse.) About sunrise we drove in the enemy's pickets and were soon near their fortifications, which had been erected to prevent our crossing. General Morgan sent in a flag of truce and demanded the surrender, but the Colonel quietly remarked: "If it was any other day he might consider the demand, but the Fourth of July was a bad day to talk about surrender, and he must therefore decline." This Colonel is a gallant man, and the entire arrangement of his defence entitles him to the highest credit for military skill. We would mark such a man in our army for promotion.

We attacked the place with two regiments, sending the remainder of our force across at another ford. The place was judiciously chosen and skilfully defended, and the result was that we were repulsed with severe loss—about twenty-five killed and twenty wounded. . . . Our march thus far has been very fatiguing—bad roads, little rest or sleep, little to eat, and a fight every day. Yet our men are cheerful, even buoyant, and to see them pressing along barefooted, hurrahing and singing, would cause one to appreciate what those who are fighting in a just and holy cause will endure.

About three o'clock, as I rode on about forty yards in advance, I heard the General exclaim something in a very excited tone, which I could not understand, and heard at the same time the report of a pistol. I turned, and, great God! to my horror I saw Captain Magennis falling from his horse, with the blood gushing out of his mouth and breast. His only remark was: "Let me down easy." In another moment his spirit had fled. He was killed by Captain Murphy because Magennis, by the direction of General Morgan, had ordered Murphy to restore a watch taken from a prisoner. Thus was the poor fellow's language of the morning dreadfully realized. I was terrible affected. I had seen blood flow freely on many a battlefield—my friends had been killed in the morning—but this caused a deeper impression and shock than any occurrence I ever witnessed. Truly this has been a sad day. General Morgan looks haggard and weary, but he never despairs. May to-morrow dawn more bright than to-day closes.

July 5th.—Another day of gloom, fatigue, and death. Moved on Lebanon at sunrise—placed our men in line. Sent around Colonel J—— with his brigade to the Danville road to cut off reënforcements, which we knew were expected from Danville. I went in with a flag of truce. It was fired on five times. Officer apologized, saying he thought it was a man with a white coat on. Very dangerous mistake, at least for me. Demanded unconditional surrender. Told Colonel Hanson we had his reënforcements cut off, and resistance was useless. He refused to surrender, and I then ordered him to send out the non-combatants, as we would be compelled to shell the town. He posted his regiment in the dépôt and in various houses, by which he was enabled to make a desperate resistance. After a fight of seven hours, General Morgan, finding the town could be taken in no other way, ordered a charge to be made. This ought to have been done at first, but General Morgan said, when it was urged on him, that he wished to avoid the destruction of private property as much as possible, and he would only permit it as a last and final resort. Colonel Hanson still held out in hopes of receiving reënforcements, and only surrendered after we had fired the buildings in which he was posted. . . .

By this surrender we obtained a sufficient quantity of guns to arm all our men who were without them; also a quantity of ammunition, of which we stood sorely in need. At the order to charge, Duke's regiment rushed forward, and poor Tommy Morgan, who was always in the lead, ran forward and cheered the men with all the enthusiasm of his bright nature. Almost at the first volley he fell back, pierced through the heart. His only words were: "Brother Cally, they have killed me." Noble youth! how deeply lamented by all who knew you! This was a crushing blow to General Morgan, as his affection for his brother exceeded the love of Jonathan to David. It caused a terrible excitement, and the men were in a state of frenzy. It required the utmost energy and promptitude on the part of the officers to prevent a scene of slaughter, which all would deeply have lamented. Our men behaved badly here, breaking open stores and plundering indiscriminately. All that officers could do was done to prevent, but in vain. These occurrences are very disgraceful, and I am truly glad that they form exceptions to the general conduct.

While I was paroling the prisoners, a courier arrived, informing me that the enemy were approaching with two regiments of cavalry and a battery of artillery, and that skirmishing was then going on with our pickets. I was therefore obliged to order the prisoners to Springfield on the double-quick. Soon after we left Lebanon, the hardest rain I ever experienced commenced to fall, and continued till nine o'clock. Arrived at Springfield at dark, when I halted the prisoners in order to parole those who were not paroled at Lebanon, and formally dismissed them. This detained me at Springfield two hours after the command had passed. Wet and chilly, worn out, horse tired and hungry. Stopped to feed her. Falling asleep, was aroused by one of the men. Started on to the command. When I reached the point on the Bardstown road where I had expected the Second brigade to encamp, was halted by a party of cavalry. Supposing them to be our own pickets, I rode up promptly to correct them for standing in full view of any one approaching, when lo! to my mortification, I found myself a prisoner. My God! how I hated it, no one can understand.

—"Journal of Lieutenant-Colonel Alston"

B. Morgan's Raid Comes to an Inglorious End

8 July, 1863. The great Ohio River, the dividing line between the North and the South, is reached. The command is crossing. Here I met Capt. Heady. The enemy are pressing us in the rear, and their gunboats kept up a steady fire on the two stern boats, in which Morgan's command is crossing.

Thoughts, hopes and anxieties chase each other in wild succession through my mind, but my Regiment is again guarding the rear and vigilance is the price of liberty. At 12 o'clock tonight, it being moonrise, the enemy pressed upon us and drove our pickets in, but again fell back.

July 9. This morning I am left with half of the Regiment one mile from the river as rear guard, and at daylight the Yankees moved down upon me. It was a critical and trying moment. By the interposition of Divine Providence, a heavy fog suddenly, and whilst hot skirmishing was going on, enveloped friends and foes, and the Yankees halted. Under this fog I crossed my command over the river. As I moved up the hills of Indiana, the enemy moved down the hills of Kentucky. We are now fairly into Yankee land. What the result will be God only knows. We attacked Corydon this evening, and, after a tolerable severe fight of two hours, took the place and several hundred prisoners. Thence to Salsberry, where we bivouacked for a few hours.

July 10. Attacked Palmyra and captured a small force of the enemy. Then moved on Salem, where, after some fighting, a considerable force surrendered to us. Here we destroyed heavy supplies, a depot, and several bridges. Then we captured Canton, tore up the railroad, and tore down the telegraph, and then rapidly moved on, like an irresistable storm, to the vicinity of Vienna, where, for a brief period, we bivouacked. The citizens seemed frightened almost to death, for Federal papers have published the wildest tales about us. The Governors of Indiana and Ohio have ordered out all able-bodied men, and we have already fought decrepit, white-haired age and buoyant, blithe boyhood.

July 11. Marched without any hindrance through Vienna, New Philadelphia, Lexington, and Paris, and came to Vernon, where we found the enemy in great force. The enemy consisted of a large force of Volunteers and Militia. We made a flank movement, tore up all the railroads around Vernon, and then traveled all night to Dupont, where we rested and fed our horses. Like an irresistable avalanche we are sweeping over this country. Man never knows his powers of endurance 'till he tries himself. The music of the enemy's balls is now as familiar and common as the carol of the spring bird which, unknowing of death and carnage around, sings today the same song that gladdened our forefathers.

July 12. We move rapidly through six or seven towns without any resistance, and tonight lie down for a little while with our bridles in our hands.

July 13. Today we reach Harrison, the most beautiful town I have yet seen in the North—a place, seemingly, where love and beauty, peace and prosperity, sanctified by true religion, might hold high carnival. Here we destroyed a magnificent bridge and saw many beautiful women. From here we moved to Miami Town, where we destroyed another splendid bridge over the Miami River. The bridge at Harrison was across Whitewater River. From Miami Town we passed through the most fertile and lovely region of Ohio. For hours the column moved at full speed, for we were now moving around Cincinnati. County seat after county seat reared itself in stately splendor, now scarcely distinguishable for the clouds of dust. Town after town and city after city are passed. A part of Morgan's command makes a feint on Cincinnati, and we move at this rate a distance of eighty-three miles, and all in sixteen hours. If there be a man who boasts of a march, let him excel this. After this Gilpin race we rested by capturing a train of cars on the Little Miami and a considerable number of prisoners. Then we surrounded Camp Dennison, captured a large train of wagons, and about two hundred mules. From there we moved on Winchester, where we destroyed a fine bridge, and thence to Jackson.

July 15. Today we traveled through several unimportant towns, destroyed one bridge, and bivouacked at Walnut Grove.

July 16. Today we find the first obstruction in our way, consisting of felled trees. The enemy are now pressing us on all sides, and the woods swarm with militia. We capture hundreds of prisoners, but, a parole being null, we can only sweep them as chaff out of our way. Today we crossed the Scioto to Piketon, and, as usual, destroyed the bridge. Thence we moved to Jackson.

July 17. Today we find our road badly blockaded and "axes to the front" is now the common command. We have today passed through many little dutch towns with which this country abounds. Tonight we halt near Pomeroy. The enemy are in considerable force in front. We attacked them and drove them from our front, and then moved rapidly in the direction of Buffington, where we intend to cross.

July 18. All are now on the qui vive, for the Ohio River is full of gunboats and transports, and an immense force of cavalry is hovering in our rear. We reached Buffington tonight. All was quiet. A dense fog wrapped this woodland scene. Early in the morning of the 19th the Yankees guarding the ford were attacked by our force, and driven away and their artillery captured. Immediately after this, and whilst we were trying the river to ascertain if it was fordable, the gunboats steamed up the river. The transports landed their infantry, thousands of cavalry moved down upon us, and the artillery commenced its deadly work. We formed and fought here to no purpose. The river was very full in consequence of a heavy rain away up the river. Shells and minie balls were ricocheting and exploding in every direction, cavalry were charging, and infantry with its slow, measured tread moved upon us, while broadside after broadside was poured upon our doomed command from the gunboats. It seemed as if our comparatively small command would be swallowed up by the innumerable horde. About half of it was here captured or killed. I made my way out by charging through the enemy's lines with about one-half the Regiment, and finally formed a juncture with the remnant of our command under Gen. Morgan, now numbering about 1,200. With these we moved towards Cheshire, traveling rapidly all night, and passing around the enemy's pickets, over cliffs and ravines, which, under ordinary circumstances, would have been considered insurmountable.

July 20. Today reached Cheshire. There Buffington was entrenched to a certain extent. The Yankees pressed us in the rear and fired on us from their gunboats in front, thus forcing us back to a high hill, where, after exhausting our ammunition, we surrendered, 700 men. I saw General Shackelford and arranged the terms of surrender. He allowed all field officers to retain side arms and horses, all others to retain private property. This proposition I announced to all the officers, and all voted to surrender, and thus ended the saddest day of my life.

—McCREARY, "The Journal of My Soldier Life"

XIX

Prisons, North and South

THIS *is doubtless the darkest chapter in the history of the war. No other, certainly, reveals so clearly American unreadiness for war or the failure to take in, early enough, its true nature or to anticipate its problems. In a sense the war took both sides by surprise. Neither government was prepared for it, neither anticipated its long duration. There was, consequently, no adequate preparation either for prisoners or for medical services. At the beginning authorities on both sides improvised prisons. The North was fairly well supplied with prisons of a sort—the existing penitentiaries, and military prisons—and others were speedily set up well behind the lines. The South used the meager facilities it already had, took over factories and warehouses, and eventually fell back on open stockades such as the notorious Andersonville.*

From the very beginning there were perplexing problems relating to the treatment of prisoners. From the strictly legal point of view all Confederates were rebels—and thus traitors—and subject to the extreme penalty. Circumstances, however, forced the Union to recognize the de facto *belligerency of the South, and Confederate prisoners were accorded the customary treatment of prisoners of war. There was a brief attempt to make an exception of sailors on privateers—to regard them as pirates—but a threat of reprisal took care of that. Some Southern officers were inclined to regard Negro troops as beyond the pale and there was a gesture of turning them over to state authorities for such treatment as was thought appropriate; this, too, yielded to the threat of reprisal and there is no evidence that Negro prisoners were maltreated. The most serious problem was that of prisoner exchange. Under the cartel of July 1862 both sides agreed to exchange or parole all prisoners within ten days, and if this cartel had been observed it would have eliminated the whole prisoner problem, for captures (up to the very end of the war) were roughly equal. Unfortunately both sides violated the cartel, and in 1863 Grant suspended further exchange of prisoners—technically on the ground of Confederate violations of the cartel but actually because the Confederacy had more to gain by exchange than the Union.*

Conditions in prisons, North and South, were uniformly bad. Most of them were overcrowded; few provided adequate food, shelter or clothing, and the medical and sanitary services were about as bad as they could be. The result was a shockingly high mortality rate. Of 194,743 Union soldiers actually imprisoned 30,128 died in captivity; of 214,865 Confederate soldiers actually imprisoned 25,976 died. The different mortality rate was a measure not of wickedness or neglect on the part of the Confederacy but of shortages of food, clothing, medical supplies, and manpower. If approximately one third of all the prisoners at Andersonville died, it must be remembered that the mortality rate in Camp Douglas in Chicago ran as high as 10 per cent a month, at times, while that at such comparatively well built camps as Elmira ran to 5 per cent a month.

1. ABNER SMALL SUFFERS IN DANVILLE PRISON

Abner Small was a boy in Waterville, Maine, when the war broke out. Enlisting as a private in the 3rd Maine Volunteers he eventually rose to be major of the 16th Maine, whose history he subsequently wrote. He fought through Fredericksburg, Chancellorsville, Gettysburg, and the Wilderness, was captured in August 1864, and imprisoned in Libby and Danville prisons in Virginia, and in Salisbury, North Carolina. His is one of the best, and one of the least embittered, accounts of prison life in the South.

[November 1864]. Our quarters were so crowded that none of us had more space to himself than he actually occupied, usually a strip of the bare, hard floor, about six feet by two. We lay in long rows, two rows of men with their heads to the side walls and two with their heads together along the center of the room, leaving narrow aisles between the rows of feet. The wall spaces were preferred, because a man could brace his back there and sit out the long day or the longer night. There was a row of posts down the center of the room, but these were too few and too narrow to give much help; I know, because I had a place by one of them.

I remember three officers, one a Yankee from Vermont, one an Irishman from New York, and one a Dutchman from Ohio, who messed together by the wall opposite me. When they came to Danville they were distinct in feature and personality. They became homesick and disheartened. They lost all interest in everything, and would sit in the same attitude hour after hour and day after day, with their backs against the wall and their gaze fixed on the floor at my feet. It grew upon me that they were gradually being merged into one man with three bodies. They looked just alike; truly, I couldn't tell them apart. And they were dying of nostalgia. . . .

Some of the prisoners played chess, checkers, and backgammon. Captain Conley and I had made a set of checkers in Libby, and we still had them, but the game palled on us. Like the ungodly majority, we killed time and escaped insanity with cards. A few of our associates, pursuing the consolations of religion, found none too much time to study the Scriptures; games had no fascinating power over them. A few others, remembering what they had learned at college, engaged in the study of classical or modern languages. Many tried to read, but reading somehow ceased to be a comfort in prison; at least, that was my experience. Our library, moreover, was a small one; it consisted of a few books and some back numbers of monthlies brought to us by the Reverend Charles K. Hall, a Methodist minister of Danville, who occasionally preached to us.

Many of our comrades developed a wonderful talent at handicraft and made hundreds of ornaments from bone and wood. Crosses, rings, and pins were artistically fashioned and most beautifully chased. Busts were carved from bricks taken from the walls. Checkers with monograms and raised figures were cut from bone and bits of wood. Altogether, there was output enough to stock a respectable museum. These objects were not made wholly in the cause of art, nor to while away the time; they were valuable for barter and exchange.

. As our money gave out, we sold the things to get more, or swapped articles of value or works of art for necessities. Boots, spurs, watches, rings, jack-knives, buttons, even toothpicks, were commodities of traffic. Boots were a quick commodity and brought high prices in debased rebel currency; but we hated to part with them. Captain Conley's pride in a pair of nice boots lasted until his luxurious habit of smoking demanded a sacrifice. The officer of the guard, an inveterate haggler with the general manner and appearance of a Malay pirate, offered one hundred Confederate dollars and finally a pair of shoes also, for the boots, and the offer was accepted. The cash was paid, and the captain, almost in tears, gave up his fine footwear. After a wait of two weeks there was passed into the prison a package addressed to Captain Conley. "My shoes!" he cried. He tore off the wrapper, and for an hour sat and swore at two old army brogans, of different sizes and both for the same foot. My own boots went for cash the day after Christmas. I fared better than Conley; I got a hundred dollars and a pair of shoes that I could wear.

All sorts of makeshifts were adopted to cover our persons as decency demanded. When I was captured, I was the proud possessor of a new staff uniform ornamented with gold lace. Five months later, my most intimate friends would have failed to recognize me in the ragged tramp who sat naked on the floor at Danville and robbed the ends of his trousers in order to reseat them. It was not until after I was paroled that I took those trousers off; I couldn't have done so before, because after sewing up the legs while I had them on, I couldn't get my feet through.

Although we all became disreputable in appearance, some of us kept up as best we could our proper relations of mutual respect. I am sorry to say that military rank was soon ignored by the majority of officers in Prison No. 3, and that selfishness and dishonesty added to our cup of humiliation and suffering; yet I know that much should be forgiven in men who had almost lost their natural humanity. Our nerves were worn ragged. The slightest of provocations would cause a quarrel. Two cavalry officers, Captain Harris and Lieutenant McGraw, fought over the possession of a few rusty cans. The captain's shirt was torn to shreds, and since it was the only shirt he had, and the remainder of his wardrobe consisted of a well-ventilated pair of trousers, he was to be pitied. . . .

Life became so unbearable, and the prospects of a general exchange so delusive, that on December 10th about a hundred of the prisoners, the most courageous, or the most wanting in judgment, made an attempt to break prison and escape, and failed miserably. Unaware of the attempt to be made, I, with five others, was walking on the ground floor for exercise when I saw two officers close in on the sentry by the door that opened into the yard, one seizing his gun and the other taking him by the throat to prevent him from giving an alarm. At the same moment another officer tried to choke into silence the sentry by the stairs, but his grip was too weak, and the brave rebel, in spite of threats, shouted, "Turn out the guard!" The cry was at once repeated outside, and muskets were thrust in through the sashless windows. I have outlived the sensation of that moment, but I know that I was never more conscious of being in the presence of death than when I caught a glimpse of eternity in the black muzzle of a gun held within six feet of my breast. The other promenaders were as helplessly exposed, and we all might have been the victims of nervous and frightened sentries, but Colonel Smith came running and shouted, "Cease firing!" He was not quick enough, however, to save the officer who had grappled with the sentry by the stairs. That unfortunate prisoner was shot through the bowels, and his wound was cruelly aggravated as he made his way up the two flights to the top floor, hurriedly helped along by some of his associates. Colonel Smith came inside, ordered a number of prisoners into close confinement, and told us that a keg of powder was buried under the prison, and that if another attempt to escape should be made, he would blow us all to hell.

—SMALL, *The Road to Richmond*

2. "THE SUFFERING AMONG THE SICK AND WOUNDED"

Capture and imprisonment was pretty much the same, East and West. This journal of an unknown Union soldier, captured after Chickamauga, tells of the hardships, the food shortages, the incompetent medical care, the dirt and disease that seemed to be the common lot of all prisoners.

STEWARD'S HOSPITAL, Sept. 20, 1863.—At nine A.M. this morning I was wounded and captured by the rebels. I was hurried to the rear as fast as possible, with quite a number of our wounded. We were taken to Steward's Hospital, which is situated some three miles from the battle-field. We were put out upon the ground, with no shelter whatever, and a great many of us had no blankets. There were some eighty of our wounded at this place. Dr. Hamilton (rebel) came round and examined our wounds; some of the worst cases washed and partially dressed. Toward evening, all that were able were marched off. . . .

Sept. 21.—Today the rebels have been so jubilant on what they term the "Yankee rout," that they have taken no notice of us whatever; the men are lying weltering in their blood, suffering beyond description.

Sept. 22.—Today we had a man die. Dr. Story (rebel) has been put in charge of all the Yankee wounded. He appears to be a gentleman, but as yet there has been nothing done for the wounded, who are suffering intensely.

Sept. 23.—Today the Doctor dressed most of the wounds. Many of the men have shattered limbs, and are suffering beyond description. We have had nothing to eat since we came here.

Sept. 24.—Two of our men died today. They had shattered limbs, and the worms had got into their wounds; had they had proper attention, they probably could have been saved.

Sept. 25.—The rebels say they have driven Rosecrans over the river, also Burnside out of East-Tennessee. The doctors are having a spree over it. No attention has been paid to us today. There are two or three hundred rebel wounded here that have to be attended to first. One man died today.

Sept. 26.—Today we drew the first rations we have had since we came here. A ration consists of half a pint of corn-meal and two ounces of beef, a miserable pittance for a hungry man. No doctor has been near today. Some of the men are suffering intensely. . . .

Sept. 27.—We lost one man by death today. Two of the boys have had limbs amputated; both will probably die. The boys are suffering a great deal from their wounds; mortification has taken place in many instances, while some have worms in their wounds. Many are very sick; no medicine to be had.

Sept. 28.—We lost two by death today; arteries burst; surgeon absent; bled to death. We have had nothing to eat today. I believe they mean to starve us to death. It is a pitiful sight to see the haggard countenances of the men. Today they have sent two hundred rebel wounded to the hospitals. . . .

Sept. 30.—Today the boys are trading their pocket-knives and every thing they can for rations. There is scarcely five dollars among us. The miserable thieves robbed us of every thing we had. Today has been a day of intense suffering among our men. It has rained all day, and we have no shelter.

Oct. 1.—It rained all night last night. We look like a set of drowned rats. Some of the boys are very sick; many must die with such treatment. The sergeant of the guard procured a tent for eight of us. Dr. Story does all he can for us. We drew our pittance of corn-meal today.

Oct. 2.—We expect to leave here today. I sincerely hope we will. I long to be in God's country once more, and behold the good old flag again. The lice and filth here are intolerable.

Oct. 3.—No signs of leaving yet. Dr. Story is doing his best to make us comfortable, but we have no bandages to dress our wounds with. Two deaths today.

Oct. 4.—Today is very cold. We have no blankets, hence there is a great deal of suffering from cold. Our rations have run out, and taking all things into consideration, it would be hard to embitter our condition.

Oct. 5.—Heavy cannonading has been going on in the front all day. The rebels say they are shelling Chattanooga. We learned today that the armistice was over, and that we would have to take a trip to Richmond. The trip will doubtless kill quite a number of us. We got our mush today. Intense suffering from cold nights.

Oct. 6.—We expected to leave today for Atlanta, but for some reason the ambulances have not come. All we have to eat is mush, with little or no salt in it. Many are suffering from diarrhoea.

Oct. 7.—Today we drew rations of flour. Captain Foster, Forty-second Illinois, is baking bread. One of our men died today. We have lost fourteen by death since we came here.

Oct. 8.—At nine A.M. this morning we were stowed in lumber-wagons and hauled to Ringgold, a distance of eight miles, over the roughest road I ever travelled. Many of the men were so sick that they could not raise their heads.

Oct. 9.—Last night they put one hundred and eight of us into box-cars and brought us to Dalton, where we stopped for the night. We had to sleep in the cars, and they gave us no supper. The night was very cold. It was heart-rending to witness the suffering among the sick and wounded. This morning we left for Dalton without breakfast, and arrived at Atlanta, Ga., at six A.M. We were then taken to a military prison, where we now lie upon the ground with no shelter or fires. Our wounds have not been dressed for three days; the stench is awful.

Oct. 10.—We are under the charge of our own doctors here, but the rebels won't furnish bandages to dress the wounds. I never suffered so from hunger in all my life. They have been promising us rations all day, and now they tell us they will be here early in the morning. The boys are selling their rings and every thing they have for something to eat.

Oct. 11.—We are a little more comfortable today; the surgeons have amputated several limbs and dressed all the wounds. One man died this morning. On the seventh instant, one of our men was shot for going too near the fence. One of our officers is here, carrying around a thirty-two pound ball and chain; several of the men are handcuffed.

—"Journal of a Union Soldier"

3. SUFFERING IN ANDERSONVILLE PRISON

Andersonville, in southwestern Georgia, was the largest and the most dreaded of Confederate prisons. The first captured Federals arrived there early in 1864; by midsummer the number of prisoners had increased to some 32,000, and this though the prison was originally designed to accommodate only 10,000. In no other prison were conditions so crowded or so wretched; the prisoners lived in tents on the bare ground or in improvised huts; the food was woefully insufficient; the water polluted; sanitary facilities wholly inadequate. By the end of the war about 50,000 prisoners—all of them privates—had been received at Andersonville, and about one third of these had died. After peace the superintendent, Captain Henry Wirz, was tried for murder and executed.

This account differs from most prison narratives in that it comes from a friendly source. Eliza Andrews was one of that notable galaxy of Confederate woman diarists who tell us so much about social life in the South during the war. After the war she wrote two books on botany and three novels.

January 27, 1865.—While going our rounds in the morning we found a very important person in Peter Louis, a paroled Yankee prisoner, in the employ of Captain Bonham. The captain keeps him out of the stockade, feeds and clothes him, and in return reaps the benefit of his skill. Peter is a French Yankee, a shoemaker by trade, and makes as beautiful shoes as I ever saw imported from France. My heart quite softened toward him when I saw his handiwork, and little Mrs. Sims was so overcome that she gave him a huge slice of her Confederate fruitcake. I talked French with him, which pleased him greatly, and Mett and I engaged him to make us each a pair of shoes. I will feel like a lady once more, with good shoes on my feet. I expect the poor Yank is glad to get away from Anderson on any terms. Although matters have improved somewhat with the cool weather, the tales that are told of the condition of things there last summer are appalling. Mrs. Brisbane heard all about it from Father Hamilton, a Roman Catholic priest from Macon, who has been working like a good Samaritan in those dens of filth and misery. It is a shame to us Protestants that we have let a Roman Catholic get so far ahead of us in this work of charity and mercy. Mrs. Brisbane says Father Hamilton told her that during the summer the wretched prisoners burrowed in the ground like moles to protect themselves from the sun. It was not safe to give them material to build shanties as they might use it for clubs to overcome the guard. These underground huts, he said, were alive with vermin and stank like charnel houses. Many of the prisoners were stark naked, having not so much as a shirt to their backs. He told a pitiful story of a Pole who had no garment but a shirt, and to make it cover him better, he put his legs into the sleeves and tied the tail around his neck. The others guyed him so on his appearance and the poor wretch was so disheartened by suffering that one day he deliberately stepped over the dead line and stood there till the guard was forced to shoot him. But what I can't understand is that a Pole, of all people in the world, should come over here and try to take away our liberty when his own country is in the hands of oppressors. One would think that the Poles, of all nations in the world, ought to sympathize with a people fighting for their liberties.

Father Hamilton said that at one time the prisoners died at the rate of a hundred and fifty a day, and he saw some of them die on the ground without a rag to lie on or a garment to cover them. Dysentery was the most fatal disease, and as they lay on the ground in their own excrements, the smell was so horrible that the good father says he was often obliged to rush from their presence to get a breath of pure air. It is dreadful. My heart aches for the poor wretches, Yankees though they are, and I am afraid God will suffer some terrible retribution to fall upon us for letting such things happen. If the Yankees ever should come to southwest Georgia and go to Anderson and see the graves there, God have mercy on the land! And yet what can we do?

The Yankees themselves are really more to blame than we, for they won't exchange these prisoners, and our poor, hard-pressed Confederacy has not the means to provide for them when our own soldiers are starving in the field. Oh, what a horrible thing war is when stripped of all its pomp and circumstance!

—ANDREWS, *The War-Time Journal of a Georgia Girl*

4. THE BRIGHT SIDE OF LIBBY PRISON

Next to Andersonville Libby was the most famous, or notorious, of Confederate prisons. Originally a vacant warehouse in Richmond, it was taken over by General Winder, provost marshal of the city, and made into a prison for commissioned officers; privates from the Virginia battles were housed at Belle Isle in the James. There were a number of spectacular escapes from Libby, and after the Dahlgren Raid of 1864, designed to free the prisoners, Libby was largely abandoned in favor of prisons farther to the south.

Frank Moran, who here tells something of the brighter side of prison life, was a captain of the 73rd New York Volunteers who was captured at Gettysburg and imprisoned first at Libby and later at Macon, Georgia, and Charleston, South Carolina.

THE building had a frontage from east to west of 145 feet, and a depth from north to south of 105 feet. It stood isolated from other buildings, with streets passing its front, rear, and west ends, and with a vacant space on the east of about sixty feet in width. The portion of the building devoted to the use of the prisoners consisted of nine rooms, each 102 feet in length by forty-five feet in breadth. The ceiling was eight feet high, except in the upper rooms, which were higher, better lighted, and better ventilated, owing to the pitch of the roof. Rickety, unbanistered stairs led from the lower to the upper rooms, and all the rooms of the upper floors were connected by doors, leaving free access from one to the other. With the exception of a few rude bunks and tables in the upper and lower west rooms, which were respectively termed "Streight's room" and "Milroy's room," and four long tables in the lower middle or "kitchen room," there was no furniture in the prison. The north windows commanded a partial view of the hilly portion of the city. From the east the prisoners could look off toward the Rocketts and City Point. The south windows looked out upon the canal and James river, with Manchester opposite and Belle Isle, while from the windows of the upper west room could be seen Castle Thunder, Jefferson Davis's mansion, and the Confederate capital.

Libby prison was a vast museum of human character, where the chances of war had brought into close communion every type and temperament; where military rank was wholly ignored, and all shared a common lot. At the time referred to, there were about 1200 Union officers there, of all ranks, and representing every loyal state. They were not men who would have sought each other's society from natural or social affinity, but men who had been involuntarily forced together by the fortunes of war, which, like politics, often "makes strange bedfellows." There were men of all sizes and nationalities. Youth and age, and titled men of Europe, who had enlisted in our cause, might be found among the captives. There were about thirty doctors, as many ministers, a score of journalists and lawyers, a few actors, and a proportionate representation from all trades and professions that engage men in civil life. Among them were travelers and scholars, who had seen the world, and could entertain audiences for hours with narratives of their journeyings; indeed, among the attractions of the prison was the pleasure derived by intimate association with men of bright and cultured minds; men who had often led their squadrons on the tough edge of battle and who in their history presented the best types of modern chivalry. It was indeed a remarkable gathering and the circumstances are not likely to arise that will reassemble its counterpart again in this generation. All in all, Libby prison, from the vast mixture of its inmates, and from all its peculiar surroundings, was doubtless the best school of human nature ever seen in this country.

It will not seem strange, therefore, that men of such varied talents, tastes, and dispositions, shipwrecked in this peculiar manner, should begin to devise ways and means to turn the tedious hours of prison life to some account. To this end meetings and consultations were held to set on foot amusements and instruction for the prisoners.

A minstrel troupe was organized, and its talent would compare favorably with some professional companies of to-day. A number of musical instruments were purchased, forming a respectable orchestra.

Refreshing music often enlivened the place when the weary-souled prisoner had laid down for the night. If there ever was a time and place when that old melody, "Home Sweet Home," touched the tenderest chords of the soldier's heart, it was on Christmas Eve of 1863, behind the barred windows of Libby prison. Chess, checkers, cards, or such other games occupied much of our time. Some busied themselves with making bone rings or ornaments, many of them carved with exquisite skill. . . .

At night the prisoners covered the floor completely, lying in straight rows like prostrate lines of battle, and when one rolled over all must necessarily do the same. It was inevitable that among such large numbers there should appear the usual infliction of snorers, whose discord at times drew a terrific broadside of boots, tin cans, and other convenient missiles, which invariably struck the wrong man. Among our number was one officer whose habit of grinding his teeth secured him a larger share of room at night than was commonly allowed to a prisoner, and his comrades hoped that a special exchange might restore him to his family; for certainly he was a man that would be missed wherever he had lodged. On a memorable night when this gentleman was entertaining us with his "tooth solo," one comrade who had been kept awake for the three previous nights, after repeatedly shouting to the nocturnal minstrel to "shut up," arose in wrath, and, picking his steps in the dark among his prostrate comrades, arrived at last near a form which he felt certain was that of the disturber of the peace. With one mighty effort, he bestowed a kick in the ribs of the victim, and hurriedly retreated to his place. Then arose the kicked officer, who was not the grinder at all, and made an address to his invisible assailant, employing terms and vigorous adjectives not seen in the New Testament, vehemently declaring in a brilliant peroration that it was enough to be compelled to spend wakeful nights beside a man who made nights hideous with serenades, without being kicked for him. He resumed his bed amid thunderous applause, during which the grinder was awakened and was for the first time made aware of the cause of the enthusiasm.

The spirit of Yankee enterprise was well illustrated by the publication of a newspaper by the energetic chaplain of a New York regiment. It was entitled *The Libby Prison Chronicle*. True, there were no printing facilities at hand, but, undaunted by this difficulty, the editor obtained and distributed quantities of manuscript paper among the prisoners who were leaders in their several professions, so that there was soon organized an extensive corps of able correspondents, local reporters, poets, punsters, and witty paragraphers, that gave the chronicle a pronounced success. Pursuant to previous announcement, the "editor" on a stated day each week, would take up his position in the center of the upper east room, and, surrounded by an audience limited only by the available space, would read the articles contributed during the week.

"The Prison Minstrels" were deservedly popular. The troupe was organized and governed by strictly professional rules. Nothing but the possession and display of positive musical or dramatic talent could command prominence, and as a natural consequence it was a common occurrence to see a second lieutenant carrying off the honors of the play, and the colonel of his regiment carrying off the chairs as a "supe." Our elephant, by the way, deserves especial mention, not only because of his peculiar construction, but because both intellectually and physically he differed from all elephants we had previously seen. The animal was composed of four United States officers, which certainly gave him unusual rank. One leg was a major, a second a naval officer, a third a captain of cavalry, and the last leg was by the happy thought of the astute manager an army surgeon. A quantity of straw formed the body; the tusks and trunk were improvised from the meager resources of our "property room." The whole was covered ingeniously by five army blankets. Indeed the elephant, seen by the "footlights" (four candles set in bottles), was pronounced by the critics of *The Libby Prison Chronicle* "a masterpiece of stage mechanism."

—Moran, "Libby's Bright Side"

5. LUTHER HOPKINS RECALLS PRISON LIFE AT POINT LOOKOUT

Prison life in the North was only a little less odious than in the South. Point Lookout, one of the largest of all Northern prisons, was at the point where the Potomac flows into Chesapeake Bay; as Luther Hopkins here tells us its location was far from salubrious, and the mortality rate was high. Charles Francis Adams, who visited it shortly after Hopkins was there, found it on the whole well run and its hospital as good as any in the North.

Hopkins was a Virginia boy who enlisted, at the age of seventeen, in Stuart's cavalry, was captured and exchanged after Gettysburg, and was captured again after Yellow Tavern, May 1864.

THE steamer on which we were placed and given such a good, substantial dinner, soon after this took its departure down the James and landed us at Fortress Monroe. . . . After remaining there a few days the Confederates were again marched aboard a steamer and taken to "Point Lookout," where a regular prison-camp had been established. I think there were about 15,000 prisoners at this camp guarded by Negro troops, which made our Southern blood boil. As the darkies used to say, "The bottom rail had got on top."

The camp was on a point of land formed by the junction of the Potomac river and Chesapeake Bay on the north side of the river. I imagine there were about 20 acres of ground, surrounded by a high board fence, probably about 14 feet high. Just below the top was built a platform about three feet wide, and on this platform the guards walked to and fro with their guns on their shoulders. From their position they could overlook the whole camp, as the ground was perfectly level. There was also a strong guard inside the camp, while artillery and regiments of infantry were stationed near the camp to guard it from outside attack, and one or more gunboats patrolled the waters that nearly surrounded the camp.

Notwithstanding this precaution, occasionally prisoners made their escape. One ingenious method that baffled our guards for a long time was the following:

The prisoners were allowed to go outside of the enclosure on the beach to bathe. And if an empty barrel or box happened to be floating on the water, a prisoner in bathing would watch his opportunity, slip his head under the barrel or box, and then as the tide drifted up the river, would follow it, keeping as near the shore as necessary until he got beyond the reach of the guard, and then take to the woods.

The punishment for trying to escape was cruel. Those who were caught at it were strung up to a pole by the thumbs, with the tips of their toes just touching the ground. Sometimes the men would faint, and had to be cut down.

Upon the whole, prison life was very monotonous. It was such an unhealthy camp that the prisoners considered that they had a better chance for their lives fighting in the army.

The water was brackish and unpleasant to the taste. The only water we had was from pumps scattered about over the camps, and during the four months that I was there the pumps were always surrounded by a thirsty crowd of from 40 to 50 prisoners, each with his tin cup, trying to wedge his way in, that he might quench his thirst.

The food, while good, was very scant. Breakfast consisted of coffee and a loaf of bread, the latter under ordinary circumstances, with vegetables and other food, would probably suffice for two meals. This loaf was given us at breakfast, and if we ate it all then we went without bread for dinner. If there was any left over we took it to our tents, laid it on the ground, and saved it for the next meal.

The dinners consisted of a tin cup of soup (generally bean or other vegetable), a small piece of meat on a tin plate, on which a little vinegar was poured to prevent scurvy. My recollection is we had no other meal, but my mind is not perfectly clear on this point. I do know, however, that we were always hungry, and the chief topic of conversation was the sumptuous meals we had sat down to in other days. . . .

We were told that the short rations were given us in retaliation for the scanty food supplied to their soldiers in Southern prisons.

The hospitals were crowded all the time, and there were many sick in the camp waiting their opportunity to go into hospitals.

We lived in what is known as Sibley tents, shaped like a bell, with an opening in the top about 15 inches in diameter.

There were 12 men to a tent, who, when they slept, arranged themselves in a circle, like the spokes of a wagon, with their feet toward the center. These tents were as close as they could stand on the ground, with wide avenues between every two rows of tents, thus allowing every tent to front on an avenue.

Every day the prisoners were called out of their tents and formed in line; roll was called and the prisoners searched. And while they were being searched, the guards were searching the tents. For just what purpose this search was done I do not know, unless it was for fear that arms might be smuggled in to be used by the prisoners for making their escape.

Many of the prisoners had a peculiar affection of the eyes, caused, perhaps, by the glare from the white tents, the sand, and the reflection from the water. There was nothing green to be seen anywhere, consequently many of the prisoners became blind for a portion of the 24 hours. Just as the sun was sinking behind the fence they would become totally blind, and had to be led by someone. As morning light came the blindness would disappear.

Some of the prisoners who were mechanics or artisans got work outside, but I believe they got no pay except full rations and the privilege of bringing things into camp, such as blocks of wood and pieces of metal. Out of these were manufactured a great many interesting little articles—small steam locomotives, wooden fans, rings from rubber buttons set with gold and silver, and sometimes gems. One ingenious fellow built a small distillery and made whiskey from potato rinds or whatever refuse he could pick up, and got drunk on the product.

All about the camp were boards on which these manufactured articles were exposed for sale. A cracker would buy a chew of tobacco. The tobacco was cut up into chews and half chews. The crackers were brought in by the men who went out to work. I cannot recall all the curious things that were exposed for sale within the camp. . . .

The nurses were all men, chosen from among the prisoners. I never saw a woman the whole time I was in prison.

The hospitals were long tents, each holding about 30 cots. As soon as a patient died, he was taken out to the dead-house, the sheets changed, and another brought in.

When I was first taken there I remarked to my neighbor that I did not think that was very prudent (meaning the placing of a new patient at once on a bed that was still warm from the body that had just been removed. He replied that the bed that I was on had been occupied by a smallpox patient, and I was put on it a few minutes after the patient was taken out.

However, there was a separate hospital for contagious diseases, and the patient had been removed as soon as the disease developed.

Most of those who went into the hospital died. The dead were all carried at once to the dead-house on stretchers, and once a day a two-horse wagon came in, and their bodies were laid in it like so much cord wood, uncoffined, taken out and buried in long trenches. The trenches were seven feet wide and three feet deep, and the bodies were laid across the trench side by side and covered with earth.

I had been in prison about four months when news came that the two Governments had agreed upon an exchange of prisoners; it only included the sick in the hospitals. Of course, every patient in the hospital was on the anxious bench, wondering whether he would be included among the fortunate ones. Some days afterward a corps of physicians came to the hospital tents to examine the different patients who lay on the cots, taking the name of one and leaving another. I happened to be among those who were selected for exchange. The object seemed to be to take only those who were not liable to be fit for service soon.

—HOPKINS, *From Bull Run to Appomattox*

6. THE AWFUL CONDITIONS AT FORT DELAWARE

Fort Delaware was the Andersonville of the North—the most dreaded of Northern prisons. Located on an island in the Delaware River, much of it was below water—which was held back by dykes—and the flimsy barracks in which the men lived were cold and damp. Unlike most prisons, Fort Delaware housed both officers and privates. Young Shotwell, whom we have met before, was captured on the eve of the Battle of Cold Harbor and imprisoned first at Point Lookout and later at Fort Delaware.

July 12, 1864.—I have just witnessed a sight that made my blood boil. When I first arrived here I made the acquaintance of a handsome young officer; Captain William H. Gordon, from West Virginia, a native of Brooke County, not far from Wheeling. After some years' service he went home on furlough and was captured while returning to the Army.

His captors were renegades, Southern born, but wearing Yankee blue; and to furnish an excuse for their malevolent treatment, they charged him with being on a recruiting expedition inside of their lines; just as I was put in irons as a spy, tho' simply on a legitimate scouting expedition with arms in my hands, and wearing our uniform.

On Saturday, Captain Gordon, and Mr. E. J. Debett, a Democrat, held as a "political prisoner," were marched out of the pen, stripped of their clothes, and dressed in the castoff blue trousers of the Yankees; after which they were put in the "Chain gang," or gang of condemned felons from the Yankee Army, undergoing sentence to hard labor for various crimes. Several hundred of this class are on the island; deserters, bounty jumpers, murderers, thieves, etc., all of whom are compelled to haul heavy loads of stone or lumber for the repair of dykes or buildings. In strange contrast of cause and effect, a handsome Gothic Chapel was built for the use of the garrison, by the labor of these miserable malefactors—hardened old sinners, who never before were inside of a church even as workmen. Into such companionship was young Gordon thrust, and today I saw his tall figure clad in shabby rags, and "paired" with a greasy looking convict, dragging at the rope of a heavy cart together with about fifty other men; while a low-browed brutal looking Yankee, with a long stick or goad, sat atop the load of bricks of granite, and continuously yelled at the team, thus: "Pull, d——n you, pull! What the h——l you hanging back for? Who's that making signs at them windows?" The last speech was meant for Captain Gordon, who as he passed our windows looked up with a sad smile as if to say: "This is hard! but I shall endure to the end." . . .

August 10th:—How strange a thing it is to be hungry! actually craving something to eat, and constantly thinking about it from morning till night, from day to day; for weeks and months!

It did not seem possible for a man thus to worry over lack of nourishment, keeping his mind continually engrossed with anger against those who starve us, and with longing for food, the German philosopher's "earnest aspirations after the unattainable."

For the past month our rations have been six, sometimes four hard crackers and 1/10 of a pound of rusty bacon (a piece the size of a hen's egg) for the twenty-four hours.

But for five days past we have not had a morsel of meat of any kind; the cooks alleging that the supply ran short and "spoiled." (For a fortnight before it ceased to be issued, the rations were so full of worms, and stank so that one had to hold his nose while eating it!) But now we receive *none at all!* Talk about Andersonville! We would gladly exchange rations with the Yankees there!

For my part I cannot swallow very fat meat, or any that is in the very least tainted, so that for a long time I have subsisted on little else than hard tack and water. And such water! There has been no rain for some time; the tanks are no longer adequate for the supply of the pen even when full; therefore the Yankees have a small vessel that is used as a water boat, and is designed to ascend the creek sufficiently far to obtain fresh water. But the

Thomas Nast

Women Working in the Fields

Illustrated London News

The Draft Riots in New York

A. R. Waud

Refugee Train Fleeing Sherman's Army

boat doesn't go above tide water, hence brings back a brackish *briny* fluid scarcely one whit better than the water from the Delaware, which oozes through the ditches in the pen.

The standing rain water of course breeds a dense swarm of animalculae, and when the hose pipes from the water boat are turned into the tanks the interior sediment is stirred up, and the whole contents become a turgid, salty, jellified mass of waggle tails, worms, dead leaves, dead fishes, and other putrescent abominations, most of which is visible to the eye in a cup of it.

The *smell* of it is enough to revolt the stomach of a fastidious person; to say nothing of the thought of making one's throat a channel for such stuff. Yet, when the tanks are empty—as they are for half a day once or oftener in the week—the cry for this briny liquid is universal, because it creates a thirst equally as much as it quenches it, but if it were not so, the intense heat which beats upon this flat, parched island would make us swallow soluble salts for temporary relief.

The surface of the Pea Patch being of alluvial mud, becomes very porous and damp in wet weather, but parched and as hard as rock in the long dry season. No shade is there, no elevation, no breeze; only a low, flat, sultry, burning oven! Today the heat is so intense that men by hundreds are seen sweltering on their backs, fairly gasping for breath, like fish dying on a sand beach.

August 11th:—Shocking reports of the ravage of pestilence both in this pen and the other. I remain so closely in my bunk, or walking to and fro in the yard that I had no idea there was so much sickness prevailing until two cases of smallpox had been taken from my own division.

Horrible to relate, the hospital is full and men are no longer taken out until dying or dead. One of the smallpox cases (since dead I learn) was poor C., who slept directly over my bunk. He was very dirty and annoying while in health, and we had some words about his stepping on my blankets with muddy boots while climbing to his bunk; but after he took the fearful disease I felt sorry for him, and helped to lift him down from his tier and carry him to the gate. Strange to say, I cannot realize the danger, though most of the prisoners are getting nervous. So are the garrison. . . .

Oct. 4th:—The catching and eating of the huge rats which infest the island has become a common thing. It is a curious sight; grown men, whiskered and uniformed officers who have already "set a squadron in the field," lurking, club in hand, near one of the many breathing holes, which the long tailed rodents have cut in the hard earth, patiently awaiting a chance to strike a blow for "fresh meat and rat soup"—for dinner! They generally succeed in getting one or more rats at a sitting. Indeed the surface of the earth in some portions of the yard seems to be honeycombed by these amphibious burrowers, which are not the ordinary house rat, but a larger species of water rat, something like the Norway variety.

They are eaten by fully a score of the officers, and apparently with relish.

When deviled or stewed, they resemble young squirrels *in looks*. I have not yet mustered stomach enough to nibble at one—though once—three years ago on the Potomac island—their brethren nibbled at me in no pleasant fashion. The flesh of these rodents is quite white, and when several are on a plate with plenty of dressing, they look so appetizing one cannot help regretting his early mis-education, or prejudice. That our antipathy to rats is all prejudice the rat eaters firmly assert. "Why," quoth one of them—"you eat wagon loads of hogs, and everybody knows a rat is cleaner than a hog. Rats are just as dainty as squirrels or chickens. Try a piece?" "No, thanks, my 'prejudices' unfortunately, are not yet abated." . . .

Oct. 9th:—Ugh! Fingers are too cold to hold the pen! Dozens of us have lain since breakfast, curled up under our blankets—thinking, thinking, and shivering with intense chilliness; not comfortable a moment in the day!

The wintry blasts sweep up the broad river, and across the flat island, with the keenness of an ocean cyclone; roaring round the prison yard, whistling through thousands of crevices in the open barracks with a chill rasping sound that increases the cold by imagination.

As for comfort, it is out of the question for the well and hearty. How much worse for the sick and debilitated! God help us this dreary winter! I dread to see night come, for then I must surrender the blankets borrowed from my comrades, and I have only half of one to sleep on and half for a covering.

And yet we are much better off than many of the poor fellows in the Privates' Pen! There are ten, or more, thousand men packed into a square of about six acres—thousands of them *barefooted*, not one in twenty supplied with underclothing. Even of those taken out to work the greater number are shoeless and hatless, and yet they gladly consent to go out and drag the heavy stone carts as long as they can stand, simply *for a few extra crusts of bread* to appease their constant, unsatisfied hunger! . . .

Stoves have been put up, one in each shed, but there is not fuel enough furnished to keep up even a semblance of fire more than half the time, and with a crowd of one hundred and ten shivering men to make a double circle around it, there is not much chance for a diffident person to get anywhere near it.

For three weeks I have not been comfortably warm during the day, nor able to sleep over two hours any night; have not tasted warm food; have not been free from the pangs of actual hunger any moment during the time. Our ration is still three hardtacks at 9 A.M. and three more at 3 P.M. with a morsel of rusty meat, and an occasional gill of rice soup. Stuff at which no ordinary respectable Negro's *dog* would condescend to sniff at, down South.

The hardships that we, officers and gentlemen, *prisoners of war*, not criminals, suffer, and which have tumbled nearly ten thousand Southerners into the pits on yonder Jersey shore, are not *necessary;* are not the result of poverty, blockade, lack of supplies, nor from necessary vigor of discipline to prevent escape. It is sheer cruelty!

—HAMILTON, ed., "The Papers of Randolph Abbott Shotwell"

7. THE PRIVATIONS OF LIFE IN ELMIRA PRISON

Elmira, opened in May 1864 to relieve pressure on the older prisons, was one of the largest of the Northern prisons, housing, by the end of the war, over 12,000 Confederates. At first the prisoners had only tents; with the coming of winter rude barracks were constructed and as these were equipped with stoves they protected the Southern boys from the worst rigors of an upstate New York winter. A feud between the commandant and the surgeon was partly responsible for bad conditions and a high sickness and mortality rate: altogether some 3,000 of Elmira's inmates died during one year of operation.

Marcus Toney was a Tennessee boy whose Privations of a Private *is one of the better of the little-known Civil War narratives.*

THE prison camp contained some forty acres of land about one mile above the city [of Elmira, New York], and near the Chemung River, a beautiful, clear, limpid mountain stream of very pure water. The stockade that surrounded the camp was much like the one at Point Lookout, but built of heavier material, and the ends of the upright planks going some eighteen inches into the ground. The planks were about sixteen feet high, and nailed to heavy sills, which were supported by large posts set deep in the ground. The stockade was about sixteen feet high, and three feet from the top was the parapet walkway or beat of the guards, who were stationed some forty feet apart, and were relieved every two hours by other guards. Commencing at nine o'clock at night, or taps, they would cry out their posts all through the hours of the night, as "Post No 1, nine o'clock; all is well," which would be taken up by all posts, and repeated all around the stockade. Inside the stockade, about fifty feet apart, were large coal oil lamps nailed near the center of the stockade, with large reflectors, which were lit after nightfall, and the guards on the parapet would be able to see any one approaching.

The tents in which we slept were struck every morning in order for inspection. The prisoners in one of the tents had a false floor laid and covered with dirt hard packed so it would have the same appearance as the ground floor in the other tents. Under this false floor was one of the prisoners digging day and night. There were six occupants of this particular tent, and by making a detail one man was digging all the time. They were tunneling to get under the fence. The tunnel was only about two feet under the ground, and they had to go about sixty feet distance to get under the fence; the only implement they had was a large knife. They had a small box to which was attached a string at both ends, and when the fellow at the farther side had filled his box he gave a pull of the string, and the other fellow just under the false floor of the tent would pull the box under the floor, pile up the dirt, and at night they would remove the false floor, gather the dirt in their hands, fill their haversacks, and scatter the dirt along the new-made streets. When they reached the upright planks of the stockade they had to go over a foot lower than the tunnel in order to get under the end of the planks. Finally the tunnel was completed, and one of the boys crawled through, poked his head on the outside, and came and reported bright moonshine, disclosed the camp of the guards under patrol across the street, and a number of pieces of artillery in position along the camp; so they waited for the moon to go down before they commenced their underground journey. The plan was that the last of the six to leave should notify as many of the prisoners as he could, in order that they might take advantage of it; but only fifteen got out, and we heard that they reached Canada in safety. . . .

In a military prison it was very difficult to get information from the outside world. No papers were allowed, and the papers received had been opened and read; if there was anything contraband, you did not get it. When you wrote a letter it was left unsealed, and when the prison authorities examined it they stamped it "Prisoner's letter, approved," and then sealed and mailed it. Money was contraband of war, for a fellow might bribe his way out; therefore, whenever a remittance came to a prisoner, it was turned over to the sutler, who opened an account with the owner, and he could purchase all he wished so long as the funds held out; but when money went, a prisoner's credit was *non est*.

Until I reached prison I did not know what a slave to habit man was. I have seen men go hungry a day and save their rations and trade them for tobacco. I have seen a prisoner discharge a quid of tobacco from his mouth and other one pick it up, dry and smoke it. They used the black navy tobacco, sold in prison at the rate of one dollar per pound. They would cut it into little squares; each square would be called a chew, and five chews five cents. We had all kinds of trade and traffics, and tobacco was one of the mediums of exchange. We had many barbers, and they would shave you for five chews of tobacco. When the barber would get more tobacco than he needed, he would sell five chews for a small loaf of bread, valued at five cents, or he could purchase a small piece of meat or a fresh rat each valued at five cents. These barbers carried square boxes with them, upon which they set their patients; and a fellow would have to be very patient, as they never used a hone or strap except their boots and shoes, and it was hard to tell which was the worst sufferer, the barber or his customer. . . .

Adjoining the cook house was a large shed with tables that would accommodate three hundred men, and there were in the shed about twenty tables which were higher than my waist when standing. . . . Seats were not allowed. The men were marched in in two ranks, and separated at the head of the table, making one rank face the other. Each man had a plate and spoon; in the plate were his bean soup and beans, by the side of his plate was a small piece of light bread, and on the bread a thin ration of salt pork. The rations were thus prepared: a baker who lived outside would come in daily and superintend the baking. In the cook house were a large number of iron kettles or caldrons in which the meat and beans were boiled. I suppose these caldrons would hold fifty gallons. The salt pork was shipped in barrels and rolled up to the caldrons, and with a pitchfork tossed in, then the beans—I have heard the boys say four beans to a gallon of water. Now when this is boiled down it gets very salty, and after three weeks of a diet of this kind a prisoner will commence to get sick. I thought for a while that the government was retaliating on us on account of Andersonville, but I afterwards believed that it was done by the army contractors. . . . I can say without hesitancy that the death rate here was higher than at any other prison North or South. . . .

A prisoner eating this diet will crave any kind of fresh meat. Marching through the camp one day was a prisoner in a barrel shirt, with placard, "I eat a dog"; another one bearing a barrel, with placard, "Dog Eater." The barrel shirt was one of the modes of punishment. The shirt was made by using a whisky or coal oil barrel, knocking out one end and in the other boring a hole so as to get the head through, and then putting on a placard to indicate the crime. It appeared that these prisoners had captured a lapdog owned by the baker who came into camp daily to bake the bread. The baker made complaint to Colonel Beall, and said that his wife and children would not have taken one hundred dollars for the dog. As the prisoners had nothing to pay with, they were treated to the barrel shirt. The punishment was a two hours' march followed by a soldier with a bayonet, and they were not allowed much rest till the two hours were completed.

I saw another barrel shirt, "I told a lie." A prisoner did not have much compunction of conscience, especially if he had lied to deceive the commandant, which he conceived to be his religious duty. A prisoner carrying a barrel shirt, "I stole my messmate's rations," was hissed all around the camp; and deservedly so, because a man who would steal from his messmates in prison deserved the most severe punishment; while the ones who carried the placard, "Dog Eater" had the sympathies of the entire camp, because many of them would have enjoyed a piece of fresh meat. When twitted about it they said: "It was not a common cur, but a Spitz, and tasted like mutton."

On account of the waste from the commissary a great many rodents from Elmira ran into the prison. As there were not any holes in which they could hide it was an easy catch for the boys by knocking them over with sticks, and there was quite a traffic in them. As there was very little currency in prison, tobacco, rats, pickles, pork, and light bread were mediums of exchange. Five chews of tobacco would buy a rat, a rat would buy five chews of tobacco, a loaf of bread would buy a rat, a rat would buy a loaf of bread, and so on. . . .

The bunks extended the length of the ward on each side, leaving an aisle in the center and two stoves in each ward, and the prisoners were not allowed to get very close to them in zero weather. With an open building, the heat was not very intense. The bunks were three high, and the boys occupying the top bunk had to do some climbing. They were wide enough to sleep two medium-sized men. Each one was allowed only a pair of blankets, and so had to sleep on the hard board; therefore, in extreme weather four slept in the space of two, using one pair of blankets to sleep on, which gave three for cover. Two of them slept with their heads toward the east, and two with their heads toward the west, and of course had to be on their sides; and when ready to change positions, one would call out, "All turn to the right"; and the next call would be, "All turn to the left." The turns had to be made as stated, or there would be collisions. Of course the men did not disrobe in extreme cold weather, and on awakening in the morning their feet would be in each other's faces.

—TONEY, *The Privations of a Private*

8. GENERAL MORGAN ESCAPES FROM THE OHIO PENITENTIARY

Famous as the "rebel raider" John Morgan was long a thorn in the side of the Union forces in the West. A veteran of the Mexican War Morgan enlisted as a scout in September 1861 and began his series of raids early the next year. Mounting success gave him overconfidence; in July 1863, as we have read, he crossed the Ohio River into Indiana and Ohio. Superior forces converged on him from all sides, and he was captured at New Lisbon, Ohio, and imprisoned in the state penitentiary at Columbus. On November 26 Morgan and a handful of his men effected one of the spectacular escapes of the war. Morgan was then given command of the Department of Southwest Virginia, and was killed in September of the following year.

There are literally hundreds of "escape" narratives; most of them follow a pattern and this one is sufficiently representative.

THEIR bedsteads were small iron stools, fastened to the wall with hinges. They could be hooked up or allowed to stand on the floor; and to prevent any suspicion, for several days before any work was attempted, they made it a habit to let them down and sit at their doors and read. Captain Hines superintended the work, while General Morgan kept watch to divert the attention of the sentinel, whose duty it was to come round during the day and observe if any thing was going on.

One day this fellow came in while Hokersmith was down under the floor boring away, and missing him said: "Where is Hokersmith?"

The General replied, "He is in my room, sick," and immediately pulled a document out of his pocket, and said to him: "Here is a memorial I have drawn up to forward to the Government at Washington; what do you think of it?"

The fellow, who perhaps could not read, being highly flattered at the General's condescension, took it and very gravely looked at it for several moments before he vouchsafed any reply; then, handing it back, he expressed himself highly pleased with it. In the mean time, Hokersmith had been signalled and came up, professing to feel "very unwell." This sentinel was the most difficult and dangerous obstacle in their progress, because there was no telling at what time he would enter during the day, and at night he came regularly every two hours to each cell, and inserted a light through the bars of their door, to see that they were quietly sleeping; and frequently, after he had completed his rounds, he would slip back in the dark, with a pair of India-rubber shoes on, to listen at their cells if any thing was going on. The General says that he would almost invariably know of his presence by a certain magnetic shudder which it would produce; but for fear that this acute sensibility might sometimes fail him, he broke up small particles of coal every morning, and sprinkled them before the cell door, which would always announce his coming.

Every thing was now ready to begin the work; so, about the latter part of October, they began to bore. All were busy—one making a rope-ladder by tearing and twisting up strips of bedtick, another making bowie-knives, and another twisting up towels. They labored perseveringly for several days, and after boring through nine inches of cement and nine thicknesses of brick placed edgewise, they began to wonder when they should reach the soft earth. Suddenly a brick fell through. What could this mean? What infernal chamber had they reached? It was immediately entered, and, to their great astonishment and joy, it proved to be an air-chamber extending the whole length of the row of cells. Here was an unexpected interposition in their favor. Hitherto they had been obliged to conceal their rubbish in their bedticks, each day burning a proportionate quantity of straw; now they had room enough for all they could dig. They at once commenced to tunnel at right angles with this air-chamber, to get through the foundation; and day after day they bored, day after day the blocks of granite were removed, and still the work before them seemed interminable.

After twenty-three days of unremitting labor, and getting through a granite wall of six feet in thickness, they reached the soil. They tunnelled up for some distance, and light began to shine. . . . This was the morning of the twenty-six day of November 1863. The next night, at twelve o'clock, was determined on as the hour at which they would attempt their liberty. Each moment that intervened was filled with dreadful anxiety and suspense, and each time the guard entered increased their apprehensions. The General says he had prayed for rain, but the morning of the twenty-seventh dawned bright and beautiful. The evening came, and clouds began to gather. How they prayed for them to increase! If rain should only begin, their chances of detection would be greatly lessened. . . . Nothing now remained to be done but for the General and Colonel Dick Morgan to change cells. The hour approached for them to be locked up. They changed coats, and each stood at the other's cell-door with his back exposed, and pretended to be engaged in making up their beds. As the turnkey entered they "turned in," and pulled their doors shut.

Six, eight, ten o'clock came. How each pulse throbbed as they quietly awaited the approach of twelve! It came—the sentinel passed his round—all well. After waiting a few moments to see if he intended to slip back, the signal was given. All quietly slipped down into the air-chamber, first stuffing their flannel-shirts and placing them in bed as they were accustomed to lie. As they moved quietly along through the dark recess to the terminus where they were to emerge from the earth, the General prepared to light a match.

As the lurid glare fell upon their countenances, a scene was presented which can never be forgotten. There were crouched seven brave men who had resolved to be free. They were armed with bowie-knives made out of case-knives. Life, in their condition, was scarcely to be desired, and the moment for the desperate chance had arrived. Suppose, as they emerged from the ground, that the dog should give the alarm—they could but die.

But few moments were spent in this kind of apprehension. The hour had arrived, and yet they came. Fortunately—yes, providentially—the night had suddenly grown dark and rainy, the dogs had retired to their kennels, and the sentinels had taken refuge under shelter. The inner wall, by the aid of the rope-ladder, was soon scaled, and now the outer one had to be attempted. Captain Taylor, (who, by the way, is a nephew of old Zack,) being a very active man, by the assistance of his comrades reached the top of the gate, and was enabled to get the rope over the wall. When the top was gained, they found a rope extending all around, which the General immediately cut, as he suspected that it might lead into the Warden's room. This turned out to be correct. They then entered the sentry-box on the wall and changed their clothes, and let themselves down the wall. In sliding down, the General skinned his hand very badly, and all were more or less bruised. Once down, they separated—Taylor and Shelton going one way, Hokersmith, Bennett, and McGee another, and General Morgan and Captain Hines proceeding immediately toward the dépôt.

The General had, by paying $15 in gold, succeeded in obtaining a paper which informed him of the schedule time of the different roads. The clock struck one, and he knew by hurrying he could reach the down-train for Cincinnati. He got there just as the train was moving off. He at once looked on to see if there were any soldiers on board, and espying a Union officer, he boldly walked up and took a seat beside him. He remarked to him that "as the night was damp and chilly, perhaps he would join him in a drink." He did so, and the party soon became very agreeable to each other.

The cars, in crossing the Scioto, have to pass within a short distance of the Penitentiary. As they passed, the officer remarked: "There's the hotel at which Morgan and his officers are spending their leisure."

"Yes," replied the General, "and I sincerely hope he will make up his mind to board there during the balance of the war, for he is a great nuisance."

When the train reached Xenia, it was detained by some accident more than an hour. Imagine his anxiety, as soldier after soldier would pass through the train, for fear that when the sentinel passed his round at two o'clock their absence might be discovered.

The train was due in Cincinnati at six o'clock. This was the hour at which they were turned out of their cells, and of course their escape would be then discovered. In a few moments after it would be known all over the country. The train, having been detained at Xenia, was running very rapidly to make up the time. It was already past six o'clock.

The General said to Captain Hines: "It's after six o'clock; if we go to the dépôt we are dead men. Now or never."

They went to the rear and put on the brakes. "Jump, Hines!" Off he went, and fell heels over head in the mud. Another severe turn of the brake, and the General jumped. He was more successful, and lighted on his feet.

There were some soldiers near, who remarked, "What in the h——l do you mean by jumping off the cars here?"

The General replied: "What in the d——l is the use of my going into town when I live here; and, besides, what business is it of yours?"

They went immediately to the river. They found a skiff, but no oars. Soon a little boy came over, and appeared to be waiting.

"What are you waiting for?" said the General.

"I am waiting for my load."

"What is the price of load?"

"Two dollars."

"Well, as we are tired and hungry, we will give you the two dollars, and you can put us over." So over he took them.

"Where does Miss —— live?"

"Just a short distance from here."

"Will you show me her house?"

"Yes, sir."

The house was reached, a fine breakfast was soon obtained, money and a horse furnished, a good woman's prayer bestowed, and off he went. From there, forward through Kentucky, every body vied with each other as to who should show him the most attention—even to the Negroes; and young ladies of refinement begged the honor to cook his meals.

—MOORE, ed., *The Rebellion Record*

XX

Behind the Lines: The North

TOTAL *war is a twentieth-century concept. The Civil War was very far from a total war, either North or South. Neither side ever mustered its full strength; neither side achieved anything like the unity we take for granted in our own time. Because the war was fought almost entirely in the South, and because the Confederacy, as the smaller and weaker of the belligerents, was required to organize a larger part of her resources, the impact of the war on the South was far deeper than it was on the North. To an extraordinary degree life went on, in the North, almost on a peacetime basis. Industry boomed; farmers expanded into the West; immigration kept up and with it city growth; colleges flourished; for the most part there was politics as usual. The war itself was fought haphazardly and inefficiently. The potential man power of the North was never effectively exploited; conscription was long delayed and, when it came, was badly administered. Business as usual was the order of the day, and profits and cost of living soared.*

What is perhaps most striking, to the contemporary student, is the pervasiveness in the North of disunity and disloyalty, fraud and corruption, incompetence and confusion in both the civilian and the military. Large segments of the population were unalterably opposed to the war; men like Vallandigham denounced it in language that was treasonable, and organizations like the Knights of the Golden Circle planned revolution, while the draft was sabotaged, bounty jumping was common, and desertion ran to over 10 per cent. Only because the Confederacy was afflicted by comparable disunity and disorganization did the Union eventually triumph.

It would require a whole volume to do justice to this large theme of the Union and the Confederacy—behind the lines. We have, of necessity, contented ourselves here with some of the more interesting and illuminating narratives.

1. WASHINGTON AS A CAMP

A political compromise dating back to the beginning of the Republic had located the capital city on the banks of the Potomac; with Maryland seething with secession sentiment and Virginia in the Confederacy, Washington was from the beginning peculiarly vulnerable, and its defense remained, throughout the war, a major strategical consideration. The location of the Confederate capital, too, was dictated by political considerations that deeply and

adversely affected military strategy; had the capital remained at Montgomery,
the whole strategy of the war, North and South, might have been different.

Noah Brooks, who here describes the capital as a camp, was a journalist
who was in Washington during the war as correspondent of the Sacramento
Union; *long-standing friendship with Lincoln gave him access to the White*
House and to many of the political leaders of the Republic. After the war
he served as editor of the New York Tribune *and the* New York Times,
and wrote a number of juveniles, the best known of which are The Boy
Emigrants *and* The Fairport Nine.

WASHINGTON was then a military camp, a city of barracks and
hospitals. The first thing that impressed the newly arrived stranger,
especially if he came, as I did, from the shores of the Peaceful Sea, where
the waves of war had not reached, was the martial aspect of the capital. Long
lines of army wagons and artillery were continually rumbling through the
streets; at all hours of the day and night the air was troubled by the clatter
of galloping squads of cavalry; and the clank of sabers, and the measured beat
of marching infantry, were ever present to the ear. The city was under
military government, and the wayfarer was liable to be halted anywhere in
public buildings, or on the outskirts of the city, by an armed sentry, who
curtly asked, "What is your business here?" Army blue was the predominat-
ing color on the sidewalks, sprinkled here and there with the gold lace of
officers. In the galleries of the Senate and House of Representatives, especially during the cold weather,—when the well-warmed Capitol was a convenient refuge for idle people,—great patches of the light blue of military
overcoats were to be marked among more somber colors of the groups of
visitors.

It was contrary to army regulations to supply soldiers with liquors, and
in most bar-rooms cards were conspicuous, bearing the legend, "Nothing sold
to soldiers." At some of the drinking-places, as if to soften the severity of the
dictum, was displayed an artistically painted group of the three arms of the
military service, over which were printed the words, "No liquors sold to."

Now and again, just after some great battle near at hand, like that of
Fredericksburg, or Chancellorsville, or Grant's long struggles in the Wilderness, the capital afforded a most distressful spectacle. Then, if at no other
time, the home-staying citizen realized something of the horrors of war.
The Washington hospitals were never empty, but at such times they were
crowded with the maimed and wounded, who arrived by hundreds as long
as the waves of sorrow came streaming back from the fields of slaughter.
One occasionally met a grim procession of the slightly wounded coming up
from the railway station at Alexandria or the steamboat landing from Aquia
Creek. They arrived in squads of a hundred or more, bandaged and limping,
ragged and disheveled, blackened with smoke and powder, and drooping
with weakness. They came groping, hobbling, and faltering, so faint and so
longing for rest that one's heart bled at the piteous sight. Here and there
were men left to make their way as best they could to the hospital, and who

were leaning on the iron railings or sitting wearily on the curbstones; but it was noticeable that all maintained the genuine American pluck in the midst of sorrow and suffering. As a rule, they were silent and unmurmuring; or if they spoke, it was to utter a grim joke at their own expense.

At the height of the war there were twenty-one hospitals in and about Washington. Some were in churches, public halls, the Patent Office, and other public buildings; but many were temporary wooden structures built for this special purpose. One of the representative hospitals was that of Harewood, erected by the government on the private grounds of W. W. Corcoran, in the outskirts of the city. There was a highly ornamented barn filled with hospital stores, clothing, and sanitary goods. A long row of cattle-sheds was boarded in and transformed into a hospital bakery. The temporary buildings constructed by the government were one story high, arranged in the form of a hollow square, row within row, and kept very neat and clean. . . .

Convalescents who had been discharged from the hospitals and who were not fit for military duty were assembled at a rendezvous in Alexandria, known as Camp Convalescent. This camp eventually became so crowded with the vast numbers of those who had been discharged from the hospitals or were stragglers from the army, that its condition was properly characterized as "infamous." More than ten thousand men, some of whom in the depth of winter were obliged to sleep on the cold ground, under canvas shelter and without fire or suitable covering, were massed together there, in the company of healthy reprobates who were "bummers," deserters, and stragglers—the riffraff of the Federal and Confederate armies. There were two of these curious improvised institutions—Camp Convalescent and Camp Straggle—both of which were crammed full. . . .

The Washington of the war was a very different city from the present stately capital. Before the war the city was as drowsy and as grass-grown as any old New England town. Squalid Negro quarters hung on the flanks of fine old mansions, and although in the centers of this "city of magnificent distances" there were handsome public buildings, with here and there a statue or some other work of art, the general aspect of things was truly rural. The war changed all that in a very few weeks. Temporary hospitals and other rude shelters arose as if by magic on every hand. The streets were crowded by night and day, and the continual passage of heavily loaded quartermasters' trains, artillery, and vehicles of kinds before unknown in Washington, churned the unpaved streets into muddy thoroughfares in winter, or cut them deep with impalpable dust in summer. It was a favorite joke of Washingtonians that "real estate was high in dry weather, as it was for the most part all in the air."

Over the flats of the Potomac rose the then unfinished white obelisk of the Washington monument, a truncated cone; and in the weather-beaten sheds around its base were stored the carved and ornamented blocks that had been contributed to the structure by foreign governments, princes, potentates, and political and social organizations. On its hill rose the unfinished dome of the Capitol, whose bare ribs were darkly limned against the sky. It was a feeling of pride, or perhaps of some tenderer sentiment, that induced the government to insist that work on the Capitol should go on in the midst of the stress and strain of civil war, just as though nothing had happened to hinder the progress of the magnificent undertaking. It is no metaphor to say that the sound of the workman's hammer never ceased on that building, even in the dark times when it was not certain that "Washington was safe." The completion of the pediments of the House and Senate wings went on without delay during all these perilous times. The colossal statue of Freedom which now adorns the apex of the central dome (designed by Crawford and cast in bronze by Clark Mills) was at first set up on a temporary base in the Capitol grounds, where it was an object of curiosity and interest to visitors. . . .

The frequent appearance in Washington of paroled rebel officers, who usually wore their own uniform with evident pride and pleasure, and sometimes with a swagger, generally threw loyalists into a fever of excitement. More than once I saw ultra-loyal newsboys or boot-blacks throw a lump of mud, or a brickbat, at the passing Confederate. One of these officers, a Lieutenant Garnett, being on parole, sent in his card to Representative Wickliffe, of Kentucky, and was by him introduced upon the floor of the House, where he attracted attention, as well as indignation, from the members present. Presently a wave of excitement seemed to sweep over the galleries, the spectators being visibly affected by the appearance of an officer in full Confederate uniform sitting on one of the sofas of the House of Representatives. This was intensified when a door-keeper spoke to the visitor, who rose from his seat, gave a profound and sweeping bow, and withdrew to the outer corridor. It appeared that the door-keeper had told the Confederate that it was contrary to the rules of the House for him to be present.

—Brooks, "Washington in Lincoln's Time"

2. WALT WHITMAN LOOKS AROUND IN WARTIME WASHINGTON

Here is another, and very different, impression of wartime Washington, and from an even more famous pen. Walt Whitman was writing for New York and Brooklyn newspapers when, in December 1862, he got word that his young brother George had been wounded at Fredericksburg. He left at once for the front, found his brother at Falmouth, Virginia; and then returned to Washington, where he earned a meager living copying documents and devoted most of his time to visiting wounded soldiers in the Washington hospitals. It was during this experience as a "wound dresser" that—so he always believed—he contracted the infection which later led to paralysis. At the very end of the war Whitman got a clerkship in the Department of the Interior, only to lose it when the Secretary discovered that he was the author of a "scandalous" book—Leaves of Grass.

Washington, March 19, 1863

DEAR NAT AND FRED GRAY:

   Since I left New York I was down in the Army of the Potomac in front
with my brother a good part of the winter, commencing time of the battle
of Fredricksburgh—have seen *"war-life,"* the real article—folded myself in
a blanket, lying down in the mud with composure—relished salt pork and
hard tack—have been on the battlefield among the wounded, the faint and
the bleeding, to give them nourishment—have gone over with a flag of truce
the next day to help direct the burial of the dead—have struck up a tremendous friendship with a young Mississippi captain (about 19) that we took
prisoner badly wounded at Fredricksburgh (he has followed me here, is in
the Emory hospital here minus a leg—he wears his confederate uniform,
proud as the devil—I met him first at Falmouth, in the Lacy house middle of
December last, his leg just cut off, and cheered him up—poor boy, he has
suffered a great deal, and still suffers—has eyes bright as a hawk, but face
pale—our affection is an affair quite romantic—sometimes when I lean over
to say I am going, he puts his arms around my neck, draws my face down,
etc., quite a scene for Rappahannock.—During January came up hither, took
a lodging room here. Did the 37th Congress, especially the night sessions the
last three weeks, explored the Capitol, meandering the gorgeous painted interminable Senate corridors, getting lost in them (a new sensation, rich and
strong, that endless painted interior at night)—got very much interested in
some particular cases in Hospitals here—go now steadily to more or less of
said Hospitals by day or night—find always the sick and dying soldiers forthwith begin to cling to me in a way that makes a fellow feel funny enough.
These Hospitals, so different from all others—these thousands, and tens and
twenties of thousands of American young men, badly wounded, all sorts of
wounds, operated on, pallid with diarrhoea, languishing, dying with fever,
pneumonia, etc., open a new world somehow to me, giving closer insights,
new things, exploring deeper mines, than any yet, showing our humanity (I
sometimes put myself in fancy in the cot, with typhoid, or under the knife)
tried by terrible, fearfullest tests, probed deepest, the living soul's, the body's
tragedies, bursting the petty bonds of art. To these, what are your dramas
and poems, even the oldest and the fearfullest? Not old Greek mighty ones;
where man contends with fate (and always yealds)—not Virgil showing
Dante on and on among the agonized and damned, approach what here I see
and take part in. For here I see, not at intervals, but quite always, how certain man, our American man—how he holds himself cool and unquestioned
master above all pains and bloody mutilations. It is immense, the best thing
of all—nourishes me of all men. This then, what frightened us all so long.
Why, it is put to flight with ignominy—a mere stuffed scarecrow of the
fields. Oh death, where is thy sting? Oh grave, where is thy victory?

   In the Patent Office, as I stood there one night, just off the cot-side of a
dying soldier, in a large ward that had received the worst cases of Second
Bull Run, Antietam, and Fredricksburgh, the surgeon, Dr. Stone (Horatio
Stone the Sculptor) told me, of all who had died in that crowded ward

the past six months, he had still to find the first man or boy who had met the approach of death with a single tremor or unmanly fear. But let me change the subject—I have given you screed enough about Death and the Hospitals—and too much—since I got started. Only I have some curious yarns I promise you my darlings and gossips, by word of mouth whene'er we meet.

Washington and its points I find bear a second and a third perusal, and doubtless many. My first impressions, architectural, etc., were not favorable: but upon the whole, the city, the spaces, buildings, etc., make no unfit emblem of our country, so far, so broadly planned, everything in plenty, money and materials staggering with plenty, but the fruit of the plans, the knit, the combination yet wanting—Determined to express ourselves greatly in a Capitol but no fit Capitol yet here (time, associations, wanting I suppose) many a hiatus yet—many a thing to be taken down and done over again yet—perhaps an entire change of base—maybe a succession of changes.

Congress does not seize very hard upon me: I studied it and its members with curiosity, and long—much gab, great fear of public opinion, plenty of low business talent, but no masterful man in Congress (probably best so). I think well of the President. He has a face like a Hoosier Michael Angelo, so awful ugly it becomes beautiful, with its strange mouth, its deep cut, crisscross lines, and its doughnut complexion.—My notion is too, that underneath his outside smutched mannerism, and stories from third-class county barrooms (it is his humor), Mr. Lincoln keeps a fountain of first-class practical telling wisdom. I do not dwell on the supposed failures of his government: he has shown, I sometimes think an almost supernatural tact in keeping the ship afloat at all, with head steady, not only not going down, and now certain not to, but with proud and resolute spirit, and flag flying in sight of the world, menacing and high as ever. I say never yet captain, never ruler, had such a perplexing dangerous task as his, the past two years. I more and more rely upon his idiomatic western genius, careless of court dress or court decorum.

Friday morning, 20th—I finish my letter in the office of Major Hapgood, a paymaster, and a friend of mine. This is a large building filled with paymasters' offices, some thirty or forty or more. This room is up on the fifth floor (a most noble and broad view from my window) curious scenes around here—a continual stream of soldiers, officers, cripples, etc., some climbing wearily up the stairs. They seek their pay—and every hour, almost every minute, has its incident, its hitch, its romance, farce or tragedy. There are two paymasters in this room. A sentry at the street door, another halfway up the stairs, another at the chief clerk's door, all with muskets and bayonets—sometimes a great swarm, hundreds around the side walk in front waiting (everybody is waiting for something here). I take a pause, look up a couple of minutes from my pen and paper—see spread, off there the Potomac, very fine, nothing pretty about it—the Washington monument, not half finished—the public grounds around it filled with ten thousand beeves on the hoof—to the left the Smithsonian with its brown turrets—to the right far across, Arlington Heights, the forts, eight or ten of them—then the long bridge, and down a ways but quite plain, the shipping of Alexandria. Opposite me and in a stone throw is the Treasury Building, and below the bustle and life of Pennsylvania Avenue. I shall hasten with my letter, and then go forth and take a stroll down "the avenue" as they call it here.

Now you boys, don't you think I have done the handsome thing by writing this astoundingly magnificent letter—certainly the longest I ever wrote in my life. Fred, I wish you to present my best respects to your father, Bloom and all; one of these days we will meet, and make up for lost time, my dearest boys.

Walt.

—Halloway, ed., *The Uncollected Poetry and Prose of Walt Whitman*

3. ANNA DICKINSON SEES THE DRAFT RIOTS IN NEW YORK CITY

The Confederacy had resort to conscription as early as April 1862; not until March 1863 did the Federal Congress enact a conscription act, and it proved so full of loopholes and exemptions as to be practically useless. The act was widely denounced as unconstitutional and despotic, and first attempts to enforce it met with resistance in various Northern cities. By all odds the worst disturbances were the great "draft riots" that swept New York City from the thirteenth to the seventeenth of July. For three or four days New York was in the grip of hoodlums who rioted, pillaged, and burned almost at will; the local authorities were all but helpless and Governor Seymour gave aid and comfort to the rioters by promising to get the obnoxious law repealed. The most disgraceful feature of the riots was the savage attack on Negroes; even the Negro Orphan Asylum was burned down by the mob.

Anna Dickinson, who here describes these outbreaks, was at the time a young woman but already well known as writer and lecturer on antislavery, temperance and woman's rights.

ON the morning of Monday, the thirteenth of July [1863], began this outbreak, unparalleled in atrocities by anything in American history and equaled only by the horrors of the worst days of the French Revolution. Gangs of men and boys, composed of railroad employees, workers in machine shops, and a vast crowd of those who lived by preying upon others, thieves, pimps, professional ruffians, the scum of the city, jailbirds, or those who were running with swift feet to enter the prison doors, began to gather on the corners and in streets and alleys where they lived; from thence issuing forth, they visited the great establishments on the line of their advance, commanding their instant close and the companionship of the workmen—many of them peaceful and orderly men—on pain of the destruction of one and a murderous assault upon the other, did not their orders meet with instant compliance.

A body of these, five or six hundred strong, gathered about one of the enrolling offices in the upper part of the city, where the draft was quietly proceeding, and opened the assault upon it by a shower of clubs, bricks, and paving stones torn from the streets, following it up by a furious rush into the office. Lists, records, books, the drafting wheel, every article of furniture or work in the room, was rent in pieces and strewn about the floor or flung into the streets, while the law officers, the newspaper reporters—who are expected to be everywhere—and the few peaceable spectators, were compelled to make a hasty retreat through an opportune rear exit, accelerated by the curses and blows of the assailants.

A safe in the room, which contained some of the hated records, was fallen upon by the men, who strove to wrench open its impregnable lock with their naked hands, and, baffled, beat them on its iron doors and sides till they were stained with blood, in a mad frenzy of senseless hate and fury. And then, finding every portable article destroyed—their thirst for ruin growing by the little drink it had had—and believing, or rather hoping, that the officers had taken refuge in the upper rooms, set fire to the house, and stood watching the slow and steady lift of flames, filling the air with demoniac shrieks and yells, while they waited for the prey to escape from some door or window, from the merciless fire to their merciless hands. One of these, who was on the other side of the street, courageously stepped forward and, telling them that they had utterly demolished all they came to seek, informed them that help-less women and little children were in the house and besought them to ex-tinguish the flames and leave the ruined premises—to disperse or at least to seek some other scene.

By his dress recognizing in him a government official, so far from hearing or heeding his humane appeal, they set upon him with sticks and clubs and beat him till his eyes were blind with blood, and he, bruised and mangled, succeeded in escaping to the handful of police who stood helpless before this howling crew, now increased to thousands. With difficulty and pain the in-offensive tenants escaped from the rapidly-spreading fire, which, having de-voured the house originally lighted, swept across the neighboring buildings till the whole block stood a mass of burning flames. The firemen came up tardily and reluctantly, many of them of the same class as the miscreants who surrounded them and who cheered at their approach, but either made no attempt to perform their duty or so feeble and farcical a one as to bring dis-grace upon a service they so generally honor and ennoble.

At last, when there was here nothing more to accomplish, the mob, swol-len to a frightful size, including myriads of wretched, drunken women and the half-grown vagabond boys of the pavements, rushed through the inter-vening streets, stopping cars and insulting peaceable citizens on their way, to an armory where were manufactured and stored carbines and guns for the government. In anticipation of the attack, this, earlier in the day, had been fortified by a police squad capable of coping with an ordinary crowd of ruf-fians, but as chaff before fire in the presence of these murderous thousands. Here, as before, the attack was begun by a rain of missiles gathered from the streets, less fatal, doubtless, than more civilized arms, but frightful in the ghastly wounds and injuries they inflicted. Of this no notice was taken by those who were stationed within. It was repeated. At last, finding they were treated with contemptuous silence and that no sign of surrender was offered the crowd swayed back, then forward, in a combined attempt to force the wide entrance doors. Heavy hammers and sledges which had been brought from forges and workshops, caught up hastily as they gathered the mechanics into their ranks, were used with frightful violence to beat them in at last successfully. The foremost assailants began to climb the stairs but were checked and for the moment driven back by the fire of the officers, who at last had been commanded to resort to their revolvers. A half-score fell wounded, and one who had been acting in some sort as their leader—a big, brutal Irish ruffian—dropped dead.

The pause was but for an instant. As the smoke cleared away there was a general and ferocious onslaught upon the armory; curses, oaths, revilings, hideous and obscene blasphemy, with terrible yells and cries, filled the air in every accent of the English tongue save that spoken by a native American. Such were there mingled with the sea of sound, but they were so few and weak as to be unnoticeable in the roar of voices. The paving stones flew like hail until the street was torn into gaps and ruts and every windowpane and sash and doorway was smashed or broken. Meanwhile divers attempts were made to fire the building but failed through haste or ineffectual materials or the vigilant watchfulness of the besieged. In the midst of this gallant defense word was brought to the defenders from headquarters that nothing could be done for their support and that if they would save their lives they must make a quick and orderly retreat. Fortunately there was a side passage with which the mob was unacquainted, and one by one they succeeded in gaining this and vanishing.

The work was begun, continued, gathering in force and fury as the day wore on. Police stations, enrolling offices, rooms or buildings used in any way by government authority or obnoxious as representing the dignity of law, were gutted, destroyed, then left to the mercy of the flames. Newspaper offices whose issues had been a fire in the rear of the nation's armies by extenuating and defending treason and through violent and incendiary appeals stirring up "lewd fellows of the baser sort" to this very carnival of ruin and blood were cheered as the crowd went by. Those that had been faithful to loyalty and law were hooted, stoned, and even stormed by the army of miscreants, who were only driven off by the gallant and determined charge of the police and in one place by the equally gallant and certainly unique defense which came from turning the boiling water from the engines upon the howling wretches, who, unprepared for any such warm reception as this, beat a precipitate and general retreat. Before night fell it was no longer one vast crowd collected in a single section, but great numbers of gatherings, scattered over the whole length and breadth of the city, some of them engaged in actual work of demolition and ruin, others, with clubs and weapons in their hands, prowling round apparently with no definite atrocity to perpetrate, but ready for any iniquity that might offer, and, by way of pastime, chasing every stray police officer or solitary soldier or inoffensive Negro who crossed the line of their vision; these three objects—the badge of a defender of the law, the uniform of the Union army, the skin of a helpless and outraged race—acted upon these madmen as water acts upon a rabid dog.

Late in the afternoon a crowd which could have numbered not less than ten thousand, the majority of whom were ragged, frowzy, drunken women, gathered about the Orphan Asylum for Colored Children—a large and beautiful building and one of the most admirable and noble charities of the city. When it became evident from the menacing cries and groans of the multitude that danger, if not destruction, was meditated to the harmless and inoffensive inmates, a flag of truce appeared, and an appeal was made in their behalf, by the principal, to every sentiment of humanity which these beings might possess—a vain appeal! Whatever human feeling had ever, if ever, filled these souls was utterly drowned and washed away in the tide of rapine and blood in which they had been steeping themselves. The few officers who stood guard over the doors and manfully faced these demoniac legions were beaten down and flung to one side, helpless and stunned, whilst the vast crowd rushed in. All the articles upon which they could seize—beds, bedding, carpets, furniture, the very garments of the fleeing inmates, some of these torn from their persons as they sped by—were carried into the streets and hurried off by the women and children who stood ready to receive the goods which their husbands, sons, and fathers flung to their care. The little ones, many of them assailed and beaten—all, orphans and caretakers, exposed to every indignity and every danger—driven on to the street, the building was fired. This had been attempted whilst the helpless children, some of them scarce more than babies, were still in their rooms; but this devilish consummation was prevented by the heroism of one man. He, the chief of the fire department, strove by voice and arm to stay the endeavor; and when, overcome by superior numbers, the brands had been lit and piled, with naked hands and in the face of threatened death he tore asunder the glowing embers and trod them underfoot. Again the effort was made and again failed through the determined and heroic opposition of this solitary soul. Then on the front steps, in the midst of these drunken and infuriated thousands, he stood up and besought them, if they cared nothing for themselves nor for those hapless orphans, that they would not bring lasting disgrace upon the city by destroying one of its noblest charities, which had for its object nothing but good.

He was answered on all sides by yells and execrations and frenzied shrieks of "Down with the nagurs!" coupled with every oath and every curse that malignant hate of the blacks could devise and drunken Irish tongues could speak. It had been decreed that this building was to be razed to the ground. The house was fired in a thousand places, and in less than two hours the walls crashed in, a mass of smoking, blackened ruins, whilst the children wandered through the streets, a prey to beings who were wild beasts in everything save the superior ingenuity of man to agonize and torture his victims.

Frightful as the day had been, the night was yet more hideous, since to the horrors which were seen was added the greater horror of deeds which might be committed in the darkness—or, if they were seen, it was by the lurid glare of burning buildings, the red flames of which, flung upon the stained and brutal faces, the torn and tattered garments, of men and women who danced and howled around the scene of ruin they had caused, made the whole aspect of affairs seem more like a gathering of fiends rejoicing in pandemonium than aught with which creatures of flesh and blood had to do. . . .

The next morning's sun rose on a city which was ruled by a reign of terror. Had the police possessed the heads of Hydra and the arms of Briareus and had these heads all seen, these arms all fought, they would have been powerless against the multitude of opposers. Outbreaks were made, crowds gathered, houses burned, streets barricaded, fights enacted, in a score of places at once. Where the officers appeared they were irretrievably beaten and overcome, their stand, were it ever so short, but inflaming the passions of the mob to fresh deeds of violence. Stores were closed, the business portion of the city deserted, the large works and factories emptied of men, who had been sent home by their employers or were swept into the ranks of the marauding bands. The city cars, omnibuses, hacks, were unable to run and remained under shelter. Every telegraph wire was cut, the posts torn up, the operators driven from their offices. The mayor, seeing that civil power was helpless to stem this tide, desired to call the military to his aid and place the city under martial law, but was opposed by the Governor—a governor who, but a few days before, had pronounced the war a failure and not only predicted but encouraged this mob rule which was now crushing everything beneath its heavy and ensanguined feet. This man, through almost two days of these awful scenes, remained at a quiet seaside retreat but a few miles from the city. Coming to it on the afternoon of the second day, instead of ordering cannon planted in the streets, giving these creatures opportunity to retire to their homes, and, in the event of refusal, blowing them there by powder and ball, he first went to the point where was collected the chiefest mob and proceeded to address them. Before him stood incendiaries, thieves, and murderers, who even then were sacking dwelling houses and butchering powerless and inoffensive beings. These wretches he apostrophized as "my friends," repeating the title again and again in the course of his harangue, assuring them that he was there as a proof of his friendship, which he had demonstrated by "sending his adjutant general to Washington to have the draft stopped," begging them to "wait for his return," "to separate now as good citizens," with the promise that they "might assemble again whenever they wished to so do"; meanwhile he would "take care of their rights." This model speech was incessantly interrupted by tremendous cheering and frantic demonstrations of delight, one great fellow almost crushing the Governor in his enthusiastic embrace.

His allies in newspaper offices attempted to throw the blame upon the loyal press and portion of the community. This was but a repetition of the cry raised by traitors in arms that the government, struggling for life in their deadly hold, was responsible for the war: "If thou wouldst but consent to be murdered peaceably, there could be no strife."

It was absurd and futile to characterize this new reign of terror as anything but an effort on the part of Northern rebels to help Southern ones at the most critical moment of the war, with the state militia and available troops absent in a neighboring commonwealth and the loyal people unprepared. These editors and their coadjutors, men of brains and ability, were of that most poisonous growth—traitors to the government and the flag of their country—renegade Americans.

—ANNA DICKINSON, *What Answer?*

4. NEVADA MINERS BID ON THE "SANITARY" FLOUR SACK

Mark Twain tried mining in a Nevada camp called Aurora, on the slopes of the Sierras. But he grew poor instead of rich, and after a while he undertook to walk 130 miles to Virginia City, where a mining boom was under way. Here he got a job on the local newspaper, the Enterprise, *and began to observe life in the wildest and most interesting city of the mountain West. In* Roughing It, *from which this passage is taken, he gives us an imcomparable picture of the Comstock Lode—its desperadoes, demagogues, gamblers, and miners, its crimes, excesses and extravagances. Everybody had money and everybody was reckless, but the people were generous, too, and exuberantly patriotic. Though there were many Confederate sympathizers in Nevada, the territory was firmly pro-Union and Lincoln saw to it that it was brought into the Union as a state in time for the 1864 election. The Sanitary Commission of the Civil War was something of a combination Red Cross, YMCA and USO.*

MONEY was wonderfully plenty. The trouble was not how to get it but how to spend it, how to lavish it, get rid of it, squander it. And so it was a happy thing that just at this juncture the news came over the wires that a great United States Sanitary Commission had been formed and money was wanted for the relief of the wounded sailors and soldiers of the Union languishing in the Eastern hospitals. Right on the heels of it came word that San Francisco had responded superbly before the telegram was half a day old. Virginia [City] rose as one man! A sanitary committee was hurriedly organized, and its chairman mounted a vacant cart in C Street and tried to make the clamorous multitude understand that the rest of the committee were flying hither and thither and working with all their might and main, and that if the town would only wait an hour, an office would be ready, books opened, and the commission prepared to receive contributions. His voice was drowned and his information lost in a ceaseless roar of cheers and demands that the money be received *now*—they swore they would not wait. The chairman pleaded and argued, but, deaf to all entreaty, men plowed their way through the throng and rained checks of gold coin into the cart and scurried away for more. Hands clutching money were thrust aloft out of the jam by men who hoped this eloquent appeal would cleave a road their strugglings could not open. The very Chinamen and Indians caught the excitement and dashed their half dollars into the cart without knowing or caring what it was all about. Women plunged into the crowd, trimly attired, fought their way to the cart with their coin, and emerged again, by and by, with their apparel in a state of hopeless dilapidation. It was the wildest mob Virginia had ever seen and the most determined and ungovernable, and when at last it abated its fury and dispersed, it had not a penny in its pocket. To use its own phraseology, it came there flush and went away busted.

After that the commission got itself into systematic working order, and for weeks the contributions flowed into its treasury in a generous stream. Individuals and all sorts of organizations levied upon themselves a regular weekly tax for the sanitary fund, graduated according to their means, and there was not another grand universal outburst till the famous "Sanitary Flour Sack" came our way. Its history is peculiar and interesting. A former schoolmate of mine, by the name of Reuel Gridley, was living at the little city of Austin in the Reese River country at this time and was the Democratic candidate for mayor. He and the Republican candidate made an agreement that the defeated man should be publicly presented with a fifty-pound sack of flour by the successful one and should carry it home on his shoulder. Gridley was defeated. The new mayor gave him the sack of flour, and he shouldered it and carried it a mile or two from lower Austin to his home in upper Austin, attended by a band of music and the whole population. Arrived there, he said he did not need the flour and asked what the people thought he had better do with it. A voice said:

"Sell it to the highest bidder for the benefit of the sanitary fund."

The suggestion was greeted with a round of applause, and Gridley mounted a drygoods box and assumed the rôle of auctioneer. The bids went higher and higher as the sympathies of the pioneers awoke and expanded, till at last the sack was knocked down to a millman at two hundred and fifty dollars and his check taken. He was asked where he would have the flour delivered, and he said:

"Nowhere—sell it again."

Now the cheers went up royally, and the multitude were fairly in the spirit of the thing. So Gridley stood there and shouted and perspired till the sun went down, and when the crowd dispersed he had sold the sack to three hundred different people and had taken in eight thousand dollars in gold. And still the flour sack was in his possession.

The news came to Virginia and a telegram went back:

"Fetch along your flour sack!"

Thirty-six hours afterward Gridley arrived, and an afternoon mass meeting was held in the opera house, and the auction began. But the sack had come sooner than it was expected; the people were not thoroughly aroused, and the sale dragged. At nightfall only five thousand dollars had been secured, and there was a crestfallen feeling in the community. However, there was no disposition to let the matter rest here and acknowledge vanquishment at the hands of the village of Austin. Till late in the night the principal citizens were at work arranging the morrow's campaign, and when they went to bed they had no fears for the result.

At eleven the next morning a procession of open carriages, attended by clamorous bands of music and adorned with a moving display of flags, filed along C Street and was soon in danger of blockade by a huzzaing multitude of citizens. In the first carriage sat Gridley, with the flour sack in prominent view, the latter splendid with bright paint and gilt lettering; also in the same carriage sat the mayor and the recorder. The other carriages contained the Common Council, the editors and reporters, and other people of imposing consequence. The crowd pressed to the corner of C and Taylor Streets, expecting the sale to begin there, but they were disappointed and also unspeakably surprised; for the cavalcade moved on as if Virginia had ceased to be of importance and took its way over the divide toward the small town of Gold Hill. Telegrams had gone ahead to Gold Hill, Silver City, and Dayton, and those communities were at fever heat and ripe for the conflict. It was a very hot day and wonderfully dusty. At the end of a short half hour we descended into Gold Hill with drums beating and colors flying, and enveloped in imposing clouds of dust. The whole population—men, women, and children, Chinamen and Indians—were massed in the main street, all the flags in town were at the masthead, and the blare of the bands was drowned in cheers. Gridley stood up and asked who would make the first bid for the National Sanitary Flour Sack. General W. said:

"The Yellow Jacket silver mining company offers a thousand dollars, coin!"

A tempest of applause followed. A telegram carried the news to Virginia, and fifteen minutes afterward that city's population was massed in the streets devouring the tidings—for it was part of the program that the bulletin boards should do a good work that day. Every few minutes a new dispatch was bulletined from Gold Hill, and still the excitement grew. Telegrams began to return to us from Virginia beseeching Gridley to bring back the flour sack, but such was not the plan of the campaign. At the end of an hour Gold Hill's small population had paid a figure for the flour sack that awoke all the enthusiasm of Virginia when the grand total was displayed upon the bulletin boards.

Then the Gridley cavalcade moved on, a giant refreshed with new lager beer and plenty of it—for the people brought it to the carriages without waiting to measure it—and within three hours more the expedition had carried Silver City and Dayton by storm and was on its way back covered with glory. Every move had been telegraphed and bulletined, and as the procession entered Virginia and filed down C Street at half past eight in the evening the town was abroad in the thoroughfares, torches were glaring, flags flying, bands playing, cheer on cheer cleaving the air, and the city ready to surrender at discretion.

The auction began; every bid was greeted with bursts of applause, and at the end of two hours and a half a population of fifteen thousand souls had paid in coin for a fifty-pound sack of flour a sum equal to forty thousand dollars in greenbacks! It was at a rate in the neighborhood of three dollars for each man, woman, and child of the population. The grand total would have been twice as large, but the streets were very narrow, and hundreds who wanted to bid could not get within a block of the stand and could not make themselves heard. These grew tired of waiting, and many of them went home long before the auction was over. This was the greatest day Virginia ever saw, perhaps.

Gridley sold the sack in Carson City and several California towns; also in San Francisco. Then he took it east and sold it in one or two Atlantic cities, I think. I am not sure of that, but I know that he finally carried it to St. Louis, where a monster sanitary fair was being held, and after selling it there for a large sum and helping on the enthusiasm by displaying the portly silver bricks which Nevada's donation had produced, he had the flour baked up into small cakes and retailed them at high prices.

It was estimated that when the flour sack's mission was ended it had been sold for a grand total of a hundred and fifty thousand dollars in greenbacks! This is probably the only instance on record where common family flour brought three thousand dollars a pound in the public market.

—MARK TWAIN, *Roughing It*

5. "O, I WILL TAKE THE PLOW, JOHN"

Southern states had seceded in full confidence that "cotton was king." But Southerners made the capital mistake of keeping their cotton at home in order to accentuate the crisis abroad; by the time they were prepared to ship it abroad the blockade was effective and Britain and France had found other sources of cotton—or learned to do without. But they could not get along without American foodstuffs. Every autumn of the war brought bumper crops of wheat and corn while Europe suffered from a succession of poor harvests; England imported fifty-fold the wheat and flour in 1862 that she had in 1859. "Old King Cotton's Dead and buried, brave young Corn is King" ran the refrain of a popular song. That the North was able to produce bumper crops with so large a part of its farm population drawn off into the armies was due to a combination of factors: the growing use of the McCormick reaper, the opening up of new land, good weather and—not least—the readiness of women to work in the fields.

Mary Livermore, who here pays tribute to the work of women, was one of the many women reformers of that day, a tireless advocate of temperance and woman suffrage, active in the work of the Sanitary Commission of the Northwest. Like Anna Dickinson she achieved popularity largely through the lecture platform.

IN the early summer of 1863, frequent calls of business took me through the extensive farming districts of Wisconsin, and Eastern Iowa, when the farmers were the busiest, gathering the wheat harvest. As we dashed along the railway, let our course lead in whatever direction it might, it took us through what seemed a continuous wheat-field. The yellow grain was waving everywhere; and two-horse reapers were cutting it down in a wholesale fashion that would have astonished Eastern farmers. Hundreds of reapers could be counted in a ride of half a dozen hours. The crops were generally good, and in some instances heavy, and every man and boy was pressed into service to secure the abundant harvest while the weather was fine.

Women were in the field everywhere, driving the reapers, binding and shocking, and loading grain, until then an unusual sight. At first, it displeased me, and I turned away in aversion. By and by, I observed how skilfully they drove the horses round and round the wheat-field, diminishing more and more its periphery at every circuit, the glittering blades of the reaper cutting wide swaths with a rapid, clicking sound, that was pleasant to hear. Then I saw that when they followed the reapers, binding, and shocking, although they did not keep up with the men, their work was done with more precision and nicety, and their sheaves had an artistic finish that those lacked made by the men. So I said to myself, "They are worthy women, and deserve praise: their husbands are probably too poor to hire help, and, like the 'helpmeets' God designed them to be, they have girt themselves to this work—and they are doing it superbly. Good wives! good women!"

One day my route took me off the railway, some twenty miles across the country. But we drove through the same golden fields of grain, and between great stretches of green waving corn. Now a river shimmered like silver through the gold of the wheat and oats, and now a growth of young timber made a dark green background for the harvest fields. Here, as everywhere, women were busy at the harvesting.

"I've got to hold up a spell, and rig up this 'ere harness," said my driver; "something's got out o' kilter." And the carriage halted opposite a field where half a dozen women and two men were harvesting. Not a little curious to know what these women reapers were like, I walked over and accosted them.

"And so you are helping gather the harvest!" I said to a woman of forty-five or fifty, who sat on the reaper to drive, as she stopped her horses for a brief breathing spell. Her face was pleasant and comely, although sunburned, with honest, straightforward eyes, a broad brow, and a mouth that indicated firmness and tenderness. Her dress, a strong calico, was worn without hoops, then thought essential on all occasions, and she was shod with stout boots, and wore a shaker bonnet.

"Yes, ma'am," she said; "the men have all gone to the war, so that my man can't hire help at any price, and I told my girls we must turn to and give him a lift with the harvestin'."

"You are not German? You are surely one of my own countrywomen—American?"

"Yes, ma'am; we moved here from Cattaraugus county, New York state, and we've done very well since we came."

"Have you sons in the army?"

"Yes," and a shadow fell over the motherly face, and the honest eyes looked out mournfully into vacancy. "All three of 'em 'listed, and Neddy, the youngest, was killed at the battle of Stone River, the last day of last year. My man, he went down to get his body, but he came back without it. There were nine thousand of our men left dead on the field there, and our Neddy's body couldn't be found among so many. It came very hard on us to let the boys go, but we felt we'd no right to hinder 'em. The country needed 'em more'n we. We've money enough to hire help if it could be had; and my man don't like to have me and the girls a-workin' out-doors; but there don't seem no help for it now."

I stepped over where the girls were binding the fallen grain. They were fine, well-built lasses, with the honest eyes and firm mouth of the mother, brown like her, and clad in the same sensible costume.

"Well, you are like your mother, not afraid to lend a hand at the harvesting, it seems!" was my opening remark.

"No, we're willing to help outdoors in these times. Harvesting isn't any harder, if it's as hard as cooking, washing, and ironing, over a red-hot stove in July and August—only we have to do both now. My three brothers went into the army, all my cousins, most of the young men about here, and the men we used to hire. So there's no help to be got but women, and the crops must be got in all the same, you know."

"One of our German women," said another of the girls, "tells us we don't know anything about war yet. For during the last war in Germany men were so scarce that she had to work three years in a blacksmith's shop. You wouldn't think it, though, if you should see her. That would be rather tough, but I tell Annie we can do anything to help along while the country's in such trouble."

"I tell mother," said the Annie referred to, standing very erect, with flashing eyes, "that as long as the country can't get along without grain, nor the army fight without food, we're serving the country just as much here in the harvest-field as our boys are on the battle-field—and that sort o' takes the edge off from this busines of doing men's work, you know." And a hearty laugh followed this statement.

Another one of the women was the wife of one of the soldier sons, with a three-year-old boy toddling beside her, tumbling among the sheaves, and getting into mischief every five minutes. His mother declared that he was "more plague than profit." From her came the same hearty assent to the work which the distress of the country had imposed on her. And she added, with a kind of homely pride, that she was considered "as good a binder as a man, and could keep up with the best of 'em."

Further conversation disclosed the fact that amid their double labor in the house and field, these women found time for the manufacture of hospital supplies, and had helped to fill box after box with shirts and drawers, dried apples and pickles, currant wine and blackberry jam, to be forwarded to the poor fellows languishing in far-off Southern hospitals. My eyes were unsealed. The women in the harvest-field were invested with a new and heroic interest, and each hard-handed, brown, toiling woman was a heroine. When the driver called to me that he had mended the broken harness, I bade the noble harvesters "good-bye," assuring them that they were the "peers of the women of the Revolution."

—LIVERMORE, *My Story of the War*

6. THE ARMY OF LOBBYISTS AND SPECULATORS

No one has ever told the full story of graft and corruption in the Civil War, but we know that it was pervasive and constant—far more so in the North than in the South, for the Confederacy offered little opportunity for large-scale corruption. Régis de Trobriand was one of those foreigners whom McClellan saluted in his Story. *He was colonel of the 54th New York Volunteers, a French unit raised in the summer of 1861, and fought bravely through the war, winning the brevet rank of major general. His* Four Years with the Army of the Potomac *was based on a diary.*

BESIDES the army formed to act against the enemy, there was another army—of lobbyists, contractors, speculators, which was continually renewed and never exhausted. These hurried to the assault on the treasury, like a cloud of locusts alighting down upon the capital to devour the substance of the country. They were everywhere; in the streets, in the hotels, in the offices, at the Capitol, and in the White House. They continually besieged the bureaus of administration, the doors of the Senate and House of Representatives, wherever there was a chance to gain something.

Government, obliged to ask the aid of private industry, for every kind of supply that the army and navy must have without delay, was really at the mercy of these hungry spoilers, who combined with one another to make the law for the government. From this arose contracts exceedingly burdensome, which impoverished the treasury, to enrich a few individuals.

As a matter of course, these latter classes, strangers to every patriotic impulse, saw in the war only an extraordinary opportunity of making a fortune. Every means for obtaining it was a good one to them; so that corruption played a great part in the business of contracting. Political protection was purchased by giving an interest in the contracts obtained. Now, as these contracts must be increased or renewed, according to the duration of the war, its prolongation became a direct advantage to a certain class of people disposing of large capital and of extended influence. What was the effect on events? It would be difficult to state precisely. But, in any case, this was evidently one of the causes which embarrassed the course of affairs, and delayed, more or less, the reëstablishment of the Union.

The government—that is, the people, who, in the end, support the weight of public expenses—was, then, fleeced by the more moderate and robbed by the more covetous. The army suffered from it directly, as the supplies, which were furnished at a price which was much above their value if they had been of a good quality, were nearly all of a fraudulent inferiority. For example, instead of heavy woollen blankets, the recruits received, at this time, light, open fabrics, made I do not know of what different substances, which protected them against neither the cold nor the rain. A very short wear changed a large part of the uniform to rags, and during the winter spent at Tenally-town the ordinary duration of a pair of shoes was no longer than twenty or thirty days.

This last fact, well attested in my regiment, was followed by energetic remonstrances, on account of which the general commanding the brigade appointed, according to the regulations, a special *Board of Inspection,* with the object of obtaining the condemnation of the defective articles. Amongst the members of the board was an officer expert in these matters, having been employed, before the war, in one of the great shoe factories of Massachusetts. The report was very precise. It showed that the shoes were made of poor leather, not having been properly tanned, that the inside of the soles was filled with gray paper, and that the heels were so poorly fastened that it needed only a little dry weather following a few days of rain to have them drop from the shoes. In fine, the fraud was flagrant in every way.

The report was duly forwarded to the superior authorities. Did it have any consideration? I never knew. However, it was necessary to exhaust the stock in hand before obtaining a new supply, and the price charged the soldier was not altered.

—De Trobriand, *Four Years with the Army of the Potomac*

7. CHARLES A. DANA HELPS STOP FRAUDS IN THE WAR DEPARTMENT

Charles A. Dana had gone from Brook Farm to the New York Tribune under Greeley, and had become, by the time of the Civil War, one of the most influential of American editors. A disagreement with Greeley led to his resignation in 1862; he was promptly appointed by the War Department a sort of field inspector, attached himself to Grant's headquarters, and did inestimable service to the Union cause by his shrewd championship of Grant and Sherman. In 1863 he became Assistant Secretary of War, dividing his time between Washington and the battle front. After the war he bought the New York Sun and lived to become the most powerful editor of his generation. The frauds he recounts here were typical of many that were being perpetrated at the time.

AT the time that I entered the War Department for regular duty, it was a very busy place. Mr. Stanton frequently worked late at night, keeping his carriage waiting for him. I never worked at night, as my eyes would not allow it. I got to my office about nine o'clock in the morning, and I stayed there nearly the whole day, for I made it a rule never to go away until my desk was cleared. When I arrived I usually found on my table a big pile of papers which were to be acted on, papers of every sort that had come to me from the different departments of the office.

The business of the War Department during the first winter that I spent in Washington was something enormous. Nearly $285,000,000 was paid out that year (from June, 1863, to June, 1864) by the quartermaster's office, and $221,000,000 stood in accounts at the end of the year awaiting examination before payment was made. We had to buy every conceivable thing that an army of men could need. We bought fuel, forage, furniture, coffins, medicine, horses, mules, telegraph wire, sugar, coffee, flour, cloth, caps, guns, powder, and thousands of other things. Sometimes our supplies came by contract; again by direct purchase; again by manufacture. Of course, by the fall of 1863 the army was pretty well supplied; still, that year we bought over 3,000,000 pairs of trousers, nearly 5,000,000 flannel shirts and drawers, some 7,000,000 pairs of stockings, 325,000 mess pans, 207,000 camp kettles, over 13,000 drums, and 14,830 fifes. It was my duty to make contracts for many of these supplies.

In making contracts for supplies of all kinds, we were obliged to take careful precautions against frauds. I had a colleague in the department, the Hon. Peter H. Watson, the distinguished patent lawyer, who had a great knack at detecting army frauds. One which Watson had spent much time in trying to ferret out came to light soon after I went into office. This was an extensive fraud in forage furnished to the Army of the Potomac. The trick of the fraud consisted in a dishonest mixture of oats and Indian corn for the horses and mules of the army. By changing the proportions of the two sorts of grain, the contractors were able to make a considerable difference in the cost of the bushel, on account of the difference in the weight and price of the grain, and it was difficult to detect the cheat. However, Watson found it out, and at once arrested the men who were most directly involved.

Soon after the arrest Watson went to New York. While he was gone, certain parties from Philadelphia interested in the swindle came to me at the War Department. Among them was the president of the Corn Exchange. They paid me thirty-three thousand dollars to cover the sum which one of the men confessed he had appropriated; thirty-two thousand dollars was the amount restored by another individual. The morning after this transaction the Philadelphians returned to me, demanding both that the villains should be released, and that the papers and funds belonging to them, taken at the time of their arrest, should be restored. It was my judgment that, instead of being released, they should be remanded to solitary confinement until they could clear up all the forage frauds and make complete justice possible. Then I should have released them, but not before. So I telegraphed to Watson what had happened, and asked him to return to prevent any false step.

Now, it happened that the men arrested were of some political importance in Pennsylvania, and eminent politicians took a hand in getting them out of the scrape. Among others, the Hon. David Wilmot, then Senator of the United States and author of the famous Wilmot proviso, was very active. He went to Mr. Lincoln and made such representations and appeals that finally the President consented to go with him over to the War Department and see Watson in his office. Wilmot remained outside, and Mr. Lincoln went in to labor with the Assistant Secretary. Watson eloquently described the nature of the fraud, and the extent to which it had already been developed by his partial investigation. The President, in reply, dwelt upon the fact that a large amount of money had been refunded by the guilty men, and urged the greater question of the safety of the cause and the necessity of preserving united the powerful support which Pennsylvania was giving to the administration in suppressing the rebellion. Watson answered:

"Very well, Mr. President, if you wish to have these men released, all that is necessary is to give the order; but I shall ask to have it in writing. In such a case as this it would not be safe for me to obey a verbal order; and let me add that if you do release them the fact and the reason will necessarily become known to the people."

Finally Mr. Lincoln took up his hat and went out. Wilmot was waiting in the corridor, and came to meet him.

"Wilmot," he said, "I can't do anything with Watson; he won't release them."

The reply which the Senator made to this remark can not be printed here, but it did not affect the judgment or the action of the President.

The men were retained for a long time afterward. The fraud was fully investigated, and future swindles of the kind were rendered impossible. If Watson could have had his way, the guilty parties—and there were some whose names never got to the public—would have been tried by military commission and sternly dealt with. But my own reflections upon the subject led me to the conclusion that the moderation of the President was wiser than the unrelenting justice of the Assistant Secretary would have been.

—Dana, *Recollections of the Civil War*

8. COLONEL BAKER OUTWITS BOUNTY JUMPERS AND BROKERS

It is difficult to imagine how the enlistment and conscription laws of the Federal government could have been drawn more badly than they were. By the law of July 1861 Congress promised a bounty of $100 for three-year enlistments, and this bounty was later extended to conscripts who agreed to serve for a long term. The act of March 3, 1863, gave a bounty of $300 to three-year enlistees. At the same time many states and localities filled their quotas by offering generous bounties. Altogether, it is estimated, the Federal government paid out some $300,000,000 in bounties, and state and local governments a comparable sum. Inevitably many soldiers enlisted just for the bounty, deserted, and re-enlisted elsewhere; some professional bounty jumpers managed to enlist and collect bounty ten or twenty times. Along with bounty jumping went bounty brokers—crooks who recruited men, and then robbed them of their bounties.

Colonel LaFayette C. Baker, who here tells us how he caught bounty jumpers and brokers red-handed, was Chief of the United States Secret Service, notorious alike for his highhanded and illegal methods and for his success in feathering his own nest while serving his government. President Johnson dismissed him for maintaining an espionage system in the White House. One historian observes that Baker's "habitual carelessness in mixing truth and fiction was not overcome in his History of the Secret Service," but, however unreliable his general account of his own distinguished services, this story of bounty jumping in January 1865 would seem to be authentic enough.

THE great demand for recruits during the war, the large bounties offered for them, and the manifold facilities for fraudulent transactions, presented temptations of great power, even to reputable citizens, to evade the plain letter of the law, and traffic in substitutes, or, by bribery and deception, personally to keep out of the hands of the recruiting officer.

The majority of the officers assigned to recruiting service were guilty of great dereliction of duty, inasmuch as, instead of endeavoring to check the growing evil, they rather pretended ignorance, or allowed it to pass unnoticed. . . .

The Department at Washington was constantly urging upon me the necessity for forming some plan, which, in a summary and successful manner, would frustrate the designs of these dishonest parties, and bring them to justice. Several attempts had been made for this purpose, but had all proved unsuccessful.

A number of plans were submitted to me, each of which I considered objectionable, on certain accounts. The shortest way to catch these deserters, which was tracking them to their haunts, it would have been folly to pursue, as such a course would result in a general alarm and stampede of the guilty. . . .

I took up my headquarters at the Astor House, and let the brokers know that I was an agent or supervisor for the interior of the State, having several large quotas to fill. I was at once besieged by applications to purchase credits. The third day I purchased sixteen sets of these enlistment-papers; and on the fourth, twenty-two, when a proposition was made by a broker to purchase forged papers, saying, those I had were such, and would answer the same purpose; that so skillfully were they prepared detection was impossible. The offer was accepted, and placed me on the most friendly terms with my associates in business. For a number of days I continued the purchase of spurious papers for less than half the price of the genuine documents. This feature of the swindling came near causing a quarrel among the brokers; some of them insisting that I should not have been informed that I bought forged papers, because I might then have paid full price. The other party contended, that by committing me to the forgery I was secured against betrayal of the cause. The former further claimed, that forged papers were worth as much to me as the genuine. These negotiations were carried on four days, when I decided to arrest the whole company. It will be understood, that the arrest of a single broker in the city would create an alarm, and end the investigation. The greatest strategy and concealment were therefore indispensable to success. The knowledge of my presence in the metropolis would have defeated my plans. On a certain day I requested nine brokers, with whom I had business, to come to my room at the same hour, bringing their papers. I had concealed, in an adjoining room, a number of my assistants. I instructed them that the signal I should use to bring them to my aid, would be a knock on the door of the apartment in which they were placed.

The illustrious nine stood around me, forged papers in hand, eagerly waiting for the checks which would bring the reward of their villainy. To fasten the guilt upon the criminals, beyond dispute, I had written receipts for the money to be paid each broker. As they walked up in line, and made their marks, for most of them could not write, I stepped to the folding-doors and gave the signal. Instantly a detective came in, and I said to my broker-friends: "Gentlemen, this joke has gone far enough; you are my prisoners. I am General Baker, the Chief of the Detective Bureau."

It would be futile for tongue or pen to attempt to describe the effect of my words upon the assemblage before me. The change that passed over it was very marked, and to me, who was the cause of it, irresistibly entertaining. The explosion of a bomb-shell in the battle-ranks could not have startled and dismayed the soldiery more suddenly than this unexpected exposure of their crimes, and the powerful grasp of justice, did the discomfited brokers, who had anticipated a very different fate. . . .

It has been sufficiently demonstrated, by incidents recorded, that monstrous frauds were perpetrated by the manufacture and sale of enlistment papers.

Indeed, it is very evident, from knowledge thus far obtained, that not a small proportion of all such documents, on which credits were given, were forged.

I shall only add to the record a few incidents, which combine in their character both comic and tragic qualities.

I had been told that soldiers would receive the bounty, re-enlist the same day, be sent to the Island, and repeat the process the day following. I was, at the time, skeptical respecting such facility in deception and incredible assurance, and to satisfy myself in regard to the truth of the matter, I dressed myself in the garb of a regular jumper and repaired, February 9th, to a recruiting office in the public square near the Astor House, New York. Assuming the air of a veteran in the business, I asked the officer what he was paying for recruits.

Before the question could be answered, the gentlemanly broker, always at hand, inquired of me my name and place of residence, which I gave him. In a low tone of voice, and with a knowing wink, he said: "Have you been through before in New York?"

I answered: "Not since last fall."

He added: "All right; come inside." And in less time than it has taken to relate the incident, I was one of "Uncle Sam's boys."

My friend gave me one hundred dollars, promising the remainder due me when I should arrive at the Island; then directing me to remain where I was for a while, he left me.

Returning within an hour, he opened the following conversation with me: "Have you ever been on the Island?"

T. D. Thulstrup

Union Field Hospital at Savage's Station

The *Monitor* and the *Merrimac*

Alonzo Chappel

I replied, "Yes."

Evidently enlightened in regard to the matter, he immediately remarked: "You know how to get off, then? When you *do,* come up to Tammany Hall, and I will put you through up town": meaning, of course, he would enlist me again.

While this conversation was passing between us another broker stepped up, and said: "Gentlemen, let us take a drink." We accepted the invitation, and they conducted me across the Park to a saloon, where I saw, at a glance, they were quite at home. Liquor was called for, and while the vender was getting it, one of the brokers quietly stepped behind the bar and addressed some conversation to him.

We then all drank to the success of the Union, or rather, all of us *appeared* to do so.

I raised the glass to my lips, and, unobserved by the rest, poured its contents into my bosom, as I had done many times before when compelled to join the convivial ring. I was convinced that my potation had been drugged. Next followed a proposition to repair to an adjoining room and engage in a game of cards.

We played until I thought it necessary to affect drowsiness and insensibility. My eyes began to close, until at length my head rested on the table in front of me, and my whole appearance indicated to my betrayers my entire helplessness in their hands.

At this juncture one of them left the room, but soon returning, exclaimed, "All right." Immediately I caught the sound of carriage wheels, and, as I anticipated, was carried to the door, and, supported by broker number one, lifted into a vehicle, and driven rapidly to the Cedar Street rendezvous. My hat was then unceremoniously pushed over my face, and I was hurried into the presence of the recruiting officer in attendance, who asked me, "Do you wish to enlist?"

Number two answered, in a tone to represent my own voice, "Ye-e-s."

I was again declared to be one of the volunteers, taken into another room, and laid on a bench, where I remained an hour, in company with three other recruits, who had been drugged in the same manner, my friends the brokers supposing they had disposed of me.

In the mean time broker number one returned, and said: "Well, old fellow, how do you feel?" to which I replied, "Very sick." Then remarking, "You'll be all right by-and-by," he left me.

I looked about me to judge of the possibility of escape. I saw at once that I could not pass out by the door, as a sentry was stationed there, and came to the conclusion that I would have to try my chances at a window.

I opened one which overlooked a back yard, sprang out, and after walking through a long passage-way, which led me into the open street, I went deliberately to my room in the Astor House.

Here I masked my face, disguised myself anew, and proceeded directly to the office of Mr. Blunt, where I offered myself to the army service, to make my third enlistment for that day.

I was hardly seated, when broker number three approached me, saying: "You want to enlist, do you?"

"Yes, I am thinking of it. What are you paying recruits now?"

"Six hundred dollars. Where are you from?"

"Steuben County. I would like to enlist if I could get a situation as clerk. I can write a pretty good hand, and am hardly able to go into the ranks."

He replied quickly, "Oh, I can fix that all right."

A conversation then followed between him and the recruiting officer, when I was made a soldier of the Union army once more. I was requested to be seated for a few moments. Soon after the broker asked me to take "a glass." I went with him to an old drinking-saloon in Cherry Street, where I found brokers numbers one and two, who immediately recognized me, but expressed no surprise at the meeting. My successful escape from the Cedar Street headquarters convinced my friends that I was an old expert in the tricks of the trade.

Their admiration for me became so great that they received me into full fellowship, regarded me as a shrewd member of the bounty jumping brotherhood, and, after freely discussing their plans and prospects, declared me to be a "perfect trump." Propositions were made to enter into partnership at once.

I was greatly amused while listening to the exploits of each, as he in turn detailed them. One related, that at a certain period he left New York, and having enlisted at Albany, Troy, Utica, Buffalo, and Chicago, returned *via* Elmira, at which place he likewise enlisted. Another had enlisted at every rendezvous from New York to Portland, Maine; while a third boasted of the amounts he had received, and mentioned those paid to recruiting officers, surgeons, brokers, and detectives. The den in which I spent the evening was a favorite haunt of the bounty jumpers. It contained a wardrobe of wearing apparel, consisting of both soldiers' and citizens' outfits. The idea of this I easily comprehended; here the jumpers could assume whatever dress they pleased, to carry out their designs. Three times that night, before two o'clock, I saw the interesting operation performed.

I selected one of my assistants to experiment in this military lottery. He dressed himself in the appropriate apparel, and in one day enlisted three times; he was sent to the Island, bought himself off, and reported for duty the following day.

The scenes described were followed by numberless arrests of bounty brokers, bounty jumpers, and others in the business, and consequently by the disclosures of their crimes, which have since attracted much public attention.

—BAKER, *The Secret Service in the Late War*

9. CONFEDERATE PLOTS AGAINST THE NORTH

It was entirely natural that the Confederacy, which was on the defensive militarily, should have sought to attack the Union from behind the lines. For in the end the only hope of Confederate victory—and it was a persistent hope—lay in encouraging discontent and disunity to the point where the Northern people would weary of the war. To this end Confederate secret agents, working closely with such treasonable organizations as the Knights of the Golden Circle and the Sons of Liberty, planned a series of attacks and uprisings in the fall of 1864. The immediate objective was to release Confederate prisoners at such places as Camp Douglas, in Chicago, and Johnson's Island, in Lake Erie, to burn Northern cities, and to distract the strength of the North by border raids; the ultimate purpose was to encourage the peace movement and defeat Lincoln in the 1864 elections. The plan to seize Camp Douglas miscarried and the leaders of the Knights implicated in the plan were captured and tried for treason. A border raid on St. Albans, Vermont, was a minor success. The two plots described in these excerpts were both fiascos.

A. A Confederate Plan to Seize Johnson's Island Is Frustrated

ON the 20th of September, 1864, the Lake cities were suddenly aroused from their imagined security by the news that a passenger steamer upon Lake Erie had been seized by a squad of Confederates, her crew overpowered, the steamer captured and her course directed to Johnson's Island, with the avowed purpose of rescuing the prisoners confined there and taking them to the Ohio shore, whence it was hoped they might make their way South through the state of Ohio. The plot was carefully planned, and perhaps might have been carried to a successful conclusion had it not been for the abundant precautions taken by the Federal forces.

The steamer, the *Philo Parsons*, left Detroit at her usual hour in the morning, and at the request of one Bennett G. Burleigh, who had come on board the night before stopped at Sandwich in Canada, nearly opposite Detroit, to take on board three friends of Burleigh, one of whom he said was lame and unable to cross the ferry. Proceeding down the river, the steamer stopped at Amherstberg, where sixteen roughish-looking men came aboard with an old trunk tied with a rope. They did not seem to be connected with Burleigh, but were supposed to be refugees from the draft returning home; and little attention was paid to them.

Nothing occurred to excite suspicion until the boat was well within American waters, when one Beall, the leader of the gang, while engaged in conversation with the mate in the pilot house, suddenly drew his revolver, and demanded possession of the boat as a Confederate officer. Recognizing the force of this argument, the mate surrendered the wheel. The crew and passengers were overpowered, driven into the cabin, and the old trunk, which proved to be a small arsenal, opened, hatchets and revolvers distributed among the conspirators, and the course of the boat continued toward Sandusky, near which lay Johnson's Island.

But at this point the success of the expedition culminated. Failing to meet a messenger who was to have been sent to meet them at Kelley's Island, on the route of the steamer, or to receive an expected signal, all the conspirators but three mutinied, refused to go farther, and returned at top speed to Amherstberg, where the boat was scuttled and abandoned and the conspirators dispersed. Another steamer was captured and scuttled on the Lake. All of the men were arrested, taken before a Justice of the Peace and discharged, although the officers were sufficiently alert to seize certain property which had been landed and detain it for customs dues.

It was fortunate the steamer turned about when she did. The officers of the *Michigan* had been apprised that the raid would be made that day. The *Michigan*, a man-of-war of fifteen guns, lay off the island, cleared for action, her guns shotted, her anchor hove short, and every preparation made to receive the expected guests. The messenger who was sent to Kelley's Island to join the conspirators had already been arrested and put in custody. There was an available force of nine hundred men at the Island to put down any insurrection. That twenty men, armed only with revolvers and hatchets, should have been able to capture the *Michigan* and release the prisoners was simply preposterous. A single broadside from the *Michigan* would probably have sunk the steamer.

—Brown, "The Lake Erie Piracy Case"

B. The Confederates Attempt to Burn New York

At 6 o'clock promptly on the evening of November 25, 1864, our party met in our cottage headquarters, two failing to report.

The bottles of Greek fire having been wrapped in paper were put in our coat pockets. Each man took ten bottles. It was agreed that after our operations were over we should secrete ourselves and meet here the next night at 6 o'clock to compare notes and agree on further plans.

I had rooms at the Astor House, City Hotel, Everett House, and the United States Hotel. Colonel Martin occupied rooms at the Hoffman, Fifth Avenue, St. Denis, and two others. Lieutenant Ashbrook was at the St. Nicholas, La Farge, and several others. Altogether nineteen hotels were fired, namely: Hoffman House, Fifth Avenue, St. Denis, St. James, La Farge, St. Nicholas, Metropolitan, Howard, Tammany, Brandreth's, Gramercy Park, Hanford, New England, Belmont, Lovejoy's, City Hotel, Astor, United States, and Everett.

I reached the Astor House at 7.20 o'clock, got my key, and went to my room in the top story. It was the lower corner front room on Broadway. After lighting the gas jet I hung the bedclothes loosely on the headboard and piled the chairs, drawers of the bureau and washstand on the bed. Then stuffed some newspapers about among the mass and poured a bottle of turpentine over it all. I concluded to unlock my door and fix the key on the outside, as I might have to get out in a hurry, for I did not know whether the Greek fire would make a noise or not. I opened a bottle carefully and quickly and spilled it on the pile of rubbish. It blazed up instantly and the whole bed seemed to be in flames, before I could get out. I locked the door and walked down the hall and stairway to the office, which was fairly crowded with people. I left the key at the office as usual and passed out.

Across at the City Hotel I proceeded in the same manner. Then in going down to the Everett House I looked over at my room in the Astor House. A bright light appeared within but there were no indications below of any alarm. After getting through at the Everett House I started to the United States Hotel, when the fire bells began to ring up town. I got through at the United States Hotel without trouble, but in leaving my key the clerk, I thought, looked at me a little curiously. It occurred to me that it had been discovered that my satchel had no baggage in it and that perhaps the clerk had it in mind to mention the fact.

As I came back to Broadway it seemed that a hundred bells were ringing, great crowds were gathering on the street, and there was general consternation. I concluded to go and see how my fires were doing. There was no panic at the Astor House, but to my surprise a great crowd was pouring out of Barnum's Museum nearly opposite the Astor. It was now a quarter after nine o'clock by the City Hall tower clock. Presently the alarm came from the City Hotel and the Everett. The surging crowds were frantic. But the greatest panic was at Barnum's Museum. People were coming out and down ladders from the second and third floor windows and the manager was crying out for help to get his animals out. It looked like people were getting hurt running over each other in the stampede, and still I could not help some astonishment for I did not suppose there was a fire in the Museum.

In accordance with our plan I went down Broadway and turned across to the North River wharf. The vessels and barges of every description were lying along close together and not more than twenty yards from the street. I picked dark spots to stand in, and jerked a bottle in six different places. They were ablaze before I left. One had struck a barge of baled hay and made a big fire. There were wild scenes here the last time I looked back. I started straight for the City Hall.

There was still a crowd around the Astor House and everywhere, but I edged through and crossed over to the City Hall, where I caught a car just starting up town. I got off on Bowery street opposite the Metropolitan Hotel to go across and see how Ashbrook and Harrington had succeeded. After walking half a square I observed a man walking ahead of me and recognized him. It was Captain Kennedy. I closed up behind him and slapped him on the shoulder. He squatted and began to draw his pistol, but I laughed and he knew me. He laughed and said he ought to shoot me for giving him such a scare.

We soon related to each other our experience. Kennedy said that after he touched off his hotels he concluded to go down to Barnum's Museum and stay until something turned up, but had only been there a few minutes when alarms began to ring all over the city. He decided to go out, and coming down the stairway it happened to be clear at a turn and the idea occurred to him that there would be fun to start a scare. He broke a bottle of Greek fire, he said, on the edge of a step like he would crack an egg. It blazed up and he got out to witness the result. He had been down there in the crowd ever since and the fires at the Astor House and the City Hotel had both been put out. But he had listened to the talk of the people and heard the opinion expressed generally that rebels were in the city to destroy it. He thought our presence must be known. Harrington had broken a bottle in the Metropolitan Theater at 8 o'clock, just after he fired the Metropolitan Hotel adjoining; and Ashbrook had done likewise in Niblo's Garden Theater adjoining the La Farge Hotel.

We went into the crowd on Broadway and stopped at those places to see what had happened. There was the wildest excitement imaginable. There was all sorts of talk about hanging the rebels to lamp posts or burning them at the stake. Still we discovered that all was surmise apparently. So far as we could learn the programme had been carried out, but it appeared that all had made a failure. It seemed to us that there was something wrong with our Greek fire.

All had observed that the fires had been put out in all the places as easily as any ordinary fire. We came to the conclusion that Longmire and his manufacturing chemist had put up a job on us after it was found that we could not be dissuaded from our purpose.

Martin and I got together as agreed and found lodging about 2 o'clock. We did not awake until 10 o'clock next day. We went into a restaurant on Broadway near Twelfth street for breakfast. It was crowded, but every one was reading a newspaper. After giving our order we got the *Herald*, *World*, *Tribune*, and *Times*, and to our surprise the entire front pages were given up to sensational accounts of the attempt to burn the city. It was plainly pointed out that rebels were at the head of the incendiary work, and quite a list of names was given of parties who had been arrested. All our fictitious names registered at the different hotels were given and interviews with the clerks described us all. The clerk of the United States Hotel especially gave a minute description of my personal appearance, clothing, manners and actions. He said I did not eat a meal at the hotel, though I had been there two days as a guest, and had nothing in my black satchel.

It was stated in the papers that the authorities had a full knowledge of the plot and the ring-leaders would be captured during the day. One paper said the baggage of two of them had been secured, and all avenues of escape being guarded the villains were sure to be caught, the detectives having a full knowledge of the rebels and their haunts.

—HEADLEY, *Confederate Operations in Canada and New York*

10. AN OHIO JUDGE UPHOLDS THE UNION CAUSE IN TANGIER

It is a bit difficult to know where to put this delectable story; certainly the episode which Frederick Seward here recounts was sufficiently behind the lines. Seward, son of the Secretary of State, was Assistant Secretary in the State Department in charge of consular relations. After the war he had a long but undistinguished career in New York politics; the volume of reminiscences from which this story is taken was published posthumously.

TANGIER is one of the few places in the world where the United States Government owns the home of its diplomatic representative. The fact that his flag has waved there undisturbed for more years than any living man can remember lends to the American Consul-General a prestige and dignity not always accorded to consuls who lodge in shabby, shifting quarters, over shops.

Trade and intercourse with America are not great, but "down along the coast of the High Barbaree" there is a traditional respect for the American flag, handed down from the days when the navy of the young Republic amazed Europe by sweeping the Barbary pirates out of the Mediterranean waters, where they had prowled and plundered for centuries.

In the year 1862, the occupant of the Consulate was Judge De Long, of Ohio. He was not much versed in Oriental wiles or modern diplomacy, but he was a zealous patriot, an honest lawyer, and an upright official. His blunt, straightforward talk was sometimes displeasing to his European colleagues, but it impressed the Moslem authorities, whose ears found it a novelty after many years of listening to glib phrases uttered in every language, from modern Parisian to ancient Sanskrit.

One February morning news was brought to the Consulate that two well-dressed Americans, with an air of authority, were sauntering through the streets of Tangier, indulging in offensive and insulting remarks about the American flag and its Consul, and expressing views in general that were highly derogatory to the honour of the United States.

Further inquiry easily discovered who they were, for they made no secret of it. One was called Tunstall and said he had been acting as United States Consul at Cadiz, until the previous summer. The other was Myers, formerly in our navy and now lieutenant of the Confederate cruiser *Sumter*, which was lying in the port of Gibraltar, where she had put in for coal.

Greatly scandalized by such proceedings, the Judge remarked: "American citizens may plot treason and rebellion at home, but they shall not do so where I am, if I have the power to prevent it." Thereupon, he promptly dispatched a messenger to Sidi Mohammed Bargash, the Minister of State, with whom he held intercourse and requested that a file of soldiers should be sent to aid him in dealing with some traitorous fellow-countrymen. . . .

When Sidi Mohammed Bargash inquired what the Consul-General wished to have done with his malefactors, he was relieved to learn that the Judge did not ask to have their heads cut off, nor to have them thrown into the dungeons of the castle, but only to have them delivered under guard at the door of the American Consulate.

The soldiers were sent. They overtook the offenders, who were leisurely proceeding toward the French steamer on which they were about to re-embark. The Moorish soldiers arrested them and marched them up to the American Consulate.

Now some explanations from them were in order. They began to expostulate. Their arrest, they declared, was absurd, an egregious blunder. They were peaceable travellers in a foreign land. True, they were at war with the United States, but Morocco was neutral soil, and nobody had a right to stop them there. They pointed out that international law, and the rules of neutrality, entitled them to immunity from arrest. In fact, according to law, the Consul could not arrest them.

The Judge's reply was succinct and to the point. He said he not only could arrest them, but that he had.

They declared they would appeal for protection to the European Powers, all of whom would demand their release.

The Judge intimated that they might appeal to all the governments in Christendom, if they chose; but that it would take considerable time. Meanwhile, they were under the jurisdiction of a Mahometan one, which was friendly to him and to the United States.

Finding him deaf to persuasion and argument, they dispatched a communication to the French Consul, stating their case. . . . They asked his interposition to end this absurd state of affairs.

The reply of the French Consul was courteous but diplomatic. He regretted their detention. But they were not French subjects, and when they left the French steamer and landed on Moorish territory, he had no right to protect them, nor to interfere in any way whatever.

A similar application to the British Minister, Mr. Drummond Hay, met with similar unsatisfactory results. . . .

The prisoners were not disheartened. Like their captor, they were quick-witted, resolute Americans, so they cast about for other help. . . . They had heard that Moorish guards sometimes were open to bribery. They mustered up a hundred dollars in gold coins and a gold watch, and with them opened negotiations.

Unluckily the Judge got wind of it, and promptly stopped the bargain. Then he sent to Sidi Mohammed Bargash for more guards, and ordered the prisoners put in irons. Someone lent them a case knife, with which Myers cut the rivets. He then jumped out of the window. But he only landed in the consular courtyard, where he was immediately caught and brought back to confinement.

But other instrumentalities were at work in their behalf. Now appeared upon the scene no less a personage than the Military Secretary of the Governor of Gibraltar.

He was the bearer of a letter to the Moorish Minister of Foreign Affairs, from the commander of the Confederate States steamer *Sumter*. It demanded the immediate release of the prisoners,—implying that terrible things would occur if the demand were not complied with. It was a trifle arrogant in tone, considering that the *Sumter* was out of coal, and was under close watch by the United States warship *Tuscarora*, which was cruising off Algeciras. But it had weight with Sidi Mohammed Bargash. He immediately sat down to write a polite note to Judge De Long, saying:

"We have received a letter from the captain of the steamer *Sumter*, from the Confederate States, in which they inform us that the two men you have seized are of the best of men, and they are guiltless,—except that they are from the separated Confederate States. We have no doubt that when you receive this letter, you will put them free."

This was couched in the politest of Arabic. The answer to it was in vigorous American.

The Judge informed his Excellency: first, that there was no government known or recognized as the "Confederate States," either by the United States or the Empire of Morocco, and that the captain and crew of the *Sumter*, as well as the men in custody, were all citizens of the United States resisting its authority; furthermore, that the *Sumter* was a Federal vessel, seized by rebels, and engaged in capturing, plundering, burning, and sinking peaceable American merchant vessels. He concluded by asking, "Shall seventy-six years of uninterrupted friendship between your government and the United States be brought to an end for the sake of pirates?"

By this time the sympathizers with the Southern cause were actively stirring up the motley nationalities in Tangier to disorder. They perceived that instead of waiting for the slow action of the Moorish and European governments they might as well deliver the prisoners themselves, by means of inflammatory speeches, indignation meetings, and a mob.

The movement was started in the market-place, where they had a table set out, with pen, ink, and paper, in the middle of the street, and began signing and pledging themselves in solemn form to force the release of the prisoners at all hazards. The mob, when gathered, would march to the Consulate, groan, howl, curse and swear, break in windows and doors, and, in the height of the tumult, would free the men in spite of their guards.

Word of the threatening state of affairs in the market-place was hastily brought to the Palace, where the Viceroy, Prince Muley el Abbas, was enjoying a quiet smoke.

The Prince listened, and, calmly removing the nargileh from his lips, remarked, "Allah is great. But what the devil have these Christians to do with the American Consul's prisoners?" He signified that it was the province of the lieutenant-governor to take troops, and disperse these riotous Christians.

And now comes another new and unexpected actor in the drama. Off the harbour appears the United States warship *Ino*, flying the American flag. She heads for the anchorage and prepares to exchange the customary salute of twenty-one guns with the Moorish forts. Her captain and officers come ashore in uniform and proceed to the Consulate and the Palace, to make the usual calls of ceremony. The Consul-General joins them.

The Prince and his ministers receive them with courtesy. Their requests are presented and are acceded to as entirely reasonable. They are, that the *Ino* shall be allowed to land thirty armed marines, who shall march the prisoners from the Consulate down to the ship. The Moorish troops will quell the mob and accompany the prisoners to the beach.

All this is speedily done, within an hour or two. The mob resolves itself into a gaping crowd of three thousand spectators, who stand gazing at the departing warship, carrying away those troublesome Americans. . . .

After his release from Fort Warren, in Boston harbour, which occurred some months later, Tunstall came to see me at the State Department. He agreed that there was a spice of grim humour in the predicament which unexpectedly overtook him and his friend at Tangier. He said he should not have much minded being captured as a prisoner of war, but that he was not quite prepared to forgive "that Ohio Judge" for putting him in irons.

—SEWARD, *Reminiscences of a War-Time Statesman and Diplomat*

XXI

Behind the Lines: The South

WHY did the Confederacy lose the war? Historians are still discussing this engrossing question, and they are still unable to agree on the answer. There is pretty general agreement, though, that the South did not lose the war on the battlefield. To be sure the Confederates were beaten at Vicksburg and Gettysburg, Chattanooga and Atlanta, decimated in the Wilderness, and shattered by Sherman's march from Atlanta to the sea and beyond. But these military defeats—so runs the argument—were consequences, not causes.

The most varied causes are assigned to explain these defeats: the blockade and shortages of essential materials; failure to win the foreign recognition so confidently anticipated; the breakdown of finance and of transportation; the incompetence of the President and of Congress; the disintegrating impact of State rights. Yet had the Confederacy used such resources of man power as it had, it might not have suffered defeat. There was food enough in the Confederacy; finances could have been controlled; the transportation system was not beyond repair; the blockade was not effective until 1863; foreign intervention would have followed upon military success and a statesmanlike policy toward such things as cotton and slavery; State rights denied to the Confederacy resources that promised victory; a wiser government would have made Lee commander in chief and permitted him to control the grand strategy of the war, and so forth. So the argument runs, and most students fall back, in the end, on the vague phrase "breakdown of morale"—a phrase which merely begs the question.

But what all this adds up to is that the Confederate cause was lost in the Confederacy itself—that is, behind the lines. The internal history of the Confederacy thus becomes a matter of paramount interest. This chapter is not designed, primarily, to illuminate the breakdown of the Confederacy, but there can be little doubt that it does so. Successive excerpts describe the inadequacy of food and of other necessities, runaway inflation, the incompetence of the medical services, the shortsighted cotton policy, the effectiveness of the blockade, the impact of invasion and of defeat on morale, dissatisfaction with the conduct of the war, the role of State rights, and the growth of defeatism.

1. RICHMOND AFTER SEVEN PINES

Seven Pines, rather than First Bull Run, brought the war home to Richmond. Bull Run had, after all, been a stunning victory; Seven Pines was, at *best, a draw. And while casualties at Bull Run had been less than 2,000, the cost of Seven Pines was over 6,000—and among them was the commanding general.*

"No city in the world was sadder than Richmond," writes Alexander Hunter, who describes here what the capital was like when the wounded and the dead were brought in from the near-by battlefield.

THE brigade moved into its former quarters, and but for the missing of old familiar faces Seven Pines would have seemed but a dream. Our camp was just as we had left it, the tents never having been taken down nor anything disturbed. For guard, the colonel had left various teamsters, convalescents, and others who always managed to get sick on the eve of any aggressive movement; and these had kept so faithfully to their posts in time of danger, we had no occasion to complain that our camp equipage had not been well protected.

In the city, busy, bustling and sad enough scenes were being enacted on every side. New regiments from the far South had just arrived and were marching through the streets, cheering and waving their hats as they passed; batteries of artillery were defiling along the thoroughfares, the drivers cracking their whips and urging their horses into a trot, all going toward the front, down Main and Broad streets into the Williamsburg road. Long lines of ambulances coming from the opposite way toiled slowly along, filled with the wounded from the battle-field, who were being carried to the various city hospitals—the long, torturing way marked by the trail of blood that oozed drop by drop from the human veins within, or else might be seen a wagonload of dead piled one upon another, their stiffened, rigid feet exposed to view, showing to the horrified spectator that for just so many the cares and sorrows of this life, its pain and misery, were passed forever.

Every vehicle from the battle-field was crowded to its utmost capacity. The more slightly wounded were made to walk, and long lines of them could be seen hobbling along the street, their wounds bound up in bloody rags. The citizens turned out in full force and did all in their power to alleviate this suffering; there was scarcely a house in Richmond wherein some wounded were not taken to be nursed with tenderest care; indeed, in some instances parlors and passages as well as chambers were converted into temporary hospitals, and everything done that unwearied nursing and gentlest attention could devise, and that for the roughest soldiers in the ranks as readily as for the highest general who wore his stars. Ladies stood in front of their homes with waiters of food and drink, luxuries and wine, which they dealt out unsparingly to wounded soldiers that passed them.

The Capitol square was filled with officers, privates and citizens; it had ever been a kind of news mart and a general rendezvous for the soldiers, while the ladies always loved to frequent its shady walks or rest on the seats beneath its trees, but the morning after the battle it was crowded. Many who were in doubt as to the fate of some loved one turned their steps to this battle park as the surest and easiest way of gaining information; comrades met and congratulated each other on escape; citizens listened to recitals of the battle; dirty, mud-covered soldiers, looking as if they had been dug out of a clay bank, were met and hugged by the whitest of arms and kissed by the sweetest of rose-bud lips; handsomely dressed and beautiful women, with tears streaming down their fair cheeks, greeted husbands, brothers and lovers. Many of those soft-eyed, soft-voiced women had dauntless souls, and when sobbing in agony at their parting they yet could murmur with pallid lips, like the Roman wives when handing their shields to their husbands and sons, "Return with them—or upon them."

It had been a time of terrible anxiety to the people of Richmond. The first battle to occur near them, they had listened all day to the thunder of the cannon with agonizing feelings, with nerves strained to the highest tension, awaiting the result. Not only did they have their own near and dear to think of, but from all the South had poured in letters from friends and relatives charging them to watch over kindred and take charge of them if wounded. Then from all quarters of the Confederacy wives had followed their husbands to the scene of action, filling with other refugees every available boarding-house, public and private in the city. To these strangers in a strange land it had been a trial of no light moment to listen to those death-dealing monsters and know *one* life was at stake. Ah, yes, this battle had thrilled the city to its depths!

Such an extraordinary call for hospital accommodations had found the Richmond authorities entirely unprepared; buildings were hastily fitted up with the barest of comforts; medical stores on hand were entirely inadequate for the demand. The city doctors were employed day and night, and as for nurses—if the women of the place, young and old, had not volunteered their services, matters would have been very much worse than they were. Soups and delicacies were sent from private houses, and so the suffering was in a measure mitigated. After some time, and throughout the war, the hospitals of Richmond were organized and better conducted, with their efficient surgeons, skilled nurses, and admirable routine; but at that time chaos reigned supreme, and many precious lives were lost from want of ordinary attention, that otherwise might have been saved.

For days and nights wagons and ambulances never ceased to empty their wretched loads before the door of each of these hastily improvised hospitals, never ceasing until the building overflowed with maimed humanity and could accommodate no more. In some instances empty stores were taken, and pallets of straw placed on the floors and counters. At the handling of wounds,—rough it must have seemed, in spite of every effort to make it gentle,—the racking of quivering nerves passing all bounds of patient endurance, screams of agony would sometimes break out upon the air with startling emphasis. Here was some poor fellow being taken from an ambulance with an arm shot so nearly off that it needed only one stroke of the knife to quite finish the work; another with a mangled leg—yes! it were better to look away from such a piteous spectacle; a boy with his face so torn by a shell that his mother would not have recognized him—and a dying soldier, his countenance already pallid in the fast-coming chill of death; and "Here one is dead, died on the way," they say as they lift a corpse from the wagon, while the passer-by, grown rapidly familiar with such fearful sights, glances hastily and passes on.

And so passed the long procession of wounded, nearly five thousand, young, middle-aged and white-haired; from the private to the highest ranks,—hurt in every conceivable manner, suffering in every way, parched, feverish, and agonized, wearing a look of mute agony no words may describe, or else lapsed in an almost fortunate unconsciousness,—men from every State, pouring out blood like water and offering up lives of sacrifice for the cause they had espoused. No city in the world was sadder than Richmond in those days; all the misery and woe of Seven Pines had been emptied into her fair streets and homes, and she had "no language but a cry"—an exceedingly bitter cry, that rose in the night to God on High, if the heavens were not brass. . . .

The people realized with a sudden shock the actualities of an internecine strife and it was brought to their very doors. Before, they had seen only its pride and pomp, and a martial showing; they had heard only the rattling of artillery over the stony streets, and the tread of passing columns; but all at once, with the sound of hostile guns, gaunt, grim-visaged war touched their hearts, and sickened their souls with horror.

It rendered them more determined, more earnest, more serious, it made them feel it was time to perform their part in the great tragedy and not waste the hours in light comedy, vain regrets or childish longings.

In one day Richmond was changed from a mirth-loving, pleasure-seeking city into a city resolute and nerved to make any sacrifice for the cause she loved.

—HUNTER, *Johnny Reb and Billy Yank*

2. A WAR CLERK SUFFERS SCARCITIES IN RICHMOND

Concentration on staple crops at the expense of grains and dairy products made the agricultural South far from self-sufficient, while industrially the South was almost wholly dependent on the North or on Britain. These basic economic factors, plus state competition for such foodstuffs and industrial products as could be found, contributed largely to the growing shortages that harassed the Confederacy.

After the war was fairly under way the Confederate government tried to meet nearly all its expenses by issues of paper money. This money steadily depreciated in value, so that every new issue was followed by a rise in prices which had to be met, in turn, by another new issue. By the end of 1864 the paper currency in circulation had reached about one billion dollars.

Other factors, too, contributed to inflation: the blockade by shutting off imports from abroad; the breakdown of the transportation system by making it hard to move merchandise; the decline in farm and factory production. All this meant that prices soared, that wages—especially the sorry wages of the soldiers—became almost worthless, and that the poor everywhere and the city-folk suffered sharp hardships.

John Beauchamp Jones, whose Rebel War Clerk's Diary *we have used before, was an editor and novelist who obtained a clerkship in the War Department for the express purpose of being at the center of things and writing about them. His book, verbose and prejudiced, is an authentic record of day-by-day life in the capital.*

May 23, 1862.—Oh, the extortioners! Meats of all kinds are selling at fifty cents per pound; butter, seventy-five cents; coffee, a dollar and half; tea, ten dollars; boots, thirty dollars per pair; shoes, eighteen dollars; ladies' shoes, fifteen dollars; shirts, six dollars each. Houses that rented for five hundred dollars last year are a thousand dollars now. Boarding, from thirty to forty dollars per month. General Winder has issued an order fixing the maximum prices of certain articles of marketing, which has only the effect of keeping a great many things out of market. The farmers have to pay the merchants and Jews their extortionate prices and complain very justly of the partiality of the general. It does more harm than good.

October 1st.—How shall we subsist this winter? There is not a supply of wood or coal in the city—and it is said that there are not adequate means of transporting it hither. Flour at sixteen dollars per barrel and bacon at seventy-five cents per pound threaten a famine. And yet there are no beggars in the streets. We must get a million of men in arms and drive the invader from our soil. We are capable of it, and we must do it. Better die in battle than die of starvation produced by the enemy.

The newspapers are printed on half sheets—and I think the publishers make money; the extras (published almost every day) are sold to the newsboys for ten cents and often sold by them for twenty-five cents. These are mere slips of paper, seldom containing more than a column—which is reproduced in the next issue. The matter of the extras is mostly made up from the Northern papers, brought hither by persons running the blockade. The supply is pretty regular, and dates are rarely more than three or four days behind the time of reception. We often get the first accounts of battles at a distance in this way, as our generals and our government are famed for a prudential reticence.

6th.— . . . This evening Custis and I expect the arrival of my family from Raleigh, N. C. We have procured for them one pound of sugar, eighty cents; four loaves of bread, as large as my fist, twenty cents each; and we have a little coffee, which is selling at two dollars and a half per pound. In the morning some one must go to market, else there will be short-commons. Washing is two dollars and a half per dozen pieces. Common soap is worth seventy-five cents per pound.

November 7th.—Yesterday I received from the agent of the City Councils fourteen pounds of salt, having seven persons in my family, including the servant. One pound to each member, per month, is allowed at five cents per pound. The extortionists sell it at seventy cents per pound. One of *them* was drawing for his family. He confessed it but said he paid fifty cents for the salt he sold at seventy cents. Profit ten dollars per bushel! I sent an article today to the *Enquirer*, suggesting that fuel, bread, meat, etc. be furnished in the same manner. We shall soon be in a state of siege.

21st.—Common shirting cotton and Yankee calico that used to sell at twelve and a half cents per yard is now a dollar seventy-five! What a temptation for the Northern manufacturers! What a rush of trade there would be if peace should occur suddenly! And what a party there would be in the South for peace (and unity with Northern Democrats) if the war were waged somewhat differently. The excesses of the Republicans *compel* our people to be almost a unit. This is all the better for us. Still, we are in quite a bad way now, God knows!

Mr. Dargan, M.C., writes to the President from Mobile that the inhabitants of that city are in an awful condition—meal is selling for three dollars and a half per bushel and wood at fifteen dollars per cord—and that the people are afraid to bring supplies, apprehending that the government agents will seize them. The President (thanks to him!) has ordered that interference with domestic trade must not be permitted.

December 1st.—God speed the day of peace! Our patriotism is mainly in the army and among the ladies of the South. The avarice and cupidity of the men at home, could only be excelled by the ravenous wolves; and most of our sufferings are fully deserved. Where a people will not have mercy on one another, how can they expect mercy? They depreciate the Confederate notes by charging from $20 to $40 per bbl. for flour; $3.50 per bushel of meal; $2 per lb. for butter; $20 per cord for wood, etc. When we shall have peace let the extortionists be remembered! let an indelible stigma be branded upon them.

A portion of the people look like vagabonds. We see men and women and children in the streets in dingy and dilapidated clothes; and some seem gaunt and pale with hunger—the speculators, and thieving quartermasters and commissaries only, looking sleek and comfortable. If this state of things continue a year or so longer, they will have their reward. There will be governmental bankruptcy, and all their gains will turn to dust and ashes, dust and ashes!

January 18, 1863.—We are now, in effect, in a state of siege, and none but the opulent, often those who have defrauded the government, can obtain a sufficiency of food and raiment. Calico, which could once be bought for twelve and a half cents per yard, is now selling at two dollars and a quarter, and a lady's dress of calico costs her about thirty dollars. Bonnets are not to be had. Common bleached cotton shirting brings a dollar and a half per yard. All other dry goods are held in the same proportion. Common tallow candles are a dollar and a quarter per pound; soap, one dollar; hams, one dollar; opossum, three dollars; turkeys, four to eleven dollars; sugar, brown, one dollar; molasses, eight dollars per gallon; potatoes, six dollars per bushel, etc.

These evils might be remedied by the government, for there is no great scarcity of any of the substantials and necessities of life in the country, if they were only equally distributed. The difficulty is in procuring transportation, and the government monopolizes the railroads and canals.

January 30th.—I cut the following from yesterday's *Dispatch:*

"The Results of Extortion and Speculation.—The state of affairs brought about by the speculating and extortion practiced upon the public cannot be better illustrated than by the following grocery bill for one week for a small family, in which the prices before the war and those of the present are compared:

1860		1863	
Bacon, 10 lbs. at 12½¢	$1.25	Bacon, 10 lbs. at $1	$10.00
Flour, 30 lbs. at 5¢	1.50	Flour, 30 lbs. at 12½¢	3.75
Sugar, 5 lbs. at 8¢	.40	Sugar, 5 lbs. at $1.15	5.75
Coffee, 4 lbs. at 12½¢	.50	Coffee, 4 lbs. at $5	20.00
Tea (green), ½ lb. at $1	.50	Tea (green), ½ lb. at $16	8.00
Lard, 4 lbs. at 12½¢	.50	Lard, 4 lbs. at $1	4.00
Butter, 3 lbs. at 25¢	.75	Butter, 3 lbs. at $1.75	5.25
Meal, 1 pk. at 25¢	.25	Meal, 1 pk. at $1	1.00
Candles, 2 lbs. at 15¢	.30	Candles, 2 lbs. at $1.25	2.50
Soap, 5 lbs. at 10¢	.50	Soap, 5 lbs. at $1.10	5.50
Pepper and salt (about)	.10	Pepper and salt (about)	2.50
Total	$6.55	Total	$68.25

"So much we owe the speculators, who have stayed at home to prey upon the necessities of their fellow-citizens."

February 11th.—Some idea may be formed of the scarcity of food in this city from the fact that, while my youngest daughter was in the kitchen to-day, a young rat came out of its hole and seemed to beg for something to eat; she held out some bread, which it ate from her hand, and seemed grateful. Several others soon appeared and were as tame as kittens. Perhaps we shall have to eat them!

18th.—One or two of the regiments of General Lee's army were in the city last night. The men were pale and haggard. They have but a quarter of a pound of meat per day. But meat has been ordered from Atlanta. I hope it is abundant there.

All the necessaries of life in the city are still going up higher in price. Butter, three dollars per pound; beef, one dollar; bacon, a dollar and a quarter; sausage meat, one dollar; and even liver is selling at fifty cents per pound.

By degrees, quite perceptibly, we are approaching the condition of famine. What effect this will produce on the community is to be seen. The army must be fed or disbanded, or else the city must be abandoned. How we, "the people," are to live is a thought of serious concern.

March 30th.—The gaunt form of wretched famine still approaches with rapid strides. Meal is now selling at twelve dollars per bushel and potatoes at sixteen. Meats have almost disappeared from the market, and none but the opulent can afford to pay three dollars and a half per pound for butter. Greens, however, of various kinds, are coming in; and as the season advances, we may expect a diminution of prices. It is strange that on the 30th of

March, even in the "sunny South," the fruit trees are as bare of blossoms and foliage as at midwinter. We shall have fire until the middle of May—six months of winter!

I am spading up my garden and hope to raise a few vegetables to eke out a miserable subsistence for my family. My daughter Ann reads Shakespeare to me o' nights, which saves my eyes.

April 17th.—Pins are so scarce and costly that it is now a pretty general practice to stoop down and pick up any found in the street. The boarding-houses are breaking up, and rooms, furnished and unfurnished, are renting out to messes. One dollar and fifty cents for beef leaves no margin for profit even at a hundred dollars per month, which is charged for board, and most of the boarders cannot afford to pay that price. Therefore they take rooms and buy their own scanty food. I am inclined to think provisions would not be deficient to an alarming extent if they were equally distributed. Wood is no scarcer than before the war, and yet thirty dollars per load (less than a cord) is demanded for it and obtained.

August 22nd.—Night before last all the clerks in the city post-office resigned, because the government did not give them salaries sufficient to subsist them. As yet their places have not been filled, and the government gets no letters—some of which lying in the office may be of such importance as to involve the safety or ruin of the government. To-morrow is Sunday, and of course the mails will not be attended to before Monday—the letters lying here four days unopened! This really looks as if we had no Postmaster-General.

October 22nd.—A poor woman yesterday applied to a merchant in Carey Street to purchase a barrel of flour. The price he demanded was $70.

"My God!" exclaimed she, "how can I pay such prices? I have seven children; what shall I do?"

"I don't know, madam," said he, coolly, "unless you eat your children."

Such is the power of cupidity—it transforms men into demons. And if this spirit prevails throughout the country, a just God will bring calamities upon the land, which will reach these cormorants, but which, it may be feared, will involve all classes in a common ruin.

January 26, 1864—The prisoners on Belle Isle (8000) have had no meat for eleven days. The Secretary says the Commissary-General informs him that they fare as well as our armies, and so he refused the commissary (Capt. Warner) of the prisoners a permit to buy and bring to the city cattle he might be able to find. An outbreak of the prisoners is apprehended: and if they were to rise, it is feared some of the inhabitants of the city would join them, for they, too, have no meat—many of them—or bread either. They believe the famine is owing to the imbecility, or worse of the government. A riot would be a dangerous occurrence now: the city battalion would not fire on the people—and if they did the army might break up, and avenge their slaughtered kindred. It is a perilous time.

March 18th.—My daughter's cat is staggering to-day, for want of animal food. Sometimes I fancy I stagger myself. We do not average two ounces of meat daily; and some do not get any for several days together. Meal is $50 per bushel. I saw adamantine candles sell at auction to-day (box) at $10 per pound; tallow, $6.50. Bacon brought $7.75 per pound by the 100 pounds.

April 8th.—Bright and warm—really a fine spring day. It is the day of *fasting*, humiliation, and prayer, and all the offices are closed. May God put it into the hearts of the extortioners to relent, and abolish, for a season, the insatiable greed for gain! I paid $25 for a half cord of wood to-day, new currency. I fear a nation of extortioners are unworthy of independence, and that we must be chastened and purified before success will be vouchsafed us.

What enormous appetites we have now, and how little illness, since food has become so high in price! I cannot afford to have more than an ounce of meat daily for each member of my family of six; and to-day Custis's parrot, which has accompanied the family in all their flights, and, it seems, will *never* die, stole the cook's ounce of fat meat and gobbled it up before it could be taken from him. He is permitted to set at one corner of the table, and has lately acquired a fondness for meat. The old cat goes staggering about from debility, although Fannie often gives him her share. We see neither rats nor mice about the premises now. This is famine. Even the pigeons watch the crusts in the hands of the children, and follow them in the yard. *And, still, there are no beggars.*

August 13th.—Flour is falling: It is now $200 per barrel—$500 a few weeks ago; and bacon is falling in price also, from $11 to $6 per pound. A commission merchant said to me, yesterday, that there was at least eighteen months' supply (for the people) of breadstuffs and meats in the city; and pointing to the upper windows at the corner of Thirteenth and Cary Streets, he revealed the ends of many barrels piled above the windows. He said that flour had been there two years, held for "still higher prices." Such is the avarice of man. Such is war. And such the greed of extortioners, even in the midst of famine—and famine in the midst of plenty!

—JONES, *A Rebel War Clerk's Diary*

3. MR. EGGLESTON RECALLS WHEN MONEY WAS PLENTIFUL

Eggleston's account of the impact of inflation on the life of the South— and especially of Richmond—parallels and supplements that of the Rebel war clerk, but is more genial and optimistic. Certainly his conclusion that municipal regulations wiped out gambling in the Confederate capital is not borne out by other evidence. George Cary Eggleston was, himself, a romantic character. Born in Indiana—brother of that Edward Eggleston who wrote the famous Hoosier Schoolmaster—*he early inherited a plantation in Amelia County, Virginia, and wholly identified himself with the life of the South. At the outbreak of the war he joined the 1st Virginia Cavalry, fought under Stuart, Fitzhugh Lee, and Longstreet and, for a time, in the South Carolina field artillery.*

After the war Eggleston had a long career as journalist and man of letters.

He was literary editor of the New York Evening Post, *served on the staff of the* New York World, *wrote scores of novels and boy's stories, compiled his recollections, and contributed a two-volume* History of the Confederate War *that is still valuable.*

THE financial system adopted by the Confederate government was singularly simple and free from technicalities. It consisted chiefly in the issue of treasury notes enough to meet all the expenses of the government, and in the present advanced state of the art of printing there was but one difficulty incident to this process; namely, the impossibility of having the notes signed in the Treasury Department as fast as they were needed. There happened, however, to be several thousand young ladies in Richmond willing to accept light and remunerative employment at their homes, and as it was really a matter of small moment whose names the notes bore, they were given out in sheets to these young ladies, who signed and returned them for a consideration. I shall not undertake to guess how many Confederate treasury notes were issued. Indeed, I am credibly informed by a gentleman who was high in office in the Treasury Department that even the secretary himself did not certainly know. The acts of Congress authorizing issues of currency were the hastily formulated thought of a not very wise body of men, and my informant tells me they were frequently susceptible of widely different construction by different officials. However that may be, it was clearly out of the power of the government ever to redeem the notes, and whatever may have been the state of affairs within the treasury, nobody outside its precincts ever cared to muddle his head in an attempt to get at exact figures.

We knew only that money was astonishingly abundant. Provisions fell short sometimes, and the supply of clothing was not always as large as we should have liked, but nobody found it difficult to get money enough. It was to be had almost for the asking. And to some extent the abundance of the currency really seemed to atone for its extreme badness. Going the rounds of the pickets on the coast of South Carolina one day in 1863, I heard a conversation between a Confederate and a Union soldier, stationed on opposite sides of a little inlet, in the course of which this point was brought out.

Union Soldier. Aren't times rather hard over there, Johnny?

Confederate Soldier. Not at all. We've all the necessaries of life.

U.S. Yes, but how about luxuries? You never see any coffee nowadays, do you?

C.S. Plenty of it.

U.S. Isn't it pretty high?

C.S. Forty dollars a pound, that's all.

U.S. Whew! Don't you call that high?

C.S. (after reflecting). Well, perhaps it is a trifle uppish, but then you never saw money so plentiful as it is with us. We hardly know what to do with it and don't mind paying high prices for things we want.

And that was the universal feeling. Money was so easily got and its value was so utterly uncertain that we were never able to determine what was a fair price for anything. We fell into the habit of paying whatever was asked, knowing that tomorrow we should have to pay more. Speculation became the easiest and surest thing imaginable. The speculator saw no risks of loss. Every article of merchandise rose in value every day, and to buy anything this week and sell it next was to make an enormous profit quite as a matter of course. So uncertain were prices, or rather so constantly did they tend upward, that when a cargo of cadet-gray cloths was brought into Charleston once, an officer in my battery, attending the sale, was able to secure enough of the cloth to make two suits of clothes without any expense whatever, merely by speculating upon an immediate advance. He became the purchaser at auction of a case of the goods and had no difficulty, as soon as the sale was over, in finding a merchant who was glad to take his bargain off his hands, giving him the cloth he wanted as a premium. The officer could not possibly have paid for the case of goods, but there was nothing surer than that he could sell again at an advance the moment the auctioneer's hammer fell on the last lot of cloths. . . .

The prices which obtained were almost fabulous, and singularly enough there seemed to be no sort of ratio existing between the values of different articles. I bought coffee at forty dollars and tea at thirty dollars a pound on the same day.

My dinner at a hotel cost me twenty dollars, while five dollars gained me a seat in the dress circle of the theater. I paid one dollar the next morning for a copy of the *Examiner*, but I might have got the *Whig, Dispatch, Enquirer*, or *Sentinel* for half that sum. For some wretched tallow candles I paid ten dollars a pound. The utter absence of proportion between these several prices is apparent, and I know of no way of explaining it except upon the theory that the unstable character of the money superinduced a reckless disregard of all value on the part of both buyers and sellers. A facetious friend used to say prices were so high that nobody could see them and that they "got mixed for want of supervision." He held, however, that the difference between the old and the new order of things was a trifling one. "Before the war," he said, "I went to market with the money in my pocket and brought back my purchases in a basket; now I take the money in the basket and bring the things home in my pocket." . . .

The effects of the extreme depreciation of the currency were sometimes almost ludicrous. One of my friends, a Richmond lady, narrowly escaped very serious trouble in an effort to practise a wise economy. Anything for which the dealers did not ask an outrageously high price seemed wonderfully cheap always, and she, at least, lacked the self-control necessary to abstain from buying largely whenever she found anything the price of which was lower than she had supposed it would be. Going into market one morning with "stimulated ideas of prices," as she phrased it, the consequence of having paid a thousand dollars for a barrel of flour, she was surprised to find nearly everything selling for considerably less than she had expected. Thinking that for some unexplained cause there was a temporary depression in prices, she purchased pretty largely in a good many directions, buying, indeed, several things for which she had almost no use at all and buying considerably more than she needed of other articles. As she was quitting the market on foot—for it had become disreputable in Richmond to ride in a carriage, and the ladies would not do it on any account—she was tapped on the shoulder by an officer who told her she was under arrest, for buying in market to sell again. As the lady was well known to prominent people she was speedily released, but she thereafter curbed her propensity to buy freely of cheap things. Buying to sell again had been forbidden under severe penalties—an absolutely necessary measure for the protection of the people against the rapacity of the hucksters, who, going early into the markets, would buy literally everything there and by agreement among themselves double or quadruple the already exorbitant rates.

It became necessary also to suppress the gambling houses in the interest of the half-starved people. At such a time, of course, gambling was a very common vice, and the gamblers made Richmond their headquarters. It was the custom of the proprietors of these establishments to set costly suppers in their parlors every night for the purpose of attracting visitors likely to become victims. For these suppers they must have the best of everything without stint, and their lavish rivalry in the poorly-stocked markets had the effect of advancing prices to a dangerous point. To suppress the gambling houses was the sole remedy, and it was only by uncommonly severe measures that the suppression could be accomplished. It was therefore enacted that any one found guilty of keeping a gambling house should be publicly whipped upon the bare back, and as the infliction of the penalty in one or two instances effectually and permanently broke up the business of gambling, even in the disorganized and demoralized state in which society then was, it may be said with confidence that whipping is the one certain remedy for this evil. Whether it be not, in ordinary cases, worse than the evil which it cures, it is not our business just now to inquire.

—Eggleston, *A Rebel's Recollections*

4. RICHMOND IS DEMORALIZED BY RUMORS

Perhaps there were no more rumors in Richmond than in Washington, but Richmond was more susceptible to them. That, at least, was the opinion of Edward Pollard, editor of the Richmond Examiner, *and historian of the war. Pollard was a curious character who had studied law, prepared for the ministry, and then ended up in journalism. An ardent secessionist, he was an equally ardent critic of Jefferson Davis, and devoted the columns of his paper to persistent and savage attacks upon the President and his policy. During and after the war he wrote a number of volumes of war history, among them this* Life of Jefferson Davis *with a "secret" history of the war. D. H. Hill charged him with "the most stupendous, wholesale plagiarism, ever perpetrated in the literary annals of the world"—a statement as extreme as those Pollard himself was accustomed to make and perhaps more accurate than most of Pollard's.*

AND here we are called to regard a most curious subject in the history of the war—the number and volume of false rumors that circulated in it. To search the origin of these rumors, to describe their flight, to inquire how the falsehoods were fledged, and to trace their effects on the spirit and conduct of the belligerents, would constitute, we believe, a chapter of entertaining and even valuable speculation. Although the two powers at war were coterminous, and although there were varied and multiplied communications between the lines of military operations, it is wonderful to notice the multitude and prevalence of false rumors which obscured the true history of the war, and tantalized, provoked, and indeed, seriously embarrassed the combatants. The prevalence of these rumors was peculiar in the South. The comparative multitude of them was due not only to the characteristically lively disposition of the people, but to a special and exceptional cause. That cause was the affected mystery with which Mr. Davis imitated some of the worst examples of government, and in the mists of which he was anxious to enlarge his own figure to most undue proportions. . . .

It would be one of the most curious volumes of modern times, a collection of all the rumors circulated in Richmond alone during the war, leaving out none of their absurdities. It would be metaphysically interesting as showing how busy and various the human fancy is. There are but two persons now who could make such a collection, even approximately, and they, through this generation, will be graphically remembered in Richmond as the rival news-hunters of a historical period. In this character they were the most notorious men in the capital.

The first, a wealthy speculator and man of leisure, was popularly known as "Long Tom," from his thin and elongated figure. This man appeared to take a morbid delight in the sole occupation of hunting news day and night; it got to be a kind of insanity with him; he scarcely ate or slept, and, at almost every hour of the day, and far into the night, he might be seen haunting the telegraph office, wandering like a weary ghost in the passage way of the War Department, or holding his hand to his ear on the skirts of every crowd on the street corners. He had no particular purpose to serve in this eaves-dropping and ear-wigging; it was his entertainment, his occupation by choice, and he was never happier than when he obtained a piece of news, good or bad, with permission to retail it.

His rival in the rumor business was a little, ferrety, incoherent man, a druggist by profession, but a "sensationist" by real occupation. He dealt only in the largest sensations. He had a habit of speaking with infinite gesture; would sometimes be lost in a perfect splutter of exclamation, when he had important news to convey; and was so dense and unintelligible in his communications, that he generally had to tell his story twice to be understood. He would sometimes break into the newspaper offices, pale and incoherent, with the most dreadful stories, nigh to bursting with news, and in such tremor from his emotions that the reporters would find it a task to calm him, and were wont to compose his nerves by a strengthening draught as a preface to his recital. Once the author recollects to have been called across the street by this little man making the most eager and dramatic gestures, and actually quivering with excitement. "Great God, have you heard the news, Mr. P.," he exclaimed thickly; "Jeff. Davis has just committed suicide!" An hour later, this news of the tragic end of the Confederate Chief had circulated all through Richmond, was wafted across the lines, and was given to the wings of the telegraph from James River to the Penobscot.

To recount even the most important of the false rumors which possessed Richmond during the war, would occupy more space than we can command. Let those who then resided in the Confederate capital but attempt to recall to memory how often Ministers from England and France had arrived with news of recognition; how often peace commissioners had come by devious ways to Richmond, with protocols and treaties; how often Beauregard crossed the Potomac in 1861; how often Washington had been captured; how often Grant's army had been defeated before Vicksburg—the stench of its dead being such that fires had to be kindled on the lines and in the streets of the town, to purify the atmosphere (so said the telegraph); in short, how often great victories were won and great defeats suffered, which never happened, or existed out of imagination!

The rumors we have described were not the least of the demoralizing consequences of Mr. Davis's unrepublican style of government. They were saps of the public spirit of the South. What is most remarkable of these rumors is that they frequently came from reputable and even semi-official sources. They did not always come from obscure authors. There were, of course, the common, paltry classes of news retailers:—the man who had just came through the lines, the "intelligent gentleman," the interesting lady refugee, and the person who mysteriously had it from "good authority." These might be listened to with contempt, or with a degree of skepticism. But in many instances in Richmond, rumors grossly false were circulated from sources so well calculated to obtain belief, that for days and weeks they would possess the public mind, and compel even the credence of newspaper men, a class which, though ambitious of news, is characteristically skeptical, and trained to estimate its probability. The fact is, the Confederate Government was so close in its confidences, so absolutely secret and secluse, that even those otherwise in close relations with it were imposed upon by false beliefs, and gave impressive endorsement to the wildest rumors.

—POLLARD, *Life of Jefferson Davis*

5. PARTHENIA HAGUE TELLS HOW WOMEN OUTWITTED THE BLOCKADE

Probably not until 1863 was the blockade really effective, but even before that date the South began to feel the pinch for ordinary domestic necessities. Now the South was paying the price for neglecting to develop even local industries. Probably the best of all accounts of what life was like for a Southern family from day to day, is that by Parthenia Hague, a Georgia lady who went to live on an Alabama plantation during the war.

AS no shoe-blacking or polish could be bought during the blockade, each family improvised its own blacking, which was soot and oil of some variety (either cottonseed, ground peas, or oil of compressed lard) mixed together. The shoes would be well painted with the mixture of soot and oil, with brushes made of the bristles of swine. Then a thin paste made of flour, bolted meal, or starch, was applied all over the blackened shoe with another brush, which paste, when dry, gave the shoe as bright and glossy an appearance as if "shined" by the best of bootblacks. Planters were very careful in killing their hogs to save a good supply of bristles, from which shapely brushes were manufactured.

The obtaining of salt became extremely difficult when the war had cut off our supply. This was true especially in regions remote from the sea-coast and border States, such as the interior of Alabama and Georgia. Here again we were obliged to have recourse to whatever expedient ingenuity suggested. All the brine left in troughs and barrels, where pork had been salted down, was carefully dipped up, boiled down, and converted into salt again. In some cases the salty soil under old smoke-houses was dug up and placed in hoppers, which resembled backwoods ash-hoppers, made for leaching ashes in the process of soap-manufacture. Water was then poured upon the soil, the brine which percolated through the hopper was boiled down to the proper point, poured into vessels, and set in the sun, which by evaporation completed the rude process. Though never of immaculate whiteness, the salt which resulted from these methods served well enough for all our purposes, and we accepted it without complaining.

Before the war there were in the South but few cotton mills. These were kept running night and day, as soon as the Confederate army was organized, and we were ourselves prevented by the blockade from purchasing clothing from the factories at the North, or clothing from France or England. The cotton which grew in the immediate vicinity of the mills kept them well supplied with raw material. Yet notwithstanding the great push of the cotton mills, they proved totally inadequate, after the war began, to our vast need for clothing of every kind. Every household now became a miniature factory in itself, with its cotton, cards, spinning-wheels, warping frames, looms, and so on. Wherever one went, the hum of the spinning wheel and the clang of the batten of the loom was borne on the ear.

Great trouble was experienced, in the beginning, to find dyes with which to color our stuffs; but in the course of time, both at the old mills and at smaller experimental factories, which were run entirely by hand, barks, leaves, roots, and berries were found containing coloring properties. I was well acquainted with a gentleman in southwestern Georgia who owned a small cotton mill, and who, when he wanted coloring substances, used to send his wagons to the woods and freight them with a shrub known as myrtle, that grew teeming in low moist places near his mill. This myrtle yielded a nice gray for woolen goods.

That the slaves might be well clad, the owners kept, according to the number of slaves owned, a number of Negro women carding and spinning, and had looms running all the time. Now and then a planter would be so fortunate as to secure a bale or more of white sheeting and osnaburgs from the cotton mills, in exchange for farm products, which would be quite a lift, and give a little breathing-spell from the almost incessant whirr, hum, and clang of the spinning wheel and loom. . . .

I have often joined with neighbors, when school hours for the day were over, in gathering roots, barks, leaves, twigs, sumach berries, and walnuts, for the hulls, which dyed wool a beautiful dark brown. Such was the variety we had to choose from, to dye our cloth and thread. We used to pull our way through the deep tangled woods, by thickly shaded streams, through broad fields, and return laden with the riches of the Southern forest! Not infrequently clusters of grapes mingled with our freight of dyes. The pine-tree's roots furnished a beautiful dye, approximating very closely to garnet, which color I chose for the sheeting for my dress. A strong decoction of the roots of the pine-tree was used. Copperas of our own production was used as the mordant. A cask or some small vessel was set convenient to the dwell-ing-house and partly filled with water, in which a small quantity of salt and vinegar had been mingled; then pieces of rusty, useless iron, such as plows too much worn to be used again, rusty broken rails, old horse-shoes, and bits of old chains were picked up and cast into the cask. The liquid copperas was always ready, and a very good substance we found it to fix colors in cloth or thread. The sheeting for the dress was folded smoothly and basted slightly so as to keep the folds in place. It was first thoroughly soaked in warm soap-suds, then dipped into the dye, and afterwards into a vessel containing liquid lye from wood-ashes; then it went again into the dye, then the lye, and so on till the garnet color was the required shade. By varying the strength of the solution any shade desirable could be obtained. My garnet-colored dress of unbleached sheeting was often mistaken for worsted delaine. . . .

One of our most difficult tasks was to find a good substitute for coffee. This palatable drink, if not a real necessary of life, is almost indispensable to the enjoyment of a good meal, and some Southerners took it three times a day. Coffee soon rose to thirty dollars per pound; from that it went to sixty and seventy dollars per pound. Good workmen received thirty dollars per day; so it took two days' hard labor to buy one pound of coffee, and scarcely any could be had even at that fabulous price. Some imagined themselves much better in health for the absence of coffee, and wondered why they had ever used it at all, and declared it good for nothing any way; but "Sour grapes" would be the reply for such as they. Others saved a few handfuls of coffee, and used it on very important occasions, and then only as an extract, so to speak, for flavoring substitutes for coffee.

There were those who planted long rows of the okra plant on the borders of their cotton or corn fields, and cultivated this with the corn and cotton. The seeds of this, when mature and nicely browned, came nearer in flavor to the real coffee than any other substitute I now remember. Yam potatoes used to be peeled, sliced thin, cut into small squares, dried and then parched brown; they were thought to be next best to okra for coffee. Browned wheat, meal, and burnt corn made passable beverages; even meal-bran was browned and used for coffee if other substitutes were not obtainable.

We had several substitutes for tea which were equally as palatable, and, I fancy, more wholesome, than much that is now sold for tea. Prominent among these substitutes were raspberry leaves. Many during the blockade planted and cultivated the raspberry-vine all around their garden palings, as much for tea as the berries for jam or pies; these leaves were considered the best substitute for tea. The leaves of the blackberry bush, huckleberry leaves, and the leaves of the holly-tree when dried in the shade, also made a palatable tea.

Persimmons dried served for dates.

Each household made its own starch, some of the bran of wheat flour. Green corn and sweet potatoes were grated in order to make starch. This process was very simple. The grated substance was placed to soak in a large tub of water; when it had passed through the process of fermentation and had risen to the surface, the grated matter was all skimmed off, the water holding the starch in solution was passed through a sieve, and then through a thin cloth to free altogether from any foreign substance. A change of clear water twice a day for three or four days was made to more thoroughly bleach the starch. It would then be put on white cloth, placed on scaffolds in the yard, and left to drip and dry. Starch of wheat bran was made in the same manner. It was as white and fine as any ever bought.

A good makeshift had soon been devised for putty and cement, and the artlessness of it will perhaps cause a smile to flit across the face of glaziers. But no cement could be bought, and this was useful in many ways, as panes of glass had to be set in, or a break to be mended; the handle broken from a pitcher to be placed on anew, or repairing done to table ware. When it was necessary to repair any such breaks, a Spanish potato (none other of the species of that esculent root answered so well) was roasted in hot ashes, peeled while yet hot, immediately mashed very fine, and mixed with about a tablespoonful of flour; it was then, while warm, applied to whatever need there was. This paste, when it had become hardened, remained fixed and firm, and was as durable as putty.

In place of kerosene for lights, the oil of cotton seed and ground peas, together with the oil of compressed lard, was used, and served well the need of the times. For lights we had also to fall back on moulding candles, which had long years lain obsolete. When beeswax was plentiful it was mixed with tallow for moulding candles. Long rows of candles so moulded would be hung on the lower limbs of widespreading oaks, where, sheltered by the dense foliage from the direct rays of the sun, they would remain suspended day and night until they were bleached as white as the sperm candles we had been wont to buy, and almost as transparent as wax candles. When there was no oil for the lamps or tallow for moulding candles, which at times befell our households, mother-wit would suggest some expedient by which the intricate problem of light could be solved.

—HAGUE, *A Blockaded Family*

6. THE CONFEDERATES BURN THEIR COTTON

Two considerations persuaded the Confederacy to try to limit cotton production: the necessity of growing enough food for her needs, and the desire to create an artificial cotton scarcity for purposes of bargaining for foreign recognition. The result of Confederate and state laws—the latter by all odds the most effective—and of invasion and the general derangement of war was a reduction in the cotton crop from over four million bales in 1861 to only three hundred thousand bales in 1864. In addition to this reduction of planting, the Confederate Congress required owners to destroy all cotton that might fall into enemy hands, and it has been estimated that some two and one half million bales were destroyed by planters or by the Confederate armies. When Farragut forced the entrance to the Mississippi on April 24, 1862, the Confederates destroyed the cotton piled up in New Orleans to prevent it falling into Federal hands.

Sarah Dawson, whom we have met elsewhere, was the daughter of Judge Thomas Gibbes Morgan, whose home in Baton Rouge was sacked by the Federals in 1862. She later married Francis Warringtone Dawson, English journalist and littérateur, who ran the blockade to join the Confederacy, fought in the Army of Northern Virginia, and later edited the famous Charleston News and Courier.

April 26, 1862.—We went this morning to see the cotton burning—a sight never before witnessed and probably never again to be seen. Wagons, drays—everything that can be driven or rolled—were loaded with the bales and taken a few squares back to burn on the commons. Negroes were running around, cutting them open, piling them up, and setting them afire. All were as busy as though their salvation depended on disappointing the Yankees. Later Charlie sent for us to come to the river and see him fire a flatboat loaded with the precious material for which the Yankees are risking their bodies and souls. Up and down the levee, as far as we could see, Negroes were rolling it down to the brink of the river where they would set the bales afire and push them in to float burning down the tide. Each sent up its wreath of smoke and looked like a tiny steamer puffing away. Only I doubt that from the source to the mouth of the river there are as many boats afloat on the Mississippi. The flatboat was piled with as many bales as it could hold without sinking. Most of them were cut open, while Negroes staved in the heads of barrels of alcohol, whisky, etc., and dashed bucketfuls over the cotton. Others built up little chimneys of pine every few feet, lined with pine knots and loose cotton, to burn more quickly. There, piled the length of the whole levee or burning in the river, lay the work of thousands of Negroes for more than a year past. It had come from every side. Men stood by who owned the cotton that was burning or waiting to burn. They either helped or looked on cheerfully. Charlie owned but sixteen bales—a matter of some fifteen hundred dollars; but he was the head man of the whole affair and burned his own as well as the property of others. A single barrel of whisky that was thrown on the cotton cost the man who gave it one hundred and twenty-five dollars. (It shows what a nation in earnest is capable of doing.) Only two men got on the flatboat with Charlie when it was ready. It was towed to the middle of the river, set afire in every place, and then they jumped into a little skiff fastened in front and rowed to land. The cotton floated down the Mississippi one sheet of living flame, even in the sunlight. It would have been grand at night. But then we will have fun watching it this evening anyway, for they cannot get through today, though no time is to be lost. Hundreds of bales remained untouched. An incredible amount of property has been destroyed today, but no one begrudges it. Every grogshop has been emptied, and gutters and pavements are floating with liquors of all kinds. So that if the Yankees are fond of strong drink, they will fare ill.

—DAWSON, *A Confederate Girl's Diary*

7. YANKEE CONTRACTORS SPECULATE IN COTTON

The reduction of the cotton crop and the blockade meant a great scarcity of cotton in the North and abroad; this in turn sent the price soaring to 31 cents a pound in 1862, 67 cents in 1863 and $1.00 in 1864. Federal law required that all cotton seized by the armies should be turned into the Treasury Department, which in turn disposed of it in the world market. The temptation to speculate in cotton was, however, irresistible. The armies of the West were accompanied by hordes of contractors who by one means or another—almost invariably illegal—obtained large quantities of cotton which they sold on their own account.

Thomas Knox was a war correspondent for the New York Herald *who made himself so obnoxious to Sherman that he was court-martialed and expelled from the army. He then took on the management of a cotton plantation in Louisiana, and it was from this vantage point that he watched the speculation in cotton. After the war he wrote a large number of juveniles.*

ON many plantations the cotton crop of 1862 was still in the field, somewhat damaged by the winter rains; but well worth gathering at the prices which then ruled the market. General Grant gave authority for the gathering of this cotton by any parties who were willing to take the contract. The contractors were required to feed the Negroes and pay them for their labor. One-half the cotton went to the Government, the balance to the contractor. There was no lack of men to undertake the collection of abandoned cotton on these terms, as the enterprise could not fail to be exceedingly remunerative.

This cotton, gathered by Government authority, was, with a few exceptions, the only cotton which could be shipped to market. There were large quantities of "old" cotton—gathered and baled in previous years—which the owners were anxious to sell, and speculators ready to buy. Numerous applications were made for shipping-permits, but nearly all were rejected. A few cases were pressed upon General Grant's attention, as deserving exception from the ordinary rule.

There was one case of two young girls, whose parents had recently died, and who were destitute of all comforts on the plantation where they lived. They had a quantity of cotton which they wished to take to Memphis, for sale in that market. Thus provided with money, they would proceed North, and remain there till the end of the war.

A speculator became interested in these girls, and plead with all his eloquence for official favor in their behalf. General Grant softened his heart and gave this man a written permit to ship whatever cotton belonged to the orphans. It was understood, and so stated in the application, that the amount was between two hundred and three hundred bales. The exact number not being known, there was no quantity specified in the permit.

The speculator soon discovered that the penniless orphans could claim two thousand instead of two hundred bales, and thought it possible they would find three thousand bales and upward. On the strength of his permit without special limit, he had purchased, or otherwise procured, all the cotton he could find in the immediate vicinity. He was allowed to make shipment of a few hundred bales; the balance was detained.

Immediately, as this transaction became known, every speculator was on the *qui vive* to discover a widow or an orphan. Each plantation was visited, and the status of the owners, if any remained, became speedily known. Orphans and widows, the former in particular, were at a high premium. Never in the history of Louisiana did the children of tender years, bereft of parents, receive such attention from strangers. A spectator might have imagined the Millennium close at hand, and the dealers in cotton about to be humbled at the feet of babes and sucklings. Widows, neither young nor comely, received the warmest attention from men of Northern birth. . . . Everywhere in that region there were men seeking "healthy orphans for adoption."

The majority of the speculators found the widows and orphans of whom they were in search. Some were able to obtain permits, while others were not. Several officers of the army became interested in these speculations, and gave their aid to obtain shipping privileges. Some who were innocent were accused of dealing in the forbidden fiber, while others, guilty of the transaction, escaped without suspicion. The temptation was great. Many refused to be concerned in the traffic; but there were some who yielded.

The contractors who gathered the abandoned cotton were enabled to accumulate small fortunes. Some of them acted honestly, but others made use of their contracts to cover large shipments of purchased or stolen cotton, baled two or three years before. The ordinary yield of an acre of ground is from a bale to a bale and a half. The contractors were sometimes able to show a yield of ten or twenty bales to the acre.

—Knox, *Camp-Fire and Cotton-Field*

8. "THE YANKEES ARE COMING"

It was the fate of the South to know invasion—and the ruth of war. Sometimes—as with Sheridan and Hunter in the Valley or Sherman in Georgia and the Carolinas—invasion meant pillaging and destruction; sometimes it was orderly enough. Occasionally, as in Mrs. Ward's account, it turned out to be merely the coming of Federal prisoners. We have met Mrs. Ward before; she was twenty-three when the events which she described took place; her description came in the form of testimony before the Congressional committee 20 years later. Of this testimony Margaret Mitchell wrote, "If I had had that book, I'm sure I would not have had to read hundreds of memoirs, letters and diaries to get the background of Gone with the Wind *accurately."*

IN the fall of 1863 we were very much menaced by General Rosecrans' army up about Dalton and Resaca, and every little while we would have an alarm that a raid was coming. A raid was a very amusing thing, or rather, it is amusing to think of now. We would wake up out of our sleep and everybody would spring out of bed saying, "The Yankees are coming; they are only 10 miles out of town; they are coming with a sword in one hand and a torch in the other." That was the watchword. Then we would all try to think what we had that was valuable, although at that time we didn't have much except the family silver and furniture, which were rapidly wearing out. The supply of bed linen was also getting small. The blankets had been all sent to the soldiers long before. Very few housekeepers had blankets as late as 1863. On these occasions the ladies would put on three or four dresses and tie around under the dresses everything that could be suspended and hidden in that way. Hams would be jerked out of the smoke-house, and holes would be dug and everything thrown in pell mell. Then we would begin to imagine that because *we* knew where those things were, the first Yankee that appeared would know, too, and often we would go and take them all up from there and dig another hole and put them in that; so that our yards came to look like graveyards. It is very funny to think of now, but it wasn't funny then—to be flying around in the middle of the night that way. Then, to add to the confusion, the children would wake up and would stare around with a vacant look, and begin saying, "What is the matter? What is the matter?" And then we would tell them "The Yankees are coming." . . .

The ideas of the children about the Yankees was very funny. As soon as they heard the Yankees were coming they would jump up and get under the bed, or run out of the house. In fact they would have no idea of what they ought to do to preserve themselves. If you told them the house was on fire of course their first impulse would have been to get out of the house, but when you told them the Yankees were coming they didn't know what to do or which way to turn—whether to run out of the house or to get under the bed or go up the chimney.

I remember one night—all these things come up to me now so vividly—I remember just such a night as I have been describing, when all the children jumped up and got under the bed. We asked what was the matter. Well, "the Yankees were coming." There was one little girl who was terribly frightened. She had no idea whether the Yankees were men, or horses, or what kind of animals they were. She just knew that they were something dreadful. That business went on through the whole of that night; we would hear that the Yankees were six miles off; that they were two miles off, and every sound we heard, whether it was the baker's cart, or anything else, we would think it was the Yankees; that they were actually in town.

On these occasions, after we had secured the things, as we thought, there would be consultations as to which of the servants would be the most trustworthy to do the manual labor—which ones we could take into our confidence, for of course it was necessary to have a Negro man around to lift things. We were obliged to take them into our confidence, and yet we mistrusted them on such occasions, because this was in 1863, and by that time there had been a great many stories told among us of the disloyalty of servants in such emergencies.

On the night I am now speaking of this excitement continued until morning came. Everybody had been up all night, and it would have been a relief to us to have known that the Yankees had come; but after awhile we ascertained that it was an unmistakable demonstration; that the Yankees were really down here about Gadsden, and that the report brought to Rome had come from a very reliable man, who had traveled all night to carry the news. The first alarm came from somebody who had heard of the matter but was not able to report the entire truth. That night and the next morning all was suspense. . . .

Just as we were all expecting the Yankees to come in, and expecting that we were just literally going to be butchered—in fact I don't know what we did think—a courier came rushing into town with the news that Forrest had captured the Yankees and was bringing them in with him as captives. Then there was a reaction, and the excitement was worse than any camp-meeting you ever saw. Everybody was flying from one end of the town to the other. Suppers that were just ready to be cooked were never cooked or eaten; there was a general jollification. Everybody in town felt relieved from a terrible pressure. Forrest came into town and every lady insisted on going up and speaking to the general and shaking hands with him and his forces. My daughter Minnie was a baby at the time, and I took her with me and went up and spoke to him and he took her and kissed her. He told us that his prisoners were coming into town, and he wanted them to eat at once. Everybody went home and there was just a regular wholesale cooking of hams and shoulders and all sorts of provisions that we had, and everything was sent down to the respective camps. We were quite willing to feed the Yankees when they had no guns.

—Testimony of Mrs. Mary A. Ward

9. "THE LIVES WHICH WOMEN HAVE LEAD SINCE TROY FELL"

The Union had no such galaxy of woman diarists and memoir writers as the Confederacy—women like Mrs. Chesnut, Sarah Morgan, Judith Mc-

Thomas Nast

The Attack on Battery Wagner

Admiral Farragut at Mobile Bay

Guire, Parthenia Hague, Eliza Andrews, and others. To this brilliant group belongs Julia LeGrand. Her father had been a colonel in the War of 1812 and one of the lordly planters of Louisiana, and Julia grew up in the world of fashion and of culture. Impoverished by her father's death, and by the war, Miss LeGrand and her sister opened a girl's school in New Orleans, and were there when the Federals captured the city. Later they took refuge in Georgia and in Texas. Only fragments of the wartime diary have been preserved.

To Mrs. Shepard Brown.

New Orleans, Nov. 17th, 1862

Dear Mrs. B——:

I have nothing to say, and might not say it if I did have it, for you know there is a heaviness prevailing in this latitude, which is not favorable to expansion of idea. I only send a line to remind you that I live and wish you to remember me. A dull and heavy anxiety has settled upon us. We hear nothing to which we can cling with comfort. Those who come in say there is much joy beyond the lines, but no one can give the why and wherefore. In the meantime we are leading the lives which women have lead since Troy fell; wearing away time with memories, regrets and fears; alternating fits of suppression, with flights, imaginary, to the red fields where great principles are contended for, lost and won; while men, more privileged, are abroad and astir, making name and fortune and helping to make a nation.

There was a frolic on board the English ship a few nights since for the benefit, the *Delta* says, of Secession women. I did not go, though Miss Betty Callender offered her services in the way of invitation. I am told that the contraband "bonny-blue flag" waved freely over seas of red wine and promontories of sugar-work. The ship represents secessiondom just now; it has not a stronghold in the city. Many a lady opened her vial of wrath, I suppose, for all were told that freedom of speech should be the order of the night. There was acting and dancing, and fish, flesh and fowl suffered in the name of our cause. Toasts were drunk to our great spirits to whom it seems the destiny of a nation is entrusted. How my heart warms to the weary, battle-stained heroes. I never fancied carpet knights even before the stern trial came.

I can't tell you what a life of suppression we lead. I feel it more because I know and feel all that is going on outside. I am like a pent-up volcano. I wish I had a field for my energies. I hate common life, a life of visiting, dressing and tattling, which seems to devolve on women, and now that there is better work to do, real tragedy, real romance and history weaving every day, I suffer, suffer, leading the life I do. . . .

Things go on just as they did. Daily life presents the same food for sorrowful reflection. Tiger, Jake and Emma hold their own within doors, and nothing has happened to prevent us from parading the streets without. A shrill horn breaks often upon my sad speculations. I rush out perhaps and sometimes find a train of striped and bestarred cavalry and sometimes only an orange cart. "What an age we live in," says philosophy, and goes in again to repine and wonder. The *Advocate* was suppressed an hour or two ago, but the pliant Jacob made haste to smooth his phrases. A quarrel is reported between the French admiral and the General. There has been a great commotion about the money sent from the New Orleans bank. Lemore has gone to prison and some others. Where are our people? Can't you contrive to let me into the secret, if you have any? You can't read if I keep on, so goodbye, with best wishes to all.

Ever your friend,

J. E. LeGrand.

—Rowland and Croxall, eds., *The Journal of Julia LeGrand*

10. "THEY MUST REAP THE WHIRLWIND"

This brief excerpt* from a letter of General Sherman's to his wife is a fitting commentary on the two preceding items. The "enmity of the women of the South" is a familiar theme in Civil War literature. Mrs. Chesnut herself wrote that "we hate our enemies and love our friends," and Stephen Vincent Benét, whose John Brown's Body *is in some ways the most faithful of all interpretations of the war, has written of*

> *The terrible hate of women's ire*
> *The smoky, the long-consuming fire.†*

To his wife.

Camp on Bear Creek, 20 Miles N.W. of Vicksburg, June 27, 1863

I doubt if history affords a parallel to the deep and bitter enmity of the women of the South. No one who sees them and hears them but must feel the intensity of their hate. Not a man is seen; nothing but women with houses plundered, fields open to the cattle and horses, pickets lounging on every porch, and desolation sown broadcast, servants all gone and women and children bred in luxury, beautiful and accomplished, begging with one breath for the soldiers' ration and in another praying that the Almighty or Joe Johnston will come and kill us, the despoilers of their homes and all that is sacred. Why cannot they look back to the day and hour when I, a stranger in Louisiana, begged and implored them to pause in their career, that secession was death, was everything fatal, and that their seizure of the public arsenals was an insult that the most abject nation must resent or pass down to future ages an object of pity and scorn? Vicksburg contains many of my old pupils and friends; should it fall into our hands I will treat them with kindness, but they have sowed the wind and must reap the whirlwind. Until

---

they lay down their arms and submit to the rightful authority of the government they must not appeal to me for mercy or favors.

—Howe, ed., *Home Letters of General Sherman*

11. GEORGIA'S GOVERNOR LAMENTS DAVIS' DESPOTISM

If Lincoln had his Seymours and Vallandighams, Davis had men like Governor Brown and Governor Vance to contend with. There was, if anything, more discontent and positive disloyalty in the Confederacy than in the Union. Part of it was inspired by sincere State-rights sentiment, part by personal hostility to President Davis, part by dissatisfaction with the conduct of the war. State-righters like Stephens and Brown and Vance thought the tyranny of Richmond worse than that of Washington; they were particularly outraged by such things as conscription and the suspension of the writ of habeas corpus. Others were sure that Davis was a monster of wickedness and of incompetence, and exhausted their energies denouncing him and his administration.

The letter given here is from the egregious Governor Brown of Georgia, the most powerful of all the state governors, and one who by his policy of putting Georgia interests first effectively sabotaged the Confederacy.

Joseph E. Brown to Alexander H. Stephens
(Private)

Canton [Georgia], Sept. 1st, 1862

Dear Sir: I have the pleasure to acknowledge the receipt of your letter of the 26th ult. and am gratified that you take the view which you have expressed about the action of Genl. Bragg in his declaration of martial law over Atlanta and his appoint[ment], as the newspapers say, of a civil governor with aids, etc.

I have viewed this proceeding as I have others of our military authorities of late with painful apprehensiveness for the future. It seems military men are assuming the whole powers of government to themselves and setting at defiance constitutions, laws, state rights, state sovereignty, and every other principle of civil liberty, and that our people engrossed in the struggle with the enemy are disposed to submit to these bold usurpations tending to military despotism without murmur, much less resistance. I should have called this proceeding into question before this time but I was hopeful from the indications which I had noted that Congress would take such action as would check these dangerous usurpations of power, and for the further reasons that I have already come almost into conflict with the Confederate authorities in vindication of what I have considered the rights of the State and people of Georgia, and I was fearful, as no other governor seems to raise these questions, that I might be considered by good and true men in and out of Congress too refractory for the times. I had therefore concluded to take no notice of this matter till the meeting of the legislature when I expect to ask the representatives of the people to define the bounds to which they desire the Governor to go in the defense of the rights and sovereignty of the state. I confess I have apprehensions that our present General Assembly does not properly reflect the sentiments of our people upon this great question, but if the Executive goes beyond the bounds where he is sustained by the representatives of the people he exposes himself to censure without the moral power to do service to the great principles involved. I fear we have much more to apprehend from military despotism than from subjugation by the enemy. I trust our generals will improve well their time while we have the advantage and the enemy are organizing another army. Hoping that your health is good and begging that you will write me when your important duties are not too pressing to permit it, I am very truly your friend.

—PHILLIPS, ed., "*The Correspondence of Robert Toombs, Alexander H. Stephens, and Howell Cobb*"

12. PEACE AT ANY PRICE

Jonathan Worth was an old-line Whig politician who fought nullification in the thirties and secession in 1861 but—like so many others—went with his state when the crisis materialized. During the war he was State Treasurer of North Carolina; in 1865 he was elected to the governorship, and re-elected again the following year.

Jonathan Worth to Jesse G. Henshaw   Raleigh Aug. 24, 1863

I hardly know whether I am in favor of the peace meetings or not. On the one hand, it is very certain that the President and his advisers will not make peace, if not forced into it by the masses and the privates in the army. Their cry echoed by almost every press is: "Independence, or the last man and the last dollar." The North will not make peace on the basis of Independence. The real question which nobody—not even Holden—will squarely present is, shall we fight on with certain desolation and impoverishment and probable ultimate defeat; or make peace on the basis of reconstruction? Nearly every public man—every journal, political and religious, and every politician, in the fervor of their patriotism, has vociferously declared in favor of "the last man and the last dollar" cry. These classes cannot be consistent unless they still cry war. Many believe the masses in their saner hours never approved the war and would rather compromise on the basis of the Constitution of the U. S. with such additional securities against any future rupture as could be agreed on. If there be any sense in peace meetings they mean reconstruction. They may rather do mischief if they are not so imposing as to force the administration to reconstruction. They will be impotent and mischievous if the army is still for war to the last man and the last dollar. I do not know the sentiments of the rank and file of the army.

I am for peace on almost any terms and fear we shall never have it until the Yankees dictate it. Upon the whole I would not go into a peace meeting now or advise others to go into one, particularly in Randolph—but I have no repugnance to them in other places and see no other chance to get to an early end of this wicked war, but by the action of the masses who have the fighting to do. If an open rupture occur between Gov. V[ance] and Mr. Holden, it will be ruinous to us. There ought to be none and I trust there will be none. There is no difference between them that justifies a breach. The Governor concedes the right of the people to hold meetings and express their wishes, but he deems such meetings inexpedient and tending to dissatisfaction and disorganization in the army and that no honorable peace can be made, after we cease to present a strong military front. The Gov. acts consistently and in the eminent difficult position he occupied, I doubt whether any pilot could manage the crippled ship in such a storm with more skill. Repress all expressions of dissatisfaction against him. He values the extravagant eulogiums of the fire-eaters at their worth. They are playing an adroit game. They would get up dissention between the Gov. and Holden and then break up the Conservative party and seize the helm of Government.

—HAMILTON, ed., *The Correspondence of Jonathan Worth*

13. "THE MAN WHO HELD HIS CONSCIENCE HIGHER THAN THEIR PRAISE"

Unionist sentiment was weaker in South Carolina than in any other Southern state and weaker, probably, in Charleston than in any other city. This epitaph on the Petigru monument in St. Michael's churchyard, Charleston, is included as evidence of the respect with which the South, even in wartime, respected honest difference of opinion. Member of a famous Charleston family, lawyer and public servant, James Petigru was probably the most distinguished of South Carolina Unionists. The toleration accorded him was a product in part of the sophistication of Charleston, in part of that class consciousness which accepted eccentricity in its aristocracy, in part of a respect for intellectual independence commoner in the Civil War generation than in our own.

JAMES LOUIS PETIGRU

Born at
Abbeville May 10th 1789
Died at Charleston March 9th 1863

JURIST. ORATOR. STATESMAN. PATRIOT.

Future times will hardly know how great a life
This simple stone commemorates—
The tradition of his Eloquence, his
Wisdom and his Wit may fade:
But he lived for ends more durable than fame,
His Eloquence was the protection of the poor and wronged;

His Learning illuminated the principles of Law—
In the admiration of his Peers,
In the respect of his People,
In the affection of his Family
His was the highest place;
The just meed
Of his kindness and forbearance
His dignity and simplicity
His brilliant genius and his unwearied industry
Unawed by Opinion,
Unseduced by Flattery,
Undismayed by Disaster,
He confronted Life with antique Courage
And Death with Christian Hope.

In the great Civil War
He withstood his People for his Country
But his People did homage to the Man
Who held his conscience higher than their praise
And his Country
Heaped her honors on the grave of the Patriot,
To whom living,
His own righteous self-respect sufficed
Alike for Motive and Reward.

"Nothing is here for tears, nothing to wail,
Or knock the breast; no weakness, no contempt,
Dispraise or blame; nothing but well and fair
And what may quiet us in a life so noble."
                    —CARSON, *Life and Letters of James Petigru*

XXII

Hospitals, Surgeons, and Nurses

THE story of Civil War medicine is only less depressing than the story of Civil War prisons; if the first is lighted by flashes of heroism, the second is ameliorated by generosity and self-sacrifice on the part of doctors and nurses. As we have seen, one reason for the high mortality rate in prisons was the low state of medical and nursing services and the primitive standards of sanitation that obtained generally. This situation reflected in part conditions in civil life, in part the wholly inadequate preparation for war, in part the conditions of medicine and public health at mid-century.

At the outbreak of the war the United States Surgeon General's office consisted of a total of 115 surgeons; 24 of these resigned to form the nucleus of the Confederate medical services. Eventually both services were vastly—but quite inadequately—expanded. Nursing services, too, were primitive. The army still relied on male nurses, most of them quite untrained. At the outbreak of the war the famous humanitarian, Dorothea Dix, hurried to Washington to offer her services; she was appointed Superintendent of Women Nurses, but never allowed any real independence. Most of the nursing service on both sides was voluntary; the United States Sanitary Commission did invaluable work in nursing and relief both at the front and in hospitals behind the line. Hospitals were mostly hastily improvised and inadequate. It is sobering to read that inspection of hospitals in the Union Army at the mid-war period (November 1862 to March 1863) reported a total of 589 as good and no less than 303 as bad or very bad, while inspections of medical officers from the beginning of the war to March 1863 found 2,727 good and 851 bad! It is to be remembered, too, when we read of the work of the surgeons and contemplate the mortality figures, that antiseptics were unknown, the relation of dirt to infection was generally not understood, anesthesia was just coming into general use, and drugs were inadequate.

It is not surprising in the light of all this that mortality from disease and wounds was far higher than from bullets, and that hospitalization was often regarded as equivalent to a death sentence. While no statistics are satisfactory and those for the Confederacy in a state of total confusion, it is a safe generalization that deaths from wounds were as numerous as deaths on the battlefield and that deaths from disease were more than twice both these combined. Perhaps the least unreliable statistics for the Union armies give 67,000 killed in action, 43,000 died of wounds, and 224,000 died of disease; an additional

24,000 are listed as dead from other causes—doubtless either wounds or disease. Confederate statistics indicate a comparable situation. Fortunately most of the soldiers were young—the largest single age group was eighteen—and from the country, and had therefore high powers of resistance and recuperation; otherwise the situation would have been even more appalling.

1. GEORGE TOWNSEND DESCRIBES THE WOUNDED ON THE PENINSULA

George Alfred Townsend was only twenty when he began to report the Civil War for the New York Herald, but he quickly established himself as one of the most brilliant of all the many war correspondents. We have already read his account of Fitz John Porter's ascent in a balloon; we shall meet him again describing the Battle of Five Forks. Townsend followed McClellan's army up the Peninsula and through that campaign to its inglorious close. There are few more graphic accounts of wounds, disease and death than those from his gifted pen.

IT was evening, as I hitched my horse to a stake near-by, and pressed up to the receptacle for the unfortunates. Sentries enclosed the pen, walking to-and-fro with loaded muskets; a throng of officers and soldiers had assembled to gratify their curiosity; and new detachments of captives came in hourly, encircled by sabremen, the Southerners being disarmed and on foot.

The scene within the area was ludicrously moving. It reminded me of the witch-scene in Macbeth, or pictures of brigands or Bohemian gypsies at rendezvous, not less than five hundred men, in motley, ragged costumes, with long hair, and lean, wild, haggard faces, were gathered in groups or in pairs, around some fagot fires. In the growing darkness their expressions were imperfectly visible; but I could see that most of them were weary, and hungry, and all were depressed and ashamed. Some were wrapped in blankets of rag-carpet, and others wore shoes of rough, untanned hide. Others were without either shoes or jackets, and their heads were bound with red handkerchiefs. Some appeared in red shirts; some in stiff beaver hats; some were attired in shreds and patches of cloth; and a few wore the soiled garments of citizen gentlemen; but the mass adhered to homespun suits of gray, or "butternut," and the coarse blue kersey common to slaves. In places I caught glimpses of red Zouave breeches and leggings; blue Federal caps, Federal buttons, or Federal blouses; these were the spoils of anterior battles, and had been stripped from the slain. Most of the captives were of the appearances denominated "scraggy" or "knotty." They were brown, brawny, and wiry, and their countenances were intense, fierce, and animal. They came from North Carolina, the poorest and least enterprising Southern State, and ignorance, with its attendant virtues, were the common facial manifestations. Some lay on the bare ground, fast asleep; others chatted nervously as if doubtful of their future treatment; a few were boisterous, and anxious to beg tobacco or coffee from idle Federals; the rest—and they comprehended the greater number—were silent, sullen, and vindictive. They met curiosity with scorn, and spite with imprecations.

A child—not more than four years of age, I think—sat sleeping in a corner upon an older comrade's lap. A gray-bearded pard was staunching a gash in his cheek with the tail of his coat. A fine-looking young fellow sat with his face in his hands, as if his heart were far off, and he wished to shut out this bitter scene. In a corner, lying morosely apart, were a Major, three Captains, and three Lieutenants,—young athletic fellows, dressed in rich gray cassimere, trimmed with black, and wearing soft black hats adorned with black ostrich-feathers. Their spurs were strapped upon elegantly fitting boots, and they looked as far above the needy, seedy privates, as lords above their vassals. . . .

I rode across the fields to the Hogan, Curtis, and Gaines mansions; for some of the wounded had meantime been deposited in each of them. All the cow-houses, wagon-sheds, hay-barracks, hen-coops, Negro cabins, and barns were turned into hospitals. The floors were littered with "corn-shucks" and fodder; and the maimed, gashed, and dying lay confusedly together. A few, slightly wounded, stood at windows, relating incidents of the battle; but at the doors sentries stood with crossed muskets, to keep out idlers and gossips. The mention of my vocation was an "open sesame," and I went unrestrained, into all the largest hospitals. In the first of these an amputation was being performed, and at the door lay a little heap of human fingers, feet, legs, and arms. I shall not soon forget the bare-armed surgeons, with bloody instruments, that leaned over the rigid and insensible figure, while the comrades of the subject looked horrifiedly at the scene.

The grating of the murderous saw drove me into the open air, but in the second hospital which I visited, a wounded man had just expired, and I encountered his body at the threshold. Within, the sickening smell of mortality was almost insupportable, but by degrees I became accustomed to it. The lanterns hanging around the room streamed fitfully upon the red eyes, and half-naked figures. All were looking up, and saying, in pleading monotone: "Is that you, doctor?" Men with their arms in slings went restlessly up and down, smarting with fever. Those who were wounded in the lower extremities, body, or head, lay upon their backs, tossing even in sleep. They listened peevishly to the wind whistling through the chinks of the barn. They followed one with their rolling eyes. They turned away from the lantern, for it seemed to sear them. Soldiers sat by the severely wounded, laving their sores with water. In many wounds the balls still remained, and the discolored flesh was swollen unnaturally. There were some who had been shot in the bowels, and now and then they were frightfully convulsed, breaking into shrieks and shouts. Some of them iterated a single word, as, "doctor," or "help," or "God," or "oh!" commencing with a loud spasmodic cry, and continuing the same word till it died away in cadence. The act of calling seemed to lull the pain. Many were unconscious and lethargic, moving their fingers and lips mechanically, but never more to open their eyes upon the light; they were already going through the valley and the shadow.

I think, still, with a shudder, of the faces of those who were told mercifully that they could not live. The unutterable agony; the plea for somebody on whom to call; the longing eyes that poured out prayers; the looking on mortal as if its resources were infinite; the fearful looking to the immortal as if it were so far off, so implacable, that the dying appeal would be in vain; the open lips, through which one could almost look at the quaking heart below; the ghastliness of brow and tangled hair; the closing pangs; the awful *quietus*. I thought of Parrhasius, in the poem, as I looked at these things:—

> "Gods!
> Could I but paint a dying groan—"

And how the keen eye of West would have turned from the reeking cockpit of the *Victory*, or the tomb of the Dead Man Restored, to this old barn, peopled with horrors. I rambled in and out, learning to look at death, studying the manifestations of pain,—quivering and sickening at times, but plying my avocation, and jotting the names for my column of mortalities. . . .

Ambulances, it may be said, incidentally, are either two-wheeled or four-wheeled. Two-wheeled ambulances are commonly called "hop, step, and jumps." They are so constructed that the forepart is either very high or very low, and may be both at intervals. The wounded occupants may be compelled to ride for hours in these carriages, with their heels elevated above their heads, and may finally be shaken out, or have their bones broken by the terrible jolting. The four-wheeled ambulances are built in shelves, or compartments, but the wounded are in danger of being smothered in them.

It was in one of these latter that I rode, sitting with the driver. We had four horses, but were thrice "swamped" on the road, and had to take out the wounded men once, till we could start the wheels. Two of these men were wounded in the face, one of them having his nose completely severed, and the other having a fragment of his jaw knocked out. A third had received a ball among the thews and muscles behind his knee, and his whole body appeared to be paralyzed. Two were wounded in the shoulders, and the sixth was shot in the breast, and was believed to be injured inwardly, as he spat blood, and suffered almost the pain of death.

The ride with these men, over twenty miles of hilly, woody country, was like one of Dante's excursions into the Shades. In the awful stillness of the dark pines, their screams frightened the hooting owls, and the whirring insects in the leaves and tree-tops quieted their songs. They heard the gurgle of the rills, and called aloud for water to quench their insatiate thirst. One of them sang a shrill, fierce, fiendish ballad, in an interval of relief, but plunged, at a sudden relapse, in prayers and curses. We heard them groaning to themselves, as we sat in front, and one man, it seemed, was quite out of his mind. These were the outward manifestations; but what chords trembled and smarted within, we could only guess. What regrets for good resolves unfulfilled, and remorse for years misspent, made hideous these sore and panting hearts? The moonlight pierced through the thick foliage of the wood, and streamed into our faces, like invitations to a better life. But the crippled and bleeding could not see or feel it,—buried in the shelves of the ambulance.

—TOWNSEND, *Campaigns of a Non-Combatant*

2. THE SANITARY COMMISSION TO THE RESCUE

The United States Sanitary Commission, the leading private relief organization of the Civil War period, was created—against strong opposition in the army—in June 1861. A distinguished Unitarian divine, the Reverend Henry W. Bellows, was President; the famous landscape architect, Frederick Law Olmsted, was Secretary; and the Commission enlisted scores of physicians and literally hundreds of public-spirited men and women. Its object, wrote Mary Livermore, "was to do what the Government could not." The "could" here is, of course, relative; it was merely that governments had not yet conceived it their responsibility to take care of the health, comfort, and general welfare of soldiers.

The Commission did a little bit of everything. Its inspectors looked into the sanitary arrangements in camps—hence its name—and brought about reforms. It reviewed matters of diet, cooking, clothing; provided private aid to soldiers and to their dependents; took care of fugitives; collected and forwarded boxes of food to the soldiers—a combination, as we have said elsewhere, of YMCA, Red Cross, and USO—and helped out even with nursing and hospital care. At the time of the Peninsular campaign the Commission obtained some hospital transports for the wounded.

We give an account here of the use of these hospital transports. Katharine Wormeley, who tells the story, was one of the many women who worked heroically for the Sanitary Commission. Born in England, the daughter of an admiral, she later distinguished herself in philanthropy and literature. She is remembered today for her remarkable translations of Balzac and of other modern French writers.

"WILSON SMALL," 5 *June*, 1862

DEAR MOTHER: I finished my last letter on the afternoon of the day when we took eighty men on the *Small*, and transferred them to the *Webster*.

We had just washed and dressed, and were writing letters when Captain Sawtelle came on board to say that several hundred wounded men were lying at the landing; that the *Daniel Webster No. 2* had been taken possession of by the medical officers, and was already half full of men, and that the surplus was being carried across her to the *Vanderbilt*; that the confusion was terrible; that there were no stores on board the *Daniel Webster No. 2* (she having been seized the moment she reached the landing on her return from Yorktown, without communicating with the Commission), nor were there any stores or preparations, not even mattresses, on board the *Vanderbilt*.

Of course the best in our power had to be done. Mrs. Griffin and I begged Mr. Olmsted not to refrain from sending us, merely because we had been up all night. He said he wouldn't send us, but if we chose to offer our services to the United States surgeon, he thought it would be merciful. Our offer was seized. We went on board; and such a scene as we entered and lived in for two days I trust never to see again. Men in every condition of horror, shattered and shrieking, were being brought in on stretchers borne by "contrabands," who dumped them anywhere, banged the stretchers against pillars and posts, and walked over the men without compassion. There was no one to direct what ward or what bed they were to go into. Men shattered in the thigh, and even cases of amputation, were shovelled into top berths without thought or mercy. The men had mostly been without food for three days, but there was *nothing* on board either boat for them; and if there had been, the cooks were only engaged to cook for the ship, and not for the hospital.

We began to do what we could. The first thing wanted by wounded men is something to drink (with the sick, stimulants are the first thing). Fortunately we had plenty of lemons, ice, and sherry on board the *Small*, and these were available at once. Dr. Ware discovered a barrel of molasses, which, with vinegar, ice, and water, made a most refreshing drink. After that we gave them crackers and milk, or tea and bread. It was hopeless to try to get them into bed; indeed, there were no mattresses on the *Vanderbilt*. All we could do at first was to try to calm the confusion, to stop some agony, to revive the fainting lives, to snatch, if possible, from immediate death with food and stimulants. Imagine a great river or Sound steamer filled on every deck,—every berth and every square inch of room covered with wounded men; even the stairs and gangways and guards filled with those who are less badly wounded; and then imagine fifty well men, on every kind of errand, rushing to and fro over them, every touch bringing agony to the poor fellows, while stretcher after stretcher came along, hoping to find an empty place; and then imagine what it was to keep calm ourselves, and make sure that every man on both those boats was properly refreshed and fed. We got through about 1 A.M., Mrs. M. and Georgy having come off other duty and reënforced us.

We were sitting for a few moments, resting and talking it over, and bitterly asking why a Government so lavish and perfect in its other arrangements should leave its wounded almost literally to take care of themselves, when a message came that one hundred and fifty men were just arriving by the cars. It was raining in torrents, and both boats were full. We went on shore again: the same scene repeated. The wretched *Vanderbilt* was slipped out, the *Kennebec* brought up, and the hundred and fifty men carried across the *Daniel Webster No. 2* to her, with the exception of some fearfully wounded ones, who could not be touched in the darkness and rain, and were therefore made as comfortable as they could be in the cars. We gave refreshment and food to all, Miss Whetten and a detail of young men from the *Spaulding* coming up in time to assist, and the officers of the *Sebago*, who had seen how hard pressed we were in the afternoon, volunteering for the night-watch. Add to this sundry Members of Congress, who, if they talked much, at least worked well. One of them, the Hon. Moses F. Odell, proposed to Mr. Olmsted that on his return to Washington he should move that the thanks of Congress be returned to us! Mr. Olmsted, mindful of our feelings, promptly declined.

We went to bed at daylight with *breakfast* on our minds, and at six o'clock we were all on board the *Daniel Webster No. 2*, and the breakfast of six hundred men was got through with in good time. Captain Sawtelle kindly sent us a large wall-tent, twelve caldrons and camp-kettles, two cooks, and a detail of six men. The tent was put up at once, Dr. Ware giving to its preparation the only hour when he might have rested during that long nightmare. We began to use it that (Tuesday) morning. It is filled with our stores; there we have cooked not only the sick-food, but *all* the food needed on the Government boats. It was hard to get it in sufficient quantity; but when everything else gave out, we broke up "hard-tack" into buckets full of hot milk and water a little sweetened,—"bread and milk" the men called it. Oh, that precious condensed milk, more precious to us at that moment than beef essence!

Tuesday was very much a repetition of Monday night. The men were cleared from the main-deck and gangways of the *Daniel Webster No. 2* onto the *Kennebec*. The feeding business was almost as hard to manage as before. But still it was done, and we got to bed at 1 A.M. Mrs. M. and I were to attend to the breakfast at 6 next morning. By some accident Mrs. M., who was ready quite as soon as I was, was carried off by the *Small*, which started suddenly to run down to the *Spaulding*. I had, therefore, to get the breakfast alone. I accomplished it, and then went ashore and fed some men who were just arriving in the cars, and others who were in tents near the landing. The horrors of that morning are too great to speak of. The men in the cars were brought on board the *Daniel Webster No. 2* and laid about the vacant main-deck and guards and on the deck of a scow that lay alongside. I must not, I ought not to tell you of the horrors of that morning. One of the least was that I saw a "contraband" step on the amputated stump of a wretched man. I took him by the arm and walked him into the tent, where I ordered them to give him other work, and forbade that he should come upon the ships again. I felt white with anger, and dared not trust myself to speak to *him*. While those awful sights pass before me I have comparatively no feeling, except the anxiety to alleviate as much as possible. I do not suffer under the sights; but oh! the sounds, the screams of men. It is when I think of it afterwards that it is so dreadful. . . .

About nine hundred wounded remain to be brought down. Mr. Olmsted says *our* boats have transported one thousand seven hundred and fifty-six since Sunday; the Government and Pennsylvania boats together about three thousand. Mr. Clement Barclay was with us on Monday night on the *Vanderbilt*. I believe he went with her to Fortress Monroe. He was working hard, with the deepest interest and skill. I went with him to attend to a little "Secesh" boy, wounded in the thigh; also to a Southern colonel, a splendid-looking man, who died, saying to Mr. Barclay, with raised hand: "Write to my wife and tell her I die penitent for the part I have taken in this war." I try to be just and kind to the Southern men. One of our men stopped me, saying: "*He's* a rebel; give that to me." I said: "But a wounded man is our brother!" (rather an obvious sentiment, if there is anything in Christianity); and they both touched their caps. The Southerners are constantly expressing surprise at one thing or another, and they are shy, but not surly, at receiving kindness. Our men are a noble set of fellows, so cheerful, uncomplaining, and generous.

Remember that in all that I have written, I have told you only about ourselves—the women. What the gentlemen have been, those of our party, those of the *Spaulding* and of the other vessels, is beyond my power to relate. Some of them fainted from time to time.

Last night, shining over blood and agony, I saw a lunar rainbow; and in the afternoon a peculiarly beautiful effect of rainbow and stormy sunset,—it flashed upon my eyes as I passed an operating-table, and raised them to avoid seeing anything as I passed.

—WORMELEY, *The Other Side of War*

3. THE BARONESS VON OLNHAUSEN NURSES AT ALEXANDRIA

One of the women who responded to Dorothea Dix's call for volunteers was Mary Phinney, who had married a German émigré, Baron Gustav von Olnhausen. On her husband's death she moved to Illinois, and from there went to nurse at the Mansion House Hospital in Alexandria. After the war she traveled in Germany, then returned to a nursing career. Her picture of conditions in the hospitals is doubtless exaggerated, yet that many of the doctors were incompetent and corrupt and that the regular medical service looked with disdain on women nurses is abundantly clear.

MISS DIX, who had been appointed by the President head of the army nurses, took me from Washington to Alexandria to the Mansion House Hospital. She told me on the journey that the surgeon in charge was determined to give her no foothold in any hospital where he reigned, and that I was to take no notice of anything that might occur, and was to make no complaint whatever might happen. She was a stern woman of few words.

There seemed to be much confusion about the Mansion House—which before the war was a famous hotel—and every part of it was crowded. She left me in the office and went in search of Dr. S. The sight of the wounded continuously carried through on stretchers, or led in as they arrived from the boats that lay at the foot of the street on which the hospital stood (this was just after that awful Cedar Mountain battle [August 1862]), seemed more than I could bear, and I thought Miss Dix would never come. At last she appeared, with Dr. S., who eyed me keenly and, it seemed to me, very savagely, and gave me in charge of an orderly to show me to the surgical ward, as it was called. It consisted of many small rooms, with a broad corridor, every room so full of cots that it was only barely possible to pass between them. Such a sorrowful sight; the men had just been taken off the battle-field, some of them had been lying three or four days almost without clothing, their wounds never dressed, so dirty and wretched. Some one gave me my charges as to what I was to do; it seemed such a hopeless task to do anything to help them that I wanted to throw myself down and give it up. Miss Dix left me, and soon the doctors came and ordered me to follow them while they examined and dressed the wounds. They seemed to me then, and afterwards I found they were, the most brutal men I ever saw. They were both volunteers, and one was a converted Jew who was constantly proclaiming it.

So I began my work, I might say night and day. The surgeon told me he had no room for me, and a nurse told me he said he would make the house so hot for me I would not stay long. When I told Miss Dix I could not remain without a room to sleep in, she, knowing the plan of driving me out, said, "My child" (I was nearly as old as herself), "you will stay where I have placed you." In the mean time McClellan's army was being landed below us from the Peninsula. Night and day the rumbling of heavy cannon, the marching of soldiers, the groaning of the sick and wounded were constantly heard; and yet in all that time I never once looked from the windows, I was so busy with the men.

One of the rooms of the ward was the operating-room, and the passing in and out of those who were to be operated upon, and the coming and going of the surgeons added so much to the general confusion. I doubt if at any time during the war there was ever such confusion as at this time. The insufficient help, the unskilful surgeons, and a general want of organization were very distressing; but I was too busy then and too tired for want of proper sleep to half realize it. Though I slept at the bedsides of the men or in a corner of the rooms, I was afraid to complain lest I be discharged. I was horribly ignorant, of course, and could only try to make the men comfortable; but the staff doctors were very friendly and occasionally helped me, and some one occasionally showed me about bandaging, so by degrees I began to do better. The worst doctor had been discharged, much to my joy, but the other one, despite his drinking habits, stayed on. After the morning visit it was no use calling upon him for anything, and I had to rely on the officer of the day if I needed help. I know now that many a life could have been saved if there had been a competent surgeon in the ward.

At this time the ward was full of very sick men and sometimes two would be dying at the same time, and both begging me to stay with them, so I got little sleep or rest. Moreover, I had no room of my own. Occasionally a nurse would extend the hospitality of the floor in hers, and I would have a straw bed dragged in on which to get a few hours' sleep. This, with a hurried bath and fresh clothes, was my only rest for weeks. It was no use to complain. The surgeon simply stormed at me and said there was no room; while Miss Dix would say, "You can bear it awhile, my child; I have placed you here and you must stay." I was at that time her only nurse in the Mansion House. Later she succeeded in getting rid of all the others and replacing them with her own.

Alexandria, March, 1863

I thought it best not to trouble you with an account of how we have been living lately,—everything cut off, nothing but coffee (so poor and with hardly ever milk) and dry bread for breakfast; for dinner bread and meat (and such meat! always the tail or neck or some other nasty part), and at night coffee and bread again. Being hungry is nothing to being so insulted. We knew we had a right to all our rations; and while Dr. S. was here we always urged Mrs. B. to ask him, and so put us out of the power of these cooks. They hate us because we are decent women and will fight for the soldiers' rights, thus cutting off their resources. For some reason she never would; she thought he would believe us selfish or something.

One day it was past all bearing. I was positively so hungry I could have eaten cat's meat. I sat over the fire after supper, tired and hungry and wondering if the good I did was balanced by my suffering (more from insults than anything else), when all at once it struck me to go to Dr. Page myself. It was eight o'clock; I found him alone, and he listened to all my story. He seemed so surprised at it, said we had not even one privilege we were entitled to, called the Steward—who is just the meanest, hatefullest (oh, help me to a word, I don't care if it *is* profane) man that ever lived—and told him that in future we were to draw our own rations and have our own cook. I felt so elated, and when I announced it next morning the women actually embraced me. . . .

When our own battles were settled, then it was time, when good feeding had given us a little strength, to put in for our patients; so last Sunday morning I opened fire. Dr. C. has that department, so I attacked him; but he was mad when I told him the patients would starve only for the nurses, who had to buy everything the sickest men ate. He denied it, and said he knew his nurse did not do it. So she was called, and said she did; then the others were called; and, at last, we had about every nurse and doctor in the house growling and snarling. Dr. C. said they had everything according to the new diet-table; some of the doctors denied it and some of them backed him up; at last we all adjourned to some underground room (the bread-room) to read the table list, when it proved that they got nothing in the quantity even that was ordered there; and as to quality, Lord help them! How I wish you could have heard the row! It went on all day; even in the evening everybody was called up and talked to; and the result is that it has been a little better this week, though far from the mark, and soon (if it grows less every day) it will be back to the old standard, for that wretch H. or somebody will miss the money and get it back if possible.

So you see our path is not all rose-leaves, and you can see, too, one of the many impositions put upon the noble fellows who are throwing away their lives for such men as these. Are all men naturally bad? That's going to be the only religious question I shall study in the future. I guess this war will make me religious, for one. I am getting a good deal more patient and forgiving than I used to be, but I'll never forgive the Rebels who kill them.

—"Diary of Mary Phinney"

4. CLARA BARTON SURMOUNTS THE FAITHLESSNESS OF UNION OFFICERS

It was not only doctors and nurses who were, at times, incompetent but army officers as well. At least so Clara Barton often thought. She was a strong-minded woman, and a bit inclined to think the worst of her superiors and associates. When the war broke out Miss Barton was working in the Patent Office in Washington. Deeply moved by the distress of the soldiers after First Bull Run she wrote a letter to the Worcester *(Massachusetts)* Spy *asking for food, clothing, and bandages for the soldiers. Provisions poured in—and she had found her mission. Never formally associated either with the Sanitary Commission or, except for a brief interlude, with the army, she conducted something of a one-woman relief organization. She carried on her beneficent activities with the Army of the Potomac, the Army of the James, around Charleston, and in and around Washington. After the war she was the moving spirit in the establishment of the American Red Cross, and for over twenty years its director.*

This excerpt comes from her war diary.

NO one has forgotten the heart-sickness which spread over the entire country as the busy wires flashed the dire tidings of the terrible destitution and suffering of the wounded of the Wilderness whom I attended as they lay in Fredericksburg. But you may never have known how many hundredfold of these ills were augmented by the conduct of improper, heartless, unfaithful officers in the immediate command of the city and upon whose actions and indecisions depended entirely the care, food, shelter, comfort, and lives of that whole city of wounded men. One of the highest officers there has since been convicted a traitor. And another, a little dapper captain quartered with the owners of one of the finest mansions in the town, boasted that he had changed his opinion since entering the city the day before; that it was in fact a pretty hard thing for refined people like the people of Fredericksburg to be compelled to open their homes and admit "these dirty, lousy, common soldiers," and that he was not going to compel it.

This I heard him say, and waited until I saw him make his words good, till I saw, crowded into one old sunken hotel, lying helpless upon its bare, wet, bloody floors, five hundred fainting men hold up their cold, bloodless, dingy hands, as I passed, and beg me in Heaven's name for a cracker to keep them from starving (and I had none); or to give them a cup that they might have something to drink water from, if they could get it (and I had no cup and could get none); till I saw two hundred six-mule army wagons in a line, ranged down the street to headquarters, and reaching so far out on the Wilderness road that I never found the end of it; every wagon crowded with wounded men, stopped, standing in the rain and mud, wrenched back and forth by the restless, hungry animals all night from four o'clock in the after-

noon till eight next morning and how much longer I know not. The dark
spot in the mud under many a wagon, told only too plainly where some poor
fellow's life had dripped out in those dreadful hours.

I remembered one man who would set it right, if he knew it, who possessed the power and who would believe me if I told him I commanded immediate conveyance back to Belle Plain. With difficulty I obtained it, and four
stout horses with a light army wagon took me ten miles at an unbroken gallop, through field and swamp and stumps and mud to Belle Plain and a steam
tug at once to Washington. Landing at dusk I sent for Henry Wilson, chairman of the Military Committee of the Senate. A messenger brought him at
eight, saddened and appalled like every other patriot in that fearful hour, at
the weight of woe under which the Nation staggered, groaned, and wept.

He listened to the story of suffering and faithlessness, and hurried from
my presence, with lips compressed and face like ashes. At ten he stood in the
War Department. They could not credit his report. He must have been deceived by some frightened villain. No official report of unusual suffering had
reached them. Nothing had been called for by the military authorities commanding Fredericksburg.

Mr. Wilson assured them that the officers in trust there were not to be
relied upon. They were faithless, overcome by the blandishments of the
wily inhabitants. Still the Department doubted. It was then that he proved
that my confidence in his firmness was not misplaced, as, facing his doubters
he replies: "One of two things will have to be done—either you will send
some one to-night with the power to investigate and correct the abuses of
our wounded men at Fredericksburg, or the Senate will send some one to-
morrow."

This threat recalled their scattered senses.

At two o'clock in the morning the Quartermaster-General and staff galloped to the 6th Street wharf under orders; at ten they were in Fredericksburg. At noon the wounded men were fed from the food of the city and the
houses were opened to the "*dirty, lousy* soldiers" of the Union Army.

Both railroad and canal were opened. In three days I returned with car-
loads of supplies.

No more jolting in army wagons! And every man who left Fredericksburg by boat or by car owes it to the firm decision of one man that his
grating bones were not dragged ten miles across the country or left to bleach
in the sands of that city.

—*The Diary of Clara Barton*

5. SUSAN BLACKFORD NURSES THE WOUNDED AT LYNCHBURG

*The South had no organization comparable to the Sanitary Commission,
but a Women's Relief Society dedicated itself to collecting money to help
sick and wounded soldiers, and thousands of Southern women volunteered
for nursing duty. Mrs. Arthur Hopkins for example not only contributed*

some $200,000 to hospital work but went to the front and was wounded at Seven Pines; others, like Mrs. Ella Newsom and Miss Kate Cumming, worked indefatigably in the makeshift hospitals of the Confederacy; Mrs. Phoebe Yates Pember—superintendent of a division of the vast Chimborazo Hospital in Richmond—was tireless in hospital and nursing home and even at the front.

Mrs. Blackford,* whom we have met before, was a member of one of Virginia's first families, wife to the distinguished Charles Blackford, judge advocate under Longstreet.

May 7th [1864]. The wounded soldiers commenced arriving on Saturday, and just as soon as I heard of it, which was before breakfast, I went to see Mrs. Spence to know what I could do for them. She said the ladies had been so shamefully treated by the surgeons that she was afraid to take any move in the matter. I told her I would go and see Dr. Randolph and ask him if we could not do something. I went down and did so at once and asked him what we could do. He said we might do anything we pleased in the way of attention to them; send or carry anything to them we wished and he would be glad of our help. As soon as I reported to Mrs. Spence what he said she started messengers in every direction to let it be known and I went to eleven places myself. We then determined to divide our provisions into two divisions: the bread, meat, and coffee to be sent to the depot, the delicacies to the hospitals. The reception of wounded soldiers here has been most hospitable. You would not believe there were so many provisions in town as have been sent to them.

On Saturday evening I went up to Burton's factory, where most of the wounded were taken, and found the committee of ladies who had been selected, of whom I was one, just going in with the supper. I went in with them. We had bountiful supplies of soup, buttermilk, tea, coffee, and loaf bread, biscuits, crackers, and wafers. It did my heart good to see how the poor men enjoyed such things. I went around and talked to them all. One man had his arm taken off just below the elbow and he was also wounded through the body, and his drawers were saturated with blood. I fixed his pillow comfortably and stroked his poor swelled and burning arm. Another I found with his hand wounded and his nose bleeding. I poured water over his face and neck, and after the blood ceased to flow wiped his pale face and wounded hand which was black from blood and powder. They were very grateful and urged us to come and see them again.

On Sunday evening news came that six hundred more would arrive and Mrs. Spence sent me word to try and do something. The servants were away and I went into the kitchen and made four quarts of flour into biscuits and two gallons of coffee, and Mrs. Spence gave me as much more barley, so I made, by mixing them, a great deal of coffee. I am very tired.

---

* Letter reprinted from *Letters from Lee's Army* by Susan Lee Blackford; copyright 1947 by Charles Scribner's Sons; used by permission of the publishers.

May 12th. My writing desk has been open all day, yet I have just found time to write to you. Mrs. Spence came after me just as I was about to begin this morning and said she had just heard that the Taliaferro's factory was full of soldiers in a deplorable condition. I went down there with a bucket of rice milk, a basin, towel, soap, etc. to see what I could do. I found the house filled with wounded men and not one thing provided for them. They were lying about the floor on a little straw. Some had been there since Tuesday and had not seen a surgeon. I washed and dressed the wounds of about fifty and poured water over the wounds of many more. The town is crowded with the poor creatures, and there is really no preparations for such a number. If it had not been for the ladies many of them would have starved to death. The poor creatures are very grateful, and it is a great pleasure to us to help them in any way. I have been hard at work ever since the wounded commenced coming. I went to the depot twice to see what I could do. I have had the cutting and distribution of twelve hundred yards of cotton cloth for bandages, and sent over three bushels of rolls of bandages, and as many more yesterday. I have never worked so hard in all my life and I would rather do that than anything else in the world. I hope no more wounded are sent here as I really do not think they could be sheltered. The doctors, of course, are doing much, and some are doing their full duty, but the majority are not. They have free access to the hospital stores and deem their own health demands that they drink up most the brandy and whiskey in stock, and, being fired up most the time, display a cruel and brutal indifference to the needs of the suffering which is a disgrace to their profession and to humanity.

—BLACKFORD, ed., *Letters from Lee's Army*

6. KATE CUMMING NURSES THE WOUNDED AFTER CHICKAMAUGA

Kate Cumming was born in Scotland but came to Alabama as a girl, and was passionately devoted to the South; when Virginia seceded, she records, she was "delirious with joy." At the outbreak of the war she offered her services as a nurse, and nursed faithfully from Corinth to the end. Her journal tells us how much nursing was a social affair rather than a medical, how much it depended on the help and generosity of the women of the South.

September 27 [1863].—A Methodist minister, Dr. Heustis, made a speech at the depot calling upon the people to send up food and nurses to Chickamauga, as General Bragg has gone after the enemy, and expects to recapture Chattanooga. All who could, went immediately to work to cook food to send off.

September 28.—This morning a meeting was held on the same subject, and Mrs. Johnston and I attended. Dr. Heustis' description of the sufferings of the men would have touched the heart of the most hardened. He said he could only tell us about our own men, and if they were suffering so much, we could guess what the prisoners were enduring. He said the principal thing needed was something to eat, and that if a basketful of biscuit were to be placed in one place where he saw some wounded men, that they would send up a shout of joy that would rend the air. He urged all who could possibly go with supplies, to do so immediately, but said there was no place there for ladies. The enemy had destroyed part of the railroad, and the wounded were taken to a place called the "Burnt Shed," some twenty miles from the battlefield, there to await transportation on the cars. Money was collected on the spot, and many promised provisions.

I made up my mind to go, though many begged me not to do so. Having friends in Ringgold, I knew I could not be very bad off; so collecting all the provisions and old linen I could, I started that afternoon. . . .

The torn-up track to Ringgold had been relaid, so we went on to that place and arrived about dark. I found what had been the Bragg hospital filled with wounded men awaiting transportation. Oh, how sad and dreary all appeared! There was not a single light in the whole building, except that which came from a fire outside, around which stood several slightly wounded soldiers shivering from cold. The balconies were filled with wounded men, wrapped in their blankets, lying on the floors. I found one room full, where all were suffering for want of water. These men were waiting to be transported to the cars. . . .

Early the next morning I hurried back to the hospital, where I was kept busy nearly all day rolling bandages. I was assisted by a young man, Mr. Dearing, from Kentucky, who was disabled by a wound in the arm. It was as much as we could do to supply the demands of the doctors. Rev. Mr. Green and my Negro servant were kept busy dressing wounds. We were seated on an upper gallery, where we could see the ambulances come in from the battlefield with their precious burdens. I saw as many as fifty come in at one time, and a dismal sight they presented. There had been no rain for some time, and the dust was so fearful that when the men were taken out of the wagons you could scarcely tell what color they were. Rolling bandages was a necessity, but it was a great trial for us, for we would so much rather have been waiting upon the wounded. At last we were told we had rolled enough for that day, and we gladly went down stairs to see what we could do.

Dr. Devine had wine and other delicacies sent to him for the soldiers from Mississippi, and he gave me an ample supply as I was leaving Newnan. I got a bucket, and nearly filling it with the wine, put in water and sugar, making a delicious drink. This, with eatables in a basket, Mr. Dearing and I carried around, and it was highly appreciated by the men. The Mississippians were more than pleased on telling them where the wine came from. By this time the soldiers had been supplied with plenty of food, so were not suffering from hunger. We also visited the cars, which were standing on the tracks filled with wounded. . . .

The next morning, the 30th, I arose bright and early, and hurriedly partaking of my breakfast, went to the hospital. . . . I had always wished to go on a battlefield—not from any idle curiosity, but from a desire to know the worst, and see if I could be of any use. While thinking over the matter, I met a Mrs. Weir, of Griffin, Ga., whose son had lost a leg in the battle, and was in a private house near the battlefield. She had come to nurse him, and said she would go with me to the battlefield if I would go out with her to see her son. Hundreds of wagons were coming in, but none returning that day. After awhile, a nice looking, covered private wagon came along, and after depositing its load of humanity, Mr. Dearing asked the owner to take us, but this, he stoutly refused to do, saying his horses were completely worn out. Mr. D. then said that one of the ladies had nursed, at least, one thousand Confederates. On hearing this, he immediately drew up and invited us all in. . . .

We traveled over the roughest roads imaginable, and the thought occurred to me that if the wounded were brought this way they must indeed suffer. The surmise proved to be correct, for we met hundreds of wagons loaded with sufferers wending their way to Ringgold. We also saw many slightly wounded on foot going the same direction.

We left Mrs. Weir at Mr. Strickland's, where her son was, and Mr. Tedford begged me to go on further, to Mr. Hunt's, where were the wounded of Hindman's division. He informed me that an excellent young lady, Mr. Hunt's daughter, was doing much for the wounded, and would be glad of my assistance. The temptation was a great one, as I had never seen a field hospital; neither had I heard anything certain about my brother, and as he was in the same brigade, I felt assured I would hear something of him. On our way I met Dr. Ray going to see a brother, whom he had just heard was badly wounded. He and several other surgeons had been wandering about for two days looking for the hospitals. They had had nothing to eat except a pig, which they had "pressed." I think he said they had been at General Cleburn's division hospital, and the first day they were there they dressed the wounds of twelve hundred men. This seems almost incredible, but we have had many more wounded than killed, and all of the wounded of the enemy were left in our hands. He also informed me that at first they had no food for the men nor rags with which to dress their wounds. I promised to send them some rags and also to visit the hospital.

I found Mr. Hunt's home a very pretty cottage in the midst of a garden, which before the battle had been filled with fine shrubbery and flowers, but was now covered with tents, flies and sheds filled with wounded. . . . Every corner of the house was filled with wounded, many of them lying upon bunks made out of the branches of trees, a hard bed at any time, but much more so for these poor wounded veterans. . . .

As we rode out of the yard, I tried to look neither to the right nor the left, for I knew that many eyes were sadly gazing at us from their comfortless sheds and tents. I could do nothing for the poor fellows, and when that is the case, I try to steel my heart against their sorrows. We could see the men cooking out in the pouring rain; a perfect war between the two elements, fire and water. All had a most cheerless aspect. As we rode on the tents of the various field hospitals came in view, and the thoughts of the inmates and their sufferings added to the gloom. I gazed in the direction of the battlefield and thought of the nameless dead who were there. A nation weeps for them; and on that day nature, like Rachel, was shedding tears for her children because they were not. The awful conflict which had so recently raged between brother and brother was vividly pictured to my mind. Oh! what a field of fratricide was there. It wrings from one the cry of the brave Falkland of old: "Peace! peace! when will it come?"

—Cumming, *Gleanings from Southland*

7. CORNELIA HANCOCK NURSES SOLDIERS AND CONTRABANDS

Of the many nursing narratives this is probably the best. Cornelia Hancock was a young lady of twenty-three when she responded to the call of her brother-in-law, Dr. Henry Child of Philadelphia, to help out as a nurse. A New Jersey Quaker, she found in nursing her vocation; after the war she worked with Southern Negroes and among the Philadelphia poor.

Her letters, covering her nursing and hospital experience from Gettysburg to the Wilderness and beyond, are simple, vivid and sincere.

Gettysburg—July 8th, 1863

My Dear Sister

We have been two days on the field; go out about eight and come in about six—go in ambulances or army buggies. The surgeons of the Second Corps had one put at our disposal. I feel assured I shall never feel horrified at anything that may happen to me hereafter. There is a great want of surgeons here; there are hundreds of brave fellows, who have not had their wounds dressed since the battle. Brave is not the word; more, more Christian fortitude never was witnessed than they exhibit, always say—"Help my neighbor first he is worse." The Second Corps did the heaviest fighting, and, of course, all who were badly wounded, were in the thickest of the fight, and, therefore, we deal with the very best class of the men—that is the bravest. My name is particularly grateful to them because it is Hancock. General Hancock is very popular with his men. The reason why they suffer more in this battle is because our army is victorious and marching on after Lee, leaving the wounded for citizens and a very few surgeons. The citizens are stripped of everything they have, so you must see the exhausting state of affairs. The Second Army Corps alone had two thousand men wounded, this I had from the Surgeon's head quarters.

I cannot write more. There is no mail that comes in, we send letters out: I believe the Government has possession of the road. I hope you will write. It would be very pleasant to have letters to read in the evening, for I am so tired I cannot write them. Get the Penn Relief to send clothing here; there are many men without anything but a shirt lying in poor shelter tents, calling on God to take them from this world of suffering; in fact the air is rent with petitions to deliver them from their sufferings. . . .

I do not know when I shall go home—it will be according to how long this hospital stays here and whether another battle comes soon. I can go right in an ambulance without being any expense to myself. The Christian Committee support us and when they get tired the Sanitary is on hand. Uncle Sam is very rich, but very slow, and if it was not for the Sanitary, much suffering would ensue. We give the men toast and eggs for breakfast, beef tea at ten o'clock, ham and bread for dinner, and jelly and bread for supper. Dried rusk would be nice if they were only here. Old sheets we would give much for. Bandages are plenty but sheets very scarce. We have plenty of woolen blankets now, in fact the hospital is well supplied, but for about five days after the battle, the men had no blankets nor scarce any shelter.

It took nearly five days for some three hundred surgeons to perform the amputations that occurred here, during which time the rebels lay in a dying condition without their wounds being dressed or scarcely any food. If the rebels did not get severely punished for this battle, then I am no judge. We have but one rebel in our camp now; he says he never fired his gun if he could help it, and, therefore, we treat him first rate. One man died this morning. I fixed him up as nicely as the place will allow; he will be buried this afternoon. We are becoming somewhat civilized here now and the men are cared for well.

On reading the news of the copperhead performance, in a tent where eight men lay with nothing but stumps (they call a leg cut off above the knee a "stump") they said if they held on a little longer they would form a stump brigade and go and fight them. We have some plucky boys in the hospital, but they suffer awfully. One had his leg cut off yesterday, and some of the ladies, newcomers, were up to see him. I told them if they had seen as many as I had they would not go far to see the sight again. I could stand by and see a man's head taken off I believe—you get so used to it here. I should be perfectly contented if I could receive my letters. I have the cooking all on my mind pretty much. I have torn almost all my clothes off of me, and Uncle Sam has given me a new suit. William says I am very popular here as I am such a contrast to some of the office-seeking women who swarm around hospitals. I am black as an Indian and dirty as a pig and as well as I ever was in my life—have a nice bunk and tent about twelve feet square. I have a bed that is made of four crotch sticks and some sticks laid across and pine boughs laid on that with blankets on top. It is equal to any mattress ever made. The tent is open at night and sometimes I have laid in the damp all night long, and got up all right in the morning.

The suffering we get used to and the nurses and doctors, stewards, etc., are very jolly and sometimes we have a good time. It is very pleasant weather now. There is all in getting to do what you *want* to do and I am doing that. . . .

Pads are terribly needed here. Bandages and lint are plenty. I would like to see seven barrels of dried rusk here. I do not know the day of the week or anything else. Business is slackening a little though—order is beginning to reign in the hospital and soon things will be right. One poor fellow is hollowing fearfully now while his wounds are being dressed.

There is no more impropriety in a *young* person being here provided they are sensible than a sexagenarian. Most polite and obliging are all the soldiers to me.

It is a very good place to meet celebrities; they come here from all parts of the United States to see their wounded. Senator Wilson, Mr. Washburn, and one of the Minnesota Senators have been here. I get beef tenderloin for dinner.—Ladies who work are favored but the dress-up palaverers are passed by on the other side. I tell you I have lost my memory almost entirely, but it is gradually returning. Dr. Child has done very good service here. All is well with me; we do not know much war news, but I know I am doing all I can, so I do not concern further. Kill the copperheads. Write everything, however trifling, it is all interest here.

From thy affectionate

C. Hancock

Contraband Hospital, Washington, Nov. 15th, 1863

My dear Sister:

I shall depict our wants in true but ardent words, hoping to affect you to some action. Here are gathered the sick from the contraband camps in the northern part of Washington. If I were to describe this hospital it would not be believed. North of Washington, in an open, muddy mire, are gathered all the colored people who have been made free by the progress of our Army. Sickness is inevitable, and to meet it these rude hospitals, only rough wooden barracks, are in use—a place where there is so much to be done you need not remain idle. We average here one birth per day, and have no baby clothes except as we wrap them up in an old piece of muslin, *that* even being scarce. Now the Army is advancing it is not uncommon to see from 40 to 50 arrivals in one day. They go at first to the Camp but many of them being *sick* from exhaustion soon come to us. They have nothing that any one in the North would call clothing. I always see them as soon as they arrive, as they come here to be vaccinated; about 25 a day are vaccinated.

This hospital is the reservoir for all cripples, diseased, aged, wounded, infirm, from whatsoever cause; all accidents happening to colored people in all employs around Washington are brought here. It is not uncommon for a colored driver to be pounded nearly to death by some of the white soldiers. We had a dreadful case of Hernia brought in today. A woman was brought here with three children by her side; said she had been on the road for some time; a more forlorn, wornout looking creature I never beheld. Her four eldest children are still in Slavery, her husband is dead. When I first saw her she laid on the floor, leaning against a bed, her children crying around her. One child died almost immediately, the other two are still sick. She seemed to need most, food and rest, and those two comforts we gave her, but clothes she still wants. I think the women are more trouble than the men. One of the white guards called to me today and asked me if I got any pay. I told him no. He said he was going to be paid soon and he would give me 5 dollars. I do not know what was running through his mind as he made no other remark. I ask for clothing for women and children, both boys and girls. Two little boys, one 3 years old, had his leg amputated above the knee the cause being his mother not being allowed to ride inside, became dizzy and had dropped him. The other had his leg broken from the same cause. This hospital consists of all the lame, halt, and blind escaped from slavery. We have a man & woman here without any feet, theirs being frozen so they had to be amputated. Almost all have scars of some description and many have very weak eyes.

There were two very fine looking slaves arrived here from Louisiana, one of them had his master's name branded on his forehead, and with him he brought all the instruments of torture that he wore at different times during 39 years of very hard slavery. I will try to send you a Photograph of him he wore an iron collar with 3 prongs standing up so he could not lay down his head; then a contrivance to render one leg entirely stiff and a chain clanking behind him with a bar weighing 50 lbs. This he wore and worked all the time hard. At night they hung a little bell upon the prongs above his head so that if he hid in any bushes it would tinkle and tell his whereabouts. The baton that was used to whip them he also had. It is so constructed that a little child could whip them till the blood streamed down their backs. This system of proceeding has been stopped in New Orleans and may God grant that it may cease all over this boasted free land, but you may readily imagine what development such a system of treatment would bring them to. With *this* class of beings, those who wish to do good to the contrabands must labor. Their standard of morality is very low.

—JAQUETTE, ed., *South after Gettysburg*

8. THE GHASTLY WORK OF THE FIELD SURGEONS

Here are three descriptions of the work of the surgeons, all of them tending to bear out the complaints of the Baroness von Olnhausen. These descriptions of heartlessness could be matched in letter after letter, diary after diary, North and South. One Kentucky editor charged that the doctors had "slain more of our troops than all of Lincoln's minions," and a Richmond one characterized the Medical Department as "unfeeling, shameful and brutal." We must remember however that it is the exceptionally bad conduct that gets recorded; routine work is taken for granted. On the whole the surgeons and nurses did about as well as they could. Certainly many of those who worked all through the war, at great peril to themselves, were distinguished members of a distinguished profession.

The first of these critics, Samuel Nichols, was an Amherst College student who enlisted in the 37th Massachusetts Volunteers; served through the war; and later edited the Pittsfield (Massachusetts) *Sun. The second is the famous politician and reformer Carl Schurz, who commanded the XI Corps at Gettys-*

burg. The third is Augustus Brown, captain in the 4th New York Heavy Artillery.

A. The Heartlessness of the Surgeons

> Hd. Qtrs. 37th Regiment Mass. Vols.
> Camp near Stafford Court House
> Nov. 23rd 1862

My Dear Cousin Phebe:

As yet only four of our number have died and some six have been discharged, two of the latter of whom were officers. Lieut. Eli T. Blackmer, a son of the Blackmer that moved from Hodges Corner in Warren, is discharged and has gone to his home in Chicopee. His health is much impaired, and his discharge was merited. Everything here concerning sickness and its management seems so repulsive that the thought of being sick or of having one of your friends in the Hospital, is filled with gloom. I will relate an instance. It is probably an instance more censurable to those having charge than usually occurs; but if the whole history of this war were brought to light more such facts would be revealed, in my mind, than would be pleasing to men (no, brutes) whose duty it is to look after the physical health of the soldier.

In our regiment was a man, private of course, who came under my notice while we were at New Baltimore, a little over one week since. He was emaciated and almost spiritless. He, to be sure, was not as cleanly as he should have been; but I know that it requires much exertion where water is scarce (and it always is in the vicinity of an army like ours) to keep decent. He looked as though he had been sick for some time. He like many others had acquired a dislike to reporting himself to the surgeons, as they have an idea the surgeons are destitute of feeling and unjust. I will not say how far this feeling is just. He at length came with those of his company who reported sick that day to the Surgeon's office within a few steps of where I sleep. I stood at the mouth of my tent and saw and heard the treatment each patient received. This fellow was treated as the rest. He took his turn and came to the front of the Doctor's tent, and received the customary question, "What's the matter with you?" (pretty question for a doctor). "What are you here for? Let's see your tongue. Shall return you to duty."

He was returned to duty. He refused to do duty and as punishment was sentenced to stand on the barrel (a very severe punishment), and added to this, to hold a heavy stone in his hand, two hours on and two off. This was the Doctor's work and not the Colonel's. I admit that it was the Colonel's duty to stop an unjust punishment if he saw one being exacted, but he would probably refer the whole case to the Doctor. To continue my story: after this I watched that young man. All energy seemed absent from him, and he acted as if he was unable to stir. I went to him and advised him to go to the Surgeon again, knowing that by tiring out the M.D. he might receive attention. I could not induce him. I saw during my conversation that he was really sick; and I was anxious to find out what ailed him, knowing if I did, I could find him medicine. I went to another regiment to get a doctor with whom I was acquainted to come and see him; but the regiment had moved that morning, and so I let the matter go for the time being. Two mornings after I saw him again at the Doctor's tent. With the usual flourishes he was reported for duty, and the next morning he was brought to the Hospital to die almost immediately. The same day he was buried with soldier's honors; and with the last volleys fired over his grave died all feelings of remissness or regret, if any such feelings were entertained.

—UNDERHILL, ed., *"Your Soldier Boy Samuel"*

B. CARL SCHURZ WATCHES THE SURGEONS AT WORK AFTER GETTYSBURG

To look after the wounded of my command, I visited the places where the surgeons were at work. At Bull Run, I had seen only on a very small scale what I was now to behold. At Gettysburg the wounded—many thousands of them—were carried to the farmsteads behind our lines. The houses, the barns, the sheds, and the open barnyards were crowded with the moaning and wailing human beings, and still an unceasing procession of stretchers and ambulances was coming in from all sides to augment the number of the sufferers. A heavy rain set in during the day—the usual rain after a battle—and large numbers had to remain unprotected in the open, there being no room left under roof. I saw long rows of men lying under the eaves of the buildings, the water pouring down upon their bodies in streams. Most of the operating tables were placed in the open where the light was best, some of them partially protected against the rain by tarpaulins or blankets stretched upon poles.

There stood the surgeons, their sleeves rolled up to the elbows, their bare arms as well as their linen aprons smeared with blood, their knives not seldom held between their teeth, while they were helping a patient on or off the table, or had their hands otherwise occupied; around them pools of blood and amputated arms or legs in heaps, sometimes more than man-high. Antiseptic methods were still unknown at that time. As a wounded man was lifted on the table, often shrieking with pain as the attendants handled him, the surgeon quickly examined the wound and resolved upon cutting off the injured limb. Some ether was administered and the body put in position in a moment. The surgeon snatched his knife from between his teeth, where it had been while his hands were busy, wiped it rapidly once or twice across his blood-stained apron, and the cutting began. The operation accomplished, the surgeon would look around with a deep sigh, and then—"Next!"

And so it went on, hour after hour, while the number of expectant patients seemed hardly to diminish. Now and then one of the wounded men would call attention to the fact that his neighbor lying on the ground had given up the ghost while waiting for his turn, and the dead body was then quietly removed. Or a surgeon, having been long at work, would put down his knife, exclaiming that his hand had grown unsteady, and that this was too

much for human endurance—not seldom hysterical tears streaming down his
face. Many of the wounded men suffered with silent fortitude, fierce determination in the knitting of their brows and the steady gaze of their bloodshot
eyes. Some would even force themselves to a grim jest about their situation
or about the "skedaddling of the rebels." But there were, too, heart-rending
groans and shrill cries of pain piercing the air, and despairing exclamations,
"Oh, Lord! Oh, Lord!" or "Let me die!" or softer murmurings in which
the words "mother" or "father" or "home" were often heard.

I saw many of my command among the sufferers, whose faces I well remembered, and who greeted me with a look or even a painful smile of
recognition, and usually with the question what I thought of their chances of
life, or whether I could do anything for them, sometimes, also, whether I
thought the enemy were well beaten. I was sadly conscious that many of
the words of cheer and encouragement I gave them were mere hollow sound,
but they might be at least some solace for the moment.

—BANCROFT AND DUNNING, eds., *The Reminiscences of Carl Schurz*

C. THE HORRORS OF THE WILDERNESS

Tuesday, May 10th [1864]. Heavy cannonading from 8 A.M. to 1 P.M.
The Pontoon train has been sent back to Fredericksburg, apparently to get
it out of the way, and the army horses are put on half-rations, that is, five
pounds of food. Ambulances and army wagons with two tiers of flooring,
loaded with wounded and drawn by four and six mule teams, pass along the
plank, or rather, corduroy road to Fredericksburg, the teamsters lashing their
teams to keep up with the train, and the wounded screaming with pain as
the wagons go jolting over the corduroy. Many of the wounds are full of
maggots. I saw one man with an arm off at the shoulder, with maggots half
an inch long crawling in the sloughing flesh, and several poor fellows were
holding stumps of legs and arms straight up in the air so as to ease the pain
the rough road and the heartless drivers subjected them to. These men had
been suffering in temporary field hospitals, as no opportunity had been
afforded to send them to the rear until we got within reach of the road running to Fredericksburg.

And this reminds me of a scene I witnessed a day or two since which
seemed to me to cap the climax of the horrors of war. Passing along a little
in the rear of the lines when a battle was raging in which my battalion was
not engaged, I came upon a field-hospital to which the stretcher-bearers were
bringing the men wounded in the conflict. Under three large "tent flies," the
center one the largest of all, stood three heavy wooden tables, around which
were grouped a number of surgeons and their assistants, the former bareheaded and clad in long linen dusters reaching nearly to the ground, which
were covered with blood from top to bottom and had the arms cut off or
rolled to the shoulders. The stretcher-bearers deposited their ghastly freight
side by side in a winrow on the ground in front of the table under the first
tent fly. Here a number of assistants took charge of the poor fellows, and as

some of them lifted a man on to the first table others moved up the winrow so that no time nor space should be lost. Then some of the surgeons administered an anaesthetic to the groaning and writhing patient, exposed his wound and passed him to the center table. There the surgeons who were operating made a hasty examination and determined what was to be done and did it, and more often than not, in a very few moments an arm or a leg or some other portion of the subject's anatomy was flung out upon a pile of similar fragments behind the hospital, which was then more than six feet wide and three feet high, and what remained of the man was passed on to the third table, where other surgeons finished the bandaging, resuscitated him and posted him off with others in an ambulance. Heaven forbid that I should ever again witness such a sight!

—Brown, *Diary of a Line Officer*

9. THE REGIMENTAL HOSPITAL

Although Charles Johnson wrote this many years after the war, it is one of the best of the comparatively few accounts of military field hospitals. Johnson had enlisted as a boy of eighteen, and was assigned to hospital duty in the West; he was with Grant in the siege of Vicksburg and later took part in the expedition into the Bayou Teche country. His account goes far to explain the failure of medical services in the war and to place responsibility not on the medical officers but on the state of medical science at the time.

IN the field the Regimental Hospital department was allowed two small tents for the officers, medicines, etc.; another small tent for the kitchen department and supplies, and a larger one for the sick. This last, known as the hospital tent, was about fourteen feet square and was capable of containing eight cots with as many patients.

In the field we almost never had sheets and white pillow cases, but made use of army blankets that were made of the coarsest, roughest fiber imaginable. In warm weather the walls of the tent were raised, which made it much more pleasant for the occupants.

However, the policy that obtained was to send those who were not likely to recover quickly to the base hospitals, though this was not always to the patient's best interests, for these larger hospitals were oftentimes centers of infection of one kind or another, especially of hospital gangrene, which seldom attacked the wounded in the field.

During a campaign our stock of medicines was necessarily limited to standard remedies, among which could be named opium, morphine, Dover's powder, quinine, rhubarb, Rochelle salts, castor oil, sugar of lead, tannin, sulphate of copper, sulphate of zinc, camphor, tincture of opium, tincture of iron, tincture opii, camphorata, syrup of squills, simple syrup, alcohol, whiskey, brandy, port wine, sherry wine, etc. Upon going into camp, where we were likely to remain a few days, these articles were unpacked and put on temporary shelves made from box-lids; and, on the other hand, when marching orders came, the medicines were again packed in boxes, the bottles protected from breaking by old papers, etc.

Practically all the medicines were administered in powder form or in the liquid state. Tablets had not yet come into use, and pills were very far from being as plentiful as they are today. The result was that most powders were stirred in water and swallowed. In the case of such medicine as quinine, Dover's powder, tannin, etc., the dose, thus prepared, was a bitter one. The bromides, sulfonal, trional and similar soporifics and sedatives, had not come in use, and asafetida, valerian and opium and its derivatives were about all the Civil War surgeon had to relieve nervousness and induce sleep.

Among the surgical supplies were chloroform, ether, brandy, aromatic spirits of ammonia, bandages, adhesive plaster, needles, silk thread for ligatures, etc. There were, also, amputating cases well supplied with catlins, artery forceps, bone forceps, scalpels, scissors, bullet probes, a tourniquet, etc. But while all the instruments were washed in water and wiped dry to keep from rusting, such an idea as making them aseptic never entered the head of the most advanced surgeon.

There was an emergency case, about the size of a soldier's knapsack, and, indeed, intended to be carried on an attendant's back like a knapsack. In this emergency case were bandages, adhesive plaster, needles, artery forceps, scalpels, spirits of ammonia, brandy, chloroform, ether, etc. This emergency case, or hospital knapsack, was always taken with the regiment when the firing-line was about to be approached, and where the First Assistant Surgeon was in charge and was ready to render first aid to any who might be wounded.

This first aid, however, never went further than staunching bleeding vessels and applying temporary dressings. Thus attended to, the wounded were taken to an ambulance, and in this conveyed to the field hospital in the rear, generally out of musket range, but almost never beyond the reach of shells and cannon balls.

Arrived at the larger field hospital the patient was cared for by the surgeons and male nurses. The wounds were examined and dressed, but never antiseptically, for no one knew the importance of antisepsis or how to put it in practise; consequently, every wound suppurated, and so-called *laudable pus* was welcomed by those in charge as an indication that the patient had reached one of the mile-posts that had to be passed on his road to recovery. Careful handwashing and nail scrubbing was never practised before operations or in dressing recent wounds. And yet, for the most part, the wounds in the end healed satisfactorily. The fact that those receiving them were, in the great majority of cases, vigorous young men had much to do with the good results. Here it may be proper to say that in the Civil War by far the largest proportion of wounds were made with bullets from what were called minie balls. These were fired, in most instances, from single-shooters and muzzle-loaders, such as the Springfield rifled musket, the Enfield rifled musket, the Austrian rifled musket, etc. These bullets weighed an ounce or more, and the guns from which they were fired would kill a man nearly a mile away, and that they produced large, ugly wounds goes without saying.

When a minie ball struck a bone it almost never failed to fracture and shatter the contiguous bony structure, and it was rarely that only a round perforation, the size of the bullet, resulted. When a joint was the part the bullet struck, the results were especially serious in Civil War days. Of course, the same was true of wounds of the abdomen and head, though to a much greater degree. Indeed, recovery from wounds of the abdomen and brain almost never occurred. One of the prime objects of the Civil War surgeon was to remove the missile, and, in doing this, he practically never failed to infect the part with his dirty hands and instrument.

When Captain William M. Colby of my company was brought from the firing-line to our Division Hospital he was in a comatose state from a bullet that had penetrated his brain through the upper portion of the occipital bone. The first thing our surgeon did was to run his index finger its full length into the wound; and this without even ordinary washing. Next he introduced a dirty bullet probe. The patient died a day or two later. . . . These facts are narrated to show the frightful handicap Civil War surgery was under from a lack of knowledge of asepsis and antisepsis; and it is needless to say that no reflection is intended to be made on our surgeon, for he was making use of the very best lights of his day, dangerous as some of these were. . . .

I think wounds from bullets were five times as frequent as those from all other sources. Shell wounds were next in frequency, and then came those from grape and canister. I never saw a wound from a bayonet thrust, and but one made by a sword in the hands of an enemy. In another chapter a reference is made to a man who received a deep wound in the upper part of his thigh, which, after some days, proved fatal. Not long after the wound was received the parts began to assume a greenish tinge and this became of a deeper hue, and when after death the parts were cut down upon, a copper tap from an exploding shell was found to be the ugly missile which had inflicted the injury that, in the end, proved fatal.

Where so many men are grouped together accidents of greater or less gravity are liable to occur. On the whole, however, our regiment was fortunate. We lost two or three by drowning and one by a steamboat explosion . . . , and I can recall but three who received accidental bullet wounds. One of these was a pistol shot of small caliber . . . , and the other was from one of the Springfield guns that was supposed not to be loaded. Looking back, I can but regard our record in this direction as especially fortunate, when the handling of so many loaded guns through so long a period is taken into account.

The only light vehicle in the regiment was our hospital ambulance, . . . a four-wheeled vehicle with bed on springs and covered with strong ducking. The rear end-gate opened with hinges at its lower part for the convenience of putting in and taking out very sick or severely injured patients. The driver of our hospital ambulance was a soldier by the name of Throgmorton, who knew his business, and attended to it. He was an expert horseman, and kept the pair of bays under his care well-groomed and properly attended to in

Action Between the *Kearsarge* and the *Alabama*

Alonzo Chappel

John R. Chapin

The Battle of Lookout Mountain

every way. They were, to a degree, spirited, and when the occasion called for it, were good steppers. Besides serving its purpose in conveying sick and wounded, our ambulance proved useful as a sort of family carriage, upon several occasions taking *certain* of us *well ones* "here-and-yon."

For service about the hospital men were detailed from the regiment to serve in the several capacities of nurses, cooks, and ambulance drivers, etc. Service of this kind was known as "special duty," and not a few came to have no little aptness in their new duties. Especially was this true of the men who cared for the sick, some of whom developed quite a little insight into disease, and were frequently able to make tolerable diagnoses and prognoses.

—JOHNSON, *Muskets and Medicine*

XXIII

The Coast and Inland Waters

SEA *power played a decisive role in the Civil War. It was the blockade, as much as any other single factor, that assured Union victory; had the Confederacy been able to break the blockade, or to persuade European nations to do so, she could probably have held out indefinitely. Almost equally important was Federal control of the major ports along the Atlantic and the Gulf coasts and of the river systems that led deep into the heart of the Confederacy. This control of coast and inland waters not only enabled the Union to supply its own forces and to move along interior lines of communication, but cut off the flow of supplies from one part of the Confederacy to another and broke Confederate lines of communication.*

In the nature of the case naval supremacy rested, from the beginning, with the Union. It was possible, after a fashion, to improvise an army, and certainly to improvise a defense; it was not possible to improvise a navy, though here the Confederacy almost did the impossible. Although the Union Navy numbered less than 40 effective vessels at the beginning of the war, it was rapidly built up to really effective strength. The Confederacy had nothing to start with—only two navy yards, no merchant marine, no seafaring population on which to draw. It was something of a miracle that the Confederacy did as well as it did on water.

The war found the Union Navy as unprepared as the army. The total number of vessels on the navy list was about 90; of these 50 were obsolete sailing ships. Most of the 40 steamers comprising the fleet were scattered around the globe; only 12 were actually available in the Home Squadron. Naval personnel was equally inadequate. Of the almost 1,500 officers, over 300 had resigned at the beginning of the war, and there were less than 7,500 seamen to man the fleet. Yet this fleet was expected to blockade over 3,000 miles of coast and co-operate with the army in attacks on coastal ports and along the inland rivers.

The Confederacy was in an even worse situation. It had no navy, and no naval personnel except such as had resigned from the Union Navy at the outbreak of the war. Both its navy yards fell to the Union before the end of the war. Yet somehow it managed to create a navy. It captured some ships, built others, raised several that had been sunk at Norfolk, converted a few merchant ships into warships, fitted out privateers, bought and built vessels abroad. At the same time it greatly strengthened its harbor defenses: Fort

Fisher did not fall until January 1865; Charleston resisted every assault by sea.

The United States Navy faced a twofold task. First it had to enforce the blockade. This actually proved less difficult than had been anticipated, for there were comparatively few ports which combined adequate harbors, harbor defenses, and connections with the interior. The most important were Norfolk (James River), Roanoke Island, New Bern (Neuse River), Beaufort, Wilmington (Cape Fear River), Charleston, Beaufort (South Carolina), Savannah, and, on the Gulf, Pensacola, Mobile, New Orleans, and Galveston. Obviously it was easier to capture these ports, once and for all, than to blockade them throughout the war, and it was to this task of reducing coastal forts and capturing ports that the Federal Army-Navy team first addressed itself.

One after another the ports fell: first Hilton Head, Port Royal, and Beaufort (South Carolina); then Roanoke Island, controlling Albemarle Sound; then—after the Monitor had forced the Merrimac to withdraw—Norfolk at the mouth of the James; and then James Island, outside Charleston. The great prize was, however, New Orleans, greatest city in the Confederacy and key to the Gulf and the Mississippi. After that the Confederacy had only a few good ports to which the swift blockade-runners could sail: Charleston, Wilmington, Mobile, and Galveston. It took longer to capture these, and Charleston was never captured from the sea, but it is no exaggeration to say that by the end of 1862 the Confederacy was pretty well bottled up.

Even more arduous was the task of clearing the Mississippi and co-operating with the army in warfare along its tributaries—the Tennessee, the Cumberland, the Arkansas, and the Red—which Federal strategy imposed upon the navy. For most of the victories in the West the army got the credit, yet without the navy the story of Fort Donelson, Shiloh, New Madrid, Vicksburg, Port Hudson, and even the Red River campaign would have been very different.

What we have here is amphibious warfare, and the problem of allocating its history to the services is a perplexing one. Certainly it does some violence to history to place the attack on Battery Wagner, for example, in a chapter devoted to the navy, or to separate the naval and the military history of the Vicksburg campaign. To break up this story, however, inserting its various segments into the history of military campaigns, would be to lose sight of the remarkable achievement of the Union Navy—and the interesting achievement of the Confederate Navy, in the war; and that would be a pity.

1. AN AMPHIBIOUS FORCE CAPTURES ROANOKE ISLAND

In September 1861 General McClellan organized what we now would call an amphibious force of three brigades and a fleet of tugboats for service along the Virginia and Carolina coasts. This force was entrusted to General Ambrose Burnside, who, early in January 1862, embarked his troops for an attack upon Roanoke Island off Albemarle Sound, North Carolina. The sound was

*strategically important not only because it afforded refuge to blockade-
runners, but because it led to New Bern, from which there was railway
connection to Goldsboro and Raleigh. The expedition, with Flag Officer
Goldsborough in command of the navy ships, ran into heavy weather, but
on February 7 it succeeded in brushing off half-hearted opposition and landed
most of its strength on Ashby's Harbor, at the center of the island. On February 8 Burnside's men fought their way through bog, mud, and water onto
Suple's Hill, and by nightfall had pressed to the northern end of the island,
bagging 2,500 prisoners and five forts. Confederate failure to strengthen the
island led to a Congressional investigation and censure of Secretary of War
Benjamin and General Huger. The next month Burnside attacked and captured New Bern and Beaufort. He was ready to move into the interior when
he was recalled to help McClellan in the Peninsular campaign.*

*The story is told by Charles Johnson, a Swedish-born boy of eighteen who
had enlisted in the New York Hawkins Zouaves.*

THE bombardment was kept up with spirit on both sides during the afternoon [of February 7]. The "Hunchback," an old ferry-boat with one
heavy gun in each end, made herself conspicuous by deliberately placing herself between the Rebel Batteries and their fleet, working one gun on each,
keeping the position till dark. A little sloop with one heavy, hundred-pound
gun placed herself inside of the line of the fleet and under full sail made her
tally of one every time she tacked. A huge column of smoke curled up about
two or three in the afternoon, from the rear of the batteries and from where
our heaviest fire was concentrated. We were conjecturing what this might
be, when the American Flag on the Flagship ran up to the maintop, which
was the signal for the troops to land.

The "Wheelbarrow" was again brought into requisition, and by eight
o'clock in the evening our Regiment was at the selected landing-place, a
very swampy point of land, some two miles below the batteries.

In landing I was separated from my Company and had to make my way
through the marsh alone. A flimsy, corduroy road of fence-rails had been
improvised, but in the darkness I could not see, and as the rails were half-
covered with mud and mire, at every other step the foot went down between,
adding the danger of breaking one's legs to the general discomfort. I finally
got through this and found the bivouac of the troops. They occupied a field
of some twenty acres around a farmhouse, which served as General Burnside's headquarters.

Ten thousand men were bivouacked on this field ranged in huddling
groups around hundreds of camp-fires, and a cold drizzling rain fell almost
incessantly during the night, keeping the mass of men in constant motion.
A few men, more enterprising than the rest, gathered evergreen branches
enough from the neighboring woods, to raise the body above the mud and
water, an experiment which I also tried with some result in sleep. The most
of the men stood talking around the fires all night. Now and then as they
moved to replenish the flames or stir the smouldering embers, long gleams of

light would flash from out the darkness, reflected from endless rows of gun-barrels and bayonets, sharp, distinct and zig-zag, like a display of lightning when unusual efforts were made at some of the fires, or faint and flickering as the rain poured harder and the flames burned lurid and low. . . .

Day dawned at last, but it brought no respite from the rain. In fact, rain has followed Burnside more or less from the time he struck Hatteras, and it does not seem ready to suspend operations yet. . . .

Quick successive reports of cannon were heard issuing from the woods not over a half a mile away, and these reports were quickly followed by volleys of musketry. There was no longer room for doubt; the ball was open in earnest.

Regiment and Regiment now formed in rapid succession and filed away into the woods in the direction of the fight, and as we waited our turn (we were of the Third Division and held in reserve) the excitement became almost unbearable. We heard a cheer once ringing clear and distinct through the woods, and without knowing whether it boded us good or ill we took it up and returned it with a will. Our good, whole-souled Lieutenant (Flemming) bestirred himself to have coffee for us before we started, which every one needed without being aware of it, and besides it helped to take up the time. At last came the welcome word of command, "Attention Battalion," and without more ado than to stop at the edge of the woods and dispense with our blankets and extra accoutrements, we filed rapidly away in the direction taken by the other Regiments.

As soon as we struck the road, a narrow one, we had to form in ranks of two from four, in order to let the string of wounded men pass on their way to the rear. They came thick and fast, and this was indeed a ghastly spectacle for us to face on the way to our maiden fight.

The poor fellows were in every imaginable condition of bodily suffering; some of them walking bravely or indifferently by themselves, with only slight wounds; others supported by comrades, pale as death from loss of blood; still others carried on stretchers, evidently in their last struggle; and some quite still—*were they already dead?*

Most of these wounded soldiers were cheerful themselves or tried to cheer us by reports from the field of how the fight was going, or such observations as they could think of that would sound well. "We advanced on them twice," a robust fellow said, and he looked as though he might advance on them again. "We are driving them back," from a young, pale-faced boy with clothes too big for his body. "You are wanted up there," feebly uttered another whose life-blood was oozing from him. "Two of their guns are taken," exclaimed one. "We are giving them Hell," shouted another. . . .

I remember after that a sort of sickening sensation as if I was going to a slaughter-house to be butchered, and as we neared the field and saw ominous shapes here and there, bodies wrapped in blankets, too deathly still for sleep, a cold shudder as of the grave passed over me. I can not believe that this was cowardly, for I know that no such idea as escape entered my mind. I was simply walking into the jaws of death for the first time, made more horrible

GENERAL MAP OF ALBEMARLE AND PAMLICO SOUNDS

by the sights and sounds around me, and I felt I must be deathly pale. This feeling made me nervous, too, for even then pride struggled to conceal my weakness; but as I looked around me to see if it was noticed by my companions, I was surprised to see the same feelings working more or less transparently through all the faces I could see back in the line. I realized the truth then, that every individual was, like myself, undergoing the same experience, and that I was not alone in looking into the awful abyss of non-existence, or trying as best I could to shake hands with Death. Strange to say, the realization of this truth gave me what I needed and that not so much courage, as sympathy for my comrades, and this took my thoughts from myself and my single individuality. It put an end to the struggle as far as I was concerned, so that when we arrived upon the field all dread or fear seemed to have passed away, and I have often thought since that I went through in that short march to the battlefield, on Roanoke, all that mortal can, but Death; that I had, in fact, looked him square in the face, and placed myself within his reach, and though I have been nearer him since, I have never felt that feeling, nor do I think I ever will. . . .

It was impossible to form in battalion line, and it was not attempted, for the trees felled in every direction would have prevented, even if the nature of the ground (a swamp) had not most effectually done so. We advanced up to a bend in the road, where a squad of the marine artillery were working one of their howitzers, when we were told to drop on account of a special volley that it seems was expected would be fired for our benefit. We disposed of ourselves without any attempt at order, on either side of the road among the other troops. All the men were crouching low behind objects of shelter and firing as fast as they could load. I took the right side of the road, looking ahead very naturally, to see what was the aim of all the shooting.

I saw a body of men moving slowly along the other end of the opening, and seeing most of the guns around me leveled in that direction, I also took aim to fire, but luckily snapped my piece. I say "luckily," because as I was in the act of repriming, the officer commanding the gun cried out to stop, "For God's sake!"—we were shooting our own men! I had been aiming like many others at a body of our men who were endeavoring to flank the enemy. Wishing, simply enough, to know "what in thunder to shoot at then," a low, broken line was pointed out to me in the edge of the wood, which I was informed was a battery behind which the enemy was posted. As I was looking, I saw some one, evidently an officer, very probably Captain Wise, jump up on the works and stand there quite bravely gesticulating, but how long he was there, I do not know, for I had no time for further observation. Just then our Bugler sounded, "Cease Firing," and then I heard the hoarse voice of our Major give the command, "Charge Bayonets," and all I know is that I was out on the road running and yelling with the rest of the men, and that with a successful leap over a wide ditch full of water, we were all together pouring pell-mell over the breastworks. When I came up and jumped into the works, there was not an enemy in sight. They must have left the moment we charged, but a dead soldier was in standing posture, slightly bent over the muzzle of one of the cannon, shot while in the act of loading. In his hands he yet clutched a charge of grape, and so lifelike did he appear that for a moment I thought he must be yet alive. One of our boys, an Irishman, and one of the first to mount the works, was so strongly under the same impression that he actually clubbed him with his musket before finding out his mistake. A wild cheer arose as our flag was planted on the fort, everybody shook hands in congratulation, all laughed and, I think, some cried, but every one was equally overjoyed at our first victory.

The enemy had left the rammers in their guns, and their knapsacks and muskets were scattered about in such confusion that it was evident they had made a hasty flight after their brave and wonderfully stubborn resistance. During the enthusiasm over our success, all order was forgotten, and I felt some apprehension that the enemy might be re-forming and come on us while we were yet in confusion. Nothing of the kind happened, however, and we were soon re-formed and in pursuit of them. . . .

Before night the enemy had surrendered some twenty-seven hundred prisoners, three or four batteries, thirty guns, and we were left masters of the Island. General Wise, the father of the brave Captain who had given his life in its defense, managed to escape with some few troops by way of Nags Head.

—Johnson, *The Long Roll*

2. THE *MERRIMAC* AND THE *MONITOR*

This is one of the half-dozen most famous engagements in American history. If it did not revolutionize naval warfare, as is often erroneously asserted, it did dramatize the advent of the revolution that had taken place—the substitution of iron or steel for oak.

When the Federals abandoned Norfolk they fired and sank a number of their ships there; among them was the 350-ton frigate, Merrimac. The Confederates raised this ship and converted her into an ironclad—renaming her, but in vain, the Virginia. Alarmed by rumors of progress on the Merrimac, the Navy Department asked for bids for the building of armored vessels. The well-known naval engineer, John Ericsson, who had been born in Sweden, was among those who submitted plans. These were accepted, and Ericsson began building his armored ship in October 1861. It was launched at the end of January, ready for sea on February 19, and sailed from New York March 6, under the command of Lieutenant John L. Worden. It arrived off Hampton Roads just in the nick of time—or perhaps a bit too late. For on March 8 the Merrimac had come out and attacked the Union fleet off Fortress Monroe.

We give here the account of the terrible destruction wrought by the Merrimac on the eighth and of the tremendous duel between the two ironclads the following day. Our first historian is Captain Van Brunt of the Minnesota; our second the intrepid Lieutenant S. Dana Greene, who succeeded the blinded Worden in command of the Monitor.

A. The *Minnesota* Fights for Her Life in Hampton Roads

United States Steamer *Minnesota,*
March 10, 1862

Sir: On Saturday, the eighth instant, at forty-five minutes after twelve o'clock P.M., three small steamers, in appearance, were discovered rounding Sewall's Point, and as soon as they came into full broadside view, I was convinced that one was the iron-plated steam-battery *Merrimac*, from the large size of her smoke-pipe. They were heading for Newport News, and I, in obedience to a signal from the senior officer present, Capt. John Marston, immediately called all hands, slipped my cables, and got under way for that point, to engage her. While rapidly passing Sewall's Point, the rebels there opened fire upon us from a rifle-battery, one shot from which going through and crippling my mainmast. I returned the fire with my broadside-guns and forecastle-pivot. We ran without further difficulty within about one and a half miles of Newport News, and there, unfortunately, grounded. The tide was running ebb, and although in the channel there was not sufficient water for this ship, which draws twenty-three feet, I knew the bottom was soft and lumpy, and endeavored to force the ship over, but found it impossible so to do. At this time it was reported to me that the *Merrimac* had passed the frigate *Congress* and run into the sloop-of-war *Cumberland*, and in fifteen minutes after, I saw the latter going down by the head. The *Merrimac* then hauled off, taking a position, and about half-past two o'clock P.M., engaged the *Congress*, throwing shot and shell into her with terrific effect, while the shot from the *Congress* glanced from her iron-plated sloping sides, without doing any apparent injury. At half-past three o'clock P.M., the *Congress* was compelled to haul down her colors. Of the extent of her loss and injury, you will be informed from the official report of her commander.

At four o'clock P.M., the *Merrimac, Jamestown* and *Patrick Henry*, bore down upon my vessel. Very fortunately, the iron battery drew too much water to come within a mile of us. She took a position on my starboard bow, but did not fire with accuracy, and only one shot passed through the ship's bow. The other two steamers took their position on my port bow and stern, and their fire did most damage in killing and wounding men, inasmuch as they fired with rifled guns; but with the heavy gun that I could bring to bear upon them, I drove them off, one of them apparently in a crippled state. I fired upon the *Merrimac* with my ten-inch pivot-gun, without any apparent effect, and at seven o'clock P.M., she too hauled off, and all three vessels steamed toward Norfolk.

The tremendous firing of my broadside guns had crowded me further upon the mud-bank, into which the ship seemed to have made for herself a cradle. From ten P.M., when the tide commenced to run flood, until four A.M., I had all hands at work, with steamtugs and hawsers, endeavoring to haul the ship off the bank; but without avail, and as the tide had then fallen considerably, I suspended further proceedings at that time.

At two A.M. the iron battery *Monitor*, Com. John L. Worden, which had arrived the previous evening at Hampton Roads, came alongside and reported for duty, and then all on board felt that we had a friend that would stand by us in our hour of trial.

At six A.M. the enemy again appeared, coming down from Craney Island, and I beat to quarters; but they ran past my ship, and were heading for Fortress Monroe, and the retreat was beaten, to allow my men to get something to eat. The *Merrimac* ran down near the Rip Raps, and then turned into the channel through which I had come. Again all hands were called to quarters, and opened upon her with my stern-guns, and made signal to the *Monitor* to attack the enemy. She immediately ran down in my wake, right within the range of the *Merrimac*, completely covering my ship, as far as was possible with her diminutive dimensions, and, much to my astonishment, laid herself right alongside of the *Merrimac*, and the contrast was that of a pigmy to a giant. Gun after gun was fired by the *Monitor*, which was returned with whole broadsides from the rebels, with no more effect, apparently, than so many pebble-stones thrown by a child. After a while they commenced manœuvring, and we could see the little battery point her bow for the rebel's, with the intention, as I thought, of sending a shot through her bow-porthole; then she would shoot by her, and rake her through her stern. In the mean time the rebels were pouring broadside after broadside, but almost all her shot flew over the little submerged propeller; and when they struck the bomb-proof tower, the shot glanced off without producing any effect, clearly establishing the fact that wooden vessels cannot contend successfully with iron-clad ones, for never before was anything like it dreamed of by the greatest enthusiast in maritime warfare.

The *Merrimac*, finding that she could make nothing of the *Monitor*, turned her attention once more to me in the morning. She had put one eleven-inch shot under my counter, near the water-line, and now, on her second approach, I opened upon her with all my broadside-guns and ten-inch pivot—a broadside which would have blown out of water any timber-built ship in the world. She returned my fire with her rifled bow-gun, with a shell which passed through the chief engineer's state-room, through the engineer's mess-room amidships, and burst in the boatswain's room, tearing four rooms all into one, in its passage exploding two charges of powder, which set the ship on fire, but it was promptly extinguished by a party headed by my first lieutenant. Her second went through the boiler of the tugboat *Dragon*, exploding it, and causing some consternation on board my ship for the moment, until the matter was explained. This time I had concentrated upon her an incessant fire from my gun-deck, spar-deck and forecastle pivot-guns, and was informed by my marine officer, who was stationed on the poop, that at least fifty solid shot struck her on her slanting side, without producing any apparent effect. By the time she had fired her third shell, the little *Monitor* had come down upon her, placing herself between us, and compelled her to change her position, in doing which she grounded, and again I poured into her all the guns which could be brought to bear upon her.

As soon as she got off, she stood down the bay, the little battery chasing her with all speed, when suddenly the *Merrimac* turned around, and ran full speed into her antagonist. For a moment I was anxious, but instantly I saw a shot plunge into the iron roof of the *Merrimac*, which surely must have damaged her, for some time after the rebels concentrated their whole battery upon the tower and pilot-house of the *Monitor*, and soon after the latter stood down for Fortress Monroe, and we thought it probable she had exhausted her supply of ammunition, or sustained some injury. Soon after the *Merrimac* and the two other steamers headed for my ship, and I then felt to the fullest extent my condition. I was hard and immovable aground, and they could take position under my stern and rake me. I had expended most of my solid shot, and my ship was badly crippled, and my officers and men were worn out with fatigue; but even in this extreme dilemma I determined never to give up the ship to the rebels, and after consulting my officers, I ordered every preparation to be made to destroy the ship, after all hope was gone to save her. On ascending the poop-deck, I observed that the enemy's vessels had changed their course, and were heading for Craney Island; then I determined to lighten the ship by throwing overboard my eight-inch guns, hoisting out provisions, starting water, etc.

At two P.M. I proceeded to make another attempt to save the ship, by the use of a number of powerful tugs and the steamer *S. R. Spaulding* . . . and succeeded in dragging her half a mile distant, and then she was again immovable, the tide having fallen. At two A.M. this morning I succeeded in getting the ship once more afloat, and am now at anchor opposite Fortress Monroe.

It gives me great pleasure to say that, during the whole of these trying scenes, the officers and men conducted themselves with great courage and coolness.

I have the honor to be your very obedient servant,

> G. J. VAN BRUNT,
> Captain U. S. N., Commanding Frigate *Minnesota*.

Hon. GIDEON WELLES,
Secretary of the Navy, Washington, D. C.

—"Report of Captain Van Brunt"

B. THE *Monitor* REPELS THE *Merrimac*

U. S. Steamer *Monitor*, Hampton Roads, Va.—At 4 P.M. [March 8, 1862] we passed Cape Henry and heard heavy firing in the direction of Fortress Monroe. As we approached, it increased, and we immediately cleared ship for action. When about halfway between Fortress Monroe and Cape Henry we spoke the pilot boat. He told us the *Cumberland* was sunk and the *Congress* was on fire and had surrendered to the *Merrimac*. We could not credit it at first, but as we approached Hampton Roads, we could see the fine old *Congress* burning brightly; and we knew it must be true. Sad indeed did we feel to think those two fine old vessels had gone to their last homes with so many of their brave crews. Our hearts were very full, and we vowed vengeance on the *Merrimac* if it should be our lot to fall in with her. At 9 P.M. we anchored near the frigate *Roanoke*, the flagship, Captain Marston. Captain Worden immediately went on board and received orders to proceed to Newport News and protect the *Minnesota* (then aground) from the *Merrimac*.

We got under way and arrived at the *Minnesota* at 11 P.M. I went on board in our cutter and asked the captain what his prospects were of getting off. He said he should try to get afloat at 2 A.M., when it was high water. I asked him if we could render him any assistance, to which he replied, "No!" I then told him we should do all in our power to protect him from the *Merrimac*. He thanked me kindly and wished us success. Just as I arrived back to the *Monitor* the *Congress* blew up, and certainly a grander sight was never seen; but it went straight to the marrow of our bones. Not a word was said, but deeply did each man think and wish we were by the side of the *Merrimac*. At 1 A.M. we anchored near the *Minnesota*. The captain and myself remained on deck, waiting for the appearance of the *Merrimac*. At 3 A.M. we thought the *Minnesota* was afloat and coming down on us; so we got under way as soon as possible and stood out of the channel. After backing and filling about for an hour, we found we were mistaken and anchored again. At daylight we discovered the *Merrimac* at anchor with several vessels under Sewall's Point. We immediately made every preparation for battle. At 8 A.M. on Sunday the *Merrimac* got under way, accompanied by several steamers, and started direct for the *Minnesota*. When a mile distant she fired two guns at her. By this time our anchor was up, the men at quarters, the guns loaded, and everything ready for action. As the *Merrimac* came close, the captain passed the word to commence firing. I triced up the port, ran out the gun, and fired the *first* gun, and thus commenced the great battle between the *Monitor* and the *Merrimac*.

Now mark the condition our men and officers were in. Since Friday morning, forty-eight hours, they had had no rest and very little food, as we could not conveniently cook. They had been hard at work all night, and nothing to eat for breakfast except hard bread, and were thoroughly worn out. As for myself, I had not slept a wink for fifty-one hours and had been on my feet almost constantly.

But after the first gun was fired we forgot all fatigues, hard work, and everything else and fought as hard as men ever fought. We loaded and fired as fast as we could. I pointed and fired the guns myself. Every shot I would ask the captain the effect, and the majority of them were encouraging. The captain was in the pilothouse, directing the movements of the vessel; Acting Master Stodder was stationed at the wheel which turns the tower but, as he could not manage it, was relieved by Steiners. The speaking trumpet from the tower to the pilothouse was broken; so we passed the word from the captain to myself on the berth deck by Paymaster Keeler and Captain's Clerk Toffey.

Five times during the engagement we touched each other, and each time I fired a gun at her, and I will vouch the hundred and sixty-eight pounds penetrated her sides. Once she tried to run us down with her iron prow but did no damage whatever. After fighting for two hours we hauled off for half an hour to hoist shot in the tower. At it we went again as hard as we could, the shot, shell, grape, canister, musket, and rifle balls flying in every direction but doing no damage. Our tower was struck several times, and though the noise was pretty loud it did not affect us any. Stodder and one of the men were carelessly leaning against the tower when a shot struck it exactly opposite them and disabled them for an hour or two.

At about 11:30 A.M. the captain sent for me. I went forward, and there stood as noble a man as lives, at the foot of the ladder to the pilothouse, his face perfectly black with powder and iron, and apparently perfectly blind. I asked him what was the matter. He said a shot had struck the pilothouse exactly opposite his eyes and blinded him, and he thought the pilothouse was damaged. He told me to take charge of the ship and use my own discretion. I led him to his room, laid him on the sofa, and then took his position. On examining the pilothouse I found the iron hatch on top, on the forward side, was completely cracked through.

We still continued firing, the tower being under the direction of Steiners. We were between two fires, the *Minnesota* on one side and the *Merrimac* on the other. The latter was retreating to Sewall's Point, and the *Minnesota* had struck us twice on the tower. I knew if another shot should strike our pilothouse in the same place, our steering apparatus would be disabled, and we should be at the mercy of the batteries on Sewell's Point. We had *strict* orders to act on the defensive and protect the *Minnesota*. We had evidently finished the *Merrimac* as far as the *Minnesota* was concerned. Our pilothouse was damaged, and we had orders *not* to follow the *Merrimac* up; therefore, after the *Merrimac* had retreated, I went to the *Minnesota* and remained by her until she was afloat. General Wool and Secretary Fox both commended me for acting as I did and said it was the strict military plan to follow. This is the reason we did not sink the *Merrimac*, and every one here capable of judging says we acted perfectly right.

—Post, ed., *Soldiers' Letters from Camp, Battle-field and Prison*

3. COMMODORE FARRAGUT CAPTURES NEW ORLEANS

From the beginning of the war the government had appreciated the paramount importance of capturing New Orleans and sealing up the Mississippi from blockade-runners. New Orleans was, however, a very tough nut to crack. Well up from the mouth of the river, it was defended by formidable forts, and across the river the Confederates had built a powerful boom consisting of chains, hulks of ships, and other obstacles.

In December 1861 the President selected David G. Farragut to command the West Gulf Blockading Squadron and directed him "to proceed up the Mississippi River and reduce the defenses which guard the approaches to New Orleans, when you will appear off that city and take possession of it."

Farragut was, at the time, sixty years old—and a veteran with 49 years of serv-ice at sea; his career, so far, had been exemplary rather than brilliant.

On February 2 Farragut sailed from Hampton Roads with 17 wooden vessels and a mortar flotilla of 20 schooners under the command of David D. Porter. On April 18, 1862, he began the bombardment of Forts Jackson and St. Philip, but was unable to make any impression on them. He then decided to run the forts, smash the boom, and sail up to New Orleans—an audacious feat which he carried through with spectacular success.

The story is told here by the New Hampshire lieutenant, George H. Perkins, of the gunboat Cayuga; *Perkins later commanded the monitor* Chick-asaw *at Mobile Bay, and retired from the navy with the rank of captain in 1881.*

NEW ORLEANS, April 27, 1862

We arrived here two days ago, after what was "the most desperate fight and greatest naval achievement on record," so every one says. Wednesday night, April 23, we were ordered to lead the way, and be ready to run by the forts at two o'clock in the morning; and at two o'clock precisely the signal was made from the *Hartford* to "get underweigh."

Captain Harrison paid me the compliment of letting me pilot the vessel, and though it was a starlight night we were not discovered until we were well under the forts; then they opened a tremendous fire on us. I was very anx-ious, for the steering of the vessel being under my charge gave me really the whole management of her. The *Cayuga* received the first fire, and the air was filled with shells and explosions which almost blinded me as I stood on the forecastle trying to see my way, for I had never been up the river before. I soon saw that the guns of the forts were all aimed for the mid-stream, so I steered close under the walls of Fort St. Philip, and although our masts and rigging got badly shot through, our hull was but little damaged.

After passing the last battery and thinking we were clear, I looked back for some of our vessels, and my heart jumped up into my mouth, when I found I could not see a *single one*. I thought they all must have been sunk by the forts. Then looking ahead I saw eleven of the enemy's gunboats com-ing down upon us, and it seemed as if we were "*gone*" sure. Three of these made a dash to board us, but a heavy charge from our eleven-inch gun settled the *Gov. Moore*, which was one of them. A ram, the *Manasses*, in attempting to butt us, just missed our stern, and we soon settled the third fellow's "hash." Just then some of our gunboats, which had passed the forts, came up, and then all sorts of things happened. There was the wildest excitement all round. The *Varuna* fired a broadside into *us*, instead of the enemy. Another of our gunboats attacked one of the *Cayuga's* prizes,—I shouted out, "Don't fire into that ship, she has surrendered!" Three of the enemy's ships had surrendered to us before any of our vessels appeared, but when they did come up we all pitched in, and settled the eleven rebel vessels, in about twenty minutes. Our short fight with the *Gov. Moore*—it used to be the *Morgan*—was very ex-citing. We were alongside of each other, and had both fired our guns, and it all depended on which should get reloaded first. The large forward gun on the *Gov. Moore* was a ten-inch shell, ours an eleven-inch, and we were so near, they were almost muzzle to muzzle.

Ours was fired first, and Beverly Kennon, the Captain of the *Gov. Moore*, is now a prisoner on board the *Cayuga*. He tells me our shot was the one that ruined him,—disabled his vessel, capsized his gun, and killed thirteen of the gun's crew. Beverly Kennon used to be an officer in our navy.

The *Cayuga* still led the way up the river, and at daylight we discovered a regiment of infantry encamped on shore. As we were very close in, I shouted to them to come on board and deliver up their arms, or we would blow them all to pieces. It seemed rather odd for a regiment on shore to be surrendering to a ship! They hauled down their colors, and the Colonel and command came on board and gave themselves up as prisoners of war. The regiment was called the Chalmette Regiment, and has been quite a famous one. The officers we released on parole and allowed them to retain their side-arms, all except one Captain, who I discovered was from New Hampshire. His name is Hickery, and he came from Portsmouth. I took his sword away from him and have kept it.

The next thing that happened was the sinking of the *Varuna*, which had been disabled by one of the enemy's vessels running into her. Soon after this the Commodore came up in the *Hartford* and ordered us all to anchor and take a little rest before attacking New Orleans, which was now within twenty miles.

By this time our ship had received forty-two shots in masts and hull, and six of our men had been wounded; one of the boys had to have one of his legs cut off. All this time, night and day, firerafts and ships loaded with burning cotton had been coming down the river and surrounded us everywhere. Besides these, the bombardment was continuous and perfectly awful. I do not believe there ever was anything like it before, and I never expect to see such a sight again. The river and shore were one blaze, and the sounds and explosions were terrific. Nothing I could say would give you any idea of these last twenty-four hours!

The next morning, April 25, we all got underweigh again, the *Cayuga* still leading, and at about nine o'clock New Orleans hove in sight. We called all hands and gave three cheers and a tiger!

There were two more fortifications still between us and New Orleans, called the Chalmette Batteries, but Captain Bailey thought they could not be of much account, and that we had best push on. When we arrived in sight of these batteries, no flag floated over them, and there was not a man to be seen—nothing but the guns, which seemed abandoned. In fact, though, there were a lot of treacherous rascals concealed in these batteries, and when we had come close enough to make them feel sure they could sink us, they opened a heavy fire. We gave them back as well as we could, but they were too much for one gunboat; so, after getting hit fourteen times, and the shot and shell striking all about us, we decided not to advance any further until some of the ships came up. Soon we had the *Hartford* on one side and the *Pensacola* on the other, and then the rebel battery was silenced very quick.

After this, there were no further obstacles between us and the city, and the fleet were soon anchored before it. The Commodore ordered Captain Bailey to go on shore, and demand its surrender, and he asked me to go with him. We took just a boat and a boat's crew, with a flag of truce, and started off. When we reached the wharf there were no officials to be seen; no one received us, although the whole city was watching our movements, and the levee was crowded in spite of a heavy rain-storm. Among the crowd were many women and children, and the women were shaking rebel flags, and being rude and noisy.

They were all shouting and hooting as we stepped on shore, but at last a man, who, I think, was a German, offered to show us the way to the council-room, where we should find the mayor of the city.

As we advanced, the mob followed us in a very excited state. They gave three cheers for Jeff Davis and Beauregard, and three groans for Lincoln. Then they began to throw things at us, and shout, "Hang them!" "Hang them!" We both thought we were in a *bad fix*, but there was nothing for us to do, but just go on.

We reached the city hall, though, in safety, and there we found the mayor and council. They seemed in a very solemn state of mind, though I must say, from what they said, they did not impress me as having much *mind* about anything, and certainly not much sense. The mayor said *he* had nothing to do with the city, as it was under martial law, and we were obliged to wait till General Lovell could arrive.

In about half an hour this gentleman appeared. He was very pompous in his manner and silly and airy in his remarks. He had about fifteen thousand troops under his command, and said he would "never surrender," but would withdraw his troops from the city as soon as possible, when the city would fall into the hands of the mayor and he could do as he pleased with it.

The mob outside had by this time become perfectly infuriated. They kicked at the doors and swore they would have us out and hang us! Of course Captain Bailey and I *felt perfectly at our ease all this while!* Indeed, every person about us, who had any sense of responsibility, was frightened for our safety. As soon as the mob found out that General Lovell was not going to surrender, they swore they would have us out anyway; but Pierre Soule and some others went out and made speeches to them, and kept them on one side of the building, while we went out the other, and were driven to the wharf in a close carriage. Finally we got on board ship all right; but of all the blackguarding I ever heard in my life that mob gave us the worst.

—BELKNAP, ed., *Letters of Capt. Geo. Hamilton Perkins*

4. NEW ORLEANS FALLS TO THE YANKEES

Farragut's fleet appeared before New Orleans about noon of April 25. The Confederate General Lovell had already fled, the coal, cotton, and ships at the levee were ablaze, the city in a state of excitement bordering on frenzy.

On the afternoon of the twenty-fifth the city surrendered; on May 1 General Benjamin Butler arrived and the control of the city was turned over to the army.

Butler's rule in New Orleans was highhanded, and possibly corrupt; it is still an article of faith throughout the South that Butler stole all the silver spoons in the city! The insults which Union soldiers suffered from the men and women of New Orleans impelled Butler to issue his notorious Order No. 28. Although there appeared to be justification for this order, it excited dismay in the North and indignation abroad. Palmerston, who made it the occasion for an unofficial protest, had to be put in his place by Minister Adams.

We give here Julia LeGrand's account of the surrender of New Orleans; General Butler's Order; Palmerston's protest against the Order; and Secretary Moran's account of the exchange between Palmerston and Adams.

A. Julia LeGrand Describes the Surrender of New Orleans

BEHOLD, what has now come to the city! Never can I forget the day that the alarm bell rang. I never felt so hopeless and forsaken. The wretched generals, left here with our troops, ran away and left them. Lovell knew not what to do; some say he was intoxicated, some say frightened. Of course the greatest confusion prevailed, and every hour, indeed almost every moment, brought its dreadful rumor. After it was known that the gunboats had actually passed, the whole city, both camp and street, was a scene of wild confusion. *The Women only* did not seem afraid. They were all in favor of resistance, *no matter how hopeless* that resistance might be.

The second day matters wore a more favorable aspect, and the Mayor and the City Council assumed a dignified position toward the enemy. Flag Officer Farragut demanded the unconditional surrender of the town. He was told that as brute force, and brute force only, gave him the power that he might come and take it. He then demanded that we, with our own hands, pull down the flag of Louisiana. This I am happy to say, was refused. Four days we waited, expecting to be shelled, but he concluded to waive the point; so he marched in his marines with two cannons and our flag was taken down and the old stars and stripes lifted in a dead silence. We made a great mistake here; we should have shot the man that brought down the flag, and as long as there was a house-top in the city left, it should have been hoisted. The French and English lay in the Gulf and a French frigate came up the river to protect French subjects.

Farragut allowed the women and children but forty-eight hours to leave the city, but the foreign consuls demanded a much longer time to move the people of their respective nations. If we had been staunch and dared them to shell, the Confederacy would have been saved. The brutal threat would never have been carried out, for England and France would never have allowed it. The delay would have enabled us to finish our boat, and besides a resistance would have showed the enemy and foreign nations, too, what stuff we were made of and how very much we were in earnest.

I never wished anything so much in my life as for resistance here. I felt no fear—only excitement. The ladies of the town signed a paper, praying that it should never be given up. We went down to put our names on the list, and met the marines marching up to the City Hall with their cannon in front of them. The blood boiled in my veins—I felt no fear—only anger. I forgot myself and called out several times: "Gentlemen, don't let the State Flag come down," and, "Oh, how can you men stand it?" Mrs. Norton was afraid of me, I believe, for she hurried me off.

I have forgotten to mention—at first, the Germans at the fort mutinied and turned their guns on their officers. In the first place, several gunboats had passed the fort at night because a traitor had failed to give the signal. He was tried and shot, and Duncan telegraphed to the city that no more should pass—then came a report that the Yankee vessels were out of powder and coal and they could not get back to their transports which they had expected to follow them. We were quite jubilant at the idea of keeping them in a sort of imprisonment, and this we could have done but for the German mutineers. The wives of these men were allowed to visit the fort, and they represented the uselessness of the struggle, because the city had already surrendered. They were told, too, that Duncan intended to blow up the fort over their heads rather than surrender. So they spiked their cannon and threatened the lives of their officers and then the Yankee fleet poured up.

These people have complimented us highly. To quell a small "rebellion," they have made preparations enough to conquer a world. This is a most cowardly struggle—these people can do nothing without gunboats. Beauregard in Tennessee can get no battle from them where they are protected by these huge block steamers. These passive instruments do their fighting for them. It is at best a dastardly way to fight. We should have had gunboats if the Government had been efficient, wise or earnest. We have lost our city, the key to this great valley, and my opinion is that we will never, never get it more, except by treaty.

—ROWLAND AND CROXALL, eds., *The Journal of Julia LeGrand*

B. GENERAL BUTLER OUTRAGES THE MORAL SENTIMENT OF THE WORLD

ORDER NO. 28

Headquarters, Department of Gulf
New-Orleans, May 15 [1862]

As officers and soldiers of the United States have been subject to repeated insults from women calling themselves ladies, of New-Orleans, in return for the most scrupulous non-interference and courtesy on our part, it is ordered hereafter, when any female shall by mere gesture or movement insult, or show contempt for any officers or soldiers of the United States, she shall be regarded and held liable to be treated as a woman about town plying her avocation.

By command of Major-Gen. BUTLER

GEO. C. STRONG, A. A. G.

—MOORE, ed., *The Rebellion Record*

C. PALMERSTON PROTESTS BUTLER'S PROCLAMATION

Brocket, 11 June, 1862

Confidential.

My Dear Sir,—I cannot refrain from taking the liberty of saying to you that it is difficult if not impossible to express adequately the disgust which must be excited in the mind of every honorable man by the general order of General Butler given in the inclosed extract from yesterday's *Times*. Even when a town is taken by assault it is the practice of the Commander of the conquering army to protect to his utmost the inhabitants and especially the female part of them, and I will venture to say that no example can be found in the history of civilized nations till the publication of this order, of a general guilty in cold blood of so infamous an act as deliberately to hand over the female inhabitants of a conquered city to the unbridled license of an unrestrained soldiery.

If the Federal Government chuses to be served by men capable of such revolting outrages, they must submit to abide by the deserved opinion which mankind will form of their conduct. My dear Sir, Yours faithfully,

PALMERSTON

—*Proceedings of the Massachusetts Historical Society*

D. "A MORE IMPUDENT PROCEEDING CANNOT BE DISCOVERED"

Wednesday, June 25, 1862. A serious correspondence has just taken place between Lord Palmerston and Mr. Adams which is destined to become historical. His Lordship with that impudence that only an Englishman can be guilty of wrote a private and confidential note to Mr. Adams on the 11th Inst., about Gen'l Butler's late order at New Orleans in which he said he could not "express adequately the disgust which must be excited in the mind of every honorable man" at that regulation "of a General guilty of so infamous an act as to deliberately hand over the female inhabitants of a conquered city to the unbridled license of an unrestrained soldiery."

Mr. Adams replied on the 12th refusing to recognise the note, unless he was assured it was official, and expressing surprise at such an unusual proceeding on the part of the Prime Minister, instead of the Minister of Foreign Affairs,—with whom Foreign Ministers carry on their correspondence on matters connected with the duties of their Mission.

To this Ld. Palmerston rejoined on the 15th by saying his note was official.

In the interview Mr. Adams saw Lord Russell and stated the case to him. He was much offended, & said Ld. Palmerston had exceeded the bounds of good behavior—a thing he had often done of late, and had no business to write such a note.

Mr. Adams renewed the subject on the 16th and after commenting on the nature of his Lordship's letter, said that "the Government he represented would visit with just indignation upon its servants abroad their tame submission to receive under the seal of privacy any indignity which it might be the disposition of the servants of any sovereign however exalted, to offer to it in that form."

Palmerston with his usual insolence answered this in a sophistical strain on the 19th, & on the 20th Mr. Adams closed the affair by a note in which he said he would decline while here to receive such communications from him. This severe reprimand had its intended effect, and his Lordship has remained silent under it.

The incident placed Mr. Adams in a very critical position, and for a few days we considered things so serious as to strongly anticipate a sudden rupture of all intercourse. Fortunately, Mr. Adams' decision saved such a result.

A more impudent proceeding than that of Palmerston in this case cannot be discovered in the whole range of political life. Knowing the brutality of his own officers and soldiers he readily imagined ours of the same stamp, and insolently presumed to lecture Mr. Adams on a thing which was not his business. His ill-manners were properly rebuked. American soldiers, he will find out, are not beasts, altho' English soldiers are; and he will also learn that it is only a debased mind that would construe Gen'l Butler's order as he has done. He has defined it according to English practice. That is all.

This proceeding of Lord Palmerston is one of the most remarkable, and probably without a parallel in Diplomatic history. Mr. Adams was placed in a most awkward predicament & managed the affair with great skill. When the story shall be made public, it will create astonishment in certain quarters. Had not Palmerston taken the course he did, it was Mr. Adams' intention to have published the correspondence privately and sent it to his colleagues so that they might know what they might at some time or other expect from his Lordship should he remain in office.

—Wallace and Gillespie, eds., *The Journal of Benjamin Moran*

5. ELLET'S STEAM RAMS SMASH THE CONFEDERATE FLEET AT MEMPHIS

At the beginning of the war Commander John Rodgers was instructed to prepare a naval force for the Mississippi. He bought three river steamers, authorized J. B. Eads of St. Louis to build seven gunboats, built a fleet of mortar boats, and prepared to co-operate with the army in its advance into the South. In January 1862 he was succeeded in command by Flag Officer Andrew Foote, who took part in the Fort Donelson expedition, and after the reduction of that fort preached in Cairo on the text "Ye believe in God; believe also in me." Foote's river fleet ran the batteries of Island No. 10 and helped reduce that island and New Madrid. Foote was disabled in action, and command of the river fleet was turned over to Captain Charles H. Davis.

Meantime an army engineer, Colonel Charles Ellet, had been authorized by the War Department to build a fleet of rams for service on the Mississippi. Two of these, the Queen of the West *and the* Monarch, *participated in the attack on the Confederate River Defense Fleet at Memphis, on June 6. Ellet himself was mortally wounded in action.*

The story of the battle is told by Colonel Ellet's brother, Alfred W. Ellet, who succeeded to the command of the rams.

UPON the startling verification of his neglected admonitions afforded by the *Merrimac*, Mr. Ellet was called to the War Department, and, after a short conference with Secretary Stanton, was given authority to purchase, refit, man, and command, with the rank of colonel, any number of vessels deemed, in his judgment, necessary to meet and defeat the fleet of iron-clad rams then known to be in process of construction on the lower Mississippi River.

Never was work more promptly or more effectually performed. Colonel Ellet purchased a number of steamboats at different points on the Ohio River, the best he could find in the short time at his disposal. He took some old and nearly worn-out boats, strengthened their hulls and bows with heavy timbers, raised bulkheads of timber around the boilers, and started them down the river to Cairo as fast as they could be got off the ways. They were the *Dick Fulton, Lancaster, Lioness, Mingo, Monarch, Queen of the West, Samson, Switzerland,* and *T. D. Horner.*

While the work was progressing, and before any one of the rams was nearly completed, information was received that the Confederate fleet had come out from under the batteries of Fort Pillow, had attacked our fleet of gun-boats lying near Craighead's Point, and had disabled two of them. Colonel Ellet received most urgent telegrams from the Secretary of War to hurry the rams forward at the earliest possible moment. In consequence of these demands, five of them were immediately dispatched down the river under my command, work upon them being continued as they proceeded and for several days after their arrival at Fort Pillow. The other rams followed, and about the 25th of May Colonel Ellet joined the fleet on board the *Switzerland*, and the ram-fleet was now ready for action.

Colonel Ellet at once conferred with Flag-Officer Charles H. Davis on the propriety of passing Fort Pillow, and engaging the enemy's fleet wherever found. Flag-Officer Davis did not approve the plan suggested, but offered no objection to Colonel Ellet's trying the experiment. Accordingly, immediate preparations were begun for running the batteries with the entire ram-fleet.

During this period of preparation, constant watch was kept upon the fort and the enemy's fleet. On the night of the 4th of June [1862] I crossed the timber point in front of the fort, and reported to the colonel commanding my conviction that the fort was being evacuated. About 2 o'clock in the morning I obtained permission, with many words of caution from Colonel

Ellet, to run down opposite the fort in a yawl and, after lying off in order to become assured that the place was abandoned, to land, with the assurance that the rams would follow in case my yawl did not return before daylight. I landed with my little band, only to find the fort entirely deserted; and after planting the National colors upon the ruins of one of the magazines, we sat down to wait for the coming of daylight and the rams. They came, followed by the entire fleet, and after a short stop all proceeded down the river, the rams taking the lead, to Fort Randolph, where they delayed long enough to plant the National flag and to examine the abandoned fortifications, the gunboats at this point taking the advance.

After leaving Fort Randolph the ram-fleet proceeded without incident to within about twenty-five miles of Memphis, where they all rounded to and tied up for the night, with orders of sailing issued to each commander; instructions to be ready to round out at the signal from the flag-ship, and that "each boat should go into the anticipated fight in the same order they maintained in sailing." At the first dawn of day (June 6th) the fleet moved down the river, and at sunrise the flag-ship rounded the bend at "Paddy's Hen and Chickens," and immediately after came in sight of the Federal gun-boats anchored in line across the river, about a mile above Memphis. Colonel Ellet promptly signaled his vessels to tie up on the Arkansas shore, in the order of their sailing, as he desired to confer with Flag-Officer Davis before passing further.

The *Queen of the West* came to first, followed by the *Monarch* and other rams in regular succession. The *Queen of the West* had made the land, and passed out line to make fast; the *Monarch* was closing in just above, but had not yet touched the shore. At this moment, and as the full orb of the sun rose above the horizon, the report of a gun was heard from around the point and down the river. It was the first gun from the Confederate River Defense Fleet moving to attack us. Colonel Ellet was standing on the hurricane-deck of the *Queen of the West*. He immediately sprang forward, and, waving his hat to attract my attention, called out: "It is a gun from the enemy! Round out and follow me! Now is our chance!" Without a moment's delay, the *Queen* moved out gracefully, and the *Monarch* followed. By this time our gun-boats had opened their batteries, and the reports of guns on both sides were heavy and rapid.

The morning was beautifully clear and perfectly still; a heavy wall of smoke was formed across the river, so that the position of our gun-boats could only be seen by the flashes of their guns. The *Queen* plunged forward, under a full head of steam, right into this wall of smoke and was lost sight of, her position being known only by her tall pipes which reached above the smoke. The *Monarch*, following, was greeted, while passing the gun-boats, with wild huzzas from our gallant tars. When freed from the smoke, those of us who were on the *Monarch* could see Colonel Ellet's tall and commanding form still standing on the hurricane-deck, waving his hat to show me which one of the enemy's vessels he desired the *Monarch* to attack,—namely, the *General Price*, which was on the right wing of their advancing line. For himself he selected the *General Lovell* and directed the *Queen* straight for her, she being about the middle of the enemy's advancing line.

The two vessels came toward each other in most gallant style, head to head, prow to prow; and had they met in that way, it is most likely that both vessels would have gone down. But at the critical moment the *General Lovell* began to turn; and that moment sealed her fate. The *Queen* came on and plunged straight into the *Lovell's* exposed broadside; the vessel was cut almost in two and disappeared under the dark waters in less time than it takes to tell the story. The *Monarch* next struck the *General Price* a glancing blow which cut her starboard wheel clean off, and completely disabled her from further participation in the fight.

As soon as the *Queen* was freed from the wreck of the sinking *Lovell*, and before she could recover headway, she was attacked on both sides by the enemy's vessels, the *Beauregard* on one side and the *Sumter* on the other. In the mêlée one of the wheels of the *Queen* was disabled so that she could not use it, and Colonel Ellet, while still standing on the hurricane-deck to view the effects of the encounter with the *General Lovell*, received a pistol-ball in his knee, and, lying prone on the deck, gave orders for the *Queen* to be run on her one remaining wheel to the Arkansas shore, whither she was soon followed by the *General Price* in a sinking condition. Colonel Ellet sent an officer and squad of men to meet the *General Price* upon her making the shore, and received her entire crew as prisoners of war. By this time consternation had seized upon the enemy's fleet, and all had turned to escape. The fight had drifted down the river, below the city.

The *Monarch*, as soon as she could recover headway after her conflict with the *General Price*, drove down upon the *Beauregard*, which vessel, after her encounter with the *Queen of the West*, was endeavoring to escape. She was thwarted by the *Monarch* coming down upon her with a well-directed blow which crushed in her side and completely disabled her from further hope of escape. Men on the deck waved a white flag in token of surrender, and the *Monarch* passed on down to intercept the *Little Rebel*, the enemy's flag-ship. She had received some injury from our gun-boats' fire, and was making for the Arkansas shore, which she reached at the moment when the *Monarch*, with very slight headway, pushed her hard and fast aground; her crew sprang upon shore and ran into the thick woods, making their escape. Leaving the *Little Rebel* fast aground, the *Monarch* turned her attention to the sinking *Beauregard*, taking the vessel in tow, and making prisoners of her crew. The *Beauregard* was towed by the *Monarch* to the bar, where she sank to her boiler-deck and finally became a total loss.

The others of the enemy's fleet were run ashore and fired by the crews before they escaped into the adjoining Arkansas swamps. The *Jeff. Thompson* burned and blew up with a tremendous report; the *General Bragg* was secured by our gun-boats before the fire gained headway, and was saved. The *Van Dorn* alone made her escape, and was afterward burned by the enemy at Liverpool Landing, upon the approach of two of our rams in Yazoo River, in order to prevent her from falling into our hands. Two other rebel boats were burned at the same time,—the *Polk* and the *Livingston.* . . .

Colonel Ellet did not rely on heavy ordnance, and did not recommend arming his rams. At the battle of Memphis there were no firearms on board the ram-fleet except a few short carbines and some pocket-revolvers; his reliance was upon the prow of his vessel. He desired, as far as possible, to protect the vulnerable parts of his ship, the boilers and engines, and with simply enough men as crew to handle the boat with certainty and dispatch, to run the gauntlet of any fire that could be precipitated upon him, and drive his ram deep into his unwieldy adversary. At the battle of Memphis the enemy concentrated their fire upon the *Queen of the West* and the *Monarch*, but their missiles passed harmlessly by. Not a splinter was raised off either of the rams, and not a man sustained the slightest injury except Colonel Ellet, whose fatal wound was received from a pistol-ball.

The battle of Memphis was, in many respects, one of the most remarkable naval victories on record. For *two* unarmed, frail, wooden river steamboats, with barely men enough on board to handle the machinery and keep the furnace-fires burning, to rush to the front, between two hostile fleets, and *into* the enemy's advancing line of eight iron-clad, heavily armed, and fully manned steam-rams, sinking one, disabling and capturing three, and carrying consternation to the others, was a sight never before witnessed.

The River Defense Fleet was composed of strong, well-built ocean steamers, well strengthened and protected with railroad iron so as to be almost invulnerable to shot when advancing. The intention was apparent to repeat at Memphis the tactics which had proved so successful at Fort Pillow,—to ram the Union gun-boats at anchor; and had the rams *Queen of the West* and *Monarch* got run through the line of gun-boats and attacked the Defense Fleet as it approached, sinking, disabling, and scattering its vessels, and thus removing the fight half a mile below, the result of the affair might have been very different. The Defense Fleet was advancing up-stream, thus exposing the strongest and best-protected portions of each vessel; the gun-boats, relying upon their guns, were at anchor, with their sterns, their most vulnerable part, pointing down-stream and consequently exposed to the tremendous attack of the enemy. Had the Confederate commanders trusted only to the strength of their vessels, ceased firing, and with every pound of steam on plunged at full speed into our anchored gun-boat fleet, who could doubt what the result would have been?

—ELLET, "Ellet and His Steam-Rams at Memphis"

6. THE *INDIANOLA* RUNS THE VICKSBURG BATTERIES

Farragut had run the Vicksburg batteries as early as June 1862, but since that time Vicksburg had been greatly strengthened. When Grant decided to approach Vicksburg from the west and south, he faced the problem of naval support in crossing the Mississippi below Vicksburg. As Port Hudson was still in Confederate hands he could not expect support from Farragut at New Orleans. The only thing was to run the Vicksburg batteries.

Here is the story, by one of the crew of the Indianola, *of how this feat was performed. Once the* Indianola *and her sister ships had shown the way, other gunboats and transports succeeded in the perilous undertaking. The* Indianola *herself was subsequently rammed, and surrendered to the Confederates.*

IT was about eleven o'clock on the night of the 13th of February, 1863, the sky being cloudy and threatening, that the *Indianola* . . . stood out into the main channel of the Mississippi and headed down the river. How many were in the secret at that hour is known only to themselves; to the writer, whose watch it was, the actual destination of the vessel was not known till the rattle of the rudder-chains and the turning of the bow down stream revealed it. Before the start, however, it was evident that we were going into action. The day before the scanty crew had been partially reinforced by detachments from other vessels of the fleet, and the ominous silence of the captain, with the still more ominous actions of the surgeon and his assistant, suggested that there was hot work ahead, and that we were to have a hand in it. As our vessel came in sight of the bluffs, the engines were checked till the great wheels moved with only enough speed to insure the proper steerage-way. Then came the final summons, which precedes and always portends hostilities, as all hands were called to quarters. This command brought the writer, then a youth of nineteen, to his place between the eleven-inch Dahlgrens in the forward turret. On the right and left of him were the guns' crews, and behind each gun the officer in command.

Not a sound broke the silence of the night, but the whispered call of the pilot, stationed outside the port, and passed along to his assistant at the wheel, "Port a little," "Starboard a little," "Steady." The great hull hardly felt the feeble tremor of the engines, and in this form the *Indianola* passed the mouth of the canal, and the lights of the mortar fleet anchored near it. Finally, a sharp order from without, "Starboard hard," followed again by the rattle of the rudder chains, indicated an approach to the sharp bend above the town; and just here a flash, followed by a dull, low rumble above, gave what seemed to be the first signs of discovery and attack. But it was a flash of lightning and its succeeding thunder from the protecting clouds above us. This false alarm was not without its effect, however, since it gave the new recruits and the youngsters a chance to determine just how they would feel when the fight actually began. This flash from the sky was followed by still denser darkness, and the only indications of an approach to the batteries were the flickering of the campfires and the higher lights of the town above.

It was afterwards reported that at last it was only an accident which discovered to the enemy the immediate presence and purpose of the *Indianola*. The story goes that a Confederate soldier, tired of his idle bivouac, happening to take up a burning brand from his replenished campfire, threw it, carelessly, into the sluggish brown current that was lapping the shore at his feet. The flash of this fire-brand, as it shot out into the night, revealed to him the presence, at almost a stone's throw from where he stood, of our vessel stealthily stealing by, like some dread intruder from the jungles upon the camp of the unsuspecting hunter. But that soldier was backed by "an army with banners," and this chance discovery was followed by the instant discharge of the picket-gun. As this signal passed along the shore line, its progress was marked by volleys of small-arms, and signal rockets shooting from point to point along the bluffs, as each battery was hastily aroused and trained for action. Then came the blinding flash and deafening boom of the great guns, rivaling the thunders of heaven, and drowning the spiteful rattle of the rifles and small-arms below. The shore battery, which was now in the rear, hastened to retrieve its lost opportunity by a vigorous, but tardy cannonade. Rapidly the flashing of guns and whistling of shells followed—now from the shore line behind, and then from the great defenses high up upon the cliffs.

These signals of our discovery were also our own signal for as marked a change of tactics. The great engines, that had been held under control so long, were now turned loose to run a race for life through this gauntlet of fire and iron hail. The great smoke stacks belched forth black smoke and crimson flame, and the paddles now thundered and beat the sluggish current as in angry protest against the resistless restraint of the preceding hours. The fun had actually begun—shot and shell screamed and burst above and beyond us, and the pilot's orders, now changed from whispered signs to vigorous commands, were heard and answered with no need of intervening messengers.

Thus the city was approached, and the *Indianola* was on the home stretch, though still in need of speed and endurance. Now appeared the wisdom of the captain's orders to hug the *left* shore, for the vessel was not touched by any of the enemy's heavy shot. The great guns on the bluffs, not being trained in the art of stooping to conquer, could not be sufficiently lowered to meet the water along our chosen line.

Thus the moments passed until the last of the batteries was left in the rear, and then the *Indianola*, having by a defiant whistle proclaimed its victory to friends and foes alike, passed beyond the wall of fire and slowly approached its first mooring, under the shadow of the cottonwoods.

—W. S. Ward, "How We Ran the Vicksburg Batteries"

7. ATTACK AND REPULSE AT BATTERY WAGNER

Throughout the war the Federals tried to capture Charleston; not until Sherman's march through South Carolina forced its evacuation did they succeed. The first major effort came in June 1862, when General Hunter landed on James Island but failed to take the fort of Secessionville (June 16). The second came on April 7, 1863, when an attempt by the Ironsides and eight monitors to break through the harbor defenses and bombard the city was repulsed with heavy loss. The third, and most substantial, was the occupation of Morris Island in the summer of 1863, and the series of land and sea assaults on Battery Wagner that finally forced its surrender.

Early in July General Gillmore, Commander of the Department of the

South, landed on the southern end of Morris Island, carried the Confederate lines by assault, and advanced on Fort (or Battery) Wagner, at the northern tip of the island and only a mile from Fort Sumter. Instead of attacking at once Gillmore waited until the following day; by that time the Confederates were ready for him, and repulsed the assault. The second attack came on July 18. The advance was led by Colonel Shaw of the famous 54th Massachusetts (Colored) Regiment; supporting him were Colonel Barton's 3rd New Hampshire, Colonel Putnam's 7th New Hampshire, Colonel Jackson's 76th Pennsylvania, Colonel Commager's 67th Ohio, and others. The attack was almost—but not quite—successful. After its failure the navy took over. In early September there was a 42-hour bombardment which eventually forced the Confederates to evacuate. Yet Charleston was still impregnable.

We give here the New York Tribune *account of the assault of July 18.*

Morris Island, S. C., July 19, 1863

Again Fort Wagner has been assaulted and again we have been repulsed, and with, I regret to say, a much more formidable loss in killed, wounded, and missing than in the first attempt. . . .

In the assault of the eleventh instant, but one brigade, and that a very small one, under the command of General Strong, were engaged; in that of last evening a whole division, consisting of three full brigades, were drawn out in line to take part in the action, but on account of some misunderstanding of orders, but two actually participated in the fight. . . .

General Gillmore designed to commence the bombardment of the Fort at daylight yesterday morning, but on account of a terrific thunderstorm, which commenced early in the evening and continued until morning, delaying the work of the engineers and dampening the ammunition, the action did not open until half-past twelve. At that hour Admiral Dahlgren signalled that he was ready, and in a few moments the *Montauk*, (his flag-ship,) the *Ironsides*, the *Catskill*, the *Nantucket*, the *Weehawken*, and the *Patapsco* moved into line in the order in which I have named them, and commenced hurling their heaviest shot and shell around, upon, and within the Fort, and, with intervals of but a very few minutes, continued this terrible fire until one hour after the sun had gone down. During all the afternoon the iron fleet lay about one mile off from the Fort, but just at the close of the engagement, and but a few moments before the first assault was made by General Strong, the Admiral ran the *Montauk* directly under the guns of Fort Wagner, and, within two hundred and eighty yards, fired round after round from his fifteen-inch gun, sending, as every shot struck, vast clouds of sand, mud, and timber high up into the air, making one huge sand-heap of that portion of the Fort facing the sea, and dismounting two of the heaviest guns. . . .

The firing was almost entirely from our own side. With the most powerful glass, but very few men could be seen in the Fort. At half-past two, a shot from one of our guns on the left cut the halyards on the flag-staff and brought the rebel flag fluttering to the ground.

In a moment, almost before we had begun to ask ourselves whether they

CHARLESTON HARBOR

had really lowered their flag, and were upon the point of surrendering or not, the old red battle-flag, which the army of the Potomac has so often had defiantly shaken in its face, was run up about ten feet above the parapet, a little cluster of men rallied around it, cheered, waved their hats, and then disappeared, and were not again seen during the day. Fort Sumter, the moment the rebel flag came to the ground, sent a shot over our heads to assure us that it had been lowered by accident and not by design. In this shot she also desired us to distinctly understand that before Fort Wagner surrendered, she herself would have to be consulted. With the exception of this little episode, almost profound silence, so far as the rebel garrison themselves could maintain it, prevailed within the Fort. . . .

For eight hours the monitors and the *Ironsides* have kept up a continuous fire, and Fort Wagner has not yet surrendered. For eight hours fifty-four guns from the land-batteries have hurled their shot and shell within her walls, and still she flaunts the red battle-flag in our face.

"Something must be done, and that, too, quickly, or in a few days we shall have the whole army in Virginia upon us," said an officer high in command. "We *must* storm the Fort to-night and carry it at the point of the bayonet!"

In a few moments signals are made from the top of the look-out, and soon generals and colonels commanding divisions and brigades were seen galloping to the headquarters of the Commanding General. . . . Officers shout, bugles sound, the word of command is given, and soon the soldiers around, upon, and under the sand-hills of Morris Island spring from their hiding-places, fall into line, march to the beach, are organized into new brigades, and in solid column stand ready to move to the deadly assault.

Not in widely extended battle-line, with cavalry and artillery at supporting distances, but in solid regimental column, on the hard ocean beach, for half a mile before reaching the Fort, in plain sight of the enemy, did these three brigades move to their appointed work.

General Strong, who has so frequently since his arrival in this department braved death in its many forms of attack, was assigned to the command of the First brigade. Colonel Putnam of the Seventh New-Hampshire . . . took command of the Second, and General Stevenson the Third, constituting the reserve. The Fifty-fourth Massachusetts, (colored regiment,) Colonel Shaw, was the advanced regiment in the First brigade, and the Second South-Carolina, (Negro,) Colonel Montgomery, was the last regiment of the reserve. . . .

Just as darkness began to close in upon the scene of the afternoon and the evening, General Strong rode to the front and ordered his brigade . . . to advance to the assault. At the instant, the line was seen slowly advancing in the dusk toward the Fort, and before a double-quick had been ordered, a tremendous fire from the barbette guns on Fort Sumter, from the batteries on Cumming's Point, and from all the guns on Fort Wagner, opened upon it. The guns from Wagner swept the beach, and those from Sumter and Cumming's Point enfiladed it on the left. In the midst of this terrible shower of shot and shell they pushed their way, reached the Fort, portions of the Fifty-fourth

Massachusetts, the Sixth Connecticut, and the Forty-eighth New-York dashed through the ditches, gained the parapet, and engaged in a hand-to-hand fight with the enemy, and for nearly half an hour held their ground, and did not fall back until nearly every commissioned officer was shot down. . . .

When the brigade made the assault General Strong gallantly rode at its head. When it fell back, broken, torn, and bleeding, Major Plimpton of the Third New-Hampshire was the highest commissioned officer to command it. General Strong, Colonel Shaw, Colonel Chatfield, Colonel Barton, Colonel Green, Colonel Jackson, all had fallen; and the list I send you will tell how many other brave officers fell with them. . . . It must be remembered, too, that this assault was made in the night—a very dark night—even the light of the stars was obscured by the blackness of a heavy thunder-storm, and the enemy could be distinguished from our own men only by the light of bursting shell and the flash of the howitzer and the musket. The Fifty-fourth Massachusetts, (Negro,) whom copperhead officers would have called cowardly if they had stormed and carried the gates of hell, went boldly into battle, for the second time, commanded by their brave Colonel, but came out of it led by no higher officer than the boy, Lieutenant Higginson.

The First brigade, under the lead of General Strong, failed to take the Fort. It was now the turn of Colonel Putnam, commanding the Second brigade, composed of the Seventh New-Hampshire, the Sixty-second Ohio, Colonel Vorhees, the Sixty-seventh Ohio, Colonel Commager, and the One Hundredth New-York, Colonel Dandy, to make the attempt. But alas! the task was too much for him. Through the same terrible fire he led his men to, over, and into the Fort, and for an hour held one half of it, fighting every moment of that time with the utmost desperation, and, as with the First brigade, it was not until he himself fell killed, and nearly all his officers wounded, and no reënforcements arriving, that his men fell back, and the rebel shout and cheer of victory was heard above the roar of Sumter and the guns from Cumming's Point. . . .

Without a doubt, many of our men fell from our own fire. The darkness was so intense, the roar of artillery so loud, the flight of grape and canister shot so rapid and destructive, that it was absolutely impossible to preserve order in the ranks of individual companies, to say nothing of the regiments.

More than half the time we were in the Fort, the fight was simply a hand-to-hand one, as the wounds received by many clearly indicate. Some have sword-thrusts, some are hacked on the head, some are stabbed with bayonets, and a few were knocked down with the butt-end of muskets, but recovered in time to get away with swollen heads. There was terrible fighting to get into the Fort, and terrible fighting to get out of it. The cowardly stood no better chance for their lives than the fearless. Even if they surrendered, the shell of Sumter were thickly falling around them in the darkness, and, as prisoners, they could not be safe, until victory, decisive and unquestioned, rested with one or the other belligerent.

The battle is over; it is midnight; the ocean beach is crowded with the dead, the dying, and the wounded. It is with difficulty you can urge your horse through to Lighthouse Inlet. Faint lights are glimmering in the sand-holes and rifle-pits to the right, as you pass down the beach. In these holes many a poor wounded and bleeding soldier has lain down to his last sleep. Friends are bending over them to staunch their wounds, or bind up their shattered limbs, but the deathly glare from sunken eyes tells that their kind services are all in vain.

—"The Attack on Fort Wagner, *New York Tribune* Account"

8. CHARLESTON UNDER FIRE

As the attack on Battery Wagner got under way, the Federal batteries on Morris Island opened fire on Charleston itself, almost five miles distant. The most powerful of the guns was the so-called Swamp Angel, an eight-inch Parrott gun mounted on piles in a swamp on Morris Island, an adjunct of James Island. In August the Swamp Angel burst, but spasmodic bombard-ment continued throughout the rest of the year and 1864. Charleston's two famous churches, St. Michael's and St. Philip's, both sustained heavy injuries.

I CAN never forget, and there are many others who can never forget, the impression which the sound of the first shell thrown into Charleston made upon the mind. It was near midnight, and, with the exception of a few of the more wakeful ones, the whole city was buried in slumber. Suddenly, and without the least premonition, a whizzing, shrieking sound was heard above the roofs of the houses, which was conjectured by some to be a rocket sent up from one of the signal-stations in the lower part of the city. A few mo-ments served to convince them of their error, for the sound was repeated, and this time with such unmistakable distinctness as to remove all doubt from the mind of even the most dubious. It was also noticed that the sound was each time preceded by the faint flash and reverberation of a gun located apparently on the southeastern extremity of James Island. The fact then be-came evident, and was soon corroborated by the shouts of the people in the streets, that the Federals were shelling the city. . . .

These first shells, it was subsequently ascertained, were thrown from the Swamp Angel Battery, located in a marsh to the southeast of James Island, the erection of which had escaped the observation of the Southern generals. This marsh, it was calculated, was four miles from the nearest point of the city, and the shells were consequently thrown a distance of four miles and a half. And yet this was by no means equal to what the Union artillerists sub-sequently attained, for when they had taken possession of Battery Wagner they sent their shells three or four blocks above Citadel Green—a distance approximating to five and a half or six miles. . . .

It was ascertained when the Union troops had obtained possession of Morris Island that they trained their guns on the city by the tall, massive steeple of St. Michael's. About no one of the numerous churches of Charles-ton do such interesting associations cluster as about this time-honored edifice.

It is reputed to have been built after a design furnished by Sir Christopher Wren, the architect of St. Paul's, London. Its organ was played at the coronation of one of the Georges; its chime of bells, by far the sweetest in the land, was originally brought from England, whither they were taken back upon the capture of the city in the Revolutionary war by the British. Here they were put up at auction, and bought in by a wealthy Englishman, who, after the war, returned them to the church. It was just in front of this church, at the corner of Broad and Meeting streets, that a statue of William Pitt used to stand, which was struck by a ball from the British batteries erected during the Revolution on James Island, and which threw their shot right into the streets of the city. The mutilated statue may still be seen standing in the grounds of the Orphan House.

During the whole of this present war the steeple of St. Michael's has been converted into an observatory. Near its top a room was constructed, fitted up with a stove to keep its occupant warm during cold weather, and furnished with a powerful telescope, through which all the movements of the Union army could be easily distinguished. Night and day the observer was kept at his post, transmitting not only frequent records of the various manœuvres of the enemy to the quarters of the general in command, but also making note of every shot fired at the city. There was imminent danger lest some one of these shot might strike the steeple and choke up the narrow passage by which alone a descent could be effected, and so a rope ladder was stretched on the outside from the observatory above to the ground beneath, by which, in case of such accident, an escape might be made. Strange to say, though the shells fell like a rain of iron all around, striking the guard-house opposite, riddling the City Hall on the north, plowing up the grave-yard on the south, and almost demolishing the Mansion House in the rear, yet this steeple was not once struck, nor was the body of the edifice injured till a short time previous to the evacuation of the city.

It was interesting to notice the varied effects of the shells in their descent into the city. Certainly one half failed to explode, the percussion shell being so arranged that it must fall at a particular angle in order to crush the cap which ignites the combustible material within. Failing to explode, they would simply drive a hole through the wall or roof against which they struck and bury themselves in the ground below. Many accidents occurred from digging up these unexploded missiles and attempting to extract the fuse. When a shell exploded on striking the noise was equal to that of a good sized piece of artillery, and it was certain to produce the greatest destruction for many rods around. I have seen almost the whole front of a two-story building torn off by a single shell.

A large shell entered the loft of a warehouse on East Bay Street, and striking the joists of the roof at a particular angle, caused the whole roof to slide off to one side. A 30-pound Parrott exploded between the roof and ceiling of one of the churches of the city, made fifteen apertures of different sizes in the ceiling, demolished a bronze chandelier over the pulpit, broke the reading-desk, split the communion-table, partially demolished two or three pews,

From the Story of the Great March by George Ward Nichols

The "Bummer"

Walton Taber

Sherman's Army Destroying Railways

The 55th Massachusetts Colored Regiment in Charleston

From The Story of the Great March by George Ward Nichols

The Burning of Columbia

and made several rents in the floor beneath—all the effect of a 30-pound Parrott, the fragments of which were afterward collected and fitted together. Another shell tore open a Bible upon the pulpit-desk of a church, leaving a leaf upon which were conspicuous the words, *"An enemy hath done this."* A large two-hundred pounder struck the Second Presbyterian Church in Charlotte Street just in the rear of the portico, and so seriously injured it that it was apprehended that the whole front of the church would fall in. But the percussion shells, though more destructive to property, were not so destructive of human life as the time fuse shells which were thrown comparatively late in the siege.

The fragment of a shell one day entered a barber's saloon and took off the head of a Negro while engaged in his work. Another Negro walking along one of the principal streets of the city, and hearing the approach of a shell ran into an alley to get clear of it, and crouched behind a door. The shell entered the alley, struck the door and killed the Negro. A couple newly married were found one morning lying dead in each other's arms. A shell had struck the house during the night, penetrated to the chamber in which they were, and extinguished the life of both at the same instant.

—W. F. G. Peck, "Four Years Under Fire at Charleston"

9. A CONFEDERATE SUBMARINE SINKS THE *HOUSATONIC*

Because the Confederacy had only a feeble navy, and was on the defensive at sea, it made more progress in torpedo and submarine warfare than the Union. Both torpedoes and submarines had been used, experimentally, in the Revolution, and Robert Fulton built at least two successful submarines, but there had been little advance in undersea warfare after his time. As early as October 1862 the Confederacy established a Naval Submarine Battery Service under the direction first of Captain Maury and then of Lieutenant Hunter Davidson; it was doubtless from him that a certain type of Confederate submarine got its name, the "David." These Davids were from 35 to 60 feet long, and were fish or cigar-shaped; generally they carried a torpedo on a spar. One of them damaged the New Ironsides *in Charleston harbor in October 1863.*

Far more spectacular, and more tragic, was the career of the Hundley. *This submarine was constructed by H. L. Hundley of Mobile, and tried out in Mobile Bay. An early experiment ended with the death of the entire crew, but the ship was raised, and sent to Charleston to operate against the Federal fleet there. Four more times the* Hundley *sank, on experimental dives or attempted attacks, each time with the loss of all or most of the crew. Yet when Beauregard called for volunteers for a fifth try, the response was instant. On February 17 the* Hundley *swam to the side of the* Housatonic, *and fired a torpedo into her side. The* Housatonic *sank, but so did the* Hundley.

Altogether Confederate torpedoes and submarines sank some 30 Federal vessels and damaged a dozen more.

IT was about this time that I saw that celebrated torpedo submarine boat, the *Hundley*, the first submarine boat ever built. As I was standing on the bank of the Stono River, I saw the boat passing along the river, where her builder, H. L. Hundley, had brought her for practice. I watched her as she disappeared around a bend of the river, and little thought of the fearful tragedy that was immediately to ensue. She made an experimental dive, stuck her nose in the mud, and drowned her entire crew. Her career was such an eventful one that I record what I recollect of it.

She was built in Mobile by Hundley, and brought on to Charleston in 1863. She was of iron, about 20 feet long, 4 feet wide, and 5 feet deep—in fact, not far from round, as I have seen it stated; and equipped with two fins, by which she could be raised or lowered in the water. The intention of her builder was that she should dive under an enemy's vessel, with a torpedo in tow, which would be dragged against the vessel, and exploded while the *Hundley*, or "*Fish*," as some called her, rose on the other side. She was worked by a hand propeller, and equipped with water tanks, which could be filled or emptied at pleasure, and thus regulate her sinking or rising. The first experiment with her was made in Mobile Bay, and she went down all right with her crew of seven men, but did not come up, and every man died, asphyxiated, as no provision had been made for storing a supply of air.

As soon as she was raised, she was brought to Charleston, and a few days after her acceptance by General Beauregard, Lieutenant Payne, of the Confederate Navy, volunteered with a crew of six men to man her and attack the Federal fleet off Charleston. While he had her at Fort Johnson, on James Island, and was making preparations for the attack, one night as she was lying at the wharf the swell of a passing steamer filled her, and she went to the bottom, carrying with her and drowning the six men. Lieutenant Payne happened to be near an open manhole at the moment, and thus he alone escaped. Notwithstanding the evidently fatal characteristics of this boat, as soon as she was raised another crew of six men volunteered under Payne and took charge of her. But only a week afterwards an exactly similar accident happened while she was alongside the wharf at Fort Sumter, and only Payne and two of his men escaped.

H. L. Hundley, her builder in Mobile, now believed that the crews did not understand how to manage the "*Fish*," and came on to Charleston to see if he could not show how it should be done. A Lieutenant Dixon, of Alabama, had made several successful experiments with the boat in Mobile Bay, and he also came on, and was put in charge, with a volunteer crew, and made several successful dives in the harbor. But one day, the day on which I saw the boat, Hundley himself took it into Stono River to practice her crew. She went down all right, but did not come up, and when she was searched for, found and raised to the surface, all of her crew were dead, asphyxiated as others had been.

After the boat was brought up to Charleston, several successful experiments were made with her, until she attempted to dive under the Confederate receiving ship *Indian Chief*, when she got entangled with an anchor chain and went to the bottom, and remained there until she was raised with every one of her crew dead, as were their predecessors.

No sooner had she been raised than a number of men begged to be allowed to give her another trial, and Lieutenant Dixon was given permission to use her in an attack on the U. S. S. *Housatonic*, a new gunboat that lay off Beach Inlet on the bar, on the condition that she should not be used as a submarine vessel, but only on the surface with a spar torpedo. On February 17, 1864, Lieutenant Dixon, with a crew of six men, made their way with the boat through the creeks behind Sullivan's Island to the inlet. The night was not very dark, and the *Housatonic* easily could be perceived lying at anchor, unmindful of danger. The "*Fish*" went direct for her victim, and her torpedo striking the side tore a tremendous hole in the *Housatonic*, which sank to the bottom in about four minutes. But as the water was not very deep her masts remained above water, and all of the crew, except four or five saved themselves by climbing and clinging to them. But the "*Fish*" was not seen again. From some unknown cause she again sank, and all her crew perished. Several years after the war, when the government was clearing the wrecks and obstructions out of Charleston harbor, the divers visited the scene of this attack, and on the sandy bottom of the sea found the hulk of the *Housatonic*, and alongside of her the shell of the "*Fish*." Within the latter were the skeletons of her devoted crew.

—FORD, *Life in the Confederate Army*

10. FARRAGUT DAMNS THE TORPEDOES AT MOBILE BAY

With the fall of New Orleans and the conquest of much of the Tennessee-Mississippi area by Federal arms, Mobile Bay assumed a position of primary importance to Confederate economy. Farragut had wanted to attack Mobile early in 1863, but had been held to Mississippi River duty by the demands of the Vicksburg and Port Hudson campaigns. After the successful reduction of Port Hudson he sailed for New York for a rest; then in January 1864 he was ordered back to the Gulf and authorized to reduce Mobile. This task required the support of land forces, and not until August 1864 were these available. Early on the morning of August 5 Farragut gave the signal for the attack, and his flotilla steamed up the broad bay, the Brooklyn *in the lead.*

John Kinney, who tells the story of that famous day, was lieutenant and signal officer on the flagship Hartford.

EXCEPT for what Farragut had already accomplished on the Mississippi, it would have been considered a foolhardy experiment for wooden vessels to attempt to pass so close to one of the strongest forts on the coast; but when to the forts were added the knowledge of the strength of the ram and the supposed deadly character of the torpedoes, it may be imagined that the coming event impressed the person taking his first glimpse of naval warfare as decidedly hazardous and unpleasant. So daring an attempt was never made in any country but ours, and was never successfully made by any commander except Farragut, who, in this, as in his previous exploits in passing the forts of the Mississippi, proved himself one of the greatest naval commanders the world has ever seen. . . .

After the reconnoissance the final council of war was held on board the *Hartford*, when the positions of the various vessels were assigned, and the order of the line was arranged. Unfortunately Captain (now Rear-Admiral) Thornton A. Jenkins was absent, his vessel, the *Richmond*, having been unavoidably delayed at Pensacola, whither she had gone for coal and to escort the monitor *Tecumseh*. Had he been present he certainly would have been selected to take the lead, in which event the perilous halt of the next day would not have occurred. Much against his own wish Admiral Farragut yielded to the unanimous advice of his captains and gave up his original determination of placing his flagship in the advance, and, in the uncertainty as to the arrival of the *Richmond*, assigned the *Brooklyn*, Captain Alden, to that position. . . .

It was the admiral's desire and intention to get underway by daylight, to take advantage of the inflowing tide; but a dense fog came on after midnight and delayed the work of forming the line.

It was a weird sight as the big ships "balanced to partners," the dim outlines slowly emerging like phantoms in the fog. The vessels were lashed together in pairs, fastened side by side by huge cables. All the vessels had been stripped for the fight, the top-hamper being left at Pensacola, and the starboard boats being either left behind or towed on the port side. The admiral's steam-launch, the *Lovall*, named after his son, steamed alongside the flag-ship on the port side.

It was a quarter of six o'clock before the fleet was in motion. Meantime a light breeze had scattered the fog and left a clear, sunny August day. The line moved slowly, and it was an hour after starting before the opening gun was fired. This was a 15-inch shell from the *Tecumseh*, and it exploded over Fort Morgan. Half an hour afterward the fleet came within range and the firing from the starboard vessels became general, the fort and the Confederate fleet replying. The fleet took position across the entrance to the bay and raked the advance vessels fore and aft, doing great damage, to which it was for a time impossible to make effective reply. Gradually the fleet came into close quarters with Fort Morgan, and the firing on both sides became terrific. The wooden vessels moved more rapidly than the monitors, and as the *Brooklyn* came opposite the fort, and approached the torpedo line, she came nearly alongside the rear monitor. To have kept on would have been to take the lead, with the ram *Tennessee* approaching and with the unknown danger of the torpedoes underneath. At this critical moment the *Brooklyn* halted and began backing and signaling with the army signals. The *Hartford* was immediately behind and the following vessels were in close proximity, and the sudden stopping of the *Brooklyn* threatened to bring the whole fleet into collision, while the strong inflowing tide was likely to carry some of the vessels to the shore under the guns of the fort. . . .

Nearly every man had his watch in his hand awaiting the first shot. To us, ignorant of everything going on above, every minute seemed an hour, and there was a feeling of great relief when the boom of the *Tecumseh's* first gun was heard. Presently one or two of our forward guns opened, and we could hear the distant sound of the guns of the fort in reply. Soon the cannon-balls began to crash through the deck above us, and then the thunder of our whole broadside of nine Dahlgren guns kept the vessel in a quiver. But as yet no wounded were sent down, and we knew we were still at comparatively long range. In the intense excitement of the occasion it seemed that hours had passed, but it was just twenty minutes from the time we went below, when an officer shouted down the hatchway: "Send up an army signal officer immediately; the *Brooklyn* is signaling."

In a moment the writer was on deck, where he found the situation as already described. Running on to the forecastle, he hastily took the *Brooklyn's* message, which imparted the unnecessary information, "The monitors are right ahead; we cannot go on without passing them."

The reply was sent at once from the admiral, "Order the monitors ahead and go on."

But still the *Brooklyn* halted, while, to add to the horror of the situation, the monitor *Tecumseh*, a few hundred yards in the advance, suddenly careened to one side and almost instantly sank to the bottom, carrying with her Captain Tunis A. M. Craven and the greater part of his crew, numbering in all 114 officers and men. . . . Meantime the *Brooklyn* failed to go ahead, and the whole fleet became a stationary point-blank target for the guns of Fort Morgan and of the rebel vessels. It was during these few perilous moments that the most fatal work of the day was done to the fleet.

Owing to the *Hartford's* position, only her few bow guns could be used, while a deadly rain of shot and shell was falling on her, and her men were being cut down by scores, unable to make reply. The sight on deck was sickening beyond the power of words to portray. Shot after shot came through the side, mowing down the men, deluging the decks with blood, and scattering mangled fragments of humanity so thickly that it was difficult to stand on the deck, so slippery was it. The old expressions of the "scuppers running blood," "the slippery deck," etc., give but the faintest idea of the spectacle on the *Hartford*. The bodies of the dead were placed in a long row on the port side, while the wounded were sent below until the surgeons' quarters would hold no more. A solid shot coming through the bow struck a gunner on the neck, completely severing head from body. One poor fellow lost both legs by a cannon-ball; as he fell he threw up both arms, just in time to have them also carried away by another shot. At one gun, all the crew on one side were swept down by a shot which came crashing through the bulwarks. A shell burst between the two forward guns in charge of Lieutenant Tyson, killing and wounding fifteen men. The mast upon which the writer was perched was twice struck, once slightly, and again just below the foretop by a heavy shell, from a rifle on the Confederate gun-boat *Selma*. . . . Looking out over the water, it was easy to trace the course of every shot, both from the guns of the *Hartford* and from the Confederate fleet.

Another signal message from the *Brooklyn* told of the sinking of the *Tecumseh*, a fact known already, and another order to "go on" was given and was not obeyed.

Soon after the fight began, Admiral Farragut, finding that the low-hanging smoke from the guns interfered with his view from the deck, went up the rigging of the mainmast as far as the futtock-shrouds, immediately below the maintop. The pilot, Martin Freeman, was in the top directly overhead, and the fleet-captain was on the deck below. Seeing the admiral in this exposed position, where, if wounded, he would be killed by falling to the deck, Fleet-Captain Drayton ordered Knowles, the signal-quartermaster, to fasten a rope around him so that he would be prevented from falling.

Finding that the *Brooklyn* failed to obey his orders, the admiral hurriedly inquired of the pilot if there was sufficient depth of water for the *Hartford* to pass to the left of the *Brooklyn*. Receiving an affirmative reply, he said: "I will take the lead," and immediately ordered the *Hartford* ahead at full speed. As he passed the *Brooklyn* a voice warned him of the torpedoes, to which he returned the contemptuous answer, "Damn the torpedoes." This is the current story, and may have some basis of truth. But as a matter of fact, there was never a moment when the din of the battle would not have drowned any attempt at conversation between the two ships, and while it is quite probable that the admiral made the remark it is doubtful if he shouted it to the *Brooklyn*.

Then was witnessed the remarkable sight of the *Hartford* and her consort, the *Metacomet*, passing over the dreaded torpedo ground and rushing ahead far in advance of the rest of the fleet, the extrication of which from the confusion caused by the *Brooklyn's* halt required many minutes of valuable time. The *Hartford* was now moving over what is called the "middle ground," with shallow water on either side, so that it was impossible to move except as the channel permitted. Taking advantage of the situation, the Confederate gunboat *Selma* kept directly in front of the flagship and raked her fore and aft, doing more damage in reality than all the rest of the enemy's fleet. The other gun-boats, the *Gaines* and the *Morgan*, were in shallow water on our starboard bow, but they received more damage from the *Hartford's* broadsides than they were able to inflict. Meanwhile the ram *Tennessee*, which up to this time had contented herself with simply firing at the approaching fleet, started for the *Hartford*, apparently with the intention of striking her amidships. She came on perhaps for half a mile, never approaching nearer than a hundred yards, and then suddenly turned and made for the fleet, which, still in front of the fort, was gradually getting straightened out and following the *Hartford*. This change of course on the part of the ram has always been a mystery. The captain of the ram, in papers published since the war, denies that any such move was made, but it was witnessed by the entire fleet, and is mentioned by both Admiral Farragut and Fleet-Captain Drayton in their official reports.

The *Hartford* had now run a mile inside the bay, and was suffering chiefly from the raking fire of the *Selma*, which was unquestionably managed more skillfully than any other Confederate vessel. Captain (now Admiral) Jouett, commanding the *Hartford's* escort, the *Metacomet*, repeatedly asked permission of the admiral to cut loose and take care of the *Selma*, and finally, at five minutes past eight, consent was given. In an instant the cables binding the two vessels were cut, and the *Metacomet*, the fastest vessel in the fleet, bounded ahead. The *Selma* was no match for her, and, recognizing her danger, endeavored to retreat up the bay. But she was speedily overhauled, and when a shot had wounded her captain and killed her first lieutenant she surrendered. Before this the *Gaines* had been crippled by the splendid marksmanship of the *Hartford's* gunners, and had run aground under the guns of the fort, where she was shortly afterward set on fire, the crew escaping to the shore. The gunboat *Morgan*, after grounding for a few moments on the shoals to the east of Navy Cove, retreated to the shallow water near the fort, whence she escaped the following night to Mobile. The *Hartford*, having reached the deep water of the bay, about three miles north of Dauphine Island, came to anchor.

Let us now return to the other vessels of the fleet, which we left massed in front of Fort Morgan by the remarkable action of the *Brooklyn* in stopping and refusing to move ahead. When the ram *Tennessee* turned away from the *Hartford*, as narrated, she made for the fleet, and in their crowded and confused condition it seemed to be a matter of no difficulty to pick out whatever victims the Confederate commander (Admiral Franklin Buchanan) might desire, as he had done in 1861 when commanding the *Merrimac* in Hampton Roads. Before he could reach them the line had become straightened, and the leading vessels had passed the fort. . . .

Whatever damage was done by the *Tennessee* to the fleet in passing the fort was by the occasional discharge of her guns. She failed to strike a single one of the Union vessels, but was herself run into by the *Monongahela*, Captain Strong, at full speed. . . . The *Monongahela* was no match for the *Tennessee*, but she had been strengthened by an artificial iron prow, and being one of the fastest—or rather, *least slow*—of the fleet, was expected to act as a ram if opportunity offered. Captain Strong waited for no orders, but seeing the huge ram coming for the fleet left his place in the line and attacked her. . . .

At last all the fleet passed the fort, and while the ram ran under its guns the vessels made their way to the *Hartford* and dropped their anchors, except the *Metacomet*, *Port Royal*, *Kennebec*, and *Itasca*. After the forts were passed, the three last named had cut loose from their escorts and gone to aid the *Metacomet* in her struggle with the *Selma* and *Morgan*. . . .

The *Tennessee*, after remaining near Fort Morgan while the fleet had made its way four miles above to its anchorage,—certainly as much as half an hour,—had suddenly decided to settle at once the question of the control of the bay. Single-handed she came on to meet the whole fleet, consisting now of ten wooden vessels and the three monitors. At that time the *Tennessee* was believed to be the strongest vessel afloat, and the safety with which she carried her crew during the battle proved that she was virtually invulnerable.

Fortunately for the Union fleet she was weakly handled, and at the end fell a victim to a stupendous blunder in her construction—the failure to protect her rudder-chains.

The spectacle afforded the Confederate soldiers, who crowded the ramparts of the two forts,—the fleet now being out of range,—was such as has very rarely been furnished in the history of the world. To the looker-on it seemed as if the fleet was at the mercy of the ram, for the monitors, which were expected to be the chief defense, were so destitute of speed and so difficult to manoeuvre that it seemed an easy task for the *Tennessee* to avoid them and sink the wooden vessels in detail.

Because of the slowness of the monitors, Admiral Farragut selected the fastest of the wooden vessels to begin the attack. While the navy signals for a general attack of the enemy were being prepared, the *Monongahela* (Captain Strong) and the *Lackawanna* (Captain Marchand) were ordered by the more rapid signal system of the army to "run down the ram," the order being immediately repeated to the monitors.

The *Monongahela*, with her prow already somewhat weakened by the previous attempt to ram, at once took the lead, as she had not yet come to anchor. The ram from the first headed for the *Hartford*, and paid no attention to her assailants, except with her guns. The *Monongahela*, going at full speed, struck the *Tennessee* amidships—a blow that would have sunk almost any vessel of the Union navy, but which inflicted not the slightest damage on the solid iron hull of the ram. (After the surrender it was almost impossible to tell where the attacking vessel had struck.) Her own iron prow and cutwater were carried away, and she was otherwise badly damaged about the stern by the collision.

The *Lackawanna* was close behind and delivered a similar blow with her wooden bow, simply causing the ram to lurch slightly to one side. As the vessels separated the *Lackawanna* swung alongside the ram, which sent two shots through her and kept on her course for the *Hartford*, which was now the next vessel in the attack. The two flag-ships approached each other, bow to bow, iron against oak. It was impossible for the *Hartford*, with her lack of speed, to circle around and strike the ram on the side; her only safety was in keeping pointed directly for the bow of her assailant. The other vessels of the fleet were unable to do anything for the defense of the admiral except to train their guns on the ram, on which as yet they had not the slightest effect.

It was a thrilling moment for the fleet, for it was evident that if the ram could strike the *Hartford* the latter must sink. But for the two vessels to strike fairly, bows on, would probably have involved the destruction of both, for the ram must have penetrated so far into the wooden ship that as the *Hartford* filled and sank she would have carried the ram under water. Whether for this reason or for some other, as the two vessels came together the *Tennessee* slightly changed her course, the port bow of the *Hartford* met the port bow of the ram, and the ships grated against each other as they passed. The *Hartford* poured her whole port broadside against the ram, but the solid shot merely dented the side and bounded into the air. The ram tried to return the salute, but owing to defective primers only one gun was discharged. This sent a shell through the berth-deck, killing five men and wounding eight. The muzzle of the gun was so close to the *Hartford* that the powder blackened her side.

The admiral stood on the quarter-deck when the vessels came together, and as he saw the result he jumped on to the port-quarter rail, holding to the mizzen-rigging, a position from which he might have jumped to the deck of the ram as she passed. Seeing him in this position, and fearing for his safety, Flag-Lieutenant Watson slipped a rope around him and secured it to the rigging, so that during the fight the admiral was twice "lashed to the rigging," each time by devoted officers who knew better than to consult him before acting. Fleet-Captain Drayton had hurried to the bow of the *Hartford* as the collision was seen to be inevitable, and expressed keen satisfaction when the ram avoided a direct blow.

The *Tennessee* now became the target for the whole fleet, all the vessels of which were making toward her, pounding her with shot, and trying to run her down. As the *Hartford* turned to make for her again, we ran in front of the *Lackawanna*, which had already turned and was moving under full headway with the same object. She struck us on our starboard side, amidships, crushing halfway through, knocking two port-holes into one, upsetting one of the Dahlgren guns, and creating general consternation. For a time it was thought that we must sink, and the cry rang out over the deck: "Save the admiral! Save the admiral!" The port boats were ordered lowered, and in their haste some of the sailors cut the "falls," and two of the cutters dropped into the water wrong side up, and floated astern. But the admiral sprang into the starboard mizzen-rigging, looked over the side of the ship, and, finding there were still a few inches to spare above the water's edge, instantly ordered the ship ahead again at full speed, after the ram.

The unfortunate *Lackawanna*, which had struck the ram a second blow, was making for her once more, and, singularly enough, again came up on our starboard side, and another collision seemed imminent. And now the admiral became a trifle excited. He had no idea of whipping the rebels to be himself sunk by a friend, nor did he realize at the moment that the *Hartford* was as much to blame as the *Lackawanna*. Turning to the writer he inquired. "Can you say 'For God's sake' by signal?"

"Yes, sir," was the reply.

"Then say to the *Lackawanna*, 'For God's sake get out of our way and anchor!' "

In my haste to send the message, I brought the end of my signal flag-staff down with considerable violence upon the head of the admiral, who was standing nearer than I thought, causing him to wince perceptibly. It was a hasty message, for the fault was equally divided, each ship being too eager to reach the enemy, and it turned out all right, by a fortunate accident, that Captain Marchand never received it. The army signal officer on the *Lackawanna*, Lieutenant Myron Adams (now pastor of Plymouth Congregational Church in Rochester, N. Y.) had taken his station in the foretop, and just as he received the first five words, "For God's sake get out"—the wind flirted the large United States flag at the mast-head around him, so that he was unable to read the conclusion of the message.

The remainder of the story is soon told. As the *Tennessee* left the *Hartford* she became the target of the entire fleet, and at last the concentration of solid shot from so many guns began to tell. The flag-staff was shot away, the smoke-stack was riddled with holes, and finally disappeared. The monitor *Chickasaw*, Lieutenant-Commander Perkins, succeeded in coming up astern and began pounding away with 11-inch solid shot, and one shot from a 15-inch gun of the *Manhattan* crushed into the side sufficiently to prove that a few more such shots would have made the casemate untenable. Finally, one of the *Chickasaw's* shots cut the rudder-chain of the ram and she would no longer mind her helm. At this time, as Admiral Farragut says in his report, "she was sore beset. The *Chickasaw* was pounding away at her stern, the *Ossipee* was approaching her at full speed, and the *Monongahela, Lackawanna*, and this ship were bearing down upon her, determined upon her destruction." From the time the *Hartford* struck her she did not fire a gun. Finally the Confederate admiral, Buchanan, was severely wounded by an iron splinter or a piece of shell, and just as the *Ossipee* was about to strike her the *Tennessee* displayed a white flag, hoisted on an improvised staff through the grating over her deck. The *Ossipee* (Captain Le Roy) reversed her engine, but was so near that a harmless collision was inevitable.

Suddenly the terrific cannonading ceased, and from every ship rang out cheer after cheer, as the weary men realized that at last the ram was conquered and the day won.

—KINNEY, "Farragut at Mobile Bay"

11. LIEUTENANT CUSHING TORPEDOES THE *ALBEMARLE*

In a war memorable for many deeds of daring, there were few more spectacular than the destruction of the Confederate ram Albemarle *by young Lieutenant William B. Cushing. A "bilged" midshipman, Cushing had managed to get into the navy as master's mate, then proceeded to distinguish himself by one heroic deed after another. He captured numerous prizes, destroyed saltworks along the Atlantic coast, captured enemy officers and couriers, and in the fall of 1864 conceived and carried through the plan to torpedo the* Albemarle. *This formidable vessel, which had already destroyed several Federal ships, was then lying at Plymouth, North Carolina, some eight miles up the Roanoke River.*

Cushing himself tells us how he attacked and sank her. For this act, of which the captain of the Albemarle *said, "a more gallant thing was not done during the war," Cushing was made lieutenant commander, at twenty-two, and given a formal vote of thanks by Congress.*

FINDING some boats building for picket duty, I selected two, and proceeded to fit them out. They were open launches, about thirty feet in length, with small engines, and propelled by a screw. A 12-pounder howitzer was fitted to the bow of each, and a boom was rigged out, some fourteen feet in length, swinging by a goose-neck hinge to the bluff of the bow. A topping lift, carried to a stanchion inboard, raised or lowered it, and the torpedo was fitted into an iron slide at the end. This was intended to be detached from the boom by means of a heel-jigger leading inboard, and to be exploded by another line, connecting with a pin, which held a grape shot over a nipple and cap. The torpedo was the invention of Engineer Lay of the navy, and was introduced by Chief-Engineer Wood. Everything being completed, we started to the southward, taking the boats through the canals to Chesapeake Bay. My best boat having been lost in going down to Norfolk, I proceeded with the other through the Chesapeake and Albemarle canal. Half-way through, the canal was filled up, but finding a small creek that emptied into it below the obstruction, I endeavored to feel my way through. Encountering a mill-dam, we waited for high water, and ran the launch over it; below she grounded, but I got a flat-boat, and, taking out gun and coal, succeeded in two days in getting her through. Passing with but seven men through the canal, where for thirty miles there was no guard or Union inhabitant, I reached the sound, and ran before a gale of wind to Roanoke Island.

In the middle of the night I steamed off into the darkness, and in the morning was out of sight. Fifty miles up the sound I found the fleet anchored off the mouth of the river, and awaiting the ram's appearance. Here, for the first time, I disclosed to my officers and men our object, and told them that they were at liberty to go or not, as they pleased. These, seven in number, all volunteered. One of them, Mr. Howarth of the *Monticello*, had been with me repeatedly in expeditions of peril.

The Roanoke River is a stream averaging 150 yards in width, and quite deep. Eight miles from the mouth was the town of Plymouth, where the ram was moored. Several thousand soldiers occupied town and forts, and held both banks of the stream. A mile below the ram was the wreck of the *Southfield*, with hurricane deck above water, and on this a guard was stationed. Thus it seemed impossible to surprise them, or to attack with hope of success.

Impossibilities are for the timid: we determined to overcome all obstacles. On the night of the 27th of October we entered the river, taking in tow a small cutter with a few men, whose duty was to dash aboard the wreck of the *Southfield* at the first hail, and prevent a rocket from being ignited.

We passed within thirty feet of the pickets without discovery, and neared the vessel. I now thought that it might be better to board her, and "take her alive," having in the two boats twenty men well armed with revolvers, cutlasses, and hand-grenades. To be sure, there were ten times our number on the ship and thousands near by; but a surprise is everything, and I thought if her fasts were cut at the instant of boarding, we might overcome those on board, take her into the stream, and use her iron sides to protect us afterward from the forts. Knowing the town, I concluded to land at the lower wharf, creep around, and suddenly dash aboard from the bank; but just as I was sheering in close to the wharf, a hail came, sharp and quick, from the ironclad, and in an instant was repeated. I at once directed the cutter to cast off, and go down to capture the guard left in our rear, and, ordering all steam, went at the dark mountain of iron in front of us. A heavy fire was at once opened upon us, not only from the ship, but from men stationed on the shore. This did not disable us, and we neared them rapidly. A large fire now blazed upon the bank, and by its light I discovered the unfortunate fact that there was a circle of logs around the *Albemarle*, boomed well out from her side, with the very intention of preventing the action of torpedoes. To examine them more closely, I ran alongside until amidships, received the enemy's fire, and sheered off for the purpose of turning, a hundred yards away, and going at the booms squarely, at right angles, trusting to their having been long enough in the water to have become slimy—in which case my boat, under full headway, would bump up against them and slip over into the pen with the ram. This was my only chance of success, and once over the obstruction my boat would never get out again. As I turned, the whole back of my coat was torn out by buckshot, and the sole of my shoe was carried away. The fire was very severe.

In a lull of the firing, the captain hailed us, again demanding what boat it was. All my men gave comical answers, and mine was a dose of canister from the howitzer. In another instant we had struck the logs and were over, with headway nearly gone, slowly forging up under the enemy's quarter-port. Ten feet from us the muzzle of a rifle gun looked into our faces, and every word of command on board was distinctly heard.

My clothing was perforated with bullets as I stood in the bow, the heel-jigger in my right hand and the exploding-line in the left. We were near enough then, and I ordered the boom lowered until the forward motion of the launch carried the torpedo under the ram's overhang. A strong pull of the detaching-line, a moment's waiting for the torpedo to rise under the hull, and I hauled in the left hand, just cut by a bullet.

The explosion took place at the same instant that 100 pounds of grape, at 10 feet range, crashed among us, and the dense mass of water thrown out by the torpedo came down with choking weight upon us.

—CUSHING, "The Destruction of the 'Albemarle' "

12. THE CONFEDERATES REPULSE AN ATTACK ON FORT FISHER

With the fall of Mobile and the effective bottling up of Charleston, Wilmington, on the Cape Fear River, was the only major port still in Confederate hands, and all through 1864 it was the chief haven of blockade-runners. With the advance of Sherman northward through the Carolinas it became important to capture the Cape Fear entrance and Wilmington in order to afford a supply base for the Union armies. The mouth of the Cape Fear was controlled by Fort Fisher, whose ramparts faced both the land and the sea. The first attack on Fort Fisher came on December 24, 1864, from a fleet of 60 vessels under Admiral Porter.

The attack, as the Confederate commander, Colonel William Lamb, here tells us, was a failure. Yet the Confederate defense, too, was something of a failure. While the defenders of the fort acquitted themselves gloriously, General Bragg with 3,500 men at near-by Wilmington made no move to strike at the troops that General Butler had landed for the attack but allowed them to get off unmolested.

Saturday, December 24, was one of those perfect winter days that are occasionally experienced in the latitude of the Cape Fear. The gale which had backed around from the northeast to the southwest had subsided the day before, and was followed by a dead calm. The air was balmy for winter, and the sun shone with almost Indian summer warmth, and the deep blue sea was calm as a lake, and broke lazily on the bar and beach.

A grander sight than the approach of Porter's formidable armada towards the fort was never witnessed on our coast. With the rising sun out of old ocean, there came upon the horizon, one after another, the vessels of the fleet, the grand frigates leading the van, followed by the ironclads,—more than fifty men-of-war, heading for the Confederate stronghold. At nine o'clock the men were beat to quarters, and silently the detachments stood by their guns. On the vessels came, growing larger and more imposing as the distance lessened between them and the resolute men who had rallied to defend their homes. The *Minnesota, Colorado,* and *Wabash,* came grandly on, floating fortresses, each mounting more guns than all the batteries on the land, and the two first, combined, carrying more shot and shell than all the magazines in the fort contained. From the left salient to the mound Fort Fisher had 44 heavy guns, and not over 3600 shot and shell, exclusive of grape and shrapnel. The Armstrong gun had only one dozen rounds of fixed ammunition, and no other projectile could be used in its delicate grooves. The order was given to fire no shot until the Columbiad at headquarters fired, and then each gun that bore on a vessel could be fired every thirty minutes, and not oftener except by special order, unless an attempt was made to cross the bar, when every gun bearing on it should be fired as rapidly as accuracy would permit, the smooth bores at ricochet.

Before coming within range, the wooden ships slowed down and the great *Ironsides* and three monitors slowly forged ahead, coming within less than a mile of the northeast salient, the other ships taking position to the right and left, the line extending more than a mile. As the *Ironsides* took her position she ran out her starboard guns, a flash was seen from the forward one, then a puff of white smoke, a deep boom was heard and over our heads came an 11-inch shell, which I saw distinctly in its passage across our flag-staff, past which it exploded harmlessly with a sharp report. . . .

This was the commencement of the most terrific bombardment from the fleet which war had ever witnessed. Ship after ship discharged its broadsides, every description of deadly missile, from a 3-inch rifle-bolt to a 15-inch shell flying widely into and over the fort until the garrison flag-staff was shattered. Most of the firing seemed directed towards it, and as it stood in the centre of the parade, all these bolts fell harmless as to human life, many of the shells, especially the rifle-shots, going over the fort and into the river in the rear. The dead calm which prevailed in nature caused the smoke to hang around the hulls of the vessels, so enveloping them as to prevent the effect of the shots our gunners were allowed to fire from being seen. It was two hours after the bombardment commenced before the flag was shot away, and in that time, although thousands of shot and shell were hurled at us, I had heard of no casualty in the works. For those two hours I had remained on the parapet of the sea face watching intently for any effort to cross the bar, and in all that time only one shell had exploded near enough to endanger my life. In the rear of the flag-staff the wooden quarters of the garrison were situated, and these were soon set on fire by the bursting shells and more than half of them were consumed. The day being balmy, most of the men had left their overcoats and blankets in their bunks and these were consumed. There was quite a quantity of naval stores,—tar and pitch near these quarters,—and they took fire and made an imposing bonfire in sympathy with the occasion.

As soon as the garrison flag was shot away, finding the staff so split and shivered that it could not be raised, I sent word to Captain Munn to raise the flag on the mound. It seems the halyards had gotten unreeved and it was necessary to climb the staff to fasten the flag. Private Christopher C. Bland volunteered for the service, and climbed the staff under heavy fire and secured the battle-flag to the masthead. At once a terrific fire was poured on the mound and the lower end of the flag having been cut loose, again that heroic soldier repeated the daring act amid the cheers of the garrison, and securely fastened the flag where it floated in triumph, although torn and rent by fragments of shell, until the victory was won. While this was being done I went to the left salient and planted a company battle-flag on the extreme left. My two hours' experience had taught me that the fleet would concentrate a heavy fire on it, and I wanted to put it where it would do the most good by causing the least harm. For five hours this tremendous hail of shot and shell was poured upon the devoted works, but with little effect. At 5.30 P.M. the fleet withdrew. . . .

In the first day's fight I had about one half of the quarters burned, three gun carriages disabled, a light artillery caisson exploded, large quantities of the earthworks torn and ploughed up, with some revetments broken and splintered, but not a single bomb proof or magazine injured. Only twenty-three men wounded, one mortally, three seriously and nineteen slightly.

Never, since the invention of gunpowder, was there so much harmlessly expended, as in the first day's attack on Fort Fisher. All was quiet during the night, but next morning, Christmas Day, at about ten o'clock, the great fleet again moved in towards the fort, being reënforced by another monitor and some additional wooden ships of war. At half-past ten the *Ironsides* opened and the fleet commenced an incessant bombardment, if possible, more noisy and furious than that of the preceding day. At about two o'clock several of the frigates came up to the bar and lowered boats, apparently to sound the entrance, but a heavy fire was immediately directed against them and they were promptly driven out. At half-past three a very gallant attempt was made by a number of barges to sound the Carolina shoals, south of the mound. A few shots from Battery Buchanan, the naval battery in my command, first cut the flag from a barge and then cut the barge in two, causing the remainder, after rescuing their comrades, to retreat rapidly.

My two 7-inch Brooke rifles both exploded in the afternoon of this day. Being manned by a detachment of sailors and situated opposite to the bar I had given the officer in charge discretion to fire upon the vessels which had approached the bar, and his fire had been more rapid than from any other guns, and with this disastrous result, the explosion wounding a number of men.

Strange as it may appear, no attempt to pass the fort was made by any of the fleet, and none except the armored vessels came within a mile of the heaviest guns. Whether the smoke obscured the fort or the gunners were untrained, it is hard to account for the wild firing of these two days. If they had tried to miss the guns on the sea face they could not have succeeded better, no gun or carriage on that face being injured by the fire of the fleet; the only two guns disabled were the two Brooke rifles, which exploded. All the disabled guns were on the land face, which was enfiladed by the fleet as well as subjected to the direct fire of the armored ships, which came within half a mile of the fort. With the exception of the Brooke Battery, and some special firing on vessels, the firing of the fort was slower and more deliberate than on the previous day, only 600 shot and shell being expended. The temptation to concentrate the whole of the available fire of the fort on a single frigate and drive her out or destroy her was very great, as I found the garrison were disappointed at having no such trophy for the first day's engagement, but I had a limited supply of ammunition, and did not know when it could be replenished. Already on the first day I had expended nearly one sixth of my supply in merely keeping the men in heart by an occasional shot. I could easily have fired every shot and shell away the first day. Admiral Porter expended nearly all of his ammunition in the two days' bombardment. The *Minnesota* fired 1982 shots and the *Colorado* 1569 shots, a total of these two frigates of 3551, about as many as we had in all the batteries of Fort Fisher. On both days I fired the last gun to let our naval visitors know that we had another shot in the locker. In the bombardment the second day, most of the remaining quarters were destroyed, more of the earthworks were displaced, but none seriously damaged, and five guns were disabled by the enemy. The greatest penetration noticed (from 15-inch shell) was five feet perpendicularly.

During the day a large fleet of transports were seen up the beach, and the Federals landed a large force at Battery Anderson, three miles from the fort. At 4.30 P.M. sharpshooters were seen on our left flank and they fired upon our gunners from the old quarters across the causeway, and killed a young courier, who had been, without my knowledge, sent out of the fort, capturing his horse. I had two pieces of artillery run out of the sallyport, and a few discharges of canister stopped the annoyance. At this time, on the 25th, my effective force had been increased to 921 regulars and 450 Junior Reserves, total 1371. At 5.30 P.M. a most furious enfilading fire against the land face and palisade line commenced, certainly never surpassed in warfare, 130 shot and shell per minute, more than two every second. I ordered my men to protect themselves behind the traverses, and removed all extra men from the chambers, with the order the moment the firing stopped, to rally to the ramparts without further orders.

As soon as this fire commenced, I saw a heavy line of skirmishers advancing on our works. Just as the naval fire ceased, the guns were manned and opened with grape and canister, and as it was becoming too dark to see the advance from the ramparts, I threw 800 men and boys behind the palisades, which had been scarcely injured. I never shall forget the gallant youths whom I rallied that night to meet the enemy. I had ordered all to man the parapets as soon as the naval fire ceased, as I supposed it would be followed by an assault. I thought the Junior Reserves were coming up too slowly and I called out rather impatiently, "Don't be cowards, boys," when one manly little officer rushed over the work followed by his companions, shouting, "We are no cowards, colonel," and manned the palisades. I ordered them not to fire until the enemy were within a few feet of the palisades, but the whistle of bullets from Butler's skirmish line so excited them that in spite of my orders they kept up a fusilade until the Federals retired.

I was determined to meet the enemy at the palisade, feeling confident the few who reached it would be easily captured or repulsed. I had the land guns, heavy and light, manned, with orders to fire grape and canister whenever they saw an advance in force, and the operators stood ready, upon my order, to explode some of the sub-terra torpedoes. I stood upon the parapet to the left of the centre sallyport, after giving directions in person to the officers on the land front. The fleet had ceased except an occasional shell from the ironclads down this face. The Federal sharpshooters were firing wildly in the darkness at our ramparts, but the bullets which were few and far between, went harmlessly over our heads. My plan was to open with grape and canister on the assaulting column, and when its front reached the palisade, to open the infantry fire and explode a line of torpedoes in their rear to stop the reënforcing line. I am confident this would have resulted in a repulse of the main body and the capture of the first line. But Butler, with wise discretion, determined not to assault. There were not enough Federal troops landed to have stormed our palisade that Christmas night. If the assaulting column could have reached the comparatively uninjured palisades through the fire of canister and grape, the explosion and infantry fire would have resulted in their capture or destruction.

My only uneasiness was from a boat attack in the rear between the Mound and Battery Buchanan, where a thousand sailors and marines could have landed with little opposition at that time and attacked us in the rear. About 3 A.M. it was reported that such an advance was being made and I sent Major Reilly with two companies to repulse them, following shortly after in person with a third company to reënforce him. A heavy wind and rain storm had arisen at midnight, and if such a movement was contemplated, it was abandoned.

Two prisoners from the 142d New York were captured in our front at night, and next morning a number of new graves were found. Our casualties for the second day were: killed, 3; wounded, mortally, 2; severely, 7; slightly, 26. Total for the two days, 3 killed and 61 wounded.

—LAMB, "The Defence of Fort Fisher"

13. "IT BEAT ANYTHING IN HISTORY"

General Lee had informed the defenders of Fort Fisher that they must hold it at all costs; otherwise he could not continue to subsist his army. For the same reason Grant was determined to reduce it. The repulse of December 24, therefore, was not accepted as final, and preparations were made for a renewal of the attack on a grander scale. On the morning of January 13, 1865, "the most formidable armada the world had ever known"—the words are those of Colonel Lamb—sailed over the horizon, 60 men-of-war under Admiral Porter and transports carrying 8,500 troops under General Terry. To beat off this force Colonel Lamb had some 1,900 men, 44 guns, and inadequate ammunition; that evil genius of the Confederacy, Braxton Bragg, kept his army of 3,500 men safely at Wilmington. The bombardment opened on the thirteenth, and continued without pause through the fourteenth. On the fifteenth an assaulting column attacked the fort from the river shore, and overwhelmed its gallant defenders. Thus fell the last available Confederate port.

Our narrator is again the "boy cannoneer," Augustus Buell.

I WOULDN'T have missed seeing that bombardment of Fort Fisher for 10 years of my life. It beat anything in history for weight of ordnance used—even greater than the bombardment of the Sebastopol forts by the English and French fleets, because the guns we used were so much heavier. I cannot describe the discharges of those 13 and 15-inch Rodman guns of the monitors, or the explosion of their great shells in the air over the fort or among its traverses. To me it seemed like firing meteors out of volcanoes. I had hitherto thought that the long percussion shell bolt of a four-and-a-half-inch Rodman siege gun, which I had "gunned" a couple of times in cannonades in the redan in the early part of the great siege was a big thing, but now I hauled down my colors. I would watch the turrets of the monitors through my glass. They would turn their iron backs on the enemy to load, and I could distinctly see the big rammer staves come out of the ports. Then they would wheel round on a line with the fort, there would be two puffs of blue smoke about the size of a thunder cloud in June, and then I could see the big shell make a black streak through the air with a tail of white smoke behind it—and then would come over the water, not the quick bark of a field gun, but a slow, quivering, overpowering roar like an earthquake, and then, away among the Rebel traverses, there would be another huge ball of mingled smoke and flame as big as a meeting house. . . .

Imagine a cold, bright day in the middle of January; a low, sandy coastline, with a dull surf combing up on the beach; a tremendous fort of the most elaborate construction, with ramparts in some places 30 feet high; huge bastions every little way; deep-throated embrasures from which frowned the muzzles of seven, eight and 10-inch Armstrong and Brooke rifled cannon and Columbiads; and the doomed flag of the gallant Confederacy floating defiantly from its tall staff!

Look, then, seaward, and see 60 steam men-of-war formed in a great arc of a circle, all steaming slowly to their anchors and rolling great volumes of smoke from their funnels. Inside of this outer arc five or six of those low, black, sullen monitors "in line abreast," as the sailors called it, slowly and steadily creeping toward the fort, no visible sign of life about them, except now and then you could see an officer's head come up over the breastwork or barbet on top of the turret.

The sullen monitors never said a word till their noses touched the beach, which was as close as they could get to their antagonist, and then—well, the like of it was never seen. From where our transport was anchored it looked as if the *Canonicus*, which was considerably nearer to the fort than any other ship, must be within 400 yards of the northeast main bastion. I kept my glass trained on her all the time. I could see the fire fly from her iron turret, deck and sides when the big bolts from the Rebel guns struck her. It did not seem possible that anything made by human hands could stand it. At this moment the three single-turreted monitors—*Canonicus, Saugus* and *Mahopac*—were in a bunch together, the *Canonicus* in the center and ahead, not 1,200 feet from the great bastion! On one flank, a little farther from the fort, was the double-turreted *Monadnock*, and on the other, still farther out, was a great, enormous mass of iron, flame and smoke, which the old Quartermaster told us was the famous *New Ironsides*, of which we had read so much in the stories of Fort Sumter. The *Ironsides* was a "broadsider," and she had 11-inch guns, of which she carried eight or nine on each side. As her guns were lighter than those of the monitors and mounted in the ordinary way, she could fire much faster than they could, and so she was pretty much a solid mass of flame all the time.

The bombardment lasted from 10 A.M. till past 2 in the afternoon. Meantime quite a force of sailors and marines had been landed below the fort, but they were not at first in sight from our anchorage. By 2 o'clock the fire from the heavy guns of the fort had ceased. Many of them were dismounted, and the shells from the fleet had driven the Confederate Cannoneers to take shelter in their bombproofs. The fleet now suddenly ceased firing and began to blow their steam whistles, which made a din almost equal to the cannonade. This was the signal for assault. At this time the infantry nearest the river had gotten up within 80 or 100 yards of the fort, and in order to get a clear view of the assault the sailors on the transport began to mount into the rigging. "Old Sig" took his station in the maintop, together with First Officer Hanscomb, and by permission of this officer I climbed up too. The ship was rolling considerably, which made the maintop a ticklish place for a landsman. . . .

The right of the line of men-of-war was now hauled in or shortened, the vessels of the right division falling into a second line astern of the center division. Probably 15 minutes elapsed between the blowing of the whistles and the grand advance of the infantry against the north face of the fort. They did not encounter so heavy a fire of musketry at first as I expected to see, but the sailors and marines who were assaulting the sea face got cold lead in big doses. From where we were it looked as if the enemy was concentrating his whole defense on the sea face. In less time than it takes to write it the infantry had mounted the parapet nearest the river and jumped down into the works. We, of course, supposed that this would finish the business, and momentarily expected the tokens of surrender. But we little understood the nature of the fort. It was so traversed and retrenched on the inside that it really amounted to a line of small redoubts inside of one large fortress, and the continuous angry crackle of musketry, with dense volumes of smoke rolling up from the inside, told that the garrison was defending every inch of the works with desperate resolution. At the time this looked like useless slaughter, though in the light of subsequent history it appears that the gallant garrison was holding out in the vain hope that Hoke's column from Wilmington would make a diversion in their favor; though they must have had a queer idea of what would have been involved in an attempt to advance infantry over that narrow sandspit, swept as it was from sea to river by the guns of 60 men-of-war!

However, the struggle inside the great fort went on until it assumed the proportions of a regular battle, lasting until after dark. The monitors kept throwing a shell now and then, but it was dangerous business as our troops had cleaned out about half the enemy's traverses and they were slowly working their way through the others. Darkness did not end the combat, but the fitful flashes kept lighting up the crest of the long sand parapet and revealing the outlines of the traverses and retrenchments inside. The monitors and *New Ironsides* also opened again with shell against the south end of the sea face, from which our sailors and marines had been repulsed, and for half or three-quarters of an hour the sight was indescribably grand. But about this time the wind lulled, so that the smoke did not drift away, and the fort and the monitors lay enveloped in a huge pall, which, added to the gloom of the night, gave a weird effect to the flashes of the 15-inch guns and the blaze of bursting shells. This lasted till about 9 o'clock at night, when the musketry ceased inside the fort, and soon after the ships began signaling with different-colored rockets, which made another beautiful spectacle. There was not much sleep that night. Shortly after the fort surrendered—say about 11 o'clock.

—BUELL, *"The Cannoneer"*

XXIV

The Blockade and the Cruisers

WE ARE *not wholly unfamiliar with the subject of this chapter. Our review of fighting along the coast and inland waters introduced us to the blockade, and our survey of British-American relations to the delicate problem of the Confederate cruisers. We record here something of the story of the blockade itself—as distinct from the attack on coastal ports—of blockade-running, and of Confederate warfare on Union shipping on the high seas.*

Lincoln had formally blockaded the whole coast of the Confederacy from the Chesapeake Bay to the Rio Grande by two proclamations of April 1861. We need not rehearse here the vexatious issue of the legality of his proclamations either in American constitutional law or in international law. Suffice it to say that the constitutionality of the blockade was sustained in the Prize Cases, and that foreign governments respected the blockade. More relevant is the question of the effectiveness of the blockade itself. And that is a very difficult question to answer.

To bottle up a dozen major ports and almost 200 minor ports and inlets the Union had, at the outbreak of the war, less than 20 vessels. By 1865 this number had been increased to over 600—and its task correspondingly diminished by the capture of all major ports. The Confederacy, of course, began at once to evade the blockade, and to persuade other nations to co-operate in this, or to break it by intervention. It had no navy with which to challenge Union control of the seas and coastal waters; the cruisers it built abroad were designed rather to prey on Union commerce than to attack Union men-of-war. Four categories of ships engaged in blockade-running: those owned by the Confederate government; those owned by state governments; those owned by private individuals or groups of speculators; and foreign ships. Of these the third and fourth categories were the most important, though government-owned blockade-runners gave a good account of themselves. It has been estimated that altogether some 600 ships were engaged, at one time or another, in the lucrative and exciting business of blockade-running, but this estimate is palpably too low; that there were, altogether, some 8,000 violations of the blockade; and that blockade-runners brought in altogether over 600,000 small arms, 550,000 pair of shoes, and large quantities of meat, coffee, saltpeter, lead, and other items. At the same time substantial quantities of supplies were brought in from Mexico, across the Rio Grande, and there was at all times a lively trade with the North: General Sherman said that Cincinnati furnished more goods to the Confederacy than Charleston!

All this would indicate that the blockade was but loosely enforced, and it cannot be denied that it was pretty ineffective in 1861 and even in 1862. Thereafter, however—what with the fall of New Orleans and of Fort Royal and the sealing up of other harbors—it became increasingly effective, and the South felt the pinch seriously. It is estimated that the chances of capture were one in ten in 1861, but one in three by 1864, and with the capture of Wilmington in January 1865 blockade-running practically ceased.

What all this adds up to is that the blockade was a decisive factor in Union victory. We cannot say that without it the Confederacy would have won, but it is clear that without it the war would have been greatly prolonged and might have ended in a stalemate. Yet it must be kept in mind that Confederate susceptibility to the blockade was enhanced by several factors, and that the blockade need not have been as injurious as it actually was. First, the Confederacy was unprepared to take advantage of the feebleness of the blockade in 1861; as the Confederates did not anticipate a long war there was no long-range buying program. Second, the blockade sent prices skyrocketing, and the Confederacy was unable to buy all that it might have obtained had it taxed more successfully or controlled prices or raised money abroad. Third, blockade-running was largely a private enterprise, and shipowners imported luxuries rather than war essentials; not until 1864 did the government assume control over it, requiring that every blockade-runner have a permit and allot at least one half of its cargo space to military essentials. Fourth, imports through Mexico and Texas were large—Galveston, for example, remained in Confederate hands—but the Federal victories on the Mississippi nullified this immense advantage.

Lacking a navy, the Confederacy early authorized letters of marque and set about outfitting privateers. Privateering had been outlawed by the Declaration of Paris, of 1856, but the United States was not a signatory to this declaration, and the Confederacy could thus claim some legal right to ignore it. There were perhaps a dozen privateers, and altogether they captured or destroyed 60 Union vessels. Far more important, for offensive purposes, were the cruisers, or commerce destroyers. As we have already seen the Confederate government sent Captain James Bulloch to Britain, at the outbreak of the war, to arrange for the purchase or construction of cruisers and rams. This service he performed with brilliant success. Altogether the Confederacy acquired 18 cruisers, of which the Alabama, *the* Florida, *the* Shenandoah, *the* Georgia, *the* Sumter, *and the* Tallahassee *were most effective. The results of the depredations of these commerce destroyers upon the American merchant marine were disastrous; not for two generations did the American fleet regain its place on the high seas, and as late as 1910 American-flag merchant ships totaled only one third the tonnage of 1860.*

We have given in this chapter something of the story of the blockade and the blockade-runners; a glimpse of privateerings; and an account of war on the high seas.

1. THE UNITED STATES NAVY BLOCKADES THE CONFEDERACY

This general account* of the Union blockade is self-explanatory. It is, however, worth underlining one point that our author makes: that the blockade of the Confederacy was "an undertaking without precedent in history." The British blockade of the continent during the Napoleonic Wars had been largely a paper affair and had not presented a task comparable to that which confronted the Navy Department in 1861. It is appropriate to recall, too, what Wait takes for granted, that Gideon Welles was one of the ablest of American Secretaries of the Navy, and that the Navy Department was, throughout the war, well run.

Horatio Wait was a paymaster in the United States Navy.

AT the beginning of the war in 1861, a perplexing question arose as to whether it would be best for the government to declare all the Southern ports of entry to be closed, or to proclaim a blockade. . . . The urgency of the case caused President Lincoln to act promptly. On April 19, 1861, six days after the surrender of Fort Sumter, he issued a proclamation declaring a blockade of the entire coast of the Confederacy, from South Carolina to Texas; and on April 27 extended it to cover Virginia and North Carolina, making a coast-line of over three thousand miles to be blockaded, greater in extent than the Atlantic coast of Europe—an undertaking without precedent in history. . . .

When Mr. Lincoln issued this proclamation we had only forty-two ships in commission in our navy. Most of them were absent on foreign stations, and only one efficient war-ship, the *Brooklyn*, was available for immediate service. The days of paper blockades had long since passed away. The universally recognized rule of international law on this subject was that "blockades, to be binding, must be effectual. There must be a squadron lying off the harbor to be blockaded, and it must be strong enough to constitute an actual blockade of the port. The neutral must have had due notice of its existence, and to affect a neutral vessel she must have been guilty of an act of violation, by passing, or attempting to pass, in or out of the port, with a cargo laden after the commencement of the blockade. The neutral must be ready to prove himself that which he professes to be; therefore he is subject to the right of visitation and search."

A more serious difficulty now presented itself. How was it possible to undertake such a blockade as this, along such a vast extent of coast, when so few ships of any kind were available, without its being open to the charge of being a mere paper blockade? In the early part of the century European powers had attempted to enforce paper blockades, but the same nations were now the first to make merry over the subject of our paper blockade. Some of the most prominent European statesmen publicly declared it a "material

---

* From *Century Magazine*. Copyright, 1898, Century Company, reprinted by permission of the publishers, Appleton-Century-Crofts, Inc.

impossibility to enforce it." To avoid any chance of technical complications, a special notice was given by our vessels at the entrance of each port actually closed by them, in addition to the general diplomatic notice, so that for a time one warning was allowed every ship touching at a blockaded port before she was liable to capture. Thus each port was brought under the full operation of the proclamation only when it was actually blockaded by one or more armed vessels.

By degrees, as the blockading force was increased, and the blockade became more extended and stringent, it was assumed that the general notice rendered the special notice unnecessary; it was finally discontinued entirely, and capture took place without warning. The magnitude of the task of establishing and maintaining the blockade was not realized by the people generally, public attention being absorbed by the raising of many large armies from the body of the people.

When the Secretary of the Navy asked the principal shipping merchants and shipowners of New York to aid him in procuring vessels for the blockade, it is related that their committees decided that thirty sailing-ships would be needed. As it took over six hundred ships, mostly steamers, to do the work, it is manifest that they had a very faint conception of what was to be done. There were twenty-eight old ships of war lying dismantled at the various navy-yards. Those that were worth repairing were fitted for sea as rapidly as possible. All the available merchant vessels that could be made to carry a battery, including tugs and old New York ferry-boats, were purchased and converted into fighting ships as hastily as the limited facilities of the Northern ports would permit. The scanty resources of the navy-yards were inadequate. All the private ship-yards were crowded with work. There were not enough skilled workmen to meet this sudden demand, and the naval officers found it necessary personally to direct the unskilled artisans, or to assist with their own hands in fitting these nondescript vessels for the mounting and working of heavy guns. As fast as the vessels could be purchased, altered, and equipped, they were stationed along the coast or sent to sea. Many such vessels, by the tact and skill of the officers in charge of them, were made to do good service. One of the most important prizes captured, the steamer *Circassian*, was taken near the harbor of Havana by one of the old Fulton Ferry boats.

The lack of men was as great an embarrassment as the want of vessels. Three hundred and twenty-two officers of the old navy joined the insurgent forces, many of them having already distinguished themselves in service. One of these, Commander John M. Brooke, rendered very important services to the Southerners by converting the ten-inch columbiads captured by them into rifled guns. They proved to be very effective pieces, and were said to be the best converted guns ever made. He also aided in devising the simplest and best of the many kinds of torpedoes and fuses used by the Confederates, as well as in designing the ram *Merrimac*.

The total number of seamen at all the Northern naval stations available for immediate detail amounted to only two hundred and seven; and it must be remembered that it was as important that they should be trained to handle

heavy guns at sea as that they should be good seamen. The true sailor will soon make himself efficient on board any ship, as far as the handling of the vessel is concerned; but in the effective use of the battery only the trained man-o'-war's-man can safely be relied upon; and there are many other minor matters, such as the division of duties, the exercise at quarters and in boats, forming essential features of the system on a man-o'-war, that are unknown outside the naval service. Officers and men from the merchant service freely offered themselves. Gunnery schools were established at the naval stations for their instruction. As fast as the volunteers could be given an elementary training in the handling of heavy guns, they were sent to sea. This was continued for three years, by which time we had six hundred and fifty vessels and over fifty thousand men afloat.

The service to be performed by this hastily improvised force was as unique as the fleet itself. The entire outer coast-line of the Confederacy was 3549 miles in extent, with several large seaports. To guard the ordinary entrances to these ports was comparatively a simple task. There was, however, a greater difficulty to be met; for the outer coast-line is only the exterior edge of a series of islands between which and the mainland there is an elaborate network of navigable sounds and passages, having numerous inlets communicating with the sea. These inlets were frequently changing under the influence of the great storms; new channels would be opened and old ones filled up. As soon as we closed a port, by stationing vessels at the main entrance thereto, the blockade-runners would slip in at some of the numerous remote inlets, reaching their destination by the inside passages; so that blockade-running flourished until we were able to procure as many blockaders as there were channels and inlets to be guarded. The extreme diversity of the services required of these blockading vessels made it difficult to obtain ships that could meet the varying necessities. They must be heavy enough to contend with the enemy's rams, or they would be driven away from the principal ports. They must be light enough to chase and capture the swift blockade-runners. They must be deep enough in the water to ride out in safety the violent winter gales, and they must be of such light draft as to be able to go near enough to the shallow inlets to blockade them efficiently.

The blockading fleets of all the important harbors were composed of several very heavy ships, with a few vessels of the lighter class; the rest of the fleet represented some of the other classes needed. But it was impossible to do this along the entire coast, and it sometimes happened that the Confederate ironclads perversely attacked the lighter vessels, as in the case of the rams at Charleston selecting for their victims the *Mercedita* and the *Keystone State*, instead of the heavier ships; while, on the other hand, the swift blockade-runners disclosed themselves most frequently to the ponderous and slow-moving ships that were least able to catch them. . . .

Many of the islands controlled by foreign governments, and lying conveniently near our coast, had good harbors that afforded admirable places of rendezvous for the blockade-runners, where they could safely refit, and remain unmolested until a favorable time came for them to slip out and make a quick run over to the forbidden port; and if unsuccessful in their illicit attempt, they could return as quickly to the protection of the neutral port. As soon as the attention of the naval authorities was drawn to the port of Nassau as a place likely to become the main depot of the contraband trade, Lieutenant-Commander Temple was sent over there privately, in the guise of a civilian, to ascertain the attitude of the officials, the state of public sentiment, and to obtain all the information possible as to the prospects of the blockade-running business. While there he manged to be present at a dinner attended by the local diplomats. There were many indications that the feeling of hostility to the United States was very general. When the old French consul was called upon to express his views, he jumped up, overflowing with an intense desire to express himself in a vigorous manner; but in spite of his profound emotions, all he could manage to utter was: "Ze American people zey sink zey are somewhat, but zey cannot!" This terse presentation of his views was received with such uproarious applause that Temple was no longer in doubt as to which way the wind blew in that place. . . .

Supplies were brought to the South from various sources, but principally from European ports. At the beginning of the war the blockade-running was carried on from Chesapeake Bay to the mouth of the Rio Grande, by vessels of all sorts, sizes, and nationalities. The steamers formerly engaged in the coasting-trade, that had been interrupted in their regular business by the war, were at first the most successful. The small sailing-vessels did well for some time before the blockade became vigorous; but as the number of our warships increased, the earlier groups of blockade-runners were either captured, destroyed, or drawn off. This diminished the volume of supplies to the Confederates just at the time when the demand was greatly increased by the emergencies of warfare, causing general distress and embarrassment in the Confederacy. Prices reached an unprecedented height. Cotton was as low as eight cents a pound in the Confederacy, as high as sixty cents a pound in England, and over one dollar a pound in New York. The moment this state of affairs became known, the science, ingenuity, and mechanical skill of the British seemed to be directed to the business of violating our blockade. Stock companies were formed, by whom the swiftest steamers in the European merchant service were quickly freighted with the supplies that would bring the highest prices in the Confederacy. Officers of rank in the royal navy, under assumed names; officers of the Confederate navy, who had but just resigned from the United States navy; and adventurous spirits from all quarters, flocked to this new and profitable, though hazardous, occupation. The Confederate government also embarked in the business, procuring swift steamers from English builders, officered with Confederate naval officers, and sailing under the British ensign. They also shipped merchandise in other vessels on government account. . . .

When the blockade-running was at its height, in 1863, a Confederate officer stated that the arrivals and departures were equal to one steamer a day, taking all of the Confederate ports together. Prior to this no such attempts had ever been made to violate a blockade. The industrial necessities of the principal maritime nations stimulated them to unusual efforts, in return for which they looked forward to a rich harvest. The British especially had abundant capital, the finest and swiftest ships ever built, manned by the most energetic seamen. They felt confident that they could monopolize the Southern cotton and the markets of the Confederacy; but when it was found that neither swift steamers, skilled officers, nor desperate efforts could give security to their best investments of capital, and that the perils to their beautiful vessels and precious cargoes increased as fast as their efforts to surmount them, ultimately becoming even greater in proportion than the enormous gains of the traffic when successful, they were at last driven off from our coast entirely, and kept at bay, though armed and supported by the greatest of foreign powers. They finally gave up the business, admitting that the blockade was a success. A Confederate officer stated that when Fort Fisher fell their last port was gone, and blockade-running was at an end.

This signal defeat of that extraordinary development of our Civil War has been spoken of as one of the great moral lessons of our struggle. After the war British officers frankly stated to our naval officers that they considered the blockade and its enforcement the great fact of the war. This was the first time in the history of naval warfare that a steam navy had been kept at sea for so long a period. The Confederates menaced the blockading fleets with nine ironclads which would have been a match for any ironclads in the French or English navy afloat at that time; therefore it becomes manifest that a fleet which could hold in check ironclads, as well as shut out blockade-runners that were the swiftest steamers built at that time, must have combined speed and power to an extent never before displayed in naval warfare. . . .

During the war our navy captured or destroyed 1504 blockade-runners, besides causing many valuable cargoes to be thrown overboard by the long-continued and close pursuit of fugitives, who escaped capture by resorting to this expedient to lighten the vessels. A Confederate officer stated that all the approaches to Wilmington harbor were as thickly paved with valuable merchandise as a certain place is said to be with "good intentions." This assertion would apply to some other harbors.

The value of prizes captured was $31,000,000. The most valuable prize taken was the English steamer *Memphis*, which brought $510,000. She was captured early in the war by the steamer *Magnolia*. The captor was herself a prize-vessel that had been bought by our government and fitted out as a gunboat. The least valuable was a sloop captured by the gunboat *Tahoma*, called the *Alligator*, which brought $50. Many of the most important prizes were taken by mere chance, or when least expected; while many a long and hard chase resulted in the overhauling of an empty vessel, the cargo having been thrown overboard in the efforts to escape.

Before the refinements of the blockade-running system began, the men-o'-war as well as the contraband vessels were all painted the conventional black; but as black objects are readily seen on the water at night, the blockade-runners were soon painted various neutral tints. Our naval authorities at once caused experiments to be made with boats painted different colors. The tint that was least conspicuous under the greatest varieties of conditions was selected, and called "Union color." It was a bluish gray; and a formula for its preparation, together with the necessary materials, was at once distributed among the blockading fleets. It was very difficult to see a vessel of this color.

—WAIT, "The Blockade of the Confederacy"

2. NOEL BLAKEMAN RECALLS THE TRIALS OF BLOCKADING

Blockade-running was exciting enough, but blockading was a monotonous affair, a matter of waiting, day after day, for some suspicious vessel to show up on the horizon. It was, as Blakeman tells us, "a condition of masterly inactivity."

Blakeman saw service on the Kingfisher *throughout most of the war.*

THE *Kingfisher* was a taut, trim little bark, with the lines and sailing qualities of a yacht and the staunchness of a regularly built warship. She had been constructed for whaling in the arctic seas, and was among the first and best purchases made by the Government from the merchant marine . . . she was, years ago, admirably adapted, with a battery of seven guns and crew of one hundred and thirty men, to the cruising service for which she was intended; and whenever the opportunity offered she never failed to give a good account of herself. . . .

Blockading was not a very attractive service, but although it was not "so easy as it looks," it was far less monotonous than was generally supposed. True, much of the time we were in a condition of masterly inactivity, but then, like the renowned Major de Boots, we were always in a warlike attitude; and then we were constantly watching and waiting like Wilkins Micawber for "something to turn up," and whether that something proved to be the appearance of a blockade runner or a hostile demonstration from the enemy, we were always ready to fight or run, as prudence or necessity required. Our swords did not rust in their scabbards, nor were we without opportunity to test the range of our guns.

Nevertheless, the pleasures of blockade service had to be experienced to be fully appreciated. There may have been an occasional spot of monotony here and there, but upon the average station the experience was as varied as it was exciting. An occasional skirmish on shore with an outlying picket of observation; a midnight alarm, which sometimes resulted in a beat to quarters merely to receive on board a boat-load of contrabands seeking refuge under cover of darkness on the "Lincum" gunboat; frequent dashes after blockade runners that somehow or other so often managed to elude our grasp; a cutting-out expedition that often resulted in the gallant capture of a very hostile fishing-smack; the destruction of salt works that increased in number the more they were destroyed; and . . . "laying low" for the monthly visit of the beef boat, that brought our supplies of fresh meat, ice, blockade sherry, and our mail, made up a round of duty that could not be fairly termed monotonous. Then it afforded a splendid opportunity for the development and study of character as well as for the exercise of qualities that under other circumstances would not have been so prominently called into requisition. If you want to find out what a man really is, go and spend a year with him on the blockade and you will discover what kind of stuff he is made of as well as what kind of a fellow you are yourself.

One of the skirmishes we had on shore was a very neat little affair. While stationed in St. Helena Sound, off the coast of South Carolina, it was deemed necessary to capture a cavalry picket that kept watch of our movements. Accordingly a night expedition was organized. We landed about half a mile from the house where the enemy was quartered, and under the guidance of an old servant of the officer in charge, who had run away and taken refuge with us, we crept stealthily up to the point of attack. The picket numbered eighteen, our force twenty-seven. The house was surrounded without our being discovered.

Three officers and the contraband walked up to the veranda and there saw the guard fast asleep, seated upon a chair. They took away his musket without awakening him, pushed the door, which was unfastened, gently open, went into the main room where the picket lay asleep upon the floor, and without raising an alarm deprived every man of his piece and carried them into the hall. As they were returning some one cried out, "Who's that?" The contraband promptly replied, "Me, Massa James," but the premature discharge of one of our muskets without, caused our whole force surrounding the house to open fire, ignoring the fact that their own officers were within. Fortunately the bullets did no harm, but the volley awoke the heavy sleepers; the man on the porch rushed in crying out that they were surrounded and his musket gone. Our officers stepped to the door and called upon them to surrender. Evidently dumbfounded at their position, they obeyed our order to fall in without resistance, were marched out of the house and down to our boats, and were afloat before they fully recovered their senses.

One of the midnight alarms of which I have spoken, although a comical affair when viewed in the past, was no laughing matter at the time. We were blockading off the Mississippi at Pass Aloutre in company with the old side-wheel frigate *Mississippi*, commanded by the elder Selfridge. From day to day and night to night we watched for the appearance of an expedition that we understood was being fitted out in New Orleans for our destruction; but for days and weeks and months we watched in vain.

Suddenly, one night between twelve and one o'clock, the much expected and welcome long roll of the drum caused every man to spring to his post. The enemy was upon us at last! We saw the occasional flash of his lights and distinctly heard the sound of his paddles, although they seemed to be a good distance off. The boarding nettings were triced down, and the Captain mounted the rigging to catch a better view, for the blackest of darkness prevailed. Every now and again he caught a glimpse of the light, but it did not seem to approach. The *Mississippi* signalled us to slip our anchor, and the splash of her paddles announced that she was under weigh. Still our skipper held on and all hands peered out into the darkness in breathless suspense. Both batteries were cast loose, with the starboard side manned, as the force of the tide laid that side next the shore.

All at once there was an ominous thump against the ship's side. "Run out and fire!" shouted the Captain to the officer in charge of No. 1, and bang it went, followed by a scratching and catching of boat-hooks and a dozen voices shouting, "O Massa, don't shoot, don't shoot," "Don't hurt this nigger," "We wants to come aboard." We breathed more freely but those ten nigger boys were never more scared in their lives. Lanterns were brought, the nettings were raised, and ten sons of Ham scrambled over the side. After hiding in the marsh for four days they had ventured to pull off to the gunboat. The paddles we heard was the noise of their oars, the light we had watched so closely must have been a will-of-the-wisp, for they had neither lantern, candle, nor matches. The retreat was sounded, we sheathed our swords and began to smile at our first encounter with the enemy.

Meanwhile the *Mississippi* had been steaming about, expecting every minute to encounter an enemy. The discharge of our gun gave the impression that we were engaged at close quarters and accordingly she came to our assistance and learned the full particulars of our bloodless victory and capture. That expected expedition from New Orleans never came down, and when we left the station Porter, Farragut, and Butler had gone up the river to try and discover its whereabouts.

The *Kingfisher* was not altogether unsuccessful in capturing prizes, and several of her chases were not altogether devoid of excitement, but a number of times she ran after those that were enabled to show us a clean pair of heels and we realized the truth of the adage that "a stern chase is a long one."

　　　—Blakeman, "Some Personal Reminiscences of the Naval Service"

3. THE *ROBERT E. LEE* RUNS THE BLOCKADE

The Robert E. Lee *was one of the most famous of all the blockade-runners. A Clyde-built iron steamer she was reputed to be the fastest afloat. Unlike most of the blockade-runners, she was owned by the Confederate government. Altogether the* Lee *ran the blockade 21 times—mostly out of Wilmington—before she was finally captured.*

John Wilkinson, who here tells his own story, was one of more than 300 naval officers who resigned, in 1861, to go with the Confederacy. He first saw duty on a shore battery in Virginia; then fought at the Battle of New Orleans, where he was captured. After his exchange he went to England, bought the ship which he christened Robert E. Lee, *and earned a reputation as the boldest of blockade-runners. In 1864 he was engaged in the attempt to capture Johnson's Island in Lake Erie; later he commanded the blockade-runner* Chickamauga.

THE *Lee* continued to make her regular trips either to Nassau or Bermuda, as circumstances required, during the summer of 1863; carrying abroad cotton and naval stores, and bringing in "hardware," as munitions of war were then invoiced. Usually the time selected for sailing was during the "dark of the moon," but upon one occasion, a new pilot had been detailed for duty on board, who failed in many efforts to get the ship over the "rip," a shifting sand bar a mile or more inside the true bar. More than a week of valuable time had thus been lost, but the exigencies of the army being at that time more than usually urgent, I determined to run what appeared to be a very great risk.

The tide serving at ten o'clock, we succeeded in crossing the rip at that hour, and as we passed over New Inlet bar, the moon rose in a cloudless sky. It was a calm night too, and the regular beat of our paddles through the smooth water sounded to our ears ominously loud. As we closely skirted the shore, the blockading vessels were plainly visible to us, some at anchor, some under way; and some of them so near to us that we saw, or fancied we saw, with our night glasses, the men on watch on their forecastles; but as we were inside of them all, and invisible against the background of the land, we passed beyond them undiscovered. The roar of the surf breaking upon the beach, prevented the noise of our paddles from being heard. The *Lee's* head was not pointed seaward, however, until we had run ten or twelve miles along the land so close to the breakers that we could almost have tossed a biscuit into them, and no vessel was to be seen in any direction.

Discovery of us by the fleet would probably have been fatal to us, but the risk was not really so great as it appeared; for, as I had been informed by a blockade-runner who had been once captured and released, being a British subject, the vigilance on board the blockading fleet was much relaxed during the moonlit nights. The vessels were sent to Beaufort to coal at these times. My informant was an officer of the British Navy, and was the guest, for a few days after his capture, of Captain Patterson then commanding the blockading fleet off the Cape Fear. Speaking of the arduous service, P. remarked to him, that he never undressed nor retired to bed, during the dark nights; but could enjoy those luxuries when the moon was shining. On this hint I acted.

It was about this time that I adopted an expedient which proved of great service on several occasions. A blockade-runner did not often pass through the fleet without receiving one or more shots, but these were always preceded by the flash of a calcium light, or by a blue light; and immediately followed by two rockets thrown in the direction of the blockade-runner. The signals were probably concerted each day for the ensuing night, as they appeared to be constantly changed; but the rockets were invariably sent up. I ordered a lot of rockets from New York. Whenever all hands were called to run through the fleet, an officer was stationed alongside of me on the bridge with the rockets. One or two minutes after our immediate pursuer had sent his rockets, I would direct ours to be discharged at a right angle to our course. The whole fleet would be misled, for even if the vessel which had discovered us were not deceived, the rest of the fleet would be baffled. . . .

We were ready to sail for Nassau on the 15th of August, 1863, and had on board, as usual, several passengers. . . .

We passed safely through the blockading fleet off the New Inlet Bar, receiving no damage from the few shots fired at us, and gained an offing from the coast of thirty miles by daylight. By this time our supply of English coal had been exhausted, and we were obliged to commence upon North Carolina coal of very inferior quality, and which smoked terribly. We commenced on this fuel a little after daylight. Very soon afterwards the vigilant look-out at the mast-head called out "Sail ho!" and in reply to the "where away" from the deck, sang out "Right astern, sir, and in chase."

The morning was very clear. Going to the mast-head I could just discern the royal of the chaser; and before I left there, say in half an hour, her topgallant sail showed above the horizon. By this time the sun had risen in a cloudless sky. It was evident our pursuer would be alongside of us by midday at the rate we were then going. The first orders given were to throw overboard the deck-load of cotton and to make more steam. The latter proved to be more easily given than executed; the chief engineer reporting that it was impossible to make steam with the wretched stuff filled with slate and dirt. A moderate breeze from the north and east had been blowing ever since daylight and every stitch of canvas on board the square-rigged steamer in our wake was drawing.

We were steering east by south, and it was clear that the chaser's advantages could only be neutralized either by bringing the *Lee* gradually head to wind or edging away to bring the wind aft. The former course would be running toward the land, besides incurring the additional risk of being intercepted and captured by some of the inshore cruisers. I began to edge away, therefore, and in two or three hours enjoyed the satisfaction of seeing our pursuer clew up and furl his sails. The breeze was still blowing as fresh as in the morning, but we were now running directly away from it, and the cruiser was going literally as fast as the wind, causing the sails to be rather a hindrance than a help. But she was still gaining on us.

A happy inspiration occurred to me when the case seemed hopeless. Sending for the chief engineer I said "Mr. S., let us try cotton, saturated with spirits of turpentine." There were on board, as part of the deck load, thirty or forty barrels of "spirits." In a very few moments, a bale of cotton was ripped open, a barrel tapped, and buckets full of the saturated material passed down into the fire-room. The result exceeded our expectations. The chief engineer, an excitable little Frenchman from Charleston, very soon made his appearance on the bridge, his eyes sparkling with triumph, and reported a full head of steam. Curious to see the effect upon our speed, I directed him to wait until the log was hove. I threw it myself, nine and a half knots. "Let her go now sir!" I said. Five minutes afterwards, I hove the log again, *thirteen and a quarter*. We now began to hold our own, and even to gain a little upon the chaser; but she was fearfully near, and I began to have visions of another residence at Fort Warren, as I saw the "big bone in the mouth" of our pertinacious friend, for she was near enough us at one time for us to

A. R. Waud

Rescuing the Wounded in the Wilderness

A. R. Waud

Distributing Ammunition to Warren's Corps

From a wartime photograph

General Grant and Staff at Bethesda Church

see distinctly the white curl of foam under her bows, called by that name among seamen. I wonder if they could have screwed another turn of speed out of her if they had known that the *Lee* had on board, in addition to her cargo of cotton, a large amount of gold shipped by the Confederate Government?

There continued to be a very slight change in our relative positions till about six o'clock in the afternoon, when the chief engineer again made his appearance, with a very ominous expression of countenance. He came to report that the burnt cotton had choked the flues, and that the steam was running down. "Only keep her going till dark, sir," I replied, "and we will give our pursuer the slip yet." A heavy bank was lying along the horizon to the south and east; and I saw a possible means of escape.

At sunset the chaser was about four miles astern and gaining upon us. Calling two of my most reliable officers, I stationed one of them on each wheel-house, with glasses, directing them to let me know the instant they lost sight of the chaser in the growing darkness. At the same time, I ordered the chief engineer to make as black a smoke as possible, and to be in readiness to cut off the smoke by closing the dampers instantly, when ordered. The twilight was soon succeeded by darkness. Both of the officers on the wheel house called out at the same moment, "We have lost sight of her," while a dense column of smoke was streaming far in our wake. "Close the dampers," I called out through the speaking tube, and at the same moment ordered the helm "hard a starboard." Our course was altered eight points, at a right angle to the previous one. I remained on deck an hour, and then retired to my state-room with a comfortable sense of security.

—WILKINSON, *The Narrative of a Blockade-Runner*

4. THE *ROB ROY* RUNS THE BLOCKADE OUT OF HAVANA

Cuba, the Bahamas, and Bermuda were the most important islands from which the blockade-runners operated. The chief ports here—especially Havana and Nassau—were friendly, transshipment to vessels bound for the British Islands convenient, and the run either to the Atlantic ports of Savannah, Charleston, and Wilmington, or to such Gulf ports as Galveston, relatively easy. The risks, to be sure, were great—but so were the profits. A captain received—so Thomas Scharf of the Confederate Navy tells us—$5,000 a month, and officers and seamen in proportion. Two successful trips usually paid the cost of the vessel; after that everything was profit, and some blockade runners made 30 or 40 trips before capture.

William Watson, who here tells of blockade-running into Galveston, is our old friend from the campaigns in Arkansas—a Scotsman who enlisted in the Confederate Army and, after capture and exchange, went into blockade-running. He appears to be the only chronicler who has left us narratives of both land and sea campaigns.

IT was already into the month of April [1864], and it was a very bad time to make a trip, owing to the lengthened days and the prevailing calms. There would be no chance of good steady winds before September, and there would be on the Texas coast about three hours more daylight each day than in winter, and the danger of capture would be very great.

On the other hand, I opined that to lay here (Havana) heavy loss was certain. The vessel not being coppered, the sea-worms would penetrate her bottom, unless often docked and painted; expenses were high, and it was almost impossible to avoid being victimized by the numerous harpies who regarded blockade runners as a legitimate prey to pick at; and I felt that if I was to lose what little I had, I would rather lose it under the guns of an honest cruiser, than have it wheedled away from me by the flattery of pretended friends; so I determined to venture a trip if I could make arrangements to do so.

The vessel was taken to the ship-yard and put on the slipdock to be thoroughly examined, caulked, and otherwise put in the best sailing trim preparative for another voyage.

As I have already said, specie money was not to be had in the Confederate States and it was not to the interest of the blockade runners to run a heavy risk on the inward trip, by taking in a valuable cargo, and many had run in with light cargoes, knowing that they could always obtain a cargo of cotton cheap, or a freight outward at very high rates.

This, however, had now been stopped by the Confederate authorities, and stringent rules had been enforced whereby all vessels entering a Confederate port must take in a full and valuable cargo.

To obtain this cargo was what I desired either as freight or on the vessel's account, and as a large part of the money we had left would be expended in the repairs of the vessel, it would be necessary—if we could not get a freight—to get some one to take a share in the adventure, and as there were so many merchants and speculators who sympathized excessively with the Confederate States and took great interest in furnishing them with supplies, I thought there would be no difficulty in making an engagement.

Applying to several of them, I found their terms to be all about the same; which was, that they were exceedingly wishful to sell me goods for a cargo, but none willing to take a share in the adventure or run any risk. . . .

I may here say that up to this time blockade running by steamers had been confined almost entirely to the Atlantic ports, while nearly the whole trade into the Gulf States had been done by sailing craft, mostly light-draught schooners. When Charleston and the other ports on the Atlantic were captured, or so closely invested that entrance to them was almost impossible, many of those steamers came to Havana to try what could be done between that port and the Gulf States, and the basis for blockade running was transferred from Nassau to Havana.

Steamers, however, were not much in favour at Havana for blockade-running purposes, and it was considered by some that their utility for this trade was more ideal than real, but of this I will speak hereafter.

Havana having now become the principal centre for blockade running, a crowd of speculators soon found their way to the place, who bought up the goods in the limited market, and ran them up to a high figure to sell to blockade runners, representing them, of course, as consignments recently got out from Europe specially selected for the Confederate market. And while trumpeting their zeal for the Confederate cause, they took special care to pocket large profits without running any risk. While to those who actually ran the blockade and incurred the risk and danger, but little accrued. . . .

About the same time my old friend Mr. R. M—— came to the yard and took a look at the *Rob Roy* as she lay on the ways.

He asked me if I had made any arrangements for a trip yet. I said I had not. He said I might come and see him the following day, and he would make me an offer.

On the following day I called upon him. He asked what value I now placed upon the vessel. I said 5,000 dollars when repaired and fitted out ready for sea.

He then said that his offer was that he would furnish a cargo equal in value to that amount, which cargo he would guarantee would satisfy the requirements of the Confederate Government as to inward cargo, and purchase much more cotton than the vessel could carry out, and the surplus would be invested in cotton bonds, which were still worth something in Havana. He would then become owner of half of the vessel, and I would be owner of half of the cargo. We would then be equal partners in the vessel and cargo, each paying his half of the disbursements, out of which he would allow me for my services as captain 500 dollars, to be paid in advance before sailing, and 7 dollars for every bale of cotton when landed in a neutral port.

The cargo which he had to put on board consisted chiefly of arms, which the Confederate Government in Texas stood much in want of at that time.

This offer I accepted, and I asked him to make a memorandum of it in writing, which he did, and handed it to me.

I then got a list of the cargo he proposed to furnish. It consisted of 200 Enfield rifles with bayonets and accoutrements, 400 Belgium muskets with bayonets, 400 cavalry swords, six cases of saddlery and accoutrements, twenty-five boxes of ammunition, a large box of cavalry currycombs and horse brushes, and several bales and cases of blankets, clothing, boots and shoes, hardware, and other goods. Besides this it was good policy to have a good supply of some things which were much esteemed by the Southern people, but which the blockade had cut off and made extremely rare, and in some parts almost unknown, such as tea, coffee, cheese, spices, etc., also thread, needles, and such furnishings. Brandies and wines as well as all spirituous liquors were forbidden to be taken in, but they were received with great thankfulness if given as donations for the use of the hospitals. All these might be entered as ship stores.

This cargo, although valuable, was far from filling up the hold of the schooner, and as I knew that a good inward cargo had great weight with the authorities in the Confederacy, I sent word to Mr. Helm, the Confederate States Consul, that I would sail in a few days for Texas, and I would take free of freight any goods which he might wish to send in.

I received a reply thanking me for the offer, and saying that he would send by my vessel 400 guns. He also said that he had some important despatches to send to General Magruder, which he would confide to my care. . . .

I was now thinking over what port I would try to enter. I was a little sick with the Brazos River on account of the troubles I had had there on last trip, and the entrance to it now was generally blockaded, and it would be impossible to enter during the day, and the bar was dangerous to enter at night without a pilot.

Captain Dave had determined to make for St. Louis Pass at the west end of Galveston Island. . . .

It was impossible, however, for the *Rob Roy* to enter there, and on the advice of Captain M. I determined to shape for Galveston, and take my chance of getting past the fleet.

Captain M. was well acquainted with all the shallow entrances to Galveston Bay, and he gave me some information as to how a light draught vessel like the *Rob Roy* might enter from the eastward or windward side. . . .

We were now all ready to sail, and I only waited for a favourable opportunity.

There were two Federal gunboats which lay between us and the Moro Castle, and which we should have to pass on the way out to sea, and I was pretty certain that they knew we had a cargo of arms on board, but they were to a considerable extent powerless, and we were cleared for Belize, Honduras.

As no vessels were allowed to leave or enter Havana harbour between sunset and sunrise, the best time to leave was just about sunset, so that if any cruisers were lying in the offing we could come to, under the guns of the Moro, until it got quite dark, and then put to sea.

Captain Dave had determined to sail at the same time that we sailed, and as I had been laughing at his vessel, he wished to bet with me a case of brandy that he would arrive in Texas before me if not captured. I did not, however, take the bet, as I intended to creep along cautiously.

I was now well manned and prepared, and my policy was—when it became calm to take down all sail, and make the vessel as inconspicuous as possible; keep a sharp look-out from the mast-head, and if anything appeared on the horizon to get out the sweeps and pull away in the opposite direction before we were observed.

Our vessel being small, the hull very low, and when the sails were down, by keeping a good look-out from the mast-head we could see a cruiser sometime before she could see us.

Everything being now ready we got what we called the mail on board. This consisted of letters for people in Texas and other parts of the Confederate States, west of the Mississippi River from all parts of the world. . . .

We now awaited a favourable wind, and were wishful to get away, as

Havana is a very bad place for a vessel's bottom fouling, and every day we lay was injuring the sailing qualities of the vessel. . . .

At last a steady breeze sprang up from the south, which freshened towards the afternoon, and we stood down the bay just before sunset.

We passed the two Federal cruisers as they lay at anchor. We saw the officers scrutinizing us with their glasses, but as neither of the vessels had steam up, it was impossible that they could follow us that night.

—WATSON, *The Adventures of a Blockade Runner*

5. RICHARD CORBIN RUNS THE BLOCKADE TO JOIN LEE'S ARMY

Richard Corbin was a young Southerner in Paris, with his family, when the war broke out. Eager to fight for his country, he finally managed to get aboard the blockade-runner Lillian *(he calls it* Lilian*), and run the blockade to Wilmington, whence he departed for Virginia.*

The captain of the Lillian *was the famous John Newland Maffit. Captain Maffit had, appropriately enough, been born at sea. Adopted by a North Carolinian, he had thrown up his commission in the United States Navy to join the Confederacy; had commanded the cruiser* Florida, *and a series of blockade-runners; and finally saw service on the ill-fated* Albemarle. *After the war he served with the Brazilian Navy, fought for the Cuban revolutionary Junta, and retired to write novels and historical articles.*

Wilmington, C.[onfederate] S.[tates], June 5, 1864

My dear Mother:

Veni, Vici, and as Julius Caesar remarked, we have gone in and won. Thank Heaven I am at last on Confederate soil, having most successfully passed through that awful ordeal yclept the blockade. There have been so many captures of late among the blockade-running squadron, that I have every reason fervently to bless my stars at having reached this haven of refuge, sound in wind and limb. I wrote to you a few minutes before sailing that the dear little *Lilian* was getting up steam for Dixie. We steamed out of St. George at six o'clock on Wednesday afternoon.

Amongst our live freight, or our live-stock—as the captain facetiously called your offspring and his travelling companions—were the amiable and accomplished correspondent of the "Thunderer," and a most amusing and jovial *bon-vivant*, who came here on a mission from the *Illustrated London News*. It is his intention to draw what he sees by field and flood, for the special amusement and edification of those indifferent John Bulls. I trust that he will be the occasion of sending to his paper the sketch of many a Yankee stampede. But to return to our muttons, in addition to these Britishers were three Confederate officers belonging to the army of the west, and who had recently effected their escape from Fort Chase. This, for a boat whose everything is sacrificed to speed and freight-carrying capacity, was an awfully big lot of passengers; so much so that there was no accomodation, in

the European sense of the word, for us. In fact at night, if the weather was
at all fine, we would have to shift for ourselves on the quarter-deck; if it was
at all squally we pigged together on the floor of our small dining room, or in
amongst the cargo.

You would have taken us without doubt for some of Lee's ragamuffins,
had you witnessed our going condition when we disembarked this morning
to report at the commanding general's head-quarters. My clothes were so
weather-stained and seedy, my physiognomy was so thickly besmeared with
a vile coating, composed of salt water and coal dust, that it required the
closest observation and very keen powers of discrimination to distinguish
this child from the very blackest of firemen. *Mais à la guerre comme à la
guerre*, and I assure you we're a very jolly albeit a very dirty set.

From the start until Friday evening everything was going on as merrily
as a marriage bell. We were rolling off with ease our fourteen knots, or
about twenty-four kilometres an hour. No Yanky was visible on the horizon,
and it was the captain's intention, had we been able to keep this speed, to
rush through the blockade on Saturday morning before sunrise.

We would have to grope our way about the coast until we saw the Cape
Fear lighthouse—for, as is often the case in the Gulf Stream, the sky was
cloudy at noon, and old Sol's countenance very indistinct; consequently an
accurate observation was out of the question. As it turned out, we would
have struck the coast twenty-five miles south of the entrance of the harbour,
had we stuck to the same course, but a portion of our engines became so
terribly heated that we were obliged to slow them. In that condition the
captain thought that his boat was not fit that night for a dash through the
fleet. He therefore determined to turn back and go out some sixty miles to
sea, and there stop the ship. As there was no more excitement in store for us
that night, I went to sleep on the deck. When I awoke next morning I found
the *Lilian* going all round the compass, performing what the sailors call
circular navigation.

To beguile the tedium of that species of navigation we devised all sorts
of pastimes, and amongst them sea-bathing. Two of the Confederate officers
jumped in, and just as I was preparing to follow suit one of the sailors
shouted out that he saw a shark. In presence of such an enemy the rebels
skedaddled in Bull Run style and hastily clambered up the sides of the boat.
In a second after, a huge shark made his appearance. He was evidently
awfully hungry, for he swam around the ship several times in quest of what
I think would not constitute a very first-class repast even for a shark; for
after six months' incarceration in a Yankee dungeon a Southerner can scarcely
be considered a very dainty morsel. The search proving fruitless, he gave his
tail a flirt suggestive of intense disgust, and made himself scarce.

This little incident had fluttered us a little, and we were gradually regaining our composure when the hand at the masthead sang out "Sail ho." All
our glasses came into play, and after a time we discovered a large steamer
straight ahead of us, that is to say between us and Wilmington. The only
thing to be done was to put about and steam away from the fellow in the

direction of Bermuda. He was bearing down upon us as fast as he could go, and at first seemed to be gaining upon us, but as the *Lilian* settled down earnestly into her working she flew through the water, and then it was evident that the pace was too much for the cruiser; she, however, pegged away after us with all the dogged tenacity characteristic of the Yankee race.

When we no longer saw her, Maffit, after a little dodging, steered back in the direction of Dixie. It was then that I became convinced that his reputation as a consummate navigator was deserved, for notwithstanding all the zigzagging and doubling which we had to execute in order to elude our pursuer he brought the *Lilian* soon after sunset, within a distance of some twelve miles off the coast and at the exact point when the steering of the ship devolved upon the pilot. We stood till nine o'clock, and then the pilot gave the order to go at full speed.

It was, I will confess, a very anxious moment, and with the exception of Maffit, who is the perfection of coolness and self-possession, and the pilot, we all looked rather nervous. As we were passing through the outer cordon of blockaders, I fancied like the Irishman that I could hear the palpitation of my heart a great many yards. They did not see, and so far we were unmolested. This gave us some confidence, and yet the hardest part was to come, for the Yankee squadron comprising the inner semi-circle, lies close to the bar, and the distance between each ship hardly averages half a mile. Whilst we were tearing along flashes of lightning now and then illuminated a dense bank of clouds ahead of us. These we took at first to be the ominous precursors of a shell or solid shot. There was of course a good deal of what the Southerners call "flickering," that is to say, bobbing and dodging of heads. Just as we were about to go over the bar we passed within a biscuit throw of what seemed to be a floating monster on our starboard side. We every moment expected a broadside, but the Yankees were napping and thanks to God we gave them the go-by. This last danger being past a frantic shaking of hands ensued, and everybody congratulated everybody else.

Whilst we were all crowding on the bridge the pilot told us to look out for a volley, as one of the enemy's launches was close to us. We all fell flat upon our faces; and whilst I was in the act of doing so I saw the boat, dropping astern of us. She appeared to be filled with armed men, and I fully expected they would pepper us with Minie bullets, but fortunately they did not take any heed of us.

Our surmise for thus escaping is that she took the *Lilian* for a Federal gunboat. Maffit now tells me that he fully expected a very warm reception; instead of which not a gun was fired at us; he is of our opinion that the vessels which ran out on the same night as we ran in must have drawn off the attention of the enemy. Without such a diversion it is impossible to understand their want of vigilance. . . . I have just heard that one of the steamers that attempted to run in that night was sunk by the Yankees.

I am most comfortably installed here, at the house of Mr. Colley, an owner of blockade ships, who lives in very good style indeed for the times. I esteem myself very fortunate at not being obliged to put up at the hotel, the filth

and nastiness of which baffles description. Here I have pleasant company,
Lawley, who is decidedly a very pleasant person, being one of Mr. Colley's
guests; a cuisine which in normal times would be pronounced very fair, and,
what is hard to procure in the Confederacy, immaculate sheets.

This is a strange prelude, is it not, to the hardships which I have been led
to expect when I undertook my journey; but this is no criterion of the
poverty and the hardships in the South, for if any place in the Confederacy
is at all thriving it ought to be Wilmington, which has the monopoly of the
blockade business. Tomorrow morning I start with Lawley for Richmond.

    —[RICHARD CORBIN], "Letters of a Confederate Officer"

6. BLOCKADE-RUNNERS SUPPLY CHARLESTON

*Here is a short account of what blockade-running meant to a city.
Charleston was pretty well bottled up, from early in the war; yet swift
blockade-runners managed to get past the Federal ships and keep the city
supplied with necessities—and with luxuries. This account describes the
situation in 1864, and is by the same pen that gave us a picture of Charleston
under fire.*

DURING those long wearisome days and weeks when the city was under
fire almost the only event of joy which would occur would be the arrival of some one of these blockade-runners. The business was finally reduced to a science. Even in the darkest night the cunning craft would work
their way in or out through the tortuous channels of the harbor. When
outward-bound the captain generally went down to Sullivan's Island upon
the evening of sailing to learn the disposition of the Union fleet and plan
the course of his exit. Lights also were always prearranged along the shores
of the island, or suspended from boats in the harbor, in order to indicate the
channel.

The most dangerous point, and that which demanded the exercise of the
greatest skill to avoid, was a narrow tongue of land which ran out from
Sullivan's Island just opposite Sumter, and which was known as the Breakwater Jetty. Here the channel is not only very narrow but takes a sudden
turn, and it was in making this turn that the vessel was in danger of getting
aground. The Union artillerists after a while learned many of the cunning
arts of the blockade-runner, and whenever they saw a light from the opposite
shore of Morris Island, which they supposed was intended for the guidance
of a vessel, they would immediately open fire. They had a way too of sending out picket-boats which would quietly allow the vessel to pass till it had
rounded the jetty and return became impossible, and then by means of
rockets would signalize the fleet outside.

The chase of a blockade-runner was the most exciting thing imaginable.
Like a hunted deer it would speed through the water, its fierce avenger after
it, every beam from stem to stern quivering through the violent pulsations
of its great iron heart, and the dash of the paddles as in their lightning-like

revolutions they would strike the water. Sometimes not only was one half of the cargo thrown overboard, but every combustible thing that could be laid hold of crowded into the furnaces to increase the steam. Some of these blockade-runners were very successful. I knew of one which had run the gauntlet no less than nineteen times, and had consequently proved a mine of wealth to its owners. When a vessel had once run the blockade it was considered to have paid for itself, and every subsequent trip was consequently clear gain. The captain generally cleared on each round trip ten thousand dollars in gold, and the pilot and mate in proportion.

To be at all connected with or interested in a blockade-runner was in those days esteemed in Charleston a signal piece of good fortune. It insured at least a partial supply of the comforts and luxuries of life; for the ladies an occasional new silk dress, the envy and admiration of the streets; for the gentlemen a good supply of Bourbon—a box or two of cigars, or a larder filled with Stilton cheese or West India fruits. By-and-by came an edict from Richmond forbidding the importation of luxuries of this kind, and restricting the cargo of a vessel entirely to those articles which the country needed in its military operations, or which contributed to the supply of the actual necessities of the people. One half of the cargo of the vessel going out was also required to be devoted to government account, and one half of the cargo of the vessel coming in. This, of course, greatly curtailed the profits of the owners, but still immense fortunes continued to be made on both sides of the water.

—PECK, "Four Years Under Fire at Charleston"

7. WILMINGTON IS TURNED TOPSY-TURVY BY THE WAR

After the fall of New Orleans Wilmington became the most important of all the Confederate ports. Two things account for this: its harbor was the most difficult of all to enter, and it was close to Lee's army in Virginia. The Federal fleet was unable to stop blockade-running into Wilmington; its capture, in January 1865, closed the last Confederate port.

It is Captain Wilkinson who here describes what the new business of blockade-running did to the little town.

THE staid old town of Wilmington was turned 'topsy turvy during the war. Here resorted the speculators from all parts of the South, to attend the weekly auctions of imported cargoes; and the town was infested with rogues and desperadoes, who made a livelihood by robbery and murder. It was unsafe to venture into the suburbs at night, and even in daylight there were frequent conflicts in the public streets, between the crews of the steamers in port and the soldiers stationed in the town, in which knives and pistols would be freely used; and not unfrequently a dead body would rise to the surface of the water in one of the docks with marks of violence upon it. The civil authorities were powerless to prevent crime. "Inter arma silent leges!" The agents and employees of different blockade-running companies lived in magnificent style, paying a king's ransom (in Confederate money) for their household expenses, and nearly monopolizing the supplies in the country market. Towards the end of the war, indeed, fresh provisions were almost beyond the reach of every one. Our family servant, newly arrived from the country in Virginia, would sometimes return from market with an empty basket, having flatly refused to pay what he called "such nonsense prices" for a bit of fresh beef, or a handful of vegetables. A quarter of lamb, at the time of which I now write, sold for $100, a pound of tea for $500. Confederate money which in September, 1861, was nearly equal to specie in value, had declined in September 1862 to 225; in the same month, in 1863, to 400, and before September, 1864, to 2,000!

Many of the permanent residents of the town had gone into the country, letting their houses at enormous prices; those who were compelled to remain kept themselves much secluded; the ladies rarely being seen upon the more public streets. Many of the fast young officers belonging to the army would get an occasional leave to come to Wilmington; and would live at free quarters on board the blockade-runners, or at one of the numerous bachelor halls ashore.

The convalescent soldiers from the Virginia hospitals were sent by the route through Wilmington to their homes in the South. The ladies of the town were organized by Mrs. De R. into a society for the purpose of ministering to the wants of these poor sufferers; the trains which carried them stopping an hour or two at the depot, that their wounds might be dressed and food and medicine supplied to them. These self-sacrificing, heroic women patiently and faithfully performed the offices of hospital nurses.

Liberal contributions were made by companies and individuals to this society, and the long tables at the depot were spread with delicacies for the sick, to be found nowhere else in the Confederacy. The remains of the meals were carried by the ladies to a camp of mere boys—home-guards outside of the town. Some of these children were scarcely able to carry a musket, and were altogether unable to endure the exposure and fatigues of field service; and they suffered fearfully from measles, and typhoid fever. Gen. Grant used a strong figure of speech, when he asserted, that "the cradle and the grave were robbed, to recruit the Confederate armies." The fact of a fearful drain upon the population was scarcely exaggerated, but with this difference in the metaphor, that those who were verging upon both the cradle and the grave, shared the hardships and dangers of war, with equal self-devotion to the cause. It is true that a class of heartless speculators infested the country, who profited by the scarcity of all sorts of supplies, but it makes the self-sacrifice of the mass of the Southern people more conspicuous, and no State made more liberal voluntary contributions to the armies, or furnished better soldiers, than North Carolina.

On the opposite side of the river from Wilmington, on a low, marshy flat, were erected the steam cotton presses, and there the blockade-runners took in their cargoes. Sentries were posted on the wharves, day and night, to prevent deserters from getting on board, and stowing themselves away; and the additional precaution of fumigating the outward bound steamers at Smithville was adopted; but in spite of this vigilance, many persons succeeded in getting a free passage abroad. These deserters, or "stowaways," were in most instances sheltered by one or more of the crew; in which event they kept their places of concealment until the steamer had arrived at her port of destination, when they would profit by the first opportunity to leave the vessel undiscovered. A small bribe would tempt the average blockade-running sailor to connive at this means of escape. The "impecunious" deserter fared more hardly; and would usually be forced by hunger and thirst to emerge from his hiding place while the steamer was on the outward voyage. A cruel device, employed by one of the captains, effectually put a stop, I believe, certainly a check to the escape of this class of "stowaways." He turned three or four of them adrift in the Gulf Stream, in an open boat, with a pair of oars, and a few days' allowance of bread and water.

—WILKINSON, *The Narrative of a Blockade Runner*

8. CONFEDERATE PRIVATEERS HARRY NORTHERN MERCHANTMEN

The Confederacy early had recourse to letters of marque, and altogether William M. Robinson, foremost authority on Confederate privateering, lists some 64 privateers of various kinds—schooners, steamers, submarines, private-armed boats, and others. These did considerable damage to Union shipping during the first year of the war, but with the rapid growth of the United States Navy and the successful establishment of the blockade, the privateer became ineffective. Privateering had been outlawed by the Declaration of Paris, but the United States was not a signatory to this Declaration and therefore in no position to protest Confederate privateering. Yet at first Federal authorities tried to treat captured privateersmen as pirates, and there was a notable trial of the crew of the Jeff Davis *for piracy. The Confederacy quickly put a stop to that policy by the threat of retaliation.*

We give here three brief excerpts illuminating the story of privateering. The first introduces us to the Ivy, *one of the earliest and most successful of the privateers, later taken into the Confederate Navy. The second is the story of the capture of the* John Welsh *by the famous* Jefferson Davis, *and is told by the master of the* John Welsh, *Captain Fitfield. The third is an entertaining acount of the recapture of another of the* Jeff Davis' *prizes, the* Enchantress, *told by Jacob Garrick, the Negro cook who engineered it.*

A. THE *Ivy* PROWLS OUTSIDE NEW ORLEANS

LAST Friday I left New Orleans for this place and boat for a little privateering—to assist in annoying the enemy's commerce; but the enemy's commerce has ceased almost to spread its wings in this latitude. On board the *Ivy* are guns and men enough to accomplish great destruction, were we called on to open with our cannon. Our human fighting material is constituted of good bone, sinew and pluck, and some of the crew having entered the privateer service with only one intent—commendable revenge on the North.

Today we succeeded in sighting a vessel of the largest dimensions, and full rigged, which proved to be the *Sarah E. Pettigrew*, which, to our sorrow, was without a cargo, there being in her hold only two or three thousand sacks of salt, from Liverpool. We soon had a prize crew on her broad decks, greatly to the muddled surprise of her officers and crew. After the formality of taking possession, your correspondent being among the boarders—we do not pay weekly—I overhauled the flag-bag, and soon had bunting in plenty for a pretty Southern Confederacy flag, which was immediately set afloat to flutter defiance to all who don't like us. The *Ivy's* capacity enables her to do her own towing, and after she had cruised around in the Gulf two or three hours to overhaul other sails, she returned to us and we turned our prows toward Pass à L'Outre, near where the *Pettigrew* now lies, awaiting to be towed to your city. The privateer *Calhoun* gave chase for the same vessel, but the *Ivy* was too fast for her.

We lie in or near the river every night, but start out soon after midnight, and keep a sharp lookout for any speck on the horizon, and when the cry of "sail-ho!" is heard the *Ivy's* "tendrils" don revolvers, swords, knives and rifles with great excitement and good nature. We have exceedingly good times and "duff" but I fear all will be closed with the appearance of the blockading force.

—Letter by M. Repard in *Daily Delta*

B. The *Jefferson Davis* Takes a Prize off Delaware

At 8:30 the privateer tacked and stood N. W., at the same time setting a French ensign, and from the fact of her having French-cut hempen sails we supposed she was a French merchant brig. In answer to her colors we set the Stars and Stripes, and thought no more of the stranger. At 9 o'clock, to our surprise, she fired a shot across our bows, when we took in the studding sails and hove the *John Welsh* to. We then supposed her to be a French man-of-war brig; but her ports were closed and the guns covered up, while but few men were to be seen on her decks.

She came within musket shot of us, and lowered a boat which was manned by expert seamen and contained Lieutenant Postell, late of the United States Navy. Just before the boat came alongside the French flag was hauled down and the Confederate flag run up. In about two minutes afterwards the armed crew was on our deck. After inquiring after my health, Lieutenant Postell desired me to show him the brig's papers. I invited him into the cabin, and after showing them, I stated the cargo was Spanish property. Said he, "You are our prize, and the Spaniards had no business to ship their cargoes in American bottoms." He then came on deck and ordered four of my men to go in the privateer's boat, and told the remainder of the crew to pack up their things and stand by to do as ordered. They immediately set to work and broke out the ship's stores and took about eight months' provisions on board of the privateer, leaving only enough to take the prize-crew back with the vessel. This occupied about five hours.

I was transferred with the remainder of my crew on board of the privateer, and they took my boat and sent theirs on board of the *John Welsh*, as mine was the best. A prize-crew corresponding in appearance and number was then put on board in charge of Prize-Master Stevens, and she was ordered to go South but I was not allowed to know of her destination. I think they will palm themselves off as the genuine crew if they fall in with the Federal cruisers. After the work of transferring the stores had been completed, Capt. Coxetter mustered all hands aft and said to them, "Boys, if you molest the crew of that brig or their things to the value of a rope yarn, I will punish you to the utmost of my power. Do you understand? Now go forward." Turning to his officers he said, "Gentlemen, I desire that you do everything in your power to make the stay of these gentlemen as agreeable as possible." He then invited me to dine with him in his cabin while my mate was taken into the officer's mess.

—CAPTAIN FITFIELD, in the *Charleston Mercury*

C. A COLORED COOK ARRANGES FOR THE RECAPTURE OF THE *Enchantress*

Soon after dinner I took my dishes to the galley and washed them. In going back to the cabin with the dishes, I saw Smith have a spy glass. I looked under the lee of the mainsail and I saw a vessel coming that I thought was a steamer. I took another look, and I saw it was a steamer. The steamer was coming right in our direction. Smith said to the men to take the flying jib off to bend; but they sang out to Smith, "You had better not bend that jib now, because if they see us making sail they will think something and come at us." He said, "Go ahead and bend it." Then they started out to bend it, and he said, "Never mind, you can let it lie." Then I heard him say, "One of you men go up and sheer over that topsail sheet." A man went up to do it and was there a considerable while. Then Lane said to me, "You can go in the forecastle, steward; and if they should come and overhaul us, and your name is called, you can answer." I said I would rather stay in the galley.

I went in the galley and watched the steamer coming. When the steamer saw us back ship, she hauled right up for us. I kept looking through from one galley door to the other, according as we would go about. We went about three or four times. The schooner was going pretty fast. I still kept looking to see how near the steamer was getting to us. I heard one of the men say, "She has hoisted her flag," and they went out and hoisted our flag. The steamer hoisted the American flag; and we hoisted our American flag.

The steamer kept coming on. I heard them say, "It is a man-of-war." When the steamer got pretty close to us, I heard a hail, "What schooner is that?" The reply was, "The *Enchantress*." "Where bound to?" "St. Jago de Cuba." As soon as that was said, I jumped out of my galley and jumped overboard, singing out that it was "a captured vessel of the privateer *Jeff*.

Davis, and they are taking her into Charleston." I sang it out so that they could hear me on board the steamer.

The steamer's boat picked me up . . . when the boat picked me up they took me on board the schooner, and then they took the prize crew off the schooner and took me on board the steamer along with them.

—*The* Jeff Davis *Piracy Case*

9. THE *GEORGIA* FIRES THE *BOLD HUNTER*

The Georgia *was one of the most successful of the commerce destroyers purchased or built in England. A swift and powerful ship of 600 tons, she was purchased by Commodore Matthew F. Maury, at Dumbarton, Scotland; obtained her guns and ordnance from the* Alar, *off the French coast, and embarked upon a brief but highly successful career as commerce destroyer. Altogether she captured and destroyed at least nine American ships.*

Here is James Morgan's account of the burning of one of them, the mis-named Bold Hunter. *Morgan was a midshipman on the* Georgia; *later he served in the Egyptian Army, engaged in journalism in South Carolina, went to Australia as consul general, and helped build the Statue of Liberty.*

ON October 9, 1863, in a light breeze and after a lively chase we brought to, with our guns, the splendid American full-rigged ship *Bold Hunter*, of Boston, from Dundee, bound to Calcutta with a heavy cargo of coal. We hove to leeward of her and brought her captain and crew over to our ship, where as usual the crew were placed in irons and below decks. Being short of coal and provisions we proceeded to supply our wants from the prize. This was easy so far as the provisions were concerned, but when it came to carrying the coal from one ship to the other in our small boats, in something of a seaway, that was another matter. After half a dozen trips one of our boats came very near being swamped, and the wind and sea rapidly rising, we gave it up as a bad job. This was about two bells (1 P.M.) in the afternoon watch. We signalled our prize-master to set fire to the *Bold Hunter* and also to come aboard the *Georgia* at once, which he did.

We had hardly finished hoisting our boats to the davits when a great cloud of smoke burst from the hatches of the *Bold Hunter*, coming from the thousands of tons of burning coal in her hold. The wind had by this time increased to a gale and the sea was running very high. As before mentioned, the wind was very light when we captured the ship and she had hove to with all sail set, even to her royals. The flames leaped from her deck to her tarry rigging and raced up the shrouds and backstays and burned away her braces—her yards swung around, her sails filled, and the floating inferno, like a mad bull, bore down on us at full speed, rushing through the water as though she was bent on having her revenge.

To avoid a collision, the order was given on the *Georgia* to go ahead at full speed. The gong in the engine-room sounded, the engine turned the screw, and the screw began to churn the water under our counter. The engine made two or three revolutions—then there was a crash—followed by yells as the engineers and oilers rushed on to the deck accompanied by a shower of lignum-vitæ cogs and broken glass from the engine-room windows. The order to make sail was instantly given, but before the gaskets which confined the furled sails to the yardarms could be cast off, the burning ship was upon us.

She had come for us with such directness that one could easily have imagined that she was being steered by some demon who had come out of the inferno which was raging in her hold. We stood with bated breath awaiting the catastrophe which seemingly was about to overtake us. The *Bold Hunter* was rated at over three thousand tons, and had inside her a burning cargo of coal of even greater weight—the *Georgia* was scarcely one-sixth her size. Onward rushed the blazing ship, presenting an awesome spectacle, with the flames leaping about her sails and rigging, while a huge mass of black smoke rolled out of her hatches. High above our heads her long, flying jib-boom passed over our poop deck as she arose on a great wave and came down on our quarter, her cutwater cleaving through the *Georgia's* fragile plates as cleanly as though they had been made out of cheese. The force of the impact pushed the *Georgia* ahead, and for a moment we congratulated ourselves that we had escaped from the fiery demon whose breath was scorching us.

But the *Bold Hunter* was not yet satisfied with the injuries she had inflicted. Recovering from the recoil she again gathered way and struck us near the place she had previously damaged, but fortunately this was a glancing blow which had the effect only of wrenching off our port quarter davits and reducing the boat which was slung to them to kindling wood.

Not yet satisfied, the apparently infuriated inanimate object made a third attempt to destroy the *Georgia*, this time, fortunately, missing her mark and passing a few yards to leeward of us. Her sails having burned, she soon lost headway and helplessly lay wallowing in the trough of the sea while the fire ate through her sides, and her tall masts, one after the other, fell with a great splash into the sea. Before she went down surrounded by a cloud of steam, we had a good view through the great holes burned in her sides of the fire raging inside her. I imagine it was a very realistic imitation of what hell looks like when the forced draughts are turned on in honour of the arrival of a distinguished sinner.

—MORGAN, *Recollections of a Rebel Reefer*

10. THE *KEARSARGE* SINKS THE *ALABAMA* OFF CHERBOURG

With the possible exception of the duel between the Monitor *and the* Merrimac, *the fight between the* Kearsarge *and the* Alabama *is the most famous naval battle of the Civil War. The* Alabama *was the most notorious of the cruisers that James Bulloch had had built at Liverpool for the Confederacy.*

Captained by the brilliant Raphael Semmes and outfitted at the Azores, in midsummer 1862, she embarked on a career of destruction unparalleled in modern naval annals. Within two years Semmes captured or destroyed over 80 merchantmen and one warship. In June 1864 his battered ship put in at the harbor of Cherbourg for repairs. There the U. S. S. Kearsarge, commanded by Captain John A. Winslow, caught up with her. Semmes accepted the challenge and steamed out to battle and destruction.

After the battle Semmes, now a rear admiral, returned to Richmond to take command of the James River Squadron. With the end of the war he served as professor of moral philosophy at Louisiana State University; then engaged in journalism and law. Commodore Winslow, whose career before this battle had been unspectacular, later commanded the Gulf Squadron.

The story of the famous battle is told here by John Kell, executive officer of the Alabama.

SOON after our arrival at Cherbourg an officer was sent on shore to ask permission of the port admiral to land our prisoners of the two captured ships. This being obtained without trouble or delay, Captain Semmes went on shore to see to the docking of the ship for repairs. Cherbourg being a naval station and the dock belonging to the government, permission had to be obtained of the emperor before we could do anything. The port admiral told us "we had better have gone into Havre, as the government might not give permission for repairs to a belligerent ship." The emperor was absent from Paris at some watering place on the coast, and would not return for some days.

Here was an impediment to our plans which gave us time for thought, and the result of such thought was the unfortunate combat between the *Alabama* and the *Kearsarge*. The latter ship was lying at Flushing when we entered Cherbourg. Two or three days after our arrival she steamed into the harbor, sent a boat on shore to communicate, steamed outside and stationed off the breakwater. While Captain Semmes had not singled her out as an antagonist, and would never have done so had he known her to be chain-clad (an armored ship), he had about made up his mind that he would cease fleeing before the foe, and meet an equal in battle when the opportunity presented itself. Our cause was weakening daily, and our ship so disabled it really seemed to us our work was almost done! We might end her career gloriously by being victorious in battle, and defeat against an equal foe we would never have allowed ourselves to anticipate.

As soon as the *Kearsarge* came into the harbor Captain Semmes sent for me to come to his cabin, and abruptly said to me: "Kell, I am going out to fight the *Kearsarge*. What do you think of it?" We then quietly talked it all over. We discussed the batteries, especially the *Kearsarge's* advantage in 11-inch guns. I reminded him of our defective powder, how our long cruise had deteriorated everything, as proven in our target-practice off the coast of Brazil on the Ship *Rockingham*, when certainly every third shot was a failure even to explode. I saw his mind was fully made up, so I simply stated these facts for myself. I had always felt ready for a fight, and I also knew that the brave young officers of the ship would not object, and the men would be not only willing, but anxious, to meet the enemy! To all outward seeming the disparity was not great between the two ships, barring the unknown (because concealed) chain armor.

The *Kearsarge* communicated with the authorities to request that our prisoners be turned over to them. Captain Semmes made an objection to her increasing her crew. He addressed our agent, Mr. Bonfils, a communication requesting him to inform Captain Winslow, through the United States Consul, that "if he would wait until the *Alabama* could coal ship he would give him battle." We began to coal and at the same to make preparation for battle. We overhauled the magazine and shell rooms, gun equipments, etc.

The *Kearsarge* was really in the fullest sense of the word a man-of-war, stanch and well built; the *Alabama* was made for flight and speed and was much more lightly constructed than her chosen antagonist. The *Alabama* had one more gun, but the *Kearsarge* carried more metal at a broadside. The seven guns of the *Kearsarge* were two 11-inch Dahlgrens, four 32-pounders, and one rifled 28-pounder. The *Alabama's* eight guns were six 32-pounders, one 8-inch and one rifled 100-pounder. The crew of the *Alabama* all told was 149 men, while that of the *Kearsarge* was 162 men.

By Saturday night, June 18th, our preparations were completed. Captain Semmes notified the admiral of the port that he would be ready to go out and meet the *Kearsarge* the following morning. Early Sunday morning the admiral sent an officer to say to us that "the ironclad Frigate *Couronne* would accompany us to protect the neutrality of French waters." . . .

Between 9 and 10 o'clock, June 19th, everything being in readiness, we got under way and proceeded to sea. We took the western entrance of the harbor. The *Couronne* accompanied us, also some French pilot-boats and an English steam yacht, the *Deerhound*, owned by a rich Englishman (as we afterward learned), who, with his wife and children, was enjoying life and leisure in his pleasure yacht. The walls and fortifications of the harbor, the heights above the town, the buildings, everything that looked seaward, was crowded with people. About seven miles from the land the *Kearsarge* was quietly awaiting our arrival.

Officers in uniforms, men at their best, Captain Semmes ordered them sent aft, and mounting a gun-carriage made them a brief address:

"Officers and seamen of the *Alabama*: You have at length another opportunity to meet the enemy, the first that has presented to you since you sank the *Hatteras*. In the meantime you have been all over the world, and it is not too much to say that you have destroyed and driven for protection under neutral flags one-half of the enemy's commerce, which at the beginning of the war covered every sea. This is an achievement of which you may well be proud, and a grateful country will not be unmindful of it. The name of your ship has become a household word wherever civilization extends. Shall that name be tarnished by defeat? [An outburst of Never! Never!] The thing is impossible. Remember that you are in the English Channel, the theatre of so much of the naval glory of our race. The eyes of all Europe are at this moment upon you! The flag that floats over you is that of a young Republic that bids defiance to her enemies, whenever and wherever found! Show the world that you know how to uphold it. Go to your quarters!"

We now prepared our guns to engage the enemy on our starboard side. When within a mile and a-quarter he wheeled, presenting his starboard battery to us. We opened on him with solid shot, to which he soon replied, and the action became active. To keep our respective broadsides bearing we were obliged to fight in a circle around a common center, preserving a distance of three quarters of a mile. When within distance of shell range we opened on him with shell. The spanker gaff was shot away and our ensign came down. We replaced it immediately at the mizzen masthead.

The firing now became very hot and heavy. Captain Semmes, who was watching the battle from the horse block, called out to me, "Mr. Kell, our shell strike the enemy's side, doing little damage, and fall off in the water; try solid shot." From this time we alternated shot and shell.

The battle lasted an hour and ten minutes. Captain Semmes said to me at this time (seeing the great apertures made in the side of the ship from their 11-inch shell, and the water rushing in rapidly), "Mr. Kell, as soon as our head points to the French coast in our circuit of action, shift your guns to port and make all sail for the coast." This evolution was beautifully performed; righting the helm, hauling aft the fore-trysail sheet, and pivoting to port, the action continuing all the time without cessation,—but it was useless, nothing could avail us.

Before doing this, and pivoting the gun, it became necessary to clear the deck of parts of the dead bodies that had been torn to pieces by the 11-inch shells of the enemy. The captain of our 8-inch gun and most of the gun's crew were killed. It became necessary to take the crew from young Anderson's gun to make up the vacancies, which I did, and placed him in command. Though a mere youth, he managed it like an old veteran.

Going to the hatchway, I called out to Brooks (one of our efficient engineers) to give the ship more steam, or we would be whipped.

He replied she "had every inch of steam that was safe to carry without being blown up!"

Young Matt O'Brien, assistant engineer, called out, "Let her have the steam; we had better blow her to hell than to let the Yankees whip us!"

The chief engineer now came on deck and reported "the furnace fires put out," whereupon Captain Semmes ordered me to go below and "see how long the ship could float."

I did so, and returning said, "Perhaps ten minutes."

"Then, sir," said Captain Semmes, "cease firing, shorten sail, and haul down the colors. It will never do in this nineteenth century for us to go down and the decks covered with our gallant wounded."

This order was promptly executed, after which the *Kearsarge* deliberately fired into us five shots! In Captain Winslow's report to the Secretary of the Navy he admits this, saying, "Uncertain whether Captain Semmes was not making some ruse, the *Kearsarge* was stopped."

Was this a time,—when disaster, defeat and death looked us in the face,—for a ship to use a ruse, a Yankee trick? I ordered the men to "stand to their quarters," and they did it heroically; not even flinching, they stood every man to his post. As soon as we got the first of these shot I told the quartermaster to show the white flag from the stern. It was done. Captain Semmes said to me, "Dispatch an officer to the *Kearsarge* and ask that they send boats to save our wounded—ours are disabled." Our little dingey was not injured, so I sent Master's Mate Fulham with the request. No boats coming, I had one of our quarter boats (the least damaged one) lowered and had the wounded put in her. Dr. Galt came on deck at this time, and was put in charge of her, with orders to take the wounded to the *Kearsarge*. They shoved off in time to save the wounded.

When I went below to inspect the sight was appalling! Assistant Surgeon Llewellyn was at his post, but the table and the patient on it had been swept away from him by an 11-inch shell, which made an aperture that was fast filling with water. This was the last time I saw Dr. Llewellyn in life. As I passed the deck to go down below a stalwart seaman with death's signet on his brow called to me. For an instant I stood beside him. He caught my hand and kissed it with such reverence and loyalty,—the look, the act, it lingers in my memory still! I reached the deck and gave the order for "every man to save himself, to jump overboard with a spar, an oar, or a grating, and get out of the vortex of the sinking ship."

As soon as all were overboard but Captain Semmes and I, his steward, Bartelli, and two of the men—the sailmaker, Alcott, and Michael Mars—we began to strip off all superfluous clothing for our battle with the waves for our lives. Poor, faithful-hearted Bartelli, we did not know he could not swim, or he might have been sent to shore—he was drowned. The men disrobed us, I to my shirt and drawers, but Captain Semmes kept on his heavy pants and vest. We together gave our swords to the briny deep and the ship we loved so well! The sad farewell look at the ship would have wrung the stoutest heart! The dead were lying on her decks, the surging, roaring waters rising through the death-wound in her side. The ship agonizing like a living thing and going down in her brave beauty, settling lower and lower, she sank fathoms deep—lost to all save love, and fame, and memory! . . .

The next thing that I remember, a voice called out, "Here's our first lieutenant," and I was pulled into a boat, in the stern sheets of which lay Captain Semmes as if dead. He had received a slight wound in his hand, which with the struggle in the water had exhausted his strength, long worn by sleeplessness, anxiety and fatigue. There were several of our crew in the boat. In a few moments we were alongside a steam yacht, which received us on her deck, and we learned it was the *Deerhound*, owned by an English gentleman, Mr. John Lancaster, who used it for the pleasure of himself and family, who were with him at this time, his sons having preferred going out with him to witness the fight to going to church with their mother, as he afterwards told us.

In looking about us I saw two French pilot boats rescuing the crew, and finally two boats from the *Kearsarge*. I was much surprised to find Mr. Fulham on the *Deerhound*, as I had dispatched him in the little dingey to ask the *Kearsarge* for boats to save our wounded. Mr. Fulham told me that "our shot had torn the casing from the chain armor of the *Kearsarge*, indenting the chain in many places." This now explained Captain Semmes' observation to me during the battle—"our shell strike the enemy's side and fall into the water." Had we been in possession of this knowledge the unequal battle between the *Alabama* and the *Kearsarge* would never have been fought, and the gallant little *Alabama* have been lost by an error. She fought valiantly as long as there was a plank to stand upon.

History has failed to explain, unless there were secret orders forbidding it, why the *Kearsarge* did not steam into the midst of the fallen foe and generously save life! The *Kearsarge* fought the battle beautifully, but she tarnished her glory when she fired on a fallen foe and made no immediate effort to save brave living men from watery graves! Both heroic commanders are now gone—before the great tribunal where "the deeds done in the body" are to be accounted for but history is history and truth is truth!

Mr. Lancaster came to Captain Semmes and said: "I think every man is saved, where shall I land you?"

He replied, "I am under English colors; the sooner you land me on English soil the better."

The little yacht, under a press of steam, moved away for Southampton. Our loss was nine killed, twenty-one wounded and ten drowned. That afternoon, the 19th of June, we were landed in Southampton and received with every demonstration of kindness and sympathy.

—KELL, *Recollections of a Naval Life*

XXV

Chickamauga and Chattanooga

WITH the fall of Vicksburg and Port Hudson the whole central Mississippi Valley fell under Union control and the fighting shifted to the margins—to Arkansas and the Red River in the West, to eastern Tennessee on the East. After Stones River Bragg had retired to Tullahoma while Rosecrans made his headquarters at Murfreesboro. Not until after Vicksburg did Rosecrans feel justified in advancing on Chattanooga. Under his command was an army of some 60,000, divided into three corps under Thomas, McCook and Crittenden, and a reserve corps under Granger. General Braxton Bragg commanded some 40,000 Confederates—over 10,000 of them cavalry—and reinforcements were soon on their way from the Army of Northern Virginia.

Again a word about geography is necessary. There was no more formidable theater of operations in the Civil War than that around Chattanooga. Chattanooga was the gateway to the East; it stood on a great bend of the Tennessee River, and on it converged the Memphis & Charleston and the Nashville & Chattanooga railroads. If the Confederates could hold it they would be able to use it as a base for offensive operations in Tennessee and Kentucky; if the Federals took it they could advance from it into Georgia. The Federals enjoyed numerical superiority, but the Confederates were favored by terrain. Between Chattanooga and Murfreesboro lay the great Cumberland plateau, a rugged mountainous area, heavily wooded and criss-crossed with streams and ravines. Chattanooga itself lay on the eastern side of a sharp bend of the Tennessee which then swerved north again and flowed in a great bend toward the southwest. This great bend was dominated by Raccoon Mountain, while immediately to the south of the city itself lay the long Lookout Mountain and to the east and south the Missionary Ridge. Southward toward Ringgold and Dalton stretched a series of heavily wooded hills and valleys cut by gorges and ravines.

Rosecrans decided to cross the Tennessee below Chattanooga. As he advanced Bragg drew back into Chattanooga. By the end of August the so-called Tullahoma campaign—a wholly bloodless one—was over, and by September 4 the Federals were across the Tennessee and below Chattanooga. If Rosecrans succeeded in cutting Bragg's communications to Atlanta, Bragg would be lost, so on September 9 he evacuated Chattanooga and retired southeastward to Chickamauga Creek. Rosecrans advanced on him in three columns, each separated from the other by mountain ridges and the two flanks some 40 miles apart. This was the moment for Bragg to strike. With that fatuousness which characterized all of his military operations, he failed to do so. He was waiting for Longstreet's divisions, which—because Burnside had moved into Knoxville—had to go the long way around through Augusta and Atlanta. Thus the golden opportunity to smash the Army of the Cumberland passed. Between September 13 and 17 Rosecrans succeeded in concentrating his scattered forces west of Chickamauga Creek.

Since—by waiting for Longstreet—Bragg had thrown away the chance to destroy Rosecrans' army piecemeal, he should have waited until both of Longstreet's divisions arrived, and then assumed the defensive. Instead he brought on battle when only half of the reinforcements had come up. There was some preliminary fighting on September 18. On the nineteenth-twentieth came the battle itself. It was, as our accounts tell us, a Confederate victory, but a curiously inconclusive one. Bragg drove in the Union right and sent it hurtling back to Rossville; he attacked the Union left and curled it up on the center. But at the center stood Thomas, who here earned his name, the Rock of Chickamauga, and when Thomas' situation was most desperate Granger came to his rescue. The Union army was beaten, but not destroyed. It retired to Chattanooga—its original objective—and Bragg invested the city.

Now, for the first time in the war, a large Federal army was besieged. Could Bragg starve it into surrender? Again we must have recourse to our maps. Railroad communications with Chattanooga from the north and the west ran through the town of Bridgeport, on the Tennessee. But Confederate batteries on Raccoon Mountain dominated Bridgeport, and Confederate guns and sharpshooters controlled the winding Tennessee. The only supply route was down the Sequatchie Valley and across the rugged Walden's Ridge; this route was raided by Wheeler and churned into mud by the autumn rains. By the end of October the situation of Rosecrans' army was critical.

Washington had already taken alarm. Rosecrans was removed and General Thomas put in temporary command. Burnside was ordered to go to his support; Grant was instructed to hurry up reinforcements; Hooker was started, with two divisions, from Virginia. During October and November Grant and Hooker converged on the Chattanooga region. Meantime Bragg did nothing effective; instead he detached Longstreet for an attack on Knoxville. By the end of October Hooker had opened the "cracker line" to Chattanooga and Thomas' army was saved. Then Grant assumed the offensive. He sent Sherman on a wide swing from Brown's Ford to the northern end of Missionary Ridge. On the twenty-fourth Hooker carried Lookout Mountain. The next day Sherman and Thomas assaulted the Confederates all along Missionary Ridge, drove them from their entrenchments, and sent them flying toward Dalton. It was one of the most spectacular victories of the war. It was also one of the most consequential. For now the Confederacy had been squeezed into the Atlantic coastal states. And with Burnside at Knoxville and Grant and Sherman at Chattanooga the way was open into Georgia and the Carolinas.

1. GENERAL BEATTY LIMNS SOME OF THE OFFICERS OF THE WEST

Here is a brief, incisive, and opinionated commentary on some of the leaders of the Army of the Cumberland. Thomas is dismissed as "modest" and "reliable"; we shall see, later, that he deserved better than this. We have met General Beatty before and he needs no further introduction.

ROSECRANS is of medium height and stout, not quite so tall as McCook and not nearly so heavy. McCook is young and very fleshy. Rousseau is by far the handsomest man in the army—tall and well proportioned, but possibly a little too bulky. R. S. Granger is a little man, with a heavy, light sandy mustache. Wood is a small man, short and slim, with dark complexion and black whiskers. Crittenden, the major general, is a spare man, medium height, lank, common sort of face, well whiskered. Major General Stanley, the cavalry man, is of good size, gentlemanly in bearing, light complexion, brown hair. McCook and Wood swear like pirates and affect the rough-and-ready style. Rousseau is given to profanity somewhat, and blusters occasionally. Rosecrans indulges in an oath now and then; but is a member of the Catholic church in good standing. Crittenden, I doubt not, swears like a trooper, and yet I have never heard him do so. He is a good drinker; and the same can be said of Rousseau. Rosecrans is an educated officer who has rubbed much against the world and has experience. Rousseau is brave, but knows little of military science. McCook is a chuckle-head. Wood and Crittenden know how to blow their own horns exceedingly well. Major General Thomas is tall, heavy, sedate; whiskers and head grayish. Puts on less style than any of those named, and is a gentlemanly, modest, reliable soldier. Rosecrans and McCook shave clean; Crittenden and Wood go the whole whisker; Thomas shaves the upper lip. Rosecrans' nose is large and curves down; Rousseau's is large and curves up; McCook has a weak nose that would do no credit to a baby. Rosecrans' laugh is not one of the free, open, hearty kind; Rousseau has a good laugh, but shows poor teeth; McCook has a grin, which excites the suspicion that he is either still very green or deficient in the upper story.

—BEATTY, *The Citizen-Soldier*

2. THE FEDERALS OPPOSE HOOD WITH DESPERATION

By September 18 Bragg had most of his army west of the Chickamauga; that day Hood arrived with three brigades. There was sharp fighting on the flanks on the eighteenth but the main attack came on the nineteenth. Thomas brought on the battle that day by attacking Forrest's dismounted cavalrymen, on the Confederate right. Soon the engagement was general. Hood struck with fury at the Union center, and pushed it back across the Lafayette road.

Negley's division counterattacked and restored the Federal position, and night fell without decisive fighting.

Captain James R. Carnahan of the 86th Indiana Volunteers here tells us how his men fought with desperation to hold Hood's assault.

NOONDAY has passed, when suddenly from out the woods to our front and left onto the open field, dashes an officer, his horse urged to its greatest speed toward our command. The men see him coming, and in an instant they are aroused to the greatest interest. "There come orders," are the words that pass from lip to lip along that line. . . . He reaches our line, and is met by our brigade commander, Colonel Geo. F. Dick, as anxious to receive the orders as he is to give them. The command comes in quick, sharp words: "The general presents his compliments, and directs that you move your brigade at once to the support of General Beard [Baird]. Take the road moving by the flank in 'double quick' to the left and into the woods, and go into line on the left of General Beatty's brigade. I am to direct you. Our men are hard pressed." The last sentence was all that was said in words as to the condition of our troops, but it told that we had read aright before he had spoken.

Scarce had the order been delivered when the command to "take arms" is heard along the line, and to drivers and cannoneers to mount. It scarcely took the time required to tell it for our brigade to get in motion, moving off the field, the artillery taking the wagon road, the infantry alongside. It was a grand scene as we moved quickly into place, closing up the column, and waiting but a moment for the command. The guns are at a right shoulder, and all have grown eager for the order—"Forward." The bugle sounds the first note of the command. Now, look along that column; the men are leaning forward for the start; you see the drivers on the artillery teams tighten the rein in the left hand, and, with the whip in the uplifted right arm, rise in their stirrups; and, as the last note of the bugle is sounded, the crack of the whips of thirty-six drivers over the backs of as many horses, and the stroke of the spurs, sends that battery of six guns and its caissons rattling and bounding over that road, while the infantry alongside are straining every nerve as they hasten to the relief of the comrades so hard pressed.

The spirits of the men grow higher and higher with each moment of the advance. The rattling of the artillery and the hoof-beats of the horses add to the excitement of the onward rush, infantry and artillery thus side by side, vieing each with the other which shall best do his part. Now, as we come nearer, the storm of the battle seems to grow greater and greater. On and yet on we press, until, reaching the designated point, the artillery is turned off to the left, on to a ridge, and go into position along its crest, while the lines of the infantry are being formed to the right of the road over which we have just been hurrying.

Our lines are scarcely formed, and the command to move forward given, when the lines which are in advance of us are broken by a terrific charge of the enemy, and are driven back in confusion onto our line—friend and foe so intermingled that we can not fire a shot without inflicting as much injury on our men as upon the enemy.

Our artillery, on the crest of the ridge back of us, have unlimbered and gone into action, and their shells are now flying over our heads into the woods, where the enemy's lines had been. Confusion seems to have taken possession of our lines, and, to add to it, the lines of our right have been broken and the enemy are sweeping past our flank. The order is given to fall back on line with the artillery. Out of the wood, under the fire of our cannon, the men hasten. Now on the crest of that ridge, without works of any kind to shelter them, our troops are again hastily formed, and none too soon. Down the gentle slope of that ridge, and away to our right and left and front stretches an open field, without tree or shrub to break the force of the balls. In our front, and at the edge of the field, two hundred yards away, runs the road parallel with our lines; beyond the road the heavy timber where the Confederate lines are formed, and well protected in their preparations for their charge.

Scarce had our lines been formed, when the sharp crack of the rifles along our front, and the whistling of the balls over our heads, give us warning that the advance of the enemy has begun, and in an instant the shots of the skirmishers are drowned by the shout that goes up from the charging column as it starts down in the woods. Our men are ready. The Seventh Indiana Battery—six guns—is on the right of my regiment; Battery M, Fourth United States Artillery, is on our left. The gunners and every man of those two batteries are at their posts of duty, the tightly drawn lines in their faces showing their purpose there to stand for duty or die. Officers pass the familiar command of caution along the line—"Steady, men, steady." The shout of the charging foe comes rapidly on; now they burst out of the woods and onto the road. As if touched by an electric cord, so quick and so in unison was it, the rifles leap to the shoulder along the ridge where waves the stars and stripes.

Now the enemy are in plain view along the road covering our entire front; you can see them, as with cap visors drawn well down over their eyes, the gun at the charge, with short, shrill shouts they come, and we see the colors of Longstreet's corps, flushed with victory, confronting us. Our men recognize the gallantry of their foe, and their pride is touched as well. All this is but the work of an instant, when, just as that long line of gray has crossed the road, quick and sharp rings out along our line the command, "Ready," "Fire!" It seems to come to infantry and artillery at the same instant, and out from the rifles of the men and the mouths of those cannons leap the death-dealing bullet and canister; again and again, with almost lightning rapidity, they pour in their deadly, merciless fire, until along that entire ridge it had become almost one continuous volley. Now that corps that had known little of defeat begins to waver; their men had fallen thick and fast about them. Again and yet again the volleys are poured into them, and the artillery on our right and left have not ceased their deadly work. No troops can long withstand such fire; their lines waver; another volley, and they are broken, and now fall back in confusion. The charge was not long in point of time, but was terrible in its results to the foe.

Along the entire line to our right and left we can hear the battle raging with increased fury. We are now on the defensive; and all can judge that the lull in our front is only the stillness that forbodes the more terrible storm that is to come. A few logs and rails are hastily gathered together to form a slight breastwork. Soon the scattering shots that began to fall about us gave us warning that our foe was again moving on us. Again we are ready, now laying behind our hastily prepared works. Again we hear the shout, as on they come with more determination than before. But with even greater courage do our men determine to hold their lines. The artillery is double shotted with canister. Again the command, "Fire!" and hotter, fiercer than before, the battle rages along our front. Shout is answered with shout, shot by shots tenfold, until again our assailants break before our fire and are again forced back.

But why repeat further the story of that Saturday afternoon. Again and again were those charges repeated along our line, only to be hurled back—broken and shattered. It did seem as though our men were more than human. The artillerymen worked as never before. Their guns—double shotted—had scarce delivered their charges, and, before the gun could complete its recoil, was caught by strong arms, made doubly strong in that fever-heat of battle; was again in position, again double shotted, and again fired into the face of the foe. The arms bared, the veins standing out in great strong lines, the hat or cap gone from the head, the eye starting almost from the socket, the teeth set, the face beaded with perspiration, balls falling all about them, those men of the Seventh Indiana Battery and Battery M seemed to be supernaturally endowed with strength.

Their comrades of the infantry vied with them in acts of heroism, and daring, and endurance. They shouted defiance at the foe with every shot; with face and hands begrimed in the smoke and dust and heat of the battle; with comrades falling about them, the survivors thought only of vengeance. All the horses on two of the guns of the Seventh Indiana Battery are shot down; another charge is beginning; those two guns might be lost; they must be gotten back. Quick as thought, a company of infantry spring to the guns, one hand holding the rifle, the other on the cannon, and, with the shot falling thick and fast in and about them, drag the guns over the brow of the ridge and down into the woods, just in the rear of our lines, and hasten back again to take their places in line, ready to meet the on-coming charge. An artillery-man is shot down; a man from the infantry takes his place and obeys orders as best he can. When the charge begins our men are lying down. Now, in the midst of it, so great has become the excitement, so intense the anxiety, all fear and prudence vanishes, and the men leap to their feet, and fire and load, and fire and load, in the wildest frenzy of desperation. They have lost all ideas of danger or the strength of the assailants. It was this absolute *desperation* of our men that held our lines.

—CARNAHAN, "Personal Recollections of Chickamauga"

3. THOMAS STANDS LIKE A ROCK AT CHICKAMAUGA

During the night of the nineteenth Longstreet came up with two more brigades, and Bragg prepared to renew the battle by a series of attacks on the attenuated Union line, from north to south. The crisis came in the afternoon of the twentieth. Fierce Confederate attacks upon the Union left led Rosecrans to weaken his right. Through some misunderstanding General Wood withdrew his division, near the center, and into the gap thus created Longstreet hurled his fresh brigades like a thunderbolt. The whole Union line cracked and broke; the right crumbled and retreated toward Rossville; the left was in desperate danger. It was then that Thomas earned for himself the title "Rock of Chickamauga"—Thomas who during the whole war never left the battlefield and never lost an engagement. It was Stones River over again, but without the artillery, without even ammunition, for at one time Thomas was forced to rely on the bayonet to hurl back the Confederate attacks. Just as the situation appeared most desperate Gordon Granger came pounding up with his reserve division and saved the day.

The story of the break-through is told here by a Confederate general and by a major in Longstreet's artillery, and the story of Thomas' stand by a brigadier attached to Rosecrans' staff. D. H. Hill was one of Lee's greatest lieutenants and needs neither introduction nor celebration. William Owen of the Washington Artillery we have met before. Thurston was a brigadier general in the Army of the Cumberland.

A. LONGSTREET BREAKS THE FEDERAL LINE

THE heavy pressure on Thomas caused Rosecrans to support him by sending the divisions of Negley and Van Cleve and Brannan's reserve brigade. In the course of these changes, an order to Wood, which Rosecrans claims was misinterpreted, led to a gap being left into which Longstreet stepped with the eight brigades which he had arranged in three lines to constitute his grand column of attack. Davis's two brigades, one of Van Cleve's, and Sheridan's entire division were caught in front and flank and driven from the field. Disregarding the order of the day, Longstreet now gave the order to wheel to the right instead of the left, and thus take in reverse the strong position of the enemy. Five of McCook's brigades were speedily driven off the field. He estimates their loss at forty per cent. Certainly that flank march was a bloody one. I have never seen the Federal dead lie so thickly on the ground, save in front of the sunken wall at Fredericksburg.

But that indomitable Virginia soldier, George H. Thomas, was there and was destined to save the Union army from total rout and ruin, by confronting with invincible pluck the forces of his friend and captain in the Mexican war. Thomas had ridden to his right to hurry up reënforcements, when he discovered a line advancing, which he thought at first was the expected succor from Sheridan, but he soon heard that it was a rebel column marching upon him. He chose a strong position on a spur of Missionary Ridge, running east and west, placed upon it Brannan's division with portions of two brigades of Negley's; Wood's division (Crittenden's) was placed on Brannan's left. These troops, with such as could be rallied from the two broken corps, were all he had to confront the forces of Longstreet, until Steedman's division of Granger's corps came to his relief about 3 P.M. Well and nobly did Thomas and his gallant troops hold their own against foes flushed with past victory and confident of future success. His new line was nearly at right angles with the line of log-works on the west side of the Rossville road, his right being an almost impregnable wall-like hill, his left nearly an inclosed fortification. Our only hope of success was to get in his rear by moving far to our right, which overlapped the Federal left.

Bushrod Johnson's three brigades in Longstreet's center were the first to fill the gap left by Wood's withdrawal from the Federal right; but the other five brigades under Hindman and Kershaw moved promptly into line as soon as space could be found for them, wheeled to the right, and engaged in the murderous flank attack. On they rushed, shouting, yelling, running over batteries, capturing trains, taking prisoners, seizing the headquarters of the Federal commander, at the Widow Glenn's, until they found themselves facing the new Federal line on Snodgrass Hill. Hindman had advanced a little later than the center, and had met great and immediate success. The brigades of Deas and Manigault charged the breastworks at double-quick, rushed over them, drove Laiboldt's Federal brigade of Sheridan's division off the field down the Rossville road; then General Patton Anderson's brigade of Hindman, having come into line, attacked and beat back the forces of Davis, Sheridan, and Wilder in their front, killed the hero and poet General Lytle, took 1100 prisoners, 27 pieces of artillery, commissary and ordnance trains, etc. Finding no more resistance on his front and left, Hindman wheeled to the right to assist the forces of the center. The divisions of Stewart, Hood, Bushrod Johnson, and Hindman came together in front of the new stronghold of the Federals.

It was now 2:30 P.M. Longstreet with his staff, was lunching on sweet-potatoes. A message came just then that the commanding general wished to see him. He found Bragg in rear of his lines, told him of the steady and satisfactory progress of the battle, that sixty pieces of artillery had been reported captured (though probably the number was over-estimated), that many prisoners and stores had been taken, and that all was going well. He then asked for additional troops to hold the ground gained, while he pursued the two broken corps down the Dry Valley road and cut off the retreat of Thomas. Bragg replied that there was no more fight in the troops of Polk's wing, that he could give Longstreet no reënforcements. . . .

Some of the severest fighting had yet to be done. . . . Hindman and Bushrod Johnson organized a column of attack upon the front and rear of the stronghold of Thomas. . . . It began at 3:30 P.M. A terrific contest ensued. The bayonet was used, and men were killed and wounded with clubbed muskets. A little after 4, the enemy was reënforced, and advanced, but was repulsed by Anderson and Kershaw.

—HILL, "Chickamauga—The Great Battle of the West"

B. "MEN, WE MUST USE THE BAYONET"

[September 20] 11:30. Our time comes at last. Latrobe gallops up and says, "Gen. Longstreet orders your division to move forward, keeping closed to the right." Trigg, Kelly, and Gracie advance, leaving our batteries to watch the enemy on the banks of the Chickamauga. We are swinging around on Polk's corps, which is now the pivot.

Our division, in advancing, passes the spot where Gen. Bragg is seated upon his horse on the Chattanooga road. He looks pale and careworn, his features rendered more haggard by a white Havelock he wears over his cap and neck.

The enemy seems to be fighting in detached bodies.

Longstreet discovers, with his soldier's eye, a gap in their already confused lines, and, forming a solid column of attack, composed of Stewart's, Hood's, Kershaw's, Johnson's, and Hindman's divisions, with Preston's as supports, breaks through and strikes the enemy, and short and bloody is the work. We move steadily forward, no halting. The men rush over the hastily-constructed breastworks of logs and rails of the foe, with the old time familiar rebel yell, and, wheeling then to the right, the column sweeps the enemy before it, and pushes along the Chattanooga road towards Missionary Ridge in pursuit. It is glorious!

We hear that Kershaw's and Hood's men are fighting, as they always do, splendidly. Several thousand prisoners and fifty pieces of artillery reported captured, General Lytle killed. At 2:45 P.M. our exultant troops are halted to rest; our division has followed on, supporting those in front who have so far done the fighting. There is no enemy left except a small force on Horseshoe Ridge, which is a very strong position; those troops of the enemy who were on Longstreet's left, when he broke through the lines, are falling back to positions of greater safety, and are flying to Chattanooga. Longstreet says "They have fought their last man and *he* is running."

3 P.M. While our division was resting at a halt, under an occasional fire of a battery posted on Horseshoe Ridge, I rode to the right and rear of our line, and there saw Gens. Longstreet and Buckner, seated on a log, eating their lunch, which their boy had brought to them. General Longstreet hailed me, and asked for a pipeful of tobacco. I produced my little bag, and he filled his meerschaum pipe. I then asked him what he thought of the battle; was the enemy beaten or not?

"Yes," he said, "all along his line; a few are holding out upon the ridge up yonder, not many though. If we had had our Virginia army here, we could have whipped them in half the time. By the by," he added, "don't you want some guns for your command? I think my men must have captured fifty to-day."

I told him I did, and would like to make a change for better ones, those we have being very indifferent.

"Well," he said, "you can have as many as you want."

"General, hadn't you better put that in writing?"

He laughed, and instructed Latrobe to write an order for the guns. . . .

It was now 4 o'clock, and the remnant of the Federal army still stubbornly held the Horseshoe Ridge, although during the day they had been assaulted by Breckenridge, Bushrod Johnson, Patton, Anderson, Hindman, and lastly by Kershaw, and all had lost heavily.

Longstreet determined to take the ridge, and sends to Bragg for some of the troops of the right wing, but Bragg says, "they have been fought out and can do him no good."

The position held by the enemy is a very Gibraltar, its sides precipitous, and difficult to climb, but the day is wearing away, and no time should be lost. Longstreet determines to put in his Tenth legion, Preston's 5,000, and sends for the General, and orders an immediate advance. "It shall be done," replies Preston, and the command Attention! is given down the lines of the three brigades. The young troops spring to their arms; it is their first baptism of fire, and if they are whipped they won't know it.

The lines are dressed, and at the commands, Forward! forward! the 5,000 move on in beautiful order. The enemy opens a terrific fire; but up the hill our men advance; now the enemy's bullets begin to tell upon the lines, and men fall to the right and left, dead and wounded; but the rest move on undismayed, firing rapidly as they advance; but the artillery and infantry fire is too hot for them, although they have fought most gallantly, and, halting under the crest where some protection is had, the lines are dressed, and General Preston, reassuring them by his presence, rides down the lines and coolly examines each man's cartridge-box, and says, "Men, we must use the bayonet,—the bayonet,—we will give them the bayonet!" The men, one and all cry out, "Go ahead, General! we are not whipped yet!" Confidence restored by the General's cool demeanor, and with the enthusiasm of the troops raised to the highest pitch, Preston rides to the front and centre of his line, and leads the way with splendid dash and bravery, waving his cap above his head, his gray hair floating in the breeze.

With fierce yells and shouts the troops advance,—Gracie on the right, Kelly the centre, and Trigg the left. It is a brave sight. Gracie and Kelly meet a determined resistance; but Trigg, who had been pushed to the enemy's right in the hope of overlapping and flanking him, sweeps down on his flank and rear, capturing 500 prisoners, the colors of the Twenty-first Ohio, the Twenty-second Michigan, and two of regiments unknown, together with Colonels Lefebvre and Carlton, and Lieut.-Col. Glenn. The enemy, assailed on front and flank, falls back, and the battle-flags of Preston's division are planted upon the summit of Horseshoe Ridge, and the battle is won.

It was now growing quite dark, and the last divisions of Rosecrans's army were soon in full retreat on the road to Chattanooga. The troops we had fought upon the ridge were under General Thomas,—the commands of

Brannan, Wood, and Granger, men of Ohio, Kentucky, and Michigan. Our tired men slept upon the field among the enemy's dead and wounded.
    —Owen, *In Camp and Battle with the Washington Artillery*

C. Thomas Holds the Horseshoe Ridge

The furious initial attack on the Federal left, on the morning of the 20th, although repulsed, unfortunately led to changes in Rosecrans's army materially affecting the results of the general conflict. Thomas, discovering his position turned and his front assaulted, hurried messengers to Rosecrans for assistance. Two aides, in rapid succession, called for reënforcements. All was still on the Federal right. The fight was raging with grand fury on the left.

Rosecrans felt that his apprehensions of the morning were to be realized. The Confederates were doubtless massing on his left. They had reached the much-coveted Chattanooga road. McCook was at once notified that Thomas was heavily pressed, that the left must be held at all hazards, and that he must be ready to reënforce Thomas at a moment's warning. Five minutes later came the order to hurry Sheridan's two brigades to the left. Negley's troops, replaced by Wood, had started. Van Cleve, with two brigades, was also sent to aid Thomas. McCook was now left with one of Sheridan's brigades and two of Jefferson C. Davis's, all depleted by Saturday's losses. They were unable to form a connected front, but joined Wood on their left. Captain Kellogg, of Thomas's staff, hurrying along the line with orders, unfortunately reported to Rosecrans that he had noticed "Brannan was out of line, and Reynolds's right exposed."

Turning to an aide Rosecrans directed him to order Wood "to close up on Reynolds as fast as possible and support him." In fact, Reynolds was *not* needing help, and Brannan was in position on his right, but slightly in rear. Wood, whose left connected with Brannan's right, passed to the rear of Brannan to reach Reynolds's position; thus a wide gap was left in the Union line. McCook had already called up Wilder to strengthen his front, and sent for the main cavalry to protect the right. The right had unexpectedly become, as it were, the *rear* of the army.

Unhappily for the National army, Bragg was *not* now massing his forces on our left. He had just been defeated and repulsed there. Bragg's main plan had failed; but in the quiet forest, within almost a stone's-throw of our right, and in the still overclouding mist, were Longstreet and Buckner, with the left wing of the Confederate army massed in battle array, impatiently awaiting the signal for attack.

Longstreet's troops were placed in column of brigades at half distance,—a masterpiece of tactics. Hood, a soldier full of energy and dash, was to lead the column, his own division being massed five brigades deep, with the brigades of Kershaw and Humphreys as additional supports.

The order to advance came at last. The deep Confederate lines suddenly appeared. The woods in our front seemed alive. On they came like an angry flood. They struck McCook's three remaining brigades, the remnants of the

Federal right. Under the daring personal exertions of McCook and Davis, they made a gallant but vain resistance. The massed lines of the enemy swarmed around their flanks. Pouring through the opening made by Wood's withdrawal, they struck his last brigade as it was leaving the line. It was slammed back like a door, and shattered. Brannan, on Wood's left, was struck in front and flank. His right was flung back; his left stood fast. Sheridan, hastening to the left with two brigades, was called back, and rushed to the rescue. His little force stayed the storm for a time. Wave after wave of Confederates came on; resistance only increased the multitude. Brannan's artillery, attacked in flank, rushed to the rear for clearer ground, and, with the Confederates at their heels, suddenly plunged into Van Cleve marching to the aid of Thomas. Disorder ensued; effective resistance was lost. The Reserve Artillery of the center, well posted in rear, unable to manoeuvre in the undergrowth, hedged around by infantry a half hour before, was now without immediate support. The sudden rush of Longstreet's compact column through the forest had foiled all plans. The astonished artillerists were swept from their guns. General Negley, with one of his brigades isolated in rear, shared the general fate of the right.

When Longstreet struck the right, Rosecrans was near McCook and Crittenden. Seeing our line swept back, he hurried to Sheridan's force for aid. With staff and escort he recklessly strove to stem the tide. They attempted to pass to the left through a storm of canister and musketry, but were driven back.

All became confusion. No order could be heard above the tempest of battle. With a wild yell the Confederates swept on far to their left. They seemed everywhere victorious. Rosecrans was borne back in the retreat. Fugitives, wounded, caissons, escort, ambulances, thronged the narrow pathways. He concluded that our whole line had given way, that the day was lost, that the next stand must be made at Chattanooga. McCook and Crittenden, caught in the same tide of retreat, seeing only rout everywhere, shared the opinion of Rosecrans, and reported to him for instructions and coöperation.

Briefly, this is the story of the disaster on our right at Chickamauga: We were overwhelmed by numbers; we were beaten in detail. Thirty minutes earlier Longstreet would have met well-organized resistance. Thirty minutes later our marching divisions could have formed beyond his column of attack. . . .

The sound of battle had lulled. No Union force was in sight. A Confederate line near by was advancing against the position. Harrison, dismounting his men, dashed at the enemy in a most effective charge. Wilder, coming up on our right, also attacked. Wilder had two regiments armed with the same repeating-rifles. They did splendid work. Longstreet told Wilder after the war that the steady and continued racket of these guns led him to think an army corps had attacked his left flank. Bragg, cautious by nature, hesitated. By the time he was ready to turn Longstreet's force against Thomas, valuable time had elapsed.

E. F. Ackermann

The Intrenchments Before Petersburg

A. R. Waud

The Battle of Winchester

Brannan, partly knocked out of line, had gathered his division on a hill at right angles to his former position, and a half mile in rear of Reynolds. General Wood came up with Harker's brigade and part of George P. Buell's, and posted them near Brannan's left. Some of Van Cleve's troops joined them, and fragments of Negley's.

General Thomas, ignorant of these movements and of the disaster to the right of the Union army, had again been attacked by Breckinridge and Forrest. They were again in Baird's rear with increased force. Thomas's reserve brigades, Willich, Grose, and Van Derveer, hurried to meet the attack. After a fierce struggle the Confederates were beaten back. Thomas, expecting the promised assistance of Sheridan, had sent Captain Kellogg to guide him to the left. Kellogg, hurrying back, reported that he had been fired on by a line of Confederates advancing in the woods in rear of Reynolds, who held the center of our general line.

The men in gray were coming on the right instead of Sheridan! Wood and Harker hoped the force advancing in the woods on their new front was a friendly one. The National flag was waved; a storm of bullets was the response. It was Stewart and Bate coming with their Tennesseeans. They had finally forced their way across the ragged edge of the Federal right, and were following Hood. Fortunately Thomas had just repulsed Breckinridge's attack on his left, and Stanley, Beatty, and Van Derveer had double-quicked across the "horseshoe" to our new right. They did not come a moment too soon. The improvised line of Federals thus hastily formed on "Battery Hill" now successfully withstood the assault of the enemy. The Union line held the crest. Longstreet was stayed at last. Gathering new forces, he soon sent a flanking column around our right. We could not extend our line to meet this attack. They had reached the summit, and were coming around still farther on through a protected ravine. For a time the fate of the Union army hung in the balance. All seemed lost, when unexpected help came from Gordon Granger and the right was saved.

—Thruston, "The Crisis at Chickamauga"

4. CHATTANOOGA UNDER SIEGE

After Chickamauga the Federals retired into Chattanooga; thus the army that had set out to capture the city ended by being caught in its own net. So serious was the situation that Grant himself came on to take charge of its relief. The immediate task was for Hooker to move into the area enclosed by the great bend of the Tennessee, between Bridgeport and Chattanooga; the second for Thomas to get control of Brown's Ferry. Then the two could link up. Had Bragg been on the alert neither of these movements could have succeeded, for Raccoon Mountain and Lookout Mountain commanded both approaches. Bragg however failed to build up adequate strength in this region south and west of Chattanooga. On October 26 Hooker crossed the Tennessee at Bridgeport and moved overland toward Brown's Ferry, and some of Thomas' forces captured Brown's Ferry and the heights above it.

The war correspondent, W. F. G. Shanks, who was with the Army of the Cumberland, here tells what life was like during the siege and how the siege was raised by opening the "cracker line."

THE siege of Chattanooga was the only one which any one of the Union armies suffered or sustained. It is a singular fact, worthy of mention just here, that the troops of the Union never abandoned a siege once begun, nor surrendered a position regularly besieged; and that, on the contrary, the rebels never carried a position regularly invested, and were compelled to surrender all those fortresses in which they were besieged. The Union armies invested and finally captured Yorktown, Fort Donelson, Corinth, Vicksburg, Island No. 10, Port Hudson, Petersburg, Atlanta, Mobile, Savannah, Charleston, Fort Fisher, Wilmington, and many other points of lesser importance and held by mere detachments, not, like those mentioned, garrisoned by entire armies. The rebels besieged Nashville, Knoxville, Chattanooga, and other minor positions held by fragments of armies and failed in all. They came nearest to success at Chattanooga. . . .

If there was little of beauty or elegance in the place when our troops retreated into it from Chickamauga, there was a great deal less a fortnight subsequently. Like many another Southern town Chattanooga grew suddenly old; one might say it turned gray during the brief but dark night of the siege. General Saint Clair Morton, the chief of Rosecrans's engineers, had no mercy; he had no idea of economy either. As one of his fellow-officers once said of him, "if Morton needed a certain quantity of earth for a fort, the fact that it was a gold mine would make no difference to him; he would only say, 'Gold dust will resist artillery—it will do.' " So laying out his line of works Morton budged from his course not an inch to spare the town. Residences were turned into block-houses; black bastions sprang up in former vineyards; rifle-pits were run through the grave-yards; and soon a long line of works stretched from the river above to the river below the city, bending crescent-like around it, as if it were a huge bow of iron, and rendering it impregnable. For a fortnight the whole army worked on the fortifications, and it became literally a walled city.

Not alone from the fact that it was shut in by the mud walls of these impregnable fortifications was the town an intrenched camp, and the engineers alone did not despoil Chattanooga of its small modicum of beauty. The winter-quarters of the troops, composed of small dog-kennel-shaped huts, built of boards and roofed over with the shelter-tents with which the soldiers were provided, were scattered all over the town in valley and on hill-side, and it was not difficult to imagine it again the little Indian town of huts and wigwams which Hanging Bird had described. The camps of the soldiers were not cantonments in the proper sense of the term. The immediate presence and threatening proximity of the enemy rendered it necessary to safety and discipline that the troops should encamp in the regular order of regiments and brigades, so as to be prepared to form at the sound of alarm, ready to repulse or to make an attack. Instead, therefore, of camping indiscriminately

CHATTANOOGA AND ITS APPROACHES

in houses as they stood, the men tore down the houses and fences, and of the frame-work built their huts, and of the bricks their chimneys and fire-places.

The veteran soldier is very ingenious, and makes himself happy on very little; and the quarters of those at Chattanooga during the siege possessed all the "modern improvements." They had curious modes of making themselves comfortable. The rebels used to call our men, when working on forts, rifle-pits, etc., "beavers in blue." The veteran was a regular beaver when building his house. He would buy, beg, or steal from the quarter-master (a species of theft recognized by the camp code of morals as entirely justifiable) the only tool he needed, an axe. With this he would cut, hew, dig, drive—any thing you like, in fact. With his axe he would cut the logs for his cabin—miniature logs, two inches in diameter—trim them to the proper length, and drive the necessary piles. With his axe he would cut the brushwood or the evergreen, and thatch his roof or cover it with his shelter-tent. With his axe he would dig a mud-hole in which to make his plaster for filling the crevices of the logs, and thus shut out the cold. Doors, chimneys, benches, chairs, tables, all the furniture of his commodious house, he would make with the same instrument.

When all was finished he would sit down to enjoy himself, sleeping on good clean straw, dining off a wooden table, drinking from glassware made from the empty ale or porter bottles from the suttler's tent, combing his whiskers before a framed looking-glass on a pine-board mantle-shelf, and looking with the air and contentedness of a millionaire on the camped world around him. These huts of the veterans were not perhaps so large and picturesque as the wigwams of the Cherokees. They really resembled more in size and appearance the huts of the beaver or prairie-dogs, and this comparison did not seem so foreign or forced as it may appear to the reader when, on the occasional bright days of the bleak siege, the gallant "war dogs" were to be seen issuing forth to bay a deep-mouthed welcome to the enterprising news-boy or faithful postman, who had run the gauntlet of rebel sharp-shooters or the embargo of mud to furnish the news from home.

Life in Chattanooga during the two months of the siege was dreary enough. There was no fighting to do; the enemy daily threw a few shells from the top of Lookout Mountain into our camps, but they were too wise to attack with infantry the works which soon encircled the city. Bragg preferred to rely for the final reduction of the garrison upon his ally Famine, and a very formidable antagonist did our men find him in the end. Bragg held the railroad line from Bridgeport to Chattanooga, thereby preventing its use by Rosecrans as a line of supplies, and compelling him to haul his provisions in wagon trains from Stevenson across the Cumberland Mountains. Every exertion of the quarter-masters failed to fully supply the army by this route, the only practicable one while the siege lasted. The animals of the army were overworked and ill-fed, and thousands died from exhaustion. It was almost impossible to obtain forage for those in Chattanooga, and the quarter-masters reported that ten thousand horses and mules died of actual starvation during the siege. Thousands were turned loose in the mountains and perished. I passed over the route from Chattanooga to Stevenson during the siege, and was never out of sight of these dead or dying "heroes whose names were never mentioned." They would frequently gather in groups around a small pool at which they could quench the thirst that consumed them, and lie down to die. Finding it impossible to obtain forage for an animal which I had in Chattanooga, and which had been latterly subsisting on the pine-board fence to which his halter was attached, I turned the poor animal loose to graze near a small stream in the town. He was too exhausted to stray away from it; lying down he picked the few blades of grass within his reach, stretched his neck to the pool for the few drops of water which it gave, and at length gave up the ghost.

The other heroes in the beleaguered town hardly suffered less. Famine became a familiar fiend; they laughed in his face, as crowds will laugh in the face of great dangers and disasters, but it was a very forced laugh. The trains of supplies for the army were frequently twenty days on the route from Stevenson, only sixty miles distant, and as the trains were not numerous naturally the supplies in the town did not increase. And many of these trains frequently came in *empty*. They could not carry full loads across the mountains with skeletons for horses; each train had to be guarded, and the guards had to be supplied from the train whose safety they secured. Most of these guards were men from the besieged city, they had been on quarter rations of fat bacon and mouldy hard bread for weeks, and they did not lose the opportunity to satisfy the cravings of their appetites when guarding the trains. It was all nonsense for quarter-masters in charge to tell them they ought to remember their starving comrades in the besieged city, to appeal to their patriotism, and to talk about discipline; if there are any periods when discipline, patriotism, and sympathy are entirely sunk in a soldier's breast they are when he is thoroughly demoralized by defeat or reckless from hunger. So it frequently happened that the guards of a train eat it *in transitu*. After the third week of the siege the men were put on quarter rations, and only two or three articles were supplied in this meagre quantity. The only meat to be had was bacon, "side bacon" or "middling," I think it is called, and a slice about the size of the three larger fingers of a man's hand, sandwiched between the two halves of a "Lincoln Platform," as the four inches square cake of "hard bread" was called, and washed down by a pint of coffee, served for a meal.

Men can not dig fortifications and fight very long on such rations; and the whole army was half famished. I have often seen hundreds of soldiers following behind the wagon trains which had just arrived, picking out of the mud the crumbs of bread, coffee, rice, etc., which were wasted from the boxes and sacks by the rattling of the wagons over the stones. Nothing was wasted in those days, and though the inspectors would frequently condemn whole wagon loads of provisions as spoiled by exposure during the trip, and order the contents to be thrown away, the soldiers or citizens always found some use for it.

The hundreds of citizens who were confined in the town at the same time suffered even more than the men. They were forced to huddle together in the centre of the town as best they could, and many of the houses occupied by them during the siege surpassed in filth, point of numbers of occupants, and general destitution, the worst tenement-house in New York city. . . .

The siege which was thus conducted was raised by strategy—the strategy of the same man who had captured the city, though he did not execute the movements. The enemy which was in reality investing the town was Famine: the way to defeat him was to find a shorter line of supplies by which the besieged army might be fed. A close study of the map had shown to Rosecrans that if Bragg could be driven from a small peninsula of land near Chattanooga, and on the south side of the Tennessee River, a very short route could be opened by the river to Bridgeport, and that by means of a couple of boats which the soldiers had built the army could be fed. Hooker's corps from the Army of the Potomac had arrived at Bridgeport on Oct. 20, and with this force the peninsula could be seized. But before he could get ready for the movement Rosecrans was relieved of the command, and General Thomas assumed control, with General Grant in chief command. In the mean time the troops in Chattanooga were on the eve of starvation. "We are issuing," said General Gordon Granger, "quarter rations for breakfast only." But Thomas, on assuming command, and being urged by Grant to hold on to the strong-hold at all hazards, had telegraphed in reply, "I will hold the town until we starve;" and the men cheerfully agreed to starve a while longer.

On the arrival of General Grant the movements which Rosecrans had planned were begun. Two columns to seize the peninsula started simultaneously—the one from Bridgeport under General Hooker, the other from Chattanooga under General W. F. Smith. Hooker moved overland along the railroad and seized upon Wauhatchie and three small hills near the mouth of Lookout Creek. Smith, with his command in pontoon boats, on the night of October 26, 1863, dropped down the Tennessee River, running past the rebel batteries to Brown's Ferry, where a prominent and commanding peak of hills on the peninsula was seized, and the boats were soon transformed into a pontoon bridge across the river at that point. General Hooker's position, which was only won after two very desperate engagements, one of which was fought at midnight, covered a road to Kelley's Ferry, a landing-place on the west side of the all-important peninsula; and the result of the whole operation was that a short and good road, only seven miles in length, was obtained from 'Chattanooga by way of Brown's Ferry to Kelley's Ferry; at which latter place the steamboats built by the troops landed supplies from Bridgeport. Supplies by this route could be very easily carried through in a day, and the army was very soon on full rations again.

—SHANKS, "Chattanooga, and How We Held It"

5. HOOKER WINS THE "BATTLE ABOVE THE CLOUDS"

As soon as the peril of the Federal position at Chattanooga was clear, Halleck ordered General Hooker to proceed west with two corps of the

*Army of the Potomac. Hooker arrived at Bridgeport early in October and,
as we have seen, crossed the river into the Raccoon Mountain region on October
26. After he had cleared this area of Confederates, his next task was to
seize control of Lookout Mountain, lying directly south of Chattanooga.
Early on the morning of November 24 his forces, 10,000 strong, began their
attack. Bragg, with characteristic imbecility, had less than 2,000 men posted
here; these put up a stiff resistance but were overwhelmed.*

The story of the "Battle above the Clouds" is told by Major Joseph Fullerton of the Army of the Cumberland.

THE morning of November 24th opened with a cold, drizzling rain.
Thick clouds of mist were settling on Lookout Mountain. At daybreak
Geary's division, and Whitaker's brigade of Cruft's division, marched up to
Wauhatchie, the nearest point at which Lookout Creek, swelled by recent
rains, could be forded, and at 8 o'clock they crossed. The heavy clouds of
mist reaching down the mountain-side hid the movement from the enemy,
who was expecting and was well prepared to resist a crossing at the Chattanooga road below. As soon as this movement was discovered, the enemy
withdrew his troops from the summit of the mountain, changed front, and
formed a new line to meet our advance, his left resting at the palisade, and
his right at the heavy works in the valley, where the road crossed the creek.
Having crossed at Wauhatchie, Whitaker's brigade, being in the advance,
drove back the enemy's pickets, and quickly ascended the mountain till it
reached the foot of the palisade. Here, firmly attaching its right, the brigade
faced left in front, with its left joined to Geary's division. Geary now moved
along the side of the mountain, and through the valley, thus covering the
crossing of the rest of Hooker's command. In the meantime Grose's brigade
was engaging the enemy at the lower road crossing, and Woods' brigade of
Osterhaus's division was building a bridge rather more than half a mile farther
up the creek. Geary, moving down the valley, reached this point at 11
o'clock, just after the bridge was finished, and as Osterhaus's division and
Grose's brigade were crossing.

Hooker's command, now united in the enemy's field, was ready to advance and sweep around the mountain. His line, hanging at the base of the
palisades like a great pendulum, reached down the side of the mountain to
the valley, where the force that had just crossed the creek was attached as its
weight. Now, as, at the command of Hooker, it swung forward in its upward movement, the artillery of the Army of the Cumberland, on Moccasin
Point, opened fire, throwing a stream of shot and shell into the enemy's rifle-pits at the foot of the mountain, and into the works thickly planted on the
"White House" plateau. At the same time the guns planted by Hooker on
the west side of the creek opened on the works which covered the enemy's
right. Then followed a gallant assault by Osterhaus and Grose. After fighting for nearly two hours, step by step up the steep mountain-side, over and
through deep gullies and ravines, over great rocks and fallen trees, the earthworks on the plateau were assaulted and carried, and the enemy was driven

out and forced to fall back. He did so slowly and reluctantly, taking advantage of the rough ground to continue the fight.

It was now 2 o'clock. A halt all along the line was ordered by General Hooker, as the clouds had grown so thick that further advance was impracticable, and as his ammunition was almost exhausted and more could not well be brought up the mountain. But all the enemy's works had been taken. Hooker had carried the mountain on the east side, had opened communication with Chattanooga, and he commanded the enemy's line of defensive works in Chattanooga Valley.

At 2 o'clock Hooker reported to General Thomas and informed him that he was out of ammunition. Thomas at once sent Carlin's brigade from the valley, each soldier taking with him all the small ammunition he could carry. At 5 o'clock Carlin was on the mountain, and Hooker's skirmishers were quickly supplied with the means of carrying on their work.

In the morning it had not been known in Chattanooga, in Sherman's army, or in Bragg's camp, that a battle was to be fought. . . . Soon after breakfast, Sherman's men at the other end of the line, intent on the north end of Missionary Ridge, and Thomas's men in the center, fretting to be let loose from their intrenchments, were startled by the sound of artillery and musketry firing in Lookout Valley. Surprise possessed the thousands who turned their anxious eyes toward the mountain. The hours slowly wore away; the roar of battle increased, as it came rolling around the point of the mountain, and the anxiety grew. A battle was being fought just before and above them. They could hear, but could not see how it was going. Finally, the wind, tossing about the clouds and mist, made a rift that for a few minutes opened a view of White House plateau. The enemy was seen to be in flight, and Hooker's men were in pursuit! Then went up a mighty cheer from the thirty thousand in the valley that was heard above the battle by their comrades on the mountain.

As the sun went down the clouds rolled away, and the night came on clear and cool. A grand sight was old Lookout that night. Not two miles apart were the parallel camp-fires of the two armies, extending from the summit of the mountain to its base, looking like streams of burning lava, while in between, the flashes from the skirmishers' muskets glowed like giant fire-flies.

—Fullerton, "The Army of the Cumberland at Chattanooga"

6. A BADGER BOY FIGHTS WITH SHERMAN AT CHATTANOOGA

Grant's plan was strategically simple but tactically complex. His purpose was to assault Bragg all along the line, drive him from his entrenchments, and, if possible, cut off his retreat and destroy him. To achieve this he planned a three-pronged operation. Sherman was to cross the Tennessee on pontoons, march up the tongue of land in front of Chattanooga, cross over to the east, and attack Bragg at the northern tip of Missionary Ridge. Once this attack was under way Thomas was to launch an attack on the center. If and when these had succeeded Hooker was to strike from the south. The attack jumped off at dawn of November 25, and all went as planned except that Sherman was held and thrown back while Thomas' supporting attack achieved victory.

Here young Jenkin Lloyd Jones, whom we have met before, records the experiences of Sherman's army during these critical days. Born in Wales Jones had been brought to Wisconsin as a baby; he enlisted at nineteen in the 6th Wisconsin Battery, fought at Corinth and Vicksburg and Chattanooga, and then marched with Sherman to the sea. After the war he became a Unitarian clergyman.

Mission Ridge, Tenn., Tuesday, Nov. 24. Marched to our position of night before last, unhitched and unharnessed. Laid down till 1 A.M. when we were awakened and ordered to hitch up. No noise allowed to be made. The pontooners marched by on quick time with axes, etc. Cogswell's Battery moved out and took position in the front. We soon followed in breathless silence, entered an open field and followed it up nearly half a mile, when we came upon the column of infantry moving along in close order and very fast. Not a breath could be heard, nothing but the grating of their feet on the gravel was to be heard. Never did a more earnest or thoughtful column move to meet the enemy. The column proceeded to the river, and we went into battery in the field thirty rods from the bank. The infantry were ferried across in the pontoon boats. One division was already across. Contrary to all expectations not a gun was fired, and we could hear nothing from our position of the advancing column. The out-post guard were gobbled up by surprise and sent over on this side. One escaped and carried the alarm that the Yankees were coming, which was not believed. But the officer of the day with seventeen men reconnoitered the grounds, and they too were "taken in out of the wet" and taken across and put in charge of the guard of the 5th Wisconsin Battery, they being stationed in a bastion on the bank. The out-post very innocently told the story that upon hearing a rustle in the brush which he challenged with a "Halt! Hush you d—— fool you, the Yankees are right here upon us! The fust thing I knew you 'uns hed me." While our Division was crossing, long trains of pontoons came up there with a long line of snow-white ambulances which caused the anxious question—"Who will he obliged to be borne in these from the field of battle?" Then came the hospital train, a wagon for each regiment in the Division, loaded with stores to establish a Division hospital.

6 A.M. Two divisions were safely across and a more beautiful scene I never witnessed. Through the gray dawn a long line of infantry could be seen drawn up on the opposite banks a mile long, while the waters were covered with boats busily going and coming, loaded with men, the regimental colors standing in the center of the boat. The bridge was now covered, boats brought up, anchored in line, and the floor laid without any delay, the 4th Division marching in the boats and the artillery covering the field. Fires were allowed to be built now and we soon had coffee. It commenced raining, as cold and disagreeable as the day could be. A steamboat was due at

4 A.M. to take us across, but did not come until 6:30 A.M. (an old rebel boat, but rebuilt). Taylor's Battery crossed the river first, and as we were not pressed we waited for the bridge to be built. It was very disagreeable, and I felt almost sick; late hours and irregular meals having brought on diarrhea, etc. A large constellation of stars were gathered on the bank, watching the progress of the bridge, among which were Sherman, Blair, W. F. Smith, chief engineer, etc. The line on the other side in one hour had a line of breast-works up and advanced out of sight to form another.

12 M. The bridge completed and we crossed it, being the second battery to do so. The dread of crossing had passed. Halted at a corn crib and the cannoneers got as much corn as they could, but the infantry was formed and advanced in column of division at secure arms. It raining very heavy. This savage-looking column moved forward with caution, crossed a forty-acre lot and halted. The skirmishers went out but not a gun was fired. Advanced again, the batteries were in column of sections. An occasional gun shot, but we advanced until we were directly under Mission Ridge. Not a reb seen and our infantry soon climbed it.

Our line formed on the brow when the artillery moved up. Battery D, 1st Missouri was the first up and soon opened fire on them from the right. Our Battery started for the left. The "smooth bores" were left on the other side of the river for want of horses, and we had four teams on a carriage, but the hill was too steep for us and two more teams were put on the pieces and the caissons left behind. A detail of two hundred men were sent to our aid with axes, the enemy sending shells over us quite thick. 1st piece failed to advance with the horses. Ropes brought forward, and it was hauled up by hand, we following with all haste.

By this time a very brisk skirmishing was going on right to our left and rear quite close, and General Matthies came down at the head of his Brigade on double quick, the old general on foot, making fine time. Captain Dillon ordered the howitzer section and Cogswell's Battery to the rear in all haste. The extra teams were unhitched and the pieces unlimbered, and with great difficulty we made a left about, the hill being so steep that it shoved our horses down amongst the infantry that were pouring down. But the cannoneers fastened a rope to the axle-tree and down we went in good earnest. Halted at the R.R. crossing in a complete jam of infantry, artillery and ambulances near General Smith's headquarters, who knew nothing of our movements and demanded by whose orders we came down. A flank movement by General Longstreet was apprehended, and we were to guard it by order of General Sherman.

We stood there in the cold damp evening for half an hour, got a feed of shelled corn from an out-house close by, when we moved back into the first field above General Matthies, and came into camp alongside of Cogswell's Battery and the 2nd and 3rd Brigades of our Division. Unhitched but did not unharness. Our rations were entirely out with the exception of coffee and some cornmeal picked up, so we ate hastily of unsifted mush and coffee.

Three drivers from each piece sent after sheaf oats for horses. I was on the detail and we rode back nearly three miles toward the river. Found the oats all gone, but plenty of good tame hay, of which we took as much as possible. Returned to camp by 9 P.M. I was nearly exhausted from cold and loss of sleep, having been up since 1 A.M. Lay down in cold and wet blankets.

Mission Ridge, Wednesday, Nov. 25. Called up before three in the morning to feed. Suffered very much from cold during the night. The blankets stiff with frost over us. Witnessed an almost total eclipse of the moon and again lay down, but no sleep. . . .

9 A.M. Not much fighting as yet, the pickets advancing and skirmishing. A reb battery shells directly over and in rear. One shell twelve-pounder time-fuse dropped ahead of our team and was dug up by the boys. A mule team came up and issued one day's rations of hard-tack.

11 A.M. The 2nd and 3rd Brigades went in on double quick followed by the 11th Corps with crescents flying, a fine looking body of men, but are looked on rather suspieciously by our sturdy veterans. They went in and advanced towards the rebels' works on Tunnel Hill, and musketry rattled very severe.

From that time [till] late in the evening a terrible struggle followed, wounded men coming back thick and fast. Our position was such that we could not witness the field and we were not permitted to leave the teams an instant. Our loss is very heavy especially in officers. The struggle on our side was for the occupation of Tunnel Hill and our line advanced up the steep side of the bluff time after time, but were obliged to fall back, the rebels being reinforced all the time, and could pick them off with ease, the lay of the land being such that they succeeded in flanking the 11th Corps, and they fell back in disorder. But they were received by the 2nd and 3rd Brigade of our Division, and soon compelled to retire.

More desperate fighting it is said by those who witnessed, they had never seen. Our line being for hours under the enemy they rolled stones upon us, wounding many. Three companies of the 5th Iowa were taken prisoners, having used up all their ammunition and would not run. Artillery could not be brought to much use, and my feelings as I staid under that hill, listening to the noise and rattle of the fight, mingled with suppressed cheers of charging parties, and the groans of the wounded as they passed in the long trains of ambulances, or the lighter wounded hobbling back a-foot with bleeding and mangled limbs I cannot describe in words. General Matthies was wounded in the head while leading his Brigade on to the charge. I saw him ride to the rear covered with blood. Colonel Putnam of the 93rd Illinois was killed instantly while waving the colors in front of his men, a noble and much loved officer. The 90th Illinois and 73rd Pennsylvania were literally cut to pieces, and their officers all killed or wounded.

The day closed, and the dark mantle of night was spread over the gory fields. We have gained nothing in the shape of ground all day, but their slaughter must be terrible. Thomas and Hooker were at them all day and it is reported gained great advantage. We had to fight the main body of the

army. Lookout was taken yesterday, 2500 prisoners and three pieces of
artillery. To-morrow if they stand, will be a final and awful test of strength.
Sherman, cool and deliberate, is ready for them. Got corn to feed on the
battle-field.

—JONES, *An Artilleryman's Diary*

7. THE ARMY OF THE CUMBERLAND CARRIES MISSIONARY RIDGE

What Pickett's charge is to the Confederacy, Thomas' attack of November 25 on Missionary Ridge is to the North, one of those moments of gallantry that seem suspended in time and are ever present and ever real. The Confederates had constructed three rows of entrenchments on rugged boulder-strewed Missionary Ridge. When Grant saw that Sherman was in trouble he asked Thomas to create a diversion by carrying the first line of entrenchments; Thomas' men carried them, and kept going to the top.

Here are three different accounts of this great dramatic event. The first is by William Morgan, a lieutenant in the 23rd Kentucky Infantry, part of Hazen's brigade. The second comes from General Fullerton, who has already told us about the Battle of Lookout Mountain. The third is from our old acquaintance, Major Connolly of the 123rd Illinois Volunteers.

A. "FIRST ONE FLAG, THEN ANOTHER, LEADS"

FROM the position occupied by my regiment, Orchard Knob was in view and all eyes were leveled in that direction. Suddenly a commotion was discernible on Orchard Knob. Officers were seen mounting their horses and riding towards the several commands. Then every man in the line knew the crucial hour had come. Intense excitement seemed to stir every soldier and officer. Excitement is followed by nervous impatience.

Time moves slowly. Here and there a soldier readjusts his accouterments or relaces his shoes. All know that many will never reach the enemy's works, yet not a countenance shows fear. The delay is becoming unbearable.

At last the first boom of the signal is heard. Men fall in and dress without command. Another gun, and nervous fingers play with gunlocks. Another and another, and each man looks into the eyes of his comrade to ascertain if he can be relied upon. The examination must have been satisfactory, for, just as the report of the fifth gun breaks upon their ears, the line is moving without a word of command from anyone, and when the sixth gun is fired the troops are well on the way, with colors unfurled and guns at "right shoulder shift." All sensations have now given way to enthusiasm. It is a sight never to be forgotten. Fifteen to twenty thousand men in well-aligned formation, with colors waving in the breeze, almost shaking the earth with cadenced tread, involuntarily move to battle.

The troops have scarcely left the rifle-pits when the guns upon the ridge open upon them. Our heavy guns in Fort Wood and the field batteries vigorously respond. We see the enemy in the rifle-pits, at the base of the ridge, looking over the works, with guns in hand, prepared to deliver fire. Why do they hesitate? We are in range. They are evidently waiting so that every shot will tell. From the enemy's lower lines now comes a storm of bullets and the air is filled with every sound of battle. The noise is terrible. Our artillery is exploding shells along the top of the ridge, and a caisson is seen to burst off to the right.

Now all feeling seems to have changed to one of determination. A terrific cheer rolls along the line. Not a rifle has yet been fired by the assaulting column. The quick step has been changed to the "double quick." Another cheer, and the enemy's first line of work at the base of the ridge is ours, together with many of his troops. Shelter is sought on the reverse side of the enemy's works, but the fire from the hilltop makes protection impossible.

Over fifty cannon, supported by veterans of many battle-fields, covered by well-built fortifications, are sending down a rain of shell, shrapnel, and rifle-bullets. The bursting projectiles seem to compress the air and one's head feels as if bound with iron bands. Unable to return the enemy's fire, the delay drives the men to desperation. To remain is to be annihilated; to retreat is as dangerous as to advance. Here and there a man leaps the works and starts towards the hilltop; small squads follow. Then someone gave the command, "Forward!" after a number of men began to advance. Officers catch the inspiration. The mounted officers dismount and stone their horses to the rear. The cry, "Forward!" is repeated along the line, and the apparent impossibility is undertaken. . . .

But little regard to formation was observed. Each battalion assumed a triangular shape, the colors at the apex surrounded by the strongest men, the flanks trailing to the rear.

First one flag passes all others and then another leads. One stand of colors, on our left, is particularly noticeable. The bearer is far ahead of his regiment and advances so rapidly that he draws the enemy's concentrated fire. Then another color-bearer dashes ahead of the line and falls. A comrade grasps the flag almost before it reaches the ground. He, too, falls. Then another picks it up, smeared with his comrade's blood, waves it defiantly, and, as if bearing a charmed life, he advances steadily towards the top. Up, up he goes, his hat pulled over his eyes, his head bent forward as if facing a storm of rain and wind. The bullets whistle about him, splintering the staff. Onward he goes, followed by the admiring cheers of his comrades, who press close behind.

As far advanced as any, Hazen's brigade struggles slowly upward. Willich's brigade on Hazen's left was somewhat in advance, but his left has met a resistance it cannot apparently overcome. On the right, Sheridan's left is considerably in the rear. This is the result of someone recalling it after it had advanced about one-fourth the way up the ridge, but before it had retreated very far the order was countermanded, and now it is forging to the front. The advance of Hazen's brigade is approaching the Rebel works. The enemy is sweeping the face of the hill with a rain of bullets, and his artillery fire crashes along the hillside from vantage-point on both flanks, killing and maiming with all the destruction of double-shotted guns. The men push upward.

Colonel Langdon, who has held his place close to the colors of his consolidated battalion, has reached a sheltered place about twenty yards from the top. Halting the colors there until he had collected about 200 men, he ordered them to fix bayonets. It is hard to tell now whose command is the most advanced. All are losing men rapidly, but not a man lags. Turchin, away to the left, closes with the enemy. His advance has evidently been stopped. Colonel Langdon rises to his feet and is shot, but before he falls he gives the command, "Forward!" The men leap forward, fire into the faces of the enemy, and the colors of the 1st Ohio and 23d Kentucky, fifty minutes after the firing of the signal-guns are planted on the works, quickly followed by the entire brigade. Of the eight corporals composing the color guard of the consolidated battalion, all fell on the hillside, and of the two sergeants who started with the colors, one is dead and the other wounded. Willich's brigade, having overcome all resistance, is over the works and his troops with a portion of Hazen's are moving along the ridge to the left. Hazen personally directs his troops along the ridge to the right, two guns taken are turned upon the enemy on our right, and discharged by firing muskets over the vent until primers could be procured.

Hooker, all this time, has been closing in on the enemy's extreme left and rear. Thus attacked on the flank, with its center pierced, a panic pervades the enemy's line, and gives Sheridan, who has had one of the steepest and highest points to climb, his opportunity, of which he promptly takes advantage. At every point now the enemy's lines begin to melt away except near Bragg's headquarters, in front of Sheridan's center. Suddenly they too give up the fight, abandon their works, and roll down the eastern slope, followed by Sheridan's division. Now cheer upon cheer greets "Old Glory" as it dots the ridge at every point and waves in triumph in the bright rays of the western sun, and the campaign, begun by the Army of the Cumberland three months before, is ended.

The loss in Hazen's brigade was 530 killed and wounded, more than one-half the loss of the entire division. It captured, during this battle, about 400 prisoners, large quantities of small-arms, sixteen to eighteen pieces of artillery, and two stands of colors, and was the first to plant its colors on the ridge.

—MORGAN, "Hazen's Brigade at Missionary Ridge"

B. "WHEN THOSE FELLOWS GET STARTED ALL HELL CAN'T STOP THEM"

None of the men of the Army of the Cumberland, who for nine weeks were buried in the trenches at Chattanooga, can ever forget the glorious night of the 24th of November. As the sun went down, the clouds rolled up the mountain, and the mist was blown out of the valley. Night came on clear, with the stars lighting up the heavens. But there followed a sight to cheer their hearts and thrill their souls. Away off to their right, and reaching skyward, Lookout Mountain was ablaze with the fires of Hooker's men, while off to their left, and reaching far above the valley, the north end of Missionary Ridge was aflame with the lights of Sherman's army. The great iron crescent that had, with threatening aspect, so long hung over them, was disappearing. The only thought that dampened their enthusiasm was that the enemy was being destroyed on the flanks, while they were tied down in the center, without a part in the victories. But late that night General Grant, thinking that General Sherman had carried Tunnel Hill, and acting in that belief, gave orders for the next day's battle. General Sherman was directed to attack the enemy at early dawn, Thomas to co-operate with him, and Hooker, to be ready to advance into Chattanooga Valley, to hold the road that zigzagged from the valley to the summit.

Early the next morning, when General Grant learned that the ridge had not been carried as far as Tunnel Hill, and that Lookout Mountain had been evacuated by the enemy, he suspended his orders, except those to Sherman, and directed Hooker to come down from the mountain, to carry the pass at Rossville, and then operate on Bragg's left and rear. Bragg's army was now concentrated on Missionary Ridge, and in the valley at the east foot. Cheatham's and Stevenson's divisions had been withdrawn from Lookout Mountain on the night of the 24th, and, marching all night, were seen at dawn the next morning moving along the summit of Missionary Ridge, on the way to reënforce Bragg's right. For several hours after daylight the flowing of this steady stream of troops continued.

Early in the morning of the 25th General Grant and General Thomas established their headquarters on Orchard Knob, a point from which the best view of the movements of the whole army could be had. At sunrise General Sherman commenced his attack, but after repeated assaults and severe fighting, it appearing to be impossible for General Sherman to take the enemy's works, operations ceased early in the afternoon.

Meanwhile Hooker was detained three hours at Chattanooga Creek, while a bridge that the retreating enemy had burned was being rebuilt. As soon as he had taken Rossville, he moved against the south end of Missionary Ridge. The ridge was quickly carried, and, sweeping northward, Hooker soon came upon Stewart's division, posted on the summit, and behind the earth-works which the Army of the Cumberland had thrown up the day after Chickamauga. Cruft's division assaulted and carried the works, thus having the good fortune of retaking the works they themselves had constructed. It was by this time nearly sundown. Hooker reached the south end of the ridge too late in the day to relieve the pressure on Sherman, who was at the north end six miles off. Bragg's right had not been turned. Success had not followed Sherman's movement. The battle as planned had not been won.

Late on this memorable afternoon there was an accident—an accident like the charge at Balaklava; though, unlike this theme for poetry, it called for greater daring, and was attended by complete success, and yielded most important results, for it led to the complete shattering of the enemy's army, and drove him from the field. On Orchard Knob, and opposite the center of Missionary Ridge, were four divisions of the Army of the Cumberland. On the left was Baird's division; then Wood's and Sheridan's divisions occupying the lines which, two days before, they had taken in their magnificent advance; on the right was R. W. Johnson's division,—all under the personal command of Thomas. It was past 3 o'clock. General Sherman had ceased operations. General Hooker's advance had not yet been felt. The day was dying, and Bragg still held the ridge. If any movement to dislodge him was to be made that day it must be made at once. At half-past three o'clock an attack was ordered by General Grant. He had changed his plan of battle. At once orders were issued that at the firing, in rapid succession, of six guns on Orchard Knob, Thomas's whole line should instantaneously move forward, Sheridan's and Wood's division in the center, Sheridan to be supported on the right by Johnson, and Wood on the left by Baird. This demonstration was to be made to relieve the pressure on Sherman. The only order given was to move forward and take the rifle-pits at the foot of the ridge. In Sheridan's division the order was, "As soon as the signal is given, the whole line will advance, and you will take what is before you."

Between Orchard Knob and Missionary Ridge was a valley, partly covered with a small growth of timber. It was wooded in front of the right of Baird's and of the whole of Wood's division. In front of Sheridan's and Johnson's it had been almost entirely cleared. At the foot of the ridge were heavy rifle-pits, which could be seen from Orchard Knob, and extending in front of them, for four and five hundred yards, the ground was covered with felled trees. There was a good plain for both direct and enfilading fire from the rifle-pits, and the approaches were commanded by the enemy's artillery. At this point the ridge is five or six hundred feet high. Its side, scored with gullies and showing but little timber, had a rough and bare appearance. Half-way up was another line of rifle-pits, and the summit was furrowed with additional lines and dotted over with epaulements, in which were placed fifty pieces of artillery. Directly in front of Orchard Knob, and on the summit of the ridge, in a small house, was Bragg's headquarters.

At twenty minutes before four the signal-guns were fired. Suddenly twenty thousand men rushed forward, moving in line of battle by brigades, with a double line of skirmishers in front, and closely followed by the reserves in mass. The big siege-guns in the Chattanooga forts roared above the light artillery and musketry in the valley. The enemy's rifle-pits were ablaze, and the whole ridge in our front had broken out like another Ætna. Not many minutes afterward our men were seen working through the felled trees and other obstructions. Though exposed to such a terrific fire, they neither fell back nor halted. By a bold and desperate push they broke through the the works in several places and opened flank and reverse fires. The enemy was thrown into confusion, and took precipitate flight up the ridge. Many prisoners and a large number of small-arms were captured. The order of the commanding general had now been fully and most successfully carried out. But it did not go far enough to satisfy these brave men, who thought the time had come to finish the battle of Chickamauga. There was a halt of but a few minutes, to take breath and to re-form lines; then, with a sudden impulse, and without orders, all started up the ridge. Officers, catching their spirit, first followed, then led. There was no thought of supports or of protecting flanks, though the enemy's line could be seen, stretching on either side.

As soon as this movement was seen from Orchard Knob, Grant quickly turned to Thomas, who stood by his side, and I heard him say angrily: "Thomas, who ordered those men up the ridge?"

Thomas replied, in his usual slow, quiet manner: "I don't know; I did not." Then, addressing General Gordon Granger, he said, "Did you order them up, Granger?"

"No," said Granger; "they started up without orders. When those fellows get started all hell can't stop them."

General Grant said something to the effect that somebody would suffer if it did not turn out well, and then, turning, stoically watched the ridge. He gave no further orders.

As soon as Granger had replied to Thomas, he turned to me, his chief-of-staff, and said: "Ride at once to Wood, and then to Sheridan, and ask them if they ordered their men up the ridge, and tell them, if they can take it, to push ahead." As I was mounting, Granger added: "It is hot over there, and you may not get through. I shall send Captain Avery to Sheridan, and other officers after both of you." As fast as my horse could carry me, I rode first to General Wood, and delivered the message. "I didn't order them up," said Wood; "they started up on their own account, and they are going up, too! Tell Granger, if we are supported, we will take and hold the ridge!"

As soon as I reached General Wood, Captain Avery got to General Sheridan, and delivered his message. "I didn't order them up," said Sheridan; "but we are going to take the ridge!" He then asked Avery for his flask and waved it at a group of Confederate officers, standing just in front of Bragg's headquarters, with the salutation, "Here's at you!" At once two guns—the "Lady Breckinridge" and the "Lady Buckner"—in front of Bragg's headquarters were fired at Sheridan and the group of officers about him. One shell struck so near as to throw dirt over Sheridan and Avery. "Ah!" said the general, "that is ungenerous; I shall take those guns for that!"

Before Sheridan received the message taken by Captain Avery, he had sent a staff-officer to Granger, to inquire whether "the order given to take the rifle-pits meant the rifle-pits at the base, or those on the top of the ridge." Granger told this officer that "the order given was to take those at the base." Conceiving this to be an order to fall back, the officer, on his way to Sheridan, gave it to General Wagner, commanding the Second Brigade of the division, which was then nearly half-way up the ridge. Wagner ordered his brigade back to the rifle-pits at the base, but it only remained there till Sheridan, seeing the mistake, ordered it forward. It again advanced under a terrific fire.

The men, fighting and climbing up the steep hill, sought the roads, ravines, and less rugged parts. The ground was so broken that it was impossible to keep a regular line of battle. At times their movements were in shape like the flight of migratory birds—sometimes in line, sometimes in mass, mostly in V-shaped groups, with the points toward the enemy. At these points regimental flags were flying, sometimes dropping as the bearers were shot, but never reaching the ground, for other brave hands were there to seize them. Sixty flags were advancing up the hill. Bragg was hurrying large bodies of men from his right to the center. They could be seen hastening along the ridge. Cheatham's division was being withdrawn from Sherman's front. Bragg and Hardee were at the center, urging their men to stand firm and drive back the advancing enemy, now so near the summit—indeed, so near that the guns, which could not be sufficiently depressed to reach them, became useless. Artillerymen were lighting the fuses of shells, and bowling them by hundreds down the hill.

The critical moment arrived when the summit was just within reach. At six different points, and almost simultaneously, Sheridan's and Wood's divisions broke over the crest,—Sheridan's first, near Bragg's headquarters; and in a few minutes Sheridan was beside the guns that had been fired at him, and claiming them as captures of his division. Baird's division took the works on Wood's left almost immediately afterward; and then Johnson came up on Sheridan's right. The enemy's guns were turned upon those who still remained in the works, and soon all were in flight down the eastern slope. Baird got on the ridge just in time to change front and oppose a large body of the enemy moving down from Bragg's right to attack our left. After a sharp engagement, that lasted till dark, he drove the enemy back beyond a high point on the north, which he at once occupied.

The sun had not yet gone down, Missionary Ridge was ours, and Bragg's army was broken and in flight!

—FULLERTON, "The Army of the Cumberland at Chattanooga"

C. "AMID THE DIN OF BATTLE 'CHICKAMAUGA' COULD BE HEARD"

Chattanooga, Dec. 7, 1863

Dear wife: . . .On Monday, Nov. 23rd our Division was ordered to move out just in front of the fortifications. We did so, and the rebels, as they looked down on us from Lookout Mountain and Mission Ridge, no doubt thought we had come out for a review. But Sheridan's Division followed us out and formed in line with us. Wonder what the rebels thought then? "Oh, a Yankee review; we'll have some fun shelling them directly." But out came Wood's Division, then Cruft's Division, then Johnson's Division, then Howard's entire Corps of "Potomacs." "What can those Yankee fools mean," Bragg must have thought, as he sat at the door of his tent on Mission Ridge and watched the long lines of blue coats and glistening guns marching around in the valley below him, almost within gun shot of his pickets, and yet not a gun fired. All was peace in Chattanooga valley that day.

The sun shone brightly, the bands played stirring airs; tattered banners that had waved on battle fields from the Potomac to the Mississippi streamed out gaily, as if proud of the battle scars they wore. Generals Grant and Hooker, and Sherman and Thomas and Logan and Reynolds and Sheridan and scores of others, with their staffs, galloped along the lines, and the scene that spread out around me like a vast panorama of war filled my heart with pride that I was a soldier and member of that great army. But what did it all mean? Bragg, from his mountain eyrie, could see what we were doing just as well as Grant who was riding around amongst us. The rebels thought they had us hemmed in so that we dared not move, and so near starved that we could not move. Two o'clock came, and all was yet quiet and peaceful, gay as a holiday review; we could see crowds of rebels watching us from Mission Ridge and Lookout Mountain, but three o'clock came, and a solitary shot away over on our left, among Wood's men, made every fellow think: "Hark"! A few moments and another shot, then a rat-tat-tat-tat made almost every one remark: "Skirmishing going on over there." Wood's line moved forward, a few volleys, still Wood's line moved forward, and Sheridan's started forward, heavy work for a few minutes then all was quiet; two important hills were gained; cheer after cheer rang out in the valley and echoed and reverberated through the gorges of Lookout and Mission Ridge; still it was only 5 o'clock Monday afternoon. The bands commenced playing and the valley was again peaceful, but we all knew there was "something up," and Bragg must have thought so too. We lay there all night, sleeping on our arms.

Tuesday, morning, Nov. 24th, broke bright and beautiful; the sun rose clear; but for whom was it a "sun of Austerlitz"? Grant or Bragg? We talked of Austerlitz and Waterloo at headquarters that morning. During the night the moon was almost totally eclipsed. We talked of that also. It was considered a bad omen among the ancients, on the eve of battle; we concluded also that it was ominous of defeat, but not for us; we concluded that it meant Bragg because he was perched on the mountain top, nearest the moon. Daylight revealed the hills which Wood and Sheridan had won the day before, bristling with cannon of sufficient calibre to reach Bragg's eyrie on Mission Ridge. About 9 o'clock in the morning some 30 heavy guns opened on Mission Ridge. It appeared then that we were to advance right down the valley and attack the rebel centre, but, hark! Away off on our right—3 miles away, on the opposite side of Lookout—we hear firing. What can that mean? Suddenly the cannon, with which we have been pounding away at Mission Ridge, are silent, and all eyes are turned westward toward Lookout Mountain. The sounds of battle increase there but it is on the other side of the mountain from us and we can see nothing, but the word passes around: "Hooker is storming Lookout"! My heart grows faint. Poor Hooker, with his Potomac boys are to be the forlorn hope! What? Storm that mountain peak 2400 feet high, so steep that a squirrel could scarcely climb it, and bristling all over with rebels, bayonets and cannon? Poor boys! far from your quiet New England homes, you have come a long way only to meet defeat on that mountain peak, and find your graves on its rugged sides! Lookout Mountain will only hereafter be known as a monument to a whole Corps of gallant New Englanders who died there for their country! But hold! Some one exclaims: "The firing comes nearer, our boys are getting up"! All eyes are turned toward the Mountain, and the stillness of death reigns among us in the valley, as we listen to the sounds of battle on the other side of the Mountain while all was quiet as a Puritan sabbath on our side of it. How hope and despair alternated in our breasts! How we prayed for their success and longed to assist them, can only be known by those of us who, in that valley, stood watching that afternoon and listening to the swelling diapason of their battle. But the firing actually did grow nearer, manifestly our men were driving them; Oh! now if they only can continue it, but we fear they cannot! I have a long telescope with which I can distinctly see everything on our side of the mountain. I scan the mountain with it closely and continuously, but not a soul can I see. After hours of anxious suspense I see a single rebel winding his way back from the firing and around to our side of the mountain.

I announce to the crowd of Generals standing around: "There goes a straggler"! and in an instant everybody's glass is to his eye, but no more stragglers are seen, still the battle rages, and the little gleam of hope, that solitary straggler raised in our breasts, dies out. Minutes drag like hours, the suspense is awful, but look! look! Here comes a crowd of stragglers! here they come by hundreds, yes by thousands! The mountain is covered with them! They are broken, running! There comes our flag around the point of the mountain! There comes one of our regiments on the double quick! Oh! such a cheer as then went up in the valley! Manly cheeks were wet with tears of joy, our bands played "Hail to the Chief," and 50 brazen throated cannon, in the very wantonness of joy, thundered out from the fortifications of Chattanooga, a salute to the old flag which was then on the mountain top. The work was done. Lookout was ours, never again to be used as a perch by rebel vultures. Didn't we of the old Army of the Cumberland feel proud though? It was one of the regiments that fought at Chickamauga that carried that first flag to the mountain top. It was a brigade of the old Chickamauga army that led the storming party up the mountain. A straggling skirmish fire was kept up along our (the Eastern) side of the mountain, which we could trace by the flashes of the guns, until 11 o'clock at night, but then all became quiet, and again we passed the night in line of battle, sleeping on our arms.

Bragg, no doubt, thought Hooker would continue to press forward across the valley from Lookout and attack his left on Mission Ridge in the morning, so he prepared for that during the night, by moving troops from his right to his left, to meet the anticipated attack of the morning, but Sherman, with his Vicksburg veterans, had all this time been lying concealed behind the hills on the North side of the Tenessee river, just North of the northern end of Mission Ridge, where Bragg's right was, awaiting the proper moment to commence his part of the stupendous plan. The time was now come.

Lookout was ours; now for Mission Ridge! Before daylight of Wednesday Nov. 25th, Sherman had his pontoons across the river, about 3 miles north of Chattanooga, and under cover of a dense fog, crossed his whole Corps and took possession of the northern extremity of Mission Ridge, finding nothing there but a few pickets, and there he fell to work fortifying. By this time

Bragg saw his mistake. The attack of Wednesday was to be on his right, at the North end of Mission Ridge, instead of his left at the South end of the Ridge, so he hurriedly countermarched his troops back from his left to his right. When the fog rose, about ten o'clock in the morning, Sherman attempted to carry the summit of the Ridge but was repulsed; again he tried it but was again repulsed, still again he tried it and was repulsed. This time the fighting was all to the left of where we were instead of to the right, as it had been the day before. Sherman, after terrible fighting, had been repulsed in three successive efforts to crush the enemy's right on the top of the Ridge, and an order came for our Division to move up the river to his support. We started. The enemy could see us from the top of the Ridge, and quickly understood (or thought they did) our design, so they commenced shelling us, as our long line of 20 regiments filed along, but we moved along until we came to where a thin strip of woodland intervened between us and the Ridge. Sheridan's Division followed us and did the same. The enemy supposed of course that we were moving on up the river to the support of Sherman, but we were not; we halted and formed line of battle in that strip of woodland, facing Mission Ridge.

This, I confess, staggered me; I couldn't understand it; it looked as though we were going to assault the Ridge, and try to carry it by storm, lined and ribbed as it was with rifle pits, and its topmost verge crowded with rebel lines, and at least 40 cannon in our immediate front frowning down on us; we never could live a moment in the open spaces of 600 yards between the strip of woods in which we were formed, and the line of rifle pits at the base of the mountain, exposed as we would be to the fire of the 40 cannon massed, and from five to eight hundred feet immediately above us, also to the infantry fire from the rifle pits. I rode down along the line of our Division, and there I found Woods Division formed on our right and facing the Ridge just as we were; I rode on and came to Sheridan's Division formed on Woods right and facing the same. Here was a line of veteran troops nearly two miles long, all facing Mission Ridge, and out of sight of the enemy. The purpose at once became plain to me, and I hurried back to my own Division, and on asking Gen. —— he replied: "When 6 guns are fired in quick succession from Fort Wood, the line advances to storm the heights and carry the Ridge if possible. Take that order to Col. ——" (commanding the third brigade of our Division) "and tell him to move forward rapidly when he hears the signal." I communicated the order at once and that was the last I saw of the brigade commander, for he was killed just as he reached the summit of the Ridge.

A few moments elapse, it is about half past three o'clock P.M., when suddenly, 6 guns are rapidly fired from Fort Wood. "Forward"! rings out along that long line of men, and forward they go, through the strip of woods, we reach the open space, say 600 yards, between the edge of the woods and the rifle pits at the foot of the Ridge. "Charge"! is shouted wildly from hundreds of throats, and with a yell such as that valley never heard before, the three Divisions (60 regiments) rushed forward; the rebels are silent a moment, but then the batteries on top of the Ridge, open all at once, and the very heavens above us seemed to be rent asunder; shells go screaming over our heads, bursting above and behind us, but they hurt nobody and the men don't notice them; about midway of the open space a shell bursts directly over my head, and so near as to make my horse frantic and almost unmanageable; he plunges and bursts breast strap and girth and off I tumble with the saddle between my legs. My orderly catches my horse at once, throws the blanket and saddle on him, gives me a "leg lift" and I am mounted again, without girth, but I hold on with my knees and catch up with our madcaps at the first rifle pits, over these we go to the second line of pits, over these we go, some of the rebels lying down to be run over, others scrambling up the hill which is becoming too steep for horses, and the General and staff are forced to abandon the direct ascent at about the second line of rifle pits; the long line of men reach the steepest part of the mountain, and they must crawl up the best way they can 150 feet more before they reach the summit, and when they do reach it, can they hold it? The rebels are there in thousands, behind breastworks, ready to hurl our brave boys back as they reach their works.

One flag bearer, on hands and knees, is seen away in advance of the whole line; he crawls and climbs toward a rebel flag he sees waving above him, he gets within a few feet of it and hides behind a fallen log while he waves his flag defiantly until it almost touches the rebel flag; his regiment follows him as fast as it can; in a few moments another flag bearer gets just as near the summit at another point, and his regiment soon gets to him, but these two regiments dare not go the next twenty feet or they would be annihilated, so they crouch there and are safe from the rebels above them, who would have to rise up, to fire down at them, and so expose themselves to the fire of our fellows who are climbing up the mountain.

The suspense is greater, if possible, than that with which we viewed the storming of Lookout. If we can gain that Ridge; if we can scale those breastworks, the rebel army is routed, everything is lost for them, but if we cannot scale the works few of us will get down this mountain side and back to the shelter of the woods. But a third flag and regiment reaches the other two; all eyes are turned there; the men away above us look like great ants crawling up, crouching on the outside of the rebel breastworks. One of our flags seems to be moving; look! look! look! Up! Up! Up! it goes and is planted on the rebel works; in a twinkling the crouching soldiers are up and over the works; apparently quicker than I can write it the 3 flags and 3 regiments are up, the close fighting is terrific; other flags go up and over at different points along the mountain top—the batteries have ceased, for friend and foe are mixed in a surging mass; in a few moments the flags of 60 Yankee regiments float along Mission Ridge from one end to the other, the enemy are plunging down the Eastern slope of the Ridge and our men in hot pursuit, but darkness comes too soon and the pursuit must cease; we go back to the summit of the Ridge and there behold our trophies—dead and wounded rebels under our feet by hundreds, cannon by scores scattered up and down the Ridge with yelling soldiers astraddle them, rebel flags lying around in profusion, and soldiers and officers completely and frantically drunk with excitement. Four hours more of daylight, after we gained that Ridge would not have left two whole pieces of Bragg's army together.

Our men, stirred by the same memories, shouted "Chickamauga"! as they scaled the works at the summit, and amid the din of battle the cry "Chickamauga"! "Chickamauga"! could be heard. That is not *fancy* it is *fact*. Indeed the plain unvarnished facts of the storming of Mission Ridge are more like romance to me now than any I have ever read in Dumas, Scott or Cooper. On that night I lay down upon the ground without blankets and slept soundly, without inquiring whether my neighbors were dead or alive, but, on waking found I was sleeping among bunches of dead rebels and Federals, and within a few rods of where Bragg slept the night before, if he slept at all.

—"Major Connolly's Letters to His Wife"

8. "THE DISASTER ADMITS OF NO PALLIATION"

Poor Braxton Bragg! He had come out of the Mexican War with a great reputation, he had won Jefferson Davis' admiration and confidence, as early as February 1861 he had been commissioned brigadier general in the new Confederate Army. But he was stiff-necked, arrogant, and quarrelsome, unpopular alike with officers and with rank and file. Victories might have made these traits bearable, but Bragg could not win victories or—if he did, as at Chickamauga—could not exploit them. After Chattanooga he asked to be relieved of his command; Davis brought him back to Richmond as military advisor.

Headquarters Army of Tennessee
Dalton, Ga., December 1, 1863

His Excellency, JEFFERSON DAVIS,
President Confederate States, Richmond:

Mr. President: I send by Lieutenant Colonel Urquhart a plain, unvarnished report of the operations at Chattanooga, resulting in my shameful discomfiture. The disaster admits of no palliation, and is justly disparaging to me as a commander. I trust, however, you may find upon full investigation that the fault is not entirely mine. Colonel Urquhart will inform you on any point not fully explained in the report. I fear we both erred in the conclusion for me to retain command here after the clamor raised against me. The warfare has been carried on successfully, and the fruits are bitter. You must make other changes here, or our success is hopeless. Breckinridge was totally unfit for any duty from the 23rd to the 27th—during all our trials—from drunkenness. The same cause prevented our complete triumph at Murfreesborough. I can bear to be sacrificed myself, but not to see my country and my friends ruined by the vices of a few profligate men who happen to have an undue popularity. General Hardee will assure you that Cheatham is equally dangerous.

May I hope, as a personal favor, that you will allow my friend Colonel Urquhart to continue with me as a part of my personal staff? He has never acted in any other capacity, and is almost a necessity in enabling me to bring up my records. I shall ever be ready to do all in my power for our common cause, but feel that some little rest will render me more efficient than I am now.

Most respectfully and truly, yours,

BRAXTON BRAGG,
General, &c.
—*War of the Rebellion . . . Official Records*

9. BURNSIDE HOLDS OUT AT KNOXVILLE

Everywhere in the West that fall and winter of 1863 saw Confederate fortunes wane. While Rosecrans was organizing his army for the Tullahoma campaign, Burnside led the Army of the Ohio into East Tennessee. The purpose of his campaign was both military and political: to cut the railroad connection between Tennessee and Virginia, and to rescue the loyal Unionists of the mountainous region of eastern Tennessee. Bragg promptly sent a corps, under General Buckner, to contest this area with him, and later sent reinforcements under Longstreet. Burnside withdrew into the fortifications of Knoxville and there awaited attack.

What happened is here told by Major Burrage of the 35th Massachusetts Volunteers. Henry S. Burrage was a student at the Newton Theological Seminary when the war broke out. He enlisted as a private and rose to a majority; he fought in Tennessee, was wounded at Cold Harbor, and captured at Petersburg. After the war he had a long and distinguished career as clergyman and historian.

ON November 13, Burnside received information that Longstreet had reached the Tennessee River at Hough's Ferry, a few miles below Loudon; and at once informing General Grant, he advised a concentration of his forces in East Tennessee for the purpose of giving battle, but expressed the opinion that the concentration should be neither in the neighborhood of Loudon nor at Kingston, but at Knoxville; thus drawing the enemy further away from Bragg, so far in fact that in case Bragg should order Longstreet to return because his assistance was needed at Chattanooga, he could not be recalled in season to render it. To this General Grant made reply: "It is of the most vital importance that East Tennessee should be held. Take immediate steps to that end. Evacuate Kingston if you think best."

Thrown thus upon his own resources, General Burnside's plan plainly was this—to draw Longstreet up the valley, checking his advance as much as possible and making Knoxville as secure as the circumstances would admit, until Grant, having grappled with Bragg at Chattanooga, should be able to send reënforcements compelling Longstreet to withdraw. . . .

At the time of the arrival of the troops on the morning of November 17, Knoxville was by no means in a defensible condition. The bastion-work occupied by Benjamin's and Buckley's batteries was not only unfinished, but was little more than begun. It required the labor of two hundred Negroes four hours to clear a place for the guns. There was also a fort in process of construction on Temperance Hill. But the work all along the line was now hurried forward with eagerness and even enthusiasm. As fast as the troops were placed in position, they commenced the construction of rifle-pits in their front, but with only a meagre supply of either spades or shovels. Though wearied by three days of marching and fighting, the troops gave themselves to the work with the energy of fresh men. As helpers, both citizens and contrabands were pressed into the service. Many of the former were loyal to the Union cause and devoted themselves to their tasks with a zeal that evinced the interest they felt in making good the defence of the town; but some of them were bitter rebels, and, as Captain Poe well remarked, "worked with a very poor grace, which blistered hands did not tend to improve." The contrabands engaged in the work with that heartiness which throughout the war characterized their labors for the Union cause. . . .

Longstreet did not leave Campbell's Station until the morning of November 17. McLaws' division led the column, and reached the vicinity of Knoxville about noon. General Burnside had ordered General Shackelford to dismount his cavalry command under General Sanders and take position on the Kingston Road a mile or more in front of the Union line of defence on that side of Knoxville. This he did, and during the forenoon of the 17th General Sanders strengthened his position in all possible ways, so that when McLaws approached, he found Sanders' little force blocking his further progress. "Part of our line," says Longstreet, "drove up in fine style and was measurably successful, but other parts, smarting under the stiff musket-fire, hesitated and lay down under such slight shelter as they could find, but close under fire,—so close that to remain inactive would endanger repulse." With such stubbornness did General Sanders contest the approach of McLaws that the latter was compelled at length to bring up his artillery; and only by the combined assault of infantry and artillery was Sanders dislodged from his position. After his men fell back, the enemy pressed forward and established lines within rifle range of our own. McLaws' division formed the Confederate right, his right extending to the river. When Jenkins came up late in the afternoon, he continued the line from McLaws' left and extending to the Tazewell Road; while Hart's and Wheeler's cavalry continued the Confederate line to the Holston River. . . .

Meanwhile Burnside's men were devoting themselves with all diligence to the labor of strengthening and completing their works around the town. For the most part, in campaigns hitherto, they had been the attacking party. So it had been at Fredericksburg, where the Ninth Corps had last faced Longstreet. Here, they were behind defensive works, and it was evident that they regarded the more advantageous position with contentment and even satisfaction. When the main line had been made reasonably secure, the usual devices in the way of obstruction received attention, such as the construction of abatis, chevaux-de-frise, to which were added wire entanglements extending from the stumps of trees, especially in front of Fort Sanders. Along a portion of the line another obstacle was formed by erecting dams on First and Second creeks, and throwing back the water. The whole constituted a series of obstructions which could not be passed in the face of a heavy fire without great difficulty and a fearful loss of life. On November 21, General Burnside telegraphed to General Grant: "We have a reasonable supply of ammunition, and the command is in good spirits. The officers and men have been indefatigable in their labors to make this place impregnable."

But the question of food-supplies was a serious one. When the siege commenced, there was in the commissary department at Knoxville little more than a day's ration for the whole of Burnside's force. Should the enemy gain possession of the south bank of the Holston, the means of subsistence for the troops at Knoxville would be cut off. Thus far Longstreet's attempts to close this part of East Tennessee to the Union forces had failed, and the whole country from the French Board to the Holston was open to our foraging-parties. . . .

At length, foiled in these attempts to seize the south bank of the Holston, Longstreet commenced the construction of a raft at Boyd's Ferry, about six miles above Knoxville. Floating this down the swift current of the river, he hoped to carry away Burnside's pontoon-bridge and thus break his communication with the country from which he was obtaining his subsistence supplies. To thwart this plan, Captain Poe commenced the construction of a boom one thousand feet in length, composed of iron bars borne up by wooden floats. This was stretched across the river above the bridge. Afterwards a boom of logs, fastened end to end by chains, was constructed further up the river. This boom was fifteen hundred feet in length. . . .

November 23, in the evening, there was a Confederate attack on the Union pickets in front of the left of the Second Division, Ninth Corps. In falling back, the pickets fired the buildings on the abandoned ground to prevent their use by the enemy's sharpshooters. Among the buildings destroyed were the arsenal and the machine-shops near the railway station. The light of the blazing buildings illuminated the town. On the following day, November 24, the Twenty-first Massachusetts and Forty-eighth Pennsylvania, under the command of Lieutenant-Colonel Hawkes of the Twenty-first, charging the Confederate line at this point, drove it back and reoccupied the abandoned position. Early in the morning of the same day also, an attack was made by the Second Michigan—numbering one hundred and ninety-seven men—on the advanced parallel which the enemy had so constructed as to envelop the northwest bastion of Fort Sanders. The works were gallantly carried, but before the supporting columns could come up, the men of the Second Michigan were repulsed by Confederate reënforcements. The Union loss, amounting to sixty-seven, included Major Byington, commanding the Second Michigan, who was left on the field mortally wounded. In anticipation of an attack that night at some point on the Union intrenchments, orders were issued that neither officers nor men, on either the outer or inner lines, should sleep. . . .

November 27 all was quiet along the lines until evening, when cheers and the strains of band-music enlivened the enemy's camps. Had reënforcements arrived, or had Grant met with reverses at Chattanooga? . . . Colonel Giltner, with his cavalry from Virginia, had reported, the first of approaching additions to Longstreet's command. As yet no word had come from Bragg to Longstreet, though there were rumors that a battle had been fought at Chattanooga. The brigades of Johnson were not yet up, and the artillery and infantry coming from Virginia were a five or six days' march away; but General Leadbetter was impatient, and an order was given by Longstreet for an assault on Fort Sanders on November 28. The weather on that day, however, proved unfavorable.

Within the Union lines it was believed that the crisis of the siege was approaching. . . . On the night of the 27th, on our left we could hear chopping across the Holston on the knob which a few days before, as Longstreet tells us, had been selected as commanding the fort and the line from the fort to the river. His men were now clearing away the trees in front of the earthwork they had constructed at that point. Would they attack at daybreak? So we thought, connecting the chopping sounds with the sound of cheering and of music in the earlier part of the night; but the morning opened as quietly as any of its predecessors. Late in the afternoon the enemy seemed to be placing troops in position in front of our lines covering Fort Sanders; and our men stood in the trenches awaiting an attack. The day passed, however, without further demonstrations.

The regiment with which I was connected was in the line between Fort Sanders and the river, and opposite the Powell house. About eleven o'clock in the evening there was a sound of heavy musketry on our right. It was a dark, cloudy night; and at the distance of only a few feet it was impossible to distinguish any object. The firing soon ceased, with the exception of an occasional shot on the picket-line. An attack had evidently been made at some point, but precisely where, or with what success, was as yet unknown. Reports soon came in. The enemy first had driven in the pickets in front of Fort Sanders, and then had attacked our line still further to the left, which also was obliged to fall back. Later we learned that the enemy had advanced along the whole line and established themselves as near as possible to our works.

It was now evident that Longstreet intended to make an attack at some point in our intrenched position. But where? All the remainder of that long, cold night—our men were without overcoats largely—we stood in the trenches pondering that question. Might not this demonstration in front of Fort Sanders be only a feint designed to draw our attention from other parts of the line where the principal blow was to be struck? So some thought. Gradually the night wore away.

In the morning, a little after six o'clock, but while it was still dark, the enemy opened a furious fire of artillery. This was directed mostly against Fort Sanders; but several shells struck the Powell house in rear of Battery Noble. Roemer immediately responded from College Hill, but Benjamin and

Buckley in Fort Sanders reserved their fire. In about twenty minutes the
enemy's fire slackened, and in its place rose the well-known rebel yell in front
of the fort. Then followed the rattle of musketry, the roar of cannon, and
the bursting of shells. The yells died away, and then rose again. Now the
roar of musketry and artillery was redoubled. It was a moment of the deepest
anxiety along our brigade front and to the right of the fort. Our straining
eyes were fixed upon the latter's dim outlines. The enemy had reached the
ditch and were now endeavoring to scale the parapet. Whose will be the
victory—oh whose? The yells again died away, and then followed three loud
Union cheers from our men in the fort—"Hurrah! hurrah! hurrah!" How
those cheers thrilled as we stood almost breathless in the trenches! They
told us in language that could not be misunderstood that Longstreet had been
repulsed and that the victory was ours. Peering through the morning mist
toward the fort only a short distance away—a glorious sight—we saw that
our flag was still there! . . .

The assault was made by three of McLaws' brigades,—Wofford's, Humphreys', and Bryan's,—with his fourth brigade in reserve. . . . In support
were the two brigades of Buckner's division commanded by General B. R.
Johnson,—they had arrived the day before,—and General Jenkins was ordered
to advance his three brigades in échelon on the left of McLaws. The brigades
were formed for attack in columns of regiments, and were directed to move
with fixed bayonets and without firing.

When the artillery fire slackened on that cold gray morning the order
for the charge was given. The salient of the northwest bastion of Fort
Sanders was the point of attack. McLaws' columns were much broken in
passing the abatis. But the wire entanglements proved a greater obstacle.
Whole companies were prostrated. Benjamin now opened his triple-shotted
guns. Nevertheless the weight of the attacking force carried the men forward, and in about two minutes from the time the charge was commenced
they had reached the ditch around the fort, and were endeavoring to scale
the parapet. The guns, which had been trained to sweep the ditch, now
opened a most destructive fire. Lieutenant Benjamin also took shells in his
hands and lighting the fuse tossed them over the parapet into the crowded
ditch. "It stilled them down," he said.

One of the Confederate reserve brigades, with added yells, now came up
in support, and in the crowded ditch the slaughter was renewed. With
desperate valor some of the men in the ditch endeavored to scale the parapet
and even planted their flags upon it, but were swept off by the muskets of
the Seventy-ninth New York (Highlanders) and of the Twenty-ninth Massachusetts. At length, satisfied of the hopelessness of their task, the survivors
in the ditch surrendered. They represented eleven regiments and numbered
nearly three hundred. Among them were seventeen commissioned officers.
Over two hundred dead and wounded, including three colonels, lay in the
ditch alone. . . . Our loss in the fort was eight men killed and five wounded,
a total of thirteen.

To us of the Ninth Corps, as well as to Longstreet's men, this assault on

Fort Sanders was Fredericksburg reversed. There, we were the attacking party. Now, we were behind a fortified line with artillery well placed, and we had an object-lesson as to the great advantage one has in a good position, strongly defended, over one who is in the attacking force. . . .

Never was a victory more complete and achieved at so slight a cost.

—BURRAGE, "Burnside's East Tennessee Campaign"

10. GENERAL MAURY DRAWS A PORTRAIT OF BEDFORD FORREST

Bedford Forrest was ubiquitous, and it is a bit difficult to know when to introduce him. He had enlisted, as a private, in 1861; when he raised his own battalion, at his own expense, he was appointed lieutenant colonel. He fought at Fort Donelson, and made good his escape; he fought with distinction at Shiloh. In July 1862 he began that career of cavalry raids which made him, in the end, the most effective Confederate officer in the West with the exception of Joseph E. Johnston himself. The whole area from Kentucky to the Gulf, and from the Mississippi to the mountains, was his theater, and throughout the last three years of the war he and his "critter company" dashed back and forth in Kentucky and Tennessee, Alabama and Mississippi, burning bridges, tearing up tracks, destroying supplies, and even—in April 1864— capturing Fort Pillow. During the period of Johnston's retreat to Atlanta Forrest was raiding widely in Tennessee, at one time reaching Paducah on the Ohio. He was in command of the Confederate cavalry during Hood's ill-fated Nashville campaign.

General Dabney H. Maury, nephew of the more famous Matthew Fontaine Maury, served as chief of staff to General Van Dorn and commander of the Gulf District in 1864-65.

WHEN the war broke out, Forrest was in the prime of his mental and physical powers. Over six feet in stature, of powerful frame, and of great activity and daring, with a personal prowess proved in many fierce encounters, he was a king among the bravest men of his time and country. He was among the first to volunteer when war broke out, and it was a matter of course that he should be the commander of the troopers who flocked to his standard. From the very outset he evinced his extraordinary capacity for war, and in his long career of great achievements no defeat or failure was ever charged to him.

When I first met him, the army of the West had been moved out of the lines about Corinth to offer battle to Halleck's forces, which was declined by that general. . . . I observed him with great interest, and felt the influence of his wonderful self-reliance. He could never brook the dictation of any commander, and he conceived and executed his own plans, moving when and where he saw work was to be done, and reporting only the successful result, which was always surprising to his enemy and to his commander. In all his long and arduous campaigns and scores of battles, he never was surprised or attacked. His successes were achieved with forces much inferior to his enemy. With unfailing daring and circumspection, he would make his tentative attack, or, as he expressed it, "I will give 'em a dare, anyhow." He was a great poker-player and illustrated some of its principles and technicalities upon the battle-field. When he found his enemy too strong for him at the point of attack, he would pull out and find a weak place, where he never failed to wade in and win his fight.

When once asked how it was he always succeeded in his battles, he replied, "I don't know, but I reckon it's because I always get there first with the most men." Unknowingly, he had announced and illustrated Napoleon's great principle of success in battle. When he found an enemy he could not attack with any hope of success, as was once the case with a strong block-house garrisoned with Negro troops and commanded by a stout-hearted Dutchman, who firmly declined to surrender and dared him to attack, he temporized and invited a parley. Forrest knew he could not carry the place without heavy loss, and that a large reinforcement was coming on the railroad to the enemy. In twenty minutes he convinced the stout-hearted colonel that he would certainly carry his works, and that if he had to do so he could not restrain his men, who would take no Negro prisoners, and the whole garrison was surrendered without firing a shot. Meantime he had sent a detachment down the road, derailed the train, and took in the reinforcements. . . .

When Forrest, with about twelve hundred men, set out in pursuit of Straight [Streight], he was more than a day behind him. Straight had several more men in the saddle than Forrest, and, being far in advance, could replace a broken-down horse by a fresh one from the farms through which his route lay, while Forrest, when he lost a horse, lost a soldier too; for no good horses were left for him. After a hot pursuit of five days and nights, during which he had lost two-thirds of his forces from broken-down horses, he overhauled his enemy and brought him to a parley. This conference took place in sight of a cut-off in the mountain road, Captain Morton and his horse artillery, which had been so long with Forrest, passing in sight along the road till they came to the cut-off, into which they would turn, re-entering the road out of view, so that it seemed that a continuous stream of artillery was passing by. Forrest had so arranged that he stood with his back to the guns, while Straight was facing them.

Forrest, in his characteristic way, described the scene to me. He said: "I seen him all the time we was talking looking over my shoulder and counting the guns. Presently he said, 'Name of God! How many guns have you got? There's fifteen I've counted already!'

"Turning my head that way, I said, 'I reckon that's all that has kept up.'

"Then he said, 'I won't surrender till you tell me how many men you've got.'

"I said, 'I've got enough to whip you out of your boots.'

"To which he said, 'I won't surrender.'

"I turned to my bugler and said, 'Sound to mount!'

"Then he cried out, 'I'll surrender!'

"I told him, 'Stack your arms right along there, Colonel, and march your men away down into that hollow.'

"When this was done," continued Forrest, "I ordered my men to come forward and take possession of the arms. When Straight saw they were barely four hundred, he did rave! demanded to have his arms back and that we should fight it out. I just laughed at him and patted him on the shoulder, and said, 'Ah, Colonel, all is fair in love and war, you know.' " . . .

When retreating, Forrest would often ride back some distance in the rear of his command, in order that he might reconnoitre the enemy for himself, and form his own estimates of his progress, etc. On one of these occasions, while crossing upper Georgia, he was galloping in haste to overtake his men, when an old woman came out of a house, and, waving her sunbonnet at him, called out, "Stop, you miserable coward! Stop and fight!" adding, as he hurried past, "If Forrest was here, he'd soon stop you!" . . .

Farragut was bombarding Fort Powell, with the intention, as I anticipated, of getting an army and fleet into Mobile Bay. Forrest telegraphed me in cipher to this effect: "The enemy has twenty-seven thousand men; has more cavalry than my whole force; I cannot check him, but with your permission will pass behind him into Memphis and destroy his stores, and thus compel him to retreat."

I replied: "Go, but come back quick. You are all I depend upon for the safety of north Mississippi."

It was more than a week before he moved. He then made a rapid march across to Oxford, and with his whole force drove back the enemy's advance, and at 4 P.M. Friday, dashed off to Memphis with two thousand horse and four guns. Saturday I first knew of his movements from the telegraph operator at Senatobia in about these words: "General Forrest has passed here at a gallop, bound for Memphis." At dawn, Sunday, came this: "Heavy cannon-firing about Memphis." He had marched ninety-four miles in thirty-six hours. Three rivers were out of their banks. He tore down houses and fences near by and bridged them and crossed his guns safely over. At crack of day, Sunday, he dashed into Memphis, and occupied the city. The commanding general fled in his night clothes from his bed, leaving his uniform, sword, etc., to the Confederates. The garrison of infantry threw themselves into the Irving Block, a strong building, from which they could not be dislodged without loss of many men. Forrest's object was fully accomplished by destroying stores and by spreading panic throughout the city, which was soon communicated by telegrams and couriers to the whole department and army of General A. J. Smith, who, on hearing that Forrest had occupied Memphis, threw up his hands, crying, "We are gone up!" and at once retreated out of Mississippi. Forrest drew his men out of the place, and by 4 P.M. was ready to go back to his own country. . . .

One evening we were sitting together in the veranda of my headquarters at Meridian, when his bodyguard came by on their way to water. I said, "General, that is a fine troop of men and horses."

"Yes, it is; and that captain is the eighth captain who has commanded it. The other seven have all been killed in battle!"

Such was the influence of his success and fame, that there were always daring applicants for vacancies in Forrest's bodyguard.

—MAURY, *Recollections of a Virginian*

From a painting by F. B. Carpenter

Lincoln Reading the Emancipation Proclamation

From mural by Hoffbauer, Courtesy of Virginia Historical Society

Lee and Some of His Lieutenants

XXVI

Atlanta and the March to the Sea

WITH Chattanooga in Federal hands and the Confederates in retreat, the way
was open to the east, and to the inauguration of that giant pincers movement
that in the end strangled the Confederacy. The Mississippi was under Federal control; in all the vast area between that river and the Appalachians only
Alabama and part of Mississippi was still held by the Confederates. What
Grant—now general of all the Union armies—planned for the spring of 1864
was a knockout blow: Meade to strike southward toward Richmond, Butler
to move up from the James River, Sigel to advance from western Virginia,
Sherman to capture Atlanta and "get into the interior of the enemy's country . . . inflicting all the damage you can against their war resources."

Sherman's march from Atlanta to the sea is probably the best known of
all Civil War campaigns—and it scarcely rose to the dignity of a campaign.
It was more nearly a glorified picnic, for Hardee, who took over the scattered
forces left in Georgia, was unable to offer any effective opposition. But the
campaign from Chattanooga to Atlanta was a different matter. It is just 100
miles between these two cities, a rugged mountainous country, crisscrossed
by rivers and valleys—poor country in which to subsist a large army. And
confronting Sherman was now Joseph E. Johnston, one of the most resourceful of all Confederate commanders, and a master of Fabian tactics.

After the debacle at Chattanooga Bragg had withdrawn to Dalton. There
he was supplanted by Johnston, who reorganized the stricken army, brought
its strength up to about 60,000, and infused it with a new fighting spirit.
Sherman, placed in command of the Grand Army of the West by Grant,
reorganized his forces into three unequal armies, commanded by Thomas,
Schofield, and McPherson. There was plenty of time for this reorganization:
winter had set in, the roads were churned into mud, and not until April
was Sherman ready to resume the offensive.

His advance was co-ordinated with Grant's offensive in the Wilderness,
and jumped off on May 7. From Dalton to Atlanta is about 85 miles. It took
Sherman two months to make that distance, and another two months to take
Atlanta. If this seems like a long time it should be remembered that Grant
enjoyed greater numerical superiority than Sherman, fought in less difficult
country and closer to his bases, and found himself at the end of four months
as far from Richmond as ever.

All the way from Dalton to Atlanta it was parry and thrust. Johnston
would get astride the railroad, or a valley; Sherman would slide around his

flank; threatened from the rear, Johnston would retire. Twice Sherman brought Johnston to battle, but both times on Johnston's terms, and both times was repulsed. Johnston was no Lee but he was the best retreater in either army. In the end the government, and public opinion, took alarm. Was Johnston going to give up Atlanta without a fight? So Davis feared, Davis who had never fully trusted him. Finally Johnston was removed from command and General Hood put in his place. A superb fighter, never happy except in battle, bearing his stump of a leg like a badge of honor, Hood was as impetuous as he was brave. He was expected to take the offensive, and he did. The results were disastrous. On September 1 Hood evacuated Atlanta. It was the first great Union victory of the year, and one that had important effects on the election that November.

What next? Where was Sherman to go? His communications were now stretched to the breaking point; Wheeler and Forrest operated in his rear. What he did was to get Grant's consent to abandon his communications and advance eastward into the heart of Georgia.

But meantime what of Hood? That general was no longer strong enough to oppose Sherman's mighty army. He decided, instead, to move westward and thus force Sherman either to return or lose Tennessee. His mind was bemused with even more ambitious plans. If Sherman marched eastward he would swing into Tennessee, reconquer Kentucky, and advance to the rescue of Lee!

But the day for all that was past. Sherman dispatched Thomas and Schofield back to Tennessee with forces which, eventually, aggregated about 50,000. And in due course of time, as we shall see, Thomas took care of Hood.

Meantime Sherman was marching to the sea. Never was such a march! If to Sherman's soldiers it was a picnic, to the Negroes it was the "day ob Jubilo."

> *How the darkeys shouted when they heard the joyful sound!*
> *How the turkeys gobbled which our commissary found!*
> *How the sweet potatoes even started from the ground,*
> *While we were marching through Georgia.*

But to the South it was such devastation and ruin as had never before been known in American warfare. Sherman cut through Georgia like a giant scythe, leaving a swath of ruined towns and plantations and railroads and bridges 60 miles wide. On December 10 he reached Savannah. He captured the city; swung north through South Carolina; burned Columbia; and continued on to the end.

1. GENERAL SHERMAN TAKES COMMAND

When Grant went to Washington to assume command of all the Union armies, he appointed Sherman to the command of the armies in the West. Though something was to be said for appointing Thomas to this position,

Sherman's claims were strong. It was not only that he had had a long and brilliant military career, but that, however unlike in character and temperament, he and Grant understood each other perfectly and worked together like a well-trained team. Indeed the great strategic plan for the destruction of the Confederacy, elaborated in the spring of 1864, was in all probability as much Sherman's as Grant's. After the war Sherman succeeded to Grant's position as commanding general of all the armies of the United States.

We have here two brief interpretations of Sherman by perspicacious observers. John Chipman Gray was barely out of the Harvard Law School when he was commissioned lieutenant in the 41st Massachusetts Volunteers. He served in the Peninsular campaign, and was then appointed judge advocate with the rank of major. He was later Story Professor of Law at the Harvard Law School and a lifelong student of the Civil War. Henry Hitchcock was another lawyer and law professor—the first dean of the St. Louis Law School. In 1863 he joined Sherman's staff, and accompanied the army on its March to the Sea.

A. "He Might Sit for a Portrait of an Ideal Yankee"

GENERAL Sherman is the most American looking man I ever saw, tall and lank, not very erect, with hair like a thatch, which he rubs up with his hands, a rusty beard trimmed close, a wrinkled face, sharp, prominent red nose, small, bright eyes, coarse red hands; black felt hat slouched over the eyes (he says when he wears anything else the soldiers cry out, as he rides along, "Hallo, the old man has got a new hat"), dirty dickey with the points wilted down, black, old-fashioned stock, brown field officer's coat with high collar and no shoulder-straps, muddy trowsers and one spur. He carries his hands in his pockets, is very awkward in his gait and motion, talks continually and with immense rapidity, and might sit to *Punch* for the portrait of an ideal Yankee. He was of course in the highest spirits and talked with an openness which was too natural not to be something more than apparent. In striving to recall his talk, I find it impossible to recall his language or indeed what he talked about, indeed it would be easier to say what he did not talk about than what he did. I never passed a more amusing or instructive day, but at his departure I felt it a relief and experienced almost an exhaustion after the excitement of his vigorous presence.

He has Savannah securely invested, his left rests securely on the Savannah River, his right at Fort McAllister, his line is within the 3 mile post from the city; he intends to throw a division across the Savannah to prevent the escape of Hardie [sic] from the city, and says he shall take his own time about reducing the city, unless he is hurried by despatches from General Grant; he has 60,000 men with him and only wishes there were more men in Savannah; he says the city is his sure game and stretches out his arm and claws his bony fingers in the air to illustrate how he has his grip on it. There is a "whip the creation" and an almost boastful confidence in himself which in an untried man would be very disgusting, but in him is intensely comic. I wish you could see him, he is a man after your own heart, like Grant he smokes constantly, and producing 6 cigars from his pocket said they were his daily allowance, but judging at the rate he travelled through them while he was on our boat, he must often exceed it. He scouted the idea of his going on ships and said he would rather march to Richmond than go there by water; he said he expected to turn North toward the latter end of December, at the same time the sun did, and that if he went through South Carolina, as he in all probability should, that his march through that state would be one of the most horrible things in the history of the world, that the devil himself could not restrain his men in that state; and I do not think that he (that is Sherman, not the devil) would try to restrain them much. He evidently purposes to make the South feel the horrors of war as much as he legitimately can, and if the men trespass beyond the strict limits of his orders he does not inquire into their cases too curiously. He told with evident delight how on his march he could look 40 miles in each direction and see the smoke rolling up as from one great bonfire.

—Letter of John Chipman Gray to John Ropes, December 14, 1864

B. "The Sort of Power Which a Flash of Lightning Suggests"

Pray don't think me likely to turn Boswell to any man's Johnson. My "chief" occupies a position and has already done things which certainly invest him with more than ordinary interest; and he impresses me as a man of power more than any man I remember. Not general intellectual power, not Websterian, but the sort of power which a flash of lightning suggests,—as clear, as intense, and as rapid. Yet with all his vigor, his Atlanta campaign showed, as his conversation and dispatches do, abundant caution and the most careful forethought.

Without any signs of arrogance, he has complete confidence in himself and—as he told me tonight he said to Grant at Vicksburg when the latter sent him out to beat off Jo Johnston's army advancing to raise the siege, warning him at the same time against J. as a most wily and dangerous adversary—"give me" said S., "men enough and time to look over the ground and I'm not afraid of the d—l." He had two days to reconnoitre and spent nearly forty hours of them in the saddle; when Johnston arrived the fords were left open for him to cross and attack—and he declined battle. The next step, as you may remember, was that Sherman pushed Johnston all the way to Jackson, and had finally to give up the chase for want of water, the rebels having spoiled all the ponds by driving cattle into them and shooting them there, and our men breaking down and giving out on the road from this cause and the summer heat. . . .

They may talk—the rebels and their friends—about "the brute Sherman," and to them while in arms against the Government they may be sure he will be nothing but a minister of wrath and vengeance, and of absolute destruction so far as the military power of the rebels and everything that is or can be used to maintain it is concerned. But as an individual and to individuals he is a straightforward, simple, kind-hearted, nay warm-hearted man, thoughtful and considerate of the feelings and scrupulously just and careful of the rights of others. I know this for I have already had unexpected opportunities of seeing it, in even trifling matters. His manner is off-hand, often almost blunt, but even in apparently harsh military measures there is often a reason not visible on the surface but founded in as much good feeling as good sense.

He ordered the establishment of an *"Indiana* State Sanitary Agent," opened in Atlanta after its fall, with a big sign hung out, etc., to be summarily closed, the goods turned over to the U. S. Quartermaster to be distributed among *all* the soldiers and strictly accounted for, and a sergeant and private whom the Agent had got detailed to keep shop for him while he went home to get more goods, were ordered back to duty. Presently came a peremptory dispatch from Secretary Stanton (based of course upon the Sanitary Agent's story of his wrongs) requiring a categorical answer as to what he did this for, and why the Agent of the State of Indiana was expelled from Atlanta, etc., etc.

"I told him why,"—said the General, relating the story to me—"told him I hadn't any *Indiana army* down there but a U. S. army—that I had already authorized two Sanitary Agents, one of the U. S. and one of the Western Sanitary Commission,—that I wasn't going to have any man come there to make distinctions among my men, and that while I was ready and willing to receive all anybody chose to give and would see that it was distributed fairly among them all *pro rata*, either among the well or the sick as they directed, I wouldn't have one man nursed because he was from Indiana and his next neighbor left to long and pine for what *he* couldn't get because he was from Ohio. And that was the last I ever heard from Mr. Secretary Stanton about the State Sanitary Agents."

Toujours perdrix, and I shall bore you with my *General*. But you see . . . precious little *here* is there to talk about else that is not contraband. I might describe my associates, but that would not be very interesting to you who never heard nor care to hear of them. I do not care to write about the signs of desolation one meets now and then,—sad but unavoidable necessities of war, for which the rebels and not we are responsible, and which will end at once whenever they lay down their arms, and neither can nor *ought* to end sooner. General Sherman is perfectly right,—the only possible way to end this unhappy conflict, in whose horrors, though he is Providentially a chief actor, no man is further from finding any pleasure, is to make it *terrible beyond endurance*.

I mean what I say, and now that I have shown my willingness to take my full share of all it involves,—Heaven knows not because I desire waste or desolation but because there is no other road to peace,—you must not find fault with me for saying so. Our enemies have shown themselves *devils* in the spirit which ever began this most unprovoked and inexcusable rebellion, and which animates its last utterance in Jeff. Davis' speech at Columbia, S. C., Oct. 4th,—and there is nothing for it but "to fight the devil with fire." Not with wanton barbarity nor with useless destruction; but it is neither barbarous nor useless but just and indispensable to utterly destroy everything, no matter whose, or what, or whom, that does or can uphold, sustain or encourage this gigantic crime. There is no peace else for this generation or the next.

—HITCHCOCK, "Letters and Diaries"

2. "THE STAR-SPANGLED BANNER" AT DALTON

After Chattanooga the Confederates retired to Dalton, where Johnston spent the winter reorganizing his stricken army. As there was no immediate danger of a Federal advance, many soldiers were furloughed home; others entertained themselves as best they could.

This reminiscence of winter quarters at Dalton comes from the Confederate Lieutenant L. D. Young of the Kentucky "Orphan Brigade."

WHO that spent the winter of '63-'64 at Dalton does not recall some circumstance or incident to remind him of the dreary "winter of discontent" spent in this mountain fastness of Northern Georgia? To many of us it seemed like an age, but withal it was a season of much needed rest and recuperation. Here in and around this little city flanked by majestic mountains, pondering over the disasters of Lookout and Missionary Ridge, we spent the time in comparative comfort and ease, some planning in mind the future campaign and its outcome, others indifferent as to the future and caring but little, willing to entrust all to those at the helm, and making the most of circumstances and the ever present, little thinking or caring for the great dangers and hardships that awaited us.

There was from the time we turned our faces Southward from Bowling Green to the very close of the war an air of indifference, a "devil may care," happy-go-lucky spirit, about these young Kentuckians that made them ready to cheerfully undertake any enterprise, no matter how dangerous or exacting the duty or perilous the undertaking. They had become so accustomed to all these things, and so thoroughly inured to hardships, that they felt themselves prepared for and rather coveted them, no matter how great or trying. While here we enjoyed more liberty and recreation than any time during or since the war began. Some of the men were furloughed and enjoyed a few days of rest with relatives and friends (if perchance they had any) in the South. The writer spent his in gay old Richmond on the James, in company with General Lewis, Captain McKendrie and other Kentuckians there assembled. All amused themselves as best they could in camp and town.

Drilling had been dispensed with—no need now for that, for in this we were perfect. Dress parade, guard mount and review were about the only exercises now required. A great sham battle broke the monotony once, and a snowball battle at another time was a diversion indulged for one day. A very pertinent question was often asked toward the close of the winter— "Who would command in the next campaign?" When at last it was given out that General Johnson would command, the spirits of the men revived and hope was again renewed. While contemplating the future, news came that the enemy were now moving Daltonward. We indulged the hope and wondered whether Sherman would undertake to force the pass in Rockyface Mountain through which the railroad and wagon road both ran. We thought of Leonidas and his Spartans and hoped for an opportunity to imitate and if possible to eclipse that immortal event at Thermopylae. But not so the wily Sherman. That "old fox" was too cunning to be caught in that or any other trap.

We were ordered out to meet him and took position in the gap and on the mountain, from which we could see extending for miles his grand encampment of infantry and artillery, the stars and stripes floating from every regimental brigade, division and corps headquarters and presenting the greatest panorama I ever beheld. Softly and sweetly the music from their bands as they played the national airs were wafted up and over the summit of the mountain. Somehow, some way, in some inexplicable and unseen manner, "Hail Columbia," "America" and "The Star Spangled Banner" sounded sweeter than I had ever before heard them, and filled my soul with feelings that I could not describe or forget. It haunted me for days, but never shook my loyalty to the Stars and Bars or relaxed my efforts in behalf of our cause.

—Young, *Reminiscences of the Orphan Brigade*

3. SHERMAN MARCHES FROM CHATTANOOGA TO ATLANTA

We begin our account of the Atlanta campaign with a general survey by its chief architect, then turn to some of its more striking episodes. There is no better account of the first phase of the campaign than that by Sherman himself. Different as Sherman was from Grant, his Memoirs have much the same qualities as those of Grant—simplicity, lucidity, and objectivity. Sherman is concerned to make clear, here, that the campaign for Atlanta was a very tough affair. He was fighting in difficult terrain, with long lines of communications, and against an able and resourceful opponent.

I NOW turn with a feeling of extreme delicacy to the conduct of that other campaign from Chattanooga to Atlanta, Savannah, and Raleigh, which with liberal discretion was committed to me by General Grant in his minute instructions of April 4th and April 19th, 1864. To all military students these letters must be familiar, because they have been published again and again, and there never was and never can be raised a question of rivalry or claim between us as to the relative merits of the manner in which we played our respective parts. We were as brothers—I the older man in years, he the higher in rank. We both believed in our heart of hearts that the success of the Union cause was not only necessary to the then generation of Americans, but to all future generations. We both professed to be gentlemen and professional soldiers, educated in the science of war by our generous Government for the very occasion which had arisen. Neither of us by nature was a combative man; but with honest hearts and a clear purpose to do what man could we embarked on that campaign, which I believe, in its strategy, in its logistics, in its grand and minor tactics, has added new luster to the old science of war. Both of us had at our front generals to whom in early life we had been taught to look up,—educated and experienced soldiers like ourselves, not likely to make any mistakes, and each of whom had as strong an army as could be collected from the mass of the Southern people,—of the same blood as ourselves, brave, confident, and well equipped; in addition to which they had the most decided advantage of operating in their own difficult country of mountain, forest, ravine, and river, affording admirable opportunities for defense, besides the other equally important advantage that we had to invade the country of our unqualified enemy and expose our long lines of supply to the guerrillas of an "exasperated people." Again, as we advanced we had to leave guards to bridges, stations, and intermediate depots, diminishing the fighting force, while our enemy gained strength by picking up his detachments as he fell back, and had railroads to bring supplies and reënforcements from his rear. I instance these facts to offset the common assertion that we of the North won the war by brute force, and not by courage and skill.

On the historic 4th day of May, 1864, the Confederate army at my front lay at Dalton, Georgia, composed, according to the best authority, of about 45,000 men, commanded by Joseph E. Johnston, who was equal in all the elements of generalship to Lee, and who was under instructions from the war powers in Richmond to assume the offensive northward as far as Nashville. But he soon discovered that he would have to conduct a defensive campaign. Coincident with the movement of the Army of the Potomac, as announced by telegraph, I advanced from our base at Chattanooga with the Army of the Ohio, 13,559 men; the Army of the Cumberland, 60,773, and the Army of the Tennessee, 24,465,—grand total, 98,797 men and 254 guns.

I had no purpose to attack Johnston's position at Dalton in front, but marched from Chattanooga to feign at his front and to make a lodgment in Resaca, eighteen miles to his rear, on "his line of communication and supply." The movement was partly, not wholly, successful; but it compelled Johnston to let go Dalton and fight us at Resaca, where, May 13th-16th, our loss was 2747 and his 2800. I fought offensively and he defensively, aided by earth parapets. He then fell back to Calhoun, Adairsville, and Cassville, where he halted for the battle of the campaign; but, for reasons given in his memoirs, he continued his retreat behind the next spur of mountains to Allatoona.

Pausing for a few days to repair the railroad without attempting Allatoona, of which I had personal knowledge acquired in 1844, I resolved to push on toward Atlanta by way of Dallas; Johnston quickly detected this, and forced me to fight him, May 25th-28th, at New Hope Church, four miles north of Dallas, with losses of 3000 to the Confederates and 2400 to us. The country was almost in a state of nature—with few or no roads, nothing that a European could understand; yet the bullet killed its victim there as surely as at Sevastopol.

Johnston had meantime picked up his detachments, and had received reënforcements from his rear which raised his aggregate strength to 62,000 men, and warranted him in claiming that he was purposely drawing us far from our base, and that when the right moment should come he would turn on us and destroy us. We were equally confident, and not the least alarmed. He then fell back to his position at Marietta, with Brush Mountain on his right, Kenesaw his center, and Lost Mountain his left. His line of ten miles was too long for his numbers, and he soon let go his flanks and concentrated on Kenesaw. We closed down in battle array, repaired the railroad up to our very camps, and then prepared for the contest. Not a day, not an hour, not a minute was there a cessation of fire. Our skirmishers were in absolute

FROM CHATTANOOGA TO ATLANTA

contact, the lines of battle and the batteries but little in rear of the skirmishers; and thus matters continued until June 27th, when I ordered a general assault, with the full coöperation of my great lieutenants, Thomas, McPherson, and Schofield, as good and true men as ever lived or died for their country's cause; but we failed, losing 3000 men, to the Confederate loss of 630. Still, the result was that within three days Johnston abandoned the strongest possible position and was in full retreat for the Chattahoochee River. We were on his heels; skirmished with his rear at Smyrna Church on the 4th day of July, and saw him fairly across the Chattahoochee on the 10th, covered and protected by the best line of field intrenchments I have ever seen, prepared long in advance. No officer or soldier who ever served under me will question the generalship of Joseph E. Johnston. His retreats were timely, in good order, and he left nothing behind. We had advanced into the enemy's country 120 miles, with a single-track railroad, which had to bring clothing, food, ammunition, everything requisite for 100,000 men and 23,000 animals. The city of Atlanta, the gate city opening the interior of the important State of Georgia, was in sight; its protecting army was shaken but not defeated, and onward we had to go,—illustrating the principle that "an army once on the offensive must maintain the offensive."

We feigned to the right, but crossed the Chattahoochee by the left, and soon confronted our enemy behind his first line of intrenchments at Peach Tree Creek, prepared in advance for this very occasion. At this critical moment the Confederate Government rendered us most valuable service. Being dissatisfied with the Fabian policy of General Johnston, it relieved him, and General Hood was substituted to command the Confederate army [July 18th]. Hood was known to us to be a "fighter," a graduate of West Point of the class of 1853, No. 44, of which class two of my army commanders, McPherson and Schofield, were No. 1 and No. 7. The character of a leader is a large factor in the game of war, and I confess I was pleased at this change, of which I had early notice. I knew that I had an army superior in numbers and *morale* to that of my antagonist; but being so far from my base, and operating in a country devoid of food and forage, I was dependent for supplies on a poorly constructed railroad back to Louisville, five hundred miles. I was willing to meet the enemy in the open country, but not behind well-constructed parapets.

Promptly, as expected, General Hood sallied from his Peach Tree line on the 20th of July, about midday, striking the Twentieth Corps (Hooker), which had just crossed Peach Tree Creek by improvised bridges. The troops became commingled and fought hand to hand desperately for about four hours, when the Confederates were driven back within their lines, leaving behind their dead and wounded. These amounted to 4796 men, to our loss of 1710. We followed up, and Hood fell back to the main lines of the city of Atlanta. We closed in, when again Hood, holding these lines with about one-half his force, with the other half made a wide circuit by night, under cover of the woods, and on the 22d of July enveloped our left flank "in air," a movement that led to the hardest battle of the campaign. He encountered the Army of the Tennessee,—skilled veterans who were always ready to fight, were not alarmed by flank or rear attacks, and met their assailants with heroic valor. The battle raged from noon to night, when the Confederates, baffled and defeated, fell back within the intrenchments of Atlanta. Their losses are reported 8499 to ours of 3641; but among these was McPherson, the commander of the Army of the Tennessee. Whilst this battle was in progress, Schofield at the center and Thomas on the right made efforts to break through the intrenchments at their fronts, but found them too strong to assault.

The Army of the Tennessee was then shifted, under its new commander (Howard), from the extreme left to the extreme right, to reach, if possible, the railroad by which Hood drew his supplies, when, on the 28th of July, he repeated his tactics of the 22d, sustaining an overwhelming defeat, losing 4632 men to our 700. These three sallies convinced him that his predecessor, General Johnston, had not erred in standing on the defensive. Thereafter the Confederate army in Atlanta clung to its parapets.

—SHERMAN, "The Grand Strategy of the War of the Rebellion"

4. JOHNSTON HALTS SHERMAN AT NEW HOPE CHURCH

Only rarely, and then when he thought his position peculiarly favorable, could Johnston afford the offensive. New Hope Church (May 25-28) was one of those occasions. Here—a few miles north of Dalton—Sherman tried to pass around Johnston's right. Johnston succeeded in stopping this, but at a cost of almost 3,000 men; nothing daunted, Sherman then slid off on Johnston's left and continued his advance.

Here Johnston himself describes the engagement at New Hope Church.

IN the mean time Jackson had given information of General Sherman's march toward the bridges near Stilesboro', and of the crossing of the leading Federal troops there on the 23d [May]. In consequence of this intelligence, Lieutenant-General Hardee was ordered to march that afternoon, by New Hope Church, to the road leading from Stilesboro', through Dallas, to Atlanta; and Lieutenant-General Polk to move to the same road, by a route farther to the left. Lieutenant-General Hood was instructed to follow Hardee on the 24th. . . . On the 25th the latter reached New Hope Church, early in the day. Intelligence was received from General Jackson's troops soon after, that the Federal army was near—its right at Dallas, and its line extending toward Alatoona.

Lieutenant-General Hood was immediately instructed to form his corps parallel with the road by which he had marched, and west of it, with the centre opposite to the church; Lieutenant-General Polk to place his in line with it, on the left, and Lieutenant-General Hardee to occupy a ridge extending from the ground allotted to Polk's corps, across the road leading from Dallas toward Atlanta—his left division, Bate's, holding that road.

As soon as his troops were in position, Lieutenant-General Hood, to "develop the enemy," sent forward Colonel Bush Jones, with his regiment and Austin's sharpshooters, in all about three hundred men. After advancing about a mile, this detachment encountered Hooker's corps. Having the written order of his corps commander to hold his ground after meeting the enemy, Colonel Jones resisted resolutely the attack of the overwhelming Federal forces. But, after a gallant, fight, he was, of course, driven back to his division—Stewart's.

An hour and a half before sunset, a brisk cannonade was opened upon Hood's centre division, Stewart's, opposite to New Hope Church. Major-General Stewart regarding this as the harbinger of assault, leaped upon his horse and rode along his line, to instruct the officers and encourage the men. He soon found the latter to be superfluous, from the confident tone in which he was addressed by his soldiers, and urged by them to lay aside all anxiety, and trust, for success, to their courage. Such pledges were well redeemed. The enemy soon appeared—Hooker's corps—in so deep order that it presented a front equal only to that of Stewart's first line—three brigades. After opening their fire, the Federal troops approached gradually but resolutely, under the fire of three brigades and sixteen field-pieces, until within fifty paces of the Confederate line. Here, however, they were compelled first to pause, and then to fall back, by the obstinate resistance they encountered. They were led forward again, advancing as resolutely, and approaching as near to the Confederate line as before, but were a second time repulsed by the firmness of their opponents, and their deliberate fire of canister-shot and musketry. The engagement was continued in this manner almost two hours, when the assailants drew off.

In this action a few of the men of Clayton's and Baker's brigades were partially sheltered by a hasty arrangement of some fallen timber which they found near their line. The other brigade engaged, Stovall's, had no such protection. Nothing entitled to the term "breastworks" had been constructed by the division. . . .

The Federal troops extended their intrenched line so rapidly to their left, that it was found necessary in the morning of the 27th to transfer Cleburne's division of Hardee's corps to our right, where it was formed on the prolongation of Polk's line. Kelly's cavalry, composed of Allen's and Hannon's Alabama brigades, together less than a thousand men, occupied the interval, of half a mile, between Cleburne's right and Little Pumpkin-Vine Creek. Martin's division (cavalry) guarded the road from Burnt Hickory to Marietta, two miles farther to the right; and Humes's the interval between Kelly's and Martin's divisions.

Between five and six o'clock in the afternoon, Kelly's skirmishers were driven in by a body of Federal cavalry, whose advance was supported by the Fourth Corps. This advance was retarded by the resistance of Kelly's troops fighting on foot behind unconnected little heaps of loose stones. As soon as the noise of this contest revealed to Major-General Cleburne the manœuvre to turn his right, he brought the right brigade of his second line, Granberry's, to Kelly's support, by forming it on the right of his first line; when the thin line of dismounted cavalry, that had been bravely resisting masses of infantry gave place to the Texan brigade.

The Fourth Corps came on in deep order, and assailed the Texans with great vigor, receiving their close and accurate fire with the fortitude always exhibited by General Sherman's troops in the actions of this campaign. They had also to endure the fire of Govan's right, including two pieces of artillery, on their right flank. At the same time, Kelly's and a part of Humes's troops, directed by General Wheeler, met the Federal left, which was following the movement of the main body, and drove back the leading brigade, taking thirty or forty prisoners. The united force continued to press forward, however, but so much delayed by the resistance of Wheeler's troops as to give time for the arrival, on that part of the field, of the Eighth and Ninth Arkansas regiments under Colonel Bancum, detached by General Govan to the assistance of the cavalry. This little body met the foremost of the Federal troops as they were reaching the prolongation of Granberry's line, and, charging gallantly, drove them back, and preserved the Texans from an attack in flank which must have been fatal. Before the Federal left could gather to overwhelm Bancum and his two regiments, Lowry's brigade, hurried by General Cleburne from its position as left of his second line, came to join them, and the two, formed abreast of Granberry's brigade, stopped the advance of the enemy's left, and successfully resisted its subsequent attacks.

The contest of the main body of the Fourth Corps with Granberry's brigade was a very fierce one. The Federal troops approached within a few yards of the Confederates, but at last were forced to give way by their storm of well-directed bullets, and fell back to the shelter of a hollow near and behind them. They left hundreds of corpses within twenty paces of the Confederate line.

When the United States troops paused in their advance, within fifteen paces of the Texan front rank, one of their color-bearers planted his colors eight or ten feet in front of his regiment, and was instantly shot dead; a soldier sprang forward to his place, and fell also, as he grasped the color-staff; a second and third followed successively, and each received death as speedily as his predecessors; a fourth, however, seized and bore back the object of soldierly devotion.

About ten o'clock at night, Granberry ascertained that many of the Federal troops were still in the hollow immediately before him, and charged and drove them from it, taking two hundred and thirty-two prisoners, seventy-two of whom were severely wounded.

—JOHNSTON, *Narrative of Military Operations*

5. ATLANTA: THE PROMISED LAND!

On July 5 Sherman and Johnston fought the minor Battle of Chatta-hoochee River; another five days and Johnston had retired to the defenses of Atlanta, Sherman on his heels. Now at last Atlanta was in sight.

What it meant to the battle-weary Union army to reach the great objec-

tive of the campaign is well expressed by our old friend Major James Connolly, one of Sherman's division inspectors.

At Chattahoochee River, July 12, 1864

Dear wife:

Mine eyes have beheld the promised land! The "domes and minarets and spires" of Atlanta are glittering in the sunlight before us, and only 8 miles distant. On the morning of the 5th, while riding at the extreme front with the General, and eagerly pressing our skirmishers forward after the rapidly retreating rebels, suddenly we came upon a high bluff overlooking the Chattahoochee, and looking southward across the river, there lay the beautiful "Gate City" in full view, and as the soldiers caught the announcement that Atlanta was in sight, such a cheer went up as must have been heard even in the entrenchments of the doomed city itself. In a very few moments Generals Sherman and Thomas (who are always with the extreme front when a sudden movement is taking place) were with us on the hill top, and the two veterans, for a moment, gazed at the glittering prize in silence. I watched the two noble soldiers—Sherman stepping nervously about, his eyes sparkling and his face aglow—casting a single glance at Atlanta, another at the River, and a dozen at the surrounding valley to see where he could best cross the River, how he best could flank them. Thomas stood there like a noble old Roman, calm, soldierly, dignified; no trace of excitement about that grand old soldier who had ruled the storm at Chickamauga. Turning quietly to my General, he said: "——, send up a couple of guns and we'll throw some shells over there," pointing to some heavy timber across the River.

In a moment I was off down the road, to the rear, to order up some artillery; the infantry column separated and opened the road, the artillery came thundering along through the long lines of men, and in fifteen minutes from the time our line of skirmishers reached that hill top, a Parrott shell went screaming from the high point, and burst beautifully on the south side of the Chattahoochee—the first since the war began. That was a glorious moment, and I felt proud that I belonged to this grand army, and that I was at the front instead of at the rear, doing "fancy duty."

—"Major Connolly's Letters to His Wife"

6. JOE JOHNSTON GIVES WAY TO HOOD

It was a fortunate day for Sherman when President Davis removed Johnston from command and appointed Hood to his place. Confronted by heavy numerical superiority Johnston had no alternative but to retreat; that he conducted his retreat in a masterly fashion is now generally admitted. Davis, however, had never fully trusted Johnston: the distrust probably dated from Johnston's protest, in 1861, against an appointment which made him only fourth in rank in the Confederate Army. Davis' suspicion of Johnston was deepened when Johnston failed either to rescue Pemberton or to strike the Federal army during the Vicksburg campaign. Johnston's appointment to Bragg's command, in December 1863, was welcomed by the officers and men of the Army of Tennessee; his dismissal was generally regarded as a calamity. When Lee was made commander in chief of Confederate armies, in February 1865, he promptly reappointed Johnston to command of what was left of his army.

We have here Davis' explanation of his dismissal of Johnston, and Johnston's defense of his strategy.

A. President Davis Removes General Johnston before Atlanta

WHEN it became known that the Army of Tennessee had been successively driven from one strong position to another, until finally it had reached the earthworks constructed for the exterior defense of Atlanta, the popular disappointment was extreme. The possible fall of the "Gate City," with its important railroad communication, vast stores, factories for the manufacture of all sorts of military supplies, rolling-mill and foundries, was now contemplated for the first time at its full value, and produced intense anxiety far and wide. From many quarters, including such as had most urged his assignment, came delegations, petitions, and letters, urging me to remove General Johnston from the command of the army, and assign that important trust to some officer who would resolutely hold and defend Atlanta.

While sharing in the keen sense of disappointment at the failure of the campaign which pervaded the whole country, I was perhaps more apprehensive than others of the disasters likely to result from it, because I was in a position to estimate more accurately their probable extent. On the railroads threatened with destruction, the armies then fighting the main battles of the war in Virginia had for some time to a great degree depended for indispensable supplies, yet I did not respond to the wishes of those who came in hottest haste for the removal of General Johnston; for here again, more fully than many others, I realized how serious it was to change commanders in the presence of the enemy. This clamor for his removal commenced immediately after it became known that the army had fallen back from Dalton, and it gathered volume with each remove toward Atlanta. Still I resisted the steadily increasing pressure which was brought to bear to induce me to revoke his assignment, and only issued the order relieving him from command when I became satisfied that his declared purpose to occupy the works at Atlanta with militia levies and withdraw his army into the open country for freer operations, would inevitably result in the loss of that important point, and where the retreat would cease could not be foretold. If the Army of Tennessee was found to be unable to hold positions of great strength like those at Dalton, Reseca, Etowah, Kenesaw, and on the Chattahoochee, I could not reasonably hope that it would be more successful in the plains below Atlanta, where it would find neither natural nor artificial advantages of position. As soon as the Secretary of War showed me the answer which he had just received in reply to his telegram to General Johnston, requesting positive information as to the General's plans and purposes, I gave my permission to issue the order relieving General Johnston and directing him to turn over to General Hood the command of the Army of Tennessee. I was so fully aware of the danger of changing commanders of an army while actively engaged with the enemy, that I only overcame the objection in view of an emergency, and in the hope that the impending danger of the loss of Atlanta might be averted.

—DAVIS, *Rise and Fall of the Confederate Government*

B. GENERAL JOHNSTON JUSTIFIES HIMSELF

Macon, Ga., September 1st, 1864

My Dear Maury:

I have been intending ever since my arrival at this place to pay a part of the epistolary debt I owe you. But you know how lazy it makes one to have nothing to do, and so with the hot weather we have been enduring here, I have absolutely devoted myself to idleness. I have been disposed to write more particularly of what concerns myself—to explain to you, as far as practicable, the operations for which I was laid on the shelf, for you are one of the last whose unfavorable opinion I would be willing to incur.

You know that the army I commanded was that which, under General Bragg, was routed at Missionary Ridge. Sherman's army was that which routed it, reinforced by the Sixteenth and Twenty-third Corps. I am censured for not taking the offensive at Dalton—where the enemy, if beaten, had a secure refuge behind the fortified gap at Ringgold, or in the fortress of Chattanooga, and where the odds against us were almost ten to four. At Resaca he received five brigades, near Kingston three, and about 3500 cavalry; at New Hope Church one; in all about 14,000 infantry and artillery. The enemy received the Seventeenth Corps and a number of garrisons and bridge guards from Tennessee and Kentucky that had been relieved by "hundred-day men."

I am blamed for not fighting. Operations commenced about the 6th of May; I was relieved on the 18th of July. In that time we fought daily, always under circumstances so favorable to us as to make it certain that the sum of the enemy's losses was five times ours, which was 10,000 men. Northern papers represented theirs up to about the end of June at 45,000. Sherman's progress was at the rate of a mile and a quarter a day. Had this style of fighting been allowed to continue, is it not clear that we would soon have been able to give battle with abundant chances of victory, and that the enemy, beaten on this side of the Chattahoochee, would have been destroyed? It is certain that Sherman's army was stronger, compared with that of Tennessee, than Grant's, compared with that of Northern Virginia. General Bragg asserts that Sherman's was absolutely stronger than Grant's. It is well known that the army of Virginia was much superior to that of Tennessee.

Why, then, should I be condemned for the defensive while General Lee was adding to his great fame by the same course? General Bragg seems to have earned at Missionary Ridge his present high position. People report at

Columbus and Montgomery that General Bragg said that my losses had been frightful; that I had disregarded the wishes and instructions of the President; that he had in vain implored me to change my course, by which I suppose is meant assume the offensive.

As these things are utterly untrue, it is not to be supposed that they were said by General Bragg. The President gave me no instructions and expressed no wishes except just before we reached the Chattahoochee, warning me not to fight with the river behind us and against crossing it, and previously he urged me not to allow Sherman to detach to Grant's aid. General Bragg passed some ten hours with me just before I was relieved, and gave me the impression that his visit to the army was casual, he being on his way further west to endeavor to get us reinforcements from Kirby Smith and Lee. I thought him satisfied with the state of things, but not so with that in Virginia. He assured me that he had always maintained in Richmond that Sherman's army was stronger than Grant's. He said nothing of the intention to relieve me, but talked with General Hood on the subject, as I learned after my removal. It is clear that his expedition had no other object than my removal and the giving proper direction to public opinion on the subject. He could have had no other object in going to Montgomery. A man of honor in his place would have communicated with me as well as with Hood on the subject. Being expected to assume the offensive, he attacked on the 20th, 22d, and 28th of July, disastrously, losing more men than I had done in seventy-two days. Since then his defensive has been at least as quiet as mine was.

Very truly yours,

J. E. JOHNSTON

Major-General MAURY

—MAURY, *Recollections of a Virginian*

7. THE UNION ARMY LEARNS TO FIGHT BEHIND FORTIFICATIONS

Atlanta proved a hard nut to crack. Hood had been appointed because he was an aggressive fighter, and he promptly took the offensive. On July 20 he struck Thomas at Peachtree Creek, but was repulsed with heavy losses. Nothing daunted he tried again two days later, this time assaulting the left of the Union line, at Decatur (the Battle of Atlanta).

This kind of fighting forced the Federals to take to entrenchments, and Henry Dwight here describes how those entrenchments were constructed, and what it was like to fight behind them. Dwight was a boy of twenty-one when he wrote this, a captain of the 20th Ohio Infantry, and aide to General Force of the XVII Corps. Later he had a distinguished career as Congregational missionary to the Near East, editor, and scholar.

HERE in the trenches before Atlanta, on this 15th day of August, I propose to give you some idea of the actual manner in which we fight. With us the pomp and show of war has become a matter of poetry rather than of fact. We need no gay dress or nodding plumes to inspire a soldier's pride. Practical utility is what we look at in matters of dress and equipment. Look at most of the pictures. Two-thirds of the pictures in books and papers represent the soldiers with enormous knapsacks neatly packed; officers leading the charge in full dress uniform, with their sabres waving in the most approved style. Now this makes a pretty picture; but let me tell you that soldiers don't put on their well-packed knapsacks to double-quick over a half mile of open ground in the hot sun at the *pas du charge*. Limited transportation soon exhausts an officer's stock of white collars. The most elegant dress uniform will become torn and spotted, and the brightly polished boots will become soiled with mud, when one is reduced to marching in line-of-battle through swamps, thickets, and brier patches, and then sleeping night after night on the bare ground with only heaven's clouds for an over-coat. Know ye, then, ladies all, yonder pretty-looking officer, with his spotless dress, resplendent with gold lace, will present a very different spectacle after a few months of campaigning. Dusty, ragged, and unshaven, his appearance is far more in accordance with his surroundings, far more becoming the earnest fighting man that you really suppose he is, than if he were arrayed as you formerly saw him, or as the pictures represent him to be.

Of course, in a war like this, upon which we all entered with the art yet to learn, the science has been progressive. Each succeeding year has developed new phases, and under such schooling our soldiers are indeed veterans; men whom practice has perfected in all the mysteries of military life. Each soldier knows that where he used to lie upon his arms all the time, in the face of the enemy, only seeking cover from the shape of the ground, he must now make a strong fortification, to enable him to hold his position, and must arrange it to stop pieces of shell from the flank as well as bullets from the front. Had the army been as experienced at Shiloh as it is now, Beauregard would have come up and broken his army to pieces on our fortifications, instead of finding our whole army lying exposed to his attacks on the open field. At Fort Donelson, too, where we had to attack fortifications, we ourselves had no sign of a work upon which we could fall back after each day's repulse; nor did the enemy seem to realize the value of his own works, for instead of quietly waiting the attack, he threw away his army by fighting outside his works.

It is now a principle with us to fight with movable breast-works, to save every man by giving him cover, from which he may resist the tremendous attacks in mass of the enemy. Thus at least we fight in Georgia, in the Atlanta campaign.

Wherever the army moves, either in gaining the enemy's work, or in taking up a new line of attack, the first duty after the halt is to create defensive fortifications—rude, indeed, but effective in enabling us to hold our ground against any force. In forming these field-works every man is to some extent his own engineer. The location of the line is selected by the officers, and each regiment fortifies its own front, each company its own ground.

Generally the situation will not allow of finishing the works at once, for the enemy will probably attack soon after you take position, which is on a commanding hill or some similar point. So you cause a hasty barricade to be constructed. The front rank take all the guns and remain on the line, while the rear rank goes off in double-quick to collect rails, logs, rocks, any thing that can assist in turning a hostile bullet. These they place on the front of the front rank, and in five minutes there is a hasty barricade, bullet-proof and breast-high, along your whole line; not a mere straight work, but one varied with its salients and re-entering angles, taking every advantage of the ground, and cross-firing on every hollow. You can do this after the enemy forms to charge you, while he is feeling you with artillery. Thus it takes just five minutes to prepare for an assault; and you can hold your line against an attack by three times your number—and that, too, with but slight loss to yourself—if your men be veteran soldiers.

It may be that when your barricade is done you have yet time. Shovels and picks are always carried by your men, and to work they go to complete the frail works. A ditch is speedily made on the inside to stand in. The earth is thrown on the outside of the barricade, and the ditch deepened, so that, standing inside, your head will be protected by the parapet. Thus you speedily have a pretty substantial earth-work, with a step inside to stand on when firing, and a ditch to stand in while loading. If you are in the woods, you want to give range to your rifles, and have all the thick undergrowth and small trees cut away for fifty paces in front. By felling these all the same way, the bushy tops all turning outward, and trimming off the smaller twigs and leaves, and tangling the tops together, you have a formidable abattis, through which it shall be next to impossible for a line to advance alone, let alone against the showers of bullets from your men at short range. This done, you can be making any amount of additions to your work as you have time, all tending to make it impregnable. Even after you have pronounced the job finished, your men will fuss and dig and tinker about the works to make them sure protection. They have no notion of taking a position, and then having it taken from them by a sudden assault. They will cut huge logs eighteen inches through, and place them on the parapet to protect the head while they shoot through a space left between the log and the parapet. They have also an ingenious plan for preventing these "head-logs" from being an injury to the service. Experience has taught them that a cannon-ball will sometimes strike one of these huge logs, and throw it off the parapet on to the troops inside. As a preventive skids, or stout poles, are placed at equal distances along the ditch. The logs being knocked off the top of the breast-work are supposed to roll along these skids, over the heads of the soldiers in the ditch, until they lodge safely on the bank beyond.

The men will also amuse themselves with devising some new entanglement or snare to annoy the advance of the enemy. They drive palisades—stakes set in the ground with their sharpened points directed outward at an angle of forty-five degrees, and so close together that a man can not pass between them. In front of the palisade they place a strong wire so arranged that it can not be seen but will trip all comers. They will then imagine how astounded will be the rebels in charging the works to be suddenly tripped up and to fall forward on the sharp palisades.

Your main works being completed you can rest secure, only putting in an embrasure for a howitzer or two here or there. These howitzers are a fine thing to repel an attack, for they throw nearly a bucketful of small balls at a charge. Your skirmish line has, in the mean time, fortified itself sufficiently for protection, and can hold an attacking column long enough for you to form line in the main works before the enemy can get there.

One reads in the papers of the assaults on earth-works, of the repulses, and yet one does not know what is contained in those words—"Assault repulsed." You make up your mind to assault the enemy's works. You have formed line of battle, with a second and third line behind you for support. You march forth filled with the determination to accomplish the object, yet feeling the magnitude of the undertaking. Two hundred yards brings you to the picket-line, and here the opposition commences. You dash across the space between the two lines, you lose a few men; and the enemy's pickets, after making as much noise as possible, run back to their main works. By this time the enemy are sure you are really coming, and open on you with artillery, besides a pretty heavy fire of musketry. This artillery throws the shell screaming through your ranks, producing more moral than physical effect, or throws shrapnell which, bursting in front, scatter myriads of small bullets around. You commence to lose men rapidly. The ball is opened. "Forward, double-quick!" again; and while the whole line of the enemy open fire from behind their works, your men, mindless of this—mindless of the death intensified, the bullets and the shells, they dash on with wild cheers.

The abattis with its tangled intricacy of sharpened branches snares your line. Tripping, falling, rising to fall again, the men struggle through this abattis. You get through this abattis, though the minutes are drawn out interminably, and though in each step are left brave men to pay for the ground. You get through a part of you and still rush on: the firing grows more fierce, the men grow more desperate. Your three lines have been almost reduced to one, and you strike another line of abattis. In this abattis are the palisades, which must be uprooted by force before a man can pass. You stumble, fall, tear your flesh on these stakes, and must stop to pull them up—stop, when every instant is an hour—stop, when you are already gasping for breath; and here open up the masked batteries, pouring the canister into that writhing, struggling, bleeding mass—so close that the flame scorches, that the smoke blinds from those guns. Is it any wonder that your three lines are torn to pieces, and have to give back before the redoubled fire of an enemy as yet uninjured comparatively? And then the slaughter of a retreat *there!* Oftentimes it is preferable to lie down and take the fire there until night rather than lose all by falling back under such circumstances.

This war has demonstrated that earth-works can be rendered nearly impregnable on either side against direct assault. An attack on fortified lines must cost a fearful price, and should be well weighed whether the cost exceed not the gain. This, then, is what an assault means—a slaughter-pen, a charnel-house, and an army of weeping mothers and sisters at home. It is inevitable. When an assault is successful, it is to be hoped that the public gain may warrant the loss of life requisite. When it is repulsed tenfold is the mourning.

It was a long time before the men could appreciate the value of these field-works. They would grumble and growl, recalling instances without number where the most charming little traps, the most elegant cross-fires, had been prepared with great labor, and had never been attacked. I saw some men most beautifully satisfied as to the necessity for defensive works the other day. On the 22d of July, before Atlanta, while these men were engaged in grumbling over some newly-finished works which the enemy would not charge, Hardee struck the Seventeenth Corps in flank and rear. His furious onset crushed the flank, and the Second Brigade of the Third Division, to which these grumblers belonged, found themselves suddenly forming the unprotected left of the corps and attacked from the rear in those very works they grumbled so about building. When this attack was made they jumped the works to the front, or outside, and fought that way. This attack repulsed, they jumped back and repulsed an attack from the outside, or real front. Thus they fought, looking for all the world like a long line of these toy-monkeys you see which jump over the end of a stick. Thus they fought for four long hours, cut off from all commanders, corps, division, and brigade, cut off from ammunition-trains, and only cheered by the noble example of General Giles A. Smith, whose command, broken by the first onset—all except one brigade—had rallied behind the works of the Third Division. Firing to front and rear, and to either flank, they held their works, only changing front by jumping over the parapet as five assaults were made upon them, successively from front, rear, or flank, until the rebel onset was checked long enough to make sure the safety of the immense wagon-trains already saved by the Sixteenth Corps.

The next works of these men I saw, and seeing them, laughed. Experience had taught the utility of fortifications, and they fortified not only the front, but facing the rear and every way, so that they could hold out if surrounded. They were not going to be caught without ammunition either; for each company had its little powder-magazine in a safe place, well stored with ammunition gathered from the battle-field. No grumbling was heard about building the works. All the spare time of the men was devoted to finishing up their pet works, standing off and regarding the effect of each addition with something of the same paternal feeling that an artist exhibits in regarding the power of each master-stroke in finishing his picture.

—Dwight, "How We Fight at Atlanta"

8. HARDEE WINS AND LOSES THE BATTLE OF ATLANTA

After Peachtree Creek Sherman sent McPherson eastward toward Decatur to cut off Hood's communications with the east and north. Hood withdrew into the defenses of Atlanta; supposing him in retreat McPherson set out "in pursuit." By a night march Hood—with Wheeler's cavalry—caught Mc-Pherson unprepared and assaulted him flank and rear. For a time disaster threatened. McPherson was killed; his army all but routed. But the Federals rallied and in the end inflicted a heavy defeat on their attackers. Confederate losses were between 7,000 and 8,000; Union less than 4,000.

Richard Tuthill, who here tells the story, was an officer of the 1st Michigan Light Artillery.

HARDEE had struck us "endways," and his men could be plainly seen occupying the works from which ours had just been driven. The battery of regulars, near the end of our line, had been captured; and Lieutenant Justin of our battery had only been able to save his guns by the exercise of great coolness and quickness of movement. No sooner had the regulars been captured than we heard the booming of their guns, and saw their shot ploughing through our line in direct enfilade.

Some one may then have ordered a change of position. I have heard it said that such an order was given. At the same time, I beg leave respectfully to doubt it. The truth is that there was no time to give orders, and I saw neither general nor staff officer there to give them. All I know is, that we limbered up our guns, and sullenly—for we were much inclined to stay where we were—moved back. Our boys loved their black steel guns, and could not endure the thought of losing one of them. The Third Ohio Battery, in our division, had twenty-pounder Parrotts,—too heavy for field service,—and had to leave at least one of them behind, though it was afterward retaken. At least twice, as we were falling back a distance of not more than two or three hundred yards, as it seems to me, we unlimbered our guns and fired at the enemy. Then the infantry would move away from us, and we would limber up and fall back a little farther, to keep on a line with them.

It is hard now to recall the sensations of twenty-five years ago, but I never can forget thinking, "Can it be possible that the Third Division, victor in a hundred battles, has at last met defeat? Is it going to leave the field while as yet few have been killed or wounded? Better, ten thousand times better, that the entire division die fighting, than to have word sent back home that without serious losses in killed and wounded, it gave up the field." "It is better, sir," said Sir Colin Campbell, "that every man of her Majesty's Guards should lie dead upon the field than that they should now turn their backs upon the enemy." Such I know were my thoughts, and such I soon, from their action, learned was the thought of that glorious and never-conquered phalanx; for in their action their country and history can read their stern, brave thoughts and high determination.

Seeing then, for the first time since the fight began, our Chief of Artillery, Captain Williams,—as nonchalant a man as I ever saw in a place of great danger,—I rode to his side and said to him, "For God's sake, Captain, let us stop falling back and fight!" By that time we had reached a position about on a line drawn at right angles to the line occupied by us when the attack was first made, running toward the east from the top of Leggett's Hill.

Captain Williams replied to my remark, "All right! stop where you are!" It was just the place to form a line of battle. Some general officer may have given an order to stop there. My own belief always has been that the boys did it of their own accord. They had been in so many fights that they did not need a general to tell them where and when to stop running and begin shooting.

Some distance to the rear of us was a rail fence. Consternation, I have been told, fell upon General Sherman, as with his glass he saw half of Leggett's division drop their guns and run to the rear. But when he saw them stop at the rail fence, and each man of them pick up two, three, and even four rails, and run back, carrying them to the place where they had left their guns, he understood what it meant, and smiled grimly. The operation was repeated; the rails were placed lengthways along their front; with bayonets, knives, and the tin plates taken from their haversacks, the earth was dug up and the rails covered, until, in less time, as it appeared to me, than it was possible to have done the same work with pick and shovel, a very fair protection for men lying on their bellies was made.

In front of us lay an open field, containing, I should think, not more than twenty acres. Beyond this were woods. Pat Cleburne's Texans,—whom Force's brigade had driven from this selfsame hillside the day before,—desperate and mad, were to make an attempt to wipe out the disgrace of their former defeat. Their line well formed, they emerged from their concealment in the woods, and yelling as only the steer-drivers of Texas could yell, charged upon our division. On the top of the hill, in the apex of the angle of the line of works facing Atlanta and our new line, was a four-gun battery of twenty-four-pounder howitzers, commanded by its boy captain, Cooper. This was Battery D, of the First Illinois Artillery, better known as "McAllister's Battery." Our six guns were also near this point, and distributed along the line for a short distance to the east of it. On came the Texans; but they were met by a continuous volley of musketry and shrapnel, shell and canister from our six-rifled Rodmans and Cooper's howitzers. It seemed as if no man of all the host who were attacking us could escape alive; and yet, still yelling, they persisted in their desperate undertaking. Their line was re-formed, and again and again they attempted the impossible,—to drive the Third Division from the line it had decided to hold.

Many of the enemy reached our line; some got across it; many were bayonetted, many killed with clubbed muskets; hand-to-hand conflicts were frequent. But not one inch did the Third Division give way. The boys obeyed Logan's well-remembered command to them at Champion Hill,— "Give them the cold steel! give them hell!"

The smell of powder was everywhere; the smoke from the guns was so dense that though a July sun was shining, there was the appearance of a dense fog. Only as the breath of a passing breeze blew the smoke away could the movements of the enemy be discerned clearly; but his unearthly *yell* could be heard above the sound of muskets and cannon. The day being very warm, men and line officers were for the most part without other clothing than hats and shoes, woollen shirts and trousers. I had left my coat and all my traps, including my letters, at the spot where I had suspended my letter-writing, and never again recovered them.

The exact sequence of events that afternoon I cannot give; nor do I believe any man can, or ever could, do so. Some time during the fight, firing was heard from the direction of Atlanta. General Cheatham's corps—as we now know—made a fierce attack upon the Seventeenth and Fifteenth corps from our west front. The smoke was so dense that the men could not at first see whence this attack came. It was remarked that our own men farther to the right, thinking the enemy had taken the position on the hill, were firing upon us. General Force called for a flag. Some frightened young officer, thinking it time to give up when we were being attacked at the same moment from all sides, and that what Force wanted was a flag of truce, ran hither and thither to get a white handkerchief, or shirt, or anything that would answer the purpose. The talk among our boys was that that quiet Christian gentle-man—now Judge Force of the Law Court of Cincinnati—was then betrayed into saying, "*Damn* you, sir! I don't want a flag of *truce;* I want the American flag!" If he did say it, we are sure that as in Uncle Tobey's case, "The accusing spirit which flew up to Heaven's chancery with the oath blushed as he gave it in; and the recording angel, as he wrote it down, dropped a tear upon the word and blotted it out forever."

A flag was soon obtained and planted upon the highest point in our earth-works, and there it remained. General Force himself was struck down by a minie-ball, which entered just at the lower outer corner of the eye, passed through his head, and came out near the base of the brain. The blood gushed from his eyes, nose, and mouth; but he uttered no moan, nor a word of com-plaint. The bones of his mouth were shattered, and he could not, in fact, speak. But from his eyes flashed a spirit unconquered and unconquerable,—the spirit of a soldier *sans peur et sans reproche*.

The attack made by Cheatham's corps from Atlanta was repulsed bloodily by Frank Blair's heroic men. But beyond the bushy ravine of which I have spoken as separating the Fifteenth Corps, where its line had been weakened by sending troops to strengthen our line fronting to the south, Cheatham had succeeded in breaking through, and was rushing in and forming in line of battle in the works from which our men had been driven. Some one asked that a part of our battery be at once sent to the ravine to shell this forming line. There was at that time comparative quiet in our immediate front, and my section of the battery hurried to the point indicated. The Confederates were there in plain sight. De Gress' battery of four twenty-pounder Parrotts had been captured, all of its horses killed, and its guns turned upon us. Tak-ing a position on the edge of the ravine, the boys of my section poured into the forming line of the enemy an enfilading fire of short-range canister—"canned hell-fire," as they used to call it—that no living thing could with-stand.

—TUTHILL, "An Artilleryman's. Recollections
of the Battle of Atlanta"

9. "YOU MIGHT AS WELL APPEAL AGAINST THE THUNDER-STORM"

Even after Peachtree Creek and the Battle of Atlanta, Hood was able to put up a stiff fight for Atlanta. Sherman fell back on his now familiar tactics of flanking the Confederates, trying to cut their supply lines to the south and the east. Late July and early August witnessed a number of stiff cavalry engagements, as Hood tried to break up these extensive flanking movements. Convinced, finally, that Hood could not be defeated by these tactics, Sherman settled down to investing Atlanta. On August 25 he put his whole army in motion to encircle the city. With his communications cut, Hood evacuated Atlanta and moved south and west, and on September 1 Sherman wired Lincoln, "Atlanta is ours, and fairly won." Already the bombardment of Atlanta had started numerous fires; when Sherman was ready to leave it for further campaigning, he ordered it destroyed. This required the evacuation of its inhabitants. Southerners looked on this as inhuman; Sherman thought it a necessary military measure, and the evacuation warning a gesture of courtesy.

What is most interesting about this letter, explaining the necessity of evacuation, is that it gives Sherman's theory of war. That Sherman inflicted heavier damage on the South than any other Union general is doubtless true; it is equally true that no other Union general was so sympathetic to the South or understood it so well.

Headquarters Military Division of the Mississippi
in the Field, Atlanta, Georgia, September 12, 1864

James M. Calhoun, Mayor, E. E. Rawson and S. C. Wells, representing City Council of Atlanta.

Gentlemen: I have your letter of the 11th, in the nature of a petition to revoke my orders removing all the inhabitants from Atlanta. I have read it carefully, and give full credit to your statements of the distress that will be occasioned, and yet shall not revoke my orders, because they were not designed to meet the humanities of the case, but to prepare for the future struggles in which millions of good people outside of Atlanta have a deep interest. We must have peace, not only at Atlanta, but in all America. To secure this, we must stop the war that now desolates our once happy and favored country. To stop war, we must defeat the rebel armies which are arrayed against the laws and Constitution that all must respect and obey. To defeat those armies, we must prepare the way to reach them in their recesses, provided with the arms and instruments which enable us to accomplish our purpose. Now, I know the vindictive nature of our enemy, that we may have many years of military operations from this quarter; and, therefore, deem it wise and prudent to prepare in time. The use of Atlanta for warlike purposes is inconsistent with its character as a home for families. There will be no manufactures, commerce, or agriculture here, for the maintenance of families, and sooner or later want will compel the inhabitants to go. Why not go now, when all the arrangements are completed for the transfer, instead of waiting till the plunging shot of contending armies will renew the scenes of the past month? Of course, I do not apprehend any such thing at this moment, but you do not suppose this army will be here until the war is over. I cannot discuss this subject with you fairly, because I cannot impart to you what we propose to do, but I assert that our military plans make it necessary for the inhabitants to go away, and I can only renew my offer of services to make their exodus in any direction as easy and comfortable as possible.

You cannot qualify war in harsher terms than I will. War is cruelty, and you cannot refine it; and those who brought war into our country deserve all the curses and maledictions a people can pour out. I know I had no hand in making this war, and I know I will make more sacrifices to-day than any of you to secure peace. But you cannot have peace and a division of our country. If the United States submits to a division now, it will not stop, but will go on until we reap the fate of Mexico, which is eternal war. The United States does and must assert its authority, wherever it once had power; for, if it relaxes one bit to pressure, it is gone, and I believe that such is the national feeling. This feeling assumes various shapes, but always comes back to that of Union. Once admit the Union, once more acknowledge the authority of the national Government, and, instead of devoting your houses and streets and roads to the dread uses of war, I and this army become at once your protectors and supporters, shielding you from danger, let it come from what quarter it may. I know that a few individuals cannot resist a torrent of error and passion, such as swept the South into rebellion, but you can point out, so that we may know those who desire a government, and those who insist on war and its desolation.

You might as well appeal against the thunder-storm as against these terrible hardships of war. They are inevitable, and the only way the people of Atlanta can hope once more to live in peace and quiet at home, is to stop the war, which can only be done by admitting that it began in error and is perpetuated in pride.

We don't want your Negroes, or your horses, or your houses, or your lands, or any thing you have, but we do want and will have a just obedience to the laws of the United States. That we will have, and if it involves the destruction of your improvements, we cannot help it.

You have heretofore read public sentiment in your newspapers, that live by falsehood and excitement; and the quicker you seek for truth in other quarters, the better. I repeat then that, by the original compact of government, the United States had certain rights in Georgia, which have never been relinquished and never will be; that the South began war by seizing forts, arsenals, mints, custom-houses, etc., etc., long before Mr. Lincoln was installed, and before the South had one jot or tittle of provocation. I myself have seen in Missouri, Kentucky, Tennessee, and Mississippi, hundreds and thousands of women and children fleeing from your armies and desperadoes, hungry and with bleeding feet. In Memphis, Vicksburg, and Mississippi, we fed thousands upon thousands of the families of rebel soldiers left on our hands, and whom we could not see starve. Now that war comes home to you, you feel very different. You deprecate its horrors, but did not feel them when you sent car-loads of soldiers and ammunition, and moulded shells and shot, to carry war into Kentucky and Tennessee, to desolate the homes of hundreds and thousands of good people who only asked to live in peace at their old homes, and under the Government of their inheritance. But these comparisons are idle. I want peace, and believe it can only be reached through union and war, and I will ever conduct war with a view to perfect an early success.

But, my dear sirs, when peace does come, you may call on me for any thing. Then will I share with you the last cracker, and watch with you to shield your homes and families against danger from every quarter.

Now you must go, and take with you the old and feeble, feed and nurse them, and build for them, in more quiet places, proper habitations to shield them against the weather until the mad passions of men cool down, and allow the Union and peace once more to settle over your old homes at Atlanta. Yours in haste,

W. T. SHERMAN, *Major-General commanding*
—Memoirs of General William T. Sherman

10. SHERMAN MARCHES FROM ATLANTA TO THE SEA

Sherman's great decision was to break his own line of communications, and live off the country. Dispatching Schofield to Knoxville and Thomas to Nashville, to take care of Hood, he set out with what was left of his army, some 62,000 men, into the heart of the Confederacy.
Once again he is the best historian of his own achievements.

ABOUT 7 A.M. of November 16th [1864] we rode out of Atlanta by the Decatur road, filled by the marching troops and wagons of the Fourteenth Corps; and reaching the hill, just outside of the old rebel works, we naturally paused to look back upon the scenes of our past battles. We stood upon the very ground whereon was fought the bloody battle of July 22d and could see the copse of wood where McPherson fell. Behind us lay Atlanta, smoldering and in ruins, the black smoke rising high in air and hanging like a pall over the ruined city. Away off in the distance, on the McDonough road, was the rear of Howard's column, the gun barrels glistening in the sun, the white-topped wagons stretching away to the south, and right before us the Fourteenth Corps, marching steadily and rapidly with a cheery look and swinging pace that made light of the thousand miles that lay between us and Richmond. Some band by accident struck up the anthem of "John Brown's soul goes marching on"; the men caught up the strain, and never before or since have I heard the chorus of "Glory, glory, hallelujah!" done with more spirit or in better harmony of time and place.

Then we turned our horses' heads to the east; Atlanta was soon lost behind the screen of trees and became a thing of the past. Around it clings many a thought of desperate battle, of hope and fear, that now seem like the memory of a dream; and I have never seen the place since. The day was extremely beautiful, clear sunlight, with bracing air, and an unusual feeling of exhilaration seemed to pervade all minds—a feeling of something to come, vague and undefined, still full of venture and intense interest. Even the common soldiers caught the inspiration, and many a group called out to me as I worked my way past them, "Uncle Billy, I guess Grant is waiting for us at Richmond!" Indeed, the general sentiment was that we were marching for Richmond and that there we should end the war, but how and when they seemed to care not; nor did they measure the distance or count the cost in life or bother their brains about the great rivers to be crossed and the food, required for man and beast, that had to be gathered by the way. There was a devil-may-care feeling pervading officers and men that made me feel the full load of responsibility, for success would be accepted as a matter of course, whereas should we fail, this march would be adjudged the wild adventure of a crazy fool. I had no purpose to march direct for Richmond by way of Augusta and Charlotte but always designed to reach the seacoast first at Savannah or Port Royal, South Carolina, and even kept in mind the alternative of Pensacola.

The first night out we camped by the roadside near Lithonia. Stone Mountain, a mass of granite, was in plain view, cut out in clear outline against the blue sky; the whole horizon was lurid with the bonfires of rail ties, and groups of men all night were carrying the heated rails to the nearest trees and bending them around the trunks. Colonel Poe had provided tools for ripping up the rails and twisting them when hot, but the best and easiest way is . . . heating the middle of the iron rails on bonfires made of the crossties and then winding them around a telegraph pole or the trunk of some convenient sapling. I attached much importance to this destruction of the railroad, gave it my personal attention, and made reiterated orders to others on the subject.

The next day we passed through the handsome town of Covington, the soldiers closing up their ranks, the color-bearers unfurling their flags, and the band striking up patriotic airs. The white people came out of their houses to behold the sight, spite of their deep hatred of the invaders, and the Negroes were simply frantic with joy. Whenever they heard my name, they clustered about my horse, shouted and prayed in their peculiar style, which had a natural eloquence that would have moved a stone. I have witnessed hundreds, if not thousands, of such scenes and can now see a poor girl, in the very ecstasy of the Methodist "shout," hugging the banner of one of the regiments and jumping up to the "feet of Jesus."

I remember, when riding around by a bystreet in Covington to avoid the crowd that followed the marching column, that some one brought me an invitation to dine with a sister of Samuel Anderson, who was a cadet at West Point with me; but the messenger reached me after we had passed the main part of the town. I asked to be excused and rode on to a place designated for camp, at the crossing of the Ulcofauhachee River, about four miles to the east of the town. Here we made our bivouac, and I walked up to a plantation house close by, where were assembled many Negroes, among them an old gray-haired man, of as fine a head as I ever saw. I asked him if he understood about the war and its progress. He said he did; that he had been looking for the "angel of the Lord" ever since he was knee-high, and though we professed to be fighting for the Union, he supposed that slavery was the cause and that our success was to be his freedom. I asked him if all the Negro slaves comprehended this fact, and he said they surely did. I then explained to him that we wanted the slaves to remain where they were and not to load us down with useless mouths, which would eat up the food needed for our fighting men, that our success was their assured freedom, that we could receive a few of their young, hearty men as pioneers, but that if they followed us in swarms of old and young, feeble and helpless, it would simply load us down and cripple us in our great task. I think Major Henry Hitchcock was with me on that occasion and made a note of the conversation, and I believe that old man spread this message to the slaves, which was carried from mouth to mouth to the very end of our journey, and that it in part saved us from the great danger we incurred of swelling our numbers so that famine would have attended our progress.

It was at this very plantation that a soldier passed me with a ham on his musket, a jug of sorghum molasses under his arm, and a big piece of honey in his hand, from which he was eating, and catching my eye, he remarked *sotto voce* and carelessly to a comrade, "Forage liberally on the country," quoting from my general orders. On this occasion, as on many others that fell under my personal observation, I reproved the man, explained that foraging must be limited to the regular parties properly detailed and that all provisions thus obtained must be delivered to the regular commissaries to be fairly distributed to the men who kept their ranks.

From Covington the Fourteeth Corps [Davis'], with which I was traveling, turned to the right for Milledgeville via Shady Dale. General Slocum was ahead at Madison with the Twentieth Corps, having torn up the railroad as far as that place, and thence had sent Geary's division on to the Oconee to burn the bridges across that stream when this corps turned south by Eatonton for Milledgeville, the common objective for the first stage of the march. We found abundance of corn, molasses, meal, bacon, and sweet potatoes. We also took a good many cows and oxen and a large number of mules. In all these the country was quite rich, never before having been visited by a hostile army; the recent crop had been excellent, had been just gathered and laid by for the winter. As a rule, we destroyed none but kept our wagons full and fed our teams bountifully.

The skill and success of the men in collecting forage was one of the features of this march. Each brigade commander had authority to detail a company of foragers, usually about fifty men, with one or two commissioned officers selected for their boldness and enterprise. This party would be dispatched before daylight with a knowledge of the intended day's march and camp, would proceed on foot five or six miles from the route traveled by their brigade, and then visit every plantation and farm within range. They would usually procure a wagon or family carriage, load it with bacon, cornmeal, turkeys, chickens, ducks, and everything that could be used as food or forage, and would then regain the main road, usually in advance of their train. When this came up, they would deliver to the brigade commissary the supplies thus gathered by the way. Often would I pass these foraging parties at the roadside, waiting for their wagons to come up, and was amused at their strange collections—mules, horses, even cattle, packed with old saddles and loaded with hams, bacon, bags of cornmeal, and poultry of every character and description. Although this foraging was attended with great danger and hard work, there seemed to be a charm about it that attracted the soldiers, and it was a privilege to be detailed on such a party. Daily they returned mounted on all sorts of beasts which were at once taken from them and appropriated to the general use, but the next day they would start out again on foot, only to repeat the experience of the day before. No doubt, many acts of pillage, robbery, and violence were committed by these parties of foragers, usually called bummers; for I have since heard of jewelry taken from women and the plunder of articles that never reached the commissary; but these acts were exceptional and incidental. I never heard of any cases of murder or rape, and no army could have carried along sufficient food and forage for a march of three hundred miles, so that foraging in some shape was necessary. The country was sparsely settled, with no magistrates or civil authorities who could respond to requisitions, as is done in all the wars of Europe, so that this system of foraging was simply indispensable to our success. By it our men were well supplied with all the essentials of life and health, while the wagons retained enough in case of unexpected delay, and our animals were well fed. Indeed, when we reached Savannah, the trains were pronounced by experts to be the finest in flesh and appearance ever seen with any army.

—*Memoirs of General William T. Sherman*

11. SHERMAN'S "BUMMERS"

The origin of the term "bummer" is a bit obscure; it was with Sherman's March to the Sea that it came into general usage. A bummer, wrote Major Nichols, "is a raider on his own account, a man who temporarily deserts his place in the ranks and starts out upon an independent foraging expedition." The term actually had more general application; cooks, orderlies, servants, were all called bummers, whether they deserved the name or not.

Here are three descriptions of this peculiar appendage to the Grand Army that marched from Atlanta to the sea. The first is by Charles Booth, a lieutenant in the 2nd Brigade of the 3rd Division. The second is by Captain Henry Dwight of the 20th Ohio Infantry, and an aide to General Force. The third is by Daniel Oakey, a captain in the 2nd Massachusetts Volunteers.

A. An Inventory of the Bummer

BUT I must close without telling you half—how our boys have marched without shoes or hats—how we have been without soap for three weeks, and obliged to cook over pitch pine fires—how, with "giant great hearts," they have waded through sloughs of despondency, and have finally secured rest, food and raiment. But I must tell you a little about a class in our army (and no inconsiderable portion of General Sherman's army do they compose) called "Bummers." Imagine a fellow with a gun and accoutrements, with a plug hat, a captured militia plume in it, a citizen's saddle, with a bed quilt or table cloth, upon an animal whose ears are the larger part of the whole. Let us take an inventory of his stock as he rides into camp at night. Poor fellow! he has rode upon that knock-kneed, shaved tail, rail fence mule over 30 miles, has fought the brush and mud, and passed through untold dangers, and all for his load, which consists of, first, a bundle of fodder for his mule; second, three hams, a sack of meal, a peck of potatoes; third, a fresh bed quilt, the old mother's coffee pot, a jug of vinegar and a bed cord. You call him an old, steady bummer. I'll give you one more picture. Here comes a squad of eighteen or nineteen, no two alike. Look at the chickens, geese, beehives; see that little fellow with a huge hog strapped upon his nag's back. There rides the commander, a Lieutenant, completely happy, for the day has been a good one, and his detail has got enough for a day's good supply for his regiment.

These "Bummers" were detailed for foragers, and upon them the army depended for subsistence; for be it known that we started with a very small stock of supplies, and our campaign was lengthened after starting from our base (Savannah), consequently the "Bummers" were the life of the army. About 5,000 strong, not a field or house or barn, but was searched by them; not a town or hamlet but the "infernal bummers" (as Kilpatrick said) managed to plunder before his cavalry came up. They met the enemy at Fayetteville, and drove him across Cape Fear river; they entered Columbia as skirmishers, not only for "Johnnies," but for meat and bread and goodies. Many outrages were committed by them. To enter a house and find the feather bed ripped open, the wardrobes ransacked, chests stripped of contents, looking glasses taken from the walls, cooking utensils gone, and all the corn meal and bacon missing, bed quilts stripped from the beds, the last jar of pickles gone, was no uncommon sight, and one to make a soldier blush with indignation. Every effort that could be made was made to check the demoralization of the foragers; but the occupation tended to demoralization, and "the army must be fed, and the Bummers must feed us." Thus we reasoned, but deprecated the means used to bring about the result. Some would discriminate, others would not, and thus the few have caused a great deal of unnecessary suffering.

CHAS. A. BOOTH

—BRADLEY, *The Star Corps*

B. A Good Word for the Bummers

Besides the fighting population of our camps there is a population constitutionally opposed to warfare—cooks, ambulance nurses, stretcher-bearers, shirks, and sometimes surgeons, who all come under the class technically called *bummers*. These are treated by the fighting men with a sort of cool contempt, no matter whether necessity or inclination keeps them to the rear, and they have a hard time. Frequently the rear of the army is a much more dangerous locality than the front line, for the missiles passing over the front line must fall somewhere, and often demoralize whole hosts of "bummers," who build miniature fortifications to live in, and collect together in crowds; for misery loves company. Any favorable ravine thus peopled immediately becomes denominated "Bummer's Roost." Here they spend their days in cooking for their nurses, if they are cooks, or attending to their own business, if their object be to escape duty and danger. Among them originate all sorts of marvelous reports of immense success or terrible disaster. They always know just what General Sherman said about the situation at any given time; and from them start many of the wild stories which penetrate the columns of our best papers.

To watch these cooks, freighted with the precious coffee for the men in the trenches, as they go out to the front three times a day, is amusing. From continually dodging the passing shells or stray bullets their forms become bent and stooping. As they approach the line, the men in the trenches commence shouting, "Hey, bummer! Run quick, bummer!" "A man was killed just there, bummer!" With such encouragements the coffee at last reaches its destination, and being distributed among the eager men the bummer is soon at liberty to hurry back to the "Roost."

—Dwight, "How We Fight at Atlanta"

C. "We Were Proud of Our Foragers"

At length, when we left Savannah and launched cheerily into the untrodden land of South Carolina, the foragers began to assume their wonted spirit. We were proud of our foragers. They constituted a picked force from each regiment, under an officer selected for the command, and were remarkable for intelligence, spirit, and daring. Before daylight, mounted on horses captured on the plantations, they were in the saddle and away, covering the country sometimes seven miles in advance. Although I have said "in the saddle," many a forager had nothing better than a bit of carpet and a rope halter; yet this simplicity of equipment did not abate his power of carrying off hams and sweet-potatoes in the face of the enemy. The foragers were also important as a sort of advance guard, for they formed virtually a curtain of mounted infantry screening us from the inquisitive eyes of parties of Wheeler's cavalry, with whom they did not hesitate to engage when it was a question of a rich plantation.

When compelled to retire, they resorted to all the tricks of infantry skirmishers, and summoned reënforcements of foragers from other regiments to help drive the "Johnnies" out. When success crowned their efforts, the plantation was promptly stripped of live stock and eatables. The natives were accustomed to bury provisions, for they feared their own soldiers quite as much as they feared ours. These subterranean stores were readily discovered by the practiced "Yankee" eye. The appearance of the ground and a little probing with a ramrod or a bayonet soon decided whether to dig. Teams were improvised; carts and vehicles of all sorts were pressed into the service and loaded with provisions. If any antiquated militia uniforms were discovered, they were promptly donned, and a comical procession escorted the valuable train of booty to the point where the brigade was expected to bivouac for the night. The regimentals of the past, even to those of revolutionary times, were often conspicuous.

On an occasion when our brigade had the advance, several parties of foragers, consolidating themselves, captured a town from the enemy's cavalry, and occupied the neighboring plantations. Before the arrival of the main column hostilities had ceased; order had been restored, and mock arrangements were made to receive the army. Our regiment in the advance was confronted by a picket dressed in continental uniform, who waved his plumed hat in response to the gibes of the men, and galloped away on his bareback mule to apprise his comrades of our approach. We marched into the town and rested on each side of the main street. Presently a forager, in ancient militia uniform indicating high rank, debouched from a side street to do the honors of the occasion. He was mounted on a raw-boned horse with a bit of carpet for a saddle. His old plumed chapeau in hand, he rode with gracious dignity through the street, as if reviewing the brigade. After him came a family carriage laden with hams, sweet-potatoes, and other provisions, and drawn by two horses, a mule, and a cow, the two latter ridden by postilions.

At Fayetteville, North Carolina, the foragers as usual had been over the ground several hours before the heads of column arrived, and the party from my regiment had found a broken-down grist-mill. Their commander, Captain Parker, an officer of great spirit and efficiency, and an expert machinist, had the old wheel hoisted into its place and put the mill in working order. Several parties from other regiments had been admitted as working members, and teams of all sorts were busy collecting and bringing in corn and carrying away meal for distribution. This bit of enterprise was so pleasing to the troops that plenty of volunteers were ready to relieve the different gangs, and the demand was so great as to keep the mill at work all night by the light of pine-knot fires and torches.

—OAKEY, "Marching Through Georgia and the Carolinas"

12. "THE HEAVENS WERE LIT UP WITH FLAMES FROM BURNING BUILDINGS"

Here is how the March to the Sea affected its victims. Dolly Lunt was a Maine girl, distantly related to Charles Sumner, who before the war went to

Covington, Georgia, to teach school, and there married a planter, Thomas
Burge. At the time Sherman's army swept through Georgia she was a widow,
still managing the plantation. Her short but moving diary has been rescued
from oblivion by Julian Street.

November 19, 1864

Slept in my clothes last night, as I heard that the Yankees went to neighbor
Montgomery's on Thursday night at one o'clock, searched his house, drank
his wine, and took his money and valuables. As we were not disturbed, I
walked after breakfast, with Sadai, up to Mr. Joe Perry's, my nearest neighbor, where the Yankees were yesterday. Saw Mrs. Laura [Perry] in the road
surrounded by her children, seeming to be looking for some one. She said
she was looking for her husband, that old Mrs. Perry had just sent her word
that the Yankees went to James Perry's the night before, plundered his house,
and drove off all his stock, and that she must drive hers into the old fields.
Before we were done talking, up came Joe and Jim Perry from their hiding-
place. Jim was very much excited. Happening to turn and look behind, as
we stood there, I saw some blue-coats coming down the hill. Jim immediately
raised his gun, swearing he would kill them anyhow.

"No, don't!" said I, and ran home as fast as I could, with Sadai.

I could hear them cry, "Halt! Halt!" and their guns went off in quick
succession. Oh God, the time of trial has come!

A man passed on his way to Covington. I hallooed to him, asking him if
he did not know the Yankees were coming.

"No—are they?"

"Yes," said I; "they are not three hundred yards from here."

"Sure enough," said he. "Well, I'll not go. I don't want them to get my
horse." And although within hearing of their guns, he would stop and look
for them. Blissful ignorance! Not knowing, not hearing, he has not suffered
the suspense, the fear, that I have for the past forty-eight hours. I walked to
the gate. There they came filing up.

I hastened back to my frightened servants and told them that they had
better hide, and then went back to the gate to claim protection and a guard.
But like demons they rush in! My yards are full. To my smoke-house, my
dairy, pantry, kitchen, and cellar, like famished wolves they come, breaking
locks and whatever is in their way. The thousand pounds of meat in my
smoke-house is gone in a twinkling, my flour, my meat, my lard, butter, eggs,
pickles of various kinds—both in vinegar and brine—wine, jars, and jugs are
all gone. My eighteen fat turkeys, my hens, chickens, and fowls, my young
pigs, are shot down in my yard and hunted as if they were rebels themselves.
Utterly powerless I ran out and appealed to the guard.

"I cannot help you, Madam, it is orders."

As I stood there, from my lot I saw driven, first, old Dutch, my dear old
buggy horse, who has carried my beloved husband so many miles, and who
would so quietly wait at the block for him to mount and dismount, and who
at last drew him to his grave; then came old Mary, my brood mare, who for

years had been too old and stiff for work, with her three-year-old colt, my two-year-old mule, and her last little baby colt. There they go! There go my mules, my sheep, and, worse than all, my boys [slaves]!

Alas! little did I think while trying to save my house from plunder and fire that they were forcing my boys from home at the point of the bayonet. One, Newton, jumped into bed in his cabin, and declared himself sick. Another crawled under the floor,—a lame boy he was,—but they pulled him out, placed him on a horse, and drove him off. Mid, poor Mid! The last I saw of him, a man had him going around the garden, looking, as I thought, for my sheep, as he was my shepherd. Jack came crying to me, the big tears coursing down his cheeks, saying they were making him go. I said:

"Stay in my room."

But a man followed in, cursing him and threatening to shoot him if he did not go; so poor Jack had to yield. . . .

My poor boys! My poor boys! What unknown trials are before you! How you have clung to your mistress and assisted her in every way you knew. . . .

Their cabins are rifled of every valuable, the soldiers swearing that their Sunday clothes were the white people's, and that they never had money to get such things as they had. Poor Frank's chest was broken open, his money and tobacco taken. He has always been a money-making and saving boy; not infrequently has his crop brought him five hundred dollars and more. All of his clothes and Rachel's clothes, which dear Lou gave her before her death and which she had packed away, were stolen from her. Ovens, skillets, coffee-mills, of which we had three, coffee-pots—not one have I left. Sifters all gone!

Seeing that the soldiers could not be restrained, the guard ordered me to have their remaining possessions brought into my house, which I did, and they all, poor things, huddled together in my room, fearing every movement that the house would be burned.

A Captain Webber from Illinois came into my house. Of him I claimed protection from the vandals who were forcing themselves into my room. . . .

He felt for me, and I give him and several others the character of gentlemen. I don't believe they would have molested women and children had they had their own way. He seemed surprised that I had not laid away in my house, flour and other provisions. I did not suppose I could secure them there, more than where I usually kept them, for in last summer's raid houses were thoroughly searched. In parting with him, I parted as with a friend.

Sherman himself and a greater portion of his army passed my house that day. All day, as the sad moments rolled on, were they passing not only in front of my house, but from behind; they tore down my garden palings, made a road through my back-yard and lot field, driving their stock and riding through, tearing down my fences and desolating my home—wantonly doing it when there was no necessity for it.

Such a day, if I live to the age of Methuselah, may God spare me from ever seeing again!

As night drew its sable curtains around us, the heavens from every point were lit up with flames from burning buildings. Dinnerless and supperless as we were, it was nothing in comparison with the fear of being driven out homeless to the dreary woods. Nothing to eat! I could give my guard no supper, so he left us. I appealed to another, asking him if he had wife, mother, or sister, and how he should feel were they in my situation. A colonel from Vermont left me two men, but they were Dutch, and I could not understand one word they said.

My Heavenly Father alone saved me from the destructive fire. My carriage-house had in it eight bales of cotton, with my carriage, buggy, and harness. On top of the cotton were some carded cotton rolls, a hundred pounds or more. These were thrown out of the blanket in which they were, and a large twist of the rolls taken and set on fire, and thrown into the boat of my carriage, which was close up to the cotton bales. Thanks to my God, the cotton only burned over, and then went out. Shall I ever forget the deliverance? . . .

The two guards came into my room and laid themselves by my fire for the night. I could not close my eyes, but kept walking to and fro, watching the fires in the distance and dreading the approaching day, which, I feared, as they had not all passed, would be but a continuation of horrors.

—LUNT, A Woman's Wartime Journal

13. ELIZA ANDREWS COMES HOME THROUGH THE BURNT COUNTRY

This is what Georgia looked like after the Yankees were through with it, as seen by a Georgia girl, Eliza Andrews. The War-Time Diary of a Georgia Girl, *from which this brief excerpt is taken, is one of the best of all Confederate diaries.*

December 24, 1864.—About three miles from Sparta we struck the "burnt country," as it is well named by the natives, and then I could better understand the wrath and desperation of these poor people. I almost felt as if I should like to hang a Yankee myself. There was hardly a fence left standing all the way from Sparta to Gordon. The fields were trampled down and the road was lined with carcasses of horses, hogs, and cattle that the invaders, unable either to consume or to carry away with them, had wantonly shot down, to starve out the people and prevent them from making their crops. The stench in some places was unbearable; every few hundred yards we had to hold our noses or stop them with the cologne Mrs. Elzey had given us, and it proved a great boon. The dwellings that were standing all showed signs of pillage, and on every plantation we saw the charred remains of the ginhouse and packing screw, while here and there lone chimney stacks, "Sherman's sentinels," told of homes laid in ashes. The infamous wretches! I couldn't wonder now that these poor people should want to put a rope round the neck of every red-handed "devil of them" they could lay their hands on. Hayricks and fodder stacks were demolished, corncribs were empty, and every bale of cotton that could be found was burnt by the savages. I saw no grain of any sort except little patches they had spilled when feeding their horses and which there was not even a chicken left in the country to eat. A bag of oats might have lain anywhere along the road without danger from the beasts of the field, though I cannot say it would have been safe from the assaults of hungry man.

Crowds of soldiers were tramping over the road in both directions; it was like traveling through the streets of a populous town all day. They were mostly on foot, and I saw numbers seated on the roadside greedily eating raw turnips, meat skins, parched corn—anything they could find, even picking up the loose grains that Sherman's horses had left. I felt tempted to stop and empty the contents of our provision baskets into their laps, but the dreadful accounts that were given of the state of the country before us made prudence get the better of our generosity.

Before crossing the Oconee at Milledgeville we ascended an immense hill, from which there was a fine view of the town, with Governor Brown's fortifications in the foreground and the river rolling at our feet. The Yankees had burnt the bridge; so we had to cross on a ferry. There was a long train of vehicles ahead of us, and it was nearly an hour before our turn came; so we had ample time to look about us. On our left was a field where thirty thousand Yankees had camped hardly three weeks before. It was strewn with the debris they had left behind, and the poor people of the neighborhood were wandering over it, seeking for anything they could find to eat, even picking up grains of corn that were scattered around where the Yankees had fed their horses. We were told that a great many valuables were found there at first, plunder that the invaders had left behind, but the place had been picked over so often by this time that little now remained except tufts of loose cotton, piles of half-rotted grain, and the carcasses of slaughtered animals, which raised a horrible stench. Some men were plowing in one part of the field, making ready for next year's crop.

—ANDREWS, *The War-Time Journal of a Georgia Girl*

14. SOUTH CAROLINA BECOMES A "HOWLING WASTE"

There was a good deal of vindictiveness in the Union ranks, and most of it was reserved for South Carolina. That state, it was felt, was chiefly responsible for the war. It had been the first to secede, and it was in Charleston harbor that the war began.

Here Captain Oakey describes the march through South Carolina.

THE beginning of our march in South Carolina was pleasant, the weather favorable, and the country productive. Sometimes at the midday halt a stray pig that had cunningly evaded the foragers would venture forth in the belief of having escaped "the cruel war," and would find his error, alas! too late, by encountering our column. Instantly an armed mob would set upon him, and his piercing shrieks would melt away in the scramble for fresh pork. But the midday sport of the main column and the happy life of the forager were sadly interrupted. The sun grew dim, and the rain came and continued. A few of our excellent foragers were reported captured by Wheeler's cavalry, while we sank deeper and deeper in the mud as we approached the Salkehatchie Swamp, which lay between us and the Charleston and Augusta railroad. As the heads of column came up, each command knew what it had to do. Generals Mower and G. A. Smith got their divisions across by swimming, wading, and floating, and effected lodgments in spite of the enemy's fire. An overwhelming mass of drenched and muddy veterans swept away the enemy, while the rest of our force got the trains and artillery over by corduroying, pontooning, and bridging. It seemed a grand day's work to have accomplished, as we sank down that night in our miry bivouac. The gallant General Wager Swayne lost his leg in this Salkehatchie encounter. Luckily for him and others we were not yet too far from our friends to send the wounded back, with a strong escort, to Pocotaligo.

We destroyed about forty miles of the Charleston and Augusta railroad, and, by threatening points beyond the route we intended to take, we deluded the enemy into concentrating at Augusta and other places, while we marched rapidly away, leaving him well behind, and nothing but Wade Hampton's cavalry, and the more formidable obstacle of the Saluda River and its swamps, between us and Columbia, our next objective. As the route of our column lay west of Columbia, I saw nothing of the oft-described and much-discussed burning of that city.

During the hasty removal of the Union prisoners from Columbia two Massachusetts officers managed to make their escape. Exhausted and almost naked, they found their way to my command. My mess begged for the privilege of caring for one of them. We gave him a mule to ride with a comfortable saddle, and scraped together an outfit for him, although our clothes were in the last stages. Our guest found the mess luxurious, as he sat down with us at the edge of a rubber blanket spread upon the ground for a table-cloth, and set with tin cups and platters. Stewed fighting-cock and bits of fried turkey were followed by fried corn-meal and sorghum. Then came our coffee and pipes, and we lay down by a roaring fire of pine-knots, to hear our guest's story of life in a rebel prison. Before daybreak the tramp of horses reminded us that our foragers were sallying forth. The red light from the countless camp-fires melted away as the dawn stole over the horizon, casting its wonderful gradations of light and color over the masses of sleeping soldiers, while the smoke from burning pine-knots befogged the chilly morning air. Then the bugles broke the impressive stillness, and the roll of drums was heard on all sides. Soon the scene was alive with blue coats and the hubbub of roll-calling, cooking, and running for water to the nearest spring or stream. The surgeons looked to the sick and footsore, and weeded from the ambulances those who no longer needed to ride.

It was not uncommon to hear shots at the head of the column. The foragers would come tumbling back, and ride alongside the regiment, adding to

SAVANNAH TO BENTONVILLE

961

the noisy talk their account of what they had seen, and dividing among their comrades such things as they had managed to bring away in their narrow escape from capture. A staff-officer would gallop down the roadside like a man who had forgotten something which must be recovered in a hurry. At the sound of the colonel's ringing voice, silence was instant and absolute. Sabers flashed from their scabbards, the men brought their guns to the "carry," and the battalion swung into line at the roadside; cats, fighting-cocks, and frying-pans passed to the rear rank; officers and sergeants buzzed around their companies to see that the guns were loaded and the men ready for action. The color-sergeant loosened the water-proof cover of the battle-flag, a battery of artillery flew past on its way to the front, following the returning staff-officer, and we soon heard the familiar bang of shells. Perhaps it did not amount to much after all, and we were soon swinging into "route step" again.

At times when suffering from thirst it was hard to resist the temptation of crystal swamp water, as it rippled along the side of a causeway, a tempting sight for the weary and unwary. In spite of oft-repeated cautions, some contrived to drink it, but these were on their backs with malarial disease at the end of the campaign, if not sooner.

After passing Columbia there was a brief season of famine. The foragers worked hard, but found nothing. They made amends, however, in a day or two, bringing in the familiar corn-meal, sweet-potatoes, and bacon.

We marched into Cheraw with music and with colors flying. Stacking arms in the main street, we proceeded to supper, while the engineers laid the pontoons across the Pedee River. The railing of the town pump, and the remains of a buggy, said to belong to Mr. Lincoln's brother-in-law, Dr. Todd, were quickly reduced to kindling-wood to boil the coffee. The necessary destruction of property was quickly accomplished, and on we went. A mile from the Lumber River the country, already flooded ankle-deep, was rendered still more inhospitable by a steady down-pour of rain. The bridges had been partly destroyed by the enemy, and partly swept away by the flood. An attempt to carry heavy army wagons and artillery across this dreary lake might have seemed rather foolhardy, but we went to work without loss of time. The engineers were promptly floated out to the river, to direct the rebuilding of bridges, and the woods all along the line of each column soon rang with the noise of axes. Trees quickly became logs, and were brought to the submerged roadway. No matter if logs disappeared in the floating mud; thousands more were coming from all sides. So, layer upon layer, the work went bravely on. Soon the artillery and wagons were jolting over our wooden causeway.

As my regiment was the rear-guard for the day, we had various offices to perform for the train, and it was midnight before we saw the last wagon over the bridge by the light of our pine torches. It seemed as if that last wagon was never to be got over. It came bouncing and bumping along, its six mules smoking and blowing in the black, misty air. The teamster, mounted on one of the wheelers, guided his team with a single rein and addressed each mule by name, reminding the animal of his faults, and accusing him of having, among other peculiarities, "a black military heart." Every sentence of his oath-adorned rhetoric was punctuated with a dexterous whip-lash. At last, drenched to the skin and covered with mud, I took my position on the bridge, seated in a chair which one of my men had presented to me, and waited for the command to "close up." . . .

As we advanced into the wild pine regions of North Carolina the natives seemed wonderfully impressed at seeing every road filled with marching troops, artillery, and wagon trains. They looked destitute enough as they stood in blank amazement gazing upon the "Yanks" marching by. The scene before us was very striking; the resin pits were on fire, and great columns of black smoke rose high into the air, spreading and mingling together in gray clouds, and suggesting the roof and pillars of a vast temple. All traces of habitation were left behind, as we marched into that giant forest with its beautiful carpet of pine-needles. The straight trunks of the pine-trees shot up to a great height, and then spread out into a green roof, which kept us in perpetual shade.

As night came on, we found that the resinous sap in the cavities cut in the trees to receive it, had been lighted by "bummers" in our advance. The effect of these peculiar watch-fires on every side, several feet above the ground, with flames licking their way up the tall trunks, was peculiarly striking and beautiful. But it was sad to see this wanton destruction of property, which, like the firing of the resin pits, was the work of "bummers," who were marauding through the country committing every sort of outrage. There was no restraint except with the column or the regular foraging parties. We had no communications, and could have no safeguards. The country was necessarily left to take care of itself, and became a "howling waste." The "coffee-coolers" of the Army of the Potomac were archangels compared to our "bummers," who often fell to the tender mercies of Wheeler's cavalry, and were never heard of again, earning a fate richly deserved.

—Oakey, "Marching through Georgia and the Carolinas"

15. THE BURNING OF COLUMBIA

Sherman reached Columbia, capital of South Carolina, on February 17. That night the city burned. Whether "Sherman burned Columbia" or not is still hotly debated. Sherman himself denied responsibility for the con-flagration, but he did say that "having utterly ruined Columbia, the right wing began its march northward." Perhaps the fire was started by accident; perhaps by the Confederates burning their cotton; perhaps by Negroes; perhaps by soldiers out of control.

We have here two accounts of the tragedy. The first comes from George Nichols, whose Story of the Great March *was the most widely read of con-temporary Civil War narratives; the second from Henry Hitchcock, whom we have already met.*

A. "A Scene of Shameful Confusion"

Columbia, February 17th [*1865*]—It is with a feeling of proud exultation that I write the date of Columbia. We have conquered and occupy the capital of the haughty state that instigated and forced forward the treason which has brought on this desolating war. The city which was to have been the capital of the Confederacy if Lee and the Rebel hosts had been driven from Richmond is now overrun by Northern soldiers. The beautiful capitol building bears the marks of Yankee shot and shell, and the old flag which the Rebels insulted at Sumter now floats freely in the air from the house-tops of the central city of South Carolina. . . .

General Sherman and General Howard were the first to cross the bridge, and entered the city, followed by their staffs. A scene of shameful confusion met their eyes. On every side were evidences of disorder; bales of cotton scattered here and there; articles of household furniture and merchandise of every description cast pell-mell in every direction by the frightened inhabitants, who had escaped from a city which they supposed was doomed to destruction. . . .

The three or four days' notice of our approach enabled the government officials to remove most of the material belonging to the branch of the Treasury Department which was located at this point; yet large quantities of paper for printing Confederate notes and bonds, with type, printing-presses, etc., has fallen into our hands. This loss is irreparable to the Rebel government.

The arsenal was found well stocked with shot, shell, fixed ammunition, powder, Enfield rifles, carbines, and other material of war. A full battery of four rifled English Blakely guns, which were in a battery commanding the bridge, was also taken, with caissons and other material. Connected with the arsenal are shops full of costly machinery for the manufacture of arms and ammunition, with founderies for all sorts of castings. A little way down the river there is a large powder-mill. All of this will be thoroughly destroyed. . . .

The store-houses are filled with all sorts of supplies—flour, meal, bacon, corn, harness, hardware, etc.—while cotton is found in every direction. As there is no treasury agent of our government to appropriate this costly material for somebody's benefit, I doubt if a very correct record of the quantity will be made before it is burned. . . .

I began to-day's record early in the evening, and while writing I noticed an unusual glare in the sky, and heard a sound of running to and fro in the streets, with the loud talk of servants that the horses must be removed to a safer place. Running out, I found, to my surprise and real sorrow, that the central part of the city, including the main business street, was in flames, while the wind, which had been blowing a hurricane all day, was driving the sparks and cinders in heavy masses over the eastern portion of the city, where the finest residences are situated. These buildings, all wooden, were instantly ignited by the flying sparks. In half an hour the conflagration was raging in every direction, and but for a providential change of the wind to the south and west, the whole city would in a few hours have been laid in ashes.

As it is, several hundred buildings, including the old State House, one or two churches, most of the carved work stored in the sheds round about the new capitol, and a large number of public store-houses, have been destroyed. In some of the public buildings the Rebels had stored shot, shell, and other ammunition, and when the flames reached these magazines we had the Atlanta experience over again—the smothered boom, the huge columns of fire shooting heavenward, the red-hot iron flying here and there. But there was one feature, pitiable indeed, which we did not find at Atlanta. Groups of men, women, and children were gathered in the streets and squares, huddled together over a trunk, a mattress, or a bundle of clothes. Our soldiers were at work with a will, removing household goods from the dwellings which were in the track of the flames, and here and there extinguishing the fire when there was hope of saving a building. General Sherman and his officers worked with their own hands until long after midnight, trying to save life and property. The house taken for headquarters is now filled with old men, women, and children who have been driven from their homes by a more pitiless enemy than the detested "Yankees."

Various causes are assigned to explain the origin of the fire. I am quite sure that it originated in sparks flying from the hundreds of bales of cotton which the Rebels had placed along the middle of the main street, and fired as they left the city. Fire from a tightly-compressed bale of cotton is unlike that of a more open material, which burns itself out. The fire lies smouldering in a bale of cotton long after it appears to be extinguished; and in this instance, when our soldiers supposed they had extinguished the fire, it suddenly broke out again with the most disastrous effect.

There were fires, however, which must have been started independent of the above-named cause. The source of these is ascribed to the desire for revenge from some two hundred of our prisoners, who had escaped from the cars as they were being conveyed from this city to Charlotte, and, with the memories of long sufferings in the miserable pens I visited yesterday on the other side of the river, sought this means of retaliation. Again, it is said that the soldiers who first entered the town, intoxicated with success and a liberal supply of bad liquor, which was freely distributed among them by designing citizens, in an insanity of exhilaration set fire to unoccupied houses.

Whatever may have been the cause of the disaster, the direful result is deprecated by General Sherman most emphatically; for however heinous the crimes of this people against our common country, we do not war against women and children and helpless persons.

—NICHOLS, *The Story of the Great March*

B. MAJOR HITCHCOCK EXPLAINS THE BURNING OF COLUMBIA

Fayetteville, North Carolina, Sunday, March 12, 1865

One word about Columbia. It was not burned by orders, but expressly against orders and in spite of the utmost effort on our part to save it. Everything seemed to conspire for its destruction. The streets were full of loose cotton, brought out and set on fire *by the rebels* before they left,—I saw it when we rode into town. A gale of wind was blowing all that day and that night, and the branches of the trees were white with cotton tufts blown about everywhere. The citizens themselves—like idiots, madmen,—brought out large quantities of liquor as soon as our troops entered and distributed it freely among them, even to the guards which Gen. Howard had immediately placed all over the city as soon as we came in. This fact is unquestionable, and was one chief cause of what followed. Here in Fayetteville a lady has told Gen. Sherman that Gen. Joe Johnson told her, yesterday morning, that the burning of Columbia was caused by liquor which the people there gave our soldiers. Besides there were 200 or 300 of "our prisoners" who had escaped from rebel hands before, and when we reached Columbia burning to revenge themselves for the cruel treatment they had received; and our own men were fully aware of the claims of Columbia to eminence as the "cradle of secession." In that same town, in 1861, a woman, a school-teacher from New England, was *tarred and feathered* and sent North "for abolition sentiments."

The result of all this was that partly by accident, from the burning cotton, partly by design by our escaped prisoners, and by our drunken men, fire was started in several places,—and once started, with the furious wind blowing, it was simply impossible to put it out. *Nothing was left undone,*—I speak advisedly—to prevent and stop it; Gen. Howard, Sherman, and other Generals and their staffs, and many other officers and hundreds of men were up and at work nearly all night, trying to do it, but in vain. The guard was changed—*three times* as many men were on guard as were ever on guard at any one time in Savannah where perfect order was preserved; our own officers shot our men down like dogs wherever they were found riotous or drunk—in short no effort was spared to stop it; and but for the liquor it might perhaps have been stopped. This is the truth; and Wade Hampton's letter to Sherman—it will be in the New York Herald if not already published North—charging him with sundry crimes at Columbia is a tissue of lies.

—Hitchcock, "Letters and Diaries"

16. GENERAL SHERMAN THINKS HIS NAME MAY LIVE

We have already read Sherman's statement to the Mayor of Atlanta on the iron necessities of war. Here is an explanation*—and a prophecy—directed to his wife. On the death of his father, Sherman had been practically adopted by Senator Ewing of Ohio. In 1850 he married Ewing's daughter Ellen. His war letters to his wife are among the most revealing and touching of Civil War letters.

* Reprinted from *Home Letters of General Sherman* edited by M. A. De Wolfe Howe; copyright 1909 by Charles Scribner's Sons, 1937 by M. A. De Wolfe Howe; used by permission of the publishers.

Savannah, January 5, 1865

John writes that I am in everybody's mouth and that even he is known as my brother, and that all the Shermans are now feted as relatives of me. Surely you and the children will not be overlooked by those who profess to honor me. I do think that in the several grand epochs of this war, my name will have a prominent part, and not least among them will be the determination I took at Atlanta to destroy that place, and march on this city, whilst Thomas, my lieutenant, should dispose of Hood. The idea, the execution and strategy are all good, and will in time be understood. I don't know that you comprehend the magnitude of the thing, but you can see the importance attached to it in England where the critics stand ready to turn against any American general who makes a mistake or fails in its execution. In my case they had time to commit themselves to the conclusion that if I succeeded I would be a great general, but if I failed I would be set down a fool. My success is already assured, so that I will be found to sustain the title. I am told that were I to go north I would be feted and petted, but as I have no intention of going, you must sustain the honors of the family. I know exactly what amount of merit attaches to my own conduct, and what will survive the clamor of time. The quiet preparation I made before the Atlanta Campaign, the rapid movement on Resaca, the crossing the Chattahoochee without loss in the face of a skillful general with a good army, the movement on Jonesboro, whereby Atlanta fell, and the resolution I made to divide my army, with one part to take Savannah and the other to meet Hood in Tennessee are all clearly mine, and will survive us both in history. I don't know that you can understand the merit of the latter, but it will stamp me in years to come, and will be more appreciated in Europe than in America. I warrant your father will find parallel in the history of the Greeks and Persians, but none on our continent. For his sake I am glad of the success that has attended me, and I know he will feel more pride in my success than you or I do. Oh that Willy were living! how his eyes would brighten and his bosom swell with honest pride if he could hear and understand these things. . . .

You will doubtless read all the details of our march and stay in Savannah in the papers, whose spies infest our camps, spite of all I can do, but I could tell you thousands of little incidents which would more interest you. The women here are, as at Memphis, disposed to usurp my time more from curiosity than business. They have been told of my burning and killing until they expected the veriest monster, but their eyes were opened when Hardee, G. W. Smith and McLaws, the three chief officers of the Rebel army, fled across the Savannah river consigning their families to my special care. There are some very elegant people here, whom I knew in better days and who do not seem ashamed to call on the 'Vandal Chief.' They regard us just as the Romans did the Goths and the parallel is not unjust. Many of my stalwart men with red beards and huge frames look like giants, and it is wonderful how smoothly all things move, for they all seem to feel implicit faith in me not because I am strong or bold, but because they think I know everything. It seems impossible for us to go anywhere without being where I have been before. My former life from 1840 to 1846 seems providential and every bit of knowledge then acquired is returned, tenfold. Should it so happen that I should approach Charleston on that very ground where I used to hunt with Jim Poyas, and Mr. Quash, and ride by moonlight to save daytime, it would be even more strange than here where I was only a visitor.

—Howe, ed., *Home Letters of General Sherman*

XXVII

The Wilderness

In February 1864 *U. S. Grant was made lieutenant general and placed in command of all the armies of the United States. For the first time it was possible to organize a unified plan of operations against the Confederacy, and this Grant promptly proceeded to do. Grant might have stayed in Washington to supervise all the complex operations which his plan involved; he preferred to accompany Meade in the crucial campaign against Lee. Thus at last these two great military chieftains were to meet in battle, a battle which ended with Lee's surrender at Appomattox just a year later. In the campaigns of 1864-65 Grant enjoyed most of the advantages. He had a numerical superiority of about two to one, and no difficulty in getting reinforcements when needed. He could count on simultaneous attacks from other quarters which would drain the Confederacy of man power, war matériel, and—in the end—the will to resist. If he did not enjoy interior lines of communication he did have command of the seas and the assistance of the navy. His armies were well fed, well clothed, and well equipped, and never lacked for munitions. As he took, and held, the offensive, he had the initiative. Lee had only the advantage of geography, and of his own military genius. The terrain over which the armies fought was well adapted to defensive operations; Lee knew it intimately; he could draw on some help from Richmond and from Beauregard on the James. But by 1864 death, disease, and desertion had reduced the Army of Northern Virginia to a point well below its strength of earlier years, and the blockade and the capture of Confederate arsenals had reduced its fighting strength. Its soldiers were hungry, ill-clad, ill-shod, and battle-weary; they knew that they could not count on reinforcement or replacement, and they knew, too, that things were going badly almost everywhere else in the Confederacy. That for a year they held off Grant's mighty hosts is a tribute to their fortitude, their fighting qualities, and their devotion to their heroic leader.*

The strategy of Grant's campaign against Lee is simple enough. His objective was not so much Richmond as Lee's army; his policy to hammer away at it until it was decimated. Lee's task was to keep Grant away from Richmond and to inflict such losses upon him that he would abandon the offensive or that the North would despair of victory and turn Lincoln out at the fall elections. With almost anyone else Lee's strategy might have worked, but in Grant he had an opponent who never knew when he was licked.

The Wilderness campaign was really one prolonged battle, from May 4, when Grant crossed the Rapidan, to June 14, when he crossed the James. The details of this battle are confusing but the general pattern is clear. To get to Richmond Grant had to whip Lee's army, or destroy it; Lee's job was to tangle him up in the Wilderness and destroy him. Imagine a diagonal line of about sixty miles, stretching roughly southeasterly from Germanna Ford on the Rapidan to Cold Harbor, just ten miles east of Richmond. Grant smashed at Lee's line, was held and thrust back, and then slid down the diagonal with Lee racing on a parallel line to stop him. Attack, repulse, slide, attack, repulse, slide—that is the tactical story of the Battle of the Wilderness, Spotsylvania, Hanover Court House, and Cold Harbor. No single battle in this campaign reached the dimensions of Gettysburg or Shiloh, but collectively they constituted the most costly campaign of the war and they embraced, too, the hottest fighting of the war. Grant's losses in the Wilderness campaign came to about 55,000; Lee's are unknown, but were probably about half that number.

Who won the Battle of the Wilderness? That is hard to say. On the face of it the victory was Lee's. He had prevented Grant from breaking his lines, had saved Richmond, had forced Grant to abandon the campaign of the direct attack from the north and fall back on siege, and had inflicted on Grant losses almost as large as the whole of Lee's own army. Yet Grant had largely achieved his own primary objective. He had so punished Lee that the Army of Northern Virginia never really recovered. He had thus prepared the way for the subsequent attack on Richmond from the south. And he ended his campaign with more men in his army than he had when he crossed the Rapidan.

1. U. S. GRANT PLANS HIS SPRING CAMPAIGN

Here is Grant's own statement of the grand strategy which he formulated for the spring of 1864; it has all his characteristic sparseness of phrase and his objectivity.

THE Union armies were now divided into nineteen departments, though four of them in the West had been concentrated into a single military division. The Army of the Potomac was a separate command, and had no territorial limits. There were thus seventeen distinct commanders. Before this time these various armies had acted separately and independently of each other, giving the enemy an opportunity, often, of depleting one command, not pressed, to reënforce another more actively engaged. I determined to stop this. To this end I regarded the Army of the Potomac as the center, and all west to Memphis, along the line described as our position at the time, and north of it, the right wing; the Army of the James, under General Butler, as the left wing, and all the troops south as a force in rear of the enemy. Some of these last were occupying positions from which they could not render service proportionate to their numerical strength. All such were depleted to the minimum necessary to hold their positions as a guard against blockade-runners; when they could not do this, their positions were abandoned altogether. In this way ten thousand men were added to the Army of the James from South Carolina alone, with General Gillmore in command. It was not contemplated that Gillmore should leave his department; but as most of his troops were taken, presumably for active service, he asked to accompany them, and was permitted to do so. Officers and soldiers on furlough, of whom there were many thousands, were ordered to their proper commands; concentration was the order of the day, and the problem was to accomplish it in time to advance at the earliest moment the roads would permit.

As a reënforcement to the Army of the Potomac, or to act in support of it, the Ninth Army Corps, over twenty thousand strong, under General Burnside, had been rendezvoused at Annapolis, Maryland. This was an admirable position for such a reënforcement. The corps could be brought at the last moment as a reënforcement to the Army of the Potomac, or it could be thrown on the sea-coast, south of Norfolk, to operate against Richmond from that direction. In fact, up to the last moment Burnside and the War Department both thought the Ninth Corps was intended for such an expedition.

My general plan now was to concentrate all the force possible against the Confederate armies in the field. There were but two such, as we have seen, east of the Mississippi River and facing north: the Army of Northern Virginia, General Robert E. Lee commanding, was on the south bank of the Rapidan, confronting the Army of the Potomac; the second, under General Joseph E. Johnston, was at Dalton, Georgia, opposed to Sherman, who was still at Chattanooga. Besides these main armies, the Confederates had to guard the Shenandoah Valley—a great storehouse to feed their armies from—and their line of communications from Richmond to Tennessee. Forrest, a brave and intrepid cavalry general, was in the West, with a large force, making a larger command necessary to hold what we had gained in middle and west Tennessee. We could not abandon any territory north of the line held by the enemy, because it would lay the Northern States open to invasion. But as the Army of the Potomac was the principal garrison for the protection of Washington, even while it was moving on to Lee, so all the forces to the West, and the Army of the James, guarded their special trusts when advancing from them as well as when remaining at them—better, indeed, for they forced the enemy to guard his own lines and resources, at a greater distance from ours and with a greater force, since small expeditions could not so well be sent out to destroy a bridge or tear up a few miles of railroad track, burn a storehouse, or inflict other little annoyances. Accordingly I arranged for a simultaneous movement all along the line.

Sherman was to move from Chattanooga, Johnston's army and Atlanta being his objective points. General George Crook, commanding in West Virginia, was to move from the mouth of the Gauley River with a cavalry force and some artillery, the Virginia and Tennessee railroad to be his objective. Either the enemy would have to keep a large force to protect their communications or see them destroyed, and a large amount of forage and provisions, which they so much needed, would fall into our hands. Sigel, who was in command in the valley of Virginia, was to advance up the valley, covering the North from an invasion through that channel as well while advancing as by remaining near Harper's Ferry. Every mile he advanced also gave us possession of stores on which Lee relied. Butler was to advance by the James River, having Richmond and Petersburg as his objective. Before the advance commenced I visited Butler at Fort Monroe. This was the first time I had ever met him. Before giving him any order as to the part he was to play in the approaching campaign I invited his views. They were very much such as I intended to direct, and as I did direct, in writing, before leaving. . . .

Banks in the Department of the Gulf was ordered to assemble all his troops at New Orleans in time to join in the general move, Mobile to be his objective.

—*Personal Memoirs of U. S. Grant*

2. LINCOLN AND GRANT PAY TRIBUTE TO EACH OTHER

Lincoln had, from the first, been attracted to Grant; when, early in the war, there was some pressure for Grant's removal Lincoln is alleged to have said, "I can't spare that man; he fights." It was Grant's habit of fighting, and of winning victories, that commended him to his commander in chief—that and his ability to avoid those personal and professional quarrels that marred the careers of so many Civil War generals. Grant had never met the President until he called on him to receive his commission as lieutenant general; at that interview Lincoln assured him that all he wanted was someone who "would take responsibility and act."

Lincoln had been informed, of course, of Grant's plans, and just before the Wilderness campaign got under way he sent Grant a note of approval and appreciation. That letter, and Grant's reply, are reproduced here.

EXECUTIVE MANSION, WASHINGTON, April 30, 1864

LIEUTENANT-GENERAL GRANT: Not expecting to see you again before the Spring campaign opens, I wish to express in this way my entire satisfaction with what you have done up to this time, so far as I understand it. The particulars of your plans I neither know or seek to know. You are vigilant and self-reliant; and, pleased with this, I wish not to obtrude any constraints or restraints upon you. While I am very anxious that any great disaster, or the capture of our men in great numbers, shall be avoided, I know these points are less likely to escape your attention than they would be mine. If there is anything wanting which is within my power to give, do not fail to let me know it. And now with a brave army, and a just cause, may God sustain you.

Yours very truly,

A. LINCOLN.

HEADQUARTERS, ARMIES OF THE UNITED STATES,
CULPEPER COURT HOUSE, VIRGINIA, May 1, 1864

THE PRESIDENT: Your very kind letter of yesterday is just received. The confidence you express for the future and satisfaction for the past in my military administration is acknowledged with pride. It shall be my earnest endeavor that you and the country shall not be disappointed. From my first entrance into the volunteer service of the country to the present day, I have never had cause of complaint—have never expressed or implied a complaint against the Administration or the Secretary of War, for throwing any embarrassment in the way of my vigorously prosecuting what appeared to be my duty. And since the promotion which placed me in command of all the armies, and in view of the great responsibility and the importance of success, I have been astonished at the readiness with which everything asked for has been yielded, without even an explanation being asked. Should my success be less than I desire and expect, the least I can say is, the fault is not with you.

Very truly, your obedient servant,

U. S. GRANT, Lieutenant-General.

—BADEAU, "Preparing for the Campaigns of '64"

3. COLONEL PORTER DRAWS A PORTRAIT OF GENERAL GRANT

This portrait of Grant is, as might be expected, a friendly one. Horace Porter left Harvard to enter West Point, and graduated third in rank in the class of 1860. He was appointed chief ordnance officer of the Army of the Potomac and then to the same position in the Army of the Cumberland, where he first made Grant's acquaintance. In November 1863 he was recalled for duty in Washington, and in April 1864 appointed aide-de-camp to Grant. He was at Grant's side all through the Wilderness and Petersburg campaigns, and his book, Campaigning with Grant, *is perhaps the best description of that chapter of Grant's military career. After the war Porter had a long and distinguished career in business and public affairs. He was vice-president of the Pullman Company, Ambassador to France, American delegate to the Hague Tribunal, and active in Republican politics and in social life.*

A DESCRIPTION of General Grant's personal appearance at this important period of his career may not be out of place here, particularly as up to that time the public had received such erroneous impressions of him. There were then few correct portraits of him in circulation. Some of the earliest pictures purporting to be photographs of him had been manufactured when he was at the distant front, never stopping in one place long enough to be "focused." Nothing daunted, the practisers of that art which is the chief solace of the vain had photographed a burly beef-contractor, and spread the pictures broadcast as representing the determined, but rather robust, features of the coming hero, and it was some time before the real photographs which followed were believed to be genuine. False impressions of him were derived, too, from the fact that he had come forth from a country leather store, and was famous chiefly for striking sledge-hammer blows in the field, and conducting relentless pursuits of his foes through the swamps of the Southwest. He was pictured in the popular mind as striding about in the most approved swash-buckler style of melodrama.

Many of us were not a little surprised to find in him a man of slim figure, slightly stooped, five feet eight inches in height, weighing only a hundred and thirty-five pounds, and of a modesty of mien and gentleness of manner which seemed to fit him more for the court than for the camp. His eyes were dark-gray, and were the most expressive of his features. Like nearly all men who speak little, he was a good listener; but his face gave little indication of his thoughts, and it was the expression of his eyes which furnished about the only response to the speaker who conversed with him. When he was about to say anything amusing, there was always a perceptible twinkle in his eyes before he began to speak, and he often laughed heartily at a witty remark or a humorous incident.

His mouth, like Washington's, was of the letter-box shape, the contact of the lips forming a nearly horizontal line. This feature was of a pattern in striking contrast with that of Napoleon, who had a bow mouth, which looked as if it had been modeled after a front view of his cocked hat. The firmness with which the general's square-shaped jaws were set when his features were in repose was highly expressive of his force of character and the strength of his will-power. His hair and beard were of a chestnut-brown color. The beard was worn full, no part of the face being shaved, but, like the hair, was always kept closely and nearly trimmed. Like Cromwell, Lincoln, and several other great men in history, he had a wart on his cheek. In his case it was small, and located on the right side just above the line of the beard.

His face was not perfectly symmetrical, the left eye being a very little lower than the right. His brow was high, broad, and rather square, and was creased with several horizontal wrinkles, which helped to emphasize the serious and somewhat careworn look which was never absent from his countenance. This expression, however, was in no wise an indication of his nature, which was always buoyant, cheerful, and hopeful. His voice was exceedingly musical, and one of the clearest in sound and most distinct in utterance that I have ever heard. It had a singular power of penetration, and sentences spoken by him in an ordinary tone in camp could be heard at a distance which was surprising.

His gait in walking might have been called decidedly unmilitary. He never carried his body erect, and having no ear for music or rhythm, he never kept step to the airs played by the bands, no matter how vigorously the bass drums emphasized the accent. When walking in company there was no attempt to keep step with others. In conversing he usually employed only two gestures; one was the stroking of his chin beard with his left hand; the other was the raising and lowering of his right hand, and resting it at intervals upon his knee or a table, the hand being held with the fingers close together and the knuckles bent, so that the back of the hand and fingers formed a right angle. When not pressed by any matter of importance he was often slow in his movements, but when roused to activity he was quick in every motion, and worked with marvelous rapidity.

He was civil to all who came in contact with him, and never attempted to snub any one, or treat anybody with less consideration on account of his inferiority in rank. With him there was none of the puppyism so often bred by power, and none of the dogmatism which Samuel Johnson characterized as puppyism grown to maturity. . . .

Throughout this memorable year (1864-5), the most important as well as the most harassing of his entire military career, General Grant never in any instance failed to manifest those traits which were the true elements of his greatness. He was always calm amid excitement, and patient under trials. He looked neither to the past with regret nor to the future with apprehension. When he could not control he endured, and in every great crisis he could "convince when others could not advise." His calmness of demeanor and unruffled temper were often a marvel even to those most familiar with him. In the midst of the most exciting scenes he rarely raised his voice above its ordinary pitch or manifested the least irritability. Whether encountered at noonday or awakened from sleep at midnight, his manner was always the same; whether receiving the report of an army commander or of a private soldier serving as a courier or a scout, he listened with equal deference and gave it the same strict attention. He could not only discipline others, but he could discipline himself. If he had lived in ancient days he might, in his wrath, have broken the two tables of stone: he never would have broken the laws which were written on them. The only manifestation of anger he had indulged in during the campaign was upon the occasion . . . when he found a teamster beating his horses near the Totopotomoy.

He never criticized an officer harshly in the presence of others. If fault had to be found with him, it was never made an occasion to humiliate him or wound his feelings. The only pointed reprimand he ever administered was in the instance mentioned in the battle of the Wilderness, when an officer left his troops and came to him to magnify the dangers which were to be feared from Lee's methods of warfare. The fact that he never "nagged" his officers, but treated them all with consideration, led them to communicate with him freely and intimately; and he thus gained much information which otherwise he might not have received. To have a well-disciplined command he did not deem it necessary to have an unhappy army. His ideas of discipline did not accord with those of the Russian officer who, one night in the Moscow campaign, reprimanded a soldier for putting a ball of snow under his head for a pillow, for the reason that indulgence in such uncalled-for luxuries would destroy the high character of the army.

It was an interesting study in human nature to watch the general's actions in camp. He would sit for hours in front of his tent, or just inside of it looking out, smoking a cigar very slowly, seldom with a paper or a map in his hands, and looking like the laziest man in camp. But at such periods his mind was working more actively than that of any one in the army. He talked less and thought more than any one in the service. He studiously avoided performing any duty which some one else could do as well or better than he, and in this respect demonstrated his rare powers of administration and executive methods. He was one of the few men holding high position who did not waste valuable hours by giving his personal attention to petty details. He never consumed his time in reading over court-martial proceedings, or figuring up the items of supplies on hand, or writing unnecessary letters or communications. He held subordinates to a strict accountability in the performance of such duties, and kept his own time for thought. It was this quiet but intense thinking, and the well-matured ideas which resulted from it, that led to the prompt and vigorous action which was constantly witnessed during this year, so pregnant with events.

—PORTER, *Campaigning with Grant*

4. FIGHTING IN THE WILDERNESS

Grant began his forward movement on the night of May 2-3, 1864. By the fourth his army was across the Rapidan and in the Wilderness. That was the way Lee wanted it. He knew of Grant's movements, and did not attempt to interfere with his crossing of the river. He preferred to tangle Grant up in the Wilderness as he had tangled Hooker up just a year earlier. For there was no better terrain for defensive operations. General Hancock described it in his report: "It was covered by a dense forest, almost impenetrable by troops in line of battle, where maneuvering was an operation of extreme difficulty and uncertainty. The undergrowth was so heavy that it was scarcely possible to see more than one hundred yards in any direction. The movements of the enemy could not be observed until the lines were almost in collision." Not only was the Wilderness covered by a dense thicket of cedar, pine, and scrub, but it was crisscrossed by small marshy streams, and the roads were mere winding trails.

Cannoneer Buell here gives us a picture of what fighting in this country was like. We have already drawn on his recollections, and need not introduce him anew.

THIS battle of the Wilderness was a singular struggle. It was contested for two days on a line approximately four miles long by about 90,000 troops on our side and 65,000 on theirs, and there was no open ground anywhere wide enough for a division to deploy on. Artillery could have been used there, but only in shelling woods and thickets at random. The battle was brought on by the Rebels moving up to us on the pike and Plank Road and striking the flank of our column as we moved along the Germania Road and the Brock, which intersect the other two at about right angles. The Rebels could have but one reasonable object in this move, and that must have been the hope of repeating Chancellorsville. It has been stated that Gen. Lee believed that he had us whipped on the night of the 6th [May], and expected that we would retreat back across the Rapidan or toward Fredericksburg. But that hope was soon shattered.

As for the fighting, it was simply bushwhacking on a grand scale in brush where all formation beyond that of regiments or companies was soon lost, and where such a thing as a consistent line of battle on either side was impossible. I knew a Wisconsin infantryman named Holmes who walked right into the Rebel skirmish line on the 6th about the time Wadsworth was killed. He surrendered, and a Rebel was sent to the rear with him. In two minutes Holmes and his guard walked right into our own lines, and that in broad daylight. After dark on the 5th four or five men who had straggled from Ayres's Brigade were halted by Bartlett's skirmishers, surrendered to them, and had been started off toward the Wilderness Tavern under guard before it was discovered that they were our own men. During the night of the 5th two men came back to the Lacey House, both slightly wounded. One was a Rebel, belonging to Hill's Corps, and the other was one of our men from Crawford's Division. They had got together in the brush; both had lost their muskets, and as the brush was getting afire they made the best of their way out of it together, taking their chances as to which of the two lines they might fall into. A man named Coombs, of the 44th New York, whom I knew, got lost in Bartlett's attack in the afternoon of the 5th, and after dark found himself away down to our left among the troops of the Second Corps, on the Brock Road, and he had passed at least two miles in the rear of the Rebel lines, and through them twice, unchallenged. He told me that when he came to the Second Corps front on the Brock Road about 10 o'clock at night and was halted, he answered: "I belong to the 44th New York; who in the —— are you?" He hadn't the remotest idea where he was. . . .

One old fellow was brought up out of the brush at the south edge of the Lacey Clearing. He belonged to the 5th Texas, of Gregg's Brigade. He had been hit in the shin by a bullet, which had temporarily paralyzed his leg without breaking the bone, at the extreme point of their advance in the afternoon of the 6th, and so was left in our hands when they fell back. Some of the boys asked him what he thought of the battle. He was a comical old cuss, and his reply was, "Battle be ——! It ain't no battle! It's a worse riot than Chickamauga was!" (He had been with Longstreet at Chickamauga the Fall before.) "You Yanks don't call this a battle, do you? At Chickamauga there was at least a rear, but here there ain't neither front nor rear. It's all a —— mess! And our two armies ain't nothin' but howlin' mobs!"

The *sang froid* of this grizzly old Texan was superb. While he sat there sopping his game leg with a wet rag and gnawing at a hardtack and piece of pork we had given him a pretty fresh youngster from one of the batteries came along and stopped to chaff with him a little. "Say, Uncle Johnny," inquired the youngster, "Haven't you fellows about made up your minds that one Southerner can't whip five Yankees?"

The venerable Rebel looked at him solemnly and responded: "Son, did you ever hear any Southern man say he could whip five Yankees?"

"N-no; I don't know that I ever did."

"Well, then, whar did you git that notion?"

"Oh, some of the men who went round up home making speeches to raise companies told us that the Johnnies bragged that one Southerner could whip five Yankees. Maybe they told us that to get our dander up!"

"I expected as much," replied Uncle Johnny. "Now let me tell you, Sonny, that that story, like a good many other things which helped to bring on this war, wasn't nothin' but a — Abolition lie!!"

—BUELL, *"The Cannoneer"*

5. PRIVATE GOSS DESCRIBES THE BATTLE OF THE WILDERNESS

Though the entire campaign from early May to mid-June is generally described as the Wilderness, it is the fighting of May 5 and 6 that is called the Battle of the Wilderness. As was so often the case in the war, neither commander wanted to bring on a general engagement that day. Grant much preferred to get out of the Wilderness, if he could, and in any event he had not yet brought Burnside up to his army; Lee was waiting for Longstreet, who, starting on the fourth, made a spectacular march of 35 miles in one day. Warren's corps, however, ran into Ewell at the Old Wilderness Tavern, and the two tangled up. Then Heth's division, of A. P. Hill's corps, advancing up the Orange Plank Road, ran into Getty, of Hancock's corps. The fighting that day was fierce but inconclusive, and it was renewed the next day on a larger scale.

Warren Goss, who here tells the story of the fighting on the fifth and the sixth, we have met before.

LEADING our right column on the morning of the 5th [May, 1864], Warren's corps resumed its prescribed march towards Parker's Store, which is on the Orange plank road. . . . Early in the morning, Ewell began his march on the same road by which Griffin was advancing. They met. The Union skirmishers were driven in. The intelligence of the meeting was conveyed to Grant, and orders suspending the movements prescribed to the different corps were at once given.

Grant and Meade both arrived at the Wilderness Tavern shortly after the initial encounter. Meade was heard to say: "They have left a division here to fool us while they concentrate and prepare a position towards the North Anna, and what I want is to prevent those fellows getting back to Mine Run." Grant, with this misconception, at once ordered an attack to brush away or capture this obtruding force.

The attack was opened by Griffin's division, which at first swept everything in its front. It had simply encountered the van of Ewell's column. . . . The disordered van of Ewell's column re-formed on a wooded hill, and resumed at once the offensive. It so happened that the right of Warren's Corps was at this time uncovered. Wright's division of the Sixth Corps, which should have covered this flank, had not come up, owing to the dense underbrush through which it was compelled to move. On this exposed flank Ewell directed his attack. On Griffin's left was Wadsworth's division. This advanced, but while beating through the dense undergrowth encountered a terrible fire from an unseen enemy. It illustrates the difficulty that beset troops operating in this tangled region, that there being no other guides, their directions were given them by the points of the compass. The orders were to advance due west. For some unknown reason Wadsworth advanced northwest, and this brought the fire of the enemy on his flank. Under this terrible flank fire the division broke in disorder. The best way to retreat was for each man to get to the rear, and not stand on the order of his going. The division of Wadsworth finally reformed in the rear and did good service during the fight which followed. . . .

In this abrupt encounter began the battle of the Wilderness. The opening was not auspicious. Warren had lost three thousand men. The enemy was in force in our front. . . .

The encounter . . . awakened Grant to the fact that the Army of Northern Virginia was in his front. He countermanded the previously ordered marches, and at once accepted Lee's challenge to battle. Here in the gloomy forest, with dogged resolution, he prepared to grapple with the enemy in this blind wrestle to the death. He at once recalled Hancock's corps from its march to Shady Grove Church. Our corps had advanced about ten miles when the order reached us, and at eleven o'clock we began our return march up the Brock road. . . .

Getty had already begun the fight before our arrival. Cheers went up from our sweat-begrimed, dusty veterans, as they came up at about three o'clock and formed in double line of battle in front of the Brock road. The road was very narrow, and densely wooded on both sides. Here we began to construct rifle-pits, by piling up logs and throwing up the soil against them. For this purpose men used their tin drinking-cups, bayonets, and case-knives, as well as the few shovels and picks which accompanied each division on pack-mules. We had not completed our rifle-pits when an order came to move on the enemy.

The scene of savage fighting with the ambushed enemy, which followed, defies description. No one could see the fight fifty feet from him. The roll and crackle of the musketry was something terrible, even to the veterans of many battles. The lines were very near each other, and from the dense underbrush and the tops of the trees came puffs of smoke, the "*ping*" of the bullets, and the yell of the enemy. It was a blind and bloody hunt to the death, in bewildering thickets, rather than a battle.

Amid the tangled, darkened woods, the "*ping! ping! ping!*" the "*pop! pop! pop!*" of the rifles, and the long roll and roar of musketry blending on our right and left, were terrible. In advancing it was next to impossible to preserve a distinct line, and we were constantly broken into small groups.

The underbrush and briars scratched our faces, tore our clothing, and tripped our feet from under us, constantly.

On our left, a few pieces of artillery, stationed on cleared high ground, beat time to the steady roar of musketry. On the Orange plank road, Rickett's battery, or Kirby's, familiar to us in so many battles, was at work with its usual vigor, adding to the uproar.

"We are playing right into these devils' hands! Bushwhacking is the game! There ain't a tree in our front, twenty feet high, but there is a reb up that tree!" said Wad Rider. Two, three, and four times we rushed upon the enemy, but were met by a murderous fire and with heavy loss from concealed enemies. As often as we rushed forward we were compelled to get back. . . .

The uproar of battle continued through the twilight hours. It was eight o'clock before the deadly crackle of musketry died gradually away, and the sad shadows of night, like a pall, fell over the dead in these ensanguined thickets. The groans and cries for water or for help from the wounded gave place to the sounds of the conflict. . . . Thus ended the first day's fighting of the Army of the Potomac under Grant.

Our lines now faced westward. Burnside's corps had arrived early in the morning, and the formation was north and south in the following order: Sedgwick on the right, then Warren's, Burnside's and Hancock's corps, in the order named. The orders given for the battle were very simple. They were these: "Attack along the entire line at five o'clock."

There was no opportunity for grand maneuvers on this difficult field. It so happened that the commanders of both armies had aggressively determined to assume the offensive early on the morning of the 6th. The plan of the Confederate commander was to overwhelm our left and compel us to retreat to the Rapidan. Longstreet had, however, not yet arrived to participate in the fight, and Lee could not deliver his decisive blow until he came up. Pending his arrival he determined to call our attention from our left by a movement against our right. It thus fell out that Lee began his movement before the hour of attack designated by Grant.

Before five o'clock the roar of musketry on our right told that Sedgwick was attacked by the enemy. Then Hancock and Warren joined in the attack, and the whole line was engaged. . . . The enemy were at once attacked with such vigor that their lines were broken at all points, and they were driven confusedly through the woods. Their dead and wounded lay thick in the jungle of scrub-oaks, pines, and underbrush, through which we rushed upon them. Squads of prisoners constantly going to the rear exchanged rough but good-natured salutations with our men. . . .

By six o'clock the rebel lines had been driven a mile and a half and were broken and disordered. The advance of our corps through swamps and tangled thickets, in this hot encounter, had broken our own lines. A proper formation of the ranks, or any control by the officers in command, in this tangled region, seemed impossible. In this disorganized condition a portion of our lines, under Birney, was brought to a stand by the firm resistance of the enemy. It had encountered the van of Longstreet's corps hastening to the fight. A halt was ordered, and the lines which had become irregular, and the brigades and regiments confusedly mixed, were reorganized.

Longstreet had, meanwhile, begun to form on the plank road, and when a further advance was attempted by the Union lines, they met this new force, and the fighting became fierce and bloody. Hancock had promptly informed Meade of the presence of some of Longstreet's men on his front. Neither was aware that he had met the entire force of that general. Intelligence had been gathered from prisoners the night previous, which led to the inference that he was moving to attack the Union left. Expecting him in this direction proved to be a great hindrance to Hancock. It was for this that he had allowed his left, under Gibbon, to remain on the Brock road. . . .

At eleven o'clock the firing died away. Burnside though constantly ordered, had not attacked. Longstreet, meanwhile, was preparing for a decisive onslaught on our front. His first blow fell on Frank's brigade of Hancock's command, which was soon swept away by the whirlwind of attack, then struck Mott's division and scattered it like leaves before the wind. Hancock answered to this by attempting to swing back his left to the plank road, and unite with his right, which was still holding its advance position.

On the right of Hancock, Wadsworth's division fought with heroic firmness. It charged the enemy several times, but was finally driven back in disorder. In this encounter General Wadsworth, while in the rear and centre of his lines cheering his men, fell mortally wounded. In the confusion which followed he was abandoned to the enemy, and died next day within their lines.

It was impossible to maneuver on account of the obstructive undergrowth, where no one could see a hundred paces in any direction. The roar of musketry alone disclosed the position of the foe, and the movements were generally learned only by actual collisions. Under these circumstances, general officers could hold but little control of their lines.

The troops fell back, in the confusion caused by the difficult field on which they fought, and re-formed in two lines behind their old intrenchments on the Brock road. Before this the tempest of the attack had ceased as suddenly as it began.

Longstreet, at the head of the assaulting column, was desperately wounded. He had, by mistake, been fired on by his own men when the tempest was at its height. This caused the halt in the attack. Lee now took command of this part of the line in person, and cautiously postponed further battle until more perfect dispositions of his troops were made. This lull in the storm lasted until four o'clock. The attack was then resumed. Then the Confederate columns came dashing on through the undergrowth until within a hundred yards of our lines. Here they halted and opened fire. Protected by their breastworks, for a time our men received but little harm. . . .

Flames sprang up in the woods in our front, where the fight of the morning had taken place. With crackling roar, like an army of fire, it came down upon the Union line. The wind drove the blinding smoke and suffocating heat into our faces. This, added to the oppressive heat of the weather, was almost unendurable. It soon became terrible. The line of fire, with resistless march, swept the thickets before its advance, then reaching out its tongue of flame, ignited the breastworks composed of resinous logs, which soon roared and crackled along their entire length. The men fought the enemy and the flames at the same time. Their hair and beards were singed and their faces blistered.

At last, blinded by the smoke and suffocated by the hot breath of the flames, with the whole length of their intrenchments a crackling mass of fire, they gave way and fell back to the second line of log intrenchments. With a shout the rebel column approached the road and attempted to seize the abandoned position. The impartial flames in turn drove them back. The fire soon consumed the logs, and the rebels planted their colors there.

The fire swept on and reached our second line of intrenchments. This, like the first, was soon consumed. The men formed at some places eight and ten ranks deep, the rear men loading the muskets for the front ranks, and thus undauntedly kept up the fight while the logs in front of them were in flames. Finally blistered, blinded, and suffocating, they gave way. The enemy yelled with exultation. They rushed forward and attempted to place their colors on this line of our defense. Their triumph was brief, for the last line of log defences was soon consumed like the first. Then, with a shout resembling the rebel yell, our men charged the enemy, and swept them back from the field. At sunset our pickets were advanced half a mile without opposition.

During the conflict our men had exhausted their ammunition and had been obliged to gather cartridges from the dead and wounded. Their rifles, in many instances, became so hot by constant firing, that they were unable to hold them in their hands. The fire was the most terrible enemy our men met that day, and few survivors will forget this attack of the flames on their lines. . . .

After sundown the Confederates made an attack on the right of Burnside's corps, creating considerable confusion. The night prevented them from following up their success. Thus ended this terrible battle, the full details of which were hid in the tangled woods and darkling forests, where its mysteries will never be disclosed.

—Goss, *Recollections of a Private*

6. "TEXANS ALWAYS MOVE THEM"

The battle of the sixth was a near disaster for Lee. Early in the morning the Federals renewed the attack, Sedgwick and Warren smashing at Ewell but making no headway against his breastworks. Meantime the fighting shifted to the Union right, where Hancock was trying to break through Hill's corps. At midafternoon Wadsworth's division rolled up Hill's right flank while Birney's division struck on the left; the Confederate line broke and the victorious Federals poured through. But Longstreet's veterans were

already coming up, Gregg's Texans in the van. Lee rallied them, and they
dashed in and saved the day for the Confederacy. This is the first of the "Lee
to the Rear" episodes.

The author of this stirring acount is unknown.

AS we stood upon this hill, Lee excited and in close consultation with Longstreet—our batteries thundering into the Wilderness below, the roar of
musketry from the undergrowth below—our men retreating in a disorganized
mass, and the Yankees pressing on and within musket shot, almost, of the hill
upon which stood our idolized chief, indeed was an exciting time, and the
emergency called for *immediate* and *determined* action upon the part of the
Confederate General. Lee was equal to the hour. Action must *not* be delayed, for in less than five minutes the enemy would be upon the hill. Longstreet's corps as it then stood in one mingled mass upon the plank road, could
not be thrown in, and time must be allowed for it to reform, and place itself
in line of battle. The cannon thundered, musketry rolled, stragglers were
fleeing, couriers riding here and there in post-haste, minnies began to sing,
the dying and wounded were jolted by the flying ambulances, and filling the
road-side, adding to the excitement the terror of death. The "Texas brigade," was in front of Fields' division—while "Humphrey's brigade" of Mississippians led the van of Kershaw's division.

The consultation ended. Gen. Gregg and Gen. Humphrey were ordered
to form their brigades in line of battle, which was quickly done, and we
found ourselves near the brow of the hill, Gregg on the left—Humphrey on
the right. "Gen. Gregg prepare to move," was the order from Gen. L.

About this time, Gen. Lee, with his staff, rode up to Gen. Gregg—"General what brigade is this?" said Lee.

"The Texas brigade," was General G's. reply.

"I am glad to see it," said Lee. "When you go in there, I wish you to give
those men the cold steel—they will stand and fire all day, and never move
unless you charge them."

"That is my experience," replied the brave Gregg.

By this time an aid from General Longstreet rode up and repeated the
order, "advance your command, Gen. Gregg." And now comes the point
upon which the interest of this "o'er true tale" hangs. "*Attention Texas Brigade*" was rung upon the morning air, by Gen. Gregg, "*the eyes of General
Lee are upon you, forward, march.*" Scarce had we moved a step, when
Gen. Lee, in front of the whole command, raised himself in his stirrups, uncovered his grey hairs, and with an earnest, yet anxious voice, exclaimed
above the din and confusion of the hour, "*Texans always move them.*"

Reader, for near four years I followed the fortunes of the Virginia army,
heard, saw and experienced much that saddened the heart or appealed in one
form or another to human passions, but never before in my lifetime or since,
did I ever witness such a scene as was enacted when Lee pronounced these
words, with the appealing look that he gave. A yell rent the air that must
have been heard for miles around, and but few eyes in that old brigade of

veterans and heroes of many a bloody field was undimmed by honest, heart-felt tears. Leonard Gee, a courier to Gen. Gregg, and riding by my side, with tears coursing down his cheeks and yells issuing from his throat exclaimed, "I would charge hell itself for that old man." It was not what Gen. Lee said that so infused and excited the men, as his tone and look, which each one of us knew were born of the dangers of the hour.

With yell after yell we moved forward, passed the brow of the hill, and moved down the declivity towards the undergrowth—a distance in all not exceeding 200 yards. After moving over half the ground we all saw that Gen. Lee was following us into battle—care and anxiety upon his countenance—refusing to come back at the request and advice of his staff. If I recollect correctly, the brigade halted when they discovered Gen. Lee's intention, and all eyes were turned upon him. Five and six of his staff would gather around him, seize him, his arms, his horse's reins, but he shook them off and moved forward. Thus did he continue until just before we reached the undergrowth, not, however, until the balls began to fill and whistle through the air. Seeing that we would do all that men could do to retrieve the misfortunes of the hour, accepting the advice of his staff, and hearkening to the protest of his advancing soldiers, he at last turned round and rode back to a position on the hill.

We reached the undergrowth—entered it with a yell, and in less than 100 yards came face to face with the advancing, triumphant, and sanguine foe—confronted only by a few brave souls who could only fire and yield their ground. The enemy were at least five or six to one of us, and death seemed to be our portion. With only 15 or 20 paces separating us, the contest waxed hot and deadlier. We gave a cheer and tried a charge, but with our handful of men our only success was to rush up to them, shoot them down, and shove them back some 10 or 15 yards. For 25 minutes we held them steady—not a foot did they advance, and at the expiration of that time more than half of our brave fellows lay around us dead, dying and wounded, and the few survivors could stand it no longer. By order of Gen. Gregg, whose manly form was seen wherever danger gloried most—I bore the order to the 5th and 1st Texas, to fall back in order.

After retreating some 50 yards, a most deafening yell was borne upon the breeze, and ere we were prepared to realize its cause, Gen. Longstreet's corps came sweeping by us, reformed, and reinforced by Gen. Anderson's division, and with a valor that stands unrivaled swept everything before them for three long miles—driving, in that long charge, the yankees from four different lines of breastworks that they had thrown up in their rear. The "Battle of the Wilderness" was won—all other fighting by the enemy that day and next was to prevent defeat from terminating in destruction. . . .

The "Texas Brigade" entered the fight 673 strong. We lost in killed and wounded over 450.—Did we or did we not do all that men could? Gen. Gregg entered the fight with at least 12 commissioned and non-commissioned on his staff. Of these, several were killed, some wounded, and only two horses untouched. Gen. G's. horse was pierced by 5 balls—each creating a mortal wound—though he rode him until we fell back—sent him to the rear where he died.

—R. C. —— in *The Land We Love*

7. THE CONFEDERATES MISS A CHANCE TO DESTROY GRANT

While the fighting of the sixth raged on the Union left, the Texans holding the breach and Mahone striking savagely at Hancock's flank, an opportunity for a punishing blow to the Federals presented itself. Gordon discovered that Sedgwick, far out on the Federal right, was "in the air" and unsupported. He planned to flank it, roll it up, get behind the Federal army and repeat Second Bull Run and Chancellorsville. But there were delays, and though Gordon won some success, it was an incomplete one. It is General Gordon himself who tells the story.

BOTH General Early and I were at Ewell's headquarters when, at about 5:30 in the afternoon [May 6], General Lee rode up and asked: "Cannot something be done on this flank to relieve the pressure upon our right?" After listening for some time to the conference which followed this pointed inquiry, I felt it my duty to acquaint General Lee with the facts as to Sedgwick's exposed flank, and with the plan of battle which had been submitted and urged in the early hours of the morning and during the day. General Early again promptly and vigorously protested as he had previously done. He still steadfastly maintained that Burnside's corps was in the woods behind Sedgwick's right; that the movement was too hazardous and must result in disaster to us. With as much earnestness as was consistent with the position of junior officer, I recounted the facts to General Lee, and assured him that General Early was mistaken; that I had ridden for several miles in Sedgwick's rear, and that neither Burnside's corps nor any other Union troops were concealed in those woods.

The details of the whole plan were laid before him. There was no doubt with him as to its feasibility. His words were few, but his silence and grim looks while the reasons for that long delay were being given, and his prompt order to me to move at once to the attack, revealed his thoughts almost as plainly as words could have done. Late as it was, he agreed in the opinion that we could bring havoc to as much of the Union line as we could reach before darkness should check us. It was near sunset, and too late to reap more than a pittance of the harvest which had so long been inviting the Confederate sickle. . . .

With my own Georgia brigade and General Robert Johnson's North Carolinians moving by the left flank, so that we should have nothing to do, when the proper point was reached, except to close up, to front face and forward, we pressed through the woods as rapidly and noiselessly as possible and halted at the point immediately opposite Sedgwick's flank. . . .

The Georgia brigade (Gordon's) was directed to make the assault, and the North Carolina brigade (Johnson's) was ordered to move farther to the Union rear and to keep as nearly as possible in touch with the attacking force and to gather up Sedgwick's men as they broke to the rear. As the sun went down these troops were ordered forward. In less than ten minutes they struck the Union flank and with thrilling yells rushed upon it and along the Union works, shattering regiments and brigades, and throwing them into wildest confusion and panic. There was practically no resistance. There could be none. The Georgians, commanded by that intrepid leader, Clement A. Evans, were on the flank, and the North Carolinians, led by a brilliant young officer, Robert Johnson, were sweeping around to the rear, without a shot in their front. There was nothing for the brave Federals to do but to fly. There was no time given them to file out from their works and form a new line of resistance. This was attempted again and again; but in every instance the swiftly moving Confederates were upon them, pouring a consuming fire into their half-formed ranks and shivering one command after another in quick succession. The gallant Union leaders, Generals Seymour and Shaler, rode among their panic-stricken troops in the heroic endeavor to form them into a new line. Their brave efforts were worse than unavailing, for both of these superb officers, with large numbers of their brigades, were quickly gathered as prisoners of war in the Confederate net; and nearly the whole of Sedgwick's corps was disorganized.

It is due to both General Ewell and General Early to say that they did all in their power to help forward the movement when once begun. There was, however, little need for help, for the North Carolina brigade, which was in the movement, had not found an opportunity to fire or to receive a shot; and the Georgia brigade as a whole had not been checked for a single moment nor suffered any serious loss. These men were literally revelling in the chase, when the unwelcome darkness put an end to it. They were so enthused by the pursuit, which they declared to me, as I rode among them, was the "finest frolic" they had ever been engaged in, that it was difficult to halt them even when it became too dark to distinguish friend from foe. With less than sixty casualties, this brigade almost single-handed had achieved these great results during the brief twilight of the 6th of May. And possibly one half of the small loss that occurred was inflicted after nightfall by Confederates who enthusiastically charged from the front upon the Union breastworks, firing as they came, and not realizing that my command in its swift movement down the flank had reached that point on Sedgwick's line. . . .

It will be seen that my troops were compelled to halt at last, not by the enemy's resistance, but solely by the darkness and the cross-fire from Confederates. Had daylight lasted one half-hour longer, there would not have been left an organized company in Sedgwick's corps. Even as it was, all accounts agree that his whole command was shaken. As I rode abreast of the Georgians, who were moving swiftly and with slight resistance, the last scene which met my eye as the curtain of night shut off the view was the crumbling of the Union lines as they bravely but vainly endeavored to file out of

The Surrender at Appomattox

W. H. Stelle

Surrender of the Army of Northern Virginia

their works and form a new line under the furious onset and withering fire of the Confederates.

—GORDON, *Reminiscences of the Civil War*

8. "THEIR DEAD AND DYING PILED HIGHER THAN THE WORKS"

On the night of May 6, Grant gave up the attempt to smash his way through Lee, and started the first of his sliding movements southward. From the seventh to the tenth he moved his great army down the Germanna Plank Road and the Brock Road toward Spotsylvania Court House. Lee anticipated his move, as he anticipated all of Grant's moves during the campaign, and had his army behind breastworks before Grant reached his objective.

By May 10 the two armies were in position, around Spotsylvania Court House, the Confederate line extending along some convenient heights in a great arc northward to the McCool house—later to be famous—and then swinging back again and stretching over two miles westward, the Union forces concentrated on either side of the angle of the Confederate line. Early on the morning of the tenth Hancock, on the Union right, threw one division across the little Po River, where it was savagely attacked by Hill and forced back. The real battle did not begin, however, until midafternoon, when Generals Warren and Wright of Hancock's corps led off with a heavy assault on the Confederate left. A little later General Upton attacked the apex of the Confederate angle, penetrated it, and threatened to take the whole Confederate line from the rear.

Once again Lee came up to rally his broken troops; once again he was prepared to lead the charge in person. This time it was Gordon and his Georgians who came to the rescue. This is the second of the "Lee to the Rear" episodes. That night the Federals drew back, and both sides licked their wounds.

Now it is our old friend Robert Stiles who tells the story.

THE 10th of May, '64, was pre-eminently a day of battle with the Army of Northern Virginia. I know, of course, that the 12th is commonly regarded as the pivotal day, the great day, and the Bloody Angle as the pivotal place, the great place, of the Spottsylvania fights, and that for an hour or so along the sides and base of that angle the musketry fire is said to have been heavier than it ever was at any other place in all the world, or for any other hour in all the tide of time. But for frequency and pertinacity of attack and repetition and constancy of repulse, I question if the left of General Lee's line on the 10th of May, 1864, has ever been surpassed. I cannot pretend to identify the separate attacks or to distinguish between them, but should think there must have been at least a dozen of them. One marked feature was that, while fresh troops poured to almost every charge, the same muskets in the hands of the same men met the first attack in the morning and the last at night; and so it was that the men, who in the early morning were so full of fight and fun that they leaped upon the breastworks and shouted to the retiring Federals to come a little closer the next time, as they did not care to go so far after the clothes and shoes and muskets, were so weary and worn and heavy at night that they could scarcely be roused to meet the charging enemy.

The troops supporting the two Napoleon guns of the Howitzers were, as I remember, the Seventh (or Eighth) Georgia and the First Texas. Toward the close of the day everything seemed to have quieted down, in a sort of implied truce. There was absolutely no fire, either of musketry or cannon. Our weary, hungry infantry stacked arms and were cooking their mean and meager little rations. Some one rose up and, looking over the works—it was shading down a little toward the dark—cried out: "Hello! What's this? Why, here come our men on a run, from—no, by Heavens! it's the Yankees!" and before any one could realize the situation or even start toward the stacked muskets the Federal column broke over the little work between our troops and their arms, bayonetted or shot two or three who were asleep before they could even awake, and dashed upon the men crouched over their low fires—with cooking utensils instead of weapons in their hands. Of course they ran. What else could they do?

The Howitzers—only the left, or Napoleon section, was there—sprang to their guns, swinging them around to bear inside our lines, double-shotted them with canister and fairly spouted it into the Federals, whose formation had been broken in the rush and the plunge over the works and who seemed to be somewhat massed and huddled and hesitating, but only a few rods away. Quicker almost than I can tell it our infantry supports, than whom there were not two better regiments in the army, had rallied and gotten to their arms, and then they opened out into a V-shape and fairly tore the head of the Federal column to pieces. In an incredibly short time those who were able to do so turned to fly and our infantry were following them over the intrenchments; but it is doubtful whether this would have been the result had it not been for the prompt and gallant action of the artillery. . . .

When it became evident that the attack had failed, I suggested to the chaplain—who happened to be with the Howitzer guns, perhaps for that sundown prayer meeting which Willy Dame mentioned—that there might be some demand for his ministrations where the enemy had broken over; so we walked up there and found their dead and dying piled higher than the works themselves. It was almost dark, but as we drew near we saw a wounded Federal soldier clutch the pantaloons of Captain Hunter, who at that moment was passing by, frying pan in hand, and heard him ask with intense eagerness: "Can you pray, sir? Can you pray?"

The old captain looked down at him with a peculiar expression, and pulled away, saying, "No, my friend, I don't wish you any harm now, but praying's not exactly my trade."

—STILES, *Four Years Under Marse Robert*

9. "BEAUTY" STUART FULFILLS HIS DESTINY

Just after the Battle of the Wilderness, Grant sent Sheridan, his new cavalry commander, on a long sweeping raid around the Confederate lines. The purpose of the raid was to disorganize Confederate communications, hold down troops in Richmond, and if possible frighten Lee into sending reinforcements to the imperiled city. The raid reached the outskirts of Richmond, but Sheridan was unable to penetrate the inner defenses. He turned northward, and it was then that Stuart met him, at Yellow Tavern.

The fighting at Yellow Tavern and the death of "Beauty" Stuart are here described by Henry B. McClellan, who was Stuart's chief of staff.

DURING this day, the 8th [May], concentrated in rear of the army and moved to the vicinity of Fredericksburg. On the morning of the 9th General P. H. Sheridan, with about twelve thousand cavalry and a large force of artillery, moved to Hamilton's Crossing, thence to the Telegraph Road, and on toward Richmond. He thus avoided all but the outer line of the Confederate pickets and patrols. The movement was promptly reported, and within two hours after his column had passed Massaponax Church Wickham's brigade was in pursuit. Wickham struck the enemy at Jarrald's Mill, and drove in the rear-guard, the 6th Ohio Cavalry, taking a number of prisoners. Here the enemy left the Telegraph Road, taking that to Beaver Dam. The 6th Ohio was now reinforced by the 1st New Jersey Cavalry, and the rear-guard, thus strengthened, made a determined stand near Mitchell's Shop. Wickham attacked promptly, but made no impression. One or two of his regiments had recoiled from the charge, when he called for Matthews' squadron of the 3d Virginia, with the remark, "I know he will go through." Matthews led his column of fours down the narrow lane and pierced the enemy's lines, but he did not return. The heavy force of the enemy closed upon the head of his column, killed five, wounded three, and captured ten men of his company. Matthews' horse was killed. While fighting on foot with his sabre, he was shot from behind and mortally wounded. His gallantry excited the admiration of his enemies, who carefully carried him to a neighboring farm-house, leaving with him one of his company who had been captured in the charge. He died that night.

At this point Stuart and Fitz Lee joined Wickham, with Lomax's and Gordon's brigades. These three brigades numbered between four and five thousand men. Leaving Fitz Lee to follow the enemy's rear toward Chilesburg, Stuart marched in the night, with Gordon's brigade, to Davinport's Bridge, where he crossed the North Anna the following morning. The brigades were united at Beaver Dam Station, where the enemy's rear was again encountered. . . . Having learned that the main column of the enemy had passed southward toward Negro Foot, with the intention of striking the Louisa or Old Mountain Road, Stuart divided his command, sending Gordon's brigade to follow the rear of the enemy, while he himself, with Fitz Lee's two brigades, marched to Hanover Junction, on his way to interpose between the enemy and Richmond. He reached the Junction some hours after dark, and proposed to prosecute his march without a stop. But Fitz Lee's men were thoroughly worn out. At the urgent request of General Lee, Stuart consented that the command should rest until one o'clock; and calling me to him, he ordered me to accompany General Lee to his bivouac, and not to close my eyes until I saw his command mounted and on the march at the appointed hour. When the troops had moved out I returned to Stuart and awoke him and the staff. . . .

Stuart's march was now directed toward the Yellow Tavern, at the intersection of the Telegraph and Old Mountain roads. As I rode by his side we conversed on many matters of personal interest. He was more quiet than usual, softer, and more communicative. It seems now that the shadow of the near future was already upon him.

He reached the Yellow Tavern at about ten o'clock, and found himself in advance of the enemy's column, and in full time to interpose between it and Richmond. Not knowing what troops were at the disposal of General Bragg, he was uncertain whether to take position in front of the enemy or to remain on the flank of his march, near the Yellow Tavern. He preferred the latter course if he could be satisfied that there was sufficient force in Richmond to hold the trenches. To ascertain this he sent me to General Bragg. I was informed by General Bragg that he had irregular troops to the number of about four thousand, and that three brigades had been ordered from the army of Petersburg, and were hourly expected. He thought he could hold the fortifications.

On my return I found that the enemy held the Brook turnpike, south of the Yellow Tavern, and I was compelled to make a *détour* through the fields to avoid capture. This somewhat delayed me, and I did not reach Stuart until after two o'clock. He told me that a heavy fight had taken place during my absence. The enemy had attempted to drive him from the Telegraph Road, but had been repulsed, after a most desperate and hand to hand fight, by the sharpshooters of Fitz Lee's brigade. The losses had been heavy. . . . He was pleased with the information I had brought from Richmond, and expressed the intention of retaining his position on Sheridan's flank, and the hope that, aided by a strong attack by the infantry in Richmond, he might be able to inflict serious disaster on the enemy's cavalry.

Thus we sat talking for more than an hour, near one of our batteries on the right of our line, north of Half-Sink. Wickham held the right, and Lomax the left. Lomax's line extended along the Telegraph Road for a short distance, then crossed it to a hill on the left, where was posted a piece of artillery. Two guns were placed immediately in the road. The whole command was dismounted except a portion of the 1st Virginia Cavalry, which was retained as a mounted reserve. . . .

About four o'clock the enemy suddenly threw a brigade of cavalry, mounted, upon our extreme left, attacking our whole line at the same time. As he always did, the general hastened to the point where the greatest danger threatened,—the point against which the enemy directed the mounted charge. . . .

The enemy's charge captured our battery on the left of our line, and drove back almost the entire left. Where Captain Dorsey was stationed—immediately on the Telegraph Road—about eighty men had collected, and among these the general threw himself, and by his personal example held them steady while the enemy charged entirely past their position. With these men he fired into their flank and rear as they passed him, in advancing and retreating, for they were met by a mounted charge of the 1st Virginia Cavalry and driven back some distance. As they retired, one man who had been dismounted in the charge, and was running out on foot, turned as he passed the general, and discharging his pistol inflicted the fatal wound.

When Captain Dorsey discovered that he was wounded he came at once to his assistance, and endeavored to lead him to the rear; but the general's horse had become so restive and unmanageable that he insisted upon being taken down, and allowed to rest against a tree. When this was done Captain Dorsey sent for another horse. While waiting the general ordered him to leave him, and return to his men and drive back the enemy. He said he feared that he was mortally wounded, and could be of no more service. Captain Dorsey told him that he could not obey that order; that he would rather sacrifice his life than leave him until he had placed him out of all danger. The situation was an exposed one. Our men were sadly scattered, and there was hardly a handful of men between that little group and the advancing enemy. But the horse arrived in time; the general was lifted on to him, and was led by Captain Dorsey to a safer place. There, by the general's order, he gave him into the charge of private Wheatly, of his company, and returned to rally his scattered men. Wheatly procured an ambulance, placed the general in it with the greatest care, and, supporting him in his arms, he was driven toward the rear.

I was hastening toward that part of the field where I had heard that he was wounded when I met the ambulance. The general had so often told me that if he were wounded I must not leave the field, but report to the officer next to him in rank, that I did not now presume to disregard his order, and the more so because I saw that Dr. Fontaine, Venable, Garnett, Hullihen, and several of his couriers were attending him. I remained with General Fitz Lee until the next morning, when he sent me to the city to see General Bragg, and I thus had an opportunity to spend an hour with my general.

As he was being driven from the field he noticed the disorganized ranks of his retreating men, and called out to them:—

"Go back! go back! and do your duty, as I have done mine, and our country will be safe. Go back! go back! I had rather die than be whipped."

These were his last words on the battle-field,—words not of idle egotism, but of soldierly entreaty. . . .

While yet in the ambulance Dr. Fontaine and Lieutenant Hullihen turned the general over on his side, in order that an examination of the wound might be made. While this was in progress he spoke to Hullihen, addressing him by the pet name which he usually employed:—

"Honey-bun, how do I look in the face?"

"General," replied Hullihen, "you are looking right well. You will be all right."

"Well," said he, "I don't know how this will turn out; but if it is God's will that I shall die I am ready." . . .

While I sat by his side the sound of cannon outside the city [Richmond] was heard. He turned to me eagerly and inquired what it meant. I explained that Gracy's brigade and other troops had moved out against the enemy's rear on the Brook turnpike, and that Fitz Lee would endeavor to oppose their advance at Meadow Bridge. He turned his eyes upward, and exclaimed earnestly, "God grant that they may be successful." Then turning his head aside, he said with a sigh,—

"But I must be prepared for another world."

The thought of duty was always uppermost in his mind; and after listening to the distant cannonading for a few moments, he said: "Major, Fitz Lee may need you." I understood his meaning, and pressed his hand in a last farewell.

As I left his chamber President Davis entered. Taking the general's hand, he asked: "General, how do you feel?"

He replied: "Easy, but willing to die, if God and my country think I have fulfilled my destiny and done my duty."

—McCLELLAN, *Life and Campaigns of J. E. B. Stuart*

10. SPOTSYLVANIA AND THE BLOODY ANGLE

The heaviest fighting of the Wilderness campaign came on May 12, when Grant came within a hairbreadth of winning the campaign and perhaps the war. The Confederates should have learned from the experience of the tenth that their salient around the McCool house was peculiarly vulnerable, but—probably because the high ground appeared to offer advantages—they failed to straighten their lines. Not only this but they withdrew their artillery from the apex of this salient, an almost fatal move. At dawn on the twelfth Hancock's divisions launched a large-scale attack on the salient, the brigades marching twenty deep. Within an hour they had breached the Confederate line, and as Hancock hurried up reinforcements, a torrent of blue poured through the break. Yet once again, as we shall see, Lee managed to plug up the gap and save the day.

Here is the story of the fighting of the twelfth as seen from Grant's headquarters; it is told by Horace Porter, whose description of Grant we have already read.

I HAD been out all night looking after the movements of the troops which were to form the assaulting columns. After they had all been placed in position I started for headquarters, in obedience to instructions, to report the situation to the general-in-chief. . . . By feeling the way for some hours I reached headquarters about daylight the next morning, May 12.

When I arrived the general was up and sitting wrapped in his overcoat close to a camp-fire which was struggling heroically to sustain its life against the assaults of wind and rain. It had been decided to move headquarters a little nearer to the center of the lines, and most of the camp equipage had been packed up ready to start. The general seemed in excellent spirits, and was even inclined to be jocose. He said to me: "We have just had our coffee, and you will find some left for you"; and then, taking a critical look at my drenched and bespattered clothes and famished appearance, added, "But perhaps you are not hungry." To disabuse the chief's mind on this score, I sent for a cup of coffee, and drank it with the relish of a shipwrecked mariner, while I related the incidents of the embarrassments encountered in Hancock's movement, and the position he had taken up. Before I had quite finished making my report the stillness was suddenly broken by artillery-firing, which came from the direction of Burnside's position. A few minutes after came the sound of cheers and the rattle of musketry from Hancock's front, telling that the main assault upon the "angle" had begun. No one could see a hundred yards from our position on account of the dense woods, and reports from the front were eagerly awaited.

It was nearly an hour before anything definite was received, but at 5:30 an officer came galloping through the woods with a report from Hancock saying he had captured the first line of the enemy's works. This officer was closely followed by another, who reported that many prisoners had been taken. Fifteen minutes later came the announcement that Hancock had captured two general officers. General Grant sent Burnside this news with a message saying, "Push on with all vigor." Wright's corps was now ordered to attack on the right of Hancock. Before six o'clock a message from Hancock's headquarters reported the capture of two thousand prisoners, and a quarter of an hour later Burnside sent word that he had driven the enemy back two miles and a half in his front. Hancock called for reinforcements, but Grant had anticipated him and had already ordered troops to his support. The scene at headquarters was now exciting in the extreme. As aides galloped up one after the other in quick succession with stirring bulletins, all bearing the glad tidings of overwhelming success, the group of staff-officers standing about the camp-fire interrupted their active work of receiving, receipting for, and answering despatches by shouts and cheers which made the forest ring.

General Grant sat unmoved upon his camp-chair, giving his constant thoughts to devising methods for making the victory complete. At times the smoke from the struggling camp-fire would for a moment blind him, and occasionally a gust of wind would blow the cape of his greatcoat over his face, and cut off his voice in the middle of a sentence. Only once during the scene he rose from his seat and paced up and down for about ten minutes. He made very few comments upon the stirring events which were crowding so closely upon one another until the reports came in regarding the prisoners. When the large numbers captured were announced, he said, with the first trace of animation he had shown: "That's the kind of news I like to hear. I had hoped that a bold dash at daylight would secure a large number of prisoners. Hancock is doing well."

This remark was eminently characteristic of the Union commander. His extreme fondness for taking prisoners was manifested in every battle he fought. When word was brought to him of a success on any part of the line, his first and most eager question was always, "Have any prisoners been

THE WILDERNESS

994

taken?" The love for capturing prisoners amounted to a passion with him. It did not seem to arise from the fact that they added so largely to the trophies of battle, and was no doubt chiefly due to his tenderness of heart, which prompted him to feel that it was always more humane to reduce the enemy's strength by captures than by slaughter. His desire in this respect was amply gratified, for during the war it fell to his lot to capture a larger number of prisoners than any general of modern times.

Meade had come over to Grant's headquarters early, and while they were engaged in discussing the situation, about 6:30 A.M., a horseman rode up wearing the uniform of a Confederate general. Halting near the camp-fire, he dismounted and walked forward, saluting the group of Union officers as he approached. His clothing was covered with mud, and a hole had been torn in the crown of his felt hat, through which a tuft of hair protruded, looking like a Sioux chief's warlock. Meade looked at him attentively for a moment, and then stepped up to him, grasped him cordially by the hand, and cried, "Why, how do you do, general?" and then turned to his general-in-chief and said, "General Grant, this is General Johnson—Edward Johnson."

General Grant shook hands warmly with the distinguished prisoner, and exclaimed, "How do you do? It is a long time since we last met."

"Yes," replied Johnson; "it is a great many years, and I had not expected to meet you under such circumstances."

"It is one of the many sad fortunes of war," answered General Grant, who offered the captured officer a cigar, and then picked up a camp-chair, placed it with his own hands near the fire, and added, "Be seated, and we will do all in our power to make you as comfortable as possible." . . .

While Generals Grant and Meade were talking with General Johnson by the camp-fire, a despatch came in from Hancock, saying, "I have finished up Johnson, and am now going into Early." General Grant passed this despatch around, but did not read it aloud, as usual, out of consideration for Johnson's feelings. Soon after came another report that Hancock had taken three thousand prisoners; then another that he had turned his captured guns upon the enemy and made a whole division prisoners, including the famous Stonewall Brigade. Burnside now reported that his right had lost its connection with Hancock's corps. General Grant sent him a brief, characteristic note in reply, saying, "Push the enemy with all your might; that's the way to connect." . . .

The battle near the "angle" was probably the most desperate engagement in the history of modern warfare, and presented features which were absolutely appalling. It was chiefly a savage hand-to-hand fight across the breastworks. Rank after rank was riddled by shot and shell and bayonet-thrusts, and finally sank, a mass of torn and mutilated corpses; then fresh troops rushed madly forward to replace the dead, and so the murderous work went on. Guns were run up close to the parapet, and double charges of canister played their part in the bloody work. The fence-rails and logs in the breastworks were shattered into splinters, and trees over a foot and a half in diameter were cut completely in two by the incessant musketry fire. A section of the trunk of a stout oak-tree thus severed was afterward sent to Washington, where it is still on exhibition at the National Museum. We had not only shot down an army, but also a forest.

The opposing flags were in places thrust against each other, and muskets were fired with muzzle against muzzle. Skulls were crushed with clubbed muskets, and men stabbed to death with swords and bayonets thrust between the logs in the parapet which separated the combatants. Wild cheers, savage yells, and frantic shrieks rose above the sighing of the wind and the pattering of the rain, and formed a demoniacal accompaniment to the booming of the guns as they hurled their missiles of death into the contending ranks. Even the darkness of night and the pitiless storm failed to stop the fierce contest, and the deadly strife did not cease till after midnight. Our troops had been under fire for twenty hours, but they still held the position which they had so dearly purchased.

My duties carried me again to the spot the next day, and the appalling sight presented was harrowing in the extreme. Our own killed were scattered over a large space near the "angle," while in front of the captured breastworks the enemy's dead, vastly more numerous than our own, were piled upon each other in some places four layers deep, exhibiting every ghastly phase of mutilation. Below the mass of fast-decaying corpses, the convulsive twitching of limbs and the writhing of bodies showed that there were wounded men still alive and struggling to extricate themselves from their horrid entombment. Every relief possible was afforded, but in too many cases it came too late. The place was well named the "Bloody Angle."

—PORTER, *Campaigning with Grant*

11. "THESE MEN HAVE NEVER FAILED YOU ON ANY FIELD"

Perhaps only once before in the history of the war had the situation been so critical to the Confederacy as it was on the morning of May 12, when the Confederate line broke: that was at Antietam. The Federal advance had not only broken through, it had enveloped General Johnson and taken him and 4,000 men prisoners. Lee tried to rally the fleeing soldiers. "Hold on!" he cried. "We are going to form a new line." But most of the men were panic-stricken, and ran to the rear. Already General Gordon had started his men forward to plug the gap—or at least hold the line. Meeting General Lee Gordon found that Lee was prepared to lead the counterattack himself.

But let Gordon tell the story—the third and the best authenticated of the "Lee to the Rear" episodes.

DURING the night Hancock had massed a large portion of General Grant's army in front of that salient, and so near to it that, with a quick rush, his column had gone over the breastworks, capturing General Edward Johnson and General George Steuart and the great body of their men before these alert officers or their trained soldiers were aware of the movement. The surprise was complete and the assault practically unresisted. In all its details—its planning, its execution, and its fearful import to Lee's army—this charge of Hancock was one of that great soldier's most brilliant achievements.

Meantime my command was rapidly moving by the flank through the woods and underbrush toward the captured salient. The mist and fog were so heavy that it was impossible to see farther than a few rods. Throwing out in front a small force to apprise us of our near approach to the enemy, I rode at the head of the main column, and by my side rode General Robert Johnson, who commanded a brigade of North Carolinians. So rapidly and silently had the enemy moved inside of our works—indeed, so much longer time had he been on the inside than the reports indicated—that before we had moved one half the distance to the salient the head of my column butted squarely against Hancock's line of battle. The men who had been placed in our front to give warning were against that battle line before they knew it. They were shot down or made prisoners. The sudden and unexpected blaze from Hancock's rifles made the dark woodland strangely lurid. General Johnson, who rode immediately at my side, was shot from his horse, severely but not, as I supposed, fatally wounded in the head. His brigade was thrown inevitably into great confusion, but did not break to the rear. As quickly as possible, I had the next ranking officer in that brigade notified of General Johnson's fall and directed him at once to assume command. He proved equal to the emergency. With great coolness and courage he promptly executed my orders.

The Federals were still advancing, and every movement of the North Carolina brigade had to be made under heavy fire. The officer in charge was directed to hastily withdraw his brigade a short distance, to change front so as to face Hancock's lines, and to deploy his whole force in close order as skirmishers, so as to stretch, if possible, across the entire front of Hancock. This done, he was ordered to charge with his line of skirmishers the solid battle lines before him. His looks indicated some amazement at the purpose to make an attack which appeared so utterly hopeless, and which would have been the very essence of rashness but for the extremity of the situation. He was, however, full of the fire of battle and too good a soldier not to yield prompt and cheerful obedience. That order was given in the hope and belief that in the fog and mists which concealed our numbers the sheer audacity of the movement would confuse and check the Union advance long enough for me to change front and form line of battle with the other brigades. The result was not disappointing except in the fact that Johnson's brigade, even when so deployed, was still too short to reach across Hancock's entire front. This fact was soon developed: not by sight, but by the direction from which the Union bullets began to come.

When the daring charge of the North Carolina brigade had temporarily checked that portion of the Federal forces struck by it, and while my brigades in the rear were being placed in position, I rode with Thomas G. Jones, the youngest member of my staff, into the intervening woods, in order, if possible, to locate Hancock more definitely. Sitting on my horse near the line of the North Carolina brigade, I was endeavoring to get a view of the Union lines, through the woods and through the gradually lifting mists. It was impossible, however, to see those lines; but, as stated, the direction from which they sent their bullets soon informed us that they were still moving and had already gone beyond our right. One of those bullets passed through my coat from side to side, just grazing my back.

Jones, who was close to me, and sitting on his horse in a not very erect posture, anxiously inquired: "General, didn't that ball hit you?"

"No," I said; "but suppose my back had been in a bow like yours? Don't you see that the bullet would have gone straight through my spine? Sit up or you'll be killed."

The sudden jerk with which he straightened himself, and the duration of the impression made, showed that this ocular demonstration of the necessity for a soldier to sit upright on his horse had been more effective than all the ordinary lessons that could have been given. It is but simple justice to say of this immature boy that even then his courage, his coolness in the presence of danger, and his strong moral and mental characteristics gave promise of his brilliant future.

The bullets from Hancock's rifles furnished the information which I was seeking as to the progress he had made within and along our earthworks. I then took advantage of this brief check given to the Union advance, and placed my troops in line for a countercharge, upon the success or failure of which the fate of the Confederate army seemed to hang. General Lee evidently thought so. His army had been cut in twain by Hancock's brilliant *coup de main*. Through that wide breach in the Confederate lines, which was becoming wider with every step, the Union forces were rushing like a swollen torrent through a broken mill-dam. General Lee knew, as did every one else who realized the momentous import of the situation, that the bulk of the Confederate army was in such imminent peril that nothing could rescue it except a counter-movement, quick, impetuous, and decisive. Lee resolved to save it, and, if need be, to save it at the sacrifice of his own life. With perfect self-poise, he rode to the margin of that breach, and appeared upon the scene just as I had completed the alignment of my troops and was in the act of moving in that crucial countercharge upon which so much depended.

As he rode majestically in front of my line of battle, with uncovered head and mounted on Old Traveller, Lee looked a very god of war. Calmly and grandly, he rode to a point near the centre of my line and turned his horse's head to the front, evidently resolved to lead in person the desperate charge and drive Hancock back or perish in the effort. I knew what he meant; and although the passing moments were of priceless value, I resolved to arrest him in his effort, and thus save to the Confederacy the life of its great leader. I was at the centre of that line when General Lee rode to it. With uncovered head, he turned his face toward Hancock's advancing column.

Instantly I spurred my horse across Old Traveller's front, and grasping his bridle in my hand, I checked him. Then, in a voice which I hoped might reach the ears of my men and command their attention, I called out, "General

Lee, you shall not lead my men in a charge. No man can do that, sir. Another is here for that purpose. These men behind you are Georgians, Virginians, and Carolinians. They have never failed you on any field. They will not fail you here. Will you, boys?" The response came like a mighty anthem that must have stirred his emotions as no other music could have done. Although the answer to those three words, "Will you, boys?" came in the monosyllables, "No, no, no; we'll not fail him," yet they were doubtless to him more eloquent because of their simplicity and momentous meaning.

But his great heart was destined to be quickly cheered by a still sublimer testimony of their deathless devotion. As this first thrilling response died away, I uttered the words for which they were now fully prepared. I shouted to General Lee, "You must go to rear." The echo, "General Lee to the rear, General Lee to the rear!" rolled back with tremendous emphasis from the throats of my men; and they gathered around him, turned his horse in the opposite direction, some clutching his bridle, some his stirrups, while others pressed close to Old Traveller's hips, ready to shove him by main force to the rear. I verily believe that, had it been necessary or possible, they would have carried on their shoulders both horse and rider to a place of safety. . . .

I turned to my men as Lee was forced to the rear, and reminding them of their pledges to him, and of the fact that the eyes of their great leader were still upon them, I ordered, "Forward!" With the fury of a cyclone, and almost with its resistless power, they rushed upon Hancock's advancing column. With their first terrific onset, the impetuosity of which was indescribable, his leading lines were shivered and hurled back upon their stalwart supports. In the inextricable confusion that followed, and before Hancock's lines could be reformed, every officer on horseback in my division, the brigade and regimental commanders, and my own superb staff, were riding among the troops, shouting in unison: "Forward, men, forward!"

But the brave line officers on foot and the enthused privates needed no additional spur to their already rapt spirits. Onward they swept, pouring their rapid volleys into Hancock's confused ranks, and swelling the deafening din of battle with their piercing shouts. Like the débris in the track of a storm, the dead and dying of both armies were left in the wake of this Confederate charge. In the meantime the magnificent troops of Ramseur and Rodes were rushing upon Hancock's dissolving corps from another point, and Long's artillery and other batteries were pouring a deadly fire into the broken Federal ranks. Hancock was repulsed and driven out. Every foot of the lost salient and earthworks was retaken, except that small stretch which the Confederate line was too short to cover.

—GORDON, *Reminiscences of the Civil War*

12. GRANT HURLS HIS MEN TO DEATH AT COLD HARBOR

Lee had saved himself by the narrowest of margins at Spotsylvania, but the Federals, too, took heavy punishment. Once more Grant pulled off on one of his sliding movements to the south. This time he headed for Hanover

Junction. Lee hurried along parallel with him, and by May 23 had taken position along the North Anna. Grant maneuvered for an attack but found Lee's defenses formidable, and decided to move on. His objective this time was Hanover Town, not far from Richmond. Lee took position on the south bank of the Totopotomy, a branch of the Pamunkey, and not far from Mechanicsville, where he had first met and defeated a Federal army. Then on June 1 the two armies shifted their positions to Cold Harbor, on the north side of the Chickahominy. On June 3 Grant decided on a head-on assault. It was probably the greatest mistake of his military career. Within a few hours he had lost about 10,000 men.

We have given here Colonel William Oates's account of the assaults, and Colonel Upton's reflections on them. Oates we have met before, notably at Gettysburg; Upton was the officer whose division made the break-through on May 10 and who later distinguished himself as one of the leading students of military science.

A. "The Dead Cover More Than Five Acres"

ON the 2nd of June [1864] Law was ordered farther down our entrenched line, with his own and Anderson's Georgia brigade, to Cold Harbor, or near it for the purpose of retaking about 300 yards of badly constructed Confederate trenches which the enemy had succeeded in capturing on General Hoke's left. . . .

None of us had slept any. The men worked all night and by day had an excellent line of defensive works completed. When day came details were sent to the rear to fill the canteens at a bold spring of pure water. They had returned, and, just before I could see the sun, I heard a volley in the woods, saw the major running up the ravine in the direction of Anderson's brigade, which lay to the right of Law's, and the skirmishers running in, pursued by a column of the enemy ten lines deep, with arms at a trail, and yelling "Huzzah! huzzah!" I ordered my men to take arms and fix bayonets. Just then I remembered that not a gun in the regiment was loaded. I ordered the men to load and the officers each to take an ax and stand to the works. I was apprehensive that the enemy would be on our works before the men could load.

As Capt. Noah B. Feagin and his skirmishers crawled over the works I thought of my piece of artillery. I called out: "Sergeant, give them double charges of canister; fire, men; fire!" the order was obeyed with alacrity. The enemy were within thirty steps. They halted and began to dodge, lie down, and recoil. The fire was terrific from my regiment, the Fourth Alabama on my immediate right, and the Thirteenth Mississippi on my left, while the piece of artillery was fired more rapidly and better handled than I ever saw one before or since. The blaze of fire from it at each shot went right into the ranks of our assailants and made frightful gaps through the dense mass of men. They endured it but for one or two minutes, when they retreated, leaving the ground covered with their dead and dying. There were 3 men in my regiment killed, 5 wounded. My piece of artillery kept up a lively fire on the enemy where they halted in the woods, with shrapnel shell.

After the lapse of about forty minutes another charge was made by the Twenty-third and Twenty-fifth Massachusetts regiments, in a column by divisions, thus presenting a front of two companies only. Bryan's Georgia brigade came up from the rear and lay down behind Law's. The charging column, which aimed to strike the Fourth Alabama, received the most destructive fire I ever saw. They were subjected to a front and flank fire from the infantry, at short range, while my piece of artillery poured double charges of canister into them. The Georgians loaded for the Alabamians to fire. I could see the dust fog out of a man's clothing in two or three places at once where as many balls would strike him at the same moment. In two minutes not a man of them was standing. All who were not shot down had lain down for protection. One little fellow raised his head to look, and I ordered him to come in. He came on a run, the Yankees over in the woods firing at him every step of the way, and as he climbed over our works one shot took effect in one of his legs. They evidently took him to be a deserter. I learned from him that there were many more out there who were not wounded. This I communicated to Colonel Perry, who was again in command, General Law having been wounded in the head during the first assault; and thereupon Perry sent a company down a ravine on our right to capture them; they soon brought the colonel who led the charge, and about one hundred other prisoners. The colonel was a brave man. He said he had been in many places, but that was the worst.

This closed their efforts against us on this field for the remainder of that day. The following night they constructed works along the edge of the woods and sharpshooting became incessant. The next day a white flag was displayed and firing was suspended. A Union officer came half-way and met a Confederate staff officer, with a request from Major-General Augur for an armistice for six hours with permission to bury the dead. It was sent to General Lee, who returned it, saying that he did not know General Augur as commander of the Army of the Potomac.

Sharp-shooting was resumed. The stench from the dead between our lines and theirs was sickening. It was so nauseating that it was almost unendurable; but we had the advantage, as the wind carried it away from us to them. The dead covered more than five acres of ground about as thickly as they could be laid. A half hour elapsed, when another white flag was displayed and another request came for an armistice for six hours, with permission to bury the dead in front of our lines, signed this time by General Grant. Lee acceded to the request and hostilities ceased for the six hours. They sent a heavy detail upon the field, and when the time expired they had to get it extended in order to finish burying, although they worked rapidly the whole time. I have no means of knowing the exact number of bodies buried, but from appearances there could not have been less than five or six hundred, and may have been a much greater number. They belonged to Baldy Smith's corps.

—OATES, *The War Between the Union and the Confederacy*

B. COLONEL UPTON DEPLORES THE BUTCHERY OF COLD HARBOR

June 4, 1864.

MY DEAR SISTER:

I am disgusted with the generalship displayed. Our men have, in many instances, been foolishly and wantonly sacrificed. Assault after assault has been ordered upon the enemy's intrenchments, when they knew nothing about the strength or position of the enemy. Thousands of lives might have been spared by the exercise of a little skill; but, as it is, the courage of the poor men is expected to obviate all difficulties. I must confess that, so long as I see such incompetency, there is no grade in the army to which I do not aspire.

Headquarters Second Brigade, *June 5, 1864.*

MY DEAR SISTER:

We are now at Cold Harbor, where we have been since June 1st. On that day we had a murderous engagement. I say *murderous*, because we were recklessly ordered to assault the enemy's intrenchments, knowing neither their strength nor position. Our loss was very heavy, and to no purpose. Our men are brave, but can not accomplish impossibilities. My brigade lost about three hundred men. My horse was killed, but I escaped unharmed. Since June 1st we have been behind rifle-pits, about three hundred yards from the enemy. A constant fusillade from both sides has been kept up, and, though but little damage has been done, it is, nevertheless, very annoying.

I am very sorry to say I have seen but little generalship during the campaign. Some of our corps commanders are not fit to be corporals. Lazy and indolent, they will not even ride along their lines; yet, without hesitancy, they will order us to attack the enemy, no matter what their position or numbers. Twenty thousand of our killed and wounded should to-day be in our ranks. But I will cease fault-finding, and express the hope that mere numbers will yet enable us to enter Richmond. Please give my love to all. I am as anxious to hear from home as you are to hear from me. The fatigue of the campaign hardly disposes one for letter-writing.

—MICHIE, *The Life and Letters of Emory Upton*

XXVIII

The Siege of Petersburg

THE *Wilderness* campaign had decimated Lee's army, but it had not destroyed it, nor had it captured Richmond. What was Grant to do? If he could not take Richmond from the north or the east, he might take it from the south; if he could not destroy Lee's army in battle, he might wear it down by siege. His next move was, therefore, logical enough. Under the protection of his gunboats he threw his army across the James and struck at Richmond from the south. Petersburg was the key to Richmond, and to the whole of eastern Virginia. Through it ran a whole network of railroads connecting with the south and west: the Petersburg & Norfolk, the Weldon, and the Southside. If Grant could cut across these, he would break Richmond's connection with the rest of the Confederacy except for the Richmond & Danville Railroad to the west. And not only would he isolate Richmond; even more important he could cut Lee's army off from its supplies.

Grant began to ferry his army across the James on June 12; by midnight of the sixteenth the movement was completed. Lee, who had anticipated this movement, was in a dilemma. If he hurried his own army across the James Grant might arrest his movement and assault Richmond with half of his force on the north, the rest on the south; either part would equal the whole of Lee's army. Lee had therefore to move with utmost caution, relying on Beauregard to hold Petersburg as long as possible and feeding him reinforcements as fast as safety permitted. Grant's movement was undoubtedly brilliantly conceived and executed but it should be remembered that it failed of its immediate objective; it neither broke the Confederate lines nor captured Petersburg.

It is often said that Grant's strategy was fundamentally that of McClellan, in 1862, and that Grant's eventual success is a vindication of McClellan. There is neither evidence nor logic to support this. McClellan at no time proposed to attack Richmond from south of the James nor did he, apparently, appreciate the importance of Petersburg as the railway focus of eastern Virginia.

Even before Grant crossed the James he ordered attacks on Richmond from Bermuda Hundred and on Petersburg; neither of these succeeded. Another opportunity to capture Petersburg presented itself on June 15 when W. F. Smith's corps was ordered to assault the thinly held Confederate lines and Hancock's corps was available for reinforcement of the attack. Once again the opportunity was fumbled. By the sixteenth Beauregard was strong _enough to resist attack, and after some ineffectual fighting Grant settled down to besiege Petersburg. His strategy was elementary but sound. With a numerical superiority of two to one, he continued to push his lines ever farther to the west, thus forcing Lee to extend his lines in turn. Eventually Lee was holding 35 miles of defensive works; with his lines stretched thin they were bound to snap somewhere, sooner or later. Because Lee showed the same superb generalship that he had showed in the Wilderness, they did not snap until the following spring, and then it was Sheridan, coming on from the Valley, who broke them._

The siege of Petersburg was the most prolonged of the war—a nine-months affair. It was punctuated by a series of battles, chiefly for the railroads leading to the south and west, and by minor diversionary battles north of the James. While no one of these battles was a major affair, all of them wore down Lee's forces by attrition. At the same time Lee's army was being reduced by sickness and desertion. That Lee was able to sustain this nine-months siege is another tribute to his resourcefulness and fortitude.

1. BUTLER'S ATTACK ON PETERSBURG FIZZLES OUT

The grand strategy which Grant had formulated earlier in the year called for a simultaneous advance on Richmond by the Army of the Potomac and the Army of the James. General Butler, commander of the Army of the James, was one of those political appointees whose career established firmly the principle that military appointments should not be made on a political basis. We have already seen how he embarrassed the administration by his command of New Orleans. Now he had a chance to redeem himself and, as usual, he muffed it. The plan which Butler proposed for the capture of Petersburg looked to an infantry assault along the City Point Road, and a cavalry attack, by General Kautz, along the Jerusalem Plank Road. Petersburg was very lightly defended, and the attack should have succeeded.

General R. E. Colston, who had been a professor at the Virginia Military Institute and fought in Stonewall Jackson's brigade, here tells why it did not.

DURING the night of June 8th-9th General Kautz and Colonel Spear, with four regiments of cavalry and 4 pieces of artillery, crossed the Appomattox on a pontoon-bridge, about 7 miles below Petersburg, and on the morning of the 9th they made their appearance in front of the left of our lines, while the Federal gun-boats opened a heavy fire upon Fort Clifton and other positions on the river. The alarm-bell was rung in the city about 9 o'clock, and every man able to shoulder a musket hurried out to the lines. Colonel F. H. Archer, a veteran of the Mexican war, who had commanded a Confederate battalion in my brigade in 1862, but now commanding the Home Guards, hastened to take position at lunettes Nos. 27 and 28 on the Jerusalem road with 125 men. This force was composed of Second Class Reserves, men exempted from active service on account of age or infirmities, and boys under conscription age, who had had no military training. Very few of them wore a uniform, and they were armed with inferior muskets and rifles, for all the best arms had to be reserved for troops in the field.

At the first sound of alarm I mounted my horse, hastened to report to General Wise and to offer my services. He thanked me warmly, saying that he was just going across the river to bring up the reserve infantry as promptly as possible, together with other reënforcements, and directed me to take command of all the forces in the lines and use them according to my judgment, with only one specific order, viz., that lunette No. 16 must be held at any hazard. He added as he turned his horse's head: "For God's sake, General, hold out till I come back, or all is lost!"

At lunette No. 16 I found the men at their guns, but the enemy were not yet in sight. They had reconnoitered from a distance the positions on our left; seeing heavy guns on the works, and not aware of the very small number of the defenders, they had continued their reconnoissance toward the right, nearly hidden from our view by the wooded and undulating character of the ground. We had no scouts or mounted men to send out for information. I had been at lunette 16 about an hour, and it was nearly 11 o'clock, when a courier arrived from Petersburg with a note from General Wise, saying that the enemy were advancing by the Jerusalem road upon Colonel Archer's position, and that reënforcements were on the way. I left my aide, Lieutenant J. T. Tosh, in command at lunette 16, with orders not to leave that position until relieved. I galloped on alone toward the Jerusalem road, and when halfway there I heard the rattle of musketry from that point. Being just then at the position of Sturdivant's section, I ordered the sergeant to bring on one of his howitzers to lunette 28, and hastened toward it, catching glimpses of Federal cavalry still moving to our right, parallel to our intrenchments. Arrived at lunettes 27 and 28 I found that Colonel Archer had disposed his small force very judiciously in the low trenches. A wagon had been overturned across the road and, together with a hastily built rail-fence, formed a pretty good barricade. A detachment of Federal cavalry had just made a spirited charge and been checked by this obstruction and by the scattering fire of the militia. Several dead horses, some sabers and carbines, and a couple of prisoners were the tokens of the repulse, and the men were in high spirits at their success in this their first fight. It was evident, however, that the enemy had only been feeling the position and were preparing for a more serious attack. Their line was visible on the edge of the woods back of the Gregory house, and our slender ranks were extended to the right and left to present an equal front. In a few minutes the howitzer that I had ordered up came in sight and was welcomed with cheers by our men. I placed it in lunette 28, and took my position in the trenches, which did not cover us more than waist-high.

Very soon an advance was made by the enemy's dismounted skirmishers, while a mounted line in close order appeared behind the Gregory house. I impressed upon the men the necessity of holding their fire until the enemy were at close range, and this direction was well observed. But the howitzer opened fire and the Federal skirmishers fell back under cover and commenced a continuous fire of small-arms. A number of their men had taken position in the Gregory house and were shooting, from the windows and from the garret, some firing through openings made by knocking off the shingles. I directed the artillery sergeant to send a few shells at the house to dislodge them, but the distance was so short that the shells passed through the building before exploding, and failed to set it on fire as I had hoped. Meanwhile the mounted line, some three hundred yards back, presented a tempting mark and I told the sergeant to give them canister. To my intense vexation he replied that he had not a single charge of canister with his piece. I then directed him to shell the mounted line, but several shells passed over the line and burst harmlessly beyond it. I now ordered him to cut the fuse at the closest notch, and, pointing the piece myself very low, I had the satisfaction of seeing the shell explode just in front of the line of cavalry and make a great gap in its ranks, causing its immediate retreat.

All this time the bullets were flying uncomfortably thick and close, but I saw no signal of another advance. Meanwhile our men, closely hugging the low breastworks and holding back their fire, were suffering no harm. In about half an hour a cannon shot was fired at us, then another, followed by others in quick succession. The enemy had paused while waiting for the arrival of their battery. So far from being dismayed, the brave civilians around me, with Colonel Archer at their head, offered to charge the battery, but I knew that the moment they left the cover of the trenches to cross the open ground they would be destroyed by the breech-loading carbines of the dismounted men supporting the battery and far overlapping our front. Our only hope was in delay. I called for a volunteer to mount my horse, find General Wise, and let him know that we could hold out but a very short time longer. A lieutenant of the Junior Reserves, Wales Hurt, a youth of eighteen, promptly offered to go, and I watched him galloping away until hidden from view by the bend of the road, while the bullets were knocking up the dust all around him and under his horse's feet.

By this time our ability to retain the position was a question of minutes only, but on these few minutes hung the rescue or the capture of the city. I knew that if we were driven in before a sufficient Confederate force recrossed the Appomattox the enemy would at once ride into the town and burn the bridges, after which they would have no difficulty in holding the place until their infantry came up, and then all of General Lee's army would be unable to force a recrossing. With the town would be lost the main lines of railway upon which our army depended almost entirely for its supplies.

But the end was very near. The enemy, sheltered by the Gregory house and the defective construction of our works, which allowed approach under cover to within fifty yards, redoubled the fire of their skirmishers and artillery; while a line in open order, overlapping both our flanks, advanced, firing rapidly. The brave militia discharged their pieces at close range. Numbers of them fell killed or wounded, and before the survivors could reload the enemy turned our left flank and more of our men fell by bullets that struck us in the rear from lunette No. 26, which we had not had men enough to occupy. Yet those heroic citizens held their ground. In the heat of the fight I picked up and discharged at the enemy two or three of the muskets dropped by our fallen men. We were now hemmed in on three sides, and only a narrow path leading through an abrupt ravine offered a way of escape. The howitzer, which continued its fire to the last, was captured while limbering up, the horses being shot in their traces, and two artillerymen killed. Some of the militia were killed or wounded with the bayonet or carbine butts, and many were captured. Our shattered remnants made their way down and across the ravine and re-formed at my command on Reservoir Hill, in order, if needed, to support Graham's battery, which had just arrived and unlimbered on the top of the hill.

After driving us from the trenches the enemy paused awhile to call in their dismounted men and to send to their rear our wounded and prisoners. They then formed in mounted column, with a few files thrown forward in open order. They advanced upon the main road, evidently expecting to enter the city without further opposition.

The moments gained at such fearful cost barely gave time for Graham's battery to cross the bridge. They came up Sycamore street at full gallop and unlimbered on the summit of Reservoir Hill just as the head of the Federal column was coming down the opposite slope into the hollow. The battery opened fire, and with rapidity and precision hurled a storm of shell and canister upon the approaching cavalry. The enemy, who thought themselves already in possession of the city, halted in surprise. But just at this moment, while they were yet hesitating, Dearing's cavalry, which had followed after Graham's battery, charged upon Kautz's and Spear's column with irresistible impetuosity. The latter wheeled about, but re-formed on the top of the next hill and gallantly endeavored to make a stand there, being joined by another column advancing upon the Blandford road. But this also was checked by a section of Sturdivant's battery, which came on their flank from another road. Under the fire of artillery and the charge of Dearing's cavalry the enemy retreated. In Jackson's field, about a mile beyond Blandford church, our cavalry captured a howitzer, complete, with its team, and in the subsequent pursuit killed or captured a number of the enemy.

—COLSTON, "Repelling the First Assault on Petersburg"

2. GRANT'S ARMY CROSSES THE JAMES

Here, in the restrained language characteristic of official reports, is Grant's own summary account of the crossing of the James, one of the notable operations of the war. For many years historians assumed that Lee was completely deceived by this movement; Douglas S. Freeman has clearly established that Lee anticipated it, prepared for it, and met it as best he could with his inadequate forces. Part of Grant's army was ferried across by ships; part of it crossed on a 2,000-foot pontoon bridge at Wilcox's Landing.

FROM the proximity of the enemy to his defenses around Richmond it was impossible by any flank movement to interpose between him and the city. I was still in a condition to either move by his left flank and invest

Richmond from the north side or continue my move by his right flank to the south side of the James. While the former might have been better as a covering for Washington, yet a full survey of all the ground satisfied me that it would be impracticable to hold a line north and east of Richmond that would protect the Fredericksburg railroad—a long, vulnerable line which would exhaust much of our strength to guard, and that would have to be protected to supply the army, and would leave open to the enemy all his lines of communication on the south side of the James. My idea, from the start, had been to beat Lee's army north of Richmond if possible; then, after destroying his lines of communication north of the James River, to transfer the army to the south side and besiege Lee in Richmond or follow him south if he should retreat. After the battle of the Wilderness it was evident that the enemy deemed it of the first importance to run no risks with the army he then had. He acted purely on the defensive behind breast-works, or feebly on the offensive immediately in front of them, and where in case of repulse he could easily retire behind them. Without a greater sacrifice of life than I was willing to make, all could not be accomplished that I had designed north of Richmond. I therefore determined to continue to hold substantially the ground we then occupied, taking advantage of any favorable circumstances that might present themselves, until the cavalry could be sent to Charlottesville and Gordonsville to effectually break up the railroad connection between Richmond and the Shenandoah Valley and Lynchburg; and when the cavalry got well off to move the army to the south side of the James River, by the enemy's right flank, where I felt I could cut off all his sources of supply except by the canal. . . .

The Second Corps commenced crossing the James River on the morning of the 14th by ferry-boats at Wilcox's Landing. The laying of the pontoon bridge was completed about midnight of the 14th, and the crossing of the balance of the army was rapidly pushed forward by both bridge and ferry. After the crossing had commenced, I proceeded by a steamer to Bermuda Hundred to give the necessary orders for the immediate capture of Petersburg. The instructions to General Butler were verbal, and were for him to send General Smith immediately, that night, with all the troops he could give him without sacrificing the position he then held. I told him that I would return at once to the Army of the Potomac, hasten its crossing, and throw it forward to Petersburg by divisions as rapidly as it could be done; that we could re-enforce our armies more rapidly there than the enemy could bring troops against us. General Smith got off as directed, and confronted the enemy's pickets near Petersburg before daylight next morning, but, for some reason that I have never been able to satisfactorily understand, did not get ready to assault his main lines until near sundown. Then, with a part of his command only, he made the assault, and carried the lines northeast of Petersburg from the Appomattox River, for a distance of over 2½ miles, capturing fifteen pieces of artillery and 300 prisoners. This was about 7 P.M. Between the line thus captured and Petersburg there were no other works, and there was no evidence that the enemy had re-enforced Petersburg with a single brigade from any source. The night was clear, the moon shining brightly, and favorable to further operations. General Hancock, with two divisions of the Second Corps, reached General Smith just after dark, and offered the service of these troops as he (Smith) might wish, waiving rank to the named commander, who he naturally supposed knew best the position of affairs and what to do with the troops. But instead of taking these troops, and pushing at once into Petersburg, he requested General Hancock to relieve a part of his line in the captured works, which was done before midnight. By the time I arrived the next morning the enemy was in force.

—"Grant's Report covering operations of all armies
of the U. S. from March, 1864 to May, 1865"

3. BEAUREGARD HOLDS THE LINES AT PETERSBURG

Grant's advance was across the James on June 14, and he ordered an attack on the feebly held Petersburg lines on the fifteenth. For this attack Smith had available some 16,000 men; Beauregard could muster no more than some 3,000. But Smith wasted the day, and before he could be joined by Hancock's corps, which had crossed the river on the fifteenth, Beauregard had rounded up enough reinforcements to hold his lines. On the sixteenth the fighting was renewed but by that time Beauregard had some 14,000 men available for defense. A series of powerful assaults by the Federals took some of the outer lines, and several of the redoubts, but the Confederates held firm on the inner lines, and by the eighteenth Lee had sent across sufficient reinforcements to make Petersburg safe. The fighting from the fifteenth to the eighteenth cost the Federals almost 10,000 in killed, wounded, and missing; there are no figures for Confederate losses, but they were less than half the Federal.

Beauregard himself tells the story of the defense of Petersburg.

THE movement of the Army of the Potomac to the south side of the James began on the evening of the 12th of June, and Smith's corps was at Bermuda Hundred in the early afternoon of the 14th. From Point of Rocks it crossed the river that night and was pushed forward without delay against Petersburg. Kautz's cavalry and Hinks's command of colored troops had been added to it.

It was with a view to thwart General Grant in the execution of such a plan that I proposed to the War Department [June 9th] the adoption—should the emergency justify it, and I thought it did—of the bold and, to me, safer plan of concentrating all the forces we could readily dispose of to give battle to Grant, and thus decide at once the fate of Richmond and of the cause we were fighting for, while we still possessed a comparatively compact, well-disciplined, and enthusiastic army in the field.

From Swift Creek, early on June 14th, I telegraphed to General Bragg: "Movement of Grant's across Chickahominy and increase of Butler's force render my position here critical. With my present forces I cannot answer for consequences. Cannot my troops sent to General Lee be returned at once? . . ." No answer came. Late in the evening of the same day, having further reason to believe that one corps at least of General Grant's army was already within Butler's lines, I telegraphed to General Lee: "A deserter from the enemy reports that Butler has been reënforced by the Eighteenth and a part of the Tenth Army Corps." To this dispatch, likewise, there came no response. But, as prompt and energetic action became more and more imperative, and as I could no longer doubt the presence of Smith's corps with Butler's forces, I sent one of my aides, Colonel Samuel B. Paul, to General Lee with instructions to explain to him the exact situation. General Lee's answer to Colonel Paul was not encouraging. He said that I must be in error in believing the enemy had thrown a large force on the south side of the James; that the troops referred to by me could be but a few of Smith's corps going back to Butler's lines. Strange to say, at the very time General Lee was thus expressing himself to Colonel Paul, the whole of Smith's corps was actually assaulting the Petersburg lines. But General Lee finally said that he had already issued orders for the return of Hoke's division; that he would do all he could to aid me, and even come himself should the necessity arise.

The Confederate forces opposed to Smith's corps on the 15th of June consisted of . . . a real effective for duty of 2200 only. These troops occupied the Petersburg line on the left from Battery No. 1 to what was called Butterworth's Bridge, toward the right, and had to be so stationed as to allow but one man for every 4½ yards. From that bridge to the Appomattox—a distance of fully 4½ miles—the line was defenseless.

Early in the morning—at about 7 o'clock—General Dearing, on the Broadway and City Point roads, reported his regiment engaged with a large force of the enemy. The stand made by our handful of cavalry, near their breastworks, was most creditable to themselves and to their gallant commander, and the enemy's ranks, at that point, were much thinned by the accurate firing of the battery under Graham. But the weight of numbers soon produced its almost inevitable result, and, in spite of the desperate efforts of our men, the cavalry breastworks were flanked and finally abandoned by us, with the loss of one howitzer. Still, Dearing's encounter with the enemy, at that moment and on that part of the field, was of incalculable advantage to the defenders of our line, inasmuch as it afforded time for additional preparation and the distribution of new orders by Wise.

At 10 o'clock A.M. the skirmishing had assumed very alarming proportions. To the urgent demands of General Wise for reënforcements, I was enabled at last to answer that part of Hoke's division was on the way from Drewry's Bluff and would be in time to save the day, if our men could stand their ordeal, hard as it was, a little while longer. Then all along the line, from one end to the other, the order was given "to hold on at all hazards!" It was obeyed with the resolute fortitude of veterans, though many of the troops thus engaged, with such odds against them, had hardly been under fire before. At 12 M., and as late a 2 P.M., our center was vigorously pressed, as though the Norfolk and Petersburg Railroad were the immediate object of the onset.

DEFENSES OF RICHMOND AND PETERSBURG

General Wise now closed the line from his right to strengthen Colonel J. T. Goode and, with him, the 34th Virginia; while, at the same time and with equal perspicacity, he hurried Wood's battalion toward the left in support of Colonel P. R. Page and his command.

The enemy, continuing to mass his columns toward the center of our line, pressed it more and more and concentrated his heaviest assaults upon Batteries Nos. 5, 6, and 7. Thinned out and exhausted as they were, General Wise's heroic forces resisted still, with such unflinching stubbornness as to equal the veterans of the Army of Northern Virginia. I was then on the field and only left it when darkness set in. Shortly after 7 P.M. the enemy entered a ravine between Batteries 6 and 7, and succeeded in flanking Battery No. 5.

But just then very opportunely appeared, advancing at double-quick, Hagood's gallant South Carolina brigade, followed soon afterward by Colquitt's, Clingman's, and, in fact, by the whole of Hoke's division. They were shown their positions, on a new line selected at that very time by my orders, a short distance in the rear of the captured works, and were kept busy the greatest part of the night throwing up a small epaulement for their additional protection.

Strange to say, General Smith contented himself with breaking into our lines, and attempted nothing further that night. All the more strange was this inaction on his part, since General Hancock, with his strong and well-equipped Second Army Corps, had also been hurried to Petersburg, and was actually there, or in the immediate vicinity of the town, on the evening of the 15th. He had informed General Smith of the arrival of his command and of the readiness of two of his divisions—Birney's and Gibbon's—to give him whatever assistance he might require. Petersburg at that hour was clearly at the mercy of the Federal commander, who had all but captured it, and only failed of final success because he could not realize the fact of the unparalleled disparity between the two contending forces. Although the result of the fighting of the 15th had demonstrated that 2200 Confederates successfully withheld nearly a whole day the repeated assaults of at least 18,000 Federals, it followed, none the less, that Hancock's corps, being now in our front, with fully 28,000 men,—which raised the enemy's force against Petersburg to a grand total of 46,000,—our chance of resistance, the next morning and in the course of the next day, even after the advent of Hoke's division, was by far too uncertain to be counted on, unless strong additional reënforcements could reach us in time. . . .

General Hancock, the ranking Federal officer present, had been instructed by General Meade not to begin operations before the arrival of Burnside's command. Hence the tardiness of the enemy's attack, which was not made till after 5 o'clock P.M., though Burnside had reached Petersburg, according to his own report, at 10 o'clock A.M. [June 16].

The engagement lasted fully three hours, much vigor being displayed by the Federals, while the Confederates confronted them with fortitude, knowing that they were fighting against overwhelming odds, constantly increasing. Birney's division of Hancock's corps finally broke into part of our line and effected a lodgment. The contest, with varying results, was carried on until after nightfall, with advantage to us on the left and some serious loss on the right. It then slackened and gradually came to an end. In the meantime Warren's corps, the Fifth, had also come up, but too late to take a part in the action of the day. Its presence before our lines swelled the enemy's aggregate to about 90,000, against which stood a barrier of not even 10,000 exhausted, half-starved men, who had gone through two days of constant hard fighting and many sleepless nights in the trenches.

Hostilities began early on the 17th. . . . The firing lasted, on the 17th, until a little after 11 o'clock P.M. Just before that time I had ordered all the camp-fires to be brightly lighted, with sentinels well thrown forward and as near as possible to the enemy's. Then, at about 12:30 A.M., on the 18th, began the retrograde movement, which, notwithstanding the exhaustion of our troops and their sore disappointment at receiving no further reënforcements, was safely and silently executed, with uncommonly good order and precision, though the greatest caution had to be used in order to retire unnoticed from so close a contact with so strong an adversary.

The digging of trenches was begun by the men as soon as they reached their new position. Axes, as well as spades; bayonets and knives, as well as axes,—in fact, every utensil that could be found,—were used. And when all was over, or nearly so, with much anxiety still, but with comparative relief, nevertheless, I hurried off this telegram to General Lee [18th, 12:40 A.M.]: "All quiet at present. I expect renewal of attack in morning. My troops are becoming much exhausted. Without immediate and strong reënforcements, results may be unfavorable. Prisoners report Grant on the field with his whole army." . . .

The evening of the 18th was quiet. There was no further attempt on the part of General Meade to assault our lines. He was "satisfied," as he said in his report, that there was "nothing more to be gained by direct attacks." The spade took the place of the musket, and the regular siege was begun. It was only raised April 2, 1865.

—BEAUREGARD, "Four Days of Battle at Petersburg"

4. "A HURRICANE OF SHOT AND SHELL"

On the night of June 17 Meade issued orders for a general assault of the Confederate lines. These assaults did not get under way early in the morning, as planned, and before they did Beauregard had been strongly reinforced by Anderson's corps and by part of Hill's corps. The Federals hurled themselves desperately against the Confederate lines, but were unable to dent them.

Here is an account of the fighting by Captain Augustus Brown of the 4th New York Artillery.

June 18 [1864]—About nine o'clock orders came to continue the charge. From the fence . . . the ground, covered with some sort of growing grain, sloped gently down for a hundred yards to a narrow belt of trees in which was the dry bed of a little stream, and beyond this belt the grade ascended gradually for some five hundred yards to the rebel works on the brow of the hill, the intervening field being covered with a luxuriant growth of corn about three feet high. Captain Vanderwiel was assigned to command a picket line which was to precede us, and the advance from this point was to be made in two lines of battle, our five companies forming part of the front line. I saw no second line of battle upon our part of the field during the earlier part of the charge, and I certainly was not informed of any in advance. The enemy had posted two pieces of artillery, perhaps more, in what appeared to be angles of its new works, and our battalion very nearly covered the front between these guns.

To those of us who had anxiously watched all the morning the preparations for our reception, and had seen some of the guns moved into position and the troops deployed behind the breastworks, it seemed perfectly evident that the charge would now prove a disastrous failure, but when the order was given, though we felt we were going to almost certain death, these five companies of artillerymen, always accustomed to obey orders, scaled the fence with a cheer, the enemy commencing to fire the moment we left the road. Reaching the belt of timber, we found the picket line halted and firing from behind trees, but the main line pushed on and out into the open cornfield.

One of my men, a good man, too, but for the moment forgetful that the question was not for him or me to decide, stopped behind a tree, and when ordered forward began to argue that we never could carry that breastwork, a proposition in which I heartily concurred, but it being no time or place for the interchange of our views I leveled my revolver at his head and he broke cover instantly. Another of my men had his musket struck by a ball and bent double like a hairpin, but straightening out his arm, which was nearly paralyzed for an instant, he picked up another musket and went on, keeping place in the line. Just at that moment Major Williams received a rifle ball in the shoulder, and falling near me, though I was not the ranking Captain on the field, directed me to assume command of the battalion, and I turned my own company over to Lieutenant Edmonston.

On assuming command, I noticed that the men in the company on the right of my own, whose Captain had allowed them a ration of whiskey just before we started, were dropping into a little ditch just outside of the line of trees, and that the Captain, who was as brave a man as ever lived, but was rather noted for his varied and vigorous vocabulary, was passing up and down the ditch poking them with his sword and with tears streaming down his face, but without an oath, was begging them to get out and keep in line and not disgrace themselves and him. Thinking to shame his men by letting them know that I, the Captain of a rival company, saw them skulking, I shouted to him to get his men out of the ditch and press forward.

I shall never forget the hurricane of shot and shell which struck us as we emerged from the belt of trees. The sound of the whizzing bullets and exploding shells, blending in awful volume, seemed like the terrific hissing of some gigantic furnace. Men, torn and bleeding, fell headlong from the ranks as the murderous hail swept through the line. A splash of blood from a man hit in the cheek struck me in the face. The shrieks of the wounded mingled with the shouts of defiance which greeted us as we neared the rebel works, and every frightful and sickening incident conspired to paint a scene which no one who survived that day will care again to witness.

This part of the charge was made across a portion of an old race course, and the belt of trees which bordered the track at that point and in which lay the dry bed of the little stream, formed a sort of arc with the ends projected toward the enemy, and as the flanks of the battalion came out in full view, and we were within about one hundred and fifty yards of the rebel line, I was astonished to see that there were no troops on either side of us, and looking back, I discovered that my five companies were the only troops of all the charging lines which were in sight, that had obeyed the order and advanced from the sunken road. Then for the first time I understood the fierceness of the fire to which we were being subjected; saw that we were receiving not only the fire from the works in our front, to which we were entitled, but a cross fire from troops and artillery on the right and left of our front which would have been directed toward other parts of the charging lines if we had been supported, and realized that with this little handful of men, being then so rapidly decimated, it was worse than useless to continue the attack. Accordingly I halted the line and gave the order to lie down, the corn being high enough to furnish some little concealment. A general break to the rear would have cost as many lives as the double-quick to the front had done, so I instantly followed my first order with another to the effect that each man should get to the rear as best he could.

When we left the sunken road the Colonel of a regiment on our left whose men, like most of our infantry after six weeks of that sort of strategy, tired of charging a breastwork three times and then going around it, had flatly refused to follow him, joined us with his color-guard and gallantly accompanied us as far as we went, and there planted his flags in the soft earth. He must have discovered the futility of a further advance about the time that I did, for just as I ordered the men down he ordered a retreat, though we were not under his command, and under the combined orders the men at once disappeared in the corn. My orders were intended to embrace the officers of the battalion as well as the men but they were not so understood, and after the men were out of sight there stood the line officers, still targets for the enemy, calmly facing him and awaiting further orders. I shall never forget my thrill of admiration for those brave men as I glanced for an instant up and down the line, but it was no time for a dress parade and I immediately ordered them down and laid down myself.

The sun was blazing straight down upon us and the surface of the ground was very hot, and added to these discomforts, the enemy was firing into the corn in the hope of hitting some of us, which no doubt was done. Although by no means overcharged with physical courage . . . I was not, up to this point, conscious of the slightest apprehension for my own personal safety, my intense anxiety for my men and my fixed determination to go over that breastwork at all hazards having probably banished all other considerations from my mind, but as I lay there broiling in the sun, normal conditions began to return, and it occurred to me that some stray bullet might possibly search me out, and, what seemed even worse,—for there is no measuring the limits and effect of personal vanity,—the reflection forced itself upon me that the rebels, and perhaps some of our own men at the rear, had seen the leader of that charge, an acting Major at least, actually hide in the corn.

That last idea settled it, and reflecting that if I should go directly to the rear I would be an easier mark than if I should go across the fire, and that a wound in the back was not considered ornamental for a soldier, I arose and deliberately walked diagonally to the rear until I came to the continuation of the ditch or runway up which, at its distant lower end, we had filed the night before to build a rifle pit, and dropping into that, worked my way down to the piece of race track just outside of the belt of trees, and crossing that reached our works in safety. Why I was not struck while making that trip is more than I can tell . . . and, as giving some idea of the severity of the fire we faced that day, I may mention that on returning to our lines I counted twenty-four shot and shell marks on the side towards the enemy of a little pine tree not more than eight inches through at the butt, and that the battalion lost, according to the company reports, one hundred and fifteen killed and wounded in this charge.

—BROWN, *The Diary of a Line Officer*

5. THE MINE AND THE BATTLE OF THE CRATER

With the failure of the assaults on the eighteenth, Grant settled down to invest Petersburg, meantime extending his lines as far to the left as he could. During the rest of June, and July, the two armies stood in their entrenchments, sniping at each other and wilting in the broiling sun. So formidable were Confederate defenses that a break-through seemed impossible. In this juncture Colonel Pleasants of the 48th Pennsylvania—a miners' regiment—proposed tunneling under the Confederate lines and breaching them by exploding a mine. The proposal was accepted, responsibility for laying the mine assigned to Colonel Pleasants' division and for breaking through the Confederate lines after the explosion to General Burnside's IX Corps. The mine was exploded at 5:00 a.m. on June 30; Union artillery opened all along the line; General Ledlie's 1st Division, minus its general, surged into the crater—and stopped.

But let our historians tell the story. The details are somewhat confused, but the outcome is clear enough. The attack—well planned as it was—failed. Federal casualties were over 4,000, Confederate around 1,000. General Ledlie resigned; charges were preferred against Burnside, who shortly resigned. Ferrero, whose colored division had borne the brunt of the fighting, was transferred to a post of less responsibility.

*Count Régis de Trobriand, whom we have met before in McClellan's
army, began the war as colonel of the 55th New York Volunteers, a French
regiment; by the end of the war he was a major general. His Four Years was
published first in Paris and subsequently translated into English.*

*John Wise, son of Virginia's Governor Henry S. Wise, was a student at
the Virginia Military Institute when he fought in the Battle of New Market;
after that engagement—whose history we will read in our next chapter—he
came east to fight for the defense of Petersburg. After the war he went into
politics, joined the Republican party, and became a cog in the Mahone political machine.*

A. Burnside Fumbles His Chance to Take Petersburg

THE mine dug under the direction of Burnside was finished and charged.
The firing of it was fixed for the next day, July 30, and was to be followed immediately by a charge of the Ninth Corps, with the support of the
Eighteenth. For this reason our division had been recalled, to relieve the
troops of General Ord in the trenches.

A few details on the manner in which this work was carried out may
be interesting here. . . .

The first notion of it occurred to Lieutenant-Colonel Henry Pleasants, an
old civil engineer, now commanding the Forty-eighth Pennsylvania. The
most advanced point of our lines was upon the lower part of a hillside
crowned by a sort of redoubt, behind which the cemetery hill commanded
the city of Petersburg. Within our lines, in a deep ravine, ran the track of
the Norfolk railroad, which was hidden from the enemy's view by our
works. This formation of the ground suggested to Colonel Pleasants the
idea of opening a horizontal gallery under the enemy's works. He proposed
it to General Potter, his division commander, who in turn submitted it to
General Burnside. The latter approved of it without hesitation, and the next
morning Colonel Pleasants set to work.

The first thing to do was to get the exact distance from the mouth of the
mine to the redoubt which it was intended to blow up. The instruments
necessary were at headquarters, but the use of them could not be obtained.
The chief engineers of the army and other authorities declared *ex cathedra*
that the project was senseless and foolish; that a mine as long as that had
never been dug; that it could not be done; that the men would be stifled by
the lack of air or crushed by the falling-in of the earth, etc. It resulted from
this that the general commanding did not approve of the undertaking, but
only tolerated it. . . .

General Burnside, who persisted in his idea, sent to Washington for an
old theodolite, which, however, enabled Colonel Pleasants to determine that
the length of the direct gallery must be five hundred and ten feet, at the end
of which lateral galleries, curving in an arc of a circle, must be dug to the
right and left, each thirty-eight feet long. It follows, of course, that all assistance was refused by the engineer corps, which did not wish to take any

part in an enterprise of which it had proclaimed the absurdity. Following suit, the superior officers of the army were greatly amused by the pleasantry.

Colonel Pleasants, left to himself without other encouragement than that of Burnside and Potter, continued his work with an unshakable perseverance. He was refused timber; he sent for it to a sawmill out of the lines. They refused him mining picks; he had the common picks in the division fixed over. They refused him wheelbarrows; he had the earth carried out in cracker boxes bound with iron taken from old fish barrels. So that he was equal to every requirement without employing a person outside of his own regiment of four hundred men, mostly recruited from among the miners in Schuylkill County, Pennsylvania.

One important point was to conceal the removed earth from the view of the enemy, who, if suspecting anything, might send some men to the tops of the trees on the hill, and discover the works, which it was important to conceal from him. For that reason, every morning, before daylight, the pioneers covered over the earth brought out of the mine during the night with branches of trees. The amount of earth removed was in all as much as eighteen thousand cubic feet.

The work, begun June 25, was finished on July 23, without accident, in spite of all predictions and of all derision. It was then necessary to change the tone. The fact must be recognized that the thing was serious. That which had been declared impossible was done. The explosion, if it succeeded, and if we knew how to get the benefit of it, must deliver Petersburg to us. . . .

Everything, then, seemed to promise success, provided that the assault should be made with vigor and in unison. That was the great point. . . .

Burnside . . . had concluded to put at the head of the column of attack his fourth division, composed of colored troops, who, more numerous and less fatigued than the others, were, taking all things into consideration, the ones on whom he could best depend. Immediately after the explosion, these two brigades were to pass through the opening made in the enemy's works, in two columns; the one to turn to the right, and the other to the left; sweep the inner side of the enemy's intrenchments and cover the flanks of the three other divisions, who would charge directly for the summit of the hill. After them would advance the Eighteenth Corps, and our success was assured. For it must be remembered that Lee, having sent five divisions to the north of the James, had but three left at Petersburg. Once established on the hill, the city was ours; the enemy was cut in two; the left, with its back to the Appomattox, would find itself surrounded, and the right could do nothing but make a prompt retreat, leaving us all the guns in the entrenchments.

The whole night was devoted to the last preparations, the attacking divisions forming at their posts as they were relieved in the trenches. Our division, which had been massed in the woods, out of sight of the enemy, during the whole day, took the place of the Eighteenth and a part of the Tenth Corps, in that part of the lines which extended from Burnside's right to the Appomattox. My brigade was the nearest to the mine, from which it was separated by a curtain of woods. My right occupied Fort Stedman, armed with ten guns, and near which were twelve mortars. My left was so near the enemy that the sharpshooters distributed along my front in a trench could easily throw stones into his advanced works. The least noise in one line was heard in the other, so that on our arrival we were saluted with a shower of shells, which did us no particular injury.

The hour set for the mine explosion was half-past three in the morning. I have stated that the principal gallery of the mine ended in a transverse gallery in the shape of an arc of a circle. In the walls of the latter eight narrow passages were made, facing each other (four on each side), leading to eight chambers, each containing a thousand pounds of power—in all, eight thousand pounds. That would make a fine explosion. So from three o'clock every one was up, the officers watch in hand, eyes fixed on the fated redan, or in that direction.

There were about two hundred men in that work, sleeping tranquilly a sleep from which they would awake in eternity. Perhaps they were dreaming of returning to their families, of the joys of the domestic fireside, at the instant when, beneath them, Colonel Pleasants (what irony in that name) was applying the fire to the match along with which they were about to consume the last minutes of their existence. Upon the parapet the motionless sentinels were watching the pale lights which began to brighten the horizon in the east. Silence reigned everywhere, but in our lines all eyes were open; in those of the enemy, nearly all were closed.

From half after three the minutes were counted.—It is still too dark, it was said.—At four o'clock it was daylight; nothing stirred as yet; at a quarter past four a murmur of impatience ran through the ranks.—What has happened? Has there been a counter-order? or an accident? Has the assault been deferred?

It had happened that the match, which was ninety feet long, had gone out at a splice about half-way of its length. It was necessary to be certain of it, and the risk was great. If the explosion took place, whoever was in the gallery was lost. Two intrepid men, Lieutenant Jacob Douty and Sergeant Henry Rees, volunteered to see what was the cause of the delay, and to re-light the match. Both returned safe and sound. The redoubt had a respite of a quarter of an hour.

Suddenly the earth trembled under our feet. An enormous mass sprang into the air. A mass without form or shape, full of red flames, and carried on a bed of lightning flashes, mounted towards heaven with a detonation of thunder. It spread out like a sheaf, like an immense mushroom whose stem seemed to be of fire and its head of smoke. Then everything appeared to break up and fall back in a rain of earth mixed with rocks, with beams, timbers, and mangled human bodies, leaving floating in the air a cloud of white smoke, which rose up in the heavens, and a cloud of gray dust, which fell slowly towards the earth. The redan had disappeared. In its place had opened a gaping gulf more than two hundred feet long by fifty wide, and twenty-five to thirty feet deep.

Immediately, as though the eruption of a volcano had poured out a tor-

rent of lava upon our lines, they were on fire from one end to the other.
All our batteries opened at once on the enemy's intrenchments. The projectiles whistled, roared, burst. Through the deafening noise of the artillery
firing was heard a cry, and the first division advanced to the assault.

It had nothing in front of it. The Confederate troops occupying the lines
to the right and the left in the immediate vicinity of the mine had fled pre-
cipitately through fright and fear of further explosions. The others, stupefied, endeavored to see what was going on while awaiting orders. The way
was completely open to the summit of the hill, which was protected by no
other line of works.

The column marched directly to the crater, and, instead of turning around
it to pursue its way, it descended into it, in the midst of the torn-up earth.
Once at the bottom, finding itself sheltered, it remained there. A part spread
out to the right and the left behind the abandoned works. The general commanding (Ledlie) the division had remained within our lines, in a bomb-
proof.

The second division, delayed at first by the obstructions, was soon mixed
up with the other. Several regiments descended into the crater, the greater
part extended towards the right without going beyond it. Only one brigade
succeeded in making its way through, so as to advance beyond. It found
itself then engaged in ground cut up by trenches, by covered ways, by
sheltered pits dug in the ground. Worse than that, the enemy, recovering
from his surprise, had already profited by the time we had lost, to place his
guns in position, and form his infantry so as to throw a concentrated fire
upon the opening made in his works. After having, with difficulty, advanced
over the natural obstacles, the brigade, more than half in confusion, seeing
that it was neither supported nor reënforced, was compelled to fall back with
loss.

The third division had not even made a like attempt. In mingling with the
first, it had simply increased the confusion, and crowded together on the left.

Time was flying; the opportunity was fast escaping us; the chances of
success were disappearing as we were looking on. Nothing could force the
troops, crowded together in the crater, or lying down behind the intrenchments, to leave their positions. The officers of spirit amongst them exhausted
themselves in vain efforts. The men would not move. Some officers ordered
without purpose, and moved around without doing anything. The greater
part remained, like the men, motionless in a state of paralysis. The mine had
been blown up two hours, and our forces had not made any advance.

Towards seven o'clock the colored division received orders to advance
in its turn. The blacks advanced resolutely, passed over the passive mass of
white troops, not a company of whom followed them, and, although their
ranks were necessarily broken by the obstacle, they charged under a deadly
fire of artillery and musketry, which reached them from all sides at once.
They even reached the enemy, took from him two hundred and fifty prisoners, captured a flag, and recovered one of ours taken by him. But they
were not sustained. They were driven back by a counter-charge, and re-

turned, running in confusion, to our lines, where, by this time, a large number of the white troops were eager to return with them.

Until then the Confederates had limited their efforts to defending the hill. Encouraged by the feeble attempts which we had made to reach it, and by the ease with which these efforts had been repulsed, they began to draw near along the intrenchments, and endeavor to retake from us the part of the lines they had abandoned. Their guns covered with their fire the space which separated the crater from our lines, where their mortars rained shell and shot. The troops which had taken shelter there found themselves so much the worse off that the cross of fire of the skirmishers rendered the rear communication more difficult.

At this time, General Meade, seeing the day lost without hope of recovery, sent orders to retreat. General Burnside endeavored in vain to obtain a suspension of the order. He still hoped, with more obstinacy than reason, not only to maintain himself on the enemy's line until night, but even to carry the hill. About noon the renewed order was promptly communicated to the troops concerned, without any manner prescribed of executing it. It was found that at this same instant the enemy, after having failed in several attempts, came out in force from a ravine where he had rallied his forces, and advanced to retake the crater. In a moment it was a general *devil take the hindmost*, a confused rush, in which those who could run fast enough and escape the rebel fire returned to our lines. Those who endeavored to resist, or were delayed, were taken prisoners.

Thus passed away the finest opportunity which could have been given us to capture Petersburg.

—De Trobriand, *Four Years with the Army of the Potomac*

B. Mahone's Division Saves the Day at the Crater

In the whole history of war, no enterprise so auspiciously begun ever resulted in a conclusion more lame and impotent. The Union troops designated for the assault, instead of drawing inspiration from the sight of the breach they had effected, actually appeared to recoil from the havoc. For some time no demonstration followed the explosion; when they finally advanced, it was not with the eagerness of grenadiers or guardsmen, but with rushes and pauses of uncertainty; and when they reached our lines, instead of treating the opening as a mere passageway to their objective point beyond, they halted, peeped, and gaped into the pit, and then, with the stupidity of sheep, *followed their bell-wethers into the crater itself*, where, huddled together, all semblance of organization vanished, and company, regimental, and brigade commanders lost all power to recognize, much less control, their respective troops. Meade, from his position a mile away, was demanding of Burnside why he did not advance beyond the crater to the Blandford cemetery. Burnside, safely in the Union lines, and separated from his assaulting columns, was replying that difficulties existed,—difficulties which he could not specify, for the double reason that he did not know what they were, and that they did not in fact exist. . . .

From our ten-inch and eight-inch mortars in the rear of the line, a most accurate fire was opened upon the troops in the breach; and our batteries to north and south began to pour a deadly storm of shell and canister upon their crowded masses. The situation looked desperate for us, nevertheless, for it was all our infantry could do to hold their lines, and not a man could be spared to meet an advance upon Blandford cemetery heights, which lay before the Union troops. At this juncture, heroic John Haskell, of South Carolina, came dashing up the plank road with two light batteries, and from a position near the cemetery began the most effective work of the day.

Exposed to the batteries and sharpshooters of the enemy, he and his men gave little heed to danger. Haskell, in his impetuous and ubiquitous gallantry, dashed and flashed about: first here, next there, like Ariel on the sinking ship. Now he darted into the covered way to seek Elliott, and implore an infantry support for his exposed guns; Elliott, responding to his appeal, was severely wounded as he attempted with a brave handful of his Carolinians to cover Haskell's position; now Haskell cheered Lampkin, who had already opened with his eight-inch mortars; now he hurried back to Flanner, where he had left him, and found him under a fire so hot that in mercy he resolved to retire all his guns but six, and call for volunteers to man them, but that was not the temper of Lee's army: every gun detachment volunteered to remain. Hurrying to the right again, he found but one group of cowards in his whole command, and these he replaced by Hampton Gibbs, and Captain Sam Preston of our brigade, whose conspicuous bravery more than atoned for the first defection; both fell desperately wounded, and were replaced by peerless Hampden Chamberlayne, who left the hospital to hurry to the fight, and won promotion by the brilliancy of his behavior. . . .

It was fully six o'clock before General Lee heard the news, from Colonel Paul, of Beauregard's staff! Colonel Paul lived in Petersburg, and, being at home that night and learning of the disaster, galloped out and informed General Lee as he was sitting down to his breakfast. Before Lee even knew of the occurrence, General Meade had had time to converse with prisoners captured at the crater, and to advise Burnside that Blandford cemetery was unprotected; that none of our troops had returned from the James; that his chance was *now;* and to implore him to move forward at all hazards, lose no time in making formations, and rush for the crest.

General Lee immediately sent Colonel Venable, of his staff, direct to Mahone, with instructions to come with two brigades of his division to Blandford cemetery to support the artillery. The urgency was so great that he did not transmit the order through General Hill, the corps commander. . . .

Meanwhile, Venable had communicated with Mahone, and Mahone, always cunning, had retired his two brigades from the lines so quietly that General Warren, opposite to him, reported that no troops had been withdrawn from his front. The Virginia and Georgia brigades of Mahone's division were the troops selected. The message to Mahone was to send them, but he insisted that he should go with them. They passed rapidly by way of a ravine from Mahone's position on the lines covering the Jerusalem plank road to a point in rear of the crater. The Virginia brigade, commanded by Weisiger, led. It was now eight o'clock. One cannot but think of what might have happened during all this time, if Burnside had acted upon Meade's urgent appeals.

The appearance of this infantry was balm and solace to the artillery blazing away upon the crest just above them. For hours they had been fighting there, almost decimated by the artillery concentrated upon them, and the distant firing of sharpshooters. They could not have withstood even a feeble assault of infantry, and had expected it during every minute they had been engaged: the coming of Mahone was their deliverance. With but an instant's pause in the ravine to strip for battle, Mahone's division, headed by their gallant little general, clambered up the slope, crossed the Jerusalem road, and passed in single file at double-quick into a covered way. There was no cheering, and no gaudy flaunting of uniforms or standards; with them, war's work had become too grim and too real for all that. In weather-worn and ragged clothes, with hats whose brims could shade their eyes for deadly aim, with bodies hardened down by march and exposure to race-horse lines, they came, not with the look or feelings of mercenaries, but like anxious, earnest men whose souls were in their work, who knew what the crisis was, and who were anxious to perform the task which that crisis demanded. Agile as cats, they sprang across the road and entered the covered way; as they skipped by, many a fellow kissed his hand to the artillerymen to right and left, or strained on tiptoe to catch sight of the ground in front, before entering the sheltered passage. For the first time during the day, a line of infantry was between our guns and the enemy; and the boys at the guns, knowing what reliance could be placed upon Mahone's veterans, took new heart and new courage, and pounded away with redoubled energy.

Venable parted with Mahone at the mouth of the covered way, and, seeking General Lee, informed him that Mahone was up, and proposed to lead his two brigades in person. The general expressed his gratification, and gave a sigh of relief. . . . The ground from the crater sloped to the north and west into a little ravine, into which the covered way, by which Mahone had entered, debouched; in this hollow Mahone formed his troops for battle, the Virginia brigade on the left.

Springing quickly from the covered way, the eight hundred Virginians lay flat upon the ground. The Georgians were forming on their right. Before the Georgians could come into position, the enemy, occupying our gorge line, succeeded in forming an attacking column, and advanced to the assault. Weisiger, commanding the Virginians, was a grim, determined man. Our boys were lying down within one hundred and sixty yards of the works, and saw within them a vast throng of Union troops, and counted eleven Union flags. A gallant Union officer, seizing a stand of Union colors, leaped upon their breastworks and called upon his men to charge. Fully realizing the paucity of his own numbers, and the danger of being overwhelmed by the mass of the enemy if they poured down upon him, Weisiger determined to anticipate the threatened movement by charging. Cautioning his men to reserve their fire, he ordered them forward. Those who saw this assault pronounce it to have been, in many respects, the most remarkable which they ever witnessed. At the command "Forward!" the men sprang to their feet; advanced at a run in perfect alignment; absolutely refrained from firing until within a few feet of the enemy; then, with their guns almost upon the bodies of their foes, delivered a deadly fire, and, rushing upon them with bayonets and clubbed muskets, drove them pell-mell back into the intrenchments which they had just left.

General Lee, when advised of this brilliant assault, remarked, "That must have been Mahone's old brigade." When news came confirming it, he again said, "I thought so." . . .

In the position gained by Mahone's old brigade, nothing intervened between them and the enemy but the pile of breastworks,—they on the outside, the enemy within the crater and gorge line. The fighting by which they established themselves was desperate and hand-to-hand.

Superb Haskell once more came to their rescue: he moved up his little Eprouvette mortars almost to our lines, and, cutting down his charge of powder to an ounce and half, so that his shell scarcely mounted fifty feet, threw a continuous hail of small shell into the pit, over the heads of our men. Our fellows seized the muskets abandoned by the retreating enemy, and threw them like pitchforks into the huddled troops over the ramparts. Screams, groans, and explosions throwing up human limbs made it a scene of awful carnage. Yet the artillery of the enemy searched every spot, and they still had a formidable force of fighting men.

The Georgia brigade, charging a little after Weisiger's, was decimated and repulsed. Our own brigade, which was engaged from first to last and never yielded a foot of ground, lost heavily, and Mahone's brigade, the "immortals" of that day, was almost annihilated. About one o'clock, the Alabama brigade of Mahone's division, under Saunders, arrived upon the scene, formed and charged, and the white flag went up from the crater. Out of it into our lines filed as prisoners eleven hundred and one Union troops, including two brigade commanders, and we captured twenty-one standards and several thousand of small arms. Over a thousand of the enemy's dead were in and about the breach, and his losses exceeded five thousand effective troops, while our lines were reestablished just where they were when the battle began.

—WISE, *The End of an Era*

6. LEE STOPS HANCOCK AT THE GATES OF RICHMOND

Sheridan's offensive in the Valley forced Lee, early in August, to send reinforcements to that threatened area. To prevent the detachment of further reinforcements Grant sent Hancock's corps north of the James to make demonstrations against Richmond and, if possible, capture Chapin's Bluff, on the James River. It was expected that this attack would take Lee by surprise, but surprise was not achieved. Yet the threat to Richmond was a serious one. During the fighting of August 16 two Confederate brigades broke and fled; "not only the day but Richmond seemed to be gone," wrote General C. W. Field.

The confused fighting from August 14 to 18 is here described by Richard Corbin, who had run the blockade in order to serve in the Confederate Army.

Headquarters, Field's Division, Petersburg, Va., August 26, 1864.—My dear mother: Some three weeks have flown by since I wrote to you from the north side of the James River, whither this division had been sent at the time of Grant's grand subterranean operation before Petersburg, the strategy of which was characterized by the fiendish ingenuity of Yankee warfare. . . . As I told you from my headquarters near Chapin's Bluff, we fully expected to pitch into the Yankees immediately on arriving on the north side of the river; but when our division had got into position the enemy had disappeared from our front. As far as the fighting was concerned, we had a little respite, but the staff did not profit much by it, for General Field having been placed ad interim in command of that division of the Richmond defenses, our duties became very onerous; but we were to a certain extent compensated by the importance it gave us, for we literally became monarchs of all we surveyed.

This comparative repose was, however, of short duration. Our scouts, a few days after, brought us the intelligence that the enemy had thrown a pontoon bridge across the river and that a large force was moving across it. We had but few troops with us, but preparations were made for a resolute defense of the line committed to our care. On Sunday they drove our skirmishers in, and in the afternoon they attempted to carry a portion of our intrenchments. For that purpose they hurled against us two divisions of their Second Corps, which rushed toward our position with yells, banners flying and bands playing. When they advanced to within about seven hundred yards of our line two twelve-pounders loaded with canister blazed away at them. Our artillery is not considered by any means the most efficient branch of our service and of late has been rather sneered at in this army, but on this occasion it did terrible execution. The Yanks advanced in four lines of battle, and a magnificent spectacle it was to witness that mighty host bearing down upon our thinly-manned breastworks. Notwithstanding my emotion, I could not refrain from admiring the sight. Our fire made wide breaches in their ranks, and after the third discharge the whole line wavered and fluttered like a flag in the wind; another shell exploding in their midst, they broke and fled in every direction without retaining a shadow of their former organization. In their frantic haste to get out of range of our murderous shots they threw away guns, equipment, and all their warlike paraphernalia. Deserters told us that they lost very heavily in that abortive charge. They again renewed the attack, but with less vigor, on our left, and were driven back with great loss by our dismounted cavalry. This was the last of that day's fighting—with the shades of night there came a cessation of hostilities.

In the morning of Tuesday the Yankees attacked us in heavy force, but we repulsed them very handsomely. Finding that these repeated assaults on that part of the line did not pay, General Hancock felt for a more vulnerable point, which he discovered on our left. After riding about ever since dawn, the general and his staff halted in a field in the rear of Wright's brigade of A. P. Hill's corps. The day was a sultry one, and the heat, superadded to other exertions, made us so weary that we got off our horses and lay down for a few moments on the grass. We had not been there many seconds when we were aroused by a terrific cannonade followed by heavy volleys of musketry. We mounted horses in a trice; presently squads of frightened men came from the front in anything but a leisurely manner. They informed us that the whole Yankee army had charged them and that they had been obliged to give way. The firing increased; the air was alive with Minié balls; the ground was torn up by shells and cannonballs, and in a few minutes the whole of Wright's brigade was stampeding toward us. We strove to rally them by entreaties and by menaces, and with pistols drawn we threatened to shoot them if they did not go back, but it was of no avail; you might as well try to argue with a flock of affrighted sheep as with a crowd of panic-stricken soldiers.

Up to this time we cannot account for this stampede. The attack, it was true, was sudden and unexpected and the force of the enemy enormous; but the men who were now flying before the Yankees had always beaten them and had invariably borne themselves on every battlefield with distinguished bravery. We are therefore much puzzled to find out what caused them to disgrace the name of their brigade in that manner. . . .

The General, finding that nothing can be got out of these men, decided to fall back, for the Federals were swooping down upon us in overwhelming numbers; it seemed as though forty thousand men would be an underestimate of the force. I was sent by him for reinforcements. I had orders to bring up without delay two brigades of our own division, viz. Laws's Alabama and Binning's Georgians. They came up at a double-quick amid a very galling fire; they were formed right under the guns of the enemy, and then they rushed in with a deafening war-whoop. It was really splendid to witness the dash of these gallant fellows. I was so carried away with enthusiasm that I cantered alongside of them, but, alas! I did not accompany them during the whole of their triumphant advance, for my faithful charger, poor Palmetto, fell under me, pierced in the left hip by a Minié ball. I was a little stunned by the fall, and when I managed to extricate myself from under him our brave boys had beaten back the foe and recaptured the position which they had taken from us. . . .

On the whole, notwithstanding the misbehavior of that brigade of Hill's corps, our achievement was a very brilliant one; for with a handful of men, say seven thousand at the outside, we drove back three of the enemy's largest corps; and as usual our division won for itself and its commander golden opinions. General Lee, toward the close of the fight, rode up and congratulated the general on the able manner in which he had handled his troops. At one time it was touch and go, and it required great coolness and skill on the part of our general to parry the attempts of the Yankees to turn our flanks; had they succeeded in accomplishing that, the consequences might have been very serious. The reverse was a very heavy one to the enemy; by sending over the best troops they evidently counted on a success. We had several small artillery and picket engagements during the rest of the week, but finally they sloped off without trumpet or drum, and on Sunday morning Hancock and Company had vamosed. Desertions from the Yankee army have been so frequent during this campaign that General Lee has desired to encourage them by circulating throughout Grant's army a paper in which kind treatment and protection is promised to those soldiers who come over to us voluntarily. This has produced the desired effect, for deserters flock into our lines at a monstrous rate, and the cry is "still they come."

—[Corbin], "Letters of a Confederate Officer"

7. THE IRON LINES OF PETERSBURG

Direct assault on the Confederates lines was out of the question; the mine had proved a ghastly failure; attacks north of the James were abortive. Grant fell back on traditional siege operations, meantime striking constantly at the Weldon and the Southside railroads, and persistently pushing his lines westward. Lee's army was stretched to the breaking point; his soldiers were tired, hungry, and dispirited; and he lost as many men by desertion as he gained by recruits and levies.

Here are three letters from a North Carolina soldier who fought through the winter in the iron lines of Petersburg.

Luther Rice Mills to John Mills

Trenches Near Crater, Petersburg, Va.
Nov. 26th [1864]

Brother John:
In my short note to you about a week ago I was unable to give you any of the army news &c. for that can only be gathered by observation. We have just passed through a spell of very hard weather. The suffering in the Trenches was much greater than it should have been. Many of the men were entirely destitute of blankets and overcoats and it was really distressing to see them shivering over a little fire made of green pine wood. Duty too is quite heavy. The men have twelve hours of Picket and twelve of Camp Guard every thirty-six hours. The effect that one cold wet night has upon the boys is a little remarkable. They are generally for *peace on any terms* toward the close of a cold wet night but after the sun is up and they get warm they are in their usual spirits. I have never seen our army so *completely whipped.* The men do not seem to fear the winter Campaign so much as they do the coming of spring. . . . I hardly know what to think of our prospect for next spring. Some men desert from our Brigade nearly every day or two, yet I

believe there will be a great many more next spring. Our army however is quite large—perhaps as large as it was last spring. . . . There is a rumor in our camp that our Division will go to Georgia. This I think extremely doubtful. One good decisive victory in the valley or Georgia would do a great deal towards cheering our men up. We have been supplied within the last few days with shoes and blankets and it is to be hoped that our men will do better. We have to carry some men to hospital for frostbites &c. Some have come in off picket crying from cold like children. In fact I have seen men in the trenches with no shoes at all. I saw Capt. John Williams a few days ago but have not been able to see Baldy yet. We are still near the old mine. I suppose that I am now within fifty yards of the spot where I was wounded. I am doing very well. My shoulder does not worry me much.

Please write soon and give me all the news.

Yours truly

L. R. Mills

Trenches Near Crater, Petersburg Va.
Jany. 3rd, 1865

Brother John:

We are still at our old position—Right of the Brigade extending just beyond Rive's Salient and Left resting near the Blowup. There is a rumor afloat that we will be relieved sometime this month and sent to the rear to rest &c. Everything seems to indicate that we are fixed up here for the winter. Our Division holds the hottest part of the entire lines. The front of Wilcox's Division immediately on our right the enemy can not be seen from the main lines. Here our Picket lines are from 50 to 200 yards from the enemy and a man dares not show his head. We have the biggest rows here some days you ever heard of. The batteries in the rear lines and the enemy's batteries get to shelling occasionally and shells fly by as thick as bats in a summer night. After a row last week some men picked up at least 500 pounds of fragments of shells within a hundred yards of my tent. It was an amusing sight to hear our boys taunting and inviting Grant's army to fight with us while they were firing salutes and rejoicing over Sherman's great victory in Georgia. Our men need a good Victory badly. It would do us a great deal of good for Grant to charge our lines. I believe every man would hail such an attack with joy. We are preparing to put out two more lines of Chevaux de Frise. The spirit of our men is improving slowly. A good many are deserting to the enemy—more than come to us. Two men of my company deserted to the enemy last Christmas night. One was a substitute from Georgetown and the other from near Wheeling. We get pit coal now instead of green pine. I guess we will be a little better now. If I could get a good big cat I could do a great deal better. We have rats and mice and something else in abundance. We can say with old Burns

"Ha! Where ye gaun ye crawlie ferties &c."

I saw a man catch a large rat and eat it about a week ago. What is it that a dirty soldier won't do? The Richmond Examiner says "Coming events cast their shadows before them" but I have not seen the shadow of that big New Year's Dinner yet. Perhaps it is not a coming event. . . . One of the men lamenting his own hard luck and Younger's good luck said five balls have struck me this campaign and the one that would have given me a furlough "I cotch in a blanket." I am in good health and doing well.

Yours truly
L. R. MILLS

Trenches Near Crater, March 2, 1865

Brother John:

Something is about to happen. I know not what. Nearly every one who will express an opinion says Gen'l Lee is about to evacuate Petersburg. The authorities are having all the cotton, tobacco &c. moved out of the place as rapidly as possible. This was commenced about the 22nd of February. Two thirds of the Artillery of our Division has been moved out. The Reserved Ordnance Train has been loaded up and is ready to move at any time. I think Gen'l Lee expects a hard fight on the right and has ordered all this simply as a precautionary measure. Since my visit to the right I have changed my opinion about the necessity for the evacuation of Petersburg. If it is evacuated Johnson's Division will be in a bad situation for getting out. Unless we are so fortunate as to give the Yankees the slip many of us will be captured. I would regret very much to have to give up the old place. The soiled and tattered Colors borne by our skeleton Regiments is sacred and dear to the hearts of every man. No one would exchange it for a new flag. So it is with us. I go down the lines, I see the marks of shot and shell, I see where fell my comrades, the Crater, the grave of fifteen hundred Yankees, when I go to the rear I see little mounds of dirt some with headboards, some with none, some with shoes protruding, some with a small pile of bones on one side near the end showing where a hand was left uncovered, in fact everything near shows desperate fighting. And here I would rather "fight it out." If Petersburg and Richmond is evacuated—from what I have seen & heard in the army—our cause will be hopeless. It is useless to conceal the truth any longer. Many of our people at home have become so demoralized that they write to their husbands, sons and brothers that desertion *now* is not *dishonorable.* It would be impossible to keep the army from straggling to a ruinous extent if we evacuate. I have just received an order from Wise to carry out on picket tonight a rifle and ten rounds of Cartridges to shoot men when they desert. The men seem to think desertion no crime & hence never shoot a deserter when he goes over—they always shoot but never hit. I am glad to say that we have not had but four desertions from our Reg't to the enemy. . . . I send you this morning "Five Months in a Yankee prison" by a Petersburg Militiaman.

Write soon.

Yours truly
L. R. MILLS
—HARMON, ed., "Letters of Luther Rice Mills"

XXIX

The Valley in 1864

THE Valley campaigns of 1864 are among the most interesting in the history of the war. There was no Stonewall Jackson to give them glamour, to be sure, but Jube Early and Phil Sheridan were not bad substitutes. Heretofore the Valley had been, chiefly, the theater for Confederate offensives; this, to some extent, it remained, but the more important offensive operations of 1864 were Federal. The final campaign of 1864 was, too, one of the most decisive of the war, for it deprived Lee's army of its major source of supply and cut it off from the west.

Grant's grand strategy, it will be remembered, called for advances up the Valley by General Sigel and from the west by Generals Averell and Crook to mesh with the major attacks by Meade and Butler. These Valley offensives got under way on time, but accomplished little; not until Sheridan took command was Grant's strategic plan vindicated.

At the end of April Averell and Crook, then along the Kanawha in western Virginia, advanced toward Lynchburg with a view to cutting the important Virginia & Tennessee Railroad. General John Morgan met them and, in a smart action, drove them back to their bases. Meantime Sigel had advanced cautiously up the Valley toward New Market. There, on May 15, he was met by Breckinridge, defeated, and hurled back. General Hunter—next to Butler the most detested of Union commanders—supplanted him and embarked on a program of systematic devastation of the Valley. His military objective was Staunton and the Virginia Central Railroad. Early in June he reached Staunton and then advanced on the town of Lexington, home of Virginia Military Institute, which he put to flames, and of Washington College, which he gutted. Lee hurried Early to the Valley to deal with this menace to his communications; Hunter retreated into western Virginia; and the Confederates were once more in undisputed control of the Valley.

Early seized the opportunity to relieve pressure on Petersburg by striking across the Potomac and at Washington. Swift marches brought him to the outskirts of Washington by July 10; as Federal forces concentrated against him he withdrew to home ground. The bold stroke had achieved its immediate objective; Grant sent large reinforcements to the Valley and appointed Sheridan to temporary command of the whole theater of operations. In two months Sheridan made a national reputation. With a numerical superiority of at least two to one, he was able to seize and hold the offensive. First he struck

Early along the Opequon; then at Winchester. These two battles all but destroyed the Confederate forces in the Valley.

Once again Lee was forced to send reinforcements, and once again the intrepid Early took the offensive, scoring what at first seemed a spectacular victory at Cedar Creek. This victory Sheridan turned into defeat. After that there was nothing to stop the deliberate and calculated destruction that Grant ordered and Sheridan willingly executed. By winter the Valley, scene of so many Confederate victories, was firmly in Union hands. And it was from the Valley that Sheridan finally rode down to the triumph of Five Forks.

1. V.M.I. BOYS FIGHT AT NEW MARKET

On April 30 General Franz Sigel, in command of the Department of West Virginia, started up the Valley toward Strasburg. Meeting no opposition he pressed on toward New Market. Breckinridge was already on his way to meet him, with a miscellaneous force including the Cadet Corps from the Virginia Military Institute—Stonewall Jackson's school—at Lexington.

John Wise, then a cadet of seventeen, here tells the story of the dash from Lexington to New Market and of "the most glorious day" of his life. The battle was a minor one, but had far-reaching consequences, for it enabled the Confederates to hold the Valley long enough to gather the harvest, so essential to Lee's hungry army.

ON the 10th of May, 1864, the Cadet Corps was the very pink of drill and discipline, and mustered 350 strong. The plebes of the last fall had passed through squad and company drill, and the battalion was now proficient in the most intricate manœuvre. The broad parade ground lay spread out like a green carpet. The far-off ranges of the Blue Ridge seemed nearer in the clear light of spring. The old guard tree, once more luxuriantly green, sheltered its watching groups of admiring girls and prattling children. . . .

Suddenly the barracks reverberated with the throbbing of drums; we awoke and recognized the long roll. Lights were up; the stoops resounded with the rush of footsteps seeking place in the ranks; the adjutant, by lantern-light, read our orders amid breathless silence. They told us that the enemy was in the valley, that Breckinridge needed help, and that we were ordered to march for Staunton at daybreak—a battalion of infantry and a section of artillery—with three days' rations. Not a sound was uttered, not a man moved from the military posture of "parade rest." Our beating hearts told us that our hour had come at last.

"Parade 's dismissed," piped the adjutant. Then came a wild halloo, as company after company broke ranks. Again in fancy I see the excited rush of that gay throng, eager as greyhounds in the leash, hurrying back and forth, preparing for the start, forgetful that it would be six hours before they should march.

Daybreak found us on the Staunton pike after a sleepless night and a breakfast by candle-light. . . . And now, fairly started upon our journey, we were plodding on right merrily, our gallant little battery rumbling behind.

At midday on the 12th of May we marched into Staunton to the tune of "The girl I left behind me." We were not quite as fresh or as neat as at the outset, but still game and saucy. . . .

Breckinridge's army, which had hurried up from south-western Virginia to meet Sigel, soon filled the town and suburbs. Now and then a bespattered trooper came up wearily from Woodstock or Harrisonburg to report the steady advance of Sigel with an army thrice the size of our own. Ever and anon the serious shook their heads and predicted hot work in store for us. Even in the hour of levity the shadow of impending bloodshed hung over all but the cadet. At evening parade the command came to move down the valley.

Morning found us promptly on the march. A few lame ducks had succumbed and were left behind, but the body of the corps were still elated and eager, although rain had overtaken us. The first day's march brought us to Harrisonburg; the second to Lacy's Springs, within ten miles of New Market. On this day evidences of the enemy's approach thickened on every hand. At short intervals upon the pike, the great artery of travel in the valley, carriages and vehicles of all sorts filled the way, laden with people and their household effects, fleeing from the hostile advance. Now and then a haggard trooper, dispirited by long skirmishing against overwhelming force, would gloomily suggest the power and numbers of the enemy. Towards nightfall, in a little grove by a church, we came upon a squad of Federal prisoners, the first that many of us had ever seen. It was a stolid lot of Germans, who eyed us with curious inquiry as we passed. Laughter and badinage had somewhat subsided when we pitched camp that night in sight of our picket-fires twinkling in the gloaming but a few miles below us down the valley. We learned, beyond doubt, that Franz Sigel and his army were sleeping within ten miles of the spot on which we rested. . . .

The day, breaking gray and gloomy, found us plodding onward in the mud. The exceedingly sober cast of our reflections was relieved by the light-heartedness of the veterans. Wharton's brigade, with smiling "Old Gabe" at their head, cheered us heartily as we came up to the spot where they were cooking breakfast by the road-side. Many were the good-natured gibes with which they restored our confidence. The old soldiers were as merry, nonchalant, and indifferent to the coming fight as if it was a daily occupation. . . .

The mile-posts on the pike scored four miles, three miles, two miles, one mile to New Market. Then the mounted skirmishers crowded past us hurrying to the front. Cheering began in our rear and was caught up by the troops along the line of march. We learned its import as Breckinridge and his staff approached, and we joined in the huzza as that soldierly man, mounted magnificently, dashed past us, uncovered, bowing, and riding like the Cid. Along the crest of the elevation in our front we beheld our line of mounted pickets and the smoldering fires of their night's bivouac. We halted with the realization that one turn in the road would bring us in full view of the enemy's position. Echols's and Wharton's brigades hurried past us. There was not so much banter then. "Forward!" was the word once more, and New Market appeared in sight.

The turn of the road displayed the whole position. A bold range of hills parallel with the mountains divides the Shenandoah Valley into two smaller valleys, and in the eastern-most of these lies New Market. . . .

Orchards skirt the village in these meadows between our position and the town, and they are filled with the enemy's skirmishers. A heavy stone fence and a deep lane run westward from the town and parallel with our line of battle. Here the enemy's infantry was posted to receive our left flank, and behind it his artillery was posted on a slope, the ground rising gradually until, a short distance beyond the town, to the left of the pike, it spreads out in an elevated plateau. The hillsides from this plateau to the pike are gradual and broken by several gullies heavily wooded by scrub-cedar.

It was Sunday morning, and 11 o'clock. In a picturesque little church-yard, right under the shadow of the village spire and among the white tomb-stones, a six-gun battery was posted in rear of the infantry line of the enemy. The moment we debouched it opened upon us.

Away off to the right, in the Luray Gap of the Massanutten range, our signal corps was telegraphing the position and numbers of the enemy. Our cavalry was moving at a gallop to the cover of the creek to attempt to flank the town. Echols's brigade was moving from the pike at a double-quick by the right flank and went into line of battle across the meadow, its left resting on the pike. Simultaneously his skirmishers were thrown forward at a run and engaged the enemy. Out of the orchards and out on the meadows arose puff after puff of blue smoke as our sharpshooters advanced, the *"pop, pop"* of their rifles ringing forth excitingly. Thundering down the pike came Mc-Laughlin with his artillery, and wheeling out into the meadows he swung into battery action left, and let fly with all his guns. The cadet section of artillery pressing a little farther forward wheeled to the left, toiled up the slope, and with a plunging fire replied to the Federal battery in the graveyard. At the first discharge of our guns a beautiful wreath of smoke shot upward and hovered over them.

The little town, which a moment before had seemed to sleep so peacefully upon that Sabbath morn, was now wreathed in battle-smoke and swarming with troops hurrying to their positions. We had their range beautifully, and every shell, striking some obstruction, exploded in the streets. Every man of our army was in sight. Every position of the enemy was plainly visible. . . .

My orders were to remain with the wagons at the bend in the pike, unless our forces were driven back; in which case we were to retire to a point of safety. When it became evident that a battle was imminent, a single thought took possession of me, and that was, that I would never be able to look my father in the face again if I sat on a baggage-wagon while my command was in its first, perhaps its only, engagement. He was a grim old fighter, at that moment commanding at Petersburg. . . . If, now that I had the opportunity, I should fail to take part in the fight I knew what was in store for me. Napoleon in Egypt pointed to the Pyramids and told his soldiers that from their heights forty centuries looked down upon them. My oration, delivered from the baggage-wagon, was not so elevated in tone, but equally emphatic. It ran about this wise:

"Boys, the enemy is in our front. Our command is about to go into action. I like fighting no better than anybody else. But I have an enemy in my rear as dreadful as any before us. If I return home and tell my father that I was on the baggage guard when my comrades were fighting I know my fate. He will kill me with worse than bullets—ridicule. I shall join the command forthwith. Any one who chooses to remain may do so."

All the guard followed. The wagon was left in charge of the black driver. Of the four who thus went, one was killed and two were wounded.

We rejoined the battalion as it marched by the left flank from the pike. Moving at double-quick we were in an instant in line of battle, our right near the turnpike. Rising ground in our immediate front concealed us from the enemy. The command was given to strip for action. Knapsacks, blankets, everything but guns, canteens, and cartridge-boxes, were thrown down upon the ground. Our boys were silent then. Every lip was tightly drawn, every cheek was pale; but not with fear. With a peculiar nervous jerk we pulled our cartridge-boxes round to the front and tightened our belts. Whistling rifled-shell screamed over us as, tipping the hill-crest in our own front, they bounded over our heads. Across the pike to our right Patton's brigade was lying down, abreast of us.

"At-ten-tion-n-n! Battalion Forward! Guide—Center-r-rr!" shouted Ship, and off we started. At that moment, from the left of the line, sprang Sergeant-Major Woodbridge, and posted himself forty paces in front of the colors as directing guide. Brave Evans, standing over six feet two, unfurled our colors that for days had hung limp and bedraggled about the staff, and every cadet in the Institute leaped forward, dressing to the ensign, elate and thrilling with the consciousness that *"This is war!"* We reached the hill-crest in our front, where we were abreast of our smoking battery and in full sight and range of the enemy. We were pressing towards him at "arms port" with the light tripping gait of the French infantry. The enemy had obtained our range, and began to drop his shell under our noses along the slope. Echols's brigade rose up and were charging on our right with the rebel yell. . . .

Down the green slope we went, answering the wild cry of our comrades as their musketry rattled out its opening volleys. In another moment we should expect a pelting rain of lead from the blue line crouching behind the stone wall at the lane. Then came a sound more stunning than thunder, that burst directly in my face; lightnings leaped; fire flashed; the earth rocked; the sky whirled round, and I stumbled. My gun pitched forward, and I fell upon my knees. Sergeant Cabell looked back at me sternly, pityingly, and called out, "Close up, men," as he passed on.

I knew no more. When consciousness returned it was raining in torrents. I was lying on the ground, which all about was torn and plowed with shell which were still screeching in the air and bounding on the earth. . . .

From this time forth I may speak of the gallant behavior of the cadets without the imputation of vanity, for I was no longer a participant in their glory. . . .

Bloody work had been done. The space between the enemy's old and new positions was dotted with their dead and wounded—shot as they fled across the open field. But this same exposed ground now lay before, and must be crossed by our own men, under a galling fire from a strong and protected position. The distance was not three hundred yards, but the ground to be traversed was a level green field of young wheat. Again the advance was ordered. Our men responded with a cheer. Poor fellows! they had already been put upon their mettle in two assaults. Exhausted, wet to ther skin, muddied to their eyebrows with the stiff clay through which they had pulled,—some of them actually shoeless after their struggle across the plowed ground,—they nevertheless advanced with great grit and eagerness; for the shouting on their right meant victory. But the foe in our front was far from conquered. As our fellows came on with a dash the enemy stood his ground most courageously. That battery, now charged with canister and shrapnel, opened upon the cadets with a murderous hail the moment they uncovered. The infantry lying behind fence-rails piled upon the ground, poured in a steady, deadly fire. . . .

The men were falling right and left. The veterans on the right of the cadets seemed to waver. Ship, our commandant, fell wounded. For the first time the cadets seemed irresolute. Some one cried out, "Lie down," and all obeyed, firing from the knee—all but Evans, the ensign, who was standing bolt upright. Poor Stanard's limbs were torn asunder and he lay there bleeding to death. Some one cried out, "Fall back, and rally on Edgar's battalion." Several boys moved as if to obey; but Pizzini, orderly of "B" company, with his Italian blood at the boiling-point, cocked his gun and swore he would shoot the first man who ran. Preston, brave and inspiring, with a smile lay down upon his only arm, remarking that he would at least save that. Collona, captain of "D," was speaking words of encouragement and bidding the boys shoot close. The boys were being decimated; manifestly they must charge or retire; and charge it was.

For at that moment, Henry A. Wise, our first captain, beloved of every boy in the command, sprung to his feet, shouted the charge, and led the Cadet Corps forward to the guns. The guns of the battery were served superbly; the musketry fairly rolled. The cadets reached the firm green-sward of the farmyard in which the battery was planted. The Federal infantry began to break and run behind the buildings. Before the order to "Limber up" could be obeyed our boys disabled the trails and were close upon the guns; the gunners dropped their sponges and sought safety in flight. Lieutenant Hanna hammered a burly gunner over the head with his cadet sword. Winder Garrett outran another and attacked him with his bayonet. The boys leaped on the guns, and the battery was theirs; while Evans was wildly waving the cadet colors from the top of a caisson. . . .

We had won a victory,—not a Manassas . . . but, for all that, a right comforting bit of news went up the pike that night to General Lee; for from where he lay, locked in the death grapple with Grant in the Wilderness, his thoughts were, doubtless, ever turning wearily and anxiously towards this flank movement in the valley.

—WISE, "The West Point of the Confederacy"

2. LEW WALLACE STOPS EARLY AT THE GATES OF WASHINGTON

As Hunter moved up the Valley, through Staunton and Lexington, and toward the all-important Virginia and Tennessee Railroad, Lee hurried re-inforcements under General Early. After some indecisive fighting at Lynch-burg Hunter retreated westward to the Kanawha. Now the Valley was clear of the invader.

Lee had already given Early discretionary authority to cross the Potomac and threaten Washington, and now Early made this plan his own. With a force of about 17,000 he pushed for the Potomac, hemmed Sigel in on Mary-land Heights, raced on to Frederick City, and appeared before Washington on July 10. Lew Wallace, who was in charge of the defenses of the city, had available only a handful of men, but the outer fortifications of the capital were formidable. Wallace's task was to delay Early until reinforcements arrived from the James. These were already on the way. Ricketts' division of the VI Corps began to arrive on the eighth; two more divisions left Peters-burg on the ninth and arrived in Washington on the eleventh. There was never any likelihood that Early could have captured the city. What he did was to relieve pressure on Petersburg and boost Southern morale.

Lew Wallace, who here tells the story of his delaying action on the eleventh, was an Indiana lawyer who had served with distinction as adjutant general of his state, fought at Fort Donelson and at Shiloh, and saved Cincin-nati from the attack by Kirby Smith. After the war he wrote The Fair God *and, while Governor General of New Mexico, the enormously popular Ben-Hur.*

July 11 [1864]:

It may be well believed that at this period of the affair I kept an eye closely on my watch. Was I not fighting for time?

When the slow-going minute-hand reached

Eleven o'Clock

I felt a thrill of gratification. Four hours gained! Four hours, and Early still in Frederick, not one step nearer his great prize than when the dawn delivered the steeples of the town from the envelope of night! Should I give notice to the authorities in Washington, and to General Grant at City Point, of what was going on? Not yet, I said to myself—not yet. For if asked, I could not have told to which city my antagonist was going, or how many men he had. Looking towards Frederick, I could see the smoke of camp-fires and wagons in park, and artillery, and a cloud of soldiers ominously sug-gestive of yet another army corps. Nevertheless, the revelations were as yet too indefinite for committal to the wires; besides which it remained to see what Ricketts and his sturdy regiments could do. I had come to have an immense confidence in him and them. How many hours additional might they not win for the Cause? Away down in my heart I was conscious of the fluttering of a hope which I was not sanguine enough to put into words.

What with anxiety and excitement my tongue had become very dry; but having put a lemon in my pocket in the morning, I was finding relief sucking it, when Colonel Catlin, near by, asked, "Are not those skirmishers I see yonder?"

"Where?"

"There, just south of the cornfield?"

I brought my glass to bear, and as promptly called Woodhull and Ross to my side, and each wrote at my dictation:

"General RICKETTS,—A line of skirmishers is advancing from the south beyond the cornfield at your left. I suggest you change front in that direction, and advance to the cornfield fence, concealing your men behind it. They will be enfiladed, but that can't be helped.

"LEW WALLACE"

"Make haste," I said to the orderly, giving him one of the duplicates and retaining the other.

Within five minutes the brigades were on their feet; within another five minutes one of them was lying down behind the fence, while the other moved leisurely to take position on its left. The manoeuvring brought both bodies into view from the west side of the river, and the gunners there were in nowise loath to profit by the advantage offered. This, of course, called Alexander and Wiegel into action.

The cannonading and the noise of bursting shells were furious—I had almost said infernal. Sympathy for the brave men under the iron rain racked me like a sharp pain; but, as said, the conditions were beyond help. The furrow had been begun; it was fast reddening under the plough; not for that, however, could I then cry stop.

Presently my attention was claimed by another sight. The cornfield of which I have spoken as on Rickett's left—his front now—was wide. How many acres it contained I cannot say; but the crop was in mid-growth, luxuriantly green and high as a man's waist. At the fence of the farther side the skirmishers disappeared; in their place there now came a line extending the length of the field, and more. Clearing the fence, the new-comers halted in the corn to regain their alignment, then advanced. I could see guidons, and several flags with pale-blue crosses on red fields, and white stars in the crosses, signifying regiments.

"They are cavalry," I said.

"That's good!" Ross replied.

"Why so?"

"Horsemen afoot are easy for infantry."

"But they may be mounted infantry."

"I don't know any difference. A horse always spoils a good soldier."

I could not help retorting, "I haven't observed that a horse had done you any hurt."

Gaps had to be made in the fence for the passage of mounted officers. These, once through, galloped to their places. Then, at a signal—a bugle-call probably—the array having attained its proper front, it started forward slowly at first; suddenly, after the passage of a space, arms were shifted, and, taking to the double-quick, the men raised their battle-cry, which, sounding across the field and intervening distance, rose to me on the height, sharper, shriller, and more like the composite yelping of wolves than I had ever heard it. And when to these were presently superadded a tempestuous tossing of guidons, waving of banners, and a furious trampling of the young corn that flew before them like splashed billows, the demonstration was more than exciting—it was really fearful; and, watching it, I understood as never before the old Vandal philosophy which taught that the sublimest inspiration of courage lay in the terrible.

A brave spectacle it was indeed; yet, as Marshal Roberts said of the charge of the Six Hundred, it was not war. I could not understand it; and whatever of admiration I felt as a beholder was lost in amazement, all because of one extraordinary feature—not a man engaged in it took time or thought it necessary to stop, though for an instant, and fire a shot! Through my glasses I could easily make out officers mounted and waving their swords, and, as I thought, cheering the line forward. What did they mean? One of them there must have been the chief; what did he mean? Did he know of what was before him? Or was he of the Southerners who, still sceptical of the courage of the North, imagined that all to be done now was to set up the yell, wave the flags, and go with a rush, and win?

My eyes dropped involuntarily to the fence—it was of rough rails—toward which the charge was coming. On the hither side of it, in the corners, I saw indistinctly what looked like daubs of blue pigment in spots darker for the shade covering them. I knew them to be soldiers—our soldiers. They lay ever so still, reminding me of hunters in a broad runway, the deer in sight and speeding down upon them. Here and there I could see men half-risen peering through the spaces between the rails—they were company officers. Behind them other figures in uniforms were standing by horses; and in them I recognized field-officers. One man was in his saddle—Ricketts. He drew all my attention. Everybody in his vicinity seemed waiting on him; and presently, like the rest, I was doing the same, waiting for the word that would call the daubs of blue pigment into life and deadly action. The bristling, noisy wave was drawing nigh and nigher. How close would he permit it to come? The word was his; was it not time to give it? He sat the horse like a block of wood, calm, indifferent. I could not see that he was even watchful. There was a noticeable fever in my blood which I tried to cool sucking more vigorously at the lemon, and saying to myself, "He knows his men, and what they can be relied upon to do."

We thus in observation were almost breathlessly silent, and for a reason;

not only did our fortunes depend upon what was about to take place; we were witnessing a rare incident which might not come to us again though we lived a hundred years. And in our minds there was a flutter of questions: "What will be the effect of the fire? Will it hush the howling? Will it stop the rush?" I felt my flesh creep, imagining the annihilation that must follow its delivery.

I heard no command given; however, up rose the figures behind the fence, up as one man. I saw the gleaming of the burnished gun-barrels as they were laid upon the upper rails. The aim taken was with deadliest intent—never more coolly. I could form no correct judgment of the distance, probably a hundred and twenty-five or thirty yards, then a ragged eruption of fire, and for an instant smoke interfered with the view.

"My God!" cried Woodhull. "They are all killed!"

With return of fair vision, we looked for the line. It had disappeared. Not a man of it was to be seen, only the green of the trodden corn, some horses galloping about riderless, and a few mounted officers bravely facing the unexpected storm.

"No," I said in reply to Woodhull, "they are not all killed. Give the fellows unhurt time to crawl along the furrows back to the fence, and you will see."

There was a cheer, no doubt by whom given. Then succeeded a firing at will. More saddles emptied, other horses rushing madly about. And ere long the thitherward fence was darkened with climbers, under whom whole sections of the rails went down, so little did the fugitives stand upon the order of their going. A few minutes more and not a living thing could be discovered in the field. Even the masterless horses were gone; while the wounded, crouching close to avoid the pitiless rain of bullets in the air above them, lay under the corn hidden as by a mantle. And they and the dead— how many were there of them?

So far victory. I sent an orderly to Ricketts with congratulations, and then consulted my watch.

—WALLACE, *An Autobiography*

3. GENERAL HUNTER DEVASTATES THE VALLEY

After New Market Sigel wired that his "retrograde" movement was carried out in good order; Halleck telegraphed in disgust to Grant, "Sigel is in full retreat on Strasburg. He will do nothing but run; never did anything else." He was relieved from command, and David Hunter appointed to his place.

No other Union general, except Butler, was so cordially detested by the South; few did so much to earn that detestation. A veteran of the Mexican War Hunter had replaced Frémont in Missouri, and been replaced, in turn, himself. He had commanded the Department of the South and issued a proclamation freeing the slaves within his lines which Lincoln was forced to repudiate. When he raised a Negro regiment the Confederate Congress proclaimed him a felon and ordered his execution if captured. Perhaps it was no wonder that he was bitter toward the South! When he replaced Sigel he embarked on a plan of systematic destruction of the Valley—a plan which Sheridan was to complete. The destruction itself was justified by those same military considerations that controlled Sherman in Georgia; what embittered Southerners was the animosity which appeared to inspire Hunter and the extent to which he exposed women and children to danger.

General John Imboden, who here describes Hunter's depredations, was a veteran of Jackson's Valley campaign, had covered the retreat at Gettysburg, and was now once more back in his familiar Valley.

FROM Brownsburg General Hunter proceeded to Lexington. . . . At Lexington he enlarged upon the burning operations begun at Staunton. On his way, and in the surrounding country, he burnt mills, furnaces, storehouses, granaries, and all farming utensils he could find, beside a great amount of fencing, and a large quantity of grain. In the town he burnt the Virginia Military Institute, and all the professors' houses except the superintendent's (General Smith's), where he had his headquarters, and found a portion of the family too sick to be removed. He had the combustibles collected to burn Washington College, the recipient of the benefactions of the Father of his Country by his will; but, yielding to the appeals of the trustees and citizens, spared the building, but destroyed the philosophical and chemical apparatus, libraries and furniture. He burned the mills and some private stores in the lower part of the town.

Captain Towns, an officer in General Hunter's army, took supper with the family of Governor John Letcher. Mrs. Letcher having heard threats that her house would be burned, spoke of it to Captain Towns, who said it could not be possible, and remarked that he would go at once to headquarters and let her know. He went, returned in a half hour, and told her that he was directed by General Hunter to assure her that the house would not be destroyed, and she might, therefore, rest easy. After this, she dismissed her fears, not believing it possible that a man occupying Hunter's position would be guilty of wilful and deliberate falsehood to a lady. It, however, turned out otherwise, for the next morning, at half-past eight o'clock, his assistant provost marshal, accompanied by a portion of his guard, rode up to the door, and Captain Berry dismounted, rang the door-bell, called for Mrs. Letcher, and informed her that General Hunter had ordered him to burn the house. She replied: "There must be some mistake," and requested to see the order. He said it was verbal. She asked if its execution could not be delayed till she could see Hunter?

He replied: "The order is peremptory, and you have five minutes to leave the house."

Mrs. Letcher then asked if she could be allowed to remove her mother's, her sister's, her own and her children's clothing. This request being refused, she left the house. In a very short time they poured camphene on the parlor floor and ignited it with a match. In the meantime Miss Lizzie Letcher was trying to remove some articles of clothing from the other end of the house, and Berry, finding these in her arms, set fire to them. The wardrobe and bureaus were then fired, and soon the house was enveloped in flames.

Governor Letcher's mother, then seventy-eight years old, lived on the adjoining lot. They fired her stable, within forty feet of the dwelling, evidently to burn it, too; but, owing to the active exertions of Captain Towns, who made his men carry water, the house was saved. While Hunter was in Lexington, Captain Mathew X. White, residing near the town, was arrested, taken about two miles, and, without trial, was shot, on the allegation that he was a bushwhacker. During the first year of the war he commanded the Rockbridge Cavalry, and was a young gentleman of generous impulses and good character. The total destruction of private property in Rockbridge county, by Hunter, was estimated and published in the local papers at the time as over $2,000,000. The burning of the Institute was a public calamity, as it was an educational establishment of great value.

From Lexington he proceeded to Buchanan, in Bottetourt county, and camped on the magnificent estate of Colonel John T. Anderson, an elder brother of General Joseph R. Anderson, of the Tredegar Works, at Richmond. Colonel Anderson's estate, on the banks of the Upper James, and his mansion, were baronial in character. The house crowned a high, wooded hill, was very large, and furnished in a style to dispense that lavish hospitality which was the pride of so many of the old-time Virginians. It was the seat of luxury and refinement, and in all respects a place to make the owner contented with his lot in this world. Colonel Anderson was old—his head as white as snow—and his wife but a few years his junior. He was in no office, and too old to fight—hence was living on his fine estate strictly the life of a private gentleman. He had often, in years gone by, filled prominent representative positions from his county. There was no military or public object on God's earth to be gained by ruining such a man. Yet Hunter, after destroying all that could be destroyed on the plantation when he left it, ordered the grand old mansion, with all its contents, to be laid in ashes.

From Buchanan he proceeded toward Lynchburg, by way of the Peaks of Otter; but on arriving within four miles of the city, where a sharp skirmish occurred between General Crook's command and three brigades under my command, at a place called the Quaker Meeting-House, he ascertained that General Early was in town with Stonewall Jackson's old corps. This was enough for him. That night he began a rapid retreat toward Salem, leaving his cavalry to make demonstrations on Early's lines long enough to give him a good day's start. . . .

I shall conclude this already long narrative by citing a few more instances of Hunter's incendiarism in the Lower Valley. It seems that, smarting under the miserable failure of his grand raid on Lynchburg, where, during a march of over two hundred miles, the largest force he encountered was under Jones at Piedmont, and he routed that, thus leaving the way open to reach Lynchburg within three days, destroy the stores there and go out through West Virginia unmolested, he had failed to do anything but inflict injury on private citizens, and he came back to the Potomac more implacable than when he left it a month before.

His first victim was the Hon. Andrew Hunter, of Charlestown, Jefferson county, his own first cousin, and named after the General's father. Mr. Hunter is a lawyer of great eminence, and a man of deservedly large influence in his county and the State. His home, eight miles from Harper's Ferry, in the suburbs of Charlestown, was the most costly and elegant in the place, and his family as refined and cultivated as any in the State. His offense, in General Hunter's eyes, was that he had gone politically with his State, and was in full sympathy with the Confederate cause. The General sent a squadron of cavalry out from Harper's Ferry, took Mr. Hunter prisoner, and held him a month in the common guard-house of his soldiers, without alleging any offense against him not common to nearly all the people of Virginia, and finally discharged him without trial or explanation, after heaping these indignities on him. Mr. Hunter was an old man, and suffered severely from confinement and exposure. While he was thus a prisoner, General Hunter ordered his elegant mansion to be burned to the ground, with all its contents, not even permitting Mrs. Hunter and her daughter to save their clothes and family pictures from the flames; and, to add to the desolation, camped his cavalry within the inclosure of the beautiful grounds, of several acres, surrounding the residence, till the horses had destroyed them.

—IMBODEN, "Fire, Sword, and the Halter"

4. GENERAL RAMSEUR FIGHTS AND DIES FOR HIS COUNTRY

There was no more gallant figure in the Confederate Army than young Stephen Dodson Ramseur of North Carolina. After graduating from West Point in 1860 he resigned a commission in the U. S. Army to go with his state the following year. His military career was meteoric: within a year he had been promoted from lieutenant to brigadier general. He fought with distinction during the Seven Days; was wounded at Malvern Hill; fought and was wounded again at Chancellorsville; recovered and fought at Gettysburg and in the Wilderness. He led the counterattack that threw Hancock back at the Bloody Angle, and there was wounded a third time. Promoted to major general, at twenty-seven, he joined Early in the Valley campaign and fought with his customary courage at Winchester and Cedar Creek.

In October 1863 Ramseur had married Ellen Richmond, and his letters to his beloved wife give a running account of the war. Those we print here describe the fighting in the Valley campaign. The day before Cedar Creek Ramseur heard that his baby had been born, and he went into battle wearing a white rose in honor of the daughter he was never to see. He was mortally wounded trying to stem Sheridan's counterattack at Cedar Creek and died the following day. "He was," wrote General Early, "a most gallant and energetic officer whom no disaster appalled, but his courage and energy seemed to gain new strength in the midst of confusion and disorder."

Staunton—Va—June 27th—1864

Have time for only a line—to tell you I am well. We have had hardest march of the war. Couldn't catch Hunter—but we hope yet to strike the Enemy a heavy blow. Do not be uneasy if you fail to hear from us. We are going still further & all communications will be cut. We hope to relieve Richmond & make Yankeedom smart. I may be pardoned for saying to *you* that I am making a reputation as a Maj. Genl. The greatest hardship is being separated from you.

Near Leesburg Va—July 15th—1864

I seize the first opportunity since our return to Va—to write &c. . . . We have been hard at work since I last wrote you—took Harpers Ferry on the 4th Inst. Marched to Frederick Md whipped the Yankees there—marched to District of Columbia & halted within five miles from Washington—(natural obstacles alone prevented our taking Washington). The heat & dust was so great that our men could not possibly march further. Time was thus given the enemy to get a sufficient force into his works to prevent our capturing them. We have however accomplished a good deal & I hope will still do good work for our Cause.

Our rumors from Richmond are very pleasing. Let us continue to pray for independence & peace.

H'dqr'ts Early's Div—July 23rd—1864

Again we have passed thro the ordeal of battle. Caleb [Genl Rs brother in law & aide de camp] & I are both safe wonderful to say. I am greatly mortified at result of battle. My men behaved shamefully. They ran from the enemy. And for the first time in my life, I am deeply mortified at the conduct of troops under my command. Had these men behaved like *my old Brigade* would have done under similar circumstances, a disgraceful retreat would have been a brilliant victory. Caleb & I are both safe wonderful to say. Do not mention to anyone the bad conduct of my troops.

Camp near Bunker Hill. Aug 28th—1864

Last night I rec'd two letters from you. Do you know how precious they are, & how much good they did me? After a long march & a sharp skirmish I had gone to bed, & was thinking of you only, when they were brought to me. I am so glad that you continue cheerful & hopeful through these terrible days. Courage my little wife—maybe I will be permitted to come & see you before long. . . . Do you know that I am beginning to believe that we may very soon have peace! Everybody seems to think that the peace party will carry the election in the north. Oh may these expectations be realized & soon may this terrible war that separates us cease. It is such a happiness to be able to write to you often—wish I had time to write more fully & more often. Is there anything you want that I can get for you. I have a bottle of fine *Old French* brandy Ill send you by first opportunity, also some money I am anxious to send you by first safe messenger.

Camp near Bunker Hill—Aug 29th—1864

This morning, much to my surprise, we are quiet—how long we will remain so is very doubtful. In fact, I have everything now ready to move. Thus, you see, our life is one of constant action—marching & counter-marching—manoeuvering & sometimes a little fighting. So far we have been very successful. God grant that we may continue to strike telling blows for our bleeding country. I am growing more hopeful about the ending of the War. Every man whose opinion I have asked & who has had an opportunity of learning the feeling of the Yankee people & soldiery, assures me that the north is tired of war & will elect an out & out, unconditional peace man at the Presidential election next November. I trust these opinions may be verified. For myself I think now, as I did several months ago, that everything depends upon the result of operations at Richmond & Atlanta. If we are enabled to baffle all of Grant's movements & to drive back Sherman, it does seem to me that the Yankee nation will be forced to conclude that the task of sub-jugating the South is more than they can accomplish. At all events we have reason for great thankfulness to the Giver of all Good for his wonderful mercy & care so continually shown toward us during this tremendous campaign. . . . Could we be permitted to see each other for even a short while how we would be encouraged & strengthened. But duty separates us—let us bear it all bravely—& the time will soon come let us hope when we will receive our rich reward—Reunion in peace, independence & happiness! . . .

Nothing new here. Will write as often as I can do not be uneasy if you do not hear regularly. Army movements & irregular mail facilities may prevent.

Camp near Winchester, Sept 6th—1864

This is certainly a time to try our souls! We see in Yankee papers that Sherman has defeated Hood & captured Atlanta. We do not wish to believe this, but are compelled to be apprehensive & anxious. Our hopes for Peace depend upon the success of our armies in the field. Even tho Sherman takes Atlanta, provided he does not destroy nor disorganize Hood's army it will still be alright as long as Gen'l Lee (God bless our old Hero!) & his glorious army continue to baffle the tremendous efforts made to capture Richmond & over run Virginia—so let us be hopeful. Our own accounts may put a different face upon northern news. You will know before this reaches you that McClellan & Pendleton are the nominees of the Chicago Convention. Their Platform is ingeniously contrived to mean either war or peace—so as to catch all of the opponents of the Lincoln administration—& to be governed by events between now & the election. If our armies can hold their own, suffer no crushing disaster before the next election. We may reasonably expect a termination of this war. Let us therefore devote all of our energies to the defense of our country—& persevere in Prayer to the Ruler of Nations. What is the news at home? I am sending you a recpt for apple butter—& as it requires no *store* things—except a few spices, it is one kind of *preserves* we can have! If our army moves forward again, I will get you a circular cloak (forget the technical name) they are "all the rage" now. If we go back up the valley as far as Strasburg soon—(as I think we will before long) & everything promises well, I intend to ask for a furlough to come to see you—dont know tho how things will be. I predict orders for a move before long. . . . We cannot use Confederate money in Maryland—& we have to give six dollars Confed. for *one* Greenback.

Camp near Winchester, Sept. 11th '64

Our campaign, tho a very active & arduous one, I think has been far more free from vexations & trials, upon our patience & endurance than the campaign around Richmond would have been. We have enjoyed a great variety of scenes—have travelled over & sojourned in the most beautiful part of the valley of Va have had pure water, a few vegetables & plenty of fresh meat. Altogether we consider ourselves very fortunate thus far. If we have an active winter campaign, we will not fare so well—tho it will be far more comfortable to campaign there this winter, than to remain in the trenches at Richmond & Petersburg. One great advantage I would have there however, that is I would be so much nearer you. I wish you could see this magnificent Valley—at this beautiful season of the year. Although plantations are ruined—& the blackened remains of once splendid mansions are to be seen on all sides yet nature is triumphant—magnificent meadows, beautiful forests & broad undulating fields rich in grass & clover! Truly it does seem sacreligious to despoil such an Eden! by the ravages of War.

I thank God that my loved ones have not yet known the terror & wretchedness caused by the presence of our mean cowardly foes, Foes who respect not helpless Age nor tender women. Surely a just God will visit upon such a nation the just indignation of His wrath! The Yankees tis true have Atlanta, & Yankee like are making a tremendous glorification over it. But Hoods Army is intact. Sherman is far away from the base of his supplies & it does seem to me that if our army *is at all energetic* his position is obliged to be a very dangerous one to him. I still hope for good news from Ga. At Richmond all efforts of Grants powerful army have heretofore been baffled—by our noble General & his gallant troops. In the "Valley District" we have forced Lincoln to send a heavy force to check our *perigrinations*. We have at least 45,000 or 50,000 men opposed to us. We have offered them battle several times on a fair field. Every offer has been declined. The Yankees hurrying behind their breast works whenever we advance. We are thus accomplishing much good by neutralizing (holding in check) this large force. We are gathering all of the wheat in this wonderfully productive valley enough to supply ourselves & to send large supplies to Gen'l Lee's Army. We have also sent Gen'l Lee several hundred fine beef cattle &c. At this time the Yankees hold less of the territory of this old Commonwealth than at any time since 1862. We learn from gentlemen recently from the North that the Peace party is growing rapidly—that McClellan will be elected & that his election will bring peace, *provided always* that we continue to *hold our own* against the Yankee Armies.

Camp near Winchester, Sept 14th—'64

I wish you could take a peep at my H'dquarters. You would observe two small tents rather the worse for wear, several wagons with their shivering mules—but the interesting & attractive feature would be a flock of ducks & chickens taking shelter under the wagons. We are really growing fat up here, with Yankee money we can buy almost anything for the table except sugar & coffee. . . . We have had no news from Richmond & the West for several days. I do hope that we may be enabled to continue to baffle Grant, & to drive back Sherman. I think everything depends upon this Fall campaign. If we whip the Yankees everywhere, or even, if we can manage to prevent their gaining any important success I surely believe that the Peace party will have grown sufficiently strong to compel a cessation of hostilities. Whatever course the North follows, *our duty is very plain*. We must fight this fight out—there must be no turning back now—too much precious blood has been shed for the maintainance of our rights! Too great a gulf has opened up between us & our foes! to allow even the thought of re-union to be entertained. No, we can & must bear & suffer all things rather than to give up to Yankees & mercenaries our glorious Birthright. If I can know you are well & hopeful & cheerful I can bear most anything—tho the separation is cruel, when I know how you need me. . . . I need some socks like those you knit for me last winter—would you like to knit me some more?

Camp near Winchester Sept 16th—1864

I do not yet give up hope of being with you soon—but I will not apply for a furlough as long as we are facing the foe. If Gen'l Early moves back to Strasburg & the Yankees do not follow us too closely, I think I may be spared to visit you if only for a few days. There is nothing new here. We are kept on the alert constantly by Yankee cavalry, who out number ours so far, that we have been unable to drive them away. We are living very well for camp life. How I wish the poor fellows in trenches at Petersburg could fare as well! Is McClellan's letter of acceptance more warlike than you anticipated? I still think everything depends upon whether we can successfully resist the Yankee thousands now being hurled against us, but if we allow the enemy to gain any great victories over us, we must expect to see the war spirit rise with renewed hope of success. Well—Beloved we must be *brave* & *patient*—with *firm faith & hope, bearing all things even unto the end*, until our independence has been achieved. I do not think we will soon again advance in this part of the Valley.

Camp near Port Republic—Sept 25th—'64

I am too tired to write. . . . The enemy with overwhelming numbers, have driven us back to this point. On the 19th our men fought splendidly at Winchester—on the 22nd the whole army stampeded without much of a fight. We lost a good many prisoners & guns—now I think we will hold the Yanks here. Caleb Richmond & I are well. He has been slightly scratched on forehead & on the leg but not badly enough hurt to quit—is now perfectly well.

Our loss has been very heavy, especially in Officers. This is a sad blow coming as it does, on the heels of the affair at Atlanta. But let us not be discouraged.

Camp near Waynesboro—Va. Sept 30th—1864

I have been too busy & too much mortified to write to you for several days. At Winchester after hard fighting, we had prevailed against the largely superior forces in our front & on our right, when the enemy's Cavalry in heavy force broke our Cavalry on the left & created a terrible disorder throughout our lines. We lost my friend Gen'l Rodes. We then fell back to Strasburg (or Fishers Hill). Here the enemy concentrated heavily on our weak point (guarded by our Cavalry) drove everything before them there, & then poured in on our left & rear. I am sorry to say that our men were very much stampeded & did not keep cool nor fight as well as they have here-to-fore done. We then retreated to Port Republic & from there to this point, 12 miles from Staunton. I am daily expecting Gen'l Early to advance. I believe if we could get enough Cavalry to even hold the Yankee Cavalry in check, that our Infantry can drive back Sheridans forces. I cannot tell you . . . how much I have thought of you during this past week. I do hope you have not given up your bright hopeful spirits. Anybody can be hopeful when everything is prosperous. *Adversity calls forth the nobler qualities of our natures.* Continue my beloved to be brave—nothing but Gods mercy has spared our lives. Cease not to pray for us & our Cause. . . .

I still feel confident of the final triumph of our Cause. It may be a long & weary time, but above all things let us never despair of the establishment of our independence. We must steel ourselves for great trials & sacrifice—& have brave hearts for any fate. . . .

I would give *anything* to be with you, but these recent battles & defeats will make it almost impossible for me to leave this army now.

Camp near Staunton Va Oct. 2nd '64

This is a very lovely quiet Sabbath day. . . . I hope that you have not allowed the bad news from the Army of the Valley District to discourage you. We must bear up bravely in the midst of disaster nor can we always hope to be successful. We must be prepared for any event, with brave hearts for any fate. . . . I hope in a few days we will be enabled to go after the Yankees & drive them down the Valley. At present we are all anxiety to hear from Richmond. We hear all sorts of rumors. I hope and pray Gen'l Lee may be enabled to overcome & drive Grant from before Richmond. Our disaster in the Valley with Hood's at Atlanta make me feel now the War Party will prevail at the North. But the peace may be a long way off—I feel that surely Justice & Right must finally triumph. We must nerve ourselves to greater exertions & prepare to endure greater privations & hardships—do our duty bravely, hoping for a happy ending of all of our troubles. Surely all true Southrons would prefer anything to submission. How I long for you to be well & happy! May we learn wisdom from our trials. Our movements may prevent my writing frequently now.

Camp near Staunton—Oct 5th '64

After the death of Gen'l Rodes I was assigned the command of his Division. This of course is very pleasing to me. Address y'r letters now "Army of the Valley"—& they will reach me sooner than old address. We have been very quiet for several days, but I expect active service before the month is out. We are very anxious about Richmond. The Yankees are said to be sending a force toward Orange Court House. They seem to stick to McClellan's plan of approaching Richmond from three directions. Everything calls for all the bravery we possess every effort in our power to meet & hurl back our foes—while we fight battles our beloved Wives, Sisters & Mothers must be constant & earnest in prayer that we may have strength courage & wisdom to overcome & drive back our powerful & cruel enemies. These are times calling for great sacrifices. We must bear separation, hardship & danger for the sake of our Country. We must dare & do in the Cause of liberty. We must never yield an inch, nor relax any effort in the defence of our home or the establishment of our nationality. We will do our duty leaving the result to God.

Camp near New Market—Oct 10th '64

I can't help feeling the most intense anxiety & solicitude on your behalf—since our disaster in the Valley, my prospect for a furlough is greatly diminished. I think my duty is plain. I ought not to leave now, even if I could do so—so my Beloved—you must be brave & cheerful without me for awhile—to be separated from you is the hardest trial of my life. . . .

Father writes me that tho discouraged by our late disasters—he is still hopeful as to the final result. I agree with you about your remarks about the "Croakers." I must confess I would be willing to take a musket & fight to the bitter end rather than submit to these miserable Yankees. I feel that they have put themselves beyond the pale of civilization by the course they have pursued in this campaign. This beautiful & fertile valley has been totally destroyed. Sheridan had some of the houses, *all* of the mills & barns, every straw & wheat stack burned. This valley is one great desert. I do not see how these people are to live. We have to haul our supplies from far up the valley. It is rumored that the Yankees are rebuilding the Manassas Gap R. R. If this is true, Sheridan will not give up his hold on the valley, & we will probably remain here for the winter—unless Gen'l Lee becomes so hard pressed that we will have to go to him. My hope now is from Hood. I do hope he may be able to overwhelm Sherman & send reinforcements to our great General Lee. The last private advices I had from Ga. were encouraging. Time is an important element. I believe that Hood can whip Sherman, & I trust he will do it quickly. I have not written you as often recently—because I have been either so constantly occupied or (I must acknowledge it) so much mortified at the recent disasters to our army of the valley that I could not write with any pleasure. There is nothing new to write about right now.

Camp near Strasburg—Va. Oct 17th—1864

My own Darling Wife—

I rec'd late last night through the Signal Corps, the telegram [announcing the birth of his baby]. It has relieved me of the greatest anxiety of my life. I hope that my darling precious wife & our darling babe too are well. . . . I cannot express my feelings. . . . I dont know how I can bear the separation from you much longer. . . . I must see you & be with you & our little Darling & The telegram did not state whether we have a son or a daughter! . . .

Tell Sister Mary for *pity's* sake if not for love's sake to write me a long letter about my little wife & baby! May God bless my Darlings & me, & soon reunite us in happiness & peace—a joyful family. Goodbye, sweetest With love inexpressible Yr devoted Husband

—RAMSEUR, Letters to his fiancée and wife

5. EARLY SURPRISES THE FEDERALS AT CEDAR CREEK

After the defeats at Opequon and Strasburg Early's slender force was shattered, and Sheridan was master of the Valley. Early retired to Port Republic, where he awaited Kershaw's brigade, which Lee was hurrying to him, as well as Rosser's cavalry. With these reinforcements the ever-sanguine Early resumed the offensive, and Sheridan withdrew beyond New Market, taking up a position along Cedar Creek, north of Strasburg. At this juncture Sheridan was called to Washington to confer with Halleck; while at Winchester he heard that Early had surprised his army at Cedar Creek and inflicted a heavy defeat upon it.

Early had indeed. On October 13 he had begun his advance northward, taking up a position at Fisher's Hill, just south of Strasburg. From the summit of this hill he could see the whole Federal camp spread out along Cedar Creek. On the nineteenth Early directed Ramseur, Gordon, and Pegram to cross the Shenandoah and attack the Federals on the flank. The attack achieved complete surprise and complete initial success; had it not been for the heroic stand of Getty's division the Union defeat might have turned into a rout.

We give here Captain Howard's account of the morning surprise, and General Stevens' recollection of the stand of Getty's division on the Union right.

A. "THE ENEMY WERE UPON US"

I WAS wakened at the first signs of day [October 19, 1864] by a terrific clap of thunder, and sprang into a sitting position and listened. The thunder was the tremendous volley that the enemy was pouring into Crook's devoted camp. The thought went through my mind like lightning that in some way the enemy had run against General Crook's corps and were getting punished for their temerity. It never occurred to me at the instant that it was possible the boot was on the other foot. I listened for the yell of our men, but, alas, it never came; instead, the Yi Yi Yi! of the Confederates, and horror of horrors,—it seemed to me as if our whole left were enveloped, enfolded, by this cry. It was like the howls of the wolves around a wagon train in the early days on the great prairies. This had taken but a moment. The camp was awake. The men sprang into line with the celerity of veterans. It was apparent to everyone from the heavy firing and the yells on our left that a great calamity impended if it had not already become a fact.

General Emory rode down in person, ordering the brigade to cross the pike, to throw a skirmish line into the timber in Crook's direction, until it met the enemy, and then to hold on as long as possible.

Away we went on a double quick through the darkness, the eastern sky at this moment showing the faint gray tinge of dawn. As we rushed along, the infernal torch on Massanutton, dire omen of impending disaster, still flashed against the southern sky. The moment the timber was reached the column came into line on the run, and skirmishers pushed rapidly forward, followed by the main body. Here we met the gallant fellows from Crook's camp who had been assailed while lying asleep and who had done the only possible thing under the circumstances,—run for their lives. They did not seem excited, only stolidly, doggedly determined to go to the rear. Many of them were only partly dressed, some wearing only underclothing, but they generally carried their muskets. An officer wearing his cap and carrying his naked sword was attired in a shirt, drawers and shoes. The flash of a musket showed him to be a man of forty with full beard, and I think I should recognize his face to-day. They passed around us, through our ranks, and almost over us, insistent, determined. They heeded none of our cries to "Turn back!" "Make a stand!" but streamed to the rear. We had little time to argue with them.

The skirmish line had not advanced a hundred yards when it ran in the darkness plump into a body of the enemy; in an instant the timber was in a blaze of light from the musketry, and we were in the midst of one of the most fearful struggles of the war. The enemy were upon us in overwhelming numbers, flushed with victory and with the capture of Crook's camps. We were a little brigade of four regiments consisting of the 12th Connecticut, 160th New York, 47th Pennsylvania and the 18th Vermont. The first two and the 8th Vermont had been brigaded together back in the Louisiana days when Godfrey Weitzel commanded us, and in many a bloody fight had we fought together. It was literally true that we had never been beaten on any field, but we were to have a new experience.

We were commanded by Colonel Stephen Thomas of the 8th Vermont, . . . the bravest man I have ever known. What Sheridan was to the army under him, Colonel Thomas was to his regiment. Many had been the critical moments in our history when his level head and iron nerve had been our salvation. More than once in the very pinch of a fight, when it seemed as if one straw more would ruin us, had we seen him on his big bay shouting in a voice which rang over the tumult of battle, "Steady, men! Old Vermont is looking at you to-day!" We had never needed him so much as now.

The 8th Vermont was on the left of our line, the most exposed position. We were hotly pressed on our front and left. The timber was ablaze with musketry and the air was filled with the yells of our confident foes. They flung themselves upon us in a mass and for a moment the struggle was hand to hand. Then came the cry "The Colors! The Colors! They've got the Colors!" and with one impulse, as if one mind had moved it, the regiment flung itself into the boiling caldron where the fight for the colors was seething and dragged them out. . . . Again and again the enemy flung many times our number against us, only to be forced back and gather for a fresh trial.

Men fought hand to hand; skulls were crushed with clubbed muskets; bayonets dripped with blood. Men actually clenched and rolled upon the ground in the desperate frenzy of the contest for the flags. Three color bearers were killed, and with one exception every member of the color-guard was killed or wounded. There was not much attempt at order. Not many orders were given. The men realized that they were in a terrible mess and fought like tigers. Stephen Thomas, "Colonel commanding" as we loved to call him, was a very present help in trouble. He raged like a lion and was everywhere present to encourage and hold fast the line. Of course only one result was possible. The time came when valor and devotion proved vain. In a moment, without warning, and as if by common consent we were being swept back, every man for himself and the enemy on every hand. I had received two severe wounds, and though not wholly disabled, was unable to make anything like good time, and I looked with envy on Captain Ford who was just in advance of me running like a buck. In an instant he went down all in a heap, but was up and off again in a second. My mental comment was, "What a lummux to fall down in such a scrape as this!" It never once entered my mind that he had been hit by one of the bullets of which the air was full. Later in the day I saw him at the hospital, and expressed my disapproval of his clumsiness under such circumstances, to which he replied, "I guess you would fall down if you were shot through both legs." . . .

Private Robert Sturgeon of my own company was a few yards in advance of me on my right, and I need not say was making good time. In an instant a tall bearded fellow in gray bounded out of the mist which overhung the field where daylight was just gaining the supremacy and ordered him to halt. They were not twenty feet apart. Sturgeon's gun was empty and his bayonet lost. He cast a startled glance over his shoulder and ran at the top of his speed. The Confederate's long legs took tremendous strides,—he sprang forward with a rush and gave a vicious lunge with his bayonet. Sturgeon swerved at the moment, but the steel caught him under the left arm, and passed through the cape of his overcoat, through the overcoat itself, through blouse and flannel shirt, between shirt and skin. It left a vivid mark along his side where the cold steel raked, but did not pierce the skin. Sturgeon stopped and threw up his hands dropping his gun. The stalwart in gray was reaching out as if to take him by the collar, when presto! one in blue, pausing in his hot haste for scarcely one second placed the muzzle of his gun hardly a foot from the Confederate's head, fired, blowing the head to fragments, and without a word was gone. Sturgeon, like a good soldier, picked up his gun and ran like a deer.

Farther back Colonel Thomas had chosen a point where he was rallying the men and making some progress toward a line; still further a skirmish line was stretched across the country to stop and collect those who were still able for duty. Challenged here, I pointed to the blood in my shoe and running down my sleeve, and passed on; passed on with greater grief and despair weighing me down than I had ever before in my life felt.

Our campaign, as I have said, had been a great success. The Shenandoah Valley, the great artery of supply, the granary of the rebellion, had the night before seemed firmly and forever in our grasp, and now before the next sunrise, I had seen it taken away from us with the fierce ruthlessness of a hurricane. There was no question about it in my mind. Harper's Ferry was the only point where the shattered army could stand. I had seen the collapse of the Eighth Corps. I had seen our whole left swept away, our camps captured, our artillery taken, our whole army forced out of its works, forced to change its line from front to left, forced far back from its proper position,—sullenly on the defensive, dangerous, but clearly out-matched. The enemy was pressing his victorious columns forward. It would be impossible to withstand him. I pictured the defense we would make of the heights of Harper's Ferry, of the weary months, perhaps years, it would take to retrieve what we had lost, and my heart beat with great throbs of grief as I dragged myself painfully to the rear. General Sheridan I well knew, was absent. . . . Unreasonably I attributed the whole disaster to General Sheridan's absence. Had he been there it could never have happened, and thereby I did injustice to the gallant Wright in command.

Pressing back to get out of danger I threw myself exhausted upon the ground a short distance south of Newtown. The country was full of men, all, it seemed to me, going to the rear; wounded men by themselves; wounded men helped by others; wounded men being carried; men strong and unhurt. Their faces were sullen, despairing, and they were turned to the north. Many halted and rested; some went to sleep, for the exhaustion of a week had been crowded into two hours. Our brigade in its struggle beyond the pike had lost more than one-third of its numbers, and the 8th Vermont, holding the left and most exposed position, had lost more than two-thirds of all the men engaged, and of the sixteen officers who gathered about our camp-fire the evening before, thirteen had been killed and wounded on this horrible hill of sacrifice.

—HOWARD, "The Morning Surprise at Cedar Creek"

B. GENERAL GETTY SAVES THE DAY

Getty's division, Second of the Sixth Corps, was camped on the extreme right of the Union infantry. Satisfied from the heavy firing on the left that the enemy was attacking in force in that quarter, General Getty lost no time in getting his troops under arms, and without waiting for orders, marched them by the left flank across the plain past the rear of the corps artillery camp, to the sound of the firing—towards the pike in front of Middletown. Neither the artillery camp, scarce two hundred yards distant, nor the other divisions, could be discerned through the fog. Already the plain was covered with fugitives, wagons and ambulances intermixed, hurrying away so eagerly and regardless of the columns marching athwart their course that many of the soldiers fixed their bayonets and, as they marched, threatened the stragglers with the points to keep them from breaking through the column. Already the whiz and ping of bullets were singing past, and the terrific noises of battle waxed louder every minute on the left. The division was formed in two lines along Meadow Brook, near the foot of the ridge, facing towards the pike; the Vermont or Second Brigade, Brigadier General L. A. Grant, in the centre; the Third Brigade, Brigadier General Daniel D. Bidwell, on the left; the First Brigade, Colonel James M. Warner, on the right. As the lines were forming, a strong force of skirmishers, consisting of the 5th and 6th regiments and a battalion of the 11th Vermont under Major Johnson of the 2nd Vermont, dashed across the brook, drove back the enemy's skirmishers through the open woods there with a rough hand, and captured several prisoners. On Getty's right, its flank within thirty yards, a well-dressed line of other Union troops extended to the right into the fog. These were of the First Division, Sixth Corps.

As soon as his lines were formed, Getty advanced across Meadow Brook and swung forward his left considerably, reaching towards the pike, and again straightened and adjusted his lines preparatory to advancing into the fight. At this moment, save an annoying skirmish fire, no attack was making on Getty, but sweeping across the fog and smoke laden plain in front, from left to right, resounded the unmistakable and awful noises of a fierce and heavy fight. The crash and crackle of musketry, the boom of guns and burst of shells, mingled with yells and cheers. Far to the right, in the fog were heard the echoing roar of the corps artillery, and the rolling musketry of the infantry. Now at last the rebel onslaught could be repulsed and hurled back, and the course of disaster stopped if not retrieved.

Thus confident that the enemy could never break through the other divisions, Getty resolved to move forward, wheeling to the right, and smite the charging Confederates in flank with the whole weight of his division. Orders were given the brigade commanders to this effect, the right brigade to commence the movement, the second and third immediately to take it up.

Getty bestrode his horse just in front of the right of his line; his staff officers galloped back to him and reported that the brigade commanders were all ready to advance, and he turned to give the final order, when the troops on his right were seen to break and fly in the utmost confusion. As far down the line as could be seen in the fog, the men were breaking successively, file after file, like a row of toppling bricks set up in play by some sportive urchin. We could see the break run along the line until it came to the last man next to the division, and he, too, sprang from his place and ran back after the others, and in a few minutes not a vestige remained of that well-ordered and apparently firm and steadfast line. Whatever may have occurred within that pall of smoke and fog, it is certain that there was no pressure to excuse the giving way of that line, as far as one could see.

Thus in the very act of delivering his well-timed, if desperate blow, Getty beheld his *point d'appui* give way, leaving his right without support, so now both flanks were in air, and the whole infantry of the army broken and driven in confusion, save only his own scanty division, while on his right front, amidst the fog and smoke appeared the enemy's battle line. In this emergency—without supports, without orders,—in the open indefensible plain where a few moments would bring the victorious Confederates charging upon his defenceless flanks, and not one ray shone amid the universal wreck and ruin,—Getty, with prompt and cool decision, moved his troops in line facing by the rear rank, back across the brook to the foot of the ridge. Then, moving up its slope he posted them in a single line extending right and left as far as possible. . . .

The withdrawal to the ridge was made with coolness and deliberation. The brigade and regimental commanders posted and adjusted their lines along the crest so as best to meet the impending attack which they coolly awaited with well-founded confidence. The skirmishers were drawn in to the foot of the ridge. . . .

Nor had they long to wait. The gray lines of Pegram's Division soon came advancing swiftly up the steep slope, and struck the troops awaiting them on the crest. The heaviest of the attack fell upon Warner's brigade. Getty's veterans coolly held their fire until the enemy was close upon them, then delivered it in their very faces, and tumbled the shattered ranks down the hill, pursued to the foot by Warner's two right regiments. . . .

The enemy's shells now began to burst over and upon the ridge, coming mostly from the high ground along the pike. The troops lay flat on the ground just behind the crest, and suffered but little, most of the shells passing over and exploding in rear of the line. It was not long before the skirmishers in front of the Vermonters and Third Brigade came running breathlessly in, and reported that the enemy was again advancing to the attack. The troops sprang to their feet, dressed their lines, fixed bayonets, moved forward a few paces to and over the crest, and met the enemy at thirty yards as he struggled, well winded and tired, up the ascent, with so well-aimed a volley, so thundering a cheer, and so sudden and spontaneous a rush forward that he fell back in great confusion to and beyond the foot of the ridge, sharply pursued by the victors half way down the slope, and a number of prisoners were taken. The troops were immediately recalled and posted again behind the crest. . . .

Early reached the skirts of Middletown just as these broken troops came tumbling back, and there met Ramseur and Pegram, who told him that the Sixth Corps was making a stand on the ridge, and urged him to throw Wharton's Division into the fight. This division having crossed Cedar Creek by the bridge with the artillery as soon as the way was cleared, and advanced along the pike, was close at hand and had not been engaged. Accordingly

Early at once ordered Wharton to attack, directing the other two division commanders to show him where to go in.

This attack fell more to the left than the preceding, more on the Third Brigade and partly on the Vermonters. Again the skirmishers ran in and gave timely warning. Again the troops rose to their feet, dressed their ranks, and gripped their muskets, with bayonets fixed; and again, at the critical moment, just as the charging line, straining up the hill, gained the summit, the steady veterans countered upon it with a terrific threefold blow, a sudden deadly volley, a fierce charge, and a mighty shout, and dashed it in pieces down the ridge. In their eagerness many of the men chased the broken troops to the foot, but the enemy's batteries in the edge of the village raked them well, inflicting some loss, and soon all were brought back to the shelter of the crest, and the line was reëstablished. In these attacks the enemy's losses must have been heavy, for at one place alone near the bend of the ridge, thirty-four of his dead were found lying on the slope the next day.

—STEVENS, "The Battle of Cedar Creek"

6. SHERIDAN RIDES DOWN THE VALLEY PIKE TO VICTORY AND FAME

The resolute stand by Getty, the confusion in Confederate ranks, and the strong defensive position to which the Federals retired, all persuaded Early to halt his own attack midway. Meantime Sheridan was riding down the Newtown and the Valley Pike from Winchester. By the time he arrived at the battlefield the Federals had steadied and were prepared to repulse Early. Sheridan speedily organized a counterattack which jumped off in midafternoon and was completely successful. Everywhere the Confederate line gave way. "They would not listen to entreaties, threats or appeals of any kind," Early reported. "A terror of the enemy's cavalry had seized them and there was no holding them." It was the end of Early—and the beginning of a legend.

Here Sheridan tells his own story.

TOWARD 6 o'clock the morning of the 19th [October], the officer on picket duty at Winchester came to my room, I being yet in bed, and reported artillery firing from the direction of Cedar Creek. I asked him if the firing was continuous or only desultory, to which he replied that it was not a sustained fire, but rather irregular and fitful. I remarked: "It's all right; Grover has gone out this morning to make a reconnoisance, and he is merely feeling the enemy." I tried to go to sleep again, but grew so restless that I could not, and soon got up and dressed myself. A little later the picket officer came back and reported that the firing, which could be distinctly heard from his line on the heights outside of Winchester, was still going on. I asked him if it sounded like a battle, and as he again said that it did not, I still inferred that the cannonading was caused by Grover's division banging away at the enemy simply to find out what he was up to. However, I went downstairs and requested that breakfast be hurried up, and at the same time ordered the horses to be saddled and in readiness, for I concluded to go to the front before any further examinations were made in regard to the defensive line.

We mounted our horses between half-past 8 and 9, and as we were proceeding up the street which leads directly through Winchester, from the Logan residence, where Edwards was quartered, to the Valley pike, I noticed that there were many women at the windows and doors of the houses, who kept shaking their skirts at us and who were otherwise markedly insolent in their demeanor, but supposing this conduct to be instigated by their well-known and perhaps natural prejudices, I ascribed to it no unusual significance. On reaching the edge of the town I halted a moment, and there heard quite distinctly the sound of artillery firing in an unceasing roar. Concluding from this that a battle was in progress, I now felt confident that the women along the street had received intelligence from the battle-field by the "grape-vine telegraph," and were in raptures over some good news, while I as yet was utterly ignorant of the actual situation. Moving on, I put my head downward toward the pommel of my saddle and listened intently, trying to locate and interpret the sound, continuing in this position till we had crossed Mill Creek, about half a mile from Winchester. The result of my efforts in the interval was the conviction that the travel of the sound was increasing too rapidly to be accounted for by my own rate of motion, and that therefore my army must be falling back.

At Mill Creek, my escort fell in behind, and we were going ahead at a regular pace, when, just as we made the crest of the rise beyond the stream, there burst upon our view the appalling spectacle of a panic-stricken army—hundreds of slightly wounded men, throngs of others unhurt but utterly demoralized, and baggage-wagons by the score, all pressing to the rear in hopeless confusion, telling only too plainly that a disaster had occurred at the front. On accosting some of the fugitives, they assured me that the army was broken up, in full retreat, and that all was lost; all this with a manner true to that peculiar indifference that takes possession of panic-stricken men. I was greatly disturbed by the sight, but at once sent word to Colonel Edwards, commanding the brigade in Winchester, to stretch his troops across the valley, near Mill Creek, and stop all fugitives, directing also that the transportation be passed through and parked on the north side of the town.

As I continued at a walk a few hundred yards farther, thinking all the time of Longstreet's telegram to Early, "Be ready when I join you and we will crush Sheridan," I was fixing in my mind what I should do. My first thought was to stop the army in the suburbs of Winchester as it came back, form a new line, and fight there; but as the situation was more maturely considered a better conception prevailed. I was sure the troops had confidence in me, for heretofore we had been successful; and as at other times they had seen me present at the slightest sign of trouble or distress, I felt that I ought to try now to restore their broken ranks, or, failing in that, to share their fate because of what they had done hitherto. . . .

For a short distance I traveled on the road, but soon found it so blocked with wagons and wounded men that my progress was impeded, and I was forced to take to the adjoining fields to make haste. When most of the wagons and wounded were past I returned to the road, which was thickly lined with unhurt men, who, having got far enough to the rear to be out of danger, had halted, without any organization, and began cooking coffee, but when they saw me they abandoned their coffee, threw up their hats, shouldered their muskets, and as I passed along turned to follow with enthusiasm and cheers. To acknowledge this exhibition of feeling I took off my hat, and with Forsyth and O'Keefe rode some distance in advance of my escort, while every mounted officer who saw me galloped out on either side of the pike to tell the men at a distance that I had come back. In this way the news was spread to the stragglers off the road, when they, too, turned their faces to the front and marched toward the enemy, changing in a moment from the depth of depression to the extreme of enthusiasm. I already knew that even in the ordinary condition of mind enthusiasm is a potent element with soldiers, but what I saw that day convinced me that if it can be excited from a state of despondency its power is almost irresistible. I said nothing except to remark, as I rode among those on the road: "If I had been with you this morning this disaster would not have happened. We must face the other way; we will go back and recover our camp."

My first halt was made just north of Newtown, where I met a chaplain digging his heels into the sides of his jaded horse, and making for the rear with all possible speed. I drew up for an instant, and inquired of him how matters were going at the front. He replied, "Everything is lost; but all will be right when you get there"; yet notwithstanding this expression of confidence in me, the parson at once resumed his breathless pace to the rear. At Newtown I was obliged to make a circuit to the left, to get round the village. I could not pass through it, the streets were so crowded, but, meeting on this détour Major McKinley, of Crook's staff, he spread the news of my return through the motley throng there.

When nearing the Valley pike, just south of Newtown I saw about three-fourths of a mile west of the pike a body of troops, which proved to be Ricketts's and Wheaton's divisions of the Sixth Corps had halted a little to the right and rear of these; but I did not stop, desiring to get to the extreme front. Continuing on parallel with the pike about midway between Newtown and Middletown I crossed to the west of it, and a little later came up in rear of Getty's division of the Sixth Corps. When I arrived this division and the cavalry were the only troops in the presence of and resisting the enemy; they were apparently acting as a rear guard at a point about three miles north of the line we held at Cedar Creek when the battle began. General Torbert was the first officer to meet me, saying as he rode up, "My God! I am glad you've come." Getty's division, when I found it, was about a mile north of Middletown, posted on the reverse slope of some slightly rising ground, holding a barricade made with fence-rails, and skirmishing slightly with the enemy's pickets.

Jumping my horse over the line of rails I rode to the crest of the elevation, and there taking off my hat, the men rose up from behind their barricade with cheers of recognition. An officer of the Vermont brigade, Colonel A. S.

Tracy, rode out to the front, and joining me, informed me that General Louis A. Grant was in command there, the regular division commander, General Getty, having taken charge of the Sixth Corps in place of Ricketts, wounded early in the action, while temporarily commanding the corps. I then turned back to the rear of Getty's division, and as I came behind it a line of regimental flags rose up out of the ground, as it seemed, to welcome me. They were mostly the colors of Crook's troops, who had been stampeded and scattered in the surprise of the morning. The color-bearers having withstood the panic, had formed behind the troops of Getty. . . . At the close of this incident I crossed the little narrow valley, or depression, in rear of Getty's line, and dismounting on the opposite crest, established that point as my headquarters. In a few minutes some of my staff joined me, and the first directions I gave were to have the Nineteenth Corps and the two divisions of Wright's corps brought to the front, so they could be formed on Getty's division, prolonged to the right; for I had already decided to attack the enemy from that line as soon as I could get matters in shape to take the offensive. Crook met me at this time, and strongly favored my idea of attacking, but said, however, that most of his troops were going. . . .

All this had consumed a good deal of time, and I concluded to visit again the point to the east of the Valley pike, from where I had first observed the enemy, to see what he was doing. Arrived there, I could plainly see him getting ready for attack, and Major Forsyth now suggested that it would be well to ride along the line of battle before the enemy assailed us, for although the troops had learned of my return, but few of them had seen me. Following his suggestion I started in behind the men, but when a few paces had been taken I crossed to the front and, hat in hand, passed along the entire length of the infantry line; and it is from this circumstance that many of the officers and men who then received me with such heartiness have since supposed that that was my first appearance on the field. But at least two hours had elapsed since I reached the ground, for it was after mid-day when this incident of riding down the front took place, and I arrived not later, certainly, than half-past 10 o'clock.

—Personal Memoirs of P. H. Sheridan

7. "THE VALLEY WILL HAVE LITTLE IN IT FOR MAN OR BEAST"

After Cedar Creek Sheridan was master of the Valley. He had already embarked on a policy of systematic destruction; now he carried that through almost without opposition. Early, to be sure, did put up a stiff fight at Middletown, on November 9, but without effect. In December, again, Rosser tried to prevent the destruction of the Virginia Central Railway, but again in vain. There was little fighting during the winter, but late in February 1865 Sheridan occupied Staunton and Charlottesville, breaking up the railways leading to the west. Meantime the Valley had suffered the fate of Georgia and South Carolina.

Here is an extract from one of Sheridan's reports to Grant.

Woodstock, October 7, 1864—9 P.M.

I have the honor to report my command at this point tonight. I commenced moving back from Port Republic, Mount Crawford, Bridgewater, and Harrisonburg yesterday morning. The grain and forage in advance of these points up to Staunton had previously been destroyed. In moving back to this point the whole country from the Blue Ridge to the North Mountains has been made untenable for a rebel army. I have destroyed over 2,000 barns filled with wheat, hay, and farming implements; over seventy mills filled with flour and wheat; have driven in front of the army over 4,000 head of stock, and have killed and have issued to the troops not less than 3,000 sheep. This destruction embraces the Luray Valley and Little Fort Valley, as well as the main valley. A large number of horses have been obtained, a proper estimate of which I cannot now make. Lieut. John R. Meigs, my engineer officer, was murdered beyond Harrisonburg, near Dayton. For this atrocious act all the houses within an area of five miles were burned. Since I came into the Valley, from Harper's Ferry up to Harrisonburg, every train, every small party, and every straggler has been bushwhacked by people, many of whom have protection papers from commanders who have been hitherto in this valley. From the vicinity of Harrisonburg over 400 wagon-loads of refugees have been sent back to Martinsburg; most of these people were Dunkers and had been conscripted. The people here are getting sick of the war; heretofore they have had no reason to complain, because they have been living in great abundance. I have not been followed by the enemy up to this point, with the exception of a small force of rebel cavalry that showed themselves some distance behind my rear guard to-day. A party of 100 of the Eighth Ohio Cavalry, which I had stationed at the bridge over the North Shenandoah, near Mount Jackson, was attacked by McNeill, with seventeen men; report they were asleep, and the whole party dispersed or captured. I think that they will all turn up; I learn that fifty-six of them have reached Winchester. McNeill was mortally wounded and fell into our hands. This was fortunate, as he was the most daring and dangerous of all the bushwhackers in this section of the country. . . . To-morrow I will continue the destruction of wheat, forage, etc., down to Fisher's Hill. When this is completed the Valley, from Winchester up to Staunton, ninety-two miles, will have but little in it for man or beast. In previous dispatches I have used "lower Valley" when I should have said "upper Valley," or, in other words, in my last dispatch I intended to say that the grain and forage from Staunton up to Lexington had been sent to Richmond, and that the grain and forage from Staunton to Strasburg had been left for the wintering of Early's army. Yesterday Colonel Powell captured a guerrilla camp on the mountains, with ten wagons and teams.

P. H. SHERIDAN
Major-General

LIEUTENANT-GENERAL GRANT

—War of the Rebellion . . . Official Records

XXX

Lee and Lincoln

SPACE *does not allow us the luxury of portraits of all the distinguished or interesting leaders, military and civilian, of the Union and Confederate causes. We must content ourselves with a presentation of the two men who, at the time and since, seemed to symbolize the two sections and causes, and who, in the end, came to be the common and cherished possession of both. It is one of the happier features of an otherwise tragic war that it left, on the whole, so little bitterness; the sectional animosities of the postwar years were rather a product of Reconstruction than of war itself. It is particularly interesting that the leading figure on each side came to be held in affection by both: this is a circumstance not common in the history of civil wars.*

Condemned by the South and, for that matter, by a substantial part of the North during his own lifetime, Lincoln came eventually to be a completely national figure, transcending section and even time. Lee was always admired, even in the North, and Northern opinion found it possible to respect his decision to go with his state while it respected, too, those Southerners like Thomas and Farragut who remained loyal to the old flag.

Since the war there has developed both a Lincoln and a Lee legend. With Lincoln the legend is almost inextricable from fact, nor is this altogether deplorable. With Lee there was less for the mythmakers to work on; while the Lee legend grows, the facts of his career are available and familiar. With Lincoln the difficulty is to separate fact and myth; with Lee to penetrate behind

> *the deadly oratory*
> *Of twenty thousand Lee Memorial Days*[*]

to reality.

That the proud and affectionate recollections of Americans should have worked on both men is a matter of gratification and good fortune. If a nation is to have heroes, it would be difficult to find better ones than these two protagonists of the cause of the Union and the cause of State rights.

Lincoln and Lee represent, in a sense, two persistent currents in American history and two strains in the American character. Just as historical legend

---

[*] From *John Brown's Body* in *The Selected Works of Stephen Vincent Benét*, published by Rinehart and Company, Inc. Copyright 1927, 1928 by Stephen Vincent Benét.

has insisted on the Puritan and the Cavalier in the founding of America—and this despite evidence to the contrary—so it has insisted on the contrast of frontier democracy and plantation aristocracy, a contrast, too, that exists in the realm of legend rather than of history. In Lincoln Americans have seen a symbol of equality and freedom; in Lee a symbol of the Cavalier spirit and chivalry. For a wonder both men fitted their legends. In apotheosizing Lincoln and Lee the American people apotheosized what was best in their character rather than what was most typical.

We do not attempt here biographies of either of these leaders; that, after all, is superfluous, for there are biographies enough, and memoirs and volumes of tributes. Our concern is the war, and the relation of these men to the war. Nor do we approach either Lincoln or Lee afresh. Almost every chapter of our history has said something about one or both of them; they do not come to us as strangers. We present them for themselves, to be sure, and as vehicles of much of the character of the contenders, but we present them in relation to the larger contest. It will be sufficient, therefore, if we introduce the chroniclers as they tell their stories.

There is an inescapable difference in these presentations. We have already seen Lee in action: the story of the Army of Northern Virginia is in a sense the story of Lee, and it is enough here to present a few glimpses of the man. He was, as Benét has said, "the prop and pillar of a state," but that role we have already seen him play. With Lincoln the situation is different. Lincoln's character can never cease to interest us, but we must be concerned with what he did, as head of the state, as well as with what he was. We have, designedly, neglected the political scene somewhat in our survey of the war; we present here some aspects of important political chapters in which Lincoln played a commanding role, notably emancipation.

1. ROBERT E. LEE GOES WITH HIS STATE

One of the momentous decisions of the war was a personal one—the decision of R. E. Lee that he could not raise his hand against his own people. No officer in the United States Army had a more brilliant record or a more distinguished career than Lee when, at the age of fifty-four, he resigned from the army to go with his state. He had performed brilliantly a number of difficult engineering assignments, fought gallantly in the Mexican War, served as Superintendent of the West Point Military Academy, and dealt effectively with Indian outbreaks along the Mexican border. Recalled to Washington early in 1861 he was informally offered command of the field forces of the United States. With deep spiritual anguish he refused this offer, resigned his commission, and accepted instead command of the military forces of Virginia. Shortly after he was appointed general in the Confederate Army. These two letters* explain his decision.

---

* From: *Recollections and Letters of General Robert E. Lee* by Robert E. Lee. Copyright 1904 by Doubleday & Company, Inc.

A. "My Relatives, My Children, My Home"

To his Sister, Mrs. Anne Marshall.

Arlington, Virginia
April 20, 1861

My Dear Sister: I am grieved at my inability to see you. . . . I have been waiting for a 'more convenient season,' which has brought to many before me deep and lasting regret. Now we are in a state of war which will yield to nothing. The whole South is in a state of revolution, into which Virginia, after a long struggle, has been drawn; and though I recognize no necessity for this state of things, and would have forborne and pleaded to the end for redress of grievances, real or supposed, yet in my own person I had to meet the question whether I should take part against my native State.

With all my devotion to the Union and the feeling of loyalty and duty of an American citizen, I have not been able to make up my mind to raise my hand against my relatives, my children, my home. I have therefore resigned my commission in the Army, and save in defense of my native State, with the sincere hope that my poor services may never be needed, I hope I may never be called on to draw my sword. I know you will blame me; but you must think as kindly of me as you can, and believe that I have endeavoured to do what I thought right.

To show you the feeling and struggle it has cost me, I send you a copy of my letter of resignation. I have no time for more. May God guard and protect you and yours, and shower upon you everlasting blessings, is the prayer of your devoted brother,

R. E. Lee

B. "I Never Desire Again to Draw My Sword"

To General Scott.

Arlington, Virginia
April 20, 1861

General: Since my interview with you on the 18th inst. I have felt that I ought no longer to retain my commission in the Army. I therefore tender my resignation, which I request you will recommend for acceptance. It would have been presented at once but for the struggle it has cost me to separate myself from a service to which I have devoted the best years of my life, and all the ability I possessed.

During the whole of that time—more than a quarter of a century—I have experienced nothing but kindness from my superiors and a most cordial friendship from my comrades. To no one, General, have I been as much indebted as to yourself for uniform kindness and consideration, and it has always been my ardent desire to merit your approbation. I shall carry to the grave the most grateful recollections of your kind consideration, and your name and fame shall always be dear to me.

Save in defense of my native State, I never desire again to draw my sword.

Be pleased to accept my most earnest wishes for the continuance of your happiness and prosperity, and believe me, most truly yours,

R. E. LEE

—LEE, *Recollections and Letters of General Robert E. Lee*

2. LEE AND JACKSON PLAN McCLELLAN'S DESTRUCTION

Here is a glimpse of Lee and Jackson discussing strategy at the beginning of the Seven Days campaign. It comes from the pen of Major Robert Stiles, member of the Richmond Howitzers, and, by now, an old friend.

ALL of us had been longing for a sight of Jackson. It is impossible to exaggerate or even to convey an adequate idea of the excitement and furor concerning him about this time, both in the army and among the people. . . .

Hearing the jingle of cavalry accouterments toward the Chickahominy, I looked up and saw a half-dozen mounted men, and riding considerably in advance a solitary horseman whom I instantly recognized as the great wizard of the marvelous Valley Campaign which had so thrilled the army and the country.

Jackson and the little sorrel stopped in the middle of the road, probably not fifty feet off, while his staff halted perhaps a hundred and fifty yards in his rear. He sat stark and stiff in the saddle. Horse and rider appeared worn down to the lowest point of flesh consistent with effective service. His hair, skin, eyes, and clothes were all one neutral dust tint, and his badges of rank so dulled and tarnished as to be scarcely perceptible. The "mangy little cadet cap" was pulled so low in front that the visor cut the glint of his eyeballs.

A ghastly scene was spread across the road hard by. . . . Jackson glanced a moment toward this scene. Not a muscle quivered as he resumed his steady gaze down the road toward Richmond. He was the ideal of concentration,—imperturbable, resistless. . . .

A moment later and his gaze was rewarded. A magnificent staff approached from the direction of Richmond, and riding at its head, superbly mounted, a born king among men. At that time General Lee was one of the handsomest of men, especially on horseback, and that morning every detail of the dress and equipment of himself and horse was absolute perfection. When he recognized Jackson he rode forward with a courier, his staff halting. As he gracefully dismounted, handing his bridle rein to his attendant, and advanced, drawing the gauntlet from his right hand, Jackson flung himself off his horse and advanced to meet Lee, the little sorrel trotting back to the staff, where a courier secured him.

The two generals greeted each other warmly, but wasted no time upon the greeting. They stood facing each other, some thirty feet from where I lay, Lee's left side and back toward me, Jackson's right and front. Jackson began talking in a jerky, impetuous way, meanwhile drawing a diagram on the ground with the toe of his right boot. He traced two sides of a triangle with promptness and decision; then starting at the end of the second line began to draw a third projected toward the first. This third line he traced slowly and with hesitation, alternately looking up at Lee's face and down at his diagram, meanwhile talking earnestly; and when at last the third line crossed the first and the triangle was complete, he raised his foot and stamped it down with emphasis, saying, "We've got him"; then signaled for his horse, and when he came, vaulted awkwardly into the saddle and was off. Lee watched him a moment, the courier brought his horse, he mounted, and he and his staff rode away.

—STILES, *Four Years under Marse Robert*

3. "A SPLENDID SPECIMEN OF AN ENGLISH GENTLEMAN"

Garnet Wolseley was a young lieutenant colonel in the British Army when, in 1862, he slipped away from a tour of duty in Canada to visit the Army of Northern Virginia. We have already enjoyed his portrait of Stonewall Jackson. Lee he admired even more than Jackson and, characteristically, his admiration found expression in extending to Lee the title "English gentleman." It was Lord Wolseley who discovered George Henderson and encouraged him to write his classic biography of Stonewall Jackson.

HAVING presented our letters to the Adjutant-General, we were in turn presented to the Commander-in-Chief. He is a strongly built man, about five feet eleven in height, and apparently not more than fifty years of age. His hair and beard are nearly white; but his dark brown eyes still shine with all the brightness of youth, and beam with a most pleasing expression. Indeed, his whole face is kindly and benevolent in the highest degree. In manner, though sufficiently conversible, he is slightly reserved; but he is a person that, wherever seen, whether in a castle or a hovel, alone or in a crowd, must at once attract attention as being a splendid specimen of an English gentleman, with one of the most rarely handsome faces I ever saw. He had had a bad fall during the Maryland expedition, from which he was not yet recovered, and which still crippled his right hand considerably.

We sat with him for a long time in his tent, conversing upon a variety of topics, the state of public affairs being of course the leading one. He talked most freely about the battle of Antietam, and assured us that at no time during that day's fight had he more than thirty-five thousand men engaged. You have only to be in his society for a very brief period to be convinced that whatever he says may be implicitly relied upon, and that he is quite incapable of departing from the truth under any circumstances. . . .

In visiting the headquarters of the Confederate generals, but particularly those of General Lee, any one accustomed to see European armies in the field cannot fail to be struck with the great absence of all the pomp and circumstance of war in and around their encampments. Lee's headquarters consisted of about seven or eight pole tents, pitched with their backs to a stake fence, upon a piece of ground so rocky that it was unpleasant to ride over it—its only recommendation being a little stream of good water which flowed close by the General's tent. In front of the tents were some three or four wheeled wagons, drawn up without any regularity, and a number of horses roamed loose about the field. The servants, who were of course slaves, and the mounted soldiers called "couriers," who always accompany each general of division in the field, were unprovided with tents, and slept in or under the waggons.

Waggons, tents, and some of the horses, were marked U.S., showing that part of that huge debt in the North has gone to furnishing even the Confederate generals with camp equipments. No guard or sentries were to be seen in the vicinity; no crowd of aides-de-camp loitering about, making themselves agreeable to visitors, and endeavouring to save their generals from receiving those who have no particular business. A large farm-house stands close by, which, in any other army, would have been the general's residence, pro tem.: but as no liberties are allowed to be taken with personal property in Lee's army, he is particular in setting a good example himself. His staff are crowded together two and three in a tent: none are allowed to carry more baggage than a small box each, and his own kit is but very little larger. Every one who approaches him does so with marked respect, although there is none of that bowing and flourishing of forage-caps which occurs in the presence of European generals: and whilst all honour him and place implicit faith in his courage and ability, those with whom he is most intimate feel for him the affection of sons to a father. Old General Scott was correct in saying that when Lee joined the Southern cause, it was worth as much as the accession of 20,000 men to the "rebels."

Since, then, every injury that it was possible to inflict, the Northerners have heaped upon him. His house on the Pamunky river was burnt to the ground and the slaves carried away, many of them by force; whilst his residence on the Arlington Heights was not only gutted of its furniture, but even the very relics of George Washington were stolen from it and paraded in triumph in the saloons of New York and Boston. Notwithstanding all these personal losses, however, when speaking of the Yankees, he neither evinced any bitterness of feeling, nor gave utterance to a single violent expression, but alluded to many of his former friends and companions amongst them in the kindest terms. He spoke as a man proud of the victories won by his country, and confident of ultimate success under the blessing of the Almighty, whom he glorified for past successes, and whose aid he invoked for all future operations. He regretted that his limited supply of tents and available accommodation would prevent him from putting us up, but he kindly placed at our disposal horses, or a two-horsed waggon, if we preferred it, to drive about in.

—[Wolseley], "A Month's Visit to the Confederate Headquarters"

4. "YOU MUST HELP DRIVE THESE PEOPLE BACK"

Here is one of those minor episodes* that illumine character. It was at the Battle of Antietam that young Captain Lee of the Rockbridge Artillery, then a lad of twenty, met his father and was sent back into battle.

Neither Lincoln nor Lee used derogatory terms in speaking of their opponents; Lee customarily referred to the Federals as "those people."

AS one of the Army of Northern Virginia, I occasionally saw the commander-in-chief on the march or passed the headquarters close enough to recognize him and members of his staff, but a private soldier in Jackson's corps did not have much time, during that campaign, for visiting, and until the battle of Sharpsburg I had no opportunity of speaking to him.

On that occasion our battery had been severely handled, losing many men and horses. Having three guns disabled, we were ordered to withdraw, and while moving back we passed General Lee and several of his staff, grouped on a little knoll near the road. Having no definite orders where to go, our captain, seeing the commanding general, halted us and rode over to get some instructions. Some others and myself went along to see and hear.

General Lee was dismounted, with some of his staff around him, a courier holding his horse. Captain Poague, commanding our battery, the Rockbridge Artillery, saluted, reported our condition and asked for instructions. The General, listening patiently, looked at us—his eyes passing over me without any sign of recognition—and then ordered Captain Poague to take the most serviceable horses and men, man the uninjured gun, send the disabled part of his command back to refit, and report to the front for duty. As Poague turned to go, I went up to speak to my father. When he found out who I was he congratulated me on being well and unhurt. I then said:

"General, are you going to send us in again?"

"Yes, my son," he replied with a smile. "You all must do what you can to help drive these people back."

—LEE, *Recollections and Letters of General Robert E. Lee*

5. "IT IS WELL WAR IS SO TERRIBLE, OR WE SHOULD GET TOO FOND OF IT"

Here is another of those little scenes that reveal character: Lee watching the repulse of the Federals at Fredericksburg. General Pendleton, who tells the story, was a West Pointer who had abandoned the army for the Church, was rector of Grace Church in Lexington, Virginia, when he joined the Rockbridge Artillery, and rose to be chief of artillery of the Army of Northern Virginia.

---

* From: *Recollections and Letters of General Robert E. Lee* by Robert E. Lee. Copyright 1904 by Doubleday & Company, Inc.

FROM prominent points in our line almost the entire scene could be taken in by the eye. And at one of these, the most commanding, where we had a few powerful guns, General Lee remained much of the day, observing the field; only too indifferent, as was his wont, to danger from the large, numerous, and well-aimed missiles hurled especially thither from the enemy's heavy batteries across the Rappahannock. Seldom, in all the wars of the world, has a spectacle been presented like that which, from this central elevation, we looked upon. More than one hundred thousand blue-coated men in the open plain, with every military appliance, in battle order, and moving in their respective subdivisions to attack our line. Although our numbers were certainly not half those of the enemy, there was misgiving, probably, in no officer or man as to the result.

Events in one quarter of the field, as it lay before us, attracted peculiar interest, and gave occasion to one of those characteristic remarks of General Lee which told at once of his capacity for enjoying the excitements of action, and of the good feeling and strong principle that kept it under control. A large force advanced rapidly to charge our right. Stonewall Jackson was there, and that he would promptly hurl them back little doubt was entertained. Still no such assault can be witnessed without earnest interest, if not concern. Nor was the shock received on our side without loss. There fell the heroic General Gregg, of the gallant and now vengeance-suffering State of South Carolina. Presently, however, as was anticipated, the spirited charge was reversed, and blue figures by thousands were seen recrossing, "double quick," with faces to the rear, the space they had traversed, and hundreds of gray pursuers hastening their speed. While younger spectators near us gave expression to their feelings by shouts, clapping of hands, &c., the gratified yet considerate and amiable commander turned to myself, and with beaming countenance said, "*It is well war is so terrible, or we should get too fond of it.*"

Not long after an incident occurred which made us shudder for our beloved chief. One of our large guns on that eminence, having to be plied continuously against another portion of the enemy's line, which was advancing to charge that part of our defences held by the good and gallant Georgian, General Tom Cobb, and being, like much hastily-cast Southern ordnance, of insufficient tenacity, finally burst with prodigious violence. None, wonderfully and happily, were struck by its fragments. And, remarkably, those who stood nearest, of whom the individual relating it to you was one, within a little over arm's length, although considerably jarred by the shock, proved to be really in less danger than others farther off. General Lee was standing perhaps fifty feet in the rear, and a large piece of the cannon, weighing, we estimated, about a third of a ton, fell just beyond him. He thus very narrowly escaped death. Like himself, however, he only looked upon the mass calmly for a moment, and then, without a syllable expressive of surprise or concern, continued the business occupying him at the time.

—PENDLETON, "Personal Recollections of General Lee"

6. LEE SENDS GENERAL McLAWS TO CALL ON SEDGWICK

Here is a scene from the Battle of Chancellorsville. It will be remembered that Hooker's plan was for his army to attack Lee at Chancellorsville while Sedgwick brushed aside Early at Fredericksburg and struck Lee on the flank. And it will be remembered, too, that the plan miscarried.

Once more it is the invaluable Stiles who tells the story.

SHORTLY after I left General McLaws he and General Lee resumed their conference, and just as they did so there occurred an incident which beautifully revealed the equipoise of General Lee's character and the charm of his manner.

If any of the minor characters mentioned in these reminiscences has a distinct personality every way worthy of approval and of remembrance, it is "Brother William," the consecrated, courageous chaplain of the Seventeenth Mississippi, or rather of Barksdale's brigade—the real hero of the great revival at Fredericksburg. He, of course, had remained behind there, with his brigade, under the general command of Early, to watch Sedgwick.

I was standing in the shade of a tree near our guns, which had been ordered to draw out on the road, head of column to the rear,—that is, toward Fredericksburg, an order and movement which we all well understood,—when my attention was called to a horseman coming at full speed from the direction in which we were heading, and as he drew near I saw it was "Brother William," and that he was greatly excited. My recollection is that he did not have a saddle, but was riding upon a blanket or cloth of some kind, and that his horse was reeking with sweat and panting from exertion. When his eye fell upon General Lee he made directly for him, and I followed as fast as I could. He dashed to the very feet of the commanding general, indeed almost upon him, and gasping for breath, his eyes starting from their sockets, began to tell of dire disaster at Fredericksburg—Sedgwick had smashed Early and was rapidly coming on in our rear.

I have never seen anything more majestically calm than General Lee was; I felt painfully the contrast between him and dear little Brother William. Something very like a grave, sweet smile began to express itself on the General's face, but he checked it, and raising his left hand gently, as if to protect himself, he interrupted the excited speaker, checking and controlling him instantly, at the same time saying very quietly:

"I thank you very much, but both you and your horse are fatigued and overheated. Take him to that shady tree yonder and you and he blow and rest a little. I'm talking to General McLaws just now. I'll call you as soon as we are through."

I said Brother William was at once dominated and controlled, and he was—but not quite satisfied. He began a mild protest: "But General!" but he did not persist in it—he simply could not. He had already dismounted, and he started back with me to the tree, leading his horse.

Unfortunately I had none of General Lee's power over him, and he began to pour out to me his recital of disaster and prediction of ruin. All was lost below, Sedgwick had stormed the heights and seized the town, the brigade had been cut off and, he feared, captured; Early had been beaten and pushed roughly aside, and at least 30,000 victorious troops were rapidly pressing on in our rear. Substantially, he alone was left to tell the tale, and had fortunately been able to secure this horse on which to come to tell it. If not already too late, it very soon would be, to do anything even to moderate the calamity.

In vain I suggested that General Lee could not be ignorant of all this; that his scouts had doubtless given him information; that General Early certainly would have found means to communicate with him; that Lee had beaten Hooker and his calm and self-reliant bearing clearly indicated that he felt himself to be master of the entire situation. But Brother William would not be comforted or reassured. General Lee had not been upon the spot and could not know; *he* had been and did know. The very calmness of the General showed he did not appreciate the gravity of the situation. While we were thus debating the matter General Lee finished with McLaws, who at once started his division on the back track to reinforce Early and help him take care of Sedgwick—and, true to his promise, Marse Robert now called for Brother William, and as he approached greeted him with a smile, saying:

"Now what were you telling us about Major Sedgwick?"

Brother William again told his tale of woe—this time with somewhat diminished intensity and less lurid coloring. When he had finished the General thanked him, saying again:

"I am very much obliged to you; the Major is a nice gentleman; I don't think he would hurt us very badly, but we are going to see about him at once. I have just sent General McLaws to make a special call upon him."

—STILES, *Four Years under Marse Robert*

7. DR. PARKS'S BOY VISITS LEE'S HEADQUARTERS

Here is a charming vignette* of Lee on the road to Gettysburg. It comes from Leighton Parks, the small boy who stood wide-eyed looking at Lee and his lieutenants. Written 40 years later, it is undoubtedly bathed in nostalgia. Yet though the conversations are suspect, the episode itself rings true enough. The Elizabethtown referred to was a small Maryland village, no longer on the map.

BEFORE the year was out we learned that the Union troops had again been driven back to Washington, and, soon after, that Lee was crossing the river at Williamsport. The report proved true. First came the cavalry. I had never supposed so many horses were to be found in the world as I now saw slowly passing through the street of Elizabethtown. They kept straight

* From *Century Magazine*. Copyright, 1905, Century Company, reprinted by permission of the publishers, Appleton-Century-Crofts, Inc.

on to the north. I asked many of the soldiers where they were going. The poor fellows knew nothing; many of them were too ignorant to know what it meant to have crossed the Potomac. Had they not crossed many rivers? What was one more than another? But the officers laughed gaily and said: "New York." Why not? What could prevent them? Was not the Army of the Potomac huddled about the defenses of Washington? "Had not Bobby Lee stolen a march on the commanding general, whoever that might be at the moment?" they added with a laugh. Indeed, the darkest hour of the war had come to the North.

So the troops passed on, thousand after thousand. The artillery followed the cavalry; then came the infantry. The impression made by the sight of so many horses was repeated by the hosts of men. It was not only the multitude that impressed those who saw that march; it was also the splendid discipline of the army. They were different from the corps we had seen the year before. These men were well clad and shod, and they came through the town with flags flying and bands playing "Dixie," "Dixie," all day long, with now and then a change to "Maryland, my Maryland" or the "Bonnie Blue Flag." We became as tired of these as we had of "Yankee Doodle" or "The Star-Spangled Banner." (But both armies marched to the tune of "The Girl I Left Behind Me.") They had the air of men who were used to conquer; they believed in the men who led them, and they did not doubt that when they saw the enemy they would drive them before them again. It was a sight such as few have seen even of those who took part in the war. Sixty thousand men, it is said, passed through Elizabethtown on the way to Gettysburg, and I can well believe it. Day after day an unbroken line passed on due north, and at night the rumble of the wagons made sleep impossible for nervous people. And who was not nervous?

Soon after the Confederates began to enter the town I met a friend of mine, the son of Dr. Doyle, who told me that his father had just been sent for to see Lee, and that I might go too if I hurried. It is needless to say that I ran as fast as my small legs could carry me, and we found the doctor just starting. Dr. Doyle was a man who had been in communication with the enemy from the beginning of the war, but had so far managed to escape the fate of many innocent men. Two of his sons had been arrested a short time before, and were lying in the jail when their friends arrived and set them free.

The doctor was in his old gig, and, being an immense man, left no room for any one else in it, so we two boys sat on the springs behind. It was on the Williamsport pike, about half a mile from the town, that we met General Lee. He had dismounted and was standing by his horse, a small sorrel mare, which, I was told, it was his custom to ride on the march. His staff was brilliant in gold lace, but he was very simply dressed. No one could have seen that man without being greatly impressed with the dignity of his bearing and the beauty of his face. His hair at this time was almost entirely white, and those who had seen him the year before said he had aged greatly in the short space of time which had elapsed since the battle of Antietam. I could not help thinking of Washington as I looked at that calm, sad face. It has been said since by those who were near him that he had no expectation of conquering the North, and that, at the most, he only hoped to win a great battle on Northern soil in order to affect public opinion in Europe, and lead to the recognition of the Southern Confederacy. However that may be, there was nothing about his bearing which looked like a great hope.

Dr. Doyle drove straight to where he was standing and announced himself as one who was sure of his welcome. General Lee came at once to the gig and thanked him politely for having come so promptly, and began at once to ask about the roads. I was astonished at the familiarity which he showed with the country, and yet he evidently wished to have his map, which he held in his hand, confirmed by an eye-witness. His questions were like those of a lawyer to a witness. What roads ran into the Lightersburg pike? Did the Cavetown pike cross the mountain? What sort of crossing was it? Could cannon be easily brought over it? His right flank, then, was protected by the Blue Ridge until he reached Gettysburg? And on his return should he come that way? Were there good roads running to the river west of the one on which he now stood? Could artillery be moved over them? Was the valley well wooded and watered all the way to Gettysburg? To all of which the answer was "Yes."

Lee had been speaking in a low tone, leaning on the shaft of the gig, with his head under the hood of it, so that we, looking in through the curtain, could see and hear everything. Suddenly Lee saw us and said: "Doctor, are these your boys?"

"One of them is," said the doctor. "The other is the son of Dr. Parks. You must have known his father in the old army."

"Is it possible!" said Lee.

Then we were called down and made our bows, and Lee said something that I could not hear; but the doctor answered, "No danger," and then added something at which Lee smiled and said, "Would you boys like to get on that horse?" pointing to his own little mare.

Of course we said, "Yes," and each in turn was lifted by General Lee up to the horse's back. I suspect that that attention was suggested by Dr. Doyle in order to divert our minds from what we had just heard. When we got back to town, he said to me: "Now run home, my boy, and tell your mother that you have seen General Lee and all that he said to you—in fact, all you can remember to have heard him say. It will interest her."

So home I ran, swelling with importance, and told my mother all the questions that General Lee had asked and what Dr. Doyle had said. Of course my mother saw at once the importance of the conversation, and charged me to keep it perfectly quiet. Which I did.

A day or two after this a friend of the family who had been very kind to me asked me if I should not like to go out to General Lee's headquarters? "To-morrow," he said, "you will see a sight that you will be able to tell as long as you live, for Lee's generals are to meet him, and the army is to move."

I boldly asked if he would lend me his horse, and he laughed and consented. So the next morning, dressed in white jacket and trousers, I started off on a brown horse, carrying a basket of raspberries to one of Lee's staff whom my mother had known since he was a lad. I remember my costume from the fact that some of the berries melted, and before I was aware of it they had made a stain on my trousers which no amount of rubbing would remove. This troubled me a good deal because I thought General Lee might think I did not know how to ride; and as I had made up my mind to ask him to let me accompany the army in some capacity not very clear to me, this gave me considerable anxiety. However, I reached the camp without further accident and found Colonel Taylor, to whom I was accredited.

Lee's headquarters were in a hickory grove about three miles from Williamsport. The grove was on the top of a small hill, and near enough to the pike for the general to see the troops as they marched by.

When I reached the camp, Colonel Taylor told me that General Lee was away, but that he would probably return before long. Indeed, it was not many minutes before we heard the trampling of horses and the guard turning out, and, on going to the door of the tent, I saw a splendid sight. First there was Lee himself riding a superb iron-gray horse, and with him were Longstreet, Ewell, and A. P. Hill. Colonel Taylor led me to General Lee and said: "General, this gentleman has brought me some raspberries, and I have asked him to take snack with us."

Lee's back was toward me when the colonel spoke, and I was startled to see how severe he looked as, wheeling sharply, he glanced quickly to right and left and then looked down. Then he smiled very pleasantly and remarked: "I have had the pleasure of meeting your friend before." And then, to my great surprise, this severe-looking man stooped down and, lifting me, kissed me. After this the generals and Colonel Taylor and I went into a large tent for "snack."

I do not remember anything that was said during the meal, nor what we had to eat. I suppose I was a good deal excited, and I know that there was a deal of laughing—I fear at my expense; for they—not Lee, but the others—asked me a great many questions, and then laughed at the answers. I suppose it was a relief to these men, who were carrying such a heavy burden, to have a child to chaff.

After luncheon we went to Lee's tent, and the general took me on his knee and talked to me until, some one having taken his attention, Hill beckoned me to come to him, which I did gladly; for, though Lee was gentle, I could not help standing in awe of him in a way that I did not of the others.

When I had been with him for a little while, Longstreet said: "Come, Hill, you've had him long enough; pass him over." So I was dragged over to Longstreet's knee and had my face well rubbed by his great brown beard. And he whispered in my ear that he had a pony he thought would carry my weight, if I should like to join his staff.

But before I could express my joy, Lee suddenly said, "Well, gentlemen," and immediately Colonel Taylor made me a sign. So I got up and said good-by; and I thought then, and think now, that they were sorry to have me go, for I suppose I brought a new element into their life. One of them— Hill, I think—called to a servant to "bring the captain's horse," at which the man grinned and untied the horse from a tree near by and led him to the front of the tent.

This placed me in a most embarrassing situation; for while I could ride very well for a boy, I was in the habit of mounting my steed by the aid of a fence. Still, I determined to do my best, and, stretching up my leg as high as it would go, managed to touch the stirrup with my toe; but, alas! when I attempted to mount into the saddle I descended to the ground, with my feet very wide apart and my jacket somewhat marked by contact with the horse's flanks. This was greeted with a good-natured laugh, which determined me to mount or die in the attempt. But I was saved either alternative, for before I had time to try again I was lifted lightly into the saddle by Lee himself, who smiled and said: "Give him time, and he'll do for the cavalry yet."

—PARKS, "What a Boy Saw of the Civil War"

8. "A SADNESS I HAD NEVER BEFORE SEEN UPON HIS FACE"

We have already seen something of Lee during and after Gettysburg, and Colonel Fremantle has given us an unforgettable picture of Lee rallying his stricken troops with the assurance that all would come right in the end. Here is perhaps a more intimate picture of Lee the night after the battle. It comes from General John Imboden, who protected the Confederate right in the advance on Gettysburg, and was detached to cover the Confederate retreat after the battle.

WHEN night closed the struggle, Lee's army was repulsed. We all knew that the day had gone against us, but the full extent of the disaster was only known in high quarters. The carnage of the day was generally understood to have been frightful, yet our army was not in retreat, and it was surmised in camp that with to-morrow's dawn would come a renewal of the struggle. All felt and appreciated the momentous consequences to the cause of Southern independence of final defeat or victory on that great field.

It was a warm summer's night; there were few camp-fires, and the weary soldiers were lying in groups on the luxuriant grass of the beautiful meadows, discussing the events of the day, speculating on the morrow, or watching that our horses did not straggle off while browsing. About 11 o'clock a horseman came to summon me to General Lee. I promptly mounted and, accompanied by Lieutenant George W. McPhail, an aide on my staff, and guided by the courier who brought the message, rode about two miles toward Gettysburg to where half a dozen small tents were pointed out, a little way from the roadside to our left, as General Lee's headquarters for the night. On inquiry I found that he was not there, but had gone to the headquarters of General A. P. Hill, about half a mile nearer to Gettysburg. When we reached the place indicated, a single flickering candle, visible from the road through the open front of a common wall-tent, exposed to view Generals Lee and Hill seated on camp-stools with a map spread upon their knees.

Dismounting, I approached on foot. After exchanging the ordinary salutations General Lee directed me to go back to his headquarters and wait for him. I did so, but he did not make his appearance until about 1 o'clock, when he came riding alone, at a slow walk, and evidently wrapped in profound thought.

When he arrived there was not even a sentinel on duty at his tent, and no one of his staff was awake. The moon was high in the clear sky and the silent scene was unusually vivid. As he approached and saw us lying on the grass under a tree, he spoke, reined in his jaded horse, and essayed to dismount. The effort to do so betrayed so much physical exhaustion that I hurriedly rose and stepped forward to assist him, but before I reached his side he had succeeded in alighting, and threw his arm across the saddle to rest, and fixing his eyes upon the ground leaned in silence and almost motionless upon his equally weary horse,—the two forming a striking and never-to-be-forgotten group. The moon shone full upon his massive features and revealed an expression of sadness that I had never before seen upon his face. Awed by his appearance I waited for him to speak until the silence became embarrassing, when, to break it and change the silent current of his thoughts, I ventured to remark, in a sympathetic tone, and in allusion to his great fatigue:

"General, this has been a hard day on you."

He looked up, and replied mournfully:

"Yes, it has been a sad, sad day to us," and immediately relapsed into his thoughtful mood and attitude. Being unwilling again to intrude upon his reflections, I said no more. After perhaps a minute or two, he suddenly straightened up to his full height, and turning to me with more animation and excitement of manner than I had ever seen in him before, for he was a man of wonderful equanimity, he said in a voice tremulous with emotion:

"I never saw troops behave more magnificently than Pickett's division of Virginians did to-day in that grand charge upon the enemy. And if they had been supported as they were to have been,—but, for some reason not yet fully explained to me, were not,—we would have held the position and the day would have been ours." After a moment's pause he added in a loud voice, in a tone almost of agony, "Too bad! *Too bad!* Oh! Too bad!"

I shall never forget his language, his manner, and his appearance of mental suffering. In a few moments all emotion was suppressed, and he spoke feelingly of several of his fallen and trusted officers; among others of Brigadier-Generals Armistead, Garnett, and Kemper of Pickett's division.

—Imboden, "The Confederate Retreat from Gettysburg"

9. LEE AND TRAVELLER REVIEW THE ARMY OF NORTHERN VIRGINIA

This picture* of a gala military review comes from August 1863, while

---

* From: *Recollections and Letters of General Robert E. Lee* by Robert E. Lee. Copyright 1904 by Doubleday & Company, Inc.

the army was recuperating after Gettysburg. It is given us by Lee's son, Captain Robert E. Lee, Jr.

DURING this period of rest, so unusual to the Army of Northern Virginia, several reviews were held before the commanding general. I remember being present when that of the Third Army Corps, General A. P. Hill commanding, took place. Some of us young cavalrymen, then stationed near the Rappahannock, rode over to Orange Court House to see this grand military pageant. From all parts of the army, officers and men who could get leave came to look on, and from all the surrounding country the people, old and young, ladies and children, came in every pattern of vehicle and on horseback, to see twenty thousand of that "incomparable infantry" of the Army of Northern Virginia pass in review before their great commander.

The General was mounted on Traveller, looking very proud of his master, who had on sash and sword, which he very rarely wore, a pair of new cavalry gauntlets, and, I think, a new hat. At any rate, he looked unusually fine, and sat his horse like a perfect picture of grace and power. The infantry was drawn up in column by divisions, with their bright muskets all glittering in the sun, their battle-flags standing straight out before the breeze, and their bands playing, awaiting the inspection of the General, before they broke into column by companies and marched past him in review.

When all was ready, General Hill and staff rode up to General Lee, and the two generals, with their respective staffs, galloped around front and rear of each of the three divisions standing motionless on the plain. As the cavalcade reached the head of each division, its commanding officer joined in and followed as far as the next division, so that there was a continual infusion of fresh groups into the original one all along the lines.

Traveller started with a long lope, and never changed his stride. His rider sat erect and calm, not noticing anything but the gray lines of men whom he knew so well. The pace was very fast, as there were nine good miles to go, and the escort began to become less and less, dropping out one by one from different causes as Traveller raced along without a check.

When the General drew up, after this nine-mile gallop, under the standard at the reviewing-stand, flushed with the exercise as well as with pride in his brave men, he raised his hat and saluted. Then arose a shout of applause and admiration from the entire assemblage, the memory of which to this day moistens the eye of every old soldier.

—LEE, *Recollections and Letters of General Robert E. Lee*

10. "HE LOOKED AS THOUGH HE WAS THE MONARCH OF THE WORLD"

We have already learned how Lee tried to lead the countercharge to close up the gap torn in his lines on the morning of the Battle of the Wilderness, May 6, 1864. Here Colonel Oates, whom we have met before, recalls for us his glimpse of Lee as the Alabamians closed up the gap.

AT about 2 o'clock A.M. on the 6th we began to move, and progressed so slowly along the devious neighborhood road that it was daylight when the head of the column reached the Plank Road, about two miles in rear of where the fighting ceased the previous evening and where, just at this moment, it recommenced with great fury. As we hurried to the front we passed quite a number of wounded Confederates lying by the side of the road, and among them Generals Cook, of Georgia, and Kirkland, of North Carolina. In anticipation that his troops would be relieved early the next morning, Hill had not prepared to receive the attack which was made on him.

Longstreet's column reached the scene of action none too soon. Hancock was just then turning Hill's right and driving his men from their position, although they were manfully contesting every inch of ground. Anderson's Georgians was the first brigade of Field's division to engage the enemy. Benning's and the Texas Brigade got into action next on the right or south side of the Plank Road, and were temporarily repulsed. We met General Benning, brought out on a litter severely wounded. Colonel Perry then formed Law's brigade, as it came up in double quick, to the left of the Plank Road with the Fourth Alabama's right resting upon it and the Fifteenth on the left of the brigade and of the line.

To reach our position we had to pass within a few feet of General Lee. He sat his fine gray horse "Traveler," with the cape of his black cloak around his shoulders, his face flushed and full of animation. The balls were flying around him from two directions. His eyes were on the fight then going on south of the Plank Road between Kershaw's division and the flanking column of the enemy. He had just returned from attempting to lead the Texas Brigade in a second charge, when those gallant men and their officers refused to allow him to do so. My friend Col. Van H. Manning, of the Third Arkansas, then in command of the brigade, did that himself, fell severely wounded while leading the charge, and was taken prisoner.

A group of General Lee's staff were on their horses just in rear of him. He turned in his saddle and called to his chief of staff in a most vigorous tone, while pointing with his finger across the road, and said: "Send an active young officer down there." I thought him at that moment the grandest specimen of manhood I ever beheld. He looked as though he ought to have been and was the monarch of the world. He glanced his eye down on the "ragged rebels" as they filed around him in quick time to their place in line, and inquired, "What troops are these?" And was answered by some private in the Fifteenth, "Law's Alabama brigade." He exclaimed in a strong voice, "God bless the Alabamians!" The men cheered and went into line with a whoop. The advance began.

—OATES, *The War Between the Union and the Confederacy*

11. "THE FIELD RESOUNDED WITH WILD SHOUTS OF LEE, LEE, LEE"

There are altogether, as we pointed out in our chapter on the Wilderness, three "Lee to the Rear" episodes. The third, and best authenticated, is that of

May 12, when Hancock broke through the salient, overran Johnson's division, and threatened the whole Confederate line. We give here Colonel Gibson's account of the crisis.

A LITTLE after dawn of the 12th [May 1864], I was aroused from a deep sleep by Frank George, one of General Gordon's orderlies, and was told by him that the Yankees had broken through our works and captured Johnson's division; and when I started to say something, he told me not to talk loud, the enemy were very close to us.

I immediately aroused up two or three men near me and told them to arouse the regiment, and tell the men to fall in as quickly and quietly as possible, without any rattling of canteens, as we were near the enemy. . . . The men fell in line about as soon as I could get mounted, and the staff officer came up a few minutes after, and guided us towards the right, and then towards the left, and after we had marched some two or three hundred yards and had come in sight of the line of unoccupied earthworks to our left, he pointed out a little farmhouse some ten or twelve hundred yards distant, and some four or five hundred yards, apparently, in rear of these works extended, as the headquarters of General Lee. He led us some hundred yards or more almost parallel to these unoccupied works, and then stopped, rather closer than the regulations required, as I thought, to a fine looking body of Confederates, dressed in nice, clean uniforms, that contrasted very strongly with the clothing of those of my brigade.

In the rear of these well-dressed troops I saw four mounted men among them; recognized General Robert E. Lee and Major-General John B. Gordon. General Lee rode towards my brigade, and as soon as I had fronted the men I turned towards him saluting for my orders. He paid no attention to me, but wheeled his horse to the right, passed through the vacancy between the brigades, took off his hat and rode Traveler grandly to the front.

He had scarcely got a dozen paces in front of our brigades when General Gordon and an officer on his left, whom I took to be his adjutant, trotted quickly after General Lee, and Gordon, as soon as he reached him seized Traveler by the right cheek of his bit, stopped him, and said to General Lee: "You must not expose yourself; your life is too valuable to the army and to the Confederacy for you to risk it so wantonly; we are Georgians, we are Virginians, we need no such encouragement." At this some of our soldiers called out, "No, No," Gordon continuing, said: "There is not a soldier in the Confederate army that would not gladly lay down his life to save you from harm;" but the men did not respond to this last proposition.

While Gordon was speaking his adjutant rode around the heads of the horses of the two generals and facing his horse in a direction opposite that of General Lee's began to tug at Traveler's bit or bridle rein. Looking through an aperture in our breastworks I saw a body of the enemy coming from our left, slowly, and cautiously approaching us.

I called out to General Lee to come back, the enemy were approaching, and that we could not fight while he was in our front. A number of our men, especially those of Company A, called out: "Come back, General Lee;

we can't fight while you are in our front;" and some members of Company A turned their right shoulders to General Lee and their backs to me, but I immediately brought these men into line by a "steady, front!" . . .

On looking out again for the enemy I noticed that they had drawn very close to our earthworks. I called out to General Lee "To come back, and come quick; that the enemy were close upon us, and that my men could not fire on the enemy without shooting him." A number of my men called out: "Come back, General Lee; we won't fight as long as you are before us; come back."

The decided call of the men seemed to produce a greater impression on General Lee than the eloquence of Gordon, and my curt suggestions. As Traveler could not be easily turned around with a mounted officer on either side of him, facing in opposite directions, the adjutant let go Traveler's bridle, Gordon turned him around to the right, and proudly started to lead him back, and as he was doing so, I called out: "Three cheers for General Lee and 'Old' Virginia," but forgot to add Gordon's name to the list, which were given with a will. Before the two generals reached the intervening space between the brigades, Gordon let go his hold of Lee's bridle and dropped behind a short space, Lee as soon as he reached the line of the brigades, turned his horse to the right, close up to mine, and Gordon and his adjutant rode up to the line of the Georgia Brigade.

When General Gordon, amid repeated shouts of "Lee, Lee to the rear!" had approached within eight or ten paces of our line, he found the interval between our two brigades blocked up. A mounted officer had stationed himself on the left of Gordon's brigade, General George Evans commanding. I had remained on the extreme right flank of Early's brigade, where I had placed myself when Lee rode to the front, and the intervening space had been crowded by men of Evans' brigade. Gordon let go his hold of Traveler's bridle, and reined up his horse to fall in behind Lee, and as he did so a member of the Warren Rifles ran forward, seized Lee's horse by the bridle reins, and amid redoubled shouts of "Lee, Lee, Lee to the rear! Lee to the rear!" led him up to the crowd and guided him through the crowders, and I backed my horse to the left to give a freer passage to the riders, and they passed through in single file, and the field of coming carnage resounded with wild shouts of "Lee, Lee, Lee!"

—Account by Colonel J. Catlett Gibson

12. LEE BIDS FAREWELL TO THE ARMY OF NORTHERN VIRGINIA

This moving document * *needs no introduction. It is relevant, however, to add a word about Lee after the war.*

Deeply convinced that the only hope for the South lay in a sincere acceptance of the verdict of Appomattox he devoted himself to healing the

---

* From: *Recollections and Letters of General Robert E. Lee* by Robert E. Lee. Copyright 1904 by Doubleday & Company, Inc.

wounds of war and training up a generation of young men who might work for the reconstruction of their section. In June 1865 he set an example to others by applying for a presidential pardon; it is mortifying to record that the pardon was never granted. In September 1865 Lee accepted the Presidency of Washington College (now Washington and Lee University), at Lexington, Virginia, and as President inaugurated a series of interesting reforms in the direction of what we would now call progressive education. Stricken with angina pectoris, he died on October 12, 1870, and was buried in Lexington.

In Benét's fine phrase, Lee had known "such glamour as can wear sheer triumph out"; if the cause for which he so valorously fought did not triumph, who can doubt that the admiration and affection in which he came to be held, North as well as South, represented a triumph that has few parallels in history?

Headquarters, Army of Northern Virginia,
April 10, 1865

After four years of arduous service, marked by unsurpassed courage and fortitude, the Army of Northern Virginia has been compelled to yield to overwhelming numbers and resources. I need not tell the survivors of so many hard-fought battles, who have remained steadfast to the last, that I have consented to this result from no distrust of them; but, feeling that valour and devotion could accomplish nothing that could compensate for the loss that would have attended the continuation of the contest, I have determined to avoid the useless sacrifice of those whose past services have endeared them to their countrymen. By the terms of the agreement, officers and men can return to their homes and remain there until exchanged. You will take with you the satisfaction that proceeds from the consciousness of duty faithfully performed; and I earnestly pray that a merciful God will extend to you His blessing and protection. With an increasing admiration of your constancy and devotion to your country, and a grateful remembrance of your kind and generous consideration of myself, I bid you an affectionate farewell.

R. E. Lee, *General.*

—Lee, *Recollections and Letters of General Robert E. Lee*

13. NATHANIEL HAWTHORNE CALLS ON PRESIDENT LINCOLN

From 1853 to 1860 Hawthorne had been in England; when he returned to his own country he was bewildered and saddened at the sectional conflict and the war. In the spring of 1862 he visited Lincoln with a delegation from Massachusetts, was disgusted by some of the politicians and lobbyists he saw about the capital, and wrote a caustic article on his observations for the Atlantic Monthly, "Chiefly about War Matters." The editor was so offended that he added a footnote: "We are compelled to omit two or three pages, in which the author describes the interview, and gives his ideas of the personal appearance and deportment of the President. The sketch ... lacks reverence, and it pains us to see a gentleman of ripe age . . . falling into the characteristic and most ominous fault of Young America." It is difficult now to understand what it was that worried editor J. T. Fields in this piece, on the whole so perceptive.

The article as Hawthorne originally wrote it appeared in his Tales, Sketches, and Other Papers.

NINE o'clock had been appointed as the time for receiving the deputation, and we were punctual to the moment; but not so the President, who sent us word that he was eating his breakfast and would come as soon as he could. His appetite, we were glad to think, must have been a pretty fair one; for we waited about half an hour in one of the antechambers, and then were ushered into a reception-room, in one corner of which sat the Secretaries of War and of the Treasury, expecting, like ourselves, the termination of the Presidential breakfast. During this interval there were several new additions to our group, one or two of whom were in a working-garb, so that we formed a very miscellaneous collection of people, mostly unknown to each other, and without any common sponsor, but all with an equal right to look our headservant in the face.

By and by there was a little stir on the staircase and in the passage-way, and in lounged a tall, loose-jointed figure, of an exaggerated Yankee port and demeanor, whom (as being about the homeliest man I ever saw, yet by no means repulsive or disagreeable) it was impossible not to recognize as Uncle Abe.

Unquestionably, Western man though he be, and Kentuckian by birth, President Lincoln is the essential representative of all Yankees, and the veritable specimen, physically, of what the world seems determined to regard as our characteristic qualities. It is the strangest and yet the fittest thing in the jumble of human vicissitudes, that he, out of so many millions, unlooked for, unselected by any intelligible process that could be based upon his genuine qualities, unknown to those who chose him, and unsuspected of what endowments may adapt him for his tremendous responsibility, should have found the way open for him to fling his lank personality into the chair of state,—where, I presume, it was his first impulse to throw his legs on the council-table and tell the Cabinet Ministers a story. There is no describing his lengthy awkwardness nor the uncouthness of his movement; and yet it seemed as if I had been in the habit of seeing him daily, and had shaken hands with him a thousand times in some village street; so true was he to the aspect of the pattern American, though with a certain extravagance which, possibly, I exaggerated still further by the delighted eagerness with which I took it in. If put to guess his calling and livelihood, I should have taken him for a country schoolmaster as soon as anything else. He was dressed in a rusty black frock-coat and pantaloons, unbrushed, and worn so faithfully that the suit had adapted itself to the curves and angularities of his figure, and had grown to be an outer skin of the man. He had shabby slippers on his feet. His hair was black, still unmixed with gray, stiff, somewhat bushy, and had apparently been acquainted with neither brush nor comb that morning, after the disarrangement of the pillow; and as to a night-cap, Uncle Abe probably knows nothing of such effeminacies. His complexion is dark and sallow, betokening, I fear, an insalubrious atmosphere around the White House; he has thick black eyebrows and an impending brow; his nose is large, and the lines about his mouth are very strongly defined.

The whole physiognomy is as coarse a one as you would meet anywhere in the length and breadth of the States; but withal, it is redeemed, illuminated, softened, and brightened by a kindly though serious look out of his eyes, and an expression of homely sagacity, that seems weighted with rich results of village experience. A great deal of native sense; no bookish cultivation, no refinement; honest at heart, and thoroughly so, and yet, in some sort, sly,—at least, endowed with a sort of tact and wisdom that are akin to craft, and would impel him, I think, to take an antagonist in flank, rather than to make a bull-run at him right in front. But, on the whole, I like this sallow, queer, sagacious visage, with the homely human sympathies that warmed it; and, for my small share in the matter, would as lief have Uncle Abe for a ruler as any man whom it would have been practicable to put in his place.

Immediately on his entrance the President accosted our member of Congress, who had us in charge, and, with a comical twist of his face, made some jocular remark about the length of his breakfast. He then greeted us all round, not waiting for an introduction, but shaking and squeezing everybody's hand with the utmost cordiality, whether the individual's name was announced to him or not. His manner towards us was wholly without pretense, but yet had a kind of natural dignity, quite sufficient to keep the forwardest of us from clapping him on the shoulder and asking him for a story.

—HAWTHORNE, *Tales, Sketches, and Other Papers*

14. AN ENGLISH VISITOR WATCHES THE PRESIDENT RECEIVE CALLERS

Busy as he was, Lincoln seemed to be on tap for anyone who wanted him; that was partly the custom of the time, partly Lincoln's own unpretentious simplicity. Here an English traveler, Robert Ferguson, tells what a typical White House day was like. The date is sometime in the fall of 1864.

ON my return from the Front to Washington I naturally felt a desire to see the man on whom the American people have, in this great crisis of their history, bestowed their confidence in so remarkable a degree. And accordingly, in company with a clergyman whom I had met at City Point, I repaired to the White House where, having ascertained at what hour the President would throw open his doors, we amused ourselves in the meantime by wandering about the public rooms; which, although tolerably spacious, are very plainly furnished and sadly in want of new carpets.

At one o'clock the door of his private room was thrown open, and all the people who had been waiting to see him, flocked in and arranged themselves on seats around the room. We found the President of the United States seated at his desk, in a plain room, which might have done for the office of a merchant or of a solicitor. According to American rule the ladies were first presented, and preferred their various requests, to most of which, generally asking for some unreasonable favour on behalf of a husband or a son, the President made answer, "Can't do it, madam; *can't* do it;" and, as the petitioner went on to urge her claim with all the fervour of female eloquence, added—"and you will not talk me into it."

With one of these cases I was rather struck. It was that of a widow lady who had one son already in the public service at Washington, and wanted to get a place for another. She stated her claims, enumerating the services of the family, the number of sons, brothers, and other relatives who had died fighting, or were still living to fight, for the republic. The expense of living at Washington where everything was, as she said, "three prices," was one of her arguments. She had already applied to the head of the department, whose answer was that he thought that she had already got her share. The President was at first disposed to be of the same opinion, but ended in making a memorandum of the case. It seemed so very curious to hear all these matters, which are done so differently with us, thus discussed in public.

Then there came a man who wanted to be allowed to go in some capacity or other to City Point, for which he had not obtained the sanction of the Commander-in-chief. "Sir," said the President, "if my own brother, or if General Washington himself, wanted to go to City Point, and General Grant didn't want to have him, he shouldn't go."

Next came a lad with a story of having been hired to bring some horses from New York, and of his employer having given him the slip and left him without funds in the streets of Washington.

"What do you want me to do?" asked the President.

"I want you to send me home."

"I have no fund which I can apply to such a purpose."

"I don't know what to do," whined the lad.

"I'll tell you what I would have done when I was a young fellow like you," replied Lincoln; "I would have worked my own way back."

Then came a man from the President's own state, with a design for a new bank note. "It's not," he explained, "like the landing of Columbus in America, or anything of that sort; no sir, it's something that everybody can understand." What it was I don't know, but the President pronounced it to be "very pretty." "Wall, I guess," said the designer, "the thing will have to stand over for a few days till we see—"

"Whether I get a new lease or not," said the President; finishing the sentence. At this last sally of Lincoln's everybody laughed, and the man sitting next to me observed that "the President was in great force today."

In the middle of the proceedings a friend came in to give him some favorable news concerning the approaching election, whereat Lincoln expressed his satisfaction in a frank and guileless manner which it did one good to see.

The next man had no favor to ask, he came, a bronzed and battered soldier in his faded uniform, simply to shake hands with the President before going home at the end of his three years' service. The President shook hands with him cordially enough, but he did not improve the occasion as Louis Napoleon would have done. He is not a master of the small graces, and had not any of those pretty phrases at hand which seemed so natural for the occasion. Pretty phrases are not the rule in America, and all he did was to ask what regiment he belonged to. In the meantime a young couple, who, as it seemed, had no other object than to add the President to the other sights of their honeymoon, had been accommodated by the master of ceremonies with chairs in a place where they could get a full view, had taken a good stare, and silently gone away.

When they had all left, my friend first introduced himself, and then, being thus duly qualified, introduced me. The President rose,—I do not flatter myself in honor of us; but to let us see that he did not want to be kept long talking. In so doing he displayed his immense height, and gaunt ungainly figure; which had not been conspicuous so long as he remained sitting. He shook hands, not with the vice-like grasp of which I had read—probably by this time he has learnt to husband his resources—but rather in a promiscuous manner, as when one shakes up a bottle. A few questions as to what we had seen in the camp, and a remark from the President that Grant was a "very determined little fellow," finished the audience.

—FERGUSON, *America during and after the War*

15. JOHN HAY LIVES WITH "THE TYCOON" IN THE WHITE HOUSE

Fresh from Brown University John Hay entered the law office of his uncle, Milton Hay, in Springfield, Illinois. Next door was the office of Lincoln and Herndon, and inevitably Lincoln came to know the young man. A mutual friend, John Nicolay, whom Lincoln had selected as his private secretary, suggested that Hay should go along as assistant private secretary, and Lincoln amiably agreed. For Hay it was the beginning of a distinguished career which led, in the end, to the Secretaryship of State.

While in the White House Hay kept a diary, and it is from this and from his letters to Nicolay that these vivacious extracts are taken.

November 13 [1861]. I wish to record what I consider a portent of evil to come. The President, Governor Seward, and I, went over to McClellan's house tonight. The servant at the door said the General was at the wedding of Col. Wheaton at General Buell's, and would soon return. We went in, and after we had waited about an hour, McC. came in and without paying any particular attention to the porter, who told him the President was waiting to see him, went up stairs, passing the door of the room where the President and Secretary of State were seated. They waited about half-an-hour, and sent once more a servant to tell the General they were there, and the answer coolly came that the General had gone to bed.

I merely record this unparalleled insolence of epaulettes without comment. It is the first indication I have yet seen of the threatened supremacy of the military authorities.

Coming home I spoke to the President about the matter but he seemed not to have noticed it specially, saying it was better at this time not to be making points of etiquette & personal dignity.

July 18, 1863. Today we spent 6 hours deciding on Court Martials, the President, Judge Holt, & I. I was amused at the eagerness with which the President caught at any fact which would justify him in saving the life of a condemned soldier. He was only merciless in cases where meanness or cruelty were shown.

Cases of cowardice he was specially averse to punishing with death. He said it would frighten the poor devils too terribly, to shoot them. On the case of a soldier who had once deserted & reinlisted he indorsed, "Let him fight instead of shooting him."

One fellow who had deserted & escaped after conviction into Mexico, he sentenced, saying, "We will condemn him as they used to sell hogs in Indiana, as they run."

To J. G. Nicolay.

EXECUTIVE MANSION, WASHINGTON, August 7, 1863

This town is as dismal now as a defaced tombstone. Everybody has gone, I am getting apathetic & write blackguardly articles for the *Chronicle* from which West extracts the dirt and fun & publishes the dreary remains. The Tycoon is in fine whack, I have rarely seen him more serene & busy. He is managing this war, the draft, foreign relations, and planning a reconstruction of the Union, all at once. I never knew with what tyrannous authority he rules the Cabinet, till now. The most important things he decides & there is no cavil. I am growing more and more firmly convinced that the good of the country absolutely demands that he should be kept where he is till this thing is over. There is no man in the country, so wise, so gentle and so firm. I believe the hand of God placed him where he is.

29 September, 1863. . . . Today came to the Executive Mansion an assembly of cold-water men & cold-water women to make a temperance speech at the Tycoon & receive a response. They filed into the East Room looking blue & thin in the keen autumnal air; Cooper, my coachman, who was about half tight, gazing at them with an air of complacent contempt and mild wonder. Three blue-skinned damsels did Love, Purity, & Fidelity in Red, White & Blue gowns. A few invalid soldiers stumped along in the dismal procession. They made a long speech at the Tycoon in which they called Intemperance the cause of our defeats. He could not see it, as the rebels drink more & worse whisky than we do. They filed off drearily to a collation of cold water & green apples, & then home to mulligrubs.

June 5, 1864. For a day or two the House has been full of patriots on the way to Baltimore who wish to pay their respects & engrave on the expectant mind of the Tycoon their images, in view of future contingencies. Among the genuine delegations have come some of the bogus & the irregular ones. Cuthbert Bullitt is here with Louisiana in his trousers pocket. He has passed thro' New York & has gotten considerably stampeded by the talk of the trading pettifoggers of politics there. He feels uneasy in his seat.

The South Carolina delegation came in yesterday. The Prest says "Let them in." "They are a swindle," I said. "They won't swindle me," quoth the Tycoon. They filed in: a few sutlers, cotton-dealers, and Negroes, presented a petition & retired.

Florida sends two delegations: neither will get in. Each attacks the other as unprincipled tricksters.

> —DENNETT, ed., *Lincoln and the Civil War in the Diaries and Letters of John Hay*

16. "MY PARAMOUNT OBJECT IS TO SAVE THE UNION"

Lincoln, and his government, were troubled from the beginning by sharp differences of opinion about the proper objectives of the war. Congress went on record, at the very beginning, that the purpose of the war was to save the Union, and not to interfere with the domestic institutions of any state. This, too, was Lincoln's position. But the Radicals were not content. They wanted—understandably enough—to end slavery, and they insisted that this object should be publicly proclaimed, regardless of consequences.

Horace Greeley, the powerful editor of the New York Tribune, *was one of the spokesmen for this group. Perhaps the greatest editor in the country, he was erratic and impulsive, and his conduct during the war often troublesome to the administration. What Greeley and his sympathizers overlooked was the effect that an abolitionist program would have on the border states.*

Greeley called this letter, which he published in the Tribune, *"The Prayer of Twenty Millions." It was certainly not that. Lincoln's reply, justifying his own temperate program, is one of the most notable of his pronouncements.*

A. "THE PRAYER OF TWENTY MILLIONS"

August 19, 1862

Dear Sir: . . . We complain that the Union cause has suffered, and is now suffering immensely, from mistaken deference to rebel Slavery. Had you, sir, in your Inaugural Address, unmistakably given notice that, in case the rebellion already commenced, were persisted in, and your efforts to preserve the Union and enforce the laws should be resisted by armed force, *you would recognize no loyal person as rightfully held in Slavery by a traitor,* we believe the rebellion would therein have received a staggering if not fatal blow. . . .

On the face of this wide earth, Mr. President, there is not one disinterested, determined, intelligent champion of the Union cause who does not feel that all attempts to put down the rebellion and at the same time uphold its inciting cause are preposterous and futile—that the rebellion, if crushed out to-morrow, would be renewed within a year if Slavery were left in full vigor—that army officers who remain to this day devoted to Slavery can at best be but half-way loyal to the Union—and that every hour of deference to Slavery is an hour of added and deepened peril to the Union. I appeal to the testimony of your ambassadors in Europe. It is freely at your service, not at mine. Ask them to tell you candidly whether the seeming subserviency of your policy to the slaveholding, slavery-upholding interest, is not the perplexity, the despair of statesmen of all parties, and be admonished by the general answer!

I close as I began with the statement that what an immense majority of the loyal millions of your countrymen require of you is a frank, declared, unqualified, ungrudging execution of the laws of the land, more especially of the Confiscation Act. That act gives freedom to the slaves of rebels coming within our lines, or whom those lines may at any time inclose—we ask you to render it due obedience by publicly requiring all your subordinates to recognize and obey it. The rebels are everywhere using the late anti-Negro riots in the North, as they have long used your officers' treatment of Negroes in the South, to convince the slaves that they have nothing to hope from a Union success—that we mean in that case to sell them into a bitter bondage to defray the cost of the war. Let them impress this as a truth on the great mass of their ignorant and credulous bondmen, and the Union will never be restored—never. We cannot conquer ten millions of people united in solid phalanx against us, powerfully aided by Northern sympathizers and European allies. We must have scouts, guides, spies, cooks, teamsters, diggers, and choppers from the blacks of the South, whether we allow them to fight for us or not, or we shall be baffled and repelled. As one of the millions who would gladly have avoided this struggle at any sacrifice but that of principle and honor, but who now feel that the triumph of the Union is indispensable not only to the existence of our country but to the well-being of mankind, I entreat you to render a hearty and unequivocal obedience to the law of the land.

Yours,

HORACE GREELEY.

—MOORE, ed., *The Rebellion Record*

B. "I Would Save the Union"

Executive Mansion, Washington, August 22, 1862

Hon. Horace Greeley:

DEAR SIR: I have just read yours of the nineteenth, addressed to myself through the New-York *Tribune*. If there be in it any statements or assumptions of fact which I may know to be erroneous, I do not now and here controvert them. If there be in it any inferences which I may believe to be falsely drawn, I do not now and here argue against them. If there be perceptible in it an impatient and dictatorial tone, I waive it in deference to an old friend, whose heart I have always supposed to be right.

As to the policy I "seem to be pursuing," as you say, I have not meant to leave any one in doubt.

I would save the Union. I would save it the shortest way under the Constitution. The sooner the National authority can be restored, the nearer the Union will be "the Union as it was." If there be those who would not save the Union unless they could at the same time *save* Slavery, I do not agree with them. If there be those who would not save the Union unless they could at the same time *destroy* Slavery, I do not agree with them. My paramount object in this struggle *is* to save the Union, and is *not* either to save or destroy Slavery. If I could save the Union without freeing *any* slave, I would do it; and if I could save it by freeing *all* the slaves, I would do it; and if I could do it by freeing some and leaving others alone, I would also do that. What I do about Slavery and the colored race, I do because I believe it helps to save this Union; and what I forbear, I forbear because I do *not* believe it would help to save the Union. I shall do *less* whenever I shall believe what I am doing hurts the cause, and I shall do *more* whenever I shall believe doing more will help the cause. I shall try to correct errors when shown to be errors; and I shall adopt new views so fast as they shall appear to be true views. I have here stated my purpose according to my view of *official* duty, and I intend no modification of my oft-expressed *personal* wish that all men, everywhere, could be free.

Yours,

A. LINCOLN.

—MOORE, ed., *The Rebellion Record*

17. "WE SHALL NOBLY SAVE OR MEANLY LOSE THE LAST, BEST HOPE OF EARTH"

Lincoln's own plan for dealing with the slave problem was compensated emancipation. Again and again he presented this to the country, to the border states, to delegations who came to plead with him. There was never much chance that it would have worked, even had Congress adopted it; even when the Confederacy was palpably collapsing, the border states refused to accept the plan.

This eloquent appeal for compensated emancipation was addressed to Congress in the annual message of December 1, 1862.

THIS plan is recommended as a means, not in exclusion of, but additional to, all others for restoring and preserving the national authority throughout the Union. The subject is presented exclusively in its economical aspect. The plan would, I am confident, secure peace more speedily and maintain it more permanently than can be done by force alone, while all it would cost, considering amounts and manner of payment and times of payment, would be easier paid than will be the additional cost of the war if we rely solely upon force. It is much, very much, that it would cost no blood at all.

The plan is proposed as permanent constitutional law. It cannot become such without the concurrence of, first, two thirds of Congress, and afterwards three fourths of the States. The requisite three fourths of the States will necessarily include seven of the slave States. Their concurrence, if obtained, will give assurance of their severally adopting emancipation at no very distant day upon the new constitutional terms. This assurance would end the struggle now and save the Union forever. . . .

Fellow-citizens, *we* can not escape history. We of this Congress and this administration will be remembered in spite of ourselves. No personal significance or insignificance can spare one or another of us. The fiery trial through which we pass will light us down in honor or dishonor to the latest generation. We *say* we are for the Union. The world will not forget that we say this. We know how to save the Union. The world knows we do know how to save it. We, even *we here*, hold the power and bear the responsibility. In *giving* freedom to the *slave* we *assure* freedom to the *free*—honorable alike in what we give and what we preserve. We shall nobly save or meanly lose the last, best hope of earth. Other means may succeed; this could not fail. The way is plain, peaceful, generous, just—a way which if followed the world will forever applaud and God must forever bless.

—LINCOLN, Annual Message of December 1, 1862

18. LINCOLN BECOMES THE GREAT EMANCIPATOR

Lincoln's Cabinet had been divided, from the beginning, on the advisability of pronouncing officially in favor of emancipation. Yet public opinion in the North was becoming increasingly insistent on some declaration of policy, and the danger of foreign intervention furnished a persuasive argument for rallying English support to the North by making the war openly one for freedom. It did not, however, seem wise to announce an emancipation policy as long as Union arms were unsuccessful; that, as Seward shrewdly remarked, would be like "our last shriek, on the retreat." Lincoln then resolved to issue the proclamation as soon as Union arms had won a victory. Antietam appeared to be such a victory, and on September 22, 1862, Lincoln presented his Cabinet with his decision. The preliminary proclamation was followed by a formal proclamation of January 1, 1863.

We give here Secretary Chase's account of the famous Cabinet meeting, and the official proclamation.

A. SECRETARY CHASE RECALLS A FAMOUS CABINET MEETING

September 22, 1862.—To department about nine. State Department messenger came with notices to heads of departments to meet at twelve. Received sundry callers. Went to the White House. All the members of the cabinet were in attendance. There was some general talk, and the President mentioned that Artemus Ward had sent him his book. Proposed to read a chapter which he thought very funny. Read it and seemed to enjoy it very much; the heads also (except Stanton). The chapter was "High-Handed Outrage at Utica."

The President then took a graver tone and said: "Gentlemen, I have, as you are aware, thought a great deal about the relation of this war to slavery, and you all remember that, several weeks ago, I read to you an order I had prepared upon the subject, which, on account of objections made by some of you, was not issued. Ever since then my mind has been much occupied with this subject, and I have thought all along that the time for acting on it might probably come. I think the time has come now. I wish it was a better time. I wish that we were in a better condition. The action of the army against the rebels has not been quite what I should have liked best. But they have been driven out of Maryland, and Pennsylvania is no longer in danger of invasion. When the rebel army was at Frederick I determined, as soon as it should be driven out of Maryland, to issue a proclamation of emancipation such as I thought most likely to be useful. I said nothing to any one, but I made a promise to myself and (hesitating a little) to my Maker. The rebel army is now driven out, and I am going to fulfill that promise. I have got you together to hear what I have written down. I do not wish your advice about the main matter, for that I have determined for myself. This I say without intending anything but respect for any one of you. But I already know the views of each on this question. They have been heretofore expressed, and I have considered them as thoroughly and carefully as I can. What I have written is that which my reflections have determined me to say. If there is anything in the expressions I use or in any minor matter which any one of you thinks had best be changed, I shall be glad to receive your suggestions. One other observation I will make. I know very well that many others might, in this matter as in others, do better than I can; and if I was satisfied that the public confidence was more fully possessed by any one of them than by me, and knew of any constitutional way in which he could be put in my place, he should have it. I would gladly yield it to him. But though I believe that I have not so much of the confidence of the people as I had some time since, I do not know that, all things considered, any other person has more; and however this may be, there is no way in which I can have any other man put where I am. I am here. I must do the best I can and bear the responsibility of taking the course which I feel I ought to take."

The President then proceeded to read his Emancipation Proclamation, making remarks on the several parts as he went on, and showing that he had fully considered the subject in all the lights under which it had been presented to him.

After he had closed, Governor Seward said: "The general question having been decided, nothing can be said further about that. Would it not, however, make the proclamation more clear and decided to leave out all reference to the act being sustained during the incumbency of the present President;

and not merely say that the Government 'recognizes' but that it will maintain the freedom it proclaims?"

I followed, saying: "What you have said, Mr. President, fully satisfies me that you have given to every proposition which has been made a kind and candid consideration. And you have now expressed the conclusion to which you have arrived clearly and distinctly. This it was your right and, under your oath of office, your duty to do. The proclamation does not, indeed, mark out the course I would myself prefer; but I am ready to take it just as it is written and to stand by it with all my heart. I think, however, the suggestions of Governor Seward very judicious, and shall be glad to have them adopted."

The President then asked us severally our opinions as to the modifications proposed, saying that he did not care much about the phrases he had used. Every one favored the modification, and it was adopted. Governor Seward then proposed that in the passage relating to colonization some language should be introduced to show that the colonization proposed was to be only with the consent of the colonists and the consent of the states in which the colonies might be attempted. This, too, was agreed to; and no other modification was proposed. Mr. Blair then said that the question having been decided, he would make no objection to issuing the proclamation; but he would ask to have his paper, presented some days since, against the policy, filed with the proclamation. The President consented to this readily. And then Mr. Blair went on to say that he was afraid of the influence of the proclamation on the border states and on the army and stated at some length the grounds of his apprehensions. He disclaimed most expressly, however, all objections to emancipation *per se*, saying he had always been personally in favor of it—always ready for immediate emancipation in the midst of slave states, rather than submit to the perpetuation of the system.

—"Diary of S. P. Chase"

B. "Forever Free"

Whereas on the 22d day of September, A.D. 1862, a proclamation was issued by the President of the United States, containing, among other things, the following, to wit:

"That on the 1st day of January, A.D. 1863, all persons held as slaves within any state or designated part of a state the people whereof shall then be in rebellion against the United States shall be then, thenceforward, and forever free; and the executive government of the United States, including the military and naval authority thereof, will recognize and maintain the freedom of such persons and will do no act or acts to repress such persons, or any of them, in any efforts they may make for their actual freedom.

"That the executive will on the 1st day of January aforesaid, by proclamation, designate the states and parts of states, if any, in which the people thereof, respectively, shall then be in rebellion against the United States; and the fact that any state or the people thereof shall on that day be in good faith represented in the Congress of the United States by members chosen thereto at elections wherein a majority of the qualified voters of such states shall have participated shall, in the absence of strong countervailing testimony, be deemed conclusive evidence that such state and the people thereof are not then in rebellion against the United States."

Now, therefore, I, Abraham Lincoln, . . . do, on this 1st day of January, A.D. 1863, . . . order and designate . . . the states and parts of states wherein the people thereof, respectively, are this day in rebellion against the United States. . . .

And by virtue of the power and for the purpose aforesaid, I do order and declare that all persons held as slaves within said designated states and parts of states are, and henceforward shall be, free; and that the executive government of the United States, including the military and naval authorities thereof, will recognize and maintain the freedom of said persons.

And I hereby enjoin upon the people so declared to be free to abstain from all violence, unless in necessary self-defense; and I recommend to them that, in all cases when allowed, they labor faithfully for reasonable wages.

And I further declare and make known that such persons of suitable condition will be received into the armed service of the United States to garrison forts, positions, stations, and other places, and to man vessels of all sorts in said service.

And upon this act, sincerely believed to be an act of justice, warranted by the Constitution upon military necessity, I invoke the considerate judgment of mankind and the gracious favor of Almighty God.

—Lincoln, "The Emancipation Proclamation"

19. LINCOLN ARRANGES FOR THE ADMISSION OF NEVADA TO THE UNION

"Lincoln," as Dana here tells us, "was a supreme politician." Yet Dana fails to give the full flavor of this particular story. Lincoln was eager to have Nevada in the Union in order to obtain its vote for the Thirteenth Amendment, to be sure. But he was not unaware of the value of Nevada's vote in the Republican Convention, or in the electoral college. Nevada got in in time to cast its vote for Lincoln. Dana we have already met, busying himself with military matters at Washington.

LINCOLN was a supreme politician. He understood politics because he understood human nature. I had an illustration of this in the spring of 1864. The administration had decided that the Constitution of the United States should be amended so that slavery should be prohibited. This was not only a change in our national policy, it was also a most important military measure. It was intended not merely as a means of abolishing slavery forever, but as a means of affecting the judgment and the feelings and the anticipations of those in rebellion. It was believed that such an amendment to the Constitution would be equivalent to new armies in the field, that it would be worth at least a million men, that it would be an intellectual army that would tend to paralyze the enemy and break the continuity of his ideas.

In order thus to amend the Constitution, it was necessary first to have the proposed amendment approved by three fourths of the States. When that question came to be considered, the issue was seen to be so close that one State more was necessary. The State of Nevada was organized and admitted into the Union to answer that purpose. I have sometimes heard people complain of Nevada as superfluous and petty, not big enough to be a State; but when I hear that complaint, I always hear Abraham Lincoln saying, "It is easier to admit Nevada than to raise another million of soldiers."

In March, 1864, the question of allowing Nevada to form a State government finally came up in the House of Representatives. There was strong opposition to it. For a long time beforehand the question had been canvassed anxiously. At last, late one afternoon, the President came into my office, in the third story of the War Department. He used to come there sometimes rather than send for me, because he was fond of walking and liked to get away from the crowds in the White House. He came in and shut the door.

"Dana," he said, "I am very anxious about this vote. It has got to be taken next week. The time is very short. It is going to be a great deal closer than I wish it was."

"There are plenty of Democrats who will vote for it," I replied. "There is James E. English, of Connecticut; I think he is sure, isn't he?"

"Oh, yes; he is sure on the merits of the question."

"Then," said I, "there's 'Sunset' Cox, of Ohio. How is he?"

"He is sure and fearless. But there are some others that I am not clear about. There are three that you can deal with better than anybody else, perhaps, as you know them all. I wish you would send for them."

He told me who they were; it isn't necessary to repeat the names here. One man was from New Jersey and two from New York.

"What will they likely to want?" I asked.

"I don't know," said the President; "I don't know. It makes no difference, though, what they want. Here is the alternative; that we carry this vote, or be compelled to raise another million, and I don't know how many more, men, and fight no one knows how long. It is a question of three votes or new armies."

"Well, sir," said I, "what shall I say to these gentlemen?"

"I don't know," said he; "but whatever promise you make to them I will perform."

I sent for the men and saw them one by one. I found that they were afraid of their party. They said that some fellows in the party would be down on them. Two of them wanted internal revenue collector's appointments. "You shall have it," I said. Another one wanted a very important appointment about the custom house of New York. I knew the man well whom he wanted to have appointed. He was a Republican, though the congressman was a Democrat. I had served with him in the Republican county committee of New York. The office was worth perhaps twenty thousand dollars a year.

When the congressman stated the case, I asked him, "Do you want that?"

"Yes," said he.

"Well," I answered, "you shall have it."

"I understand, of course," said he, "that you are not saying this on your own authority?"

"Oh, no," said I; "I am saying it on the authority of the President."

Well, these men voted that Nevada be allowed to form a State government, and thus they helped secure the vote which was required. The next October the President signed the proclamation admitting the State. In the February following Nevada was one of the States which ratified the Thirteenth Amendment, by which slavery was abolished by constitutional prohibition in all of the United States. I have always felt that this little piece of side politics was one of the most judicious, humane, and wise uses of executive authority that I have ever assisted in or witnessed.

—DANA, *Recollections of the Civil War*

20. LINCOLN AND HAY FOLLOW THE ELECTION RETURNS

It is almost inconceivable to us, now, that Lincoln should not have been re-elected in 1864. Yet the prospects, in the summer of that year, were dim. Grant was getting nowhere in the Wilderness or at Petersburg; Sherman did not take Atlanta until September and then started on what many critics were pleased to call a "retreat." Frémont was nominated by a group of disgruntled abolitionists and War Democrats, and on August 29 the Democrats nominated McClellan on a platform declaring that the war was a failure. As late as August 18 Horace Greeley wrote that Lincoln's defeat was inevitable and called for another candidate to save the Union. And on August 23 Lincoln presented his Cabinet with a folded sheet of paper, and asked them to sign on the blank side; the other side contained this statement:

"This morning as for some days past, it seems exceedingly probable that this administration will not be re-elected. Then it will be my duty to so co-operate with the President-elect as to save the Union between the election and the inauguration; as he will have secured his election on such ground that he cannot possibly save it afterward."

Yet in the end the tide turned. Atlanta fell and Sherman marched triumphantly to the sea; Farragut won at Mobile Bay; Grant whittled away Lee's army in front of Petersburg. The election returns of 1864 gave Lincoln 2,216,067, McClellan 1,808,725 votes, and Lincoln's electoral vote was 212, McClellan's 21.

Once more it is Hay who tells the story of Lincoln and the election.

Nov. 8, 1864. The house has been still and almost deserted today. Everybody in Washington, not at home voting, seems ashamed of it and stays away from the President.

I was talking with him to-day. He said, "It is a little singular that I, who am not a vindictive man, should have always been before the people for election in canvasses marked for their bitterness; always but once; when I came to Congress it was a quiet time. But always besides that the contests in which I have been prominent have been marked with great rancor."

At noon Butler sent a despatch simply saying, "The quietest city ever seen."

Butler was sent to New York by Stanton. The President had nothing to do with it. Thurlow Weed was nervous about his coming, thought it would harm us and even as late as Sunday wrote saying that Butler's presence was on the whole injurious, in spite of his admirable General Order.

Hoffman sent a very cheering despatch giving a rose-coloured estimate of the forenoon's voting in Baltimore. "I shall be glad if that holds," said the President, "because I had rather feared that in the increased vote over that on the Constitution, the increase would rather be against us."

During the afternoon few despatches were received.

At night, at 7 o'clock we started over to the War Department to spend the evening. Just as we started we received the first gun from Indianapolis, showing a majority of 8,000 there, a gain of 1,500 over Morton's vote. The vote itself seemed an enormous one for a town of that size and can only be accounted for by considering the great influx since the war of voting men from the country into the State centres where a great deal of Army business is done. There was less significance in this vote on account of the October victory which had disheartened the enemy and destroyed their incentive to work.

The night was rainy, steamy and dark. We splashed through the grounds to the side door of the War Department where a soaked and smoking sentinel was standing in his own vapor with his huddled-up frame covered with a rubber cloak. Inside a half-dozen idle orderlies, up-stairs the clerks of the telegraph. As the President entered they handed him a despatch from Forney claiming ten thousand Union majority in Philadelphia. "Forney is a little excitable." Another comes from Felton, Baltimore giving us "15,000 in the city, 5,000 in the state. All Hail, Free Maryland." That is superb. A message from Rice to Fox, followed instantly by one from Sumner to Lincoln, claiming Boston by 5,000, and Rice's & Hooper's elections by majorities of 4,000 apiece. A magnificent advance on the chilly dozens of 1862.

Eckert came in shaking the rain from his cloak, with trousers very disreputably muddy. We sternly demanded an explanation. He had slipped, he said, & tumbled prone, crossing the street. He had done it watching a fellow-being ahead and chuckling at his uncertain footing.

Which reminded the Tycoon, of course. The President said, "For such an awkward fellow, I am pretty sure-footed. It used to take a pretty dextrous man to throw me. I remember, the evening of the day in 1858, that decided the contest for the Senate between Mr Douglas and myself, was something like this, dark, rainy and gloomy. I had been reading the returns, and had ascertained that we had lost the Legislature and started to go home. The path had been worn hog-back & was slippery. My foot slipped from under me, knocking the other one out of the way, but I recovered myself & lit square, and I said to myself, 'It's a slip and not a fall.' "

The President sent over the first fruits to Mrs. Lincoln. He said, "She is more anxious than I."

We went into the Secretary's room. Mr. Welles and Fox soon came in. They were especially happy over the election of Rice, regarding it as a great triumph for the Navy Department. Says Fox, "There are two fellows that have been especially malignant to us, and retribution has come upon them both. Hale and Winter Davis."

"You have more of that feeling of personal resentment than I," said Lincoln. "Perhaps I may have too little of it, but I never thought it paid. A man has not time to spend half his life in quarrels. If any man ceases to attack me, I never remember the past against him. It has seemed to me recently that Winter Davis was growing more sensible to his own true interests and has ceased wasting his time by attacking me. I hope for his own good he has. He has been very malicious against me but has only injured himself by it. His conduct has been very strange to me. I came here, his friend, wishing to continue so. I had heard nothing but good of him; he was the cousin of my intimate friend Judge Davis. But he had scarcely been elected when I began to learn of his attacking me on all possible occasions. It is very much the same with Hickman. I was much disappointed that he had failed to be my friend. But my greatest disappointment of all has been with Grimes. Before I came here, I certainly expected to rely upon Grimes more than any other one man in the Senate. I like him very much. He is a great strong fellow. He is a valuable friend, a dangerous enemy. He carries too many guns not to be respected in any point of view. But he got wrong against me, I do not clearly know how, and has always been cool and almost hostile to me. I am glad he has always been the friend of the Navy and generally of the Administration."

Despatches kept coming in all the evening showing a splendid triumph in Indiana, showing steady, small gains all over Pennsylvania, enough to give a fair majority this time on the home vote. Guesses from New York and Albany which boiled down to about the estimated majority against us in the city, 35,000, and left the result in the State still doubtful.

A despatch from Butler was picked up & sent by Sanford, saying that the City had gone 35,000 McC. & the State 40,000. This looked impossible. The State had been carefully canvassed & such a result was impossible except in view of some monstrous and undreamed of frauds. After a while another came from Sanford correcting former one & giving us the 40,000 in the State.

Sanford's despatches all the evening continued most jubilant: especially when he announced that most startling majority of 80,000 in Massachusetts.

General Eaton came in and waited for news with us. I had not before known that he was with us. His denunciations of Seymour were especially hearty and vigorous.

Towards midnight we had supper, provided by Eckert. The President went awkwardly and hospitably to work shoveling out the fried oysters. He was most agreeable and genial all the evening in fact. Fox was abusing the coffee for being so hot—saying quaintly, it kept hot all the way down to the bottom of the cup as a piece of ice staid cold till you finished eating it.

We got later in the evening a scattering despatch from the West, giving us Michigan, one from Fox promising Missouri certainly, but a loss in the first district from that miserable split of Knox & Johnson, one promising Delaware, and one, too good for ready credence, saying Raymond & Dodge & Darling had been elected in New York City.

Capt. Thomas came up with a band about half-past two, and made some music and a small hifalute.

The President answered from the window with rather unusual dignity and effect & we came home.

W. H. L[amon] came to my room to talk over the Chief Justiceship; he goes in for Stanton & thinks, as I am inclined to think, that the President cannot afford to place an enemy in a position so momentous for good or evil.

He took a glass of whiskey and then, refusing my offer of a bed, went out &, rolling himself up in his cloak, lay down at the President's door; passing the night in that attitude of. touching and dumb fidelity, with a small arsenal of pistols and bowie knives around him. In the morning he went away leaving my blankets at my door, before I or the President were awake.

—Dennett, ed., *Lincoln and the Civil War in the Diaries and Letters of John Hay*

21. LINCOLN REPLIES TO A SERENADE

On November 10, two days after the election, when the returns were in, Lincoln was serenaded at the White House by some enthusiastic countrymen. He took the occasion to make one of the more thoughtful of his short addresses, one which pointed the significance of the election as a commentary on democracy in wartime.

IT has long been a grave question whether any government, not too strong for the liberties of its people, can be strong enough to maintain its existence in great emergencies. On this point the present rebellion brought our republic to a severe test, and a presidential election occurring in regular course during the rebellion, added not a little to the strain.

If the loyal people united were put to the utmost of their strength by the rebellion, must they not fail when divided and partially paralyzed by a political war among themselves? But the election was a necessity. We cannot have free government without elections; and if the rebellion could force us to forego or postpone a national election, it might fairly claim to have already conquered and ruined us. The strife of the election is but human nature practically applied to the facts of the case. What has occurred in this case must ever recur in similar cases. Human nature will not change. In any future great national trial, compared with the men of this, we shall have as weak and as strong, as silly and as wise, as bad and as good. Let us, therefore, study the incidents of this as philosophy to learn wisdom from, and none of them as wrongs to be revenged. But the election, along with its incidental and undesirable strife, has done good too. It has demonstrated that a people's government can sustain a national election in the midst of a great civil war. Until now, it has not been known to the world that this was a possibility. It shows that, even among candidates of the same party, he who is most devoted to the Union and most opposed to treason can receive most of the people's votes. It shows, also, to the extent yet known, that we have more men now than we had when the war began. Gold is good in its place, but living, brave, patriotic men are better than gold.

But the rebellion continues, and now that the election is over, may not all having a common interest reunite in a common effort to save our common country? For my own part, I have striven and shall strive to avoid placing any obstacle in the way. So long as I have been here I have not willingly planted a thorn in any man's bosom. While I am deeply sensible to the high compliment of a reëlection, and duly grateful, as I trust, to almighty God for having directed my countrymen to a right conclusion, as I think, for their own good, it adds nothing to my satisfaction that any other man may be disappointed or pained by the result.

May I ask those who have not differed with me to join with me in this same spirit toward those who have? And now let me close by asking three hearty cheers for our brave soldiers and seamen and their gallant and skilful commanders.

—*Complete Works of Abraham Lincoln*

22. LINCOLN VISITS THE COLORED SOLDIERS AT CITY POINT

Lincoln got to the army as often as possible, and sometimes to the embarrassment of officers and soldiers alike; Justice Oliver Wendell Holmes once recalled the occasion when he had cried out to the tall, absent-minded President, "Get down, you damn fool," and John Hay tells us of the time when Lincoln waited patiently for McClellan, who had gone up to bed and refused to see him. Probably no visit that Lincoln ever paid to his soldiers was more gratifying than this one that General Porter describes.

ON Tuesday, June 21 [1864], a white river-steamer arrived at the wharf, bringing President Lincoln, who had embraced this opportunity to visit for the first time the armies under General Grant's immediate command. As the boat neared the shore, the general and several of us who were with him at the time walked down to the wharf, in order that the general-in-chief might meet his distinguished visitor and extend a greeting to him as soon as the boat made the landing. As our party stepped aboard, the President came down from the upper deck, where he had been standing, to the after-gangway, and reaching out his long, angular arm, he wrung General Grant's hand vigorously, and held it in his for some time, while he uttered in rapid words his congratulations and expressions of appreciation of the great task which had been accomplished since he and the general had parted in Washington.

The group then went into the after-cabin. General Grant said: "I hope you are very well, Mr. President."

"Yes, I am in very good health," Mr. Lincoln replied; "but I don't feel very comfortable after my trip last night on the bay. It was rough, and I was considerably shaken up. My stomach has not yet entirely recovered from the effects."

An officer of the party now saw that an opportunity had arisen to make this scene the supreme moment of his life, in giving him a chance to soothe the digestive organs of the Chief Magistrate of the nation. He said: "Try a glass of champagne, Mr. President. That is always a certain cure for sea-sickness."

Mr. Lincoln looked at him for a moment, his face lighting up with a smile, and then remarked: "No, my friend; I have seen too many fellows seasick ashore from drinking that very stuff." This was a knockdown for the officer, and in the laugh at his expense Mr. Lincoln and the general both both joined heartily.

General Grant now said: "I know it would be a great satisfaction for the troops to have an opportunity of seeing you, Mr. President; and I am sure your presence among them would have a very gratifying effect. I can furnish you a good horse, and will be most happy to escort you to points of interest along the line."

Mr. Lincoln replied: "Why, yes; I had fully intended to go out and take a look at the brave fellows who have fought their way down to Petersburg in this wonderful campaign, and I am ready to start at any time."

General Grant presented to Mr. Lincoln the officers of the staff who were present, and he had for each one a cordial greeting and a pleasant word. There was a kindliness in his tone and a hearty manner of expression which went far to captivate all who met him. The President soon stepped ashore, and after sitting awhile at headquarters mounted the large bay horse "Cincinnati," while the general rode with him on "Jeff Davis." Three of us of the staff accompanied them, and the scenes encountered in visiting Butler's and Meade's commands were most interesting. Mr. Lincoln wore a very high black silk hat and black trousers and frock-coat. Like most men who had been brought up in the West, he had good command of a horse, but it must be acknowledged that in appearance he was not a very dashing rider. On this occasion, by the time he had reached the troops he was completely covered with dust, and the black color of his clothes had changed to Confederate gray. As he had no straps, his trousers gradually worked up above his ankles, and gave him the appearance of a country farmer riding into town wearing his Sunday clothes. A citizen on horseback is always an odd sight in the midst of a uniformed army, and the picture presented by the President bordered upon the grotesque.

However, the troops were so lost in admiration of the man that the humorous aspect did not seem to strike them. The soldiers rapidly passed the word along the line that "Uncle Abe" had joined them, and cheers broke forth from all the commands, and enthusiastic shouts and even words of familiar greeting met him on all sides.

After a while General Grant said: "Mr. President, let us ride on and see the colored troops, who behaved so handsomely in Smith's attack on the works in front of Petersburg last week."

"Oh, yes," replied Mr. Lincoln; "I want to take a look at those boys. I read with the greatest delight the account given in Mr. Dana's despatch to the Secretary of War of how gallantly they behaved. He said they took six out of the sixteen guns captured that day. I was opposed on nearly every side when I first favored the raising of colored regiments; but they have proved their efficiency, and I am glad they have kept pace with the white troops in the recent assaults. When we wanted every able-bodied man who could be spared to go to the front, and my opposers kept objecting to the Negroes, I used to tell them that at such times it was just as well to be a little color-blind. I think, general, we can say of the black boys what a country fellow who was an old-time abolitionist in Illinois said when he went to a theater in Chicago and saw Forrest playing *Othello*. He was not very well up in Shakspere, and didn't know that the tragedian was a white man who had blacked up for the purpose. After the play was over the folks who had invited him to go to the show wanted to know what he thought of the actors, and he said: 'Wall, layin' aside all sectional prejudices and any partiality I may have for the race, derned ef I don't think the nigger held his own with any on 'em.' " The Western dialect employed in this story was perfect.

The camp of the colored troops of the Eighteenth Corps was soon reached, and a scene now occurred which defies description. They beheld for the first time the liberator of their race—the man who by a stroke of his pen had struck the shackles from the limbs of their fellow-bondmen and proclaimed liberty to the enslaved. Always impressionable, the enthusiasm of the blacks now knew no limits. They cheered, laughed, cried, sang hymns of praise, and shouted in their Negro dialect, "God bress Massa Linkum!" "De Lord save Fader Abraham!" "De day ob jubilee am come, shuah." They crowded about him and fondled his horse; some of them kissed his hands, while others ran off crying in triumph to their comrades that they had touched his clothes. The President rode with bared head; the tears had started to his eyes, and his voice was so broken by emotion that he could scarcely articulate the words of thanks and congratulation which he tried to speak to the humble and devoted men through whose ranks he rode. The scene was affecting in the extreme, and no one could have witnessed it unmoved.

—PORTER, *Campaigning with Grant*

23. "WITH MALICE TOWARD NONE"

Comment on Lincoln's noble second Inaugural Address is as superfluous as comment on his Gettysburg Address. It is, however, relevant to remark that the magnanimous policy which he here suggested for reconstruction was repudiated by Congress during his lifetime and after his death, and that this repudiation embittered sectional relations for half a century.

FELLOW countrymen: At this second appearing to take the oath of the presidential office there is less occasion for an extended address than there was at the first. Then a statement somewhat in detail of a course to be pursued seemed fitting and proper. Now, at the expiration of four years, during which public declarations have been constantly called forth on every point and phase of the great contest which still absorbs the attention and engrosses the energies of the nation, little that is new could be presented. The progress of our arms, upon which all else chiefly depends, is as well known to the public as to myself, and it is, I trust, reasonably satisfactory and encouraging to all. With high hope for the future, no prediction in regard to it is ventured.

On the occasion corresponding to this four years ago all thoughts were anxiously directed to an impending civil war. All dreaded it, all sought to avert it. While the inaugural address was being delivered from this place, devoted altogether to *saving* the Union without war, insurgent agents were in the city seeking to *destroy* it without war—seeking to dissolve the Union and divide effects by negotiation. Both parties deprecated war, but one of them would *make* war rather than let the nation survive, and the other would *accept* war rather than let it perish, and the war came.

One eighth of the whole population was colored slaves, not distributed generally over the Union, but localized in the southern part of it. These slaves constituted a peculiar and powerful interest. All knew that this interest was somehow the cause of the war. To strengthen, perpetuate, and extend this interest was the object for which the insurgents would rend the Union even by war, while the government claimed no right to do more than to restrict the territorial enlargement of it. Neither party expected for the war the magnitude or the duration which it has already attained. Neither anticipated that the *cause* of the conflict might cease with or even before the conflict itself should cease. Each looked for an easier triumph and a result less fundamental and astounding. Both read the same Bible and pray to the same God, and each invokes His aid against the other. It may seem strange that any men should dare to ask a just God's assistance in wringing their bread from the sweat of other men's faces, but let us judge not, that we be not judged. The prayers of both could not be answered. That of neither has been answered fully. The Almighty has His own purposes. "Woe unto the world because of offenses; for it must needs be that offenses come, but woe to that man by whom the offense cometh." If we shall suppose that American slavery is one of those offenses which, in the providence of God, must needs come, but which, having continued through His appointed time, He now wills to remove, and that He gives to both North and South this terrible war as the woe due to those by whom the offense came, shall we discern therein any departure from those divine attributes which the believers in a living God always ascribe to Him? Fondly do we hope, fervently do we pray, that this mighty scourge of war may speedily pass away. Yet, if God wills that it continue until all the wealth piled by the bondsman's two hundred and fifty years of unrequited toil shall be sunk, and until every drop of blood drawn with the lash shall be paid by another drawn with the sword, as was said three thousand years ago, so still it must be said, "The judgments of the Lord are true and righteous altogether."

With malice toward none, with charity for all, with firmness in the right as God gives us to see the right, let us strive on to finish the work we are in, to bind up the nation's wounds, to care for him who shall have borne the battle and for his widow and his orphan, to do all which may achieve and cherish a just and lasting peace among ourselves and with all nations.

—LINCOLN, "Second Inaugural Address"

24. ABRAHAM LINCOLN IS ASSASSINATED

Lincoln had gone to Richmond the day after the Confederates had evacuated it—calling, while there, on Mrs. Pickett—and then had returned to Washington in time to make a memorable address on reconstruction. On the evening of April 14 he went to Ford's Theater to see Laura Keene in an English comedy, Our American Cousin. *John Wilkes Booth, brother of the more famous Edwin Booth, had concocted a plot to assassinate all the principal officers of the government; a Southern sympathizer, he thought that this might undo the work of the Union armies and save the South. Entering Lincoln's box he sent a ball through the President's head; then leaped to the stage, shouting, "Sic semper tyrannis!" and made good his escape.*

The moving story of Lincoln's death is told by the sorrowing Gideon Welles.

I HAD retired to bed about half past-ten on the evening of the 14th of April, and was just getting asleep when Mrs. Welles, my wife, said some one was at our door. Sitting up in bed, I heard a voice twice call to John, my son, whose sleeping-room was on the second floor directly over the front entrance. I arose at once and raised a window, when my messenger, James Smith, called to me that Mr. Lincoln, the President, had been shot, and said Secretary Seward and his son, Assistant Secretary Frederick Seward, were assassinated. James was much alarmed and excited. I told him his story was very incoherent and improbable, that he was associating men who were not together and liable to attack at the same time. "Where," I inquired, "was the President when shot?" James said he was at Ford's Theatre on 10th Street. "Well," said I, "Secretary Seward is an invalid in bed in his house yonder on 15th Street." James said he had been there, stopped in at the house to make inquiry before alarming me.

I immediately dressed myself, and, against the earnest remonstrance and appeals of my wife, went directly to Mr. Seward's, whose residence was on the east side of the square, mine being on the north. James accompanied me. As we were crossing 15th Street, I saw four or five men in earnest consultation, standing under the lamp on the corner by St. John's Church. Before I had got half across the street, the lamp was suddenly extinguished and the knot of persons rapidly dispersed. For a moment, and but a moment I was disconcerted to find myself in darkness, but recollecting that it was late and about time for the moon to rise, I proceeded on, not having lost five steps, merely making a pause without stopping. Hurrying forward into 15th Street, I found it pretty full of people, especially so near the residence of Secretary Seward, where there were many soldiers as well as citizens already gathered.

Entering the house, I found the lower hall and office full of persons, and among them most of the foreign legations, all anxiously inquiring what truth there was in the horrible rumors afloat. I replied that my object was to ascertain the facts. Proceeding through the hall to the stairs, I found one, and I think two, of the servants there holding the crowd in check. The servants were frightened and appeared relieved to see me. I hastily asked what truth there was in the story that an assassin or assassins had entered the house and assaulted the Secretary. They said it was true, and that Mr. Frederick was also badly injured. They wished me to go up, but no others. . . . As I entered, I met Miss Fanny Seward, with whom I exchanged a single word, and proceeded to the foot of the bed. Dr. Verdi and, I think, two others were there. The bed was saturated with blood. The Secretary was lying on his back, the upper part of his head covered by a cloth, which extended down over his eyes. His mouth was open, the lower jaw dropping down. I exchange a few whispered words with Dr. V. Secretary Stanton, who came after but almost simultaneously with me, made inquiries in a louder tone till admonished by a word from one of the physicians. We almost immediately withdrew and went into the adjoining front room, where lay Frederick Seward. His eyes were open but he did not move them, nor a limb, nor did he speak. Doctor White, who was in attendance, told me he was unconscious and more dangerously injured than his father.

As we descended the stairs, I asked Stanton what he had heard in regard to the President that was reliable. He said the President was shot at Ford's Theatre, that he had seen a man who was present and witnessed the occurrence. I said I would go immediately to the White House. Stanton told me the President was not there but was at the theatre. "Then," said I, "let us go immediately there." . . .

The President had been carried across the street from the theatre, to the house of a Mr. Peterson. We entered by ascending a flight of steps above the basement and passing through a long hall to the rear, where the President lay extended on a bed, breathing heavily. Several surgeons were present, at least six, I should think more. Among them I was glad to observe Dr. Hall, who, however, soon left. I inquired of Dr. H., as I entered, the true condition of the President. He replied the President was dead to all intents, although he might live three hours or perhaps longer.

The giant sufferer lay extended diagonally across the bed, which was not long enough for him. He had been stripped of his clothes. His large arms, which were occasionally exposed, were of a size which one would scarce have expected from his spare appearance. His slow, full respiration lifted the clothes with each breath that he took. His features were calm and striking. I had never seen them appear to better advantage than for the first hour, perhaps, that I was there. After that, his right eye began to swell and that part of his face became discolored.

Senator Sumner was there, I think, when I entered. If not he came in soon after, as did Speaker Colfax, Mr. Secretary McCulloch, and the other members of the Cabinet, with the exception of Mr. Seward. A double guard was stationed at the door and on the sidewalk, to repress the crowd, which was of course highly excited and anxious. The room was small and over-crowded. The surgeons and members of the Cabinet were as many as should have been in the room, but there were many more, and the hall and other rooms in the front or main house were full. One of these rooms was occupied by Mrs. Lincoln and her attendants, with Miss Harris. Mr. Dixon and Mrs. Kinney came to her about twelve o'clock. About once an hour Mrs. Lincoln would repair to the bedside of her dying husband and with lamentation and tears remain until overcome by emotion.

(April 15.) A door which opened upon a porch or gallery, and also the windows, were kept open for fresh air. The night was dark, cloudy, and damp, and about six it began to rain. I remained in the room until then without sitting or leaving it, when, there being a vacant chair which some one left at the foot of the bed, I occupied it for nearly two hours, listening to the heavy groans, and witnessing the wasting life of the good and great man who was expiring before me.

About 6 A.M. I experienced a feeling of faintness and for the first time after entering the room, a little past eleven, I left it and the house, and took a short walk in the open air. It was a dark and gloomy morning, and rain set in before I returned to the house, some fifteen minutes [later]. Large groups of people were gathered every few rods, all anxious and solicitous. Some one or more from each group stepped forward as I passed, to inquire into the condition of the President, and to ask if there was no hope. Intense grief was on every countenance when I replied that the President could survive but a short time. The colored people especially—and there were at this time more of them, perhaps, than of whites—were overwhelmed with grief. . . .

A little before seven, I went into the room where the dying President was rapidly drawing near the closing moments. His wife soon after made her last visit to him. The death-struggle had begun. Robert, his son, stood with several others at the head of the bed. He bore himself well, but on two occasions gave way to overpowering grief and sobbed aloud, turning his head and leaning on the shoulder of Senator Sumner. The respiration of the President became suspended at intervals, and at last entirely ceased at twenty-two minutes past seven. . . .

I went after breakfast to the Executive Mansion. There was a cheerless cold rain and everything seemed gloomy. On the Avenue in front of the White House were several hundred colored people, mostly women and children, weeping and wailing their loss. This crowd did not appear to diminish through the whole of that cold, wet day; they seemed not to know what was to be their fate since their great benefactor was dead, and their hopeless grief affected me more than almost anything else, though strong and brave men wept when I met them.

—Diary of Gideon Welles

25. "YES, HE HAD LIVED TO SHAME ME FROM MY SNEER"

American tributes to Lincoln are innumerable; let us close with a tribute from an Englishman who repented his malign attacks on the martyred President and was courageous enough to say so. Tom Taylor was the son of a laborer, and one might have expected from him some understanding of Lincoln, and of the Union cause. A man of varied talents—he had studied law, was art critic for the Times, *and had written several score plays—he is remembered as editor of* Punch. *Throughout the war* Punch *was ceaselessly critical of the North, and of Lincoln.*

Here is Tom Taylor's mea culpa.

ABRAHAM LINCOLN
Foully Assassinated April, 14, 1865

You lay a wreath on murdered Lincoln's bier,
   You, who with mocking pencil wont to trace
Broad for the self-complacent British sneer
   His length of shambling limb, his furrowed face,

His gaunt, gnarled hands, his unkempt, bristling hair,
   His garb uncouth, his bearing ill at ease;
His lack of all we prize as debonair,
   Of power or will to shine, of art to please.

You, whose smart pen backed up the pencil's laugh,
   Judging each step, as though the way were plain;
Reckless, so it could point its paragraph
   Of chief's perplexity or people's pain.

Beside this corps, that beats for winding sheet
   The Stars and Stripes he lived to rear anew,
Between the mourners at his head and feet,
   Say, scurril-jester, is there room for you?

Yes, he had lived to shame me from my sneer,
   To lame my pencil, and confute my pen—
To make me own this hind of princes peer,
   This rail-splitter a true-born king of men. . . .

The Old World and the New, from sea to sea,
  Utter one voice of sympathy and shame!
Sore heart, so stopped when it at last beat high,
  Sad life, cut short just as its triumph came.

A deed accurst! Strokes have been struck before
  By the assassin's hand, whereof men doubt
If more of horror or disgrace they bore;
  But thy foul crime, like Cain's, stands darkly out.

Vile hand, that brandest murder on a strife,
  Whate'er its grounds, stoutly and nobly striven;
And with the martyr's crown crownest a life
  With much to praise, little to be forgiven!
                              —Tom Taylor

XXXI

The Sunset of the Confederacy

AND so we come to the last chapter of the history of the war, a chapter which none can read without emotion. It is a long and ragged chapter, embracing action in Tennessee, the Carolinas, and Virginia over a period of five months. But it has a coherent pattern—the pattern of Confederate disintegration and collapse.

The closing month of 1864 saw the Confederacy in desperate straits. Sheridan had swept up the Valley, shattering Early's army and closing the door on that storehouse for Lee's army. Thomas destroyed Hood at Nashville, and the pitiful remnants of the once mighty Army of Tennessee were limping into Alabama and Mississippi. Sherman had taken Savannah and turned northward to spread ruin through South Carolina. Grant was hammering at the Petersburg lines, and Lee thrust in vain against the iron ring that the Union commander had forged around him. The blockade, too, was ever tighter. Mobile had fallen in August; Fort Fisher, the last Confederate port, was captured in January. At the beginning of 1865 only two Confederate armies were still in the field as fighting forces: Johnston's forces in the Carolinas, and Lee's Army of Northern Virginia. All through the winter months of 1865 these were decimated by battle, disease, and desertion. With spring came the final blows. Sherman pursued Johnston into North Carolina and shattered him at Bentonville; Sheridan rode down from the Valley to join Grant south of Petersburg and overwhelmed Pickett at Five Forks; Grant broke through the lines of Petersburg. Lee abandoned the city he had held for nine grim months, gave up Richmond, and fled along the Appomattox toward the west. It was the end.

In a sense it is true that the Confederacy was not beaten on the battlefield until the very end of the war when, in all theaters of operation, the Union forces held a two-to-one numerical superiority, and enjoyed the inestimable advantage of continuous reinforcement. To this day it is argued that the Confederates succumbed not to the armed might of the North but to other forces. There were enough men to fill the depleted ranks—so it is asserted; there was food enough for the hungry soldiers, and clothing enough in the warehouses; there were arms and munitions sufficient for the needs of the armed forces; there was everything but the will to continue the fight.

But this argument begs the crucial question—why the will to fight had been fatally weakened by 1865? Why did state officials connive with draft evasion? Why did the armies melt away by desertion? Why did the com-

missary, the transportation system, the economy itself, collapse? A comprehensive answer to these questions would involve a review of the whole war,
but a simple answer is not wholly unsatisfactory: these things failed because
the Federal armies had overrun most of the South, because they had destroyed
so much of the war potential, because they had laid waste the land, killed and
wounded the soldiers. The South did not lose because morale was low; morale
was low because the South was palpably losing.

The accounts of the collapse of the Confederacy which we include here
tell their own story and require little introduction or explanation. What we
are witnessing, here, is the working out of the grand strategy that Grant
formulated in 1864. Once that strategy had been planned, and backed up
with the immense resources available to the North, there was no hope for
the South except perhaps in war-weariness and a change of administration in
the North. Hood's ambitious attempt to achieve a vast flanking movement
against the Union armies was foredoomed to failure; after Atlanta there was
nothing left to oppose Sherman; sooner or later the combined armies in Virginia were bound to break Lee's defenses and force him to evacuate Richmond.

Yet to the end two possibilities glimmered in the imaginations of some of
the last-ditch Confederates. Lee might have broken away from Petersburg,
joined Johnston somewhere in western Virginia or North Carolina, and
fought out a last campaign there. Or Lee and Johnston might have encouraged their soldiers to make good their escape and wage a long guerrilla warfare against the invader. Neither possibility had anything to offer. Even had
Lee and Johnston joined forces there is no likelihood that they could have
opposed successfully the combined armies of Sherman and Grant—or, for
that matter, either of them. And guerrilla warfare would have condemned
the South to months and possibly years of devastating warfare without advancing in any way the cause of Southern independence.

Lee and Johnston recognized this, and were realistic enough to know, too,
when the end had come. President Davis was less realistic. As late as April 4
he issued an address to the people of the Confederacy asserting that "nothing
was now needed to render our triumph certain but the exhibition of our un-
quenchable resolve." Even after the surrender of Lee, Davis wanted to hold
out, but was dissuaded by Johnston and Beauregard and by some of his
civilian advisers. None can doubt, now, that these were right in their conclusion that the verdict of Appomattox was final.

1. THOMAS ANNIHILATES HOOD AT NASHVILLE

It will be remembered that after Atlanta Hood moved into western
Georgia with a view to striking at Sherman's communications. By November
Sherman gave up what appeared to be a futile pursuit, and turned eastward.
Hood and Davis then conceived an ambitious but visionary plan to recover
Tennessee and Kentucky and help Lee in Virginia. Hood was to strike north-
ward across the Tennessee, destroy Sherman's communications, advance into

Kentucky, and with such recruits as rallied to his banner, move eastward into Virginia. For this proposed campaign Hood had some 40,000 effectives.

The first part of the operation went according to plan. By the end of October Hood's army was at Florence, Alabama, and on November 19 it began its forward movement across the Tennessee. As yet neither Thomas nor Schofield were strong enough to oppose Hood, but reinforcements were on the way. On November 29 Hood caught up with Schofield at Spring Hill, just south of Franklin; that night while Hood was asleep Schofield escaped through the Confederate lines to Franklin where he threw up entrenchments and awaited the Confederate advance. Hood came up next day, and hurled his divisions against the Union entrenchments in a series of assaults as gallant as those of Gettysburg. He was unable to break Schofield's lines, however, and Franklin proved a costly defeat, Confederate losses running to some 6,000.

After Franklin Schofield withdrew to Nashville, where Thomas was rapidly building up a force strong enough to take the offensive. Hood followed, and on December 2 had his army in position south and east of the city, astride the Franklin Pike and the railroad to Chattanooga. The reinforcements which Grant had arranged for were coming in rapidly, and within a few days Thomas had a force of close to 50,000 men to deal with about half that number under Hood. Grant wanted Thomas to attack at once, but Thomas was, as usual, deliberate; quite rightly he was determined to mount and equip his cavalry before undertaking an offensive which—so he hoped—would require a pursuit. By December 8 Thomas was ready for action; then bad weather intervened and he delayed. Meantime—as General Wilson tells us—Grant had become impatient to the point of ordering Logan to proceed to Nashville to supersede Thomas. On the fourteenth the weather cleared, and Thomas moved out for the kill. Nashville was perhaps the most complete victory of the entire war, for it utterly destroyed Hood's army. Wilson pursued the stricken remnants across the Tennessee; Hood resigned; and the Army of Tennessee was no more.

This account* of the battle is by Thomas' brilliant young cavalry commander, General James Wilson.

O N December 9, as a result of daily conferences, Thomas ordered me to break camp at Edgefield, to recross the Cumberland with my entire force, and to take position within the defenses of Nashville between the Hillsboro and Harding turnpikes so as to be ready to join in the attack against Hood the next day. But a heavy rain setting in about the time the movement should have begun my orders were countermanded till further notice. Rain, snow, and sleet in abundance followed by intense cold covered the ground that night with such a glare of snow and ice as to render it impossible to move cavalry not especially rough-shod for the occasion. In fact, neither infantry nor cavalry could have made any progress whatever over a battlefield so undulating and broken and so covered with ice and frozen snow as was that

---

* From *Under the Old Flag*, Vol. II, by James Harrison Wilson. Reprinted by permission of the publishers, Appleton-Century-Crofts, Inc.

which separated our lines from those of the enemy. There cannot be the slightest doubt that the prevailing conditions made it necessary to suspend operations and were a full justification for every hour of delay that followed this remarkable storm. It was at its greatest intensity when Grant telegraphed positive orders directing Thomas to attack the enemy without further delay, and it was after it had spent its full force that Thomas, on the evening of December 10, invited his corps commanders to his headquarters for the purpose of reciting his orders, making known his reply, and asking their views as to the action he had taken entirely on his own responsibility in the emergency then at hand. . . .

As the others were withdrawing Thomas asked me to remain for further conference, and this I did with great pleasure. As soon as we were alone he said, with much feeling:

"Wilson, the Washington authorities treat me as if I were a boy. They seem to think me incapable of planning a campaign or of fighting a battle, but if they will just let me alone till thawing weather begins and the ground is in condition for us to move at all I will show them what we can do. I am sure my plan of operations is correct, and that we shall lick the enemy, if he only stays to receive our attack." . . .

Everything was astir, breakfast was over, and the cavalry corps ready to move out by daylight the next morning [December 15], but, owing to a dense fog which followed the change in the weather, the cavalry as well as the infantry was compelled to delay the advance till half past eight, by which time it had cleared sufficiently to enable each organization to move against the enemy as directed. In spite, however, of every precaution, McArthur's division of Smith's corps, instead of marching to its position on the left by my rear, as Smith had promised, deliberately crossed my front, thereby delaying not only my advance but the advance of the rest of the army till nearly ten o'clock. Had the enemy been specially alert, this unnecessary delay might have greatly deranged our plan of attack. As it was it cost the entire army an hour and a half, which, in the short days of December, could ill be spared, and might have been of inestimable value in our operations of that afternoon.

Simultaneously with the advance of the infantry, the cavalry moved out as directed, though Hatch's division was further delayed after beginning its march by the fact that McArthur's infantry still blocked its way. Finally having got a clear road, it advanced rapidly under the cover of a strong line of skirmishers. Brushing away the enemy's pickets, it soon encountered Ector's brigade of infantry on the farther side of Richland Creek, strongly entrenched on commanding ground. Without a moment's hesitation, Stewart's brigade threw itself headlong against the enemy, broke through his line, and drove him rapidly beyond Harding's House. . . .

Having by this brilliant operation cleared his front and put the enemy's cavalry to flight, Hatch pushed his first brigade by flank rapidly to the left to join his second brigade. This done, the division found itself on the flank of a four-gun battery, posted in a redoubt which formed the left of the enemy's position. Sending his own battery "I," First Illinois Light Artillery, still farther to the right to a position from which it could enfilade the enemy's entrenchments, Hatch threw forward Coon's brigade, dismounted, broke through the enemy's infantry, and captured the redoubt with four guns. Turning the captured guns upon the enemy occupying a higher hill farther on, Hatch promptly threw forward his second brigade, supported by his first, and swept over a second redoubt, capturing four guns and two hundred and fifty prisoners. This operation was conducted in sight of the infantry, which had never seen dismounted cavalry assault a fortified position before. To men less brave and determined than these dismounted horsemen it would have seemed like madness to attack such entrenchments, but armed with magazine carbines the strong line of skirmishers made light of the work before them. In spite of the steep acclivity and of the withering fire both of artillery and musketry, the dismounted cavalrymen swept over the next redoubt and, putting the enemy to flight, captured still another four-gun battery which the enemy abandoned in the valley beyond. It was now almost dark, and the cavalrymen, having been fighting on foot swinging on a long

FRANKLIN AND NASHVILLE

radius from hill to hill, over rough and muddy ground, had become exceedingly fatigued. Besides, night was at hand, and Hatch was, therefore, directed to bring forward his horses and bivouac on the Hillsboro turnpike, connecting with Schofield's right and covering it from the enemy. . . .

The cavalry operations still farther to our right had been equally successful. Croxton's brigade and Johnson's division, although delayed by McArthur's infantry, had found the enemy posted behind Richland Creek, but, pressing him vigorously in front and flank, they brushed him quickly out of the way. Croxton, after following him several miles, also turned to the left, skirmishing heavily with the enemy, and finally went into bivouac near the sixth mile post on the Hillsboro turnpike. Both he and Johnson had swept everything before them, thus making it easy to concentrate the entire mounted force within supporting distance of each other on the left and rear of the enemy's position.

From this condensed account, it will be seen that the cavalry corps had driven back the enemy's entire left wing an average of over four miles, and had placed itself in a position from which it was enabled to renew the attack against the enemy's left and rear the next day with deadly effect. . . .

Shortly after dawn of the 16th, the enemy drove in Hammond's pickets and took possession of the Granny White pike. This was the initial movement of the day, but Hammond, a gallant soldier, realizing the importance of that turnpike, without waiting for orders threw out the dismounted men of his entire brigade, drove the enemy back in turn, and regained firm possession of the turnpike. . . .

But by noon our skirmishers, not less than four thousand in number, had pushed their way slowly through the underbrush and woods up the hills in a curved line from Schofield's right, across the Granny White pike, to a position parallel with the enemy's line and facing Nashville. There was no longer any uncertainty as to which flank we ought to be on, for all was now going well. Led and directed by their gallant officers, the men of the two divisions, skirmishing heavily, pressed the enemy steadily back from the start at every point.

In the midst of the heaviest fighting, one of our detachments captured a courier from Hood, carrying a dispatch to Chalmers, directing him "for God's sake to drive the Yankee cavalry from our left and rear or all is lost." Regarding this dispatch as of the first importance, I sent it at once to Thomas without even making a copy of it. Having already informed both Thomas and Schofield by courier of my success and of the steady progress my troopers were making, I sent three staff officers, one after the other, urging Schofield to attack the enemy in front and finish up the day's work with victory. But nothing whatever was done as yet from the right of the infantry line to support my movement.

Finally, fearing that nothing would be done, and that night would come on again before the enemy could be shaken out of his position, by the efforts of the dismounted cavalry alone, I rode around the enemy's left flank to Thomas's headquarters, which I found on the turnpike about two miles from my own. This was between three and four o'clock, and, as it was a cloudy, rainy day, it was already growing dark. Thomas and Schofield were standing together on the reverse side of a small hill, over the top of which the enemy's line on a still higher elevation could be plainly seen less than a mile away. What was of still more importance was that my dismounted men, with their guidons fluttering in the air, flanked and covered by two batteries of horse artillery, were in plain sight moving against the left and rear of the enemy's line. Shots from their batteries aimed too high but passing over the enemy's heads were falling in front of Schofield's corps. And yet he gave no orders to advance.

Pointing out the favorable condition of affairs, I urged Thomas, with ill-concealed impatience, to order the infantry forward without further delay. Still the stately chieftain was unmoved. Apparently doubting that the situation could be as I represented it, he lifted his field glasses and coolly scanned what I clearly showed him. It was a stirring sight, and, gazing at it, as I thought, with unnecessary deliberation, he finally satisfied himself. Pausing only to ask me if I was sure that the men entering the left of the enemy's works above us were mine, and receiving the assurance that I was dead certain of it, he turned to Schofield and as calmly as if on parade directed him to move to the attack with his entire corps.

Fully realizing that the crisis was now on, I galloped as rapidly as my good gray, Sheridan, could carry me back to my own command, but when I reached its front the enemy had already broken and was in full but disorderly retreat by the only turnpike left in his possession. This was shortly after 4 P.M.

The dismounted troopers had closed in upon the enemy's entrenchments and entered them from the rear before the infantry reached them in front. They had captured fifteen more field guns, thus bringing their score up to twenty-seven for the two days, and had picked up several hundred prisoners. . . . It was now raining heavily, mist was gathering, and dark was closing down like a pall over both victor and vanquished. . . .

Meanwhile, the Confederate commander had committed his final and fatal mistake and had lost out forever. His flank was turned and taken in reverse and his line was irretrievably broken. The most he could hope to do now was to save his army by flight from total destruction and capture. And in this his most potent allies were darkness, rain, snow, sleet, mud, and rising rivers, all of which he was to have in succession for the next two weeks. With the beginning of darkness he was in full retreat along the two turnpikes and we were thundering at his heels.

—WILSON, *Under the Old Flag*

2. "THE LAST CHANCE OF THE CONFEDERACY"

Sherman had entered Savannah on December 21, 1864, and then turned north, through the heart of South Carolina. Against his army of veterans Hardee—now in command of Confederate forces in Georgia and South Caro-

lina—could oppose only delaying actions. Columbia fell on February 18, 1865, and that same day the Confederates evacuated Charleston. By the beginning of March Sherman was into North Carolina, moving on Fayette-ville and striking toward Raleigh, the capital of the state.

Meantime Grant had decided to open up communications with Sherman by water, and provide him with a convenient Atlantic port for a supply base. Wilmington was the last major port of the Confederacy. It was commanded by Fort Fisher, and after a desperate struggle Federal amphibious forces cap-tured this fort—and Wilmington—in mid-January. New Bern, at the mouth of the Neuse River and with direct railroad connections to Goldsboro and Raleigh, was equally important. Burnside had seized this place in 1862; now Schofield came on from Tennessee to direct an advance along the Neuse to-ward Goldsboro and an eventual junction with Sherman coming up from the south.

One of Lee's first acts as commander in chief of the Confederate armies had been to restore Joseph Johnston to command of all armies opposing Sherman. Johnston sent Bragg to hold Schofield and on March 8-10 there was sharp fighting west of the great Dover Swamp. Bragg retired on Golds-boro, and Johnston prepared to move out to attack Sherman before his army and Schofield's could link up. Sherman's Grand Army of the West was strung out in several columns along many miles of road, and it was Johnston's plan to strike its vanguard. The opportunity came at Bentonville on March 19. It was "the last chance of the Confederacy"—and not a very good one. Actually even had Johnston succeeded in breaking Slocum's advance divi-sions, his position would still have been hopeless, for Sherman and Schofield together could muster some 90,000 to his own 35,000.

Alexander McClurg, who tells the story of the Battle of Bentonville, was a Chicago bookdealer who had helped organize the Crosby Guards at the beginning of the war, fought at Perryville, Chickamauga, and Chattanooga, and marched with Sherman to the sea and through the Carolinas, as chief of staff to General J. C. Davis. He later became one of America's famous book-sellers and publishers.

GENERAL SHERMAN had himself been marching for several days with the left and exposed wing, and on the night of the 18th his headquar-ters, as well as those of General Slocum, who commanded the left wing, had been pitched within the lines of the Fourteenth Army Corps. On the morn-ing of the 19th . . . when the strains of Old Hundred had ceased, and the men had had their accustomed breakfast of coffee and hardtack, varied here and there with a piece of cold chicken or ham, or a baked sweet potato, foraged from the country, the regiments of the first division—General W. P. Carlin's—of the Fourteenth Corps filed out upon the road, and began the advance. This was about seven o'clock. For the first time almost in weeks, the sun was shining, and there was promise of a beautiful day; and the men strode on vigorously and cheerily.

They found in their front, as they always did, the enemy's cavalry, watching their movements and opposing their advance. But there was of course "nothing but cavalry," and the men pressed on, light-hearted, anticipating the rest they should have at Goldsboro, and then the last march toward Richmond and home. But the cavalry in front were stubborn. They did not yield a foot of ground before it was wrested from them. They were inclined to fight; and the old expression of the Atlanta campaign was brought out for use again: "They don't drive worth a damn." Even the organized parties of foragers, the historical "bummers" of Sherman's army, men who generally made short work of getting through a thin curtain of cavalry, when chickens and pigs and corn and sweet potatoes were on the other side,—even these renowned troopers fell back, dispirited, behind our skirmishers, and lined the roadsides.

At length the whole of the first brigade—General H. C. Hobart's—was deployed and pushed vigorously forward; but still the resistance of the enemy was determined and the advance slow. It began to be evident that they had some reason for this unusual opposition. Ten o'clock came, and we had gained but five miles. General Hobart was hotly engaged. The second brigade—Colonel George P. Buell's—was ordered to make a detour to the left, and take the enemy's line in the flank; but meanwhile our own right flank was becoming exposed to a similar fate, as the enemy overlapped us in that direction, and the third brigade—Lieutenant-Colonel Miles's—was deployed on the right of the first.

Thus the whole of General Carlin's division was now deployed and in line of battle; yet everywhere it found the enemy in front strong and stubborn. The right and left of our line were ordered to advance and develop his strength. They did advance right gallantly, but they soon encountered a strong line of infantry. This was pressed back several hundred yards, after severe fighting; and our men dashed, all unprepared, against a line of earthworks, manned with infantry and strengthened with artillery. The enemy opened upon them such a destructive fire that they were compelled to fall back, with severe loss. Many men and officers and two regimental commanders had fallen, and the whole line was severely shattered; but very important information had been gained. Observations and the reports of prisoners captured left little reason to doubt that General Johnston's whole army was in position in our immediate front, and the persistent fighting of the cavalry had been intended to give time for ample preparation.

It was now about half past one o'clock, and Generals Slocum and Davis were together in consultation, in the woods to the left of the road, when a deserter from the enemy was sent to them by General Carlin. . . . This man told a straight but startling story. It was to the effect that General Johnston's whole army, consisting of over thirty thousand men, had by night marches been concentrated in our immediate front, and was strongly entrenched. He said that General Johnston, accompanied by Generals Hardee and Cheatham and Hoke, had just ridden around among his troops, in the highest spirits, and that he had heard him address a portion of them, telling them that "at last the long-wished-for opportunity had occurred;" that they were "concentrated and in position, while General Sherman's army was scattered over miles of country, separated by almost impassable roads." . . .

The news had come none too soon, for our little command was again preparing to attack. . . . Two divisions and a brigade, with a battery of artillery,—in all, less than ten thousand men,—were face to face with an overwhelming force of the enemy, who had chosen their own ground, strengthened it with field-works, and placed their artillery in position. Confident and prepared, they awaited the order to advance, while we were deceived and surprised.

It was certain that they would lose no time, but attack at once and in overwhelming numbers. Up to this time General Slocum had shared the belief of General Sherman that the force in our front was inconsiderable. He was now thoroughly undeceived, and he went energetically to work to prepare for the most vigorous defensive fighting possible. Every precaution was taken, and the men all along our line were in the act of throwing up hasty field-works, when the attack came upon us like a whirlwind. . . .

Almost immediately I met masses of men slowly and doggedly falling back along the road, and through the fields and open woods on the left of the road. They were retreating, and evidently with good cause; but there was nothing of the panic and rout so often seen on battlefields earlier in the war. They were retreating, but they were not demoralized. Minié-balls were whizzing in every direction, although I was then far from the front line as I had left it only a short time before. Pushing on through these retreating men, and down the road, I met two pieces of artillery,—a section of the 19th Indiana battery,— and was dashing past it, when the lieutenant in command called out, "For Heaven's sake, don't go down there! I am the last man of the command. Everything is gone in front of you. The lieutenant commanding my battery and most of the men and horses are killed, and four guns are captured. These two guns are all we have left."

Checking my horse, I saw the rebel regiments in front in full view, stretching through the fields to the left as far as the eye could reach, advancing rapidly, and firing as they came. Everything seemed hopeless on our centre and left; but in the swampy woods on the right of the road our line seemed still to be holding its position. An overwhelming force had struck Carlin's entire division and Robinson's brigade, and was driving them off the field. The onward sweep of the rebel lines was like the waves of the ocean, resistless. . . . General Morgan's division, on the right, had also been heavily assailed; but it was better situated, and not being at this time out-flanked, it held its position.

One of Morgan's brigades,—that of General Fearing,—being in reserve, had not been engaged. When the left first began to give way, General Davis sent Colonel Litchfield to Fearing, with instructions to hold his brigade in readiness to march in any direction. A few moments later, when the left was falling back, and the rebel line was sweeping after them in hot pursuit, General Davis came plunging through the swamp on his fiery white mare toward the reserve. "Where is that brigade, Litchfield?"

"Here it is, sir, ready to march." It was in column of regiments, faced to the front.

Ordering it swung around to the left, General Davis shouted, "Advance upon their flank, Fearing! Deploy as you go! Strike them wherever you find them! Give them the best you've got, and we'll whip them yet!" All this was uttered with an emphasis and fire known only upon the field of battle.

The men caught up the closing words, and shouted back, "Hurrah for old Jeff! We'll whip 'em yet!" as they swung off through the woods at a rattling pace. Officers and men, from General Fearing down, were alike inspired with the spirit of their commander, and "We'll whip them yet!" might well be considered their battle-cry. They struck the successful enemy with resist-less impetuosity, and were quickly engaged in a desperate conflict. Upon this movement, in all probability, turned the fortunes of the day. It was the right thing, done at the right time.

Seeing at once that, as Fearing advanced, his right flank must in turn become exposed, General Davis sent to General Slocum, begging for another brigade to move in upon Fearing's right and support him. Fortunately, Coggs-well's fine brigade of the Twentieth Corps arrived not long after upon the field, and it was ordered to report to General Davis for that purpose. . . . It was splendidly done. The men of these two brigades—Fearing's and Coggs-well's—seemed to divine that upon them had devolved the desperate honor of stemming the tide of defeat, and turning it into victory; and magnificently they responded. Finer spirit and enthusiasm could not be shown by troops, and it is no wonder that, after a fierce and bloody contest, the flushed and victorious troops of the enemy, thus taken in the flank, gave way, and in their turn fell back in confusion. So stunned and bewildered were they by this sudden and unexpected attack that their whole line withdrew from all the ground they had gained, and apparently reëntered their works.

And now there was a lull along the whole front, which gave invaluable time for the re-formation of our shattered lines. . . .

To the surprise of every one, a full hour was allowed by the enemy for these new dispositions; and it was about five o'clock before their long line was again seen emerging from the pine woods and swampy thickets in front, and sweeping across the open fields. As soon as they appeared, our artil-lery opened upon them with most destructive effect. Still they pressed gal-lantly on, but only to be met with a well-delivered fire from our infantry, securely posted behind hastily improvised field-works, such as our troops were then well skilled in throwing up in a very brief time, and of which they had dearly learned the value. Attack after attack was gallantly met and re-pulsed, and the golden opportunity of the enemy upon our left was lost. . . .

Morgan's whole division was now stretched out over such an extent of ground that all his troops were in the front line, and he had no men left for a second line or a reserve. As all old troops were wont to do at that time, when in the presence of the enemy, they had at once fallen to build such field-works as could be hastily thrown up with rails and light timber. As one of their officers expressed it, they had often attacked works, but they had rarely had the pleasure of fighting behind them themselves, and they rather enjoyed the prospect. They were there, and they meant to stay. Their skirmishers were heavily engaged from the time they took position, and they found the enemy in front in force, and shielded by well-constructed works. They were fighting more or less severely until about half-past four o'clock in the afternoon, when the enemy attempted to carry their position by assault. The charge was desperate and persistent, and the roar of musketry, as it rolled up from that low wood, was incessant. For half an hour it continued, and the commander of the corps, General Davis, sat uneasily on his horse, a short distance in the rear, and listened to it. . . .

After a while, a slight cessation was noticed in the firing; and by direction of General Davis, I rode forward toward the line to ascertain definitely how matters stood. The ground was swampy, and here and there were openings through the trees, while generally bushes and thickets obstructed the view. I had gone but a few rods, when I caught a glimpse through a vista, obliquely to the left, of a column of men moving to the right, straight across my path and directly in the rear of our line, though out of sight of it. They looked like rebels, and my sharp-sighted orderly, Batterson, said they were "rebs;" but the view was obscured by smoke, and the idea that the enemy could be in that position was preposterous. I hesitated but a moment, and pressed on. A hundred yards further through the bushes, and I broke out suddenly into a large, nearly circular, open space, containing perhaps half an acre. Here the view was not a cheerful one. On the opposite side of the opening, at perhaps twenty-five yards' distance, was a body of unmistakably rebel troops, marching by the flank in column of fours, toward the right. Beyond the column, under a wide-spreading tree, dismounted, stood a group of Confederate officers, whose appearance and uniforms indicated high rank. . . .

Mitchell's brigade had already discovered the intruders in their rear, who at first were thought by them to be reinforcements. . . . Fortunately, all was now quiet in front, and General Morgan quickly got his men to the reverse of their own works. In other words, they were now in front of their works, and prepared to sustain an attack from the rear. . . .

The enemy attacked vigorously, but instead of taking Morgan by surprise, he found him ready. Again the struggle was sharp and bloody, but brief. Nothing could stand that day before the veterans of the old second division. Truly they were enjoying the novelty of fighting behind works. Hardee was repulsed, with severe loss. . . .

Considering the great disaster which was imminent, and which was averted, it is not too much to claim for this engagement that it was one of the most decisive of the lesser battles of the war. When Johnston, with skillful strategy, and with wonderful celerity and secrecy, massed his scattered troops near the little hamlet of Bentonsville, and placed them, unknown to his great adversary, in a strong position directly across the road upon which two "light divisions," as he expressed it, were marching, he proposed to himself nothing less than to sweep these two divisions from the field, in the first furious onset; and then, hurrying on with flushed and victorious troops, to attack, in deep column and undeployed, the two divisions of the Twentieth Corps, which, through heavy and miry roads, would be hastening to the assistance of their comrades. These divisions he expected to crush easily, while General Sherman and the right wing were many miles from the field. Then, with half his army destroyed, with supplies exhausted, and far from any base, he believed General Sherman and his right wing only would no longer be a match for his elated and eager troops.

Never before, in all the long struggle, had fortune and circumstance so united to favor him, and never before had hope shone so brightly. If Sherman's army were destroyed, the Confederacy would be inspired with new spirit, and ultimate success would be at last probable. Doubtless such dreams as these flitted through General Johnston's mind on that Sunday morning, when his well-laid plans seemed so sure of execution. With what a sad and heavy heart he turned at night from the hard-fought field, realizing that the last great opportunity was lost, we can only imagine. As the sun went down that night, it undoubtedly carried with it, in the mind of General Johnston, at least, the last hopes of the Southern Confederacy.

—McClurg, "The Last Chance of the Confederacy"

3. THE DESPERATE GAMBLE OF FORT STEDMAN

After Johnston's defeat in North Carolina it was clear that Lee's only hope was to give up Richmond, withdraw from Petersburg, and try to join up with the remnants of Johnston's army somewhere in southern Virginia. But before he abandoned what he had fought for so long and so gallantly, he tried one last desperate gamble. That was the attack on Fort Stedman. This fort was less than a mile south of the Appomattox, and its capture would, Lee hoped, open the road to Grant's supply base at City Point. If the attack were successful Grant would have to bring up some of the divisions on his left, or shorten his lines; either action would make it easier for Lee to evacuate his lines, when that became necessary, and join Johnston.

To the break-through at Fort Stedman Lee was prepared to commit half of his entire force. General Gordon, always bold and aggressive, was to spearhead the attack. It jumped off early in the morning of March 25, met with initial success, and then—as Gordon tells us—with disastrous failure. The Confederates lost no fewer than 2,783 prisoners, and losses in killed and wounded were heavy.

General James A. Walker, who here recalls the fateful attack, was a brigadier in Gordon's corps; after the war he was a Congressman from Virginia.

ONE morning in March, 1865, General John B. Gordon, my corps commander, requested me to ride with him, and we crossed the Pocahontas bridge, and rode to a point on the hills on the left bank of the Appomattox river opposite the enemy's second line of fortifications on the right bank of the river in front of Hare's Hill or Fort Stedman. We spent an hour or more examining the enemy's position through our field glasses, when General Gordon turned to me and very carelessly inquired what I thought of the position occupied by my division, and whether I thought I could hold it against an assault by the enemy in force.

I replied that I did not think I could hold my position against an assault because the enemy's lines were so close they could dash over our works any night before we were aware of their coming, and I added: "I can take their front line any morning before breakfast."

General Gordon smiled and remarked: "Don't you forget what you have said; I may call on you to make your words good." He then told me that he had suggested to General Lee the idea of making an assault upon the enemy's works in his front and would know in a few days whether it would be adopted. A few days later Gordon sent for his three division commanders and informed us that the attack would be made; and the time and manner of the assault were then determined on. My division was to attack Fort Stedman and the other two designated points on the right of the fort.

The attacks were to be made simultaneously by each division, the signal for the assault to be three musket or pistol shots fired in quick succession.

Each division was to be preceded by a storming party consisting of fifty picked men carrying axes to clear away the *chevaux de frise*, and one hundred picked infantry men armed with muskets, commanded by a captain and one lieutenant, on whose courage and coolness we could confidently rely; each division to follow closely behind the storming party, marching by the right flank.

The preparations for the movement were simple, but required some little time. In the first place, rations for three days had to be issued, cooked, brought up, and distributed. The cartridge boxes had to be examined and filled up with cartridges; muskets had to be inspected; the sick and disabled sent to hospitals; the storming party selected, and instructed as to what was required of them.

After all these things were looked after, we had to wait for night to begin the movement. The entire corps, three divisions, had to be marched out of the trenches so as to give room to form their separate columns, and then to march back to the breastworks so as to bring the head of the columns to the spot where our works were to be crossed.

This was done quietly and with the least possible noise. No commands were given, but the words were passed in low tones from man to man. About an hour before daylight my storming party pressed cautiously and silently one by one over the breastworks, and crept up close to one of our solitary pickets in his pit and lay down on the ground. . . .

When all was ready, we awaited the signal in breathless suspense, but the suspense was relieved when General Gordon came down the line to where the head of my column rested, and, finding my command ready to move, stepped to one side and fired three pistol shots in rapid succession. The last report was scarcely heard before the recumbent figures sprang to their feet and Captain Anderson commanded, "Forward! Double-quick!" and his men moved off at a trail arms, and not a word was spoken or a sound heard except the regular beat of their feet as they stepped out at a double-quick.

I have read many accounts, both in history and fiction, of such attacks, and my blood has been stirred in reading them; but I never read an account of one so dashing, so orderly, and so quiet as this. The cool, frosty morning made every sound distinct and clear, and the only sound heard was the tramp! tramp! of the men as they kept step as regularly as if on drill, and the cries of of the Federal picket as he ran with all speed into the fort, shouting: "The Rebels are coming! The Rebels are coming!" Our men were instructed not to try to capture or harm the "Yank," but to follow the path he took, and it would carry us to the opening in the enemy's *chevaux de frise*, and not to cheer until they were on the enemy's breastworks; and then to cheer as loudly as possible as a signal for the division to follow, and to fire as rapidly as they could reload, in every direction, through the fort, to confuse the Federals and prevent them from rallying and forming before our main body should come up.

The gallant little band came to a halt as they reached the obstructions, and a galling fire from muskets inside the fort met them at that point, and a number of them were killed and wounded during the pause.

The halt was a short one, for sharp axes wielded by strong arms were at work, and the heavy blows rang out on the frosty air like the blows of giants, and in a few seconds more the "Rebel yell" made the welkin ring, announcing to our expectant ears that Fort Stedman was carried, and that our boys were inside the enemy's works.

They proceeded at once to make it lively by firing promiscuously in every direction wherever they could see a blue coat to fire at.

The enemy were taken entirely by surprise and all were asleep except the thin line which guarded the side of the redoubt which faced our lines. . . .

As soon as the wild cheering of our boys gave the signal, the head of the column was put in motion, and crossing our breastworks, moved rapidly across the intervening space and into the captured fort. . . .

As the head of the column entered Fort Stedman the resistance wholly ceased, and in the dim light of the coming dawn the fleeing enemy could be seen on every side, hastening to the protection of the second line of forts.

Our being in possession of Fort Stedman made the enemy's breastworks on either side and as far as the neighboring forts untenable and they were rapidly abandoned. . . .

The attacks by the other Confederate columns were either not made, or if made, were unsuccessful, and these troops came to my aid in the neighborhood of Fort Stedman. By the time the sun was above the horizon the enemy had poured forth from their camps in rear, and filled the forts and breastworks of the second line with troops, both infantry and artillery. They sent out a heavy skirmish line which engaged ours and a brisk and angry skirmish fire was kept up until our troops were withdrawn.

Their artillery, too, came into play, and the guns of their forts in the second line and on our right and left concentrated their fire on Fort Stedman, and such a storm of shot and shell as fell into and around the old fort has seldom been seen. We had failed to carry the second line by surprise; it was manned by four times our numbers, and our task was hopeless. Nothing remained but to withdraw to our breastworks.

—WALKER, "Gordon's Assault on Fort Stedman"

4. "NOW RICHMOND ROCKED IN HER HIGH TOWERS TO WATCH THE IMPENDING ISSUE"

With the failure of the attack on Fort Stedman Lee's position became critical. On March 26 he notified President Davis that Richmond must be abandoned. He himself could not give up Petersburg at once; it took time to collect supplies for an army on the move, and to make the necessary dispositions. Yet every hour that he stayed on in the trenches of Petersburg the situation became more dangerous. Already Grant had issued orders for a general assault on the twenty-ninth; already Sheridan had come on from the Valley to the north bank of the James; already Lincoln and Sherman had arrived at City Point to witness the grand climax of the campaign and plan for armistice and peace.

By the end of March Grant had pushed his lines across the Weldon Railroad and the Quaker road and along the White Oak road toward Five Forks. On the twenty-ninth Lee struck at the Federals at Gravelly Run, but failed to break through. If the Federal line extended farther west, it could curve northward and cut off Lee's retreat along the Appomattox. This was precisely what Grant was planning. On the twenty-ninth Grant sent Sheridan to Five Forks via Dinwiddie Court House, and Lee started Fitzhugh Lee and Pickett after him. Pickett and Fitz Lee entrenched at Five Forks; then the two generals went off to a shad bake. At four in the afternoon of April 1 Sheridan struck. It was the greatest disaster that the Army of Northern Virginia ever knew; it was the Waterloo of the Confederacy.

George Alfred Townsend, with whose remarkable literary talents we are already familiar, is once again our historian.

WE must start with the supposition that our own men far outnumbered the Rebels. The latter were widely separated from their comrades before Petersburg, and the adjustment of our infantry as well as the great movable force at Sheridan's disposal, renders it doubtful that they could have returned. At any rate they did not do so, whether from choice or necessity, and it was a part of our scheme to push them back into their entrenchments. This work was delegated to the cavalry entirely, but, as I have said before, mounted carbineers, are no match for stubborn, bayoneted infantry. So when the horsemen were close up to the Rebels, they were dismounted, and acted as infantry to all intents. A portion of them, under Gregg and Mackenzie, still adhered to the saddle, that they might be put in rapid motion for flanking and charging purposes; but fully five thousand indurated men, who had seen service in the Shenandoah and elsewhere, were formed in line of battle on foot, and by charge and deploy essayed the difficult work of pressing back the entire Rebel column. This they were to do so evenly and ingeniously, that the Rebels should go no farther than their works, either to escape eastward or to discover the whereabouts of Warren's forces, which were already forming. Had they espied the latter they might have become so discouraged as to break and take to the woods; and Sheridan's object was to capture them as well as to rout them. So, all the afternoon, the cavalry pushed them hard, and the strife went on uninterruptedly and terrifically. . . .

A colonel with a shattered regiment came down upon us in a charge. The bayonets were fixed; the men came on with a yell; their gray uniforms seemed black amidst the smoke; their preserved colors, torn by grape and ball, waved yet defiantly; twice they halted, and poured in volleys, but came on again like the surge from the fog, depleted, but determined; yet, in the hot faces of the carbineers, they read a purpose as resolute, but more calm, and, while they pressed along, swept all the while by scathing volleys, a group of horsemen took them in flank. It was an awful instant; the horses recoiled; the charging column trembled like a single thing, but at once the Rebels, with rare organization, fell into a hollow square, and with solid sheets of steel defied our centaurs. The horsemen rode around them in vain; no charge could break the shining squares, until our dismounted carbineers poured in their volleys afresh, making gaps in the spent ranks, and then in their wavering time the cavalry thundered down. The Rebels could stand no more; they reeled and swayed, and fell back broken and beaten. And on the ground their colonel lay, sealing his devotion with his life.

Through wood and brake and swamp, across field and trench, we pushed the fighting defenders steadily. For a part of the time, Sheridan himself was there, short and broad, and active, waving his hat, giving orders, seldom out of fire, but never stationary, and close by fell the long yellow locks of Custer, sabre extended, fighting like a Viking, though he was worn and haggard with much work. At four o'clock the Rebels were behind their wooden walls at Five Forks, and still the cavalry pressed them hard, in feint rather than solemn effort, while a battalion dismounted, charged squarely upon the face of their breastworks which lay in the main on the north side of the White Oak road. Then, while the cavalry worked round toward the rear, the infantry of Warren, though commanded by Sheridan, prepared to take part in the battle.

The genius of Sheridan's movement lay in his disposition of the infantry. The skill with which he arranged it, and the difficult manoeuvres he projected and so well executed, should place him as high in infantry tactics as he has heretofore shown himself superior in cavalry. The infantry which had marched at 2½ P.M. from the house of Boisseau, on the Boydtown plank-road, was drawn up in four battle lines, a mile or more in length, and in the beginning facing the White Oak road obliquely; the left or pivot was the division of General Ayres, Crawford had the center and Griffin the right. These advanced from the Boydtown plank-road, at ten o'clock, while Sheridan was thundering away with the cavalry, mounted and dismounted, and deluding the Rebels with the idea that he was the sole attacking party; they lay concealed in the woods behind the Gravelly Run meeting-house, but their left was not a half-mile distant from the Rebel works, though their right reached so far off that a novice would have criticized the position sharply. Little by little, Sheridan, extending his lines, drove the whole Rebel force into their breastworks; then he dismounted the mass of his cavalry and charged the works straight in the front, still thundering on their flank. At last, every Rebel was safe behind his intrenchments. Then the signal was given, and the concealed infantry, many thousand strong, sprang up and advanced by eçhelon to the right. Imagine a great barndoor shutting to, and you have the movement, if you can also imagine the door itself, hinge and all, moving forward also. This was the door:—

AYRES—CRAWFORD—GRIFFIN.

Stick a pin through Ayres and turn Griffin and Crawford forward as you would a spoke in a wheel, but move your pin up also a very little. In this way Ayres will advance, say half a mile, and Griffin, to describe a quarter revolution, will move through a radius of four miles. But to complicate this movement by eçhelon, we must imagine the right when half way advanced cutting across the centre and reforming, while Crawford became the right and Griffin the middle of the line of battle. Warren was with Crawford on this march. Gregory commanded the skirmishers. Ayres was so close to the Rebel left that he might be said to hinge upon it; and at 6 o'clock the whole corps column came crash upon the full flank of the astonished Rebels. Now came the pitch of the battle.

We were already on the Rebel right in force, and thinly in their rear. Our carbineers were making feint to charge in direct front, and our infantry, four deep, hemmed in their entire left. All this they did not for an instant note, so thorough was their confusion; but seeing it directly, they, so far from giving up, concentrated all their energy and fought like fiends. They had a battery in position, which belched incessantly, and over the breastworks their musketry made one unbroken roll, while against Sheridan's prowlers on their left, by skirmish and sortie, they stuck to their sinking fortunes, so as to win unwilling applause from mouths of wisest censure.

It was just at the coming up of the infantry that Sheridan's little band was pushed the hardest. At one time, indeed, they seemed about to undergo extermination; not that they wavered, but that they were so vastly over-powered. It will remain to the latest time a matter of marvel that so paltry a cavalry force could press back sixteen thousand infantry; but when the infantry blew like a great barndoor—the simile best applicable—upon the enemy's left, the victory that was to come had passed the region of strategy and resolved to an affair of personal courage. We had met the enemy; were they to be ours? To expedite this consummation every officer fought as if he were the forlorn hope. Mounted on his black pony, the same which he rode at Winchester, Sheridan galloped everywhere, his flushed face all the redder, and his plethoric, but nervous figure all the more ubiquitous. He galloped once straight down the Rebel front, with but a handful of his staff. A dozen bullets whistled for him together; one grazed his arm, at which a faithful orderly rode; the black pony leaped high, in fright, and Sheridan was untouched, but the orderly lay dead in the field, and the saddle dashed afar empty. . . .

The fight, as we closed upon the Rebels, was singularly free from great losses on our side, though desperate as any contest ever fought on the continent. One prolonged roar of rifle shook the afternoon; we carried no artillery, and the Rebel battery, until its capture, raked us like an irrepressible demon, and at every foot of the entrenchments a true man fought both in front and behind. The birds of the forest fled afar; the smoke ascended to heaven; locked in so mad a frenzy, none saw the sequel of the closing day. Now Richmond rocked in her high towers to watch the impending issue, but soon the day began to look gray, and a pale moon came tremulously out to watch the meeting squadrons. Imagine along a line of a full mile, thirty thousand men struggling for life and prestige; the woods gathering about them—but yesterday the home of hermit hawks and chipmonks—now ablaze with bursting shells, and showing in the dusk the curl of flames in the tangled grass, and, rising up the boles of the pine trees, the scaling, scorching tongues. Seven hours this terrible spectacle had been enacted, but the finale of it had almost come.

It was by all account in this hour of victory when the modest and brave General Winthrop of the first brigade, Ayres division, was mortally wounded. He was riding along the breastworks, and in the act as I am assured, of saving a friend's life, was shot through to the left lung. He fell at once, and his men, who loved him, gathered around and took him tenderly to the rear, where he died before the stretcher on which he lay could be deposited beside the meeting-house door. On the way from the field to the hospital he wandered in mind at times, crying out, "Captain Weaver how is that line? Has the attack succeeded?" . . .

At seven o'clock the Rebels came to the conclusion that they were outflanked and whipped. They had been so busily engaged that they were a long time finding out how desperate were their circumstances; but now, wearied with persistent assaults in front, they fell back to the left, only to see four close lines of battle waiting to drive them across the field, decimated. At the right the horsemen charged them in their vain attempt to fight "out," and in the rear straggling foot and cavalry began also to assemble; slant fire, cross fire, and direct fire, by file and volley rolled in perpetually, cutting down their bravest officers and strewing the fields with bleeding men; groans resounded in the intervals of exploding powder, and to add to their terror and despair, their own artillery, captured from them, threw into their own ranks, from its old position, ungrateful grape and canister, enfilading their breastworks, whizzing and plunging by air line and ricochet, and at last bodies of cavalry fairly mounted their intrenchments, and charged down the parapet, slashing and trampling them, and producing inexplicable confusion. They had no commanders, at least no orders, and looked in vain for some guiding hand to lead them out of a toil into which they had fallen so bravely and so blindly. A few more volleys, a new and irresistible charge, a shrill and warning command to die or surrender, and, with a sullen and tearful impulse, five thousand muskets are flung upon the ground, and five thousand hot, exhausted, and impotent men are Sheridan's prisoners of war.

　　　　　　　　　　—TOWNSEND, *Campaigns of a Non-Combatant*

5. "THE MOST SUPERB SOLDIER IN ALL THE WORLD" FALLS AT FIVE FORKS

One by one, in that last bitter year, the Army of Northern Virginia was losing its most dashing leaders. Jeb Stuart had fallen at Yellow Tavern, Robert Rodes at Winchester, Stephen Ramseur at Cedar Creek, General John Pegram, one of the youngest and most brilliant of brigadiers, in the fighting at Petersburg. A. P. Hill, to whom both Jackson and Lee called on their deathbeds, fell the day after Five Forks. One of the most heartbreaking of the losses of Five Forks was that of young William Pegram, the "boy" colonel of artillery—he was just twenty-three—who was admired and beloved as Pelham and Stuart and Ramseur had been.

The tragic event is here recorded by Pegram's adjutant, Gordon McCabe; after the war McCabe became one of the nation's great schoolmasters.

April 1st [1865]. Had nothing to eat, so parched some corn taken from horses' feed. Henry Lee, an old University friend of ours and Ass't Adj't. Gen'l Payne's Brigade, afterwards sent us some meat and bread. At 10 o'clk. we put 3 guns, 1 of Ellett's and Early's section, in position in the centre, and Ellett's other 3 on the right commanding a field. Soon afterwards the enemy's cavalry appeared in front of our right at the distance of 800 yds. We could plainly see them and their pennons flying in the wind. We opened at once with our guns. I told one of the gunners to fire on their colours, on which they were forming. He made a splendid shot, bursting a shell just in front of the colours. The whole line fell back into the woods, but their skirmishers occupied the yard of the Gillem House, and we continued to give them an occasional shot. Skirmishing now broke out in the centre and Col. P[egram] and myself rode down to our guns there. The skirmishing was quite heavy, and Col. ordered Lt. Early to dismount, as we were the only officers mounted on the field. He ordered me to dismount, but he wouldn't, so I wouldn't. We fired a few rounds and the skirmishing soon died out. Col. and myself went back to the right, where we expected the attack to be made. We lay down at the foot of a tree, as everything was now quiet, and he soon fell asleep.

At about 4½ the enemy attacked him, and we mounted and rode rapidly to the centre. When we reached our guns the enemy were only 30 yds. from them, and the infantry fire terrific beyond anything I have ever seen. We were the only mounted officers at that point. The officers, Lts. Hollis and Early, were as cool as on parade, and the men were serving their guns with a precision and rapidity beyond all praise. Pickett's Divn. were fighting well too. We had not been in the battery very long, when Col. P. riding between Lt. Early's guns reeled out of his saddle, shot through his left arm and left side. He cried out, 'Oh, Gordon, I'm mortally wounded, take me off the field.' His last order was, 'Fire your canister low.' I put him on a stretcher and sent him to the rear, and then went back among the guns to give the order. I ran back to the stretcher, and he took my hand and gave me a message for his mother and sisters. He begged me to remain with him, wh. I intended anyhow to do. When I got him to the ambulance, our skirmishers were falling back, square in our rear, and a line of battle pressing them. We were now completely enveloped, our left having been turned and the enemy in our rear. Our guns were carried within 3 minutes, Lt. Early killed and Lt. Hollis captured and the whole line rolled up.

The rout now became general, with the exception of Corse's Brigade, which had not been heavily engaged. This brigade opened to the right and left and let the rout pass through, and then closed up and came off with their integrity of organization unimpaired. I took Col. in my arms and made the ambulance drive between 2 parallel lines-of-battle of the enemy for 4 or 5 hundred yds. I carried him to Ford's Depot on S. S. R. R. about 10 miles from the field. While in the ambulance we prayed together and he was perfectly resigned to die. At about 10 o'clk we reached Ford's and I obtained a bed for him at a Mr Pegram's. I had given him morphine in small quantities until he was easier, and he soon fell into a doze. The enemy advanced on the place about 12 o'clk, and I was left alone with him. I sent off our sabres, horses, spurs, etc. as I felt sure that we w'd be captured. I shall never forget that night of watching. I could only pray. He breathed heavily through the night, and passed into a stupor. I bound up his wounds as well as I knew how and moistened his lips with water. At about Sunday morning April 2nd, he died as gently as possible.

Thus died the truest Christian, the most faithful friend and the most superb soldier in all the world. He was, indeed, my Jonathon, pure in heart, brave in deed, chivalric until it bordered on Quixotism, generous and utterly unselfish, he was the Havelock of the Army of Northern Virginia. I laid him out, helped to dig his grave, buried him in a blanket, and then read the Episcopal service over him.

      —GORDON, *Memories and Memorials of William Gordon McCabe*

6. THE CONFEDERATES ABANDON RICHMOND

After Five Forks the abandonment of Richmond was inevitable. To give President Davis time to move government offices and archives Lee clung to his lines at Petersburg for another day. Early on the morning of April 2 Grant assaulted the Confederate lines, carrying the first line of entrenchments. Lee retired to the suburbs of the city; Grant attacked and carried Forts Gregg and Whitworth—the last strongholds. A final assault was planned for the morning of the third, but that night Lee's army slipped away and be-

gan the race to the west. Meantime the Confederate government had evacuated Richmond; on the morning of the third the capital was formally surrendered to General Weitzel, and Federal troops moved in to restore order and put out the flames that were threatening to destroy the city.

We have here two descriptions of the evacuation of Richmond and its occupation by the Federals. The first* comes from the brilliant Constance Cary, later Mrs. Burton Harrison, whose husband was private secretary to President Davis. The second account is by a Yankee—Lieutenant R. B. Prescott, who was one of the first of the conquerors to enter the stricken city.

A. "A Great Burst of Sobbing All Over the Church"

GRACE STREET, RICHMOND, *April 4, 1865*

MY PRECIOUS MOTHER AND BROTHER:

I write you this jointly, because I can have no idea where Clarence is. Can't you imagine with what a heavy heart I begin it—? The last two days have added long years to my life. I have cried until no more tears will come, and my heart throbs to bursting night and day. When I bade you good-bye, dear, and walked home alone, I could not trust myself to give another look after you. All that evening the air was full of farewells as if to the dead. Hardly anybody went to bed. We walked through the streets like lost spirits till nearly daybreak. My dearest mother, it is a special Providence that has spared you this! Your going to nurse poor Bert at this crisis has saved you a shock I never can forget. With the din of the enemy's wagon trains, bands, trampling horses, fifes, hurrahs and cannon ever in my ears, I can hardly write coherently. As you desired, in case of trouble, I left our quarters and came over here to be under my uncle's wing. In Aunt M.'s serious illness the house is overflowing; there was not a room or a bed to give me, but that made no difference, they insisted on my staying all the same. Up under the roof there was a lumber-room with two windows and I paid an old darkey with some wrecks of food left from our housekeeping, to clear it out, and scrub floor and walls and windows, till all was absolutely clean. A cot was found and some old chairs and tables—our own bed linen was brought over, and here I write in comparative comfort, so don't bother about me!

Hardly had I seemed to have dropped upon my bed that dreadful Sunday night—or morning rather—when I was wakened suddenly by four terrific explosions, one after the other, making the windows of my garret shake. It was the blowing up, by Admiral Semmes, by order of the Secretary of the Navy, of our gunboats on the James, the signal for an all-day carnival of thundering noise and flames. Soon the fire spread, shells in the burning arsenals began to explode, and a smoke arose that shrouded the whole town, shutting out every vestige of blue sky and April sunshine. Flakes of fire fell

---

* Reprinted from *Recollections Grave and Gay* by Mrs. Burton Harrison; copyright 1911 by Charles Scribner's Sons, 1939 by Fairfax Harrison; used by permission of the publishers.

around us, glass was shattered, and chimneys fell, even so far as Grace Street from the scene. . . .

Edith and I . . . set out for the Capitol Square, taking our courage in both hands. Looking down from the upper end of the square, we saw a huge wall of fire blocking out the horizon. In a few hours no trace was left of Main, Cary, and Canal Streets, from 8th to 18th Streets, except tottering walls and smouldering ruins. The War Department was sending up jets of flame. Along the middle of the streets smouldered a long pile, like street-sweepings, of papers torn from the different departments' archives of our beloved Government, from which soldiers in blue were picking out letters and documents that caught their fancy. The Custom House was the sole building that defied the fire amongst those environing the Square. The marble Statesman on the Monument looked upon queer doings that day, inside the enclosure from which all green was soon scorched out, or trampled down by the hoofs of cavalry horses picketted at intervals about it. Mr. Reed's Church, Mrs. Stanard's house, the Prestons' house, are all burned; luckily the Lee house and that side of Franklin stand uninjured. General Lee's house has a guard camped in the front yard.

We went on to the head-quarters of the Yankee General in charge of Richmond, that day of doom, and I must say were treated with perfect courtesy and consideration. We saw many people we knew on the same errand as ourselves. We heard stately Mrs. —— and the ——'s were there to ask for food, as their families were starving. Thank God, we have not fallen to that! Certainly, her face looked like a tragic mask carved out of stone.

A courteous young lieutenant . . . was sent to pilot us out of the confusion, and identify the house, over which a guard was immediately placed. Already the town wore the aspect of one in the Middle Ages smitten by pestilence. The streets filled with smoke and flying fire were empty of the respectable class of inhabitants, the doors and shutters of every house tight closed. . . .

The ending of the first day of occupation was truly horrible. Some Negroes of the lowest grade, their heads turned by the prospect of wealth and equality, together with a mob of miserable poor whites, drank themselves mad with liquor scooped from the gutters. Reinforced, it was said, by convicts escaped from the penitentiary, they tore through the streets, carrying loot from the burnt district. (For days after, even the kitchens and cabins of the better class of darkies displayed handsome oil paintings and mirrors, rolls of stuff, rare books, and barrels of sugar and whiskey.) One gang of drunken rioters dragged coffins sacked from undertakers, filled with spoils from the speculators' shops, howling so madly one expected to hear them break into the Carmagnole. Thanks to our trim Yankee guard in the basement, we felt safe enough, but the experience was not pleasant.

Through all this strain of anguish ran like a gleam of gold the mad vain hope that Lee would yet make a stand somewhere—that Lee's dear soldiers would give us back our liberty.

Dr. Minnegerode has been allowed to continue his daily services and I never knew anything more painful and touching than that of this morning when the Litany was *sobbed out* by the whole congregation.

A service we went to the same evening at the old Monumental I never shall forget. When the rector prayed for 'the sick and wounded soldiers and all in distress of mind or body,' there was a brief pause, filled with a sound of weeping all over the church. He then gave out the hymn: 'When gathering clouds around I view.' There was no organ and a voice that started the hymn broke down in tears. Another took it up, and failed likewise. I, then, with a tremendous struggle for self-control, stood up in the corner of the pew and sang alone. At the words, 'Thou Saviour see'st the tears I shed,' there was again a great burst of crying and sobbing all over the church. I wanted to break down dreadfully, but I held on and carried the hymn to the end. As we left the church, many people came up and squeezed my hand and tried to speak, but could not. Just then a splendid military band was passing, the like of which we had not heard in years. The great swell of its triumphant music seemed to mock the shabby broken-spirited congregation defiling out of the gray old church buried in shadows, where in early Richmond days a theatre with many well-known citizens was burned! That was one of the tremendous moments of feeling I experienced that week.
  —HARRISON, *Recollections Grave and Gay*

B. "THE POOR COLORED PEOPLE THANKED GOD THAT THEIR SUFFERINGS WERE ENDED"

Every moment the light we had seen over Richmond on starting became more and more brilliant. Above it hung great clouds of heavy smoke, and as we drew nearer there arose a confused murmur now swelling into a loud roar and then subsiding, and again swelling into a great tumult of excited voices, while at frequent intervals short, sharp explosions were heard as of the discharge of field artillery. Weary, breathless, hungry, begrimed with dust and perspiration, but eager and excited, we pushed on, and at half-past six o'clock in the morning I stood with about two-thirds of my men on the summit of a hill and looked down upon the grandest and most appalling sight that my eyes ever beheld. Richmond was literally a sea of flame, out of which the church steeples could be seen protruding here and there, while over all hung a canopy of dense black smoke, lighted up now and then by the bursting shells from the numerous arsenals scattered throughout the city. I waited here until the stragglers of my command had come up, then marched down the hill until we came to a little creek, crossed by a few planks which alone separated us from the city. Two mounted cavalry-men stood upon this bridge who said that they had been sent there by General Weitzel with orders to allow no one to cross the bridge until he came up. So there was nothing to do but to wait.

The men stacked arms and threw themselves upon the ground. While resting, a rebel iron-clad lying in the James River in full sight blew up with a terrific crash, scattering fragments of iron and timbers all about us, but fortunately no one was hurt. In a few moments more a carriage appeared coming from the city, and stopped directly before us. Beckoning me to approach, the occupant asked if I was in command of the men lying about, and on being answered in the affirmative, he said that he was the mayor of Richmond, and that he wished to make a formal surrender of the city. At the same time he placed in my hands a large package, containing, I presume, official papers, the city seal, keys and other property. I told him that General Weitzel, commanding the department, would be present in a short time and that he would be a proper person to treat with. Even while we were speaking the general and his staff appeared at the top of the hill, and the mayor rode forward to meet him. The whole party shortly returned, and General Weitzel ordered me to follow him into the city.

This I did, but we had not advanced many rods before the smoke became so thick as to make it impossible to see even a few feet in advance, and for this reason, I suppose, I missed the general, he turning to the right towards the upper part of the city, and I to the left towards the river. We had not gone far before I discovered that I had become separated from him and was uncertain how to proceed, when on a lamp-post at a corner I read the words, "Main Street." Thinking this would at least conduct us to the central part of the city and assist in finding the capitol grounds, I turned into it.

The scene that met our eyes here almost baffles description. Pandemonium reigned supreme. Two large iron-clads near by in the river exploded with a deafening crash, the concussion sweeping numbers of people off their feet. The street we were in was one compact mass of frenzied people, and it was only with the greatest difficulty that we were able to force our way along. Had they been hostile our lives would not have been worth a moment's purchase.

But the poor colored people hailed our appearance with the most extravagant expressions of joy. They crowded into the ranks and besought permission to carry the soldiers' knapsacks and muskets. They clapped them on the back, hung about their necks, and "God bless you," and "Thank God, the Yankees have come," resounded on every side. Women, emaciated, barefoot, with but one scanty skirt made from old bags, fell on their knees in the street, and with clasped hands and streaming eyes thanked God that their sufferings were ended at last. Others with little children, wretched little skeletons, clinging to their scanty skirts and crying with hunger and fright, pressed into the ranks and begged most piteously for food. One woman, I distinctly remember, with three little pale, starved girls clinging about her, herself barefoot, bareheaded, thinly and miserably clad, seized my arm with a vise-like grip, and begged for the love of God, for just a morsel for her starving children. They had tasted nothing since Sunday morning, and then only a spoonful of dry meal. I gave her the contents of my haversack, and one man in the ranks, a great, rough, swearing fellow, poured into her lap his entire three days' rations of pork and hard bread, thrust a ten dollar greenback, all the money he possessed, into her hand, swearing like a pirate all the while as a means of relief to his overcharged feelings, their intensity being abundantly evident by the tears which coursed rapidly down his cheeks. . . .

The gutters literally ran whiskey. The members of the City Council, foreseeing the mischief that would ensue should the liquor shops be sacked, had rolled all the barrels to the curbstone, knocked in their heads, and emptied their contents into the gutters. The poisonous flood rolled like a river of death rapidly on into the sewers, while the atmosphere fairly reeked with its unsavory odor. The rougher element of the population, white and black alike, were dipping up the vile stuff with their hands, and pouring it down their throats. The shrill whistle of locomotives sounded loud and frequent in the near distance, as train after train hurried away bearing frantic citizens with what valuables they had time to secure. Bands of thieves and rascals of every degree, broken loose from the penitentiary, were entering the stores on either side the street and stealing whatever they could lay their hands upon, while the entire black population seemed out of doors and crazy with delight. Tumult, violence, riot, pillage, everywhere prevailed, and as if these were not enough to illustrate the horrors of war, the roar of the flames, the clanging of bells, and general uproar and confusion were sufficient to appall the stoutest heart.

Fearing violence from some unexpected source in the midst of such fearful scenes, I looked about for some avenue of escape into a less crowded street, where I could more easily keep the soldiers apart from the populace, but none presented itself. At length the heat became so great that we could proceed no further. Our hair and beards were scorched, our clothing smoked, the air we breathed was like a furnace blast, and many of the men, weighed down as they were with musket, knapsacks, blanket, ammunition, and other accoutrements, were well-nigh exhausted. Three fire engines were burning in the street immediately before us. On the sidewalk near by lay the bodies of three young girls burnt to a crisp. People jumped from the windows of burning buildings; others with wildly waving arms shrieked for help, not daring to take the fatal leap.

On a lamp-post just at my right, I read the words "Fourteenth Street," and turning to a citizen who stood in a porch on the corner, I asked him to direct me to the capitol.

"Turn right up here," he said, "go straight on for two or three streets, and you will see it just on your left." He also added that General Early, at the head of a body of Confederate cavalry, had passed along only a moment before, and with out-stretched hand showed us through the smoke the rearmost rank. . . .

The same tumultuous scenes just described were visible throughout the city. The spacious capitol grounds afforded the only spot of refuge, and these were crowded with women and children, bearing in their arms and upon their heads their most cherished possessions. Piles of furniture lay scattered in every direction, and about them clustered the hungry and destitute family groups, clinging to each other with the energy of despair. One of the most touching sights amid these accumulated horrors, was that of a little girl—a toddling infant—holding her kitten tightly under her arm, a dilapidated rag doll in one hand and grasping her mother's gown with the other, as they sought shelter from the showers of cinders, under the capitol steps.

The constant explosion of ammunition in the arsenals seemed almost like a battle. Many citizens were killed by the flying fragments. Many were burned to death. In one house seventeen people perished from the flames. The sick, the aged, helpless and infirm, left to themselves in the general panic, could only pray for deliverance, which came to them when the flames had stifled their prayers in death.

Seven hundred and fifty thousand loaded shells in the arsenals, exploding from the heat, tore their way through houses, ploughed up the streets and the gardens, and spread death and destruction on every hand. The whole city jarred and vibrated with horrid sounds, while warehouses, stores, mills, bridges, depots, and dwellings went down by scores and hundreds. The streets leading to the railroad stations were filled with a frantic mob, pushing, struggling, cursing, trampling each other without mercy in their efforts to get away with what plunder they could carry. No troops of either army were in sight, only rebel stragglers, whose long familiarity with similar scenes rendered them, no doubt, the only cool-headed and indifferent spectators of these appalling sights. Over and above all the terrible roar of the conflagration as it leaped from building to building, from street to street, filled the whole city with its scorching breath, and lent added horrors to the scene.

—Prescott, "The Capture of Richmond"

7. THE WHITE FLAG AT APPOMATTOX

On the night of April 2-3, Lee withdrew from Petersburg along the northern bank of the little Appomattox; at the same time Mahone abandoned his lines at Bermuda Hundred, and Ewell retreated from north of the James. The objective of Lee's army was Danville, where there were abundant supplies and from which he might yet hope to link up with Johnston; if he were cut off from Danville he hoped to make Lynchburg and the Valley. Grant, however, was hot in pursuit, Sheridan's cavalry in the lead. Lee planned to concentrate and provision his forces at Amelia Court House, some 30 miles west of Petersburg; when he got there, on April 4 and 5, however, he found no supplies, and a day was lost in foraging for provisions.

Meantime Sheridan's cavalry had reached Jetersville, west of Amelia Court House. Lee turned north, planning to swing around Sheridan and get to Farmville. Meade's infantry came up, however, and at Sayler's Creek inflicted a heavy defeat on the shattered Confederates. By the seventh Lee's army was reduced to two infantry and one cavalry corps, and had lost most of its wagon trains. This diminished force reached Farmville on that day, where it was once again required to fight. That night Lee resumed his retreat toward Lynchburg, but Sheridan raced ahead to Appomattox Court House and blocked his advance.

Already some of his officers were advising surrender, but Lee determined on one final try. He instructed Gordon to move against Sheridan; if he should find only cavalry he was to fight; if he found an army in front of him, he was to abandon the attempt to break through.

Early on the morning of the ninth the dauntless Gordon moved out to the attack. Only Sheridan's cavalry was in front of him, and he assailed it with fury; for a moment he was, miraculously, successful. Then, about 9 a.m. the Union V and XXIV Corps reached the battlefield, and Gordon withdrew.

Already Grant had opened discussions looking to the surrender of the Army of Northern Virginia. With the failure of Gordon to break through, Lee was now ready to discuss surrender.

We give here Joshua Chamberlain's description of the fighting on the morning of the ninth, and the "white flag, earnestly borne, like a wraith of morning mist." Chamberlain we have met in the fighting at Fredericksburg and Gettysburg. A clergyman, and professor at Bowdoin College, he enlisted as lieutenant colonel in the 20th Maine, fought in over 20 engagements, was six times wounded, received the Congressional Medal of Honor for his gallantry, and in the Appomattox campaign commanded two brigades of the V Army Corps. After the war he served as Governor of Maine and President of Bowdoin College.

THE darkest hours before the dawn of April 9, 1865, shrouded the Fifth Corps sunk in feverish sleep by the roadside six miles away from Appomattox Station on the Southside Road. Scarcely is the first broken dream begun when a cavalryman comes splashing down the road and vigorously dismounts, pulling from his jacket-front a crumpled note. The sentinel standing watch by his commander, worn in body but alert in every sense, touches your shoulder. "Orders, sir, I think." You rise on elbow, strike a match, and with smarting, streaming eyes read the brief, thrilling note, sent back by Sheridan to us infantry commanders. Like this, as I remember: "I have cut across the enemy at Appomattox Station, and captured three of his trains. If you can possibly push your infantry up here to-night, we will have great results in the morning."

Ah, sleep no more. The startling bugle notes ring out "The General"— "To the march." Word is sent for the men to take a bite of such as they have for food: the promised rations will not be up till noon, and by that time we shall be perhaps too far away for such greeting. A few try to eat, no matter what. Meanwhile, almost with one foot in the stirrup, you take from the hands of the black boy a tin plate of nondescript food and a dipper of miscalled coffee;—all equally black, like the night around. You eat and drink at a swallow; mount, and away to get to the head of the column before you shout the "Forward." They are there—the men: shivering to their senses as if risen out of the earth, but something in them not of it. Now sounds the "Forward," for the last time in our long-drawn strife. And they move— these men—sleepless, supperless, breakfastless, sore-footed, stiff-jointed, sense-benumbed, but with flushed faces pressing for the front.

By sunrise we have reached Appomattox Station, where Sheridan has left the captured trains. A staff officer is here to turn us square to the right, to the Appomattox River, cutting across Lee's retreat. Already we hear the sharp ring of the horse-artillery, answered ever and anon by heavier field

PETERSBURG TO APPOMATTOX

guns; and drawing nearer, the crack of cavalry carbines; and unmistakably, too, the graver roll of musketry of opposing infantry. There is no mistake. Sheridan is square across the enemy's front, and with that glorious cavalry alone is holding at bay all that is left of the proudest army of the Confederacy. It has come at last,—the supreme hour. No thought of human wants or weakness now: all for the front; all for the flag, for the final stroke to make its meaning real—these men of the Potomac and the James, side by side, at the double in time and column, now one and now the other in the road or the fields beside. One striking feature I can never forget,—Birney's black men abreast with us, pressing forward to save the white man's country.

We did not know exactly what was going on. We did know that our cavalry had been doing splendid work all night, and in fact now was holding at bay Lee's whole remaining army. . . .

I was therefore in about the middle of our Fifth Corps column. The boom of the battle thickened ahead of us. We were intent for the front. Suddenly I am accosted by a cavalry staff officer dashing out of a rough wood road leading off to our right. "General, you command this column?"

"Two brigades of it, sir; about half the First Division, Fifth Corps."

"Sir, General Sheridan wishes you to break off from this column and come to his support. The rebel infantry is pressing him hard. Our men are falling back. Don't wait for orders through the regular channels, but act on this at once."

Of course I obey, without question. . . .

Sharp work now. Pushing through the woods at cavalry speed, we come out right upon Sheridan's battle flag gleaming amidst the smoke of his batteries in the edge of the open field. Weird-looking flag it is: fork-tailed, red and white, the two bands that composed it each charged with a star of the contrasting color; two eyes sternly glaring through the cannon-cloud. Beneath it, that storm-center spirit, that form of condensed energies, mounted on the grim charger, Rienzi, that turned the battle of the Shenandoah,—both, rider and steed, of an unearthly shade of darkness, terrible to look upon, as if masking some unknown powers.

Right before us, our cavalry, Devins' division, gallantly stemming the surges of the old Stonewall brigade, desperate to beat its way through. I ride straight to Sheridan. A dark smile and impetuous gesture are my old orders. Forward into double lines of battle, past Sheridan, his guns, his cavalry, and on for the quivering crest! For a moment it is a glorious sight: every arm of the service in full play,—cavalry, artillery, infantry; then a sudden shifting scene as the cavalry, disengaged by successive squadrons, rally under their bugle-calls with beautiful precision and promptitude, and sweep like a storm-cloud beyond our right to close in on the enemy's left and complete the fateful envelopment.

Ord's troops are now square across the Lynchburg Pike. Ayres and Bartlett have joined them on their right, and all are in for it sharp. In this new front we take up the battle. Gregory follows in on my left. It is a formidable front we make. The scene darkens. In a few minutes the tide is turned; the incoming wave is at flood; the barrier recedes. In truth, the Stonewall men hardly show their well-proved mettle. They seem astonished to see before them these familiar flags of their old antagonists, not having thought it possible that we could match our cavalry and march around and across their pressing columns.

Their last hope is gone,—to break through our cavalry before our infantry can get up. Neither to Danville nor to Lynchburg can they cut their way; and close upon their rear, five miles away, are pressing the Second and Sixth Corps of the Army of the Potomac. It is the end! They are now giving way, but keep good front, by force of old habit. Halfway up the slope they make a stand, with what perhaps they think a good omen,—behind a stone wall. I try a little artillery on them, which directs their thoughts towards the crest behind them, and stiffen my lines for a rush, anxious for that crest myself. My intensity may have seemed like excitement. For Griffin comes up, quizzing me in his queer way of hitting off our weak points when we get a little too serious; accusing me of mistaking a blooming peach tree for a rebel flag, where I was dropping a few shells into a rallying crowd. I apologize—I was a little near-sighted, and hadn't been experienced in long-range fighting. But as for peaches, I was going to get some if the pits didn't sit too hard on our stomachs. . . .

But now comes up Ord with a positive order: "Don't expose your lines on that crest. The enemy have massed their guns to give it a raking fire the moment you set foot there." I thought I saw a qualifying look as he turned away. But left alone, youth struggled with prudence. My troops were in a bad position down here. I did not like to be "the under dog." It was much better to be on top and at least know what there was beyond. So I thought of Grant and his permission to "push things" when we got them going; and of Sheridan and his last words as he rode away with his cavalry, smiting his hands together—"Now smash 'em, I tell you; smash 'em!" So we took this for orders, and on the crest we stood. One booming cannon-shot passed close along our front, and in the next moment all was still.

We had done it,—had "exposed ourselves to the view of the enemy." But it was an exposure that worked two ways. For there burst upon our vision a mighty scene, fit cadence of the story of tumultuous years. Encompassed by the cordon of steel that crowned the heights about the Court House, on the slopes of the valley formed by the sources of the Appomattox, lay the remnants of that far-famed counterpart and companion of our own in momentous history,—the Army of Northern Virginia—Lee's army! . . .

It was hilly, broken ground, in effect a vast amphitheater, stretching a mile perhaps from crest to crest. On the several confronting slopes before us dusky masses of infantry suddenly resting in place; blocks of artillery, standing fast in a column or mechanically swung into park; clouds of cavalry small and great, slowly moving, in simple restlessness;—all without apparent attempt at offense or defence, or even military order.

In the hollow is the Appomattox,—which we had made the dead-line for our baffled foe, for its whole length, a hundred miles; here but a rivulet that might almost be stepped over dry-shod, and at the road crossing not thought worth while to bridge. Around its edges, now trodden to mire, swarms an indescribable crowd: worn-out soldier struggling to the front; demoralized citizen and denizen, white, black, and all shades between,—following Lee's army, or flying before these suddenly confronted terrible Yankees pictured to them as demon-shaped and bent; animals, too, of all forms and grades; vehicles of every description and non-description,—public and domestic, four-wheeled, or two, or one,—heading and moving in every direction, a swarming mass of chaotic confusion.

All this within sight of every eye on our bristling crest. Had one the heart to strike at beings so helpless, the Appomattox would quickly become a surpassing Red Sea horror. But the very spectacle brings every foot to an instinctive halt. We seem the possession of a dream. We are lost in a vision of human tragedy. But our light-twelve Napoleon guns come rattling up behind us to go into battery; we catch the glitter of the cavalry blades and brasses beneath the oak groves away to our right, and the ominous closing in on the fated foe. . . .

Watching intently, my eye was caught by the figure of a horseman riding out between those lines, soon joined by another, and taking a direction across the cavalry front towards our position. They were nearly a mile away, and I curiously watched them till lost from sight in the nearer broken ground and copses between.

Suddenly rose to sight another form, close in our own front,—a soldierly young figure, a Confederate staff officer undoubtedly. Now I see the white flag earnestly borne, and its possible purport sweeps before my inner vision like a wraith of morning mist. He comes steadily on, the mysterious form in gray, my mood so whimsically sensitive that I could even smile at the material of the flag,—wondering where in either army was found a towel, and one so white. But it bore a mighty message,—that simple emblem of homely service, wafted hitherward above the dark and crimsoned streams that never can wash themselves away.

The messenger draws near, dismounts; with graceful salutation and hardly suppressed emotion delivers his message: "Sir, I am from General Gordon. General Lee desires a cessation of hostilities until he can hear from General Grant as to the proposed surrender."

What word is this! so long so dearly fought for, so feverishly dreamed, but ever snatched away, held hidden and aloof; now smiting the senses with a dizzy flash! "Surrender?" We had no rumor of this from the messages that had been passing between Grant and Lee, for now these two days, behind us. "Surrender?" It takes a moment to gather one's speech. "Sir," I answer, "that matter exceeds my authority. I will send to my superior. General Lee is right. He can do no more." All this with a forced calmness, covering a tumult of heart and brain. I bid him wait a while, and the message goes up to my corps commander, General Griffin, leaving me mazed at the boding change.

Now from the right come foaming up in cavalry fashion the two forms I had watched from away beyond. A white flag again, held strong aloft, making straight for the little group beneath our battle-flag, high borne also,—the red Maltese cross on a field of white, that had thrilled hearts long ago. I see now that it is one of our cavalry staff in lead,—indeed I recognize him, Colonel Whitaker of Custer's staff; and, hardly keeping pace with him, a Confederate staff officer. Without dismounting, without salutation, the cavalryman shouts: "This is unconditional surrender! This is the end!" Then he hastily introduces his companion, and adds: "I am just from Gordon and Longstreet. Gordon says 'For God's sake, stop this infantry, or hell will be to pay!' I'll go to Sheridan," he adds, and dashes away with the white flag, leaving Longstreet's aide with me.

I was doubtful of my duty. The flag of truce was in, but I had no right to act upon it without orders. There was still some firing from various quarters, lulling a little where the white flag passed near. But I did not press things quite so hard. Just then a last cannon-shot from the edge of the town plunges through the breast of a gallant and dear young officer in my front line,—Lieutenant Clark, of the 185th New York,—the last man killed in the Army of the Potomac, if not the last in the Appomattox lines. Not a strange thing for war,—this swift stroke of the mortal; but coming after the truce was in, it seemed a cruel fate for one so deserving to share his country's joy, and a sad peace-offering for us all.

Shortly comes the order, in due form, to cease firing and to halt. There was not much firing to cease from; but "halt," then and there? It is beyond human power to stop the men, whose one word and thought and action through crimsoned years had been but forward. They had seen the flag of truce, and could divine its outcome. But the habit was too strong; they cared not for points of direction, it was forward still,—forward to the end; forward to the new beginning; forward to the Nation's second birth!

—CHAMBERLAIN, *The Passing of the Armies*

8. GENERAL LEE SURRENDERS AT APPOMATTOX

The story of the surrender needs no further introduction. As early as April 7 Grant had suggested to Lee the propriety of surrender, in order to avoid further bloodshed. Lee, as we have seen, was not yet ready to give up. But when he found his sadly decimated army surrounded, on the ninth, he knew that the end had come. "There is nothing left for me to do but go and see General Grant," said Lee, "and I would rather die a thousand deaths." But there was no alternative; that afternoon Lee rode Traveller to the McLean house in Appomattox Court House and accepted Grant's terms of surrender.

We give here Colonel Charles Marshall's account of the famous scene in the McLean house.

WE struck up the hill towards Appomattox Court House. There was a man named McLean who used to live on the first battle field of Manassas, at a house about a mile from Manassas Junction. He did n't like the war, and having seen the first battle of Manassas, he thought he would get away where there would n't be any more fighting, so he moved down to Appomattox Court House. General Lee told me to go forward and find a house where he could meet General Grant, and of all people, whom should I meet but McLean. I rode up to him and said, "Can you show me a house where General Lee and General Grant can meet together?" He took me into a house that was all dilapidated and that had no furniture in it. I told him it would n't do.

Then he said, "Maybe my house will do!" He lived in a very comfortable house, and I told him I thought that would suit. I had taken the orderly along with me, and I sent him back to bring General Lee and Babcock, who were coming on behind. I went into the house and sat down, and after a while General Lee and Babcock came in. Colonel Babcock told his orderly that he was to meet General Grant, who was coming on the road, and turn him in when he came along. So General Lee, Babcock and myself sat down in McLean's parlour and talked in the most friendly and affable way.

In about half an hour we heard horses, and the first thing I knew General Grant walked into the room. There were with him General Sheridan, General Ord, Colonel Badeau, General Porter, Colonel Parker, and quite a number of other officers whose names I do not recall.

General Lee was standing at the end of the room opposite the door when General Grant walked in. General Grant had on a sack coat, a loose fatigue coat, but he had no side arms. He looked as though he had had a pretty hard time. He had been riding and his clothes were somewhat dusty and a little soiled. He walked up to General Lee and Lee recognized him at once. He had known him in the Mexican war. General Grant greeted him in the most cordial manner, and talked about the weather and other things in a very friendly way. Then General Grant brought up his officers and introduced them to General Lee.

I remember that General Lee asked for General Lawrence Williams, of the Army of the Potomac. That very morning General Williams had sent word by somebody to General Lee that Custis Lee, who had been captured at Sailor Creek and was reported killed, was not hurt, and General Lee asked General Grant where General Williams was, and if he could not send for him to come and see him. General Grant sent somebody out for General Williams, and when he came, General Lee thanked him for having sent him word about the safety of his son.

After a very free talk General Lee said to General Grant: "General, I have come to meet you in accordance with my letter to you this morning, to treat about the surrender of my army, and I think the best way would be for you to put your terms in writing."

General Grant said: "Yes; I believe it will."

So a Colonel Parker, General Grant's Aide-de-Camp, brought a little table over from a corner of the room, and General Grant wrote the terms and conditions of surrender on what we call field note paper, that is, a paper that makes a copy at the same time as the note is written. After he had written it, he took it over to General Lee.

General Lee was sitting at the side of the room; he rose and went to meet General Grant to take that paper and read it over. When he came to the part in which only public property was to be surrendered, and the officers were to retain their side arms and personal baggage, General Lee said: "That will have a very happy effect."

General Lee then said to General Grant: "General, our cavalrymen furnish their own horses; they are not Government horses, some of them may be, but of course you will find them out—any property that is public property, you will ascertain that, but it is nearly all private property, and these men will want to plough ground and plant corn."

General Grant answered that as the terms were written, only the officers were permitted to take their private property, but almost immediately he added that he supposed that most of the men in the ranks were small farmers, and that the United States did not want their horses. He would give orders to allow every man who claimed to own a horse or mule to take the animal home.

General Lee having again said that this would have an excellent effect, once more looked over the letter, and being satisfied with it, told me to write a reply. General Grant told Colonel Parker to copy his letter, which was written in pencil, and put it in ink. Colonel Parker took the table and carried it back to a corner of the room, leaving General Grant and General Lee facing each other and talking together. There was no ink in McLean's inkstand, except some thick stuff that was very much like pitch, but I had a screw boxwood inkstand that I always carried with me in a little satchel that I had at my side, and I gave that to Colonel Parker, and he copied General Grant's letter with the aid of my inkstand and my pen.

There was another table right against the wall, and a sofa next to it. I was sitting on the arm of the sofa near the table, and General Sheridan was on the sofa next to me. While Colonel Parker was copying the letter, General Sheridan said to me, "This is very pretty country."

I said, "General, I have n't seen it by daylight. All my observations have been made by night and I have n't seen the country at all myself."

He laughed at my remark, and while we were talking I heard General Grant say this: "Sheridan, how many rations have you?"

General Sheridan said: "How many do you want?" and General Grant said, "General Lee has about a thousand or fifteen hundred of our people prisoners, and they are faring the same as his men, but he tells me his have n't anything. Can you send them some rations?"

"Yes," he answered. They had gotten some of our rations, having captured a train.

General Grant said: "How many can you send?" and he replied "Twenty-five thousand rations."

General Grant asked if that would be enough, and General Lee replied "Plenty; plenty; an abundance;" and General Grant said to Sheridan "Order your commissary to send to the Confederate Commissary twenty-five thousand rations for our men and his men."

After a while Colonel Parker got through with his copy of General Grant's letter and I sat down to write a reply. I began it in the usual way: "I have the honor to acknowledge the receipt of your letter of such a date," and then went on to say the terms were satisfactory.

I took the letter over to General Lee, and he read it and said: "Don't say, 'I have the honor to acknowledge the receipt of your letter of such a date'; he is here; just say, 'I accept these terms.' "

Then I wrote:—

HEADQUARTERS OF THE ARMY OF NORTHERN VIRGINIA
April 9, 1865

I received your letter of this date containing the terms of the surrender of the Army of Northern Virginia proposed by you. As they are substantially the same as those expressed in your letter of the 8th instant, they are accepted. I will proceed to designate the proper officers to carry the stipulations into effect.

Then General Grant signed his letter, and I turned over my letter to General Lee and he signed it. Parker handed me General Grant's letter, and I handed him General Lee's reply, and the surrender was accomplished. There was no theatrical display about it. It was in itself perhaps the greatest tragedy that ever occurred in the history of the world, but it was the simplest, plainest, and most thoroughly devoid of any attempt at effect, that you can imagine.

The story of General Grant returning General Lee's sword to him is absurd, because General Grant proposed in his letter that the officers of the Confederate Army should retain their side-arms. Why, in the name of common sense, anybody should imagine that General Lee, after receiving a letter which said that he should retain his side-arms, yet should offer to surrender his sword to General Grant, is hard to understand. The only thing of the kind that occurred in the whole course of the transaction—which occupied perhaps an hour—was this: General Lee was in full uniform. He had on the handsomest uniform I ever saw him wear; and he had on a sword with a gold, a very handsome gold and leather, scabbard that had been presented to him by English ladies. General Grant excused himself to General Lee towards the close of the conversation between them, for not having his side arms with him; he told him that when he got his letter he was about four miles from his wagon in which his arms and uniform were, and he said that he had thought that General Lee would rather receive him as he was, than be detained, while he sent back to get his sword and uniform. General Lee told him he was very much obliged to him and was very glad indeed that he had n't done it.

—SIR FREDERICK MAURICE, ed., *An Aide-de-Camp of Lee*

9. "THE WHOLE COLUMN SEEMED CROWNED WITH RED"

The day after the surrender Grant rode over to Lee's headquarters to discuss with him the formalities of surrender; later that day Meade rode over to pay his respects. Already the leaders of the grand armies were binding up the wounds of war, taking the road to reunion. Formal surrender was arranged for the twelfth, and General Chamberlain was designated to receive it on behalf of Grant. Grant, Meade, and Sheridan had all left Appomattox by that day, but Lee stayed on to the bitter end, though he did not witness the actual stacking of arms.

The description of that ceremony comes, appropriately enough, from Chamberlain himself.

IT was now the morning of the 12th of April. I had been ordered to have my lines formed for the ceremony at sunrise. It was a chill gray morning, depressing to the senses. . . . We formed along the principal street, from the bluff bank of the stream to near the Court House on the left,—to face the last line of battle, and receive the last remnant of the arms and colors of that great army which ours had been created to confront for all that death can do for life. . . .

Our earnest eyes scan the busy groups on the opposite slopes, breaking camp for the last time, taking down their little shelter-tents and folding them carefully as precious things, then slowly forming ranks as for unwelcome duty. And now they move. The dusky swarms forge forward into gray columns of march. On they come, with the old swinging route step and swaying battle-flags. In the van, the proud Confederate ensign—the great field of white with canton of star-strewn cross of blue on a field of red, the regimental battle-flags with the same escutcheon following on, crowded so thick, by thinning out of men, that the whole column seemed crowned with red. At the right of our line our little group mounted beneath our flags, the red Maltese cross on a field of white, erewhile so bravely borne through many a field more crimson than itself, its mystic meaning now ruling all.

The momentous meaning of this occasion impressed me deeply. I resolved to mark it by some token of recognition, which could be no other than a salute of arms. Well aware of the responsibility assumed, and of the criticisms that would follow, as the sequel proved, nothing of that kind could move me in the least. The act could be defended, if needful, by the suggestion that such a salute was not to the cause for which the flag of the Confederacy stood, but to its going down before the flag of the Union. My main reason, however, was one for which I sought no authority nor asked forgiveness. Before us in proud humiliation stood the embodiment of manhood: men whom neither toils and sufferings, nor the fact of death, nor disaster, nor hopelessness could bend from their resolve; standing before us now, thin, worn, and famished, but erect, and with eyes looking level into ours, waking memories that bound us together as no other bond;—was not such manhood to be welcomed back into a Union so tested and assured?

Instruction had been given; and when the head of each division column comes opposite our group, our bugle sounds the signal and instantly our whole line from right to left, regiment by regiment in succession, gives the soldier's salutation, from the "order arms" to the old "carry"—the marching salute. Gordon at the head of the column, riding with heavy spirit and downcast face, catches the sound of shifting arms, looks up, and, taking the meaning, wheels superbly, making with himself and his horse one uplifted figure, with profound salutation as he drops the point of his sword to the boot toe; then facing to his own command, gives word for his successive brigades to pass us with the same position of the manual,—honor answering honor. On our part not a sound of trumpet more, nor roll of drum; not a cheer, nor word nor whisper of vain-glorying, nor motion of man standing again at the order, but an awed stillness rather, and breath-holding, as if it were the passing of the dead!

As each successive division masks our own, it halts, the men face inward towards us across the road, twelve feet away; then carefully "dress" their line, each captain taking pains for the good appearance of his company, worn and half starved as they were. The field and staff take their positions in the intervals of regiments; generals in rear of their commands. They fix bayonets, stack arms; then, hesitatingly, remove cartridge-boxes and lay them down. Lastly,—reluctantly, with agony of expression,—they tenderly fold their flags, battle-worn and torn, blood-stained, heart-holding colors, and lay them down; some frenziedly rushing from the ranks, kneeling over them, clinging to them, pressing them to their lips with burning tears. And only the Flag of the Union greets the sky!

What visions thronged as we looked into each other's eyes! Here pass the men of Antietam, the Bloody Lane, the Sunken Road, the Cornfield, the Burnside-Bridge; the men whom Stonewall Jackson on the second night at Fredericksburg begged Lee to let him take and crush the two corps of the Army of the Potomac huddled in the streets in darkness and confusion; the men who swept away the Eleventh Corps at Chancellorsville; who left six thousand of their companions around the bases of Culp's and Cemetery Hills at Gettysburg; these survivors of the terrible Wilderness, the Bloody-Angle at Spottsylvania, the slaughter pen of Cold Harbor, the whirlpool of Bethesda Church!

Here comes Cobb's Georgia Legion, which held the stone wall on Marye's Heights at Fredericksburg, close before which we piled our dead for breastworks so that the living might stay and live.

Here too come Gordon's Georgians and Hoke's North Carolinians, who stood before the terrific mine explosion at Petersburg, and advancing retook the smoking crater and the dismal heaps of dead—ours more than theirs—huddled in the ghastly chasm.

Here are the men of McGowan, Hunton, and Scales, who broke the Fifth Corps lines on the White Oak Road, and were so desperately driven back on that forlorn night of March 31st by my thrice-decimated brigade.

Now comes Anderson's Fourth Corps, only Bushrod Johnson's Division left, and this the remnant of those we fought so fiercely on the Quaker Road two weeks ago, with Wise's Legion, too fierce for its own good.

Here passes the proud remnant of Ransom's North Carolinians which we swept through Five Forks ten days ago,—and all the little that was left of this division in the sharp passages at Sailor's Creek five days thereafter.

Now makes its last front A. P. Hill's old Corps, Heth now at the head, since Hill had gone too far forward ever to return: the men who poured destruction into our division at Shepardstown Ford, Antietam, in 1862, when Hill reported the Potomac running blue with our bodies; the men who opened the desperate first day's fight at Gettysburg, where withstanding them so stubbornly our Robinson's Brigades lost 1185 men, and the Iron Brigade alone 1153,—these men of Heth's Division here too losing 2850 men, companions of these now looking into our faces so differently.

What is this but the remnant of Mahone's Division, last seen by us at the North Anna? its thinned ranks of worn, bright-eyed men recalling scenes of costly valor and ever-remembered history.

Now the sad great pageant—Longstreet and his men! What shall we give them for greeting that has not already been spoken in volleys of thunder and written in lines of fire on all the river-banks of Virginia? Shall we go back to Gaines' Mill and Malvern Hill? Or to the Antietam of Maryland, or Gettysburg of Pennsylvania?—deepest graven of all. For here is what remains of Kershaw's Division, which left 40 per cent. of its men at Antietam, and at Gettysburg with Barksdale's and Semmes' Brigades tore through the Peach Orchard, rolling up the right of our gallant Third Corps, sweeping over the proud batteries of Massachusetts—Bigelow and Philips,—where under the smoke we saw the earth brown and blue with prostrate bodies of horses and men, and the tongues of overturned cannon and caissons pointing grim and stark in the air.

Then in the Wilderness, at Spottsylvania and thereafter, Kershaw's Division again, in deeds of awful glory, held their name and fame, until fate met them at Sailor's Creek, where Kershaw himself, and Ewell, and so many more, gave up their arms and hopes,—all, indeed, but manhood's honor.

With what strange emotion I look into these faces before which in the mad assault on Rives' Salient, June 18, 1864, I was left for dead under their eyes! It is by miracles we have lived to see this day,—any of us standing here.

Now comes the sinewy remnant of fierce Hood's Division, which at Gettysburg we saw pouring through the Devil's Den, and the Plum Run gorge; turning again by the left our stubborn Third Corps, then swarming up the rocky bastions of Round Top, to be met there by equal valor, which changed Lee's whole plan of battle and perhaps the story of Gettysburg.

Ah, is this Pickett's Division?—this little group left of those who on the lurid last day of Gettysburg breasted level cross-fire and thunderbolts of storm, to be strewn back drifting wrecks, where after that awful, futile, pitiful charge we buried them in graves a furlong wide, with name unknown!

Met again in the terrible cyclone-sweep over the breastworks at Five Forks; met now, so thin, so pale, purged of the mortal,—as if knowing pain or joy no more. How could we help falling on our knees, all of us together, and praying God to pity and forgive us all!

—CHAMBERLAIN, *The Passing of the Armies*

10. "THE SHATTERED REMAINS OF LEE'S ARMY"

Some 28,000 soldiers of the Army of Northern Virginia were paroled at Appomattox; the others had melted away. When Johnston surrendered, on April 14, some 37,000 were paroled. Taylor's forces in Alabama did not surrender until May 4, and Kirby Smith, who commanded the Trans-Mississippi area, held out until May 26. Long before that, however, the process of disintegration was under way, soldiers streaming back to their homes.

Here our Georgia girl, Eliza Andrews, describes the disintegration of the armies and the home-coming of the soldiers.

April 24, 1865. Monday.—The shattered remains of Lee's army are beginning to arrive. There is an endless stream passing between the transportation office and the depot, and trains are going and coming at all hours. The soldiers bring all sorts of rumors and keep us stirred up in a state of never-ending excitement. Our avenue leads from the principal street on which they pass, and great numbers stop to rest in the grove. Emily is kept busy cooking rations for them, and pinched as we are ourselves for supplies, it is impossible to refuse anything to the men that have been fighting for us. Even when they don't ask for anything the poor fellows look so tired and hungry that we feel tempted to give them everything we have.

Two nice-looking officers came to the kitchen door this afternoon while I was in there making some sorghum cakes to send to General Elzey's camp. They then walked slowly through the back yard and seemed reluctant to tear themselves away from such a sweet, beautiful place. Nearly everybody that passes the street gate stops and looks up the avenue, and I know they can't help thinking what a beautiful place it is. The Cherokee rose hedge is white with blooms. It is glorious. A great many of the soldiers camp in the grove, though Colonel Weems has located a public camping ground for them farther out of town. The officers often ask for a night's lodging, but our house is always so full of friends who have a nearer claim that a great many have to be refused. It hurts my conscience ever to turn off a Confederate soldier on any account, but we are so overwhelmed with company—friends and people bringing letters of introduction—that the house, big as it is, will hardly hold us all, and members of the family have to pack together like sardines. Captain John Nightingale's servant came in this afternoon—the "little Johnny Nightingale" I used to play with down on the old Tallasee plantation—but reports that he does not know where his master is. He says the Yankees captured him (the Negro) and took away his master's horse that he was tending, but as soon as night came on he made his escape on another horse that he took from them, and put out for home. He says he don't like the Yankees because they "didn't show no respec' for his feelin's." He talks with a strong salt-water brogue and they laughed at him, which he thought very ill-mannered. Father sent him round to the Negro quarters to wait till his master turns up.

May 1st, Monday.— . . . The conduct of a Texas regiment in the streets this afternoon gave us a sample of the chaos and general demoralization that may be expected to follow the breaking up of our government. They raised a riot about their rations, in which they were joined by all the disorderly elements among both soldiers and citizens. First they plundered the commissary department and then turned loose on the quartermaster's stores. Paper, pens, buttons, tape, cloth—everything in the building—was seized and strewn about on the ground. Negroes and children joined the mob and grabbed what they could of the plunder. Colonel Weems's provost guard refused to interfere, saying they were too good soldiers to fire on their comrades, and so the plundering went on unopposed. Nobody seemed to care much, as we all know the Yankees will get it in the end, anyway, if our men don't.

I was at Miss Maria Randolph's when the disturbance began, but by keeping to the back streets I avoided the worst of the row, though I encountered a number of stragglers running away with their booty. The soldiers were very generous with their "confiscated" goods, giving away paper, pens, tape, etc., to anybody they happened to meet. One of them poked a handful of pen staves at me; another, staggering under an armful of stationery, threw me a ream of paper, saying, "There, take that and write to your sweetheart on it." I took no notice of any of them but hurried on home as fast as I could, all the way meeting Negroes, children, and men loaded with plunder.

When I reached home I found some of our own servants with their arms full of thread, paper, and pens which they offered to sell me, and one of them gave me several reams of paper. I carried them to Father, and he collected all the other booty he could find, intending to return it to headquarters, but he was told that there is no one to receive it, no place to send it to—in fact, there seemed to be no longer any headquarters nor any other semblance of authority. Father saved one box of bacon for Colonel Weems by hauling it away in his wagon and concealing it in his smokehouse. All of Johnston's army and the greater portion of Lee's are still to pass through, and since the rioters have destroyed so much of the forage and provisions intended for their use, there will be great difficulty in feeding them. They did not stop at food but helped themselves to all the horses and mules they needed. A band of them made a raid on General Elzey's camp and took nine of his mules. They excused themselves by saying that all government stores will be seized by the Yankees in a few days, anyway, if left alone, and our own soldiers might as well get the good of them while they can. This would be true if there were not so many others yet to come who ought to have their share.

Our back yard and kitchen have been filled all day, as usual, with soldiers waiting to have their rations cooked. One of them, who had a wounded arm, came into the house to have it dressed and said that he was at Salisbury when

Garnett was shot and saw him fall. He told some miraculous stories about the valorous deeds of "the Colonel," and although they were so exaggerated that I set them down as apocryphal, I gave him a piece of cake, notwithstanding, to pay him for telling them.

May 2, Tuesday,— . . . It seems as if all the people I ever heard of, or never heard of, either, for that matter, are passing through Washington. Some of our friends pass on without stopping to see us because they say they are too ragged and dirty to show themselves. Poor fellows! if they only knew how honorable rags and dirt are now, in our eyes, when endured in the service of their country, they would not be ashamed of them. The son of the richest man in New Orleans trudged through the other day with no coat to his back, no shoes on his feet. The town is full of celebrities, and many poor fugitives whose necks are in danger meet here to concert plans for escape; and I put it in my prayers every night that they may be successful. General Wigfall started for the West some days ago, but his mules were stolen, and he had to return. He is frantic, they say, with rage and disappointment. General Toombs left tonight, but old Governor Brown, it is said, has determined not to desert his post. I am glad he has done something to deserve respect and hope he may get off yet, as soon as the Yankees appoint a military governor. Clement Clay is believed to be well on his way to the Trans-Mississippi, the land of promise now, or rather the city of refuge from which it is hoped a door of escape may be found to Mexico or Cuba. The most terrible part of the war is now to come, the "bloody assizes." "Kirke's lambs," in the shape of Yankee troopers, are closing in upon us; our own disbanded armies, ragged, starving, hopeless, reckless, are roaming about without order or leaders, making their way to their far-off homes as best they can. The props that held society up are broken. Everything is in a state of disorganization and tumult. We have no currency, no law save the primitive code that might makes right. We are in a transition state from war to subjugation, and it is far worse than was the transition from peace to war. The suspense and anxiety in which we live are terrible.

—ANDREWS, *The War-Time Journal of a Georgia Girl*

11. THE STARS AND STRIPES ARE RAISED OVER FORT SUMTER

When the Confederate forces evacuated Charleston in February 1865, and Union troops entered, the first thought of the captors was to hold a ceremonial reraising of the flag over the fort. The event was set for April 14, the anniversary of the surrender four years before, and the flag was hoisted by Robert Anderson, who was in command in 1861.

This moving scene is described by Mary Cadwalader Jones, daughter of a well-known Philadelphia attorney, and granddaughter of Horace Binney.

ON March 18, 1865, Edwin M. Stanton, Lincoln's last Secretary of War, wrote to brevet Major General Robert Anderson:

"I have the pleasure of communicating to you the inclosed order of the President, directing the flag of the United States to be raised and planted upon the ruins of Fort Sumter by your hands, on the 14th day of April next, the fourth anniversary of the evacuation of that post by the United States forces under your command."

It was my good fortune to be there. . . .

Sailing from New York in the end of February, 1865, we landed at Hilton Head and reached Charleston by way of Savannah in the last days of March or beginning of April. To one who had never seen the actual effects of war, the city was a melancholy spectacle. Our bombardment had left its marks everywhere, even on church steeples and on gravestones in the cemeteries. One heavy Parrott gun, called by our men the "Swamp Angel" which had been planted in a marsh five miles inland, did a great deal of damage before she burst, and was looked upon by the Charlestonians with a mixture of wrath and amazement.

Every one who could possibly get away had left the city before our troops entered it; the streets were deserted except for our sentries, strolling soldiers and sailors, and bands of Negroes who had floated down on flatboats from distant plantations, many of them never having seen a large town before in their lives. Almost without exception the house and body servants had stuck to their masters and mistresses; these were field hands, and they gaped and laughed like careless children. As their new freedom did not feed them, they lived chiefly on the good-natured charity of our troops and at night camped in the empty cotton warehouses, with the natural result of frequent fires.

Heavy cloth-of-gold roses hung over garden walls and on the porches of closely-shuttered houses; occasionally an old servant would creep furtively from a back door; but there was no sign of ordinary everyday life—the men were all at the war and the women and children either away or in hiding. It had been different in the less aristocratic Savannah, which the Federal troops had occupied since December; when I walked about there, always with an officer or an orderly, the girls would run up their high steps and turn their backs sharply on the hated blue uniform, but if I looked round quickly after I had gone a little farther I usually caught them gazing eagerly at the back of my frock. Fashions were four years old in the Confederacy; it was worth while to run the blockade for rifles or quinine, but not for furbelows. Charleston was, however, too proud and too sad to care about fashions.

The ceremony was to be at noon punctually; four or five thousand people wanted to go; and there was no regular communication between Sumter and the town. The big visiting steamship ferried her own passengers, and the boats belonging to the blockading squadron plied busily to and fro, as temporary landings and steps had been put up on all sides of the fort walls. The entire management was in the hands of the Navy, and everything went like clockwork.

The ceremony began with a short prayer by the old army chaplain who had prayed when the flag was hoisted over Fort Sumter on December 27, 1860. Next a Brooklyn clergyman read parts of several Psalms, expecting the company to read alternate verses, as in church; but that was not very effective, because if any copies were printed, there were not enough of them to go round. Then Sergeant Hart, who had held up the flag when its staff was shot through in the first attack, came forward quietly and drew the selfsame flag out of an ordinary leather mail bag. We all held our breath for a second, and then we gave a queer cry, between a cheer and a yell; nobody started and nobody led it; I never heard anything like it before or since, but I can hear it now. It stopped suddenly, for we saw that a couple of the sailors who had been in the first fight were fastening the flag to its new halyards with a little wreath of laurel on top. General Anderson stood up, bareheaded, took the halyards in his hands, and began to speak. At first I could not hear him, for his voice came thickly, but in a moment he said clearly, "I thank God that I have lived to see this day," and after a few more words he began to hoist the flag. It went up slowly and hung limp against the staff, a weather-beaten, frayed, and shell-torn old flag, not fit for much more work, but when it had crept clear of the shelter of the walls a sudden breath of wind caught it, and it shook its folds and flew straight out above us, while every soldier and sailor instinctively saluted.

I don't know just what we did next, but I remember looking on either side of me and seeing my father's eyelids brimming over and that Admiral Dahlgren's lips were trembling. I think we stood up, somebody started "The Star-Spangled Banner," and we sang the first verse, which is all that most people know. But it did not make much difference, for a great gun was fired close to us from the fort itself, followed, in obedience to the President's order, "by a national salute from every fort and battery that fired upon Fort Sumter." The measured, solemn booming came from Fort Moultrie, from the batteries on Sullivan and Folly Islands, and from Fort Wagner. . . . When the forts were done it was the turn of the fleet, and all our warships from the largest—which would look tiny today—down to the smallest monitor, fired and fired in regular order until the air was thick and black with smoke and one's ears ached with the overlapping vibrations.

—JONES, *Lantern Slides*

12. "BOW DOWN, DEAR LAND, FOR THOU HAST FOUND RELEASE"

In July 1865 Harvard College held commemoration services for Harvard men who had given their lives to the preservation of the Union. Altogether 138 Harvard men had been killed, or died, in the Union armies—and 64 in the Confederate armies. James Russell Lowell, then a Professor at Harvard College, was called on to write an appropriate ode. "The ode itself," he said later, "was an improvisation . . . the whole thing came out of me with a rush." It is, by common consent, the finest of Lowell's poems, and probably the most noble and moving poem to come out of the Civil War.

XI

Not in anger, not in pride,
Pure from passion's mixture rude
Ever to base earth allied,
But with far-heard gratitude,
Still with heart and voice renewed,
To heroes living and dear martyrs dead,
The strain should close that consecrates our brave.
Lift the heart and lift the head!
Lofty be its mood and grave,
Not without a martial ring,
Not without a prouder tread
And a peal of exultation:
Little right has he to sing
Through whose heart in such an hour
Beats no march of conscious power,
Sweeps no tumult of elation!
'T is no Man we celebrate,
By his country's victories great,
A hero half, and half the whim of Fate,
But the pith and marrow of a Nation
Drawing force from all her men,
Highest, humblest, weakest, all,
For her time of need, and then
Pulsing it again through them,
Till the basest can no longer cower,
Feeling his soul spring up divinely tall,
Touched but in passing by her mantle-hem.
Come back, then, noble pride, for 't is her dower!
How could poet ever tower,
If his passions, hopes, and fears,
If his triumphs and his tears,
Kept not measure with his people?
Boom, cannon, boom to all the winds and waves!
Clash out, glad bells, from every rocking steeple!
Banners, advance with triumph, bend your staves!
And from every mountain-peak
Let beacon-fire to answering beacon speak,
Katahdin tell Monadnock, Whiteface he,
And so leap on in light from sea to sea,
Till the glad news be sent
Across a kindling continent,
Making earth feel more firm and air breathe braver:
"Be proud! for she is saved, and all have helped to save her!
She that lifts up the manhood of the poor,

She of the open soul and open door,
With room about her hearth for all mankind!
The fire is dreadful in her eyes no more;
From her bold front the helm she doth unbind,
Sends all her handmaid armies back to spin,
And bids her navies, that so lately hurled
Their crashing battle, hold their thunders in,
Swimming like birds of calm along the unharmful shore.
No challenge sends she to the elder world,
That looked askance and hated; a light scorn
Plays o'er her mouth, as round her mighty knees
She calls her children back, and waits the morn
Of nobler day, enthroned between her subject seas."

XII

Bow down, dear Land, for thou hast found release!
Thy God, in these distempered days,
Hath taught thee the sure wisdom of His ways,
And through thine enemies hath wrought thy peace!
Bow down in prayer and praise!
No poorest in thy borders but may now
Lift to the juster skies a man's enfranchised brow.
O Beautiful! my Country! ours once more!
Smoothing thy gold of war-dishevelled hair
O'er such sweet brows as never other wore,
And letting thy set lips,
Freed from wrath's pale eclipse,
The rosy edges of their smile lay bare,
What words divine of lover or of poet
Could tell our love and make thee know it,
Among the Nations bright beyond compare?
What were our lives without thee?
What all our lives to save thee?
We reck not what we gave thee;
We will not dare to doubt thee,
But ask whatever else, and we will dare!

—JAMES RUSSELL LOWELL, "Ode Recited at the
Harvard Commemoration," July 31, 1865

BIBLIOGRAPHY AND INDEX

BIBLIOGRAPHY AND ACKNOWLEDGMENTS

CHAPTER I. DARKENING CLOUDS

1. Abraham Lincoln Is Nominated in the Wigwam.

   Murat Halstead, *Caucuses of 1860.* Columbus, Ohio, 1860. Pp. 141-154.

2. "First Gallant South Carolina Nobly Made the Stand."

   A. South Carolina Ordinance of Secession. In Frank Moore, ed., *The Rebellion Record: A Diary of American Events, with Documents, Narratives, Illustrative Incidents, Poetry, etc.* New York, 1861. I, 2.

   B. South Carolina Declaration of Causes of Secession. *Ibid.,* pp. 3 ff.

3. "She Has Left Us in Passion and Pride."

   Oliver Wendell Holmes, "Brother Jonathan's Lament for Sister Caroline," *Poems.* Boston: Ticknor & Fields, 1862.

4. Lincoln Refuses to Compromise on Slavery.

   A. Letter to E. B. Washburne. Nicolay and Hay, eds., *The Complete Works of Abraham Lincoln.* New York: The Century Co., 1894. I, 658. (By permission of Appleton-Century-Crofts, Inc.)

   B. Letter to James T. Hale. *Ibid.,* p. 664.

   C. Letter to W. H. Seward. *Ibid.,* p. 668.

5. Lincoln Writes His Inaugural Address.

   William H. Herndon and Jesse W. Weik, *Herndon's Lincoln: The True Story of a Great Life.* Chicago: Belford, Clark & Co., 1889. III, 478, 482-485.

6. Lincoln Is Inaugurated.

   A. Herndon Describes the Inauguration. William H. Herndon and Jesse W. Weik, *Herndon's Lincoln: The True Story of a Great Life.* Chicago: Belford, Clark & Co., 1889. III, 493-497.

   B. Wilder Dwight Sees Lincoln Inaugurated. Elizabeth A. W. Dwight, *The Life and Letters of Wilder Dwight.* Boston: Ticknor & Fields, 1868. Pp. 33-34.

   C. The Public Man Attends the Inauguration. Allen Thorndike Rice, ed., "The Diary of a Public Man," *North American Review,* CXXIXX (1879), 382-385.

7. "We Are Not Enemies But Friends."

   Abraham Lincoln, "First Inaugural Address," in James D. Richardson, ed., *A Compilation of the Messages and Papers of the Presidents, 1789-1902.* New York, 1904. VI, 5-12.

8. Mr. Lincoln Hammers Out a Cabinet.

   Harriet A. Weed, ed., *The Autobiography of Thurlow Weed.* Boston: Houghton, Mifflin & Co., 1893. Pp. 605-607.

9. Secretary Seward Tries to Take Charge of the Lincoln Administration.

   A. Memorandum from Secretary Seward. Nicolay and Hay, eds., *The Complete Works of Abraham Lincoln.* New York: The Century Co., 1894. I, 29. (By permission of Appleton-Century-Crofts, Inc.)

   B. Reply to Secretary Seward's Memorandum. *Ibid.,* p. 30.

10. The Confederacy Organizes at Montgomery.

    T. C. DeLeon, *Four Years in Rebel Capitals.* Mobile, Ala.: The Gossip Printing Co., 1890, 1892. Pp. 23-27.

11. A War Clerk Describes Davis and His Cabinet.

    John B. Jones, *A Rebel War Clerk's Diary at the Confederate States Capital.* Philadelphia: J. B. Lippincott Co., 1866. I, 36-40.

12. **A State Agent Calls on the Confederate Leaders.**

John Lewis Peyton, *The American Crisis; or, Pages from the Note-Book of a State Agent During the Civil War.* London: Saunders, Otley, & Co., 1867. I, 114-147, *passim.*

CHAPTER II. THE CONFLICT PRECIPITATED

1. **Mrs. Chesnut Watches the Attack on Fort Sumter.**

Mary Boykin Chesnut, *A Diary from Dixie*, Isabella D. Martin and Myrta Lockett Avary, eds. New York: D. Appleton & Co., 1905. Pp. 32-40. (By permission of Appleton-Century-Crofts, Inc.)

2. **Abner Doubleday Defends Fort Sumter.**

Abner Doubleday, *Reminiscences of Forts Sumter and Moultrie, 1860-1861.* New York: Harper & Bros., 1876. Pp. 142-173, *passim.*

3. **Major Anderson Surrenders Fort Sumter.**

"Reports of Major Anderson," in *The War of the Rebellion: A Compilation of the Official Records of the Union and Confederate Armies.* Washington, 1880. Series I, vol. I, 12.

4. **"The Heather Is on Fire."**

A. An Indiana Farm Boy Hears the News. Oscar Osburn Winther, ed., *With Sherman to the Sea, Journal of Theodore Upson.* Baton Rouge, La.: Louisiana State University Press, 1943. Pp. 9-11. (By permission of Louisiana State University Press.)
B. "There Never Was Anything Like It." Anna Ticknor and George S. Hillard, eds., *Life, Letters, and Journals of George Ticknor.* Boston: Osgood, 1876. II, 433-434.
C. "There Is But One Thought—The Stars and Stripes." Charles Chauncey Binney, *The Life of Horace Binney.* Philadelphia: J. B. Lippincott Co., 1903. Pp. 330-333. (By permission of Marie Sorchan Binney.)
D. "One Great Eagle-Scream." G. W. Bacon and E. W. Howland, eds., *Letters of a Family During the War for the Union, 1861-1865.* New Haven, Conn.: Privately printed, 1899. I, 66-71.

5. **"The Spirit of Virginia Cannot Be Crushed."**

Lyon G. Tyler, *Letters and Times of the Tylers.* Richmond, 1884. II, 641-642, 651-652.

6. **"I Am Filled with Horror at the Condition of Our Country."**

J. G. de Roulhac Hamilton, ed., *The Correspondence of Jonathan Worth.* Raleigh, N. C.: North Carolina Historical Commission, 1909. I, 145-148. (By permission of State of North Carolina Department of Archives and History.)

7. **A Northern Democrat Urges Peaceful Separation.**

John Bigelow, ed., *Letters and Literary Memorials of Samuel J. Tilden.* New York: Harper & Bros., 1908. I, 157-159. (By permission of Harper & Bros.)

8. **"The Race of Philip Sidneys Is Not Extinct."**

George William Curtis, ed., *The Correspondence of John Lothrop Motley.* New York: Harper & Bros., 1889. II, 40-43.

9. **A Young Poet Explains the Significance of the War.**

Laura Stedman and George M. Gould, *Life and Letters of Edmund Clarence Stedman.* New York: Moffat, Yard & Co., 1910. I, 240-244.

10. **The Supreme Court Upholds the Constitution.**

Prize Cases, 67 United States Supreme Court Reports 635 (1863).

CHAPTER III. THE GATHERING OF THE HOSTS

1. "Our People Are All United."

Arney Robinson Childs, ed., *The Private Journal of Henry William Ravenel, 1859-1887.* Columbia, S. C.: University of South Carolina Press, 1947. Pp. 65-67. (By permission of University of South Carolina Press.)

2. Southern Ladies Send Their Men Off to War.

Testimony of Mrs. Mary A. Ward, *Report of the Committee of the Senate upon the Relations between Labor and Capital, and Testimony Taken by the Committee.* Washington: U. S. Government Printing Office, 1885. IV, 331-332.

3. Two English Visitors Describe the Confederate Army.

A. "The Personnel of the Army Is Very Varied." "A Month with the 'Rebels,' " *Blackwood's Edinburgh Magazine*, XC (1861), 764-765.

B. "The High Standards of Intelligence." "Ten Days in Richmond," *Ibid.*, XCII (1862), 392-393.

4. The North Builds a Vast Army Overnight.

Edward Dicey, *Six Months in the Federal States.* London and Cambridge: Macmillan, 1863. II, 5-12.

5. Northern Boys Join the Ranks.

A. Warren Goss Enlists in the Union Army. Warren Lee Goss, *Recollections of a Private, A Story of the Army of the Potomac.* New York: Thomas Y. Crowell Co., 1890. Pp. 1-5.

B. Lieutenant Favill Raises a Company and Gets a Commission. Josiah Marshall Favill, *The Diary of a Young Officer.* Chicago: R. R. Donnelley & Sons, 1909. Pp. 42 ff.

C. Recruiting a Battalion of "Savages." Captain John G. B. Adams, "Sunshine and Shadows of Army Life," in *Civil War Papers . . . Massachusetts Military Order of the Loyal Legion of the U. S.* Boston: Printed for the Commandery, 1900. II, 448-449, 451. (By permission of Massachusetts Commandery, Military Order of the Loyal Legion of the United States.)

D. "We Thought the Rebellion Would Be Over Before Our Chance Would Come." Michael H. Fitch, *Echoes of the Civil War as I Hear Them.* New York: R. F. Fenno & Co., 1905. Pp. 17-20. (By permission of Mr. H. C. Fenno.)

6. The Reverend James T. Ayers Recruits Negro Soldiers in Tennessee.

John Hope Franklin, ed., *The Diary of James T. Ayers.* Springfield, Ill.: Illinois State Historical Society, 1947. Pp. 19-24. (By permission of John Hope Franklin and Illinois State Historical Library.)

7. Baltimore Mobs Attack the Sixth Massachusetts.

Frederic Emory, "The Baltimore Riots," in *The Annals of the War, Written by Leading Participants North and South, Originally Published in the Philadelphia Weekly Times.* Philadelphia: The Times Publishing Co., 1879. Pp. 775 ff.

8. How the Seventh Regiment Got from New York to Washington.

Fitz-James O'Brien in the *New York Times*, in Frank Moore, ed., *The Rebellion Record.* New York, 1861. I, 148-154.

9. Frank Wilkeson Goes South with Blackguards, Thieves, and Bounty Jumpers.

Frank Wilkeson, *Recollections of a Private Soldier in the Army of the Potomac.* New York: G. P. Putnam's Sons, 1887. Pp. 1-11.

10. Supplying the Confederacy with Arms and Ammunition.

E. P. Alexander, *Military Memoirs of a Confederate.* New York: Charles Scribner's Sons, 1907. Pp. 52-54. (By permission of Charles Scribner's Sons.)

11. How the Army of Northern Virginia Got Its Ordnance.

Col. William Allan, "Reminiscences of Field Ordnance Service with the Army of Northern Virginia—1863-'5," *Southern Historical Society Papers*, XIV (1886), 138-145.

12. The Tredegar Iron Works Serve the Confederate Armies.

T. C. DeLeon, *Four Years in Rebel Capitals.* Mobile, Ala.: The Gossip Printing Co., 1890, 1892. Pp. 91-92.

13. Secretary Benjamin Recalls the Mistakes of the Confederate Congress.

Sir Frederick Maurice, ed., *An Aide-de-Camp of Lee, Papers of Charles Marshall.* Boston: Little, Brown & Co., 1927. Pp. 14-18. (By permission of Sir Frederick Maurice.)

14. Northern Ordnance.

Comte de Paris, *History of the Civil War in America.* Philadelphia: Porter & Coates, 1875. I, 298-301.

CHAPTER IV. BULL RUN AND THE PENINSULAR CAMPAIGN

1. A Confederate Doctor Describes the Victory at First Bull Run.

Letter of Dr. J. C. Nott, in Frank Moore, ed., *The Rebellion Record.* New York, 1862. II, 93-94.

2. "Bull Run Russell" Reports the Rout of the Federals.

William Howard Russell, *My Diary North and South.* London: Bradbury & Evans, 1863. II, 210-254.

3. How the Women Took the News of Bull Run.

Charles Minor Blackford, III, ed., *Letters from Lee's Army; or, Memoirs of Life In and Out of the Army in Virginia During the War Between the States, Compiled by Susan Leigh Blackford from original and contemporaneous memoirs, correspondence and diaries.* New York: Charles Scribner's Sons, 1947. Pp. 36-37. (By permission of Charles Scribner's Sons.)

4. Stonewall Jackson Credits God with the Victory.

Mary Anna Jackson, *Life and Letters of General Thomas J. Jackson.* New York: Harper & Bros., 1891. Pp. 177-178.

5. "The Capture of Washington Seems Inevitable."

Allen Thorndike Rice, ed., "A Page of Political Correspondence, Unpublished Letters of Mr. Stanton to Mr. Buchanan," *North American Review*, CXXIX (1879), 482-483.

6. The Yankees Suffer Disaster at Ball's Bluff.

Randolph Abbott Shotwell, "Three Years in Battle," J. G. de Roulhac Hamilton, ed., *The Papers of Randolph Abbott Shotwell.* Raleigh, N. C.: North Carolina Historical Commission, 1929. I, 113-119. (By permission of State of North Carolina Department of Archives and History.)

7. McClellan Opens the Peninsular Campaign.

George B. McClellan, *McClellan's Own Story.* New York: Charles L. Webster & Co., 1887. Pp. 352-353.

8. General Wool Takes Norfolk.

Egbert L. Viele, "A Trip with Lincoln, Chase, and Stanton," *Scribner's Monthly*, XVI (1878), 819-822.

9. The Army of the Potomac Marches to Meet McClellan.

[Sallie Putnam], *Richmond During the War, Four Years of Personal Observation by a Richmond Lady.* New York: G. W. Carleton, 1867. Pp. 119-120.

10. R. E. Lee Takes Command.

General Evander M. Law, "The Fight for Richmond," *Southern Bivouac*, II (April 1867), 649 ff.

11. "Beauty" Stuart Rides Around McClellan's Army.

John Esten Cooke, *Wearing of the Gray; Being Personal Portraits, Scenes, and Adventures of the War.* New York: E. B. Treat & Co., 1867. Pp. 179 ff.

12. President Davis Visits the Battlefield at Mechanicsville.

Constance Cary Harrison, "Richmond Scenes in '62," in *Battles and Leaders of the Civil War*. New York: The Century Co., 1884, 1887, 1888. II, 446-448.

13. The Fighting at Gaines' Mill.

A. Hood's Texans Capture a Battery at Gaines' Mill. J. B. Polley, *A Soldier's Letters to Charming Nellie*. New York: The Neale Publishing Co., 1908. Pp. 54-60.

B. Oliver Norton Fights Like a Madman at Gaines' Mill. Oliver Willcox Norton, *Army Letters, 1861-1865*. Chicago: Privately printed, 1903. Pp. 92 ff.

14. The End of Seven Days.

A. The Federals Are Forced Back at White Oak Swamp. Thomas L. Livermore, *Days and Events, 1860-1866*. Boston: Houghton Mifflin Co., 1920. Pp. 86-90. (By permission of U. W. Harris Livermore Estate.)

B. Captain Livermore Fights at Malvern Hill. *Ibid.*, pp. 94-98.

15. Richard Auchmuty Reviews the Peninsular Campaign.

E. S. A., ed., *Letters of Richard Tylden Auchmuty, Fifth Corps Army of the Potomac*. Privately printed, n.p., n.d. Pp. 68-72.

CHAPTER V. STONEWALL JACKSON AND THE VALLEY CAMPAIGN

1. Stonewall Jackson Breaks the Sabbath.

Mary Anna Jackson, *Life and Letters of General Thomas J. Jackson*. New York: Harper & Bros., 1891. Pp. 248-249.

2. Dick Taylor Campaigns with Jackson in the Valley.

Richard Taylor, *Destruction and Reconstruction: Personal Experiences of the Late War*. New York: D. Appleton & Co., 1879, 1900. Pp. 44-59.

3. Taylor's Irishmen Capture a Battery at Port Republic.

Richard Taylor, *Destruction and Reconstruction*. New York: D. Appleton & Co., 1879, 1900. Pp. 72-76.

4. General Law Describes Jackson at Seven Days.

General Evander M. Law, "The Fight for Richmond," *Southern Bivouac*, II (April 1867), 649 ff.

5. Colonel Wolseley Visits Stonewall Jackson.

[Col. Garnet Wolseley], "A Month's Visit to Confederate Headquarters," *Blackwood's Edinburgh Magazine*, XCIII (January-June 1863), 21.

6. Stonewall Jackson Gets a New Uniform.

Heros von Borcke, *Memoirs of the Confederate War for Independence*. London, 1866. I, 295-297.

7. Henry Kyd Douglas Remembers Stonewall Jackson.

Henry Kyd Douglas, *I Rode with Stonewall*. Chapel Hill, N. C.: University of North Carolina Press, 1940. Pp. 234-235, 103-121, *passim*, 196. (By permission of University of North Carolina Press.)

CHAPTER VI. SECOND BULL RUN AND ANTIETAM

1. "Who Could Not Conquer With Such Troops as These?"

R. L. Dabney, *Life and Campaigns of Lt. Gen. Thomas J. Jackson*. New York: Blelock & Co., 1866. Pp. 516-518.

2. Jackson Outsmarts and Outfights Pope at Manassas.

[John Hampden Chamberlayne], "Narrative by a Rebel Lieutenant," in Frank Moore, ed., *The Rebellion Record*. New York, 1863. V, 402-404.

3. Pope Wastes His Strength on Jackson.

D. H. Strother, "Personal Recollections of the War," *Harper's New Monthly Magazine*, XXXV (1867), 713 ff.

4. General Gregg Exhorts His Men to Die in Their Tracks.

Edward McCrady, Jr., "Gregg's Brigade in the Second Battle of Manassas," *Southern Historical Society Papers*, XIII (1885), 32-39.

5. Longstreet Overwhelms Pope at Manassas.

Alexander Hunter, *Johnny Reb and Billy Yank*. New York: The Neale Publishing Co., 1905. Pp. 244-245.

6. Stevens and Kearny Are Killed at Chantilly.

Charles F. Walcott, "The Battle of Chantilly," in Theodore F. Dwight, ed., *The Virginia Campaign of 1862 Under General Pope*. (Published for The Military Historical Society of Massachusetts.) Boston: Houghton, Mifflin & Co., 1895. Pp. 145-160. (By permission of Houghton Mifflin Company.)

7. "Little Mac" Is Reappointed to Command.

A. "To Fight Is Not His Forte." *Diary of Gideon Welles, Secretary of the Navy Under Lincoln and Johnson*. Boston: Houghton Mifflin Co., 1911. I, 107-108. (By permission of Houghton Mifflin Company.)

B. General Sherman Explains Why He Cannot Like McClellan. M. A. De Wolfe Howe, ed., *Home Letters of General Sherman*. New York: Charles Scribner's Sons, 1909. Pp. 314-316. (By permission of Charles Scribner's Sons.)

C. "Little Mac's A-Coming." Oliver Willcox Norton, *Army Letters, 1861-1865*. Chicago: Privately printed, 1903. Pp. 101-102.

8. McClellan "Saves His Country" Twice.

George B. McClellan, *McClellan's Own Story*. New York: Charles L. Webster & Co., 1887. Pp. 308-660, *passim*.

9. McClellan Finds the Lost Order.

Letter of the Secretary of War, Organization of the Army of the Potomac, and of its Campaigns in Virginia and Maryland under the command of Maj. Gen. George B. McClellan, from July 26, 1861 to November 7, 1862. Washington: Government Printing Office, 1864. Pp. 188-189.

10. McClellan Forces Turner's Gap and Crampton's Gap.

D. H. Strother, "Personal Recollections of the War. By a Virginian," *Harper's New Monthly Magazine*, XXXVI (1868), 275-278.

11. The Bloodiest Day of the War.

D. H. Strother, "Personal Recollections of the War. By a Virginian," *Harper's New Monthly Magazine*, XXXVI (1868), 281-284.

12. Hooker Hammers the Confederate Left—In Vain.

A. Wisconsin Boys Are Slaughtered in the Cornfield. Rufus R. Dawes, *Service with the Sixth Wisconsin Volunteers*. Marietta, Ohio: E. R. Alderman & Sons, 1890. Pp. 90-92.

B. McLaws to the Rescue of Hood. James A. Graham, "Twenty-Seventh Regiment," in Walter Clark, ed., *Histories of the Several Regiments and Battalions from North Carolina in the Great War 1861-'65*. Raleigh, N.C.: North Carolina Historical Commission, n.d. II, 433-437.

C. Longstreet Turns a Battery on the Federals. James Longstreet, "The Invasion of Maryland," in *Battles and Leaders of the Civil War*. New York: The Century Co., 1884, 1887, 1888. II, 669-670.

13. The Desperate Fighting along Bloody Lane.

A. Thomas Livermore Puts on His War Paint. Thomas L. Livermore, *Days and Events, 1860-1866*. Boston: Houghton Mifflin Co., 1920. Pp. 137-141, 146. (By permission of U. W. Harris Livermore Estate.)

B. General Gordon Is Wounded Five Times at Antietam. General John B. Gordon, *Reminiscences of the Civil War*. New York: Charles Scribner's Sons, 1903. Pp. 81-90. (By permission of Charles Scribner's Sons.)

14. "The Whole Landscape Turns Red" at Antietam.

David I. Thompson, "With Burnside at Antietam," in *Battles and Leaders of the Civil War*. New York: The Century Co., 1884, 1887, 1888. II, 661-662.

CHAPTER VII. FREDERICKSBURG AND CHANCELLORSVILLE

1. Lincoln Urges McClellan to Advance.

Lincoln to McClellan, in *The War of the Rebellion . . . Official Records*. Ser. I, vol. XIX, pt. 1, 13 ff.

2. A Day of Rebel Rule in Chambersburg.

A. K. McClure, "The Invasion of Pennsylvania," in Frank Moore, ed., *The Rebellion Record*. New York, 1863. VI, 1-4.

3. Burnside Blunders at Fredericksburg.

A. The Yankees Attack Marye's Heights. William M. Owen, "A Hot Day on Marye's Heights," in *Battles and Leaders of the Civil War*. New York: The Century Co., 1884, 1888. III, 97-99.

B. "Fredericksburg Was a Trap." *Cincinnati Commercial*, in Frank Moore, ed., *The Rebellion Record*. New York, 1863. VI, 96-100.

4. The Assault on Marye's Hill.

A. The Irish Brigade Is Repulsed on Marye's Hill. J. B. Polley, *A Soldier's Letters to Charming Nellie*. New York: The Neale Publishing Co., 1908. Pp. 88 ff.

B. The 5th New Hampshire to the Rescue. Captain John R. McCrillis, in William Child, *A History of the Fifth Regiment New Hampshire Volunteers, in the American Civil War, 1861-1865*. Bristol, N. H.: R. W. Musgrove, 1893. I, 155-157.

5. The Gallant Pelham at Fredericksburg.

John Esten Cooke, *Wearing of the Gray; Being Personal Portraits, Scenes, and Adventures of the War*. New York: E. B. Treat & Co., 1867. Pp. 137-138, 133-134.

6. Night on the Field of Fredericksburg.

General J. L. Chamberlain, "Night on the Field of Fredericksburg," in W. C. King and W. P. Derby, eds., *Camp-Fire Sketches and Battle-Field Echoes*. Springfield, Mass.: W. C. King & Co., 1887. Pp. 127-130.

7. Lincoln Appoints Hooker to the Command of the Army.

Lincoln to Hooker, in *The War of the Rebellion . . . Official Records*. Ser. I, vol. XL, 4.

8. Lee Whips Hooker at Chancellorsville.

Charles Fessenden Morse, *Letters Written During the Civil War, 1861-1865*. Boston: Privately printed, 1898. Pp. 127-138.

9. Pleasonton Stops the Confederates at Hazel Grove.

Alfred Pleasonton, "The Successes and Failures of Chancellorsville," in *Battles and Leaders of the Civil War*. New York: The Century Co., 1884. III, 177-181.

10. Captain Livermore Holds the Lines Against Jackson.

Thomas L. Livermore, *Days and Events, 1860-1866*. Boston: Houghton Mifflin Co., 1920. Pp. 200-203. (By permission of U. W. Harris Livermore Estate.)

11. Stuart and Anderson Link Up at Chancellorsville.

Heros von Borcke, *Memoirs of the Confederate War for Independence*. London, 1866. II, 234-241.

12. Lee Loses His Right Arm.

Rev. James P. Smith, "Stonewall Jackson's Last Battle," in *Battles and Leaders of the Civil War*. New York: The Century Co., 1884, 1888. III, 211-214.

CHAPTER VIII. HOW THE SOLDIERS LIVED: EASTERN FRONT

1. Theodore Winthrop Recalls a Typical Day at Camp Cameron.

   Theodore Winthrop, *Life in the Open Air, and Other Papers*. Boston: Ticknor & Fields, 1863. Pp. 271-276.

2. Daily Life in Camp Millington.

   Lawrence Van Alstyne, *Diary of an Enlisted Man*. New Haven, Conn.: The Tuttle, Morehouse & Taylor Co., 1910. Pp. 29-31.

3. Abner Small Paints a Portrait of a Private in the Army of the Potomac.

   Harold A. Small, ed., *The Road to Richmond; The Civil War Memoirs of Major Abner R. Small of the Sixteenth Maine Volunteers. Together with the Diary which he kept when he was a Prisoner of War*. Berkeley: University of California Press, 1939. Pp. 192-193, 196-197. (By permission of University of California Press.)

4. Life with the Thirteenth Massachusetts.

   Charles E. Davis, *Three Years in the Army: The Story of the Thirteenth Massachusetts Volunteers*. Boston: Estes & Lauriat, 1894. Pp. 3-99, *passim*. (By permission of L. C. Page & Company, Inc.)

5. Minutiae of Soldier Life in the Army of Northern Virginia.

   Carlton McCarthy, *Detailed Minutiae of Soldier Life in the Army of Northern Virginia, 1861-1865*. Richmond: Carlton McCarthy & Co., 1882. Pp. 16-28.

6. Getting a Haircut in the Army.

   William Meade Dame, *From the Rapidan to Richmond and the Spottsylvania Campaign; A Sketch in Personal Narrative of the Scenes a Soldier Saw*. Baltimore: Green-Lucas Co., 1920. Pp. 38-44.

7. Inventions and Gadgets Used by the Soldiers.

   John D. Billings, *Hardtack and Coffee, or, The Unwritten Story of Army Life*. Boston: George M. Smith & Co., 1887. Pp. 272 ff.

8. Shoemaking and Tailoring in Winter Quarters.

   McHenry Howard, *Recollections of a Maryland Confederate Soldier and Staff Officer under Johnston, Jackson and Lee*. Baltimore: Williams & Wilkins Co., 1914. Pp. 248-253.

9. How the Soldiers Marched.

   Joel Cook, *The Siege of Richmond*. Philadelphia: George W. Childs, 1862. Pp. 82-85.

10. Hardtack and Coffee.

    John D. Billings, *Hardtack and Coffee, or, The Unwritten Story of Army Life*. Boston: George M. Smith & Co., 1887. Pp. 110 ff.

11. "Starvation, Rags, Dirt, and Vermin."

    Randolph Abbott Shotwell, "Three Years in Battle," J. G. de Roulhac Hamilton, ed., *The Papers of Randolph Abbott Shotwell*. Raleigh, N. C.: North Carolina Historical Commission, 1929. I, 314-316. (By permission of State of North Carolina Department of Archives and History.)

12. Voting in the Field.

    A. Electioneering in the Camps. R. G. Plumb, ed., "James A. Leonard, Letters of a Fifth Wisconsin Volunteer," *Wisconsin Magazine of History*, III (1919-1920), 63-64. (By permission of State Historical Society of Wisconsin.)

    B. President Lincoln Needs the Soldier Vote. Letter of Lincoln to General Sherman. Nicolay and Hay, eds., *The Complete Works of Abraham Lincoln*. New York: The Century Co., 1894. II, 577-578. (By permission of Appleton-Century-Crofts, Inc.)

    C. Voting for McClellan. "George Breck's Civil War Letters from the 'Reynolds Battery,'" in Blake McKelvey, ed., *Rochester in the Civil War*. Rochester, N. Y.: Rochester Historical Society Publications, 1944. Pp. 140-141. (By permission of Rochester Historical Society.)

13. Red Tape, North and South.

A. Dunn Browne Has Trouble with the War Department. [Samuel Fiske], *Mr. Dunn Browne's Experiences in the Army.* Boston: Nichols & Noyes, 1866. Pp. 372-375.

B. A Confederate Lieutenant Complains That Red-Tapeism Will Lose the War. Randolph Abbott Shotwell, "Three Years in Battle," J. G. de Roulhac Hamilton, ed., *The Papers of Randolph Abbott Shotwell.* Raleigh, N. C.: North Carolina Historical Commission, 1929. I, 382-385. (By permission of State of North Carolina Department of Archives and History.)

14. The Confederates Get Religion.

A. Religion in the Confederate Army. Benjamin W. Jones, *Under the Stars and Bars; A History of the Surry Light Artillery.* Richmond: Everett Waddey Co., 1909. Pp. 80 ff.

B. John Dooley Describes Prayer Meetings. Joseph T. Durkin, ed., *John Dooley, Confederate Soldier: His War Journal.* Washington: Georgetown University Press, 1945. P. 58. (By permission of Georgetown University Press.)

CHAPTER IX. INCIDENTS OF ARMY LIFE: EASTERN FRONT

1. How It Feels to Be under Fire.

Frank Holsinger, "How Does One Feel Under Fire?" in *War Talks in Kansas . . . Kansas Commandery of the Military Order of the Loyal Legion of the United States.* Kansas City, Mo.: Franklin Hudson Publishing Co., 1906. I, 301-304. (By permission of Kansas Commandery, Military Order of the Loyal Legion of the United States.)

2. The Third Ohio Is Flooded Out in West Virginia.

John Beatty, *The Citizen-Soldier; or Memoirs of a Volunteer.* Cincinnati: Wilstach, Baldwin & Co., 1879. Pp. 58-62.

3. Fitz John Porter Views the Confederates from a Balloon.

George Alfred Townsend, *Campaigns of a Non-Combatant, And His Romaunt Abroad During the War.* New York: Blelock & Co., 1866. Pp. 115-118.

4. Stuart's Ball Is Interrupted by the Yankees.

Heros von Borcke, *Memoirs of the Confederate War for Independence.* London, 1866. I, 193-198.

5. Major R—— Whips the Yankees Singlehanded.

John Esten Cooke, *Wearing of the Gray; Being Personal Portraits, Scenes, and Adventures of the War.* New York: E. B. Treat & Co., 1867. Pp. 279 ff.

6. Foreigners Fight in the Northern Army.

George B. McClellan, *McClellan's Own Story.* New York: Charles L. Webster & Co., 1887. Pp. 141-145.

7. The Mud Campaign.

[Samuel Fiske], *Mr. Dunn Browne's Experiences in the Army.* Boston: Nichols & Noyes, 1866. Pp. 115-118.

8. With "Extra Billy" Smith at York.

Robert Stiles, *Four Years Under Marse Robert.* New York: The Neale Publishing Co., 1903. Pp. 202-206.

9. Blue and Gray Fraternize on the Picket Line.

Alexander Hunter, *Johnny Reb and Billy Yank.* New York: The Neale Publishing Co., 1905. Pp. 429-431.

10. Life With the Mosby Guerrillas.

John W. Munson, *Reminiscences of a Mosby Guerrilla.* Boston: Moffat, Yard & Co., 1906. Pp. 21 ff.

11. Thomas Wentworth Higginson Celebrates Life in a Black Regiment.

T. W. Higginson, *Army Life in a Black Regiment*. Boston: Lee & Shepard, 1890. Pp. 131 ff.

12. Rebel and Yankee Yells.

J. Harvie Dew, "The Yankee and Rebel Yells," *Century Illustrated Magazine*, XLIII (April 1892), 954-955.

13. Death on the Battlefield.

Henry N. Blake, *Three Years in the Army of the Potomac*. Boston: Lee & Shepard, 1865. Pp. 80-82.

CHAPTER X. FROM FORT DONELSON TO STONES RIVER

1. U. S. Grant Applies for a Job.

[Ulysses S. Grant], *Personal Memoirs of U. S. Grant*. New York: Charles L. Webster & Co., 1885. I, 239-240.

2. Grant Wins His Spurs at Belmont.

Eugene Lawrence, "Grant on the Battle-Field," *Harper's New Monthly Magazine*, XXXIX (1869), 212.

3. U. S. Grant Becomes Unconditional Surrender Grant.

[Ulysses S. Grant], *Personal Memoirs of U. S. Grant*. New York: Charles L. Webster & Co., 1885. I, 296-313.

4. General Pope Captures New Madrid.

William E. and Ophia D. Smith, *Colonel A. W. Gilbert, Citizen-Soldier of Cincinnati*. Cincinnati: Historical and Philosophical Society of Ohio, 1934. Pp. 84-86. (By permission of Historical and Philosophical Society of Ohio.)

5. Henry Stanley Fights with the Dixie Grays at Shiloh.

Dorothy Stanley, ed., *The Autobiography of Sir Henry Morton Stanley*. Boston and New York: Houghton Mifflin Co., 1909. Pp. 187-200. (By permission of Houghton Mifflin Company.)

6. An Illinois Private Fights at the Hornet's Nest.

Leander Stillwell, *The Story of a Common Soldier of Army Life in the Civil War, 1861-1865*. 2nd ed.; Kansas City, Mo.: Franklin Hudson Publishing Co., 1920. Pp. 42-52.

7. Rosecrans Whips Van Dorn at Corinth.

Oscar L. Jackson, *The Colonel's Diary: Journals kept before and during the Civil War by the late Colonel Oscar L. Jackson of New Castle, Pennsylvania, sometime Commander of the 63 Regiment O.V.I.* Privately printed, n.d., n.p., Foreword dated May, 1922. Pp. 70-76.

8. The Orphan Brigade Is Shattered at Stones River.

L. D. Young, *Reminiscences of a Soldier in the Orphan Brigade*. Paris, Ky.: Privately printed, n.d. Pp. 47-51.

CHAPTER XI. THE STRUGGLE FOR MISSOURI AND THE WEST

1. How the Arms Were Taken from the St. Louis Arsenal.

Chicago Tribune, in Frank Moore, ed., *The Rebellion Record*. New York, 1861. I, 147-148.

2. Cotton Is King at the Battle of Lexington.

Samuel Phillips Day, *Down South*. London: Hurst & Blackett, Publishers, 1862. II, 181-188.

3. Guerrilla Warfare in Missouri.

A. "The Contemptable Jay Hawkers." Max H. Guyer, ed., "Journal and Letters of Corporal William O. Gulick," *Iowa Journal of History and Politics*, XXVIII (April 1930), 425 ff. (By permission of State Historical Society of Iowa.)

B. The Displaced Persons of Southern Missouri. Col. William Monks, "A History of Southern Missouri and Northern Arkansas," in William E. Connelley, *Quantrill and the Border Wars*. Cedar Rapids, Iowa: The Torch Press, 1910. Pp. 213-217.

4. The Tide Turns at Pea Ridge.

Franz Sigel, "The Pea Ridge Campaign," in *Battles and Leaders of the Civil War*. New York: The Century Co., 1884-1887. I, 327-329.

5. The Confederates Scatter after Pea Ridge.

William Watson, *Life in the Confederate Army; Being the Observations and Experiences of an Alien in the South during the American Civil War*. New York: Scribner & Welford, 1888. Pp. 320-339, *passim*.

6. Quantrill and His Guerrillas Sack Lawrence.

Narrative by Gurdon Grovenor, in William E. Connelley, *Quantrill and the Border Wars*. Cedar Rapids, Iowa: The Torch Press, 1910. Pp. 362-365.

7. Colonel Bailey Dams the Red River.

Letter from Rear Admiral Porter to Gideon Welles, May 16, 1864, in W. J. Tenney, *The Military and Naval History of the Rebellion*. New York: D. Appleton & Co., 1865. Pp. 513-514.

8. Defeat and Retreat on the Red River.

Lawrence Van Alstyne, *Diary of an Enlisted Man*. New Haven, Conn.: The Tuttle, Morehouse & Taylor Co., 1910. Pp. 327-331.

9. Price Invades the North and Is Defeated at Westport.

Wiley Britton, "Resumé of Military Operations in Missouri and Arkansas, 1864-65," in *Battles and Leaders of the Civil War*. New York: The Century Co., 1884, 1887, 1888. IV, 375-377.

10. The Confederates Win an Empty Victory at Glorietta Pass.

Col. W. R. Scurry, "Report of the Battle of Glorietta," in *Official Reports of Battles, as published by the order of the Confederate Congress at Richmond*. New York: Charles B. Richardson, 1863. Pp. 186-189.

CHAPTER XII.   HOW THE SOLDIERS LIVED: WESTERN FRONT

1. John Chipman Gray Views the Western Soldier.

Worthington C. Ford, ed., *War Letters, 1862-1865, of John Chipman Gray and John Codman Ropes*. Boston: Houghton Mifflin Co., 1927. Pp. 364-366. (By permission of Massachusetts Historical Society.)

2. A Wisconsin Boy Complains of the Hardships of Training.

Chauncey H. Cooke, "Letters of a Badger Boy in Blue: Into the Southland," *Wisconsin Magazine of History*, IV (1920-1921), 209-210. (By permission of State Historical Society of Wisconsin.)

3. An Officer's Quarters in Camp Curtis.

"Civil War Letters of Brigadier General William Ward Orme, 1862-1866," *Illinois State Historical Journal*, XXIII (1930-1931), 261-263. (By permission of Illinois State Historical Journal.)

4. Religion and Play in the Army of the Tennessee.

Jenkin Lloyd Jones, *An Artilleryman's Diary*. Madison, Wis.: Wisconsin Historical Commission, 1914. Pp. 166-210, *passim*. (By permission of Wisconsin Historical Commission.)

5. The Great Revival in the Army of Tennessee.

Mary A. H. Gay, *Life in Dixie During the War*. 3rd ed., Atlanta, Ga.: Charles P. Boyd, 1892. Pp. 79-86.

6. From Reveille to Taps.

Brevet Major George Ward Nichols, *The Story of the Great March, from the Diary of a Staff Officer*. New York: Harper & Bros., 1865. Pp. 48-55.

7. Forced Marches in the Teche Country.

John William De Forest, "Forced Marches," *Galaxy*, V (1868), 708 ff.

8. An Indiana Boy Reassures His Mother about Morals in the Army.

Oscar Osburn Winther, ed., *With Sherman to the Sea, Journal of Theodore Upson*. Baton Rouge, La.: Louisiana State University Press, 1943. Pp. 102-105. (By permission of Louisiana State University Press.)

9. An Illinois Private Complains of Bad Cooking.

Leander Stillwell, *The Story of a Common Soldier of Army Life in the Civil War, 1861-1865*. 2nd ed., Kansas City, Mo.: Franklin Hudson Publishing Co., 1920. Pp. 35-37.

10. How to Make Money in the Army.

E. W. Locke, *Three Years in Camp and Hospital*. Boston: G. D. Russell & Co., 1870. Pp. 297-307.

11. Graft and Corruption in the Confederate Commissary.

William Watson, *Life in the Confederate Army*. New York: Scribner & Welford, 1888. Pp. 164-166.

12. The Soldiers Get Paid and the Sutler Gets the Money.

Charles Beneulyn Johnson, *Muskets and Medicine, or Army Life in the Sixties*. Philadelphia: F. A. Davis Co., 1917. Pp. 197-200. (By permission of F. A. Davis Company.)

13. Song and Play in the Army of Tennessee.

Bromfield L. Ridley, *Battles and Sketches of the Army of Tennessee*. Mexico, Mo.: Missouri Printing & Publishing Co., 1906. Pp. 461-463.

CHAPTER XIII. INCIDENTS OF ARMY LIFE: WESTERN FRONT

1. Mark Twain Recalls a Campaign That Failed.

Mark Twain, "The Private History of a Campaign That Failed," *Century Magazine*, XXXI (December 1885), 194 ff.

2. Major Connolly Loses Faith in the Chivalry of the South.

"Major Connolly's Letters to His Wife, 1862-1865," *Transactions of the Illinois State Historical Society for the year 1928*. ("Publications of the Illinois State Historical Library," No. 35.) Springfield, Ill., 1928. Pp. 220-224. (By permission of Illinois State Historical Society.)

3. The Great Locomotive Chase in Georgia.

William Pittenger, "The Locomotive Chase in Georgia," *Century Magazine*, XIV (May 1888), 141-146.

4. Captain Canfield Tries to Free Slaves.

Captain S. S. Canfield, *History of the 21st Regiment Ohio Volunteer Infantry*. Toledo: Vrooman, Anderson & Bateman, 1893. Pp. 53-56.

5. A Badger Boy Meets the Originals of *Uncle Tom's Cabin*.

Chauncey H. Cooke, "Letters of a Badger Boy in Blue: Into the Southland," *Wisconsin Magazine of History*, IV (1920-1921), 324-325, 328-329. (By permission of State Historical Society of Wisconsin.)

6. Incidents of the Picket Line at Chattanooga.

J. B. Polley, *A Soldier's Letters to Charming Nellie.* New York: The Neale Publishing Co., 1908. Pp. 142-148.

7. The Confederates Escape in the Teche Country.

John William De Forest, "Forced Marches," *Galaxy,* V (1868), 708 ff.

8. Forrest's Cavalrymen Capture a Colt.

John Milton Hubbard, *Notes of a Private.* St. Louis: Nixon-Jones Printing Co., 1913. Pp. 174-177.

9. General Wilson Raises His Cavalry the Hard Way.

James Harrison Wilson, *Under the Old Flag: Recollections of Military Operations in the War for the Union, the Spanish War, the Boxer Rebellion, etc.* New York: D. Appleton & Co., 1912. II, 32-34. (By permission of Appleton-Century-Crofts, Inc.)

CHAPTER XIV.   THE PROBLEM OF DISCIPLINE

1. Thomas Wentworth Higginson Explains the Value of Trained Officers.

T. W. Higginson, "Regular and Volunteer Officers," *Atlantic Monthly,* XIV (September 1864), 348-357.

2. The New York Seventy-Ninth Mutinies.

War Letters of William Thompson Lusk, Captain, Assistant Adjutant-General United States Volunteers, 1861-1863. New York: Privately printed, 1911. Pp. 72-76.

3. "It Does Not Suit Our Fellows to Be Commanded Much."

Charles F. Johnson, *The Long Roll; being a Journal of the Civil War, as set down during the years 1861-1863 by Charles F. Johnson, sometime of Hawkins Zouaves.* East Aurora, N. Y.: The Roycrofters, 1911. Pp. 63-64.

4. Griping in the Union Army.

"Civil War Letters of Samuel S. Partridge," in Blake McKelvey, ed., *Rochester in the Civil War.* Rochester, N. Y.: Rochester Historical Society Publications, 1944. Pp. 82-84. (By permission of Rochester Historical Society.)

5. A Camp of Skulkers at Cedar Mountain.

George Alfred Townsend, *Campaigns of a Non-Combatant, And His Romaunt Abroad During the War.* New York: Blelock & Co., 1866. Pp. 264-265.

6. "The Army Is Becoming Awfully Depraved."

Charles W. Wills, *Army Life of an Illinois Soldier.* Washington: Globe Printing Co., 1906. Pp. 135-136, 209.

7. Robert Gould Shaw Complains That War Is a Dirty Business.

Letter of Robert Gould Shaw in Lydia Minturn Post, ed., *Soldiers' Letters from Camp, Battle-field and Prison.* Published for the U. S. Sanitary Commission. New York: Bunce & Huntington, 1865. Pp. 249 ff.

8. The Yankee Invaders Pillage and Burn.

A. The Yankees Sack the Page House in Williamsburg. [David Edward Cronin], *The Evolution of a Life—Described in the Memoirs of Major Seth Eyland* (pseud.). New York, 1884. Pp. 205-207.

B. "The Soldiers Delight in Destroying Everything." "Civil War Letters of Francis Edwin Pierce," in Blake McKelvey, ed., *Rochester in the Civil War.* Rochester, N. Y.: Rochester Historical Society Publications, 1944. Pp. 160-161. (By permission of Rochester Historical Society.)

C. The Yankees Sack Sarah Morgan's Home. Sarah Morgan Dawson, *A Confederate Girl's Diary,* Warrington Dawson, ed. Boston: Houghton Mifflin Co., 1913. Pp. 174-202, *passim.* (By permission of Mr. Warrington Dawson.)

D. Grierson's Raiders on a Rampage. Mrs. W. F. Smith, ed., "The Yankees in New Albany: Letter of Elizabeth Jane Beach, July 29, 1864," *The Journal of Mississippi History*, II (1940), 42-48. (By permission of Mississippi Historical Society.)

9. Punishments in the Union and Confederate Armies.

A. Maintaining Discipline in the Army of the Potomac. Elizabeth A. W. Dwight, *Life and Letters of Wilder Dwight*. Boston: Ticknor & Fields, 1868. Pp. 94-95.

B. Punishments in the Army of the Potomac. Frank Wilkeson, *Recollections of a Private Soldier in the Army of the Potomac*. New York: G. P. Putnam's Sons, 1887. Pp. 30-36.

C. Punishments in the Army of Northern Virginia. Joseph T. Durkin, ed., *John Dooley, Confederate Soldier: His War Journal*. Washington: Georgetown University Press, 1945. Pp. 73-74, 83. (By permission of Georgetown University Press.)

10. Executing Deserters.

A. General Sheridan Executes Two Deserters at Chattanooga. "Civil War Letters of Washington Gardner," *Michigan History Magazine*, I (1917), 8-9. (By permission of Michigan Historical Commission.)

B. Executing Deserters from the Confederate Army. Spencer Glasgow Welch, *A Confederate Surgeon's Letters to his Wife—by Spencer Glasgow Welch, Surgeon 13th South Carolina Volunteers, McGowan's Brigade*. New York and Washington: The Neale Publishing Co., 1911. Pp. 44-45, 79-80.

11. General Lee Discusses the Problem of Discipline.

Douglas Southall Freeman, ed., *Lee's Confidential Dispatches . . . to Jefferson Davis and the War Department of the Confederate States of America, 1862-1865*. New York: G. P. Putnam's Sons, 1915. Pp. 154-158. (By permission of Mr. W. W. De Renne.)

12. An Englishman Praises the Good Conduct of American Soldiers.

Edward Dicey, *Six Months in the Federal States*. London and Cambridge: Macmillan, 1863. II, 242-243.

CHAPTER XV.   GREAT BRITAIN AND THE AMERICAN CIVIL WAR

1. Henry Ravenel Expects Foreign Intervention.

Arney Robinson Childs, ed., *The Private Journal of Henry William Ravenel, 1859-1887*. Columbia, S. C.: University of South Carolina Press, 1947. P. 59. (By permission of University of South Carolina Press.)

2. *Blackwood's Edinburgh Magazine* Rejoices in the Break-Up of the Union.

"Democracy Teaching by Example," *Blackwood's Edinburgh Magazine*, XC (October 1861), 401-402.

3. Yancey and Mann Plead the Confederate Cause.

John Lewis Peyton, *The American Crisis; or, Pages from the Note-Book of a State Agent During the Civil War*. London: Saunders, Otley, & Co., 1867. II, 1-20, *passim*.

4. Northerners Invoke English Understanding.

A. August Belmont Warns of Bitter Feeling between America and England. August Belmont, *Letters, Speeches, and Addresses*. Privately printed, n.p., 1890. Pp. 48-50.

B. George Ticknor Explains the War to His English Friends. Anna Ticknor and George S. Hillard, eds., *Life, Letters, and Journals of George Ticknor*. Boston: Osgood, 1876. II, 446-448.

5. Captain Wilkes Seizes Mason and Slidell.

D. Macneill Fairfax, "Captain Wilkes's Seizure of Mason and Slidell," in *Battles and Leaders of the Civil War*. New York: The Century Co., 1884, 1887, 1888. II, 135-141.

6. "Shall It Be Love, or Hate, John?"

James Russell Lowell, "Jonathan to John," *Poems*, many editions.

7. Commons Debates the Recognition of the Confederacy.

Sarah Agnes Wallace and Frances Elma Gillespie, eds., *The Journal of Benjamin Moran, 1857-1865*. Chicago: University of Chicago Press, 1949. II, 1040-1044. (By permission of University of Chicago Press.)

8. Palmerston and Russell Discuss Intervention.

Spencer Walpole, *The Life of Lord John Russell*. London: Longmans, Green & Co., 1889. II, 349-350; and E. D. Adams, *Great Britain and the American Civil War*. New York: Longmans, Green & Co., 1925. II, 43-44. (By permission of Longmans, Green & Co., Inc.)

9. "An Error, the Most Singular and Palpable."

John Morley, *The Life of William Ewart Gladstone*. New York: The Macmillan Co., 1903. II, 81-83. (By permission of The Macmillan Company and Mr. Guy E. Morley.)

10. John Bright Deplores the Policy of His Government.

Letter from John Bright to Charles Sumner, *Proceedings of the Massachusetts Historical Society* (Boston), XLVI (1913), 108-109. (By permission of Massachusetts Historical Society.)

11. The English Press Condemns the Emancipation Proclamation.

A. "This Is a Very Sad Document." *The Times* (London), October 7, 1862.

B. "Monstrous, Reckless, Devilish." *Blackwood's Edinburgh Magazine*, XCII (November 1862), 636-645, *passim*.

12. Manchester Workingmen Stand by the Union.

A. "We Are Truly One People." Address to President Lincoln by the Working-Men of Manchester, in Frank Moore, ed., *The Rebellion Record*. New York, 1864. VI, 344.

B. "An Instance of Sublime Christian Heroism." Lincoln's Reply to the Working-Men of Manchester, in Nicolay and Hay, eds., *The Complete Works of Abraham Lincoln*. New York: The Century Co., 1894. II, 301-302. (By permission of Appleton-Century-Crofts, Inc.)

13. "Count" Gurowski Rages against the English.

Adam Gurowski, *Diary, From November 18, 1862, To October 18, 1863*. New York: G. W. Carleton, 1864. II, 5, 24, 59, 70, 89, 171, 186, 191.

14. Richard Cobden Rejoices in the Emancipation Proclamation.

Edward L. Pierce, contributor, "Letters of Richard Cobden to Charles Sumner," *American Historical Review*, II (1896-1897), 308-309. (By permission of American Historical Association.)

15. English Aristocrats Organize for Southern Independence.

Goldwin Smith, *Letter to a Whig Member of the Southern Independence Association*. London, 1864. Pp. 28-31.

16. Minister Adams Points Out That This Is War.

Great Britain. Parliament. *Accounts and Papers. State Papers, North America* (1864) 62: 17-18.

CHAPTER XVI. SONGS THE SOLDIERS SANG

1. "Dixie," by Daniel E. Emmett.

2. "The Bonnie Blue Flag," by Harry McCarthy.

3. "John Brown's Body," by Thomas B. Bishop(?).

4. "All Quiet Along the Potomac," by Ethel Lynn Beers.

5. "Marching Along," by William Batchelder Bradbury.

6. "Maryland! My Maryland!" by James R. Randall.

7. "Ye Cavaliers of Dixie," by Benjamin F. Porter.

8. "Stonewall Jackson's Way," by John Williamson Palmer.

9. The Battle Hymn of the Republic.

   A. Writing "The Battle Hymn of the Republic." Julia Ward Howe, *Reminiscences, 1819-1899.* Boston: Houghton, Mifflin & Co., 1899. Pp. 273-276.
   B. "The Battle Hymn of the Republic," by Julia Ward Howe.
   C. "The Battle Hymn of the Republic" in Libby Prison. Laura E. Richards and Maud Howe Elliott, *Julia Ward Howe, 1819-1910.* Boston: Houghton Mifflin Co., 1916. I, 188-189. (By permission of Houghton Mifflin Company.)

10. "We Are Coming, Father Abraham," by James Sloan Gibbons.

11. "The Battle-Cry of Freedom," by George F. Root.

12. "Tramp, Tramp, Tramp," by George F. Root.

13. "Just Before the Battle, Mother," by George F. Root.

14. "Tenting Tonight," by Walter Kittredge.

15. Weeping, Sad and Lonely.

    A. "Weeping, Sad and Lonely," by Charles C. Sawyer.
    B. "The Faded Coat of Blue," by J. H. McNaughton.
    C. "The Vacant Chair," by George F. Root.
    D. "Sleeping for the Flag," by Henry Clay Work.

16. "Marching through Georgia," by Henry Clay Work.

17. Mister, Here's Your Mule.

    A. "Mister, Here's Your Mule" (Author Unknown).
    B. "Do They Miss Me in the Trenches?" by J. W. Naff.
    C. "We Are the Boys of Potomac's Ranks" (Author Unknown).
    D. "Goober Peas," by A. Pender.
    E. "Grafted into the Army," by Henry Clay Work.

18. "Lorena," by H. D. L. Webster(?).

19. "When Johnny Comes Marching Home," by Patrick S. Gilmore(?).

BIBLIOGRAPHICAL NOTE

It is impossible to give satisfactory bibliographical listings for particular Civil War songs. These songs appear, for the most part, in variant forms in a great miscellany of collections. It can rarely be said that any one form is the correct one. In some cases the authorship of popular songs is unknown, in many cases it is in dispute. We have thought it most helpful, therefore, merely to list the most useful of the many volumes of Civil War songs—altogether almost one hundred were published during or after the war—from which our own selection has been drawn.

American War Songs; published under supervision of the National Committee for the Preservation of Existing Records of the National Society of the Colonial Dames of America. Philadelphia: Privately printed, 1925. 202 pp.

Bill, Ledyard, ed., *Lyrics, Incidents, and Sketches of the Rebellion.* 2nd ed.; New York: C. A. Alvord, 1864. Part I, Lyrics of the War. 100 pp.

Browne, Francis Fisher, ed., *Bugle-echoes; a Collection of Poems of the Civil War, Northern and Southern.* New York: White, Stokes & Allen, 1886. 336 pp.

Collection of War Songs of the South. Atlanta: Franklin Printing & Publishing Co., 1895. Cover title: "*Southern War Songs.*"

Davidson, Nora F. M., comp., *Cullings from the Confederacy.* Washington: Rufus H. Darby Printing Co., 1903. 163 pp.

Duganne, Augustine J. H., *Ballads of the War.* New York: J. Robbins, 1862.

Eggleston, [George Cary], *American War Ballads and Lyrics: a Collection of Songs and Ballads of the Colonial Wars, the Revolution, the War of 1812-15, the War with Mexico, and the Civil War.* New York: G. P. Putnam's Sons, 1889. 2 vols.

Fagan, William Long, ed., *Southern War Songs, Camp-Fire, Patriotic and Sentimental.* New York: M. T. Richardson & Co., 1890. 389 pp.

Hewes, George Whitfield, *Ballads of the War.* New York: Carleton, 1862. 147 pp.

Hubner, Charles W., ed., *War Poets of the South and Confederate Camp-Fire Songs.* Atlanta: U. P. Byrd, 1896. 207 pp.

Mason, Emily V., ed., *The Southern Poems of the War.* Baltimore: J. Murphy & Co., 1867. 456 pp.

Miles, Dudley, H., ed., *Poetry and Eloquence of Blue and Gray.* Foreword by William P. Trent, with an appendix "Songs of the War Days" edited by Jeanne Robert Foster. (F. T. Miller, ed., *The Photographic History of the Civil War,* Vol. IX.) New York: The Review of Reviews Co., 1911. 352 pp.

Moore, Frank, ed., *The Civil War in Song and Story, 1860-1865.* New York: P. F. Collier, 1889. 560 pp.

——, ed., *Lyrics of Loyalty.* New York: G. P. Putnam, 1864. 336 pp.

——, ed., *Songs and Ballads of the Southern People, 1861-1865.* New York: D. Appleton & Co., 1886.

Our National War Songs: a Complete Collection of Grand Old War Songs, Battle Songs, National Hymns, Memorial Hymns, Decoration Day Songs . . . Chicago: S. Brainard's Sons Co., [cop. 1892]. 223 pp.

Putnam, Sallie A. Brock, ed., *The Southern Amaranth, a Carefully Selected Collection of Poems Growing out of and in Reference to the Late War.* New York: G. S. Wilcox, 1869. 651 pp.

Simms, William Gilmore, ed., *War Poetry of the South.* New York: Richardson & Co., 1867. 482 pp.

War Songs of the Blue and the Gray, As Sung by the Brave Soldiers of the Union and Confederate Armies in Camp, on the March, and in Garrison; with a preface by Prof. Henry L. Williams. New York: Hurst & Co., 1905. 215 pp.

Wharton, H. M., ed., *War Songs and Poems of the Southern Confederacy, 1861-1865; a collection of the most popular and impressive songs and poems of war times . . .* Philadelphia: n.p. 1904. 412 pp.

CHAPTER XVII. GETTYSBURG

1. General Lee Decides to Take the Offensive.

   The War of the Rebellion . . . Official Records. Ser. I, vol. XXVII, pt. III, 868-869; ser. I, vol. XXVII, pt. III, 880-882; ser. I, vol. XXVII, pt. II, 305.

2. Ewell Whips the Federals at Winchester.

   John O. Casler, *Four Years in the Stonewall Brigade.* Guthrie, Okla.: Capital State Printing Co., 1893. Pp. 239-244.

3. General Lee Invades Pennsylvania.

   Letter of William S. Christian, in Frank Moore, ed., *The Rebellion Record.* New York, 1864. VII, 325.

4. The Armies Converge on Gettysburg.

Henry J. Hunt, "The First Day at Gettysburg," in *Battles and Leaders of the Civil War.* New York. The Century Co., 1884, 1888. III, 271 ff.

5. Buford and Reynolds Hold Up the Confederate Advance.

Major Joseph G. Rosengarten, "General Reynolds' Last Battle," in *The Annals of the War, Written by Leading Participants North and South . . . in the Philadelphia Weekly Times.* Philadelphia: The Times Publishing Co., 1879. Pp. 62-64.

6. A Boy Cannoneer Describes Hard Fighting on the First Day.

Augustus Buell, *"The Cannoneer." Recollections of Service in the Army of the Potomac. By "A Detached Volunteer" in the Regular Artillery.* Washington: The National Tribune, 1890. Pp. 63-73, *passim.*

7. The Struggle for Little Round Top.

A. General Hood Wants to Outflank the Union Left. Letter from J. B. Hood to James Longstreet, June 28th, 1875, in *Southern Historical Society Papers,* IV (1877), 147-150.

B. General Warren Seizes Little Round Top. "Reminiscences of the 140th Regiment, New York Volunteer Infantry, by Porter Farley," in Blake McKelvey, ed., *Rochester in the Civil War.* Rochester: Rochester Historical Society, 1944. Pp. 218-223. (By permission of Rochester Historical Society.)

C. Colonel Oates Almost Captures Little Round Top. William C. Oates, *The War Between the Union and the Confederacy and Its Lost Opportunities, with a history of the 15th Alabama Regiment and the forty-eight battles in which it was engaged.* New York: The Neale Publishing Co., 1905. Pp. 210-211, 212, 218-221.

D. The 20th Maine Saves Little Round Top. Theodore Gerrish, *Army Life: A Private's Reminiscences of the Civil War.* Portland, Me.: Hoyt, Fogg & Donham, 1882. Pp. 104-111.

8. Ewell Fails to Take Culp's Hill.

Randolph H. McKim, *A Soldier's Recollections: Leaves from the Diary of a Young Confederate, With an Oration on the Motives and Aims of the Soldiers of the South.* New York: Longmans, Green & Co., 1910. Pp. 195-206.

9. High Tide at Gettysburg.

A. Alexander Gives the Signal to Start. Letter from E. P. Alexander to the Rev. J. Wm. Jones, in *Southern Historical Society Papers,* IV (1877), 102-109, *passim.*

B. Armistead Falls Beside the Enemy's Battery. James Longstreet, *From Manassas to Appomattox: Memoirs of the Civil War in America.* 2nd ed., rev.; Philadelphia: J. B. Lippincott Co., 1903. Pp. 391-394. (By permission of Mrs. Helen Dortch Longstreet.)

C. "The Crest Is Safe." Frank Aretas Haskell, *The Battle of Gettysburg.* ("Wisconsin History Commission Reprints," No. 1.) Wisconsin History Commission, November 1908. Pp. 107 ff. (By permission of Wisconsin Historical Commission.)

D. "All This Will Come Right in the End." [Arthur J. L. Fremantle], "The Battle of Gettysburg and the Campaign in Pennsylvania," *Blackwood's Edinburgh Magazine,* XCIV (1863), 380-382.

10. Lee Retreats from Gettysburg.

[Napier Bartlett], *A Soldier's Story of the War; Including the Marches and Battles of the Washington Artillery and of other Louisiana Troops.* New Orleans, 1874. Pp. 192-196.

11. General Lee Offers to Resign after Gettysburg.

The War of the Rebellion . . . Official Records. Ser. I, vol. LI, pt. II, 752-753; vol. XXIX, pt. II, 639-640.

12. "Bells Are Ringing Wildly."

War Letters of William Thompson Lusk. New York: Privately printed, 1911. Pp. 284-285.

13. "A New Birth of Freedom."

Abraham Lincoln, "The Gettysburg Address," November 19, 1863, Nicolay and Hay, eds., *The Complete Works of Abraham Lincoln*. New York: The Century Co., 1894. II, 439. (By permission of Appleton-Century-Crofts, Inc.)

CHAPTER XVIII. VICKSBURG AND PORT HUDSON

1. Sherman Fails at Chickasaw Bluffs.

[William T. Sherman], *Memoirs of General William T. Sherman*. New York: D. Appleton & Co., 1875. I, 289-294.

2. "Onward to Vicksburg."

Edgar L. Erickson, ed., "With Grant at Vicksburg—From the Civil War Diary of Captain Charles E. Wilcox," *Journal of the Illinois State Historical Society*, XXX (January 1938), 463-497, *passim*. (By permission of Illinois State Historical Society.)

3. Colonel Grierson Discovers That the Confederacy Is a Hollow Shell.

"Reports of Col. Benjamin H. Grierson," in *The War of the Rebellion . . . Official Records*. Ser. I, vol. XXIV, pt. I, 522 ff.

4. A Union Woman Suffers through the Siege of Vicksburg.

George W. Cable, ed., "A Woman's Diary of the Siege of Vicksburg. Under Fire from the Gunboats," *Century Illustrated Magazine*, VIII (1885), 767-775.

5. Vicksburg Surrenders.

U. S. Grant, "The Vicksburg Campaign," in *Battles and Leaders of the Civil War*. New York: The Century Co., 1884, 1888. III, 530-536.

6. General Banks Takes Port Hudson.

A. Banks Is Repulsed at Port Hudson. L. Carroll Root, ed., "Private Journal of William H. Root, Second Lieutenant, Seventy-Fifth New York Volunteers, April 1—June 14, 1863," *Louisiana Historical Quarterly*, XIX (July 1936), 666-667. (By permission of Louisiana Historical Society.)

B. Eating Mules at Port Hudson. *Port Hudson—Its History from an Interior Point of View, as Sketched from the Diary of an Officer*. St. Francisville, La., 1938. (By permission of Mr. Elrie Robinson.)

C. Blue and Gray Fraternize after the Surrender of Port Hudson. *Ibid.*

7. "The Father of Waters Again Goes Unvexed to the Sea."

Letter of Lincoln to James C. Conkling. Nicolay and Hay, eds., *The Complete Works of Abraham Lincoln*. New York: The Century Co., 1894. II, 398-399. (By permission of Appleton-Century-Crofts, Inc.)

8. General Morgan Invades the North.

A. Morgan's Cavalrymen Sweep Through Kentucky. "Journal of Lieutenant-Colonel Alston," in Frank Moore, ed., *The Rebellion Record*. New York, 1864. VII, 358-360.

B. Morgan's Raid Comes to an Inglorious End. James Bennett McCreary, "The Journal of My Soldier Life," *Register of the Kentucky State Historical Society*, XXXIII (July 1935), 198-200. (By permission of Kentucky State Historical Society.)

CHAPTER XIX. PRISONS, NORTH AND SOUTH

1. Abner Small Suffers in Danville Prison.

Harold A. Small, ed., *The Road to Richmond; The Civil War Memoirs of Major Abner R. Small of the Sixteenth Maine Volunteers. Together with the Diary which he kept when he was a Prisoner of War*. Berkeley: University of California Press, 1939. Pp. 171-176. (By permission of University of California Press.)

2. "The Suffering Among the Sick and Wounded."

"Journal of a Union Soldier," in Frank Moore, ed., *The Rebellion Record.* New York, 1864. VII, 594-596.

3. Suffering in Andersonville Prison.

Eliza Frances Andrews, *The War-Time Journal of a Georgia Girl, 1864-1865.* New York: D. Appleton & Co., 1908. Pp. 76-79.

4. The Bright Side of Libby Prison.

Frank E. Moran, "Libby's Bright Side: A Silver Lining in the Dark Cloud of Prison Life," in W. C. King and W. P. Derby, eds., *Camp-Fire Sketches and Battle-Field Echoes.* Springfield, Mass.: W. C. King & Co., 1887. Pp. 180-181, 183-185.

5. Luther Hopkins Recalls Prison Life at Point Lookout.

Luther W. Hopkins, *From Bull Run to Appomattox, A Boy's View.* Baltimore: Fleet-McGinley Co., 1908. Pp. 169-180.

6. The Awful Conditions at Fort Delaware.

Randolph Abbott Shotwell, "Three Years in Battle," J. G. de Roulhac Hamilton, ed., *The Papers of Randolph Abbott Shotwell.* Raleigh, N. C.: North Carolina Historical Commission, 1931. II, 149-182, *passim.* (By permission of State of North Carolina Department of Archives and History.)

7. The Privations of Life in Elmira Prison.

Marcus B. Toney, *The Privations of a Private.* Nashville, Tenn.: Methodist Episcopal Church South, 1905. Pp. 93-104, *passim.*

8. General Morgan Escapes from the Ohio Penitentiary.

"Rebel Account," in Frank Moore, ed., *The Rebellion Record.* New York, 1871. VIII, 318-320.

CHAPTER XX. BEHIND THE LINES: THE NORTH

1. Washington as a Camp.

Noah Brooks, "Washington in Lincoln's Time," *Century Illustrated Magazine,* XXVII (November 1894), 140-141. (By permission of Appleton-Century-Crofts, Inc.)

2. Walt Whitman Looks Around in Wartime Washington.

Emory Halloway, ed., *The Uncollected Poetry and Prose of Walt Whitman.* New York: Doubleday, Page & Co., 1921. II, 21 ff. (By permission of Doubleday & Company, Inc.)

3. Anna Dickinson Sees the Draft Riots in New York City.

Anna Elizabeth Dickinson, *What Answer?* Boston: Ticknor & Fields, 1868. Pp. 243-256.

4. Nevada Miners Bid on the "Sanitary" Flour Sack.

Mark Twain, *Roughing It.* Hartford, Conn., 1871, and many editions.

5. "O, I Will Take the Plow, John."

Mary A. Livermore, *My Story of the War.* Hartford, Conn.: A. D. Worthington & Co., 1888. Pp. 145-149.

6. The Army of Lobbyists and Speculators.

Régis de Trobriand, *Four Years with the Army of the Potomac.* Trans. by George K. Dauchy. Boston: Ticknor & Co., 1889. Pp. 134-136.

7. Charles A. Dana Helps Stop Frauds in the War Department.

Charles A. Dana, *Recollections of the Civil War.* New York: D. Appleton & Co., 1898. Pp. 161-164. (By permission of Appleton-Century-Crofts, Inc.)

8. Colonel Baker Outwits Bounty Jumpers and Brokers.

LaFayette C. Baker, *The Secret Service in the Late War.* Philadelphia: John E. Potter & Co., 1874. Pp. 249-267, *passim.*

9. Confederate Plots Against the North.

A. A Confederate Plan to Seize Johnson's Island Is Frustrated. Hon. H. B. Brown, "The Lake Erie Piracy Case," *The Green Bag*, XXI (April 1909), 143-147.

B. The Confederates Attempt to Burn New York. John W. Headley, *Confederate Operations in Canada and New York*. New York: The Neale Publishing Co., 1906. Pp. 274-277.

10. An Ohio Judge Upholds the Union Cause in Tangier.

Frederick W. Seward, *Reminiscences of a War-Time Statesman and Diplomat, 1830-1915*. New York & London: G. P. Putnam's Sons, 1916. Pp. 219-226.

CHAPTER XXI. BEHIND THE LINES: THE SOUTH

1. Richmond after Seven Pines.

Alexander Hunter, *Johnny Reb and Billy Yank*. New York: The Neale Publishing Co., 1905. Pp. 155-158.

2. A War Clerk Suffers Scarcities in Richmond.

John B. Jones, *A Rebel War Clerk's Diary at the Confederate States Capital*. Philadelphia: J. B. Lippincott Co., 1866. Vols. I and II, *passim*.

3. Mr. Eggleston Recalls When Money Was Plentiful.

George Cary Eggleston, *A Rebel's Recollections*. New York, 1874. Pp. 78-84, 100-109.

4. Richmond Is Demoralized by Rumors.

Edward A. Pollard, *Life of Jefferson Davis, with a Secret History of the Southern Confederacy*. Philadelphia: National Publishing Co., 1869. Pp. 315, 319-321.

5. Parthenia Hague Tells How Women Outwitted the Blockade.

Parthenia Antoinette Hague, *A Blockaded Family: Life in Southern Alabama During the Civil War*. Boston: Houghton, Mifflin & Co., 1888. Pp. 37-42, 100-105.

6. The Confederates Burn Their Cotton.

Sarah Morgan Dawson, *A Confederate Girl's Diary*, Warrington Dawson, ed. Boston: Houghton Mifflin Co., 1913. Pp. 16-18. (By permission of Mr. Warrington Dawson.)

7. Yankee Contractors Speculate in Cotton.

Thomas W. Knox, *Camp-Fire and Cotton-Field: Southern Adventure in Time of War. Life with the Union Armies, and Residence on a Louisiana Plantation*. New York: Blelock & Co., 1865. Pp. 307-309, 311-317.

8. "The Yankees Are Coming."

Testimony of Mrs. Mary A. Ward, *Report of the Committee of the Senate upon the Relations between Labor and Capital, and Testimony Taken by the Committee*. Washington: Government Printing Office, 1885. IV, 334-336.

9. "The Lives Which Women Have Lead Since Troy Fell."

Kate Mason Rowland and Mrs. Morris L. Croxall, eds., *The Journal of Julia LeGrand, New Orleans, 1862-1863*. Richmond: Everett Waddey Co., 1911. Pp. 51-54.

10. "They Must Reap the Whirlwind."

M. A. De Wolfe Howe, ed., *Home Letters of General Sherman*. New York: Charles Scribner's Sons, 1909. Pp. 268-269. (By permission of Charles Scribner's Sons.)

11. Georgia's Governor Laments Davis' Despotism.

Ulrich B. Phillips, ed., "The Correspondence of Robert Toombs, Alexander H. Stephens, and Howell Cobb," *Annual Report of the American Historical Society for the year of 1911*. Washington: Government Printing Office, 1913, II, 605-606. (By permission of American Historical Society.)

12. Peace at Any Price.

J. G. de Roulhac Hamilton, ed., *The Correspondence of Jonathan Worth.* Raleigh, N. C.: North Carolina Historical Commission, 1909. I, 257-258. (By permission of State of North Carolina Department of Archives and History.)

13. "The Man Who Held His Conscience Higher Than Their Praise."

James Petigru Carson, *Life, Letters and Speeches of James Louis Petigru, The Union Man of South Carolina.* Washington: W. H. Loudermilk & Co., 1920. P. 487.

CHAPTER XXII.   HOSPITALS, SURGEONS, AND NURSES

1. George Townsend Describes the Wounded on the Peninsula.

George Alfred Townsend, *Campaigns of a Non-Combatant, And His Romaunt Abroad During the War.* New York: Blelock & Co., 1866. Pp. 103-118.

2. The Sanitary Commission to the Rescue.

Katherine Wormeley, *The Other Side of War; With the Army of the Potomac. Letters from the Headquarters of the United States Sanitary Commission during the Peninsular Campaign in Virginia in 1862.* Boston: Ticknor & Co., 1889. Pp. 102-111.

3. The Baroness von Olnhausen Nurses at Alexandria.

James Phinney Monroe, ed., *Adventures of an Army Nurse. Edited from the Diary and Correspondence of Mary Phinney, Baroness von Olnhausen.* Boston: Little, Brown & Co., 1903. Pp. 32-35, 39-46, *passim.*

4. Clara Barton Surmounts the Faithlessness of Union Officers.

William E. Barton, *The Life of Clara Barton, Founder of the American Red Cross.* Boston: Houghton Mifflin Co., 1922. I, 277-279. (By permission of Mr. Bruce Barton.)

5. Susan Blackford Nurses the Wounded at Lynchburg.

Charles Minor Blackford, III, ed., *Letters from Lee's Army; or, Memoirs of Life In and Out of the Army in Virginia During the War Between the States. Compiled by Susan Leigh Blackford from original and contemporaneous memoirs, correspondence and diaries.* New York: Charles Scribner's Sons, 1947. Pp. 259-261. (By permission of Charles Scribner's Sons.)

6. Kate Cumming Nurses the Wounded after Chickamauga.

Kate Cumming, *Gleanings from Southland; Sketches of Life and Manners of the People of the South Before, During and After the War of Secession.* Birmingham: Roberts & Co., 1895. Pp. 135-144.

7. Cornelia Hancock Nurses Soldiers and Contrabands.

Henrietta Stratton Jaquette, ed., *South After Gettysburg, Letters of Cornelia Hancock from the Army of the Potomac, 1863-1865.* Philadelphia: University of Pennsylvania Press, 1937. Pp. 8-12, 31-32. (By permission of University of Pennsylvania Press.)

8. The Ghastly Work of the Field Surgeons.

A. The Heartlessness of the Surgeons. Charles Sterling Underhill, ed., *"Your Soldier Boy Samuel"—Civil War Letters of Lieut. Samuel Edmund Nichols, Amherst '65 of the 37th Regiment Massachusetts Volunteers.* Privately printed, 1929. Pp. 50-52. (By permission of Mrs. I. S. Underhill.)

B. Carl Schurz Watches the Surgeons at Work after Gettysburg. Frederic Bancroft and William A. Dunning, eds., *The Reminiscences of Carl Schurz, With a Sketch of his life and public services from 1869 to 1906.* New York: The McClure Co., 1908. III, 38-40.

C. The Horrors of the Wilderness. Augustus C. Brown, *The Diary of a Line Officer.* New York: Privately printed, 1906. Pp. 43-44.

9. The Regimental Hospital.

Charles Beneulyn Johnson, *Muskets and Medicine, or Army Life in the Sixties.* Philadelphia: F. A. Davis Co., 1917. Pp. 129-134. (By permission of F. A. Davis Company.)

CHAPTER XXIII. THE COAST AND INLAND WATERS

1. An Amphibious Force Captures Roanoke Island.

Charles F. Johnson, *The Long Roll; being a Journal of the Civil War, as set down during the years 1861-1863.* East Aurora, N. Y.: The Roycrofters, 1911. Pp. 90-96.

2. The *Merrimac* and the *Monitor.*

A. The *Minnesota* Fights for Her Life in Hampton Roads. "Report of Captain Van Brunt," in Frank Moore, ed., *The Rebellion Record.* New York, 1863. IV, 267-268.

B. The *Monitor* Repels the *Merrimac.* S. D. Greene to His Parents, March 14, 1862, in Lydia Minturn Post, ed., *Soldiers' Letters from Camp, Battle-field and Prison.* New York: Bunce & Huntington, 1865. Pp. 109-113.

3. Commodore Farragut Captures New Orleans.

Susan Perkins, ed., *Letters of Capt. Geo. Hamilton Perkins, U. S. N. . . . Also a Sketch of His Life.* Concord, N. H.: Privately printed, 1886. Pp. 67-71.

4. New Orleans Falls to the Yankees.

A. Julia LeGrand Describes the Surrender of New Orleans. Kate Mason Rowland and Mrs. Morris L. Croxall, eds., *The Journal of Julia LeGrand, New Orleans, 1862-1863.* Richmond: Everett Waddey Co., 1911. Pp. 39-43.

B. General Butler Outrages the Moral Sentiment of the World. General Butler's Order No. 28, in Frank Moore, ed., *The Rebellion Record.* New York, 1863. V, 136.

C. Palmerston Protests Butler's Proclamation. Palmerston to Charles Francis Adams, *Proceedings of the Massachusetts Historical Society* (Boston), XLV (1911-1912), 257. (By permission of Massachusetts Historical Society.)

D. "A More Impudent Proceeding Cannot Be Discovered." Sarah Agnes Wallace and Frances Elma Gillespie, eds., *The Journal of Benjamin Moran, 1857-1865.* Chicago: University of Chicago Press, 1949. II, 1027-1029. (By permission of University of Chicago Press.)

5. Ellet's Steam Rams Smash the Confederate Fleet at Memphis.

Alfred W. Ellet, "Ellet and His Steam-Rams at Memphis," in *Battles and Leaders of the Civil War.* New York: The Century Co., 1884-1887. I, 453-459.

6. The *Indianola* Runs the Vicksburg Batteries.

W. S. Ward, "How We Ran the Vicksburg Batteries," *Magazine of History,* XIV (1885), 602-604.

7. Attack and Repulse at Battery Wagner.

"The Attack on Fort Wagner. New York 'Tribune' Account," in Frank Moore, ed., *The Rebellion Record.* New York, 1864, VII, 211-214.

8. Charleston under Fire.

W. F. G. Peck, "Four Years Under Fire at Charleston," *Harper's New Monthly Magazine,* XXXI (1865), 358-366.

9. A Confederate Submarine Sinks the *Housatonic.*

Arthur P. Ford, *Life in the Confederate Army: Being Personal Experiences of a Private Soldier in the Confederate Army.* New York: The Neale Publishing Co., 1905. Pp. 24-27.

10. Farragut Damns the Torpedoes at Mobile Bay.

John C. Kinney, "Farragut at Mobile Bay," in *Battles and Leaders of the Civil War.* New York: The Century Co., 1884, 1887, 1888. IV, 382 ff.

11. Lieutenant Cushing Torpedoes the *Albemarle.*

W. B. Cushing, "The Destruction of the 'Albemarle,' " in *Battles and Leaders of the Civil War.* New York: The Century Co., 1884, 1887, 1888. IV, 634-637.

12. The Confederates Repulse an Attack on Fort Fisher.

William Lamb, "The Defence of Fort Fisher, North Carolina," *Papers of the Military Historical Society of Massachusetts* (Boston), IX (1912), 361-368. (By permission of Military Historical Society of Massachusetts.)

13. "It Beat Anything in History."

Augustus Buell, "*The Cannoneer." Recollections of Service in the Army of the Potomac. By "A Detached Volunteer" in the Regular Artillery.* Washington: The National Tribune, 1890. Pp. 328-333.

CHAPTER XXIV. THE BLOCKADE AND THE CRUISERS

1. The United States Navy Blockades the Confederacy.

Horatio L. Wait, "The Blockade of the Confederacy," *The Century Illustrated Magazine,* XXXIV (1898), 914-920, *passim.* (By permission of Appleton-Century-Crofts, Inc.)

2. Noel Blakeman Recalls the Trials of Blockading.

A. Noel Blakeman, "Some Personal Reminiscences of the Naval Service," in A. Noel Blakeman, ed., *Personal Recollections of the War of the Rebellion, Second Series.* (Military Order of the Loyal Legion of the United States, New York Commandery.) New York: G. P. Putnam, 1897. Pp. 235-239.

3. The *Robert E. Lee* Runs the Blockade.

John Wilkinson, *The Narrative of a Blockade-Runner.* New York: Sheldon & Co., 1877. Pp. 162-171.

4. The *Rob Roy* Runs the Blockade out of Havana.

William Watson, *The Adventures of a Blockade Runner; or, Trade in Time of War.* London: T. Fisher Unwin, 1892. Pp. 141-159.

5. Richard Corbin Runs the Blockade to Join Lee's Army.

[Richard Corbin], "Letters of a Confederate Officer to His Family in Europe during the Last Year of the War of Secession," reprinted by William Abbatt, *Magazine of History,* Extra No. 24, 1913. Pp. 23-29.

6. Blockade-Runners Supply Charleston.

W. F. G. Peck, "Four Years Under Fire at Charleston," *Harper's New Monthly Magazine,* XXXI (1865), 364.

7. Wilmington Is Turned Topsy-Turvy by the War.

John Wilkinson, *The Narrative of a Blockade-Runner.* New York: Sheldon & Co., 1877. Pp. 464-466.

8. Confederate Privateers Harry Northern Merchantmen.

A. The *Ivy* Prowls Outside New Orleans. Letter of M. Repard, in *New Orleans Delta,* May 26, 1861, in William Morrison Robinson, Jr., *The Confederate Privateers.* New Haven, Conn.: Yale University Press, 1928. Pp. 45-46. (By permission of Yale University Press.)

B. The *Jefferson Davis* Takes a Prize off Delaware. Captain Fitfield, in *The Charleston Mercury,* July 23, 1861, *Ibid.,* 67-69.

C. A Colored Cook Arranges for the Recapture of the *Enchantress. The* Jeff Davis *Piracy Case. Full report of trial of William Smith for piracy as one of Crew of Confederate privateer* Jeff Davis. Philadelphia: King & Baird, 1861, *Ibid.,* 82-84.

9. The *Georgia* Fires the *Bold Hunter.*

James Morris Morgan, *Recollections of a Rebel Reefer.* London: Constable & Co., Ltd., 1918. Pp. 154-156. Boston: Houghton Mifflin Co., 1917. (By permission of Mrs. Daniel Hunter Wallace.)

10. The *Kearsarge* Sinks the *Alabama* off Cherbourg.

John McIntosh Kell, *Recollections of a Naval Life, including the Cruises of the Confederate States Steamers "Sumter" and "Alabama."* New York: The Neale Publishing Co., 1900. Pp. 244-251.

CHAPTER XXV. CHICKAMAUGA AND CHATTANOOGA

1. General Beatty Limns Some of the Officers of the West.

John Beatty, *The Citizen-Soldier; or Memoirs of a Volunteer.* Cincinnati: Wilstach, Baldwin & Co., 1879. Pp. 235-236.

2. The Federals Oppose Hood with Desperation.

James R. Carnahan, "Personal Recollections of Chickamauga," in *Sketches of War History, 1861-65 . . . Ohio Commandery of the Military Order of the Loyal Legion of the United States.* Cincinnati: Robert Clarke & Co., 1888. I, 410-417.

3. Thomas Stands Like a Rock at Chickamauga.

A. Longstreet Breaks the Federal Line. Daniel H. Hill, "Chickamauga—The Great Battle of the West," in *Battles and Leaders of the Civil War.* New York: The Century Co., 1884, 1888. III, 657-660.

B. "Men, We Must Use the Bayonet." Wm. Miller Owen, *In Camp and Battle with the Washington Artillery of New Orleans.* Boston: Ticknor & Co., 1885. Pp. 278-284.

C. Thomas Holds the Horseshoe Ridge. Gates P. Thruston, "The Crisis at Chickamauga," in *Battles and Leaders of the Civil War.* New York: The Century Co., 1884, 1888. III, 663-664.

4. Chattanooga under Siege.

W. F. G. Shanks, "Chattanooga, And How We Held It," *Harper's New Monthly Magazine,* XXXVI (1867-1868), 142-146, 148-149.

5. Hooker Wins the "Battle above the Clouds."

Joseph G. Fullerton, "The Army of the Cumberland at Chattanooga," in *Battles and Leaders of the Civil War.* New York: The Century Co., 1884, 1888. III, 721-723.

6. A Badger Boy Fights with Sherman at Chattanooga.

Jenkin Lloyd Jones, *An Artilleryman's Diary.* Madison, Wis.: Wisconsin History Commission, 1914. Pp. 132-142. (By permission of Wisconsin Historical Commission.)

7. The Army of the Cumberland Carries Missionary Ridge.

A. "First One Flag, Then Another, Leads." William A. Morgan, "Hazen's Brigade at Missionary Ridge," in *War Talks in Kansas . . . Commandery of Kansas, Military Order of the Loyal Legion of the United States.* Kansas City, Mo.: Franklin Hudson Publishing Co., 1906. I, 271-275. (By permission of Kansas Commandery, Military Order of the Loyal Legion of the United States.)

B. "When Those Fellows Get Started All Hell Can't Stop Them." Joseph G. Fullerton, "The Army of the Cumberland at Chattanooga," in *Battles and Leaders of the Civil War.* New York: The Century Co., 1884, 1888. III, 723-726.

C. "Amid the Din of Battle 'Chickamauga' Could Be Heard." "Major Connolly's Letters to His Wife, 1862-1865," *Transactions of the Illinois State Historical Society.* ("Publications of the Illinois State Historical Library," No. 35.) Springfield, Ill.: 1928. Pp. 298-303. (By permission of Illinois State Historical Society.)

8. "The Disaster Admits of No Palliation."

Braxton Bragg to Jefferson Davis, in *The War of the Rebellion . . . Official Records.* Ser. I, vol. LII, pt. II, 745-746.

9. Burnside Holds Out at Knoxville.

Henry S. Burrage, "Burnside's East Tennessee Campaign," *Papers of the Military Historical Society of Massachusetts* (Boston), VIII (1910), 574-595, *passim*. (By permission of Military Historical Society of Massachusetts.)

10. General Maury Draws a Portrait of Bedford Forrest.

General Dabney H. Maury, *Recollections of a Virginian*. New York: Charles Scribner's Sons, 1897. Pp. 204-218, *passim*.

CHAPTER XXVI. ATLANTA AND THE MARCH TO THE SEA

1. General Sherman Takes Command

A. "He Might Sit for a Portrait of an Ideal Yankee." John Chipman Gray to John Ropes, in Roland Gray, "Memoir of John Chipman Gray," *Proceedings of the Massachusetts Historical Society* (Boston), XLIX (1915-1916), 393-394. (By permission of Massachusetts Historical Society.)

B. "The Sort of Power Which a Flash of Lightning Suggests." M. A. De Wolfe Howe, ed., *Marching with Sherman, Passages from the Letters and Campaign Diaries of Henry Hitchcock*. New Haven, Conn.: Yale University Press, 1927. Pp. 30, 34-36. (By permission of Yale University Press.)

2. "The Star-Spangled Banner" at Dalton.

L. D. Young, *Reminiscences of a Soldier of the Orphan Brigade*. Paris, Ky.: Privately printed, n.d. Pp. 75-76.

3. Sherman Marches from Chattanooga to Atlanta.

W. T. Sherman, "The Grand Strategy of the War of the Rebellion," *Century Illustrated Magazine*, XIII (February 1888), 593-595.

4. Johnston Halts Sherman at New Hope Church.

Joseph E. Johnston, *Narrative of Military Operations, Directed, During the Late War Between the States*. New York: D. Appleton & Co., 1874. Pp. 326-331.

5. Atlanta: The Promised Land!

"Major Connolly's Letters to His Wife, 1862-1865," *Transactions of the Illinois State Historical Society*. ("Publications of the Illinois State Historical Library," No. 35.) Springfield, Ill.: 1928. Pp. 346-347. (By permission of Illinois State Historical Society.)

6. Joe Johnston Gives Way to Hood.

A. President Davis Removes General Johnston before Atlanta. Jefferson Davis, *Rise and Fall of the Confederate Government*. New York: D. Appleton & Co., 1881. II, 556-557.

B. General Johnston Justifies Himself. Letter from Johnston to Maury, in Dabney H. Maury, *Recollections of a Virginian*. New York: Charles Scribner's Sons, 1897. Pp. 146-148.

7. The Union Army Learns to Fight behind Fortifications.

Henry O. Dwight, "How We Fight at Atlanta," *Harper's New Monthly Magazine*, XXIX (1864), 663-666.

8. Hardee Wins and Loses the Battle of Atlanta.

Richard S. Tuthill, "An Artilleryman's Recollections of the Battle of Atlanta," in *Military Essays and Recollections . . . Military Order of the Loyal Legion, Illinois Commandery*. Chicago: A. C. McClurg & Co., 1891. I, 302-306.

9. "You Might as Well Appeal against the Thunder-Storm."

[William T. Sherman], *Memoirs of General William T. Sherman*. New York: D. Appleton & Co., 1875. II, 125-127.

10. Sherman Marches from Atlanta to the Sea.

[William T. Sherman], *Memoirs of General William T. Sherman*. New York: D. Appleton & Co., 1875. II, 178 ff.

11. Sherman's "Bummers."

A. An Inventory of the Bummer. Letter of Charles A. Booth, March 27, 1865, in G. S. Bradley, *The Star Corps; or, Notes of an Army Chaplain, during Sherman's Famous "March to the Sea."* Milwaukee, 1865. Pp. 274-276.

B. A Good Word for the Bummers. Henry O. Dwight, "How We Fight at Atlanta," *Harper's New Monthly Magazine*, XXIX (1864), 666.

C. "We Were Proud of Our Foragers." Daniel Oakey, "Marching Through Georgia and the Carolinas," in *Battles and Leaders of the Civil War*. New York: The Century Co., 1884, 1887, 1888. IV, 672-673.

12. "The Heavens Were Lit Up with Flames from Burning Buildings."

Dolly Sumner Lunt, *A Woman's Wartime Journal . . . With an introduction and Notes by Julian Street*. New York: The Century Co., 1918. Pp. 20-32, *passim*. (By permission of Mrs. L. D. Bolton.)

13. Eliza Andrews Comes Home through the Burnt Country.

Eliza Frances Andrews, *The War-Time Journal of a Georgia Girl*. New York: D. Appleton & Co., 1908. Pp. 32-33, 38.

14. South Carolina Becomes a "Howling Waste."

Daniel Oakey, "Marching Through Georgia and the Carolinas," in *Battles and Leaders of the Civil War*. New York: The Century Co., 1884, 1887, 1888. IV, 675-678.

15. The Burning of Columbia.

A. "A Scene of Shameful Confusion." Brevet Major George Ward Nichols, Aide-de-Camp to General Sherman, *The Story of the Great March, from the Diary of a Staff Officer*. New York: Harper & Bros., 1865. Pp. 160-166.

B. Major Hitchcock Explains the Burning of Columbia. M. A. De Wolfe Howe, ed., *Marching with Sherman, Passages from the Letters and Campaign Diaries of Henry Hitchcock*. New Haven: Yale University Press, 1927. Pp. 265-270. (By permission of Yale University Press.)

16. General Sherman Thinks His Name May Live.

M. A. De Wolfe Howe, ed., *Home Letters of General Sherman*. New York: Charles Scribner's Sons, 1909. Pp. 324-327. (By permission of Charles Scribner's Sons.)

CHAPTER XXVII. THE WILDERNESS

1. U. S. Grant Plans His Spring Campaign.

[Ulysses S. Grant], *Personal Memoirs of U. S. Grant*. New York: Charles L. Webster & Co., 1886. II, 127 ff.

2. Lincoln and Grant Pay Tribute to Each Other.

Adam Badeau, "Preparing for the Campaigns of '64," in *Battles and Leaders of the Civil War*. New York: The Century Co., 1884, 1887, 1888. IV, 113.

3. Colonel Porter Draws a Portrait of General Grant.

General Horace Porter, *Campaigning with Grant*. New York: The Century Co., 1897. Pp. 13-16, 248-250.

4. Fighting in the Wilderness.

Augustus Buell, *"The Cannoneer." Recollections of Service in the Army of the Potomac. By "A Detached Volunteer" in the Regular Artillery*. Washington: The National Tribune, 1890. Pp. 167-169.

5. Private Goss Describes the Battle of the Wilderness.

Warren Lee Goss, *Recollections of a Private. A Story of the Army of the Potomac.* New York: Thomas Y. Crowell & Co., 1890. Pp. 268-277.

6. "Texans Always Move Them."

R. C. ——, of 'Hood's Texas Brigade,' "Gen. Lee at the 'Wilderness,'" in *The Land We Love,* V (1868), 484-486.

7. The Confederates Miss a Chance to Destroy Grant.

General John B. Gordon, *Reminiscences of the Civil War.* New York: Charles Scribner's Sons, 1903. Pp. 258, 248-251. (By permission of Charles Scribner's Sons.)

8. "Their Dead and Dying Piled Higher Than the Works."

Robert Stiles, *Four Years Under Marse Robert.* New York: The Neale Publishing Co., 1910. Pp. 253-255, 263-264.

9. "Beauty" Stuart Fulfills His Destiny.

H. B. McClellan, *The Life and Campaigns of Major-General J. E. B. Stuart . . .* Boston: Houghton, Mifflin & Co., 1885. Pp. 409-417.

10. Spotsylvania and the Bloody Angle.

General Horace Porter, *Campaigning with Grant.* New York: The Century Co., 1897. Pp. 101-111.

11. "These Men Have Never Failed You on Any Field."

General John B. Gordon, *Reminiscences of the Civil War.* New York: Charles Scribner's Sons, 1903. Pp. 275-281. (By permission of Charles Scribner's Sons.)

12. Grant Hurls His Men to Death at Cold Harbor.

A. "The Dead Cover More Than Five Acres." William C. Oates, *The War Between the Union and the Confederacy and Its Lost Opportunities.* New York: The Neale Publishing Co., 1905. Pp. 365-368.

B. General Upton Deplores the Butchery at Cold Harbor. Peter S. Michie, *The Life and Letters of Emory Upton, Colonel of the Fourth Regiment of Artillery, and Brevet Major-General, U. S. Army.* New York: D. Appleton & Co., 1885. P. 108.

CHAPTER XXVIII. THE SIEGE OF PETERSBURG

1. Butler's Attack on Petersburg Fizzles Out.

R. E. Colston, "Repelling the First Assault on Petersburg," in *Battles and Leaders of the Civil War.* New York: The Century Co., 1884, 1887, 1888. IV, 636-637.

2. Grant's Army Crosses the James.

"Grant's Report covering operations of all armies of the U. S. from March, 1864 to May, 1865," in *The War of the Rebellion . . . Official Records.* Ser. I, vol. XXXVI, pt. I, 22-25.

3. Beauregard Holds the Lines at Petersburg.

G. T. Beauregard, "Four Days of Battle at Petersburg," in *Battles and Leaders of the Civil War.* New York: The Century Co., 1884, 1887, 1888. IV, 540-544.

4. "A Hurricane of Shot and Shell."

Captain Augustus C. Brown, *The Diary of a Line Officer.* New York: Privately printed, 1906. Pp. 77-82.

5. The Mine and the Battle of the Crater.

A. Burnside Fumbles His Chance to Take Petersburg. Régis de Trobriand, *Four Years with the Army of the Potomac.* Trans. by George K. Dauchy. Boston: Ticknor & Co., 1889. Pp. 608 ff.

B. Mahone's Division Saves the Day at the Crater. John S. Wise, *The End of an Era.* Boston: Houghton, Mifflin & Co., 1899. Pp. 357-366.

6. Lee Stops Hancock at the Gates of Richmond.

[Richard Corbin], "Letters of a Confederate Officer to His Family in Europe during the Last Year of the War of Secession," reprinted by William Abbatt, *Magazine of History*, Extra No. 24, 1913. Pp. 57-62.

7. The Iron Lines of Petersburg.

George D. Harmon, ed., "Letters of Luther Rice Mills—a Confederate Soldier," *North Carolina Historical Review*, IV (July 1927), 303-308. (By permission of State of North Carolina Department of Archives and History.)

CHAPTER XXIX. THE VALLEY IN 1864

1. V.M.I. Boys Fight at New Market.

John S. Wise, "The West Point of the Confederacy," *Century Illustrated Magazine*, XXXVII (1888-1889), 464-470.

2. Lew Wallace Stops Early at the Gates of Washington.

Lew Wallace, An Autobiography. New York: Harper & Bros., 1906. Pp. 765-772, *passim*. (By permission of Harper and Brothers.)

3. General Hunter Devastates the Valley.

General J. D. Imboden, "Fire, Sword, and the Halter," in *The Annals of the War, Written by Leading Participants North and South . . . in the Philadelphia Weekly Times*. Philadelphia: The Times Publishing Co., 1879. Pp. 177-181.

4. General Ramseur Fights and Dies for His Country.

Letters of Ramseur to his fiancée and wife, Ramseur Manuscripts, University of North Carolina. (By permission of Messrs. Paul W. Schenck, Jr., and David Schenck.)

5. Early Surprises the Federals at Cedar Creek.

A. "The Enemy Were upon Us." Captain S. E. Howard, "The Morning Surprise at Cedar Creek," in *Civil War Papers . . . Massachusetts Commandery, Military Order of the Loyal Legion of the United States*. Boston: Printed for the Commandery, 1900. II, 417-422. (By permission of Massachusetts Commandery, Military Order of the Loyal Legion of the United States.)

B. General Getty Saves the Day. General Hazard Stevens, "The Battle of Cedar Creek, Oct. 19, 1864," *Ibid*. I, 210-215. (By permission of Massachusetts Commandery, Military Order of the Loyal Legion of the United States.)

6. Sheridan Rides down the Valley Pike to Victory and Fame.

[Philip H. Sheridan], *Personal Memoirs of P. H. Sheridan*. New York: Charles L. Webster & Co., 1888. II, 68-86.

7. "The Valley Will Have Little in It for Man or Beast."

Letter of General Sheridan, in *The War of the Rebellion . . . Official Records*, Ser. I, vol. XLIII, pt. 1, 30-31.

CHAPTER XXX. LEE AND LINCOLN

1. Robert E. Lee Goes with His State.

A. "My Relatives, My Children, My Home." Lee to his sister, Mrs. Anne Marshall, in Robert E. Lee [Jr.], *Recollections and Letters of General Robert E. Lee*. New York: Doubleday, Page & Co., 1904. Pp. 25-26. (By permission of Doubleday & Company, Inc.)

B. "I Never Desire Again to Draw My Sword." Lee to General Scott, *Ibid.*, 24-25.

2. Lee and Jackson Plan McClellan's Destruction.

Robert Stiles, *Four Years Under Marse Robert*. New York: The Neale Publishing Co., 1910. Pp. 97-99.

3. "A Splendid Specimen of an English Gentleman."

[Col. Garnet Wolseley], "A Month's Visit to the Confederate Headquarters," *Blackwood's Edinburgh Magazine*, XCIII (January-June 1863), 18, 20-21.

4. "You Must Help Drive These People Back."

Robert E. Lee [Jr.], *Recollections and Letters of General Robert E. Lee*. New York: Doubleday, Page & Co., 1904. Pp. 77-78. (By permission of Doubleday & Company, Inc.)

5. "It Is Well War Is So Terrible or We Should Get Too Fond of It."

W. N. Pendleton, "Personal Recollections of General Lee," *Southern Magazine*, XV (1874), 620-621.

6. Lee Sends General McLaws to Call on Sedgwick.

Robert Stiles, *Four Years Under Marse Robert*. New York: The Neale Publishing Co., 1910. Pp. 176-178.

7. Dr. Parks's Boy Visits Lee's Headquarters.

Leighton Parks, "What a Boy Saw of the Civil War; with Glimpses of General Lee," *Century Illustrated Magazine*, LXX (1905), 258-264. (By permission of Appleton-Century-Crofts, Inc.)

8. "A Sadness I Had Never Before Seen upon His Face."

J. D. Imboden, "The Confederate Retreat from Gettysburg," in *Battles and Leaders of the Civil War*. New York: The Century Co., 1884, 1888. III, 420-421.

9. Lee and Traveller Review the Army of Northern Virginia.

Robert E. Lee [Jr.], *Recollections and Letters of General Robert E. Lee*. New York: Doubleday, Page & Co., 1904. Pp. 106-107. (By permission of Doubleday & Company, Inc.)

10. "He Looked as Though He Was the Monarch of the World."

William C. Oates, *The War Between the Union and the Confederacy and Its Lost Opportunities*. New York: The Neale Publishing Co., 1905. Pp. 343-344.

11. "The Field Resounded with Wild Shouts of Lee, Lee, Lee."

Account by Colonel J. Catlett Gibson, *Southern Historical Society Papers*, XXXI (1903), 200-203. (By permission of Southern Historical Society.)

12. Lee Bids Farewell to the Army of Northern Virginia.

Robert E. Lee [Jr.], *Recollections and Letters of General Robert E. Lee*. New York: Doubleday, Page & Co., 1904. Pp. 153-154. (By permission of Doubleday & Company, Inc.)

13. Nathaniel Hawthorne Calls on President Lincoln.

Nathaniel Hawthorne, *Tales, Sketches, and Other Papers*, many editions.

14. An English Visitor Watches the President Receive Callers.

Robert Ferguson, *America During and After the War*. London, 1866. Pp. 114 ff.

15. John Hay Lives with "The Tycoon" in the White House.

Tyler Dennett, ed., John Hay, *Lincoln and the Civil War in the Diaries and Letters of John Hay*. New York: Dodd, Mead & Co., 1939. Pp. 34-35, 68-69, 76, 96, 185. (By permission of Dodd, Mead & Company, Inc.)

16. "My Paramount Object Is to Save the Union."

A. "The Prayer of Twenty Millions." Greeley to Lincoln, in Frank Moore, ed., *The Rebellion Record*. New York, 1871. XII, 480 ff.

B. "I Would Save the Union." Lincoln to Greeley, *Ibid*.

17. "We Shall Nobly Save or Meanly Lose the Last, Best Hope of Earth."

Abraham Lincoln, "Annual Message of Dec. 1, 1862," in James D. Richardson, ed., *Messages and Papers of the Presidents*. New York, 1904. VI, 126 ff.

18. Lincoln Becomes the Great Emancipator.

A. Secretary Chase Recalls a Famous Cabinet Meeting. J. W. Shuckers, *The Life and Public Services of Salmon Portland Chase.* New York: D. Appleton & Co., 1874. Pp. 453-455.

B. "Forever Free." Abraham Lincoln, "The Emancipation Proclamation," in James D. Richardson, ed., *Messages and Papers of the Presidents.* New York, 1904. VI, 157 ff.

19. Lincoln Arranges for the Admission of Nevada to the Union.

Charles A. Dana, *Recollections of the Civil War.* New York: D. Appleton & Co., 1898. Pp. 174-177. (By permission of Appleton-Century-Crofts, Inc.)

20. Lincoln and Hay Follow the Election Returns.

Tyler Dennett, ed., John Hay, *Lincoln and the Civil War in the Diaries and Letters of John Hay.* New York: Dodd, Mead & Co., 1939. Pp. 232-236. (By permission of Dodd, Mead & Company, Inc.)

21. Lincoln Replies to a Serenade.

Nicolay and Hay, eds., *The Complete Works of Abraham Lincoln.* New York: The Century Co., 1894. II, 595-596. (By permission of Appleton-Century-Crofts, Inc.)

22. Lincoln Visits the Colored Soldiers at City Point.

General Horace Porter, *Campaigning with Grant.* New York: The Century Co., 1897. Pp. 216-220.

23. "With Malice Toward None."

Abraham Lincoln, "Second Inaugural Address," in James D. Richardson, ed., *Messages and Papers of the Presidents.* New York, 1904. VI, 276-277.

24. Abraham Lincoln Is Assassinated.

Diary of Gideon Welles. Boston: Houghton Mifflin Co., 1911. II, 283 ff. (By permission of Houghton Mifflin Company.)

25. "Yes, He Had Lived to Shame Me from My Sneer."

Tom Taylor, "Abraham Lincoln," *Punch* (London), XLVIII (May 6, 1865), 182.

CHAPTER XXXI. THE SUNSET OF THE CONFEDERACY

1. Thomas Annihilates Hood at Nashville.

James Harrison Wilson, *Under the Old Flag; Recollections of Military Operations in the War for the Union, the Spanish War, the Boxer Rebellion, etc.* New York: D. Appleton & Co., 1912. II, 99-121, *passim.* (By permission of Appleton-Century-Crofts, Inc.)

2. "The Last Chance of the Confederacy."

Alexander C. McClurg, "The Last Chance of the Confederacy," *Atlantic Monthly,* L (September 1882), 389 ff.

3. The Desperate Gamble of Fort Stedman.

General James A. Walker, "Gordon's Assault on Fort Stedman," *Southern Historical Society Papers,* XXXI (1903), 23-29. (By permission of Southern Historical Society.)

4. "Now Richmond Rocked in Her High Towers to Watch the Impending Issue."

George Alfred Townsend, *Campaigns of a Non-Combatant, And His Romaunt Abroad During the War.* New York: Blelock & Co., 1866. Pp. 318-326.

5. "The Most Superb Soldier in All the World" Falls at Five Forks.

Armistead Churchill Gordon, *Memories and Memorials of William Gordon McCabe.* Richmond, Va.: Old Dominion Press, Inc., 1925. I, 164-166. (By permission of Mr. W. Gordon McCabe II and Brigadier General E. R. Warner McCabe.)

6. The Confederates Abandon Richmond.

A. "A Great Burst of Sobbing All Over the Church." Mrs. Burton Harrison, *Recollections Grave and Gay.* New York: Charles Scribner's Sons, 1916. Pp. 210-219. (By permission of Charles Scribner's Sons.)

B. "The Poor Colored People Thanked God That Their Sufferings Were Ended." R. B. Prescott, "The Capture of Richmond," in *Civil War Papers . . . Massachusetts Commandery, Military Order of the Loyal Legion of the United States.* Boston: Printed for the Commandery, 1900. I, 64-70. (By permission of Massachusetts Commandery, Military Order of the Loyal Legion of the United States.)

7. The White Flag at Appomattox.

Joshua Lawrence Chamberlain, *The Passing of the Armies, An Account of the Final Campaign of the Army of the Potomac, Based upon Personal Reminiscences of the Fifth Army Còrps.* New York: G. P. Putnam's Sons, 1915. Pp. 230-242.

8. General Lee Surrenders at Appomattox.

Sir Frederick Maurice, ed., *An Aide-de-Camp of Lee; being the Papers of Colonel Charles Marshall.* Boston: Little, Brown & Co., 1927. Pp. 268-274. (By permission of Sir Frederick Maurice.)

9. "The Whole Column Seemed Crowned with Red."

Joshua Lawrence Chamberlain, *The Passing of the Armies, An Account of the Final Campaign of the Army of the Potomac, Based upon Personal Reminiscences of the Fifth Army Corps.* New York: G. P. Putnam's Sons, 1915. Pp. 248, 258-265.

10. "The Shattered Remains of Lee's Army."

Eliza Frances Andrews, *The War-Time Journal of a Georgia Girl.* New York: D. Appleton & Co., 1908. Pp. 181-198, *passim.*

11. The Stars and Stripes Are Raised over Fort Sumter.

Mary Cadwalader Jones, *Lantern Slides.* Boston: Privately printed, 1937. (By permission of Mrs. Max Farrand.)

12. "Bow Down, Dear Land, for Thou Hast Found Release."

James Russell Lowell, "Ode Recited at the Harvard Commemoration," *Poems,* many editions.

INDEX